THE TIMES

Guide to Golf Courses of Britain & Ireland

THE TIMES

Guide to
Golf Courses
of
Britain & Ireland

Compiled by Mark Rowlinson

Foreword by John Hopkins

hamlyn

First published in Great Britain in 2001 by
Hamlyn, a division of Octopus Publishing Group Ltd
2–4 Heron Quays, London E14 4JP

ISBN 0 600 60372 5

A CIP catalogue record for this book is available from the British Library

Printed and bound in Italy

10 9 8 7 6 5 4 3 2 1

Every effort has been made to ensure that the information given in this book is as accurate as possible. However, golf courses are frequently adjusted and redesigned and new courses appear all the time. The Publishers will be grateful for any information that will assist them in updating future editions.

Contents

Foreword

Anyone who has played golf for any length of time will have experienced moments such as this. In 25 minutes time you are due on the 1st tee of a golf course with which you are not familiar. You suspect you are 30 minutes away, but you are not sure because you do not know where the course is. In your frustration you aim the bonnet of your car at a set of traffic lights in the hope they will remain green only to have to jam on the brakes when they change to red. As you brake hard you hear your irons rattling around in the boot and they remind you that one of your New Year's resolutions was to be more organized, to plan routes in advance, to allow more time for journeys. You peer out of the window in mounting frustration. Where is that golf course? Where is the turn off? Where is the B719 that is supposed to come up on the left as you head south. Perhaps you are going north? And so the panic builds up until, finally, somehow, you turn the last corner and see the course and a sense of relief descends.

It is equally likely that this book will be a source of reference to anyone going on holiday and wanting to know about golf courses nearby. You might know that Silloth is a terrific course – you ought to anyway because it is – but you might not be so well acquainted with the fact that it has narrow fairways, large sand dunes and was designed by a trio that included Willie Park Junior, the son of the winner of the first Open, in 1860 at Prestwick, and the great Alister Mackenzie whose imprint is evident in so many courses around the world.

Mark Rowlinson's qualifications to write this thorough, fact-filled guide include a knowledge of music, which helped him retain a sense of composure during weeks of preparation, and a background in the arts and broadcasting. This has helped him discover some facts that might not be included in traditional guide books. It takes a wider-than-usual approach to unearth the fact that Barnes Wallis first tested the bouncing bomb, with which he would later make his name, on the lake at Silvermere, now played as the 17th and 18th holes, or that he had a wartime study in the clubhouse at Burhill. Rowlinson has found out that a ghost haunts the clubhouse at Flint, that the clubhouse at Chestfield, near Whitstable in Kent, dates from the 15th century and that the composer, Sir Edward Elgar was once a member of the Worcestershire. Oh yes, and that Arctic skuas nest on the fairways of Sanday, one of only three courses on Orkney.

Rowlinson is a lifelong golfer who has a handicap of 14.7 at Conway in north Wales. The inspiration for this book may well have been born in his early days. 'When I was a kid my father pointed out that the golf course was of far greater interest than my golf over it,' he said. 'I have a train spotter's mentality for sillinesses, such as two bunkers on the outside of a dogleg.' He was also one of the team that produced the *World Atlas of Golf*, which was first published in 1976 and is revered by many people, me included. Thus in some of the entries in *The Times Guide to Golf Courses of Britain and Ireland* you will see the sort of neat line drawings that were present in the *World Atlas*. Nor will you be surprised at the amount of detail included in some of the course entries. Consider this, for example, in reference to the Alwoodley and Dr Mackenzie's role in designing it. 'Alwoodley is an early example of the genius of ... Mackenzie, the designer of Augusta National, Cypress Point and Royal Melbourne. At the time,' Rowlinson continues, 'he was Alwoodley's first Hon. Secretary. He could not resist becoming involved in the design process and he quickly impressed the consultant, Harry Colt, with his breadth of vision and architectural flair.'

I travel throughout Britain, Ireland and mainland Europe as golf correspondent of *The Times*. A nice line of work, I know. I have been attending golf tournaments for several decades now and there are still many courses with which I am not familiar and many places I have not visited, never mind played golf there. This book, therefore, will never be far from the glove compartment of my car or from the desk in my study. It is invaluable.

Introduction

British golf is unique. In what other sport is it possible to tread the very same ground that the giants of the game have graced only the day before? The ordinary person can only dream of playing a set of tennis at Wimbledon, taking spot kicks at Old Trafford, riding a thoroughbred at Ascot, or walking out to bat at Lord's. But, for the payment of a green fee (not insubstantial, it has to be admitted), an ordinary golfer can tee the ball up on the 1st at St Andrews, Royal Lytham or Wentworth and attempt to emulate the feats of the greats. For sure, it will take advance planning, and it may not be possible easily to comply with handicap restrictions, but, for thousands of golfers from home and abroad every year, the dream becomes a reality. Of the current regular European Tour venues only Loch Lomond is off limits, being a strictly members only club. And for those whose golfing memories stretch back for more than a decade or two there are some hallowed fairways available for a very modest sum indeed. For instance, PGA Championships were held at Maesdu, Ashburnham, Thorndon Park and Dunbar, with Peter Alliss, Dai Rees, Brian Huggett and David Talbot amongst the winners. As recently as 1989 the Benson and Hedges Open was still being played at Fulford, that immaculately maintained jewel at York, with a star-studded winners' board resplendent with the names of Tony Jacklin, Tom Weiskopf, Greg Norman, Lee Trevino, and Sandy Lyle, amongst others, and that very famous tree overlooking the 17th green up which the agile Bernhard Langer once climbed in order to play his third shot. There are hundreds of courses around these islands on which some such memorable event has occurred, and almost all of them are open to all golfers.

In this book are listed over 2,500 clubs, and around 3,000 courses, complete with all the essential information the potential visitor may require. Green fees are those charged for a single mid-week round by an adult visitor during the 2001 season. Most of the information has been supplied by the clubs themselves, but it has to be said that golf club secretaries, managers and administrators come in two kinds: those who could not be more helpful, and those who simply cannot be bothered to respond to letters, faxes, telephone calls or even personal visits! The itinerant golfer will find that welcomes are also of two kinds, some clubs bending over backwards to accommodate visitors, greeting them warmly, while other clubs appear to despise visitors as much as vermin (yet they are ready enough to pocket their green fee payments). Much is revealed by a preliminary telephone call and, given that most courses are now extremely busy, advance booking is essential, even at many pay-and-play or public courses. Corporate and society golf is an important part of many clubs' activities (and a welcome source of income) and bookings should be made well in advance. Handicap certificates are nominally required of individual visitors or parties at an increasing number of clubs. In practice, few clubs actually bother to check, except for open competition competitors.

As the 21st century opens golf has reached a crossroads. There are more golfers than ever, and, given the perilous state of agriculture, many farmers are taking the risk of getting out of potatoes and into Pinnacles. So, happily, there are more and more simple pay-and-play or inexpensive proprietary courses coming on stream. They are vital to the future of the game, because they are the only way many can get a first foothold in the game, especially the young. The cost of joining a long-established members' club of some standing is prohibitive to many, and will remain so when incomes continue to rocket in certain trades and professions while in others they languish far behind or the financial uncertainty of unemployment looms. Golf club memberships are ageing and, with so many active seniors, there are few vacancies for new members. Many of the new courses provide the solution. They may have no more than a few straightforward holes, a caravan to take green fees, and a couple of chemical lavatories, but it is remarkable how quickly the green fees add up, enabling the proprietor to improve the property, perhaps replacing the caravan with a log cabin with changing facilities. Grants are frequently available to plant trees, and some of the courses opened only a few years ago are already important refuges for wildlife. Golf has had a poor ecological press in recent years, but there is much good work going on, and a thoughtfully managed golf course can be a very valuable haven for rare or endangered plants and creatures.

There is an extraordinary variety to the courses scattered all across these islands. Brief descriptions therefore are given to enable the visiting golfer to select courses which might suit the reader's pocket and temperament, for it has to be said that one golfer's idea of heaven (an ancient links with narrow fairways lined with impenetrable gorse, littered with bunkers, and subject to a wind devastating to even the most robust swing) is another's idea of absolute purgatory. In a book of this nature it has only been possible to give thumbnail sketches of most clubs and courses, but 50 of the top courses have been singled out for special treatment, with a detailed description, course map and card of the course (see pages 10–59). Naturally, they include the Open Championship courses, Ryder Cup venues, and so on. A further 500 courses of interest have been highlighted throughout the Gazetteer, giving a broad geographical spread and a considerable variety of style, cost, and accessibility, from lavish resort courses to quiet country courses, £190 green fees to £10. For convenience they are marked individually on the accompanying maps (see pages 417–432).

Nobody could hope to visit every single golf course there is, so the author has been grateful for the advice of a number of knowledgeable correspondents and for the help of many club secretaries. But golf clubs are living organisms, growing and developing almost daily, so it is almost certain that as soon as it is stated authoritatively that 'This course has the longest par 5 in Staffordshire' some other club has already rebuilt a hole to exceed it. Clubs are listed by the county in which they play competitive golf, which occasionally leads to anomalies between the clubs' addresses and where they are listed in the gazetteer. While every care has been taken to make this book as accurate as possible, the author is grateful to have any errors or omissions pointed out by the secretary or captain of any clubs misrepresented, so that corrections can be made in future editions.

The Alwoodley

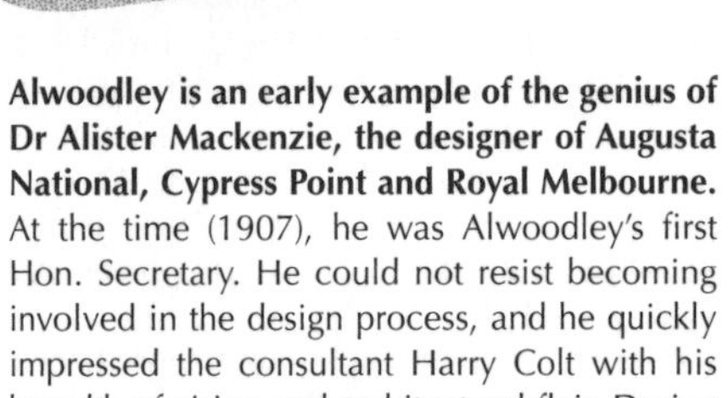

Alwoodley is an early example of the genius of Dr Alister Mackenzie, the designer of Augusta National, Cypress Point and Royal Melbourne. At the time (1907), he was Alwoodley's first Hon. Secretary. He could not resist becoming involved in the design process, and he quickly impressed the consultant Harry Colt with his breadth of vision and architectural flair. During a recent lengthening of the course, tees were moved back much as Mackenzie had originally envisaged, and this has further strengthened an already outstanding heathland course. Course maintenance is a matter of great pride at Alwoodley, and its good drainage makes for enjoyable winter golf.

All but one of the greens are in Mackenzie's original positions. They call for a wide variety of approach shots, and some deft rescue work if they are missed. The longest hole, the 8th, is a dog-leg curving round a wood, and it needs long, accurate driving and a cool nerve if attack is the order of the day. Certainly the prettiest holes are among the most memorable: the short par-5 10th, for example, is said to have been the prototype for the 13th at Augusta; and the par-3 11th boasts a tightly bunkered green cunningly located at the top of a deceptive rise.

Stamina is needed to return a good score at Alwoodley, because, as you head for home from the 13th, the course turns into the wind with a succession of big par 4s interrupted only by a par 3, itself of some length. At 470 yards from the championship tee, with eight bunkers and plentiful heather and gorse, the 18th keeps the pressure up to the very end.

CARD OF THE COURSE

	yards	par		yards	par
1	404	4	10	475	5
2	305	4	11	167	3
3	514	5	12	365	4
4	478	4	13	402	4
5	369	4	14	206	3
6	455	4	15	409	4
7	143	3	16	414	4
8	584	5	17	434	4
9	191	3	18	470	4
Out	3,443	36	In	3,342	35
Total	6,785 yards		par 71		

Ballybunion

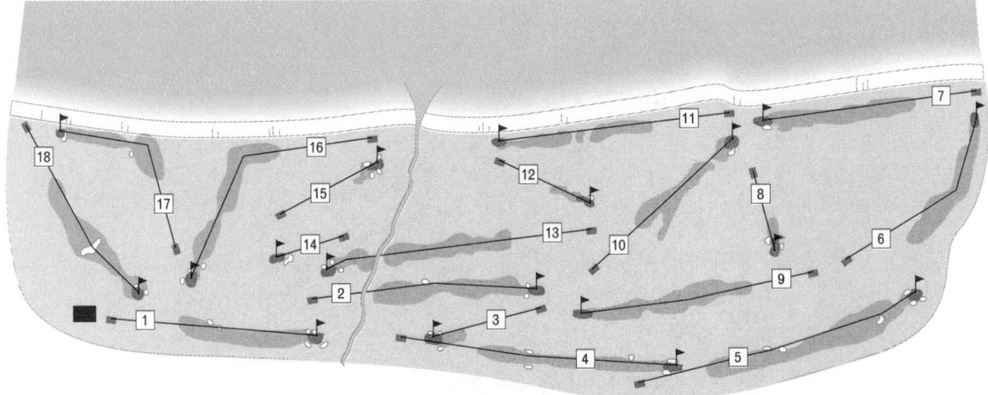

Ballybunion is universally acknowledged as one of the world's great courses. Although golf had been played there since the late 19th century, it was not until 1926 that the 18-hole layout now known as the Old course was built. Being situated in a remote part of western Ireland, it remained familiar to only a few until the Irish Amateur Championship was held there in 1937 – the eminent golf architect Tom Simpson having been called in to make whatever alterations he felt were necessary to equip Ballybunion for its first big event. All Simpson had to do was tinker with three greens and add one bunker – and little has been done since. If proof of its greatness were needed, it can be found in the much-quoted eulogies of Tom Watson, the first of the great Americans to visit it regularly. Byron Nelson, Jack Nicklaus, Peter Thomson, Phil Mickelson and many other distinguished players have followed in Watson's footsteps and fallen for its charms.

What is so remarkable about the Old course is its abundant personality, running through the dunes, along them and up over them. There is so much life in the ground that every shot requires careful consideration, especially pitches to the raised greens. The first few holes are relatively prosaic, but, breaking out on to the top of the dunes at the 6th green, the course moves into top gear. Magical holes such as the 11th, 16th and 17th, and the brilliant par 3s – the 8th and 15th – are what make Ballybunion incomparable.

CARD OF THE OLD COURSE

	yards	par		yards	par
1	400	4	10	361	4
2	439	4	11	451	4
3	220	3	12	200	3
4	529	5	13	486	5
5	552	5	14	135	3
6	382	4	15	212	3
7	420	4	16	499	5
8	154	3	17	376	4
9	456	4	18	379	4

Out	3,552 yards	par 36
In	3,099 yards	par 35
Total	6,651 yards	par 71

Ballyliffin

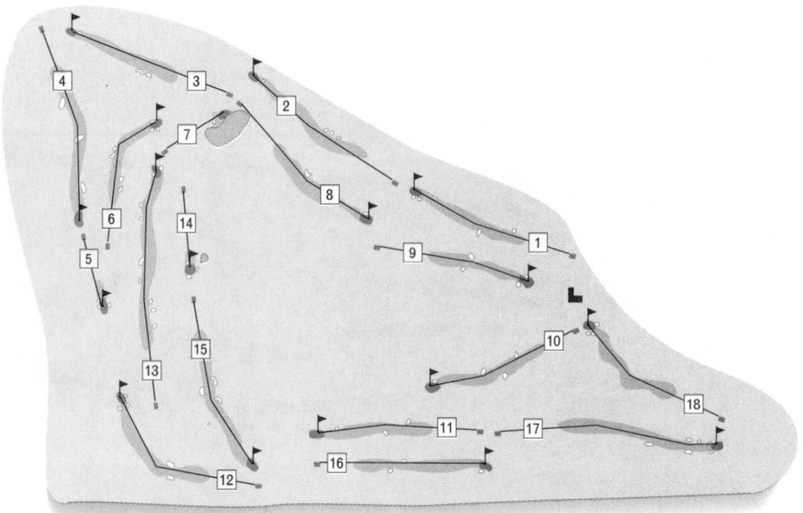

For many years, knowledgeable golfers have made the pilgrimage to County Donegal but only fairly recently have they been drawn to Ballyliffin. One such pilgrim was Nick Faldo, who visited in 1993 and was immediately smitten. Although he was playing the Old Course at that time, diggers were already at work shaping the fairways of a second course, Glashedy Links, of championship standard, designed by Pat Ruddy and Tom Craddock. This shares with the Old Course the stunning seascapes from Malin Head past Glashedy Rock (Ballyliffin's equivalent of Ailsa Craig) to Fanad Head, while inland the scene is dominated by the hills, Crockaughrim, Buluba and Binion.

Glashedy Links would be a fine test on the stillest of days, because of its great length, any number of deep, revetted bunkers, large, undulating greens, punishing rough and plenty of movement in the land. The wind, however, is very rarely absent, and the skilful golfer must keep the ball low, simply to survive. The start is serious with three tough par 4s heading for the dunes. Respite of a kind follows in a short par 5 but it is well bunkered, and that is certainly true of the short 5th. A climb on to the top of the dunes is rewarded with magnificent views from the 7th tee. The club is particularly proud of the sequence of holes starting at the 12th, a sharp dog-leg. Plenty of stamina is required for the 13th – the longest of the par 5s – and the 15th – the toughest of the par 4s.

CARD OF THE COURSE

	yards	par		yards	par
1	426	4	10	397	4
2	432	4	11	419	4
3	428	4	12	448	4
4	479	5	13	572	5
5	177	3	14	183	3
6	361	4	15	440	4
7	183	3	16	426	4
8	422	4	17	549	5
9	382	4	18	411	4
Out	3,290 yards	par 35			
In	3,845 yards	par 37			
Total	7,135 yards	par 72			

The Belfry

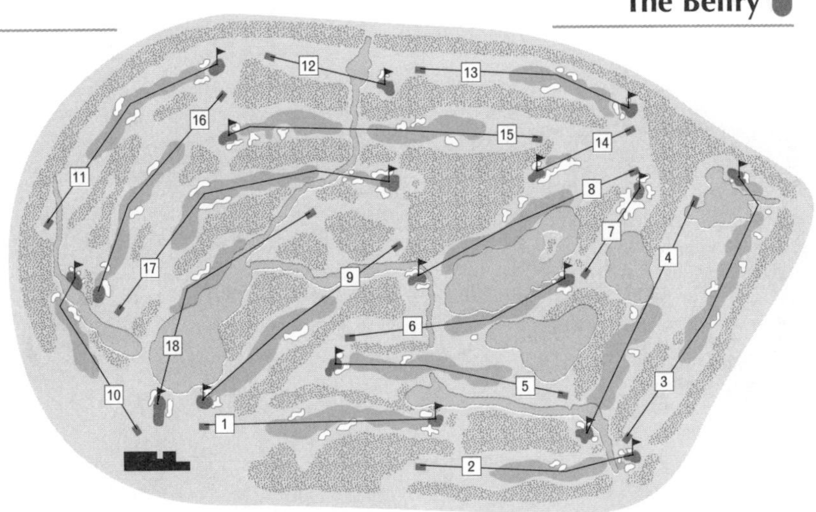

Only The Brabazon at The Belfry has hosted four Ryder Cup matches – no other course has hosted more than two. Since the 1993 Ryder Cup, more than £2 million has been spent on preparing the course for the 2001 matches. Major surgery has been carried out, with the substantial redesign of a number of holes, plus smaller, but no less significant, alterations to the many ponds and streams, reshaping of bunkers and greens, planting of more trees and improvement of spectator facilities. The three previous Ryder Cups at The Belfry have been full of drama, and the revised course's professional debut in 2000 lived up to its reputation, when Padraig Harrington – the leader at the start of the last day of the Benson and Hedges International – was disqualified for failing to sign his card. Jose-Maria Olazabal then went on to win, with a score of 275, 13 under par.

Although, on The Brabazon, professionals expect to reach the par-5 15th and 17th in two shots, they risk losing the hole at a crucial stage if they fail to place their drive in the exact spot required. The 18th is one of the great finishing holes in golf, a long par 4 with two compulsory water carries. There is nowhere to bale out and, for those whose Ryder Cup match has reached this hole, the drive must flirt with the water along the left, to take some of the pressure off the very demanding approach shot. The 10th is another all-or-nothing hole on which the daring (and strong) may drive the green, but there is no margin for error.

Of the completely new holes, the par-5 3rd provides excitement for spectators when the professionals go for glory with a long carry over a lake to an angled green, hoping for that heroic eagle putt.

CARD OF THE BRABAZON COURSE

	yards	par		yards	par
1	411	4	10	311	4
2	379	4	11	419	4
3	538	5	12	208	3
4	442	4	13	384	4
5	408	4	14	190	3
6	395	4	15	545	5
7	177	3	16	413	4
8	428	4	17	564	5
9	433	4	18	473	4
Out	3,611	36	In	3,507	36
Total	7,118 yards	par 72			

The Berkshire

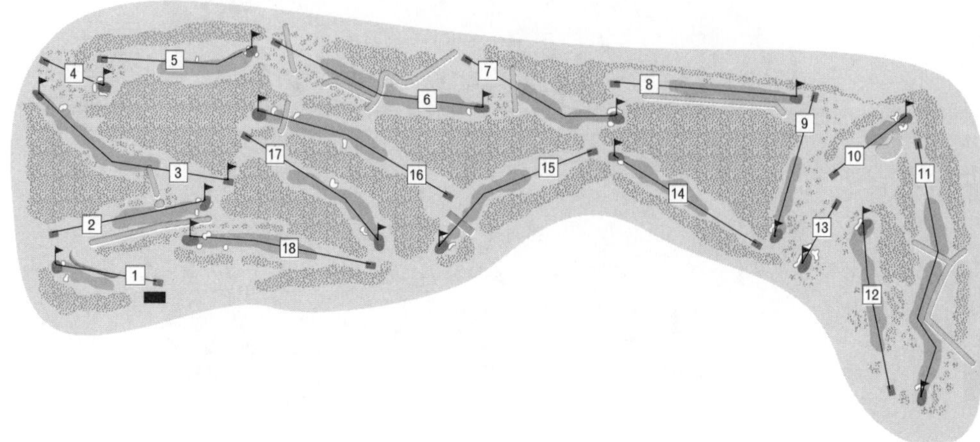

The Berkshire is privileged to have two courses of equal standing, laid out on Crown land in the late 1920s by Herbert Fowler. This was once a royal hunting forest, and the courses' barrel bridges are a legacy of Queen Anne's reign, enabling her carriage to cross streams while following the hunt. The Berkshire is closely associated with amateur golf – its own Berkshire Trophy is one of the highlights of the amateur year – and therefore the temptation has always been resisted to lengthen either course unnaturally. The courses, however, are no easier than their longer neighbours, such as Wentworth, because most of the fairways are narrowed between trees or bunkers at driving length.

The Red Course is just slightly longer than the Blue, and is unusual in having six par 5s and six par 3s. Two of its short holes are celebrated. The 10th is a 188-yard, all-or-nothing shot across a valley to a narrow, angled green surrounded by steep drops. The 16th is even longer, 221 yards from the white plates, with a narrow entrance between bunkers. Of the par 4s, the 4th and 8th with their raised greens stand out.

The Blue Course is slightly more conventional in the disposition of its holes, yet its 1st is by far the harder, a long compulsory carry over a heathery valley to a distant green. There are some excellent, shorter par 4s, such as the 7th with its fairway curving sharply round a mound as it heads for a green attractively framed by the trees. The sequence of closing par 4s is handsome and demanding, especially the sterling 16th with its difficult carry over bunkers and a stream to a raised green.

CARD OF THE BLUE COURSE

	yards	par		yards	par
1	217	3	10	199	3
2	344	4	11	477	5
3	475	5	12	355	4
4	153	3	13	154	3
5	330	4	14	363	4
6	476	5	15	406	4
7	364	4	16	452	4
8	404	4	17	378	4
9	310	4	18	403	4
Out	3,073	36	In	3,187	35
Total	6,260 yards	par 71			

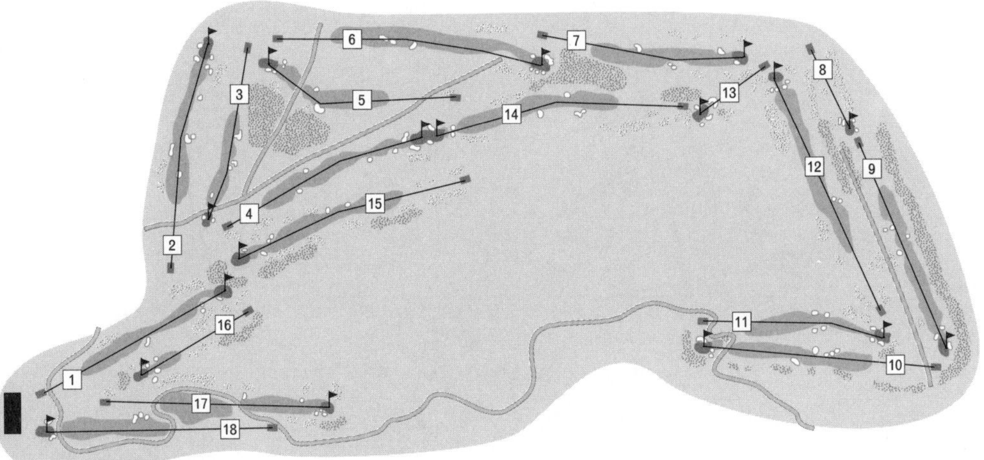

Since the first time it hosted the Open Championship, in 1931, Carnoustie has had a reputation as the toughest of all the Open courses. This was reinforced in the 1999 Open, when the course had been set up – controversially – with excessively narrow fairways and impossibly deep rough, and great players were reduced to hacking like beginners.

Golf is thought to have been played at Carnoustie for 500 years, the Championship course evolving slowly since the mid-19th century until it acquired its current form in 1926, when James Braid made the last major alterations. It is long – well over 7,300 yards for the Open – and exceptionally tight and, to score well, straightness is of even greater value than length off the tee. The ground is flat, and there are none of the towering sand hills of other famous links to offer shelter from the wind, which must be faced from every angle – the only stretch of consecutive holes running in more or less the same direction is that from the 13th to the 16th.

There are few weaknesses in the Carnoustie defensive armament. Braid's bunkering pressurizes every tee shot, and there are some difficult decisions to be made, such as whether to risk the narrow Hogan's Alley on the long 6th, with the danger of going out-of-bounds, or to drive safely to the right but then having to play the second shot to the narrowest part of the fairway where a burn cuts in from the right. The Barry Burn makes the finish fearsome, snaking back and forth across the 17th and 18th fairways. It was in its murky waters that Jean Van de Velde's Open Championship aspirations were literally washed away in 1999. Discretion is essential to survive at Carnoustie.

CARD OF THE CHAMPIONSHIP COURSE

	yards	par		yards	par
1	407	4	10	466	4
2	462	4	11	383	4
3	342	4	12	479	4
4	412	4	13	169	3
5	411	4	14	515	5
6	578	5	15	472	4
7	412	4	16	250	3
8	183	3	17	459	4
9	474	4	18	487	4
Out	3,681	36	In	3,680	35
Total	7,361 yards	par 71			

50

Celtic Manor

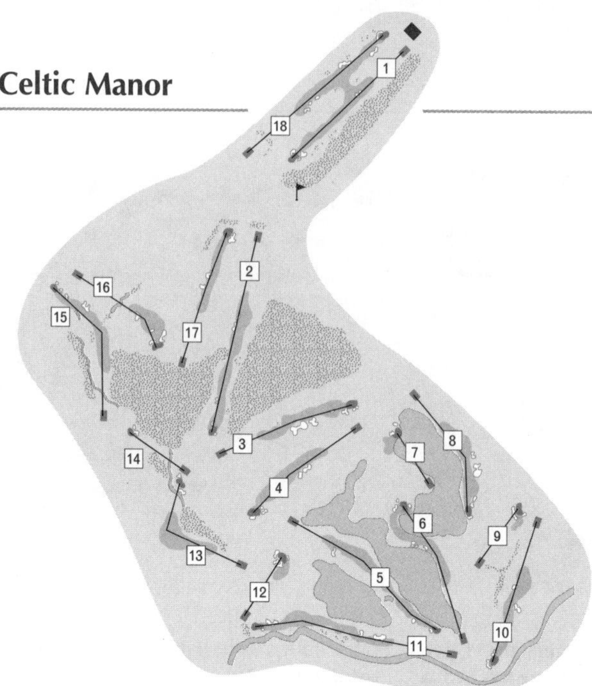

Wentwood Hills at Celtic Manor was one of the last courses to be opened in the 20th century. It is a fitting memorial to the designer Robert Trent Jones Senior, who died in the summer of 2000, at the age of 93. Jones was one of the greatest, most prolific and influential of all golf architects, and for Wentwood Hills he collaborated with his son, Robert II, himself a very prominent golf designer. No fewer than 20 US Opens and 12 USPGAs have been played on Jones Senior's courses – an unrivalled tally. Of Welsh ancestry, Jones contributed three thought-provoking designs at Celtic Manor: Coldra Woods, Roman Road and Wentwood Hills.

One of the most spectacular courses ever built in the UK, Wentwood Hills is laid out over a remarkable site, beginning and ending on rolling high ground with entrancing views. The middle part of the round is played through a series of lakes and ponds beside a tidal river. Linking these two elements are a number of mountainous holes, which first plunge spectacularly and then climb steeply through the woods. Everything is on a gargantuan scale: the course is 6,661 yards long from the forward yellow tees, though two of the most fascinating holes are the shortest par 4s. The 13th is an energetic dog-leg laid out in such a way as to tempt the big hitter to cut off all of the curve – almost certainly suicidally – while the 16th climbs over a bunker-plagued hill. Star billing, probably, must be reserved for the subtle 6th, a strategic par 4 involving two water carries, an impish hole on which all is not revealed at once.

CARD OF THE WENTWOOD HILLS COURSE

	yards	par		yards	par
1	471	4	10	440	4
2	613	5	11	621	5
3	440	4	12	211	3
4	413	4	13	395	4
5	565	5	14	206	3
6	436	4	15	456	4
7	190	3	16	340	4
8	416	4	17	423	4
9	213	3	18	554	5
Out	3,757	36	In	3,646	36
Total	7,403 yards	par 72			

County Louth

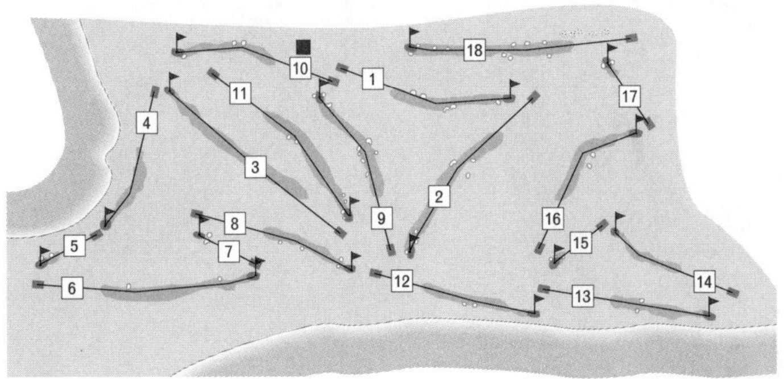

Ireland's leading 72-hole amateur strokeplay event, the East of Ireland Championship, has been held at County Louth ever since 1941. Right from the start it became almost the personal property of the great Irish amateur Joe Carr, who won this event no fewer than 12 times. Although the club was founded in the 1890s, the present course dates from the late 1930s, when the flamboyant Tom Simpson made the most of the natural resources of this archetypal linksland, which feels surprisingly remote despite being only just off the main Dublin-Belfast road outside Drogheda.

To succeed on a Simpson-designed course, guile must be added to skill and strength. This strategy is exemplified on the shortest of the par 4s, the 14th, which is one of the star holes despite needing only a drive and pitch, and being bunkerless. The tiny green is raised up above heaving ground and, unless the pitch is precisely judged, anxious scrambling will surely follow. The par 3s, too, seem not to need great length for their defence, the longest of them being only 179 yards from the very back. Again, just to miss the green by a whisker is likely to call for the deftest of touches with the pitch shot simply to hold the ball on these firm and speedy putting surfaces.

At County Louth, the present-day order of play has ensured an even spread of the finest holes throughout the round, with the 1st and 3rd standing out early on. The run along the coast from the 12th is seaside golf of the highest order, with the narrow approaches to the 12th and 13th particularly demanding. Bunkering in such terrain is often superfluous, so the six traps governing the drive at the tough 9th come as a rude shock, as does the one guarding the right front of the green.

CARD OF THE COURSE

	yards	par		yards	par
1	433	4	10	398	4
2	482	5	11	481	5
3	544	5	12	410	4
4	344	4	13	421	4
5	158	3	14	332	4
6	531	5	15	152	3
7	163	3	16	388	4
8	407	4	17	179	3
9	419	4	18	541	5
Out	3,481	37	In	3,302	36
Total	6,783 yards	par 73			

Cruden Bay

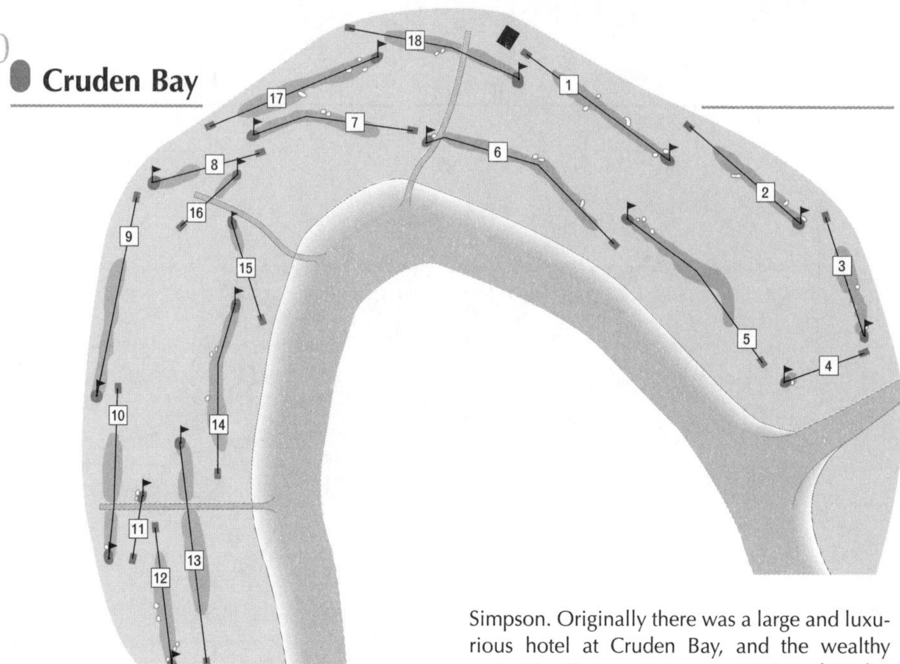

Cruden Bay is a period piece. No one would design holes in quite the same way today – there are blind shots, for example – but its qualities are such that the thinking golfer will feel a real sense of achievement at solving some of the many problems posed by its designer, Tom Simpson. Originally there was a large and luxurious hotel at Cruden Bay, and the wealthy eccentric Simpson was commissioned to lay out a golf course as one of the facilities for its guests. Many players reckon this to be Simpson's finest work, which is high praise indeed, for a number of his courses in France and Belgium are certainly of the first rank. The hotel did not survive the Second World War but, thankfully, the golf course was saved.

The course runs through the sand dunes in a figure of eight so that both the inward and outward holes enjoy proximity to the sea, and at many points throughout the round there are inspiring views. The player, however, must concentrate on the golf, for Simpson's cunning is much in evidence. He himself described the 8th as 'mischievous, subtle and provocative'. It may be only 258 yards long, and, although a par 4, has been played as a par 3, but there is serious trouble down the hill to the right. Both long holes cross streams, and on the 6th the water and a deep bunker guard the front of the green, making the approach tricky from any range. There are blind shots to the greens on the 14th and 15th, and the final hole was one of Simpson's favourites; it is not the most spectacular at Cruden Bay but is a genuine seaside special, with humps and hollows deflecting weak shots.

CARD OF THE COURSE

	yards	par		yards	par
1	416	4	10	385	4
2	339	4	11	149	3
3	286	4	12	320	4
4	193	3	13	550	5
5	454	4	14	397	4
6	529	5	15	239	3
7	392	4	16	182	3
8	258	4	17	428	4
9	462	4	18	416	4
Out	3,329	36	In	3,066	34
Total	6,395 yards	par 70			

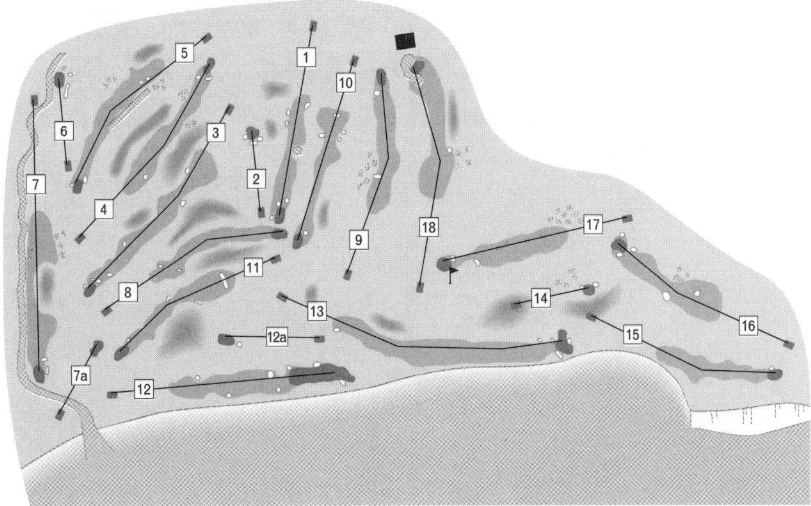

Although it opened only in 1993, The European has already had its 7th hole included in the world's 100 greatest holes. It has also been ranked among the best courses not only in Ireland but also the world, being placed world 28th by *Golfer's Companion*. After 30 years as a golf writer and course designer, Pat Ruddy decided he wanted to own his own golf course, so he built The European. The chosen site was ideal, with its towering sand dunes and marshlands, and the opportunity to route holes along the cliffs, beside the beach and into Hades itself. Aware that genuine linksland is a rare commodity, Ruddy's philosophy has been to keep human intervention well hidden, utilizing natural features to deceive the golfer's eye on the length of a shot or the width of a fairway. Ruddy's original thinking is apparent in his building of 20 holes. Why waste good golfing land once you have reached 18 holes? Why not stay out in the fresh air a little longer?

The par-4 7th may be the star hole tactically, but the 10th is also a hole on which intelligent golf pays off. There, despite the width of the fairway, the player needs to place the drive precisely, to open up the green through a narrow gap in the dunes. On the par-4 12th, the green has been lengthened to 127 yards, apparently to encourage three-putting, while the green on the enormously long 13th is far wider than it is deep, making some very tricky pin positions available. The one concession to modern course architecture is the horseshoe-shaped lake enveloping the left side of the final green. Water, in the form of the Irish Sea, also threatens the slice on holes 12, 13 and 15.

CARD OF THE COURSE:

	yards	par		yards	par
1	392	4	10	417	4
2	160	3	11	389	4
3	499	5	12	459	4
4	452	4	13	596	5
5	409	4	14	165	3
6	187	3	15	401	4
7	470	4	16	415	4
8	415	4	17	391	4
9	427	4	18	445	4
Out	3411	35	In	3678	36
Total	7089 yards	par 71			

Formby

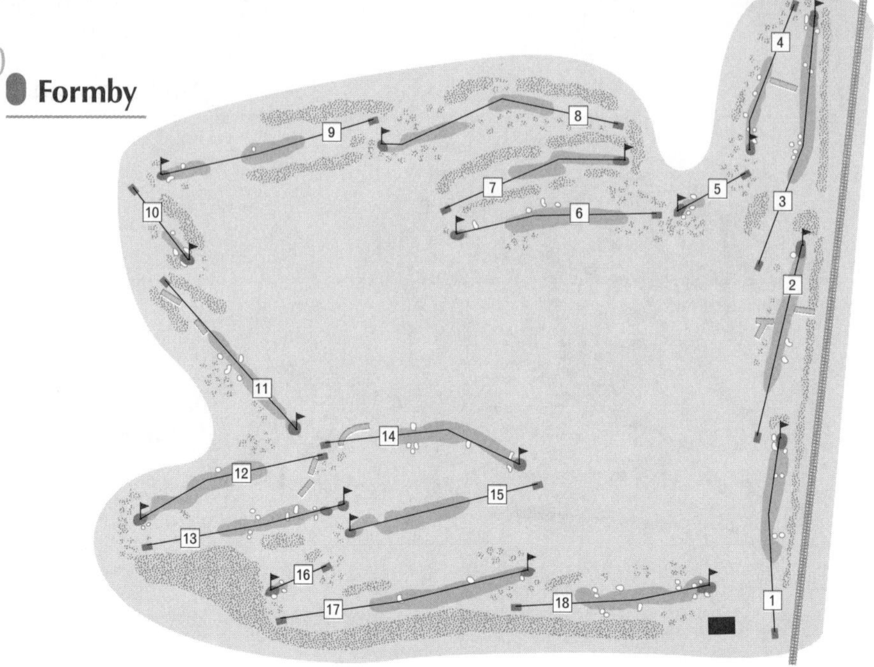

Formby is unquestionably the most beautiful of the many top rate links courses between Liverpool and Southport, running through heather and sand dunes and set against a backdrop of pines. There is an imposing grandeur to its enormous clubhouse, too, however much it may resemble a Victorian railway station. Members of long-standing might mourn the passing of the old holes, abandoned in the face of coastal erosion, but their replacements are some of the best Formby has to offer. From the championship tees, ten of the twelve par 4s are more than 400 yards long, yet length alone will not conquer the course. Wiliness is needed to overcome the tight bunkering and gentle undulations of the original holes, while only the most committed play will avoid punishment on the hillier new holes as they twist and turn through the pines.

The course builds gradually, beginning on gentle, heathery ground alongside the railway, before the short 5th leads off into wilder country. When driving on the 7th, courage is needed to believe the marker post as the fairway tilts wildly and the steeply sloping green can only be found on the correct line. It is much the same approaching the 8th green, which is cunningly protected by its elevation and a shoulder of the dunes. It needs no bunker. Shaping shots according to the lie of the land is made more complicated by the frequent changes of direction, bringing the wind into play from all angles, and each green is protected in a different manner: for example, the 6th is on the far side of mounds, the 11th raised up, and the 15th beyond the dunes.

CARD OF THE COURSE

	yards	par		yards	par
1	435	4	10	215	3
2	403	4	11	422	4
3	538	5	12	421	4
4	312	4	13	431	4
5	183	3	14	431	4
6	428	4	15	403	4
7	388	4	16	127	3
8	493	5	17	494	5
9	450	4	18	419	4
Out	3,630	37	In	3,363	35
Total	6,993 yards	par 72			

Ganton

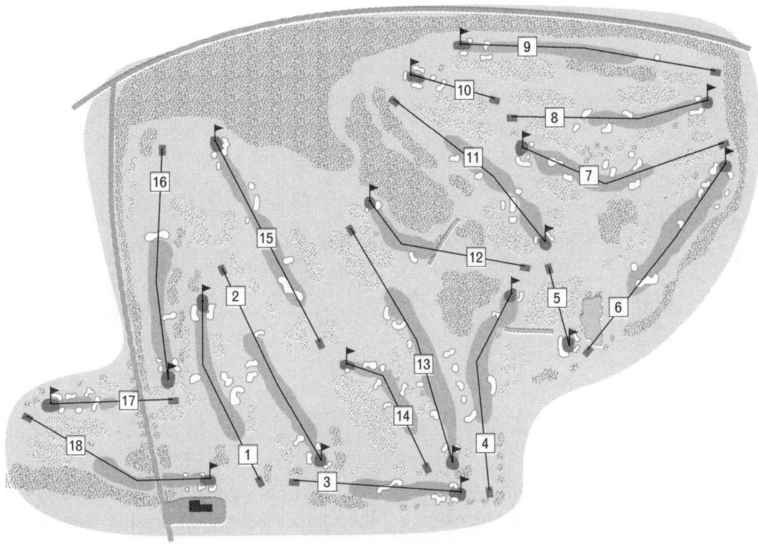

There are few more blessed places to play golf than Ganton, in all respects a seaside links, despite its rural setting in the peaceful Vale of Pickering. Ganton is the only inland course ever to host the Amateur Championship (which it has done three times), and the presence there of the Ryder Cup (1949), Curtis Cup (2000) and Walker Cup (2003) confirms its undoubted pedigree. Ganton's championship examination paper is one of persistent and intelligent probing – not outright assault – and its immediate charms lull many a golfer into a false sense of security.

As collections of bunkers go, Ganton's is rarely equalled, either for depth or for quantity. There is also its length, of course, and only the strongest will aspire to reaching the greens of the par-4 6th or 15th in two shots, and the par-3 17th in an even more improbable single blow. It is, however, the subtle challenge of holes such as the 3rd with its cunningly bunkered green, the 4th with a lovely carry across a devious depression or the 11th with its cross-bunkers, which gain the immediate praises of golfers of all abilities. Even the shortest of par 4s, the 14th, is no giveaway with its penal bunkering, while the 12th invites an overambitious skirmish with the trees. Everything is summed up in a brilliant final hole: although not the strongest hole on the card, this is a clever test of wisdom and nerve under competition conditions. It is a classic 'cape' hole on which the best line for the drive over a sandy waste offers the least margin for error, with tall trees closing in on either side.

CARD OF THE COURSE

	yards	par		yards	par
1	373	4	10	168	3
2	445	4	11	417	4
3	334	4	12	363	4
4	406	4	13	524	5
5	157	3	14	282	4
6	470	4	15	461	4
7	435	4	16	448	4
8	414	4	17	249	3
9	504	5	18	434	4
Out	3,538	36	In	3,346	35
Total	6,884 yards	par 71			

Gleneagles

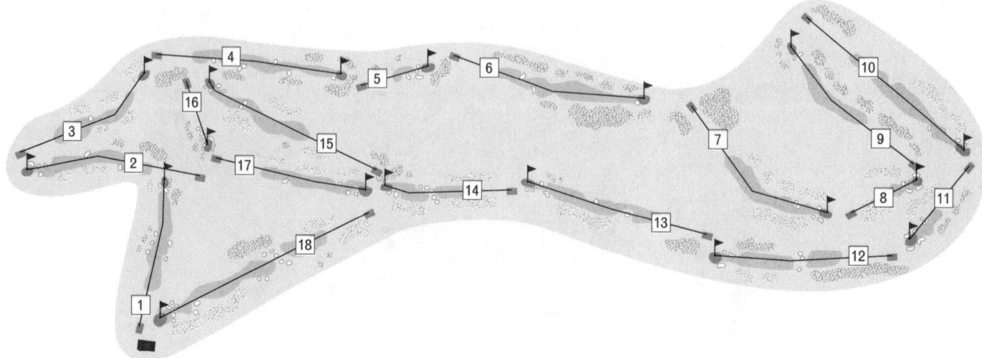

Television has made the closing holes of the King's course at Gleneagles familiar to many people, especially the par-5 18th, which careers down the hillside in front of a truly grand hotel. It was the General Manager of the Caledonian Railway Company, Donald Matheson, who conceived the idea of this hotel, a 'Riviera in the Highlands' to which royalty, the nobility and the simply wealthy would travel along his railway lines. The project was interrupted by the First World War, and the hotel did not officially open until 1924, but by then James Braid had finished work on two of his masterpieces, the King's and Queen's courses. Many professional tournaments have been held over the King's, but it was as he stood on the 1st tee of the Queen's that Lee Trevino famously remarked, 'If Heaven is as good as this, I sure hope they have some tee times left.' Jack Nicklaus designed a third course, the PGA Centenary, which was opened in 1993; it is in excess of 7,000 yards in length.

The King's course boasts a magnificent mountain setting, with ravishing views on every hole. One of the toughest holes is undoubtedly the 4th, a very long par 4 that climbs through a narrow valley. Not everything is as stiff, though, with engaging shorter par 4s such as the tumbling 3rd and entertaining 14th to amuse. The 13th, Braid's Brawest, is renowned, a long par 4 on which the drive must avoid a ridge and bunker if there is to be any hope of finding the plateau green abundantly protected with yet more ridges and sand – ridges being a feature of Gleneagles fairways. To the professionals, the 18th is only a drive and pitch, since they have no difficulty in clearing the bunker-lined ridge 250 yards out from the tee.

CARD OF THE KING'S COURSE

	yards	par		yards	par
1	362	4	10	499	5
2	436	4	11	230	3
3	374	4	12	442	4
4	466	4	13	464	4
5	178	3	14	309	4
6	480	5	15	459	4
7	444	4	16	158	3
8	178	3	17	377	4
9	409	4	18	525	5
Out	3,327	35	In	3,463	36
Total	6,790 yards	par 71			

Gullane

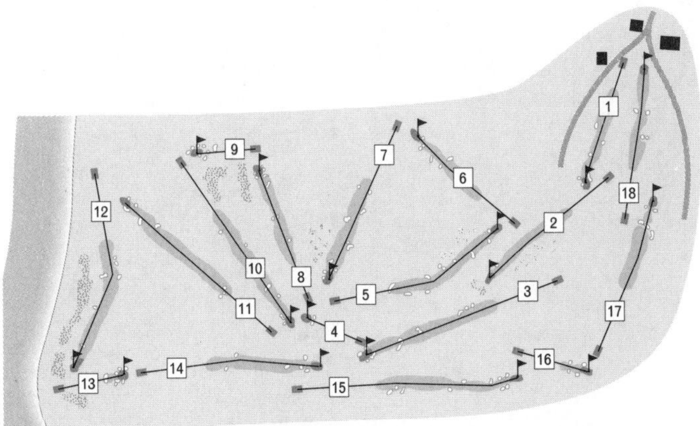

Gullane's turf is reputed to be the finest in all Scotland, and its No. 1 course will pleasantly surprise many who visit the ancient golfing village of Gullane for the first time. It could not be more different from its illustrious – but flat and relatively featureless – neighbours Muirfield and Luffness New, because it bestrides an outcrop of basalt rock to give what Bernard Darwin described as 'the best view in golf'. This unusually hilly linksland was formed centuries ago when the wind blew sand from the shores of Aberlady Bay to cover the rock, its saltiness contributing to the establishment of the traditional seaside grasses, marrams, bents and fescues. The No. 1 has been a frequent final qualifying course when the Open Championship has been held at Muirfield, as has the No. 2, a slightly shorter course in length but not in character.

The 1st, a short par 4, starts beside the village street, a hole the great amateur Joe Carr once drove during Open qualifying. Gradually the length builds as the hill is climbed until, standing on the 7th tee, the summit has been reached and a particularly inviting downhill drive follows. Time, however, should be made to drink in the celebrated views over the gentle hills and farmlands of the Lothians, and over the Firth of Forth northwards towards the hills of Fife. The golf then moves towards the shore with the 10th, 11th and 12th covering almost a mile between them, a notably demanding stretch. The short holes are all tightly bunkered, and the 16th, along a ridge, often deceives for length. Another inspiring downhill drive awaits on the 17th before the round ends as it began, in the heart of the village.

CARD OF THE NO. 1 COURSE

	yards	par		yards	par
1	302	4	10	466	4
2	379	4	11	471	4
3	496	5	12	480	5
4	144	3	13	170	3
5	450	4	14	435	4
6	324	4	15	537	5
7	398	4	16	186	3
8	332	4	17	390	4
9	151	3	18	355	4
Out	2,976	35	In	3,490	36
Total	6,466 yards	par 71			

Hillside

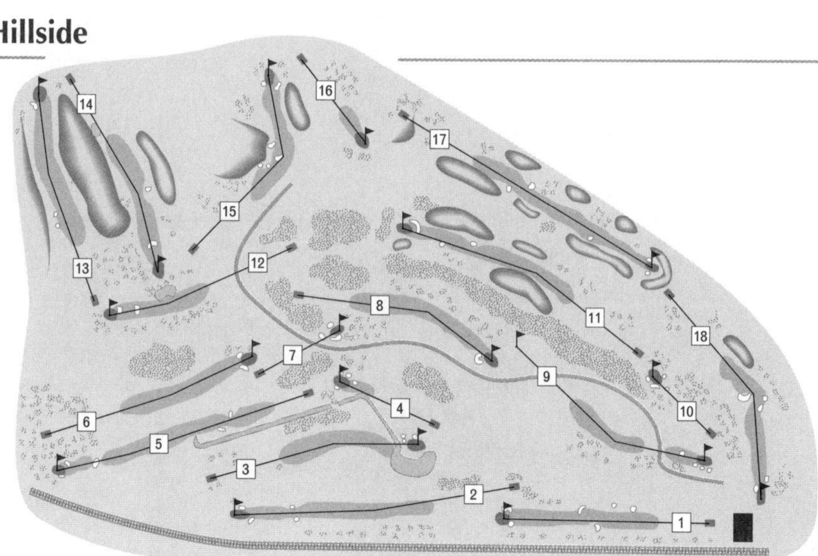

Hillside is one of Southport's triumvirate of great courses. It is separated from Royal Birkdale by only a footpath, and from Southport and Ainsdale by a railway line, putting it right in the heart of that wonderful eruption of sand hills stretching from Southport almost to the very gates of Liverpool. Hillside staged the 1979 Amateur Championship and the 1982 PGA Championship, which saw Tony Jacklin win his last professional title.

The railway is a constant threat over the first couple of holes, on relatively flat ground, while the 3rd is quite a tough proposition with a tricky drive to a curving fairway followed by a demanding approach over a ditch to a well-bunkered green above a pond. Good position from the tee is required on all holes, and especially on the dog-legs that give the 6th, 8th and 9th much character.

After the turn, it is off into the sand hills with a vengeance. The lovely 10th, set off against a stand of pines, is surrounded by exceedingly deep bunkers. Views are stunning as the 11th tee is reached: out to the right are Birkdale, a heaving mass of dunes, and the breaking waves of the Irish Sea beyond. Far below is the thin ribbon of fairway curving through its own private valley to a green far in the distance. A pond to the right of the 12th is all too easily driven, and the green is cunningly protected by a ridge and bunkers. Bunkers in the corner of the dog-leg are a feature of the attractive 15th fairway, while the impressive 16th needs no bunker at all, so skilfully is it sited. Another magnificent vista and another star hole await on the 17th tee, while the 18th is on the flat, bunkered to ensure a long final shot.

CARD OF THE CHAMPIONSHIP COURSE

	yards	par		yards	par
1	399	4	10	147	3
2	525	5	11	508	5
3	402	4	12	399	4
4	195	3	13	398	4
5	504	5	14	400	4
6	413	4	15	422	4
7	176	3	16	199	3
8	405	4	17	548	5
9	433	4	18	440	4
Out	3,452	36	In	3,461	36
Total	6,913 yards		par 72		

Hunstanton

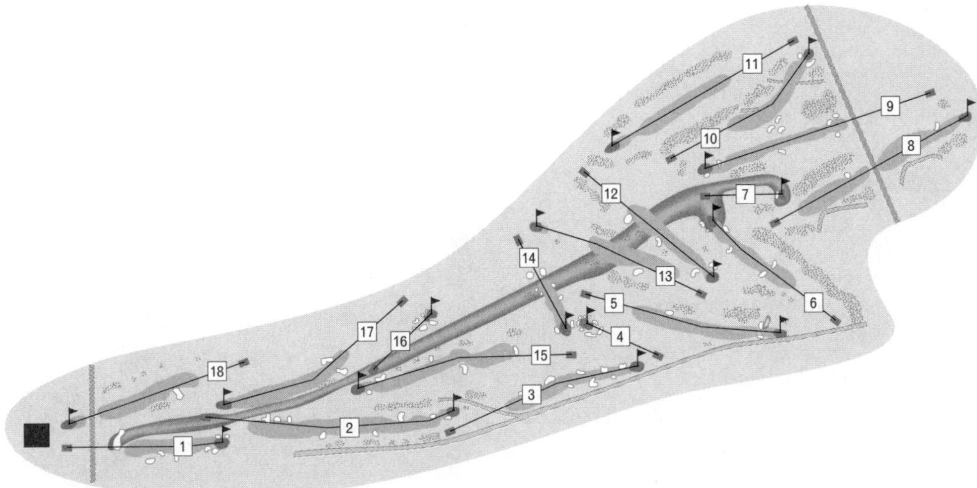

Hunstanton's greens may well be the quickest and truest in England, day in, day out. They put a strict premium on approach work on this demanding links, which is laid out along a spine of dunes overlooking the Wash.

The start is critical, with a substantial carry over a gaping bunker to an undulating fairway. Then, for a time, the golf is inland in character, although the waters of the River Hun punish the slice on these lengthy holes. On the 6th, play reverts to the dunes in impressive style, with a precision pitch to a domed green attended by big drops. The par-3 7th is equally uncompromising, with a compulsory carry over a chasm, a broad, steep-faced bunker on the direct line, and all manner of horrors to either side. Taking play out to the far end of the course, the 8th ought not to trouble unduly, but it is easy to slice out of bounds and those who know the quirks of the green have a considerable advantage.

Into the wind the carry to the 9th fairway is formidable, with bunkers either side of the fairway the least of the perils. The contours of the 10th green are likely to confound many, while the narrow fairway of the 11th is located only by the straightest of hitters.

However, Hunstanton is remembered most for the stretch from the 12th to the 14th, gloriously old-fashioned holes straddling the dunes. The 13th is one of the great idiosyncrasies of golf, yet a hole that seems utterly right in this context. From there, the finish is splendid: the 15th narrow along a valley fairway, the 16th a heavily bunkered downhill par 3, the 17th a superb two-shotter climbing on to the dunes, and the home hole with its tricky approach across low ground.

CARD OF THE COURSE

	yards	par		yards	par
1	343	4	10	375	4
2	532	5	11	439	4
3	443	4	12	358	4
4	172	3	13	387	4
5	436	4	14	219	3
6	337	4	15	478	5
7	166	3	16	189	3
8	505	5	17	445	4
9	513	5	18	398	4
Out	3,447	37	In	3,288	35

Total 6,735 yards par 72

The K Club

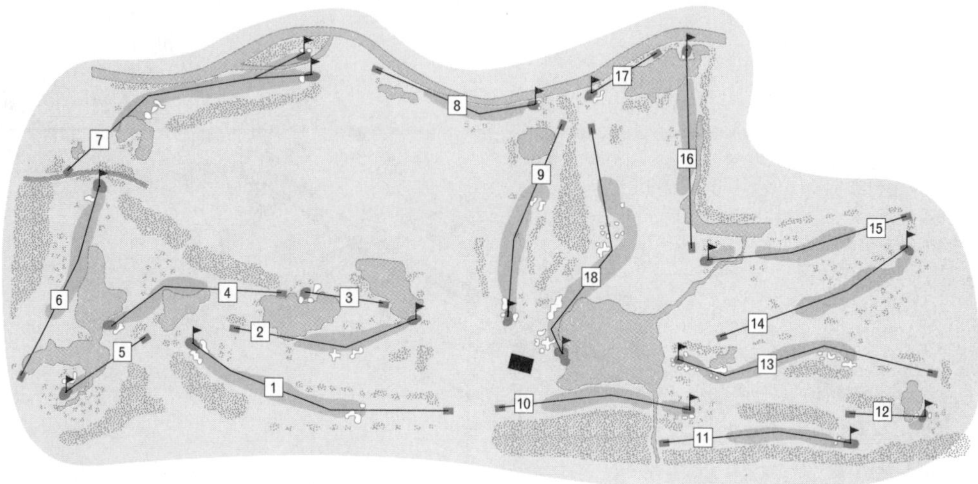

When in 2005 the Ryder Cup comes to the K Club, it will be the first time the Cup has been staged in Ireland, and Arnold Palmer's course is well suited to provide the risk-taking drama that is such a feature of these matches. Like all good courses, it will succumb to great play, as was demonstrated by Darren Clarke's course record 60, scored during the 1999 European Open. The K Club, or Kildare Hotel and Country Club, is not just about professional golfers and their daring deeds, however. Outside tournament time, this is one of the most peaceful spots on earth – a historic parkland along the banks of the River Liffey, in the heart of Kildare racing country.

The Liffey comes into play on several holes, as do lakes, ponds, streams, waterfalls, ancient trees and extravagantly sculpted bunkers – the condition of the course being commensurate with the green fee, one of the highest in Europe. Palmer is commemorated on the 13th, the sort of hole that, in his prime, he would have attacked. This par 5 needs a daring carry from the tee over a bunker-riddled hill if there is to be any chance of reaching the tightly trapped green in two. Even longer is the 7th, a monster hole finishing with a pitch over the Liffey to a green set on an island in its limpid waters. The 8th, a crescent-shaped hole of the utmost simplicity – and danger – also skirts the river. Fittingly, Palmer contrived to end the round with a death-or-glory hole, a par 5 at the sort of length every professional expects to reach in two. The green juts out into a lake and is guarded by sand on the other side. Under the pressures of a tournament, it provides a nail-biting finish.

CARD OF THE COURSE

	yards	par		yards	par
1	584	5	10	418	4
2	408	4	11	413	4
3	173	3	12	170	3
4	402	4	13	568	5
5	213	3	14	416	4
6	446	4	15	447	4
7	606	5	16	395	4
8	375	4	17	173	3
9	434	4	18	537	5
Out	3,641	36	In	3,537	36
Total	7,178 yards	par 72			

Killarney

No golf course in Ireland can quite match Killarney for the magic of its setting. Its courses wind through the gentle woodlands of the Western Demesne, part of what was once the vast estate of the Earl of Kenmare. Beyond, the splendour of the Kerry Mountains is reflected in the crystal clear waters of Lough Leane on whose shores some of the prettiest of all golf holes are laid out.

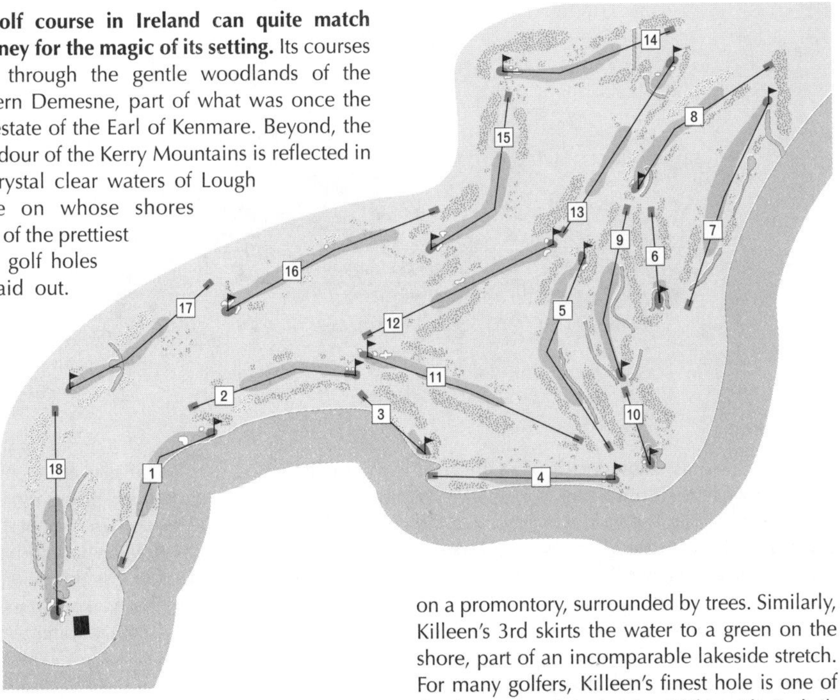

No wonder Henry Longhurst said of Killarney, 'What a lovely place to die!'

Today's courses have their origins in one opened in 1939, designed by Sir Guy Campbell. At about that time, Lord Castlerosse, the larger-than-life London newspaper columnist and socialite, succeeded to the Kenmare title and immediately threw himself into developing the golf course. Although he did not live to see his changes come to fruition, he did create several superb holes that have survived to the present day. He also sowed the seeds of expansion, which was done in the 1970s when the Mahony's Point and Killeen courses came into being, and it was over the Killeen Course that Nick Faldo won the 1991 and 1992 Irish Opens.

Campbell's original closing holes now end the round on Mahony's Point, with the 18th one of the most famous of all finishing holes, a 196-yard par 3, all carry across a bay to a green set on a promontory, surrounded by trees. Similarly, Killeen's 3rd skirts the water to a green on the shore, part of an incomparable lakeside stretch. For many golfers, Killeen's finest hole is one of Castlerosse's originals, the 13th, with its brilliantly sited green beyond a stream.

CARD OF THE KILLEEN COURSE

	yards	par		yards	par
1	380	4	10	170	3
2	380	4	11	509	5
3	196	3	12	475	4
4	414	4	13	442	4
5	470	4	14	386	4
6	201	3	15	421	4
7	488	5	16	520	5
8	414	4	17	387	4
9	382	4	18	450	4
Out	3,325	35	In	3,760	37
Total	7,085 yards	par 72			

Lahinch

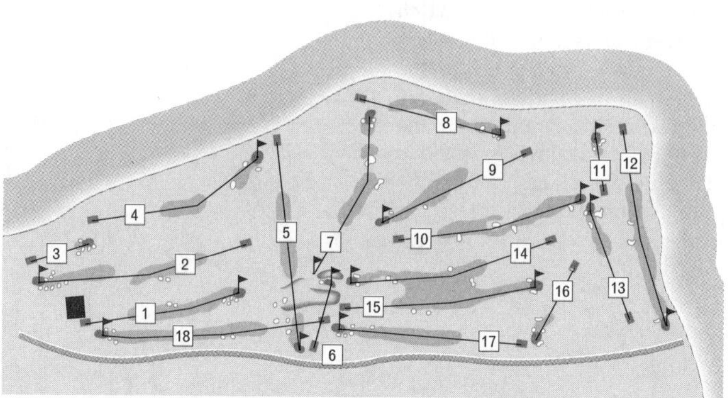

Lahinch is the most idiosyncratic of all the great links courses in the British Isles. It is often nicknamed the Irish St Andrews, which gives a fair impression of a course which is so distinctive that there is absolutely nothing else like it, and a town that eats, breathes and sleeps golf. Tradition also inhabits the local weather-forecasting, which consists simply of observing the goats. If they are somewhere out on the course there is a chance of finishing the round in the dry. If they are up by the clubhouse a drenching is probable.

CARD OF THE COURSE

	yards	par		yards	par
1	385	4	10	451	4
2	512	5	11	138	3
3	151	3	12	475	4
4	428	4	13	274	4
5	483	5	14	488	5
6	156	3	15	462	4
7	399	4	16	195	3
8	350	4	17	438	4
9	384	4	18	533	5
Out	3,248	36	In	3,454	36
Total	6,702 yards	par 72			

The two most famous holes at Lahinch – the 5th and 6th – are blind period pieces the like of which have been removed from most other prominent courses, yet here should remain preserved in aspic. The only problem with the par-5 5th, Klondyke, is that you may be hit by players driving from the 18th tee, the two fairways crossing. Those who detest blind shots will grumble about their second over a vast sand hill, but, with a little research, it is perfectly possible to deduce what is required.

The par-3 6th, the Dell, is no less controversial. The only indication of where the ball should be hit is a white stone set on the summit of what has been described as a three-storey dune. The green is wide but outrageously shallow and, it must be assumed, in the low ground on the far side. This is probably the only unaltered vestige of Tom Morris's original course, laid out in the 1890s. Dr Alister Mackenzie revised the course substantially in the 1920s, and the eccentricities of the 5th and 6th should not detract from the excellence of holes such as the 4th, 7th, 9th and 11th.

Muirfield

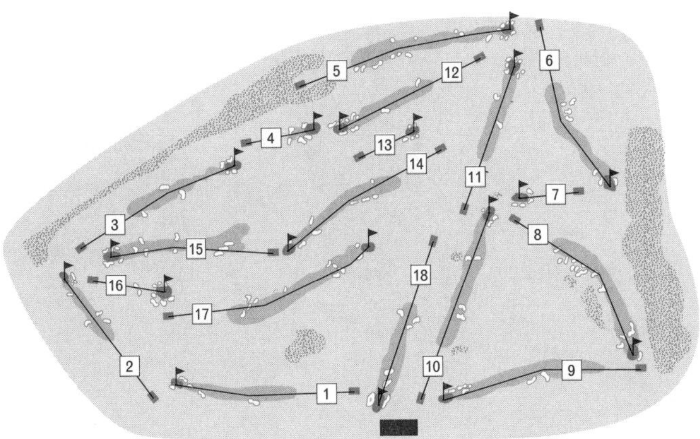

With only one blind drive, Muirfield is reckoned to be among the fairest of our great links. As Jack Nicklaus once described it, 'You can see where you are going and you get what you hit.'

The Honourable Company of Edinburgh Golfers, which first codified the rules of golf, dates back to 1744, and it played courses at Leith and Musselburgh before moving to its new course at Muirfield in 1891. It staged its inaugural Open Championship the following year, the first to be played over 72 holes, and in it the great English amateur Harold Hilton triumphed with a score of 305. The list of Muirfield Open Champions after Hilton is stunning: Harry Vardon (1896), James Braid (1901, 1906), Ted Ray (1912), Walter Hagen (1929), Alf Perry (1935), Henry Cotton (1948), Gary Player (1959), Jack Nicklaus (1966), Lee Trevino (1972), Tom Watson (1980), Nick Faldo (1987, 1992).

Muirfield was ahead of its time in being laid out in two concentric loops. These play in opposite directions, unlike the traditional out-and-back links, and, so, few consecutive holes run in the same direction. The wind must therefore be tackled from every quarter, with frequent changes. Lacking enormous dunes, it gives the impression of a gentleness that is somewhat misleading – the bunkering is imaginative and severe, the rough more verdant and clinging than might be expected.

Bunkering in the angles of the dog-legs makes holes such as the 6th and 8th particularly demanding from the tee, though straightness is equally imperative on the short holes, each of them with a very narrow green attended by exceptionally deep bunkers. Although the back nine is thought to be slightly easier than the front nine, it opens with a stern hole with penal rough, which 'still throbs from the thrashings of the great man's death throes' – after it had thwarted Arnold Palmer during the 1966 Open.

CARD OF THE MEDAL COURSE

	yards	par		yards	par
1	446	4	10	473	5
2	347	4	11	354	4
3	377	4	12	380	4
4	182	3	13	156	3
5	510	5	14	449	4
6	443	4	15	394	4
7	147	3	16	186	3
8	443	4	17	506	5
9	465	4	18	415	4
Out	3,360	35	In	3,313	36
Total	6,673 yards	par 71			

Nairn

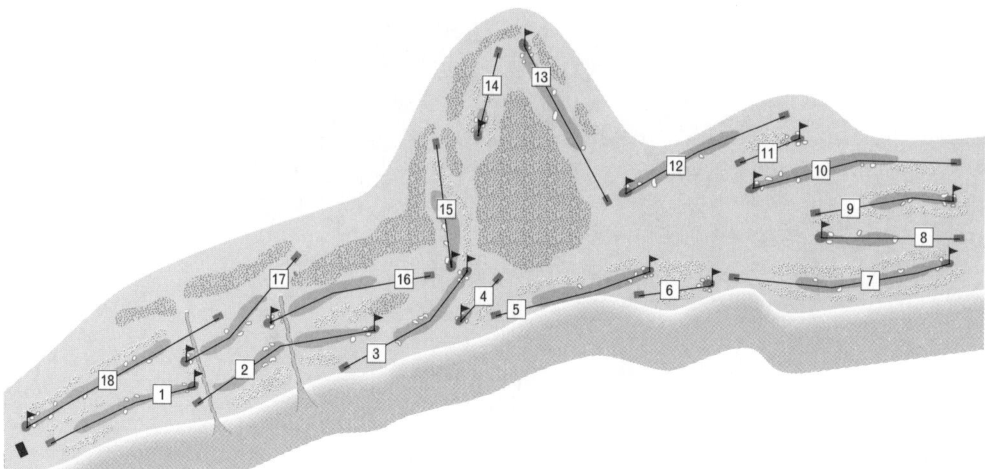

The beauty and fine golfing qualities of Nairn were brought to a vast audience when the 1999 Walker Cup was televised from there. Outstanding play on the second day enabled the Great Britain & Ireland team to come from behind to beat the Americans by a record margin of 15 points to 9. For that match the 7th, normally a par 5, was reduced to a 487-yard par 4, a tough proposition even for these talented players. For lesser mortals, it is quite possible to slice into the sea on six of the first seven holes, especially as they are usually played into the wind. Views across the Moray Firth to Black Isle are complemented nearer at hand by the purple heather and golden gorse, which await those who fail to find Nairn's narrow fairways. An excursion inland brings a contrasting touch of heathland to several holes on the back nine.

Scoring is said to be slightly easier going out, the par 4s not being overlong, though plentiful bunkers and a raised, sloping green call for solid shot-making on the 3rd, while the 5th fairway is perilously close to the beach. Tight bunkering is a feature of many greens, and the putting surface on the 8th slopes down from front to back, making it a difficult green to hit and hold. The hardest holes come together, from the 12th to the 14th. The par-4 12th fairway is threatened by bushes. There is trouble on both sides of the 13th fairway and the long, uphill approach to the green is frequently complicated by a cross-wind. Though downhill, the par-3 14th is also tough, exposed to the wind and with a very difficult green. On paper, the 15th appears to offer relief, but this par 4 features the tightest of drives and a tricky short pitch.

CARD OF THE COURSE

	yards	par		yards	par
1	395	4	10	536	5
2	486	5	11	160	3
3	396	4	12	444	4
4	144	3	13	431	4
5	385	4	14	219	3
6	183	3	15	306	4
7	550	5	16	425	4
8	355	4	17	377	4
9	359	4	18	554	5
Out	3,253	36	In	3,452	36
Total	6,705 yards	par 72			

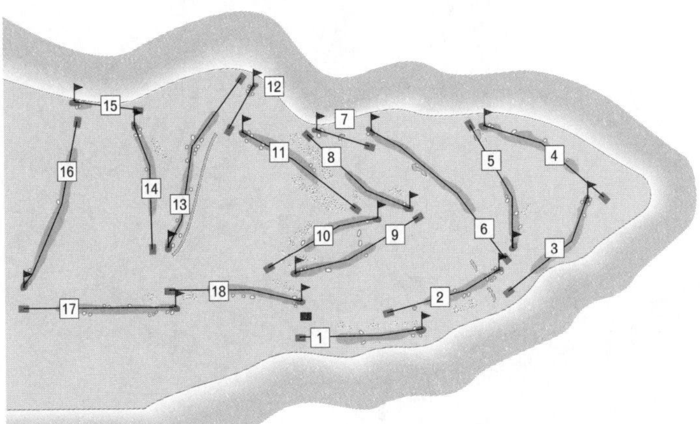

Portmarnock is one of the best tournament venues in the world, an opinion readily endorsed by the cream of the professionals who have competed there. The links at Portmarnock is almost an island, and in its early days it could be reached only by boat or, at low tide, by horse-drawn carriage. The Irish whiskey family, the Jamesons, had their own private golf course there – one of the earliest in Ireland. In 1894 they were approached by W.C. Pickeman and George Ross to lease the land for the construction of a first-class links. Terms were agreed and the first golf on the new course was played on Boxing Day of that year. By 1896 the course had been expanded to a full 18 holes and, as at Muirfield, it abandoned the traditional out-and-back principle of so many early courses, making the wind a very considerable factor in the defences of the course. Portmarnock still retains this layout, which has been judiciously upgraded over the years.

It is a long course and yet two of its most acclaimed holes are not outrageously so. Many would agree with Henry Cotton that the finest hole is the 14th, praise indeed from a man who lost an Irish Open by taking 7 here. The greatness lies in the elevation of the green beyond a ridge with two perfectly placed bunkers complicating the approach, whatever its length. Arnold Palmer holds the 15th in high regard, an awe-inspiring hole so close to the (out-of-bounds) beach that, when the wind is off the sea, the shot must be struck out over the sands to swing back towards the green. The putting surface is a narrow table top above tricky depressions and deep bunkers, so this hole has been the downfall of many fine golfers.

CARD OF THE COURSE

	yards	par		yards	par
1	394	4	10	370	4
2	411	4	11	428	4
3	398	4	12	155	3
4	474	4	13	566	5
5	397	4	14	411	4
6	603	5	15	190	3
7	184	3	16	578	5
8	401	4	17	473	4
9	438	4	18	411	4
Out	3,700	36	In	3,582	36
Total	7,282 yards		par 72		

Royal Birkdale

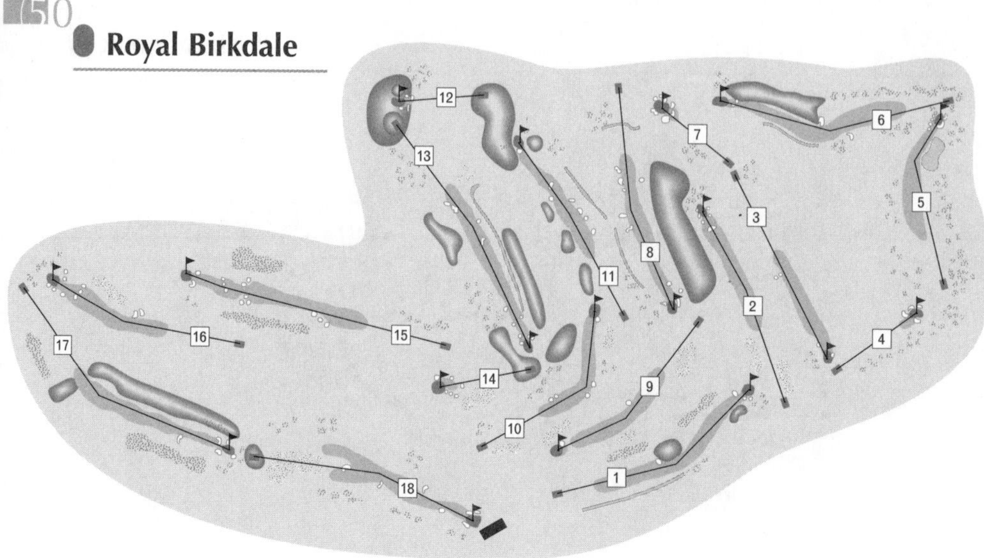

Birkdale was immediately acclaimed for its fairness and exceptional spectator viewing when, in 1954, it first hosted the Open Championship. This praise reflected the novel way in which the course had been laid out along the flat bottoms of the valleys between the dunes. Players' stances are rarely less than perfect, which is why the professionals rate Birkdale so highly. The Hawtree family, one of the great architectural dynasties, have long been associated with Birkdale, and Martin Hawtree redesigned and relaid all 18 greens for the 1998 Open. Each one is subtly borrowed, and many have potential for notably difficult pin positions.

One of the toughest holes opens the round. This par 4 features a tight drive between a mound and an out-of-bounds fence followed by an approach through mounds and bunkers to a secretive green. The dunes provide attractive situations for many greens and that on the 2nd is an example, delightfully framed in the folds of the land, backed by trees and raised up between its attendant bunkers. A bunker in mid-fairway 40 yards short of the putting surface is a major threat to the handicap golfer. Hawtree's remodelling of the 6th green has further strengthened an already difficult hole, a par 4 for the professionals but a par 5 for members and visitors. Only a drive of considerable length makes it past a big mound on the right, around which the fairway bends. Even then, there will be at least 200 yards to the green, high up on a bank behind bunkers – the shot almost certainly directly into the wind. Professionals record few birdies here. The wind is likely to oppose on the 15th and 16th, too, though, mercifully, it should assist on the two substantial finishing holes.

CARD OF THE COURSE

	yards	par		yards	par
1	449	4	10	403	4
2	421	4	11	408	4
3	407	4	12	183	3
4	203	3	13	498	4
5	344	4	14	198	3
6	480	4	15	544	5
7	177	3	16	416	4
8	457	4	17	547	5
9	411	4	18	472	4
Out	3,349	34	In	3,669	36
Total	7,018 yards	par 70			

Royal County Down

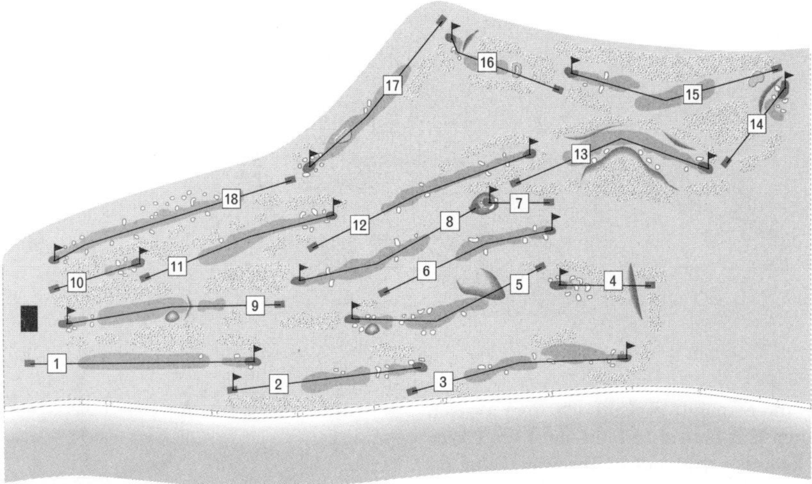

No golfer visiting Newcastle could fail to be astounded by the majesty of the Royal County Down's setting. Slieve Donard and the rest of the Mourne Mountains form the most imposing of backcloths, while Dundrum Bay and the Irish Sea sparkle out to the east, and the narrowest ribbons of fairway thread a tentative path through as impressive a set of sand dunes as could be imagined. Nor would any golfer with an ounce of wit fail to recognize the enormity of the challenge set by the course itself. As Donald Steel wrote, 'The Open Championship has been staged on courses that are not as good.'

Old Tom Morris received four golden guineas to lay out the course in 1889, and to this day many features from that time remain, not least a number of blind shots both from the tee and approaching the green. The fairways are surrounded by purple heather and golden gorse, beautiful to look at but savagely punishing. Innumerable bunkers litter the course, deep caverns topped off with bushy eyebrows of seaside grasses. Many greens, invariably swift, are slightly domed, immediately rejecting the wavering approach shot. Newcastle is very much the place for the traditional, bump-and-run approach.

Tom Watson rates the first 15 holes very highly in his affections, and few would disagree, when there are so many strong holes. Its collection of par 3s is as good as any, three of them with long carries over a sea of gorse and the 7th a tiny hill-top target. The par 4s are equally outstanding: on the 5th, for example, the daring are rewarded for clearing a high dune from the tee; and the 13th calls for a long straight drive or else a desperate blind approach over another sandy mountain.

CARD OF THE COURSE

	yards	par		yards	par
1	506	5	10	197	3
2	421	4	11	438	4
3	474	4	12	525	5
4	212	3	13	443	4
5	438	4	14	213	3
6	396	4	15	464	4
7	145	3	16	276	4
8	429	4	17	427	4
9	486	4	18	547	5
Out	3,507	35	In	3,530	36
Total	7,037 yards	par 71			

50

Royal Dornoch

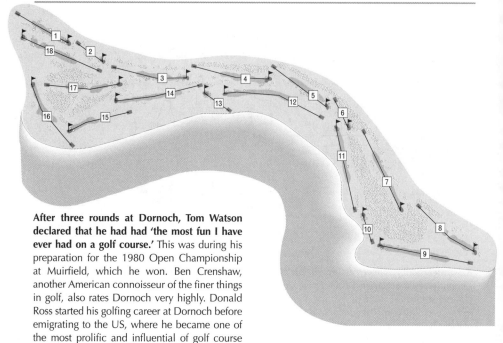

After three rounds at Dornoch, Tom Watson declared that he had had 'the most fun I have ever had on a golf course.' This was during his preparation for the 1980 Open Championship at Muirfield, which he won. Ben Crenshaw, another American connoisseur of the finer things in golf, also rates Dornoch very highly. Donald Ross started his golfing career at Dornoch before emigrating to the US, where he became one of the most prolific and influential of golf course architects in the early years of the 20th century. His designs reflected best Scottish practice.

The distinctive Dornoch feature that Ross exported was the raised green, as typified by those at Pinehurst No. 2. For this, the approach shot must be perfectly lined and weighted or it will surely be deflected into the bunkers and swales that surround these greens. Though Dornoch has been remodelled several times, principally under the guidance of Club Secretary John Sutherland, the character of the course has never been compromised, and there remains much of the historic atmosphere of the links first recorded in 1616.

One of Watson's favourite holes is the 5th. Although not a particularly long par 4, it calls for a precise tee shot to a well-bunkered, sloping fairway, to leave a reasonable pitch to the long, narrow green angled across the line of approach. All the short holes are first rate: the 2nd is very unforgiving if the green is missed, and the 6th lies on a hillside plateau among the gorse. Most famous of all is the 14th, Foxy, a long, bunkerless par 4 on which the fairway is narrow between mounds, and the green raised up across the line of play, so it is the very devil to find.

CARD OF THE COURSE

	yards	par		yards	par
1	331	4	10	177	3
2	184	3	11	450	4
3	414	4	12	557	5
4	427	4	13	180	3
5	354	4	14	445	4
6	163	3	15	358	4
7	463	4	16	402	4
8	437	4	17	405	4
9	529	5	18	456	4
Out	3,302	35	In	3,430	35
Total	6,732 yards	par 70			

Royal Liverpool

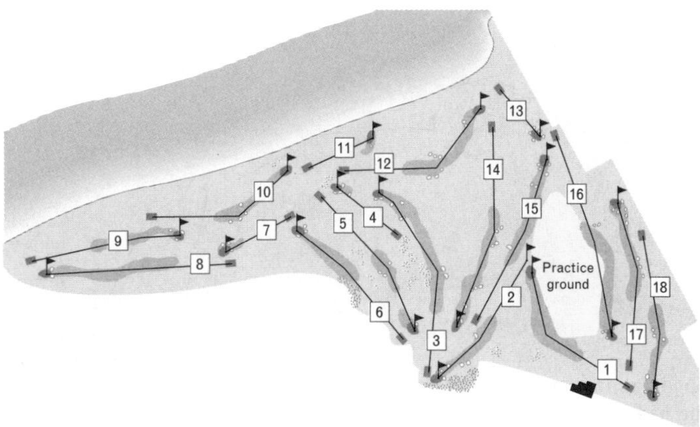

Royal Liverpool has been restored to the Open Championship roster. This welcome news, announced by the Royal & Ancient Golf Club in February 2001, will bring golf's premier tournament back to Hoylake for the first time since 1967, when Roberto de Vicenzo proved a popular winner. Unfortunately, since then, there was not sufficient space within the course boundaries to house the tented villages and media parks that are such a feature of modern championships. However, the recent purchase of land on a neighbouring site and the construction of an extensive practice ground on the other side of Meols Drive have at last provided that space.

Few alterations have had to be made to the course itself, one of the most complete examinations of a golfer's technique and courage imaginable. Donald Steel, the consultant architect, has reshaped only two holes – largely in the interests of safety – constructed a new 18th green and slightly revised the bunkering. Many will regret the demise of the old 17th, with its green so close to the road that it was possible to putt out-of-bounds, but the new hole retains much of the fear factor of the old.

Indeed, fear is a factor on many holes, such as the 1st on which it is all too easy to slice out-of-bounds on both the drive and second shot. Equally intimidating is the drive on the 6th, over the corner of an out-of-bounds orchard – a terrifying carry when the hole is played directly into the wind, as it frequently is. Length is at a premium throughout, and the new course will measure in excess of 7,200 yards, with only a single par 4 under 400 yards, the 9th, which is part of a lovely sequence in tumbling dunes at the far end of the course.

CARD OF THE COURSE

	yards	par		yards	par
1	429	4	10	412	4
2	413	4	11	200	3
3	525	5	12	455	4
4	200	3	13	159	3
5	448	4	14	547	5
6	422	4	15	459	4
7	198	3	16	558	5
8	525	5	17	435	4
9	392	4	18	430	4
Out	3,552	36	In	3,655	36
Total	7,207 yards	par 72			

50

Royal Lytham and St Annes

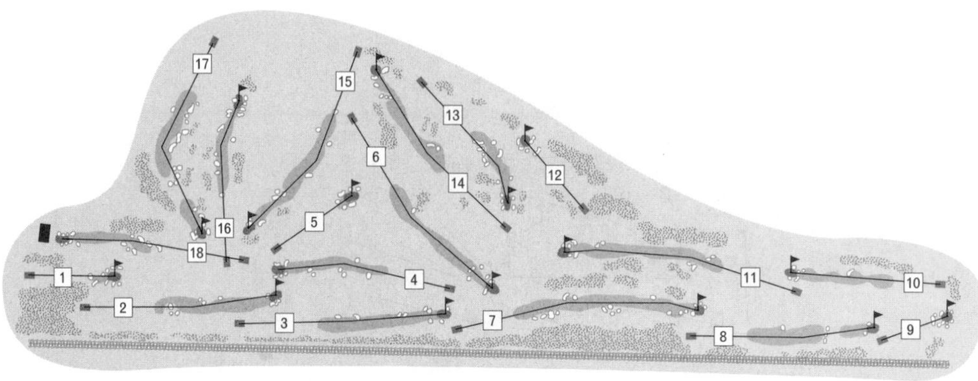

Royal Lytham enjoyed a fairy tale start to its long Open Championship history. A miraculous recovery shot on the 17th by Bobby Jones enabled him to overcome the challenges of Al Watrous and Walter Hagen to take the 1926 title. It was 70 years before another American, Tom Lehman, lifted the Claret Jug at Lytham. Miraculous recoveries were even more a part of the first Open won by Severiano Ballesteros, in 1979, when his driving took him to parts of the Lytham course few – other than the greenkeepers – had ever visited. After Tony Jacklin's 1969 Open victory there, European golfers had the confidence to believe that they could once again challenge the best Americans, South Africans and Australians, who had so dominated the majors since the Second World War.

Strangely, Lytham does not look like a typical Open venue, being a mile inland from the sea and surrounded by houses and a railway line. On a winter's day, with the wind howling across this barren landscape, it is bleak indeed. Lytham is also unusual in having a generous allocation of short par 4s, and yet a study of the record books shows that its winning scores have not been noticeably lower than at any of the other regular Open venues – with the obvious exception of Carnoustie in 1999.

The course is remorseless, especially over the back nine, with its exceptionally demanding 14th, 15th and 17th. Indeed, the final hole has wrecked the hopes and chances of a remarkable list of distinguished Championship contenders. The foundation of a good professional score is made on the way out, but, for the amateur, these holes are hardly easier, with a substantial par 3 to open the round, and out-of-bounds a real threat on the 2nd, 3rd and 8th – all strong two-shotters.

CARD OF THE COURSE

	yards	par		yards	par
1	206	3	10	334	4
2	437	4	11	542	5
3	457	4	12	198	3
4	393	4	13	342	4
5	212	3	14	445	4
6	490	5	15	463	4
7	553	5	16	357	4
8	418	4	17	467	4
9	164	3	18	414	4
Out	3,330	35	In	3,562	36
Total	6,892 yards	par 71			

Royal Porthcawl

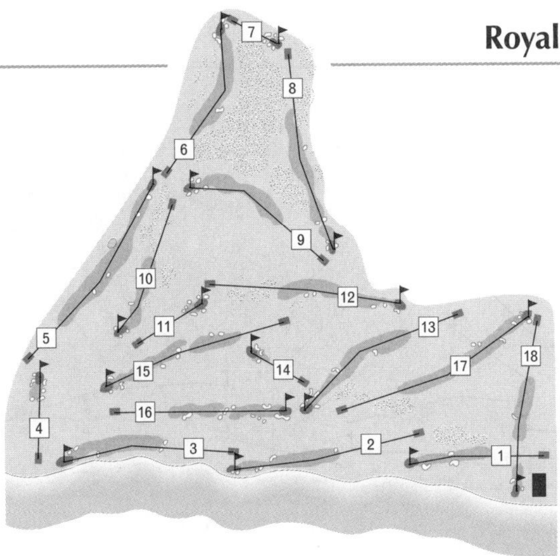

Royal Porthcawl is the jewel in a brilliant crown, having glorious Southerndown and demanding Pyle and Kenfig as its near neighbours. Such is the challenge of golf at Porthcawl that it has staged just about every significant event in the amateur and professional game in Britain except the Open Championship. Its most recent honour was to host the 1995 Walker Cup, when the home side comfortably defeated an American team that included the future tour stars Notah Begay and Tiger Woods.

Porthcawl's overall length may not seem excessive – well below that apparently compulsory figure of 7,000 yards – but many of the par 4s are considerably over 400 yards, particularly on the daunting back nine. Unusually, the sea is visible from every single hole. After the climb to higher ground on the 5th, the golf is, for a while, more akin to heathland than true links, with heather, broom and gorse lining the narrow fairways.

The first three holes skirt the shore, the 2nd and 3rd greens being elusive targets perilously close to the beach. The excellent 4th is surrounded by deep, troublesome bunkers. Shorter even than Royal Troon's Postage Stamp, Porthcawl's 7th can prove ruinous if the narrow, undulating putting surface is not found, while the medium length 9th is unexpectedly tough, its green at the top of a rise and surrounded by bunkers and treacherous slopes.

Coming home, the 13th and 15th are often played into the wind, ensuring that even long hitters are at full stretch, and the 15th and 16th fairways are both interrupted by cross-bunkers at an awkward length. The downhill approach to the final green deceives many. With the three-level green sloping down to the beach, the shot is rarely played with confidence.

CARD OF THE COURSE

	yards	par		yards	par
1	327	4	10	336	4
2	454	4	11	186	3
3	421	4	12	468	5
4	196	3	13	441	4
5	515	5	14	150	3
6	389	4	15	464	4
7	124	3	16	433	4
8	475	5	17	511	5
9	384	4	18	411	4
Out	3,285	36	In	3,400	36
Total	6,685 yards	par 72			

Royal Portrush

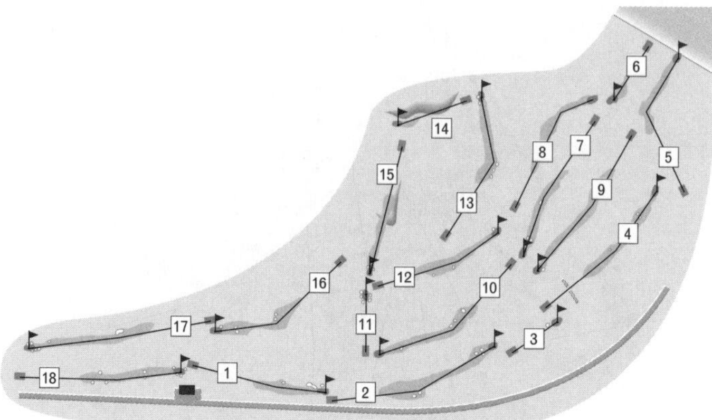

The Open Championship has been held outside England and Scotland only once, in 1951 when Max Faulkner triumphed at Royal Portrush. It is theoretically possible that the Championship may one day return, but much still depends on the Irish political situation and improved hotel provision. However, there is little doubting the suitability of the Dunluce course for the purpose, the club's Valley course also being a good test, and there are excellent potential final qualifying venues in neighbouring Portstewart, Castlerock and Ballycastle.

CARD OF THE DUNLUCE COURSE

	yards	par		yards	par
1	392	4	10	478	5
2	505	5	11	170	3
3	155	3	12	392	4
4	457	4	13	386	4
5	384	4	14	210	3
6	189	3	15	365	4
7	431	4	16	428	4
8	384	4	17	548	5
9	475	5	18	469	4
Out	3,372	36	In	3,446	36
Total	6,818 yards	par 72			

Today's Dunluce course is mainly a product of the 1930s, when Harry Colt transformed a newly acquired tract of tumbling dunes, although golf had been played at Portrush since 1888. With so much natural movement in the ground, Colt was clearly inspired in choosing the ideal locations for his greens. He raised them up sufficiently to put a real premium on approach work and relied on subtle undulations to pose all sorts of putting problems. With deep rough and uneven lies just off the narrow fairways, there was little need of bunkers or other man-made punishments.

The sense of anticipation on the 5th tee is great, with a drive over much rough country to an angled fairway, followed by a pitch to one of the most magnificently sited greens in all golf, clinging to the edge of the cliffs above the pounding ocean. P.G. Stevenson, club professional for 55 years, is commemorated on the 7th, a fine two-shotter. The notorious par-3 14th, Calamity Corner, involves a long carry over unwelcoming, low ground with unthinkable horrors down the hill to the right, while the 15th, Purgatory, is appropriately named for a hole that punishes the hook mercilessly. Whatever the outcome of the golf, relief can always be found afterwards at nearby Bushmills Distillery.

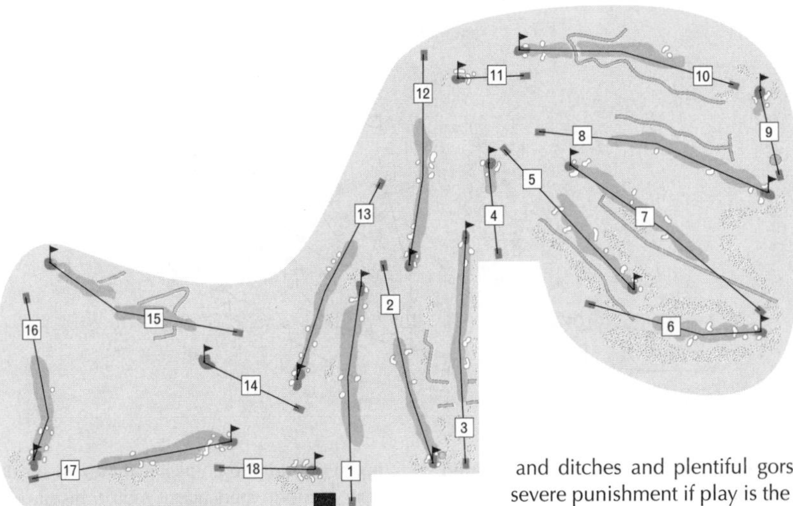

Harlech is a wonderful place for golf, down among the wild orchids in the dunes below the forbidding castle on its commanding rocky outcrop. The whole scene is backed dramatically by the peaks of Snowdonia. It is incongruous, then, that a links as renowned as Royal St David's should have been begun almost by accident by a boomerang-throwing Australian (Harold Finch-Hatton) and a man who knew nothing about golf (W.H. More). The Club has since hosted many of the most important championships and international matches in the amateur calendar. It is too far from the major centres of population to attract modern professional tournaments, yet many professionals have gone there to play for recreation, since Harlech's reputation as a serious examination of a golfer's technique is considerable. Par is only 69, but standard scratch is 73 – a stark indication of the testing nature of the links.

Although the course moves into substantial dunes towards the end of the round, the early holes are flattish, offering no escape from the wind. When the wind is up, even the strongest players are hard put to get up in two on some of the many lengthy par 4s. The bunkering has been kept relevant to the contemporary game, and ditches and plentiful gorse inflict severe punishment if play is the least bit erratic. A run of big, strong holes from the 10th returns play towards the clubhouse and the closing loop among the dunes. The par-3 14th, despite its lack of bunkers, is a real handful, often played into the wind, when it can be unreachable. Some very uncertain lies are to be found in the humps and bumps surrounding this green. Also bunkerless is the 15th, probably the finest hole, with a narrow fairway and semi-blind approach.

CARD OF THE COURSE

	yards	par		yards	par
	443	4	10	453	4
2	376	4	11	153	3
3	468	4	12	436	4
4	188	3	13	450	4
5	378	4	14	222	3
6	403	4	15	432	4
7	494	5	16	354	4
8	517	5	17	428	4
9	175	3	18	201	3
Out	3,442	36	In	3,129	33
Total	6,571 yards		par 69		

Royal St George's

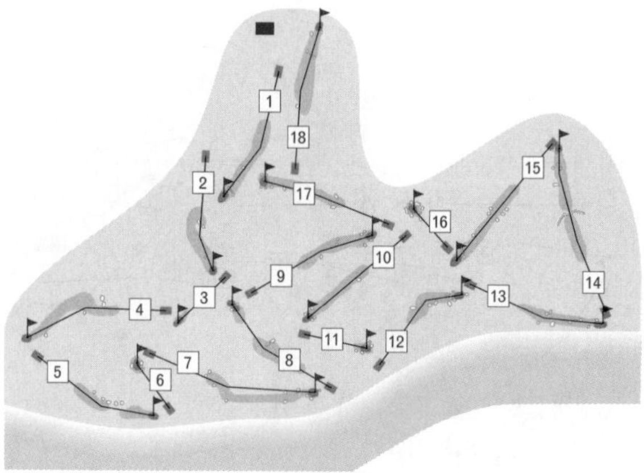

Royal St George's is, in many ways, England's premier links. It was the first course outside Scotland to host the Open Championship, which it did in 1894. In 2003 it will stage the event for the 13th time, more than any other English club. It is also the only club in the south of England to retain its Open status since the Second World War.

A couple of Scottish golfers, Dr Laidlaw Purves and Henry Lamb, disenchanted with their muddy course in London, searched the south coast of England in the 1880s looking for a patch of traditional linksland over which they might lay out something rather better. They spotted their goal from the vantage point of the tower of Sandwich church, the most spectacular dunes in south-east England.

It is thought that Purves himself designed the first course, which was opened in 1887. At around 6,000 yards, heavily bunkered and exceptionally narrow, it was a severe test, particularly as there were a great many blind shots. Nevertheless, Harry Vardon, during the 1904 Open, tamed the course with a round of 69, the first time a score under 70 was recorded in the Championship.

Today's course follows much the same route as the original, although a number of totally blind holes such as The Maiden have been superseded. Courage and confidence are still required driving on the big holes through the sand hills, such as on the 4th, 5th and 7th. Similarly, the approach shots to many greens can be nerve-wracking - the sunken 8th, elevated 10th and cross-bunkered 15th. Many Championship contenders have come to grief by slicing out-of-bounds on the treacherous 14th, while the final green is threatened by a deep bunker on the right and the notorious Duncan's Hollow on the left.

CARD OF THE COURSE

	yards	par		yards	par
1	441	4	10	413	4
2	376	4	11	216	3
3	210	3	12	365	4
4	468	4	13	443	4
5	421	4	14	551	5
6	172	3	15	478	4
7	530	5	16	163	3
8	418	4	17	425	4
9	389	4	18	468	4
Out	3,425	35	In	3,522	35
Total	6,947 yards	par 70			

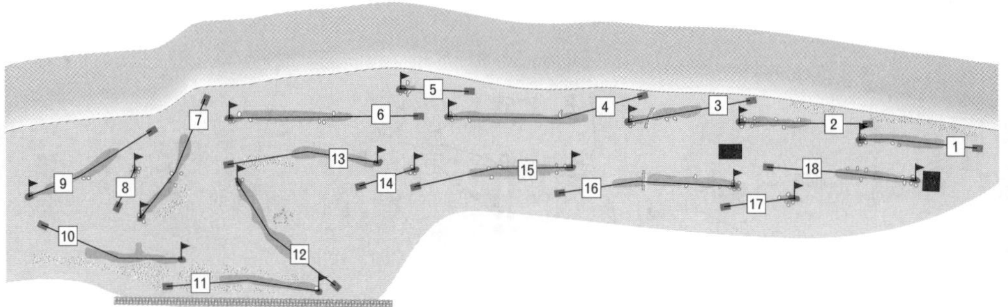

Royal Troon has a habit of exacting revenge for precocious play. In Greg Norman's case, it was a fairway bunker 300 yards out from the last tee, during the four-hole play-off for the 1989 Open Championship, which brought him back to earth with a bump. It could, however, have been anywhere on the back nine, for Troon's homeward run is fearsome. Before his setback, Norman had already birdied the first six holes at Royal Troon on his way to a course record 64 and a tie for the lead on the final afternoon.

Troon's opening is indeed gentle, with a series of shortish par 4s alongside the shore. These are the holes – especially the 5th on top of the dunes – to savour the views across the Firth of Clyde to the mountains of the Isle of Arran and down the coast, past Ayr, to distant Ailsa Craig. There is a splendid panorama from the 7th tee, but the course is tightening up and this hole is a beauty with its curving fairway laid out below. The 8th, the famous Postage Stamp, is the shortest hole in Open Championship golf, being only 126 yards long, yet the prospect from its tee causes concern. The green is a tiny ledge on the side of a sand hill, surrounded by bunkers and hostile country beyond. When it is windy, club selection can seem impossible.

From the 10th tee, low down, there is a blind drive to a narrow fairway high above – the back nine has now started in earnest. Open contenders play the 11th as a formidable par 4, with a huge carry over gorse to a narrow fairway, the green hard up against the railway. The 13th and 15th are brutal par 4s and the table-top 17th green a most elusive target.

CARD OF THE OPEN CHAMPIONSHIP COURSE

	yards	par		yards	par
1	364	4	10	438	4
2	391	4	11	463	4
3	379	4	12	431	4
4	557	5	13	465	4
5	210	3	14	179	3
6	577	5	15	457	4
7	402	4	16	542	5
8	126	3	17	223	3
9	423	4	18	452	4
Out	3,429	36	In	3,650	35
Total	7,079 yards	par 71			

Royal West Norfolk

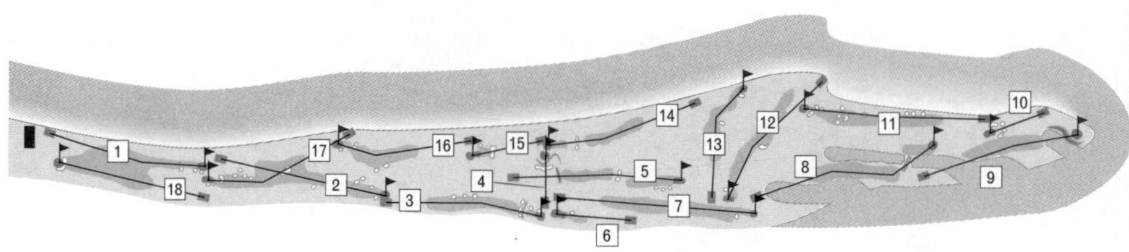

Golf at Royal West Norfolk is for romantic spirits who can revel in the timelessness of the ancient links. The course occupies a narrow strip of dunes squeezed between salt marshes and the sea, becoming an island when the tides are at their highest. Since the course was first laid out in the 1890s, there have been changes mainly through the loss of holes to erosion, yet its characteristic qualities of crisp natural links turf, huge sleeper-faced bunkers and small, rapid greens are unaltered. The difficulty of finding and holding these greens makes this a place for the skilled craftsman who can manufacture shots to order.

The back nine is shorter on paper but is often played into the wind, and, being higher in the dunes, is more exposed. Right from the first tee, the golf is serious, with a substantial carry over wild country to a fairway shared with the 18th. A big bunker threatens the next drive – out-of-bounds, too. The 3rd really tests the golfer's resolve, with its green perched on top of a mound, a wall of sleepers to be carried and straightness is of the essence with the big drops into sand or, worse, on either side. The 4th may be only 122 yards long, yet the green is a mere 21 yards deep, and raised high above the ubiquitous wooden fortifications.

Two of the most brilliant holes come at the far end of the course. Crossing two stretches of tidal marsh, the 8th is a par 5 reachable in two but only if the golf has been heroic. The 9th is its par-4 equivalent, with the need to take the most daring line from the tee in order to ease the approach shot, which is played over another stretch of marsh and wooden ramparts.

CARD OF THE COURSE

	yards	par		yards	par
1	413	4	10	147	3
2	442	4	11	474	5
3	401	4	12	377	4
4	122	3	13	304	4
5	415	4	14	428	4
6	182	3	15	186	3
7	481	5	16	335	4
8	492	5	17	390	4
9	403	4	18	379	4
Out	3,351	36	In	3,020	35
Total	6,371 yards	par 71			

Royal Worlington and Newmarket

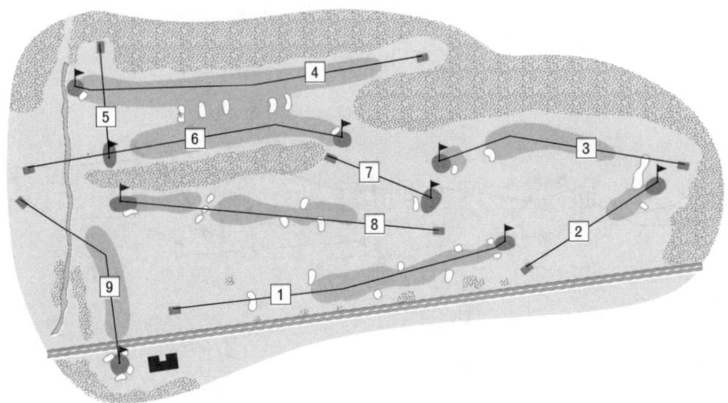

Royal Worlington and Newmarket is often cited as the finest nine-hole golf course in England, if not the world. It runs over an outcrop of sandy soil, giving brilliant drainage, especially in winter, and ensuring links-like fairway turf and lightning-fast putting surfaces. With subtle ridges and mounds guarding the greens, the key to a good score at Royal Worlington is being able to improvise approach shots, a skill somewhat in decline since the advent elsewhere of holding greens and lob wedges. The course has hardly been altered since it was laid out in 1891 and, fittingly, matchplay is the order of the day, with three- and four-ball play forbidden.

The opening hole is comparatively gentle, a short par 5, but the problems of the 2nd are not easily solved, the domed putting surface repelling all but the most perfectly weighted shots on this substantial par 3. A ditch and bunkers characterize the 3rd, while straight hitting is required on the 4th with its tee back in the woods. There is a nasty ridge just in front of this green, making the approach shot awkward whatever its length.

The short 5th is a devilish hole, falling away into grassy hollows on either side. It may be bunkerless but its capacity for reducing grown men to tears is legendary. Two very strong par 4s, the 6th and 8th, run in parallel on either side of a row of firs, and, between them, the 7th often deceives for length. While the strong may aspire to drive the final green, it is for most golfers a first-rate 'cape' hole, inviting bravado but punishing the slightest blemish unmercifully. On most nine-hole courses there is a sense of anticlimax to tackling the same holes a second time, but at Royal Worlington eager anticipation is the norm.

CARD OF THE COURSE

	yards	par
1	486	5
2	224	3
3	361	4
4	495	5
5	157	3
6	458	4
7	165	3
8	460	4
9	299	4
Total	3,105	35

Saunton

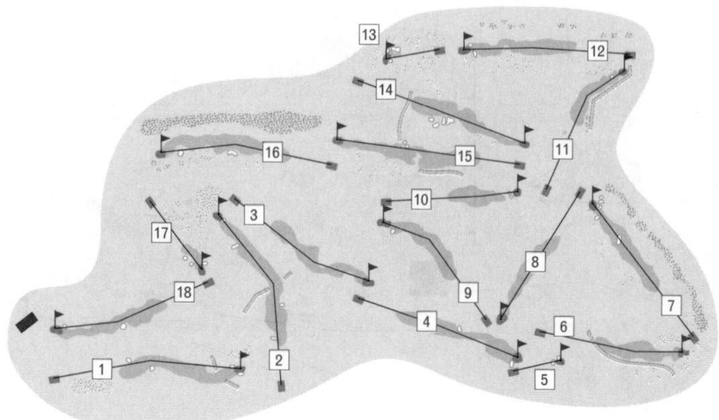

The East Course at Saunton has been recognized as one of England's top courses since it opened in 1919. This Devonian club, however, also possesses a second outstanding links course, the West, which was revived in the 1970s and is now pretty much the equal of the East. A few miles west of Barnstaple, where the River Taw enters the sea, is an expanse of sand hills almost on a par with those on the Lancashire coast. The two courses at Saunton occupy but a fraction of it, contributing greatly to the pleasing sense of escape that playing there gives.

As far as today's longest hitters are concerned, one possible weakness in both courses is the lack of a genuine, three-shot par 5, yet there is strength enough in the longer par 4s to test even them. The 7th on the West may be the toughest of all the par 4s, an unforgiving dog-leg on which the drive is seriously threatened by a ditch.

Herbert Fowler (architect of the East Course) and Frank Pennink (West Course) took full advantage of what God provided, using the natural features to create holes with considerable individuality. Consequently, neither course is over-reliant on bunkers for defence. The West's 7th has no need of sand, and the East's 3rd is also bunkerless – and one of the finest holes on that course. This wonderfully natural hole, comparable in its way with the Dornoch's 14th, Foxy, runs down a valley between the dunes, curving at the length of a decent drive, and its green is protected in front by a mound. Around the turn, the East is flatter, but by the 16th the sand hills have grown again to make this one of the great English two-shotters, part of a sterling finish.

CARD OF THE EAST COURSE

	yards	par		yards	par
1	478	4	10	337	4
2	476	5	11	362	4
3	402	4	12	414	4
4	441	4	13	145	3
5	122	3	14	455	4
6	370	4	15	478	5
7	428	4	16	434	4
8	380	4	17	207	3
9	392	4	18	408	4
Out	3,489	36	In	3,240	35
Total	6,729 yards	par 71			

Slaley Hall

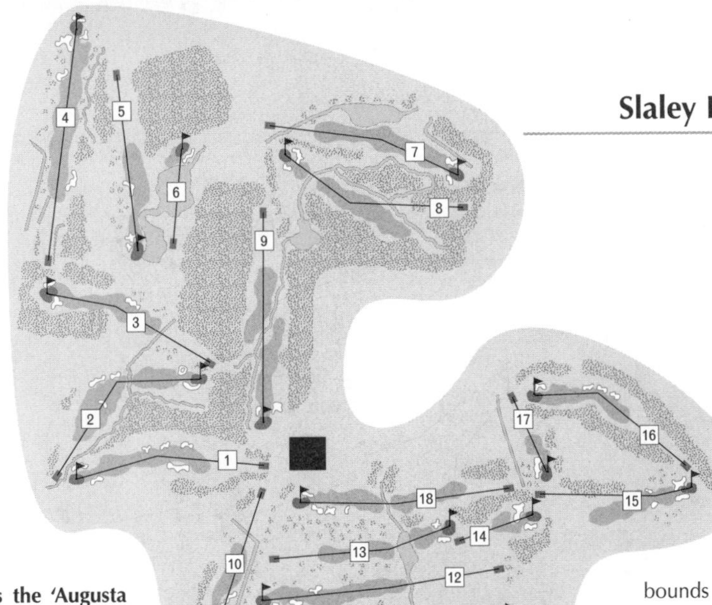

Known as the 'Augusta of the North', Slaley Hall is at its most beautiful in June, when the rhododendrons are in full bloom, adding great splashes of brilliant scarlet to an already handsome setting. June is also when the cream of Europe's professional golfers arrive, to compete in the Compaq European Grand Prix.

Dave Thomas designed the Hunting Course (over which the European Tour events are played), and many say that it is his finest – praise indeed, given the distinction of so many of his creations. In terms of difficulty there is little to choose between this and the complementary Priestman Course, which was laid out on higher ground by Neil Coles – both are man-sized tests, full of character.

There is great individuality to each hole on the Hunting Course, with the 9th taking pride of place. Climbing steadily, this par 4 plays far longer than its measured length of 453 yards. The drive is threatened by trees, rhododendrons and a stream, which closes in from the left, before cutting across the fairway. The view back down the fairway from the green is ravishing. Strong holes abound, such as the mischievous 2nd, which runs downhill towards a stream before turning sharp right, up past bunkers to the green set in the trees. The 3rd green, too, is handsomely framed in the woods, while the 4th bounds downhill to give delightful views over the Northumberland countryside (and professional golfers the chance to hit monster drives). Streams and ditches tighten the drives on the 7th and 8th, on both of which long hitters can cut off some of the dog-leg. The back nine moves on to more open ground, its par 4s generally shorter, though a stream restricts driving length on the two hardest holes on this half, the 13th and 18th.

CARD OF THE HUNTING COURSE

	yards	par		yards	par
1	429	4	10	362	4
2	429	4	11	562	5
3	412	4	12	531	5
4	521	5	13	395	4
5	382	4	14	179	3
6	205	3	15	331	4
7	432	4	16	395	4
8	423	4	17	184	3
9	453	4	18	463	4
Out	3,686	36	In	3,402	36
Total	7,088 yards		par 72		

Southerness

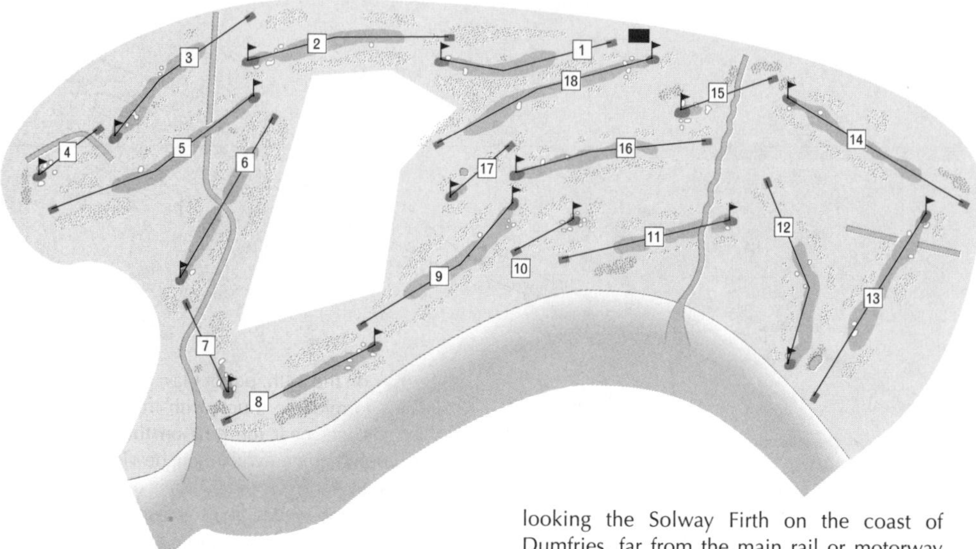

The unspoiled nature of Southerness is one of its most treasured qualities. Having been groomed for 50 years by a wise ground staff, with no excessive use of fertilizers, the fairways uphold the true links qualities sought after by connoisseurs of the traditional game. Another attraction is its relatively remote location, overlooking the Solway Firth on the coast of Dumfries, far from the main rail or motorway networks. This has ensured that Southerness is today as peaceful as it must have been when it first opened in June 1947. The course, which cost no more than £2,000 to build, was designed by Philip Mackenzie Ross at much the same time as he restored Turnberry after its wartime ravages.

A standard scratch score of four shots above par gives some indication of the challenge facing the golfer at Southerness, and, with eight of the eleven par 4s over 400 yards long, length is at a premium. Length at Southerness, however, must be combined with accuracy, since each fairway is lined with heather, bracken or gorse, from which escape is far from certain. Another feature of the layout is that the wind must be tackled from every quarter. Into the prevailing wind, the opening stretch can be daunting, not least the task of trying to find the tightly bunkered green of the 450-yard 2nd. The lovely par-3 7th leads to a delightful stretch parallel to the shore, culminating in the magnificent 12th, calling for a big drive to avoid fairway bunkers and a long approach shot, probably into the wind, to a green perched on a shelf above the beach. With its views across the sea to the Lakeland fells, it is an unrivalled spot.

CARD OF THE COURSE

	yards	par		yards	par
1	393	4	10	168	3
2	450	4	11	390	4
3	408	4	12	421	4
4	169	3	13	467	4
5	496	5	14	458	4
6	405	4	15	217	3
7	215	3	16	433	4
8	371	4	17	175	3
9	435	4	18	495	5
Out	3,342	35	In	3,224	34
Total	6,566 yards	par 69			

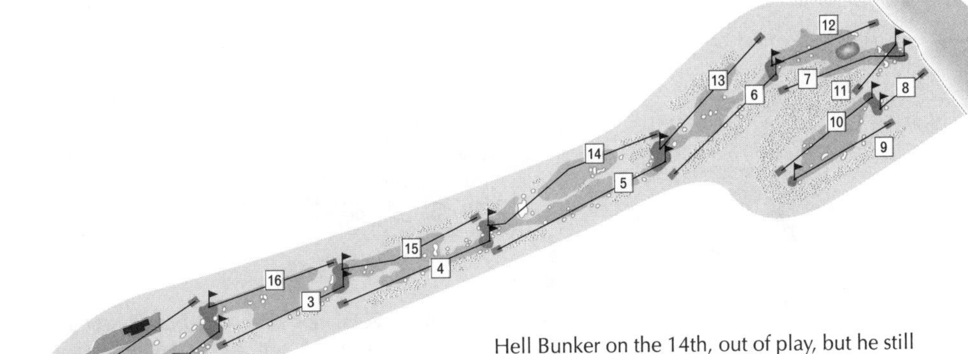

The Old Course at St Andrews is like an incurable disease. Not everyone catches it – there are some who find little good to say about it – but those who once fall under its spell never lose their addiction. This historic course dates back to at least the 15th century, and has been closely associated with the government of the game worldwide, through the Royal & Ancient Golf Club. It boasts imperishable links with every great golfer of the last 150 years, who has played some miraculous shot here or come to grief there. To what other course would golfers willingly travel half way round the world, actually looking forward to playing a hole as hideously ugly and outrageously capricious as the 17th, the Road Hole?

Whatever its anachronisms, the Old Course supremely rewards thought. Nick Faldo plotted his way to victory in the 1990 Open Championship, and in 2000 Tiger Woods' game plan contrived that he did not visit a single bunker during all four rounds. Woods' great power took many famous obstacles, such as Hell Bunker on the 14th, out of play, but he still needed his formidable touch with improvised short shots to get near the pins on these gargantuan double-greens with their bewildering contours. At St Andrews, the 6-iron is of greater value than the lob wedge at 50 yards.

A number of options exist on most holes, with the left-hand route usually less hazardous from the tee, but then the approach shot may well be trickier. Nevertheless, it is not unusual for canny golfers deliberately to drive on to the 6th fairway when playing the 13th, or to use the 5th fairway to avoid Hell Bunker on the 14th. Only the right-hand route will do on the 17th, the Road Hole, however.

CARD OF THE OLD COURSE

	yards	par		yards	par
1	376	4	10	379	4
2	413	4	11	174	3
3	397	4	12	314	4
4	464	4	13	430	4
5	568	5	14	581	5
6	412	4	15	456	4
7	388	4	16	424	4
8	175	3	17	455	4
9	352	4	18	357	4
Out	3,545	36	In	3,570	36
Total	7,115 yards	par 72			

St Enodoc

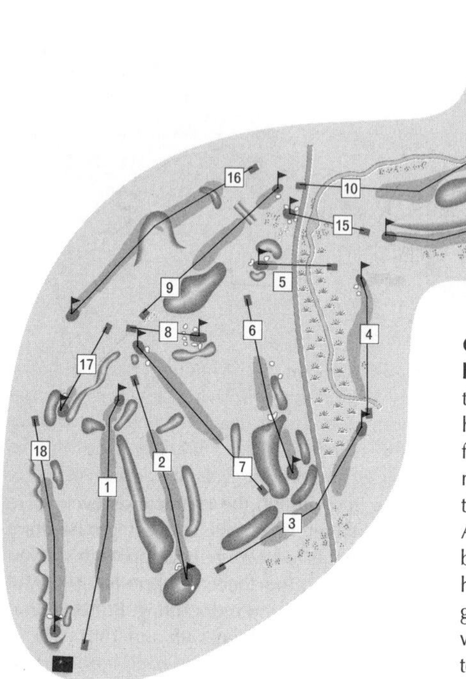

Golf at St Enodoc used to be played over a 27-hole course, 18 out and 9 home, although there are no surviving records to show exactly how it was done. James Braid was responsible for the 18-hole layout, returning occasionally to make revisions, and that course is essentially the one played today. There are times when Atlantic gales, funnelled up the Camel estuary, batter the golfer incessantly and 18 of Braid's holes feel more like 27. Even though it is of no great length, it can be physically demanding, with many hills to be climbed and deep valleys to be crossed. There is probably not a level piece of ground on the course. The 6th has possibly the highest sand hill on any course in Britain – the Himalayas – which rises 80 feet above the fairway with a monumental bunker set in its face.

The start at St Enodoc is pure links golf, a fine par 5 with a testing approach shot followed by a first-rate par 4 to a plateau green. Suddenly the character changes with a drive over the road, and the first encounter with St Enodoc's stone wall, which marks the out-of-bounds. The green is perilously close to it, and the 4th, short though it may be, is all about driving as far as possible over the wall. After a return to the central links, the course moves into new territory on the 10th, a dangerous, narrow par 4 alongside a stream. The holes then form a loop encircling the little church of St Enodoc, which once had to be dug out of the sands and is now the resting place of Sir John Betjeman. The final three holes, in the heart of the dunes, are as good as any.

CARD OF THE COURSE

	yards	par		yardsd	par
1	518	5	10	457	4
2	438	4	11	205	3
3	436	4	12	386	4
4	292	4	13	360	4
5	161	3	14	355	4
6	378	4	15	168	3
7	394	4	16	495	5
8	155	3	17	206	3
9	393	4	18	446	4
Out	3,165	35	In	3,078	34
Total	6,243 yards		par 69		

St George's Hill

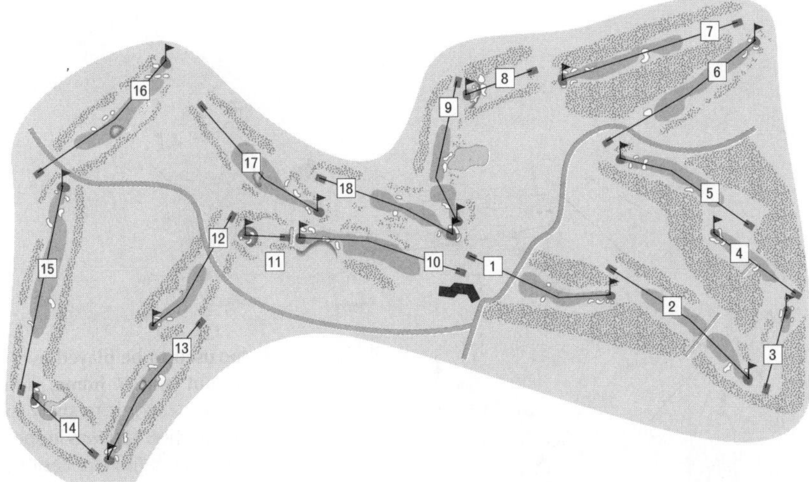

St George's Hill was the very first golf course constructed as an integral part of a superior housing development. With great foresight, George Tarrant, a local builder, seized the opportunity when this vast estate became available in 1911. The site was conducive to imaginative design with its pine-clad hills and well-drained, sandy subsoil on which heather thrives, and, he made a wise choice of course architect – employing Harry Colt. Tarrant also built a magnificent pavilion on top of one of the hills, giving majestic views out over the course and deep into Surrey.

Originally there were 36 holes, but only 27 survive, the 9-hole Green Course being rather shorter and perhaps more feminine than its big brother, the Red and Blue Course, though its 2nd is a match for any par 3 anywhere. Where the longer Red and Blue Course impresses is in the variety of the challenges it sets. The 1st hole strikes out into a wooded valley before climbing and twisting to a hill-top green. The 2nd is more open, crossing a stream as it descends towards the green. The green of the short 3rd is on two levels, higher on the right than the left, and so on.

After the exceptional 8th, a very rugged short hole, the 9th sweeps in a graceful arc as it rises to a tricky, sloping green set below the clubhouse. If anything, the character is even more individual after the turn, with a high, heathery hill to be cleared with a long approach shot on the 10th, and four deep bunkers lying in wait for those who are found wanting. Bunkers short of the greens make the 13th and 16th particularly tough par 4s from the back tees, and on the minuscule 11th the slightest error is punished severely.

CARD OF THE RED AND BLUE COURSE

	yards	par		yards	par
1	384	4	10	434	4
2	458	4	11	110	3
3	197	3	12	347	4
4	271	4	13	423	4
5	390	4	14	208	3
6	468	4	15	534	5
7	476	5	16	440	4
8	177	3	17	417	4
9	372	4	18	390	4
Out	3,193	35	In	3,303	35
Total	6,496 yards	par 70			

Sunningdale

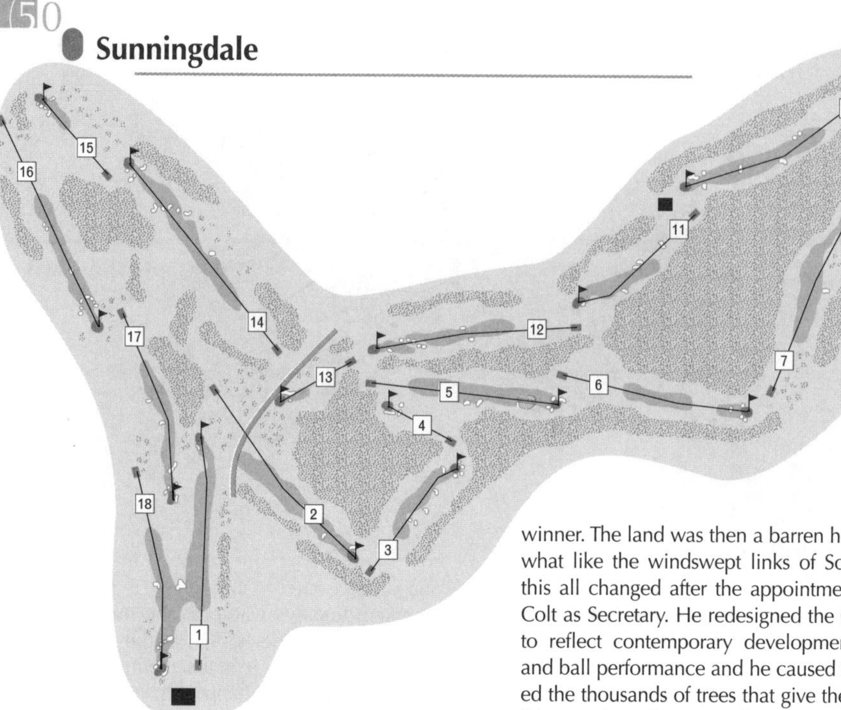

Sunningdale was not the first course built in Surrey's heath-and-heather belt, but it was the first great one. Opened in 1901, the Old Course was designed by Willie Park Jnr, son of the inaugural Open Champion and himself a two-times winner. The land was then a barren heath, somewhat like the windswept links of Scotland, but this all changed after the appointment of Harry Colt as Secretary. He redesigned the Old Course to reflect contemporary developments in club and ball performance and he caused to be planted the thousands of trees that give the individual fairways their pleasant seclusion. Colt also added a second course, the New, which opened in 1922. Both courses are first class and of similar length; the New, however, is slightly less wooded but, arguably, has even better short holes.

The par 4s on the Old Course are not quite testing enough for the modern professionals, so scoring in recent tournaments has been remarkably low. In winning the 1988 European Open, Ian Woosnam averaged only 65 shots per round, and Karrie Webb recorded a 63 in her runaway victory in the 1997 Women's British Open. The Old Course is plenty long enough for amateurs, however, and it is often the shorter par 4s that ruin a potentially good card. The 11th is certainly in that category, with its sloping fairway and a devious, little green conducive to indecisive pitching.

High on everyone's list of favourites is the par-5 10th, an inspiring hole played from an elevated tee with panoramic views. The sequence of three holes from the 5th is warmly regarded, too: the 5th with its approach over one of the earliest artificial water hazards, and the 7th to a charming green in a dell.

CARD OF THE OLD COURSE

	yards	par		yards	par
1	494	5	10	478	5
2	489	5	11	325	4
3	319	4	12	451	4
4	161	3	13	185	3
5	419	4	14	509	5
6	415	4	15	226	3
7	402	4	16	438	4
8	182	3	17	421	4
9	273	4	18	432	4
Out	3,154	36	In	3,465	36
Total	6,619 yards	par 72			

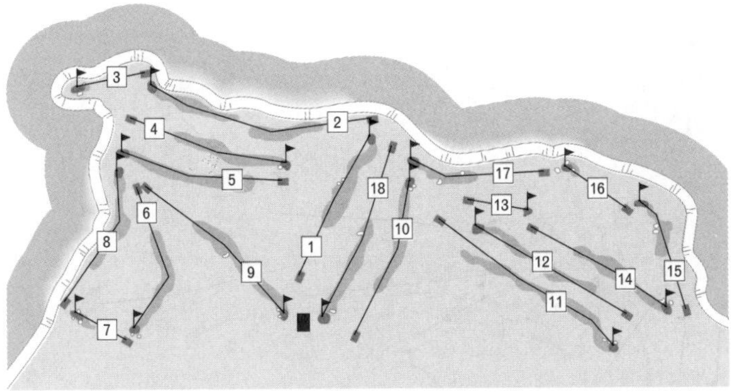

Arnold Palmer's first Irish essay was the spectacular links on the shores of the Atlantic Ocean at Tralee. A later Palmer jewel, the K Club on the banks of the River Liffey, has been given great prominence by its award of the 2005 Ryder Cup matches. Time, however, may well award the greater accolades to Tralee. It is a breathtaking site, terrifying to golfers of all abilities in any sort of wind, for in such rugged country there is no place to hide if the centre of the fairway cannot be found with confidence. The 1968 film, Ryan's Daughter, captured the essence of this coastline, scenes for it being filmed on the beach beside what is now the 2nd fairway. And, if the historians are to be believed, it was from these waters that St. Brendan set out for the unknown some time in the 6th Century. Perhaps he discovered the Hebrides – or perhaps it was America. No golfer who has taken on Tralee in a gale and survived will have anything but the highest respect for Brendan and his crew in their primitive boats.

Palmer reckoned that he designed the first nine and that God did the rest. Those first nine are comparatively flat, but rarely far from the sea and all too often a shot which is nearly good enough finds its way onto the rocks or into the breakers on holes such as the 3rd or 8th. On the back nine it is the mountainous terrain which sorts the sheep from the goats with a number of intimidating carries across inhospitable ravines, such as the short 13th. The 12th may be the hardest hole on the course, but it was of the 11th that Jeff Sluman remarked that it was a hole that "even Tiger can't reach in two."

CARD OF THE COURSE

	yards	par		yards	par
1	402	4	10	427	4
2	594	5	11	570	5
3	194	3	12	444	4
4	425	4	13	158	3
5	428	4	14	400	4
6	416	4	15	303	4
7	154	3	16	196	3
8	382	4	17	351	4
9	493	5	18	462	4
Out	3,488	36	In	3,311	35
Total	6,799 yards	par 71			

Turnberry

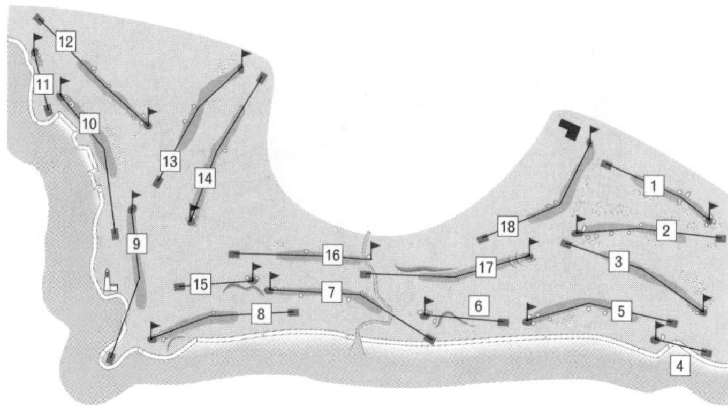

What sets Turnberry's Ailsa Course apart is its incomparable stretch of seaside holes from the 4th to the 11th, which hug the cliffs in dramatic fashion. This most scenic of Open venues took the stage by storm, its first Open being the remarkable 'Duel in the sun' of 1977, when Tom Watson and Jack Nicklaus gave a breathtaking display of brilliant golf and great sportsmanship. Greg Norman was the next champion, in 1986 when he posted a 63 in the second round to announce his intentions. Nick Price was no less spectacular a winner in 1994, closing with a remarkable 31 for his final nine holes, to sneak a one-shot victory from Jesper Parnevik. Turnberry provides a wealth of golfing drama against a background never more spectacular than when the crimson sun sinks into the sea past Ailsa Craig with the Mull of Kintyre and Northern Ireland beyond.

On the seaside holes, the most arresting moment comes when the golfer sets foot on the 9th tee, built on a rocky promontory high above the waves, with a 200-yard carry across the sea to a hog's-back fairway. These are all fine holes with the curving fairways of the 5th, 7th and 8th, the long carry to the 6th green and the enchanting sweep of the 10th fairway down towards the beach all outstanding. Any sense of anticlimax at then moving inland is countered by the difficulty of the tough 14th, the uncompromising carry to the 15th and the devious little burn that crosses the 16th at an awkward spot, just in front of the green. The 17th is a birdie hope for all, and the 18th blessedly straightforward.

CARD OF THE AILSA COURSE

	yards	par		yards	par
1	350	4	10	452	4
2	430	4	11	174	3
3	462	4	12	446	4
4	165	3	13	412	4
5	442	4	14	449	4
6	231	3	15	209	3
7	529	5	16	409	4
8	431	4	17	497	5
9	454	4	18	434	4
Out	3,494	35	In	3,482	35
Total	6,976 yards	par 70			

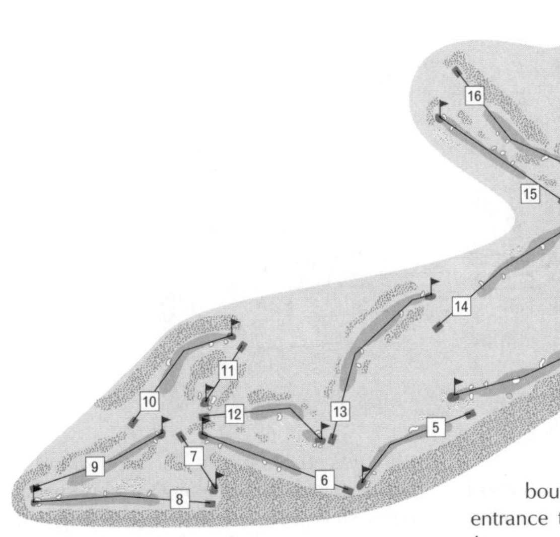

Unusually, the Old Course begins with a par 3, but it is a very full-length example at 235 yards, with out-of-bounds on both sides and a narrow entrance to the green between bunkers. Play then moves out onto the wide spaces of the heath for a series of fine par 4s, of which the 5th stands out for the attractive sweep of its ever-narrowing fairway as it runs downhill towards the angled green. The finish is impressive, too, with the 16th particularly renowned, swinging up towards a hilltop green raised above a wicked bunker.

Walton Heath boasts two magnificant heathland courses on the grand scale, which were completed by Herbert Fowler before the First World War. Since then, it has hosted many important professional tournaments, not least the 1981 Ryder Cup and five European Opens. A composite course, drawn from the Old and New, is used for such big events, serving to demonstrate the almost equal standing of each. The heath provides excellent drainage, making for fast-running fairways and firm, speedy greens. It also grows heather to perfection, and a very serious hazard it can prove to the golfer who is not on top of his game. Outcrops of gorse and bracken and, in parts, trees are the other major problems off the fairways, while a profusion of expansive, heather-encrusted bunkers dictate strategy throughout the round.

After a quiet start, the New Course suddenly tightens up on the 3rd, its fairway constricted by a bunker at the length of a good drive. There is a similar interruption to the fairway on the 9th, both holes then calling for seriously long approach shots to narrow greens. From the championship tee, the 16th plays to a daunting 581 yards, making it the longest hole on either course.

CARD OF THE OLD COURSE

	yards	par		yards	par
1	235	3	10	417	4
2	458	4	11	198	3
3	289	4	12	396	4
4	441	4	13	529	5
5	437	4	14	569	5
6	440	4	15	426	4
7	183	3	16	510	5
8	494	5	17	193	3
9	400	4	18	404	4
Out	3,377	35	In	3,642	37
Total	7,019 yards	par 72			

Waterville

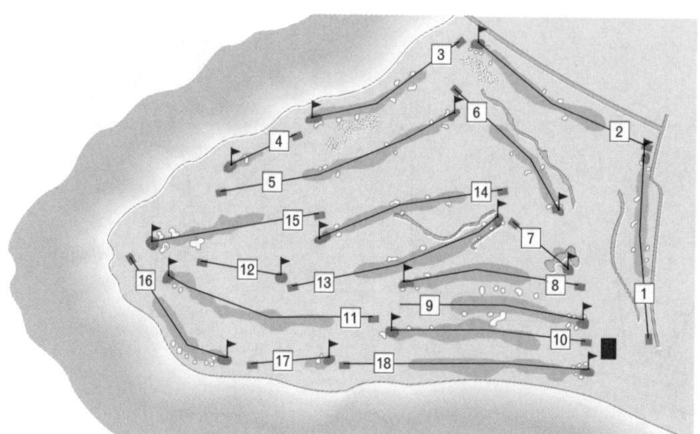

The great Sam Snead once described Waterville's challenging links as "The beautiful monster – one of the golfing wonders of the world". It seems particularly appropriate when playing from the blue tees – the course stretching to more than 7,200 yards. Golf has been played at Waterville since 1889, hardly surprising considering the extent of the sand hills alongside Ballinskelligs Bay. The site itself is steeped in history, Noah's granddaughter, Cessair, apparently landing on these very shores 'shortly after the flood', according to the 'Book of Invasions' of AD 1000.

It was not until the early 1970s, however, that the true golfing potential of this glorious spot was revealed by John Mulcahy, an Irish-American returning to his roots. To do this, he enlisted the services of the Irish course designer Eddie Hackett as well as past Masters champion Claude Harmon. Hackett was a great exponent of simple course architecture, and he looked first to nature and only later to the digger in exploiting the natural resources of a tract of land, to the benefit of both the client's purse and the cards of succeeding generations of golfers. He need not have extended himself at Waterville, for it is a place of outstanding beauty, a promontory jutting into the ocean with the mountains of Kerry as a backdrop – but that was hardly Hackett's style.

No one will forget the magnificent views afforded on the 17th tee, yet it is the short par-5 11th – one of the simplest holes – that appeals immediately to golfers of all abilities. Restraint is of the essence, everything being governed by the angles of the dunes through which the narrow fairway curves, earning from Gary Player the accolade of 'the most beautiful and satisfying par 5 of them all.'

CARD OF THE COURSE

	yards	par		yards	par
1	430	4	10	475	4
2	469	4	11	506	5
3	417	4	12	200	3
4	179	3	13	518	5
5	595	5	14	456	4
6	387	4	15	407	4
7	178	3	16	350	4
8	435	4	17	196	3
9	445	4	18	582	5
Out	3,535	35	In	3,690	37
Total	7,225 yards	par 72			

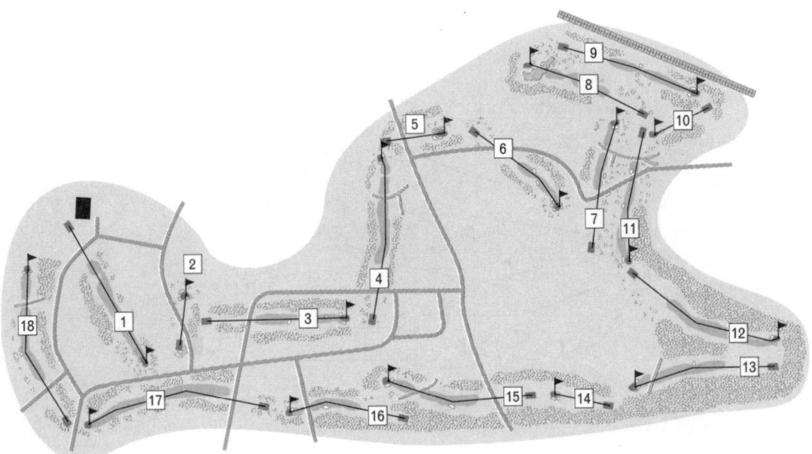

Three choice golf courses weave their way between the mansions of the rich and famous on the opulent estate that is Wentworth. The best golfers in Europe go there each May for the PGA Championship, and 12 of the best golfers in the world return each October for the World Match Play Championship, which has been held there for more than 30 years. The earliest big tournaments took place on the East Course, and there are some who rate it at least as highly as the West. Recently John Jacobs, Gary Player and Bernard Gallagher joined forces to construct the Edinburgh Course, of considerable length and with contemporary challenges in a style that does not conflict with Harry Colt's existing courses. However, it is the West Course, the so-called Burma Road, with which all armchair golf-watchers are so familiar.

Such is the power of modern professional golfers that the Burma Road nickname no longer seems appropriate. They are certainly not frightened to attack the course, and a score in the low 270s is usually required to ensure victory in the PGA. This West Course is more subtle than daunting, which is why it really comes into its own for matchplay. Many holes are lost when a casual approach shot is played to the wrong part of the green. Seemingly innocuous holes such as the 16th have greens that can confound even the hottest putter, while the crafty slopes of the 15th green make it regular three-putt territory.

On paper the front nine appears easier, but the average professional score on the 7th, for example, is above par. Once again, it is the difficulty of hitting the approach to the correct part of the green which makes this hole so fascinating. White knuckles accompany a downhill putt on the 3rd, too.

CARD OF THE WEST COURSE

	yards	par		yards	par
1	473	5	10	184	3
2	154	3	11	403	4
3	447	4	12	509	5
4	497	5	13	442	4
5	191	3	14	179	3
6	354	4	15	481	4
7	396	4	16	383	4
8	400	4	17	571	5
9	452	4	18	531	5
Out	3,364	36	In	3,683	37
Total	7,047 yards	par 73			

West Sussex

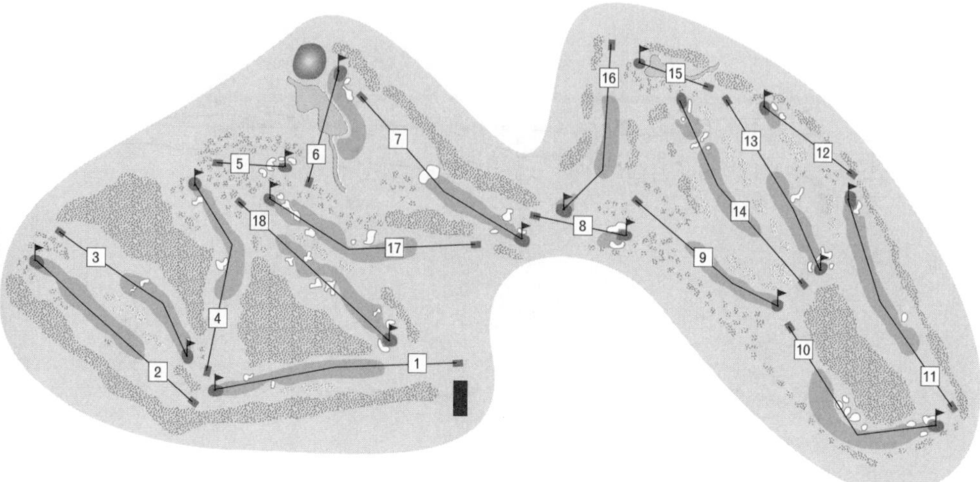

For the good amateur, West Sussex provokes thought on every stroke, yet it makes no claim to be a championship test – the overall length disposing of that. West Sussex occupies a rare patch of prime golfing land, an outcrop of heathland sheltering under the Downs amid the clays and marshes of this corner of Sussex. Such is the disposition of the holes that shots of all lengths and all shapes are required during a round, and the enchanting woodland surroundings cannot fail to lift the hearts of all players.

There is a degree of notoriety to the par-3 6th, with its almighty carry over a pond and marsh. These are not its only indignities, for there are two serious bunkers on one side of the green and a heathery hill on the other. True, there is an alternative route for the timid, but how would they cope on the 7th? There the tee shot must clear a wall of sand and a sea of heather covering the hill in front, a carry of about 200 yards. Only then does the fairway begin.

Bunkers in profusion dictate strategy on the remarkable 10th, and the 11th is a splendid par 4 with an approach over low ground to an angled, raised green. Around there, the golfer begins to disbelieve the stated facts about this being a short course. The 12th is all carry over heather, the 13th involves a testing approach over bunkers, and the 14th is fascinating with its downhill approach over cross-bunkers. This is indeed serious golf. Perhaps the pretty 15th and 16th offer a breather, but the 17th demands long, straight driving with its tee shot over heather to a sloping fairway. Once again, there is originality about the bunkering, putting much pressure on the shot to the green.

CARD OF THE COURSE

	yards	par		yards	par
1	485	5	10	401	4
2	413	4	11	448	4
3	360	4	12	219	3
4	388	4	13	382	4
5	144	3	14	429	4
6	224	3	15	143	3
7	440	4	16	364	4
8	187	3	17	441	4
9	351	4	18	402	4
Out	2,992	34	In	3,229	34
Total	6,221 yards	par 68			

Western Gailes

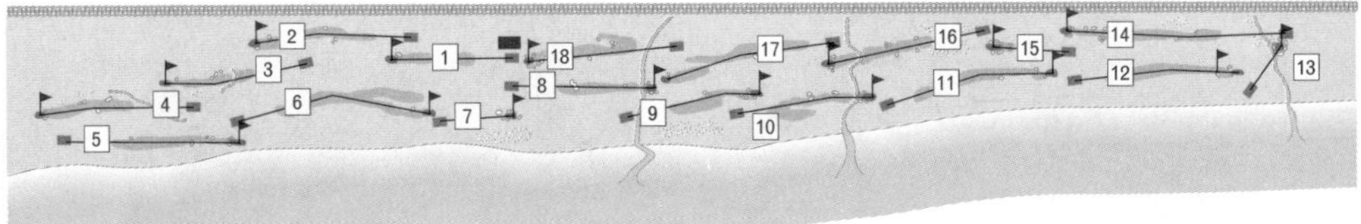

Western Gailes might be said to encapsulate the best features of the golfing riches that abound on the Ayrshire coast – of Turnberry, Prestwick, Royal Troon, Barassie, Glasgow Gailes and Irvine, among others. It is situated on a narrow strip of linksland – no more than the width of two fairways – between the railway and the sea. Regular host to Open qualifying, it has also seen Curtis Cup action in 1972 and the PGA Championship in 1964. Its confined site could hardly accommodate the modern professional game, though the test set by the course itself is a distinctly good one.

The main delight of Western Gailes is in the variety of its challenges with par 4s of every length. This ensures that each club in the bag will be required, particularly as many greens are finely contoured and engagingly set into folds in the dunes. The layout in two out-and-back loops is organized so that both long holes run in opposite directions and, if the long stretch from the 4th to the 13th plays more or less into the wind, at least it comes in the middle of the round before fatigue sets in. The fairways undulate attractively, but the sand hills are not overfacing.

Typical of its ingeniously situated greens is the 6th, set in a hollow in the dunes, requiring a perfectly judged approach shot. What adds spice to it is the distinct hump on the right of the putting surface. The short 7th is a beauty, nestling in its own private hollow by the beach and well bunkered. Several greens are found just beyond burns, and there is always the threat of straying on to the railway line down the closing stretch, though heather and gorse are the main destroyers on this charming links.

CARD OF THE COURSE

	yards	par		yards	par
1	309	4	10	348	4
2	434	4	11	445	4
3	365	4	12	436	4
4	400	4	13	141	3
5	453	4	14	562	5
6	506	5	15	194	3
7	196	3	16	404	4
8	365	4	17	443	4
9	336	4	18	377	4
Out	3,364	36	In	3,350	35
Total	6,714 yards	par 71			

Woburn

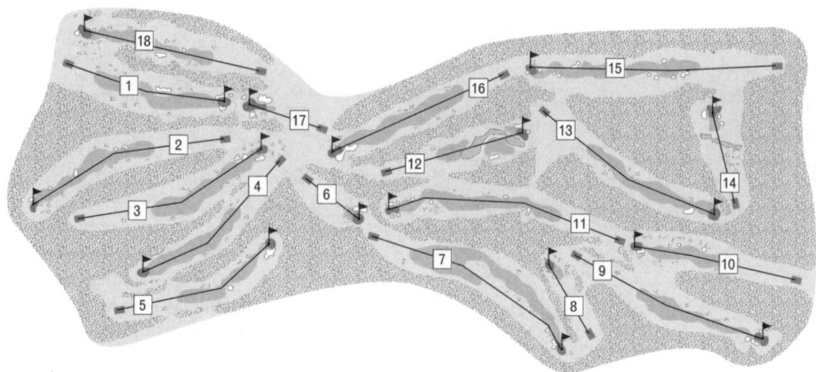

The Marquess Course at Woburn is the latest and most challenging of the beautiful woodland courses on the Duke of Bedford's estate. For 25 years the Duke's and Duchess Courses carried Woburn's flag proudly, hosting no fewer than 36 professional tournaments and championships between them. Now the honour of hosting tour events has been taken on by the Marquess Course, which opened for play in 2000.

This has been designed to encourage bravery. The 7th, for example, is a par 5 that is reachable in two by the professionals, but they must drive to the right of a line of pine trees splitting the fairway, with no room for error. Their second shot is then all carry – well over 200 yards – across a valley and deep bunkers with all manner of evils in wait should they fail. There is an easier route to the left of the pines, but then the green is out of range of the second shot. The outward half ends with an inspiring, long approach played over a valley to an angled green framed by oaks and rhododendrons.

From the back tee, the drive at the short par-4 12th must carry more than 250 yards to clear a pond, leaving only a lob-wedge shot to the green, but accuracy is equally important with a stream on the left of the fairway and a big bunker on the right. The finish from there is tough, with subtle use made of individual trees to dictate strategy. Play left from the tee on the 13th and the second shot will be blocked out by the trees directly in front, and a large oak at the front left of the 17th green necessitates a shot drawn round behind it, if the pin is located on the left of the putting surface.

CARD OF THE MARQUESS COURSE

	yards	par		yards	par
1	395	4	10	374	4
2	506	5	11	579	5
3	473	4	12	343	4
4	425	4	13	467	4
5	415	4	14	219	3
6	159	3	15	575	5
7	538	5	16	450	4
8	188	3	17	176	3
9	473	4	18	425	4
Out	3,572	36	In	3,608	36
Total	7,180 yards	par 72			

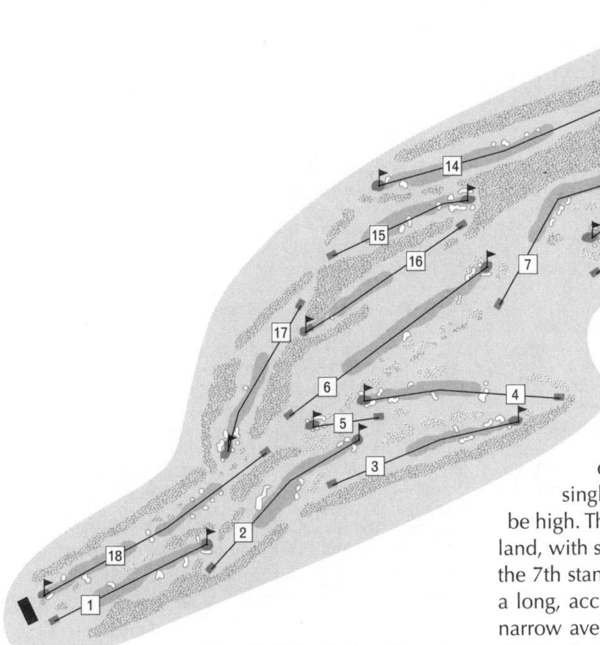

Woodhall Spa's already considerable profile was raised further when the English Golf Union bought it in 1995. It was a controversial action, but the EGU have invested heavily, for example by building a second course, The Bracken. The original course was then named The Hotchkin, in honour of Colonel S.V. Hotchkin, who rebuilt it during the 1920s, in the form we now know. The courses make a cleverly complementary pair. The Hotchkin, the world-famous championship course, is heathland in nature, with an enormous number of formidable bunkers, narrow fairways and firm, fast greens of a traditional type. The Bracken is a mixture of parkland and woodland with plenty of water hazards, bunkering in a more American style and greens laid to USGA specifications.

On the outward nine of The Bracken, water is an important feature. It is a very significant part of the strategy on the huge par-5 4th and short par-5 8th, but it is the island green of the short 16th that most players are thankful to leave unscathed.

On The Hotchkin course, heather and gorse devour wayward shots, while the deep bunkers are so numerous and perfectly positioned that golfers of all standards are made to think on every single shot, and the price of failure can be high. The first half is golf of the open heathland, with substantial par 4s and 5s from which the 7th stands out for the premium it places on a long, accurate drive. Coming home, through narrow avenues of trees, the par 4s tend to be shorter, but the 11th and 13th are exceptions, being tough and handsome holes. The 18th is a jewel – a par 5 with an intimidating drive from a tee back in the trees and a prominent oak tree to thwart the merest slice.

CARD OF THE HOTCHKIN COURSE

	yards	par		yards	par
1	361	4	10	338	4
2	442	4	11	437	4
3	415	4	12	172	3
4	414	4	13	451	4
5	148	3	14	521	5
6	526	5	15	321	4
7	470	4	16	395	4
8	209	3	17	336	4
9	584	5	18	540	5
Out	3,569	36	In	3,511	37
Total	7,080 yards	par 73			

EAST ENGLAND

The golfing bureaucrats have deemed that the East of England is in reality two distinct regions, with Middlesex, Hertfordshire and parts of Essex representing the bulk of golf in North and East London, while the remainder consists of largely rural East Anglia, principally Norfolk and Suffolk. Despite recent additions, the number of courses in these two counties is small, yet the quality is impressively high. Inevitably, those courses in and around the sprawl of London and its suburbs are busy all year round and it may take a number of telephone calls before a casual round of golf can be set up at short notice. On the plus side, green fees at many of these clubs are not excessive given their proximity to London. Happily, too, the geology of this part of the country ensures many a pleasant surprise, with even some of the Essex courses climbing significantly, and many of them giving expansive views.

Moor Park has hosted numerous important professional tournaments over the years, and there were a great many favourable comments from the international field of young amateurs who contested the 2001 Carris Trophy over its lovely, rolling High Course. Hanbury Manor, just outside Ware, has seen a number of recent European Tour events with Darren Clarke and Lee Westwood amongst the winners. It is said that good players win on good courses, and certainly the variety of challenges set on Nicklaus Junior's course is impressive, and there are fine views over the verdant Hertfordshire countryside from the front nine.

In complete contrast are a number of strongly traditional courses in East Anglia which shun the glittering lights, on which matchplay takes precedence over strokeplay, and on which no three- or four-ball play is permitted: Aldeburgh, Hunstanton, Royal West Norfolk and Royal Worlington & Newmarket head this list. All those fed up with the slow pace of play on so many of our golf courses should make every effort to experience their delights. All four enjoy brilliant architecture and superb greens, Hunstanton and Royal West Norfolk being fine genuine links courses, the other two inland, although sharing many links-like characteristics. There are also superb seaside tests at Felixstowe Ferry, Great Yarmouth, Royal Cromer and Sheringham, yet some of the finest golf is to be found inland, on well drained heathland. Ipswich boasts two such courses, at Purdis Heath and at Rushmere. Woodbridge has 27 particularly attractive holes running through heather and gorse, while the courses at Thetford and King's Lynn are more forested, both of them lengthy, testing and stunningly beautiful.

New courses are springing up throughout the region, in many welcome cases adding to the number of pay-and-play facilities of what had once been a rather golf-starved area. Modern construction techniques have opened up the possibilities of building courses amidst the dykes and drains of fenland, and water hazards to rival those of the fabled gator-ridden tracks of Florida now beckon here and there. Bring plenty of spare balls!

BEDFORDSHIRE

ASPLEY GUISE & WOBURN SANDS GOLF CLUB

West Hill, Aspley Guise, Milton Keynes, Bedfordshire MK17 8DX
✆ 01908 583596 Fax 01908 583596
Map 8, F8
M1 Jct 13, 2 miles W
Founded 1914
Sandy Herd's original 9 holes were expanded to 18 by Robert Sandow in 1972-4. Length on paper is not exceptional, but good use has been made of rolling countryside to locate elevated greens on holes such as the par-5 8th and 14th. The short 10th is a beauty.
18 holes, 6079 yards
par 71, S.S.S 70
Designer Sandy Herd, Robert Sandow
Green fees £26
Catering, changing room/showers, bar, trolley hire, shop, practice facilities
Visitors welcome weekdays
Handicap certificate required
Societies welcome by prior arrangement

AYLESBURY VALE GOLF CLUB

Stewkley Road, Wing, Leighton Buzzard, Bedfordshire LU7 OUJ
✆ 01525 240196 Fax 01525 240848
Map 8, E9
www.aylesburyvalegolfclub.i12.com
4 miles W of Leighton Buzzard
Founded 1990
Lengthy parkland course with a stream intersecting several holes, notably the 420-yard 13th. Good off-course facilities, and a friendly welcome.
18 holes, 6612 yards
par 72, S.S.S 72
Designer Don Wright
Green fees £13
Catering, changing room/showers, bar, club, trolley and buggy hire, shop, driving range, conference facilities
Visitors welcome
Societies welcome by prior arrangement
Heath Park House, 291 Heath Road, Leighton Buzzard, Beds, Bedfordshire
✆ 01523 381646

BEADLOW MANOR HOTEL GOLF & COUNTRY CLUB

Beadlow, Shefford, Bedfordshire SG17 5PH
✆ 01525 860800 Fax 01525 861345
Map 8, G8
A507, 2 miles W of Shefford
Founded 1973
Two American-style parkland courses with many water hazards.
Baron Course: 18 holes, 6691 yards, par 73, S.S.S 72
Baroness Course: 18 holes, 6072 yards, par 71, S.S.S 69
Green fees £16
Catering, changing room/showers, bar, accommodation, club, trolley and buggy hire, shop, driving range, practice facilities
Visitors welcome
Handicap certificate required
Societies welcome by prior arrangement
Beadlow Manor Hotel, Beadlow, Shefford, Bedfordshire
✆ 01525 860800

BEDFORD & COUNTY GOLF CLUB

Green Lane, Clapham, Bedford, Bedfordshire MK41 6ET
✆ 01234 359189 Fax 01234 357195
Map 8, F8
olga@bedcounty.fsnet.co.uk
www.bedfordandcountygolfclub.co.uk
A6, 2 miles NW of Bedford

Founded 1912
Pleasantly undulating course with a brook running across the 7th, 10th and 11th, and a particularly tough 470-yard par 4 at the 15th.
18 holes, 6399 yards
par 70, S.S.S 70
Green fees £24
Catering, changing room/showers, bar, trolley hire, shop, practice facilities
Visitors welcome weekdays
Handicap certificate required
Societies welcome by prior arrangement
Woodlands Manor, Green Lane, Clapham, Bedford, Bedfordshire MK41 6EP
01234 363281

THE BEDFORD GOLF CLUB

Carnoustie Drive, Great Denham Golf Village, Biddenham, Bedfordshire MK40 4FF
01234 320022 Fax 01234 320023
Map 8, F8
thebedford1@ukonline.co.uk
www.kolvengolf.com
A428, 2 miles W of Bedford
Founded 1999
A very new course, links-like in nature, on well-drained ground, in a part of the country not noted for its wet-weather play.
18 holes, 6478 yards
par 72, S.S.S 72
Green fees £25
Catering, changing room/showers, bar, club, trolley and buggy hire, shop, practice facilities, conference facilities
Visitors welcome weekdays
Societies welcome by prior arrangement
Shakespeare Hotel, Shakespeare Road, Bedford, Bedfordshire
01234 213147

BEDFORDSHIRE GOLF CLUB

Spring Lane, Stagsden, Bedford, Bedfordshire MK43 8SR
01234 822555 Fax 01234 825052
Map 8, F8
A422, 3 miles W of Bedford
Founded 1891
Trees both enhance the visual attraction of the course and provide many strategic hazards.
18 holes, 6565 yards
par 70, S.S.S 72
Green fees £24
Changing room/showers, trolley and buggy hire, shop
Visitors welcome weekdays
Societies welcome by prior arrangement

CHALGRAVE MANOR GOLF CLUB

Dunstable Road, Toddington, Dunstable, Bedfordshire LU5 6JN
01525 876556 Fax 01525 876556
Map 8, F9
A5120, M1 Jct 12, 2 miles W
Founded 1994
An undulating meadowland course with a 621-yard par-5 9th, which even exceeds 600 yards from the yellow plates.
18 holes, 6398 yards
par 72, S.S.S 70
Designer Mike Palmer
Green fees £15
Catering, changing room/showers, bar, trolley and buggy hire, shop, practice facilities
Visitors welcome – restricted weekends
Societies welcome by prior arrangement

COLMWORTH GOLF CLUB

New Road, Colmworth, Bedfordshire MK44 2NV
01234 378181 Fax 01234 376235
Map 8, F7
Off B660, 7 miles N of Bedford
Founded 1992
A wide open parkland course with a number of ponds.
18 holes, 6435 yards
par 72, S.S.S 71
Designer John Glasgow
Green fees £12
Changing room/showers, club, trolley and buggy hire, shop, driving range, practice facilities, par 3 course, fishing
Visitors welcome only as members' guests
Societies welcome by prior arrangement

COLWORTH GOLF CLUB

Unilver Research, Sharnbrook, Bedford, Bedfordshire MK44 1LQ
01933 353269 **Map 8, F7**
Off A6, 10 miles N of Bedford
Founded 1985
A private club attached to the Unilver Research establishment.
9 holes, 2626 yards
par 68, S.S.S 66
Green fees £6.50
Visitors-members' guests only
No societies

DUNSTABLE DOWNS GOLF CLUB

Whipsnade Road, Dunstable, Bedfordshire LU6 2NB
01582 604472 Fax 01582 478700
Map 8, F9
B4541, 2 miles S of Dunstable
Founded 1907
With nine holes in a valley, and nine on the downs, there is great variety to Dunstable Downs – and splendid views, too. The card is unusual, with eight par 4s and a solitary short hole on the back nine. Five long par 4s and the 572-yard 3rd test seriously.
18 holes, 6251 yards
par 70, S.S.S 70
Designer James Braid
Green fees £22.50
Catering, changing room/showers, bar, trolley hire, shop, practice facilities
Visitors welcome weekdays, restricted
Handicap certificate required
Societies welcome by prior arrangement
Kitt's Inn, 306 High Street North, Dunstable, Bedfordshire
01582 66231

GRIFFIN GOLF CLUB

Chaul End Road, Caddington, Bedfordshire LU1 4AX
01582 415573 Fax 01582 415314
Map 8, F9
A505, (M1 Jct 11)
Founded 1985
Ponds and lakes are a recurring hazard.
18 holes, 6240 yards
par 71, S.S.S 70
Green fees £13
Catering, changing room/showers, bar
Visitors welcome weekdays
Societies welcome by prior arrangement

JOHN O' GAUNT GOLF CLUB

Sutton Park, Sandy, Biggleswade, Bedfordshire SG19 2LY
01767 260360 Fax 01767 262834
Map 8, G8
B1040, 3 miles NE of Biggleswade
Founded 1948
Two contrasting courses on historic land. John O'Gaunt explores comparatively level parkland, with several very long par 4s of considerable difficulty, especially the 5th, 6th and 13th. Though shorter, Carthagena is equally full of character, with strong two-shotters at the 5th and 7th, and a distinctive finish to the round.
John O'Gaunt: 18 holes, 6513 yards, par 71, S.S.S 71
Designer F.W. Hawtree
Carthagena: 18 holes, 5869 yards, par 69, S.S.S 69
Designer Club members
Green fees £45
Catering, changing room/showers, bar, trolley and buggy hire, shop, practice facilities

Visitors welcome weekdays
Handicap certificate required
Societies welcome by prior arrangement

LEIGHTON BUZZARD GOLF CLUB

Plantation Road, Leighton Buzzard, Bedfordshire LU7 7JF
☎ 01525 373811/373812 **Map 8, F9**
Off A4146, 1½ miles N of Leighton Buzzard
Founded 1925
A parkland course with a challenging finish.
18 holes, 6101 yards
par 71, S.S.S 70
Green fees £20
Catering, changing room/showers, bar, club, trolley and buggy hire, shop, practice facilities
Visitors welcome weekdays, except Tuesday
Handicap certificate required
Societies welcome by prior arrangement

LYSHOTT HEATH GOLF CLUB

Ampthill, Bedfordshire MK45 2JB
☎ 01525 840252 Fax 01525 406249
Map 8, F8
www.lyshott-heath.com
A507, 4 miles from M1 Jct 12
Founded 1980
A long parkland course overlooking the Bedford Plain.
18 holes, 7021 yards
par 74, S.S.S 73
Designer William Sutherland
Green fees £20
Catering, changing room/showers, bar, trolley hire, shop, practice facilities
Visitors welcome, restricted Thursday and weekend
Societies welcome by prior arrangement

MOUNT PLEASANT

Station Road, Lower Stondon, Henlow, Bedfordshire SG16 6JL
☎ 01462 850999 **Map 8, G9**
davidsimsmpgolf@aol.com
Off A600 at 'Bird in Hand', 4 miles N of Hitchin
Founded 1992
As its name suggests, a pleasant parkland layout renowned for its presentation and maintenance. 18 tees give variation second time round.
9 holes, 6003 yards
par 70, S.S.S 69
Designer Derek Young
Green fees £13
Catering, changing room/showers, bar, club and trolley hire, shop, practice facilities
Visitors welcome – advance booking system
Societies welcome by prior arrangement
🏨 Sun Hotel, Sun Street, Hitchin, Hertfordshire
☎ 01462 436411

MOWSBURY GOLF CLUB

Kimbolton Road, Bedford, Bedfordshire MK41 8DQ
☎ 01234 216374/771041 **Map 8, F8**
B660, 2 miles N of Bedford
Founded 1975
A well-designed municipal course with excellent facilities.
18 holes, 6514 yards
par 72, S.S.S 71
Designer Hawtree
Green fees £7.50
Club and trolley hire, shop, driving range, squash
Visitors welcome
Societies welcome by prior arrangement

PAVENHAM PARK GOLF CLUB

Pavenham, Bedford, Bedfordshire MK43 7PE
☎ 01234 822202 Fax 01234 826602
Map 8, F8
Off A6, 4 miles NW of Bedford
Founded 1994
A parkland course designed by the club's professional Zac Thompson.
18 holes, 6353 yards
par 72, S.S.S 71
Designer Zac Thompson
Green fees £19
Catering, changing room/showers, bar, club, trolley and buggy hire, shop, practice facilities
Visitors welcome, weekdays
Societies welcome by prior arrangement

RAF HENLOW GOLF CLUB

RAF Henlow Camp, Henlow, Bedfordshire SG16 6DN
☎ 01462 851515 x7083 Fax 01462 816780 **Map 8, G8**
A600, 3 miles SE of Shefford
Founded 1985
A military course unavailable to the general public.
9 holes, 5618 yards
S.S.S 67
Green fees £10
Visitors welcome only as members' guests
No societies

SOUTH BEDS GOLF CLUB

Warden Hill Road, Luton, Bedfordshire LU2 7AE
☎ 01582 575201 Fax 01582 495381
Map 8, F9
Off A6, 2 miles N of Luton
Founded 1892
Undulating downland courses.
Galley Course: 18 holes, 6389 yards, par 71, S.S.S 71
Warden Course: 9 holes, 2424 yards, par 32, S.S.S 32
Green fees £20
Catering, changing room/showers, bar, trolley hire, shop, practice facilities
Visitors welcome weekdays
Handicap certificate required
Societies welcome by prior arrangement

STOCKWOOD PARK GOLF CLUB

Stockwood Park, London Road, Luton, Bedfordshire LU1 4LX
☎ 01582 413704 Fax 01582 481001
Map 8, F9
A6, 1 mile S of Bedford
Founded 1973
An expansive, municipal, parkland course, backed up with good practice facilities.
18 holes, 6049 yards
par 69, S.S.S 69
Green fees £8.70
Catering, changing room/showers, bar, club, trolley and buggy hire, shop, driving range, practice facilities
Visitors welcome
Societies welcome by prior arrangement

TILSWORTH GOLF CENTRE

Dunstable Road, Tilsworth, near Leighton Buzzard, Bedfordshire LU7 9PU
☎ 01525 210721 Fax 01525 210465
Map 8, F9
info@tilsworthgolf.co.uk
www.tilsworthgolf.co.uk
A5, close to Travelodge, M1 Jct 12
Founded 1975
Short parkland course with views of six counties from the 6th tee. Good facilities.
18 holes, 5306 yards
par 69, S.S.S 67
Green fees £12
Catering, changing room/showers, bar, club, trolley and buggy hire, shop, driving range, conference and function facilities
Visitors welcome
Societies welcome by prior arrangement
🏨 Travelodge, Watling Street, Hockliffe, Leighton Buzzard, Bedfordshire
☎ 08700 850950

WYBOSTON LAKES GOLF COURSE

Wyboston Lakes Business and Leisure Village, Wyboston, Bedfordshire MK44 3AL
✆ 01480 212625 Fax 01480 223000
Map 8, G7
golf@wybostonlakes.co.uk
www.wybostonlakes.co.uk
Jct A1 and A428 East, 1 mile S of St Neots
Founded 1978
A flat parkland course with five lakes, and bordered by the Great Ouse. Abundant wildlife.
18 holes, 5955 yards
par 70, S.S.S 70
Designer N. Oakden
Green fees £13
Catering, changing room/showers, bar, accommodation, club, trolley and buggy hire, shop, driving range, practice facilities, fishing, watersports, conference and training facilities
Visitors welcome – booking required for weekend
Societies welcome by prior arrangement
🏨 Premier Lodge, Great North Road, Eaton Socon, St Neots, Cambridgeshire PE19 3EN
✆ 0870 7001368

CAMBRIDGESHIRE

ABBOTSLEY GOLF HOTEL & COUNTRY CLUB

Eynesbury Hardwicke, St Neots, Cambridgeshire PE19 4XN
✆ 01480 477669 Fax 01480 471018
Map 8, G7
abbotsley@americangolf.uk.com
B1046, 2 miles S of St Neots
Founded 1976
An enterprising golf development, with plenty of water and trees. The Abbotsley is the harder course. Green fees are less for the Cromwell. Course designer, Vivien Saunders, is a past Women's British Open champion.
Abbotsley Course: 18 holes, 6311 yards, par 73, S.S.S 72
Designer Vivien Saunders
Cromwell Course: 18 holes, 6087yards, par 70, S.S.S 69
Green fees £19
Catering, changing room/showers, bar, accommodation, club, trolley and buggy hire, shop, driving range, practice facilities, fitness centre, squash courts, holistic health and beauty centre
Visitors welcome
Societies welcome by prior arrangement
🏨 Abbotsley Golf Hotel, Eynesbury Hardwicke, St Neots, Cambridgeshire PE19 6XN
✆ 01480 474000 Fax 01480 471018

BOURN GOLF CLUB

Toft Road, Bourn, Cambridge, Cambridgeshire CB3 7TT
✆ 01954 718057 Fax 01954 718908
Map 9, A7
Off B1046, M11 Jct 12
Founded 1991
An undulating parkland course with water features.
18 holes, 6417 yards
S.S.S 71
Green fees £16
Catering, changing room/showers, bar, club and trolley hire, shop, practice facilities
Visitors welcome weekdays
Societies welcome by prior arrangement

BRAMPTON PARK GOLF CLUB

Buckden Road, Brampton, Huntingdon, Cambridgeshire PE18 8NF
✆ 01480 434700 Fax 01480 411145
Map 8, G7
Off A1/A14, 3 miles W of Huntingdon
Founded 1991
A very attractive course with rivers, lakes and tall trees. With the presence of the Great Ouse and Lane Rivers, plus the Brampton Brook, there is an abundance of wildlife, including one of the biggest colonies of badgers in the region.
18 holes, 6300 yards
par 71, S.S.S 72
Designer Simon Gidman
Green fees £25
Catering, changing room/showers, bar, trolley hire, shop, practice facilities
Visitors welcome
Societies welcome by prior arrangement

CAMBRIDGE GOLF CLUB

Station Road, Longstanton, Cambridge, Cambridgeshire CB4 5DR
✆ 01954 789388 **Map 9, A7**
Off A14 at Bar Hill Junction W of Cambridge
Founded 1993
A long, rolling parkland course.
18 holes, 6800 yards
par 72, S.S.S 72
Green fees £13
Catering, changing room/showers, bar, club, trolley and buggy hire, driving range, practice facilities, conference facilities
Visitors welcome
Societies welcome by prior arrangement

CAMBRIDGE MERIDIAN GOLF CLUB

Comberton Road, Toft, Cambridge, Cambridgeshire CB3 7RY
✆ 01223 264700 Fax 01233 264701
Map 9, A7
www.golfsocieties.com
B1046 in Toft Village (access from M11 Jct 12 via A 603)
Founded 1994
From the very back tees the course extends to 7,200 yards, with the 200-yard 5th reckoned to be one of the hardest par 3s, with a four-tier green.
18 holes, 6707 yards
par 73, S.S.S 72
Designer Peter Alliss, Clive Clark
Green fees £17.50
Catering, changing room/showers, bar, club, trolley and buggy hire, shop, practice facilities, conference facilities
Visitors welcome
Societies welcome by prior arrangement

CAMBRIDGESHIRE MOAT HOUSE GOLF CLUB

Bar Hill, Cambridge, Cambridgeshire CB3 8EU
✆ 01954 780098 Fax 01954 780010
Map 9, A7
www.cambridgeshiregolf.co.uk
A14, 5 miles NW of Cambridge
Founded 1974
The trees have grown in a quarter of a century to enhance the seclusion of individual fairways and cut off some of the noise from the busy A14. There is considerable challenge to the design.
18 holes, 6734 yards
par 72, S.S.S 73
Green fees £21
Catering, changing room/showers, bar, accommodation, club, trolley and buggy hire, shop, practice facilities, conference & banqueting facilities
Visitors welcome with restrictions
Societies welcome by prior arrangement
🏨 Cambridgeshire Moat House, Bar Hill, Cambridgeshire
✆ 01954 249988

ELTON FURZE GOLF CLUB

Bullock Road, Haddon, Peterborough, Cambridgeshire PE7 3TT
✆ 01832 280189 Fax 01832 280299
Map 8, G5
secretary@eltonfurzegolfclub.co.uk
www.eltonfurzegolfclub.co.uk

Off A605, 4 miles W of Peterborough
Founded 1992
Attractive, wooded parkland course with ponds, ditches and slopes giving a good test of golf.
18 holes, 6279 yards
par 70, S.S.S 71
Designer Roger Fitton
Green fees £22
Catering, changing room/showers, bar, trolley and buggy hire, shop, driving range, practice facilities, available for functions
Visitors welcome – handicap preferred
Societies welcome by prior arrangement
🏨 Bell Inn, High Street, Stilton, Nr Peterborough, Cambridgeshire
✆ 01733 241066

ELY CITY GOLF CLUB

107 Cambridge Road, Ely, Cambridgeshire CB7 4HX
✆ 01353 663317 Fax 01353 668636
Map 9, B6
elygolf@lineone.net
www.elygolf.co.uk
1 mile S of City Centre
Founded 1961
A lengthy course, mature parkland, with views towards Ely Cathedral, a frequent host to county matches – an indication of its quality. Very friendly club.
18 holes, 6627 yards
par 72, S.S.S 72
Designer Sir Henry Cotton
Green fees £30
Catering, changing room/showers, bar, club and trolley hire, shop, practice facilities, snooker
Visitors welcome
Handicap certificate required
Societies welcome by prior arrangement
🏨 Nyton Hotel, Barton Road, Ely, Cambridgeshire
✆ 01353 662459

GIRTON GOLF CLUB

Dodford Lane, Girton, cambridge, Cambridgeshire CB3 OQE
✆ 01223 276991 Fax 01223 277150
Map 9, A7
secretary@girtongolfclub.sagehost.co.uk
www.girtongolfclub.sagenet.co.uk
2 miles N of Cambridge
Founded 1936
A mature parkland course, quite tight amongst the trees and bushes, and with excellent greens. The short holes are testing, and the closing stretch culminates in the 565-yard 18th.
18 holes, 6012 yards
par 69, S.S.S 69
Designer Allan Gow
Green fees £20
Catering, changing room/showers, bar, club and trolley hire, shop, practice facilities
Visitors welcome weekdays
Societies welcome Tuesday to Friday by prior arrangement
🏨 Post House, Lake View, Impington, Cambridge, Cambridgeshire
✆ 0870 400 9015

THE GOG MAGOG GOLF CLUB

Shelford Bottom, Cambridge, Cambridgeshire CB2 4AB
✆ 01223 247626 Fax 01223 414990
Map 9, B7
www.gogmagog.co.uk
A1307, 2 miles S of Cambridge
Founded 1901
The high ground of both courses gives superb views over Cambridge and the Fens, plus unrivalled drainage. After its opening stiff climb, the Old Course plays much like an inland links, being littered with bunkers, supplemented by many ridges and hollows, as typified by the par-5 7th and 8th.
Old Course: 18 holes, 6398 yards, par 70, S.S.S 70
Wandlebury: 18 holes, 6735 yards, par 72, S.S.S 72
Designer Martin Hawtree
Green fees £35
Catering, changing room/showers, bar, club and trolley hire, shop, driving range, practice facilities
Visitors welcome weekdays
Handicap certificate required
Societies welcome by prior arrangement

HEMINGFORD ABBOTTS GOLF CLUB

New Farm Lodge, Cambridge Road, Hemingford Abbotts, Cambridgeshire PE18 9HQ
✆ 01480 495000 Fax 01480 496149
Map 9, A7
A14, signposted Hemingford Abbotts
Founded 1991
Water hazards enliven this testing 9-hole course.
9 holes, 5468 yards
par 68, S.S.S 68
Designer Ray Paton
Green fees £12
Catering, changing room/showers, bar, club and trolley hire, shop, driving range
Visitors welcome, restricted weekends
Societies welcome by prior arrangement

HEYDON GRANGE GOLF & COUNTRY CLUB

Heydon, Royston, Cambridgeshire SG8 7NS
✆ 01763 208988 Fax 01763 208926
Map 9, A8
A505, near Duxford, M11 Jct 10
Founded 1994
Attractive, almost links-like courses in open country with good views and serious rough.
18 holes, 6512 yards,
par 72, S.S.S 72
Designer Cameron Sinclair
9 holes, 3249 yards,
par 36, S.S.S 36
Green fees £15
Catering, changing room/showers, bar, club, trolley and buggy hire, shop, driving range, practice facilities
Visitors welcome
Societies welcome by prior arrangement

LAKESIDE LODGE GOLF CENTRE

Fen Road, Pidley, Huntingdon, Cambridgeshire PE28 3DF
✆ 01487 740540 Fax 01487 740852
Map 8, G6
info@lakeside-lodge.co.uk
www.lakeside-lodge.co.uk
Off A141, NE of Huntingdon (signposted)
Founded 1992
Everything from an indoor golf simulator to a full-length course with eight lakes and 15,000 trees. Manor Course in process of extension.
Lodge Course: 18 holes, 6865 yards, par 72, S.S.S 73
Manor Course: 9 holes, 2601 yards, par 68
Designer A. Headley
Green fees £12
Catering, changing room/showers, bar, accommodation, club, trolley and buggy hire, shop, driving range, practice facilities, full conference facilities, indoor golf simulator,bowling, pitch and putt
Visitors welcome
Societies welcome by prior arrangement
🏨 Lakeside Lodge, Pidley, Huntingdon, Cambridgeshire PE28 3DF
✆ 01487 740540

MALTON GOLF CLUB

Malton Lane, Meldreth, Royston, Hertfordshire SG8 6PE
✆ 01763 262200 Fax 01763 262209
Map 9, A8
desk@maltongolf.co.uk
www.maltongolf.co.uk
Off A10, 4 miles N of Royston,

between Orwell and Meldreth
Founded 1994
With the River Cam running through the course, this is a haven for wildlife in the surrounding woodlands and wetlands. Beware the dangerous 7th!
18 holes, 6708 yards
par 72, S.S.S 72
Green fees £10
Catering, changing room/showers, bar, club, trolley and buggy hire, shop, driving range, practice facilities
Visitors welcome
Societies welcome by prior arrangement
🏨 Chiswick House, Meldreth, Royston, Hertfordshire SG8 6LZ
✆ 01763 260242

MARCH GOLF CLUB

Frogs Abbey, Grange Road, March, Cambridgeshire PE15 OYH
✆ 01354 652364 **Map 9, A5**
Off A141, March bypass
Founded 1922
Very flat, but not easy, 9-holer with the par-4 8th as the hardest hole.
9 holes, 6210 yards
par 70, S.S.S 70
Green fees £17
Catering, changing room/showers, bar, trolley hire, shop
Visitors welcome weekdays
Societies welcome by prior arrangement

OLD NENE GOLF & COUNTRY CLUB

Muchwood Lane, Bodsey, Ramsey, Cambridgeshire PE26 2XQ
✆ 01487 813519 **Map 8, H6**
1 mile N of Ramsey
Founded 1992
Typical of the new breed of East Anglian course, flat (inevitably) and making much use of water in its defences.
9 holes, 5605 yards
par 68, S.S.S 68
Designer Richard Edrich
Green fees £10
Catering, changing room/showers, bar, club, trolley and buggy hire, shop, driving range, practice facilities
Visitors welcome
Societies welcome by prior arrangement

ORTON MEADOWS GOLF CLUB

Ham Lane, Peterborough, Cambridgeshire PE2 5UU
✆ 01733 237478 **Map 8, G5**
www.ortonmeadowsgolfcourse.co.uk
A605, 3 miles SW of Peterborough
Founded 1987
Unusually challenging for a public course, with many water hazards to inhibit the diffident beginner.
18 holes, 5664 yards
par 67, S.S.S 68
Designer D. & R. Fitton
Green fees £10.50
Catering, changing room/showers, bar, club and trolley hire, shop, practice facilities, pitch & putt course
Visitors welcome
Societies welcome by prior arrangement

PETERBOROUGH MILTON GOLF CLUB

Milton Ferry, Peterborough, Cambridgeshire PE6 7AG
✆ 01733 380489 Fax 01733 380489
Map 8, G5
Off A47, 4 miles W of Peterborough
Founded 1937
Built to prevent urban development, this is one of James Braid's last courses. Among many strengths are the several dog-legs which put pressure on placing the drive – the 10th and 15th, for instance. The short holes are fascinating, and a new lake has added spice to the 1st and 18th.
18 holes, 6479 yards
par 71, S.S.S 72
Designer James Braid
Green fees £25
Catering, changing room/showers, bar, trolley hire, shop, driving range, conference facilities
Visitors welcome weekdays
Handicap certificate required
Societies welcome by prior arrangement

RAMSEY GOLF CLUB

4 Abbey Terrace, Ramsey, Huntingdon, Cambridgeshire PE26 1DD
✆ 01487 812600 Fax 01487 815746
Map 8, H6
admin@ramseygolf.com
Off A1, onto B660 into Ramsey
Founded 1922
Parkland course exposed to the wind. Trees and water hazards define strategy. Well maintained.
18 holes, 6163 yards
par 71, S.S.S 70
Green fees £25
Catering, changing room/showers, bar, club and trolley hire, shop, practice facilities
Visitors welcome weekdays
Handicap certificate required
Societies welcome by prior arrangement
🏨 Anchor Inn, Sutton Gault, Cambridgeshire CB6 2BD
✆ 01353 778537 Fax 01353 776180
anchor-sutton-gault@compuserve.com

ST IVES GOLF CLUB

St Ives, Huntingdon, Cambridgeshire PE27 6DH
✆ 01480 64459 Fax 01480 468392
Map 8, H7
Off A1123, W of St Ives
Founded 1923
A parkland course.
9 holes, 6180 yards
par 70, S.S.S 70
Green fees £20
Catering, changing room/showers, bar, club and trolley hire, shop
Visitors welcome weekdays
Handicap certificate required
Societies welcome by prior arrangement
🏨 Abbotsley Golf Hotel, Eynesbury Hardwicke, St Neots, Cambridgeshire PE19 6XN
✆ 01480 474000 Fax 1480 471018

ST NEOTS GOLF CLUB

Crosshall Road, St Neots, Cambridgeshire PE19 7AE
✆ 01480 472363 Fax 01480 472363
Map 8, G7
office@stneots-golfclub.co.uk
www.stneots-golfclub.co.uk
A1, at B1048 junction to Higham Ferrars.
Founded 1890
The oldest club in Cambridgeshire, with the River Kym and a number of ponds much in evidence, particularly on the front nine.
18 holes, 6033 yards
par 69, S.S.S 69
Designer Harry Vardon
Green fees £25
Catering, changing room/showers, bar, club, trolley and buggy hire, shop, practice facilities
Visitors welcome weekdays
Handicap certificate required
Societies welcome by prior arrangement
🏨 Eaton Oak, Great North Road, St Neots, Cambridgeshire
✆ 01480 219555

THORNEY GOLF CENTRE

English Drove, Thorney, Peterborough, Cambridgeshire PE6 OTJ
✆ 01733 270570 Fax 01733 270842
Map 8, G5
A47, E of Peterborough, signposted from Thorney village
Founded 1991
Two fenland courses, of which the Lakes Course is somewhat harder,

particularly given its many water features.
Lakes: 18 holes, 6402 yards, par 71, S.S.S 70
Fen: 18 holes, 6104 yards, par 70, S.S.S 69
Designer Alan Hind, Ian Matthews, Angus Dow
Green fees £11.50
Catering, changing room/showers, bar, club, trolley and buggy hire, shop, driving range, practice facilities, gym, function facilities, additional 9-hole course
Visitors welcome
Societies welcome by prior arrangement

THORPE WOOD GOLF CLUB

Nene Parkway, Peterborough, Cambridgeshire PE3 6SE
✆ 01733 267701 Fax 01733 332774
Map 8, G5
www.thorpewoodgolfcourse.co.uk
A47, 3 miles W of Peterborough
Founded 1975
A remarkable public course, of enormous length and seriously testing, representing astonishing value for money.
18 holes, 7086 yards
par 73, S.S.S 74
Designer Peter Alliss, Dave Thomas
Green fees £10.70
Catering, changing room/showers, bar, club and trolley hire, shop, practice facilities
Visitors welcome – prior booking system
Societies welcome by prior arrangement

TYDD ST GILES

Kirkgate, Tydd St Giles, Wisbech, Cambridgeshire PE13 5NZ
✆ 01945 871007 Fax 01945 870566
Map 9, A4
Off A1101, 4 miles NW of Wisbech
Founded 1994
A new course, one of the few in The Fens.
18 holes, 6226 yards
par 70, S.S.S 70
Green fees £8.50
Visitors welcome by prior arrangement
Societies welcome by prior arrangement

WATERBEACH GOLF CLUB

Waterbeach Barracks, Waterbeach, Cambridge, Cambridgeshire CB5 9PA
✆ 01223 575260 Fax 01223 511525
Map 9, B7
Off A10, NE of Cambridge
Founded 1968
A private club attached to the old military barracks.
9 holes, 6236 yards
par 70, S.S.S 70
Green fees £10
Visitors only as members' guests
No societies

ESSEX

ABRIDGE GOLF & COUNTRY CLUB

Epping Lane, Stapleford Tawney, Essex RM4 1ST
✆ 01708 688396 Fax 01708 688550
Map 16, G4
www.abridgegolfclub.co.uk
M11 Jct 6, M25 Jct 27
Founded 1964
One of only a handful of British courses designed by Henry Cotton, Abridge begins to turn the screw after the turn when a run of long par 4s culminates in the 471-yard 14th, its green on the far side of a pond. The dog-leg 3rd is almost as demanding.
18 holes, 6686 yards
par 72, S.S.S 72
Designer Henry Cotton
Green fees £30
Catering, changing room/showers, bar, club, trolley and buggy hire, shop, driving range, practice facilities, swimming pool, sauna, conference and wedding facilities
Visitors welcome weekdays
Handicap certificate required
Societies welcome by prior arrangement

BALLARDS GORE GOLF & COUNTRY CLUB

Gore Road, Canewdon, Rochford, Essex SS4 2DA
✆ 01702 258917 Fax 01702 258571
Map 5, E1
2 miles NE of Rochford
Founded 1980
A long parkland course with many water hazards.
18 holes, 6874 yards
par 73, S.S.S 73
Designer D.T. J. Caton
Green fees £20
Catering, changing room/showers, bar, trolley and buggy hire, shop, practice facilities
Visitors welcome weekdays
Societies welcome by prior arrangement

BASILDON GOLF CLUB

Clayhill Lane, Sparrow's Hearne, Basildon, Essex SS16 5JP
✆ 01286 533297 Fax 01208 533849
Map 5, D2
Off A176, 1 mile S of Basildon
Founded 1967
A mature parkland course.
18 holes, 6236 yards
par 72, S.S.S 70
Green fees £9
Catering, changing room/showers, bar, club, trolley and buggy hire, shop, practice facilities
Visitors welcome
Societies welcome by prior arrangement

BELFAIRS GOLF CLUB

Eastwood Road North, Leigh-on-Sea, Essex SS9 4LR
✆ 01702 52345 **Map 5, D2**
Off A127
Founded 1926
A very valuable commodity, a Colt-designed municipal course of some difficulty.
18 holes, 5802 yards
par 70, S.S.S 68
Designer Harry Colt
Green fees £11
Catering, changing room/showers, bar, club and trolley hire, shop, tennis, pitch & putt
Visitors welcome
Societies welcome by prior arrangement

BELHUS PARK GOLF CLUB

Belhus Park, South Ockendon, Essex RM15 4QR
✆ 01708 854260 **Map 16, H6**
N of A13, Avely turn, M25 Jct 30
Founded 1975
A mature parkland course with the full facilities of a leisure centre.
18 holes, 5604 yards
par 69, S.S.S 68
Green fees £14
Catering, changing room/showers, bar, club and trolley hire, shop, driving range, leisure centre, swimming pool, large function facilities
Visitors welcome
Societies welcome by prior arrangement
Thurrock Hotel, South Ockendon, Aveley, Essex

BENTLEY GOLF CLUB

Ongar Road, Brentwood, Essex CM15 9SS
✆ 01277 373179 Fax 01277 375097
Map 16, H3
A128, between Brentwood and Ongar, M25 Jct 8
Founded 1973
A parkland course with water hazards, both ponds and ditches, coming into play on 11 holes. Two of the par 3s are over 200 yards long, and the mid-length par-3 12th has a lake and two ditches to protect the

green.
18 holes, 6709 yards
par 72, S.S.S 72
Designer Alec Swan
Green fees £22
Catering, changing room/showers, bar, trolley and buggy hire, shop, practice facilities
Visitors welcome weekdays
Societies welcome by prior arrangement
🏨 Forte Posthouse, Brook Street, Brentwood, Essex
✆ 01277 260260

BENTON HALL GOLF CLUB

Wickham Hill, Witham, Essex CM8 3LH
✆ 01376 502454 Fax 01376 521050
Map 9, D10
m.orwin@clubhaus.com
www.clubhaus.com
A12, 8 miles NE of Chelmsford, M25 Jct 28
Founded 1992
With the River Blackwater flowing through the course, supplemented by ponds and ditches, water affects play on eleven holes of this handsome but testing course. On the back nine a number of holes climb quite steeply.
18 holes, 6495 yards
par 72, S.S.S 72
Designer Alan Walker, Chris Cox
Green fees £11
Catering, changing room/showers, bar, club, trolley and buggy hire, shop, driving range, practice facilities, 9-hole, par-3 course, extensive function facilities
Visitors welcome, subject to restrictions
Societies welcome by prior arrangement
🏨 White Hart, Coggeshall, near Colchester, Essex CO6 1NH
✆ 01376 561654 Fax 01376 561789

BIRCH GROVE GOLF CLUB

Layer Road, Kingsford, Colchester, Essex CO2 0HS
✆ 01206 734276 Fax 01206 734276
Map 9, E9
B1026, 2 miles S of Colchester
Founded 1970
Attractive course, on which the dog-leg 6th stands out, running through woodland, with water hazards and out-of-bounds threatening.
9 holes, 4532 yards
par 66, S.S.S 63
Designer M. Marston
Green fees £12
Catering, changing room/showers, bar, trolley hire, shop, practice facilities, small conference room
Visitors welcome – restricted Sunday mornings
Societies welcome by prior arrangement
🏨 Kingsford Park Hotel, Layer Road, Colchester, Essex
✆ 01206 734301

BOYCE HILL GOLF CLUB

Vicarage Hill, Benfleet, Essex SS7 1PD
✆ 01268 793625 Fax 01268 750497
Map 5, D2
boycehill@hotmail.com
4 miles W of Southend
Founded 1922
Unusually hilly for an Essex course, with resultant good views over the Thames Estuary, Boyce Hill puts a premium on skilled shotmaking with its inevitable uphill, downhill and sidehill lies. The club, happily, maintains the old practice of naming its holes.
18 holes, 6003 yards
par 68, S.S.S 68
Designer James Braid
Green fees £25
Catering, changing room/showers, bar, trolley hire, shop
Visitors welcome weekdays
Handicap certificate required
Societies welcome by prior arrangement, Thursdays only
🏨 Post House, Basildon, Essex
✆ 01904 620033

BRAINTREE GOLF CLUB

Kings Lane, Stisted, Braintree, Essex CM7 8DA
✆ 01376 346079 Fax 01376 348677
Map 9, C9
manager@braintreegolfclub.freeserve.co.uk
www.braintreegolfclub.co.uk
Off A120, 2 miles NE of Braintree
Founded 1891
Laid out to make the most of the wonderful trees in the Stisted Hall estate (to which the club moved in 1973) and with views of the River Blackwater, Braintree enjoys glorious surroundings. A newly extended clubhouse makes this a particularly enjoyable environment for golf for member and visitor alike.
18 holes, 6175 yards
par 70, S.S.S 69
Designer Hawtree
Green fees £25
Catering, changing room/showers, bar, trolley and buggy hire, shop, practice facilities
Visitors welcome – subject to restrictions
Handicap certificate required
Societies welcome by prior arrangement
🏨 White Hart, Coggeshall, Near Colchester, Essex CO6 1NH
✆ 01376 561654 Fax 01376 561789

BRAXTED PARK GOLF CLUB

Braxted Park, Witham, Essex CM8 3EN
✆ 01376 572372 Fax 01621 892840
Map 9, D10
A12, NE of Witham
Founded 1953
A pay and play course of some age in a handsome parkland setting.
9 holes, 2940 yards
par 70, S.S.S 68
Designer Sir Allen Clark
Green fees £12
Catering, changing room/showers, bar, trolley hire, shop, fishing
Visitors welcome weekdays
Societies welcome by prior arrangement

BUNSAY DOWNS GOLF CLUB

Little Baddow Road, Woodham Walter, Maldon, Essex CM9 6RW
✆ 01245 412648 **Map 9, C10**
Off A414, E of Chelmsford
Founded 1982
A short public course which can boast Mickey Walker as its professional.
9 holes, 2913 yards
par 70, S.S.S 68
Green fees £10
Catering, changing room/showers, bar, club, trolley and buggy hire, shop, driving range, practice facilities, par 3 course
Visitors welcome weekdays
Societies welcome by prior arrangement

BURNHAM-ON-CROUCH GOLF CLUB

Ferry Road, Burnham-on-Crouch, Essex CM10 8PQ
✆ 01621 782282 Fax 01621 784489
Map 5, E1
burnhamgolf@hotmail.com
B1010, 1 mile W of Burnham
Founded 1923
A parkland course overlooking the River Crouch with some of the finest views on any Essex course. Surprisingly hilly in parts, the course can seem difficult when the wind gets up.
18 holes, 6056 yards
par 70, S.S.S 69
Designer Howard Swann
Green fees £26
Catering, changing room/showers, bar, trolley and buggy hire, practice facilities
Visitors welcome weekdays
Societies welcome by prior arrangement
🏨 White Hart Hotel, The Quay,

Burbham-on-Crouch, Essex
CM0 8AS
☎ 01621 782106

THE BURSTEAD GOLF CLUB

Tye Common Road, Little Burstead, Billericay, Essex CM12 9SS
☎ 01277 631171 Fax 01277 632766
Map, C11
Off A176, 2 miles S of Billericay
Founded 1995
A testing new course in pretty parkland, with water hazards.
18 holes, 6275 yards
par 71, S.S.S 70
Designer Patrick Tallack
Green fees £19
Catering, changing room/showers, bar, trolley and buggy hire, shop, practice facilities
Visitors welcome weekday
Handicap certificate required
Societies welcome by prior arrangement

CANONS BROOK GOLF CLUB

Elizabeth Way, Harlow, Essex CM19 5BE **Map 16, F2**
☎ 01279 421 482 Fax 01279 626 393
M11 Jct 7
Founded 1962
A challenging course, not only long but also requiring considerable accuracy. The eponymous Canons Brook affects the 1st, 17th and 18th, with the 17th one of the star holes.
18 holes, 6763 yards
par 73, S.S.S 73
Designer Henry Cotton
Green fees £23
Catering, changing room/showers, bar, club, trolley and buggy hire, shop, practice facilities
Visitors welcome weekdays
Societies welcome by prior arrangement

CASTLE POINT GOLF CLUB

Waterside Farm, Somnes Avenue, Canvey Island, Essex SS8 9FG
☎ 01268 510830 **Map 5, D2**
A130, on Canvey Island
Founded 1988
Very exposed to the wind which whistles up the Thames Estuary, and with considerable use of water hazards, an exacting test.
18 holes, 6153 yards
par 71, S.S.S 69
Green fees £9
Catering, changing room/showers, bar, club, trolley and buggy hire, shop, driving range
Visitors welcome
Societies welcome by prior arrangement

CHANNELS GOLF CLUB

Belsteads Farm Lane, Little Waltham, Chelmsford, Essex CM3 3PT
☎ 01245 440005 Fax 01245 442032
Map 9, C10
www.channelsgolf.co.uk
Off A130, 3 miles N of Chelmsford
Founded 1975
A brilliant use of reclaimed gravel workings. As the name implies, water is a major factor on the Channels Course, while Belsteads is less intimidating for the beginner. The par-3 17th on the Channels Course is a do-or-die water hole, all carry, and the 330-yard 6th is equally uncompromising.
Channels Course: 18 holes, 6402 yards, par 71, S.S.S 71
Designer Sir Henry Cotton, Howard Swan
Belsteads Course: 9 holes, 4779 yards, par 67, S.S.S 63
Designer Howard Swan
Green fees £27
Catering, changing room/showers, bar, trolley and buggy hire, shop, driving range, practice facilities, conference, wedding, function facilities
Visitors welcome, weekdays only (Channels); every day (Belsteads)
Societies welcome by prior arrangement

CHELMSFORD GOLF CLUB

Widford, Chelmsford, Essex CM2 9AP
☎ 01245 256483 Fax 01245 256483
Map 9, C10
Office@chelmsfordgc.sagehost.co.uk
www.chelmsfordgc.sagehost.co.uk
Off A12, A1016 towards Widford
Founded 1893
A charming, well wooded course, surprisingly hilly, with highly-reputed fast greens. Matching par is far from easy with many dog-legs and a good number of lengthy par 4s. The 3rd, for example, is a tight 468-yard par 4 curving through the trees with its fairway interrupted by a stream.
18 holes, 5981 yards
par 68, S.S.S 69
Designer Harry Colt
Green fees £35
Catering, changing room/showers, bar, trolley and buggy hire, shop, practice facilities
Visitors welcome weekdays
Handicap certificate required
Societies welcome by prior arrangement

CHIGWELL GOLF CLUB

High Road, Chigwell, Essex IG7 5BH
☎ 020 8500 2059 Fax 020 8501 3410 **Map 16, F4**
info@chigwellgolfclub.co.uk
www.chigwellgolfclub.co.uk
A113, M11 Jct 4
Founded 1925
A remarkably undulating and attractive parkland course, with very long par 4s at the 1st and 15th.
18 holes, 6279 yards
par 71, S.S.S 70
Designer F. Hawtree, J.H. Taylor
Green fees £35
Catering, changing room/showers, bar, club and trolley hire, shop, practice facilities
Visitors welcome weekdays
Handicap certificate required
Societies welcome by prior arrangement
Prince Regent Hotel, Manor Road, Woodford Bridge, Essex IG8 8AE
☎ 020 8505 9966

CLACTON-ON-SEA GOLF CLUB

West Road, Clacton-on-Sea, Essex CO15 1AJ
☎ 01255 421919 Fax 01255 424602
Map 9, F10
www.clactongolfclub.com
On sea front SW of town centre
Founded 1892
A flat course, exposed to the wind, behind the sea wall. Fleets (ditches) threaten many holes and lakes feature on the 1st/16th, 15th and 17th. Big par 4s occupy the first five stroke rankings, with the 360-yard 14th next, a tricky hole, through fleets to a two-level green.
18 holes, 6532 yards
par 71, S.S.S 71
Green fees £20
Changing room/showers, club, trolley and buggy hire, shop
Visitors welcome
Handicap certificate required
Societies welcome by prior arrangement

COLCHESTER GOLF CLUB

Braiswick, Colchester, Essex CO4 5AU
☎ 01206 853396 Fax 01206 852698
Map 9, E9
B1508, NW of town centre
Founded 1909
One of the best courses in Essex, yet it is hard to reconcile today's course with what was left at the end of the Second World War: a military training ground. Trees give individuality and a degree of seclusion to each hole. The final two

holes constitute a testing finish.
18 holes, 6347 yards
par 70, S.S.S 70
Designer James Braid
Green fees £25
Catering, changing room/showers, bar, trolley hire, shop, driving range
Visitors welcome weekdays
Handicap certificate required
Societies welcome by prior arrangement

COLNE VALLEY GOLF CLUB

Station Road, Earls Colne, Colchester, Essex CO6 2LT
✆ 01787 224343 Fax 01787 224126
Map 9, D9
A1124 at Earls Colne, between Halstead and Colchester.
Founded 1991
Plentiful water hazards, not least the River Colne, and USGA standard greens enhance this parkland course in pretty countryside.
18 holes, 6303 yards
par 70, S.S.S 70
Designer Howard Swan
Green fees £18
Catering, changing room/showers, bar, trolley and buggy hire, shop, practice facilities, function suite, snooker, pool
Visitors welcome, restricted weekends
Societies welcome by prior arrangement

CRONDON PARK GOLF CLUB

Stock Road, Stock, Essex CM4 9DP
✆ 01277 841115 Fax 01277 841356
Map 9, C10
B1007, off A12, 5 miles S of Chelmsford.
Founded 1994
Water hazards feature widely on this appealing parkland course.
18 holes, 6585 yards
par 72, S.S.S 71
Designer Martin Gillett
Green fees £17
Catering, changing room/showers, bar, trolley and buggy hire, shop, driving range, 9-hole course
Visitors welcome weekdays
Societies welcome by prior arrangement

ELSENHAM GOLF CENTRE

Hall Road, Elsenham, Bishop's Stortford, Essex CM22 6DH
✆ 01279 812865 Fax 01279 816970
Map 9, B9
B1051, off M11, close to Stansted Airport
Founded 1997
The ideal relaxation while waiting for that long delayed holiday flight?
9 holes, 5854 yards
par 70
Green fees £10
Visitors welcome
Societies welcome by prior arrangement

EPPING FOREST GOLF & COUNTRY CLUB

Woolston Manor, Abridge Road, Chigwell, Essex IG7 6BX
✆ 020 8500 2549 Fax 020 8501 5452 **Map 16, F4**
M11 Jct 5
Founded 1994
Neil Coles has been one of the early advocates of stadium golf designs, and all his layouts show comtemporary design features.
18 holes, 6408 yards
S.S.S 71
Designer Neil Coles
Green fees £28
Catering, changing room/showers, bar, trolley hire, shop, driving range
Visitors welcome weekdays
Handicap certificate required
Societies welcome by prior arrangement

ESSEX GOLF COMPLEX

Garon Park, Eastern Avenue, Southend-on-Sea, Essex SS2 4PT
✆ 01702 601701 Fax 01702 601033
Map 5, E2
www.essexgolfcentre.com
A127 towards Southend, signposted
Founded 1993
Admirably, the short course is maintained to the same level as the main course. 9 new holes are under construction. 12 lakes come into play on the current main course.
18 holes, 6237 yards, par 70, S.S.S 70
Designer Alan Walker, Charles Cox
9 holes, 948 yards, par 27, S.S.S 27
Green fees £16
Catering, changing room/showers, bar, club, trolley and buggy hire, shop, driving range, practice facilities
Visitors welcome
Societies welcome by prior arrangement

THE ESSEX GOLF & COUNTRY CLUB

Earls Colne, Colchester, Essex CO6 2NS
✆ 01787 224466 Fax 01787 224410
Map 9, D9
B1024, off A120
Founded 1991
Extensive sporting facilities constructed on the site of a famous Second World War airfield.
County Course: 18 holes, 6982 yards, par 73, S.S.S 73
Designer Reg Plumbridge
Garden Course: 9 holes, 2771 yards, par 34, S.S.S 34
Green fees £25
Catering, changing room/showers, bar, club, trolley and buggy hire, shop, driving range, practice facilities, tennis, swimming, fishing, gym, health club, conference and function facilities
Visitors welcome
Societies welcome by prior arrangement

FAIRLOP WATERS GOLF CLUB

Forest Road, Barkingside, Ilford, Essex IG6 3JA
✆ 020 8500 9911 **Map 16, F5**
2 miles from end of M11, Fairlop underground station
Founded 1987
A parkland course.
18 holes, 6288 yards
S.S.S 72
Green fees £7.50
Driving range, par 3 course
Visitors welcome
Societies welcome by prior arrangement

FIVE LAKES HOTEL GOLF & COUNTRY CLUB

Colchester Road, Tolleshunt Knights, Maldon, Essex CM9 8HX
✆ 01621 868888 Fax 01621 869696
Map 9, D10
B1026, 8 miles S of Colchester
Founded 1974
Both courses feature plentiful water hazards, with fine views towards the River Blackwater. Once known as Quietwaters and, before that, Manifold.
Lakes Course: 18 holes, 6767 yards, par 72, S.S.S 72
Designer Neil Coles
Links Course: 18 holes, 6250 yards, par 71, S.S.S 70
Green fees £18
Catering, changing room/showers, bar, accommodation, club, trolley and buggy hire, shop, driving range, full hotel, conference & function facilities, swimming pool, squash, gym
Visitors welcome
Societies welcome by prior arrangement
Five Lakes Hotel, Colchester Road, Tolleshunt Knights, Maldon, Essex CM9 8HX
✆ 01621 868888

FORRESTER PARK GOLF CLUB

Beckingham Road, Great Totham, Near Maldon, Essex CM9 8EA
✆ 01621 891406 Fax 01621 891406
Map 9, D10

B1022 near Maldon.
Founded 1968
A parkland course with a historic clubhouse and lovely views.
18 holes, 6073 yards
par 71, S.S.S 72
Designer Forrester-Muir, Everett
Green fees £18
Catering, changing room/showers, bar, trolley and buggy hire, shop, driving range, practice facilities, conference and function facilities, tennis
Visitors welcome, restricted weekends
Societies welcome by prior arrangement
🏨 Rivenhall Motor Inn, Rivenhall, Essex
✆ 01376 516969

FRINTON GOLF CLUB

1 The Esplanade, Frinton-on-Sea, Essex CO13 9EP
✆ 01255 674618 Fax 01255 674618
Map 9, F9
SW of town centre
Founded 1895
As at neighbouring Clacton, ditches cross many fairways where golfers would prefer they did not. The wind is rarely absent.
Long Course: 18 holes, 6259 yards, par 71, S.S.S 70
Designer Willie Park, Harry Colt
Short Course: 9 holes, 2508 yards,
Green fees £26
Catering, changing room/showers, bar, club, trolley and buggy hire, shop, practice facilities
Visitors welcome weekdays, restricted weekends
Handicap certificate required
Societies welcome by prior arrangement

GOSFIELD LAKE GOLF CLUB

The Manor House, Gosfield, Halstead, Essex CO9 1SE
✆ 01787 474747 Fax 01787 476044
Map 9, C9
B1017, 7 miles N of Braintree
Founded 1986
The Lakes course lives up to its name with water entering play on many holes. The Meadows course is a much gentler affair.
Lakes Course: 18 holes, 6756 yards, par 72, S.S.S 72
Designer Sir Henry Cotton, Howard Swann
Meadows Course: 9 holes, 4180 yards, par 66, S.S.S 63
Green fees £30
Catering, changing room/showers, bar, trolley and buggy hire, shop, practice facilities
Visitors welcome
Handicap certificate required for Lakes Course
Societies welcome by prior arrangement

HAINAULT FOREST GOLF COMPLEX

Romford Road, Chigwell Row, Essex IG7 4QW
✆ 0208 500 2131 Fax 0208 501 5196 **Map 16, F4**
www.essexgolfcentre.com
A1112, off A12 from M25 Jct 29
Founded 1904
Public courses of some antiquity, hilly, and scenic.
Lower Course: 18 holes, 6545 yards, par 72, S.S.S 72
Upper Course: 18 holes, 5886 yards, par 70, S.S.S 68
Designer J.H. Taylor, F. Hawtree
Green fees £15
Catering, changing room/showers, bar, club, trolley and buggy hire, shop, driving range, practice facilities, conference facilities
Visitors welcome
Societies welcome by prior arrangement

HARTSWOOD GOLF CLUB

King George's Playing Fields, Ingrave Road, Brentwood, Essex CM14 5AE
✆ 01277 214830 **Map 16, H4**
A128, 1 mile S of Brentwood
Founded 1971
A private members' club playing over a municipal golf course. The private club hosts society visits.
18 holes, 6192 yards
par 70, S.S.S 69
Green fees £10
Catering, changing room/showers, bar, trolley hire, shop
Visitors welcome
Societies welcome by prior arrangement
🏨 Post House, London Road, Brentwood, Essex CM14 5NF
✆ 0870 400 9012

HARWICH & DOVERCOURT GOLF CLUB

Station Road, Parkeston, Harwich, Essex CO12 4NZ
✆ 01255 503616 Fax 01255 503323
Map 9, F9
Off A120, near ferry terminal
Founded 1906
A compact 9-hole course, long established, close to the busy ferry port.
9 holes, 2950 yards
par 70, S.S.S 69
Green fees £17
Catering, changing room/showers, bar, trolley hire
Visitors welcome weekdays.
Handicap certificate required
Societies welcome by prior arrangement

HIGH BEECH GOLF COURSE

Wellington Hill, Loughton, Essex IG10 4AH
✆ 020 8508 7323 **Map 16, E4**
M11 to Loughton or M25 to Waltham Abbey
Founded 1963
A par-3 course set in the heart of Epping Forest.
9 holes, 1477 yards
par 27
Green fees £3.70
Club and trolley hire, shop
Visitors welcome
Societies welcome by prior arrangement

ILFORD GOLF CLUB

291 Wanstead Park Road, Ilford, Essex IG1 3TR
✆ 020 8554 0094 Fax 020 8554 0822 **Map 16, F5**
www.ilfordgolfclub.co.uk
M11 end, A406, A12 East, The Drive.
Founded 1907
A compact, but testing course on which three holes cross the River Roding.
18 holes, 5299 yards
par 67, S.S.S 66
Green fees £15
Catering, changing room/showers, bar, trolley hire, shop
Visitors welcome weekdays
Societies welcome by prior arrangement
🏨 Forte Ilford Travelodge, Beehive Harvester, Gants Hill, Ilford, Essex
✆ 0870 90 56343

LANGDON HILLS GOLF CENTRE

Lower Dunton Road, Bulphan, Essex RM14 3TY
✆ 01268 548444 Fax 01268 490084
Map 16, H5
Off A128 between A13 and A127 (M25 Jct 29)
Founded 1991
From one of the few hills in Essex there are expansive views over the city of London.
Bulphan Course: 9 holes, 3372 yards, par 37,
Horndon Course: 9 holes, 3054 yards, par 36,
Langdon Course: 9 holes, 3132 yards, par 35,
Green fees £14.85
Catering, changing room/showers, bar, trolley and buggy hire, shop, driving range, practice facilities

Visitors welcome
Societies welcome by prior arrangement

LEXDEN WOOD GOLF CLUB

Bakers Lane, Colchester, Essex CO3 4AU
☎ 01206 843333 Fax 01706 854775
Map 9, E9
Off A12/A133
Founded 1995
Perhaps the most commendable feature of this complex is its Junior Golf Academy, at which juniors are given free tuition. New clubhouse and professional facilities on stream.
18 holes, 5608 yards
par 67, S.S.S 64
Green fees £18
Catering, changing room/showers, bar, club, trolley and buggy hire, shop, driving range, practice facilities, par 3 Executive course
Visitors welcome
Societies welcome by prior arrangement
Post House, Abbots Lane, 8 Ash Green, Colchester, Essex
☎ 0870 400 9020

LOUGHTON GOLF CLUB

Clays Lane, Debden Green, Loughton, Essex IG10 2RZ
☎ 0208 302 2923 **Map 16, E4**
M25 Jct 26
Founded 1986
There is heathland character to this parkland course on the edge of Epping Forest. Great views.
9 holes, 4652 yards
par 66, S.S.S 63
Green fees £13
Catering, changing room/showers, bar, club and trolley hire, shop, practice facilities
Visitors welcome
Societies welcome by prior arrangement

MALDON GOLF CLUB

Beeleigh Langford, Maldon, Essex CM9 6LL
☎ 01621 853212 **Map 9, D10**
Off B1019, NW of Maldon
Founded 1891
By using alternative tees for the back nine, considerable variety is obtained for this parkland course, almost surrounded by waterways.
9 holes, 6253 yards
par 71, S.S.S 70
Green fees £15
Catering, changing room/showers, bar
Visitors welcome weekdays
Handicap certificate required
Societies welcome by prior arrangement

MAYLANDS GOLF CLUB

Harold Park, Romford, Essex RM3 0AZ
☎ 017083 42055 Fax 017083 73080
Map 16, G5
A12, close to M25 Jct 28
Founded 1936
One of Colt's later courses, in unspoiled rolling parkland.
18 holes, 6351 yards
par 71, S.S.S 70
Designer Harry Colt
Green fees £20
Catering, changing room/showers, bar, club, trolley and buggy hire, shop, practice facilities
Visitors welcome weekdays
Handicap certificate required
Societies welcome by prior arrangement

NAZEING GOLF CLUB

Middle Street, Nazeing, Essex EN9 2LW
☎ 01992 893798 Fax 01992 893882
Map 16, F2
M11 Jct 7, 2 miles SW of Harlow
Founded 1992
A contemporary-styled course with much use made of water hazards.
18 holes, 6598 yards
par 72, S.S.S 71
Designer Martin Gillett
Green fees £20
Catering, changing room/showers, bar, trolley and buggy hire, shop, driving range, practice facilities
Visitors welcome weekdays
Handicap certificate required
Societies welcome by prior arrangement

NORTH WEALD GOLF CLUB

Rayley Lane, North Weald, Epping, Essex CM16 6AR
☎ 01992 522118 Fax 01992 522881
Map 16, G3
M11 Jct 7 1 mile E
Founded 1996
Part of the Barrelfield Group Network, which allows members free midweek access to other group courses, North Weald boasts a number of exciting water holes such as the 4th, 8th and 10th. Only two par 4s are over 400 yards, but the par-5 6th and 18th are over 550.
18 holes, 6311 yards
par 71, S.S.S 70
Designer David Williams
Green fees £20
Catering, changing room/showers, bar, trolley and buggy hire, shop, driving range, practice facilities
Visitors welcome
Handicap certificate required
Societies welcome by prior arrangement

ORSETT GOLF CLUB

Brentwood Road, Orsett, Essex RM16 3DS
☎ 01375 891352 Fax 01375 892471
Map 5, D2
Junction of A13 and A128
Founded 1899
A regular host to Open Championship qualifying, Orsett provides links-like turf and an abundance of gorse. There are only four par 4s over 400 yards in length, and the par 5s are reachable in two by good players, but, with the wind off the Thames, the gorse is very threatening.
18 holes, 6603 yards
par 72, S.S.S 72
Designer James Braid
Green fees £25
Catering, changing room/showers, bar, trolley and buggy hire, shop, practice facilities
Visitors welcome weekdays
Handicap certificate required
Societies welcome by prior arrangement

REGIMENT WAY GOLF CENTRE

Back Lane, Little Waltham, Chelmsford, Essex CM3 3PR
☎ 01245 261100 **Map 9, C10**
A130, 3 miles NE of Chelmsford
Founded 1995
A shortland parkland course with floodlit driving range.
9 holes, 4887 yards
par 65, S.S.S 64
Green fees £8
Shop, driving range
Visitors welcome
Societies welcome by prior arrangement

RISEBRIDGE GOLF CENTRE

Risebridge Chase, Lower Bedfords Road, Romford, Essex RM1 4DG
☎ 01708 741429 **Map 16, G5**
Off A12, 2 miles from M25 Jct 28
Founded 1972
A Hawtree-designed course with water hazards.
18 holes, 6394 yards
par 71, S.S.S 70
Designer F. Hawtree
Green fees £12
Catering, changing room/showers, bar, club and trolley hire, shop, driving range, 9 hole, par 3
Visitors welcome
Societies welcome by prior arrangement

ROCHFORD HUNDRED GOLF CLUB

Rochford Hall, Hall Road, Rochford, Essex SS4 1NW

✆ 01702 544302 **Map 9, D11**
3 miles N of Southend-on-Sea
Founded 1893
An old club with a number of historic features, such as the church located between the 17th and 18th fairways, and Grade I listed Rochford Hall, serving as the clubhouse.
18 holes, 6256 yards
par 72, S.S.S 70
Designer James Braid
Green fees £30
Catering, changing room/showers, bar, trolley and buggy hire, shop
Visitors welcome, restricted Tuesdays and Sundays
Handicap certificate required
Societies welcome by prior arrangement

ROMFORD GOLF CLUB

Heath Drive, Gidea Park, Romford, Essex RM2 5QB
✆ 01708 740007 Fax 01708 752157
Map 16, G5
A118, 1 mile E of Romford
Founded 1894
Reputation has it that there is one bunker for every day of the year, a feature only Fairhaven in Lancashire could once proudly boast. Whatever the truth, it certainly seems that way.
18 holes, 6395 yards
par 72, S.S.S 70
Designer Harry Colt
Green fees £25
Catering, changing room/showers, bar, trolley hire, shop
Visitors welcome, restricted weekends
Handicap certificate required
Societies welcome by prior arrangement

ROYAL EPPING FOREST GOLF CLUB

Forest Approach, Station Road, Chingford, London E4 7AZ
✆ 020 8529 6407 Fax 020 8559 4664 **Map 16, E4**
S of Chingford station
Founded 1888
One of the best public courses around London, with a delightful woodland layout. It is also one of a number of London courses on which it is compulsory to wear red outer garments to warn members of the public to keep well clear!
18 holes, 6342 yards
par 71, S.S.S 70
Green fees £10.70
Club and trolley hire, shop
Visitors welcome by prior arrangement – booking system
Societies welcome by prior arrangement

SAFFRON WALDEN GOLF CLUB

Windmill Hill, Saffron Walden, Essex CB10 1BX
✆ 01799 522786 Fax 01799 522786
Map 9, B9
office@swgc.com
www.swgc.com
B184, M11 Jct 9
Founded 1919
There are lovely views over Saffron Walden and Audley End House from this parkland course, one of the longest in the locality.
18 holes, 6606 yards
par 72, S.S.S 72
Green fees £35
Catering, changing room/showers, bar, club, trolley and buggy hire, shop, driving range, practice facilities
Visitors welcome weekdays
Handicap certificate required – limit: 28 men, 45 women
Societies welcome by prior arrangement
🏨 The Saffron Hotel, High Street, Saffron Walden, Essex
✆ 01799 522676

ST CLERE'S GOLF CLUB

St Clere's Hall, Stanford-le-Hope, Essex SS17 0LX
✆ 01375 673007 **Map 5, D2**
On A13, 5 miles E of M25 Jct 30/31
Parkland course with views over Tilbury and the Thames Estuary.
18 holes, 6474 yards
par 72, S.S.S 71
Designer Adrian Stiff
Green fees £15
Catering, changing room/showers, bar, club, trolley and buggy hire, shop, driving range
Visitors welcome
Handicap certificate required
Societies welcome by prior arrangement

STAPLEFORD ABBOTTS GOLF CLUB

Horseman's Side, Tysea Hill, Stapleford Abbotts, Essex RM4 1JU
✆ 01708 381278 Fax 01708 386345
Map 16, G4
3 miles N of Romford, M25 Jct 28
Founded 1989
Three contemporary courses complemented by a restored 18th Century barn which serves as the atmospheric clubhouse. Green fees on Priors and Par 3 courses are less.
Abbots: 18 holes, 6501 yards, par 72, S.S.S 71
Designer Howard Swann
Priors: 18 holes, 5878 yards, par 70, S.S.S 69
Designer Howard Swann
Par 3: 9 holes, 1140 yards,
Green fees £27
Catering, changing room/showers, bar, club, trolley and buggy hire, shop, practice facilities, conference, wedding, function facilities
Visitors welcome – restricted Abbots Course weekends
Societies welcome by prior arrangement

THE STOCK BROOK COUNTRY CLUB

Queen's Park Avenue, Stock, Billericay, Essex CM12 0SP
✆ 01277 653616 Fax 01277 633063
Map 9, C10
B1007, 5 miles S of Chelmsford
Founded 1992
Six lakes are a menacing feature on several holes of this gently undulating course in unspoiled countryside.
Stock Brook Course: 18 holes, 6905 yards, par 72, S.S.S 72
Designer Martin Gillett
Manor Course: 9 holes, 2997 yards, par 35
Green fees £25
Catering, changing room/showers, bar, club, trolley and buggy hire, shop, driving range, practice facilities, conference, wedding & banquetting facilities, tennis, swimming, bowls
Visitors welcome, with restrictions.
Handicap certificate required – limit: limit: 28 men, 45 women
Societies welcome by prior arrangement
🏨 Brentwood Post House, Brook Street , Brentwood, Essex CM14 5NF
✆ 0870 400 9012

THEYDON BOIS GOLF CLUB

Theydon Bois, Epping, Essex CM16 4EH
✆ 01992 813054 Fax 01992 813054
Map 16, F3
M25 Jct 26, 1 mile S of Epping
Founded 1897
An exceedingly handsome course in Epping Forest.
18 holes, 5480 yards
par 68, S.S.S 68
Designer James Braid
Green fees £25
Catering, changing room/showers, bar, club and trolley hire, shop
Visitors welcome, restricted Wednesday, Thursday and weekends
Societies welcome by prior arrangement

THORNDON PARK GOLF CLUB
Ingrave, Brentwood, Essex CM13 3RH
☎ 0277 810345 **Map 5, C1**
Off A128, 2 miles SE of Brentwood
Founded 1920
Laid out in the Deer Park of magnificent Thorndon Hall, ancestral home of the Petre family, the course is reckoned by many to be the finest in Essex, certainly one of the most beautiful. A lake, stream and ravines feature on many holes, with the 3rd and 8th particularly difficult.
18 holes, 6492 yards
par 71, S.S.S 71
Designer Harry Colt, Charles Alison
Green fees £40
Catering, changing room/showers, bar, club and trolley hire, shop, practice facilities
Visitors welcome weekdays
Handicap certificate required
Societies welcome by prior arrangement

THORPE HALL GOLF CLUB
Thorpe Hall Avenue, Thorpe Bay, Essex SS1 3AT
☎ 01702 582205 Fax 01702 582205
Map 5, E2
Off A13, 2 miles E of Southend.
Founded 1907
A breeding ground for the great: Sir Micahel Bonallack, Peter Dawson (Sir Michael's successor at the R&A), and England player Richard McEvoy all began their golf here. Lengthy driving is an advantage on the 458-yard 6th and 554-yard 8th, the imperative throughout being on accurate positional play.
18 holes, 6319 yards
par 71, S.S.S 71
Green fees £32
Catering, changing room/showers, bar, club, trolley and buggy hire, shop, practice facilities, squash, sauna
Visitors welcome by prior arrangement
Handicap certificate required
Societies Fridays only, by prior arrangement

THREE RIVERS GOLF & COUNTRY CLUB
Stow Road, Cold Norton, Chelmsford, Essex CM3 6RR
☎ 01621 828631 Fax 01621 828060
Map 9, C10
d.evers@clubhouse.com
www.clubhaus.com
5 miles S of Maldon
Founded 1972
The Kings Course has matured over the years, a Hawtree design in the English tradition. The Jubilee, although much shorter and less challenging, offers an inexpensive introduction to American-style architecture.
Kings: 18 holes, 6536 yards, par 72, S.S.S 71
Designer Fred Hawtree
Jubilee: 18 holes, 4503 yards, par 64, S.S.S 62
Green fees £20
Catering, changing room/showers, bar, club, trolley and buggy hire, shop, practice facilities, conference and function facilities
Visitors welcome with restrictions
Societies welcome by prior arrangement

TOOT HILL GOLF CLUB
School Road, Toot Hill, Ongar, Essex CM5 9PU
☎ 01277 365747 **Map 16, G3**
Off A414, 7 miles SE of Harlow
Founded 1991
A parkland course with views into Epping Forest.
18 holes, 6053 yards
par 70, S.S.S 69
Designer Martin Gilett
Green fees £30
Catering, changing room/showers, bar, club, trolley and buggy hire, shop, driving range, practice facilities
Visitors welcome, weekends restricted
Handicap certificate required
Societies welcome by prior arrangement

TOP MEADOW GOLF CLUB
Fen Lane, North Ockendon, Upminster, Essex RM14 3PR
☎ 01708 852239 **Map 16, H5**
info@topmeadow.co.uk
www.topmeadow.co.uk
B186, S of A127. M25 Jct 29
Founded 1985
One of the more elevated of Essex courses, giving good urban and rural views and a testing round of golf.
18 holes, 6227 yards
par 72, S.S.S 71
Designer D. Stock
Green fees £12
Catering, changing room/showers, bar, accommodation, trolley and buggy hire, shop, driving range, practice facilities
Visitors welcome weekdays
Societies welcome by prior arrangement
Top Meadow Golf Club, Fen Lane, North Ockendon, Upminster, Essex
☎ 01708 852239

TOWERLANDS GOLF CLUB
Panfield Road, Braintree, Essex CM7 5BJ
☎ 01376 326802 Fax 01376 552487
Map 9, C9
B1053, 1 mile NW of Braintree
Founded 1985
Part of a complex offering a number of sports.
9 holes, 5559 yards
par 68, S.S.S 66
Green fees £10
Catering, changing room/showers, bar, club and trolley hire, shop, driving range, practice facilities, squash & gymnasium, sports hall
Visitors welcome restricted weekends
Societies welcome by prior arrangement

UPMINSTER GOLF CLUB
114 Hall Lane, Upminster, Essex RM14 1AU
☎ 01708 220000 **Map 16, H5**
S of A127 W towards Romford.
Founded 1928
Not only a good parkland course with heathland characteristics, but also an 11th-century clubhouse with a registered ghost.
18 holes, 6082 yards
par 69, S.S.S 69
Green fees £25
Catering, changing room/showers, bar, club and trolley hire, shop, county standard bowling green
Visitors welcome by prior arrangement – restrictions Tuesday and weekend
Handicap certificate required
Societies welcome by prior arrangement

WANSTEAD GOLF CLUB
Overton Drive, Wanstead, London E11 2LW
☎ 0208 989 3938 Fax 0208 532 9138 **Map 16, G5**
wgclub@aol.com
Off A12 at Wanstead
Founded 1893
A parkland course constructed on the Wanstad House estate.
18 holes, 6015 yards
par 69, S.S.S 69
Designer James Braid
Green fees £28
Catering, changing room/showers, bar, club, trolley and buggy hire, shop, conference and function facilities
Visitors welcome weekdays
Handicap certificate required
Societies welcome by prior arrangement

Forte Ilford Travelodge, Beehive Harvester, Gants Hill, Ilford, Essex
0870 90 56343

WARLEY PARK GOLF CLUB

Magpie Lane, Little Warley, Brentwood, Essex CM13 3DX
01277 224891 Fax 01277 200679
Map 16, H4
enquiries@warleyparkgc.com
M 25 Jct 29, 2 miles S of Brentwood
Founded 1975
Parkland course with plentiful water.
27 holes, 6250 yards
par 71, S.S.S 70
Designer Reg Plumrose
Green fees £30
Catering, changing room/showers, bar, trolley and buggy hire, shop, practice facilities
Visitors welcome weekdays. Handicap certificate required
Societies welcome by prior arrangement
Post House, London Road, Brentwood, Essex CM14 5NF
0870 400 9012

WARREN GOLF CLUB

Woodham Walter, Maldon, Essex CM9 6RW
01245 223258 Fax 01245 223989
Map 9, C10
Off A414, 7 miles E of Chelmsford
Founded 1932
Another of the courses at which the distinguished Mickey Walker is professional, a scenic parkland course laid out in a 17th-century deer park with a history traceable back to Roman times.
18 holes, 6211 yards
par 70, S.S.S 69
Green fees £30
Catering, changing room/showers, bar, club, trolley and buggy hire, shop, driving range
Visitors welcome, restricted weekends
Societies welcome by prior arrangement

WEALD PARK GOLF CLUB

Coxtie Green Road, South Weald, Brentwood, Essex CM14 5RJ
01277 375101 Fax 01277 374888
Map 16, H4
www.americangolf.com
A1023, M25 Jct 28, 3 miles towards Brentwood
Founded 1994
Lakes and ponds and judiciously retained oak trees feature on this testing course.
18 holes, 6612 yards
par 71, S.S.S 72
Designer Reg Plumbridge
Green fees £18
Catering, changing room/showers, bar, trolley and buggy hire, shop, driving range, practice facilities
Visitors welcome
Societies welcome by prior arrangement

WEST ESSEX GOLF CLUB

Bury Road, Sewardstonebury, Chingford, London E4 7QL
020 8529 4367 Fax 020 8524 7870 **Map 16, F4**
sec@westessexgolfclub.co.uk
www.westessexgolfclub.co.uk
M25 Jct 26, A121 towards Chingford, then A112
Founded 1900
From the high ground of this handsome course there are excellent views of the City of London, Essex, Hertfordshire and Middlesex.
18 holes, 6289 yards
par 71, S.S.S 70
Designer James Braid
Green fees £28
Catering, changing room/showers, bar, trolley and buggy hire, shop, driving range, practice facilities, large banquet room
Visitors welcome weekdays, except Tusday am and Thursday pm. Handicap certificate required
Societies welcome by prior arrangement
County Hotel Epping Forest, 30 Oak Hill, Woodford Green, Essex IG8 9NY
020 8787 9988 Fax 0208 5060941

WOODFORD GOLF CLUB

2 Sunset Avenue, Woodford Green, Essex IG8 0ST
020 8504 0553 Fax 020 8559 0504 **Map 16, E4**
Off A104, NW Woodford Green
Founded 1890
Parkland course on the edge of Epping Forest.
9 holes, 5867 yards
par 70, S.S.S 68
Designer Tom Dunn
Green fees £10
Catering, changing room/showers, bar, shop
Visitors welcome, with restrictions
Societies welcome by prior arrangement

HERTFORDSHIRE

ABBEY VIEW GOLF CLUB

Westminster Lodge Leisure Centre, Hollywell Hill, St Albans, Hertfordshire AL1 2DL
01727 868227 Fax 01727 863017
Map 16, C3
Off Holywell Hill, centre of St Albans
An executive length public course.
9 holes, 1383 yards
par 29
Catering, changing room/showers, bar, club and trolley hire, shop, tennis courts, swimming pool
Visitors welcome
Societies welcome by prior arrangement

ALDENHAM GOLF & COUNTRY CLUB

Church Lane, Aldenham, watford, Hertfordshire WD2 8AL
01923 853929 Fax 01923 858472
Map 16, C4
Off B462, 3 miles E of Watford
Founded 1975
Parkland courses with fine views.
18 holes, 6500 yards, par 70, S.S.S 71
9 holes, 2350 yards, par 33, S.S.S 33
Green fees £25
Catering, changing room/showers, bar, club, trolley and buggy hire, shop
Visitors welcome
Societies welcome by prior arrangement

ALDWICKBURY PARK GOLF CLUB

Piggottshill Lane, Harpenden, Hertfordshire AL5 1AB
01582 760112 Fax 01582 760113
Map 16, C2
enquiries@aldwickburyparkgolfclub.com
www.aldwickburyparkgolfclub.com
M1 Jct 9, between Wheathampstead and Harpenden
Founded 1995
Having been equipped with USGA specification greens, drainage is good in winter. Trees add to the beauty.
18 holes, 6532 yards
par 71, S.S.S 70
Designer Martin Gillett, Ken Brown
Green fees £24
Catering, changing room/showers, bar, club, trolley and buggy hire, shop, practice facilities, 9-hole, par-3 course, function room (winter)
Visitors welcome – restricted weekends
Societies welcome by prior arrangement
Hertfordshire Moat House, London Road, Markyate, Hertfordshire AL3 8HH
01582 449988

ARKLEY GOLF CLUB

Rowley Green Road, Barnet, Hertfordshire EN5 3HL
020 8449 0394 Fax 020 8440

5214 **Map 16, D4**
denisreedagc@aol.com
www.arkleygolfclub.co.uk
Off A1(M), N of Barnet
Founded 1909
9 holes of charming parkland golf are enlivened by 18 tees, giving considerable change of approach first and second time round.
9 holes, 6117 yards
par 69, S.S.S 69
Designer James Braid
Green fees £22
Catering, bar, trolley hire, shop, practice facilities
Visitors welcome weekdays
Societies welcome by prior arrangement
West Lodge Park, Cockfosters Road, Hadley Wood, Barnet, Hertfordshire EN4 0PY
020 8216 3900 Fax 0208 2163937
beales_westlodgepark@compuserve.com

ASH VALLEY GOLF CLUB

Much Hadham Lane, Much Hadham, Hertfordshire SG10 6HD
01279 843253 Fax 01920 842389
Map 9, A9
Off A120 at Much Hadham
An undulating course, a haven for wild flowers and birds, with views as far as Canary Wharf. The 2nd is a tough, uphill par 4 of 437 yards, but the reward is its backdrop, full of bluebells in May, golden brown in autumn. The par-5 10th has a corkscrew fairway.
18 holes, 6586 yards
par 72, S.S.S 71
Designer Martin Gillett
Green fees £9
Catering, changing room/showers, bar, club and trolley hire, shop, practice facilities
Visitors welcome
Societies welcome by prior arrangement

ASHRIDGE GOLF CLUB

Little Gaddesden, Berkhamsted, Hertfordshire HP4 1LY
01442 842244 Fax 01442 843770
Map 8, F10
info@ashridgegolfclub.ltd.uk
www.ashridgegolfclub.ltd.uk
B4506, 4 miles N of Berkhamstead
Founded 1932
Thrice Open Champion, Henry Cotton, was for a time professional at this elegant and tastefully restrained course. He is commemorated on the 9th, a mid-length par 4 on which he discovered the exact line which enabled him to drive the green – an astonishing feat even with today's clubs and balls.
18 holes, 6547 yards
par 72, S.S.S 71
Designer C.K. Hutchison, Sir Guy Campbell, S.V. Hotchkin, Tom Simpson
Green fees On application
Catering, changing room/showers, bar, club and trolley hire, shop, driving range, practice facilities
Visitors welcome with restrictions
Handicap certificate required – limit: 28 men, 36 women
Societies welcome by prior arrangement
Hemel Hempsted Travel Inn, Stoney Lane, Bourne End, Hemel Hempsted, Hertfordshire
01442 879149

BARKWAY PARK GOLF CLUB

Nuthampstead Road, Barkway, Royston, Hertfordshire SG8 8EN
01763 849070 **Map 9, A9**
B1368, 5 miles SE of Royston
Founded 1992
A long course in the Hertfordshire countryside, one of the few in this country designed by a woman, Vivien Saunders, winner of the 1977 Ladies British Open.
18 holes, 6997 yards
par 74, S.S.S 74
Designer Vivien Saunders
Green fees £10
Catering, changing room/showers, bar, trolley and buggy hire, shop, practice facilities
Visitors welcome
Societies welcome by prior arrangement

BATCHWOOD HALL GOLF CLUB

Batchwood Drive, St Albans, Hertfordshire AL3 5XA
01727 833349 Fax 01582 793215
Map 16, C3
A5081, NW of St Albans, M1 Jct 9
Founded 1935
Pay-and-play facility designed by one of the Great Triumvirate, J.H. Taylor.
18 holes, 6487 yards
par 71, S.S.S 71
Designer J.H. Taylor
Green fees £9
Catering, changing room/showers, bar, club and trolley hire, shop
Visitors welcome weekdays
Societies welcome by prior arrangement

BATCHWORTH PARK GOLF CLUB

London Road, Rickmansworth, Hertfordshire WD3 1JS
01923 711400 Fax 01923 710200
Map 16, B4
A404, SE of Rickmansworth, M25 Jct 18
Founded 1996
A new Dave Thomas course, but, as a private club, available to members and their guests only.
18 holes, 6723 yards
par 72, S.S.S 72
Designer Dave Thomas
Catering, changing room/showers, bar, trolley hire, shop, practice facilities
Visitors welcome only as members' guests
No societies

BERKHAMSTED GOLF CLUB

The Common, Berkhamsted, Hertfordshire HP4 2QB
01442 865851 Fax 01442 863730
Map 8, F10
clubhouse@berkhamsted.golfagent.co.uk
www.golfagent.com/clubsites/berkhamsted
2 miles N of Berkhamsted
Founded 1890
Berkhamsted may have no sand bunkers, but bracken, heather, and gorse and, particularly, moundwork make it a considerable challenge. The most emphatic of the mounds is the prehistoric earthwork, Grim's Dyke, which constitutes a formidable obstacle on several holes. Chalky soil gives excellent drainage and, therefore, very good winter golf.
18 holes, 6605 yards
par 71, S.S.S 72
Designer Harry Colt, James Braid
Green fees £30
Catering, changing room/showers, bar, trolley hire, shop, practice facilities
Visitors welcome – restricted
Handicap certificate required – limit: 24
Societies welcome by prior arrangement
Hemel Hempstead Travel Inn, Stoney Lane, Bourne End, Hemel Hempstead, Hertfordshire
01442 879149

BISHOP'S STORTFORD GOLF CLUB

Dunmow Road, Bishop's Stortford, Hertfordshire CM23 5HP
01279 654715 Fax 01279 655215
Map 9, B9
bishopstortfordgc@hotmail.com
www.bsgc.co.uk
A1250, ½ mile W of M11 Jct 8
Founded 1910
A well-established, gently undulating parkland course providing a true test. Splendid new clubhouse.
18 holes, 6404 yards

par 71, S.S.S 71
Designer James Braid
Green fees £27
Catering, changing room/showers, bar, club, trolley and buggy hire, shop, practice facilities, conference, wedding, function facilities, snooker
Visitors welcome weekdays
Handicap certificate required
Societies welcome by prior arrangement
Down Hall Hotel, Hatfield Heath, Hertfordshire
01279 731441

BOXMOOR GOLF CLUB

18 Box Lane, Hemel Hempstead, Hertfordshire HP2 0DJ
01442 242434 **Map 16, B3**
B4505, W of Hemel Hempstead
Founded 1890
A short, but tricky, moorland course.
9 holes, 4854 yards
par 64, S.S.S 63
Green fees £15
Catering, changing room/showers, bar
Visitors welcome restricted Sundays
Societies welcome by prior arrangement

BRICKENDON GRANGE GOLF CLUB

Pembridge Lane, Brickendon, Hertford, Hertfordshire SG13 8PD
01992 511258 Fax 01992 511411
Map 16, E2
genman@brickendongrangegc.co.uk
www.brickendongrangegc.co.uk
3 miles S of Hertford
Founded 1967
A highly respected design, giving challenging, but enjoyable golf. The 17th is particularly fine.
18 holes, 6403 yards
par 71, S.S.S 70
Designer C.K. Cotton
Green fees £28
Catering, changing room/showers, bar, club, trolley and buggy hire, shop, practice facilities
Visitors welcome weekdays
Societies welcome by prior arrangement

BRIDGEDOWN GOLF CLUB

St Albans Road, Barnet, Hertfordshire EN5 4RE
020 8448 4120 Fax 020 8441 7649 **Map 16, D3**
A1081, 1 mile S of South Mimms, M25 Jct 23
Founded 1994
A parkland course.
18 holes, 6626 yards
par 72, S.S.S 72
Designer Howard Swann
Green fees £15
Shop, practice facilities
Visitors welcome
Societies welcome by prior arrangement

BRIGGENS HOUSE HOTEL GOLF CLUB

Briggens Park, Stanstead Road, Stanstead Abbotts, Ware, Hertfordshire SG12 8LD
01279 793685 **Map 16, F2**
Off A414, E of Harlow.
Founded 1988
Attractive parkland course open to non-residents at a reasonable green fee.
9 holes, 5582 yards
par 72, S.S.S 69
Green fees £14
Catering, changing room/showers, bar, accommodation, club, trolley and buggy hire, shop, practice facilities, full hotel, conference and function facilities
Visitors welcome – restricted Sunday morning
Societies welcome by prior arrangement
Briggens House Hotel, Stanstead Abbotts, Ware, Hertfordshire SG12 8LD
01279 829955

BROCKET HALL GOLF CLUB

Welwyn, Hertfordshire AL8 7XG
01707 390063 **Map 16, D2**
B653, E of Welwyn Garden City
A1(M) Jct 4
Founded 1992
Although Brocket Hall does not accept casual visitors, corporate events are possible. Two impressive contemporary courses.
Palmerston Course: 18 holes, 6925 yards, S.S.S 73
Designer Donald Steel
Melbourne Course: 18 holes, 6616 yards, S.S.S 72
Designer Peter Alliss, Clive Clark
Catering, changing room/showers, bar, club, trolley and buggy hire, shop, driving range
Visitors welcome, only as members' guests
Handicap certificate required
Societies welcome by prior arrangement

BROOKMANS PARK GOLF CLUB

Brookmans Park, Hatfield, Hertfordshire AL9 7AT
01707 652487 Fax 01707 661851
Map 16, D3
Off A1000, 3 miles S of Hatfield
Founded 1930
Popular with societies and casual visitors who are looking for a round of golf in the country, without being too far from London, testing the good player without embarrassing the mid- to high-handicapper.
18 holes, 6473 yards
par 71, S.S.S 71
Designer Hawtree/Taylor
Green fees £30
Catering, changing room/showers, trolley and buggy hire, shop
Visitors welcome weekdays
Handicap certificate required
Societies welcome by prior arrangement

BUSHEY GOLF & COUNTRY CLUB

High Street, Bushey, Hertfordshire WD2 1BJ
020 8950 2283 Fax 020 8386 1181 **Map 16, C4**
A4008, 2 miles S of Watford
Founded 1980
A charming 9-hole course of fair length.
9 holes, 3000 yards, S.S.S 69
Green fees £10
Catering, changing room/showers, bar, club, trolley and buggy hire, shop, practice facilities, sauna & gymnasium
Visitors welcome except Wednesday
Societies welcome by prior arrangement

BUSHEY HALL GOLF CLUB

Bushey Hall Drive, Bushey, Hertfordshire WD23 2EP
01923 22253 Fax 01923 229759
Map 16, C4
busheyhallgolf@aol.com
www.golfclubuk.co.uk
M1 Jct 5, A41 towards Harrow. At 1st roundabout, Hartspring Lane (3rd exit), straight across next lights, then 4th exit at roundabout.
Founded 1890
A long-established, and welcoming, club with a recently refurbished course. The 1930s clubhouse is both atmospheric and comfortable.
18 holes, 6099 yards
par 70, S.S.S 69
Green fees £20
Catering, changing room/showers, bar, club, trolley and buggy hire, shop, practice facilities, conference facilities
Visitors welcome with restrictions
Societies welcome by prior arrangement
Jarvis International Hotel, Watford, Hertfordshire WD23 8HQ
020 8901 0100

CHADWELL SPRINGS GOLF CLUB

Hertford Road, Ware, Hertfordshire SG12 9LE
✆ 01920 462075 Fax 01920 461447
Map 16, E2
A119, 2 miles W of Ware
Founded 1899
On well-drained soil, the course is seldom closed because of the weather. Its greens are particularly well reputed.
9 holes, 6480 yards
par 72, S.S.S 71
Catering, changing room/showers, bar, trolley hire, shop, practice facilities, conference and function facilities
Visitors welcome
Societies welcome by prior arrangement
🏨 Salisbury Arms, Fore Street, Hertford, Hertfordshire SG14 1BZ
✆ 01992 583091 Fax 01992 552510

CHESFIELD DOWNS GOLF CLUB

Jack's Hill, Graveley, Stevenage, Hertfordshire SG4 7EQ
✆ 01462 482929 Fax 01462 482930
Map 8, G9
B197, A1(M) Jct 8
Founded 1991
With full facilities designed to encourage all comers into golf, the course itself is a big, wide-open layout of some challenge.
18 holes, 6646 yards
par 71, S.S.S 72
Designer Jonathan Gaunt
Green fees £16
Catering, changing room/showers, bar, club, trolley and buggy hire, shop, driving range, practice facilities, 9-hole, par-3 course
Visitors welcome
Societies welcome by prior arrangement

CHESHUNT GOLF CLUB

Park Lane, Cheshunt, Hertfordshire EN7 6QD
✆ 01992 29777 **Map 16, E3**
Off B156, 1½ miles NW of Cheshunt, M25 Jct 25
Founded 1976
Perhaps the Hawtree family's most impressive skill, their great exploits at Birkdale and elsewhere notwithstanding, is their ability to create good simple layouts, to a limited budget, encouraging to the beginner, yet challenging to the expert. This is but one example.
18 holes, 6608 yards
par 71, S.S.S 71
Designer Hawtree
Green fees £9.50
Catering, changing room/showers, bar, club, trolley and buggy hire, shop, practice facilities
Visitors welcome – booking system
Societies welcome by prior arrangement

CHORLEYWOOD GOLF CLUB

Common Road, Chorleywood, Hertfordshire WD3 5LN
✆ 01923 282009 Fax 01923 286739
Map 16, B4
chorleywood.gc@btclick.com
M25 Jct 18, A404 towards Amersham. 2nd traffic lights turn left, signposted Chorleywood Town, club on right 2/3 mile.
Founded 1890
The oldest golf club in Hertfordshire with a pretty course, part heathland, part woodland, "influenced" by James Braid.
9 holes, 5712 yards
par 68, S.S.S 67
Designer James Braid
Green fees £16
Catering, changing room/showers, bar
Visitors welcome – with restrictions
Societies welcome by prior arrangement
🏨 Sportsman Hotel, Station Approach, Chorleywood, Hertfordshire
✆ 01923 285155

DANESBURY PARK GOLF CLUB

Codicote Road, Old Welwyn, Hertfordshire AL6 9SD
✆ 01438 840100 Fax 01438 840768
Map 16, D2
B656 N of Welwyn, A1 (M) Jct 6
Founded 1991
To restore the body after golf there is a beauty and holistic clinic catering for men and women alike.
9 holes, 4414 yards
par 64, S.S.S 62
Designer D. Snowdon
Green fees £12.50
Catering, changing room/showers, bar, practice facilities
Visitors welcome
Societies welcome by prior arrangement
🏨 Quality Inn, The Link Road, Old Welwyn, Hertfordshire
✆ 01438 716911

DYRHAM PARK COUNTRY CLUB

Galley Lane, Barnet, Hertfordshire EN5 4RA
✆ 020 8440 3361 Fax 020 84419836
Map 16, D4
Off A1081, M25 Jct 23
Founded 1963
As with a number of private clubs around London, Dyrham Park does not accommodate casual visitors, but will accept a limited number of society or corporate events, when the glories of its fine parkland course become evident to a wider audience.
18 holes, 6422 yards
par 71, S.S.S 70
Designer C.K. Cotton
Catering, changing room/showers, bar, club, trolley and buggy hire, shop, tennis courts, fishing & caddies
Visitors welcome only as members' guests
Societies welcome Wednesdays by prior arrangement

EAST HERTS GOLF CLUB

Hamels Park, Buntingford, Hertfordshire SG9 9NA
✆ 01920 821922 Fax 01920 823700
Map 9, A9
A10 at Puckeridge
Founded 1899
The numerous magnificent specimen trees make this a particularly delightful parkland course.
18 holes, 6456 yards
par 71, S.S.S 71
Green fees £35
Catering, changing room/showers, bar, club, trolley and buggy hire, shop, practice facilities
Visitors welcome with restrictions
Handicap certificate required
Societies welcome by prior arrangement
🏨 Vintage Hotel, Puckeridge, Hertfordshire

ELSTREE GOLF CLUB

Watling Street, Elstree, Hertfordshire WD6 3AA
✆ 020 8953 6115 Fax 020 8207 6390 **Map 16, C4**
kathy@elstree-golf.co.uk
A5183, 1 mile N of Elstree.
Founded 1984
A Donald Steel designed parkland course famous for its friendly welcome.
18 holes, 6556 yards
par 73, S.S.S 72
Designer Donald Steel
Green fees £27.50
Catering, changing room/showers, bar, club, trolley and buggy hire, shop, driving range, practice facilities, conference, wedding, function facilities
Visitors welcome – restricted weekends
Societies welcome by prior arrangement

FOREST HILLS GOLF CLUB

Newgate Street, Hertfordshire SG13 8EW
☎ 01707 876825 Fax 01707 876825
Map 8, H10
Off B197,1 mile NW of Cuffley
Founded 1994
The USGA specification greens may be tricky to putt on, but succour is on hand in the excellent Szechuan/Thai cuisine available in the clubhouse.
9 holes, 6440 yards
par 72, S.S.S 71
Designer Mel Flannigan
Green fees £15
Catering, changing room/showers, bar, trolley hire, shop
Visitors welcome weekdays
Societies welcome by prior arrangement
Marriott, Waltham Abbey, Hertfordshire

GREAT HADHAM GOLF & COUNTRY CLUB

Great Hadham Road, Bishop's Stortford, Hertfordshire SG10 6JE
☎ 01279 843558 Fax 01279 842122
Map 9, B9
B1004, 3 miles SW of Bishops Stortford
Founded 1993
An open course with some links characteristics.
18 holes, 6854 yards
par 72, S.S.S 73
Green fees £19
Catering, changing room/showers, bar, club and trolley hire, shop, driving range, practice facilities, full gymnasium
Visitors welcome, with weekend restrictions
Societies welcome by prior arrangement
Down Hall Hotel, Hatfield Heath, Hertfordshire CM22 7AS

HADLEY WOOD GOLF CLUB

Beech Hill, Hadley Wood, Barnet, Hertfordshire EN4 0JJ
☎ 020 8449 4328 Fax 020 8364 8633 **Map 16, D4**
gen.mgr@hadleywoodgc
www.hadleywoodgc.com
M25 Jct 24, A111 to Cockfosters
Founded 1922
The splendid Georgian clubhouse, dating back to 1781, looks out over an immaculately kept course with typical Mackenzie touches, for ever deceiving the unwary. One commentary speaks, very pertinently, of the course as being 'landscaped like a garden'.
18 holes, 6506 yards
par 72, S.S.S 71
Designer Alister Mackenzie
Green fees £40
Catering, changing room/showers, bar, club and trolley hire, shop, driving range, practice facilities
Visitors welcome weekdays
Handicap certificate required
Societies welcome by prior arrangement
West Lodge Park, Cockfosters Road, Hadley Wood, Barnet, Hertfordshire EN4 0PY
☎ 0208 2163900 Fax 0208 2163937
beales_westlodgepark@compuserve.com
www.bealeshotels.co.uk

MARRIOTT HANBURY MANOR GOLF & COUNTRY CLUB

Ware, Hertfordshire SG12 0SD
☎ 01920 487722 Fax 01920 487692
Map 9, A10
A10, N of Ware, M25 Jct 25
Founded 1990
Two contrasting nines were laid out by Jack Nicklaus II, the early holes on rolling ground in the Hertfordshire countryside, while the back nine occupy old parkland. Water is a significant threat on several holes, especially the two star par 4s, the 8th and 13th, and the par-5 17th.
18 holes, 7016 yards
par 72, S.S.S 74
Designer Jack Nicklaus II
Green fees £75
Catering, changing room/showers, bar, accommodation, club, trolley and buggy hire, shop, driving range, practice facilities, full hotel, conference, function, and wedding facilities
Visitors welcome only as hotel guest or guest of member
Societies welcome by prior arrangement
Marriott Hanbury Manor Hotel Golf and Country Club, Ware, Hertfordshire
☎ 01920 487722

HARPENDEN COMMON GOLF CLUB

East Common, Harpenden, Hertfordshire AL5 1BL
☎ 01582 460655 Fax 01582 715959
Map 8, G10
hcgc@hcommon.freeserve.co.uk
A1081, 4 miles N of Harpenden
Founded 1931
An old course updated by TV pundit Ken Brown.
18 holes, 6214 yards
par 70, S.S.S 70
Designer Ken Brown
Green fees £25
Catering, changing room/showers, bar, club and trolley hire, shop, practice facilities
Visitors welcome
Handicap certificate required
Societies welcome by prior arrangement
Harpenden House Hotel, 18 Southdown Road, Harpenden, Hertfordshire
☎ 01582 449955

HARPENDEN GOLF CLUB

Hammonds End, Redbourn Lane, Harpenden, Hertfordshire AL5 2AX
☎ 01582 767124 Fax 01582 712725
Map 8, G10
harpgolf@hammonds94.freeserve.co.uk
B487 E of Harpenden, M1 Jct 9
Founded 1894
Confirmation of Harpenden's standing as a good parkland test has come with its selection by the PGA to host the regional finals of the Lombard Trophy two years running.
18 holes, 6381 yards
par 70, S.S.S 70
Designer F. Hawtree, J.H. Taylor
Green fees £27
Catering, changing room/showers, bar, club and trolley hire, shop, practice facilities
Visitors welcome
Handicap certificate required
Societies welcome by prior arangement
Milton Hotel, 25 Milton Road, Harpenden, Hertfordshire
☎ 01582 762914

HARTSBOURNE GOLF & COUNTRY CLUB

Hartsbourne Avenue, Bushey Heath, Hertfordshire WD2 1JW
☎ 020 8950 1133 Fax 020 8950 5357 **Map 16, C4**
Off A4008, 5 miles SE of Watford
Founded 1946
One of the first country clubs established with the coming of peace after the Second World War.
18 holes, 6385 yards, par 71, S.S.S 70
Designer Hawtree/Taylor
9 holes, 5773 yards, par 70, S.S.S 68
Catering, changing room/showers, bar, club, trolley and buggy hire, shop, practice facilities
Visitors welcome only as members' guests
Societies welcome by prior arrangement

HATFIELD LONDON COUNTRY CLUB

Bedwell Park, Essendon, Hatfield, Hertfordshire AL9 6JA
☎ 01707 663131 Fax 01707 278475
Map 16, D2
B158, 4 miles E of Hatfield, A1(M) Jct 4
Founded 1976
Fred Hawtree's challenging course from the 1970s has been joined by a 1990s 7,000 yard course which the members are able to keep to themselves.
Pay-and-play course: 18 holes, 6808 yards, par 72, S.S.S 72
Designer Fred Hawtree
Members' Course: 18 holes, 7091 yards, par 72, S.S.S 74
Designer Landscape Design Company
Green fees £17
Catering, changing room/showers, bar, club, trolley and buggy hire, shop, practice facilities, conference and wedding facilities, par-3 course, tennis
Visitors welcome on pay-and-play course only
Societies welcome by prior arrangement on pay-and-play course

THE HERTFORDSHIRE GOLF CLUB

Broxbournebury Mansion, White Stubbs Lane, Broxbourne, Hertfordshire EN10 7PY
☎ 01992 466666 Fax 01992 470326
Map 16, E3
Off A10, 8 miles N of M25 Jct 25
Founded 1995
The first Nicklaus pay-and-play facility in England, with all the characteristic bunkers, water hazards, and huge, highly contoured greens. The front nine is particularly good.
18 holes, 6388 yards
par 70, S.S.S 70
Designer Jack Nicklaus II
Green fees £21
Catering, changing room/showers, bar, club, trolley and buggy hire, shop, driving range, practice facilities
Visitors welcome
Handicap certificate required
Societies welcome by prior arrangement

KINGSWAY GOLF CENTRE

Cambridge Road, Melbourn, Royston, Hertfordshire SG8 6EY
☎ 01763 262727 Fax 01763 263298
Map 9, A8
Off A10, N of Royston
Founded 1991
Tricky little short course.
9 holes, 2500 yards
par 33, S.S.S 32
Green fees £5
Changing room/showers, bar, shop, driving range, 9-hole, par-3 course
Visitors welcome
Societies welcome by prior arrangement

KNEBWORTH GOLF CLUB

Deards End Lane, Knebworth, Hertfordshire SG3 6NL
☎ 01438 812752 Fax 01438 8152216 **Map 8, G9**
B197, 1 mile S of Stevenage
Founded 1908
Rolling parkland course with several holes running parallel with the East Coast main line railway.
18 holes, 6492 yards
par 71, S.S.S 71
Designer Willie Park
Green fees £30
Catering, changing room/showers, bar, trolley and buggy hire, shop
Visitors welcome weekdays
Handicap certificate required
Societies welcome by prior arrangement

LAMERWOOD GOLF CLUB

Codicote Road, Wheathampstead, Hertfordshire AL4 8GB
☎ 01582 833013 Fax 01582 832604
Map 8, G10
B653 W of A1(M) Jct 4
Founded 1996
A new course, almost 7,000 yards long, a mixture of woodland and parkland. Amongst the full facilities is a Japanese restaurant.
18 holes, 6953 yards
par 72
Designer Cameron Sinclair
Green fees £22
Catering, changing room/showers, bar, club, trolley and buggy hire, shop, driving range, practice facilities
Visitors welcome
Societies welcome by prior arrangement

LETCHWORTH GOLF CLUB

Letchworth Lane, Letchworth, Hertfordshire SG6 3NQ
☎ 01462 682713 **Map 8, G9**
Off A505, S of Letchworth
Founded 1905
One of the loveliest of all Hertfordshire courses, having matured over almost a century.
18 holes, 6181 yards
par 70, S.S.S 69
Designer Harry Vardon
Green fees £27
Catering, changing room/showers, bar, trolley hire, shop, practice facilities
Visitors welcome weekdays
Handicap certificate required
Societies welcome by prior arrangement

LITTLE HAY GOLF COMPLEX

Box Lane, Bovingdon, Hemel Hempstead, Hertfordshire HP3 0DQ
☎ 01442 833798 **Map 8, F10**
B4505, 2 miles W of Hemel Hempstead
Founded 1977
A parkland course, Hawtree-designed, and of considerable length.
18 holes, 6678 yards
par 72, S.S.S 72
Designer Hawtree
Green fees £11
Catering, changing room/showers, bar, club and trolley hire, shop, driving range, practice facilities, pitch and putt course
Visitors welcome
Societies welcome by prior arrangement

MANOR OF GROVES GOLF & COUNTRY CLUB

High Wych, Sawbridgeworth, Hertfordshire CM21 0LA
☎ 01279 722333 Fax 01279 726972
Map 16, F2
1 mile N of Harlow
Founded 1991
A parkland course laid out in the grounds of its parent hotel.
18 holes, 6280 yards
par 71, S.S.S 70
Designer S Sharer
Green fees £20
Catering, changing room/showers, bar, club, trolley and buggy hire, shop, practice facilities
Visitors welcome
Societies welcome by prior arrangement
Manor of Groves Hotel Golf and Country Club, High Wych, Sawbridgeworth, Hertfordshire
☎ 01279 722333

MID HERTS GOLF CLUB

Gustard Wood, Wheathampstead, Hertfordshire AL4 8RS
☎ 01582 832242 Fax 01582 834834
Map 8, G10
B651, 6 miles N of St Albans
Founded 1892
One of the few heathland courses in Hertfordshire.
18 holes, 6060 yards
par 69, S.S.S 69
Green fees £35
Catering, changing room/showers, bar, trolley hire, shop, practice

facilities
Visitors welcome weekdays with restrictions
Societies welcome by prior arrangement

MILL GREEN GOLF CLUB

Gypsy Lane, Mill Green, Welwyn Garden City, Hertfordshire AL7 4TY
☎ 01707 276900 Fax 01707 276898
Map 16. D2
Off A414, S of Welwyn Garden City
Founded 1994
A parkland course with lakes and woods.
18 holes, 6615 yards
par 72, S.S.S 72
Designer Clive Clark, Peter Alliss
Green fees £19
Catering, changing room/showers, bar, club, trolley and buggy hire, shop, driving range, 9-hole, par-3 course
Visitors welcome weekdays
Societies welcome by prior arrangement

MOOR PARK GOLF CLUB

Rickmansworth, Hertfordshire WD3 1QN
☎ 01923 773146 Fax 01923 777109
Map 16, B4
moorparkgolfclub@aol.com
www.moorparkgolf.co.uk
M25 Jct 17/18 – 2 miles
Founded 1924
Two distinguished old courses in keeping with the grandeur of the Duke of Monmouth's mansion, now serving as the magnificent clubhouse. Colt utilised the natural undulations of the parkland to create a number of first rate holes, such as the par-4 8th and 14th on the championship High Course.
High Course: 18 holes, 6713 yards, par 72, S.S.S 72
Designer Harry Colt
West Course: 18 holes, 5823 yards, par 69, S.S.S 68
Green fees £60
Catering, changing room/showers, bar, club, trolley and buggy hire, shop, driving range, practice facilities, full conference, function and wedding facilities, tennis
Visitors welcome weekdays
Handicap certificate required
Societies welcome by prior arrangement
🏨 Long Island Exchange, Rickmansworth, Hertfordshire
☎ 01923 775211

OLD FOLD MANOR GOLF CLUB

Old Fold Lane, Hadley Green, Barnet, Hertfordshire EN5 4QN
☎ 020 8440 9185 Fax 020 8441 4863 **Map 16, D4**
A1000, 1 mile N of Barnet
Founded 1910
Good value heathland golf inside the M25.
18 holes, 6466 yards
par 71, S.S.S 71
Green fees £20
Catering, changing room/showers, bar, club, trolley and buggy hire, shop, practice facilities
Visitors welcome weekdays, with restrictions
Handicap certificate required
Societies welcome by prior arrangement

OXHEY PARK GOLF CLUB

Prestwick Road, South Oxhey, Watford, Hertfordshire WD19 7EX
☎ 01923 248213 Fax 01923 248213
Map 16, B4
2 miles SW of Watford, M1 Jct 5
Short course with driving range.
9 holes, 1637 yards
par 58
Green fees £5
Shop, driving range
Visitors welcome
Societies welcome by prior arrangement

PANSHANGER GOLF COMPLEX

Old Herns Lane, Welwyn Garden City, Hertfordshire AL7 2ED
☎ 01707 333312 **Map 16, D2**
B1000, N of Welwyn Garden City, A1(M) Jct 6
Founded 1976
Undulating parkland course.
18 holes, 6167 yards
par 72, S.S.S 70
Green fees £13
Catering, changing room/showers, bar, club, trolley and buggy hire, squash, 9-hole, par-3 course
Visitors welcome
Societies welcome by prior arrangement

PORTERS PARK GOLF CLUB

Shenley Hill, Radlett, Hertfordshire WD7 7AZ
☎ 01923 854127 Fax 01923 855475
Map 8, G10
E of Radlett on Shenley road, M25 Jct 22
Founded 1899
One of the best tests of golf in this part of the county, undulating parkland with considerable variety. Streams front a number of greens, many fairways lean one way or the other, and the closing stretch of strong par 4s demands good play.
18 holes, 6313 yards
par 70, S.S.S 70
Designer C.S. Butchart, J.H. Taylor
Green fees £30
Catering, changing room/showers, bar, club and trolley hire, shop, driving range
Visitors welcome weekdays, restricted weekends
Handicap certificate required
Societies welcome by prior arrangement

POTTERS BAR GOLF CLUB

Darkes Lane, Potters Bar, Hertfordshire EN6 1DE
☎ 01707 652020 Fax 01707 655051
Map 16, D3
info@pottersbargolfclub.com
A1000, N of Potters Bar, M25 Jct 24
Founded 1923
Tony Jacklin represented Potters Bar when he won the Open Championship in 1969. Streams cross many fairways although, generally, they are well short of greens and do not affect approach shots. The two streams which cross the par-5 16th, however, are very much a factor on the second shot.
18 holes, 6291 yards
par 71, S.S.S 70
Designer James Braid
Green fees £25
Catering, changing room/showers, bar, club, trolley and buggy hire, shop, practice facilities
Visitors welcome weekdays
Handicap certificate required
Societies welcome by prior arrangement

REDBOURN GOLF CLUB

Luton Lane, Redbourn, St Albans, Hertfordshire AL3 7QA
☎ 01582 793493 Fax 01582 794362
Map 16, C2
enquiries@redbourngolfclub.com
www.redbourngolfclub.com
M1 Jct 9, A5183 towards Redbourn
Founded 1971
With six par 4s over 400 yards, and a 619-yard par 5, there is serious golf to be played here. A useful 9-holer complements the main course.
18 holes, 6506 yards
par 70, S.S.S 71
9-hole, par-3 course
Green fees £30
Catering, changing room/showers, bar, club, trolley and buggy hire, shop, driving range, practice facilities
Visitors welcome – restricted weekends
Societies welcome by prior arrangement
🏨 Hertfordshire Moat House, London Road, Markyate,

Hertfordshire AL3 8HH
☎ 01582 449988

RICKMANSWORTH GOLF COURSE

Moor Lane, Rickmansworth, Hertfordshire WD3 1QL
☎ 01923 775278 Fax 01923 775278
Map 16, B4
Off A4145, 2 miles S of town. M25 Jct 18
Founded 1937
Hilly parkland course in the shadow of Moor Park.
18 holes, 4493 yards
par 63, S.S.S 62
Designer Harry Colt
Green fees £10
Catering, changing room/showers, bar, club, trolley and buggy hire, shop
Visitors welcome
Societies welcome by prior arrangement

ROYSTON GOLF CLUB

Baldock Road, Royston, Hertfordshire SG8 5BG
☎ 01763 243476 Fax 01763 246910
Map 9, A8
roystongolf@btconnect.com
A505, SW of Royston
Founded 1892
Distinctive, hilly course, recently voted Britain's 4th best winter course in a golfing magazine. Nick Faldo won Royston's Junior Open in 1972.
18 holes, 6086 yards
par 70, S.S.S 70
Designer Harry Vardon
Green fees £25
Catering, changing room/showers, bar, club and trolley hire, shop, practice facilities
Visitors welcome weekdays
Handicap certificate required – limit: 28
Societies welcome by prior arrangement
🏨 Chiswick House, Meldreth, Royston, Cambridgeshire SG8 6LZ
☎ 01763 260242

SANDY LODGE GOLF CLUB

Sandy Lodge Lane, Northwood, Middx, HA6 2JD
☎ 01923 825429 Fax 01923 824319
Map 16, B4
Off A404, beside Moor Park underground station
Founded 1910
A fine heathland course, having sandy soil with links-like qualities.
18 holes, 6347 yards
par 71, S.S.S 71
Designer Harry Vardon
Green fees £31
Catering, changing room/showers, bar, trolley hire, shop, driving range
Visitors welcome, restricted weekends
Handicap certificate required
Societies welcome by prior arrangement

SHENDISH MANOR GOLF CLUB

Shendish House, Apsley, Hemel Hempstead, Hertfordshire HP3 0AA
☎ 01442 251806 Fax 01442 230683
Map 8, F10
Off A41, S of Hemel Hemstead
Founded 1984
Laid out on hilly ground, a course to test players at all handicap levels, with fine views.
18 holes, 5660 yards
par 70, S.S.S 68
Designer Henry Cotton, Donald Steel
Green fees £15
Catering, changing room/showers, bar, club, trolley and buggy hire, shop, practice facilities, sauna, gymnasium, pitch-and-putt course
Visitors welcome
Societies welcome by prior arrangement

SOUTH HERTS GOLF CLUB

Links Drive, Totteridge, London N20 8QU
☎ 020 8445 2035 Fax 020 8445 7569 **Map 16, D4**
www.southherts.co.uk
Off A1 at Apex Corner, via Totteridge Lane
Founded 1899
Between them Harry Vardon and Dai Rees served for over 70 years as the very distinguished professionals at South Herts, and much of the design is Vardon's. Narrow entrances to the greens, subtle breaks on their putting surfaces, and the gentle hilliness of the rolling, tree-lined fairways restrict scoring effectively.
18 holes, 6432 yards
par 72, S.S.S 71
Designer Willie Park Jnr, Harry Vardon
Green fees £30
Catering, changing room/showers, bar, club, trolley and buggy hire, shop, practice facilities
Visitors welcome weekdays
Handicap certificate required
Societies welcome by prior arrangement

STEVENAGE GOLF CENTRE

Aston Lane, Stevenage, Hertfordshire SG2 7EL
☎ 01438 880424 **Map 8, G9**
Off B5169, 4 miles SE of Stevenage
Founded 1980
Pleasantly wooded, and with a number of water hazards.
18 holes, 6451 yards
par 72, S.S.S 71
Designer John Jacobs
Green fees £11
Catering, changing room/showers, bar, club, trolley and buggy hire, shop, driving range
Visitors welcome
Societies welcome by prior arrangement

STOCKS HOTEL GOLF & COUNTRY CLUB

Stocks Road, Aldbury, Tring, Hertfordshire HP23 5RX
☎ 01442 851341 Fax 01442 851253
Map 8, F9
2 miles E of Tring
Founded 1994
A parkland course of very considerable length.
18 holes, 7016 yards
par 72, S.S.S 74
Designer Mike Billcliffe
Green fees £25
Catering, changing room/showers, bar, accommodation, club, trolley and buggy hire, shop, practice facilities, full hotel facilities
Visitors welcome
Handicap certificate required
Societies welcome by prior arrangement
🏨 Stocks Hotel, Stocks Road, Aldbury, Tring, Hertfordshire
☎ 01442 851341 Fax 01442 851253

VERULAM GOLF CLUB

London Road, St Albans, Hertfordshire AL1 1JG
☎ 01727 853327 Fax 01727 812201
Map 16, C3
www.verulamgolf.co.uk
Off A1081, 1 mile from M25 Jct 22.
Founded 1905
Samuel Ryder, who presented the Ryder Cup, was Captain of Verulam and his personal professional, Abe Mitchell, is represented on top of the trophy. There are fine views from the course, especially that of St Albans Abbey from the 11th tee. Out-of-bounds potentially threatens on no fewer than fourteen holes.
18 holes, 6448 yards
par 72, S.S.S 71
Designer James Braid, Donald Steel
Green fees £25
Catering, changing room/showers, bar, club and trolley hire, shop, practice facilities
Visitors welcome weekdays
Handicap certificate required
Societies welcome by prior arrangement

WELWYN GARDEN CITY GOLF CLUB

Mannicotts, High Oaks Road, Welwyn Garden City, Hertfordshire AL8 7BP
☎ 01923 236484 Fax 01923 222300
Map 16, D2
B197, A1 (M) Jct 4
Founded 1922
A parkland course, an early stamping ground of Nick Faldo.
18 holes, 6100 yards
par 69, S.S.S 69
Designer Hawtree
Green fees £30
Catering, changing room/showers, bar, trolley and buggy hire, shop
Visitors welcome weekdays
Handicap certificate required
Societies welcome by prior arrangement

WEST HERTS GOLF CLUB

Cassiobury Park, Watford, Hertfordshire WD3 3GG
☎ 01923 236484 Fax 01923 222300
Map 16, B4
Off A412 W of Watford
Founded 1890
'A fine day at Cassiobury comes within a measurable distance of heaven'. Bernard Darwin's remark of 1910 is equally valid today. Over £1 million has been spent recently in refurbishment of the clubhouse and practice facilities, making it a very well-equipped (and good value) club for members and visitors alike.
18 holes, 6528 yards
par 72, S.S.S 71
Designer Tom Morris, Alister Mackenzie
Green fees £26
Catering, changing room/showers, bar, club, trolley and buggy hire, shop, practice facilities, indoor teaching, Golf Foundation Starter Centre
Visitors welcome
Societies welcome by prior arrangement
🏨 White House Hotel, Upton Raod, Watford, Hertfordshire
☎ 01923 429988

WHIPSNADE PARK GOLF CLUB

Studham Lane, Dagnall, Hertfordshire HP4 1RH
☎ 01442 842330 Fax 01442 842090
Map 8, F9
www.whipsnadeparkgc.com
Off A4147, 8 miles N of Hemel Hempstead
Founded 1974
A long parkland/downland course, adjoining Whipsnade Zoo, with fine views towards the Chilterns.
18 holes, 6812 yards
par 73, S.S.S 72
Green fees £26
Catering, changing room/showers, bar, club, trolley and buggy hire, shop, practice facilities
Visitors welcome weekdays
Societies welcome by prior arrangement

WHITEHILL GOLF CLUB

Dane End, Ware, Hertfordshire SG12 0JS
☎ 01920 438495 Fax 01920 438891
Map 9, A9
Off A10, 4 miles N of Ware
Founded 1990
A parkland course with a number of significant water hazards.
18 holes, 6636 yards
par 72, S.S.S 72
Green fees £19.50
Catering, changing room/showers, bar, club and trolley hire, shop, driving range
Visitors welcome
Handicap certificate required
Societies welcome by prior arrangment

MIDDLESEX

AIRLINKS GOLF CLUB

Southall Lane, Hounslow, Middlesex TW5 9PE
☎ 020 8561 1418 Fax 020 8813 6284 **Map 16, C6**
Off M4 Jct 3, W of Hounslow
Founded 1984
Attached to the David Lloyd Tennis Centre, a public parkland course designed by Peter Alliss and Dave Thomas.
18 holes, 6001 yards
par 71, S.S.S 69
Designer Peter Alliss, Dave Thomas
Green fees £10
Catering, changing room/showers, bar, club, trolley and buggy hire, shop, driving range, practice facilities, tennis
Visitors welcome
Societies welcome by prior arrangement

AMERICAN GOLF AT SUNBURY

Charlton Lane, Shepperton, Middlesex TW17 8QA
☎ 01932 772898 Fax 01932 789300
Map 16, B7
sunbury@americangolf.uk.com
www.americangolf.com
M3 Jct 1, A308 towards Staines. At 4th lights take Littleton Road. Charlton Lane is in Charlton Village.
Founded 1991
The usual comprehensive pay-and-play facilities are complemented by a converted 16th-century barn which makes a fine venue for functions.
18 holes, 5540 yards, par 68, S.S.S 65
9 holes, 2607 yards, par 33, S.S.S 32
Green fees £14
Catering, changing room/showers, bar, club, trolley and buggy hire, shop, driving range, function suite
Visitors welcome
Societies welcome by prior arrangement

ASHFORD MANOR GOLF CLUB

Fordbridge Road, Ashford, Middlesex TW15 3RT
☎ 01784 255490 Fax 01784 424649
Map 16, B7
www.amgc.co.uk
A308, M25 Jct 13, M3 Jct 1
Founded 1898
A long-established parkland course with excellent greens. There is plenty of strength in the longer par 4s, with the 7th, 10th and 17th each measuring over 450 yards.
18 holes, 6352 yards
par 70, S.S.S 70
Green fees £30
Catering, changing room/showers, bar, trolley hire, shop, practice facilities, small meeting/function room
Visitors welcome weekdays
Handicap certificate required
Societies welcome by prior arrangement
🏨 The Anchor, Church Square, Shepperton, Middlesex TW17 9JZ
☎ 01932 221618

BRENT VALLEY GOLF CLUB

138 Church Road, Hanwell, London W7 3BE
☎ 020 8567 4230 **Map 16, C6**
Off A4020 Uxbridge Road.
Founded 1938
A public parkland course through which flows the River Brent.
18 holes, 5426 yards
par 67, S.S.S 66
Green fees £10
Catering, changing room/showers, bar, club and trolley hire, shop
Visitors welcome
Societies welcome by prior arrangement

BUSH HILL PARK GOLF CLUB

Bush Hill, Winchmore Hill, London N21 2BU
☎ 020 8360 5738 Fax 020 8360 5583 **Map 16, E4**

www.bushhillparkgolfclub.co.uk
1 mile S of Enfield
Founded 1895
A parkland course, well-wooded and extensively bunkered.
18 holes, 5825 yards
par 70, S.S.S 68
Green fees £25
Changing room/showers, trolley hire, shop
Visitors welcome, restricted Wednesday and weekends
Handicap certificate required
Societies welcome by prior arrangement

C & L GOLF & COUNTRY CLUB

West End Road, Northolt, Middlesex UB5 6RD
☎ 020 8845 5662 **Map 16, B5**
Off A40, opposite Northolt Airport
Founded 1991
One of many sports facilities available at this club.
9 holes, 4440 yards
par 64, S.S.S 62
Designer Patrick Tallack
Green fees £10
Catering, changing room/showers, bar, practice facilities, tennis & swimming pool, squash
Visitors welcome
Societies welcome by prior arrangement

CREWS HILL GOLF CLUB

Cattlegate Road, Crews Hill, Enfield, Middlesex EN2 8AZ
☎ 020 8366 7422 Fax 020 8364 5641 **Map 16, E4**
M25 Jct 24, towards Enfield
Founded 1920
One of the best courses in the area, with a heathland front nine, and much tighter, if shorter, back nine somewhat troubled by a river.
18 holes, 6244 yards
par 70, S.S.S 70
Designer Harry Colt
Green fees £23
Catering, changing room/showers, bar, trolley and buggy hire, shop
Visitors welcome. Handicap certificate required
Societies welcome by prior arrangement
🏨 Royal Chase Hotel, The Ridgeway, Enfield, Middlesex EN2 8AR
☎ 020 8366 6500

EALING GOLF CLUB

Perivale Lane, Greenford, Middlesex UB6 8SS
☎ 0208 997 0937 Fax 0208 998 0756 **Map 16, C5**
Off A40, opposite Hoover Building.
Founded 1898
Ealing has a remarkable record in amateur golf, having been European Club Champions in 1989 and 1990. For a course that is not long on paper, there are some remarkably long individual holes, including three par 3s at over 200 yards, while the 6th is a 465-yard par 4.
18 holes, 6216 yards
par 70, S.S.S 70
Designer Harry Colt
Green fees £30
Catering, changing room/showers, bar, club and trolley hire, shop, practice facilities
Visitors welcome weekdays.
Handicap certificate required
Societies welcome by prior arrangement

ENFIELD GOLF CLUB

Old Park Road South, Enfield, Middlesex EN2 7DA
☎ 020 8363 3970 Fax 020 8342 0381 **Map 16, E4**
enfieldgolfclub@dial.pipex.com
www.enfieldgolfclub.co.uk
M25 Jct 24, A1005 towards Enfield
Founded 1893
One of London's older clubs. Salmons Brook runs through the course.
18 holes, 6154 yards
par 72, S.S.S 70
Designer James Braid
Green fees £27
Catering, changing room/showers, bar, trolley hire, shop
Visitors welcome – must telephone first
Handicap certificate required
Societies welcome by prior arrangement
🏨 West Lodge Park, Cockfosters Road, Hadley Wood, Barnet, Hertfordshire EN4 0PY
☎ 020 8216 3900 Fax 020 8216 3937
beales_westlodgepark@compuserve.com
www.bealeshotels.co.uk

FINCHLEY GOLF CLUB

Nether Court, Frith Lane, London NW7 1PU
☎ 020 8346 2436 Fax 020 8343 4205 **Map 16, D4**
secretary@finchleygolfclub.co.uk
www.finchleygolfclub.co.uk
A1 northbound at North Circular Road
Founded 1929
Parkland course particularly renowned for its back nine, which is played through the delightful grounds of a Victorian mansion, now the clubhouse.
18 holes, 6536 yards
par 72, S.S.S 71
Designer James Braid
Green fees £25
Catering, changing room/showers, bar, club, trolley and buggy hire, shop, practice facilities
Visitors welcome – restricted certain mornings
Societies welcome by prior arrangement
🏨 Hendon Hall Hotel, Sanders Lane, Hendon, Middlesex
☎ 020 8203 3341

FULWELL GOLF CLUB

Wellington Road, Hampton Hill, Middlesex TW12 1JY
☎ 0208 977 2733 Fax 0208 977 7732 **Map 16, C6**
A311, 2 miles S of Twickenham
Founded 1904
The present course dates from 1958 and calls for good positional play. A stream in front of the green of the par-5 5th makes it a testing hole for those contemplating reaching the green in two. The approach to the final green is similar, needing great accuracy and nerve.
18 holes, 6544 yards
par 71, S.S.S 71
Designer John Morrison
Green fees £30
Catering, changing room/showers, bar, club, trolley and buggy hire, shop, practice facilities
Visitors welcome weekdays (not Tuesday)
Handicap certificate required
Societies welcome by prior arrangement

GRIM'S DYKE GOLF CLUB

Oxhey Lane, Hatch End, Pinner, Middlesex HA5 4AL
☎ 020 8428 4093 Fax 020 8421 5494 **Map 16, C4**
A4008, 3 miles N of Harrow
Founded 1910
A rolling parkland course, taking its name from a prehistoric earthwork.
18 holes, 5600 yards
par 69, S.S.S 67
Designer James Braid
Green fees £25
Catering, changing room/showers, bar, club and trolley hire, shop
Visitors welcome, restricted weekends
Societies welcome by prior arrangement

HAMPSTEAD GOLF CLUB

Winnington Road, London N2 0TU
☎ 020 8455 0203 Fax 020 8731 6194 **Map 16, D5**

Close to Kenwood House, E of Hampstead.
Founded 1893
Said to be the nearest proper course to Charing Cross, Hampstead is a charming 9-holer, with a delightful clubhouse. Three strenuous par 4s, the 465-yard 2nd, 463-yard 6th, and 420-yard 7th, are offset by gentler holes, although, measuring only 106 yards, the 3rd demands total precision.
9 holes, 5822 yards
par 68, S.S.S 68
Designer Tom Dunn
Green fees £30
Catering, changing room/showers, bar, club and trolley hire, shop, practice facilities
Visitors welcome – limited numbers
Handicap certificate required
Societies welcome by prior arrangement.

HARROW SCHOOL GOLF CLUB

Harrow School, High Street, Harrow-on-the-Hill, Middlesex HA1 3JT
☎ 020 872 8000 **Map 16, D4**
Off A40
Founded 1978
A marvellous asset set in the beautiful grounds of this distinguished school. From the 4th tee there are extensive views over London.
9 holes, 3690 yards
par 57, S.S.S 57
Designer Donald Steel
Green fees £7
Changing room/showers, practice facilities
Visitors welcome only as members' guests
Handicap certificate required – limit: 36
No societies

HASTE HILL GOLF CLUB

The Drive, Northwood, Middlesex HA6 1HN
☎ 01923 825224 Fax 01923 826485
Map 16, B4
Off A404
Founded 1933
A very pretty parkland course, well-wooded, in gently hilly country.
18 holes, 5736 yards
par 68, S.S.S 68
Green fees £12.50
Club, trolley and buggy hire, shop
Visitors welcome
Societies welcome by prior arrangement

HEATH PARK GOLF CLUB

Stockley Road, West Drayton, Middlesex UB7 9NA
☎ 01895 444232 Fax 01895 445122
Map 16, B6
www.hpgc.co.uk
Off A408, 1 mile SE of West Drayton
Founded 1975
A short, but hilly course with excellent off-course facilities.
9 holes, 3800 yards
par 64, S.S.S 62
Designer Neil Coles
Green fees £7
Catering, changing room/showers, bar, club and trolley hire, shop, practice facilities, indoor swimming pool, sauna, gymnasium
Visitors welcome, with restrictions
Societies welcome by prior arrangement
🏨 Crown Plaza Hotel, Stockley Road, West Drayton, Middlesex
☎ 01895 445555458

HENDON GOLF CLUB

Ashley Walk, Devonshire Road, London NW7 1DG
☎ 020 8346 6023 Fax 020 8343 1974 **Map 16, D4**
hendongolf@talk21.com
www.hendongolfclub.co.uk
M1 Jct 2, then 1st left at lights (Holders Jill Road). 1st left at next roundabout into Devonshire Road, then left into Ashley Walk.
Founded 1903
Seclusion and privacy is given to individual fairways by an enormous variety of trees. Colt's design, and the bunkering in particular, gives considerable challenge.
18 holes, 6289 yards
par 70, S.S.S 70
Designer Harry Colt
Green fees £30
Catering, changing room/showers, bar, club and trolley hire, shop, practice facilities
Visitors welcome weekdays – restricted weekends
Handicap certificate required – limit: 28 men, 36 women
Societies welcome by prior arrangement
🏨 Hendon Hall Hotel, Sanders Lane, Hendon, Middlesex
☎ 020 8203 3341

HIGHGATE GOLF CLUB

Denewood Road, Highgate, London N6 4AH
☎ 020 8340 1906 Fax 020 8348 9152 **Map 16, D5**
www.highgategolfclub.freeserve.co.uk
Off Sheldon Avenue, Highgate
Founded 1904
Tight parkland course with several holes played across an enclosed reservoir.
18 holes, 5964 yards
par 69, S.S.S 69
Designer Cuthbert Butchart
Green fees £30
Changing room/showers, club and trolley hire, shop
Visitors welcome weekdays with restrictions
Societies welcome by prior arrangement

HILLINGDON GOLF CLUB

18 Dorset Way, Hillingdon, Uxbridge, Middlesex UB10 0JR
☎ 01895 239810 Fax 01895 233956
Map 16, B5
Off A4020, W side of town, opposite St John's Church
Founded 1892
Gently undulating parkland course.
9 holes, 5459 yards
par 68, S.S.S 67
Green fees £15
Catering, changing room/showers, bar, trolley hire, shop
Visitors welcome weekdays, with restrictions
Societies welcome by prior arrangement

HORSENDEN HILL GOLF COURSE

Woodland Rise, Greenford, Middlesex UB6 0RD
☎ 020 8902 4555 **Map 16, D5**
Close to Sudbury Town tube station
Founded 1935
A short course on hilly ground with distant views of the London Eye and Wembley Stadium.
9 holes, 3000 yards
par 56, S.S.S 55
Green fees £11.65
Catering, changing room/showers, bar, club and trolley hire, shop, practice facilities
Visitors welcome
No societies

HOUNSLOW HEATH GOLF CLUB

Staines Road, Hounslow, Middlesex TW4 5DS
☎ 020 8570 5271 **Map 16, C6**
A315, between Hounslow and Bedfont
Founded 1979
Attractive, partially wooded, heathland course.
18 holes, 5901 yards
par 69, S.S.S 68
Designer Fraser Middleton
Green fees £8.40
Catering, changing room/showers, bar, club and trolley hire, shop, practice facilities
Visitors welcome weekdays

Societies welcome by prior arrangement

LEE VALLEY LEISURE GOLF COURSE

Picketts Lock Lane, Edmonton, London N9 0AS
✆ 020 8803 3611 **Map 16, E4**
1 mile N of North Circular Road
Founded 1973
Water, in the form of the River Lee and a lake, is a threat on many holes.
18 holes, 4902 yards
par 66, S.S.S 64
Green fees £10
Catering, changing room/showers, bar, club and trolley hire, shop, driving range, heated indoor swimming pool, squash, gymnasium
Visitors welcome
Societies welcome by prior arrangement

LONDON GOLF CENTRE

Ruislip Road, Northolt, Middlesex UB5 6QZ
✆ 020 8841 6162 Fax 020 8842 2097 **Map 16, B5**
Off A40 at Polish War Memorial
Founded 1984
Also known as Lime Trees Park, one of a number of welcome new facilities close to the A40 in West London.
9 holes, 5838 yards
par 71, S.S.S 69
Green fees £5
Catering, changing room/showers, bar, club and trolley hire, shop, driving range
Visitors welcome
Societies welcome by prior arrangement

MILL HILL GOLF CLUB

100 Barnet Way, Mill Hill, London NW7 3AL
✆ 020 8959 2282 Fax 020 8906 0731 **Map 16, D4**
A1 southbound, ½ mile N of Apex Corner
Founded 1925
Sandwiched between the M1 and A1, Mill Hill is a handsome, wooded course benefiting from the past attentions of two master architects, Abercromby and Colt. Ponds add spice to the 2nd, 10th and 17th, and the big par 4s, the 6th, 12th and 15th, complement a number of shorter two-shotters.
18 holes, 6247 yards
par 70, S.S.S 70
Designer J.F. Abercromby, Harry Colt
Green fees £25
Catering, changing room/showers, bar, club and trolley hire, shop, practice facilities
Visitors welcome weekdays
Handicap certificate required
Societies welcome by prior arrangement

MUSWELL HILL GOLF CLUB

Rhodes Avenue, Wood Green, London N22 7UT
✆ 020 8888 2044 Fax 020 8889 9380 **Map 16, D4**
1 mile from Bounds Green Station, 1 mile N of North Circular Road
Founded 1893
A parkland course with water hazards – strongly testing.
18 holes, 6494 yards
par 71, S.S.S 71
Designer James Braid
Green fees £23
Catering, changing room/showers, bar, club, trolley and buggy hire, shop
Visitors welcome weekdays
Societies welcome by prior arrangement

NORTH MIDDLESEX GOLF CLUB

The Manor House, Friern Barnet Lane, Whetstone, London N20 0NL
✆ 020 8445 1604 Fax 020 8445 5023 **Map 16, C4**
office@northmiddlesexgc.co.uk
www.northmiddlesex.co.uk
5 miles S of M25 Jct 23
Founded 1904
The greens are rated as some of the best in the region. The 5th and 18th are tough par 3s, and the par-4 14th needs a carry of 190 yards over a stream.
18 holes, 5625 yards
par 69, S.S.S 67
Designer Willie Park Jnr.
Green fees £23
Catering, changing room/showers, bar, trolley hire, shop
Visitors welcome – restricted weekends
Handicap certificate required
Societies welcome by prior arrangement
🏨 West Lodge Park, Cockfosters Road, Hadley Wood, Barnet, Hertfordshire EN4 0PY
✆ 020 8216 3900 Fax 2082163937
beales_westlodgepark@compuserve.com
www.bealeshotels.co.uk

NORTHOLT GOLF CENTRE

Huxley Close, Northolt, Middlesex UB5 5UL
✆ 020 8841 5550 **Map 16, B5**
M40, Target roundabout
Founded 1991
A short course attached to a long-established driving range.
9 holes
par 56, S.S.S 55
Green fees £5
Club and trolley hire, shop, driving range
Visitors welcome
Societies welcome by prior arrangement

NORTHWOOD GOLF CLUB

Rickmansworth Road, Northwood, Middlesex HA6 2QW
✆ 01923 825329 Fax 01923 840150 **Map 16, B4**
A404, 3 miles SE of Rickmansworth
Founded 1891
An old club with a parkland course verging on heathland in nature. The 10th used to be one of the most famous all-or-nothing long par 3s, but is now a little easier as a drive-and-pitch par 4.
18 holes, 6553 yards
par 71, S.S.S 71
Designer James Braid
Green fees £27
Catering, changing room/showers, bar, club and trolley hire, shop, practice facilities
Visitors welcome weekdays
Handicap certificate required
Societies welcome by prior arrangement

PERIVALE PARK GOLF CLUB

Stockdove Way, Argyle Road, Greenford, Middlesex UB6 8EN
✆ 020 8575 7116 **Map 16, C5**
Off A40, 1 mile E of Greenford
Founded 1932
Municipal parkland course beside the River Brent.
9 holes, 5296 yards
par 68, S.S.S 67
Green fees £4.40
Changing room/showers, club and trolley hire, shop
Visitors welcome
Societies welcome by prior arrangement

PINNER HILL GOLF CLUB

Southview Road, Pinner Hill, Middlesex HA6 1JT
✆ 0208 866 0963 Fax 0208 868 4817 **Map 16, C5**
pinnerhillgc@ukz.net
www.pinnerhillgc.co.uk
Off Pinner Hill Road
Founded 1928
The views from this wooded parkland course extend across London to Canary Wharf, the London Eye, and the North Downs.
18 holes, 6330 yards
par 71, S.S.S 70

Designer J.H. Taylor, Hawtree
Green fees £35
Catering, changing room/showers, bar, club, trolley and buggy hire, shop, practice facilities
Visitors welcome with restrictions
Societies welcome by prior arrangment

RUISLIP GOLF CLUB
Ickenham Road, Ruislip, Middlesex HA4 7DQ
✆ 01895 638835 Fax 01895 622172 **Map 16, C5**
B466, SW of Ruislip
Founded 1936
Attractive parkland course beside the Marylebone railway line.
18 holes, 5571 yards
par 69, S.S.S 67
Designer Sandy Herd
Green fees £12.50
Catering, changing room/showers, bar, club, trolley and buggy hire, shop, driving range
Visitors welcome
Societies welcome by prior arrangement

STANMORE GOLF CLUB
29 Gordon Avenue, Stanmore, Middlesex HA7 2RL
✆ 020 8954 2599 Fax 020 8954 6418 **Map 16, B6**
Off Old Church Lane, between Stanmore and Belmont
Founded 1893
Partially wooded parkland course.
18 holes, 5860 yards
par 68, S.S.S 68
Green fees £28.50
Catering, changing room/showers, bar, trolley hire, shop, practice facilities
Visitors welcome weekdays, restricted weekends
Handicap certificate required
Societies welcome by prior arrangement

STOCKLEY PARK GOLF CLUB
The Clubhouse, Stockley Park, Uxbridge, Middlesex UB11 1AQ
✆ 0208 813 5700 Fax 0208 813 5655 **Map 16, B6**
info@stockleyparkgolf.com
www.stockleyparkgolf.com
A 408, M4 Jct 4
Founded 1993
One of the few Trent Jones courses in England, and an excellent example of his technique, making the golfer think on every shot. Cunning bunkering affects players of all abilities, the greens are full of movement, many raised up tellingly, and the undulations of the site have been exploited strategically.
18 holes, 6754 yards
par 72, S.S.S 72
Designer Robert Trent Jones
Green fees £24
Catering, changing room/showers, bar, club, trolley and buggy hire, shop, practice facilities, full conference facilities
Visitors welcome
Societies welcome by prior arrangement

STRAWBERRY HILL GOLF CLUB
Wellesley Road, Strawberry Hill, Twickenham, Middlesex TW2 5SD
✆ 020 8894 1246 **Map 16, C6**
Off A311, S side of town centre
Founded 1900
A compact 9-hole parkland course alongside the railway line to Hampton and Sunbury.
9 holes, 4762 yards
par 64, S.S.S 62
Designer J.H. Taylor
Green fees £20
Catering, changing room/showers, bar, trolley hire, shop
Visitors welcome weekdays, restriced weekends
Societies welcome by prior arrangement

SUDBURY GOLF CLUB
Bridgewater Road, Wembley, Middlesex HA10 1AL
✆ 020 8902 3713 Fax 020 8903 2966 **Map 16, C5**
A4090, SW of Wembley
Founded 1920
A Colt-designed parkland course adjoining the Grand Union Canal and Horsenden Hill Golf Course.
18 holes, 6282 yards
par 69, S.S.S 70
Designer Harry Colt
Green fees £30
Catering, changing room/showers, bar, trolley and buggy hire, shop
Visitors welcome weekdays
Handicap certificate required
Societies welcome by prior arrangement

TRENT PARK GOLF CLUB
Bramley Road, Southgate, London N14 4UT
✆ 020 8366 7432 Fax 020 8368 3823 **Map 16, D4**
A110, near Oakwood underground station
Founded 1973
Many holes are troubled by the Merryhills Brook which flows through the middle of the course.
18 holes, 6008 yards
par 70, S.S.S 69
Green fees £10.60
Catering, changing room/showers, bar, club and trolley hire, shop, driving range
Visitors welcome weekdays
Societies welcome by prior arrangement

TWICKENHAM GOLF CLUB
Staines Road, Twickenham, Middlesex TW2 5JD
✆ 020 8783 1698 Fax 020 8941 9134 **Map 16, C6**
A305, 2 miles W of Twickenham
Founded 1977
Adjacent to Fulwell Golf Club, and sharing many of its verdant qualities.
9 holes, 6014 yards
par 72, S.S.S 69
Designer Charles Lawrie
Green fees £6.50
Catering, changing room/showers, bar, club and trolley hire, shop, driving range, putting green
Visitors welcome
Societies welcome by prior arrangement

UXBRIDGE GOLF CLUB
The Drive, Harefield Place, Uxbridge, Middlesex UB10 8PA
✆ 01895 231169 Fax 01895 810262
Map 16, B5
Off B467, 2 miles N of Uxbridge
Founded 1947
Attractive parkland course.
18 holes, 5711 yards
par 68, S.S.S 68
Green fees £12.50
Catering, changing room/showers, bar, club, trolley and buggy hire, shop, practice facilities
Visitors welcome
Societies welcome by prior arrangement

WEST MIDDLESEX GOLF CLUB
Greenford Road, Southall, Middlesex UB1 3EE
✆ 020 8574 3450 Fax 020 8574 2383 **Map 16, C5**
A4127, off A4020, between Hanwell and Southall
Founded 1891
Visitor green fees (already good value) are reduced on Mondays and Wednesdays at this James Braid-designed parkland course in the Brent Valley.
18 holes, 6119 yards
par 69, S.S.S 69
Designer James Braid
Green fees £15.50
Catering, changing room/showers, bar, trolley hire, shop
Visitors welcome – restricted weekends

Societies welcome by prior arrangement

WHITEWEBBS GOLF COURSE

Beggars Hollow, Clay Hill, Enfield, Middlesex EN2 9JN
☎ 020 8363 2951 **Map 16, E4**
1 mile N of Enfield
Founded 1932
A public parkland course, attractive with trees and a stream.
18 holes, 5863 yards
par 68, S.S.S 68
Green fees £10
Catering, changing room/showers, bar, club and trolley hire, shop, practice facilities
Visitors welcome
Societies welcome by prior arrangement

WYKE GREEN GOLF CLUB

Syon Lane, Isleworth, Osterley, Middlesex TW7 5PT
☎ 020 8560 8777 Fax 020 8569 8392 **Map 16, C6**
office@wykegreen.golfagent.co.uk
www.wykegreengolfclub.co.uk
A4 to Gillette Corner, N onto Syon Lane
Founded 1928
The first golf course many visitors to England see, for the Piccadilly Line runs through the middle of the course on its way from Heathrow Airport. Although it is flat, with many parallel holes, it is far from a beginner's course with seven par 4 holes over 420 yards long.
18 holes, 6211 yards
par 69, S.S.S 70
Designer F.G. Hawtree
Green fees £25
Catering, changing room/showers, bar, club, trolley and buggy hire, shop, practice facilities
Visitors welcome with weekend restrictions
Societies welcome by prior arrangement
🏨 Four Pillars Hotel, Great West Road, Osterley, Middlesex

NORFOLK

BARNHAM BROOM HOTEL GOLF CLUB

Honingham Road, Barnham Broom, Norwich, Norfolk NR9 4DD
☎ 01603 759393 Fax 01603 758224
Map 9, E5
enquiry@barnhambroomhotelco.uk
www.barnham-broom.co.uk
Off A47, 10 miles SW of Norwich
Founded 1977
Lucky is the hotel which can offer its guests two contrasting courses, the Valley running through the valley of the River Yare, and the Hill, as might be expected, on higher ground, with good views.
Hill Course: 18 holes, 6495 yards, par 71, S.S.S 71
Designer Donald Steel
Valley Course: 18 holes, 6603 yards, par 72, S.S.S 72
Designer Frank Pennink
Green fees £20
Catering, changing room/showers, bar, accommodation, club, trolley and buggy hire, shop, driving range, full hotel facilities
Visitors welcome
Societies welcome by prior arrangement
🏨 Barnham Broom Hotel, Honingham Road, Barnham Broom, Norfolk NR9 4DD
☎ 01603 759393 Fax 01603 758224
enquiry@barnhambroomhotel.co.uk
www.barnham-broom.co.uk

BAWBURGH GOLF CLUB

Glen Lodge, Marlingford, Bawburgh, Norwich, Norfolk NR9 3LU
☎ 01603 740404 Fax 01603 740403
Map 9, F5
info@bawburgh.com
www.bawburgh.com
Off A47, Norwich southern by-pass, at Norfolk Showground exit.
Founded 1979
A mixture of parkland and heathland. The 18th is considered one of the best holes in the county, a 460-yard par 4. Other strong holes include the 446-yard 8th, and 568-yard 13th.
18 holes, 6231 yards
par 70, S.S.S 70
Designer Shaun Manser
Green fees £20
Catering, changing room/showers, bar, trolley and buggy hire, shop, driving range, practice facilities, driving range, discount golf shop
Visitors welcome, restricted weekends
Societies welcome by prior arangement
🏨 Park Farm Hotel, Hethersett, Norwich, Norfolk
☎ 01603 810264

CALDECOTT HALL GOLF CLUB

Caldecott Hall, Beccles Road, Fritton, Norfolk NR31 9EY
☎ 01493 4888488 Fax 01493 488561 **Map 9, G5**
A143, 5 miles SW of Gt Yarmouth
Founded 1994
Many hundreds of acres of woodland hacking are available to riders. There is a similar exilharating sense of rural delight in the golf course, dog-legging its way over hills and through pine woods.
18 holes, 6572 yards
par 72, S.S.S 71
Green fees £15
Catering, changing room/showers, bar, club, trolley and buggy hire, shop, driving range, practice facilities, 9-hole, par-3 course, equestrian centre
Visitors welcome
Handicap certificate required
Societies welcome by prior arrangement

COSTESSEY PARK GOLF CLUB

Costessey Park, Costessey, Norwich, Norfolk NR8 5AL
☎ 01603 746333 Fax 01603 746185
Map 9, F4
Off A47, 3 miles W of Norwich
Founded 1983
A parkland course with rivers and lakes very much in play.
18 holes, 5900 yards
par 71, S.S.S 69
Green fees £20
Catering, changing room/showers, bar, club, trolley and buggy hire, shop
Visitors welcome
Societies welcome by prior arrangement

DEREHAM GOLF CLUB

Quebec Road, Dereham, Norfolk NR19 2DS
☎ 01362 695900 **Map 9, D4**
derehamgolfclub@dgolfclub.freeserve.co.uk
B1146 Fakenham road, ½ mile from Dereham
Founded 1934
A mature parkland course of decent length close to the town centre.
9 holes, 6225 yards
par 71, S.S.S 70
Green fees £15
Catering, changing room/showers, bar, trolley and buggy hire, shop, practice facilities
Visitors welcome – restrictions
Handicap certificate required
Societies welcome by prior arrangement
🏨 Phoenix Hotel, Dereham, Norfolk
☎ 01362 692276

DUNHAM GOLF CLUB

Little Dunham, King's Lynn, Norfolk PE32 2DF
☎ 01328 701718 Fax 01328 701906
Map 9, D4
Off A47, 4 miles NE of Swaffham
Founded 1987
A short parkland course with lakes.
9 holes, 2269 yards
S.S.S 62

Designer Cecil Denny
Green fees £9
Catering, changing room/showers, bar, club and trolley hire, shop, practice facilities
Visitors welcome
Societies welcome by prior arrangement

DE VERE DUNSTON HALL HOTEL GOLF CLUB

Ipswich Road, Dunston, Norwich, Norfolk NR14 8PQ
✆ 01508 470444 Fax 01508 470689
Map 9, F5
A140, S of Norwich
Founded 1994
Typical of the new breed of hotel course, with plenty of visual interest (not least water), sufficient challenge for the good player, yet not too dispiriting for the novice.
18 holes, 6319 yards
par 71, S.S.S 70
Designer M. Shaw
Green fees £20
Catering, changing room/showers, bar, accommodation, club, trolley and buggy hire, shop, driving range, practice facilities, full hotel, leisure, conference and function facilities
Visitors welcome – priority to hotel guests
Societies welcome by prior arrangement

EAGLES GOLF CLUB

39 School Road, Tilney All Saints, Kings Lynn, Norfolk PE34 4RS
✆ 01553 827147 Fax 01553 829777
Map 9, B4
shop@eagles-golf-tennis.co.uk
www.eagles-golf-tennis.co.uk
A47 between Kings Lynn and Wisbech
Founded 1985
A multi-sports complex with water coming into play on the main course.
9 holes, 4284 yards
par 64, S.S.S 61
Designer D.W. Horn
Green fees £7.50
Catering, changing room/showers, bar, club and trolley hire, shop, driving range, practice facilities, par 3 course, tennis, floodlit football
Visitors welcome
Societies welcome by prior arrangement
🏨 Butterfly Hotel, Hardwick Narrows, King's Lynn, Norfolk
✆ 01553 771707

EATON GOLF CLUB

Newmarket Road, Norwich, Norfolk NR4 6SF
✆ 01603 451686 Fax 01603 451686
Map 9, F5
www.eatongc.co.uk
A11, S of Norwich
Founded 1910
Well-wooded, challenging course with some of the best greens in the area. The club prides itself on drawing its members from all walks of life, free of the old-school-tie nature of many other clubs.
18 holes, 6114 yards
par 70, S.S.S 70
Green fees £30
Catering, changing room/showers, bar, club and trolley hire, shop, practice facilities
Visitors welcome, with restrictions
Handicap certificate required
Societies welcome by prior arrangement
🏨 Annesley Hotel, Newmarker Road, Norwich, Norfolk
✆ 01603 624553

FAKENHAM GOLF CLUB

The Race Course, Fakenham, Norfolk NR21 7NY
✆ 01328 862867 **Map 9, D3**
B1146 or A1967, at Fakenham racecourse
Founded 1973
Parkland course.
9 holes, 6174 yards
par 71, S.S.S 70
Designer Charles Lawrie
Green fees £14
Catering, changing room/showers, bar, trolley hire, shop, practice facilities, tennis courts, squash
Visitors welcome weekdays
Societies welcome by prior arrangement

FELTWELL GOLF CLUB

Thor Avenue, off Wilton Road, Wilton Road, Feltwell, Norfolk IP26 4AY
✆ 01842 827644 **Map 9, C6**
B1112, 1 mile S of Feltwell, 3 miles NW of Brandon.
Founded 1976
Playing conditions resemble those of a links with fast running fairways and exposure to the wind.
9 holes, 6488 yards
par 72, S.S.S 71
Green fees £15
Catering, changing room/showers, bar, trolley hire, shop, practice facilities
Visitors welcome, with restrictions
Societies welcome by prior arrangement
🏨 Brandon House Hotel, 79 High Street, Brandon, Suffolk, Norfolk
✆ 01842 8101711

GORLESTON GOLF CLUB

Warren Road, Gorleston on Sea, Great Yarmouth, Norfolk NR31 6JT
✆ 01493 661911 Fax 01493 661911
Map 9, H5
Off A12 between Great Yarmouth and Lowestoft
Founded 1906
Standing on the 7th green, the most easterly in Britain, there is no land between it and the North Pole! Set along the clifftops, erosion has been a constant threat, but a rescue, some twenty years ago, has preserved these coastal holes for the enjoyment of future generations of golfers.
18 holes, 6391 yards
par 71, S.S.S 71
Designer J.H. Taylor
Green fees £21
Catering, changing room/showers, bar, club and trolley hire, shop
Visitors welcome
Handicap certificate required
Societies welcome by prior arrangement

GREAT YARMOUTH & CAISTER GOLF CLUB

Beach House, Caister-on-Sea, Great Yarmouth, Norfolk NR30 5TD
✆ 01493 661911 Fax 01493 661911
Map 9, H14
Off A149, ½ mile N
Founded 1882
A historic links running in and out of the race course, with many outcrops of gorse, tough seaside grasses, as well as humps and hollows. The 4th and 8th are big two-shotters running in opposite directions, vulnerable to the wind, well-bunkered, and with their fairways narrowed short of the green.
18 holes, 6330 yards
par 70, S.S.S 70
Designer Harry Colt
Green fees £27
Catering, changing room/showers, bar, trolley hire, shop
Visitors welcome, restricted weekends
Societies welcome by prior arrangement

HUNSTANTON GOLF CLUB

Golf Course Road, Old Hunstanton, Norfolk PE36 6JQ
✆ 01485 532811 Fax 01485 532319
Map 9, C3
hunstanton.golf@eidosnet.co.uk
Off A149 in village of Old Hunstanton
Founded 1891
See Top 50 Courses, page 25
18 holes, 6911 yards
par 72, S.S.S 74

Designer George Fernie, James Braid, James Sherlock
Green fees £55
Catering, changing room/showers, bar, club, trolley and buggy hire, shop, practice facilities
Visitors welcome – restricted weekends, 2-ball play only
Handicap certificate required
Societies welcome by prior arrangement – no company days
Le Strange Arms, Old Hunstanton, Norfolk
01485 534411

KING'S LYNN GOLF CLUB

Castle Rising, King's Lynn, Norfolk PE31 6BD
01553 631654 Fax 01553 631036
Map 9, C4
klgc@eidosnet.co.uk
www.playandstay.net
Off A149, 4 miles NE of King's Lynn
Founded 1923
An exceptionally handsome course roaming the woods of Castle Rising. The trees which frame every hole give a wonderful sense of seclusion but they also punish wayward hitting severely. Ditches and a pond threaten on the 2nd, the longest of the par 4s, and the dog-leg 10th is highly regarded.
18 holes, 6609 yards
par 72, S.S.S 73
Designer Peter Alliss, Dave Thomas
Green fees £40
Catering, changing room/showers, bar, trolley hire, shop
Visitors welcome
Societies welcome by prior arrangement

THE LINKS COUNTRY PARK GOLF CLUB

Sandy Lane, West Runton, Norfolk NE27 9QH
01263 838215 Fax 01263 838264
Map 9, E4
sales@links-hotel.co.uk
www.links-hotel.co.uk
Off A149, W of Cromer
Founded 1899
Charming, short course attached to 'towers-and-turrets' hotel – good views.
9 holes, 4814 yards
par 66, S.S.S 64
Designer J.H. Taylor
Green fees £25
Catering, changing room/showers, bar, accommodation, club, trolley and buggy hire, shop, practice facilities, swimming pool (indoor), sauna, tennis, conference facilities
Visitors welcome
Societies welcome by prior arrangement
Links Hotel, Sandy Lane, West Runton, Norfolk NR27 9QH
01263 838383

MATTISHALL GOLF CLUB

South Green, Mattishall, Dereham, Norfolk NR20 3JZ
01362 850464 **Map 9, E4**
Off B1063, 6 miles E of Dereham
Founded 1990
What might seem just another parkland course is elevated to notoriety by having the longest hole in Norfolk – a 625-yard monster of a par 5.
9 holes, 6218 yards
par 72, S.S.S 69
Designer B.C. Todd
Green fees £8
Changing room/showers, bar, club and trolley hire, 9-hole pitch-and-putt
Visitors welcome, restricted weekends.
Societies welcome by prior arrangement

MIDDLETON HALL GOLF CLUB

Hall Orchards, Middleton, King's Lynn, Norfolk PE32 1RH
01553 841800 Fax 01553 841800
Map 9, C4
middleton-hall@btclick.com
www.middletonhall.co.uk
A47, 3 miles E of King's Lynn
Founded 1989
Set in the gently undulating grounds of 17th-century Middleton Hall, with its splendid specimen trees. Views over the Norfolk countryside are a bonus.
18 holes, 6007 yards
par 71, S.S.S 69
Designer R. Scott
Green fees £25
Catering, changing room/showers, bar, trolley and buggy hire, shop, driving range
Visitors welcome
Societies welcome by prior arrangement
Butterfly Hotel, Hardwick Narrows, King's Lynn, Norfolk
01553 771707

MUNDESLEY GOLF CLUB

Links Road, Mundesley, Norwich, Norfolk NR11 8ES
01263 720279 Fax 01263 7202799, F3
5 miles SE of Cromer
Founded 1901
It was on Mundesley's par-3 7th that Harry Vardon scored his only hole-in-one. There are extensive views over the countryside.
9 holes, 5377 yards
par 68, S.S.S 66
Designer Harry Vardon
Green fees £18
Catering, changing room/showers, bar, trolley hire, shop, driving range, practice facilities
Visitors welcome, with restrictions
Handicap certificate required
Societies welcome by prior arrangement
Manor Hotel, Beach Road, Mundesley, Norwich, Norfolk
01263 720309

THE NORFOLK GOLF & COUNTRY CLUB

Hingham Road, Reymerston, Norwich, Norfolk NR9 4QQ
01362 850297 Fax 01362 850614
Map 9, E4
Off B1135, 12 miles W of Norwich
Founded 1993
Formerly known as Reymerston Golf Club, a very attractive course laid out in rolling countryside. The greens are vast, as are the bunkers, and good ecological management is a feature of the philosophy.
18 holes, 6603 yards
par 72, S.S.S 72
Green fees £20
Catering, changing room/showers, bar, club, trolley and buggy hire, shop, driving range, heated swimming pool, sauna & gymnasium
Visitors welcome with prior booking
Societies welcome by prior arrangement

RAF MARHAM GOLF CLUB

RAF Marham, King's Lynn, Norfolk PE33 9NP
01760 337261 Ext.650
Map 9, E4
SE of King's Lynn
Founded 1974
Over the years the members of several active RAF stations have laid out golf courses in areas of spare land within the site. Access is restricted, and has to be conditional on operational requirements.
9 holes, 5244 yards
S.S.S 66
Visitors welcome by prior arrangement – restricted
No societies

RICHMOND PARK GOLF CLUB

Saham Road, Watton, Thetford, Norfolk IP25 6EA
01953 881803 Fax 01953 881817
Map 9, D5
info@richmondpark.co.uk
www.richmondpark.co.uk
Off A1075, ½ mile NW of Watton town centre.

Founded 1990
Set in 100 acres of parkland with trees and the Little Wissey River as the principle features.
18 holes, 6289 yards
par 71, S.S.S 70
Designer Scott/Jessup
Green fees £20
Catering, changing room/showers, bar, accommodation, club, trolley and buggy hire, shop, driving range, practice facilities
Visitors welcome, with restrictions
Societies welcome by prior arrangement
Richmond Park Holiday Apartments, Watton, Norfolk
01953 881803

ROYAL CROMER GOLF CLUB

145 Overstrand Road, Cromer, Norfolk NR27 0JH
01263 512884 Fax 01263 512430
Map 9, F3
general.manager@royal-cromer.com
www.royal-cromer.com
B1159, 1 mile E of Cromer
Founded 1888
Cromer is an old club with links to the foundation of the Curtis Cup. The front nine, on low ground, has many strong par 4s, especially the 6th and 7th, but the most memorable holes are those on the cliffs by the lighthouse, from the short 13th to the 15th.
18 holes, 6509 yards
par 72, S.S.S 72
Designer Tom Morris, J.H. Taylor, James Braid, Frank Pennink
Green fees £37
Catering, changing room/showers, bar, trolley and buggy hire, shop, practice facilities
Visitors welcome
Handicap certificate required
Societies welcome by prior arrangement
Sea Marge, Overstrand, Norfolk
01263 579579

ROYAL NORWICH GOLF CLUB

Drayton High Road, Hellesdon, Norwich, Norfolk NR6 5AH
01603 429928 Fax 01603 417945
Map 9, F4
www.royalnorwichgolf.co.uk
A1067, 2½ miles NW of town centre
Founded 1893
With undulating, tree-lined fairways this is a handsome course, and Braid's layout makes the most of these natural hazards to provide an engaging test. A particular delight is the charm and challenge of the shorter par 4s, while holes such as the 463-yard 2nd are a match for anybody.
18 holes, 6506 yards
par 72, S.S.S 72
Designer James Braid
Green fees £30
Catering, changing room/showers, bar
Visitors welcome – ring first
Handicap certificate required
Societies welcome by prior arrangement

ROYAL WEST NORFOLK GOLF CLUB

Brancaster, Near King's Lynn, Norfolk PE31 8AX
01485 210087 Fax 01485 210087
Map 9, C2
A149, E of Hunstanton
Founded 1892
See Top 50 Courses, page 42
18 holes, 6427 yards
par 71, S.S.S 71
Designer Horace Hutchinson, Holcombe Ingleby
Green fees £60
Catering, changing room/showers, bar, club and trolley hire, shop, practice facilities
Visitors welcome – restrictions
Handicap certificate required
Societies welcome by prior arrangement – numbers limited
The Hoste Arms, Burnham Market, Norfolk
01328 738257

RYSTON PARK GOLF CLUB

Ely Road, Denver, Downham Market, Norfolk PE38 0HH
01366 382133 Fax 01366 383834
Map 9, B5
A10, 1 mile S of Downham Market
Founded 1933
Set out in beautiful parkland with some of the best greens in Norfolk.
9 holes, 6310 yards
par 70, S.S.S 70
Designer James Braid
Green fees £20
Catering, changing room/showers, bar, club, trolley and buggy hire, practice facilities
Visitors welcome weekdays
Handicap certificate required
Societies welcome by prior arrangement
Castle Hotel, Downham Market, Norfolk
01366 384311

SHERINGHAM GOLF CLUB

Weybourne Road, Sheringham, Norfolk NR26 8HG
01263 823488 Fax 01263 825189
Map 9, E2
sgc.sec@care4free.net
www.sheringhamgolfclub.co.uk
A149, W of Sheringham
Founded 1891
A wondrously varied course enjoying stunning views from its clifftop site. The most spectacular holes are those at the very edge of the cliffs, the 5th, 6th, and 7th, but, as the course edges inland, gorse becomes a persistent threat. Bunkering throughout is serious and the greens are a joy.
18 holes, 6495 yards
par 70, S.S.S 71
Designer Tom Dunn
Green fees £40
Catering, changing room/showers, bar, trolley and buggy hire, shop, practice facilities
Visitors welcome
Handicap certificate required
Societies welcome by prior arrangement
Southlands Hotel, South Street, Sheringham, Norfolk
01263 822679

MARRIOTT SPROWSTON MANOR HOTEL & COUNTRY CLUB

Wroxham Road, Sprowston, Norwich, Norfolk NR7 8RP
01603 254290 Fax 01603 788884
Map 9, F4
Off A1151, 4 miles NE of Norwich
Founded 1980
A well-wooded parkland course rewarding accuracy. The lime tree, called Seven Sisters, behind the 6th green was planted on the day King Charles I was beheaded.
18 holes, 5673 yards
par 70, S.S.S 68
Green fees £21
Catering, changing room/showers, bar, accommodation, club, trolley and buggy hire, shop, driving range, practice facilities, full hotel, leisure, conference and function facilities, swimming, gym, beauty salon
Visitors welcome
Handicap certificate required – limit: 28 men, 45 women
Societies welcome by prior arrangement
Marriott Sprowston Manor Hotel, Wroxham Road, Sprowston, Norfolk NR7 8RP
01603 410871

SWAFFHAM GOLF CLUB

Cley Road, Swaffham, Norfolk PE37 8AE
01760 721621 Fax 01760 721621
Map 9, D4
swaffhamgc@supanet.com
1½ miles S of Swaffham
Founded 1922
Pretty country course and wildlife

habitat.
18 holes, 6550 yards
par 71, S.S.S 71
Designer Jonathan Gaunt
Green fees £20
Catering, changing room/showers, bar, club and trolley hire, shop, practice facilities
Visitors welcome weekdays
Handicap certificate required
Societies welcome by prior arrangement

THETFORD GOLF CLUB

Brandon Road, Thetford, Norfolk IP24 3NE
✆ 01842 752169 Fax 01842 766212
Map 9, D6
www.club-noticeboard.co.uk
B1107, 3 miles W of Thetford
Founded 1912
Five new holes introduced in 1988 added serious length without losing the charm of the original holes, with their fast-running heathland fairways cut through Breckland forest. The long par 4s, such as the 8th and 18th, stretch everyone, while the bunkering of the undulating 380-yard 5th is simply brilliant.
18 holes, 6849 yards
par 72, S.S.S 73
Designer C.H. Mayo, Donald Steel
Green fees £34
Catering, changing room/showers, bar, club and trolley hire, shop, practice facilities
Visitors welcome
Handicap certificate required
Societies welcome by prior arrangement
🏨 Bell Hotel, Bridge Street, Thetford, Norfolk
✆ 01842 754455

WENSUM VALLEY HOTEL GOLF & COUNTRY CLUB

Beech Avenue, Taverham, Norwich, Norfolk NR8 6HP
✆ 01603 261012 Fax 01603 261664
Map 9, F4
www.wensumvalley.co.uk
A1067, 4 miles NW of Norwich
Founded 1990
Attractive courses laid out along and across a valley. Visitors usually find the greens difficult to read, although perfectly fair. The drive to the par-4 12th on the Valley Course is the high spot, from an elevated tee, far above the distant fairway.
Valley Course: 18 holes, 6172 yards, par 71, S.S.S 69
Designer B.C. Todd
Wensum Course: 9 holes, 5812 yards, par 70, S.S.S 68
Green fees £18
Catering, changing room/showers, bar, accommodation, club, trolley and buggy hire, shop, driving range, practice facilities, fishing
Visitors welcome
Societies welcome by prior arrangement
🏨 Wensum Valley Hotel, Beech Avenue, Taverham, Norfolk
✆ 01603 261012 Fax 01603 261664

WESTON PARK GOLF CLUB

Weston Longville, Norwich, Norfolk NR9 5JW
✆ 01603 872363 Fax 01603 873040
Map 9, E4
www.weston-park.co.uk
Off A1067, 7 miles NW of Norwich
Founded 1993
A most appealing course, wending its way through the tall trees of a long-established parkland.
18 holes, 6603 yards
par 72, S.S.S 72
Designer John Glasgow
Green fees £27
Catering, changing room/showers, bar, trolley and buggy hire, shop, practice facilities, tennis
Visitors welcome
Societies welcome by prior arrangement

SUFFOLK

ALDEBURGH GOLF CLUB

Saxmundham Road, Aldeburgh, Suffolk IP15 5PE
✆ 01728 452890 Fax 01728 452937
Map 9, G7
info@aldeburghgolfclub.co.uk
www.aldeburghgolfclub.co.uk
A1094, W of town centre
Founded 1893
Narrow, gorse-lined fairways, innumerable deep bunkers (some of them sleeper-faced), lightning-fast greens and a high proportion of long par 4s make Aldeburgh a serious examination even for the best players. Brilliant drainage makes for excellent winter golf, and the club maintains a traditional atmosphere especially in its two-ball only policy.
Ideburgh: 18 holes, 6349 yards, par 68, S.S.S 71
Designer John Thompson, Willie Fernie, J.H. Taylor
River: 9 holes, 2114 yards, par 64, S.S.S 61
A*Green fees* £45
Catering, changing room/showers, bar, club and trolley hire, shop, practice facilities
Visitors welcome
Handicap certificate required on main course, unlimited on River Course
Societies welcome by prior arrangement
🏨 White Lion Hotel, Aldeburgh, Suffolk
✆ 01728 452720

ALNESBOURNE PRIORY GOLF CLUB

Priory Park, Ipswich, Suffolk IP10 0JT
✆ 01473 727393 Fax 01473 278372
Map 9, F8
Off A14, travelling E, first exit after Orwell Bridge, left, left again, cross over A14 into Priory Park
Founded 1986
Very handsome woodland, executive-length course with superb views across the River Orwell.
9 holes, 1700 yards
par 29
Green fees £10
Catering, changing room/showers, bar, club hire, conference and wedding facilities, caravan parking
Visitors welcome – closed Tuesday
Societies welcome by prior arrangement
🏨 Courtyard Marriott, The Havens, Ransomes Europark, Ipswich, Suffolk
✆ 01473 272244

BECCLES GOLF CLUB

The Common, Beccles, Suffolk NR34 9BX
✆ 01502 712244 **Map 9, G5**
Off A146, 10 miles W of Lowestoft
Founded 1899
Rather an endearing course, typical of a earlier age, when golf courses were laid out on common land. Gorse is a persistent hazard.
9 holes, 5562 yards
par 68, S.S.S 67
Green fees £8
Catering, changing room/showers, bar, club and trolley hire, shop
Visitors welcome weekdays, restricted Sundays
Societies welcome by prior arrangement

BRETT VALE GOLF CLUB

Noakes Road, Raydon, Ipswich, Suffolk IP7 5LR
✆ 01473 310718 Fax 01473 312270
Map 9, E8
info@brettvalegolfgolf.com
www.brettvalegolfgolf.com
From A12 take B1070 tawards Hadleigh. Turn left in Raydon – water tower marks the spot!
Founded 1993
Glorious views of Constable countryside abound at Brett Vale.
18 holes, 5797 yards
par 70, S.S.S 69

Designer Howard Swann
Green fees £20
Catering, changing room/showers, bar, club, trolley and buggy hire, shop, driving range, practice facilities, conference facilities
Visitors welcome
Societies welcome by prior arrangement
Marlborough Hotel, Henley Road, Ipswich, Suffolk
01473 257677

BUNGAY & WAVENEY VALLEY GOLF CLUB

Outney Common, Bungay, Suffolk NR35 1DS
01986 892337 Fax 01986 892222
Map 9, F5
bungaygolf@aol.com
www.club-noticeboard.co.uk
½ mile W of Bungay
Founded 1889
Attractive James Braid course with five demanding par 4s averaging 425 yards, the 3rd, 6th, 8th, 11th and 13th.
18 holes, 6044 yards
par 69, S.S.S 69
Designer James Braid
Green fees £24
Catering, changing room/showers, bar, club, trolley and buggy hire, shop, practice facilities
Visitors welcome weekdays
Societies welcome by prior arrangement
Castles Hotel, 35 Earsham Street, Bungay, Suffolk NR35 1AF
01986 892283

BURY ST EDMUNDS GOLF CLUB

Tut Hill, Bury St Edmunds, Suffolk IP28 6LG
01284 755979 Fax 01284 763288
Map 9, D7
Off A14, 2 miles W of Bury St Edmunds
Founded 1922
A parkland course which has been gradually updated over the years until, now, it presents a long and fascinating test.
18 holes, 6669 yards, par 72, S.S.S 72
Designer Ted Ray, Frank Pennink
9 holes, 4434 yards, par 62, S.S.S 62
Designer Hawtree
Green fees £24
Catering, changing room/showers, bar, club and trolley hire, shop, practice facilities
Visitors welcome weekdays
Societies welcome by prior arrangement

CRETINGHAM GOLF CLUB

Grove Farm, Cretingham, Woodbridge, Suffolk IP13 7BA
01728 685275 Fax 01728 685037
Map 9, F8
Off A1120, 2 miles SE of Earl Soham
Founded 1984
A parkland course of modest length, but with good off-course facilities. Plans are afoot to extend to 18 holes and a length of around 6500 yards.
9 holes, 4552 yards
par 66, S.S.S 64
Green fees £7
Catering, changing room/showers, bar, club, trolley and buggy hire, shop, driving range, practice facilities, swimming, tennis, pitch-and-putt, caravan park
Visitors welcome
Societies welcome by prior arrangement

DISS GOLF CLUB

Stuston Common, Diss, Suffolk IP22 4AA
01379 641025 Fax 01379 644586
Map 9, E6
Off A140
Founded 1903
A challenging course, and regular host of county events. A 215-yard par 3 makes for a tricky opening, and dog-legs at the 5th, 8th and 14th demand precise positional play. Hardest of all is the 460-yard par-4 13th, with mounds to be cleared on the second shot.
18 holes, 6262 yards
par 70, S.S.S 70
Designer M.Pinner
Green fees £25
Catering, changing room/showers, bar, club and trolley hire, shop, practice facilities
Visitors welcome weekdays
Societies welcome by prior arrangement
Park Hotel, Diss, Suffolk
01379 642244

FELIXSTOWE FERRY GOLF CLUB

Ferry Road, Felixstowe, Suffolk IP4 9RY
01394 283060 Fax 01394 273679
Map 9, F8
www.felixstowegolf.co.uk
A14 to Felixstowe, 2 miles NE of town
Founded 1880
A very old and distinguished club whose course was rebuilt in traditional manner after the Second World War by Henry Cotton. The opening and closing sequences are on genuine linksland, with perhaps the 17th just the best of an inspiring, classic collection. Slightly inland, the mid-round holes involve plentiful water.
Martello Course: 18 holes, 6308 yards, par 72, S.S.S 70
Designer Henry Cotton
Kingsfleet Course: 9 holes, 2986 yards, par 35,
Green fees £26
Catering, changing room/showers, bar, trolley hire, shop, practice facilities
Visitors welcome weekdays (all week on 9-hole course)
Societies welcome by prior arrangement

FLEMPTON GOLF CLUB

Bury St Edmunds, Suffolk IP28 6HQ
01284 728291 **Map 9, D7**
A1101, 4 miles NE of Bury St Edmunds
Founded 1895
Flempton has begun to achieve a widespread reputation, hardly challenging Mildenhall, but, rightly, recognising the superior qualities of this 9-hole jewel.
9 holes, 6240 yards
par 70, S.S.S 70
Designer J.H. Taylor
Green fees £22
Catering, changing room/showers, bar, trolley hire, shop, practice facilities
Visitors welcome weekdays
Handicap certificate required
Societies welcome by prior arrangement

FYNN VALLEY GOLF CLUB

Witnesham, Ipswich, Suffolk IP6 9JA
01473 785267 Fax 01473 785632
Map 9 F8
enquiries@fynn-valley.co.uk
www.fynn-valley.co.uk
B1077, 2 miles N of Ipswich
Founded 1991
An undulating parkland course running along a river valley, with wickedly contoured greens.
18 holes, 6310 yards
par 70, S.S.S 71
Designer Tony Tyrrell
Green fees £22
Catering, changing room/showers, bar, club, trolley and buggy hire, shop, driving range, 9-hole, par-3 course, conference and banquetting facilities
Visitors welcome, restricted weekends
Societies welcome by prior arrangement
Marlborough Hotel, Henley Road, Ipswich, Suffolk
01473 257677

HALESWORTH GOLF CLUB

Bramfield Road, Halesworth, Suffolk IP19 9XA
☎ 01986 875567 Fax 01986 874565
Map 9, G6
A144, off A12.
Founded 1990
Begun as the St Helena Golf Club, an expansive 27-hole parkland layout with full off-course facilities.
Blythe Course: 18 holes, 6580 yards, par 72, S.S.S 72
Designer J.W. Johnson
Valley Course: 9 holes, 2398 yards, par 33, S.S.S 33
Green fees £15
Catering, changing room/showers, bar, club, trolley and buggy hire, shop, driving range, practice facilities, 9-hole course
Visitors welcome
Handicap certificate required on 18-hole course
Societies welcome by prior arrangement

HAVERHILL GOLF CLUB

Coupals Road, Haverhill, Suffolk CB9 7UW
☎ 01440 712628 Fax 01440 761951
Map 9, C8
haverhillgolf@coupalsraod.fsnet.co.uk
www.club-noticeboard.co.uk
Off A1107, 1 mile E of Haverhill
Founded 1976
For the most part a gently undulating course running down to the river marking the Essex-Suffolk border, but when the course was expanded to 18 holes the opportunity was taken to construct holes alongside (and over) a gully.
18 holes, 5929 yards
par 70, S.S.S 69
Designer Charles Lawrie, Philip Pilgrim
Green fees £22
Catering, changing room/showers, bar, club and trolley hire, shop, practice facilities
Visitors welcome, subject to restrictions
Societies welcome by prior arrangement

HINTLESHAM HALL GOLF CLUB

Hintlesham, Ipswich, Suffolk IP8 3NS
☎ 01473 652761 Fax 01473 652750
Map 9, E8
office@hintleshamhallgolfclub.com
www.hintleshamhall.com
A1070, 4 miles W of Ipswich
Founded 1991
A very attractive and thoroughly testing course laid out over well-wooded, undulating parkland. The 4th is said to be the toughest par 3 in East Anglia.
18 holes, 6602 yards
par 72, S.S.S 72
Designer Hawtree
Green fees £30
Catering, changing room/showers, bar, accommodation, club, trolley and buggy hire, shop, driving range, practice facilities, full hotel facilities at Hintlesham Hall
Visitors welcome weekdays
Handicap certificate required
Societies welcome by prior arrangement
🏨 Hintlesham Hall, Hintlesham, Ipswich, Suffolk IP8 3NS
☎ 01473 652334

IPSWICH (PURDIS HEATH) GOLF CLUB

Purdis Heath, Bucklesham Road, Ipswich, Suffolk IP3 8UQ
☎ 01473 728941 Fax 01473 715236
Map 9, F8
mail@ipswichgolfclub.com
www.ipswichgolfclub.com
3 miles E of Ipswich
Founded 1895
Ecological course management has retained the heathland characteristics of this fascinating course, which was laid out by James Braid in 1927. Little has been altered since, apart from opening out a pond to enliven the short 15th. The tricky 9-hole second course is run as a valuable public facility.
Main Course: 18 holes, 6435 yards, par 71, S.S.S 71
Designer James Braid
9-hole Course: 9 holes, 1930 yards, par 31,
Green fees £40
Catering, changing room/showers, bar, club and trolley hire, shop, practice facilities
Visitors welcome – unrestricted on 9-hole Course
Handicap certificate required on Main Course
Societies welcome by prior arrangement
🏨 Courtyard Marriott, The Havens, Ransomes Europark, Ipswich, Suffolk
☎ 01473 272244

LINKS (NEWMARKET) GOLF CLUB

Cambridge Road, Newmarket, Suffolk CB8 0TG
☎ 01638 663000 Fax 01638 661476
Map 9, C7
A1034, 1 mile SW of Newmarket
Founded 1902
A parkland course, its title notwithstanding, on a gently undulating site in the very heart of racing country.
18 holes, 6424 yards
par 72, S.S.S 71
Designer Col. Hotchkin
Green fees £30
Catering, changing room/showers, bar, club and trolley hire, shop, practice facilities
Visitors welcome – restricted weekends
Handicap certificate required
Societies welcome by prior arrangement

NEWTON GREEN GOLF CLUB

Newton Green, Sudbury, Suffolk CO10 0QN
☎ 01787 377215 Fax 01787 377547
Map 9, D8
secretary@newtongreengolfclub.fsnet.co.uk
www.newtongreengolfclub.fsnet.co.uk
A134, 3 miles S of Sudbury
Founded 1907
A course of two distinct halves, the front nine quite open, well-bunkered and with a lake. The back nine features gorse, ditches, and interesting greens.
18 holes, 5973 yards
par 69, S.S.S 68
Green fees £17.50
Catering, changing room/showers, bar, club and trolley hire, shop, practice facilities
Visitors welcome weekdays
Societies welcome by prior arrangement
🏨 Hill Lodge Hotel, Newton Road, Sudbury, Suffolk
☎ 01787 377568

ROOKERY PARK GOLF CLUB

Carlton Colville, Lowestoft, Suffolk NR33 8HJ
☎ 01502 515103 Fax 01502 560380
Map 9, G5
A146, 2 miles W of Lowestoft
Founded 1975
A long parkland course with full off-course facilities, including a par-3 course.
18 holes, 6714 yards
par 72, S.S.S 72
Designer Charles Lawrie
Green fees £30
Catering, changing room/showers, bar, club and trolley hire, shop, practice facilities, 9-hole, par-3 course
Visitors welcome, with restrictions
Societies welcome by prior arrangement

ROYAL WORLINGTON & NEWMARKET GOLF CLUB
Golf Links Road, Worlington, Bury St Edmunds, Suffolk IP28 8SD
☎ 01638 712216 Fax 01638 717787
Map 9, C6
Off A11, 6 miles NE of Newmarket (signposted)
Founded 1893
See Top 50 Courses, page 43
9 holes, 6210 yards
par 70, S.S.S 71
Designer Tom Dunn, Captain A.M. Ross
Green fees £45
Catering, changing room/showers, bar, club and trolley hire, shop, practice facilities
Visitors welcome weekdays by prior arrangement (2-ball play only)
Handicap certificate required
Societies welcome by prior arrangement

RUSHMERE GOLF CLUB
Rushmere Heath, Ipswich, Suffolk IP4 5QQ
☎ 01473 728076 Fax 01473 725648
Map 9, F8
Off A1214, 3 miles E of Ipswich.
Founded 1927
A private club playing over (mostly) common land, with an abundance of gorse in addition to plentiful oaks. From the outset the gauntlet is thrown down, a narrow 433-yard dog-leg through the gorse bushes. Only one hole is bunkerless (the 12th), and the 18th is an unforgiving finishing hole.
18 holes, 6262 yards
par 70, S.S.S 70
Green fees £25
Catering, changing room/showers, bar, club and trolley hire, shop, practice facilities
Visitors welcome, restricted weekends
Handicap certificate required
Societies welcome by prior arrangement

SECKFORD GOLF CLUB
Seckford Hall Road, Great Bealings, Woodbridge, Suffolk IP13 6NT
☎ 01394 388000 Fax 01394 3828189 **Map 9, F8**
www.seckfordgolf.co.uk
Off A12, 3 miles W of Woodbridge
Founded 1991
Quite a challenging course – its diminutive yardage meaning little – with hilly holes and plentiful water hazards.
18 holes, 5303 yards
par 68, S.S.S 66
Designer J. Johnson
Green fees £16
Catering, changing room/showers, bar, club and trolley hire, shop, driving range, practice facilities
Visitors welcome
Societies welcome by prior arrangement

SOUTHWOLD GOLF CLUB
The Common, Southwold, Suffolk IP18 6TB
☎ 01502 723790 Fax 01502 723790
Map 9, G6
A1095 or B1126 entering Southwold.
Founded 1884
Heathland course on common land with views to the sea.
9 holes, 6052 yards
par 70, S.S.S 69
Green fees £20
Catering, changing room/showers, bar, club and trolley hire, shop, practice facilities
Visitors welcome
Societies welcome by prior arrangement
The Swan, Southwold, Suffolk
☎ 01502 722186

THE STOKE-BY-NAYLAND CLUB
Keepers Lane, Leavenheath, Colchester, Essex, Suffolk CO6 4PZ
☎ 01206 262836 Fax 01206 263356
Map 9, D8
info@golf-club.co.uk
www.stokebynayland.co.uk
B1068, off A134, 6 miles from Colchester.
Founded 1972
Two fine courses in famous artistic countryside. Of many challenging holes the palm goes to the 10th on the Gainsborough with its double water crossing. Both courses end with formidable drives over water.
Constable: 18 holes, 6544 yards, par 72, S.S.S 71
Gainsborough: 18 holes, 6498 yards, par 72, S.S.S 71
Green fees £25
Catering, changing room/showers, bar, accommodation, trolley and buggy hire, shop, driving range, practice facilities, wedding licence, conference facilities, gymnasium, swimming pool, squash
Visitors welcome
Handicap certificate required at weekends
Societies welcome by prior arrangement
Stoke-by-Nayland Club, Keepers Lane, Leavenheath, Colchester, Suffolk CO6 4PZ
☎ 01206 262836

STOWMARKET GOLF CLUB
Lower Road, Onehouse, Stowmarket, Suffolk IP14 3DA
☎ 01449 736392 Fax 01449 736826
Map 9, E7
mail@stowmarketgc.sagehost.co.uk
www.club-noticeboard.co.uk/stowmarket
Off B1115, SW of Stowmarket
Founded 1962
A testing parkland course designed by its founder members, with a 250-yard par 3, making it the longest short hole in Suffolk (and, for that matter, one of the longest anywhere). The standard scratch score of 69 is rarely beaten by much.
18 holes, 6107 yards
par 69, S.S.S 69
Designer Founder members
Green fees £25
Catering, changing room/showers, bar, club, trolley and buggy hire, shop, driving range, practice facilities
Visitors welcome
Handicap certificate required
Societies welcome by prior arrangement
Cedars Hotel, Needham Road, Stowmarket, Suffolk
☎ 01449 612668

THE SUFFOLK GOLF & COUNTRY CLUB
St John's Hill Plantation, The Street, Fornham All Saints, Suffolk IP28 6JQ
☎ 01284 706777 Fax 01284 706721
Map 9, D7
B1106, off A14
Founded 1974
Re-created out of the Fornham Park course, a handsome parkland course with the River Lark and a number of ponds coming into play. It is owned by the same leisure group as The Norfolk.
18 holes, 6321 yards
par 72, S.S.S 71
Designer Howard Swann
Green fees £25
Catering, changing room/showers, bar, club, trolley and buggy hire, shop, driving range, practice facilities, swimming pool, gym, leisure facilities
Visitors welcome – advance booking system
Societies welcome by prior arrangement

THORPENESS HOTEL GOLF & COUNTRY CLUB
Lakeside Avenue, Thorpeness, Aldeburgh, Suffolk IP16 4NH
☎ 01728 452176 Fax 01728 453868

Map 9, G7
info@thorpeness.co.uk
www.thorpeness.co.uk
B1069, in Thorpeness.
Founded 1922
Thorpeness was created as a complete holiday village between 1910 and 1930. Only two holes of James Braid's original course have been changed, and, with eight par 4s at 400 yards or longer, it is quite a handful in the omnipresent wind. Heather and gorse are punishing to inaccurate play.
18 holes, 6281 yards
par 69, S.S.S 70
Designer James Braid
Green fees £25
Catering, changing room/showers, bar, accommodation, club, trolley and buggy hire, shop, practice facilities, full hotel facilities
Visitors welcome
Handicap certificate required
Societies welcome by prior arrangement
The Hotel and Golf Club, Thorpeness, Aldeburgh, Suffolk IP16 4NH
01728 452176 Fax 01728 453868
info@thorpeness.co.uk
www.thorpeness.co.uk

UFFORD PARK HOTEL GOLF & LEISURE CLUB

Yarmouth Road, Ufford, Woodbridge, Suffolk IP12 1QW
01394 382836 **Map 9, F8**
B1438, 2 miles N of Woodbridge
Founded 1992
An impressive parkland course with a great many water hazards.
18 holes, 6325 yards
par 71, S.S.S 71
Designer Phil Pilgrim
Green fees £18
Catering, changing room/showers, bar, accommodation, club, trolley and buggy hire, shop, driving range, practice facilities, full hotel and leisure facilities
Visitors welcome – advisable to book
Societies welcome by prior arrangement

WALDRINGFIELD HEATH GOLF CLUB

Newbourne Road, Waldringfield, Woodbridge, Suffolk IP12 4PT
01473 736768 Fax 01473 736436
Map 9, F8
3 miles NE of Ipswich
Founded 1983
A testing heathland course with gorse and bracken threatening inaccurate play. The hardest holes are probably the par-3 9th with water almost surrounding the green and the 464-yard 16th, usually played into the wind.
18 holes, 6141 yards
par 71, S.S.S 69
Designer Peter Pilgrim
Green fees £15
Catering, changing room/showers, bar, club, trolley and buggy hire, shop, practice facilities, conference and function facilities
Visitors welcome weekdays without restrictions – weekends with member or handicap certificate
Societies welcome by prior arrangement

WOODBRIDGE GOLF CLUB

Bromeswell Heath, Woodbridge, Suffolk IP12 2PF
01394 382038 Fax 01394 3823920 **9, F8**
A1152, E of Woodbridge
Founded 1893
Returned to peace and quiet since the demise of Woodbridge as an air base, both courses offer rewarding golf in delightful surroundings. While some holes are those of the open heath, others weave through undulating avenues of trees giving charm and variety, and hole lengths ensure welcome change of pace.
Main Course: 18 holes, 6299 yards, par 70, S.S.S 70
Designer David Howie
Forest Course: 9 holes, 6382 yards, par 70, S.S.S 70
Designer F.W. Hawtree
Green fees £32
Catering, changing room/showers, bar, trolley hire, shop, practice facilities
Visitors welcome weekdays – unlimited Forest Course
Handicap certificate required on Main Course
Societies welcome by prior arrangement

MIDLANDS

In the early days, before today's knowledge of the techniques of major earth moving, complex drainage and irrigation, and the development of hybrid grass strains, the Midland counties must have presented the golf course architect with a formidable challenge. Thus all the old Midland courses of any standing were sited on outcrops of quick-draining sand or gravel amidst the predominant clays and loams – Little Aston, Sherwood Forest, Beau Desert, Notts and Woodhall Spa. Just how restricted some of these outcrops are is exemplified by Woodhall Spa, where the old Hotchkin Course occupies almost all of this prime land, whereas the new Bracken Course is very different in nature, having been constructed out of meadowland and woods.

Of the Midland counties only Lincolnshire has a coastline, and, indeed, it can boast one of the very few true links courses on the English coast north of The Wash – Seacroft, a real gem. Lincolnshire's other old courses of real charm, such as Lincoln and Blankney, have more recently been joined by modern layouts worthy of exploration, notably Forest Pines, Belton Park and Belton Woods, both just outside Grantham. In the late 20th century they were contemporary courses which brought the big-money professional game to the Midlands, following where Collingtree Park, Forest of Arden and The Belfry had lead the way. The Belfry is much more than simply three 18-hole courses, being a huge golf industry in its own right. In one way at least the Brabazon is head and shoulders above any other course on either side of the Atlantic, having, uniquely, hosted four Ryder Cup Matches. Amongst players, and the golfing press in particular, the Brabazon has both enthusiasts and detractors, but its record for providing brilliantly exciting head-to-head contests cannot be denied. The vision of those who realized that a dull potato field would one day become one of the world's great golfing battlegrounds can only be applauded.

Shropshire, Worcestershire and Herefordshire are three of England's loveliest counties, their countryside still miraculously unspoiled. Between them they have few golf clubs, but what many of these courses can offer is that unhurried, relaxed quality that some of us can remember from the 1950s and '60s, invariably in delightful surroundings. Further east, the country courses of Leicestershire, Northamptonshire and Rutland share a similar pastoral charm which soothes the troubled breast of the golfer who has done battle with Charnwood Forest, Northamptonshire County or Luffenham Heath and lost. Warwickshire's most testing courses tend to be closer to Birmingham and Coventry but, again, there are many charms to be discovered in and around Shakespeare's England.

Derbyshire and Staffordshire both venture into the southern uplands of the Pennines, with courses such as Leek, Cavendish and Sickleholme. Staffordshire also embraces parts of the industrial West Midlands, where many of its best courses are to be found – Beau Desert, Whittington Heath, Enville and majestic Little Aston.

DERBYSHIRE

ALFRETON GOLF CLUB

Wingfield Road, Oakerthorpe,
Alfreton, Derbyshire DE55 7LH
✆ 01773 832070 **Map 8, C2**
A615, 1 mile W of Alfreton
Founded 1892
An unusual course, having 11 compact holes.
11 holes, 5393 yards
par 67, S.S.S 66
Catering, changing room/showers, bar, shop
Visitors welcome
Societies welcome by prior arrangement

ALLESTREE PARK GOLF CLUB

Allestree Hall, Allestree, Derby,
Derbyshire DE22 2EU
✆ 01332 550616 **Map 8, B3**
1 mile N of A6/A38 junction, 4 miles N of Derby
Founded 1947
Attractive, rolling parkland course with good views.
18 holes, 5806 yards
par 68, S.S.S 68
Catering, changing room/showers, bar, club and trolley hire, shop, practice facilities
Visitors welcome – booking system
Societies welcome by prior arrangement

ASHBOURNE GOLF CLUB

Wyaston Road, Ashbourne,
Derbyshire DE6 1NB
✆ 01335 342078 Fax 01335 347937
Map 8, A2
www.ashbournegolfclub.co.uk
A515, A52, 2 miles W of Ashbourne
Founded 1886
A hilly parkland course with good views over the delightful surrounding countryside as well as Ashbourne's beautiful "Cathedral of the Peak".
18 holes, 6402 yards
par 72, S.S.S 72
Designer David Hemstock
Green fees £20
Catering, changing room/showers, bar, trolley hire, shop
Visitors welcome weekdays
Societies welcome by prior arrangement

BAKEWELL GOLF CLUB

Station Road, Bakewell, Derbyshire
DE45 1GB
✆ 01629 812307 **Map 8, A1**
Bakewell – off Sheffield Road
Founded 1899
Hilly parkland course in attractive surroundings above charming town.
9 holes, 5240 yards
par 68, S.S.S 66
Green fees £15
Catering, changing room/showers, bar, practice facilities
Visitors welcome, subject to competitions
Handicap certificate required

BIRCH HALL GOLF CLUB

Sheffield Road, Unstone, Derbyshire
S18 5DH
✆ 01246 291979 **Map 11, A11**
Off A61 between Sheffield and Chesterfield, at Unstone.
Founded 1992
Demanding moorland/parkland course, with undulating lies and plenty of gorse.
18 holes, 6509 yards
par 73, S.S.S 71
Designer David Tucker
Green fees £10
Catering, changing room/showers, bar
Visitors welcome, with restrictions
Societies welcome by prior arrangement

BLUE CIRCLE GOLF CLUB

Cement Works, Hope, Derbyshire
S33 2RP

☎ 01433 622315 **Map 10, H10**
Cement Works, Hope
Founded 1985
A private club
9 holes, 5350 yards
S.S.S 66
Visitors welcome only as members' guests
No societies

BONDHAY GOLF CLUB

Bondhay Lane, Whitwell, Worksop, Derbyshire S80 3EH
☎ 01909 723608 Fax 01909 720226
Map 11, B 11
Off A619, 5m W of Worksop
Founded 1991
A big course with many distinctive holes designed around – or over – lakes.
18 holes, 6785 yards
par 72, S.S.S 74
Designer Donald Steel
Green fees £16
Catering, changing room/showers, bar, club, trolley and buggy hire, shop, driving range, practice facilities, 9-hole, par-3 course, fishing
Visitors welcome by prior arrangement
Societies welcome by prior arrangement

BRAILSFORD GOLF CLUB

Pools Head Lane, Brailsford, Ashbourne, Derbyshire DE6 3BU
☎ 01355 360096 **Map 8, B3**
A52 between Ashbourne and Derby
Founded 1991
Recent parkland course with lakes and other water hazards. New clubhouse will offer further golfing and conference facilities.
9 holes, 6292 yards
par 72, S.S.S 70
Designer A.F. Simms
Green fees £13.50
Catering, bar, club, trolley and buggy hire, shop, driving range
Visitors welcome
Societies welcome by prior arrangement
🏨 Yew Tree Inn and Lodge, Ednaston, Brailsford, Ashbourne, Derbyshire DE6 6FE
☎ 01335 360433

MARRIOTT BREADSALL PRIORY HOTEL GOLF & COUNTRY CLUB

Moor Road, Morley, Derby, Derbyshire DE7 6DL
☎ 01332 836016 Fax 01332 833509
Map 8, B3
www.marriotthotels.co.uk
Village of Breadsall, near Derby
Founded 1979
Two courses set in the grounds of an old priory. The Moorland Course (which rarely closes) features stone walls and wind-swept moorland.
Priory Course: 18 holes, 6120 yards, par 72, S.S.S 69
Moorland Course: 18 holes, 6028 yards, par 70, S.S.S 69
Designer Donald Steel
Green fees £25
Catering, changing room/showers, bar, accommodation, club, trolley and buggy hire, shop, driving range, practice facilities, full conference and leisure facilities
Visitors welcome
Societies welcome by prior arrangement
🏨 Breadsall Priory Hotel and CC, Moor Road, Morley, Derbyshire DE7 6DL
☎ 01332 832235 Fax 01332 833509
www.marriott.com/marriott/emags

BROUGHTON HEATH GOLF CLUB

Bent Lane, Church Broughton, Derbyshire DE65 5BA
☎ 01283 521235 Fax 01283 521235
Map 8, A3
Off A516 near Hatton/Church Broughton
A par-3 course.
18 holes, 3087 yards
par 54, S.S.S 53
Green fees £8
Changing room/showers, club and trolley hire, shop, practice facilities
Visitors welcome – booking system
Societies welcome by prior arrangement

BUXTON & HIGH PEAK GOLF CLUB

Townend, Buxton, Derbyshire SK17 7EN
☎ 01298 23453 Fax 01298 26333
Map 10, G11
Off A6 NE of Buxton
Founded 1887
A rugged moorland course on the north edge of Buxton, in glorious Peak District scenery. The course straddles the A6, and there is particularly serious rough.
18 holes, 5954 yards
par 69, S.S.S 69
Green fees £22
Catering, changing room/showers, bar, club, trolley and buggy hire, shop, driving range
Visitors welcome
Societies welcome by prior arrangement

CARSINGTON WATER GOLF CLUB

Carsington, Wirksworth, Derbyshire
☎ 01629 85650 **Map 8, B2**
Off B5035, 8 miles NE of Ashbourne
Founded 1994
Overlooking Carsington Water, near Cromford and its associated industrial revolution sites.
9 holes, 6000 yards
S.S.S 66
Designer John Ludlow
Visitors welcome
Societies welcome by prior arrangement

CAVENDISH GOLF CLUB

Gadley Lane, Buxton, Derbyshire SK17 6XD
☎ 01298 23494 Fax 01298 79708
Map 10, G11
Off A53, W of Buxton
Founded 1925
Handsome, and deceptively tricky, Mackenzie course with uplifting views towards the Peak District. Four comparatively gentle holes open proceedings, but the 5th is another matter, uphill and with a stream troubling the drive. The two big par 4s just after the turn are not easily overcome, nor is the 18th.
18 holes, 5721 yards
par 68, S.S.S 68
Designer Alister Mackenzie
Green fees £26
Catering, changing room/showers, bar, club and trolley hire, shop, practice facilities
Visitors welcome
Handicap certificate required
Societies welcome by prior arrangement

CHAPEL-EN-LE-FRITH GOLF CLUB

The Cockyard, Manchester Road, Chapel en le Frith, Derbyshire SK23 9UH
☎ 01298 812118 Fax 01298 814990
Map 10, G10
www.chapelgolf.co.uk
Off B5470, between Whaley Bridge and Chapel-en-le-Frith
Founded 1905
A very scenic course in the heart of the Peak District, although it is relatively level and walking is, therefore, easy.
18 holes, 6054 yards
par 70, S.S.S 69
Green fees £26
Catering, changing room/showers, bar, club and trolley hire, shop, practice facilities
Visitors welcome
Societies welcome by prior arrangement

CHESTERFIELD GOLF CLUB

Walton, Chesterfield, Derbyshire S42 7LA
☎ 01246 279256 Fax 01246 276622
Map 11, B11
A632 Matlock Road, SW of Chesterfield
Founded 1897
A testing parkland course with more than a hint of moorland characteristics. Extensive views.
18 holes, 6247 yards
par 71, S.S.S 70
Green fees £26
Catering, changing room/showers, bar, trolley hire, shop, practice facilities
Visitors welcome
Handicap certificate required
Societies welcome by prior arrangement

CHESTERFIELD MUNICIPAL GOLF CLUB

Murray House, Crow Lane, Chesterfield, Derbyshire S41 0EQ
☎ 01246 273887 Fax 01246 558024
Map 11, B11
½ mile E of Chesterfield Station
Founded 1934
A parkland course with good views of Chesterfield's twisted spire.
18 holes, 6013 yards
par 71, S.S.S 69
Green fees £5.80
Changing room/showers, club hire, shop, 9-hole course
Visitors welcome
Societies welcome by prior arrangement

CHEVIN GOLF CLUB

Duffield, Derby, Derbyshire DE56 4EE
☎ 01332 841864 Fax 01332 841864
Map 8, B3
Off A6, 5 miles N of Derby
Founded 1894
A hilly moorland course, the slopes compounding the need for accuracy.
18 holes, 6057 yards
par 69, S.S.S 69
Green fees £27
Catering, changing room/showers, bar, club and trolley hire, shop, practice facilities
Visitors welcome weekdays with restrictions
Societies welcome by prior arrangement

DERBY SINFIN GOLF COURSE

Wilmore Road, Sinfin, Derby, Derbyshire DE24 9HD
☎ 01332 766323 **Map 8, B3**
Off A52, 1 mile S of Derby
Founded 1923
A long-established parkland course, with generous fairways and easy walking.
18 holes, 6163 yards
par 70, S.S.S 69
Catering, changing room/showers, bar, club and trolley hire, shop, practice facilities
Visitors welcome
Societies welcome by prior arrangement

EREWASH VALLEY GOLF CLUB

Golf Club Road, Stanton-by-Dale, Derbyshire DE7 4QR
☎ 0115 9324667 **Map 8, C3**
M1 Jct 25, N of Stanton-by-Dale village.
Founded 1905
One of the longer courses in Derbyshire, overlooking the M1, Erewash Valley's most individual holes are those played in an old quarry.
18 holes, 6557 yards
par 72, S.S.S 71
Designer Hawtree
Green fees £24.50
Catering, changing room/showers, bar, trolley and buggy hire, shop, driving range, practice facilities
Visitors welcome
Handicap certificate required
Societies welcome by prior arrangement
🏨 Risley Lodge Hotel, Derby Road, Risley, Derbyshire

GLOSSOP & DISTRICT GOLF CLUB

Sheffield Road, Glossop, Derbyshire SK13 7PU
☎ 01457 865247 **Map 10, G10**
Off A57, 1 mile E of Glossop
Founded 1894
Vigorous course, climbing towards the Snake Pass and descending once again. For the fit, it gives rewarding views.
11 holes, 5800 yards
par 68, S.S.S 68
Green fees £15
Catering, changing room/showers, bar, trolley hire, shop
Visitors welcome weekdays
Societies welcome by prior arrangement

GRASSMOOR GOLF CENTRE

North Wingfield Road, Grassmoor, Chesterfield, Derbyshire S42 5EA
☎ 01246 856044 Fax 01246 853486
Map 11, B11
Off B6038, 2 miles S of Chesterfield
Founded 1992
Quite a difficult course incorporating water features, with excellent practice facilities.
18 holes, 5723 yards
par 69, S.S.S 69
Designer Martin Hawtree
Green fees £10
Catering, changing room/showers, bar, club and trolley hire, shop, driving range, practice facilities
Visitors welcome with advance booking
Societies welcome by prior arrangement

HORSLEY LODGE GOLF CLUB

Smalley Mill Road, Horsley, Derbyshire DE21 5BL
☎ 01332 780838 Fax 01332 781118
Map 8, B3
Off A38, 4 miles N of Derby
Founded 1992
Peter McEvoy is designing some of the most challenging of contemporary courses, particurlarly in Ireland. This is one of his earlier essays on English soil.
18 holes, 6336 yards
par 72, S.S.S 71
Designer Peter McEvoy
Green fees £28
Catering, changing room/showers, bar, accommodation, club, trolley and buggy hire, shop, driving range
Visitors welcome weekdays
Societies welcome by prior arrangement
🏨 Horsley Lodge, Smalley Mill Road, Horsley, Derbyshire
☎ 01332 780838

ILKESTON GOLF COURSE

West End Drive, Ilkeston, Derbyshire DE7 5GH
☎ 0115 930 4550 **Map 8 C3**
½ mile E of Ilkeston
Founded 1929
A short municipal parkland course
9 holes, 4116 yards
par 62, S.S.S 60
Green fees £6.50
Visitors welcome weekdays
Societies welcome by prior arrangment

KEDLESTON PARK GOLF CLUB

Kedleston, Quarndon, Derby, Derbyshire DE22 5JD
☎ 01332 840035 Fax 01332 840035
Map 8, B3
Off A38, 4 miles N of Derby
Founded 1947
An air of nobility attends the golf, with the course laid out through avenues of tall trees, adjoining Kedleston Hall. It is a good test for the amateur player, too, with seven par 4s over 400 yards long, and the difficult holes evenly distributed between the front and back nines.
18 holes, 6675 yards

par 72, S.S.S 72
Designer James Braid
Green fees £30
Catering, changing room/showers, bar, club, trolley and buggy hire, shop, practice facilities
Visitors welcome weekdays with prior booking
Societies welcome by prior arrangement

MATLOCK GOLF CLUB

Chesterfield Road, Matlock Moor, Matlock, Derbyshire DE4 5LZ
☎ 01629 582191 **Map 8, B1**
A632, 1 mile N of Matlock
Founded 1906
A sweeping hillside course with good views.
18 holes, 5804 yards
par 70, S.S.S 68
Designer Tom Williamson
Green fees £25
Catering, changing room/showers, bar, trolley hire, shop
Visitors welcome weekdays with restrictions
Societies welcome by prior arrangement

MAYWOOD GOLF CLUB

Rushy Lane, Risley, Derbyshire DE7 3ST
☎ 0115 939 2306 **Map 8, C3**
Off A52, close M1 Jct 25
Founded 1990
A parkland course with plenty of water.
18 holes, 6424 yards
par 72, S.S.S 71
Designer P. Moon
Green fees £22
Catering, changing room/showers, bar, trolley hire, shop, practice facilities
Visitors welcome weekdays, restricted weekends
Societies welcome by prior arrangement

MICKLEOVER GOLF CLUB

Uttoxeter Road, Mickleover, Derbyshire DE3 5AD
☎ 01332 518662 Fax 01332 512092
Map 8, B3
A516/B5020, 3 miles W of Derby
Founded 1923
A charming, undulating, parkland course with good rural views.
18 holes, 5702 yards
par 68, S.S.S 68
Designer Charles Knight
Green fees £22
Catering, changing room/showers, bar, club and trolley hire, shop, practice facilities
Visitors welcome – handicap certificate required at weekend
Societies welcome by prior arrangement
🏨 Mickleover Court Hotel, Etwall Road, Mickleover, Derbyshire

MORLEY HAYES GOLF CLUB

Main Road, Morley, Derbyshire DE7 6DG
☎ 01332 782000 Fax 01332 781094
Map 8, B3
enquiries@morleyhayes.com
www.morleyhayes.com
A608, 3 miles N of Derby
Founded 1992
A lengthy pay-and-play course surrounded by mature woodland and a deer park, itself well-wooded and with several water features.
Manor Course: 18 holes, 6477 yards, par 72, S.S.S 72
Tower Course: 9 holes, 1614 yards, par 30
Green fees £16.50
Catering, changing room/showers, bar, club, trolley and buggy hire, shop, driving range, conference facilities
Visitors welcome
Societies welcome by prior arrangement
🏨 Express Holiday Inn, Pride Park, Derby, Derbyshire
☎ 01332 388000

NEW MILLS GOLF CLUB

Shaw Marsh, New Mills, High Peak, Derbyshire SK22 4QE
☎ 01663 743485 **Map 10, G10**
Off B6101, off A6 in New Mills
Founded 1907
A moorland course with good views.
9 holes, 5633 yards
par 68, S.S.S 67
Designer David Williams
Green fees £12
Catering, changing room/showers, bar, club, trolley and buggy hire, shop, practice facilities
Visitors welcome weekdays
Societies welcome by prior arrangement

ORMONDE FIELDS GOLF & COUNTRY CLUB

Nottingham Road, Codnor, Ripley, Derbyshire DE5 9RG
☎ 01773 742987 Fax 01773 740293
Map 8, C2
A610, 2 miles from M1 Jct 26
Founded 1906
Undulating parkland course.
18 holes, 6504 yards
par 71, S.S.S 72
Designer John Fearn
Green fees £17.50
Catering, changing room/showers, bar, trolley hire, shop, practice facilities
Visitors welcome
Societies welcome by prior arrangment

PASTURES GOLF CLUB

Off Merlin Way, Mickleover Country Park, Mickleover, Derbyshire DE3 5DQ
☎ 01332 516700 **Map 8, B3**
A516, 4 miles W of Derby
Founded 1969
As might be expected of a Pennink design, this is a trickier proposition than the statistics alone imply. Fine views over the Trent Valley.
9 holes, 5014 yards
par 64, S.S.S 64
Designer Frank Pennink
Green fees £18
Catering, changing room/showers, bar, club and trolley hire, practice facilities
Visitors welcome, with restrictions
Handicap certificate required
Societies welcome by prior arrangement
🏨 Mickleover Court Hotel, Etwall Road, Mickleover, Derbyshire

SHIRLAND GOLF CLUB

Lower Delves, Shirland, Near Alfreton, Derbyshire DE55 6AU
☎ 01773 834935 **Map 8, C2**
Off A61 opposite Shirland Church
Founded 1977
Panoramic views over the Derbyshire countryside from most parts of the course enhance golf at Shirland.
18 holes, 6072 yards
par 71, S.S.S 70
Green fees £17
Catering, changing room/showers, bar, club, trolley and buggy hire, shop, practice facilities, conference and function facilities
Visitors welcome – restricted weekends
Societies welcome by prior arrangement
🏨 Riber Hall, Matlock, Derbyshire
☎ 01629 582795

SICKLEHOLME GOLF CLUB

Bamford, Sheffield, Derbyshire S33 0BH
☎ 01433 651306 **Map 11, A10**
Off A6013, by Bamford station
Founded 1898
In the very heart of the Peak District, Sickleholme is exceptionally handsome. With four par 4s under 300 yards in length the course may appear short on paper, but there are hills to be climbed and ravines to be crossed, and holes such as the 452-yard 6th are stern.
18 holes, 6064 yards

par 69, S.S.S 69
Green fees £26
Catering, changing room/showers, bar, trolley hire, shop, practice facilities
Visitors welcome, restricted Wednesday and weekends
Societies welcome by prior arrangement

STANEDGE GOLF CLUB

Walton Hay Farm, Stanedge, Ashover, Chesterfield, Derbyshire S45 0LW
✆ 01246 566156 **Map 8, B1**
B5057 near Red Lion pub
Founded 1934
The 2nd tee is 1000 ft above sea level, and there are views over four counties, yet walking is comfortable at this small, friendly club.
9 holes, 5786 yards
par 68, S.S.S 68
Green fees £15
Changing room/showers, bar, practice facilities, meals by arrangement
Visitors welcome weekday mornings – with member at other times
Societies welcome by prior arrangement
Sandpiper Hotel, Sheffield Road, Sheepbridge, Chesterfield, Derbyshire
✆ 01246 450550

HEREFORDSHIRE

BELMONT LODGE & GOLF CLUB

Belmont, Hereford, Herefordshire HR2 9SA
✆ 01432 352666 Fax 01432 358090
Map 7, D8
info@belmontlodge.co.uk
www.belmontlodge.co.uk
A465, S of Hereford
Founded 1982
In lovely countryside, the front nine is on high ground with views to the Malvern Hills, while the back nine is played alongside the River Wye.
18 holes, 6511 yards
par 72, S.S.S 71
Green fees £19
Catering, changing room/showers, bar, accommodation, trolley and buggy hire, shop, practice facilities, coarse and salmon fishing, bowls, tennis, hotel and conference facilities
Visitors welcome
Societies welcome by prior arrangement
Belmont Lodge, Belmont, Hereford, Herefordshire HR2 9SA
✆ 01432 352666 Fax 01432 358090
info@belmontlodge.co.uk
www.belmontlodge.co.uk

BURGHILL VALLEY GOLF CLUB

Tillington Road, Burghill, Hereford, Herefordshire HR4 7RW
✆ 01432 760456 Fax 01432 761654
Map 7, D8
www.bvgc.co.uk
Off A4110, 4 miles N of Hereford
Founded 1991
An interesting parkland course weaving through cider orchards, the aroma of which can be quite intoxicating in autumn.
18 holes, 6239 yards
par 71, S.S.S 70
Green fees £20
Changing room/showers, bar, trolley and buggy hire, shop, practice facilities
Visitors welcome
Societies welcome by prior arrangement

CADMORE LODGE GOLF CLUB

Berrington Green, Tenbury Wells, Worcester, Worcestershire WR15 8TQ
✆ 01584 810044 Fax 01584 810044
Map 7, E7
info@cadmorelodge.demon.co.uk
www.cadmorelodge.demon.co.uk
Off A4112, Tenbury Wells–Leominster road
Founded 1990
Several spectacular water holes contrast remarkably with the peace and quiet of the charming countryside.
9 holes, 5146 yards
par 68, S.S.S 65
Green fees £10
Catering, changing room/showers, bar, accommodation, full hotel facilities
Visitors welcome
Societies welcome by prior arrangement
Cadmore Lodge Hotel, Tenbury Wells, Herefordshire WR15 8TQ
✆ 01584 810044

HEREFORD MUNICIPAL GOLF COURSE

Holmer Road, Hereford, Herefordshire HR4 9UD
✆ 01432 344376 Fax 01432 266281
Map 7, D8
Off A49, in centre of race course
Founded 1983
Laid out in the middle of the race course, quite a challenging municipal facility, adjacent to a leisure centre.
9 holes, 6120 yards
par 70, S.S.S 69
Green fees £6.75
Catering, changing room/showers, bar, club and trolley hire, shop, practice facilities
Visitors welcome, except race days
Societies welcome by prior arrangement

HEREFORDSHIRE GOLF CLUB

Raven's Causeway, Wormsley, Hereford, Herefordshire HR4 8LY
✆ 01432 830219 Fax 01432 830095
Map 7, D8
5 miles NW of Hereford
Founded 1896
A parkland course deep in the glorious Herefordshire countryside.
18 holes, 6069 yards
par 70, S.S.S 69
Designer James Braid
Green fees £20
Catering, changing room/showers, bar, club, trolley and buggy hire, shop, practice facilities
Visitors welcome
Societies welcome by prior arrangement

KINGTON GOLF CLUB

Bradnor Hill, Kington, Herefordshire HR5 3RE
✆ 01544 230340 Fax 01544 340270
Map 7, C7
Off B4355, N of Kington
Founded 1926
The highest 18-hole golf course in England, with sheep-cropped turf and magnificent views into the Radnor Forest and over a great deal of unspoiled Herefordshire. Constructed on a naturally well drained site, golf is surprisingly good up here even in winter, when there are special packages available for visitors.
18 holes, 5840 yards
par 70, S.S.S 68
Designer C.K. Hutchinson
Green fees £15
Catering, changing room/showers, bar, club and trolley hire, shop, practice facilities
Visitors welcome
Societies welcome by prior arrangement

LEOMINSTER GOLF CLUB

Ford Bridge, Leominster, Herefordshire HR6 0LE
✆ 01568 610055 Fax 01568 610055
Map 7, D8
leominstergolf@freeuk.com
Off A49, 3 miles S of Leominster (signposted)
Founded 1967
The lower holes of this undulating parkland course run beside the River

Lugg, while the higher holes give wonderful views over one of the most unspoiled parts of England.
18 holes, 6026 yards
par 70, S.S.S 69
Designer Bob Sandow
Green fees £8
Catering, changing room/showers, bar, trolley hire, shop, driving range, practice facilities
Visitors welcome
Societies welcome by prior arrangement
Talbot Hotel, West Street, Leominster, Herefordshire HR6 8EP
01568 616347

ROSS-ON-WYE GOLF CLUB

Two Park, Gorsley, Ross-on-Wye, Herefordshire HR9 7UT
01989 720267 Fax 01989 720212
Map 7, E9
secretary@therossonwyegolfclub.co.uk
www.therossonwyegolfclub.co.uk
M50 Jct 3
Founded 1903
Hewn from dense woodland in the early 1960s – with most of the work being done by members – Ross-on-Wye is immensely attractive at all times of year. The trees punish inaccurate golf, especially on the four substantial par 4s on the back nine. However, there are several drive-and-pitch holes to compensate.
18 holes, 6451 yards
par 72, S.S.S 73
Designer C K Cotton
Green fees £32
Catering, changing room/showers, bar, club and trolley hire, shop, practice facilities
Visitors welcome with restrictions
Societies welcome by prior arrangement

SAPEY GOLF CLUB

Upper Sapey, Worcester, Worcestshire WR6 6XT
01886 853288 Fax 01886 853485
Map 7, E7
anybody@sapeygolf.co.uk
www.sapeygolf.co.uk
M5 Jct 5. A38 to Droitwich. A443 to Great Witley. Then B4203 for 5 miles.
Founded 1989
A parkland course with trees, ditches and water, and oustanding views to the Malvern Hills.
18 holes, 5935 yards
par 69, S.S.S 68
Designer Ross McMurray
Green fees £18
Catering, changing room/showers, bar, club, trolley and buggy hire, shop, 9-hole, par-3 course, bowling green
Visitors welcome – restricted weekends
Societies welcome by prior arrangement
The Granary, Church House Farm, Collington, Bromyard, Herefordshire
01885 410345

SOUTH HEREFORDSHIRE GOLF CLUB

Twin Lakes, Upton Bishop, Ross-on-Wye, Herefordshire HR9 7UA
01989 780535 Fax 01989 740611
Map 7, E9
M50 Jct 4, 3 miles NE of Ross-on-Wye
Founded 1992
A spacious parkland course in beautiful countryside, with off course facilities to match.
18 holes, 6672 yards
par 71, S.S.S 72
Designer John Day
Green fees £15
Catering, changing room/showers, bar, club, trolley and buggy hire, shop, driving range, practice facilities, 9-hole, par-3 course
Visitors welcome
Societies welcome by prior arrangement

LEICESTERSHIRE

BEEDLES LAKE GOLF CLUB

170 Broome Lane, East Goscote, Leicestershire LE7 3WQ
0116 260 6759 **Map 8, D4**
Off A46, 4 miles N of Leicester
Founded 1993
A parkland course overlooking a lake.
18 holes, 6732 yards
par 72, S.S.S 72
Designer David Tucker
Green fees £10
Changing room/showers, bar, club and trolley hire, shop, driving range, fishing
Visitors welcome
Societies welcome by prior arrangement

BIRSTALL GOLF CLUB

Station Road, Birstall, Leicester, Leicestershire LE4 3BB
0116 2675245 Fax 0116 2674322,
Map 8, D4
A6, 3 miles N of Leicester
Founded 1901
A long-established parkland course with the usual trees and water hazards, plus the unusual distraction of a steam-operated railway line adjacent.
18 holes, 6230 yards
par 70, S.S.S 70
Green fees £25
Catering, changing room/showers, bar, club and trolley hire, shop, practice facilities, snooker, small conference room
Visitors welcome, with restrictions
Handicap certificate required
Societies welcome by prior arrangement
Premier Lodge, The Heathley Park, Groby Road, Leicester, Leicestershire
0870 7001420

BLABY GOLF CLUB

Lutterworth Road, Blaby, Leicestershire LE8 3DB
0116 278 4804 **Map 8, D5**
Blaby Village, 3 miles S of Leicester
Founded 1991
A parkland course with large driving range and crazy golf.
9 holes, 5312 yards
par 68, S.S.S 68
Green fees £6
Catering, changing room/showers, bar, club and trolley hire, shop, driving range, practice facilities
Visitors welcome
Societies welcome by prior arrangement

BREEDON PRIORY GOLF CLUB

Green Lane, Wilson, Derby, Leicestershire DE73 1LG
01332 863081 Fax 01332 863081
Map 8, B4
M1 Jct 23A, A453 towards Melbourne
Founded 1990
A parkland course close to the bustle of Donnington Park race track and the sublime peace of ancient Breedon-on-the-Hill Church.
18 holes, 5777 yards
par 69, S.S.S 68
Designer David Snell
Green fees £18
Catering, changing room/showers, bar, trolley hire, shop, practice facilities
Visitors welcome weekdays
Societies welcome by prior arrangement

CHARNWOOD FOREST GOLF CLUB

Breakback Road, Woodhouse Eaves, Loughborough, Leicestershire LE12 8TA
01509 890259 Fax 01509 890925
Map 8, C4

M1 Jct 22/23.
Founded 1890
One of the most beautiful 9-hole courses in existence. This, the oldest club in Leicestershire, is laid out on high ground overlooking the Quorn country. Golf is played against a background of the craggy granite Hanging Stone Rocks, and an excellent challenge it is, tough enough without a single bunker.
9 holes, 5970 yards
par 69, S.S.S 69
Designer James Braid
Green fees £20
Catering, changing room/showers, bar
Visitors welcome weekdays
Handicap certificate required
Societies welcome by prior arrangement

COSBY GOLF CLUB

Chapel Lane, Cosby, Leicester, Leicestershire LE9 1RG
☎ 0116 2848275 Fax 0116 2864484
Map 8, C5
secretary@cosby-golf-club.co.uk
www.cosby-golf-club.co.uk
Of B4114, M1 (M69) Jct 21
Founded 1895
A challenging course, often used for county matches. On paper the par 4s appear relatively short, but dog-legs, out-of-bounds and a stream are but some of the punishing hazards. Stroke 1 is the formidable 12th.
18 holes, 6410 yards
par 71, S.S.S 71
Designer Hawtree
Green fees £18
Catering, changing room/showers, bar, trolley hire, shop, practice facilities
Visitors welcome weekdays
Handicap certificate required
Societies welcome by prior arrangement
🏨 Spindle Lodge, Leicester, Leicestershire
☎ 0116 2338801

ENDERBY GOLF CLUB

Mill Lane, Enderby, Leicester, Leicestershire LE9 5NW
☎ 0116 284 9388 **Map 8, C5**
M1 Jct 21, 2 miles from Enderby
Founded 1986
A simple parkland course attached to a leisure centre.
9 holes, 4356 yards
S.S.S 61
Green fees £6.10
Catering, changing room/showers, club and trolley hire, shop, leisure facilities including swimming
Visitors welcome
Societies welcome by prior arrangement

FOREST HILL GOLF CLUB

Markfield Lane, Botcheston, Leicestershire LE9 9FJ
☎ 01455 824800 **Map 8, C5**
gerry@hyde14.fsnet.co.uk
M1 Jct 22, A50, follow signs to Desford and Thornton.
Founded 1991
A parkland course in the heart of Leicestershire. The 15th is a particularly difficult par 4 with water in front of the green.
18 holes, 6039 yards
par 71, S.S.S 69
Green fees £22
Catering, changing room/showers, bar, club and trolley hire, shop, driving range, practice facilities, conference facilities
Visitors welcome, subject to restrictions
Societies welcome by prior arrangement
🏨 Rothley Court Hotel, Westfield Lane, Rothley, Leicestershire
☎ 011623 74483

GLEN GORSE GOLF CLUB

Glen Road, Oadby, Leicester, Leicestershire LE2 4RF
☎ 0116271 3748 Fax 0116271 4159
Map 8, D5
www.ukcourses.co.uk/glengorse/index.htm
A6, 5 miles SE of Leicester
Founded 1933
Despite the name, it will be the lakes on the 6th and 7th which visiting golfers will be pleased to pass unscathed. Ridges and furrows cause the golfer to adapt on the 2nd, 3rd, 10th, 14th and 16th, and there are tough challenges after the turn. The views are delightful.
18 holes, 6648 yards
par 72, S.S.S 72
Green fees £25
Catering, changing room/showers, bar, trolley hire, shop, practice facilities
Visitors welcome, with restrictions
Handicap certificate required
Societies welcome by prior arrangement
🏨 Premier Lodge, The Heathley Park, Groby Road, Leicester, Leicestershire
☎ 0870 7001420

HINCKLEY GOLF CLUB

Leicester Road, Hinckley, Leicestershire LE10 3DR
☎ 01455 615014 Fax 01455 615014
Map 8, C5
proshop@hinckleygolfclub.com
www.hinckleygolfclub.com
B4668, ½ mile E of Hinckley, M69 Jct 1
Founded 1894
Hinckley runs to an 'Amen Corner' worthy of the title – three holes from the 11th. Nine lakes come into play throughout the round.
18 holes, 6529 yards
par 71, S.S.S 71
Green fees £25
Catering, changing room/showers, bar, trolley and buggy hire, shop, practice facilities, conference facilities, Computerised teaching academy
Visitors welcome
Handicap certificate required
Societies welcome by prior arrangement
🏨 Chapel House, Friar's Gate, Atherstone, Warwickshire CV9 1EY
☎ 01827 718949 Fax 01827 717702

HUMBERSTONE HEIGHTS GOLF CLUB

Gipsy Lane, Leicester, Leicestershire LE5 0TB
☎ 0116 299 5570 **Map 8, D5**
A563 Leicester Ring Road, E of city centre.
Founded 1978
Extensive facilities. Meals by prior arrangement.
18 holes, 6343 yards
par 70, S.S.S 70
Designer Hawtree
Green fees £11
Catering, changing room/showers, bar, club, trolley and buggy hire, shop, driving range, practice facilities, 9-hole pitch-and-putt
Visitors welcome
Societies welcome by prior arrangement
🏨 Spindle Lodge, Leicester, Leicestershire
☎ 0116 2338801

KIBWORTH GOLF CLUB

Weir Road, Kibworth Beauchamp, Leicester, Leicestershire LE8 0LP
☎ 0116 2792301 Fax 0116 2796434
Map 8, D5
A6, 8 miles SE of Leicester.
Founded 1904
Kibworth Beauchamp is a picturesque village, with an appropriately scenic golf course, with tree-lined fairways and a meandering stream. Good facilities include a 350-yard driving range and modern clubhouse.
18 holes, 6333 yards
par 71, S.S.S 70
Green fees £23
Catering, changing room/showers, bar, club and trolley hire, shop,

driving range, practice facilities
Visitors welcome weekdays
Handicap certificate required
Societies welcome by prior arrangement
Three Swans, High Street, Market Harborough, Leicestershire

KILWORTH SPRINGS GOLF CLUB

South Kilworth Road, North Kilworth, Lutterworth, Leicestershire LE17 6HJ
01858 575082 Fax 01858 575078
Map 8, D6
A4304, M1 Jct 20
Founded 1993
A tough course, the front nine resembling an inland links, the back nine more parkland in nature with lakes.
18 holes, 6718 yards
par 72, S.S.S 72
Designer Ray Baldwin
Green fees £18
Catering, changing room/showers, bar, trolley and buggy hire, shop, driving range, conference facilities
Visitors welcome with restrictions
Societies welcome by prior arrangement

KIRBY MUXLOE GOLF CLUB

Station Road, Kirby Muxloe, Leicester, Leicestershire LE9 2EP
0116 239 3457 Fax 0116 239 3457 **Map 8, C5**
B5380, S of Kirby Muxloe
Founded 1893
Two distinctly long par 4s, the 4th and 6th, are especially demanding early in the round, both featuring approaches played over a ditch. There are plenty of shorter par 4s in compensation, often tight dog-legs on which position is vital. A lake protects the green of the par-5 17th.
18 holes, 6279 yards
par 71, S.S.S 70
Green fees £25
Catering, changing room/showers, bar, club and trolley hire, shop, practice facilities
Visitors welcome with restrictions
Handicap certificate required
Societies welcome by prior arrangement

LANGTON PARK GOLF & COUNTRY CLUB

Langton Hall, Leicester, Leicestershire LE16 7TY
01858 545374 Fax 01858 545358
Map 8, D5
Off A6, 2 miles N of Market Harborough
Founded 1994
A new parkland course in the Leicester countryside near Market Harborough.
18 holes, 6724 yards
S.S.S 72
Designer Martin Hawtree
Catering, changing room/showers, bar, practice facilities
Visitors welcome
Handicap certificate required
Societies welcome by prior arrangement

THE LEICESTERSHIRE GOLF CLUB

Evington Lane, Leicester, Leicestershire LE5 6DJ
0116 273 8825 Fax 0116 273 1900 **Map 8, D5**
theleicestershiregolfclub@hotmail.com
Off A6030 E of City Centre
Founded 1890
Of good length, yet without a single par 5, it is immediately apparent that the Leicestershire's great strength is its collection of substantial par 4s. With the 461-yard 5th playing uphill, and dog-legs toughening the 455-yard 9th, 453-yard 11th and 442-yard 15th, long hitting is advantageous.
18 holes, 6329 yards
par 68, S.S.S 71
Designer Charles Mackenzie, C.K. Cotton
Green fees £24
Catering, changing room/showers, bar, trolley hire, shop, practice facilities
Visitors welcome weekdays
Handicap certificate required
Societies welcome by prior arrangement

LINGDALE GOLF CLUB

Joe Moon's Lane, Woodhouse Eaves, Loughborough, Leicestershire LE12 8TF
01509 890703 Fax 01509 890703
Map 8, C4
Off B5300, M1 Jct 22
Founded 1967
On the edge of Charnwood Forest, a hilly parkland course with many tough holes.
18 holes, 6545 yards
par 71, S.S.S 71
Designer David Tucker
Green fees £22
Catering, changing room/showers, bar, trolley hire, shop, practice facilities
Visitors welcome
Societies welcome by prior arrangement

LONGCLIFFE GOLF CLUB

Snells Nook Lane, Nanpantan, Loughborough, Leicestershire LE11 3YA
01509 239129 Fax 01509 231286
Map 8, C4
longcliffe@btconnect.com
www.longcliffegolf.co.uk
M1 Jct 23
Founded 1906
An EGU championship course, selected by the Curtis Cup team in 1994 and 1998 as their preparation course. Henry Cotton praised the 7th as one of the best inland holes in England.
18 holes, 6625 yards
par 72, S.S.S 72
Green fees £29
Catering, changing room/showers, bar, trolley hire, shop, practice facilities, conference and banquetting facilities
Visitors welcome weekdays
Handicap certificate required
Societies welcome by prior arrangement
Quality Hotel, Ashby Road, Loughborough, Leicestershire
01509 211800

LUTTERWORTH GOLF CLUB

Rugby Road, Lutterworth, Leicestershire LE17 4HN
01455 552532 Fax 01455 533586
Map 8, C6
A426, M1 Jct 20.
Founded 1904
An attractive course running in and out of the valley of the River Swift.
18 holes, 6226 yards
par 70, S.S.S 70
Designer David Snell
Green fees £20
Catering, changing room/showers, bar, club, trolley and buggy hire, shop, driving range, practice facilities
Visitors welcome weekdays
Societies welcome by prior arrangement

MARKET HARBOROUGH GOLF CLUB

Great Oxendon Road, Market Harborough, Leicestershire LE16 8NF
01858 463684 Fax 01858 432906
Map 8, D6
A508, 1 mile S of Market Harborough
Founded 1898
A pretty parkland course with plenty of water.
18 holes, 6022 yards
par 70, S.S.S 69
Designer Howard Swann
Green fees £20

Catering, changing room/showers, bar, trolley hire, shop, practice facilities
Visitors welcome weekdays
Societies welcome by prior arrangement

MELTON MOWBRAY GOLF CLUB

Waltham Road, Thorpe Arnold, Melton Mowbray, Leicestershire LE14 4SD
☎ 01664 562118 Fax 01664 562118
Map 8, E4
A607, 2 miles NE of Melton Mowbray.
Founded 1925
A parkland course just outside the pork pie capital of England.
18 holes, 6222 yards
par 70, S.S.S 70
Green fees £20
Catering, changing room/showers, bar, club and trolley hire, shop, practice facilities
Visitors welcome with restrictions
Societies welcome by prior arrangement

OADBY GOLF CLUB

Leicester Road, Oadby, Leicester, Leicestershire LE2 4AJ
☎ 0116 270 9052 **Map 8, D5**
A6, SE of Leicester
Founded 1974
A municipal parkland course with 9 holes inside the race course.
18 holes, 6311 yards
par 72, S.S.S 70
Green fees £7
Catering, changing room/showers, bar, club and trolley hire, shop, practice facilities
Visitors welcome
Societies welcome by prior arrangement

PARK HILL GOLF CLUB

Park Hill, Seagrave, Leicestershire LE12 7NG
☎ 01509 815454 Fax 01509 816062
Map 8, D4
mail@parkhillgolf.co.uk
www.parkhillgolf.co.uk
A46, 6 miles N of Leicester (M1 Jct 21a)
Founded 1994
With lovely views over the Charnwood Forest, this is a parkland course on the grand scale, with rolling fairways, five huge par 5s, and the almost inevitable water, especially surrounding the 18th green.
18 holes, 7219 yards
par 73, S.S.S 75
Green fees £20
Catering, changing room/showers, bar, trolley hire, shop, practice facilities, function & conference facilities
Visitors welcome
Societies welcome by prior arrangement
🏨 Willoughby Lodge, Willoughby, Leicestershire

ROTHLEY PARK GOLF CLUB

Westfield Lane, Rothley, Leicester, Leicestershire LE7 7LH
☎ 01162 302809 Fax 01162 302809
Map 8, C4
secretary@rothleypark.co.uk
www.rothleypark.com
2 miles W of A6, N of Leicester
Founded 1912
Parkland course in the Leicestershire countryside.
18 holes, 6477 yards
par 71, S.S.S 71
Green fees £25
Catering, changing room/showers, bar, club and trolley hire, shop, practice facilities
Visitors welcome – restricted Tuesday and weekends
Handicap certificate required
Societies welcome by prior arrangement
🏨 Rothley Court Hotel, Westfield Lane, Rothley, Leicestershire
☎ 0116 2374483

SCRAPTOFT GOLF CLUB

Beeby Road, Scraptoft, Leicester, Leicestershire LE7 9SJ
☎ 0116 241 9000 Fax 0116 241 8863 **Map 8, D5**
Off A47
Founded 1928
A quiet parkland course.
18 holes, 6235 yards
par 70, S.S.S 70
Green fees £20
Catering, changing room/showers, bar, club and trolley hire, shop, practice facilities
Visitors welcome weekdays
Handicap certificate required
Societies welcome by prior arrangement

SIX HILLS GOLF CLUB

Six Hills, Melton Mowbray, Leicestershire LE14 3PR
☎ 01509 881225 Fax 01509 889090
Map 8, D4
Off A46, 10 miles N of Leicester
Founded 1986
A parkland course.
18 holes, 5758 yards
par 71, S.S.S 69
Green fees £10
Changing room/showers, shop
Visitors welcome
Societies welcome – no advance booking system

STAPLEFORD PARK HOTEL, SPA, GOLF & SPORTING ESTATE

Stapleford Park, Near Melton Mowbray, Leicestershire, LE14 2EF
☎ 01572 787522 Fax 01572 787651
Map 8, E4
reservations@stapleford.co.uk
www.stapleford.co.uk
3 miles E of Melton Mowbray, off A606 or B676
Founded 2001
A stunning new course laid out in the peaceful Capability Brown grounds of a sumptuous hotel dating back to the 14th century. The design, in two extended loops never more than two holes wide, makes strategic use of streams, ponds and mature woodland, enjoying delightful country views.
18 holes, 6915 yards
par 73, S.S.S. 73
Designer Donald Steel
Full hotel and leisure facilities, including shooting, riding, falconry, and spa, wedding, banqueting and corporate function facilities, driving range, club hire, trolley hire
Visitors - hotel guests and corporate members only
Handicap certificate required
🏨 Stapleford Park Hotel, Spa, Golf and Sporting Estate
Stapleford Park, Near Melton Mowbray, Leicestershire, LE14 2EF
☎ 01572 787522 Fax 01572 787651
reservations@stapleford.co.uk
www.stapleford.co.uk

ULLESTHORPE COURT HOTEL GOLF CLUB

Frolesworth Road, Ullesthorpe, Lutterworth, Leicestershire LE17 5BZ
☎ 01455 209023 Fax 01455 202537
Map 8, D6
www.ullesthorpecourt.co.uk
Off A5, close to M69 Jct 1, M1 Jct 20.
Founded 1976
A parkland course of good length and challenge, popular with visitors and societies who take advantage of the many inclusive residential packages.
18 holes, 6650 yards
par 72, S.S.S 72
Green fees £18
Catering, changing room/showers, bar, accommodation, club, trolley and buggy hire, shop, practice facilities, full hotel facilities, tennis, swimming and gym
Visitors welcome weekdays
Societies welcome by prior

arrangement
Ullesthorpe Court Country Hotel, Frolesworth Road, Ullesthorpe, Leicestershire
01455 209023

WESTERN PARK GOLF COURSE

Scudamore Road, Leicester, Leicestershire LE3 1UQ
0116 287 2339 **Map 8, C5**
Off A47, 2 miles W of city centre
Founded 1920
Despite its length, a parkland course which is not too discouraging to the beginner while still giving satisfaction to the competent player.
18 holes, 6532 yards
par 72, S.S.S 71
Green fees £8.99
Catering, changing room/showers, bar, club and trolley hire, shop, practice facilities
Visitors welcome
Societies welcome by prior arrangement

WHETSTONE GOLF CLUB

Cambridge Road, Cosby, Leicester, Leicestershire LE9 5SH
0116 286 1424 Fax 0116 286 1424 **Map 8, C5**
Between A426 and B4114, between Cosby and Whetstone.
Founded 1965
A parkland course with some water coming into play – good value.
18 holes, 5795 yards
par 68, S.S.S 68
Designer E. Callaway
Green fees £15
Catering, changing room/showers, bar, club, trolley and buggy hire, shop, driving range, practice facilities
Visitors welcome
Societies welcome by prior arrangement

WILLESLEY PARK GOLF CLUB

Measham Road, Ashby-de-la-Zouch, Leicestershire LE65 2PF
01530 414596 Fax 01530 414596
Map 8, B4
B5006, between A42 and Ashby.
Founded 1921
From the opening drive, through an avenue of trees, to the challenging closing stretch, Willesley Park demands consistently accurate golf.
18 holes, 6304 yards
par 70, S.S.S 70
Designer James Braid
Green fees £30
Catering, changing room/showers, bar, trolley hire, shop, practice facilities
Visitors welcome, restricted weekends
Handicap certificate required
Societies welcome by prior arrangement
Royal Hotel, Station Road, Ashby de la Zouch, Leicestershire LE65 2GP
01530 412833

LINCOLNSHIRE

ASHBY DECOY GOLF CLUB

Ashby Decoy, Burringham Road, Scunthorpe, Lincolnshire DN17 2AB
01724 842913 Fax 01724271708
Map 11, D9
B1450, 2 miles SW of Scunthorpe
Founded 1936
A flat parkland course.
18 holes, 6281 yards
par 71, S.S.S 71
Green fees £18
Catering, changing room/showers, bar, trolley and buggy hire, shop, practice facilities
Visitors welcome weekdays
Handicap certificate required
Societies welcome by prior arrangement

BELTON PARK GOLF CLUB

Belton Lane, Londonsthorpe Road, Grantham, Lincolnshire NG31 9SH
01496 567399 Fax 01496 592078
Map 8, F3
www.greatgolfatbeltonpark.co.uk
A607, 2 miles NE of Grantham
Founded 1890
Golf has been played in the attractive grounds of Lord Brownlow's estate since 1890, the current 27 holes being the work of Peter Alliss. He has retained the classical landscape of oak and pine parkland while providing a contemporary test of golf. Society packages and catering are particularly good value.
Ancaster Course: 18 holes, 6325 yards, par 70, S.S.S 70
Designer Tom Williamson, Peter Alliss
Belmont Course: 18 holes, 6075 yards, par 69, S.S.S 69
Brownlow Course: 18 holes, 6472 yards, par 71, S.S.S 71
Designer Tom Williamson,Peter Alliss
Green fees £26
Catering, changing room/showers, bar, club and trolley hire, shop, practice facilities
Visitors welcome with restrictions
Handicap certificate required
Societies welcome by prior arrangement

BELTON WOODS HOTEL GOLF CLUB

Belton, Grantham, Lincolnshire NG32 2LN
01476 593200 Fax 01476 547547
Map 8, F3
A607, 2 miles N of Grantham
Founded 1991
Two long and testing parkland courses and a short course are but a part of the many facilities of this country hotel.
Lakes Course: 18 holes, 6833 yards, par 72, S.S.S 72
Red Arrows Course: 9 holes, 1116 yards, par 27, S.S.S 27
Woodside Course: 18 holes, 6623 yards, par 73, S.S.S 73
Green fees £27
Catering, changing room/showers, bar, accommodation, club, trolley and buggy hire, shop, driving range, practice facilities, full hotel function, leisure and conference facilities
Visitors welcome
Societies welcome by prior arrangement
Belton Woods Hotel, Belton, Nr Grantham, Lincolnshire
01476 593200

BLANKNEY GOLF CLUB

Blankney, Lincoln, Lincolnshire LN4 3AZ
01526 320263 Fax 01526 323521
Map 8, F1
B1188, 10 miles SE of Lincoln.
Founded 1903
A very attractive parkland course with trees and a lake, maintained in fine condition, which was judiciously upgraded by Cameron Sinclair to provide an exacting test, even though only two par 4s exceed 400 yards. A useful facility is an on-site bungalow which can be hired by small visiting parties.
18 holes, 6638 yards
par 72, S.S.S 73
Designer Cameron Sinclair
Green fees £20
Catering, changing room/showers, bar, accommodation, club and trolley hire, shop, practice facilities
Visitors welcome
Handicap certificate required
Societies welcome by prior arrangement

BOSTON GOLF CLUB

Cowbridge, Horncastle Road, Boston, Lincolnshire PE22 7EL
01205 350589 Fax 01205 350589
Map 8, H2
B1183, 2 miles from Boston
Founded 1900
Very flat course with plenty of water.
18 holes, 6490 yards

par 72, S.S.S 71
Green fees £19
Catering, changing room/showers, bar, club, trolley and buggy hire, shop, practice facilities
Visitors welcome
Handicap certificate required
Societies welcome by prior arrangement

BOSTON WEST GOLF CLUB

Hubbert's Bridge, Boston, Lincolnshire PE20 3QX
☎ 01205 290670 Fax 01205 290725
Map 8, H2
B1192, 2 miles W of Boston
Founded 1995
A flat parkland course.
18 holes, 6199 yards
par 71, S.S.S 70
Designer Michael Zara
Green fees £11
Catering, changing room/showers, bar, club and trolley hire, shop, practice facilities
Visitors welcome
Societies welcome by prior arrangement

BURGHLEY PARK (STAMFORD) GOLF CLUB

St Martin's Without, Stamford, Lincolnshire PE9 3JX
☎ 01780 762100 Fax 01780 753789
Map 8, F5
burghley.golf@lineone.com
B1081, 1 mile S of Stamford
Founded 1890
Laid out in the aristocratic surroundings of Burghley Park, a beautiful parkland course with highly reputed greens.
18 holes, 6230 yards
par 70, S.S.S 70
Designer Rev. J.D. Day
Green fees £24
Catering, changing room/showers, bar, club, trolley and buggy hire, shop, practice facilities
Visitors welcome weekdays
Handicap certificate required
Societies welcome by prior arrangement
🏨 The Garden House, St Martin's, Stamford, Lincolnshire PE9 2LP
☎ 01780 763359

CANWICK PARK GOLF CLUB

Canwick Park, Washingborough Road, Lincoln, Lincolnshire LN4 1EF
☎ 01522 536870 Fax 01522 542912
Map 11, E11
secretary@canwickpark.co.uk
www.canwickpark.co.uk
B1188, 1 mile E of Lincoln
Founded 1893
A very old club with a Hawtree course from the 1970s. Two of the short holes, the 5th and 13th, are over 200 yards in length, the 13th set off against the imposing backdrop of Lincoln Cathedral.
18 holes, 6160 yards
par 70, S.S.S 69
Designer Hawtree
Green fees £17
Catering, changing room/showers, bar, trolley and buggy hire, shop, practice facilities
Visitors welcome, restricted weekends
Societies welcome by prior arrangement
🏨 D'Isney Place, Eastgate, Lincoln, Lincolnshire LN2 4AA
☎ 01522 538881 Fax 01522 511321
info@disney-place.freeserve.co.uk
www.disney-place.freeserve.co.uk

CARHOLME GOLF CLUB

Carholme Road, Lincoln, Lincolnshire LN1 1SE
☎ 01522 536811/523725 Fax 01522 5333733 **Map 11, E11**
info@carholme-golfclub.co.uk
www.carholme-golfclub.co.uk
A57, beside racecourse
Founded 1906
A freindly club with a well-kept parkland course in sight of Lincoln Cathedral. The 406-yard 5th is quite a handful, with ponds and trees to be avoided on this demanding dog-leg.
18 holes, 6215 yards
par 71, S.S.S 70
Green fees £18
Catering, changing room/showers, bar, shop, practice facilities
Visitors welcome with weekend restrictions
Societies welcome by prior arrangement

CLEETHORPES GOLF CLUB

Kings Road, Cleethorpes, Lincolnshire DN35 0PN
☎ 01472 814060 **Map 11, G9**
Off A1301, 1 mile S of Cleethorpes
Founded 1894
Little remains of Harry Vardon's old course but the character is preserved, that of a flat parkland layout, crisscrossed by drainage dykes.
18 holes, 6349 yards
par 70, S.S.S 69
Designer Harry Vardon
Green fees £20
Catering, changing room/showers, bar, trolley hire, shop, practice facilities
Visitors welcome
Societies welcome by prior arrangement

ELSHAM GOLF CLUB

Barton Road, Elsham, Brigg, Lincolnshire DN20 0LS
☎ 01652 680291 Fax 01652 680308
Map 11, E9
B1206, 2 miles N of Brigg
Founded 1900
A pretty course secreted away in the Lincolnshire woodlands. The start is encouraging, with three shortish par 4s, but the 2nd, for instance, needs accuracy from the tee if the dog-leg is to be overcome. Length is more significant later on, with four par 4s exceeding 400 yards coming home.
18 holes, 6402 yards
par 71, S.S.S 71
Green fees £18
Catering, changing room/showers, bar, trolley and buggy hire, shop, practice facilities
Visitors welcome weekdays
Societies welcome by prior arrangement

FOREST PINES HOTEL GOLF COURSE & SPA

Ermine Street, Broughton, near Brigg, Lincolnshire DN20 0AQ
☎ 01652 650756 Fax 01652 650495
Map 11, E9
enquiries@forestpines.co.uk
www.forestpines.co.uk
M180 Jct 4
Founded 1996
In the flatlands of Lincolnshire there are many golfing surprises, not least Woodhall Spa. Forest Pines is almost a piece of classic Surrey heathland translated to the gates of Scunthorpe. Its 27 holes are surprisingly mature for a course so young, well wooded, and a challenge for the good player.
Beeches: 9 holes, 3102 yards, par 35,
Designer John Morgan
Forest: 9 holes, 3291 yards, par 36,
Pines: 9 holes, 3591 yards, par 37,
Green fees £30
Catering, changing room/showers, bar, accommodation, club, trolley and buggy hire, shop, driving range, practice facilities, full function facilities
Visitors welcome, but ring first
Societies welcome by prior arrangement
🏨 Forest Pines Hotel, Golf Course, & Spa, Ermine Street, Broughton, Near Brigg, Lincolnshire DN20 0AQ
☎ 01652 650770 Fax 016526 50495
enquiries@forestpines.co.uk
www.forestpines.co.uk

GAINSBOROUGH GOLF CLUB

The Belt Road, Thonock, Gainsborough, Lincolnshire DN21 1PZ
☎ 01427 613088 Fax 01427 810172
Map 11, D10
Off A631 (signposted)
Founded 1894
Owned by the Ping company, the original course was known simply as Thonock, and has been much revised by Brian Waites. Karsten Lakes is the new course and, as might be expected from the name, involves many water hazards.
Thonock Park: 18 holes, 6266 yards, par 72, S.S.S 69
Designer Brian Waites
Karsten Lakes: 18 holes, 6900 yards, par 72, S.S.S 72
Designer Neil Coles
Green fees £25
Catering, changing room/showers, bar, accommodation, club, trolley and buggy hire, shop, driving range, practice facilities, 2 self-contained flats for hire, conference facilities, Ping club-fitting centre
Visitors welcome
Societies welcome by prior arrangement
Hickman Hill Hotel, Hickman Hill, Gainsborough, Lincolnshire

GEDNEY HILL GOLF & COUNTRY CLUB

West Drove, Gedney Hill, Spalding, Lincolnshire PE12 0NT
☎ 01406 330922 Fax 01406 330323
Map 8, H4
B1166, 17 miles NE of Peterborough
Founded 1989
An inland links with no escape from the wind.
18 holes, 5285 yards
par 70, S.S.S 66
Designer Monkwise
Green fees £11
Catering, changing room/showers, bar, club, trolley and buggy hire, shop, driving range, practice facilities, bowls, Snooker etc
Visitors welcome
Societies welcome by prior arrangement

GRANGE PARK GOLF COURSE

Butterwick Road, Messingham, Scunthorpe, Lincolnshire DN17 3PP
☎ 01724 762945 **Map 11, E9**
1½ miles from Messingham
Founded 1991
A simple pay-and-play layout with good off-course facilities.
13 holes, 4149 yards
par 49, S.S.S 48
Designer R.W. Price
Green fees £6.50
Changing room/showers, club and trolley hire, shop, driving range, practice facilities, 9-hole, par-3 course, tennis, bowls, fishimg, caravan site
Visitors welcome
Societies welcome by prior arrangement

GRIMSBY GOLF CLUB

Littlecoates Road, Grimsby, Lincolnshire DN34 4LU
☎ 01472 267727 Fax 01472 505510
Map 11, G9
Off A46, 1 mile W of town centre
Founded 1922
A parkland course with slightly more undulation than is usual in coastal Lincolnshire.
18 holes, 6057 yards
par 70, S.S.S 69
Designer Harry Colt
Green fees £22
Catering, changing room/showers, bar, trolley and buggy hire, shop, practice facilities
Visitors welcome weekdays
Societies welcome by prior arrangement

HIRST PRIORY PARK GOLF COURSE

Crowle, near Scunthorpe, Lincolnshire DN17 4BU
☎ 01724 711619 **Map 11, D9**
hirstpriory@aol.com
Off A161, near M180 Jct 2
Founded 1995
A flat parkland course with some use of water.
18 holes, 6283 yards
par 71, S.S.S 69
Designer David Baxter
Green fees £12
Catering, changing room/showers, bar, club and trolley hire, shop, practice facilities
Visitors welcome
Societies welcome by prior arrangement
Red Lion Hotel, Market Place, Epworth, Near Scunthorpe, Lincolnshire DN9 1EU
☎ 01427 872208

HOLME HALL GOLF CLUB

Holme Lane, Bottesford, Scunthorpe, Lincolnshire DN16 3RF
☎ 01724 862078 Fax 01724 862078
Map 11, E9
Off A818, close to M180 Jct 4
Founded 1908
A mixture of heathland and parkland, brilliantly drained, giving good winter golf, even if the wind from the east can be bitter.
18 holes, 6475 yards
par 71, S.S.S 71
Green fees £20
Catering, changing room/showers, bar, club, trolley and buggy hire, shop
Visitors welcome weekdays
Societies welcome by prior arrangement

HORNCASTLE GOLF CLUB

West Ashby, Horncastle, Lincolnshire LN9 5PP
☎ 01507 526800 **Map 11, G11**
A158, 1 mile N of Hornacastle
Founded 1990
Plentiful water hazards make the golf challenging, and the wildlife abundant. Clubhouse is "Golfer's Arms".
18 holes, 5717 yards
par 70, S.S.S 68
Designer E.C. Wright
Green fees £15
Catering, changing room/showers, bar, club and trolley hire, driving range, practice facilities, fishing, wedding, function and conference facilities
Visitors welcome
Societies welcome by prior arrangement
Admiral Rodney Hotel, Horncastle, Lincolnshire
☎ 01507 523131

HUMBERSTON PARK GOLF CLUB

Humberston Avenue, Humberston, Lincolnshire DN36 4SJ
☎ 01472 210404 **Map 11, G9**
A1031, 3 miles S of Grimsby
A developing course and facilities, with profits from green fees ploughed back into the upgrade.
9 holes, 3670 yards
par 60, S.S.S 57
Designer T. Barraclough
Green fees £8
Changing room/showers, bar
Visitors welcome with restrictions
Societies welcome by prior arrangement

IMMINGHAM GOLF CLUB

St Andrews Lane, Church Lane, Immingham, Lincolnshire DN42 2EU
☎ 01469 575298 Fax 01469 577636
Map 11, F8
admin@immgc.com
www.immgc.com
Near St Andrew's Church, off Bluestone Lane
Founded 1975
A flat course, but made interesting and testing by ditches and ponds and tree-lined dog-legs.
18 holes, 6215 yards
par 71, S.S.S 70

Designer Hawtree
Green fees £12
Catering, changing room/showers, bar, shop, practice facilities
Visitors welcome
Societies welcome by prior arrangement
Oaklands Hotel, Laceby Roundabout, Laceby, Grimsby, Lincolnshire

KENWICK PARK GOLF CLUB

Kenwick Hall, Louth, Lincolnshire LN11 8NY
01507 607161 Fax 01507 606556
Map 11, G10
golfatkenwick@nascr.net
www.louthnet.co.uk
Off A157, 1 mile S of Louth
Founded 1992
Parkland course designed by Patrick Tallack.
18 holes, 6782 yards
par 72, S.S.S 73
Designer Patrick Tallack
Green fees £27
Catering, changing room/showers, bar, accommodation, club, trolley and buggy hire, shop, driving range, practice facilities, conference facilities
Visitors welcome
Handicap certificate required
Societies welcome by prior arrangement
Kenwick Park Hotel, Kenwick, Louth, Lincolnshire
01507 608806

KINGSWAY GOLF CLUB

Kingsway, Scunthorpe, Lincolnshire DN15 7ER
01724 840945 **Map 11, E9**
Off A18, between Berkeley and Queensway roundabouts
Founded 1971
A parkland course of executive length.
9 holes, 1915 yards
par 58, S.S.S 59
Green fees £3.60
Changing room/showers, club and trolley hire, shop
Visitors welcome
Societies welcome by prior arrangement

KIRTON HOLME GOLF CLUB

Holme Road, Kirton Holme, Boston, Lincolnshire PE20 1SY
01205 290669 **Map 8, H3**
4 miles W of Boston, signposted off A52
Founded 1992
The Boston Stump, the second highest church tower in England, dominates the skyline of this young, flat course.
9 holes, 5778 yards
par 70, S.S.S 68
Designer D.W. Welberry
Green fees £5
Catering, changing room/showers, bar, club and trolley hire, practice facilities
Visitors welcome
Societies welcome by prior arrangement
The Poachers Inn, Surieshead Road, Kirton Holme, Boston, Lincolnshire
01205 290310

LINCOLN GOLF CLUB

Torksey, Lincoln, Lincolnshire LN1 2EG
01427 718721 Fax 01427 718721
Map 11, D10
Off A156, 12 miles NW of Lincoln
Founded 1891
Undulating fairways, crisp turf, gorse and heather give a links-like feel to many holes, contrasting with the tree-lined parkland holes. A sequence of long par 4s around the turn is particularly demanding, and the handsome 17th, played over a pond and prominent bunkers, is the pick of the short holes.
18 holes, 6438 yards
par 71, S.S.S 71
Green fees £26
Catering, changing room/showers, bar, trolley hire, shop
Visitors welcome weekdays
Handicap certificate required
Societies welcome by prior arrangement

LOUTH GOLF CLUB

Crowtree Lane, Louth, Lincolnshire LN11 9LJ
01507 603681 Fax 01507 608501
Map 11, G10
louthgolfclub1992@btinternet.com
www.louthgolfclub.com
Off A16, W of Louth
Founded 1965
Fairways are threaded through wooded, rolling hills. There are a number of long par 4s and several solid par 5s. Attractive country panoramas.
18 holes, 6430 yards
par 72, S.S.S 71
Green fees £18
Catering, changing room/showers, bar, trolley and buggy hire, shop, driving range, practice facilities, squash courts
Visitors welcome – restricted weekends
Societies welcome by prior arrangement
Lincolnshire Poacher, 211 Eastgate, Louth, Lincolnshire
01507 603657

THE MANOR GOLF CLUB

Laceby Manor, Laceby, Grimsby, Lincolnshire DN37 7EA
01472 873468 Fax 01472 276706
Map 11, F9
judith@manorgolf.com
www.manorgolf.com
A18, W of Grimsby
Founded 1992
A mixture of wooded and wide open fairways. The 16th green is surrounded by water.
18 holes, 6343 yards
par 72, S.S.S 70
Designer Sports Turf Research Institute
Green fees £18
Catering, changing room/showers, bar, trolley and buggy hire, shop, practice facilities, conference facilities
Visitors welcome
Societies welcome by prior arrangement
Oaklands Hotel, Laceby Roundabout, Laceby, Grimsby, Lincolnshire
01472 872248

MARKET RASEN & DISTRICT GOLF CLUB

Legsby Road, Market Rasen, Lincolnshire LN8 3DZ
01673 842319 **Map 11, F10**
B631, 1 mile E of Market Rasen
Founded 1912
Quite a challenging heathland course with lovely views over the Lincolnshire Wolds.
18 holes, 6209 yards
par 70, S.S.S 70
Designer Hawtree
Green fees £18
Catering, changing room/showers, bar, trolley hire, shop, practice facilities
Visitors welcome weekdays
Handicap certificate required
Societies welcome by prior arrangement, Tuesday and Friday
Lincolnshire Poacher, 211 Eastgate, Louth, Lincolnshire
01507 603657

MARKET RASEN RACE COURSE

Legsby Road, Market Rasen, Lincolnshire LN8 3EA
01673 843434 Fax 01673 844532
Map 11, F10
In centre of race course
Founded 1989
Well drained on sandy soil, this public course makes good use of

the spare land within the race course.
9 holes, 2350 yards
par 32
Green fees £4
Club hire
Visitors welcome
Societies welcome by prior arrangement

MARTIN MOOR GOLF CLUB

Martin Road, Blankney, Lincolnshire LN4 3BE
☎ 01526 378243 Fax 01526 378243
Map 8, F1
B1189, 6 miles from Woodhall Spa
Founded 1992
Given the success of Woodhall Spa, it is hardly surprising that other spots of Lincolnshire heathland are being sought on which to build golf courses.
9 holes, 6325 yards
par 72, S.S.S 70
Green fees £9.50
Changing room/showers, bar, club and trolley hire, shop, practice facilities
Visitors welcome
Societies welcome by prior arrangement
Eagle Lodge Hotel, The Broadway, Woodhall Spa, Lincolnshire LN10 6SP
☎ 01526 353231 Fax 01526 352797

MILLFIELD GOLF CLUB

Laugherton, Lincoln, Lincolnshire LN1 2LB
☎ 01427 718473 Fax 01427 718473
Map 11, D11
A1133, W of Lincoln near Torksey
Founded 1985
A wide range of facilities with the Milfield course designed to test experienced golfers, while others learn on the complementary courses.
The Millfield Course: 18 holes, 6004 yards, par 72, S.S.S 69
The Grenville Green: 18 holes, 4485 yards, par 65,
Designer C. Watson
Green fees £5
Catering, changing room/showers, bar, trolley and buggy hire, shop, driving range, practice facilities, 9-hole, par-3 course
Visitors welcome
Societies welcome by prior arrangement

NORMANBY HALL GOLF CLUB

Normanby, Scunthorpe, Lincolnshire DN15 9HU
☎ 01724 720226 **Map 11, E8**
dmac1066@aol.com
B1130, 5 miles N of Scunthorpe. Follow signs for Normanby Hall Country Park.
Founded 1978
A fine parkland course with plenty of challenge.
18 holes, 6547 yards
par 72, S.S.S 71
Green fees £12.50
Catering, changing room/showers, bar, club, trolley and buggy hire, shop, practice facilities
Visitors welcome – restricted weekends
Societies welcome by prior arrangement
Forest Pines Hotel, Golf Course, & Spa, Ermine Street, Broughton, near Brigg, Lincolnshire DN20 0AQ
☎ 01652 650770 Fax 01652 650495
enquiries@forestpines.co.uk
www.forestpines.co.uk

NORTH SHORE HOTEL & GOLF COURSE

North Shore Road, Skegness, Lincolnshire PE25 1DN
☎ 01754 763298 Fax 01754 761902
Map 9, B1
golf@north-shore.co.uk
www.north-shore.co.uk
A52, 1 mile N of town centre
Founded 1910
Part links, part parkland, with the 5th hole particularly demanding, having a narrow fairway running beside the beach.
18 holes, 6257 yards
par 71, S.S.S 71
Designer James Braid
Green fees £22
Catering, changing room/showers, bar, accommodation, trolley and buggy hire, shop, conference and banquetting facilities
Visitors welcome
Societies welcome by prior arrangement
North Shore Hotel, North Shore Road, Skegness, Lincolnshire
☎ 01754 763298

POTTERGATE GOLF CLUB

Moor Lane, Branston, Lincoln, Lincolnshire
☎ 01522 794867 **Map 8, F1**
B1188, 3 miles SE of Lincoln
Founded 1992
A short parkland course.
9 holes, 5164 yards
par 68, S.S.S 65
Designer W.T. Bailey
Green fees £8
Bar, shop
Visitors welcome
Societies welcome by prior arrangement

RAF CONINGSBY GOLF CLUB

RAF Coningsby, Lincoln, Lincolnshire LN4 4FE
☎ 01526 342581 Ext 6828 **Map 8, G2**
B1192 between Woodhall Spa and Coningsby
Built around the old 617 Squadron (Dambusters) airfield, now home to the Battle of Britain Memorial Flight.
9 holes, 5354 yards
par 68, S.S.S 66
Green fees £6
Changing room/showers, trolley hire, practice facilities
Visitors welcome weekdays
Societies welcome by prior arangement
Golf Hotel, Woodhall Spa, Lincolnshire
☎ 01526 353535

RAF WADDINGTON GOLF CLUB

Waddington, Lincoln, Lincolnshire LN5 9NB
☎ 01522 720271 (Ext.7958)
Map 8, F1
Off A15, 3 miles S of Lincoln
Founded 1972
A brilliant use of spare ground within the airfield – quite tricky!
9 holes, 5519 yards
S.S.S 69
Visitors welcome only as members' guests
Societies welcome by prior arrangement

SANDILANDS GOLF CLUB

Sandilands, Sutton-on-Sea, Lincolnshire LN12 2RJ
☎ 01507 441432 **Map 11, H10**
Off A52, 1 mile S of Sutton-on-Sea.
Founded 1900
Seacroft is often cited as the only links course between The Wash and The Tees, but that is to overlook the genuine links qualities of Sandilands, a few miles up the coast.
18 holes, 5995 yards
par 70, S.S.S 69
Green fees £15
Catering, changing room/showers, bar, club, trolley and buggy hire
Visitors welcome
Societies welcome by prior arrangement

SEACROFT GOLF CLUB

Drummond Road, Seacroft, Skegness, Lincolnshire PE25 3AU
☎ 01754 763020 Fax 01754 763020
V9, B1
richard@seacroft-golfclub.co.uk
www.seacroft-golfclub.co.uk
S of Skegness town centre
Founded 1895

The many traditional features of blind shots, tight, fine seaside grass, abundant bunkers, and savage rough, only serve to reinforce the feeling that this was surely how true links golf was meant to be played. It is possible to slice out of bounds on 14 holes. Seacroft is a classic.
18 holes, 6479 yards
par 71, S.S.S 71
Designer Willie Fernie, Herbert Fowler, C.K. Cotton
Green fees £27
Catering, changing room/showers, bar, club, trolley and buggy hire, shop, practice facilities
Visitors welcome
Handicap certificate required
Societies welcome by prior arrangement
Crown Hotel, Drummond Road, Seacroft, Skegness, Lincolnshire
01754 610760

SLEAFORD GOLF CLUB
Willoughby Road, South Rauceby, Sleaford, Lincolnshire NG34 8PL
01529 488644 Fax 01529 488326
Map 8, F2
sleafordgolfclub@btinternet.com
A153, 2 miles W of Sleaford
Founded 1905
Usually described as an 'inland links', this is one of the driest courses in Lincolnshire – a pleasure even in winter.
18 holes, 6443 yards
par 72, S.S.S 71
Designer Tom Williamson
Green fees £18
Catering, changing room/showers, bar, club, trolley and buggy hire, shop, practice facilities, 6-hole short course
Visitors welcome – restricted weekends
Handicap certificate required
Societies welcome by prior arrangement
Carre Arms Hotel, 1 Mareham Road, Sleaford, Lincolnshire
01529 303156

SOUTH KYME GOLF CLUB
Skinners Lane, South Kyme, Lincoln, Lincolnshire LN4 4AT
01526 861113 Fax 01526 861080
Map 8, G2
B1395, 6 miles E of Sleaford.
Founded 1990
Probably best described as an inland links, the challenging course is under constant development, with 21,000 tons of soil being used for recent landscaping. Excellent greens.
18 holes, 6597 yards
par 72, S.S.S 71
Designer G. Bradley
Green fees £15
Catering, changing room/showers, bar, trolley and buggy hire, shop, practice facilities
Visitors welcome
Societies welcome by prior arrangement
The Leagate Inn, Leagate Road, Coningsby, Lincoln, Lincolnshire
01526 6342370

SPALDING GOLF CLUB
Surfleet, Spalding, Lincolnshire PE11 4EA
01775 680386 Fax 01775 680988
Map 8, G3
Off A16, 4 miles N of Spalding
Founded 1907
A remarkable course, designed and built in-house. The River Glen and Blue Gowt Drain plus ponds mean that only a few holes are not threatened by water. The wicked 2nd tempts the golfer's vanity. Stroke 1 is the 428-yard 4th, curving left, with the river awaiting the merest slice.
18 holes, 6492 yards
par 72, S.S.S 71
Designer Joe Price, Tony Ward, John Spencer
Green fees £20
Catering, changing room/showers, bar, trolley hire, shop, practice facilities
Visitors welcome – restricted competition days
Handicap certificate required
Societies welcome by prior arrangement
Woodlands Hotel, Pinchbeck Road, Spalding, Lincolnshire
01775 769333 Fax 01775 711369

STOKE ROCHFORD GOLF CLUB
Great North Road, Grantham, Lincolnshire NG33 5EW
01476 530275 **Map 8, F3**
Off A1, S of Grantham
Founded 1924
A parkland course overlooking the Great North Road.
18 holes, 6252 yards
par 70, S.S.S 70
Designer C. Turner, Major Hotchkin
Green fees £22
Changing room/showers, trolley and buggy hire, shop
Visitors welcome weekdays with restrictions
Societies welcome by prior arrangement

SUDBROOK MOOR GOLF CLUB
Charity Lane, Carlton Scroop, Grantham, Lincolnshire NG32 3AT
01400 250796 **Map 8, F2**
info@sudbrookmoor.co.uk
www.sudbrookmoor.co.uk
A607, Grantham–Lincoln road.
Founded 1986
A pretty 9-hole course with 18 pin positions, twelve par 4s and six par 3s.
9 holes, 4827 yards
par 66, S.S.S 64
Designer Tim Hutton
Green fees £7
Catering, changing room/showers, club and trolley hire, shop, practice facilities, 3-hole, par-3 course
Visitors welcome
No societies
Old Barn Hotel, Toll Bar Road, Marston, Grantham, Lincolnshire
01400 250909

SUTTON BRIDGE GOLF CLUB
New Road, Sutton Bridge, Spalding, Lincolnshire PE12 9RQ
01406 350323 **Map 9, B4**
Off A17 between Kings Lynn and Long Sutton
Founded 1914
A unique golf course, built around a Victorian dock basin, beside the River Nene.
9 holes, 5822 yards
par 70, S.S.S 69
Green fees £18
Catering, changing room/showers, bar, club and trolley hire, shop, practice facilities
Visitors welcome weekdays
Handicap certificate required
Societies welcome by prior arrangement
Bridge Hotel, Bridge Road, Sutton Bridge, Spalding, Lincolnshire
01406 350222

TETNEY GOLF CLUB
Station Road, Tetney, Near Grimsby, Lincolnshire DN36 5HY
01472 211644 Fax 01472 211644
Map 11, F9
Off A16 between Grimsby and Louth
Founded 1994
A parkland course with a number of water hazards and views of the Lincolnshire Wolds.
18 holes, 6100 yards
par 71, S.S.S 69
Designer S. Grant
Green fees £10
Catering, changing room/showers, bar, club, trolley and buggy hire, shop, driving range, practice facilities
Visitors welcome
Societies welcome by prior arrangement
Oaklands Hotel, Laceby

Roundabout, Laceby, Grimsby, Lincolnshire
☎ 01472 872248

TOFT HOTEL GOLF CLUB

Toft, Bourne, Lincolnshire PE10 0JT
☎ 01778 590616 Fax 01778 590264
Map 8, F4
A6121, 6 miles NE of Stamford
Founded 1988
A very striking parkland course making much use of water both in its defences and for beauty.
18 holes, 6486 yards
par 72, S.S.S 71
Designer Derek & Roger Fitton
Green fees £20
Catering, changing room/showers, bar, accommodation, club, trolley and buggy hire, shop, driving range
Visitors welcome
Societies welcome by prior arrangement
Toft Hotel, Toft, Nr Bourne, Lincolnshire
☎ 01778 590614

WALTHAM WINDMILL GOLF CLUB

Cheapside, Waltham, Grimsby, Lincolnshire DN37 0HT
☎ 01472 824109 Fax 01472 828391
Map 11, G9
Off A16, 2 miles S of Grimsby
Founded 1997
A parkland course designed by Jim Payne, former distinguished Lincolnshire amateur, later a winner on the European Tour.
18 holes, 6400 yards
par 71, S.S.S 70
Designer Jim Payne
Green fees £18
Catering, bar, practice facilities
Visitors welcome weekdays
Societies welcome by prior arrangement

WOODHALL SPA GOLF CLUB

The National Golf Centre, The Broadway, Woodhall Spa, Lincolnshire LN10 6PU
☎ 01526 352511 Fax 01526 351817
Map 8, G1
booking@englishgolfunion.org
www.englishgolfuntion.org
B1191 – E of Woodhall Spa
Founded 1905
See Top 50 Courses. page 59
Hotchkin: 18 holes, 7080 yards, par 73, S.S.S 75
Designer S.V. Hotchkin
Bracken: 18 holes, 6735 yards, par 72, S.S.S 73
Designer Donald Steel
Green fees £55
Catering, changing room/showers, bar, trolley hire, shop, driving range, practice facilities, self-catering house
Visitors welcome
Handicap certificate required – limit: 24
Societies welcome by prior arrangement
Petwood Hotel, Woodhall Spa, Lincolnshire LN10 6QF
☎ 01526 352411 Fax 01526 353473

WOODTHORPE HALL GOLF CLUB

Woodthorpe, Alford, Lincolnshire LN13 0DD
☎ 01507 450000 Fax 01507 450000
Map 11, H11
info@woodthorpehall.co.uk
www.woodthorpehall.co.uk
Off B1373, N of Alford
Founded 1986
A parkland course.
18 holes, 5140 yards
par 67, S.S.S 65
Green fees £10
Catering, changing room/showers, bar, fishing
Visitors welcome
Societies welcome by prior arrangement

NORTHAMPTONSHIRE

BRAMPTON HEATH GOLF CLUB

Sandy Lane, Church Brampton, Northamptonshire NN6 8AX
☎ 01604 843939 Fax 01604 843885
Map 8, D7
slawrence@bhgc.co.uk
www.bhgc.co.uk
Off A5119, 3 miles N of Northampton
Founded 1995
A heathland course similar in soil and drainage to Northamptonshire County, next door, but with a more contemporary design.
18 holes, 6366 yards
par 71, S.S.S 70
Designer David Snell
Green fees £13
Catering, changing room/showers, bar, club, trolley and buggy hire, shop, driving range, short course par 3
Visitors welcome
Societies welcome by prior arrangement

COLD ASHBY GOLF CLUB

Stanford Road, Cold Ashby, Northampton, Northamptonshire NN6 6EP
☎ 01604 740548 Fax 01604 740548
Map 8, D6
coldashby.golfclub@virgin.net
www.coldashbygolfclub.com
Near A5199/A14 Jct 1, N of Northampton
Founded 1974
Variety is easy to achieve when it is possible to make up three different courses from 27 holes. A fine set of courses with wonderful views.
Ashby-Elkington Course: 18 holes, 6308 yards, par 72, S.S.S 70
Designer David Croxton
Elkington-Winwick Course: 18 holes, 6250 yards, par 70, S.S.S 70
Winwick-Ashby Course: 18 holes, 6004 yards, par 70, S.S.S 69
Green fees £14
Catering, changing room/showers, bar, club and trolley hire, shop, practice facilities
Visitors welcome weekdays, with weekend restrictions
Societies welcome by prior arrangement

COLLINGTREE PARK GOLF CLUB

Windingbrook Lane, Northampton, Northamptonshire NN4 0XN
☎ 01604 700000 Fax 01604 702600
Map 8, E7
info@collingtreepark.com
www.collingtreeparkgolf.com
M1 Jct 15
Founded 1990
Probably the best value American-style course in the country, past host to two European Tour events. Johnny Miller's design makes good use of water, not least on the 600-yard 18th, with a lake running the length of the fairway on the left, and the green totally surrounded by water.
18 holes, 6908 yards
par 72, S.S.S 73
Designer Johnny Miller
Green fees £20
Catering, changing room/showers, bar, club, trolley and buggy hire, shop, driving range, practice facilities, corporate entertainment facilities
Visitors welcome
Handicap certificate required
Societies welcome by prior arrangement

DAVENTRY & DISTRICT GOLF CLUB

Norton Road, Daventry, Northamptonshire NN11 5LS
☎ 01327 702829 **Map 8, C7**
N of town, next to BBC station
Founded 1911
An undulating course next to the BBC's World Service transmitters. Golfers may find a broadcast in Swahili emerging from a 6-iron held

at just the right angle!
9 holes, 5812 yards
par 69, S.S.S 68
Green fees £10
Catering, changing room/showers, bar
Visitors welcome with restrictions
Societies welcome by prior arrangement

DELAPRE GOLF COMPLEX

Eagle Drive, Nene Valley Way, Northampton, Northamptonshire NN4 7DU
✆ 01604 764036 Fax 01604 706378
Map 8, E7
A508/A45, 3 miles from M1 Jct 15
Founded 1976
A huge municipal golf complex with every imaginable facility.
Main Course: 18 holes, 6293 yards, par 70, S.S.S 70
Hardingstone Course: 9 holes, 2146 yards, par 32, S.S.S 32
Designer John Jacobs, John Corby
Green fees £10
Catering, changing room/showers, bar, club and trolley hire, shop, driving range, practice facilities
Visitors welcome
Societies welcome by prior arrangement

EMBANKMENT GOLF CLUB

The Embankment, Wellingborough, Northamptonshire NN8 1LD
✆ 01933 228465 **Map 8, E7**
SE of Wellingborough
Founded 1975
As the name implies, laid out on the embankment of the river as it flows through Wellingborough.
9 holes, 3400 yards
S.S.S 57
Designer T.H. Neal
Green fees £4
Bar
Visitors welcome as members' guests
No Societies

FARTHINGSTONE HOTEL GOLF CLUB

Farthingstone, Towcester, Northamptonshire NN12 8HA
✆ 01327 361291 Fax 01327 361645
Map 8, D7
www.farthingstone.co.uk
4 miles W of A5, M1 Jct 16
Founded 1974
A very pretty country course.
18 holes, 6299 yards
par 70, S.S.S 70
Designer Mike Gallagher
Green fees £15
Catering, changing room/showers, bar, accommodation, club, trolley and buggy hire, shop, practice facilities, squash
Visitors welcome
Societies welcome by prior arrangement
🏨 Farthingstone Hotel, Farthingstone Towcester, Northants, Northamptonshire
✆ 01327 361560

HELLIDON LAKES HOTEL & COUNTRY CLUB

Hellidon, Daventry, Northamptonshire NN11 5LS
✆ 01327 262550 Fax 01327 262559
Map 8, C7
stay@hellidon.demon.co.uk
www.hellidon.co.uk
Off A361, S of Daventry
Founded 1991
A very challenging parkland course, undulating and, in many places, breathtaking.
18 holes, 6700 yards, par 72, S.S.S 72
9 holes, 5582 yards, par 67, S.S.S 67
Designer David Snell
Green fees £20
Catering, changing room/showers, bar, accommodation, club, trolley and buggy hire, shop, practice facilities, swimming, fishing, tenpin bowling and tennis
Visitors welcome
Handicap certificate required
Societies welcome by prior arrangement
🏨 Hellidon Lakes Hotel, Hellidon, Daventry, Northamptonshire
✆ 01327 262550

KETTERING GOLF CLUB

Headlands, Kettering, Northamptonshire NN15 6XA
✆ 01536 511104 Fax 01536 511104
Map 8, E6
A14, S of Kettering
Founded 1891
A gentle parkland course.
18 holes, 6081 yards
par 69, S.S.S 69
Designer Tom Morris
Green fees £24
Catering, changing room/showers, bar, club and trolley hire, shop, practice facilities
Visitors welcome weekdays
Societies welcome by prior arrangement

KINGFISHER COUNTRY CLUB

Buckingham Road, Deanshanger, Milton Keynes, Northamptonshire MK18 6DG
✆ 01908 562332 Fax 01908 260857
Map 8, E8
A422, 7 miles NW of Milton Keynes
Founded 1994
A pleasant pay and play course with a number of water hazards.
9 holes, 5471 yards
par 70, S.S.S 67
Designer Donald Steel
Green fees £6.50
Catering, changing room/showers, bar, club and trolley hire, shop, driving range, practice facilities, fishing, model steam railway, function rooms
Visitors welcome
Societies welcome by prior arrangement

KINGSTHORPE GOLF CLUB

Kingsley Road, Northampton, Northamptonshire NN2 7BU
✆ 01604 719602 Fax 01604 710610
Map 8, E7
kingsthorpe.gc@lineone.net
2 miles n of Northampton, off A508
Founded 1908
Renowned for its warm welcome for visitors, and the challenging nature of a number of its holes.
18 holes, 5918 yards
par 69, S.S.S 69
Designer C.H. Alison, Harry Colt
Green fees £25
Catering, changing room/showers, bar, trolley hire, shop
Visitors welcome, with restrictions
Handicap certificate required
Societies welcome by prior arrangement
🏨 Coach House Hotel, 8-10 East Park Parade, Northampton, Northamptonshire
✆ 01604 250981

NORTHAMPTON GOLF CLUB

Harlestone, Northampton, Northamptonshire NN7 4EF
✆ 01604 845102 Fax 01604 820262
Map 8, D7
A428, 4 miles NW of Northampton
Founded 1893
A parkland course on rolling countryside with a number of water features and sweeping views.
18 holes, 6615 yards
par 72, S.S.S 72
Designer Donald Steel
Green fees £32
Catering, changing room/showers, bar, trolley hire, shop, practice facilities, banqueting & function facilities
Visitors welcome weekdays
Handicap certificate required
Societies welcome by prior arrangement

NORTHAMPTONSHIRE COUNTY GOLF CLUB

Golf Lane, Church Brampton, Northampton, Northamptonshire

NN6 8AZ
☎ 01604 843025 Fax 01604 843463
Map 8, D7
In village of Church Brampton, off A428
Founded 1909
Travellers on the railway line from Northampton to Rugby are granted an unrivalled view of this inviting and peacefully secluded course. One of the holes they see, the 11th, is one of the best, climbing to a green that is tricky to hold. The last three holes yield few birdies.
18 holes, 6505 yards
par 70, S.S.S 72
Designer Harry Colt
Green fees £45
Catering, changing room/showers, bar, club and trolley hire, shop, driving range, practice facilities
Visitors welcome, subject to restrictions
Handicap certificate required
Societies welcome by prior arrangement, Wednesday and Thursday only
Broomhill Country House Hotel, Holdenby Road, Spratton, Northampton, Northamptonshire NN6 8LD
☎ 01604 845959

OUNDLE GOLF CLUB

Benefield Road, Oundle, Peterborough PE8 4EZ
☎ 01832 272273 Fax 01832 273 267
Map 8, F5
office@oundlegolfclub.fsnet.co.uk
A427 W of Oundle
Founded 1893
A stream, running through the middle of this gently undulating parkland course, affects several holes. A friendly welcome is assured.
18 holes, 6235 yards
par 72, S.S.S 70
Green fees £25
Catering, changing room/showers, bar, club and trolley hire, shop, practice facilities
Visitors welcome, with restrictions
Handicap certificate required
Societies welcome by prior arrangement
The Talbot, New Street, Oundle, Northamptonshire
☎ 01832 273621

OVERSTONE PARK GOLF CLUB

Watermark Leisure, Billing Lane, Northampton, Northamptonshire NN6 0AP
☎ 01604 647666 Fax 01604 642635
Map 8, E7
M1 Jct 15, A45 to Billing Aquadrome
Founded 1994
Set on rolling parkland, there are good views from Donald Steel's challenging course.
18 holes, 6602 yards
par 72, S.S.S 72
Designer Donald Steel
Green fees £26
Catering, changing room/showers, bar, club, trolley and buggy hire, shop, driving range, practice facilities
Visitors welcome weekdays
Societies welcome by prior arrangement

PRIORS HALL GOLF COURSE

Weldon Road, Corby, Northamptonshire NN17 3JH
☎ 01536 260756 **Map 8, E6**
A43, 1 mile E of Corby
Founded 1965
One of the best designed municipal courses of its era. The country needs more of them!
18 holes, 6631 yards
par 72, S.S.S 72
Designer Hawtree & Sons
Green fees £13.70
Catering, changing room/showers, bar, accommodation, club and trolley hire, shop, practice facilities
Visitors welcome
Handicap certificate required
Societies welcome by prior arrangement
The George Hotel, 5 Stamford Road, Weldon, Northamptonshire
☎ 01536 267810

RUSHDEN GOLF CLUB

Kimbolton Road, Chelveston, Wellingborough, Northamptonshire NN9 6AN
☎ 01933 418511 **Map 8, F7**
A45, 2 miles E of Higham Ferrers
Founded 1919
An undulating parkland course crossed by a stream.
10 holes, 6335 yards
par 71, S.S.S 70
Green fees £18
Catering, changing room/showers, bar
Visitors welcome weekdays with restrictions
Societies welcome by prior arrangement

STAVERTON PARK GOLF CLUB

Staverton Park, Staverton, Daventry, Northamptonshire NN11 6JT
☎ 01327 302000 Fax 01327 311428
Map 8, C7
A425, 1 mile W of Daventry
Founded 1977
A parkland course with a good challenge and plentiful views.
18 holes, 6602 yards
par 71, S.S.S 72
Designer John Harris
Green fees £25
Catering, changing room/showers, bar, club, trolley and buggy hire, shop, driving range
Visitors welcome
Societies welcome by prior arrangement

STOKE ALBANY GOLF CLUB

Ashley Road, Stoke Albany, Market Harborough, Northamptonshire LE16 8PL
☎ 01858 535208 Fax 01858 535505
Map 8, E6
info@stokealbanygolfclub.co.uk
www.stokealbanygolfclub.co.uk
Off A14, N of Rothwell
Founded 1995
Located in the Welland Valley, with fine views of the surrounding countryside, and a typically challenging Hawtree design.
18 holes, 6132 yards
par 71, S.S.S 69
Designer Martin Hawtree
Green fees £13
Catering, changing room/showers, bar, trolley hire, driving range, practice facilities
Visitors welcome
Societies welcome by prior arrangement

WELLINGBOROUGH GOLF CLUB

Harrowden Hall, Great Harrowden, Wellingborough, Northamptonshire NN9 5AD
☎ 01933 677234 Fax 01933 679379
Map 8, E7
A509, 2 miles N of Wellingborough
Founded 1893
Harrowden Hall is one of the most impressive clubhouses in English golf, with a known history dating back to 1511 and connections with the Gunpowder Plot. Early in the 18th century the house was rebuilt in its present classical style. The challenging course is of good length in rolling parkland.
18 holes, 6619 yards
par 72, S.S.S 72
Designer Hawtree
Green fees £30
Catering, changing room/showers, bar, club, trolley and buggy hire, shop, practice facilities, conference and function facilities, swimming pool, snooker
Visitors welcome weekdays – with restrictions
Societies welcome by prior arrangement

🏨 Kettering Park Hotel, Kettering Venture Park, Kettering, Northamptonshire
✆ 01536 416666

WHITTLEBURY PARK GOLF & COUNTRY CLUB

Whittlebury, Towcester, Northamptonshire NN12 8XW
✆ 01327 858092 Fax 01327 858009
Map 8, D8
A413, 3 miles S of Towcester
Founded 1992
The Grand Prix course is laid out alongside the Silverstone motor racing track, and 1905 is a reconstruction of a former course on this site. Various combination of holes can be arranged to provide different levels of challenge.
1905: 9 holes, 3256 yards, par 36, S.S.S 36
Grand Prix: 9 holes, 3339 yards, par 36, S.S.S 36
Royal Whittlewood: 9 holes, 3323 yards, par 36, S.S.S 36
Green fees £18
Catering, changing room/showers, bar, club, trolley and buggy hire, shop, driving range, practice facilities, hospitality and function suites, croquet, clay piegon shooting, archery and 9-hole short course
Visitors welcome
Handicap certificate required
Societies welcome by prior arrangement

NOTTINGHAMSHIRE

BEESTON FIELDS GOLF CLUB

Beeston, Nottingham, Nottinghamshire NG9 3DD
✆ 0115 925 7062 Fax 0115 925 4280 **Map 8, C3**
Off A52 (M1 Jct 25), 5 miles SW of Nottingham.
Founded 1923
Tom Williamson designed many of the best courses in the Nottinghamshire area, and at one time could claim to have worked on all but one of the courses within a 50-mile radius of the city centre. Beeston Fields is a charming undulating parkland course.
18 holes, 6404 yards
par 71, S.S.S 71
Designer Tom Williamson
Green fees £26
Catering, changing room/showers, bar, club and trolley hire, shop, practice facilities
Visitors welcome weekdays
Societies welcome by prior arrangement

BRAMCOTE HILLS GOLF COURSE

Thoresby Road, Bramcote, Nottinghamshire NG9 3EP
✆ 0115 928 1880 **Map 8, C3**
Off A52 between Nottingham and Derby
Founded 1981
Entertaining par-3 course – quite testing.
18 holes, 1501 yards
par 54
Green fees £7
Club hire
Visitors welcome
Societies welcome by prior arrangement – no companies
🏨 The Priory, Derby Road, Bramcote, Nottingham, Nottinghamshire
✆ 0115 922 1691

BRIERLEY FOREST GOLF CLUB

Main Street, Huthwaite, Sutton-in-Ashfield, Nottinghamshire NG17 2LG
✆ 01623 550761 Fax 01623 550761
Map 8, C2
M1 Jct 28, 2 miles W of Sutton-in-Ashfield.
Founded 1993
Undulating parkland course in the heart of the Nottinghamshire coal field. Old Hardwick Hall is visible from the 9th tee, and the 18th is the highest hole in the county.
18 holes, 6008 yards
par 72, S.S.S 69
Designer Dave Hibbert, Phil Roberts
Green fees £11.50
Catering, bar, club hire
Visitors welcome
Societies welcome by prior arrangement
🏨 Swallows Hotel, Carter Lane East, South Normanton, Derby, Nottinghamshire
✆ 01773 812000

BULWELL FOREST GOLF CLUB

Hucknall Road, Bulwell, Nottingham, Nottinghamshire NG6 9LQ
✆ 0115 977 0576 Fax 0115 976 3172 **Map 8, C3**
A661, near M1 Jct 26
Founded 1902
A public course with all the difficulties off the fairways of a true heathland course
18 holes, 5746 yards
par 68, S.S.S 68
Green fees £11
Catering, changing room/showers, bar, club and trolley hire, shop
Visitors welcome
Societies welcome by prior arrangement

CHILWELL MANOR GOLF CLUB

Meadow Lane, Chilwell, Nottingham, Nottinghamshire NG9 5AE
✆ 0115 925 8958 Fax 0115 9220575
Map 8, C3
chilwellmanorgolfclub@barbox.net
A6005, 4 miles W of Nottingham
Founded 1906
A parkland course.
18 holes, 6395 yards
par 70, S.S.S 71
Designer Tom Williamson
Green fees £20
Catering, changing room/showers, bar, trolley hire, shop, practice facilities
Visitors welcome
Handicap certificate required
Societies welcome by prior arrangement
🏨 Village Hotel, Chilwell Retail Park, Brailsford Way, Chilwell, Nottinghamshire
✆ 0115 9469422

COLLEGE PINES GOLF CLUB

Worksop College Drive, Worksop, Nottinghamshire S80 3AP
✆ 01909 501431 Fax 01909 481227
Map 11, C11
www.collegepinesgolfclub.co.uk
B6034, 1 mile SE of Worksop
Founded 1994
A (rare) contemporary heathland course with such brilliant drainage that temporary greens or tees are never used, the club priding itself on being 'the home of all year round golf'.
18 holes, 6716 yards
par 73, S.S.S 72
Designer David Snell
Green fees £12
Catering, changing room/showers, bar, club, trolley and buggy hire, shop, driving range, practice facilities
Visitors welcome
Societies welcome by prior arrangement
🏨 Lion Hotel, Bridge Street, Worksop, Nottinghamshire
✆ 01909 477925

COTGRAVE PLACE GOLF & COUNTRY CLUB

Stragglethorpe, Nottinghamshire NG12 3HB
✆ 0115 933 3344 Fax 0115 933 4567 **Map 8, C3**
A52, 5 miles SE of Nottingham
Founded 1992
Two parkland courses, partly designed by Peter Alliss, with names referring to two of the Majors. There is little similarity with St Andrews or Augusta, but the greens are big and

difficult to read.
Open Course: 18 holes, 6303 yards, par 71, S.S.S 70
Masters Course: 18 holes, 5887 yards, par 69, S.S.S 68
Green fees £15
Catering, changing room/showers, bar, club, trolley and buggy hire, shop, driving range, practice facilities
Visitors welcome
Societies welcome by prior arrangement

COXMOOR GOLF CLUB

Coxmoor Road, Sutton-in-Ashfield, Nottinghamshire NG17 5LF
✆ 01623 557359 Fax 01623 557359 **Map 8, C2**
A661, 2 miles S of Mansfield
Founded 1913
Coxmoor shares many of the championship honours in this part of the country with Sherwood Forest, only a few miles away. It is a thoroughly testing heathland course with much servere punishment awaiting thoughtless golf.
18 holes, 6571 yards
par 73, S.S.S 72
Green fees £30
Catering, changing room/showers, bar, trolley hire, shop, practice facilities
Visitors welcome weekdays, with restrictions
Handicap certificate required
Societies welcome by prior arrangement

EDWALTON GOLF CLUB

Edwalton, Nottingham, Nottinghamshire NG12 4AS
✆ 0115 923 4775 **Map 8, C3**
Off A606, 2 miles S of Nottingham
Founded 1982
A 9-hole municipal course of good length and with good supplementary facilities.
9 holes, 3336 yards
par 36, S.S.S 36
Designer Frank Pennink
Green fees £4.90
Catering, changing room/showers, bar, club and trolley hire, shop, 9-hole, par-3 course
Visitors welcome
Societies welcome by prior arrangement

KILTON FOREST GOLF CLUB

Blyth Road, Worksop, Nottinghamshire S81 0TL
✆ 01909 486563 Fax 01909 486563 **Map 11, C10**
1 mile NE of Worksop
Founded 1978
Highly regarded public course on the edge of Sherwood Forest. Good course, well maintained.
18 holes, 6424 yards
par 72, S.S.S 71
Green fees £9
Catering, changing room/showers, bar, club, trolley and buggy hire, shop, practice facilities
Visitors welcome with weekend restrictions
Societies welcome by prior arrangement

LEEN VALLEY GOLF CENTRE

Wigwam Lane, Hucknall, Nottinghamshire NG15 7TA
✆ 0115 964 2037 Fax 0115 964 2724 **Map 8, C2**
leen-jackbarker@btinternet.com
www.123.ndirect.co.uk/jb
½ mile from Hucknall town centre – follow signs for railway station.
Founded 1994
The challenge of Leen Valley is summed up in a brook, a river, and several lakes – handsome and unforgiving.
18 holes, 6330 yards
par 72, S.S.S 70
Designer Tom Hodgetts
Green fees £9.50
Catering, changing room/showers, bar, club, trolley and buggy hire, shop, practice facilities, 9-hole, par-3 course
Visitors welcome
Societies welcome by prior arrangement

MANSFIELD WOODHOUSE GOLF CLUB

Leeming Lane North, Mansfield Woodhouse, Nottinghamshire NG19 9EU
✆ 01623 23521 **Map 8, C1**
Off A60, 2 miles N of Mansfield
Founded 1973
A parkland/heathland public course.
9 holes, 4892 yards
par 68, S.S.S 65
Green fees £3
Catering, changing room/showers, bar, club hire, shop
Visitors welcome
Societies welcome by prior arrangement

MAPPERLEY GOLF CLUB

Central Avenue, Plains Road, Mapperely, Nottingham, Nottinghamshire NG3 5RH
✆ 0115 9556672 Fax 0115 9556670 **Map 8, C3**
Off B684, 3 miles NE of Nottingham
Founded 1907
Meadowland course enjoying pleasing views across the Vale of Belvoir.
18 holes, 6303 yards
par 71, S.S.S 70
Designer J. Mason
Green fees £17
Catering, changing room/showers, bar, club, trolley and buggy hire, shop, practice facilities
Visitors welcome, restricted weekends
Societies welcome by prior arrangement
🏨 Langar Hall, Langar, Nottingham, Nottinghamshire NG13 9HG
✆ 01949 860559 Fax 01949 861045
langarhall-hotel@ndirect.co.uk

NEWARK GOLF CLUB

Kelwick, Coddington, Newark, Nottinghamshire NG24 2QX
✆ 01636 626241 Fax 01636 626497 **Map 8, E2**
A17, 4 miles E of Newark
Founded 1901
A charming parkland course, hidden away behind trees. The cares of the world are readily forgotten here.
18 holes, 6457 yards
par 71, S.S.S 71
Designer Tom Williamson
Green fees £22
Catering, changing room/showers, bar, trolley hire, shop, practice facilities
Visitors welcome weekdays
Handicap certificate required
Societies welcome by prior arrangement

NORWOOD PARK GOLF COURSE

Norwood Park, Southwell, Nottinghamshire NG25 0PW
✆ 01636 816626 Fax 01636 815702 **Map 8, D2**
norwoodgolf@mail.com
www.norwoodpark.org.uk
½ mile W of Southwell, on Kirklington road.
Founded 1999
Nine further holes are under construction at this expansive, American-style layout, with big, undulating greens and plentiful water, in the grounds of a distinguished country house.
9 holes, 6666 yards
par 72, S.S.S 71
Designer Clyde B Johnston
Green fees £7.50
Catering, changing room/showers, club, trolley and buggy hire, shop, driving range, practice facilities, conference, function and wedding facilities at Norwood Hall
Visitors welcome
Societies welcome by prior arrangement
🏨 The Reindeer Inn, Westgate,

Southwell, Nottinghamshire
✆ 01636 813257

NOTTINGHAM CITY GOLF CLUB

Lawton Drive, Bulwell, Nottingham, Nottinghamshire NG6 8BL
✆ 0115 927 8021 Fax 0115 927 6916 **Map 8, C3**
M1 Jct 26, follow signs to Bulwell
Founded 1910
A municipal course, also played over by a private club. There are links with Bulwell Forest, enabling visitors to use the facilities of both courses on the same day.
18 holes, 6218 yards
par 69, S.S.S 70
Green fees £11
Catering, changing room/showers, bar, club and trolley hire, shop
Visitors welcome
Societies welcome by prior arrangement

NOTTS GOLF CLUB

Hollinwell, Kirkby-in-Ashfield, Nottinghamshire NG17 7QR
✆ 01623 753225 Fax 01623 753655
Map 8, C2
Off A611, S of Mansfield.
Founded 1887
A great course, of considerable length, with hole after hole posing a new strategic problem. The 8th, with its drive through trees over a lake, and the 228-yard downhill 13th are particularly renowned, but then the 2nd and 4th, 12th, 15th and 18th are rival candidates for star billing.
18 holes, 7098 yards
par 72, S.S.S 75
Designer Willie Park, J.H. Teylor
Green fees £45
Catering, changing room/showers, bar, trolley and buggy hire, shop, driving range, practice facilities
Visitors welcome weekdays – restrictions Friday
Handicap certificate required
Societies welcome by prior arrangement
Holly Lodge, Ravenhead, Nottinghamshire
✆ 01623 793853

OAKMERE PARK GOLF CLUB

Oaks Lane, Oxton, Nottinghamshire NG25 0RH
✆ 0115 965 3545 Fax 0115 965 5628 **Map 8, D2**
oakmere@ukgolf.net
A614, NE of Nottingham
Founded 1974
Two parkland courses with good off course facilities.
18 holes, 6617 yards, par 72, S.S.S 72
9 holes, 6407 yards, par 72, S.S.S 71
Designer Frank Pennink
Green fees £18
Catering, changing room/showers, bar, club, trolley and buggy hire, shop, driving range, practice facilities
Visitors welcome – restricted weekends
Societies welcome by prior arrangement
Travel Inn, Nottingham, Nottinghamshire
✆ 0115 951 9971 Fax 0115 977 0113

RADCLIFFE-ON-TRENT GOLF CLUB

Dewberry Lane, Cropwell Road, Radcliffe-on-Trent, Nottinghamshire NG12 2JH
✆ 0115 933 3000 Fax 0115 911 6991 **Map 8, D3**
A52, E of Nottingham
Founded 1909
A flat course in the Trent Valley with many interesting and testing holes.
18 holes, 6381 yards
par 70, S.S.S 71
Designer Tom Williamson
Green fees £23
Catering, changing room/showers, bar, club and trolley hire, shop, practice facilities
Visitors welcome with restrictions
Societies welcome by prior arrangement

RAMSDALE PARK GOLF CENTRE

Oxton Road, Calverton, Nottinghamshire NG14 6NU
✆ 0115 965 5600 Fax 0115 965 4105 **Map 8, D2**
ramsdale@burhillgolf.net
www.burhillgolf.net
B6386, 10 miles NE of Nottingham
Founded 1992
One of the best pay-and-play tests in the country, with splendid views from the hilly ground. The par-5 15th involves an intimidating carry over water and dangerous rough.
High Course: 18 holes, 6546 yards, par 71, S.S.S 71
Low Course: 18 holes, 2844 yards, par 54,
Designer Hawtree
Green fees £18.50
Catering, changing room/showers, bar, club, trolley and buggy hire, shop, driving range
Visitors welcome
Societies welcome by prior arrangement
Premier Lodge, Nottingham North, Mansfield Road, Arnold, Nottinghamshire NG5 6BH
✆ 0870 7001532

RETFORD GOLF CLUB

Brecks Road, Ordsall, Retford, Nottinghamshire DN22 7UA
✆ 01777 703733 Fax 01777 710412
Map 11, C10
A620, 1½ miles S Retford
Founded 1921
A parkland course designed by the ubiquitous Tom Williamson.
18 holes, 6409 yards
par 72, S.S.S 72
Designer Tom Williamson
Green fees £15
Catering, changing room/showers, bar, club, trolley and buggy hire, shop, practice facilities
Visitors welcome weekdays
Societies welcome by prior arrangement

RUDDINGTON GRANGE GOLF CLUB

Wilford Road, Ruddington, Nottingham, Nottinghamshire NG11 6NB
✆ 0115 984 6141 Fax 0115 984 5165 **Map 8, C3**
A52/A60, 5 miles S of Nottingham.
Founded 1988
A parkland course on which the majority of holes are troubled in some way by water.
18 holes, 6543 yards
par 72, S.S.S 72
Green fees £16
Catering, changing room/showers, bar, trolley hire, shop, driving range, practice facilities
Visitors welcome
Handicap certificate required
Societies welcome by prior arrangement

RUFFORD PARK GOLF CENTRE

Rufford Lane, Rufford, Newark, Nottinghamshire NG22 9DG
✆ 01623 825253 Fax 01623 825254
Map 8, D1
enquiries@ruffordpark.co.uk
Off A614, 2 miles S of Ollerton roundabout
Founded 1993
Set in the heart of Sherwood Forest, with glorious views of Rufford Abbey and Lake, the course is built on sandy soil, giving fine winter golf.
18 holes, 6200 yards
par 69, S.S.S 69
Green fees £15
Catering, changing room/showers, bar, club, trolley and buggy hire, shop, driving range, practice facilities, function, wedding, conference facilities

Visitors welcome, restricted weekends
Societies welcome by prior arrangement
The Grand St Leger Hotel, Bennethorpe, Doncaster, East Yorkshire DN2 6AX
01302 364111

RUSHCLIFFE GOLF CLUB

Stocking Lane, East Leake, Nottinghamshire LE12 5RL
01509 852701 Fax 01509 852688
Map 8, C3
rushcliffegc@netscapeonline.co.uk
M1 Jct 24, 5 miles E of Kegworth
Founded 1910
Attractive parkland course in the Nottingham hinterland.
18 holes, 6009 yards
par 70, S.S.S 69
Green fees £25
Catering, changing room/showers, bar, shop, driving range, practice facilities
Visitors welcome, with restrictions
Handicap certificate required
Societies welcome by prior arrangement

SERLBY PARK GOLF CLUB

Serlby, Nottinghamshire DN10 6BA
01777 818268 **Map 11, C10**
Between A614 and A638, S of Bawtry
Founded 1906
A private members' club with a short parkland course.
9 holes, 5370 yards
par 66, S.S.S 66
Catering, changing room/showers, bar
Visitors welcome only as members' guests
Societies welcome by prior arrangement

SHERWOOD FOREST GOLF CLUB

Eakring Road, Mansfield, Nottinghamshire NG18 3EW
01623 626689 Fax 01623 420412
Map 8, D1
sherwood@forest43.freeserve.co.uk
A617, 2 miles E of Mansfield
Founded 1895
Sherwood Forest has, undoubtedly, one of the best collections of par 4s in the land, with seven playing to 400 yards or longer, and the run from the 11th to the 14th stretching a mile between them – all but two yards! Visually, its woodland setting contributes an equally lasting impression.
18 holes, 6849 yards
par 71, S.S.S 74
Designer Harry Colt, James Braid
Green fees £40
Catering, changing room/showers, bar, trolley hire, shop, practice facilities, snooker
Visitors welcome weekdays
Handicap certificate required
Societies welcome by prior arrangement

SOUTHWELL GOLF CLUB

Southwell Race Course, Rolleston, Newark, Nottinghamshire NG25 0TS
01636 815294 Fax 01636 812271
Map 8, D2
A617, 6 miles W of Newark
Founded 1993
A parkland course adjacent to Southwell Race Course, close to the enchanting little town of Southwell, dominated by its very attractive Minster.
18 holes, 5763 yards
par 70, S.S.S 68
Green fees £15
Shop
Visitors welcome
Societies welcome by prior arrangement

SPRINGWATER GOLF CLUB

Moor Lane, Calverton, Nottingham, Nottinghamshire NG14 6FZ
0115 965 2129 **Map 8, D2**
Off A6097, between Lowdham and Oxton.
Founded 1991
A parkland course with delightful views over the Trent Valley.
9 holes, 3203 yards
par 72, S.S.S 71
Green fees £9
Catering, changing room/showers, bar, club, trolley and buggy hire, shop, driving range
Visitors welcome
Societies welcome by prior arrangement

STANTON-ON-THE-WOLDS GOLF CLUB

Golf Road, Stanton-on-the-Wolds, Nottingham, Nottinghamshire NG12 5BH
0115 9374885 Fax 0115 9374885
Map 8, D3
1 mile W of A606, 7 miles SE of Nottingham
Founded 1906
A stream enlivens this parkland course.
18 holes, 6437 yards
par 73, S.S.S 71
Designer Tom Williamson
Green fees £23
Catering, changing room/showers, bar, trolley hire, shop, practice facilities
Visitors welcome weekdays
Handicap certificate required
Societies welcome by prior arrangement
Rufford Hotel, 53 Melton Road, West Bridgford, Nottingham, Nottinghamshire
0115 9814202

TRENT LOCK GOLF CENTRE

Lock Lane, Sawley, Long Eaton, Nottinghamshire NG10 3DD
0115 946 4398 Fax 0115 946 1183 **Map 8, C3**
M1 Jct 25, S of Long Eaton
Founded 1991
With 3 holes running alongside the River Trent and a number of other water hazards, the main course is quite testing.
18 holes, 5730 yards, par 69, S.S.S 68
9 holes, 2908 yards, par 36,
Green fees £12.50
Catering, changing room/showers, bar, club, trolley and buggy hire, shop, driving range, practice facilities
Visitors welcome
Societies welcome by prior arrangement

WOLLATON PARK GOLF CLUB

Lime Tree Avenue, Wollaton Park, Nottingham, Nottinghamshire NG8 1BT
0115 978 7574 Fax 0115 970 0736 **Map 8, C3**
wollatonparkgc@aol.com
Entrance on slip road from Derby Road (A52) onto northbound carriageway of Nottingham Ring Road
Founded 1927
Overlooked by 17th-century Wollaton Hall, the handsome course is roamed by deer.
18 holes, 6445 yards
par 71, S.S.S 71
Designer Tom Williamson
Green fees £28.50
Catering, changing room/showers, bar, club and trolley hire, shop, practice facilities
Visitors welcome
Societies welcome by prior arrangement
The Priory, Derby Road, Bramcote, Nottingham, Nottinghamshire
0115 9221691

WORKSOP GOLF CLUB

Windmill Lane, Worksop, Nottinghamshire S80 2SQ
01909 472696 Fax 01909 477731
Map 11, C11
B6034, off A57 ring road, S of

Worksop
Founded 1911
With gorse and mature trees, fast fairways and firm greens, this is a first rate heathland course.
18 holes, 6660 yards
par 72, S.S.S 73
Green fees £26
Catering, changing room/showers, bar, trolley hire, shop, practice facilities
Visitors welcome by prior arrangement
Societies welcome by prior arrangement

RUTLAND

GREETHAM VALLEY GOLF CLUB

Wood Lane, Greetham, Oakham, Rutland LE15 7NP
☎ 01780 460004 Fax 01780 460623
Map 8, F4
gvgc@rutnet.co.uk
www.greethamvalleygolf.co.uk
From A1 take B668 towards Greetham – signposted.
Founded 1990
Two 18-hole courses and a pay-and-play par-3 course in verdant Rutland countryside. Both big courses make considerable strategic use of water features, providing especially mischievous finishing holes.
Lakes: 18 holes, 6736 yards, par 72, S.S.S 72
Designer Ben Stephens
Valley: 18 holes, 5595 yards, par 68, S.S.S 67
Green fees £24
Catering, changing room/showers, bar, club, trolley and buggy hire, shop, driving range, par-3 course, conference and function facilities, archery, 4-wheel drive course
Visitors welcome
Societies welcome by prior arrangement
🏨 Barnsdale Lodge Hotel, The Avenue, Rutland Water, Oakham, Rutland
☎ 01572 724678

LUFFENHAM HEATH GOLF CLUB

Ketton, Stamford, Lincolnshire PE9 3UU
☎ 01780 720205 Fax 01780 722416
Map 8, F5
A6121, 5 miles W of Stamford
Founded 1911
An inland jewel which remains remarkably little known, despite its many excellent qualities. Two plunging holes, the par-4 4th and short 17th, have great visual appeal, but it is the strength of the longer par-4s which most attracts the good player, notably the 2nd, 11th, 13th and 16th.
18 holes, 6273 yards
par 70, S.S.S 70
Designer James Braid
Green fees £35
Catering, changing room/showers, bar, club and trolley hire, shop, practice facilities
Visitors welcome by prior arrangement
Societies welcome by prior arrangement

RAF COTTESMORE GOLF CLUB

Oakham, Rutland LE15 7BL
☎ 01572 812241 (Ext.6706) **Map 8, F4**
Off A1, NW of Stamford
Founded 1982
A private course within an active military base.
9 holes, 5767 yards
S.S.S 67
Visitors welcome only as member's guests

RAF NORTH LUFFENHAM GOLF CLUB

RAF North Luffenham, Oakham, Rutland LE15 8RL
☎ 01780 720041 (Ext 7523) Fax 7200 **Map 8, F5**
Off A6121, SW of Stamford
Founded 1975
Said by those who have played it to be the best of the courses on RAF bases, but only a few members of the public can ever find out.
9 holes, 6048 yards
par 70, S.S.S 69
Visitors welcome only as members' guests

RUTLAND COUNTY GOLF & LEISURE CLUB

Great Casterton, Stamford, Lincs PE9 4AQ
☎ 01780 460330 Fax 01780 460437
Map 8, F4
Off A1, 3 miles N of Stamford
Founded 1991
An 'inland links' set in the heart of England's smallest county.
18 holes, 6401 yards
par 71, S.S.S 71
Designer Cameron Sinclair
Green fees £25
Catering, changing room/showers, bar, club, trolley and buggy hire, shop, driving range, practice facilities, conference suite
Visitors welcome – restricted weekends
Handicap certificate required
Societies welcome by prior arrangement
🏨 White Horse Hotel, Empingham, Oakham, Rutland
☎ 01780 460221

SHROPSHIRE

AQUALATE GOLF CLUB

Stafford Road, Newport, Shropshire TF10 9JT
☎ 01952 811699 Fax 01592 825343
Map 7, F4
www.aqualegolf.f2s.com
Off A518, 1 mile E of Newport
Founded 1995
A parkland course close to Aqualate Mere, between Newport and Gnosall.
18 holes, 5659 yards
par 69, S.S.S 67
Green fees £12
Catering, changing room/showers, shop, driving range
Visitors welcome
Societies welcome by prior arrangement

ARSCOTT GOLF CLUB

Arscott, Pontesbury, Shrewsbury, Shropshire SY3 0XP
☎ 01743 860114 Fax 01743 860114
Map 7, D5
Off A488, 5 miles SW of Shrewsbury
Founded 1992
A remarkable new course, seriously challenging, and giving views to the glorious Shropshire hills, Stiperstones, Long Mynd, and Corndon.
18 holes, 6112 yards
par 70, S.S.S 69
Designer Martin Hamer
Green fees £16
Catering, changing room/showers, bar, shop
Visitors welcome weekdays
Societies welcome by prior arrangement

BRIDGNORTH GOLF CLUB

Stanley Lane, Bridgnorth, Shropshire WV16 4SF
☎ 01746 763315 Fax 01746 761381
Map 7, F5
bridgnorth-golf@supanet.com
www.18global
Through town centre following signs to Broseley. ½ mile from town centre.
Founded 1889
Quite a long course, mostly flat alongside the River Severn, but one or two holes are surprisingly hilly.
18 holes, 6675 yards
par 72, S.S.S 72
Green fees £26
Catering, changing room/showers,

bar, club and trolley hire, shop, practice facilities
Visitors welcome – restricted weekends
Handicap certificate required
Societies welcome by prior arrangement
Old Vicarage, Worfield, Bridgnorth, Shropshire WV15 5JZ
01746 716497 Fax 01746 716552
admin@the-old-vicarage.demon.co.uk
www.oldvicarageworfield.com

CHESTERTON VALLEY GOLF CLUB

Chesterton, Near Worfield, Bridgnorth, Shropshire WV15 5NX
01746 783682 **Map 7, F5**
B4176, Dudley-Telford road between Bridgnorth and Wolverhampton.
Founded 1993
Renowned for its good drainage, Chesterton Valley has little need of temporary greens.
18 holes, 5671 yards
par 69, S.S.S 67
Designer Len Vains
Green fees £14.50
Changing room/showers, bar, trolley hire, shop
Visitors welcome
Societies welcome by prior arrangement
Old Vicarage, Worfield, Bridgnorth, Shropshire WV15 5JZ
01746 716497 Fax 01746 716552
admin@the-old-vicarage.demon.co.uk
www.oldvicarageworfield.com

CHURCH STRETTON GOLF CLUB

Trevor Hill, Church Stretton, Shropshire SY6 6JH
01694 722281 Fax 01694 722633
Map 7, D5
Off A49, W of Church Stretton
Founded 1898
A mountainous course on which worldy cares disappear when play takes place on the slopes of the Long Mynd, deep in the heart of A.E. Housman's Shropshire Lad *country. The views are magnificent, the situation thrilling, and holes such as the 4th and 9th fully challenge golfers of every ability.*
18 holes, 5024 yards
par 66, S.S.S 65
Designer James Braid
Green fees £14
Catering, changing room/showers, bar, shop
Visitors welcome
Handicap certificate required
Societies welcome by prior arrangement

CLEOBURY MORTIMER GOLF CLUB

Wyre Common, Cleobury Mortimer, Shropshire DY14 8HQ
01299 271112 Fax 01299 271468
Map 7, F6
www.cleoburygolfclub.com
A4117, SW of Kidderminster
Founded 1993
Three loops of 9 holes looking onto the lovely Shropshire hill country.
Badgers Sett: 9 holes, 3271 yards, par 36, S.S.S 36
Deer Park: 9 holes, 3167 yards, par 35, S.S.S 35
Foxes Run: 9 holes, 2980 yards, par 34, S.S.S 34
Green fees £18.50
Catering, changing room/showers, bar, trolley and buggy hire, shop, driving range
Visitors welcome
Societies welcome by prior arrangement

HAWKSTONE PARK HOTEL, GOLF, FOLLIES & HISTORIC PARK

Weston-under-Redcastle, Shrewsbury, Shropshire SY4 5UY
01939 200611 Fax 01939 200311
Map 7, E3
info@hawkstone.co.uk
www.hawkstone.co.uk
Off A49, N of Shrewsbury
Founded 1920
It was at Hawkstone Park that Sandy Lyle's prodigious game was nurtured. The original Hawkstone Course is a traditional parkland layout flowing through avenues of oak and birch, with magnificent views. Brian Huggett designed the Windmill Course in a more contemporary style, and it, too, enjoys lovely views over Shropshire.
Windmill Course: 18 holes, 6764 yards, par 72, S.S.S 72
Designer Brian Huggett
Hawkstone Course: 18 holes, 6491 yards, par 72, S.S.S 71
Designer James Braid
Green fees £28
Catering, changing room/showers, bar, accommodation, club, trolley and buggy hire, shop, driving range, practice facilities
Visitors welcome
Handicap certificate required
Societies welcome by prior arrangement
Hawkstone Park Hotel, Weston-under-Redcastle, Shrewsbury, Shropshire SY4 5UY
01939 200611 Fax 01939 200311
info@hawkstone.co.uk
www.hawkstone.co.uk

HILL VALLEY GOLF & COUNTRY CLUB

Terrick Road, Whitchurch, Shropshire SY13 4JZ
01948 663 584 Fax 01948 665927
Map 7, E3
Off A49, Whitchurch bypass
Founded 1975
One of the early Alliss/Thomas courses, the Emerald is a contemporary challenge in a quiet country location. Thought is required on every shot, with plenty of water in the form of ponds and streams, very often at a nagging length, while many greens are cunningly angled. Exceptionally good value.
Emerald: 18 holes, 6685 yards, par 73, S.S.S 72
Sapphire: 18 holes, 4801 yards, par 66, S.S.S 64
Designer Peter Alliss, Dave Thomas
Green fees £20
Catering, changing room/showers, bar, club, trolley and buggy hire, shop, driving range, practice facilities
Visitors welcome
Societies welcome by prior arrangement

LILLESHALL HALL GOLF CLUB

Abbey Road, Lilleshall, Newport, Shropshire TF10 9AS
01952 603840 Fax 01952 604776
Map 7, F4
Off A41, via B4379, 3 miles S of Newport
Founded 1937
The back nine, Colt's original course, enjoys the seclusion of glorious woodland and cunning golfing challenges. It is one of those places where the flowers must be smelled, the birdsong enjoyed, and the peace of rural Britain taken in. The early holes are on meadowland, interrupted by several watery pits.
18 holes, 5906 yards
par 68, S.S.S 68
Designer Harry Colt
Green fees £20
Catering, changing room/showers, bar, club and trolley hire, shop
Visitors welcome weekdays
Societies welcome by prior arrangement

LLANYMYNECH GOLF CLUB

Pant, Near Oswestry, Shropshire SY10 8LB
01691 830983 **Map 7, C4**
A483, 6 miles S of Oswestry
Founded 1933
Inspiring upland golf with spectacular views over vast areas of England and Wales. Amongst several testing par 4s, the 12th

excels, with its tight drive along a narrow hilltop and a dangerously sited green just over a ridge. The course crosses the national boundary twice and adjoins historic Offa's Dyke.
18 holes, 6047 yards
par 70, S.S.S 69
Green fees £20
Catering, changing room/showers, bar, trolley hire, shop, practice facilities
Visitors welcome subject to restrictions
Societies welcome by prior arrangement
Pen-y-Dyffryn, Rhydycroesau, Oswestry, Shropshire SY10 7JD
01691 653700 Fax 01691 650066
penydyffryn@go2.co.uk
www.go2.co.uk/penydyffryn

LUDLOW GOLF CLUB

Broomfield, Ludlow, Shropshire SY8 2BT
01584 856285 **Map 7, D6**
ludlowgolfclub@talk21.com
Off A49/B4365, 2 miles N of Ludlow
Founded 1889
Laid out around Ludlow race course this flat course is surrounded by beautiful countryside. Its sandy soil gives fine turf and excellent greens all year round. With bracken and gorse and two reservoirs coming into play it can be remarkably unforgiving. The par-3 14th is a full carry over water.
18 holes, 6277 yards
par 70, S.S.S 70
Green fees £18
Catering, changing room/showers, bar, club and trolley hire, shop, practice facilities
Visitors welcome
Societies welcome by prior arrangement

MARKET DRAYTON GOLF CLUB

Sutton, Market Drayton, Shropshire TF9 1LX
01630 652266 Fax 01630 652266
Map 7, E3
Between A41 and A529, 1 mile S of Market Drayton
Founded 1911
An undulating, well-wooded parkland course in agricultural north Shropshire.
18 holes, 6290 yards
par 71, S.S.S 71
Green fees £24
Catering, changing room/showers, bar, trolley hire, shop
Visitors welcome weekdays
Societies welcome by prior arrangement

MEOLE BRACE GOLF CLUB

Meole Brace, Shrewsbury, Shropshire SY2 6QQ
01743 364050 Fax 01743 364050
Map 7, D4
Off A49, 1 mile S of Shrewsbury
Founded 1976
A municipal course to the south of Shrewsbury with occasional water hazards.
9 holes, 5830 yards
par 68, S.S.S 68
Green fees £14
Club and trolley hire, shop, pitch & putt course
Visitors welcome weekdays
Societies welcome by prior arrangement

MILE END GOLF CLUB

Old Shrewsbury Road, Oswestry, Shropshire SY11 4JE
01691 671246 Fax 01691 670580
Map 7, C3
mileendgc@aol.com
Off A5, 1 mile SE of Oswestry
Founded 1992
Good facilities, excellent value for money, and a notably friendly welcome at this country course. Water protects the par-3 3rd and 17th, and the 542-yard 14th is the longest hole.
18 holes, 6194 yards
par 71, S.S.S 69
Designer Price, Gough
Green fees £15
Catering, changing room/showers, bar, trolley hire, shop, driving range, practice facilities
Visitors welcome
Societies welcome by prior arrangement
Moreton Park Lodge, Gledrid, Chirk, Wrexham LL14 5DG
01691 776666

OSWESTRY GOLF CLUB

Aston Park, Oswestry, Shropshire SY11 4JJ
01691 610448 Fax 01691 610535
Map 7, C3
www.oswestrygolfclub.co.uk
A5, 3 miles SE of Oswestry
Founded 1903
Easy walking parkland course with the Welsh hills as an ever-present backdrop.
18 holes, 6024 yards
par 70, S.S.S 69
Designer James Braid
Green fees £23
Catering, changing room/showers, bar, trolley hire, shop, practice facilities, snooker
Visitors welcome
Handicap certificate required
Societies welcome by prior arrangement
The Wynnstay, Church Street, Oswestry, Shropshire SY11 2SZ
01691 655261 Fax 01691 670606

PATSHULL PARK HOTEL GOLF & COUNTRY CLUB

Pattingham, Shropshire WV6 7HR
01902 700100 Fax 01902 700874
Map 7, F5
www.patshullpark.co.uk
Off A464, W of Wolverhampton
Founded 1980
Patshull was laid out by former Ryder Cup Captain, John Jacobs, in the Capability Brown grounds of what was once the home of the Earls of Dartmouth. 75 acres of lakes provide a backdrop to the course (and good fishing), while a 17th-century Doric arch forms an impressive hotel entrance.
18 holes, 6412 yards
par 72, S.S.S 71
Designer John Jacobs
Green fees £25
Catering, changing room/showers, bar, accommodation, club, trolley and buggy hire, shop, driving range, practice facilities
Visitors welcome
Handicap certificate required
Societies welcome by prior arrangement
Patshull Park Hotel, Pattingham, Shropshire
01902 700100

SEVERN MEADOWS GOLF CLUB

Highley, Bridgnorth, Shropshire WV16 6HZ
01746 862212 **Map 7, F6**
B4555, 5 miles S of Bridgnorth
Founded 1990
A hilly parkland course overlooking the Severn Valley.
18 holes, 6357 yards
par 72, S.S.S 70
Green fees £12
Catering, changing room/showers, bar
Visitors welcome weekdays
Societies welcome by prior arrangement

SHIFNAL GOLF CLUB

Decker Hill, Shifnal, Shropshire TF11 8QL
01952 460467 Fax 01952 460330
Map 7, F4
B4379, 1 mile N of Shifnal
Founded 1929
The epitome of parkland golf, laid out in the estate of a mansion house which now serves as the elegant clubhouse.
18 holes, 6468 yards

par 71, S.S.S 71
Designer Frank Pennink
Green fees £25
Catering, changing room/showers, bar, trolley hire, shop, practice facilities
Visitors welcome weekdays
Societies welcome by prior arrangement

SHREWSBURY GOLF CLUB

Condover, Shrewsbury, Shropshire SY5 7BL
✆ 01743 872976 Fax 01743 874647
Map 7, D5
www.shrewsbury-golf-club.co.uk
A49, 5 miles S of Shrewsbury
Founded 1891
A parkland course, partially undulating, with lovely views south to the Long Mynd.
18 holes, 6300 yards
par 70, S.S.S 70
Designer C.K. Cotton & partners
Green fees £19
Catering, changing room/showers, bar, trolley hire, shop, practice facilities
Visitors welcome
Handicap certificate required
Societies welcome by prior arrangement

THE SHROPSHIRE GOLF CLUB

Muxton Lane, Muxton, Telford, Shropshire TF7 5NJ
✆ 01952 677800 Fax 01952 677622
Map 7, F4
golf@theshropshire.co.uk
www.theshropshire.co.uk
M54 Jct 4, B5060 signposted to The Shropshire.
Founded 1992
With many water hazards this is a particularly challenging course, especially from the back tees.
Blue/Silver, 18 holes, 6589 yards, par 71, S.S.S 71
Silver/Gold, 18 holes, 6637 yards, par 72, S.S.S. 72
Blue/Gold, 18 holes, 6620 yards, par 71, S.S.S. 71
Designer Martin Hawtree
Green fees £18
Catering, changing room/showers, bar, club, trolley and buggy hire, shop, driving range, practice facilities, conference and function facilities
Visitors welcome
Societies welcome by prior arrangement
🏨 Holiday Inn, St Quentin Gate, Telford, Shropshire TF3 4EH
✆ 01952 527000 Fax 01952 291949

TELFORD GOLF & COUNTRY CLUB

Great Hay, Sutton Heights, Telford, Shropshire TF7 4DT
✆ 01952 429977 Fax 01952 586602
Map 7, F5
Off A442, 4 miles S of Telford
Founded 1976
A parkland course noted for its lakes and large bunkers.
18 holes, 6761 yards
par 72, S.S.S 72
Designer John Harris
Green fees £25
Catering, changing room/showers, bar, accommodation, club, trolley and buggy hire, shop, driving range, practice facilities
Visitors welcome
Handicap certificate required
Societies welcome by prior arrangement
🏨 Telford Golf & Country Club, Great Hay, Sutton Heights, Shropshire
✆ 01952 429977

WORFIELD GOLF CLUB

Worfield, Bridgnorth, Shropshire WV15 5HE
✆ 01746 716541 Fax 01746 716302
Map 7, F5
A454, 3 miles E of Bridgnorth
Founded 1991
An attractive parkland course with several lakes.
18 holes, 6801 yards
par 73, S.S.S 73
Designer T. Williams, D. Gough
Green fees £16
Catering, changing room/showers, bar, trolley and buggy hire, shop, practice facilities
Visitors welcome weekdays
Societies welcome by prior arrangement

WREKIN GOLF CLUB

Wellington, Telford, Shropshire TF6 5BX
✆ 01952 244032 Fax 01952 252906
Map 7, E4
Off B5061, S of Wellington
Founded 1905
An exceedingly hilly course perched on the end of The Wrekin. It is doubtful if there is a level lie anywhere on the course, but the stunning views are more than fair compensation.
18 holes, 5570 yards
par 67, S.S.S 67
Green fees £20
Catering, changing room/showers, bar, trolley hire, shop
Visitors welcome weekdays
Societies welcome by prior arrangement

STAFFORDSHIRE

ALSAGER GOLF & COUNTRY CLUB

Audley Road, Alsager, Stoke-on-Trent, Staffordshire ST7 2UR
✆ 01270 875700 Fax 01270 882207
Map 7, F2
business@alsagergolfclub.com
www.alsagergolfclub.com
J16 (M6)
Well-designed parkland course with an excursion into the hills on the back nine giving fine views, and needing some puff!
18 holes, 6225 yards
par 70, S.S.S 70
Green fees £35
Catering, changing room/showers, bar, club and trolley hire, shop, practice facilities, conference & function facilities
Visitors welcome, with restrictions
Handicap certificate required
Societies welcome by prior arrangement
🏨 Manor House Hotel, Audley Road, Alsager, Stoke-upon-Trent, Staffordshire
✆ 01270 884000 Fax 01270 882483

ASTON WOOD GOLF CLUB

Blake Street, Sutton Coldfield B74 4EU
✆ 0121 580 7803 Fax 0121 353 0354 **Map 7, H5**
kenheathcote.astonwoodgolfclub.co.uk
www.astonwoodgolfclub.co.uk
A4026 Blake Street at Little Aston
Founded 1994
A tough modern course with a number of exciting water holes especially on the back 9.
18 holes, 6457 yards
par 71, S.S.S 71
Designer Peter Alliss, Clive Clark
Green fees £22
Catering, changing room/showers, bar, club, trolley and buggy hire, shop, driving range, practice facilities, conference facilities
Visitors welcome
Societies welcome by prior arrangement
🏨 Fairlawns Hotel, Little Aston Road, Aldridge, Staffordshire WS9 0NU
✆ 01922 455122

BARLASTON GOLF CLUB

Meaford Road, Stone, Staffordshire ST15 8UX
✆ 01782 372795 Fax 01782 372867
Map 7, G3
barlaston.gc@virgin.net
Off A34 between Stone and

Trentham, M6 Jct 15
Founded 1974
A parkland course designed by Peter Alliss.
18 holes, 5801 yards
par 69, S.S.S 68
Designer Peter Alliss
Green fees £20
Catering, changing room/showers, bar, trolley hire, shop, practice facilities
Visitors welcome – restricted weekends
Societies welcome by prior arrangement

BEAU DESERT GOLF CLUB

Rugeley Road, Hazel Slade, Cannock, Staffordshire WS12 5PJ
☎ 01543 422626 Fax 01543 451137
Map 7, G4
From Cannock, A460 towards Rugeley. Take right turn to Hazel Slade in Hednesford.
Founded 1921
Excellent Herbert Fowler heathland course full of guile, and host to innumerable Open Championship qualifying rounds. First rate par 4s include the 5th, with a drive over wild country to an angled fairway and steep climb to a 3-level green. The 12th is a brilliant double dog-leg two-shot hole.
18 holes, 6310 yards
par 70, S.S.S 71
Designer Herbert Fowler
Green fees £38
Catering, changing room/showers, bar, trolley hire, shop, driving range, practice facilities, conference and corporate facilities
Visitors welcome – restricted weekends
Handicap certificate required – limit: 24 men, 36 women
Societies welcome by prior arrangement
🏨 Roman Way Hotel, Watling Street, Cannock, Staffordshire
☎ 01543 572121

BLOXWICH GOLF CLUB

136 Stafford Road, Bloxwich, Walsall WS3 3PQ
☎ 01922 476593 Fax 01922 493449
Map 7, G5
bloxwich.golf-club@virgin.net
M6 Jct 10, turn right for Walsall, left onto A34 for Cannock. Club *c.* 3 miles, on right.
Founded 1924
Well-reputed parkland course, tight enough to make matching par always quite an achievement. The par 3s are notable, and there are a couple of first rate par 4s.
18 holes, 6257 yards
par 71, S.S.S 71
Green fees £20
Catering, changing room/showers, bar, trolley hire, shop
Visitors welcome weekdays
Handicap certificate required
Societies welcome by prior arrangement
🏨 Fairlawns Hotel, Little Aston Road, Aldridge, Staffordshire WS9 0NU
☎ 01922 455122

BRANSTON GOLF & COUNTRY CLUB

Burton Road, Branston, Burton-upon-Trent, Staffordshire DE14 3DP
☎ 01283 543207 Fax 01283 566984
Map 8, B4
golfacademy@bramston-golf-club.co.uk
www.branston-golf-club.co.uk
Close to A38 'Burton South' exit
Founded 1975
A Jonathan Gaunt design introducing water on 12 holes. Very much the country club concept.
18 holes, 6697 yards
par 72, S.S.S 72
Designer Jonathan Gaunt
Green fees £28
Catering, changing room/showers, bar, club and trolley hire, shop, driving range, comprehensive fitness and leisure facilities
Country club
Visitors welcome, weekend restrictions
Handicap certificate required
Societies welcome by prior arrangement
🏨 Ye Olde Dog & Partridge Hotel, High Street, Tutbury, Burton-upon-Trent, Staffordshire DE13 9LS
☎ 01283 813030 Fax 01283 813178

BROCTON HALL GOLF CLUB

Brocton, Stafford, Staffordshire ST17 0TH
☎ 01785 662627 Fax 01785 661591
Map 7, G4
A34, 4 miles SE of Stafford
Founded 1894
A gentle parkland course on the outskirts of Stafford.
18 holes, 6064 yards
par 69, S.S.S 69
Designer Harry Vardon
Green fees £33
Catering, changing room/showers, bar, club, trolley and buggy hire, shop, practice facilities
Visitors welcome
Handicap certificate required
Societies welcome by prior arrangement

BURSLEM GOLF CLUB

Wood Farm, High Lane, Stoke-on-Trent, Staffordshire ST6 7JT
☎ 01782 837006 **Map 7, G2**
B5049, 4 miles N of city centre
Founded 1907
An undulating moorland course with a number of climbs.
9 holes, 5274 yards
par 66, S.S.S 66
Green fees £16
Catering, changing room/showers, bar
Visitors welcome weekdays
Societies welcome by prior arrangement

BURTON ON TRENT GOLF CLUB

43 Ashby Road East, Burton-upon-Trent, Staffordshire DE15 0PS
☎ 01283 568708 Fax 01283 544551
Map 8, B4
burtongolfclub@telk21.com
A511, 3 miles from Burton
Founded 1894
A Colt-designed parkland course on which golf is often played in the heady atmosphere generated by England's brewing capital. The round ends with an Augusta-like hole.
18 holes, 6579 yards
par 71, S.S.S 71
Designer Harry Colt
Green fees £28
Catering, changing room/showers, bar, club and trolley hire, shop, practice facilities, private meeting room
Visitors welcome, with restrictions.
Handicap certificate required
Societies welcome by prior arrangement
🏨 Newton Park, Newton Solney, Near Burton-upon-Trent, Staffordshire
☎ 01283 703568

CALDERFIELDS GOLF CLUB

Aldridge Road, Walsall WS4 2JS
☎ 01922 632243 Fax 01922 638787
Map 7, G5
www.calderfieldsgolf.com
M6 Jct 10, follow signs for Walsall Arboretum. Left at arboretum island, 2nd exit at next island. Calderfields right at next island.
Founded 1981
A tranquil course in the busy West Midlands, further enhanced by its lake views. Beware the par-4 8th, with its unforgiving approach played over water.
18 holes, 6509 yards
par 73, S.S.S 71
Designer J. Spooner, C. Andrews
Green fees £18

Catering, changing room/showers, bar, club, trolley and buggy hire, shop, driving range, practice facilities
Visitors welcome
Societies welcome by prior arrangement
Friendly Hotel, Wolverhampton Road West, Walsall, Staffordshire WS2 0BS
01922 724444

CANNOCK PARK GOLF CLUB

Stafford Road, Cannock, Staffordshire WS11 2AL
01543 578850 Fax 01543 578850
Map 7, G4
A34, ½ mile N of Cannock
Founded 1993
Quite short, but benefiting from the fine scenery of Cannock Chase.
18 holes, 5048 yards
par 67, S.S.S 65
Designer John Mainland
Green fees £9
Catering, changing room/showers, bar, club and trolley hire, shop
Visitors welcome
Societies welcome by prior arrangement

THE CHASE GOLF CLUB

Pottall Pool Road, Penkridge, Stafford, Staffordshire ST19 5RN
01785 712191 Fax 01785 712692
Map 7, G4
thechase@btinternet.com
www.crownsportsplc.com
M6 Jct 12 or 13. A449 to Penkridge, then B5012 to Cannock. Then Rugeley Road.
Founded 1994
A members' club which operates as a pay-and-play facility for visitors. The links-like course, with views to the Welsh hills, is complemented by good off-course facilities.
18 holes, 6707 yards
par 73, S.S.S 72
Green fees £14.50
Catering, changing room/showers, bar, club, trolley and buggy hire, shop, driving range, practice facilities, function and conference facilities
Visitors welcome, with restrictions
Societies welcome by prior arrangement
Quality Hotel Stafford, Pinfold Lane, Penkridge, Staffordshire ST19 5QP
01785 712459

THE CRAYTHORNE GOLF GOLF CLUB

Craythorne Road, Stretton, Burton-upon-Trent, Staffordshire DE13 0AZ
01283 533745 Fax 01283 511908
Map 8, B3
admin@craythorne.co.uk
www.craythorne.co.uk
Off A38/A5121, 1½ miles N of Burton
Founded 1975
A shortish course, but the par 3s are not easily tamed, and the par-5 14th is exacting. The Pub/Restaurant is open to the public.
18 holes, 5400 yards
par 68, S.S.S 67
Designer C. Johnson, A. Wright
Green fees £22
Catering, changing room/showers, bar, club, trolley and buggy hire, shop, driving range, practice facilities, full conference and function facilities
Visitors welcome
Handicap certificate required
Societies welcome by prior arrangement
Mill House, Cornmill Lane, Tutbury, Burton-upon-Trent, Staffordshire DE13 9HA
01283 813634

DARTMOUTH GOLF CLUB

Vale Street, West Bromwich B71 4DW
0121 588 2131 **Map 7, G5**
Off A4041, E of town centre
Founded 1910
Extraordinary old course in the heart of industrial West Bromwich, with a 617-yard par 5 to open the round, the longest opening hole in the country?
9 holes, 6036 yards
par 71, S.S.S 71
Green fees £20
Catering, changing room/showers, bar, club and trolley hire, shop
Visitors welcome weekdays
Societies welcome by prior arrangement

DENSTONE COLLEGE GOLF CLUB

Denstone, Uttoxeter, Staffordshire ST14 5HN
01889 590484 **Map 8, A3**
6 miles N of Uttoxeter
A parkland course laid out in the grounds of a public school.
9 holes, 4404 yards
par 64, S.S.S 62
Designer M.P. Raisbeck
Green fees £5
Visitors only as members' guests
Societies welcome by prior arrangement

DRAYTON PARK GOLF CLUB

Drayton Park, Tamworth, Staffordshire B78 3TN
01827 251139 Fax 01827 284035
Map 8, A5
A4091, 2 miles S of Tamworth
Founded 1897
An old parkland course now rather caught up in the trappings of the Drayton Manor Leisure Park.
18 holes, 6401 yards
par 71, S.S.S 71
Designer James Braid
Green fees £33
Catering, changing room/showers, bar, trolley hire, shop
Visitors welcome weekdays, with restrictions
Handicap certificate required
Societies welcome by prior arrangement

DRUIDS HEATH GOLF CLUB

Stonnall Road, Aldridge, Walsall WS9 9JZ
01922 455595 Fax 01922 452887
Map 7, H5
M6 Jct 12, A5 to Brownhills, A452 two miles past Brownhills.
Founded 1974
A testing heathland course with good views of Staffordshire and the City of Birmingham.
18 holes, 6661 yards
par 72, S.S.S 73
Catering, changing room/showers, bar, trolley hire, shop, practice facilities
Visitors welcome – restrictions
Handicap certificate required
Societies welcome by prior arrangement
Fairlawns Hotel, Little Aston Road, Aldridge, Staffordshire WS9 0NU
01922 455122

ENVILLE GOLF CLUB

Highgate Common, Enville, Stourbridge DY7 5BN
01384 872074 Fax 01384 873396
Map 7, F6
enville@egolfclub.freeserve.co.uk
A458, 6 miles W of Stourbridge.
Founded 1935
Since 1983 Enville has enjoyed the use of two full length 18-hole courses, arranged so that they each have nine heathland holes and nine in the woods. With two 215-yard par 3s and a number of very strong par 4s the Highgate Course is an excellent golfing test.
Highgate Course: 18 holes, 6531 yards, par 72, S.S.S 72
Lodge Course: 18 holes, 6290 yards, par 70, S.S.S 70
Green fees £30
Catering, changing room/showers, bar, trolley and buggy hire, shop
Visitors welcome weekdays
Societies welcome by prior arrangement

GOLDENHILL GOLF CLUB

Mobberley Road, Goldenhill, Stoke-on-Trent, Staffordshire ST6 5SS
✆ 01782 784715 Fax 01782 775940
Map 7, F2
Off A50, between Tunstall and Kidsgrove
Founded 1983
Laid out on the site of an old mine, an undulating course with plentiful water hazards.
18 holes, 5957 yards
par 71, S.S.S 69
Green fees £6
Catering, changing room/showers, bar, club and trolley hire, shop
Visitors welcome
Societies welcome by prior arrangement

GREAT BARR GOLF CLUB

Chapel Lane, Birmingham B43 7BA
✆ 0121 357 1232 **Map 7, H5**
M6 Jct 7, 6 miles NW of Birmingham
Founded 1961
Constructed in the 1960s at a time when there was little development in golf, a great asset, only 6 miles from the centre of Birmingham.
18 holes, 6459 yards
par 72, S.S.S 71
Green fees £30
Catering, changing room/showers, bar, trolley hire, shop
Visitors welcome weekdays
Societies welcome by prior arrangement

GREENWAY HALL GOLF CLUB

Stockton Brook, Stoke-on-Trent, Staffordshire ST9 9LJ
✆ 01782 503158 **Map 7, G2**
Off A53, 5 miles N of Stoke
Founded 1908
On hilly ground, north-east of Stoke City Centre, with good views of the Pennine foothills.
18 holes, 5676 yards
par 68, S.S.S 67
Green fees £14
Catering, changing room/showers, bar, shop
Visitors welcome weekdays
Societies welcome by prior arrangement

HANDSWORTH GOLF CLUB

11 Sunningdale Close, Handsworth Wood, Birmingham B20 1NP
✆ 0121 554 3387 Fax 0121 554 3387 **Map 7, H6**
Off A4040, NW of city centre.
Founded 1895
A parkland course in the heart of the City of Birmingham.
18 holes, 6267 yards
par 70, S.S.S 70
Green fees £30
Catering, changing room/showers, bar, trolley hire, shop, practice facilities, squash
Visitors welcome weekdays
Societies welcome by prior arangement

HIMLEY HALL GOLF CENTRE

Himley Hall Park, Himley Road, Dudley DY3 4DF
✆ 01902 895207 **Map 7, G6**
Off A449 at Himley
Founded 1979
A public course of good length, with enjoyable views from its undulating parkland site.
9 holes, 6380 yards
par 70, S.S.S 70
Designer Baker
Green fees £6.50
Catering, trolley hire, shop, driving range, practice facilities
Visitors welcome
Societies welcome by prior arrangement
🏨 Himley House Hotel, Himley, Staffordshire
✆ 01902 892468

INGESTRE PARK GOLF CLUB

Ingestre, Stafford, Staffordshire ST18 0RE
✆ 01889 270845 Fax 01889 270845
Map 7, G4
6 miles E of Stafford, M6 Jct 13/14
Founded 1977
Laid out in the grounds of the former home of the Earl of Shrewsbury, Ingestre Park is secluded and peaceful, and enjoys views over delightful countryside.
18 holes, 6268 yards
par 70, S.S.S 70
Designer Hawtree
Green fees £25
Catering, changing room/showers, bar, club, trolley and buggy hire, shop, practice facilities
Visitors welcome weekdays
Handicap certificate required
Societies welcome by prior arrangement

IZAAK WALTON GOLF CLUB

Cold Norton, Stone, Staffordshire ST15 0NS
✆ 01785 760900 **Map 7, F3**
B2056, 7 miles NW of Stafford
Founded 1992
Given its name, it could hardly be otherwise: there are streams and ponds aplenty at Izaak Walton.
18 holes, 6281 yards
par 72, S.S.S 72
Designer Mike Lowe
Green fees £15
Catering, changing room/showers, bar, trolley hire, shop, driving range
Visitors welcome
Societies welcome by prior arrangement

KEELE GOLF COURSE

Newcastle Road, Keele, Newcastle-under-Lyme, Staffordshire ST5 5AB
✆ 01782 627596 **Map 7, F2**
A525 Whitchurch road, 2 miles W of Newcastle.
Founded 1975
In open parkland, on the side of a hill close to Keele University.
18 holes, 6300 yards
par 71, S.S.S 70
Green fees £8.50
Catering, bar, club, trolley and buggy hire, shop, driving range
Visitors welcome
Societies welcome by prior arrangement
🏨 Comfort Inn, Liverpool Road, Newcastle-under-Lyme, Staffordshire
✆ 01782 717000

LAKESIDE GOLF CLUB

Rugeley Power Station, Rugeley WS15 1PR
✆ 01889 575667 **Map 7, H4**
A513, 2 miles SE of Rugeley
Founded 1969
Golfers travelling on the West Coast main line will be familar with this course, almost all of which is visible from the train: tight fairways, small greens, and a threatening river.
18 holes, 5765 yards
par 71, S.S.S 69
Visitors only as members' guests

LEEK GOLF CLUB

Cheddleton Road, Birchall, Leek, Staffordshire ST13 5RE
✆ 01538 384779 Fax 01538 384535
Map 7, G2
A520, ½ mile S of Leek
Founded 1892
Renowned for its velvet fairways and testing greens, today's course bears testament to the conditioning work put in – and prolific tree planting – over the last 40 years. Some of its previous moorland qualities survive, however. The challenge of the short holes is reflected in their rating in the stroke index.
18 holes, 6218 yards
par 70, S.S.S 70
Green fees £24
Catering, changing room/showers, bar, trolley hire, shop
Visitors welcome
Handicap certificate required
Societies welcome by prior arrangement

LITTLE ASTON GOLF CLUB

Streetly, Sutton Coldfield B74 3AN
☎ 0121 353 2066 Fax 0121 580 8387 **Map 7, H5**
manager@littleastongolf.co.uk
www.littleastongolf.co.uk
Off A454, 4 miles NW of Sutton Coldfield
Founded 1908
An aristocratic parkland course, this handsome layout continues to challenge all comers despite the relative lack of long par 4s. Abundant bunkering, cunning use of natural undulations and ungenerous greens are the main defences. The double dog-leg 10th is tough, but the lakeside 17th must be the prettiest of all.
18 holes, 6670 yards
par 72, S.S.S 73
Designer Harry Vardon
Green fees £50
Catering, changing room/showers, bar, trolley hire, shop, practice facilities
Visitors welcome weekdays
Handicap certificate required
Societies welcome by prior arrangement
🏨 Fairlawns Hotel, Little Aston Road, Aldridge, Staffordshire WS9 0NU
☎ 01922 455122

MANOR (KINGSTONE) GOLF CLUB

Leese Hill, Kingstone, Uttoxeter, Staffordshire ST14 8QT
☎ 01889 563234 Fax 01889 563234
Map 7, H3
A518, 4 miles SW of Uttoxeter
Founded 1991
A parkland course in pretty country.
18 holes, 6060 yards
par 71, S.S.S 69
Green fees £12
Catering, bar, driving range, practice facilities, fishing
Visitors welcome
Societies welcome by prior arrangement

NEWCASTLE-UNDER-LYME GOLF CLUB

Whitmore Road, Newcastle-under-Lyme, Staffordshire ST5 2QB
☎ 01782 616585 Fax 01782 617006
Map 7, F2
A53, 2 miles SW of Newcastle-under-Lyme
Founded 1908
A parkland course in undulating country close to the M6.
18 holes, 6317 yards
par 72, S.S.S 71
Green fees £26
Catering, changing room/showers, bar, club and trolley hire, shop
Visitors welcome weekdays
Societies welcome by prior arrangement

ONNELEY GOLF CLUB

Onneley, Crewe, Cheshire CW5 5QF
☎ 01782 750577 **Map 7, F3**
Off A525, 8 miles W of Newcastle
Founded 1968
A meadowland course in gently rolling country.
9 holes, 5584 yards
par 70, S.S.S 67
Green fees £20
Catering, changing room/showers, bar
Visitors welcome weekdays
Societies welcome by prior arrangement

OXLEY PARK GOLF CLUB

Stafford Road, Bushbury, Wolverhampton WV10 6DE
☎ 01902 425892 Fax 01902 712241
Map 7, G5
A449, 1 mile N of Wolverhampton
Founded 1913
An undulating parkland course beside the railway line in the suburbs of Wolverhampton.
18 holes, 6226 yards
par 71, S.S.S 70
Designer Harry Colt
Green fees £25
Catering, changing room/showers, bar, trolley hire, shop
Visitors welcome, with restrictions
Societies welcome by prior arrangement

PARKHALL GOLF CLUB

Hulme Road, Weston Coyney, Stoke-on-Trent, Staffordshire ST3 5BH
☎ 01782 599584 **Map 7, G2**
A50, 3 miles SW of Stoke-on-Trent
Founded 1989
A public course of no great length, yet enjoying the views and peculiar difficulties of rolling moorland.
18 holes, 4770 yards
S.S.S 54
Green fees £6
Shop
Visitors welcome
Societies welcome by prior arrangment

PENN GOLF CLUB

Penn Common, Wolverhampton WV4 5JN
☎ 01902 330472 Fax 01902 620504
Map 7, G5
Off A449, 2 miles S of Wolverhampton
Founded 1908
A rugged heathland course on which it pays not to stray from the fairways.
18 holes, 6462 yards
par 70, S.S.S 72
Green fees £25
Catering, changing room/showers, bar, trolley hire, shop
Visitors welcome weekdays
Handicap certificate required
Societies welcome by prior arrangement

PERTON PARK GOLF CLUB

Wrottesley Park Road, Perton, Wolverhampton, Staffordshire WV6 7HL
☎ 01902 380103 Fax 01902 326219
Map 7, F5
Off A454, 6 miles W of Wolverhampton
Founded 1990
Perhaps Wolverhampton's greatest merit is that it is only a matter of minutes by car from the city centre to the most glorious countryside. Perton is but 6 miles from the centre, and proves the point.
18 holes, 6620 yards
par 72, S.S.S 72
Green fees £12
Catering, changing room/showers, bar, club, trolley and buggy hire, shop, driving range, tennis courts, grreen bowls
Visitors welcome
Societies welcome by prior arrangement

SANDWELL PARK GOLF CLUB

Birmingham Road, West Bromwich B71 4JJ
☎ 0121 553 4637 Fax 0121 525 1651 **Map 7, G5**
secretary@sandwellparkgolfclub.co.uk
www.sandwellparkgolfclub.co.uk
M5 Jct 1, 200 yards along A41
Founded 1895
A standard scratch score two strokes above par is some indication of the considerable challenge of this fine course, miraculously secluded, despite being so close to Birmingham City Centre.
18 holes, 6468 yards
par 71, S.S.S 73
Designer Harry Colt
Green fees £31
Catering, changing room/showers, bar, trolley hire, shop, practice facilities
Visitors welcome weekdays
Handicap certificate required
Societies welcome by prior arrangement
🏨 Birmingham West Bromwich Moat House, Birmingham Road,

West Bromwich B70 6RS
☎ 0121 609 9988

SEDGLEY GOLF CENTRE

Sandyfields Road, Sedgley, Dudley DY3 3DL
☎ 01902 880503 **Map 7, G5**
Off A463 half a mile from Sedgley
Founded 1989
Extensive views south and west to the Malverns and Clee Hills.
9 holes, 3147 yards
par 36, S.S.S 70
Designer W.G. Cox
Green fees £6.50
Trolley and buggy hire, shop, driving range, practice facilities
Visitors welcome
Societies welcome by prior arrangement, no company days
🏨 Park Hall Hotel, Park Drive, Goldthorne Park, Wolverhampton WV4 5AJ
☎ 01902 331121

SEEDY MILL GOLF CLUB

Tennals Lane, Elmhurst, Lichfield, Staffordshire WS13 8HE
☎ 01543 417333 Fax 01543 418098
Map 8, A4
k.denver@clubhaus.com
www.clubhaus.com
Off A515 Lichfield-Ashbourne road.
Founded 1991
An interesting contrast with Whittington Heath, Lichfield's older and rather sterner championship course. Seedy Mill's lakes and rolling greens have more of a contemporary, almost American, feel.
18 holes, 6305 yards
par 62, S.S.S 70
Designer Hawtree
Green fees £22
Catering, changing room/showers, bar, club, trolley and buggy hire, shop, driving range, practice facilities, 9-hole, par-3 course, conference, wedding and function facilities, Restaurant open to public
Visitors welcome – restricted weekends
Societies welcome by prior arrangement
🏨 Little Barrow, Beacon Street, Lichfield, Staffordshire WS13 7AR
☎ 01543 414500

THE SOUTH STAFFORDSHIRE GOLF CLUB

Danescourt Road, Tettenhall, Wolverhampton WV6 9BQ
T 01902 751065 Fax 01902 741753
Map 7, G5
Off A41, 3 miles W of Wolverhampton
Founded 1892
Quietly hidden away in a pleasant suburb of Wolverhampton, South Staffordshire has hosted many important events, amateur and professional, over the years. A run of big par 4s from the 9th to the 14th, interrupted only by the short 11th, favours the strong player. Two drive-and-pitch holes end the round.
18 holes, 6500 yards
par 71, S.S.S 71
Designer Harry Vardon
Green fees £34
Catering, changing room/showers, bar, trolley and buggy hire, shop
Visitors welcome weekdays
Societies welcome by prior arrangement

ST THOMAS'S PRIORY GOLF CLUB

Armitage Lane, Armitage, near Rugeley WS15 1ED
☎ 01543 491116 Fax 01543 492244
Map 7, H4
A513, 1 mile SE of Rugeley.
Founded 1995
A recent parkland course.
18 holes, 5969 yards
par 70, S.S.S 70
Green fees £20
Catering, changing room/showers, bar, club, trolley and buggy hire, shop, practice facilities
Visitors welcome – with restrictions
Handicap certificate required
Societies welcome by prior arrangement

STAFFORD CASTLE GOLF CLUB

Newport Road, Stafford, Staffordshire ST16 1BP
☎ 01785 223821 **Map 7, G4**
staffordcastlegolfclub@fsmail.net
A518, W of Stafford town centre
Founded 1906
Lengthy 9-hole course in the lee of Stafford Castle.
9 holes, 6382 yards
par 71, S.S.S 70
Green fees £16
Catering, changing room/showers, bar, practice facilities
Visitors welcome – not Sunday morning
Societies welcome by prior arrangement
🏨 Garth Hotel, Moss Pit, Stafford, Staffordshire
☎ 01785 256124

STONE GOLF CLUB

The Fillybrooks, Stone, Staffordshire ST15 0NB
☎ 01785 813103 **Map 7, G3**
A34, W of town centre
Founded 1896
A pleasant parkland course overlooking the town of Stone, which apparently got its name from the pile of stones erected to cover the bodies of two early Christian princes, murdered by their pagan father.
9 holes, 6299 yards
par 71, S.S.S 70
Green fees £15
Catering, changing room/showers, bar, trolley hire, practice facilities
Visitors welcome weekdays
Handicap certificate required
Societies small parties welcome by prior arrangement
🏨 Haydon House, Stoke-on-Trent, Staffordshire
☎ 01782 711311

SWINDON GOLF CLUB

Bridgnorth Road, Swindon, Dudley DY3 4PU
☎ 01902 897031 Fax 01902 326219
Map 7, G5
B4176, 5 miles SW of Wolverhampton
Founded 1976
One of a number of recent developments in this corner of Staffordshire, close to the main industrial heartland, yet utterly rural. The views are quite outstanding.
18 holes, 6088 yards
par 71, S.S.S 69
Green fees £18
Catering, changing room/showers, bar, trolley and buggy hire, shop, driving range, fishing, 9-hole, par-3 course
Visitors welcome weekdays
Societies welcome by prior arrangement

TAMWORTH GOLF CLUB

Eagle Drive, Amington, Tamworth, Staffordshire B77 4EG
☎ 01827 709303 Fax 01827 709304
Map 8, B5
M42 Jct 10, A5 towards Amington
Founded 1975
Highly regarded public course with excellent facilities. Expansive views over Staffordshire and Derbyshire.
18 holes, 6605 yards
par 73, S.S.S 72
Green fees £13
Catering, changing room/showers, bar, club, trolley and buggy hire, shop, driving range, practice facilities, conference facilities
Visitors welcome
Societies welcome by prior arrangement
🏨 Travel Inn, Bonehill Road, Bitterscote, Tamworth, Staffordshire B78 3HQ

THREE HAMMERS GOLF CENTRE

Old Stafford Road, Coven, Wolverhampton WV10 7PP
☎ 01902 790428 **Map 7, G5**
A449, N of M54 Jct 2
One of the earliest driving ranges in the country attracted Henry Cotton to lay out its modest, but ingeniously testing, par-3 course.
18 holes, 1438 yards
par 54, S.S.S 54
Designer Henry Cotton
Green fees £6
Catering, changing room/showers, bar, club hire, driving range, practice facilities
Visitors welcome
Societies welcome by prior arrangement

TRENTHAM GOLF CLUB

14 Barlaston Old Road, Trentham, Stoke-on-Trent, Staffordshire ST4 8HB
☎ 01782 658109 Fax 01782 644024
Map 7, F3
secretary@trenthamgolf.org
www.trenthamgolf.org
A 5035, 3 miles M6 Jct 15 via A500 and A34
Founded 1894
Set on part of the Duke of Sutherland's estate, Trentham is both handsome and challenging. It hosted the 1994 English Open Mid-Amateur, and is a frequent venue for county matches. The trees and lakes which contribute to the beauty are an equal part of the design. Ecology is taken seriously.
18 holes, 6619 yards
par 72, S.S.S 72
Designer Harry Colt, Hugh Alison
Green fees £30
Catering, changing room/showers, bar, club and trolley hire, shop, practice facilities
Visitors welcome weekdays. Handicap certificate required
Societies welcome by prior arrangement

TRENTHAM PARK GOLF CLUB

Trentham Park, Stoke-on-Trent, Staffordshire ST4 8AE
☎ 01782 658800 Fax 01782 658800
Map 7, F3
A34 close to M6 Jct 15
Founded 1936
Familiar to regular travellers on the M6, who get a good impression of this rolling parkland course even at 70 mph. Like neighbouring Trentham, it is laid out in part of the former estate of the Duke of Sutherland. The opening drive, skirting a waterfall and lake, requires confident striking.
18 holes, 6425 yards
par 71, S.S.S 71
Green fees £22.50
Catering, changing room/showers, bar, trolley and buggy hire, shop
Visitors welcome
Societies welcome by prior arrangement

UTTOXETER GOLF CLUB

Woodgate Farm, Wood Lane, Uttoxeter, Staffordshire ST14 8JR
☎ 01889 564884 Fax 01889 567501
Map 7, H3
uttoxetergolfclub@talk21.com
Off A50, past entrance to Uttoxeter race course
Founded 1972
A picturesque course overlooking the Dove Valley, and racing at Uttoxeter.
18 holes, 5801 yards
par 70, S.S.S 69
Designer G. Rothera
Green fees £20
Catering, changing room/showers, bar, trolley and buggy hire, shop, practice facilities
Visitors welcome – prior booking at weekends
Societies welcome by prior arrangment
🏨 Oldroyd Guest House, 18-20 Bridge Street, Uttoxeter, Staffordshire ST14 8AD
☎ 01889 562763 Fax 01889 568916
www.page-net.co.uk/web-sites/oldroyd

WALSALL GOLF CLUB

Broadway, Walsall WS1 3EY
☎ 01922 613512 Fax 01922 616460
Map 7, G5
Off A34, 1 mile S of Walsall
Founded 1907
Perhaps taking his inspiration from Walsall's famous Arboretum, Mackenzie has here laid out a course more parkland in nature than most we associate with him – that is, before he embarked on Augusta.
18 holes, 6259 yards
par 70, S.S.S 70
Designer Alister Mackenzie
Green fees £33
Catering, changing room/showers, bar, trolley hire, shop
Visitors welcome weekdays
Societies welcome by prior arrangement

WERGS GOLF CLUB

Keepers Lane, Tettenhall, Wolverhampton, Staffordshire WV8 2DH
☎ 01902 742225 Fax 01902 744748
Map 7, G5
Off A41, W of Wolverhampton
Founded 1990
A full length course on the boundary between the industrial West Midlands and gloriously unspoiled Shropshire.
18 holes, 6949 yards
par 72, S.S.S 73
Designer C.W. Moseley
Green fees £15
Catering, changing room/showers, bar, trolley and buggy hire, shop, practice facilities
Visitors welcome
Societies welcome by prior arrangement

WESTWOOD GOLF CLUB

Newcastle Road, Leek, Staffordshire ST13 7AA
☎ 01538 398897 Fax 01538 382485
Map 7, G2
A53, 1½ miles from Leek town centre.
Founded 1923
In a quiet location with wonderful views, the course is a good test of golf, with the River Churnet affecting play.
18 holes, 6086 yards
par 70, S.S.S 69
Green fees £18
Catering, changing room/showers, bar, trolley hire, shop, practice facilities, rooms available for conferences etc
Visitors welcome
Societies welcome by prior arrangement
🏨 Abbey Inn, Abbey Green Road, Leek, Staffordshire ST13 8SA
☎ 01538 382865

WHISTON HALL GOLF CLUB

Whiston, Cheadle, Staffordshire ST10 2HZ
☎ 01538 266260 **Map 7, G2**
Off A52, E of Stoke-on-Trent
Founded 1971
Rather a good test, not exceptionally long, but full of golfing problems. The ideal retreat for sensitive adults while their brash offspring overcome the challenges of nearby Alton Towers.
18 holes, 5742 yards
par 71, S.S.S 69
Green fees £10
Catering, changing room/showers, bar, trolley hire, fishing
Visitors welcome
Societies welcome by prior arrangment

WHITTINGTON HEATH GOLF CLUB

Tamworth Road, Lichfield, Staffordshire WS14 9PW

☎ 01543 432317 Fax 01543 432317
Map 8, A5
A51, E of Lichfield
Founded 1886
Heather, gorse, birches, oaks and imaginatively positioned bunkers combine to give Whittington its considerable strength. The shortest par 4s, the 5th and 6th, require unfailing precision, while the back nine has four tough two-shotters, the 12th, 14th, 17th and 18th. Notably pretty is the sylvan setting of the 7th green.
18 holes, 6458 yards
par 70, S.S.S 71
Designer Harry Colt
Green fees £40
Catering, changing room/showers, bar, trolley hire, shop, practice facilities
Visitors welcome weekdays
Handicap certificate required
Societies welcome by prior arrangement
Swinfen Hall Hotel, Swinfen, Near Lichfield, Staffordshire WS14 9RS
☎ 01543 481494

WOLSTANTON GOLF CLUB

Dinsdale Old Hall, Hassam Parade, Wolstanton, Newcastle, Staffordshire ST5 9DR
☎ 0172 616995 **Map 7, F2**
Off A34, 1½ miles NW of Newcastle
Founded 1904
Rather an unusual course – suburban moorland. It is also unusual in the high proportion of par 3 holes, many of which are exceptionally demanding.
18 holes, 5807 yards
par 68, S.S.S 68
Green fees £20
Catering, changing room/showers, bar, trolley hire, shop
Visitors welcome weekdays
Handicap certificate required
Societies welcome by prior arrangement

WARWICKSHIRE

ANSTY GOLF CLUB

Brinklow Road, Ansty, Coventry, Warwickshire CV7 9JH
☎ 02476 621341 Fax 02476 602671
Map 8, C6
www.coventry.co.uk/anstygolfclub
1 mile from M6/M69 Jct 2
Founded 1990
The Oxford Canal, which passes through the course provides a diversion to golfers on this pretty country course.
27 holes, 6079 yards
par 71, S.S.S 69
Designer David Morgan
Green fees £10
Catering, changing room/showers, bar, club, trolley and buggy hire, shop, driving range, practice facilities, conference facilities
Visitors welcome
Societies welcome by prior arrangement
Ansty Hall Hotel, Brinklow Road, Ansty, Warwickshire
☎ 01203 612222

ATHERSTONE GOLF CLUB

The Outwoods, Coleshill Road, Atherstone, Warwickshire CV9 2RL
☎ 01827 713110 Fax 01827 715686
Map 8, B5
B4116, ½ mile S of Atherstone
Founded 1894
An undulating parkland course.
18 holes, 6012 yards
par 72, S.S.S 70
Green fees £20
Catering, changing room/showers, bar, trolley hire
Visitors welcome weekdays, with restrictions
Societies welcome by prior arrangement

THE BELFRY

Lichfield Road, Wishaw, Warwickshire B76 9PR
☎ 01675 470301 Fax 01675 470174
Map 8, A5
enquiries@thebelfry.com
www.thebelfry.com
A446, 2 miles from M42 Jct 9
Founded 1976
See Top 50 Courses, page 11
Brabazon: 18 holes, 7118 yards, par 72, S.S.S 74
Designer Peter Alliss, Dave Thomas
PGA National: 18 holes, 7053 yards, par 72, S.S.S 74
Designer Dave Thomas
Derby: 18 holes, 6009 yards, par 69, S.S.S 69
Designer Peter Alliss, Dave Thomas
Green fees £120
Catering, changing room/showers, bar, accommodation, club, trolley and buggy hire, shop, driving range, practice facilities, full hotel facilities, extensive conference and function facilities
Visitors welcome
Handicap certificate required
Societies welcome by prior arrangement
De Vere Belfry Hotel, Wishaw, Warwickshire
☎ 01675 470301

BIDFORD GRANGE GOLF CLUB

Stratford Road, Bidford-on-Avon, Warwickshire B50 4LY
☎ 01789 490319 Fax 01789 778184
Map 8, A8
B439, W of Stratford-upon-Avon
Founded 1992
A course of immense length with plenty of water hazards.
18 holes, 7233 yards
par 72, S.S.S 74
Designer Howard Swan, Paul Tillman
Green fees £12
Catering, changing room/showers, bar, accommodation, club, trolley and buggy hire, shop, driving range, fishing
Visitors welcome
Societies welcome by prior arrangment
Bidford Grange, Stratford Road, Bidford-on-Avon, Warwickshire
☎ 01789 490319 Fax 01789 778184

BOLDMERE GOLF CLUB

Monmouth Drive, Sutton Coldfield, Birmingham BJ3 6JR
☎ 0121 354 3379 **Map 8, A5**
1 mile W of Sutton Coldfield
Founded 1936
A pretty parkland course alongside a lake, with an abundance of short holes.
18 holes, 4463 yards
par 63, S.S.S 62
Green fees £9
Catering, changing room/showers, bar, club and trolley hire, shop
Visitors welcome
Societies welcome by prior arrangment

BRAMCOTE WATERS GOLF CLUB

Bazzard Road, Bramcote, Nuneaton, Warwickshire CV11 6QJ
☎ 01455 220807 Fax 01203 388776
Map 8, C6
Off B4114, 4 miles SE of Nuneaton
Founded 1995
A short pay and play course.
9 holes, 4995 yards
par 66, S.S.S 64
Designer David Snell
Green fees £10
Visitors welcome
Societies welcome by prior arrangement

CITY OF COVENTRY (BRANDON WOOD) GOLF CLUB

Brandon Lane, Coventry, Warwickshire CV8 3GQ
☎ 024 7654 3141 Fax 024 76545108
Map 8, C6

Off A45, 6 miles SE of Coventry
Founded 1977
A long public course running beside the River Avon.
18 holes, 6610 yards
par 72, S.S.S 72
Designer Frank Pennink
Green fees £8.45
Catering, changing room/showers, bar, club, trolley and buggy hire, shop, driving range, practice facilities
Visitors welcome
Societies welcome by prior arrangement

COPT HEATH GOLF CLUB

1220 Warwick Road, Knowle, Solihull B93 9LN
✆ 01564 772650 Fax 01564 771022
Map 8, A6
A 4141 2 miles S of Solihull
Founded 1907
Copt Heath is one of the strongest courses in the area, with 100 or so bunkers dominating play throughout the round. It is a handsome course, too, with trees lining many fairways, frequently thwarting the ambitions of the wayward. The start is daunting, with two meaty par 4s in succession.
18 holes, 6517 yards
par 71, S.S.S 71
Designer Harry Vardon, Harry Colt
Green fees £40
Catering, changing room/showers, bar, trolley and buggy hire, shop, driving range
Visitors welcome weekdays
Handicap certificate required
Societies by prior arrangement

COVENTRY GOLF CLUB

St Martins Road, Finham Park, Coventry, Warwickshire CV3 6RJ
✆ 024 7641 1123 Fax 024 7669 0131 **Map 8, B6**
A444/B4113, 2 miles S of Coventry
Founded 1887
Coventry's standing is reflected in its staging of the 1960 PGA Championship, 1988 PGA Assistants' Championship and 1993 Club Professionals' Championship, amongst other events. The course's length comes mostly from its having five par 5s, but the 15th and 17th are both par 3s well over 200 yards long.
18 holes, 6601 yards
par 73, S.S.S 73
Designer Harry Vardon, Hawtree
Green fees £35
Catering, changing room/showers, bar, shop
Visitors welcome weekdays
Handicap certificate required
Societies welcome by prior arrangement

COVENTRY HEARSALL GOLF CLUB

Beechwood Avenue, Coventry, Warwickshire CV5 6DF
✆ 024 76713470 Fax 024 7669 1534
Map 8, B6
Off A45, 1½ miles S of Coventry
Founded 1894
A gentle parkland course.
18 holes, 6005 yards
par 70, S.S.S 69
Green fees £25
Catering, changing room/showers, bar, shop
Visitors welcome weekdays
Societies welcome by prior arrangement

EDGBASTON GOLF CLUB

Church Road, Edgbaston, Birmingham B15 3TB
✆ 0121 454 1736 Fax 0121 454 2395 **Map 7, H6**
Off A38, 1½ miles S of Birmingham
Founded 1896
A place of remarkable seclusion and beauty only 2 miles from Birmingham City Centre. Colt utilised the fine specimen trees of Capability Brown's Edgbaston Park to give each hole great charm, and the 12th and 13th, running alongside a lake, are particularly handsome. That 13th is also a tactical gem.
18 holes, 6106 yards
par 69, S.S.S 69
Designer Harry Colt
Green fees £37.50
Catering, changing room/showers, bar, club, trolley and buggy hire, shop
Visitors welcome
Handicap certificate required
Societies welcome by prior arrangement

MARRIOTT FOREST OF ARDEN HOTEL GOLF CLUB

Maxstoke Lane, Meriden, Coventry, Warwickshire CV7 7HR
✆ 01676 522335 Fax 01676 523711
Map 8, B6
Off A45, 9 miles W of Coventry
Founded 1970
The Arden is a regular venue on the European Tour, a course of two very different characters. The front nine is on level ground punctuated by trout ponds, but the back nine has the freedom of a historic and gorgeous deer park, the 12th, 16th and 17th holes standing out.
Arden: 18 holes, 7173 yards, par 72, S.S.S 73
Designer Donald Steel
Aylesford: 18 holes, 6525 yards, par 72, S.S.S 71
Green fees £35
Catering, changing room/showers, bar, accommodation, club, trolley and buggy hire, shop, driving range, practice facilities, full hotel facilities
Visitors welcome weekdays
Societies welcome by prior arrangement
🏨 Marriott Forest of Arden Hotel, Maxstoke Lane, Meriden, Coventry, Warwickshire CV7 7HR
✆ 01676 522335

HARBORNE CHURCH FARM GOLF CLUB

Vicarage Road, Harborne, Birmingham B17 0SN
✆ 0121 427 1204 Fax 0121 428 3126 **Map 7, G6**
www.learnaboutgolf.co.uk
Off A4040, SW of city centre
Founded 1926
Quite tricky, despite its length, with a number of water hazards.
9 holes, 4882 yards
par 66, S.S.S 64
Green fees £6
Catering, changing room/showers, bar, club and trolley hire, shop
Visitors welcome
Societies welcome by prior arrangement

HARBORNE GOLF CLUB

40 Tennal Road, Harborne, Birmingham B32 2JE
✆ 0121 427 1728 Fax 012127 4039
Map 7, G6
3 miles SW of Birmingham, M5 Jct 3
Founded 1893
A parkland course with pleasant views from the higher ground.
18 holes, 6210 yards
par 70, S.S.S 70
Designer Harry Colt
Green fees £30
Catering, changing room/showers, bar, club and trolley hire, shop
Visitors welcome weekdays
Societies welcome by prior arrangement

HATCHFORD BROOK GOLF CLUB

Coventry Road, Sheldon, Birmingham B26 3PY
✆ 0121 743 9821 Fax 0121 743 3420 **Map 8, A6**
mhampton@hbgc18.fsbusiness.co.uk
www.golfpro-direct.co.uk
A45, adjacent to Birmingham International Airport (M42 Jct 6).
Founded 1969
A useful public facility for those with a few hours' break from duties at the NEC, or, perhaps, those whose holiday flight has been seriously delayed.

18 holes, 6160 yards
par 70, S.S.S 69
Green fees £11.50
Catering, changing room/showers, bar, club and trolley hire, shop, practice facilities
Visitors welcome, with restrictions
Societies welcome by prior arrangement
Forte Posthouse Hotel, Coventry Road, Birmingham International Airport B26 3QW
01217 826141 Fax 01217 822476

HENLEY GOLF & COUNTRY CLUB

Birmingham Road, Henley-in-Arden, Warwickshire B95 5QA
01564 793715 Fax 01564 795754
Map 8, A7
A3400, off M40 Jct 16.
Founded 1994
A long parkland course on which visitors may book up to seven days in advance.
18 holes, 6933 yards
par 73, S.S.S 73
Designer N. Selwyn-Smith
Green fees £20
Catering, changing room/showers, bar, club and trolley hire, shop
Visitors welcome
Societies welcome by prior arrangement

HILLTOP GOLF CLUB

Park Lane, Handsworth, Birmingham B21 8LJ
0121 554 4463 **Map 7, G5**
A41, 1 mile from M5 Jct 1
Founded 1979
A parkland course in a city conservation area.
18 holes, 6208 yards
par 71, S.S.S 69
Green fees £9
Catering, changing room/showers, bar, club and trolley hire, shop
Visitors welcome
Societies welcome by prior arrangement

INGON MANOR GOLF & COUNTRY CLUB

Ingon Lane, Snitterfield, Stratford-upon-Avon, Warwickshire CV37 0QE
01789 731857 **Map 8, A7**
Off A46, 3 miles N of Stratford-upon-Avon
Founded 1993
A parkland course.
18 holes, 6575 yards
par 73, S.S.S 71
Designer David Hemstock
Green fees £20
Catering, changing room/showers, bar, accommodation, club, trolley and buggy hire, shop, driving range, practice facilities
Visitors welcome
Handicap certificate required
Societies welcome by prior arrangement
Ingon Manor Hotel, Ingon Lane, Snitterfield, nr Stratford-upon-Avon, Warwickshire
01789 731857

KENILWORTH GOLF CLUB

Crewe Lane, Kenilworth, Warwickshire CV8 2EA
01926 858517 Fax 01926 864453
Map 8, B6
info@kenilworthgolfclub.tsnet.co.uk
www.kenilworthgolfclub.co.uk
Off A46, signposted
Founded 1889
A parkland course.
18 holes, 6400 yards
par 73, S.S.S 71
Designer Hawtree
Green fees £30
Catering, changing room/showers, bar, club and trolley hire, shop, driving range, practice facilities, conference facilities
Visitors welcome
Handicap certificate required
Societies welcome by prior arrangement
Chesford Grange Hotel, Chesford Bridge, Kenilworth, Warwickshire CV8 2LD
01926 859331

LADBROOK PARK GOLF CLUB

Poolhead Lane, Tanworth-in-Arden, Warwickshire B94 5ED
01564 742264 Fax 01564 742909
Map 8, A7
secretary@ladbrookparkgolfclub.fsnet.co.uk
M42 Jct 3
Founded 1908
A typically fascinating Colt design wandering through the Warwickshire countryside, featuring undulating parkland, mature trees, flowing streams, with perhaps the 17th hole staying longest in the memory.
18 holes, 6427 yards
par 71, S.S.S 71
Designer Harry Colt
Green fees £25
Catering, changing room/showers, bar, club and trolley hire, shop, practice facilities
Visitors welcome weekdays
Handicap certificate required
Societies welcome by prior arrangement
The Limes, Forshaw Heath Road, Earlswood, Solihull, Warwickshire B94 5JZ
01564 703715

LEAMINGTON & COUNTY GOLF CLUB

Golf Lane, Whitmarsh, Leamington Spa, Warwickshire CV31 2QA
01926 425961 Fax 01926 425961
Map 8, B7
M40 Jct 13, 1½ miles S of Leamington Spa
Founded 1908
The most interesting holes are those which cross undulating ground near the club house. With holes on flatter ground at the far end of the course there is plenty of variety to the nature of the challenge.
18 holes, 6439 yards
par 71, S.S.S 71
Designer Harry Colt
Green fees £27
Catering, changing room/showers, bar, trolley and buggy hire, shop
Visitors welcome
Societies welcome by prior arrangement

MARCONI (GRANGE GC) GOLF CLUB

Copsewood, Coventry, Warwickshire CV3 1HS
024 7656 3339 **Map 8, B6**
A428, 2½ miles E of Coventry
Founded 1924
A parkland course.
9 holes, 6048 yards
S.S.S 71
Designer T.J. McAuley
Green fees £10
Catering
Visitors welcome weekdays with restrictions
Societies welcome by prior arrangement

MAXSTOKE PARK GOLF CLUB

Castle Lane, Coleshill, Birmingham B46 2RD
01675 466743 Fax 01675 466743
Map 8, B6
sec@maxstokepark.co.uk
3 miles SE of Coleshill
Founded 1898
Deep in the countryside, Maxstoke Park is unusual in having an inhabited castle in the centre of the course.
18 holes, 6442 yards
par 71, S.S.S 71
Green fees £27.50
Catering, changing room/showers, bar, trolley and buggy hire, shop, driving range, practice facilities
Visitors welcome
Societies welcome by prior arrangement
Maxstoke Castle, Castle Lane, Coleshill, Birmingham B46 2RD
01675 466743 Fax 01675 466743
sec@maxstokepar.co.uk

MOOR HALL GOLF CLUB

Moor Hall Drive, Four Oaks, Sutton Coldfield B75 6LN
☎ 0121 308 5106 Fax 0121 308 6130 **Map 8, A5**
manager@moorhallgolfclub.fsnet.co.uk
www.18gobal.com
Four Oaks, off A453.
Founded 1932
A vintage Hawtree and Taylor parkland course, the trees having matured for some 70 years, not only enhancing the environment but also enforcing the need for pinpoint accuracy. Three fairways are crossed by a stream, and the 14th is highly regarded, far and wide, for its more than considerable challenge.
18 holes, 6249 yards
par 70, S.S.S 70
Designer F. Hawtree, J.H. Taylor
Green fees £30
Catering, changing room/showers, bar, accommodation, club and trolley hire, shop, practice facilities
Visitors welcome, with weekend restrictions
Handicap certificate required
Societies welcome by prior arrangement
🏨 Moor Hall Hotel, Moor Hall Drive, Four Oaks, Sutton Coldfield, Warwickshire B75 6LN
☎ 01213 083751 Fax 01213 088974

NEWBOLD COMYN GOLF CLUB

Newbold Terrace East, Leamington Spa, Warwickshire CV32 4 EW
☎ 01926 421157 **Map 8, B7**
Off B4099, E of town centre
Founded 1973
A hilly municipal course.
18 holes, 6315 yards
par 70, S.S.S 70
Green fees £8
Catering, changing room/showers, bar, club and trolley hire, shop, indoor swimming pool, gymnasium
Visitors welcome
Societies welcome by prior arrangement

NORTH WARWICKSHIRE GOLF CLUB

Hampton Lane, Meriden Warwickshire CV7 7LL
☎ 01676 522464 Fax 01676 522915 **Map 8, B6**
Off A45, 6 miles W of Coventry
Founded 1894
A parkland course.
9 holes, 6390 yards
par 72, S.S.S 71
Green fees £18
Catering, changing room/showers, bar, trolley hire, shop
Visitors welcome weekdays
Societies welcome by prior arrangement

NUNEATON GOLF CLUB

Golf Drive, Whitestone, Nuneaton, Warwickshire CV11 6QF
☎ 024 7634 7810 Fax 024 7632 7563 **Map 8, B5**
Off B4114, 2 miles SE of Nuneaton
Founded 1905
A well wooded parkland course.
18 holes, 6429 yards
par 71, S.S.S 71
Green fees £25
Catering, changing room/showers, bar, trolley and buggy hire, shop
Visitors welcome weekdays
Societies welcome by prior arrangement

OAKRIDGE GOLF CLUB

Arley Lane, Ansley Village, Nuneaton, Warwickshire CV10 9PH
☎ 01676 541389 Fax 01676 542709 **Map 8, B5**
Off B4112, W of Nuneaton
Founded 1993
A challenging parkland course with a number of water hazards.
18 holes, 6242 yards
par 71, S.S.S 70
Designer Algie Jayes
Green fees £15
Catering, changing room/showers, bar, club, trolley and buggy hire, shop
Visitors welcome weekdays
Societies welcome by prior arrangement

OLTON GOLF CLUB

Mirfield Road, Solihull B91 1JH
☎ 0121 705 1083 Fax 0121 711 2010 **Map 8, A6**
A41, 7 miles SE of Birmingham
Founded 1893
A parkland course.
18 holes, 6232 yards
par 69, S.S.S 71
Green fees £25
Catering, changing room/showers, bar, club and trolley hire, shop
Visitors welcome weekdays
Societies welcome by prior arrangement

PURLEY CHASE GOLF & COUNTRY CLUB

Pipers Lane, Ridge Lane, Nuneaton, Warwickshire CV10 0RB
☎ 024 7639 3118 **Map 8, B5**
Off B4114, 2 miles NW
Founded 1980
Water hazards threaten a great number of holes on this parkland course.
18 holes, 6772 yards
par 72, S.S.S 72
Designer B. Tomlinson
Green fees £15
Catering, changing room/showers, bar, club, trolley and buggy hire, shop, driving range
Visitors welcome
Societies welcome by prior arrangement

PYPE HAYES GOLF CLUB

Eachelhurst Road, Walmley, Sutton Coldfield B76 1EP
☎ 0121 351 1014 **Map 8, A5**
M6 Jct 6, following signs to Lichfield, then Walmley.
Founded 1934
Pype Hayes is said to be the most played municipal golf course in England.
18 holes, 5996 yards
par 71, S.S.S 69
Green fees £11
Catering, changing room/showers, club, trolley and buggy hire, shop, practice facilities, conference facilities
Visitors welcome
Societies welcome by prior arrangement
🏨 Clover Hotel, Chester Road, Erdington, Birmingham, Warwickshire

ROBIN HOOD GOLF CLUB

St Bernards Road, Solihull B92 7DJ
☎ 0121 706 0159 Fax 0121 706 0806 **Map 8, A6**
robin.hood.golf.club@dial.pipex.com
Off B4025, 2 miles W of Solihull
Founded 1893
An attractive, well wooded, parkland course. A mid-fairway tree 80 yards short of the green adds to the difficulties of the 457-yard 4th, and another governs play on the huge par-5 13th. Streams are a factor driving on the 7th and 12th, and the closing holes are challenging.
18 holes, 6635 yards
par 72, S.S.S 72
Designer Harry Colt
Green fees £29
Catering, changing room/showers, bar, club and trolley hire, shop, driving range
Visitors welcome weekdays
Societies welcome by prior arrangement

RUGBY GOLF CLUB

Clifton Road, Rugby, Warwickshire CV21 3RD
☎ 01788 544637 Fax 01788 542306 **Map 8, C6**
B5414, 1 mile E of Rugby
Founded 1891
A compact parkland course divided

by a railway viaduct.
18 holes, 5614 yards
par 68, S.S.S 67
Green fees £20
Catering, changing room/showers, bar, club and trolley hire, shop
Visitors welcome weekdays
Societies welcome by prior arrangement

SHIRLEY GOLF CLUB

Stratford Road, Solihull B90 4EW
✆ 0121 744 6001 Fax 0121 745 8220 **Map 8, A6**
shirleygolfclub@btclick.com
M42 Jct 4
Founded 1955
An undulating parkland course, with many tricky dog-legs. Pride of place goes to the 436-yard 15th which turns through a right angle, leaving a 175-yard uphill approach to the green with a threatening out-of-bounds.
18 holes, 6507 yards
par 72, S.S.S 71
Green fees £25
Catering, changing room/showers, bar, club and trolley hire, shop, practice facilities
Visitors welcome weekdays
Handicap certificate required
Societies welcome by prior arrangement
🏨 Travel Inn, Stratford Road, Shirley, Solihull
✆ 0121 744 2942

SPHINX GOLF CLUB

Sphinx Drive, Coventry, Warwickshire CV3 1WA
✆ 024 7645 1361 **Map 8, B6**
4 miles S of Coventry
Founded 1948
A parkland course.
9 holes, 4262 yards
S.S.S 60
Green fees £8
Catering, bar
Visitors welcome weekdays
Societies welcome by prior arrangement

STONEBRIDGE GOLF CENTRE

Somers Road, Meriden, Warwickshire CV7 7PL
✆ 01676 522 442 **Map 8, B6**
A452, then B4102, M42 Jct 6
Founded 1996
A remarkably challenging course not unlike the front nine at neighbouring Forest of Arden.
18 holes, 6240 yards
par 70, S.S.S 70
Designer M. Jones
Green fees £14.50
Catering, changing room/showers, bar, club, trolley and buggy hire, shop, driving range, conference and wedding facilities
Visitors welcome
Societies welcome by prior arrangement
🏨 Strawberry Bank Hotel, Meriden, Warwickshire
✆ 01676 522117 Fax 01676 523804

STONELEIGH DEER PARK GOLF CLUB

Coventry Road, Stoneleigh, Warwickshire CV8 3DR
✆ 02476 639991 Fax 02476 511533 **Map 8, B6**
Off A46 between Warwick and Coventry
Founded 1991
As the name suggests, laid out in a handsome old deer park beside the River Avon.
18 holes, 6056 yards
par 72, S.S.S 71
Green fees £16.00
Catering, changing room/showers, bar, club, trolley and buggy hire, shop, practice facilities, 9-hole, par-3 course
Visitors welcome
Handicap certificate required
Societies welcome by prior arrangements
🏨 Eaton Court Hotel, Leamington Spa, Warwickshire
✆ 01926 885848

STRATFORD OAKS GOLF CLUB

Bearley Road, Snitterfield, Stratford-upon-Avon, Warwickshire CV37 0EZ
✆ 01789 731982 Fax 01789 731981 **Map 8, A7**
Off A46, 3 miles N of Stratford
Founded 1991
One of a number of new, almost American-style, golf courses in this part of Warwickshire, with the inevitable water hazards much in evidence.
18 holes, 6100 yards
par 71, S.S.S 69
Designer Howard Swann
Green fees £15
Catering, changing room/showers, bar, club and trolley hire, shop, driving range
Visitors welcome
Societies welcome by prior arrangement

STRATFORD-ON-AVON GOLF CLUB

Tiddington Road, Stratford-upon-Avon, Warwickshire CV37 7BA
✆ 01789 205749 Fax 01789 414909 **Map 8, B7**
www.stratfordgolf.co.uk
B4086, ½ mile E of Stratford-upon-Avon
Founded 1894
A lovely old parkland course with a very demanding finish.
18 holes, 6311 yards
par 72, S.S.S 70
Designer J.H. Taylor
Green fees £35
Catering, changing room/showers, bar, club, trolley and buggy hire, shop, practice facilities
Visitors welcome with restrictions
Societies welcome by prior arrangement

SUTTON COLDFIELD GOLF CLUB

110 Thornhill Road, Sutton Coldfield B74 3ER
✆ 0121 353 9633 Fax 0121 353 5503 **Map 8, A5**
Off B4138, 9 miles N of Birmingham
Founded 1889
A venerable club, laid out by Dr Mackenzie after the First World War on a prime piece of heathland in Sutton Park. A Roman road, the Icknield Way, crosses several holes, and Mackenzie's vision brings the customary great individuality. Unusually three par 5s follow consecutively from the 5th to 7th.
18 holes, 6549 yards
par 72, S.S.S 71
Designer Alister Mackenzie.
Green fees £25
Catering, changing room/showers, bar, trolley hire, shop, practice facilities
Visitors welcome – ring first
Handicap certificate required
Societies welcome by prior arrangement

TIDBURY GREEN GOLF CLUB

Tilehouse Lane, Shirley, Solihull B90 1HP
✆ 01564 824460 **Map 8, A6**
M42 Jct, near Earlswood Lakes
Founded 1994
A short parkland course.
9 holes, 2473 yards
par 34
Designer Derek Stevenson
Green fees £6
Shop, driving range
Visitors welcome
Societies welcome by prior arrangement

WALMLEY GOLF CLUB

Brooks Road, Wylde Green, Sutton Coldfield B72 1HR
✆ 0121 377 7272 Fax 0121 377 7272 **Map 8, A5**
walmleygolfclub@aol.com
M6 Jct 5 or 6, then A452 or A5127. Off A5127 at Wylde Green.

Founded 1902
A well-wooded parkland course with lakes affecting play on the 4th, 5th and 6th. The par-4 9th is highly regarded.
18 holes, 6585 yards
par 72, S.S.S 72
Green fees £30
Catering, changing room/showers, bar, trolley hire, shop, practice facilities
Visitors welcome weekdays
Handicap certificate required
Societies welcome by prior arrangement

WARWICK GOLF CENTRE

Warwick Race Course, Warwick, Warwickshire CV34 6HW
☎ 01926 494316 **Map 8, B7**
Founded 1886
Golf had been played at Warwick since 1886, but the current public facility was re-founded in 1971.
9 holes, 5364 yards
par 68, S.S.S 66
Designer D.G. Dunkley
Green fees £5
Changing room/showers, bar, club and trolley hire, shop, driving range
Visitors welcome, restricted Sunday morning.
Societies welcome by prior arrangement, no company days
🏨 Warwick Arms Hotel, 17 High Street, Warwick, Warwickshire
☎ 01926 492759

THE WARWICKSHIRE GOLF CLUB

Leek Wootton, Warwick, Warwickshire CV35 7QT
☎ 01926 409409 Fax 01926 408409
Map 8, B7
wwshire@waverider.co.uk
www.clubhaus.com
M40 Jct 15, A46 to Coventry, signs to Leek Wootton.
Founded 1993
Karl Litten's design of four 9-hole loops gives six possible 18-hole courses, while multiple tees allow for great variation in overall length. From the white tees each nine features seriously long par 5s and substantial par 4s, but, in recompense, there are also several genuinely short par 3s.
South/East: 18 holes, 7154 yards, par 72, S.S.S 73
Designer Karl Litten
West/North: 18 holes, 7178 yards, par 72, S.S.S 74
Green fees £45
Catering, changing room/showers, bar, club, trolley and buggy hire, shop, driving range, practice facilities, conference and wedding facilities, 9-hole short course
Visitors welcome – 7-day booking system
Societies welcome with prior booking

WELCOMBE HOTEL GOLF CLUB

Warwick Road, Stratford-upon-Avon, Warwickshire CV37 0NR
☎ 01789 413800 Fax 01789 262028
Map 8, B7
laurad@welcombe.co.uk
www.welcombe.co.uk
Exit M40 Jct 15 follow signs to Stratford on A439
Founded 1607
The hotel is a vast Victorian mansion in the heart of Shakespeare Country. It looks out onto a rolling parkland course with lakes, and to the Cotswolds beyond.
18 holes, 6288 yards
par 70, S.S.S 69
Designer T. McAuley
Green fees £40
Catering, changing room/showers, bar, accommodation, club, trolley and buggy hire, shop, driving range, practice facilities, conference & Wedding facilities
Visitors welcome, with restrictions
Handicap certificate required – limit: 28 men, 36 women
Societies welcome by prior arrangement
🏨 Welcombe Hotel, Warwick Road, Stratford-upon-Avon, Warwickshire CV37 0NR
☎ 01789 295252 Fax 01789 414666
sales@welcombe.co.uk
www.welcombe.co.uk

WHITEFIELDS HOTEL GOLF & COUNTRY CLUB

Coventry Road, Thurlaston, Rugby, Warwickshire CV23 9JR
☎ 01788 815555 Fax 01788 815555
Map 8, C6
www.whitefields/hotel.co.uk
M45/A45 junction
Founded 1992
Well drained parkland course overlooking the expanse of Draycote Water. 6th, 7th and 13th are long par 4s demanding strong hitting.
18 holes, 6233 yards
par 71, S.S.S 70
Green fees £24
Catering, changing room/showers, bar, accommodation, club, trolley and buggy hire, shop, driving range, practice facilities, extensive conference, function and wedding facilities
Visitors welcome
Societies welcome by prior arrangement
🏨 Whitefields Hotel Golf and Country Club, Coventry Road, Thurlaston, Warwickshire
☎ 01788 521800

WIDNEY MANOR GOLF CLUB

Saintbury Drive, Widney Manor, Solihull B91 3SZ
☎ 0121 711 3646 Fax 0121 711 3691 **Map 8, A6**
markharrhy@aol.com
M42 Jct 4, follow signs to Monkspath
Founded 1990
What was rather a plain and basic course alongside the M42 is being substantially upgraded under new management, with USGA-specification greens, and a major drainage project. Good things are promised.
18 holes, 5060 yards
par 68, S.S.S 65
Green fees £9.95
Catering, changing room/showers, bar, trolley and buggy hire, shop, driving range, practice facilities
Visitors welcome
Societies welcome by prior arrangement
🏨 Regency Hotel, Stratford Road, Shirley, Solihull
☎ 0121 745 6119

WINDMILL VILLAGE HOTEL GOLF & LEISURE CLUB

Birmingham Road, Allesley, Coventry, Warwickshire CV5 9AL
☎ 024 7640 4041 Fax 024 7640 7016 **Map 8, B6**
A45, 3 miles W of Coventry
Founded 1990
Although the overall length is not great there are two lakes which must be cleared with full shots on this surprisingly challenging course.
18 holes, 5213 yards
par 70, S.S.S 67
Designer Robert Hunter, John Harrhy
Green fees £9.95
Catering, changing room/showers, bar, accommodation, club, trolley and buggy hire, shop, tennis courts, swimming, fishing & gym
Visitors welcome
Societies welcome by prior arrangement
🏨 Windmill Village Hotel, Birmingham Road, Allesley, Coventry, Warwickshire
☎ 024 7640 4041

WISHAW GOLF CLUB

Bulls Lane, Wishaw, Sutton Coldfield B76 9AA
☎ 0121 313 2110 **Map 8, A5**
3 miles NW of M42 Jct 9

Founded 1995
A short parkland course.
18 holes, 5397 yards
par 71, S.S.S 66
Green fees £12
Catering, changing room/showers, bar, trolley and buggy hire, shop
Visitors welcome
Societies welcome by prior arrangement

WORCESTERSHIRE

ABBEY HOTEL GOLF & COUNTRY CLUB

Dagnell End Road, Redditch B98 7BD
✆ 01527 63918 Fax 01527 584112
Map 7, G7
A441, N of Redditch
Founded 1985
A parkland course with extensive woodlands and a number of lakes.
18 holes, 6499 yards
par 72, S.S.S 72
Designer Donald Steel
Green fees £15
Catering, changing room/showers, bar, accommodation, club, trolley and buggy hire, shop, driving range, practice facilities, fishing, swimming pool, sauna
Visitors welcome weekdays
Societies welcome by prior arrangement
Abbey Hotel, Dagnell End Road, Redditch, Worcestershire
✆ 01527 63918

BLACKWELL GOLF CLUB

Blackwell, Bromsgrove B60 1PY
✆ 0121 445 1994 Fax 0121445 4911
Map 7, G6
M42 Jct 1, E of Bromsgrove
Founded 1893
A venerable parkland course on hilly ground giving good views.
18 holes, 6230 yards
par 70, S.S.S 71
Designer H. Fowler, T. Simpson
Green fees £50
Catering, changing room/showers, bar, club, trolley and buggy hire, shop
Visitors welcome weekdays
Handicap certificate required
Societies welcome by prior arrangement

BRANDHALL GOLF CLUB

Heron Road, Oldbury, Warley B68 8AQ
✆ 0121 552 7475 **Map 7, G5**
Off A4123, W of Birmingham city centre
Founded 1946
An undulating parkland course.
18 holes, 5813 yards
par 70, S.S.S 68
Green fees £11
Catering, bar, club and trolley hire, shop
Visitors welcome restricted weekends
Societies welcome by prior arrangement

BRANSFORD GOLF CLUB

Bransford Road, Worcester WR6 5JD
✆ 01886 833545 Fax 01886 822465
Map 7, F8
info@bransfordgolfclub.co.uk
M5 Jct 7, then A4103, 3 miles from Worcester
Founded 1990
With 14 lakes, Florida has come to Worcestershire. The 16th is a genuine island hole, andf there are superb views of Worcester and the Malvern Hills.
18 holes, 6204 yards
par 72, S.S.S 72
Designer Bob Sandow
Green fees £25
Catering, changing room/showers, bar, accommodation, club, trolley and buggy hire, shop, driving range, practice facilities
Visitors welcome
Societies welcome by prior arrangement
Bank House Hotel, Bransford Road, Worcester WR6 5JD
✆ 01886 833551

BROMSGROVE GOLF CENTRE

Stratford Road, Bromsgrove B60 1LD
✆ 01527 570505 Fax 01527 570964
Map 7, G6
www.bromsgrovegolfcentre.co.uk
2 miles from M42 Jct 1
Founded 1993
It may be pay-and-play, but do not underestimate the challenge of the par-3 16th, across a lake, and the undulations of the greens.
18 holes, 5880 yards
par 68, S.S.S 68
Designer Hawtree
Green fees £14.50
Catering, changing room/showers, bar, club, trolley and buggy hire, shop, driving range, practice facilities, conference facilities
Visitors welcome
Societies welcome by prior arrangement
Hanover International Hotel, Kidderminster Road, Bromsgrove
✆ 01527 576600

CHURCHILL & BLAKEDOWN GOLF CLUB

Churchill Lane, Blakedown, Kidderminster, Worcestershire DY10 3NB
✆ 01562 700018 **Map 7, G6**
A456, 3 miles N of Kidderminster
Founded 1926
An undulating parkland course.
9 holes, 6472 yards
par 72, S.S.S 71
Green fees £20
Catering, changing room/showers, bar, trolley hire, shop
Visitors welcome weekdays
Societies welcome by prior arrangement

COCKS MOOR WOODS GOLF CLUB

Alcester Road, King's Heath, Birmingham B14 6ER
✆ 0121 444 3584 **Map 7, H6**
A435, 6 miles S of Birmingham
Founded 1926
A well wooded parkland course.
18 holes, 5769 yards
par 69, S.S.S 68
Green fees £9
Catering, changing room/showers, bar, club and trolley hire, shop, heated swimming pool, gymnasium
Visitors welcome
Societies welcome by prior arrangement

DROITWICH GOLF & COUNTRY CLUB

Ford Lane, Droitwich, Worcestershire WR9 0BQ
✆ 01905 774344 Fax 01905 797290
Map 7, G7
Off A38 (M5 Jct 5) 1 mile N of Droitwich
Founded 1897
A compact, hilly course in lovely countryside.
18 holes, 6058 yards
par 70, S.S.S 69
Designer James Braid, G. Franks
Green fees £26
Catering, changing room/showers, bar, trolley hire, shop
Visitors welcome weekdays
Societies welcome by prior arrangement

DUDLEY GOLF CLUB

Turners Hill, Rowley Regis, Worcestershire B65 9BP
✆ 01384 253709 Fax 01384 233877
Map 7, G5
Off B4171, 2 miles S of town centre
Founded 1893
A hilly course with views of the Black Country.
18 holes, 5714 yards
par 69, S.S.S 68

Green fees £25
Catering, changing room/showers, bar, trolley hire, shop
Visitors welcome weekdays
Societies welcome by prior arrangement

EVESHAM GOLF CLUB

Craycombe Links, Fladbury, Pershore, Worcestershire WR10 2QS
☎ 01386 860395 Fax 01386 861356
Map 7, G8
A4538 Evesham-Pershore road
Founded 1894
Good length parkland 9-hole course laid out in pretty countryside beside the River Avon, with views across to the Malvern Hills.
9 holes, 6408 yards
par 72, S.S.S 71
Green fees £20
Catering, changing room/showers, bar, trolley and buggy hire, shop, practice facilities
Visitors welcome weekdays
Handicap certificate required
Societies welcome by prior arrangement – not company days
Chequers Inn, Fladbury, Pershore, Worcestershire
☎ 01396 765566

FULFORD HEATH GOLF CLUB

Tanners Green Lane, Wythall, Birmingham B47 6BH
☎ 01564 824758 Fax 01564 822629
Map 7, H6
M42 Jct 3
Founded 1933
Lakes and streams dictate play on many holes, and out-of-bounds lurks on the left of each outward hole. Streams at driving length cross the 7th, 9th, and 10th. Cool nerves are needed to negotiate the water on the 2nd and 12th, and again on the 166-yard par-3 16th.
18 holes, 6179 yards
par 70, S.S.S 70
Designer James Braid, Martin Hawtree
Green fees £34
Catering, changing room/showers, bar, trolley hire, shop
Visitors welcome weekdays
Handicap certificate required
Societies welcome by prior arrangement

GAY HILL GOLF CLUB

Hollywood Lane, Birmingham B47 5PP
☎ 0121 430 6523 Fax 0121 436 7796 **Map 7, H6**
A435, 7 miles S of Birmingham
Founded 1913
A parkland course in the southern suburbs of Birmingham.
18 holes, 6532 yards
par 72, S.S.S 71
Green fees £28.50
Catering, changing room/showers, bar, club and trolley hire, shop
Visitors welcome weekdays
Societies welcome by prior arrangement

HABBERLEY GOLF CLUB

Low Habberley, Kidderminster, Worcestershire DY11 5RG
☎ 01562 745756 Fax 01562 745756
Map 7, F6
2 miles NW of Kidderminster
Founded 1924
A hilly parkland course in very attractive countryside.
9 holes, 5440 yards
par 69, S.S.S 67
Green fees £10
Catering, changing room/showers, bar
Visitors welcome weekdays
Societies welcome by prior arrangement

HAGLEY GOLF & COUNTRY CLUB

Wassell Grove, Hagley, Stourbridge, Worcestershire DY9 9JW
☎ 01562 883701 Fax 01562 887518
Map 7, G6
Off A456, 1 mile E of Hagley
Founded 1980
Fine views prevail on this parkland course set on the Clent Hills.
18 holes, 6353 yards
par 72, S.S.S 72
Green fees £22.50
Catering, changing room/showers, bar, trolley hire, shop
Visitors welcome weekdays with restrictions
Societies welcome by prior arrangement

HALESOWEN GOLF CLUB

The Leasowes, Halesowen B62 8QF
☎ 0121 501 3606 Fax 0121 501 3606 **Map 7, G6**
A456, 2 miles NE of Kidderminster
Founded 1906
A course laid out in a famous old park.
18 holes, 5754 yards
par 69, S.S.S 69
Green fees £25
Catering, changing room/showers, bar, club and trolley hire, shop
Visitors welcome weekdays
Societies welcome by prior arrangement

KIDDERMINSTER GOLF CLUB

Russell Road, Kidderminster, Worcestershire DY10 3HT
☎ 01562 822303 Fax 01562 827866
Map 7, F7
Off A449, Wolverhampton-Worcester Road
Founded 1909
A parkland course.
18 holes, 6405 yards
par 72, S.S.S 71
Green fees £30
Catering, changing room/showers, bar, club and trolley hire, shop
Visitors welcome weekdays
Handicap certificate required
Societies welcome by prior arrangement

KINGS NORTON GOLF CLUB

Brockhill Lane, Weatheroak, Alvechurch, Birmingham B48 7ED
☎ 01564 826789 Fax 01564 826955
Map 7, H6
www.kingsnortongc.demon.co.uk
Off A435, 1 mile N of M42 Jct 3.
Founded 1892
Three loops of nine holes, each finishing with a par 5, were constructed when the club moved to this site in 1970. Long par 4s feature on the Blue Course, two meaty par 5s on the Red Course, as well as water to the right of the 7th and 8th.
Blue Course: 9 holes, 3544 yards, par 36, S.S.S 36
Designer Fred Hawtree
Red Course: 9 holes, 3475 yards, par 36, S.S.S 36
Yellow Course: 9 holes, 3307 yards, par 36, S.S.S 36
Green fees £31
Catering, changing room/showers, bar, club, trolley and buggy hire, shop
Visitors welcome weekdays
Societies welcome by prior arrangement

LICKEY HILLS GOLF CLUB

Lickey Hills, Rednal, Birmingham B45 8RR
☎ 0121 453 3159 **Map 7, G6**
B4096, off A38, 2 miles N of Bromsgrove
Founded 1927
A hilly parkland course with fine views of the City of Birmingham.
18 holes, 5835 yards
par 68, S.S.S 68
Designer Carl Bretherton
Green fees £9
Changing room/showers, club hire, shop, tennis courts
Visitors welcome
Societies welcome by prior arrangement

LITTLE LAKES GOLF CLUB

Lye Head, Bewdley, Worcester DY12 2UZ

☎ 01299 266385 Fax 01299 266398
Map 7, F6
www.littlelakes.co.uk
Off A456, 3 miles W of Bewdley
Founded 1975
In a lovely part of the English countryside, with wildlife abounding, and splendid views, this parkland course has some links characteristics.
18 holes, 6100 yards
par 69, S.S.S 68
Designer M. Laing
Green fees £15
Catering, changing room/showers, bar, club, trolley and buggy hire, shop, practice facilities, conference facilites, tennis, swimming
Visitors welcome, with restrictions
Societies welcome by prior arrangement
🏨 Jarvis Heath Hotel and Country Club, Habberley Road, Bewdley, Worcestershire DY12 1LJ
☎ 01299 406401 Fax 01299 406400

MOSELEY GOLF CLUB

Springfield Road, Kings Heath, Birmingham B14 7DX
☎ 0121 444 4957 Fax 0121 441 4662 **Map 7, H6**
admin@mosgolf.freeserve.co.uk
www.wugc.co.uk/moseley
A435 (M42 Jct 3) to Kings Heath. Course adjoins outer Ring Road
Founded 1892
A proud old club with a well-wooded parkland course and several water hazards. A secluded rural retreat, yet only five miles from the centre of Birmingham.
18 holes, 6315 yards
par 70, S.S.S 71
Designer Harry Colt
Green fees £37
Catering, changing room/showers, bar, trolley hire, shop, practice facilities
Visitors – weekdays only by prior arrangement
Handicap certificate required
Societies welcome by prior arrangement
🏨 St John's Swallow, Solihull
☎ 0121 711 3000

NORTH WORCESTERSHIRE GOLF CLUB

Frankley Beeches Road, Northfield, Birmingham B31 5LP
☎ 0121 475 5721 Fax 0121 476 8681 **Map 7, G6**
northworcs@freeserve.co.uk
M5 Jct 4, A38 towards Birmingham
Founded 1907
A charming old parkland course in the leafy suburbs of south Birmingham.
18 holes, 5950 yards
par 69, S.S.S 68
Designer James Braid
Green fees £25
Catering, changing room/showers, bar, trolley hire, shop, practice facilities
Visitors welcome weekdays
Handicap certificate required
Societies welcome by prior arrangement
🏨 Outside Inn, Birmingham Great Park, Bristol Road South, Rubery, Birmingham
☎ 0121 460 1988

OMBERSLEY GOLF CLUB

Bishopswood Road, Ombersley, Droitwich, Worcestershire WR9 0LE
☎ 01905 620747 Fax 01905 620047
Map 7, F7
Off A449, 6 miles N of Worcester
Founded 1991
Extensive facilities and good views towards the Severn Valley.
18 holes, 6139 yards
par 72, S.S.S 69
Designer David Morgan
Green fees £11.50
Catering, changing room/showers, bar, club, trolley and buggy hire, shop, driving range
Visitors welcome
Societies welcome by prior arrangement

PERDISWELL PARK GOLF CLUB

Bilford Road, Worcester WR3 8DX
☎ 01905 75668 Fax 01905 756608
Map 7, F7
Off A38, N of Worcester
Founded 1981
A parkland course.
18 holes, 5297 yards
par 68, S.S.S 68
Green fees £5
Catering, bar
Visitors welcome
Societies welcome by prior arrangement

PITCHEROAK GOLF CLUB

Plymouth Road, Redditch B97 4PB
☎ 01527 541054 **Map 7, G7**
Off A448, SW of Redditch
Founded 1973
A hilly parkland course.
9 holes, 4584 yards
par 65, S.S.S 62
Green fees £7.85
Catering, changing room/showers, bar, club and trolley hire, shop, practice facilities
Visitors welcome
Societies welcome by prior arrangement

RAVENMEADOW GOLF CLUB

Hindlip Lane, Claines, Worcester WR3 8SA
☎ 01905 757525 Fax 01905 759184
Map 7, F7
Off A38, 3 miles N of Worcester
Founded 1996
A parkland course.
9 holes, 5440 yards
par 67
Green fees £10.75
Catering, bar, shop, driving range, practice facilities
Visitors welcome
Societies welcome by prior arrangement

REDDITCH GOLF CLUB

Lower Grinsty, Green Lane, Callow Hill, Redditch B97 5PJ
☎ 01527 543079 Fax 01527 547413
Map 7, G7
Off A441, 3 miles SW of Redditch
Founded 1913
A pleasantly wooded parkland course with water hazards.
18 holes, 6494 yards
par 72, S.S.S 72
Designer Frank Pennink
Green fees £28
Catering, changing room/showers, bar, club, trolley and buggy hire, shop, practice facilities
Visitors welcome weekdays
Societies welcome by prior arrangement

STOURBRIDGE GOLF CLUB

Worcester Lane, Pedmore, Stourbridge, Worcestershire DY8 2RB
☎ 01384 395566 Fax 01384 4444660 **Map 7, G6**
www.stourbridge-golf-club.co.uk
B4187, 1 mile S of Stourbridge
Founded 1892
A gently undulating parkland course, which the Guinness Book of Records use to list as "the longest yardage on the smallest acreage."
18 holes, 6231 yards
par 70, S.S.S 69
Green fees £30
Catering, changing room/showers, bar, club and trolley hire, shop, practice facilities
Visitors welcome weekdays – with restrictions. Handicap certificate required
Societies welcome by prior arrangement
🏨 Travelodge, Birmingham Road, Hagley
☎ 01562 883120

TOLLADINE GOLF CLUB

The Fairway, Tolladine Road, Worcester WR4 9BA

☎ 01905 21074 **Map 7, F7**
M5 Jct 6 towards Worcester city centre
Founded 1898
A parkland course.
9 holes, 5174 yards
S.S.S 67
Green fees £10
Catering, changing room/showers, bar
Visitors welcome weekdays, with restrictions
Societies welcome by prior arrangement

THE VALE GOLF & COUNTRY CLUB

Bishampton, Pershore, Worcestershire WR10 2LZ
☎ 01386 462781 Fax 01386 462597
Map 7, G8
www.tv.gch.co.uk
Off A538, 6 miles NW of Evesham, M5 Jct 6
Founded 1991
An 18-hole course of enormous length on rolling Worcestershire farmland with extensive views.
International Course: 18 holes, 7114 yards, par 74, S.S.S 74
Lenches Course: 9 holes, 2918 yards, par 35, S.S.S 34
Designer M. Sandow
Green fees £20
Catering, changing room/showers, bar, club, trolley and buggy hire, shop, driving range, practice facilities
Visitors welcome weekdays
Societies welcome by prior arrangement

WARLEY GOLF CLUB

Lightwoods Hill, Warley B67 5EQ
☎ 0121 429 2440 **Map 7, G6**
Off A456, 5 miles W of Birmingham
Founded 1921
Well wooded parkland course.
9 holes, 5346 yards
par 68, S.S.S 66
Green fees £10
Catering, changing room/showers, bar, club and trolley hire, shop
Visitors welcome
Societies welcome by prior arrangement

WHARTON PARK GOLF CLUB

Longbank, Bewdley, Worcestershire DY12 2QW
☎ 01299 405163 Fax 01299 405121
Map 7, F6
A456 near Bewdley
Founded 1992
A very challenging course in the heart of the Worcestershire countryside.
18 holes, 6435 yards
par 72, S.S.S 71
Designer Mike Huston
Green fees £20
Catering, changing room/showers, bar, trolley and buggy hire, shop, practice facilities, function and conference facilities
Visitors welcome, restricted weekends
Societies welcome by prior arrangement
🏨 Jarvis Heath Hotel and Country Club, Habberley Road, Bewdley, Worcestershire DY12 1LJ
☎ 01299 406401 Fax 01299 406400

WORCESTER GOLF & COUNTRY CLUB

Boughton Park, Bransford Road, Worcester WR2 4EZ
T 01905 421132 Fax 01905 749090
Map 7, F8
A4103, 1 mile W of Worcester
Founded 1898
Part of Mackenzie's layout remains, laid out in level parkland with mature trees.
18 holes, 6251 yards
par 70, S.S.S 70
Designer Alister Mackenzie
Green fees £25
Catering, changing room/showers, bar, trolley hire, shop, tennis courts, squash
Visitors welcome weekdays. Handicap certificate required
Societies welcome by prior arrangement

WORCESTERSHIRE GOLF CLUB

Wood Farm, Malvern Wells, Worcestershire WR14 4PP
☎ 01684 575992 Fax 01684 575992
Map 7, F8
Off A449/B4209, 2 miles S of Gt Malvern
Founded 1879
The oldest club in the Midlands, counting the composer Sir Edward Elgar among its early members, the Worcestershire enjoys lovely views over the Severn Valley from its rolling site on the side of the Malvern Hills. The par-4 10th is the hardest hole, 441 yards to an elevated green.
18 holes, 6500 yards
par 71, S.S.S 72
Green fees £32
Catering, changing room/showers, bar, trolley hire, shop
Visitors welcome weekdays
Handicap certificate required
Societies welcome by prior arrangement

WYRE FOREST GOLF CENTRE

Zortech Avenue, Kidderminster, Worcestershire DY11 7EX
☎ 01299 822682 Fax 01299 879433
Map 7, F6
simonprice@wyreforestgolf.com
wyreforestgolf.co.uk
Off A451 between Kidderminster and Stourport
Founded 1995
Despite the title, this is more of an inland links, an exceptionally well-drained, relatively open course. There are good views over the surrounding countryside, and the 6th, 12th and 16th are singled out for their challenge.
18 holes, 5790 yards
par 70, S.S.S 68
Green fees £10
Catering, changing room/showers, bar, club, trolley and buggy hire, shop, driving range, practice facilities
Visitors welcome
Societies welcome by prior arrangement
🏨 Swan Hotel, High Street, Stourport on Severn, Worcestershire DY13 8BX
☎ 01299 871661

NORTH ENGLAND

A huge region, with an enormous number of golf courses of extraordinary diversity, the North can boast no fewer than three Open Championship venues: Royal Birkdale, Royal Lytham and, back on the roster after a lengthy gap, Royal Liverpool. They are the greatest of the many magnificent links courses along the Irish Sea coast, a list that includes Wallasey, West Lancashire, Formby, Southport & Ainsdale, Hillside, Seascale and Silloth-on-Solway – all top-flight courses. The East Coast is somewhat different, with only one true links course in Yorkshire (Cleveland at Redcar), a brilliant specimen in Durham (at Seaton Carew), and a number of charmers on the Northumberland coast. Perversely, the finest links course on this side of the country, Ganton, is located not on the coast at all, but some 12 miles inland, in the heart of rural Yorkshire.

The North, however, is not only about its top-flight links courses. In the northern suburbs of the city of Leeds, for instance, are found, side by side, Alwoodley, Moortown and Sand Moor, three of the best inland courses in England, with Headingley, Moor Allerton, Harrogate, Pannal and a host of others almost within walking distance. A mere stone's throw from the centre of the great mediæval city of York is Fulford, one of the best conditioned courses in the country, and, for many years, a host to the world's golfing greats who used to come here to play in the prestigious Benson & Hedges tournament. Today, a classy field is always assembled for the annual European Tour visit to Slaley Hall in Northumberland, a resort which somehow manages to satisfy the contradictory needs of corporate entertainment and promotional activities with those of the golfer who wants a terrific test in glorious surroundings without the vulgarity that unfortunately so often accompanies the former.

The Pennines offer many an uncompromising moorland test, from the engaging Brampton, almost on Hadrian's Wall itself, south to Huddersfield and Hallamshire on the outskirts of two of the northern industrial conurbations. On the other side of the city of Sheffield from Hallamshire is Lindrick, one of Yorkshire's historic heathland courses, which once brought Greg Norman, when at the height of his powers, to his knees.

Add to these the inland delights of Lancashire (Bolton Old Links, Clitheroe, Fairhaven, Manchester, Ormskirk and Pleasington), the diverse and largely unsung delights of Cheshire (Caldy, Carden Park, Delamere Forest, Dunham Forest, Heswall, Mere, Prestbury, Sandiway and Wilmslow), further challenges in Cumbria (Carlisle, Penrith and Windermere, for instance), fine inland courses in Durham (with Brancepeth Castle leading a distinguished field), infinite variety in Northumberland (never less than picturesque from Hexham to Berwick), and the stunning seascapes of just about every course on the Isle of Man (with Castletown, which has water on three sides, amongst the most engaging of all our links courses). Good golf is rarely far away in the North of England.

CHESHIRE

ADLINGTON GOLF CENTRE

Sandy Hey Farm, London Road, Adlington, Macclesfield, Cheshire SK10 4NG
✆ 01625 850660 Fax 01625 850960
Map 10, F10
davidmoss@adlingtongolfcentre.com
www.adlingtongolfcentre.com
A523 London Road, ½ mile south of Poynton signs for industrial estate. Golf centre signposted.
Founded 1993
Clever par-3 course which tests the competent golfer's approach game thoroughly but does not overface the beginner. 27 further holes are planned.
9 holes, 660 yards
par 27
Designer Hawtree
Green fees £6
Catering, bar, club hire, shop, driving range, practice facilities
Visitors welcome at all times
Societies welcome by prior arrangement

ALDER ROOT GOLF CLUB

Alder Root Lane, Winwick, Warrington, Cheshire WA2 8RZ
✆ 01925 291919 Fax 01925 291919
Map 10, E10
M62 Jct 9, take A49 northbound for 800 yards. Left at lights, then first right.
Founded 1993
Well wooded course, undulating, and with several water hazards.
10 holes, 5820 yards
par 69, S.S.S 68
Designer Millington/Lander
Green fees £16
Catering, changing room/showers, bar, trolley and buggy hire, shop
Visitors welcome weekdays
Societies welcome by arrangement

ALDERLEY EDGE GOLF CLUB

Brook Lane, Alderley Edge, Cheshire SK9 7RU
✆ 01625 585583 **Map 10, F11**
B5085 Alderley Edge-Knutsford Road, ½ mile on right
Founded 1907
Challenging 9-hole layout with strong par-4 opening holes and testing short 8th.
9 holes, 5823 yards
par 68, S.S.S 68
Designer T.G.Renouf
Green fees £20
Catering, changing room/showers, bar, shop, practice facilities
Visitors welcome weekdays
Societies thursdays by prior arrangement

ALDERSEY GREEN GOLF CLUB

Aldersey, Chester, Cheshire CH3 9EH
✆ 01829 782157 **Map 7, D2**
Off A41 S of Chester
Founded 1993
A new parkland course.
18 holes, 6150 yards
par 70
Green fees £12
Bar, shop
Visitors welcome
Societies welcome by prior arrangement

ALTRINCHAM GOLF CLUB

Stockport Road, Timperley, Altrincham, Cheshire WA15 7LP
✆ 0161 928 0761 **Map 10, F10**
A 560, 1 mile E of Altrincham
Founded 1893
Pleasant old parkland course, but can be very busy – keep an eye out for errant drives!
18 holes, 6204 yards
par 71, S.S.S 69
Green fees £8.40
Shop, driving range
Visitors welcome, but wise to book

in advance
Societies by prior arrangement

ALVASTON HALL GOLF CLUB

Middlewich Road, Nantwich, Cheshire CW5 6PD
✆ 01270 628473 Fax 01270 623395
Map 7, E2
A 530, 2 miles E of Nantwich
Founded 1992
Entertaining executive-length course with enough challenge to interest the competent player.
9 holes, 3708 yards
par 64, S.S.S 59
Green fees £10
Catering, changing room/showers, bar, accommodation, club and trolley hire, shop, extensive leisure and function facilities
Visitors – adults only
Handicap certificate required
Societies welcome by prior arrangement
🏨 Alvaston Hall Hotel and Country Club, Middlewich Road, Nantwich, Cheshire CW5 6PD
✆ 01270 628473 Fax 01270 623395

ANTROBUS GOLF CLUB

Foggs Lane, Antrobus, Northwich, Cheshire CW9 6JQ
✆ 01925 730890 Fax 01925 730100
Map 10, E10
www.amtrobusgolfclub.co.uk
A559, close to M56 Jct 10
Founded 1993
Very flat, but techincally demanding with water affecting play on almost every shot.
18 holes, 6220 yards
par 72, S.S.S 72
Designer Michael Slater
Green fees £20
Catering, changing room/showers, bar, shop, driving range
Visitors welcome
Handicap certificate required
Societies welcome by prior arrangement

ASHTON-ON-MERSEY GOLF CLUB

Church Lane, Sale, Cheshire M33 5QQ
✆ 0161 976 4390 Fax 0161 976 4390 **Map 10, F10**
M60 Jct 7, A56 south, take first right (Glebelands Road), after *c.* 1 mile turn right into Church Lane
Founded 1897
Characterful course with several interesting holes on the banks of the River Mersey.
9 holes, 6146 yards
par 71, S.S.S 69
Green fees £20
Catering, changing room/showers, bar, shop
Visitors welcome weekdays except Tuesday
Handicap certificate required
Societies Thursdays, by prior arrangement

ASTBURY GOLF CLUB

Peel Lane, Astbury, Congleton, Cheshire CW12 4RE
✆ 01260 298663 Fax 01260 291000
Map 7, F1
admin@astburygolfclub.com
A34, S of Congleton turn into Astbury village, course about 1 mile further on
Founded 1922
Gentle parkland course alongside canal with two particularly challenging long holes (3rd and 12th).
18 holes, 6296 yards
par 71, S.S.S 70
Green fees £30
Catering, changing room/showers, bar, club and trolley hire, shop, practice facilities
Visitors welcome weekdays
Handicap certificate required
Societies welcome by prior arrangement

AVRO GOLF CLUB

Old Hall Lane, Woodford, Cheshire SK7 1QR
✆ 0161 439 2709 **Map 10, F10**
A5102, W of Woodford
Interesting 9-hole layout at end of British Aerospace runways. Several distinctive holes.
9 holes, 5735 yards
par 69, S.S.S 68
Changing room/showers
Visitors welcome by prior arrangement, restricted weekends and competition days
No societies

BIRCHWOOD GOLF CLUB

Kelvin Close, Birchwood, Warrington, Cheshire WA3 7PB
✆ 01925 818819 Fax 01925 822403
Map 10, E10
M62 Jct 11, follow signs for Science Park North
Founded 1979
A long, contemporary course with much strategic use of water. Despite its location, in the midst of a factory estate, there is good seclusion to most fairways. The 9th, 11th and 14th are parcticularly memorable, with their do-or-die skirmishes with water. Trees in mid fairway complicate the par-5 8th.
18 holes, 6727 yards
par 71, S.S.S 73
Designer Tom Macauley
Green fees £20
Catering, changing room/showers, bar, trolley hire, shop
Visitors welcome, but telephone first
Societies Monday, Wednesday, Thursday, by prior arrangement

BRAMALL PARK GOLF CLUB

20 Manor Road, Bramhall, Stockport, Cheshire SK7 3LY
✆ 0161 485 7101 Fax 0161 485 7101 **Map 10, F10**
North of Bramhall village centre, Ack Lane for *c.* 1 mile, right at roundabout into Manor Road, club on right
Founded 1894
A handsome parkland course on which a stream complicates the approach to the 1st and 8th greens. Testing longer par 4s occur at the 10th and 11th. The par-3 7th and 15th can be uncompromising, and the par-5 6th plays very long, albeit downhill over the run in.
18 holes, 6214 yards
par 70, S.S.S 69
Green fees £25
Catering, changing room/showers, bar, trolley hire, shop, practice facilities
Visitors welcome weekdays
Handicap certificate required
Societies welcome by prior arrangement

BRAMHALL GOLF CLUB

Ladythorn Road, Bramhall, Stockport, Cheshire SK7 2EY
✆ 0161 439 6092 Fax 0161 439 0264 **Map 10, F10**
Off A5102, E of Bramhall village centre
Founded 1905
Charming parkland course on which many holes are cleverly defended by depressions and pits. Good views towards Peak District.
18 holes, 6136 yards
par 70, S.S.S 70
Green fees £32
Catering, changing room/showers, bar, club and trolley hire, shop, practice facilities
Visitors welcome – restrictions
Handicap certificate required– limit: 24 men, 36 women
Societies welcome by prior arrangement
🏨 County Hotel, Bramhall Lane South, Bramhall, Stockport, Cheshire
✆ 0161 4559988

GARDEN PARK HOTEL GOLF CLUB

Carden, Chester, Cheshire CH3 9DQ
✆ 01829 731000 Fax 01829 731032

Map 7, D2
A 534, 10 miles south of Chester
Founded 1992
Two contrasting courses in the heart of beautiful countryside. The Cheshire course is at its best where it climbs through woodland and over a sandstone outcrop. The flatter Nicklaus course is longer and includes several strategic water holes which appeal to the good player who is prepared to take risks.
Nicklaus Course: 18 holes, 7045 yards, par 72, S.S.S 73
Designer Jack and Steve Nicklaus
Cheshire Course: 18 holes, 6824 yards, par 72, S.S.S 72
Designer Alan Higgins
Green fees £60 (Nicklaus), £40 (Cheshire)
Catering, changing room/showers, bar, club and trolley hire, shop
Visitors welcome by prior arrangement
Handicap certificate required for Nicklaus course
Soft spikes only
Societies welcome by prior arrangement
Carden Park Hotel, Chester, Cheshire CH3 9DQ
0182 9731600

CHEADLE GOLF CLUB
Shiers Drive, Cheadle Road, Cheadle, Cheshire SK8 1HW
0161 491 4452 **Map 10, F10**
Between Cheadle and Cheadle Hulme off A5149
Founded 1885
Very old club with pretty course. Several fine holes crossing streams.
9 holes, 5006 yards
par 64, S.S.S 65
Designer T. Renouf
Green fees £20
Catering, changing room/showers, bar, trolley hire, shop
Visitors welcome Monday, Wednesday, Friday and Sunday (restricted)
Handicap certificate required
Societies by prior arrangement

CHESTER GOLF CLUB
Curzon Park, Chester, Cheshire CH4 8AR
01244 677760 Fax 01244 676667
Map 7, D1
Curzon Park North, off A6104
Founded 1901
Parkland course overlooking River Dee, the best holes plunging from an escarpment.
18 holes, 6508 yards
par 72, S.S.S 71
Green fees £25
Catering, changing room/showers, bar, club and trolley hire, shop
Visitors welcome, but contact in advance
Handicap certificate required
Societies welcome by prior arrangement

CONGLETON GOLF CLUB
Biddulph Road, Congleton, Cheshire CW12 3LZ
01260 273540 **Map 7, G1**
A527 1 mile SE of Congleton
Founded 1898
Energetic, but pretty, 9-hole course on hilly site. Club selection can be tricky. Fine views.
9 holes, 5103 yards
par 68, S.S.S 65
Green fees £21
Catering, changing room/showers, bar, shop
Visitors welcome, but contact club first
Handicap certificate required
Societies welcome by prior arrangement

CREWE GOLF CLUB
Fields Road, Haslington, Crewe, Cheshire CW1 5TB
01270 584099 Fax 01270 584099
Map 7, F2
www.crewegolfclub.co.uk
Off A534, SE of Haslington village
Founded 1911
Interesting parkland course secreted away in the countryside. There is enjoyable variety about the holes, some undulating, others flat, some governed by water hazards, others involving tight drives one side or the other of mid-fairway trees. The early holes playing in and out of a river valley are particularly appealing.
18 holes, 6424 yards
par 71, S.S.S 71
Green fees £27
Catering, changing room/showers, bar, trolley hire, shop, practice facilities
Visitors welcome weekdays
Societies welcome Tuesdays by prior arrangement

DAVENPORT GOLF CLUB
Worth Hall, Middlewood Road, Poynton, Cheshire SK12 1TS
01625 876951 Fax 01625 877489
Map 10, G10
A523 Stockport-Macclesfield road, turn at Poynton traffic lights into Park Lane. Keep left at fork into Middlewood Road. Club on left.
Founded 1913
Excellent views from this challenging, hilly course. Many strong par 4s, especially 17th.
18 holes, 6027 yards
par 69, S.S.S 69
Green fees £27
Catering, changing room/showers, bar, club and trolley hire, shop, practice facilities
Visitors welcome except Wednesday and Saturday
Societies welcome Tuesday and Thursday – apply in advance

DELAMERE FOREST GOLF CLUB
Station Road, Delamere, Northwich, Cheshire CW8 2JE
01606 883264 Fax 01606 883800
Map 7, E1
Off B5152, 10 miles E of Chestger
Founded 1910
Inspiring Herbert Fowler layout with many tough par 4s, especially on the front nine. Holes such as the 1st and 8th require substantial carries across low ground, and the 2nd and 7th need muscle. Though shorter, the back nine is no less fascinating, especially the gorgeous 14th, and idiosyncratic 15th.
18 holes, 6328 yards
par 69, S.S.S 71
Designer Herbert Fowler
Green fees £30
Catering, changing room/showers, bar, trolley and buggy hire, shop
Visitors welcome, advisable to phone in advance
2-ball only at weekend
Societies apply in advance

DISLEY GOLF CLUB
Stanley Hall Lane, Disley, Stockport, Cheshire SK12 2JX
01663 762071 Fax 01663 762678
Map 10, G10
Off A6, at Disley village, turning left at traffic lights, Jacksons Edge Road. Golf club 2nd turning on right.
Founded 1889
Upland course, though not ridiculously hilly, giving splendid panoramas and some fine holes. New holes under construction.
18 holes, 5942 yards
par 70, S.S.S 69
Green fees £25
Catering, changing room/showers, bar, club and trolley hire, shop, practice facilities
Visitors welcome weekdays, restricted Thursday and weekend
Societies by prior arrangement
Hilton Moorside, Mudhurst Lane, Higher Disley, Stockport, Cheshire
01663 764151

DUKINFIELD GOLF CLUB
Yew Tree Lane, Dukinfield, Cheshire SK16 5DB
0161 338 2340 **Map 10, G9**

Off B6175, S of Dukinfield and Stalybridge
Founded 1913
Short and compact, but by no means uninteresting course overlooking Manchester.
18 holes, 5303 yards
par 67, S.S.S 66
Green fees £16.50
Catering, changing room/showers, bar, trolley hire, shop
Visitors welcome weekdays except Wednesday afternoon
Societies welcome by prior arrangement

DUNHAM FOREST GOLF CLUB

Oldfield Lane, Altrincham, Cheshire WA14 4TY
☎ 0161 928 2727 Fax 0161 929 8975 **Map 10, F10**
dunham@absonline.net
Off A56, S of Altrincham
Founded 1961
Beautiful course, much of it running through mature beech woods. The 1st and 5th pass an ancient burial mound, and there are demanding long par 4s at the 4th and 17th. With many fairways curving through the trees accurate placing of the drive is the main priority. Exceptionally comfortable clubhouse.
18 holes, 6636 yards
par 72, S.S.S 72
Designer John Day
Green fees £40
Catering, changing room/showers, bar, club, trolley and buggy hire, shop, driving range, practice facilities
Visitors welcome weekdays by prior arrangement
Societies welcome by prior arrangement
Quality Hotel, Bowdon, Cheshire
☎ 01619 287121

EATON GOLF CLUB

Guy Lane, Waverton, Chester, Cheshire CH3 7PH
☎ 01244 335885 Fax 01244 335782 **Map 7, D1**
Off A41,SE of Chester
Founded 1965
New course built when club moved to this site in early 1990s. Clever design demands thoughtful play.
18 holes, 6562 yards
par 72, S.S.S 71
Designer Donald Steel
Catering, changing room/showers, bar, club, trolley and buggy hire, shop
Visitors welcome, but contact in advance
Handicap certificate required
Societies welcome, not Wednesday or weekends. Contact in advance.

ELLESMERE PORT GOLF CLUB

Chester Road, Childer Thornton, South Wirral, Cheshire CH66 1QF
☎ 0151 339 7689 Fax 0151 339 7689 **Map 10, D11**
A41, NE of Ellesmere Port centre
Founded 1971
One of the better public courses in Cheshire, with a tough finish.
18 holes, 6432 yards
par 71, S.S.S 70
Designer Cotton, Pennink, Lawrie
Green fees £6.90
Catering, changing room/showers, bar, club and trolley hire, shop, squash
Visitors welcome, but arrange with professional for weekends
Societies by prior arrangement

FRODSHAM GOLF CLUB

Simons Lane, Frodsham, Cheshire WA6 6HE
☎ 01928 732159 Fax 01928 734070 **Map 10, D11**
www.frodshamgolfclub.co.uk
A56, 9 miles Ne of Chester, M56 Jct 12
Founded 1990
On high ground, giving attractive panoramas. Many thought-provoking holes.
18 holes, 6298 yards
par 70, S.S.S 70
Designer John Day
Green fees £30
Catering, changing room/showers, bar, club and trolley hire, shop
Visitors welcome weekdays, book in advance
Societies book in advance

GATLEY GOLF CLUB

Waterfall Farm, Styal Road, Heald Green, Cheshire SK8 3TW
☎ 0161 436 2830 **Map 10, F10**
Off B5166, S of Gatley
Founded 1910
Quite a challenging 9-hole course with a demanding start and finish.
9 holes, 5909 yards
par 68, S.S.S 68
Green fees £21
Catering, changing room/showers, bar, shop, practice facilities
Visitors welcome weekdays
Handicap certificate required
Societies by prior arrangement
Etrop Grange, Bailey Lane, Manchester Airport, Cheshire
☎ 0161 499 0500

HALE GOLF CLUB

Rappax Road, Hale, Cheshire WA15 0NU
☎ 0161 980 4225 **Map 10, F10**
Off Bankhall Lane, S of Hale
Founded 1903
Charming, peaceful, 9-holer, many holes full of individual character, especially those close to the River Bollin.
9 holes, 5780 yards
par 68, S.S.S 68
Green fees £20
Catering, changing room/showers, bar, shop
Visitors welcome weekdays, but not before 4.30 Thursday
Societies by prior arrangement

HAZEL GROVE GOLF CLUB

Buxton Road, Hazel Grove, Stockport, Cheshire SK7 6LU
☎ 0161 483 3978 **Map 10, G10**
Off A6, 3 miles S of Stockport
Founded 1912
Surviving classic Mackenzie holes intermingled with more contemporary Macauley holes providing a well varied test.
18 holes, 6310 yards
par 71, S.S.S 71
Designer Alister Mackenzie, Tom Macauley
Green fees £30
Catering, changing room/showers, bar, club and trolley hire, shop
Visitors welcome, apply in advance
Societies Thursday and Friday by prior arrangement

HEATON MOOR GOLF CLUB

Mauldeth Road, Heaton Mersey, Stockport, Cheshire SK4 3NX
☎ 0161 432 2134 Fax 0161 432 2134 **Map 10, F10**
hmgc@ukgateway.net
M60 Jct 1, A5145 towards Didsbury. Turn right at Mauldeth Road.
Founded 1892
Gentle parkland course playing around Chinese Embassy buildings, with interesting dog-leg 3rd, 5th, and 15th, and provocative 1st.
18 holes, 5968 yards
par 70, S.S.S 69
Green fees £23
Catering, changing room/showers, bar, club and trolley hire, shop, practice facilities
Visitors welcome, with restrictions
Societies welcome by prior arrangement
Rudyard Hotel, 271 Wellington Road North, Heaton Chapel, Stockport, Cheshire
☎ 0161 432 2753

HELSBY GOLF CLUB

Tower's Lane, Helsby, Frodsham, Cheshire WA6 0JB
☎ 01928 722021 Fax 01928 725384

Map 10, D11
A56, S of Helsby, M56 Jct 14
Founded 1901
Pleasant country course with stern finish from the 13th.
18 holes, 6229 yards
par 70, S.S.S 70
Green fees £25
Catering, changing room/showers, bar, club and trolley hire, shop
Visitors welcome weekdays with prior arrangement
Handicap certificate required
Societies Tuesdays and Thursdays by prior arrangement

HEYROSE GOLF CLUB

Budworth Road, Tabley, Near Knutsford, Cheshire WA16 0HZ
✆ 01565 733664 Fax 01565 734578
Map 10, E11
secretary@heyrosegolfclub.fsnet.co.uk
M6 Jct 19, take Pickmere Road at Windmill Pub, club signposted, *c.* 1 mile.
Founded 1989
Deceptively testing meadowland course with wicked 16th, a 230-yard par 3 through trees to a green beside a brook.
18 holes, 6515 yards
par 73, S.S.S 71
Designer C.N. Bridge
Green fees £19
Catering, changing room/showers, bar, club and trolley hire, shop, practice facilities, conference facilities for 40, dining for 150, restaurant open to public
Visitors welcome, not before 3.30 Saturday, ladies priority Wednesday, seniors Thursday morning.
Societies welcome by prior arrangement

THE HIGH LEGH GOLF CLUB

Warrington Road, Mere and High Legh, Knutsford, Cheshire WA16 0WA
✆ 01565 830888 Fax 01565 830999
Map 10, E10
www.foregolfathighlegh.co.uk
A50, at High Legh, midway between M6 Jct 20 and Mere
Designed by Ryder Cup Captain, Mark James, new tees will stretch this country-club style layout to 7,200 yards. An additional 9-hole course has been constructed but is not yet in play.
18 holes, 6253 yards
par 70, S.S.S 70
Designer Mark James
Green fees £20
Catering, changing room/showers, bar, club, trolley and buggy hire, shop, driving range, practice facilities, indoor golf swing room
Visitors casual guests restricted – phone first
Societies welcome by prior arrangement
Mere Court Hotel, Warrington Road, Mere, Knutsford, Cheshire
✆ 01565 831000
sales@merecourt.co.uk
www.merecourt.co.uk

HOULDSWORTH GOLF CLUB

Houldsworth Park, Reddish, Stockport, Cheshire SK5 6BN
✆ 0161 442 9611 Fax 0161 442 1712 **Map 10, F9**
Off A6 at North Reddish
Founded 1910
Dave Thomas reworking of a valuable parkland course only 4 miles from the centre of Manchester.
18 holes, 6209 yards
par 71, S.S.S 70
Designer Dave Thomas
Green fees £20
Catering, changing room/showers, bar, club and trolley hire, shop
Visitors welcome, but only by prior arrangement at weekends or bank holidays
Societies welcome by prior arrangement

KNIGHTS GRANGE GOLF CLUB

Grange Lane, Winsford, Cheshire CW7 2PT
✆ 01606 552780 **Map 7, E1**
Off A54 in town centre, signposted to sports complex, M6 Jct 18/19
Founded 1983
Pleasantly rural on north edge of Winsford, recently expanded to 18 holes.
18 holes, 6253 yards
S.S.S 70
Green fees £5
Changing room/showers, club and trolley hire, shop
Visitors welcome, with advance booking system
Societies welcome by prior arrangement

THE KNUTSFORD GOLF CLUB

Mereheath Lane, Knutsford, Cheshire WA16 6HS
✆ 01565 633355 **Map 10, E10**
Mereheath Lane, just N of town centre, beside Tatton Park
Founded 1891
Laid out in handsome woodlands on the edge of Tatton Park, with deer for company over the first two holes, both fine par 4s. The 4th is a charming dog-leg, the 8th a stern two-shotter, with a drive over ponds, and there are separate 9th and 18th holes to finish.
10 holes, 6288 yards
par 70, S.S.S 70
Green fees £25
Catering, changing room/showers, bar, trolley hire, shop, practice facilities
Visitors welcome by prior arrangement, but restricted Wednesday and weekends
Handicap certificate required
Societies Thursdays only, by prior arrangement
Belle Epoque, 60 King Street, Knutsford, Cheshire WA16 6DT
✆ 01565 633060 Fax 01565 634150
belleepoque@compuserve.com

LEIGH GOLF CLUB

Kenyon Hall, Broseley Lane, Culceth, Cheshire WA3 4BG
✆ 01925 762943 Fax 01925 765097
Map 10, E10
Off A579, NW of Culcheth
Founded 1906
Narrow tree-lined fairways, several dog-legs, and occasional streams make this a tricky course. Gorgeous clubhouse.
18 holes, 5884 yards
par 69, S.S.S 68
Designer James Braid
Green fees £26
Catering, changing room/showers, bar, trolley hire, shop
Visitors welcome, but book in advance
Handicap certificate required
Societies Mondays and Tuesdays by prior arrangement

LYMM GOLF CLUB

Whitbarrow Road, Lymm, Cheshire WA13 9AN
✆ 01925 752177 Fax 01925 755020
Map 10, E10
mail@lymmgolfclub.fsnet.co.uk
www.lymm-golf-club.co.uk
Off A6144, SE of Warrington
Founded 1907
Rolling holes alongside Manchester Ship Canal are pretty, while ponds and ditches affect lower-lying holes.
18 holes, 6304 yards
par 71, S.S.S 70
Green fees £22
Changing room/showers, trolley hire, shop
Visitors welcome weekdays
Handicap certificate required
Societies wednesdays only by prior arrangement

MACCLESFIELD GOLF CLUB

The Hollins, Macclesfield, Cheshire SK11 7EA

☎ 01625 619952 Fax 01625 260061
Map 10, G11
secretary@maccgolfclub.co.uk
www.maccgolfclub.co.uk
At S end of main Silk Road take Windmill Street
Founded 1889
Sporting course on hilly ground overlooking Macclesfield, a great deal of Cheshire, and a further six counties.
18 holes, 5700 yards
par 70, S.S.S 68
Designer Hawtree
Green fees £25
Catering, changing room/showers, bar, club and trolley hire, shop, practice facilities
Visitors welcome weekdays
Handicap certificate required
Societies welcome by prior arrangement
Sutton Hall, Bullocks Lane, Sutton, Macclesfield, Cheshire
☎ 01260 253211

MALKINS BANK GOLF CLUB

Betchton Road, Malkins Bank, Sandbach, Cheshire CW11 4XN
☎ 01270 765931 Fax 01270 764730
Map 7, F2
Off A533, SE of Sandbach
Founded 1980
Gently undulating, with several teasing holes, such as the dog-leg 4th threatened by a stream, and exceptionally narrow 13th.
18 holes, 6024 yards
par 70, S.S.S 69
Designer Hawtree
Green fees £8.60
Catering, changing room/showers, bar, club and trolley hire, shop, practice facilities
Visitors welcome
Societies welcome by prior arrangement
Chimney House Hotel, Church Lane, Sandbach, Cheshire
☎ 01270 764141

MARPLE GOLF CLUB

Barnsfold Road, Hawk Green, Marple, Cheshire SK6 7EL
☎ 0161 427 2311 Fax 0161 427 1125 **Map 10, G10**
Off A6, 2 miles from High Lane North. From central Marple take Church Lane, right into Hibbert Lane, at Hawk Green take Barnsfold Road to golf club.
Founded 1892
Very compact course with one or two crossing holes. Glorious views over Cheshire.
18 holes, 5552 yards
par 68, S.S.S 67
Green fees £20
Catering, changing room/showers, bar, trolley hire, shop
Visitors welcome, but restricted Thursday afternoons and weekends
Societies welcome by prior arrangement

MARTON MEADOWS GOLF CLUB

New House Farm, Marton, Macclesfield, Cheshire SK11 9HF
☎ 01260 224330 **Map 7, F1**
A34, behind Marton village church
Founded 2000
Pleasant executive length course (one par 4) in heart of Cheshire countryside.
9 holes, 2488 yards
par 56, S.S.S n/a
Green fees £5
Practice facilities, club room available for functions
Visitors welcome at all times, dress code applies, children to be accompanied by adult
Societies welcome by arrangement

MELLOR AND TOWNSCLIFFE GOLF CLUB

Gibb Lane, Tarden, Mellor, Stockport, Cheshire SK6 5NA
☎ 0161 427 2208 Fax 0161 427 0103 **Map 10, G10**
www.mandtgc.demon.co.uk
Off A626, at Marple Bridge taking Longhurst Lane, then Gibb Lane at Mellor.
Founded 1894
Splendid upland golf for the fit, with some of the best holes on the highest ground.
18 holes, 5925 yards
par 70, S.S.S 69
Green fees £20
Catering, changing room/showers, bar, trolley hire, shop
Visitors welcome weekdays
Societies welcome by prior arrangement

MERE GOLF AND COUNTRY CLUB

Chester Road, Mere, Knutsford, Cheshire WA16 6LJ
☎ 01565 830155 Fax 01565 830713
Map 10, F10
enquiries@meregolf.co.uk
www.meregolf.co.uk
A556 at Mere. M6 Jct 19 1 mile. M56 Jct 7 2 miles.
Founded 1934
The last word in opulence, both on the course and in the luxurious clubhouse and leisure facilities. The condition of the course is invariably excellent. From the back tees it is a good challenge, growing in difficulty after the turn, and particularly over the closing four holes by the lake.
18 holes, 6817 yards
par 71, S.S.S 73
Designer James Braid
Green fees £70
Catering, changing room/showers, bar, club, trolley and buggy hire, shop, driving range, practice facilities, full function and conference facilities, other outdoor pursuits available include cross-country driving and falconry
Visitors welcome Monday, Tuesday and Thursday only
Handicap certificate required
Societies welcome by prior arrangement
Mere Court Hotel, Warrington Road, Mere, Knutsford, Cheshire
☎ 01565 831000
sales@merecourt.co.uk
www.merecourt.co.uk

MERSEY VALLEY GOLF CLUB

Warrington Road, Bold Heath, Widnes, Cheshire WA8 3XL
☎ 0151 424 6060 Fax 0151 424 6060 **Map 10, D10**
M62 Jct 7, 2 miles
Founded 1995
A well varied course with par 4s ranging from 287 to 449 yards and short holes from 130 to 225 yards.
18 holes, 6374 yards
par 72, S.S.S 70
Designer R.M.R. Bush
Green fees £18
Bar, shop, practice facilities
Visitors welcome
Societies welcome with prior booking

MOBBERLEY GOLF CLUB

Burleyhurst Lane, Mobberley, Knutsford, Cheshire WA16 7JZ
☎ 01565 880188 Fax 01565 880178
Map 10, F10
Off B5085, M56 Jct 6, taking Newton Hall Lane at Bird in Hand pub. Golf club on right after c. 1 mile.
Founded 1995
Boasts one of the longest opening holes in the country at 599 yards, and USGA specification greens.
9 holes, 5542 yards
par 67, S.S.S 67
Green fees £17
Catering, changing room/showers, bar, club, trolley and buggy hire, shop, practice facilities, indoor teaching academy
Visitors welcome
Societies welcome by prior arrangement
Four Seasons, Hale Road, Hale Barns, Cheshire
☎ 0161 904 0301

MOLLINGTON GRANGE GOLF CLUB

Townfield Lane, Mollington, Chester, Cheshire CH1 6NJ
☎ 01244 851185 **Map 7, D1**
A540, 2 miles N of Chester, close to end of M56
Founded 1999
New course in rolling parkland with 650-yard 7th. New par-3 17th to island green under construction.
18 holes, 6696 yards
par 72, S.S.S 72
Green fees £25
Catering, changing room/showers, bar, trolley hire, shop, practice facilities
Visitors welcome weekdays, weekend afternoons
Societies welcome weekdays with prior arrangement

DE VERE MOTTRAM HALL HOTEL GOLF & COUNTRY CLUB

Wilmslow Road, Mottram St Andrew, Prestbury, Cheshire SK10 4QT
☎ 01625 828135 Fax 01625 828950
Map 10, F11
DMH.Sales@devere-hotels.com
A538, 4 miles SE of Wilmslow
Founded 1991
Advantage must be taken of the relatively straightforward front nine on level ground, for the back nine is tough, with three very serious par 4s in the 12th, 13th and 17th, and a couple of par 3s substantially over 200 yards in length. Surroundings on this undulating part are handsome indeed.
18 holes, 7006 yards
par 72, S.S.S 74
Designer Dave Thomas
Green fees £39
Catering, changing room/showers, bar, accommodation, club, trolley and buggy hire, shop, driving range, practice facilities, full leisure, conference and banqueting facilities
Visitors welcome
Handicap certificate required
Societies welcome by prior arrangement
🏨 De Vere Mottram Hall Hotel, Wilmslow Road, Mottram St Andrew, Prestbury, Cheshire SK10 4QT
☎ 01625 828135

PEOVER GOLF CLUB

Plumley Moor Road, Lower Peover, near Knutsford, Cheshire WA16 9SE
☎ 01565 723337 Fax 01565 723311
Map 10, F11
mail@peovergolfclub.co.uk
www.peovergolfclub.co.uk
A556 (2 miles S of M6 Jct 19), turn at Smoker pub for Plumley Moor Road. Golf club on right.
Founded 1996
Meadowland course made trickier by streams, especially the strong par-4 10th and 11th. Handsome clubhouse.
18 holes, 6702 yards
par 72, S.S.S 72
Designer Peter Naylor
Green fees £18
Catering, changing room/showers, bar, trolley and buggy hire, shop, practice facilities, function, wedding facilities, beauty/body conditioning
Visitors welcome
Societies welcome by prior arrangement
🏨 Golden Pheasant, Plumley Moor Road, Plumley, Near Knutsford, Cheshire
☎ 01565 722261

PORTAL GOLF & COUNTRY CLUB

Cobblers Cross Lane, Tarporley, Cheshire CW6 0DJ
☎ 01829 733933 Fax 01829 733928
Map 7, E1
www.portalgolf.co.uk
A51, 11 miles SE of Chester
Founded 1992
Expansive and challenging Donald Steel layout, with some very long holes as played from the championship tees. Hilly ground gives superb views and also complicates club selection. Signature hole, 14th, is picturesque par 3 over water to tiny green, and 437-yard 17th toughest, uphill with water to be carried.
Championship Course: 18 holes, 7037 yards, par 73, S.S.S 74
Designer Donald Steel
Arderne Course: 9 holes, 1724 yards, par 30
Green fees £40
Catering, changing room/showers, bar, club, trolley and buggy hire, shop, driving range, largest indoor teaching academy in Britain
Visitors welcome, but advisable to book in advance
Handicap certificate required
Societies welcome by prior arrangement

PORTAL PREMIER GOLF CLUB

Forest Road, Tarporley, Cheshire CW6 0JA
☎ 01829 733884 Fax 01829 733666
Map 7, E1
portal@aol.co.uk
A49, 1 mile N of Tarporley
Founded 1990
Former Oaklands course now in Portal stable, with similar fine views and many searching two-shotters.
18 holes, 6538 yards
par 71, S.S.S 72
Designer Tim Rouse
Green fees £30
Catering, changing room/showers, bar, club, trolley and buggy hire, shop, driving range, practice facilities, conference, wedding, function facilities, sauna, snooker
Visitors welcome
Societies welcome by prior arrangement
🏨 Wild Boar Hotel, Whitchurch Road, Beeston, Near Tarporley, Cheshire
☎ 01829 260309

POULTON PARK GOLF CLUB

Dig Lane, Cinnamon Brow, Warrington, Cheshire WA2 0SH
☎ 01925 822802 Fax 01925 822802
Map 10, E10
Off A574, Crab Lane
Founded 1980
Admirable use of narrow strip of land between housing and M6/M62, short but tactical.
9 holes, 4978 metres
par 68, S.S.S 66
Green fees £18
Catering, changing room/showers, bar, shop
Visitors welcome weekdays, but not 5-6 p.m.
Societies welcome by prior arrangement

PRESTBURY GOLF CLUB

Macclesfield Road, Prestbury, Cheshire SK10 4BJ
☎ 01625 828241 Fax 01625 828241
Map 10, F11
www.prestburygolfclub.com
Macclesfield Road from Prestbury village centre, club on right
Founded 1920
Handsome, wooded, hilly course. Colt's masterly design calls for intelligent play, particularly approaching the many tellingly raised greens. Toughest of all is 9th, a lengthy dog-leg par 4 climbing to a three-level green, and there are exhilarating shots across a valley at 14th and 17th. 16th is a bunkerless gem.
18 holes, 6359 yards
par 71, S.S.S 71
Designer Harry Colt
Green fees £42
Catering, changing room/showers, bar, trolley hire, shop, driving range, practice facilities, conference facilities
Visitors welcome weekdays.
Handicap certificate required – limit:

28
Societies welcome by prior arrangement
White House Manor, New Road, Prestbury, Macclesfield, Cheshire SK10 4HP
01625 829376 Fax 01625 828627

PRYORS HAYES GOLF CLUB

Willington Road, Oscroft, Tarvin, Cheshire CH3 8NL
01829 741250 Fax 01829 749077
Map 7, D1
www.pryor-hayes.co.uk
A51, 5 miles E of Chester
Founded 1993
Rapidly maturing meadowland course given golfing challenge by strategic use of trees and water.
18 holes, 6054 yards
par 69, S.S.S 69
Designer John Day
Green fees £20
Catering, changing room/showers, bar, trolley and buggy hire, shop
Visitors welcome
Societies welcome by prior arrangement

QUEEN'S PARK GOLF CLUB

Queens Park Drive, Crewe, Cheshire CW2 7SB
01270 662378 Fax 01270 569902
Map 7, F2
SW of Crewe centre, off A532 Coppenhall Lane and Victoria Avenue
Founded 1985
Pretty municipal course with many short, but tight par 4s, and one very testing hole, 452-yard par 4 7th.
9 holes, 4920 yards
par 68, S.S.S 64
Green fees £6.50
Catering, changing room/showers, bar, club and trolley hire, shop
Visitors welcome, except Wednesday or Sunday mornings
Societies welcome by prior arrangement

REASEHEATH GOLF CLUB

Reaseheath College, Reaseheath, Nantwich, Cheshire CW5 6DF
01270 625131 Fax 01270 625665
Map 7, E2
On A51, 1 mile NE of Nantwich
Founded 1987
The classroom for this major centre for greenkeeper training, providing an ever changing, but fascinating little course.
9 holes, 3726 yards
par 62, S.S.S 58
Designer Dennis Mortram
Green fees £6
Catering
Visitors only with member
Societies welcome weekdays only by prior arrangement

REDDISH VALE GOLF CLUB

Southcliffe Road, Reddish, Stockport, Cheshire SK2 7LN
0161 480 2359 Fax 0161 477 8242 **Map 10, F10**
admin@reddishvalegolfclub.co.uk
www.reddishvalegolfclub.co.uk
1 mile NE of Stockport, M60 Jct 13
Founded 1912
Alister Mackenzie gem hidden away in an unfashionable corner of Stockport. Even the early holes on flattish ground offer strategic challenge, but when the 6th plunges spectacularly down to the banks of the River Tame the golf moves into top gear. Several thoroughly uncompromising holes are balanced by subtler challenges.
18 holes, 6086 yards
par 69, S.S.S 69
Designer Alister Mackenzie
Green fees £22
Catering, changing room/showers, bar, trolley hire, shop, practice facilities
Visitors welcome weekdays
Societies welcome weekdays by prior arrangement
Bredbury Hall Hotel, Dark Lane, Goyt Valley, Bredbury, Cheshire SK6 2DH
0161 430 7421 Fax 0161 439 5079

RINGWAY GOLF CLUB

Hale Mount, Hale Barns, Altrincham, Cheshire WA15 8SW
0161 980 8432 **Map 10, F10**
A538, 1 mile from M56 Jct 6
Founded 1909
A good test for the accomplished golfer, with a high proportion of longer par 4s, many of which curve through avenues of mature trees, calling for precise driving. Plentiful bunkers complicate the approaches to the excellent 7th and 15th, and a stream adds charm (and difficulty) to the pretty 11th.
18 holes, 6494 yards
par 71, S.S.S 71
Designer Harry Colt, James Braid
Green fees £35
Catering, changing room/showers, bar, club and trolley hire, shop, practice facilities
Visitors welcome weekdays, with restrictions
Societies welcome Thursdays, May-September, by prior arrangement

ROMILEY GOLF CLUB

Goosehouse Green, Romiley, Cheshire SK6 4LJ
0161 430 2392 Fax 0161 430 7258 **Map 10, G10**
B6104 Stockport Road, Romiley, take Sandy Lane (east of railway bridge). Right at fork into Barlow Fold Road, Goosehouse Green on left.
Founded 1897
Splendid upland golf on the edge of the Peak District, hilly, but not exhaustingly so. Precise drives are required to set up feasible approaches to cleverly sited greens, none more strikingly so than the 6th, high above mounds and sand. Each hole has welcome individuality and the views are superb.
18 holes, 6412 yards
par 70, S.S.S 71
Green fees £30
Catering, changing room/showers, bar, trolley hire, shop
Visitors welcome, but restricted Thursday and Saturday
Societies welcome Tuesday and Wednesday with prior reservation

RUNCORN GOLF CLUB

Clifton Road, Runcorn, Cheshire WA7 4SU
01928 574214 Fax 01928 574214
Map 10, D10
S of Runcorn Station
Founded 1909
Mixture of old and new holes, 10th and 17th best of the old, 11th and 12th most interesting of the new.
18 holes, 6035 yards
par 69, S.S.S 69
Green fees £20
Catering, changing room/showers, bar, trolley hire, shop
Visitors welcome weekdays, with restrictions
Handicap certificate required
Societies welcome by prior arrangement

SALE GOLF CLUB

Sale Lodge, Golf Road, sale, Cheshire M33 2XU
0161 973 1638 Fax 0161 962 4217 **Map 10, F10**
M60 Jct 8, take A6144 towards Sale. Left at lights into Wythenshawe Road, left into Maizefield Road, left into Fairy Lane, left (over bridge) into Golf Road
Founded 1913
Arguably the best of the many courses along the Mersey Valley, with strong woodland holes to start and the tricky 13th, over streams, also notable. The Mersey threatens the 4th, 5th and 6th. Club professional, Dick Burton, won the last Open Championship to be held

before the Second World War.
18 holes, 6351 yards
par 71, S.S.S 70
Green fees £28
Catering, changing room/showers, bar, trolley hire, shop
Visitors welcome weekdays
Societies welcome weekdays by prior arrangement

SANDBACH GOLF CLUB

117 Middlewich Road, Sandbach, Cheshire CW11 1FH
✆ 01270 762117 **Map 7, F2**
A533 Middlewich Road, NW of town centre.
Founded 1895
Compact 9-holer with long par 4s at 4th and 5th, and pretty short 2nd beside a pond.
9 holes, 5598 yards
par 68, S.S.S 67
Green fees £20
Catering, changing room/showers, bar, buggy hire, practice facilities
Visitors welcome weekdays
Societies welcome by prior arrangement
🏨 Poplar Mount, 2 Station Road, Elworth, Sandbach, Cheshire

SANDIWAY GOLF CLUB

Chester Road, Sandiway, Cheshire CW8 2DJ
✆ 01606 883247 Fax 01606 888548 **Map 7, E1**
A556, E of Sandiway
Founded 1921
A fine course, justly respected by professionals and top amateurs. The long par-4 10th, 12th and 14th are particularly testing. Downhill drives at the 1st, 5th and 15th encourage, but deceptively sloping fairways complicate driving at the par-5 4th and 16th, while the short par-4 17th teases.
18 holes, 6435 yards
par 70, S.S.S 72
Designer Ted Ray
Green fees £35
Catering, changing room/showers, bar, club and trolley hire, shop, practice facilities
Visitors welcome but book in advance
Handicap certificate required
Societies welcome by prior arrangement

SHRIGLEY HALL HOTEL GOLF CLUB

Shrigley Park, Pott Shrigley, Near Macclesfield, Cheshire SK10 5SB
✆ 01625 575757 Fax 01625 575437 **Map 10, G11**
shrigleyhallgolf@paramount-hotels.co.uk
www.paramount-hotels.co.uk
A523 Macclesfield-Stockport Road, traffic lights at Legh Arms pub, signposted to Adlington and Pott Shrigley. Hotel/golf course signposted, on left after c. 1 mile.
Founded 1989
In a stunning location, on a hillside overlooking the Cheshire plain, Shrigley Hall is full of character. The hills make many yardages irrelevant, and the par-5 7th is well-nigh impossible for all but the longest hitters, but the views are so magnificent that such minor grudges are readily forgiven.
18 holes, 6281 yards
par 71, S.S.S 71
Designer Donald Steel
Green fees £36
Catering, changing room/showers, bar, accommodation, club, trolley and buggy hire, shop, driving range, practice facilities, 154-room 4-star hotel, award winning restaurant, full leisure and conference facilities, many other outdoor sporting pursuits available
Visitors welcome, but contact in advance
Societies welcome by prior arrangement
🏨 Shrigley Hall Hotel, Shrigley Park, Pott Shrigley, Cheshire
✆ 01625 575757

ST MICHAELS JUBILEE GOLF CLUB

Dundalk Road, Widnes, Cheshire WA8 8BS
✆ 0151 424 6230 Fax 0151 495 2124 **Map 10, D10**
Off A568, towards Widnes town centre, immediately turning left at next roundabout, left again at next roundabout, course on left.
Founded 1977
Gently undulating course split by main Speke Road, the golf the more interesting for the intervention of a stream.
18 holes, 5612 yards
par 69, S.S.S 67
Green fees tba
Catering, changing room/showers, bar, shop
Visitors welcome
Societies welcome by prior arrangement

STAMFORD GOLF CLUB

Oakfield House, Huddersfield Road, Heyheads, Stalybridge, Cheshire SK15 3PY
✆ 01457 836550 **Map 10, G9**
stamford.golfclub@totalise.co.uk
B6175 NE of Stalybridge town centre
Founded 1901
Tricky moorland course with many demanding holes, such as the unforgiving 8th and 13th.
18 holes, 5701 yards
par 70, S.S.S 68
Green fees £20
Catering, changing room/showers, bar, trolley hire, shop, function and conference facilities
Visitors welcome, restricted weekends and competition days
Societies welcome by prior arrangement

STOCKPORT GOLF CLUB

Offerton Road, Offerton, Stockport, Cheshire SK2 5HL
✆ 0161 427 8369 Fax 0161 449 8293 **Map 10, G10**
A627, SE of Stockport
Founded 1905
A one-time open moorland course transformed 40 years ago by the planting of thousands of trees, making this an attractive and secluded place. Apart from the 463-yard par-4 1st, length is not generally a problem, but the trees narrow many fairways and the excellent greens are cleverly defended.
18 holes, 6326 yards
par 71, S.S.S 71
Designer Peter Barrie, Sandy Herd, James Braid
Green fees £35
Catering, changing room/showers, bar, club and trolley hire, shop
Visitors welcome, but contact professional first
Societies welcome weekdays by prior arrangement

STYAL GOLF CLUB AND DRIVING RANGE

Station Road, Styal, Cheshire SK9 4JN
✆ 01625 531359 Fax 01625 530063 **Map 10, F10**
www.styalgolf.co.uk
M56 Jct 5, or A34
Founded 1994
Very flat, but deceptively tricky course with ponds, streams, trees and hedges. New par-3 course.
Styal: 18 holes, 6301 yards, par 70, S.S.S 70
Designer T Holmes
Styal Par-3 Course: 9 holes, 1242 yards, par 27, S.S.S 27
Designer T. Holmes, G. Traynor
Green fees £17
Catering, changing room/showers, bar, club, trolley and buggy hire, shop, driving range, Cheshire Golf Academy tuition centre, restaurant open to public

Visitors welcome
Societies welcome with prior reservation
Stanneylands Hotel, Stanneylands Road, Wilmslow, Cheshire
01625 525225

SUTTON HALL GOLF CLUB

Aston Lane, Sutton Weaver, Runcorn, Cheshire WA7 3ED
01928 790747 Fax 01928 759174
Map 10, E10
A56, 3 miles S of M56 Jct 12
Founded 1995
Good value, lengthy, parkland course overlooking the Weaver Valley, with many ditches and ponds.
18 holes, 6608 yards
par 72, S.S.S 72
Designer Steve Wundke
Green fees £18
Catering, changing room/showers, bar, club and trolley hire, shop, practice facilities
Visitors welcome
Societies welcome by prior arrangement

THE TYTHERINGTON CLUB

Dorchester Way, Tytherington, Macclesfield, Cheshire SK10 2JP
01625 506000 Fax 01625 506040
Map 10, G11
c.rogers@clubhaus.com
www.clubhaus.com
A 523 Silk Road, N from Macclesfield, left at Hurdsfield roundabout, right at lights. Club is on left (signposted).
Founded 1986
Modern parkland course which has hosted ladies professional tour events. Water hazards augment searching design.
18 holes, 6765 yards
par 72, S.S.S 73
Designer Patrick Dawson, Dave Thomas
Green fees £32
Catering, changing room/showers, bar, club, trolley and buggy hire, shop, driving range, practice facilities, country club and conference facilities, fitness complex
Visitors welcome
Handicap certificate required
Societies welcome by prior arrangement
Belgrade Hotel, Jackson Lane, Kerridge, Macclesfield, Cheshire SK10 5BG
01625 573246

UPTON-BY-CHESTER GOLF CLUB

Upton Lane, Chester, Cheshire CH2 1EE
01244 381183 Fax 01244 376955
Map 7, D1
A41, N from city centre, or via A5116 Liverpool Road
Founded 1934
Pleasant parkland course in Chester suburbs, with attractive clubhouse. Finish from 14th is lively.
18 holes, 5808 yards
par 69, S.S.S 68
Green fees £25
Catering, changing room/showers, bar, trolley hire, shop, practice facilities
Visitors welcome, but check first
Societies welcome weekdays by arrangement

VALE ROYAL ABBEY GOLF CLUB

Whitegate, Near Northwich, Cheshire CW8 2BA
01606 301291 Fax 10606 301414
Map 7, E1
Off A556
Founded 1998
Spacious new layout in historic parkland, with several very challenging par 4s, including 466-yard 7th to green by lake.
18 holes, 6357 yards
par 71, S.S.S 70
Designer Simon Gidman
Green fees £15
Catering, changing room/showers, bar, club and trolley hire, shop, practice facilities
Visitors welcome only as members' guests
No societies

VICARS CROSS GOLF CLUB

Tarvin Road, Great Barrow, Chester, Cheshire CH3 7HN
01244 335174 Fax 01244 335686
Map 7, D1
A51, 4 miles E of Chester
Founded 1939
Gentle country course with many short- to medium-length par 4s, but some tight dog-legs which are far from easily overcome.
18 holes, 6428 yards
par 72, S.S.S 71
Designer Eric Parr
Green fees £25
Catering, changing room/showers, bar, club and trolley hire, shop, practice facilities
Visitors welcome, but not on competition days or Wednesdays
Societies Tuesday or Thursday by arrangement

WALTON HALL GOLF CLUB

Warrington Road, Higher Walton, Warrington, Cheshire WA4 5LU
01925 263061 **Map 10, E10**
Off A56 Chester New Road, 2 miles S of Warrington
Founded 1972
Long, demanding public course which poses many tough questions even for the expert, particularly over the back nine.
18 holes, 6843 yards
par 72, S.S.S 73
Designer Dave Thomas, Peter Alliss
Green fees £9
Catering, changing room/showers, bar, club, trolley and buggy hire, shop
Visitors welcome, but wise to book in advance
Societies by prior arrangement

WARRINGTON GOLF CLUB

Hill Warren, Appleton, Warrington, Cheshire WA4 5HR
01925 261775 Fax 01925 265933
Map 10, E10
A49, 3 miles S of Warrington
Founded 1903
Appealing hillside course giving lovely views, and some fascinating golf on holes such as the spectacular 7th.
18 holes, 6305 yards
par 72, S.S.S 70
Designer James Braid
Green fees £27
Catering, changing room/showers, bar, club and trolley hire, shop, practice facilities
Visitors welcome weekdays
Societies welcome by prior arrangement

WERNETH LOW GOLF CLUB

Werneth Low Road, Gee Cross, Hyde, Cheshire SK14 3AF
0161 368 2503 Fax 0161 320 0053 **Map 10, G10**
Off A560 at Gee Cross, M67 Jct 4
Founded 1912
In good weather the views alone reward a visit, but, despite its modest length, the course is not easily tamed.
11 holes, 6113 yards
par 70, S.S.S 69
Green fees £18
Catering, changing room/showers, bar, trolley hire
Visitors welcome, but not Tuesday morning, Thursday afternoon or Sunday, by prior arrangement only Saturday
Societies welcome by prior arrangement

WIDNES GOLF CLUB

Highfield Road, Widnes, Cheshire WA8 7DT
0151 424 2440 Fax 0151 495 2849 **Map 10, D10**
A658 Kingsway, ½ mile from station, M62 Jct 7
Founded 1924
Fairly flat, compact site bounded by railway and houses, but streams, trees and narrow fairways punish the errant.
18 holes, 5719 yards
par 69, S.S.S 68
Green fees £22
Catering, changing room/showers, bar, trolley hire, shop, practice facilities
Visitors welcome, with restrictions – phone first
Societies welcome by prior arrangement

THE WILMSLOW GOLF CLUB

Great Warford, Mobberley, Knutsford, Cheshire WA16 7AY
01565 872148 Fax 01565 872172
Map 10, F10
wilmslowgolfclub@ukf.net
www.wilmslowgolfclub.ukf.net
Off B5085, Wilmslow-Knutsford road, turning opposite sign for Plough and Flail pub.
Founded 1889
A charming old country course, past host to European Tour events and Open Championship Qualifying. Condition, even in winter, impressive. The entrances to many greens are narrow. Long, shaped drives are necessary to overcome the 2nd and 15th, ordinarily the toughest par 4s. The par-3 14th is uncompromising.
18 holes, 6607 yards
par 72, S.S.S 72
Designer Sandy Herd, James Braid, Tom Simpson, George Duncan, Fred Hawtree, Cotton, Pennink, Lawrie, Dave Thomas
Green fees £40
Catering, changing room/showers, bar, club and trolley hire, shop, practice facilities
Visitors welcome, not Wednesday or during competitions
Societies welcome by prior arrangement
Belle Epoque, 60 King Street, Knutsford, Cheshire WA16 6DT
01565 633060 Fax 01565 634150
belleepoque@compuserve.com

CUMBRIA

ALSTON MOOR GOLF CLUB

The Hermitage, Alston, Cumbria CA9 3DB
01434 381675 Fax 01434 381675
Map 10, E1
B6277, 2 miles S of Alston
Founded 1905
A fell course capable of testing all handicap levels. The scenery of the northern Pennines and Tyne Valley is incomparable.
10 holes, 5518 yards
par 68, S.S.S 67
Designer Club members
Green fees £9
Catering, changing room/showers, bar
Visitors welcome
Societies welcome by prior arrangement
Lovelady Shield, Nenthead Road, Alston, Cumbria CA9 3LF
01434 381203 Fax 01434 381515
enquiries@lovelady.co.uk
www.lovelady.co.uk

APPLEBY GOLF CLUB

Brackenber Moor, Appleby, Cumbria CA16 6LP
017683 51432 Fax 017683 52773
Map 10, E2
Off A66, 2 miles SE of Appleby
Founded 1903
Moorland golf at its best, with excellent greens and outstanding views of the Pennine and Lakeland Fells.
18 holes, 5901 yards
par 68, S.S.S 68
Designer Willie Fernie
Green fees £18
Catering, changing room/showers, bar, club and trolley hire, shop, practice facilities
Visitors welcome
Handicap certificate required
Societies welcome by prior arrangement
Tufton Arms Hotel, Market Square, Appleby-in-Westmorland, Cumbria CA16 6XA
01768 351593

BARROW GOLF CLUB

Rakesmoor Lane, Hawcoat, Barrow-in-Furness, Cumbria LA14 4QB
01229 825444 **Map 10, C5**
Off A590, follow industrial route, 3 miles before Barrow.
Founded 1921
A parkland course on the outskirts of industrial Barrow enjoying excellent views of the Southern Fells.
18 holes, 6184 yards
par 71, S.S.S 70
Green fees £20
Catering, changing room/showers, bar, trolley hire, shop, practice facilities
Visitors welcome weekdays
Handicap certificate required
Societies welcome by prior arrangement

BRAMPTON (TALKIN TARN) GOLF CLUB

Brampton, Cumbria CA8 1HN
016977 2255 Fax 016977 41487
Map 13, C10
B6473, off A69, 1 mile S of Brampton
Founded 1907
On a fine day the views from the higher parts of Brampton are unbeatable – towards the Lakeland Hills and far into Scotland. At the start and finish of the round the holes are pleasantly rolling, their undulations mere mole hills in comparison with the twelve extraordinary, but exciting, highland holes,
18 holes, 6407 yards
par 72, S.S.S 71
Designer James Braid
Green fees £22
Catering, changing room/showers, bar, club and trolley hire, shop, practice facilities
Visitors welcome
Societies welcome by prior arrangement

BRAYTON PARK GOLF CLUB

Lakeside Inn, Brayton Park, Aspatria, Cumbria CA5 3TD
016973 20840 **Map 10, B1**
Off A916,1 mile N of Aspatria
Founded 1986
An inexpensive parkland course.
9 holes, 5402 yards
S.S.S 65
Green fees £5
Catering, changing room/showers, bar, club hire, shop
Visitors welcome
Societies welcome by prior arrangement

CARLISLE GOLF CLUB

Aglionby, Carlisle, Cumbria CA4 8AG
01228 510164 Fax 01228 513303
Map 13, C11
A69, ½ mile E of M6 Jct 43
Founded 1908
Surrounded by beech and pine woods, and intersected by streams, Carlisle is attractive. The 11th is full of character, a 384-yard dog-leg on which the second shot is played through a gap in the trees. Though none of the par 3s is particularly long

they are highly thought of.
18 holes, 6223 yards
par 71, S.S.S 70
Designer Mackenzie Ross
Green fees £25
Catering, changing room/showers, bar, club, trolley and buggy hire, shop, practice facilities
Visitors welcome – restrictions at weekend
Handicap certificate required
Societies welcome by prior arrangement
Crown Hotel, Wetheral, Carlisle, Cumbria
01228 561888

CARUS GREEN GOLF CLUB

Kendal, Cumbria LA9 6EB
01539 721097 Fax 01539 721097
Map 10, D4
fred-eileen@hotmail.com
M6 Jct 36, A6 towards Kendal. At N end of Kendal bypass follow sign for Burneside.
Founded 1995
A lowland course surrounded by the Lakeland Fells and, to a large extent, by the River Kent.
18 holes, 5716 yards
par 70, S.S.S 68
Designer W. Adamson
Green fees £12
Catering, changing room/showers, bar, club and trolley hire, shop, practice facilities
Visitors welcome
Societies welcome by prior arrangement
Castle Green Hotel, Sedbergh Road, Kendal, Cumbria
01539 734000

CASTERTON GOLF COURSE

Sedbergh Road, Casterton, Near Kirkby Lonsdale, Cumbria LA6 2LA
015242 71592 Fax 015242 74387
Map 10, E5
castertongc@hotmail.com
A683, Kirkby Lonsdale-Sedbergh road
Founded 1992
With marvellous views of historic Kirkby Lonsdale, the course also offers two holiday flats with half-price golf for guests.
9 holes, 5726 yards
par 70, S.S.S 68
Designer W. Adams
Green fees £10
Catering, changing room/showers, bar, accommodation, club and trolley hire, shop, practice facilities
Visitors welcome
Societies welcome by prior arrangement
Pheasant Inn, Casterton, near Kirkby Lonsdale, Cumbria LA6 2LA
01524 271230

COCKERMOUTH GOLF CLUB

Embleton, Cockermouth, Cumbria CA13 9SG
017687 76223 Fax 017687 76491
Map 10, B2
Off A66
Founded 1896
Sited high in the mountains, surrounded by spectacular Lakeland Fell scenery.
18 holes, 5496 yards
par 69, S.S.S 67
Designer James Braid
Green fees £15
Catering, changing room/showers, bar, trolley hire
Visitors welcome with restrictions
Societies welcome by prior arrangement
Derwent Lodge Hotel, Embleton, Cockermouth, Cumbria
01765 776606

DALSTON HALL GOLF CLUB

Dalston Hall, Dalston, Carlisle, Cumbria CA5 7JX
01228 710165 **Map 13, C11**
M46 Jct 42
Founded 1990
A parkland course south west of Carlisle.
9 holes, 2700 yards
S.S.S 67
Green fees £5
Catering, changing room/showers, bar
Visitors welcome
Societies welcome by prior arrangement

THE DUNNERHOLME GOLF CLUB

Duddon Road, Askam-in-Furness, Cumbria LA16 7AW
01229 462675 **Map 10, B5**
Off A595, crossing railway
Founded 1990
A genuine links course, also enjoying views of the Furness Fells.
10 holes, 6154 yards
par 72, S.S.S 70
Green fees £10
Changing room/showers, bar
Visitors welcome
Societies welcome by prior arrangement

EDEN GOLF CLUB

Crosby-on-Eden, Carlisle, Cumbria CA6 4RA
01228 573003 Fax 01228 818435
Map 13, C10
www.edengolf.co.uk
A689, M6 Jct 44
Founded 1991
Taking its name from the river which it follows, this seriously testing course makes use of a large number of water hazards. Good off-course facilities.
18 holes, 6500 yards
par 72, S.S.S 72
Green fees £30
Catering, changing room/showers, bar, club and trolley hire, shop, driving range, practice facilities
Visitors welcome
Societies welcome by prior arrangement
Crosby Lodge Hotel, High Crosby, Crosby-on-Eden, Carlisle, Cumbria

FURNESS GOLF CLUB

Walney Island, Barrow-in-Furness, Cumbria LA14 3LN
01229 471232 **Map 10, B6**
Off A590, on Walney Island.
Founded 1872
A links course very much exposed to the wind with superb views, which deserves to be better known than it is.
18 holes, 6363 yards
par 71, S.S.S 71
Green fees £17
Catering, changing room/showers, bar, trolley hire, shop, practice facilities
Visitors welcome
Handicap certificate required
Societies welcome by prior arrangement

GRANGE FELL GOLF CLUB

Fell Road, Grange-over-Sands, Cumbria LA11 6HB
015395 32536 **Map 10, D5**
Off B5278, between Grange-over-Sands and Cartmel.
Founded 1952
A 9-hole course of enormous character as it climbs over Grange Fell, with several memorable holes and magnificent views.
9 holes, 5312 yards
par 70, S.S.S 66
Green fees £12
Changing room/showers
Visitors welcome
Societies welcome by prior arrangement

GRANGE-OVER-SANDS GOLF CLUB

Meathop Road, Grange-over-Sands, Cumbria LA11 6QX
015395 33180 Fax 015395 33754
Map 10, D5
Off B5277
Founded 1919
A very flat piece of parkland

overlooking Morecambe Bay, transformed by Alister Mackenzie, who documented it in his classic treatise 'Golf Architecture'. The short holes are especially admired.
18 holes, 5938 yards
S.S.S 69
Designer Alister Mackenzie
Green fees £20
Catering, changing room/showers, bar, club and trolley hire, shop, practice facilities
Visitors welcome
Handicap certificate required
Societies welcome by prior arrangement

HALTWHISTLE GOLF CLUB

Wallend Farm, Greenhead, Carlisle, Cumbria CA6 7HN
☎ 01697 747367 Fax 01434 344311
Map 13, D10
Off A69, N of Haltwhistle
Founded 1967
Almost on Hadrian's Wall, with fine views of the Border country.
18 holes, 5522 yards
par 69, S.S.S 67
Designer Andrew Mair
Green fees £12
Catering, changing room/showers, bar
Visitors welcome
Societies welcome by prior arrangement

KENDAL GOLF CLUB

The Heights, Kendal, Cumbria LA9 4PQ
☎ 01539 724079 Fax 01539 733708
Map 10, D4
Off A6, 1 mile W of Kendal
Founded 1891
A moorland course with excellent views outside the busy town of Kendal.
18 holes, 5769 yards
par 70, S.S.S 68
Green fees £20
Catering, changing room/showers, bar, club and trolley hire, shop
Visitors welcome
Handicap certificate required
Societies welcome by prior arrangement

KESWICK GOLF CLUB

Threlkeld Hall, Threlkeld, Keswick, Cumbria CA12 4SX
☎ 017687 79010 Fax 017687 79861
Map 10, C2
secretary@keswickgolfclub.com
www.keswickgolfclub.com
A66, 4 miles E of Keswick
Founded 1979
Surrounded by breathtakingly beautiful scenery, the course is a tribute to the dedication of the members who largely built it by hand.
18 holes, 6225 yards
par 71, S.S.S 72
Designer Eric Brown
Green fees £20
Catering, changing room/showers, bar, club and trolley hire, shop, practice facilities, bowls
Visitors welcome (restrictions Thursday and Sunday)
Handicap certificate required
Societies welcome by prior arrangement
🏨 The Grange, Manor Brow, Keswick, Cumbria CA12 4BA
☎ 01768 772500

KIRKBY LONSDALE GOLF CLUB

Scaleber Lane, Barbon, Carnforth, Cumbria LA6 2LJ
☎ 015242 76365 Fax 015242 76503
Map 10, E5
www.klgolf.dial.pipex.com
A683, N of Kirkby Lonsdale
Founded 1991
Laid out in gentle countryside in the valley of the River Lune.
18 holes, 6481 yards
par 72, S.S.S 71
Designer W. Squires
Green fees £20
Catering, changing room/showers, bar, club and trolley hire, shop, practice facilities
Visitors welcome
Societies welcome by prior arrangement

MARYPORT GOLF CLUB

Bank End, Maryport, Cumbria CA15 6PA
☎ 01900 812605 Fax 01900 815626
Map 10, B2
B5300, 1½ miles N of Maryport
Founded 1905
With lovely views across the Solway Firth to the hills of Galloway, the course is part-links, part parkland.
18 holes, 6088 yards
par 70, S.S.S 69
Green fees £17
Catering, changing room/showers, bar, trolley hire, practice facilities
Visitors welcome, restricted weekends
Societies welcome by prior arrangement
🏨 Ellenbank Hotel, Birkby, Maryport, Cumbria
☎ 01900 815233

PENRITH GOLF CLUB

Salkeld Road, Penrith, Cumbria CA11 8SG
☎ 01768 891919 Fax 01768 891919
Map 10, D2
Off A6, ½ mile NE of Penrith
Founded 1890
Good value green fees are reduced for guests of several local hotels and guest houses. With fine views of the Lakeland fells from its elevated site, Penrith offers the best of upland golf, without exhausting climbing. The card displays a considerable variety in hole lengths, from 105 to 516 yards.
18 holes, 6047 yards
par 69, S.S.S 69
Green fees £20
Catering, changing room/showers, bar, club and trolley hire, shop, driving range, practice facilities
Visitors welcome
Handicap certificate required
Societies welcome by prior arrangement
🏨 Hornby Hall, Brougham, Penrith, Cumbria CA10 2 AR
☎ 01768 891114 Fax 1768891114

SEASCALE GOLF CLUB

The Banks, Seascale, Cumbria CA20 1QL
☎ 019467 28202 Fax 019467 28202
Map 10, B4
secretary@seascalegolfclub.org
www.seascalegolfclub.org
In Seascale village
Founded 1893
Despite the brooding presence of Sellafield at the end of the course, Seascale offers a rarely encountered grandeur and robustness. The early holes, on high heathland, tumble vigorously, the 3rd particularly demanding, and the brilliant 9th plunges to a green beside a stream. Hardest of all is the linksland 16th.
18 holes, 6419 yards
par 71, S.S.S 71
Designer Willie Campbell, George Lowe
Green fees £24
Catering, changing room/showers, bar, club and trolley hire, shop, driving range, practice facilities, conference facilities
Visitors welcome
Societies welcome by prior arrangement
🏨 Calder House, The Banks, Seascale, Cumbria
☎ 01946 728538 Fax 01946 724230

SEDBERGH GOLF CLUB

Dent Road, Sedbergh, Cumbria LA10 5SS
☎ 015396 20993 Fax 01539620993
Map 10, E4
sedberghgc@btinternet.com
1½ miles from Sedbergh on Dent Road, M6 Jct 37
Founded 1896

18 tees give a variety to the second time round on this scenic course in the Yorkshire Dales National Park.
9 holes, 5624 yards
par 70, S.S.S 68
Designer W.G.Squires
Green fees £14
Catering, changing room/showers, bar, club and trolley hire, shop, practice facilities
Visitors welcome – prior booking essential
Societies welcome by prior arrangement
George & Dragon, Dent, Sedbergh, Cumbria
015396 25256

SILECROFT GOLF CLUB

Silecroft, Millom, Cumbria, Cumbria
01229 774250 **Map 10, B5**
Off A5093, 2 miles W of Millom
Founded 1903
A remote links with magnificent seascapes.
9 holes, 5877 yards
par 68, S.S.S 68
Green fees £15
Catering, changing room/showers, bar
Visitors welcome weekdays
Societies welcome by prior arrangement

SILLOTH-ON-SOLWAY GOLF CLUB

Silloth, Wigton, Cumbria CA7 4BL
016973 31304 Fax 016973 31782
Map 13, A11
West end of sea front
Founded 1892
Silloth's reputation as one of the finest links courses in the country is at last reaching the golfing public at large. With the front nine twisting and turning through the dunes, and the finish beset by gorse, the course embraces every seaside virtue, with the par-5 13th quite outstanding.
18 holes, 6626 yards
par 72, S.S.S 73
Designer David Grant, Willie Park, Alister Mackenzie
Green fees £26
Catering, changing room/showers, bar, club and trolley hire, shop, practice facilities
Visitors welcome – restricted
Handicap certificate required
Societies welcome by prior arrangement

ST BEES GOLF CLUB

Peckmill, Beach Road, St Bees, Cumbria CA27 0AD
01946 822515 **Map 10, A3**
Off B5345, 3 miles S of Whitehaven
Founded 1929
On hilly ground overlooking the sea with views towards St Bees Head.
9 holes, 5122 yards
par 64, S.S.S 65
Green fees £12
Visitors welcome weekdays
Societies welcome by prior arrangement

STONY HOLME GOLF CLUB

St Aidan's Road, Carlisle, Cumbria CA7 1LS
01228 625511 **Map 13, C10**
M6 Jct 43, A69 towards Carlisle.
Founded 1974
Well equipped municipal course on the banks of the River Eden.
18 holes, 5775 yards
par 69, S.S.S 68
Designer Frank Pennink
Green fees £7.80
Catering, changing room/showers, bar, club, trolley and buggy hire, shop, driving range, practice facilities, 9-hole short course
Visitors welcome
Societies welcome by prior arrangement

ULVERSTON GOLF CLUB

Bardsea Park, Ulverston, Cumbria LA12 9QJ
01229 582824 **Map 10, C5**
Off A5087, 2 miles S of Ulverston
Founded 1895
A fascinating parkland course overlooking Morecambe Bay, with a famous quarry hole.
18 holes, 6201 yards
par 71, S.S.S 70
Designer Alex Herd, Harry Colt.
Green fees £25
Catering, changing room/showers, bar, club and trolley hire, shop, practice facilities
Visitors welcome
Handicap certificate required
Societies welcome by prior arrangement

WINDERMEREGOLF CLUB

Cleabarrow, Windermere, Cumbria LA23 3NG
015394 43123 Fax 015394 43123
Map 10, D4
B5284, 1 mile E of Bowness
Founded 1891
One of the most beautiful courses in England. With superb views of the Lakeland Fells and Morecambe Bay, Windermere is remarkably challenging for a course so short. Rocky outcrops, heather and bracken can inflict serious damage on a potentially good score, and even the shortest par 4s demand considerable accuracy.
18 holes, 5132 yards
par 67, S.S.S 65
Designer George Lowe
Green fees £24
Catering, changing room/showers, bar, club and trolley hire, shop
Visitors welcome
Handicap certificate required
Societies welcome by prior arrangement

WORKINGTON GOLF CLUB

Branthwaite Road, Workington, Cumbria CA14 4SS
01900 603460 Fax 01900 607122
Map 10, A2
Between A595 and A596, 1 mile E of Workington
Founded 1893
A parkland course on high ground giving fine views and something of a challenge, particularly on the back nine.
18 holes, 6252 yards
par 72, S.S.S 70
Designer James Braid
Green fees £20
Catering, changing room/showers, bar, trolley and buggy hire, shop, practice facilities
Visitors welcome
Handicap certificate required
Societies welcome by prior arrangement

DURHAM

BARNARD CASTLE GOLF CLUB

Harmire Road, Barnard Castle, Durham DL12 8QN
01833 638355 Fax 01833 695551
Map 10, G3
christine.sec@talk21.com
www.barnardcastlegolfclub.org.uk
B6278, 1 mile N of town centre
Founded 1898
With expansive views in open country, the course is crossed by a number of streams which enliven many of the shorter par 4s, including the inviting 1st. The 6th and 13th are long and distinctive par 5s, while the short par-4 16th and 17th are entertaining but potentially ruinous.
18 holes, 6406 yards
par 73, S.S.S 71
Green fees £20
Catering, changing room/showers, bar, club and trolley hire, shop, practice facilities
Visitors welcome
Handicap certificate required
Societies welcome by prior arrangement
Jersey Farm Hotel, Barnard Castle, Durham
01833 638223

BEAMISH PARK GOLF CLUB

Beamish, near Stanley, Durham DH9 0RH
✆ 0191 3701382 Fax 0191 3702937
Map 11, A1
beamishpark@beamishparkgc.fsbusiness.co.uk
www.beamishparkgc@beamishparkgc.fsbusiness.co.uk
Adjacent to Beamish Open Air Museum, between Chester le Street and Stanley
Founded 1951
Laid out in the Deer Park of Beamish Hall, once the home of the Shafto family, celebrated in the popular song about Bobby.
18 holes, 6220 yards
par 71, S.S.S 70
Designer Sir Henry Cotton
Green fees £16
Catering, changing room/showers, bar, club and trolley hire, shop, practice facilities
Visitors welcome – restricted weekends
Societies welcome by prior arrangement
🏨 Lumley Castle, Chester-le-Street, Durham DH3 4NX
✆ 0191 389 1111 Fax 0191 389 1881

BILLINGHAM GOLF CLUB

Sandy Lane, Billingham, Durham TS22 5NA
✆ 01642 557060 Fax 01642 533816
Map 11, B2
eddiedouglas@billgolfclub.fsnet.co.uk
Western boundary of Billingham
Founded 1967
A welcoming club with an undulating parkland course. Skills are tested against the long par-3 5th and difficult par-4 13th.
18 holes, 6404 yards
par 73, S.S.S 71
Designer Frank Pennink
Green fees £25
Catering, changing room/showers, bar, club and trolley hire, shop, practice facilities
Visitors welcome, restricted weekends
Societies welcome by prior arrangement
🏨 Marine Hotel, The Front, Seaton Carew, Hartlepool, Durham
✆ 01429 864144

BISHOP AUCKLAND GOLF CLUB

High Plains, Durham Road, Bishop Auckland, Durham DL14 8DL
✆ 01388 663648 Fax 01388 607005
Map 11, A2
enquiries@bagc.co.uk
www.bagc.co.uk
A689, 1 mile from Bishop Auckland Market Place
Founded 1894
A hilly parkland course with an unusual run of three par 5s in succession. The par-3 7th and 8th are both played over gullies to target greens, and the 221-yard 12th is unforgiving. Views from the high ground are splendid, including glimpses of the Bishop of Durham's Palace.
18 holes, 6402 yards
par 72, S.S.S 71
Designer James Kay
Green fees £22
Catering, changing room/showers, bar, club and trolley hire, shop, practice facilities
Visitors welcome, closed Good Friday and Christmas
Societies welcome by prior arrangement
🏨 Park Head Hotel, New Coundon, Bishop Auckland, Durham
✆ 01388 661727

BLACKWELL GRANGE GOLF CLUB

Briar Close, Blackwell, Darlington, Durham DL3 8QX
✆ 01325 464458 Fax 01325 464458
Map 11, A3
secretary@blackwell-grange.demon.co.uk
Off A66, 1 mile W of town centre
Founded 1930
Parkland course on outskirts of Darlington.
18 holes, 5621 yards
par 68, S.S.S 67
Designer Frank Pennink
Green fees £20
Catering, changing room/showers, bar, club and trolley hire, shop, practice facilities
Visitors welcome
Handicap certificate required
Societies welcome by prior arrangement
🏨 Blackwell Grange, Grange Road, Darlington, Durham DL3 8QH
✆ 01325 509955

BRANCEPETH CASTLE GOLF CLUB

Brancepeth Village, Durham, Durham DH7 8EA
✆ 0191 3780075 Fax 01913780075
Map 10, H1
brancepethcastle@btclick.com
A690, 6 miles W of Durham
Founded 1924
One of the loveliest inland courses in England. Seriously deep ravines trouble a great many tee shots and the back-to-back par 3s around the turn are amongst the best of their kind, both involving compulsory carries of around 200 yards. Historic St Brandon's Church and Brancepeth Castle overlook the course.
18 holes, 6400 yards
par 70, S.S.S 70
Designer Harry Colt
Green fees £30
Catering, changing room/showers, bar, trolley hire, shop, practice facilities
Visitors welcome weekdays
Handicap certificate required
Societies welcome by prior arrangement
🏨 Georgian Town House, 10 Crossgate, Durham, Durham DH1 4PS
✆ 0191 3868070 Fax 0191 3868070

CASTLE EDEN & PETERLEE GOLF CLUB

Castle Eden, Hartlepool, Durham TS27 4SS
✆ 01429 836220 **Map 11, B1**
www.ceden-golf.co.uk
A19, 10 miles S of Sunderland
Founded 1927
Very attractive rolling parkland course.
18 holes, 6262 yards
par 70, S.S.S 70
Designer Sir Henry Cotton
Green fees £22
Catering, changing room/showers, bar, club and trolley hire, shop, practice facilities
Visitors welcome
Societies welcome by prior arrangement

CHESTER-LE-STREET GOLF CLUB

Lumley Park, Chester-le-Street, Durham DH3 4NS
✆ 0191 388 3218 Fax 0191388 1220
Map 11, A1
B1284/A167, 1 mile E of Chester-le-Street
Founded 1908
A parkland course in the grounds of Lumley Castle.
18 holes, 6437 yards
par 71, S.S.S 71
Designer J.H. Taylor
Green fees £20
Changing room/showers, bar, club and trolley hire, shop
Visitors welcome weekdays with restrictions
Handicap certificate required
Societies welcome by prior arrangement
🏨 Lumley Castle, Chester-le-Street, Durham DH3 4NX
✆ 0191 3891111 Fax 0191 3891881

CONSETT & DISTRICT GOLF CLUB

Elmfield Road, Consett, Durham DH8 5NN
✆ 01207 502186 Fax 01207 505060
Map 10, H1
secretary@consettgolfclub.SAFC.co.uk
www.derwentside.org.uk/consettgolfclub
A691, E of town centre
Founded 1911
Good value, as with so many courses in County Durham. The views over the Derwent Valley towards the Cheviots are panoramic.
18 holes, 6020 yards
par 71, S.S.S 69
Designer Harry Vardon
Green fees £18
Catering, changing room/showers, bar, trolley hire, shop
Visitors welcome, restricted weekends
Handicap certificate required
Societies welcome by prior arrangement
🏨 Raven Country Hotel, Broomhill, Ebchester, Durham
✆ 01207 562562

CROOK GOLF CLUB

Low Job's Hill, Crook, Durham DL15 9AA
✆ 01388 762429 Fax 01388 767926
Map 10, H1
Off A690, ½ mile E of Crook
Founded 1919
A mixture of parkland and heathland with splendid views and 'greens to test the best'.
18 holes, 6076 yards
par 70, S.S.S 69
Green fees £16
Catering, changing room/showers, bar, practice facilities, conference/function facilities
Visitors welcome
Societies welcome by prior arrangement
🏨 The Old Manor House Hotel and Country Club, The Green, West Auckland, Durham
✆ 01388 834834

DARLINGTON GOLF CLUB

Haughton Grange, Darlington, Durham DL1 3JD
✆ 01325 355324 Fax 01325 488126
Map 11, A3
Off A167/A1150, NE of Darlington
Founded 1908
A beautifully conditioned parkland course.
18 holes, 6270 yards
par 71, S.S.S 70
Designer Alister Mackenzie
Green fees £22
Catering, changing room/showers, club and trolley hire, shop, practice facilities
Visitors welcome weekdays – with restrictions
Societies welcome by prior arrangement

DINSDALE SPA GOLF CLUB

Middleton St George, Darlington, Durham DL2 1DW
✆ 01325 332297 Fax 01325 332297
Map 11, A3
5 miles SE of Darlington, between Middleton St George and Neasham
Founded 1910
Parkland course, mainly straightforward, but with a couple of interesting holes in and out of a valley.
18 holes, 6099 yards
par 71, S.S.S 69
Green fees £25
Catering, changing room/showers, bar, trolley hire, shop, practice facilities
Visitors welcome with restrictions Tuesday and weekends
Societies welcome by prior arrangement
🏨 Croft Spa Hotel, Croft on Tees, Darlington, Durham

DURHAM CITY GOLF CLUB

Littleburn, Langley Moor, Durham, Durham DH7 8HL
✆ 0191 378 0069 Fax 0191 378 4265 **Map 11, A1**
Off A690, 1½ miles W of Durham
Founded 1887
A parkland course alongside a river.
18 holes, 6326 yards
par 71, S.S.S 70
Designer C.C. Stanton
Green fees £22
Catering, changing room/showers, bar, trolley and buggy hire, shop, practice facilities
Visitors welcome weekdays
Societies welcome by prior arrangement

EAGLESCLIFFE GOLF CLUB

Yarm Road, Eaglescliffe, Stockton-on-Tees, Durham TS16 0DQ
✆ 01642 780238 Fax 01642 780238
Map 11, B3
egcsec@lineone.net
A135, S of Stockton-on-Tees
Founded 1914
Set on a hilly site beside the River Tees, giving fine views of the Cleveland Hills.
18 holes, 6275 yards
par 72, S.S.S 70
Designer James Braid, Sir Henry Cotton
Green fees £26
Catering, changing room/showers, bar, club and trolley hire, shop, practice facilities
Visitors welcome subject to restrictions
Handicap certificate required
Societies welcome by prior arrangement
🏨 Sunnyside Hotel, 580-582 Yarm Road, Eaglescliffe, Stockton-on-Tees, Durham TS16 0DF
✆ 01642 780075

HALL GARTH GOLF AND COUNTRY CLUB HOTEL

Coatham Mundeville, Darlington, Durham DL1 3LU
✆ 01325 320 246 Fax 01325 310 083 **Map 11, A3**
A167 towards Darlington, A1 (M) Jct 59.
Founded 1995
A lengthy 9-hole course with a number of tricky water holes.
9 holes, 6621 yards
par 72, S.S.S 72
Designer Brian Moore
Green fees £12.50
Catering, changing room/showers, bar, accommodation, club and trolley hire, shop, practice facilities
Visitors welcome – with restrictions
Societies welcome by prior arrangement
🏨 Hall Garth Hotel, Coatham Mundeville, Darlington, Durham
✆ 01325 300400

HARTLEPOOL GOLF CLUB

Hart Warren, Hartlepool, Durham TS24 9QF
✆ 01429 274398 Fax 01429 274129
Map 11, B2
www.hartlepoolgolfclub.co.uk
Off A1086, N of Hartlepool
Founded 1906
An attractive mix of seaside and genuine links holes, not unduly long, but there are tough holes such as the par-4 8th and 14th, and the unforgiving short par-3 7th, over a deep ravine. James Braid's 367-yard 10th is a club favourite, albeit to a hidden green.
18 holes, 6202 yards
par 70, S.S.S 70
Designer James Braid
Green fees £24
Catering, changing room/showers, bar, club and trolley hire, shop
Visitors welcome weekdays
Societies welcome by prior arrangement

HIGH THROSTON GOLF CLUB

Hart Lane, Hartlepool, Durham TS26 0UG

☎ 01429 275325 **Map 11, B2**
A179, off A19, 2 miles NW of Hartlepool.
Founded 1997
A parkland course.
18 holes, 6247 yards
par 71, S.S.S 70
Designer Jonathan Gaunt
Green fees £16
Changing room/showers
Visitors welcome
Societies welcome by prior arrangement

HOBSON MUNICIPAL GOLF CLUB

Hobson, Burnopfield, Newcastle-upon-Tyne, Durham NE16 6BZ
☎ 01207 271605 **Map 13, G10**
A692, 6 miles SW of Newcastle
Founded 1978
A parkland course.
18 holes, 6403 yards
S.S.S 71
Green fees £13
Catering, changing room/showers, bar, club and trolley hire, shop
Visitors welcome
Societies welcome by prior arrangement

KNOTTY HILL GOLF CENTRE

Sedgefield, Stockton-on-Tees, Durham TS21 2BB
☎ 01740 620320 Fax 01740 622227
Map 11, A2
A1(M) Jct 60, 1 mile N of Sedgefield on A177
Founded 1992
Rather impressive young courses, making the most of their natural resources of woodland and water.
Princes Course: 18 holes, 6577 yards, par 72, S.S.S 71
Bishops Course: 18 holes, 5859 yards, par 70,
Designer C. Stanton
Green fees £13
Catering, changing room/showers, accommodation, trolley and buggy hire, shop, driving range, practice facilities, conference facilities
Visitors welcome
Societies welcome by prior arrangement
🏨 Hardwick Hall Hotel, Sedgefield, Stockton on Tees, Durham TS21 2EH
☎ 01740 620253

MOUNT OSWALD MANOR AND GOLF COURSE

South Road, Durham, Durham DH1 3TQ
☎ 0191 3867527 Fax 0191 3860975
Map 11, A1
information@mountoswald.co.uk
www.mountoswald.co.uk
Of A177, 1 mile SW of city centre.
Founded 1924
Exceedingly good value for a well-established parkland course close to a city centre. The extensive facilities of the impressive listed Georgian mansion house are available for a wide range of functions.
18 holes, 6101 yards
par 71, S.S.S 69
Green fees £12.50
Catering, changing room/showers, bar, club and trolley hire, practice facilities, extensive conference and function facilities
Visitors welcome
Societies welcome by prior arrangement
🏨 Swallow Three Tuns Hotel, New Elvet, Durham, Durham DH1 3AQ
☎ 0191 386 4326

NORTON GOLF COURSE

Junction Road, Norton, Stockton-on-Tees, Durham TS20 1HN
☎ 01642 676385 Fax 01642 608467
Map 11, B2
1 mile E of A177, from A19
Founded 1989
Inexpensive pay-and-play course with a demanding 2nd hole, a 124-yard full carry over water.
18 holes, 5855 yards
par 70, S.S.S 71
Designer T. Harper
Green fees £10
Catering, trolley hire, practice facilities, garden centre, bowling green
Visitors welcome
Societies welcome weekdays
🏨 Swallow Hotel, High Street, Stockton, Durham

OAKLEAF GOLF COMPLEX

School Aycliffe Lane, Newton Aycliffe, Durham DL5 6QZ
☎ 01325 310820 Fax 01325 310820
Map 11, A2
A1 Jct 59
Founded 1993
A mature parkland course offering excellent value for money.
18 holes, 5818 yards
par 70, S.S.S 68
Green fees £9
Catering, changing room/showers, bar, club and trolley hire, shop, driving range, conference facilities, many other sports facilities
Visitors welcome
Societies welcome by prior arrangement
🏨 Redworth Hall Hotel, Redworth, Heighton, Durham
☎ 01388 770600

RAMSIDE HALL GOLF CLUB

Ramside Hall Hotel, Carrville, Durham, Durham DH1 1TD
☎ 0191 386 9514 Fax 0191 386 9519 **Map 11, A1**
A690, 2 miles E of Durham
Founded 1995
3 loops of 9 holes, much interrupted by water, part of the comprehensive golfing facilities that are available at this hotel.
Bishops Course: 9 holes, 3285 yards, par 36
Designer Jonathan Gaunt
Cathedral Course: 9 holes, 2874 yards, par 34
Princes Course: 9 holes, 3235 yards, par 36, S.S.S 36
Green fees £28
Catering, changing room/showers, bar, accommodation, club, trolley and buggy hire, shop, driving range, practice facilities
Visitors welcome
Societies welcome by prior arrangement
🏨 Ramside Hall Hotel, Carville, Durham, Durham
☎ 0191 386 5282

ROSEBERRY GRANGE GOLF CLUB

Grange Villa, Chester-le-Street, Durham DH2 3NF
☎ 0191 370 0670 Fax 0191 370 2047 **Map 11, A1**
A693, 3 miles W of Chester-le-Street
Founded 1986
Quite a challenging public course.
18 holes, 5892 yards
par 70, S.S.S 68
Green fees £12
Catering, changing room/showers, bar, club and trolley hire, shop, driving range
Visitors welcome
Societies welcome by prior arrangement

RYHOPE GOLF CLUB

Leechmere Way, Hollycarrside, Ryhope, Sunderland, Durham SR2 0DH
☎ 0191 523 7333 Fax 0191 521 3811 **Map 13, H11**
Off A19, 3 miles S of Sunderland
Founded 1992
A public parkland course.
18 holes, 4601 yards
par 65, S.S.S 63
Designer Jonathan Gaunt
Green fees £6
Changing room/showers, bar, club hire, shop
Visitors welcome
Societies welcome by prior arrangement

SEAHAM GOLF CLUB

Shrewsbury Street, Dawdon, Seaham, Durham SR7 7RD
☎ 0191 581 2354 **Map 11, B1**
Off A19
Founded 1908
A heathland course with good views close to the sea.
18 holes, 6017 yards
par 70, S.S.S 69
Designer Alister Mackenzie
Green fees £18
Catering, changing room/showers, bar, club and trolley hire, shop
Visitors welcome
Societies welcome by prior arrangement

SEATON CAREW GOLF CLUB

Tees Road, Hartlepool, Durham TS25 1DE
☎ 01429 890660 **Map 11, B2**
www.seatoncarewgolfclub.org.uk
On sea front, S of Seaton Carew (via A19/A689)
Founded 1874
22 holes can be configured in two forms. It hardly matters which, for this is undoubtedly one of the most testing championship links in England, good enough to host the Brabazon Trophy. Critics may denounce the industrial skyline, but when the golf is of this quality who notices the surroundings?
Old: 18 holes, 6613 yards, par 72, S.S.S 72
Designer Dr. McCuaig, Alister Mackenzie
Brabazon: 18 holes, 6855 yards, par 73, S.S.S 73
Designer Dr. McCuaig, Alister Mackenzie, Frank Pennink
Green fees £32
Catering, changing room/showers, bar, club, trolley and buggy hire, shop, practice facilities
Visitors welcome – restrictions weekends
Handicap certificate required
Societies welcome by prior arrangement
🏨 Marine Hotel, The Front, Seaton Carew, Hartlepool, Durham
☎ 01429 864144

SOUTH MOOR GOLF CLUB

The Middles, Craghead, Stanley, Durham DH9 6AG
☎ 01207 232848 Fax 01207 284616
Map 10, H1
www.southmoor-golfclub.co.uk
B6532, 1 mile S of Stanley
Founded 1923
Heather and gorse are amongst the threats lying off the fairways on this testing, hilly course.
18 holes, 6271 yards
par 72, S.S.S 70
Designer Alister Mackenzie
Green fees £15
Catering, changing room/showers, bar, club, trolley and buggy hire, shop, practice facilities
Visitors welcome – restricted weekends
Handicap certificate required
Societies welcome by prior arrangement
🏨 Lumley Castle, Chester-le-Street, Durham DH3 4NX
☎ 0191 389 1111 Fax 1913891881

STRESSHOLME GOLF CLUB

Snipe Lane, Darlington, Durham DL2 2SA
☎ 01325 461002 Fax 01325 351826
Map 11, A3
Off A67, SW of Darlington
Founded 1976
A long and well equipped municipal course.
18 holes, 6511 yards
par 70, S.S.S 71
Green fees £9.50
Catering, changing room/showers, bar, club and trolley hire, shop, driving range
Visitors welcome
Societies welcome by prior arrangement

WOODHAM GOLF AND COUNTRY CLUB

Burnhill Way, Newton Aycliffe, Durham DH5 4PN
☎ 01325 320574 Fax 01325 315254
Map 11, A2
1 mile S of A689 at Newton Aycliffe
Founded 1981
Excellent value for such an entertaining, well-wooded course.
18 holes, 6719 yards
par 73, S.S.S 72
Designer J Hamilton Stutt
Green fees £16.50
Catering, changing room/showers, bar, club, trolley and buggy hire, shop, practice facilities, function room
Visitors welcome – restricted weekends
Societies welcome by prior arrangement
🏨 Eden Arms Hotel, Rushyford, Durham
☎ 01388 720541

THE WYNYARD CLUB

Wellington Drive, Wynyard Park, Billingham, Durham TS22 5QJ
☎ 01740 644399 Fax 01740 644058
Map 11, B2
Off A689, E of Sedgefield
Founded 1996
Laid out in the grounds of the former home of the Marquesses of Londonderry, the Wellington Course can be stretched to over 7,000 yards. Two of the short holes, the 3rd and 12th, involve compulsory carries over lakes, and water makes the 15th and 16th exciting for the big hitter.
18 holes, 6851 yards
par 72, S.S.S 73
Designer Hawtree
Catering, changing room/showers, bar, club, trolley and buggy hire, shop, driving range, practice facilities
Visitors welcome only as members' guests
Societies welcome by prior arrangement

GREATER MANCHESTER

BLACKLEY GOLF CLUB

Victoria Avenue East, Manchesterr M9 7HW
☎ 0161 643 2980 **Map 10, F9**
A6104, NE Manchester
Founded 1907
A parkland course alongside the recently opened M60 Manchester Ring Road.
18 holes, 6235 yards
par 70, S.S.S 70
Green fees £24
Catering, changing room/showers, bar, trolley and buggy hire, shop
Visitors welcome weekdays – with restrictions
Societies welcome by prior arrangement

CHORLTON-CUM-HARDY GOLF CLUB

Barlow Hall, Barlow Hall Road, Manchester M21 7JJ
☎ 0161 881 3139 Fax 0161 881 4532 **Map 10, F10**
chorltongolf@hotmail.com
www.chorltoncumhardygolfclub.sagenet.co.uk
Off M56/A5103, at Barlow Moor Road, SW Manchester
Founded 1902
Characterful course alongside River Mersey, with a historic, half-timbered clubhouse, with its resident ghost.
18 holes, 5980 yards
par 70, S.S.S 69
Green fees £25
Catering, changing room/showers, bar, club and trolley hire, shop, practice facilities
Visitors welcome
Societies welcome by prior arrangement

🏨 Britannia Country House Hotel, Palatine Road, Didsbury, Greater Manchester
✆ 0161 434 3411

DAVYHULME PARK GOLF CLUB

Gleneagles Road, Davyhulme, Manchester M41 8SA
✆ 0161 748 2260 Fax 0161 747 4067 **Map 10, F10**
M60 Jct 9, heading for Urmston. Take Moorside Road past Trafford General Hospital, right into Gleneagles Road.
Founded 1910
A parkland course. The club was origanally called Entwisle Golf Club, founded in 1893.
18 holes, 6237 yards
par 72, S.S.S 70
Green fees £26
Catering, changing room/showers, bar, club and trolley hire, shop, practice facilities
Visitors welcome weekdays – restrictions
Handicap certificate required
Societies welcome by prior arrangement

DENTON GOLF CLUB

Manchester Road, Denton, Manchester M34 2GF
✆ 0161 336 3218 Fax 0161 336 4751 **Map 10, F9**
M60 Jct 24, A57, E of Manchester
Founded 1909
Parkland course overlooking Audenshaw Reservoirs.
18 holes, 6496 yards
par 71, S.S.S 71
Green fees £25
Catering, changing room/showers, bar, trolley hire, shop, practice facilities
Visitors welcome – restricted weekends
Handicap certificate required
Societies welcome by prior arrangement
🏨 Malmaison, Piccadilly, Manchester, Greater Manchester M1 3AQ
✆ 0161 278 1000 Fax 0161 278 1002

DIDSBURY GOLF CLUB

Ford Lane, Northenden, Manchester, Greater Manchester M22 4NQ
✆ 0161 998 9278 Fax 0161 998 9278 **Map 10, F10**
6 miles S of Manchester, M63 Jct 9
Founded 1891
A course in two parts, either side of M60. Easy walking on flat ground along the banks of the River Mersey.
18 holes, 6273 yards
par 70, S.S.S 70
Green fees £26
Catering, changing room/showers, bar, trolley hire, shop
Visitors welcome weekdays
Handicap certificate required
Societies welcome by prior arrangment

ELLESMERE GOLF CLUB

Old Clough Lane, Worsley, Manchester M28 7HZ
✆ 0161 790 8591 **Map 10, F9**
honsec@ellesmeregolf.fsnet.co.uk
www.ellesmeregolf.co.uk
A580 Eastbound (turn left just before M60 Northbound Junction)
Founded 1913
With four new holes the club has the luxury of different winter and summer courses. Two streams affect 11 holes, and one hole even has its own disused mine-shaft.
18 holes, 6247 yards
par 70, S.S.S 70
Green fees £22
Catering, changing room/showers, bar, trolley hire, shop, practice facilities
Visitors welcome – restrictions competition days
Handicap certificate required
Societies welcome by prior arrangement
🏨 Novotel, Worsley, Manchester, Greater Manchester

FAIRFIELD GOLF AND SAILING CLUB

Booth Road, Audenshaw, Manchester M34 5GA
✆ 0161 370 1641 **Map 10, F9**
Off A635, SE of Manchester
Founded 1892
Laid out alongside a reservoir.
18 holes, 5664 yards
par 68, S.S.S 68
Green fees £18
Catering, changing room/showers, bar, trolley hire, shop
Visitors welcome weekdays
Societies welcome by prior arrangement

FLIXTON GOLF CLUB

Church Road, Flixton, Manchester M41 6EP
✆ 0161 746 7160 Fax 0161 748 2116 **Map 10, F9**
M60 Jct 10, follow signs to Urmston. Follow Church Road to Flixton
Founded 1893
One of the longest 9-hole courses in the UK, well maintained, and a good test of golf.
9 holes, 6410 yards
par 71, S.S.S 71
Green fees £16
Catering, changing room/showers, bar, trolley hire, shop, practice facilities
Visitors welcome weekdays, except Wednesday
Societies welcome by prior arrangement
🏨 Manor Hey, Stretford Road, Urmston, Manchester, Greater Manchester
✆ 0161 748 3896

THE GREAT LEVER & FARNWORTH GOLF CLUB

Plodder Lane, Farnworth, Bolton, Greater Manchester BL4 0LQ
✆ 01204 656650 Fax 01204 656137 **Map 10, F9**
M61 Jct 4 or A666, 2 miles S of Bolton.
Founded 1901
A parkland course.
18 holes, 6064 yards
par 70, S.S.S 69
Green fees £20
Catering, changing room/showers, bar, club and trolley hire, shop, practice facilities
Visitors welcome – subject to restrictions
Handicap certificate required
Societies welcome by prior arrangement
🏨 Bolton Moat House, 1 Higher Bridge Street, Bolton, Greater Manchester
✆ 01204 879988

HEATON PARK GOLF CLUB

Heaton Park, Prestwich, Manchester M25 5SW
✆ 0161 654 9899 **Map 10, F9**
M60 Jct 19
Founded 1912
Much exciting golf on this municipal course full of character, especially the water holes.
18 holes, 5815 yards
par 70, S.S.S 70
Designer J.H. Taylor
Green fees £10
Catering, changing room/showers, bar, club and trolley hire, shop, driving range, practice facilities
Visitors welcome
Societies welcome by prior arrangement

THE MANCHESTER GOLF CLUB

Hopwood Cottage, Rochdale Road, Middleton, Manchester M24 6QP
✆ 0161 643 3202 Fax 0161 643 9174 **Map 10, F9**
mgc@zen.co.uk
www.manchestergc.co.uk
M62 Jct 20, A 627(M) towards Middleton/Oldham, A664 to

Middleton
Founded 1882
An old and distinguished club with an expansive layout and excellent facilities. Tough moorland rough and many a steep drop await the ball hit off line, and three of the short holes are played across valleys. To miss a green such as the 12th by mere inches can be disastrous.
18 holes, 6519 yards
par 72, S.S.S 72
Designer Harry Colt
Green fees £30
Catering, changing room/showers, bar, trolley and buggy hire, shop, driving range, practice facilities, conference, banquet, wedding, and exhibition facilities
Visitors welcome – with restrictions
Handicap certificate required
Societies welcome by prior arrangement
Norton Grange, Manchester Road, Rochdale, Greater Manchester
01706 630788

MANOR GOLF CLUB

Moss Lane, Kearsley, Greater Manchester BL4 8SF
01204 701027 Fax 01204 796914
Map 10, F9
M62 Jct 17.
Founded 1995
A parkland pay and play course with a driving range adjacent.
18 holes, 5010 yards
par 66, S.S.S 64
Designer Jeff Yates
Green fees £5
Catering, changing room/showers, bar, club and trolley hire, shop, driving range
Visitors welcome
Societies welcome by prior arrangement

NORTH MANCHESTER GOLF CLUB

Rhodes House, Manchester Old Road, Middleton, Manchester M24 4PE
0161 643 9033 Fax 0161 643 7775 **Map 10, F9**
www.nmgc.co.uk
Off A6104, M60 Jct 19/20
Founded 1894
Adventurous, hilly course with a number of very challenging water holes, not least the18th, a long par 3 all carry over a lake. In fact water threatens right from the start with an uphill drive over a pond. The long par-4 10th is a brilliant, unforgiving cape hole.
18 holes, 6598 yards
par 72, S.S.S 72
Designer A. Compston
Green fees £25
Catering, changing room/showers, bar, trolley hire, shop, practice facilities
Visitors welcome
Societies welcome by prior arrangement

NORTHENDEN GOLF CLUB

Palatine Road, Manchester M22 4FR
0161 998 4738 Fax 0161 945 5592 **Map 10, F10**
Off M56/Parkway 5 miles SW of Manchester.
Founded 1913
One of the best of Manchester's Mersey courses with a notoriously difficult start along its banks.
18 holes, 6503 yards
par 72, S.S.S 71
Designer T.G. Renouf
Green fees £27
Catering, changing room/showers, bar, club and trolley hire, shop, practice facilities
Visitors welcome
Societies welcome by prior arrangement
Britannia Country House Hotel, Palatine Road, Didsbury, Greater Manchester
0161 434 3411

PIKE FOLD GOLF CLUB

Hills Lane, Unsworth, Bury, Greater Manchester BL9 8QP
0161 766 3561 Fax 0161 796 3569 **Map 10, F9**
M66 Jct 3. from slip road turn left at lights (Pillsworth Road). Turn left at Hollins Lane. Turn left at Pole Lane, follow signs to club.
Founded 1921
A lengthy 9-hole course with USGA-specification greens giving good playing conditions all year round.
9 holes, 6312 yards
par 72, S.S.S 72
Designer Steve Marnoch
Green fees £20
Catering, changing room/showers, bar, club and trolley hire, shop, practice facilities, function/wedding/conference room
Visitors welcome – subject to restrictions. Handicap certificate required
Societies welcome by prior arrangement

PRESTWICH GOLF CLUB

Hilton Lane, Prestwich, Greater Manchester M25 9XB
0161 773 2544 Fax 0161 772 0700 **Map 10, F9**
M60 Jct 17, A56 towards Manchester
Founded 1908
A short but tight parkland course.
18 holes, 4806 yards
par 64, S.S.S 64
Green fees £20
Catering, changing room/showers, bar, club and trolley hire, shop
Visitors welcome weekdays.
Handicap certificate required
Societies welcome by prior arrangement

STAND GOLF CLUB

The Dales, Ashbourne Grove, Whitefield, Manchester M45 7NL
T 0161 766 2388 Fax 0161 796 3234
Map 10, F9
M60 Jct 17, A665 off A56
Founded 1904
Although parkland in nature and bounded by roads and housing, there is a moorland feel to the golf with excellent use made of the many natural undulations to create a testing and satisfying course.
18 holes, 6411 yards
par 72, S.S.S 71
Designer Alex Herd
Green fees £25
Catering, changing room/showers, bar, club and trolley hire, shop, practice facilities
Visitors welcome weekdays
Societies welcome by prior arrangement

SWINTON PARK GOLF CLUB

East Lancs Road, Swinton, Manchester M27 5LX
0161 794 0861 Fax 0161 281 0698 **Map 10, F9**
A580 (East Lancs Road), 5 miles from centre of Manchester
Founded 1926
A long parkland course, and one on which the visitor does not feel cheated having to play from yellow markers – there is very little difference in the white and yellow cards.
18 holes, 6726 yards
par 73, S.S.S 72
Green fees £25
Catering, changing room/showers, bar, trolley hire, shop, practice facilities, conference and function facilities
Visitors welcome weekdays.
Handicap certificate required
Societies welcome by prior arrangement

WHITEFIELD GOLF CLUB

Higher Lane, Whitefield, Manchester M45 7EZ
0161 351 2700 Fax 0161 351 2712 **Map 10, F9**
M60 Jct 17, off A56

Founded 1932
A parkland course.
18 holes, 6045 yards
par 69, S.S.S 69
Green fees £25
Catering, changing room/showers, bar, club and trolley hire, shop, practice facilities, tennis courts
Visitors welcome with restrictions
Societies welcome by prior arrangement

WILLIAM WROE GOLF COURSE

Pennybridge Lane, Flixton, Manchester M31 3DL
☎ 0161 748 8680 **Map 10, F9**
B5158, M6 Jct 4
Founded 1973
A flat parkland course west of Manchester city centre.
18 holes, 4395 yards
par 68, S.S.S 65
Green fees £7.90
Catering, changing room/showers, bar, club hire, shop
Visitors welcome – with restrictions
Societies welcome by prior arrangement

WITHINGTON GOLF CLUB

243 Palatine Road, West Didsbury, Manchester M20 2UE
☎ 0161 445 9544 Fax 0161 445 5210 **Map 10, F10**
On Palatine Road, between Northenden and Withington.
Founded 1892
On flat ground beside the Mersey, with the 5th and the finish from the tigerish 14th as the star holes.
18 holes, 6364 yards
par 71, S.S.S 70
Green fees £26
Catering, changing room/showers, bar, club and trolley hire, shop, practice facilities
Visitors welcome weekdays
Handicap certificate required.
Societies welcome by prior arrangement
🏨 Britannia Country House Hotel, Palatine Road, Didsbury, Greater Manchester
☎ 0161 434 3411

WORSLEY GOLF CLUB

Stableford Avenue, Monton Green, Eccles, Manchester M30 8AP
☎ 0161 789 4202 Fax 0161 789 3200 **Map 10, F9**
Off A572, M60 Jct 13
Founded 1894
A parkland course.
18 holes, 6252 yards
par 71, S.S.S 70
Designer James Braid
Green fees £20
Catering, changing room/showers, bar, club and trolley hire, shop, practice facilities
Visitors welcome with restrictions
Societies welcome by prior arrangement

MARRIOTT WORSLEY PARK HOTEL & COUNTRY CLUB

Worsley Park, Worsley, Greater Manchester M28 2QT
☎ 0161 975 2043 Fax 0161 799 6341 **Map 10, F10**
www.marriotthotels.com/mangs
A575, close to M60 Jct 13
Founded 1999
Set in over 200 acres of parkland, with 8 lakes and 70 bunkers, this welcome addition to the otherwise rather dull golfing provision in West Manchester calls on brains at least as much as muscle to achieve a good score.
18 holes, 6611 yards
par 71, S.S.S 72
Designer Ross McMurray
Green fees £50
Catering, changing room/showers, bar, accommodation, club, trolley and buggy hire, shop, driving range, practice facilities, full hotel, leisure, conference, health and beauty and function facilities
Visitors welcome, subject to restrictions
Handicap certificate required
Societies welcome by prior arrangement
🏨 Marriott Worsley Park Hotel and Country Club, Worsley Park, Worsley, Manchester M28 2QT
☎ 0161 975 2000 Fax 0161 799 6341

ISLE OF MAN

CASTLETOWN HOTEL GOLF CLUB

Fort Island, Derbyhaven, Isle of Man IM9 1UA
☎ 01624 822201 Fax 01624 824633
At Derbyhaven close to airport
Founded 1892
An exhilarating seaside course with one of the most exciting finishes imaginable. The last three holes run along the rocks, with a big carry over the waves called for on the 17th tee. It is easy enough to finish in the sea on the approach to the final green, too.
18 holes, 6711 yards
par 72, S.S.S 72
Designer Mackenzie Ross
Green fees £28
Catering, changing room/showers, bar, accommodation, club, trolley and buggy hire, shop
Visitors welcome
Societies welcome by prior arrangement
🏨 Castletown Golf Links Hotel, Fort Island, Castletown, Isle of Man
☎ 01624 822201

DOUGLAS MUNICIPAL GOLF CLUB

Pulrose Park, Douglas, Isle of Man IM2 1AE
☎ 01624 675952
1 mile from Douglas, close to power station
Founded 1927
The only municipal course on the Isle of Man, with most holes on hilly ground giving good views but seriously punishing the inaccurate.
18 holes, 5922 yards
par 69, S.S.S 69
Designer Alister Mackenzie
Green fees £10
Catering, changing room/showers, bar, club and trolley hire, shop
Visitors welcome
Societies welcome by prior arrangement

KING EDWARD BAY GOLF CLUB

Groudle Road, Howstrake, Onchan, Isle of Man IM3 2JR
☎ 01624 672709 Fax 01624 827724
N from Douglas Promenade on coast road, turning into Harbour Road, then Groudle Road
Founded 1893
A heroic effort rescued the old Howstrake club from extinction in the 1980s. Some of Tom Morris's original holes were lost, but new holes have been created, running through the gorse towards Groudle Bay. Stunning scenery, testing golf.
18 holes, 5284 yards
par 67, S.S.S 66
Designer Tom Morris
Green fees £14
Catering, changing room/showers, bar, club, trolley and buggy hire, shop, practice facilities, conference room, restaurant available for banquets, functions
Visitors welcome
Handicap certificate required.
Societies welcome by prior arrangement
🏨 Imperial Hotel, Central Promenade, Douglas, Isle of Man IM2 4LU
☎ 01624 621656 Fax 1624 672160

MOUNT MURRAY GOLF AND COUNTRY CLUB

Santon, Isle of Man IM4 2HT
☎ 01624 661111 Fax 01624 611116

hotel@enterprise.net
www.mountmurray.com
At Santon off Douglas-Castletown road
Founded 1975
A modern design, yet many of the hazards are of the traditional kind, principally gorse, streams, and ponds, but also an indigenous threat, the Manx hedge. Views from the high ground are splendid and the golfer is invited to gamble on dog-legs and the pond of the closing par 5.
18 holes, 6715 yards
par 73, S.S.S 73
Designer Bingley Sports Turf Research
Green fees £25
Catering, changing room/showers, bar, accommodation, club, trolley and buggy hire, shop, driving range, practice facilities, full hotel facilities
Visitors welcome
Societies welcome by prior arrangement
Mount Murray Hotel, Santon, Isle of Man IM4 2HT
0162 4661111

PEEL GOLF CLUB

Rheast Lane, Peel, Isle of Man IM5 1BG
01624 843456 Fax 01624 843456
peelgolfclub@manx.net
www.geocities.com/peelgc
Entering Peel on A1 from St Johns, first left after High School
Founded 1895
A vintage James Braid course, not long but requiring intelligent play, with particularly interesting greens. Heather, gorse and a stream are the main problems, with the 8th and 11th notably strong holes.
18 holes, 5850 yards
par 69, S.S.S 69
Designer James Braid
Green fees £18
Catering, changing room/showers, bar, club and trolley hire, shop, practice facilities, snooker
Visitors welcome, subject to restrictions for club events, particularly Saturdays
Societies welcome by prior arrangement
Hilton, Central Promenade, Douglas, Isle of Man
01624 625535

PORT ST MARY GOLF CLUB

Kallow Road, Port St Mary, Isle of Man IM9 5EJ
01624 834932
Signposted from Port St Mary
Founded 1936
A hilly course, renowned for its excellent greens and marvellous views.
9 holes, 5418 yards
par 68, S.S.S 66
Designer George Duncan
Green fees £11
Catering, changing room/showers, bar, club and trolley hire, shop
Visitors welcome with restrictions
Societies welcome by prior arrangement

RAMSEY GOLF CLUB

Brookfield, Ramsey, Isle of Man IM8 2AH
01624 812244 Fax 01624 815833
ramsey.golfclub@iofm.net
Brookfield Avenue, off Parliament Square/Mountain Road
Founded 1891
The oldest course on the Isle of Man, on which racing driver Nigel Mansell won the club championship in 1990. Delightful surroundings.
18 holes, 5960 yards
par 70, S.S.S 69
Designer James Braid
Green fees £22
Catering, changing room/showers, bar, club and trolley hire, shop, practice facilities
Visitors welcome weekdays
Handicap certificate required
Societies welcome by prior arrangement
Grand Island Hotel, Bride Road, Ramsey, Isle of Man
01624 812455

ROWANY GOLF CLUB

Rowany Drive, Port Erin, Isle of Man IM9 6LN
01624 834072 Fax 01624 834072
At Port Erin
Founded 1895
A friendly club, with a short but sporting course close to Bradda Head. Many an outcrop of prickly gorse and a central rocky hillock provide the most exciting golf. The par-5 5th involves a blind approach to a hilltop green, and the 12th and 14th are full of character.
18 holes, 5970 yards
par 70, S.S.S 68
Green fees £14
Catering, changing room/showers, bar, club, trolley and buggy hire, shop, practice facilities, pitch-and-putt course
Visitors welcome
Societies welcome by prior arrangement
Ocean Castle, Promenade, Port Erin, Isle of Man IM9 6LH
01624 836399 Fax 01624 836537

LANCASHIRE

ACCRINGTON AND DISTRICT GOLF CLUB

Devon Avenue, Oswaldwistle, Accrington, Lancashire BB5 4LS
01254 231091 Fax 01254 233273
Map 10, F8
info@accrington-golf-club.fsnet.co.uk
www.accrington-golf-club.fsnet.co.uk
M65 Jct 6/7
Founded 1893
A picturesque course on rolling moorland. The gravel-based greens give good surfaces all year round.
18 holes, 6060 yards
par 70, S.S.S 69
Designer James Birtwistle
Green fees £22
Catering, changing room/showers, bar, club, trolley and buggy hire, shop, practice facilities, clubhouse available for meetings and functions
Visitors welcome – restricted weekends
Handicap certificate required
Societies welcome by prior arrangement
Dunkenhalgh Hotel, Blackburn Road, Clayton-le-Moors, Lancashire
01254 398021

ASHTON & LEA GOLF CLUB

Tudor Avenue, Lea, Preston, Lancashire PR4 0XA
01772 735282 Fax 01772 735762
Map 10, D8
ashtonleagolf@supanet.com
www.ukgolfer.org
A5085, 3 miles W of Preston
Founded 1913
A good foil for the stern links courses of Lytham a few miles to the west. Quite a testing parkland course.
18 holes, 6334 yards
par 71, S.S.S 70
Designer J. Steer
Green fees £23
Catering, changing room/showers, bar, trolley hire, shop, practice facilities, conference/meeting facilities
Visitors welcome with restrictions
Societies welcome by prior arrangement

ASHTON-IN-MAKERFIELD GOLF CLUB

Garswood Park, Liverpool Road, Ashton-in-Makerfield, Lancashire WN4 0YT
01942 719330 **Map 10, E9**
M6 Jct 24 – southbound only. M6 Jct 23 northbound, A580

westbound. Follow A58 signs for Wigan & Ashton.
Founded 1902
Well secluded course, pretty when the trees are in leaf.
18 holes, 6205 yards
par 70, S.S.S 70
Green fees £28
Catering, changing room/showers, bar, club and trolley hire, shop, practice facilities
Visitors welcome weekdays.
Handicap certificate required
Societies welcome by prior arrangement
Haydock Thistle Hotel, Penny Lane, Haydock, St Helens, Lancashire
01942 272000

ASHTON-UNDER-LYNE GOLF CLUB

Gorsey Way, Ashton-under-Lyne, Lancashire OL6 9HT
0161 330 1537 Fax 0161 330 6673 **Map 10, G9**
Off B6194, 8 miles E of Manchester
Founded 1913
Rugged upland course with a fine short hole over a ravine to close the round.
18 holes, 6209 yards
par 70, S.S.S 70
Green fees £25
Catering, changing room/showers, bar, trolley hire, shop
Visitors welcome weekdays
Handicap certificate required
Societies welcome by prior arrangement
Broadoak Hotel, Broadoak Road, Ashton-under-Lyne, Lancashire
0161 330 2764

BACUP GOLF CLUB

Maden Road, Bankside Lane, Bacup, Lancashire OL13 8HN
01706 873170 Fax 01706 867726
Map 10, F8
A671, S of Bacup
Founded 1910
A moorland course.
9 holes, 6008 yards
par 70, S.S.S 69
Green fees £
Changing room/showers
Visitors welcome
Societies welcome by prior arrangement

BAXENDEN & DISTRICT GOLF CLUB

Top o' th' Meadow, Baxenden, Accrington, Lancashire BB5 2EA
01254 234555 **Map 10, F8**
www.baxendengolf.co.uk
Off M65 Jct 7/8, A56 following signs from Baxenden
Founded 1913
A moorland course with pleasant views.
9 holes, 5740 yards
par 70, S.S.S 68
Green fees £15
Catering, changing room/showers, bar
Visitors welcome weekdays
Societies welcome by prior arrangement

BEACON PARK GOLF CLUB

Beacon Lane, Dalton, Up Holland, Lancashire WN8 7RU
01695 627500 **Map 10, D9**
Off A577 at Up Holland
Founded 1982
Interesting and challenging parkland course close to the M6, pleasantly undulating.
18 holes, 5927 yards
par 72, S.S.S 69
Designer Donald Steel
Catering, changing room/showers, bar, club and trolley hire, shop, driving range, practice facilities
Visitors welcome with booking system
Societies welcome by prior arrangement

BLACKBURN GOLF CLUB

Beardwood Brow, Blackburn, Lancashire BB2 7AX
01254 51122 Fax 01254 665578
Map 10, E8
Off A677, 1 mile NW of Blackburn
Founded 1894
Good views of the Lancashire countryside and Pennines from this elevated site.
18 holes, 6144 yards
par 71, S.S.S 70
Green fees £24
Catering, changing room/showers, bar, trolley hire, shop, practice facilities
Visitors welcome, restricted weekends
Societies welcome by prior arrangement

DE VERE BLACKPOOL HOTEL GOLF CLUB

East Park Drive, Blackpool, Lancashire FY3 8LL
01253 766156 Fax 01253 798800
Map 10, C7
Next to Stanley Park
Founded 1994
A typical modern hotel course, also known as Heron's Reach, with a good deal of water to appeal to the vanity of the big hitter.
18 holes, 6628 yards
par 72, S.S.S 71
Designer Peter Alliss, Clive Clark
Green fees £35
Catering, changing room/showers, bar, accommodation, club, trolley and buggy hire, shop, driving range, practice facilities
Visitors welcome
Handicap certificate required
Societies welcome by prior arrangement
De Vere Blackpool Hotel, East Park.Drive, Blackpool, Lancashire
01253 838866

BLACKPOOL NORTH SHORE GOLF CLUB

Devonshire Road, Blackpool, Lancashire FY2 0RD
01253 352054 Fax 01253 591240
Map 10, C7
B5124 off Promenade
Founded 1904
Blackpool North Shore was for many years a final qualifying venue when the Open Championship was held at Royal Lytham. It is set on the cliffs north of the town centre, its turf perhaps more parkland than links in nature, and many problems are set by the course's considerable undulations.
18 holes, 6431 yards
par 71, S.S.S 71
Green fees £30
Catering, changing room/showers, bar, club and trolley hire, shop, practice facilities, dining facilities for up to 100
Visitors welcome weekdays
Handicap certificate required
Societies welcome by prior arrangement
Travel Inn Red Lion, Devonshire Road, Bispham, Blackpool, Lancashire
01253 354942

BLACKPOOL PARK GOLF CLUB

North Park Drive, Blackpool, Lancashire FY3 8LS
01253 397916 Fax 01253 397916
Map 10, C7
2 miles E of Blackpool, M55
Founded 1925
A municipal course, open to all, with a design by the great Dr. Mackenzie.
18 holes, 6087 yards
par 70, S.S.S 69
Designer Alister Mackenzie
Green fees £10.50
Catering, changing room/showers, bar, club and trolley hire, shop
Visitors welcome
Societies welcome by prior arrangement

BOLTON GOLF CLUB

Lostock Park, Bolton, Lancashire BL6 4AJ
☎ 01204 843067 Fax 0204 843067
Map 10, E9
HMS@boltongolf.golfagent.co.uk
www.golfagent.com/clubsites/bolton_golf_club
M61 Jct 6, follow directions for Horwich and Bolton
Founded 1891
An old club with a challenging heathland course
18 holes, 6237 yards
par 70, S.S.S 70
Green fees £30
Catering, changing room/showers, bar, trolley hire, shop, practice facilities
Visitors welcome
Handicap certificate required
Societies welcome by prior arrangement

BOLTON OLD LINKS GOLF CLUB

Chorley Old Road, Montserrat, Bolton, Lancashire BL1 5SU
☎ 01204 842307 Fax 01204 842307
Map 10, E9
B6626, 3 miles N of Bolton
Founded 1891
With only two par 4s exceeding 400 yards Bolton Old Links might, on paper, appear slightly short for the contemporary golfer. That is to ignore the considerable effect of the rolling terrain, and the brilliance of Alister Mackenzie, whose designs continue to challenge to this day. Fascinating golf. Uplifting surroundings.
18 holes, 6406 yards
par 72, S.S.S 72
Designer Alister Mackenzie
Green fees £30
Catering, changing room/showers, bar, trolley hire, shop, practice facilities, function rooms
Visitors welcome – with restrictions
Handicap certificate required
Societies welcome by prior arrangement
🏨 De Vere Whites Hotel, The Reebok Stadium, De Havilland Way, Lostock, Bolton, Lancashire
☎ 01204 667788

BOLTON OPEN GOLF

Longsight Park, Longsight Lane, Harwood, Lancashire BL2 4JX
☎ 0161 790 6076 **Map 10, E9**
A666, 3 miles NE of Bolton
A 9-hole pay-and-play course with driving range.
9 holes
Green fees £6.50
Visitors welcome
Societies welcome by prior arrangement

BRACKLEY MUNICIPAL GOLF COURSE

Bullows Road, Little Hulton, Worsley, Lancashire M38 9TR
☎ 0161 790 6076 **Map 10, F9**
Off A6, NW of Manchester
Founded 1977
A parkland course.
9 holes, 6006 yards
par 70, S.S.S 69
Green fees £4
Shop
Visitors welcome
Societies welcome by prior arrangement

BREIGHTMET GOLF CLUB

Red Bridge, Ainsworth, Bolton, Lancashire BL2 5PA
☎ 01204 527381 **Map 10, F9**
Off A58, E of Bolton
Founded 1911
An unusually long 9-hole course.
9 holes, 6416 yards
par 72, S.S.S 71
Green fees £15
Catering, changing room/showers, bar
Visitors welcome weekdays
Handicap certificate required
Societies welcome by prior arrangement

BROOKDALE GOLF CLUB

Medlock Road, Woodhouses, Failsworth, Lancashire M35 9WQ
☎ 0161 681 4534 Fax 0161 688 6872 **Map 10, F9**
www.chadys.freeserve.co.uk
Off A62, between Manchester and Oldham.
Founded 1896
A parkland course with several problems posed by a river.
18 holes, 5841 yards
par 68, S.S.S 68
Green fees £22
Catering, changing room/showers, bar, trolley hire, shop
Visitors welcome weekdays
Societies welcome by prior arrangement

BURNLEY GOLF CLUB

Glen View, Burnley, Lancashire BB11 3RW
☎ 01282 421045 Fax 01282 451281
Map 10, F7
www.burnley-golf.co.uk
Off A646, S of Burnley
Founded 1905
An upland course with pleasant views.
18 holes, 5911 yards
par 69, S.S.S 69
Green fees £20
Catering, changing room/showers, bar, trolley hire, shop
Visitors welcome
Societies welcome by prior arrangement

BURY GOLF CLUB

Unsworth Hall, Blackford Bridge, Bury, Lancashire BL9 9TJ
☎ 0161 766 4897 Fax 0161 796 3480 **Map 10, F9**
Off A56, M60 Jct 17
Founded 1890
Not particularly long but correspondingly tight, calling for accurate play.
18 holes, 5927 yards
par 69, S.S.S 69
Designer Alister Mackenzie
Green fees £26
Catering, changing room/showers, bar, trolley hire, shop
Visitors welcome weekdays
Societies welcome by prior arrangement

CASTLE HAWK GOLF CLUB

Chadwick lane, Castleton, Rochdale, Lancashire OL11 3BY
☎ 01706 640841 Fax 01706 860587
Map 10, G9
M62 Jct 20, at Castleton
Founded 1975
An unusual layout giving two short courses rather than one longer, and perhaps less interesting, course.
18 holes, 5398 yards, par 68, S.S.S 68
9 holes, 3158 yards, par 55, S.S.S 55
Green fees £7
Catering, changing room/showers, bar, club and trolley hire, shop, driving range
Visitors welcome
Societies welcome by prior arrangement

CHARNOCK RICHARD GOLF CLUB

Preston Road, Charnock Richard, Chorley, Lancashire PR7 5LE
☎ 01257 470707 Fax 01257 794343
Map 10, D8
A49, adjacent to Camelot Park
A parkland course beside the Camelot pleasure park.
18 holes, 6234 yards
par 71, S.S.S 70
Designer Chris Court
Green fees £15
Changing room/showers, bar, trolley and buggy hire
Visitors welcome weekdays with restrictions

Societies welcome by prior arrangement

CHORLEY GOLF CLUB

Hall o' th' Hill, Heath Charnock, Chorley, Lancashire PR6 9HX
☎ 01257 480263 Fax 01257 480722
Map 10, E8
secretary@chorleygolfclub.freeserve.co.uk
www.chorleygolfclub.co.uk
A6 Jct A673, 6 miles S of Chorley
Founded 1897
A friendly club with a newly extended clubhouse in a lovely upland spot with good views.
18 holes, 6240 yards
par 71, S.S.S 70
Designer J.A. Steer
Green fees £29
Catering, changing room/showers, bar, trolley and buggy hire, shop
Visitors welcome weekdays
Handicap certificate required.
Societies welcome by prior arrangement
The Coach House, The Ridges, Weavers Brow, Limbrick, Chorley, Lancashire PR6 9EB
☎ 01257270081

CLITHEROE GOLF CLUB

Whalley Road, Pendleton, Clitheroe, Lancashire BB7 1PP
☎ 01200 424242 Fax 01200 422292
Map 10, F7
From A59 take A671 towards Clitheroe, turn left (signposted Barrow, Whalley). Club on right.
Founded 1891
An engaging collection of pretty parkland holes set off against the imposing backdrop of Pendle Hill and the Bowland Fells. The short 17th, not unlike the 12th at Augusta, is the most eye-catching hole, while strong par 4s such as the 3rd, 7th and 12th are a match for all.
18 holes, 6326 yards
par 71, S.S.S 71
Designer James Braid
Green fees £33
Catering, changing room/showers, bar, club and trolley hire, shop, driving range, practice facilities, snooker, small conference room
Visitors welcome, restricted weekends
Handicap certificate required
Societies welcome by prior arrangement
Northcote Manor, Northcote Road, Langho, Blackburn, Lancashire BB6 8BE
☎ 01254 240555 Fax 01254 246568
admin@ncotemanor.demon.co.uk
www.ncotemanor.demon.co.uk

COLNE GOLF CLUB

Law Farm, Skipton Old Road, Colne, Lancashire BB8 7EB
☎ 01282 863391 **Map 10, F7**
Off A56, E of Colne
Founded 1901
A moorland course with good views.
9 holes, 5961 yards
par 70, S.S.S 69
Green fees £20
Catering, changing room/showers, bar, practice facilities
Visitors welcome with restrictions
Societies welcome by prior arrangement

CROMPTON AND ROYTON GOLF CLUB

High Barn, Royton, Oldham, Lancashire OL2 6RW
☎ 0161 624 0986 Fax 0161 652 4711 **Map 10, G9**
M62 jct 20, A627(M) towards Oldham. Then A663 and A671 towards Royton. Turn right at Royton Centre traffic lights.
Founded 1911
Vigorous upland golf with a number of testing longer par 4s.
18 holes, 6214 yards
par 70, S.S.S 70
Green fees £18
Catering, changing room/showers, bar, club and trolley hire, shop
Visitors welcome
Handicap certificate required
Societies welcome by prior arrangement
John Milne Travel Lodge, Newhay Road, Milnrow, Lancashire

DARWEN GOLF CLUB

Winter Hill, Duddon Avenue, Darwen, Lancashire BB3 0LB
☎ 01254 701287 Fax 01254 773833
Map 10, F8
Off A666, 1 mile N of Darwen
Founded 1893
A mixture of moorland and parkland holes.
18 holes, 5863 yards
par 69, S.S.S 68
Green fees £25
Catering, changing room/showers, bar, shop, practice facilities
Visitors welcome with restrictions
Societies welcome by prior arrangement

DEAN WOOD GOLF CLUB

Lafford Lane, Up Holland, Wigan, Lancashire WN8 0QZ
☎ 01695 627480 Fax 01695 622245
Map 10, D9
office@dwgc.fsnet.co.uk
M6 Jct 26, A577, signposted Up Holland.
Founded 1922
Well presented, pretty, parkland course with plenty of variety, having a flat front half, and hilly back nine.
18 holes, 6147 yards
par 70, S.S.S 71
Designer James Braid
Green fees £30
Catering, changing room/showers, bar, club and trolley hire, shop, practice facilities
Visitors welcome weekdays
Societies welcome by prior arrangement
Holland Hall Hotel, Up Holland, Lancashire
☎ 01695 624426

DEANE GOLF CLUB

Off Junction Road, Deane, Bolton, Lancashire BL3 4NS
☎ 01204 61944 **Map 10, E9**
M61 Jct 5
Founded 1906
A parkland course with hills and ravines.
18 holes, 5652 yards
par 68, S.S.S 67
Green fees £20
Catering, changing room/showers, bar, trolley hire, shop
Visitors welcome weekdays
Societies welcome by prior arrangement

DUNSCAR GOLF CLUB

Longworth Lane, Bromley Cross, Bolton, Lancashire BL7 9QY
☎ 01204 592992 Fax 01204 303321
Map 10, E9
Off A666, 3 miles N of Bolton
Founded 1908
With fine views of the Pennines, the course boasts several interesting holes, including the par-3 16th, set in an old quarry.
18 holes, 6085 yards
par 71, S.S.S 69
Green fees £20
Catering, changing room/showers, bar, club and trolley hire, shop, practice facilities
Visitors welcome with restrictions
Societies welcome by prior arrangement
Last Drop Village Hotel, Hospital Road, Bromley Cross, Bolton, Lancashire BL7 9PZ
☎ 01204 591131

DUXBURY PARK GOLF COURSE

Duxbury Hall Road, Duxbury Park, Chorley, Lancashire PR7 4AS
☎ 01257 265380 Fax 01257 241378
Map 10, E8
A5106, off A6 S of Chorley
Founded 1975
A parkland course.

18 holes, 6270 yards
par 71, S.S.S 70
Designer Hawtree
Green fees £8
Changing room/showers, club and trolley hire, shop
Visitors welcome – booking system
Societies welcome by prior arrangement

FAIRHAVEN GOLF CLUB

Lytham Hall Park, Ansdell, Lytham St Annes, Lancashire FY8 4JU
☎ 01253 736741 Fax 01253 731461
Map 10, C8
B5261, E of Lytham
Founded 1895
Despite being almost next door to Royal Lytham this is an exceptionally flat parkland course, renowned for its condition. The trees which frame each hole add to the beauty and punish the wayward, and the bunkering is profuse. Six par 5s give the course its length and high par rating.
18 holes, 6883 yards
par 74, S.S.S 73
Designer J.A. Steer, James Braid
Green fees £33
Catering, changing room/showers, bar, trolley hire, shop, practice facilities
Visitors welcome weekdays with restrictions
Societies welcome by prior arrangement

FISHWICK HALL GOLF CLUB

Glenluce Drive, Farringdon Park, Preston, Lancashire PR1 5TD
☎ 01772 798300 Fax 01772 704600
Map 10, E8
A59, M6 Jct 31
Founded 1912
Parkland course overlooking the River Ribble.
18 holes, 6045 yards
par 70, S.S.S 69
Green fees £26
Catering, changing room/showers, bar, trolley hire, shop
Visitors welcome by prior arrangement
Societies welcome by prior arrangement

FLEETWOOD GOLF CLUB

Golf House, Princes Way, Fleetwood, Lancashire FY7 8AH
☎ 01253 773573 Fax 01253 773573
Map 10, C7
fleetwoodgc@aol.com
www.fleetwoodgolfclub.org.uk
1 mile W of Fleetwood, on sea front
Founded 1932
Fleetwood is said by many to be the toughest course after Royal Lytham on the Fylde coast. The 176-yard 8th is very hard in a wind, and the 16th and 17th are strong par 4s when played from the white plates. There are good views of the Lakeland fells.
18 holes, 6557 yards
par 72, S.S.S 71
Designer A. Steer
Green fees £24
Catering, changing room/showers, bar, club and trolley hire, shop, practice facilities
Visitors welcome
Handicap certificate required – limit: 24
Societies welcome by prior arrangement
🏨 North Euston Hotel, The Esplanade, Fleetwood, Lancashire FY7 6BN
☎ 01253 876525

GARSTANG COUNTRY HOTEL AND GOLF CLUB

Garstang Road, Bowgreave, Garstang, Lancashire PR3 1YE
☎ 01995 600100 Fax 01995 600950
Map 10, D7
reception@garstanghotelandgolf.co.uk
www.garstanghotelandgolf.co.uk
B6430, 1 mile of Garstang
Bordered by the Rivers Wyre and Calder and overlooked by the Bowland Fells, a gentle parkland course which builds to a tough finish.
18 holes, 6050 yards
par 68
Designer Richard Bradbeer
Green fees £18
Catering, changing room/showers, bar, club hire, shop, driving range, practice facilities
Visitors welcome
Societies welcome by prior arrangement
🏨 Garstang Country Hotel, Bowgreave, Garstang, Lancashire PR3 1YE
☎ 01995 600100 Fax 01995 600950
reception@garstanghotelandgolf.co.uk
www.garstanghotelandgolf.co.uk

GATHURST GOLF CLUB

Miles Lane, Shevington, Wigan, Lancashire WN8 0NL
☎ 01257 255882 Fax 01257 261226
Map 10, D9
gathurst.golfclub@genie.co.uk
1 mile S of M6 Jct 27
Founded 1913
A parkland course only a mile from the M6. There is a reduction for guests of the Moathouse.
18 holes, 6063 yards
par 70, S.S.S 69
Designer Neville Pearson
Green fees £26
Catering, changing room/showers, bar, shop, practice facilities
Visitors welcome, subject to restrictions
Handicap certificate required
Societies welcome by prior arrangement
🏨 Wigan and Standish Moathouse, Almond Brook Road, Standish, Wigan, Lancashire WN6 0SR
☎ 01257 499988

GHYLL GOLF CLUB

Ghyll Brow, Barnoldswick, Colne, Lancashire BB18 6JH
☎ 01282 842466 **Map 10, F7**
B6252, off A56, 6 miles W of Skipton.
Founded 1907
A course on the Lancashire/Yorkshire border with fine views towards Ingleborough and Pen-y-Ghent.
9 holes, 5708 yards
par 68, S.S.S 68
Green fees £15
Catering, changing room/showers
Visitors welcome
Societies welcome by prior arrangement

GREAT HARWOOD GOLF CLUB

Harwood Bar, Great Harwood, Lancashire BB6 7TE
☎ 01254 884391 Fax 01254 879495
Map 10, E7
Off A59, between Blackburn and Clitheroe
Founded 1896
A parkland course surrounded by handsome hill country.
9 holes, 6413 yards
par 71, S.S.S 71
Green fees £16
Catering, changing room/showers, bar
Visitors welcome
Societies welcome by prior arrangement

GREEN HAWORTH GOLF CLUB

Green Haworth, Accrington, Lancashire BB5 3SL
☎ 01254 237580 Fax 01254 396176
Map 10, F8
Off A680, S of Accrington
Founded 1914
A robust moorland course.
9 holes, 5556 yards
par 68, S.S.S 67
Catering, changing room/showers, bar
Visitors welcome weekdays – with restrictions

Societies welcome by prior arrangement

GREENMOUNT GOLF CLUB

Greenmount, Bury, Lancashire BL8 4LH
☎ 01204 883712 **Map 10, F8**
Holcombe Village between Bury and Ramsbottom.
Founded 1920
Hilly parkland course.
9 holes, 5230 yards
S.S.S 66
Green fees £15
Catering, changing room/showers, bar, shop
Visitors welcome weekdays
Societies welcome by prior arrangement

HAIGH HALL GOLF CLUB

Haigh Hall Country Park, Haigh, Wigan, Lancashire WN2 1PE
☎ 01942 833337 Fax 01942 831417
Map 10, E9
2 miles NW of Wigan, M6 Jct 27
Founded 1972
First rate municipal course which has been used for a number of important tournaments.
18 holes, 6423 yards
par 70, S.S.S 71
Designer Frank Pennink
Green fees £7
Catering, changing room/showers, bar, club and trolley hire, shop, practice facilities
Visitors welcome
Societies welcome by prior arrangement

HARWOOD GOLF CLUB

Springfield, Roading Brook Road, Bolton, Lancashire BL2 4JD
☎ 01204 524233 Fax 01204 524233
Map 10, F9
B6391, 4 miles NE of town centre
Founded 1926
Parkland course on the outskirts of Bolton.
18 holes, 5778 yards
par 70, S.S.S 68
Designer G. Shuttleworth
Green fees £20
Catering, changing room/showers, bar, shop, practice facilities
Visitors welcome weekdays
Societies welcome by prior arrangement
🏨 Last Drop Village Hotel, Hospital Road, Bromley Cross, Bolton, Lancashire BL7 9PZ
☎ 01204 591131

HEYSHAM GOLF CLUB

Trumacar Park, Middleton Road, Heysham, Morecambe, Lancashire LA3 3JH
☎ 01524 852000 Fax 01524 853030
Map 10, D6
Off A683, signed for Middleton
Founded 1910
From the elevated part of the course there are superb views of Morecambe Bay and the Lakeland Fells.
18 holes, 5989 yards
par 68, S.S.S 69
Designer Alec Herd
Green fees £22
Catering, changing room/showers, bar, trolley hire, shop, practice facilities
Visitors welcome
Handicap certificate required.
Societies welcome by prior arrangement
🏨 Headway Hotel, Marine Road East, Morecambe, Lancashire
☎ 01524 412525

HINDLEY HALL GOLF CLUB

Hall Lane, Hindley, Wigan, Lancashire WN2 2SQ
☎ 01942 525020 Fax 01942 253871
Map 10, E9
M61 Jct 5 or 6
Founded 1905
A parkland course.
18 holes, 5913 yards
par 69, S.S.S 68
Green fees £20
Catering, changing room/showers, bar, trolley hire, shop, practice facilities
Visitors welcome
Societies welcome by prior arrangement

HORWICH GOLF CLUB

Victoria Road, Horwich, Lancashire BL6 5PH
☎ 01204 696980 Fax 01942 205316
Map 10, E9
M61 Jct 6
Founded 1895
A parkland course with views towards Winter Hill.
9 holes, 5404 yards
S.S.S 67
Designer George Lowe
Green fees £16
Catering, changing room/showers, bar, shop
Visitors welcome only as members' guests or by prior arrangement
Societies welcome by prior arrangement

HURLSTON HALL GOLF CLUB

Hurlston Gate, 56 Moorfield Lane, Scarisbrick, Lancashire L40 8JD
☎ 01704 840400 Fax 01704 841404
Map 10, D9
hurlstonhall@btinternet.com
www.hurlstonehall.co.uk
A570, 2 miles NW of Ormskirk, M58 Jct 3
Founded 1993
A challenging parkland course with seven lakes and two streams. Hurlston Hall has been designated the North-West Regional Training Centre for juniors by the EGU.
18 holes, 6746 yards
par 72, S.S.S 72
Designer Donald Steel
Green fees £28
Catering, changing room/showers, bar, club, trolley and buggy hire, shop, driving range, practice facilities, function rooms, fishing
Visitors welcome
Handicap certificate required
Societies welcome by prior arrangement
🏨 Beaufort Hotel, High Lane, Burscough, Ormskirk, Lancashire L40 7SN
☎ 01704 895135

INGOL GOLF CLUB

Tanterton Hall Road, Ingol, Preston, Lancashire PR2 7BY
☎ 01772 734556 Fax 01772 729815
Map 10, D7
ingol@golfers.net
www.ingolgolfclub.co.uk
1½ miles NW of Preston off A46, M6 Jct 32
Founded 1981
Attractive parkland course with out-of-bounds threatening on almost every shot. The 400-yard 2nd and 527-yard 15th are both right-hand dog-legs with an all-or-nothing approach to the green over water, hardly surprisingly Stroke 1 and 2, respectively. Two short par 4s, the 5th and 11th, tempt the big hitter.
18 holes, 6294 yards
par 72, S.S.S 70
Designer Sir Henry Cotton, Michael Bonallack
Green fees £20
Catering, changing room/showers, bar, club, trolley and buggy hire, shop, practice facilities
Visitors welcome
Handicap certificate required
Societies welcome by prior arrangement
🏨 Barton Grange Hotel, Garstang Road, Preston, Lancashire PR3 5AA

KNOTT END GOLF CLUB

Wyreside, Knott End-On-Sea, Lancashire FY6 0AA
☎ 01253 810576 Fax 01253 813446
Map 10, C7
M55 Jct 3, A585, B5377 to Knott End.
Founded 1910
Part links, part parkland, Knott End

is a wonderfully remote place for golf, despite being close to Blackpool and Fleetwood. Very exposed to the elements, but extensive views over Morecambe Bay are a reward.
18 holes, 5832 yards
par 69, S.S.S 68
Designer James Braid
Green fees £22
Catering, changing room/showers, bar, trolley hire, shop, practice facilities
Visitors welcome – restricted weekends
Societies welcome by prior arrangement
🏨 Springfield House Hotel, Wheel Lane, Pilling, Lancashire PR3 6HL
✆ 01253 790301

LANCASTER GOLF CLUB

Ashton Hall, Ashton-with-Stodday, Lancaster, Lancashire LA2 0AJ
✆ 01524 751247 Fax 01524 752742
Map 10, D6
Off A588, 1 mile SW of Lancaster
Founded 1932
With a magnificent clubhouse, dating back to mediaeval times, this parkland course overlooks the Lune Estuary, very exposed to the winds whipping in off the Irish Sea. The dog-leg 9th and 437-yard 17th are the toughest holes, and the par-3 18th can wreck a card.
18 holes, 6500 yards
par 71, S.S.S 71
Designer James Braid
Green fees £32
Catering, changing room/showers, bar, accommodation, club and trolley hire, shop, practice facilities, Dormy House
Visitors welcome weekdays
Handicap certificate required
Societies welcome by prior arrangement
🏨 Lancaster Golf Club Dormy House, Ashton Hall, Ashton-with-Stodday, Lancaster, Lancashire LA2 0AJ
✆ 01524 751247 Fax 01524 754742

LANSIL GOLF CLUB

Caton Road, Lancaster, Lancashire LA4 3PE
✆ 01524 39269 **Map 10, D6**
A683, E of Lancaster
Founded 1947
A compact and, therefore, tight and demanding parkland course.
9 holes, 5608 yards
par 70, S.S.S 67
Green fees £12
Changing room/showers
Visitors welcome weekdays with restrictions
Societies welcome by prior arrangement

LEYLAND GOLF CLUB

Wigan Road, Leyland, Lancashire PR5 2UD
✆ 01772 436457 Fax 01772 436457
Map 10, D8
www.leylandgolfclub.com
A49, M6 Jct 28
Founded 1923
A parkland course.
18 holes, 6123 yards
par 69, S.S.S 70
Green fees £25
Catering, changing room/showers, bar, trolley hire, shop, practice facilities
Visitors welcome weekdays
Societies welcome by prior arrangement

LOBDEN GOLF CLUB

Whitworth, Rochdale, Lancashire OL12 8XJ
✆ 01706 3432280 Fax 01706 343228 **Map 10, F8**
A671 from Rochdale, turning right in Whitworth at Dog & Partridge.
Founded 1888
Exposed, moorland course with the highest tee in Lancashire (6th).
9 holes, 5697 yards
par 70, S.S.S 68
Green fees £15
Catering, changing room/showers, bar, practice facilities, snooker
Visitors welcome, restricted Saturdays
Societies welcome by prior arrangement

LONGRIDGE GOLF CLUB

Fell Barn, Jeffrey Hill, Longridge, Preston, Lancashire PR3 2TU
✆ 01772 783291 Fax 01772 783022
Map 10, E7
M6 Jct 31a, to Longridge, course 1 mile NE of town.
Founded 1877
Superb views from the high ground compensate for some exhausting hill climbing below the clubhouse.
18 holes, 5969 yards
par 70, S.S.S 69
Green fees £15
Catering, changing room/showers, bar, trolley hire, shop
Visitors welcome
Societies welcome by prior arrangement

LOWES PARK GOLF CLUB

Hilltop, Lowes Road, Bury, Lancashire BL9 6SU
✆ 0161 764 1231 Fax 0161 763 9503 **Map 10, F9**
Off A56, N of Bury – turn at Sundial Inn
Founded 1915
Moorland course with expansive views.
9 holes, 6006 yards
par 70, S.S.S 68
Green fees £15
Catering, changing room/showers, bar, practice facilities
Visitors welcome, with restrictions weekends
Societies welcome by prior arrangement
🏨 Red Hall, Manchester Road, Walmersley, Bury, Lancashire
✆ 01706 822476

LYTHAM GREEN DRIVE GOLF CLUB

Ballam Road, Lytham, Lancashire FY8 4LE
✆ 01253 737379 Fax 01253 731350
Map 10, C8
www.ukgolfer.org
A5853, M55 Jct 4
Founded 1922
For many years an Open Qualifying venue, Green Drive is a flat, but pretty, parkland course on which accuracy is a priority, with a good number of drive-and-pitch par 4s. However, the 5th and 10th are substantial two-shotters, and the 8th and 13th lengthy par 3s. A very welcoming club.
18 holes, 6163 yards
par 70, S.S.S 69
Designer J.A. Steer
Green fees £27
Catering, changing room/showers, bar, trolley hire, shop, practice facilities
Visitors welcome weekdays
Societies welcome by prior arrangement
🏨 Fernlea Hotel, 11-17 South Promenade, Lytham St Annes, Near Blackpool, Lancashire
✆ 01253 726726

MARLAND GOLF CLUB

Springfield Park, Bolton Road, Rochdale, Lancashire OL11 4RE
✆ 01706 49801 Fax 01706 49801
Map 10, F9
M62 Jct 19/20
Founded 1928
A parkland course.
18 holes, 5237 yards
S.S.S 66
Green fees £7
Shop
Visitors welcome weekdays
Societies welcome by prior arrangement

MARSDEN PARK GOLF CLUB

Townhouse Road, Nelson,
Lancashire BB9 8DG
✆ 01282 661912 **Map 10, G9**
Off M65 Jct 13 towards Nelson
Founded 1969
True, there are some hills on the course, but the effort is worth it for the fine views to Pendle Hill and the Yorkshire Dales.
18 holes, 5813 yards
par 70, S.S.S 68
Green fees £10
Catering, changing room/showers, bar, club and trolley hire, shop
Visitors welcome with restrictions
Societies welcome by prior arrangement

MORECAMBE GOLF CLUB

Marine Road East, Bare,
Morecambe, Lancashire LA4 6AJ
✆ 01524 412841 Fax 01524 400088
Map 10, D6
morecambegolf@btconnect.com
A589, Carnforth road
Founded 1945
Over the years the course has taken on something of a parkland nature, particularly with the planting of trees, and introduction and enlargement of water hazards. Lovely views.
18 holes, 5770 yards
par 67, S.S.S 69
Designer Alister Mackenzie
Green fees £23
Catering, changing room/showers, bar, trolley hire, shop, practice facilities, function and conference facilities
Visitors welcome
Handicap certificate required
Societies welcome by prior arrangement
🏨 The Elms Hotel, Bare, Morecambe, Lancashire LA4 6DD
✆ 01524 411501 Fax 01524 831979

MOSSOCK HALL GOLF CLUB

Liverpool Road, Bickerstaffe,
Lancashire L39 0EE
✆ 01695 421717 Fax 01695 424969
Map 10, D9
M58 Jct 2, 1 mile
Founded 1996
From an elevated tee to a heavily bunkered green, set off against trees, with a stream meandering through, the 11th is one of the prettiest holes in Lancashire.
18 holes, 6475 yards
par 71, S.S.S 70
Designer Steve Marnoch
Green fees £25
Catering, changing room/showers, bar, trolley hire, shop, practice facilities
Visitors welcome
Handicap certificate required
Societies welcome by prior arrangement
🏨 Kilhey Court Hotel, Worthington, Haigh, Wigan, Lancashire

MYTTON FOLD HOTEL GOLF CLUB

Whalley Road, Langho, Lancashire
BB6 8AB
✆ 01254 240662 Fax 01254 248119
Map 10, E7
www.smoothhound.co.uk/hotels/mytton
A59, 3 miles N of Blackburn
Founded 1994
An attractive hotel course in the scenic Ribble Valley, quite testing.
18 holes, 6082 yards
par 72, S.S.S 69
Designer Frank Hargreaves
Green fees £14
Catering, changing room/showers, bar, accommodation, trolley and buggy hire, shop, practice facilities, full hotel, conference and function facilities
Visitors welcome
Societies welcome by prior arrangement
🏨 Mytton Fold Hotel, Whalley Road, Langho, Lancashire
✆ 01254 240662

NELSON GOLF CLUB

Kings Causeway, Brierfield, Nelson,
Lancashire BB9 0EU
✆ 01282 611834 Fax 01282 606226
Map 10, F7
Off A682 2 miles N of Burnley, M65 Jct 12
Founded 1902
Mackenzie's clever design makes the most of this upland site without tiring hill climbing. The par 3s hold the key to good scoring, while the 419-yard 14th is the most testing hole.
18 holes, 5977 yards
par 70, S.S.S 69
Designer Alsiter Mackenzie
Green fees £25
Catering, changing room/showers, bar, trolley hire, shop, practice facilities
Visitors welcome – restricted Thursday and Saturday
Handicap certificate required
Societies welcome by prior arrangement
🏨 Spread Eagle, Sawley, Clitheroe, Lancashire BB7 4NH
✆ 01200 441202 Fax 01200 441973

OLDHAM GOLF CLUB

Lees New Road, Oldham,
Lancashire OL4 5PN
✆ 0161 624 4986 **Map 10, G9**
Off A669, 2 miles E of Oldham
Founded 1892
Undulating moorland course.
18 holes, 5122 yards
par 66, S.S.S 65
Green fees £16
Catering, changing room/showers, bar, trolley hire, shop
Visitors welcome
Societies welcome by prior arrangement

ORMSKIRK GOLF CLUB

Cranes Lane, Lathom, Ormskirk,
Lancashire L40 5UJ
✆ 01695 572112 **Map 10, D9**
Off A577, 2 miles E of Ormskirk, M58 Jct 3, at Hulton Castle public house, right at next junction.
Founded 1899
Parkland golf at its most peaceful, but testing enough to be a frequent Open Qualifying venue. Three long par 4s, the 3rd, 7th and 8th, feature on the spacious front nine. On Harold Hilton's original course, now the back nine, the holes are generally shorter, running charmingly through the woods.
18 holes, 6480 yards
par 70, S.S.S 71
Designer Harold Hilton
Green fees £35
Catering, changing room/showers, bar, trolley hire, shop, practice facilities
Visitors welcome weekdays
Societies welcome by prior arrangement

PENNINGTON GOLF CLUB

Pennington Country Park, Leigh,
Lancashire WN7 3PA
✆ 01942 682852 **Map 10, E9**
Off A579, SW of Leigh
Founded 1975
Streams and ponds add interest here.
9 holes, 5516 yards
par 70, S.S.S 68
Green fees £3.35
Changing room/showers, shop
Visitors welcome
Societies welcome by prior arrangement

PENWORTHAM GOLF CLUB

Blundell Lane, Penwortham,
Preston, Lancashire PR1 0AX
✆ 01772 744630 Fax 01772 740172
Map 10, D8
penworthamgolfclub@supanet.com
www.penwortham@ukgolfer.org
Off A59, 1 mile W of Preston
Founded 1908
A parkland course on the banks of the River Ribble.
18 holes, 6056 yards

par 69, S.S.S 69
Green fees £25
Catering, changing room/showers, bar, trolley hire, shop, practice facilities, small meeting room
Visitors welcome, subject to club competitions
Handicap certificate required
Societies welcome by prior arrangement
Tickled Trout, Preston New Road, Samlesbury, Near Preston, Lancashire
01772 877671

PLEASINGTON GOLF CLUB

Pleasington Lane, Pleasington, Blackburn, Lancashire BB2 5JF
01254 202177 Fax 01254 201028
Map 10, E8
Off A674/A675 W of Blackburn
Founded 1891
Yardages are almost irrelevant in hilly country and rarely is a green here approached on the level. The surrounding scenery is superb, and the course condition noteworthy. The 11th is a monster par 5 of 574 yards from the back and the 13th a daunting par 4 of 460 yards.
18 holes, 6541 yards
par 71, S.S.S 72
Green fees £36
Catering, changing room/showers, bar, trolley and buggy hire, shop, practice facilities
Visitors welcome
Handicap certificate required
Societies welcome by prior arrangement
Fernhurst Lodgings & Public House, Bolton Road, Blackburn, Lancashire
01254 693541

POULTON-LE-FYLDE GOLF CLUB

Myrtle Farm, Breck Road, Poulton-le-Fylde, Lancashire FY6 7HJ
01253 892444 **Map 10, C7**
Off A586, N of Poulton
Founded 1982
Streams and ditches enliven this public facility.
9 holes, 6000 yards
par 70, S.S.S 69
Green fees £11
Catering, changing room/showers, bar, club and trolley hire, shop, practice facilities, heated indoor swimming pool
Visitors welcome
Societies welcome by prior arrangement

PRESTON GOLF CLUB

Fulwood Hall Lane, Fulwood, Preston, Lancashire PR2 8DD
01772 700011 Fax 01772 794234
Map 10, D7
M6 Jct 32, N of town centre
Founded 1892
Charming old parkland course with feature holes at the 14th (201-yard par 3) and 17th (539-yard par 5).
18 holes, 6312 yards
par 71, S.S.S 71
Designer James Braid
Green fees £27
Catering, changing room/showers, bar, club and trolley hire, shop, driving range, practice facilities, conference facilities
Visitors welcome, with restrictions
Handicap certificate required
Societies welcome by prior arrangement
Preston Marriott Hotel, Garstang Road, Preston, Lancashire PR3 5JB
01772 864087

REGENT PARK (BOLTON) GOLF CLUB

Links Road, Chorley New Road, Bolton, Lancashire BL6 4AF
01204 844170 **Map 10, E9**
A673, 3 miles W of Bolton
Founded 1931
A parkland course.
18 holes, 6130 yards
par 70, S.S.S 69
Green fees £8
Catering, changing room/showers, club and trolley hire, shop
Visitors welcome weekdays
Societies welcome by prior arrangement

RISHTON GOLF CLUB

Eachill Links, Hawthorn Drive, Rishton, Lancashire BB1 4HG
01254 884442 Fax 01254 51946
Map 10, E8
Off A678, E of Blackburn
Founded 1927
Hilly moorland course.
9 holes, 6097 yards
par 70, S.S.S 69
Green fees £12
Catering, changing room/showers, bar
Visitors welcome weekdays
Societies welcome by prior arrangement

ROCHDALE GOLF CLUB

Edenfield Road, Bagslate, Rochdale, Lancashire OL11 5YR
01706 646024 Fax 01706 861113
Map 10, F9
A680, 2 miles W of Rochdale
Founded 1888
A pleasantly wooded parkland course.
18 holes, 6050 yards
par 71, S.S.S 69
Designer George Lowe
Green fees £23
Catering, changing room/showers, bar, club and trolley hire, shop
Visitors welcome
Societies welcome by prior arrangement

ROSSENDALE GOLF CLUB

Ewood Lane Head, Haslingden, Rochdale, Lancashire BB4 6LH
01706 831339 Fax 01706 228669
Map 10, F8
Off A56, close to end of M66
Founded 1903
A new clubhouse has enhanced the facilities at this course laid out on high ground with expansive views.
18 holes, 6293 yards
par 72, S.S.S 71
Green fees £25
Catering, changing room/showers, bar, trolley hire, shop
Visitors welcome weekdays
Societies welcome by prior arrangement

ROYAL LYTHAM AND ST ANNES GOLF CLUB

Links Gate, Lytham St Annes, Lancashire FY8 3LQ
01253 724206 Fax 01253 780946
Map 10, C8
½ mile E of St Annes
Founded 1886
See Top 50 Courses, page
18 holes, 6892 yards
par 71, S.S.S 74
Designer George Lowe, Harry Colt, Tom Simpson, C.K. Cotton, Colin Maclaine
Green fees £95
Catering, changing room/showers, bar, accommodation, trolley hire, shop, practice facilities
Visitors welcome weekdays
Societies welcome by prior arrangement

SADDLEWORTH GOLF CLUB

Mountain Ash, Uppermill, Oldham, Lancashire OL3 6LT
01457 873653 Fax 01457 820647
Map 10, G9
A670, E of Saddleworth
Founded 1904
A moorland course high in the Pennines, very exposed to the weather, but when the sun shines the views are incomparable and the air most invigorating.
18 holes, 5976 yards
par 71, S.S.S 69
Designer George Lowe, Alister Mackenzie
Green fees £23
Catering, changing room/showers, bar, club, trolley and buggy hire,

shop, practice facilities
Visitors welcome
Societies welcome by prior arrangement

SHAW HILL HOTEL GOLF AND COUNTRY CLUB

Preston Road, Whittle-le-Woods, Chorley, Lancashire PR6 7PP
☎ 01257 269221 Fax 01257 261223
Map 10, E8
A6, 1 mile N of Chorley
Founded 1925
Challenging parkland course with a number of exciting water holes. Several holes run beside an ordnance factory – beware sudden noises!
18 holes, 6246 yards
par 72, S.S.S 70
Designer Tom McAuley
Green fees £30
Catering, changing room/showers, bar, accommodation, club, trolley and buggy hire, shop, driving range, practice facilities, full hotel facilities, heated indoor swimming pool
Visitors welcome weekdays
Handicap certificate required
Societies welcome by prior arrangement
🏨 Shaw Hill Hotel, Preston Road, Whittle-le-Woods, Chorley, Lancashire
☎ 01257 269221

SILVERDALE GOLF CLUB

Redbridge Lane, Silverdale, Carnforth, Lancashire LA5 0SP
☎ 01524 701300 Fax 01524 702074
Map 10, D5
M6 Jct 35 (Carnforth), 4 miles W, opposite Silverdale Station.
Founded 1906
This very challenging course with heathland and rocky outcrops is currently being extended to 18 holes with a new practice area. Wonderful scenery.
12 holes, 5210 yards
par 69, S.S.S 66
Green fees £15
Catering, changing room/showers, bar, club and trolley hire, shop
Visitors welcome, restricted Sundays
Handicap certificate required
Societies welcome by prior arrangement
🏨 Silverdale Hotel, Silverdale, Carnforth, Lancashire
☎ 01524 701206

SPRINGFIELD PARK GOLF CLUB

Springfield Park, Bolton Road, Rochdale, Lancashire OL11 5YR
☎ 01706 656401 **Map 10, F9**
Off A58, 2 miles SW of Rochdale
Founded 1927
An attractive course in the valley of the River Roch.
18 holes, 5237 yards
par 67, S.S.S 66
Green fees £6
Club hire
Visitors welcome
Societies welcome by prior arrangement

ST ANNES OLD LINKS GOLF CLUB

Highbury Road East, St Annes on Sea, Lancashire FY8 2LD
☎ 01253 723597 Fax 01253 781506
Map 10, C8
sectysaolgc@cybermail.uk.com
www.saolgc.uk.com
Off A 584 N of St Annes
Founded 1901
A famous old links, regularly used for Open Championship final qualifying. Very exposed to the wind, and with fast and true greens, it has a cruel finish with two lengthy par 5s. The par-3 9th is well known, but the hardest hole is the 7th, a 447-yard brute.
18 holes, 6750 yards
par 72, S.S.S 72
Designer George Lowe, Sandy Herd
Green fees £38
Catering, changing room/showers, bar, club and trolley hire, shop, practice facilities
Visitors welcome
Handicap certificate required
Societies welcome by prior arrangement
🏨 Fernlea Hotel, 11-17 South Promenade, Lytham St Annes, near Blackpool, Lancashire
☎ 01253 726726

STANDISH COURT GOLF CLUB

Rectory Lane, Standish, Wigan, Lancashire WN6 0XD
☎ 01257 425777 Fax 01257 425888
Map 10, E9
info@standishgolf.co.uk
www.standishgolf.co.uk
M6 Jct 27/M61 Jct 6
Founded 1995
A short course renowned for its condition. Good facilities.
18 holes, 5266 yards
par 68, S.S.S 66
Designer Patrick Dawson
Green fees £10
Catering, changing room/showers, bar, club and trolley hire, shop, driving range, practice facilities
Visitors welcome
Societies welcome by prior arrangement
🏨 Charnley Arms, Standish, Wigan, Lancashire

STONYHURST PARK GOLF CLUB

Stonyhurst, Hurst Green, Blackburn, Lancashire BB6 9QB
☎ 01254 826478 **Map 10, E7**
B6243, 5 miles SW of Clitheroe
Founded 1980
A parkland course in glorious countryside.
9 holes, 5529 yards
S.S.S 66
Green fees £12
Visitors welcome weekdays
Societies welcome by prior arrangement

TOWNELEY GOLF CLUB

Towneley Park, Todmorden Road, Burnley, Lancashire BB11 3ED
☎ 01282 438473 **Map 10, F7**
A671, 1½ miles E of Burnley
Founded 1932
A public parkland facility. Beware the internal out-of-bounds!
18 holes, 5811 yards
par 70, S.S.S 68
Green fees £10.65
Catering, changing room/showers, bar, trolley hire, shop, practice facilities, tennis, bowls
Visitors welcome
Societies welcome by prior arrangement

TUNSHILL GOLF CLUB

Kiln Lane, Milnrow, Rochdale, Lancashire OL16 3TS
☎ 01706 342095 **Map 10, G9**
At Milnrow, 1 mile M62 Jct 21
Founded 1901
A tumbling moorland course with rocky outcrops, very punishing in parts.
9 holes, 5743 yards
par 70, S.S.S 68
Green fees £15
Catering, changing room/showers, bar
Visitors welcome weekdays
Societies welcome by prior arrangement

TURTON GOLF CLUB

Wood End Farm, Chapeltown Road, Bromley Cross, Bolton, Lancashire BL7 9QH
☎ 01204 852235 **Map 10, F9**
Off B6472, 3½ miles N of Bolton
Founded 1908
From Turton's elevated moorland setting there are fine views to the Pennines and as far as Cheshire.
18 holes, 6124 yards

par 70, S.S.S 69
Green fees £20
Catering, changing room/showers, bar, practice facilities, function/conference facilities
Visitors welcome, restricted Wednesday and Saturday
Societies welcome by prior arrangement
🏨 Last Drop Village Hotel, Hospital Road, Bromley Cross, Bolton, Lancashire BL7 9PZ
✆ 01204 591131

WALMERSLEY GOLF CLUB

Garrett's Close, Walmersley, Bury, Lancashire BL9 6TE
✆ 0161 764 7770 Fax 01706 827618
Map 10, F8
OscarGoldstein@excite.co.uk
Off A56, 2 miles N of Bury
Founded 1906
Generous fairways and greens on this moorland course. Magnificent views from 7th tee.
18 holes, 5341 yards
par 69, S.S.S 66
Designer Steve Marnoch
Green fees £20
Catering, changing room/showers, bar, trolley hire, shop, practice facilities
Visitors welcome, with restrictions
Societies welcome by prior arrangement
🏨 Red Hall, Manchester Road, Walmersley, Bury, Lancashire
✆ 01706 822476

WERNETH GOLF CLUB

Green Lane, Garden Suburb, Oldham, Lancashire OL8 3AZ
✆ 0161 624 1190 **Map 10, G9**
A627, S of Oldham
Founded 1908
A moorland course with hazards such as streams and gullies.
18 holes, 5363 yards
par 68, S.S.S 66
Designer Sandy Herd
Green fees £18
Catering, changing room/showers, bar, trolley hire, shop
Visitors welcome weekdays
Societies welcome by prior arrangement

WESTHOUGHTON GOLF CLUB

Long Island, Westhoughton, Bolton, Lancashire BL5 2BR
✆ 01942 811085 **Map 10, E9**
A58, 4 miles SW of Bolton
Founded 1929
A parkland course.
9 holes, 5834 yards
par 70, S.S.S 68
Green fees £16
Catering, changing room/showers, bar, shop
Visitors welcome weekdays
Societies welcome by prior arrangement

WHALLEY GOLF CLUB

Long Leese Barn, Clerk Hill Road, Whalley, Clitheroe, Lancashire BB7 9DR
✆ 01254 824766 **Map 10, E7**
1 mile S of A59
Founded 1912
Parkland course with delightful views over the Ribble Valley and Pendle Hill
9 holes, 6258 yards
par 72, S.S.S 71
Green fees £16
Catering, changing room/showers, bar, trolley hire, shop, practice facilities
Visitors welcome
Societies welcome with prior booking
🏨 Higher Trapp Hotel, Trapp Lane, Simontone, Burnley, Lancashire
✆ 01282 772781

WHITTAKER GOLF CLUB

Littleborough, Lancashire OL5 0LH
✆ 01706 378310 **Map 10, G8**
Off A58, 1½ miles N of Littleborough
Founded 1906
A moorland course with spectacular views.
9 holes, 5576 yards
par 68, S.S.S 67
Designer N.P. Stott
Green fees £12
Changing room/showers
Visitors welcome weekdays
Societies welcome by prior arrangement

WIGAN GOLF CLUB

Arley Hall, Arley Lane, Haigh, Near Wigan, Lancashire WN1 2UH
✆ 01257 421360 **Map 10, E9**
www.wigangolfclub.co.uk
Off B5239 4 miles N of Wigan, M6 Jct 27
Founded 1898
Recently extended to 18 holes, the club's pride and joy is its 17th-century clubhouse, surrounded by a 12th-century moat on which black swans glide.
18 holes, 6008 yards
par 70, S.S.S 69
Designer Gaunt & Marnoch
Green fees £25
Catering, changing room/showers, bar
Visitors welcome – not Saturdays
Handicap certificate required
Societies welcome by prior arrangement
🏨 Kilhey Court Hotel, Worthington, Haigh, Wigan, Lancashire

WILPSHIRE GOLF CLUB

72 Whalley Road, Wilpshire, Blackburn, Lancashire BB1 9LF
✆ 01254 248260 Fax 01254 246475
Map 10. E7
A666, 3 miles NE of Blackburn
Founded 1890
A very scenic course, with splendid views of the Ribble Valley and surrounding hill country.
18 holes, 5911 yards
par 69, S.S.S 69
Designer James Braid
Green fees £25.50
Catering, changing room/showers, bar, trolley hire, shop, practice facilities
Visitors welcome
Handicap certificate required
Societies welcome by prior arrangement
🏨 Millstone Hotel, Church Lane, Mellor, Blackburn, Lancashire

MERSEYSIDE

ALLERTON MUNICIPAL GOLF CLUB

Allerton Road, Liverpool, Merseyside L18 3JT
✆ 0151 428 1046 **Map 10, D10**
A562, 5 miles SE of city centre
Founded 1934
A parkland course in the suburbs of Liverpool.
18 holes, 5494 yards
par 67, S.S.S 65
Club and trolley hire, shop
Visitors welcome
Societies welcome by prior arrangement

ARROWE PARK GOLF CLUB

Arrowe Park, Birkenhead, Merseyside CH49 5LW
✆ 0151 677 1527 **Map 10, C10**
From Mersey Tunnel via Borough Road
Founded 1932
One of the best of the several good public courses on the Wirral, with tree-lined fairways running through gentle parkland.
18 holes, 6396 yards
par 71, S.S.S 71
Green fees £7.50
Catering, club and trolley hire, shop, practice facilities, 9-hole pitch and putt
Visitors welcome – restricted weekends
Societies welcome by prior arrangement

Village Hotel & Leisure Club, Pool Lane, Bebington, Wirral, Merseyside
0151 643 1616

BIDSTON GOLF CLUB
Bidston Link Road, Wallasey, Merseyside L44 2HR
0151 638 3412 **Map 10, C10**
M53 Jct 1
Founded 1913
Very flat and somewhat bleak, but a number of testing holes are played alongside or over drainage dykes, with no room for error.
18 holes, 6140 yards
par 70, S.S.S 71
Green fees £22
Catering, changing room/showers, bar, shop
Visitors welcome weekdays
Societies welcome by prior arrangement

BLUNDELLS HILL GOLF CLUB
Blundells Lane, Rainhill, Merseyside L35 6NA
0151 430 0100 Fax 0151 426 5256 **Map 10, D10**
info@blundellshill.demon.co.uk
www.blundellshill.co.uk
M62 Jct 7, A57 towards Prescot
Founded 1994
A parkland course.
18 holes, 6347 yards
par 71, S.S.S 70
Designer Steve Marnoch
Green fees £25
Catering, changing room/showers, bar, trolley and buggy hire, shop, driving range
Visitors welcome
Societies welcome by prior arrangement

BOOTLE GOLF CLUB
Dunnings Bridge Road, Bootle, Merseyside L30 2PP
0151 928 1371 **Map 10, C10**
5 miles N of Liverpool, 1 mile W of M57/M58
Founded 1934
Amazing value for money – 18 holes on a thoroughly testing course for less than £10.
18 holes, 6263 yards
par 70, S.S.S 70
Designer Fred Stevens
Green fees £7.20
Catering, changing room/showers, bar, trolley hire, shop
Visitors welcome, restricted weekends
Societies welcome by prior arrangement
Park Hotel, Dunnings Bridge Road, Bootle, Merseyside

BOWRING GOLF CLUB
Bowring Park, Roby Road, Huyton, Merseyside L36 4HD
0151 489 1901 **Map 10, D10**
M62 Jct 5
Founded 1913
A parkland course on either side of the M62.
9 holes, 5592 yards
par 70, S.S.S 66
Green fees £6
Catering, shop
Visitors welcome
Societies welcome by prior arrangement

BRACKENWOOD GOLF CLUB
Brackenwood Lane, Bebington, Wirral, Merseyside L63 2LY
0151 608 3093 **Map 10, C10**
Near M53 Jct 4
Founded 1933
A sense of space all too rare on a municipal course, inviting views onto the Denbigh Hills, and sound design make this excellent value.
18 holes, 6131 yards
par 70, S.S.S 70
Green fees £7.50
Catering, changing room/showers, bar, club and trolley hire, shop
Visitors welcome
Societies welcome by prior arrangement

BROMBOROUGH GOLF CLUB
Raby Hall Road, Bromborough, Wirral, Merseyside CH63 0NW
0151 334 4499 Fax 0151 334 7300 **Map 10, C10**
sec@bromborough-golf-club.freeserve.co.uk
www.bromborough-golf-club.freeserve.co.uk
Off A41 N of M53 Jct 5
Founded 1903
Many long par 4s cross a central valley, making this a good test for the better player, with a notably demanding finish. The short holes are particularly good.
18 holes, 6603 yards
par 72, S.S.S 72
Green fees £28
Catering, changing room/showers, bar, club, trolley and buggy hire, shop, practice facilities
Visitors welcome, with restrictions
Societies welcome by prior arrangement
Raby House Hotel, Benty Heath Lane, Willaston, Wirral, Merseyside CH64 1SB
0151 327 1900

CALDY GOLF CLUB
Links Hey Road, Caldy, Wirral, Merseyside CH48 1NB
0151 625 5660 Fax 0151 625 7394 **Map 10, C10**
A540, signposted at junction with A551
Founded 1907
Caldy has everything, with a mix of parkland, downland, and links holes providing an excellent day's golf in a superb location overlooking the Dee Estuary with the Welsh Hills beyond. The run of seaside holes from the 3rd to the 10th is magical, with the par-4 6th the pick.
18 holes, 6675 yards
par 72, S.S.S 73
Designer Jack Morris, Donald Steel
Green fees £40
Catering, changing room/showers, bar, trolley and buggy hire, shop, practice facilities
Visitors welcome weekdays by prior arrangement
Societies welcome by prior arrangement

CHILDWALL GOLF CLUB
Naylor's Road, Gateacre, Liverpool, Merseyside L27 2YB
0151 487 0654 Fax 0151 487 0882 **Map 10, C10**
B1578, 2 miles from M62 Jct 6
Founded 1913
A good mature parkland course calling for intelligent play.
18 holes, 6425 yards
par 72, S.S.S 71
Designer James Braid
Green fees £26
Catering, changing room/showers, bar, club and trolley hire, shop, practice facilities
Visitors welcome with restrictions
Societies welcome by prior arrangement

EASTHAM LODGE GOLF CLUB
117 Ferry Road, Eastham, Wirral, Merseyside CH62 0AP
0151 327 3003 Fax 0151 327 3003 **Map 10, C10**
A41 6 miles S of Birkenhead, M53 Jct 5
Founded 1973
Constructed in stages and a model for aspiring course designers in how to get a quart out of a pint pot.
18 holes, 5706 yards
par 68, S.S.S 68
Designer Hawtree, David Hemstock
Green fees £22.50
Catering, changing room/showers, bar, trolley hire, shop, practice facilities, snooker
Visitors welcome weekdays

Societies welcome by prior arrangement
Village Hotel & Leisure Club, Pool Lane, Bebington, Wirral, Merseyside
0151 643 1616

ECCLESTON PARK GOLF CLUB

Rainhill Road, Liverpool, Merseyside L35 4PG
0151 493 0033 Fax 0151 493 0044 **Map 10, D10**
M62 Jct 7
A new parkland course.
18 holes, 6495 yards
par 70
Catering, changing room/showers, bar, trolley hire, shop
Visitors welcome by prior arrangement
Societies welcome by prior arrrangement

FORMBY GOLF CLUB

Golf Road, Formby, Liverpool, Merseyside L37 1LQ
01704 872164 Fax 01704 833028
Map 10, C9
info@formbygolfclub.co.uk
www.formbygolfclub.co.uk
By Freshfield Station, off A565
Founded 1884
See Top 50 Courses, page
18 holes, 6993 yards
par 72, S.S.S 74
Designer Willie Park, Harry Colt, Frank Pennink, Donald Steel
Green fees £65
Catering, changing room/showers, bar, accommodation, trolley hire, shop, practice facilities
Visitors welcome
Handicap certificate required
Societies welcome by prior arrangement
Treetops Hotel, Southport Old Road, Formby, Merseyside
01704 572430

FORMBY HALL GOLF CLUB

Southport Old Road, Formby, Merseyside L37 0AB
01704 875699 **Map 10, C9**
Off Formby bypass, opposite Woodvale Aerodrome.
Founded 1996
A new club with a lavish course, already receiving very favourable notices. Eleven lakes add to the considerable difficulties of the layout. The ground is flat, and many trees have been planted to give a little shelter from the wind, and soften the aspect.
18 holes, 6892 yards
par 73, S.S.S 73
Designer Alex Higgins
Green fees £35
Catering, changing room/showers, bar, trolley and buggy hire, shop, driving range, practice facilities
Visitors welcome weekdays
Societies welcome by prior arrangement

FORMBY LADIES' GOLF CLUB

Golf Road, Formby, Liverpool, Merseyside L37 1YH
01704 874127 Fax 01704 873493
Map 10, C9
Off A565, by Freshfield Station
Founded 1896
Formby Ladies' is one of only three ladies' clubs in England. The course, a charming and demanding links, is entirely encircled by the famous championship links, although the ladies have their own club house. A super course, not to be missed.
18 holes, 5426 yards
par 71, S.S.S 71
Green fees £30
Catering, changing room/showers, bar, trolley hire, shop, practice facilities
Visitors welcome by prior arrangement
Societies welcome by prior arrangement

GRANGE PARK GOLF CLUB

Prescot Road, St Helens, Merseyside WA10 3AD
01744 22980 Fax 01744 26318
Map 10, D10
A58, 1½ miles SW of St Helens
Founded 1891
A fine James Braid course which, somehow, has escaped wider national acclaim, which is surprising given the quality of the course.
18 holes, 6446 yards
par 72, S.S.S 71
Designer James Braid
Green fees £26
Catering, changing room/showers, bar, trolley hire, shop, practice facilities
Visitors welcome with restrictions
Societies welcome by prior arrangement

HAYDOCK PARK GOLF CLUB

Golborne Park, Newton Lane, Newton-le-Willows, Merseyside WA12 0HX
01925 224389 Fax 01925 228525
Map 10, E10
Off A49/A580, 1 mile E of M6 Jct 23
Founded 1877
An attractive parkland course, well drained and always in fine fettle. Close to the famous race course, the ground rolls enough to add significantly to the problems posed.
18 holes, 6058 yards
par 70, S.S.S 69
Designer James Braid
Green fees £27
Catering, changing room/showers, bar, trolley hire, shop, practice facilities
Visitors welcome – with restrictions
Societies welcome by prior arrangement

THE HESKETH GOLF CLUB

Cockle Dick's Lane, Cambridge Road, Southport, Merseyside PR9 9QQ
01704 536897 Fax 01704 539250
Map 10, C8
secretary@heskethgolf.golfagent.co.uk
www.ukgolfer.org
Off A565 (Cambridge Road), 1 mile N of Southport
Founded 1885
A frequent host to final qualifying for the Open Championship, Hesketh is the oldest of Southport's several distinguished courses. The holes around the attractive clubhouse have greater linksland characteristics, with the 15th perhaps the pick. Over the road the holes are plainer, although the 449-yard 6th is notoriously difficult.
18 holes, 6587 yards
par 72, S.S.S 72
Designer Jack Morris
Green fees £40
Catering, changing room/showers, bar, club and trolley hire, shop, practice facilities
Visitors welcome – restricted weekends
Handicap certificate required
Societies welcome by prior arrangement
Metropole Hotel, 3 Portland Street, Southport, Merseyside PR8 1LL
01704 536836

HESWALL GOLF CLUB

Cottage Lane, Gayton, Heswall, Merseyside CH60 8PB
0151 342 1237 Fax 0151 342 6140 **Map 10, C10**
A540 at Gayton, 8 miles NW of Chester
Founded 1902
Heswall's parkland fairways run down to the salt marshes of the Dee Estuary, where ditches and ponds complicate matters, notably on the testing 7th and 14th. Further inland there is more movement in the ground, with the first two holes sweeping up and down significantly. The secluded setting is magical.
18 holes, 6554 yards
par 72, S.S.S 72

Green fees £35
Catering, changing room/showers, bar, club, trolley and buggy hire, shop, practice facilities
Visitors welcome
Handicap certificate required
Societies by prior arrangement – Wednesday and Friday

HILLSIDE GOLF CLUB

Hastings Road, Hillside, Southport, Merseyside PR8 2LU
☎ 01704 567169 Fax 01704 563192
Map 10, C8
hillside@ukgolfer.org
www.ukgolfer.org
A565, 3 miles S of Southport, close to Hillside Railway Station.
Founded 1911
See Top 50 Courses, page
18 holes, 6850 yards
par 72, S.S.S 74
Designer Fred Hawtree
Green fees £50
Catering, changing room/showers, bar, trolley and buggy hire, shop, practice facilities, dining facilities for 150
Visitors welcome, by arrangement with Secretary
Handicap certificate required – limit: 28 men, 40 women
Societies welcome by prior arrangement
Scarisbrick Hotel, Lord Street, Southport, Merseyside
☎ 01704 543000

HOUGHWOOD GOLF CLUB

Billinge Hill, Crank Road, Crank, St Helens, Merseyside WA11 8RL
☎ 01744 894444 Fax 01744 894754
Map 10, D10
Off A580, 3 miles N of St Helens, M6 Jct 26
Founded 1996
Houghwood has attracted enthusiastic notices in its first years, not only for its test of golf but also for its wonderful views, over Lancashire and on into the Welsh Hills.
18 holes, 6202 yards
par 70, S.S.S 71
Designer Neville Pearson
Green fees £17.50
Catering, changing room/showers, bar, trolley and buggy hire, shop, practice facilities, conference and banquetting facilities, Indoor golf simulator
Visitors welcome
Societies welcome by prior arrangement
Haydock Thistle Hotel, Penny Lane, Haydock, St Helens, Lancashire
☎ 01942 272000

HOYLAKE MUNICIPAL GOLF COURSE

Carr Lane, Hoylake, Wirral, Merseyside L47 4BQ
☎ 0151 632 2956 **Map 10, C10**
Off A540, SW of town centre
Founded 1933
Although the course is flat it enjoys links-like qualities with firm, true greens. Genuine pot bunkers, streams and ditches feature widely.
18 holes, 6313 yards
par 70, S.S.S 70
Designer James Braid
Green fees £7
Catering, changing room/showers, bar, club, trolley and buggy hire, shop
Visitors welcome
Societies welcome by prior arrangement

HUYTON & PRESCOT GOLF CLUB

Hurst Park, Huyton Lane, Huyton, Merseyside L36 1UA
☎ 0151 489 1138 Fax 0151 489 0797 **Map 10, D10**
Off B5199, close to M57 Jct 2
Founded 1905
An enjoyable parkland course, well wooded, quite challenging.
18 holes, 5839 yards
par 68, S.S.S 68
Green fees £24
Catering, changing room/showers, bar, trolley hire, shop
Visitors welcome weekdays
Societies welcome by prior arrangement

LEASOWE GOLF CLUB

Leasowe Road, Moreton, Wirral, Merseyside CH46 3RD
☎ 0151 677 5852 Fax 0151 677 5852 **Map 10, C10**
A5551, behind Leasowe Castle
Founded 1891
For the most part a flat course hidden below the sea wall, but the few links holes around the "Castle" are more entertaining.
18 holes, 5969 yards
par 72, S.S.S 70
Designer John Ball Jnr
Green fees £22.50
Catering, changing room/showers, bar, trolley hire, shop
Visitors welcome with restrictions
Societies welcome by prior arrangement
Leasowe Castle Hotel, Leasowe Road, Moreton, Wirral, Merseyside CH46 3RD

LEE PARK GOLF CLUB

Childwall Valley Road, Gateacre, Liverpool, Merseyside L27 3YA
☎ 0151 487 9861 **Map 10, D10**
B5178, 1 mile from M62 Jct 5
Founded 1954
A parkland course close to Knowlsey Safari Park.
18 holes, 6024 yards
par 72, S.S.S 69
Catering, changing room/showers, bar, trolley hire
Visitors welcome
Societies welcome by prior arrangement

LIVERPOOL MUNICIPAL GOLF COURSE

Ingoe Lane, Kirkby, Liverpool, Merseyside L32 4SS
☎ 0151 546 5435 **Map 10, D10**
M57 Jct 6
Founded 1967
A long flat municipal course close to the world famous Aintree race course.
18 holes, 6706 yards
par 72, S.S.S 72
Green fees £6.90
Catering, changing room/showers, bar, club and trolley hire, shop, practice facilities
Visitors welcome
Societies welcome by prior arrangement

PRENTON GOLF CLUB

Golf Links Road, Prenton, Birkenhead, Merseyside CH42 8LW
☎ 0151 608 **Map 10, C10**
M53 Jct 3, then Wood Church Road, Prenton Hall Road and Golf Links Road
Founded 1905
A sweeping parkland course very exposed to the wind. Not all of Mackenzie's work survives, but there are many fascinating holes, such as the 4th which crosses not only a stream but also a Roman road. The short par-4 1st is deceptive, with water and bunkers frequently causing indecision.
18 holes, 6429 yards
par 71, S.S.S 71
Designer Alister Mackenzie
Green fees £30
Catering, changing room/showers, bar, club and trolley hire, shop, practice facilities
Visitors welcome
Societies welcome by prior arrangement

ROYAL BIRKDALE GOLF CLUB (THE)

Waterloo Road, Birkdale, Southport, Merseyside PR8 2LX
☎ 01704 567920 Fax 01704 562327
Map 10, C8
royalbirkdale@dial.pipex.com

www.royalbirkdale.com
A565, 1½ miles S of Southport
Founded 1889
See Top 50 Courses, page
18 holes, 6690 yards
par 72, S.S.S 73
Designer George Lowe, J.H. Taylor, F.G. Hawtree, F.W. Hawtree, Martin Hawtree
Green fees £108
Catering, changing room/showers, bar, club and trolley hire, shop, practice facilities
Visitors welcome, subject to restrictions
Handicap certificate required
Societies welcome by prior arrangement
Prince of Wales, Lord Street, Southport, Merseyside
01704 536688

ROYAL LIVERPOOL GOLF CLUB

Meols Drive, Hoylake, Wirral, Merseyside CH47 4AL
0151 632 3101 Fax 0151 632 6737 **Map 10, C10**
sec@royal-liverpoolgolf.com
www.royal-liverpool-golf.com
A540 between Hoylake and West Kirby
Founded 1869
See Top 50 Courses, page
18 holes, 7128 yards
par 72, S.S.S 76
Designer Robert Chambers, George Morris, Donald Steel
Green fees £70
Catering, changing room/showers, bar, club and trolley hire, shop, driving range, practice facilities
Visitors welcome by prior arrangement
Handicap certificate required – limit: 24
Societies welcome by prior arrangement
Kings Gap Court Hotel, The Kings Gap, Hoylake, Wirral, Merseyside
0151 632 2073

SHERDLEY PARK MUNICIPAL GOLF CLUB

Sherdley Park, St Helens, Merseyside WA9 5DE
01744 813149 Fax 01744 817967
Map 10, D10
Off A570, 2 miles S of St Helens
Founded 1973
A hilly parkland course.
18 holes, 5974 yards
par 70, S.S.S 69
Green fees £7.20
Changing room/showers, club hire, driving range, practice facilities
Visitors welcome
Societies welcome by prior arrangement

SOUTHPORT AND AINSDALE GOLF CLUB

Bradshaws Lane, Ainsdale, Southport, Merseyside PR8 3LG
01704 578000 Fax 01704 570896
Map 10, C9
secretary@sandagolfclub.co.uk
www.sandagolfclub.co.uk
3 miles S of Southport
Founded 1906
At one time the foremost of the great Southport links, hosting the Ryder Cups of 1933 and 1937. It is separated from Hillside only by a railway line, although it does not enjoy quite such overwhelming sandhills. The par-5 16th, Gumbleys, with its exacting second shot, is world famous.
18 holes, 6685 yards
par 72, S.S.S 73
Designer James Braid
Green fees £45
Catering, changing room/showers, bar, club and trolley hire, shop, practice facilities
Visitors welcome, restricted weekends
Handicap certificate required
Societies welcome by prior arrangement
Scarisbrick Hotel, Lord Street, Southport, Merseyside
01704 543000

SOUTHPORT MUNICIPAL GOLF CLUB

Park Road West, Southport, Merseyside PR9 0JS
01704 535286 **Map 10, C8**
Off A565, N end of Promenade
Founded 1914
A genuine links course.
18 holes, 6253 yards
par 70, S.S.S 69
Green fees £6
Catering, changing room/showers, bar, club, trolley and buggy hire, shop
Visitors welcome
Societies welcome by prior arrangement

SOUTHPORT OLD LINKS GOLF CLUB

Moss Lane, Southport, Merseyside PR9 7QS
01704 228207 Fax 01704 505353
Map 10, C8
Off A5267, N of town centre
Founded 1926
A proper links course – if only there were room for 9 more holes!
9 holes, 6349 yards
par 72, S.S.S 71
Green fees £20
Catering, changing room/showers, bar
Visitors welcome weekdays
Societies welcome by prior arrangement

WALLASEY GOLF CLUB

Bayswater Road, Wallasey, Merseyside CH45 9LA
0151 691 1024 Fax 0151 638 8988 **Map 10, C10**
wallaseygc@aol.com
M53 Jct 1, follow signs for New Brighton A554.
Founded 1891
Huge sandhills make for a wonderful opening sequence leading to a spectacular panoramic tee on the 4th. The same dunes make the holes just after the turn and the finish from the 16th equally special. That 16th is a long par 3 with a formidable carry to an elevated green.
18 holes, 6607 yards
par 72, S.S.S 73
Designer Tom Morris
Green fees £45
Catering, changing room/showers, bar, club and trolley hire, shop, practice facilities
Visitors welcome
Handicap certificate required – limit: 24 men, 36 women
Societies welcome by prior arrangement
Leasowe Castle Hotel, Leasowe Road, Moreton, Wirral, Merseyside CH46 3RD

WARREN GOLF CLUB

Grove Road, Wallasey, Wirral, Merseyside CH45 0JA
0151 639 8323 **Map 10, C10**
www.warrengc.freeserve.co.uk
Just inland of King's Parade
Founded 1911
Potentially splendid little genuine links, with two really old-fashioned blind holes, but much conditioning is required.
9 holes, 5890 yards
par 72, S.S.S 69
Green fees £6.40
Club and trolley hire, shop
Visitors welcome
Societies welcome by prior arrangement

WEST DERBY GOLF CLUB

Yew Tree Lane, Liverpool, Merseyside L12 9HQ
0151 254 1034 Fax 0151 259 0505 **Map 10, D10**
pmilne@westderbygc.freeserve.co.uk
2 miles N of Liverpool end of M62
Founded 1896

The Deysbrook, which meanders through the course, presents a threat over the first eight holes.
18 holes, 6277 yards
par 72, S.S.S 70
Green fees £27
Catering, changing room/showers, bar, trolley hire, shop
Visitors welcome weekdays
Societies welcome by prior arrangement
Derby Lodge Hotel, Roby Road, Huyton, Liverpool, Merseyside
0151 480 4440

WEST LANCASHIRE GOLF CLUB

Hall Road West, Blundellsands, Liverpool, Merseyside L23 8SZ
0151 924 4115 Fax 0151 931 4448 **Map 10, C9**
Next to Hall Road Station, 1 mile NW of Crosby
Founded 1873
A first-rate links course at the southern end of the line of dunes stretching all the way from Southport, and a regular final qualifying venue for the Open. The architecture is subtle rather than brutal, though the 440-yard 14th is an exception, a big dog-leg to a woodside green.
18 holes, 6768 yards
par 72, S.S.S 73
Designer C.K. Cotton
Green fees £45
Catering, changing room/showers, bar, trolley hire, shop, practice facilities
Visitors welcome weekdays
Handicap certificate required
Societies welcome by prior arrangement

WIRRAL LADIES' GOLF CLUB

93 Bidston Road, Birkenhead, Wirral, Merseyside CH43 6TS
0151 652 1255 Fax 0151 653 4323 **Map 10, C9**
1 mile NE of M53 Jct 3
Founded 1894
A brilliant little course, made up mostly of teasing shorter par 4s, for a man rarely more than a mid-iron and a pitch, but that pitch will have to be inch-perfect. Cleverly raised greens, deceptive moundwork and narrow fairways lined with thick rough are complemented by high standards of greenkeeping.
18 holes, 4948 yards
par 69, S.S.S 69
Designer Harold Hilton
Green fees £25
Catering, changing room/showers, bar, club and trolley hire, shop, practice facilities
Visitors welcome
Handicap certificate required

Societies welcome by prior arrangement

WOOLTON GOLF CLUB

Doe Park, Speke Road, Woolton, Liverpool, Merseyside L25 7TZ
0151 486 1601 Fax 0151 486 1664 **Map 10, D10**
1 mile NW of Ford motor works
Founded 1901
A parkland course.
18 holes, 5706 yards
par 69, S.S.S 68
Green fees £24
Catering, changing room/showers, bar, trolley and buggy hire, shop
Visitors welcome with restrictions
Societies welcome by prior arrangement

NORTHUMBERLAND

ALLENDALE GOLF CLUB

High Studdon, Allendale, Hexham, Northumberland NE47 9DH
01434 683926 **Map 13, E10**
pmasoncd@aol.com
B6295 1½ S of Allendale
Founded 1962
From 18 tees, play is along hilly meadowland fairways to 9 greens. Side slopes effectively narrow some holes, and the lovely scenery may well distract the golfer's concentration.
9 holes, 4501 yards
par 66, S.S.S 64
Designer Members
Green fees £12
Changing room/showers, bar
Visitors welcome
Societies welcome by prior arrangement
Kings Head Hotel, Market Place, Allendale, Northumberland,
01434 683681

ALNMOUTH GOLF CLUB

Foxton Hall, Alnmouth, Northumberland NE66 3BE
01665 830231 Fax 01665 830922 **Map 13, G7**
secretary@alnmouthgolfclub.com
www.alnmouthgolfclub.com
5 miles SE of Alnwick
Founded 1869
Founded in 1869, Alnmouth is the 4th oldest club in England. Its present course was laid out in 1930 by Harry Colt. Although the course overlooks Alnmouth Bay, with the 6th green hard by the shore, the turf is more parkland in nature. The Dormy House sleeps up to 18.
18 holes, 6484 yards
par 71, S.S.S 71
Designer Harry Colt
Green fees £22
Catering, changing room/showers, bar, accommodation, club, trolley and buggy hire, shop
Visitors welcome – with restrictions
Societies welcome by prior arrangement – with restrictions
Foxton Hall Dormy House, Foxton Hall, Lesbury, Alnmouth, Northumberland
01665 830231

ALNMOUTH VILLAGE GOLF CLUB

Marine Road, Alnmouth, Northumberland NE66 2RZ
01665 830370 Fax 01665 602096 **Map 13, G7**
From Alnmouth on A1068
Founded 1869
An undulating seaside course.
9 holes, 6020 yards
par 70, S.S.S 70
Green fees £15
Catering, changing room/showers, bar
Visitors welcome
Handicap certificate required
Societies welcome by prior arrangement

ALNWICK GOLF CLUB

Swansfield Park, Alnwick, Northumberland NE66 1AB
01665 602632 **Map 13, G7**
A1 (northbound)
Founded 1907
Extended to 18 holes in 1995, Alnwick is a mixture of mature parkland and gorse-lined open country, with panoramic views out to sea. The 16th green is built on the site of an old fort.
18 holes, 6250 yards
par 70, S.S.S 70
Designer George Rochester, Rae
Green fees £20
Catering, changing room/showers, bar, trolley hire
Visitors welcome, restricted competition days
Societies welcome by prior arrangement
White Swan Hotel, Bondgate Within, Alnwick, Northumberland NE66 1PP
01665 602109

ARCOT HALL GOLF CLUB

Dudley, Cramlington, Northumberland NE23 7QP
0191 2362794 Fax 0191 2170370 **Map 13, G9**
www.arcothallgolfclub.com
Off A1, 7 miles N of Newcastle

Founded 1909
James Braid's charming parkland course, running through avenues of ancient beech and oak trees, is complemented by a magnificent Grade II listed mansion as its well-appointed clubhouse.
18 holes, 6400 yards
par 70, S.S.S 70
Designer James Braid
Green fees £26
Catering, changing room/showers, bar, club, trolley and buggy hire, shop, practice facilities, conference room
Visitors welcome – subject to restrictions
Handicap certificate required – limit: 28
Societies welcome by prior arrangement
🏨 Holiday Inn, Great North Road, Seaton Burn, Northumberland

BAMBURGH CASTLE GOLF CLUB

The Club House, 40 The Wynding, Bamburgh, Northumberland NE69 7DE
✆ 01668 214378 Fax 01668 214607
Map 13, G6
bamburghcastlegolfclub@hotmail.com
3 miles E of A1
Founded 1904
Bamburgh is one of the most romantic courses in the north of England, with five castles and a wonderful stretch of coastline visible from the course. More heathland than links in nature, there are many fascinating holes, not least the unforgiving 224-yard 6th, with a green surrounded by rocks.
18 holes, 5621 yards
par 68, S.S.S 67
Designer George Rochester
Green fees £25
Catering, changing room/showers, bar, trolley and buggy hire, practice facilities
Visitors welcome
Handicap certificate required
Societies welcome by prior arrangement

BEDLINGTONSHIRE GOLF COURSE

Acorn Bank, Bedlington, Northumberland NE22 5SY
✆ 01670 822457 **Map 13, G9**
A1068, N of Newcastle
Founded 1972
A long, testing parkland course.
18 holes, 6813 yards
par 73, S.S.S 73
Designer Frank Pennink
Green fees £15
Catering, changing room/showers, bar, club and trolley hire, shop
Visitors welcome
Societies welcome by prior arrangement

BELFORD GOLF CLUB

South Road, Belford, Northumberland NE70 7HY
✆ 01668 213433 Fax 01668 213919
Map 13, G6
Off A1 midway between Alnwick and Berwick
Founded 1993
A 9-hole course of good length enjoying uplifting views over the Northumbrian coast.
9 holes, 6304 yards
par 72, S.S.S 70
Designer Nigel Williams
Green fees £10
Catering, changing room/showers, bar, club, trolley and buggy hire, shop, driving range
Visitors welcome
Societies welcome by prior arrangement
🏨 The Blue Bell, Market Place, Belford, Northumberland NE70 7NE
✆ 01668 213543

BELLINGHAM GOLF CLUB

Boggle Hole, Bellingham, Hexham, Northumberland NE48 2DT
✆ 01434 220152 Fax 01434 220160
Map 13, E9
secretary-bellinghamgc@hotmail.com
www.bellinghamgolfclub.co.uk
B6320, northern outskirts of Bellingham
Founded 1893
A very welcoming club – 7 days a week – in the delightful North Tyne Valley. Bellingham was the first course in Britain to receive Lottery funding (for its development into an 18-hole layout).
18 holes, 6093 yards
par 70, S.S.S 70
Designer E. Johnson, Ian Wilson
Green fees £20
Catering, changing room/showers, bar, club, trolley and buggy hire, driving range
Visitors welcome
Societies welcome by prior arrangement
🏨 Riverdale Hall Hotel, Bellingham, Hexham, Northumberland NE48 2JT
✆ 01434 220254

BERWICK-UPON-TWEED GOLF CLUB

Goswick, Berwick-upon-Tweed, Northumberland TD15 2RW
✆ 01289 387380 Fax 01289 387334
Map 13, F5
goswickgc@btconnect.com
www.goswicklinksgc.co.uk
A1, 5 miles S of Berwick.
Founded 1889
A very welcoming club whose traditional links course boasts rippling fairways, fast greens, and even the odd blind shot to the pin. But there is nothing unfair about it, and it provides an excellent test of golf in lovely surroundings. The views along the coast and to Lindisfarne are uplifting.
18 holes, 6452 yards
par 72, S.S.S 71
Designer James Braid, Frank Pennink, Donald Steel
Green fees £25
Catering, changing room/showers, bar, club, trolley and buggy hire, shop, driving range, practice facilities
Visitors welcome weekdays, restricted weekends
Societies welcome by prior arrangement
🏨 The Blue Bell, Market Place, Belford, Northumberland NE70 7NE
✆ 01668 213543

BLYTH GOLF CLUB

New Delaval, Blyth, Northumberland NE24 4DB
✆ 01670 356514 Fax 01670 540134
Map 13, H9
blythgc@lineone.net
www.blythgolf.co.uk
From A1061 take B1532
Founded 1905
Dog-legs feature significantly on Hamilton Stutt's cunning design. Placing of the tee shot is of greater importance than outright length.
18 holes, 6456 yards
par 72, S.S.S 71
Designer J. Hamilton Stutt
Green fees £19
Catering, changing room/showers, bar, shop, practice facilities
Visitors welcome weekdays
Societies welcome by prior arrangement
🏨 Waterford Arms, Collywell Bay Road, Seaton Sluice, Northumberland
✆ 0191 237 0450

BURGHAM PARK GOLF CLUB

Felton, Morpeth, Northumberland NE65 8QP
✆ 01670 787 898 Fax 01670 787 164 **Map 13, G8**
A1, N of Morpeth
Founded 1994
A parkland course of good length.
18 holes, 6751 yards
par 72, S.S.S 72
Designer Andrew Mair

Green fees £18
Catering, changing room/showers, bar, trolley hire, shop, practice facilities. Visitors welcome
Societies welcome by prior arrangement

CLOSE HOUSE GOLF CLUB

Close House, Heddon-on-the-Wall, Newcastle-upon-Tyne, Northumberland NE15 0HT
✆ 0191 4886515 Fax 0191 4886515
Map 13, G10
physical-recreation-sport@ncl.ac.uk
www.ncl.ac.uk/~nprs/index.html
Off A69 near Wylam
Founded 1965
In the idyllic Tyne Valley, a pleasant parkland course in the grounds of a magnificent mansion which is visible from much of the course.
18 holes, 5606 yards
par 68, S.S.S 67
Designer Hawtree
Green fees £18
Catering, changing room/showers, conference & wedding facilities
Visitors welcome only as members' guests
Societies welcome by prior arrangement
🏨 Close House Mansion, Close House, Heddon on the Wall, Newcastle upon Tyne, Northumberland
✆ 01661 852255

DUNSTANBURGH CASTLE GOLF CLUB

Embleton, Northumberland NE66 3XQ
✆ 01665 576562 **Map 13, G7**
Off A1, 7 miles NE of Alnwick
Founded 1900
Overlooked by the castle, the course sweeps in a great arc – rarely more than two fairways wide – alongside Embleton Bay giving majestic views. With 14 par 4s ranging from 289 to 444 yards every sort of approach shot will be required, and the wind must be tackled from every quarter.
18 holes, 6298 yards
par 70, S.S.S 70
Designer James Braid
Green fees £16
Catering, changing room/showers, bar, club and trolley hire, shop
Visitors welcome
Societies welcome by prior arrangement

HEXHAM GOLF CLUB

Spital Park, Hexham, Northumberland NE46 3RZ
✆ 01434 603072 Fax 01434 601865
Map 13, F10
hexham.golf.club@talk21.com
www.hexhamgolfclub.ntb.org.uk
B6531, 1 mile W of Hexham (off A69)
Founded 1892
Set in the grounds of a handsome Georgian house surrounded by the glorious scenery of the Tyne Valley, Hexham is a delight. Magnificent specimen trees frame many fairways and constant changes of level ensure refreshing individuality to the holes. The inviting downhill sweep of the 18th makes a fitting conclusion.
18 holes, 6301 yards
par 70, S.S.S 70
Designer Harry Vardon, James Caird
Green fees £30
Catering, changing room/showers, bar, club and trolley hire, shop, practice facilities, squash club, meeting rooms
Visitors welcome
Societies welcome by prior arrangement
🏨 Beaumont Hotel, Beaumont Street, Hexham, Northumberland NE46 3LT
✆ 01434 602331

LINDEN HALL

Longhorsley, Morpeth, Northumberland NE65 8XF
✆ 01670 500011 Fax 01670 500001
Map 13, G8
golf@lindenhall.co.uk
www.lindenhall.co.uk
A697, 8 miles NW of Morpeth
Founded 1997
With the course built around a charming old country house now a hotel, Jonathan Gaunt seems to have achieved the impossible – a course which tests the good golfer from the back tees, yet is not too daunting for the less accomplished.
18 holes, 6846 yards
par 72, S.S.S 73
Designer Jonathan Gaunt
Green fees £20
Catering, changing room/showers, bar, accommodation, club, trolley and buggy hire, shop, driving range, full leisure, conference and banqueting facilities, swimming, tennis, gym
Visitors welcome – restricted weekends
Societies welcome by prior arrangement
🏨 Linden Hall Hotel, Longhorsley, Morpeth, Northumberland NE65 8XF
✆ 01670 500000

LONGHIRST HALL GOLF CLUB

Longhirst Hall, Longhirst, Northumberland NE61 3LL
✆ 01670 791 505 Fax 01670 791768
Map 13, G9
www.longhirstgolf.co.uk
4 miles NE of Morpeth
Founded 1997
A challenging parkland course with many lakes, a touch of Florida in the Northumberland countryside.
18 holes, 6570 yards
par 72, S.S.S 72
Designer B. Poole
Green fees £16
Catering, changing room/showers, bar, accommodation, shop, practice facilities, 9-hole short course
Visitors welcome
Societies welcome by prior arrangement

MAGDALENE FIELDS GOLF CLUB

Magdalene Fields, Berwick-upon-Tweed, Northumberland TD15 1NE
✆ 01289 306384 Fax 01289 306130
Map 13, F5
mfgc@firefly.club24.co.uk
www.magdalene-fields.co.uk
Berwick town centre, just off A1
Founded 1903
This most northerly course in England sweeps handsomely over the cliff-tops towards the sea. Indeed, the short 8th is played over a cove. The outward half is the harder, culminating in the heart-stopping 9th, but the 16th is aptly named 'The Destroyer', played from a tee on the beach.
18 holes, 6407 yards
par 72, S.S.S 71
Designer Willie Park Jnr
Green fees £17
Catering, changing room/showers, bar, club, trolley and buggy hire, shop, practice facilities
Visitors welcome – with restrictions
Societies welcome by prior arrangement
🏨 Kings Arms Hotel, Hide Hill, Berwick-upon-Tweed, Northumberland
✆ 01289 307454

MATFEN HALL COUNTRY HOUSE HOTEL AND GOLF CLUB

Matfen, Near Newcastle-upon-Tyne, Northumberland NE20 0RH
✆ 01661 886400 Fax 01661 886055
Map 13, F10
info@matfenhall.com
www.matfenhall.com
Off B5318, 5 miles N of Corbridge
Founded 1994
A handsome, rolling course in one of the loveliest corners of England. A lake and the River Pont are brought into play on several holes, not least the very unforgiving 222-yard 17th.

Strong par 4s at the 4th, 9th, 12th and 14th are counterbalanced by several gentler drive-and-pitch holes.
18 holes, 6534 yards
par 72, S.S.S 71
Designer Andrew Mair, Jonathan Gaunt
Green fees £25
Catering, changing room/showers, bar, accommodation, club, trolley and buggy hire, shop, driving range, practice facilities, full hotel, conference and function facilities, par-3 golf course
Visitors welcome – restricted weekend mornings
Societies welcome by prior arrangement
Matfen Hall Country House Hotel and Golf Club, Matfen, Near Newcastle-upon-Tyne, Northumberland NE20 0RH
01661 886500

MORPETH GOLF CLUB

The Clubhouse, Morpeth, Northumberland NE61 2BT
01670 504942 Fax 01670 504918
Map 13, G9
A197, 1 mile S of Morpeth
Founded 1906
A lovely old parkland course with open views to the Cheviot Hills.
18 holes, 6207 yards
par 71, S.S.S 69
Designer Harry Vardon
Green fees £20
Catering, changing room/showers, bar, trolley hire, shop
Visitors welcome
Handicap certificate required
Societies welcome by prior arrangement

NEWBIGGIN GOLF CLUB

Newbiggin-by-the-Sea, Northumberland NE64 6DW
01670 817344 Fax 01670 520236
Map 13, H9
Off A197
Founded 1884
A links course which deserves to be better known than it is.
18 holes, 6452 yards
par 72, S.S.S 71
Designer Willie Park
Green fees £15
Catering, changing room/showers, bar, club and trolley hire, shop
Visitors welcome – with restrictions
Societies welcome by prior arrangement

PONTELAND GOLF CLUB

53 Bell Villas, Ponteland, Newcastle-upon-Tyne, Northumberland NE20 9BD
01661 822689 Fax 01661 860077
Map 13, G10
A696, 1 mile from entrance to Newcastle Airport
Founded 1927
A genuine championship course, hosting the 2000 English Open Mid-Amateur amongst others, with renowned, fine turf. The 9th and 16th challenge even the best golfers.
18 holes, 6523 yards
par 72, S.S.S 71
Designer Harry Fernie
Green fees £25
Catering, changing room/showers, bar, club and trolley hire, shop, practice facilities
Visitors welcome weekdays
Handicap certificate required
Societies welcome by prior arrangement
Novotel Newcastle, Ponteland Road, Kenton, Newcastle-upon-Tyne, Northumberland
0191 214 0303

PRUDHOE GOLF CLUB

Eastwood Park, Prudhoe-on-Tyne, Northumberland NE42 5DX
01661 832466 **Map 13, G10**
A695, 12 miles W of Newcastle
Founded 1930
Rolling parkland course.
18 holes, 5862 yards
par 69, S.S.S 68
Green fees £20
Catering, changing room/showers, bar, trolley hire, shop
Visitors welcome weekdays
Societies welcome by prior arrangement

ROTHBURY GOLF CLUB

Old Race Course, Thropton Road, Rothbury, Morpeth, Northumberland NE65 7TR
01669 621271 **Map 13, F8**
15 miles N of Morpeth, via A697
Founded 1891
Gentle 9-hole course on the edge of the Northumberland National Park.
9 holes, 5681 yards
par 68, S.S.S 67
Green fees £11
Catering, changing room/showers, bar
Visitors welcome – restricted weekends
Societies welcome by prior arrangement – no company days
Queens Head Hotel, Townfoot, Rothbury, Morpeth, Northumberland NE65 7SR
01669 620470

SEAHOUSES GOLF CLUB

Beadnell Road, Seahouses, Northumberland NE68 7XT
01665 720794 Fax 01665 721994
Map 13, G6
B1340, just S of Seahouses village.
Founded 1913
One of those deceptive courses on which the yardage gives little indication of the challenge ahead – standard scratch is rarely bettered. Despite the apparent lack of length, Seahouses has been good enough to host many county events and boasts two of the finest short holes in the North of England.
18 holes, 5516 yards
par 67, S.S.S 67
Green fees £18
Catering, changing room/showers, bar, trolley hire, practice facilities
Visitors welcome
Societies welcome by prior arrangement
Links Hotel, King Street, Seahouses, Northumberland
01665 720062

DE VERE SLALEY HALL

Slaley, Hexham, Northumberland NE47 0BY
01434 673154 Fax 01434 673152
Map 13, F10
slaley.hall@devere-hotels.com
Off B6306 at Slaley, 3 miles SE of Hexham
Founded 1990
See Top 50 Courses, page
Hunting Course: 18 holes, 7088 yards, par 72, S.S.S 74
Designer Dave Thomas
Priestman Course: 18 holes, 6951 yards, par 72, S.S.S 73
Designer Neil Coles
Green fees £60
Catering, changing room/showers, bar, accommodation, club, trolley and buggy hire, shop, driving range, practice facilities, full hotel leisure, function and conference facilities
Visitors welcome
Societies welcome by prior arrangement
De Vere Slaley Hall, Slaley, Near Hexham, Northumberland NE47 0BY
01434 673350 Fax 01434 673962
slaley.hall@devere-hotels.com

STOCKSFIELD GOLF CLUB

New Ridley, Stocksfield, Northumberland NE43 7RE
01661 843041 Fax 01661 843046
Map 13, F10
info@sgcgolf.co.uk
www.sgcgolf.co.uk
Off A68, 2 miles S of Stocksfield
Founded 1913
An attractive, well-wooded parkland course. Pennink's design calls for thoughtful play, especially on the

outward half where a stream affects several holes.
18 holes, 6015 yards
par 70, S.S.S 70
Designer Frank Pennink
Green fees £25
Catering, changing room/showers, bar, club and trolley hire, shop, driving range, practice facilities, snooker
Visitors welcome – restricted Saturday
Societies welcome by prior arrangement
🏨 Royal Derwent Hotel, Allensford, Northumberland DH8 9BB
✆ 01207 592000

SWARLAND HALL GOLF CLUB

Coast View, Swarland, Morpeth, Northumberland NE65 9JG
✆ 01670 787010 **Map 13, G8**
1 mile off A1, 8 miles S of Alnwick
Founded 1993
A lengthy parkland course on high ground giving extensive views to the Simonside Hills in the west and the North Sea coast in the east.
18 holes, 6628 yards
par 72, S.S.S 72
Green fees £15
Catering, changing room/showers, bar, club, trolley and buggy hire, shop, practice facilities, dining/meeting room
Visitors welcome
Societies welcome by prior arrangement
🏨 White Swan Hotel, Bondgate Within, Alnwick, Northumberland NE66 1PP
✆ 01665 602109

TYNEDALE GOLF COURSE

Tyne Green, Hexham, Northumberland NE46 3HQ
✆ 01434 608154 **Map 13, F10**
A69, S of River Tyne
Founded 1908
A short public course in the Tyne Valley.
9 holes, 5706 yards
S.S.S 68
Green fees £10
Catering, changing room/showers, shop
Visitors welcome with restrictions
Societies welcome by prior arrangement

WARKWORTH GOLF CLUB

The Links, Warkworth, Morpeth, Northumberland NE65 0SW
✆ 01665 711596 **Map 13, G8**
Off A1068, 9 miles SE of Alnwick
Founded 1891
Charming old links course.
9 holes, 5986 yards
par 70, S.S.S 68
Designer Old Tom Morris
Green fees £12
Catering, changing room/showers, bar, shop
Visitors welcome – with restrictions
Societies welcome by prior arrangement

WOOLER GOLF CLUB

Dodd Law, Doddington, Wooler, Northumberland NE71 6EA
✆ 01668 282135 **Map 13, F7**
B6525, 3 miles N of Wooler
Founded 1976
A tribute to the members themselves who designed this jewel in a prime location with panoramic views into the Cheviots and Border Country, and out to the North Sea.
9 holes, 6411 yards
par 72, S.S.S 71
Designer Members
Green fees £10
Catering, changing room/showers, bar, buggy hire
Visitors welcome
Societies welcome by prior arrangement
🏨 Wheatsheaf Hotel, Market Place, Wooler, Northumberland

TYNE AND WEAR

BACKWORTH GOLF CLUB

The Hall, Backworth, Shiremoor, Newcastle, Tyne and Wear NE27 0AH
✆ 0191 268 1048 **Map 13, H10**
B1322, off Tyne Tunnel link road
Founded 1937
Parkland course between Newcastle and Blyth.
9 holes, 5930 yards
par 71, S.S.S 69
Green fees £14
Catering, changing room/showers, bar, bowling green
Visitors welcome – with restrictions
Societies welcome by prior arrangement

BIRTLEY (PORTOBELLO) GOLF CLUB

Birtley Lane, Birtley, Tyne and Wear DH3 2LR
✆ 0191 410 2207 **Map 13, G10**
Off A167, 3 miles from A1 (M)
Founded 1922
Parkland course between Washington and Gateshead.
9 holes, 5662 yards
par 67, S.S.S 67
Green fees £12
Changing room/showers, bar
Visitors welcome, restrictions weekend
Societies welcome by prior arrangement – no company days
🏨 Swallow Hotel, Gateshead, Tyne and Wear
✆ 0191 477 1105

BOLDON GOLF CLUB

Dipe Lane, East Boldon, Tyne and Wear NE36 0PQ
✆ 0191 536 4082 Fax 0191 537 2270 **Map 13, H10**
www.boldongolfclub.co.uk
Off A184, SE of Boldon
Founded 1912
A parkland course designed by Harry Vardon.
18 holes, 6348 yards
par 72, S.S.S 70
Designer Harry Vardon
Green fees £18
Catering, changing room/showers, bar, club and trolley hire, shop, driving range
Visitors welcome weekdays
Societies welcome by prior arrangement

CITY OF NEWCASTLE GOLF CLUB

Three Mile Bridge, Gosforth, Newcastle-upon-Tyne, Tyne and Wear NE3 2DR
✆ 0191 285 1775 Fax 0191 284 0700 **Map 13, G10**
B1318, 3 miles N of city centre
Founded 1891
Only three miles from the city centre, yet there is a real country feeling to this attractive parkland course, with fairways well separated and plentiful trees. Only one par 4 exceeds 400 yards, the 442-yard 16th, which is appropriately named Vardon's Best, commemorating the course architect and Open Champion.
18 holes, 6528 yards
par 72, S.S.S 71
Designer Harry Vardon
Green fees £24
Catering, changing room/showers, bar, club and trolley hire, shop, practice facilities, conference facilities
Visitors welcome
Societies welcome by prior arrangement
🏨 Imperial Swallow Hotel, Jesmond Road, Jesmond, Newcastle upon Tyne, Tyne and Wear

ELEMORE GOLF COURSE

Easington Lane, Houghton-le-Spring, Tyne and Wear
✆ 0191 5173057 Fax 0191 5173054
Map 13, H11
5 miles E of Durham
Founded 1994

A fine pay-and-play layout with a number of water holes.
18 holes, 5947 yards
par 69, S.S.S 69
Designer Jonathan Gaunt
Green fees £9
Catering, changing room/showers, bar, club, trolley and buggy hire, shop, practice facilities
Visitors welcome
Societies welcome by prior arrangement

GARESFIELD GOLF CLUB

Chopwell, Tyne and Wear NE17 7AP
☎ 01207 561278 Fax 01207 561309
Map 13, G10
Off A1/A694 at Rowlands Gill (B6315)
Founded 1922
A well-wooded, undulating parkland course.
18 holes, 6458 yards
par 72, S.S.S 71
Green fees £17
Catering, changing room/showers, bar, club and trolley hire, shop
Visitors welcome weekdays
Societies welcome by prior arrangement

GEORGE WASHINGTON COUNTY HOTEL, GOLF AND COUNTRY CLUB

Stone Cellar Road, High Unsworth, District 12, Washington, Tyne and Wear NE37 1PH
☎ 0191 4029988 Fax 0191 4151166
Map 13, G11
Signposted from A1(M) and A194.
Founded 1990
A demanding course, part of extensive facilities at this hotel and country club.
18 holes, 6604 yards
par 73, S.S.S 72
Designer Eric Watson
Green fees £20
Catering, changing room/showers, bar, accommodation, club, trolley and buggy hire, shop, driving range, practice facilities, full hotel facilities, 9-hole pitch & putt
Visitors welcome
Societies welcome by prior arrangement
🏨 George Washington County Hotel, Stonecellar Road, Washington, Tyne and Wear
☎ 0191 402 9988

GOSFORTH GOLF CLUB

Broadway East, Gosforth, Newcastle-upon-Tyne, Tyne and Wear NE3 5ER
☎ 0191 285 0553 Fax 0191 284 6274 **Map 13, G10**
gosgolf@gosforth.fsbusiness.co
Off A6125, 3 miles N of Newcastle
Founded 1906
Parkland course with water features on 4th, 15th and 18th holes.
18 holes, 6024 yards
par 69, S.S.S 69
Green fees £24
Catering, changing room/showers, bar, trolley hire, shop, practice facilities
Visitors welcome
Handicap certificate required
Societies welcome by prior arrangement
🏨 Gosforth Park Hotel, Gosforth, Newcastle-upon-Tyne, Tyne and Wear

HETTON-LE-HOLE GOLF CLUB

Elemore Golf Course, Elemore Lane, Hetton-le-Hole, Tyne and Wear DH5 0EX
☎ 0191 5173057 Fax 0191 5173054
Map 13, H11
4 miles E of A1(M) Jct 62
A testing parkland course, the par-3 3rd and par-4 6th both being water holes.
18 holes, 5947 yards
par 69, S.S.S 69
Green fees £9
Catering, changing room/showers, bar, club, trolley and buggy hire, shop, practice facilities
Visitors welcome
Societies welcome by prior arrangement

HEWORTH GOLF CLUB

Gingling Lane, Heworth, Gateshead, Tyne and Wear NE10 8XY
☎ 0191 469 9832 **Map 13, G10**
A1(M)/A195, SE of Gateshead
Founded 1912
A wooded parkland course.
18 holes, 6404 yards
par 72, S.S.S 71
Green fees £15
Catering, changing room/showers, bar, practice facilities
Visitors welcome weekdays
Societies welcome by prior arrangement

HOUGHTON-LE-SPRING GOLF CLUB

Copt Hill, Houghton-le-Spring, Tyne and Wear DH5 8LU
☎ 0191 584 1198 **Map 13, H11**
A1085, ½ mile E of Houghton
Founded 1908
A hillside course with good views.
18 holes, 6416 yards
par 72, S.S.S 71
Green fees £20
Catering, changing room/showers, bar, shop
Visitors welcome – restricted Sundays
Societies welcome by prior arrangement

NEWCASTLE UNITED GOLF CLUB

Ponteland Road, Cowgate, Newcastle-upon-Tyne, Tyne and Wear NE5 3JW
☎ 0191 286 4693 **Map 13, G10**
Off A6127, NW of city centre
Founded 1892
An undulating moorland course.
18 holes, 6617 yards
par 72, S.S.S 72
Catering, changing room/showers, bar, club and trolley hire, shop
Visitors welcome weekdays
Societies welcome by prior arrangement

THE NORTHUMBERLAND GOLF CLUB

High Gosforth Park, Newcastle-upon-Tyne, Tyne and Wear NE3 5HT
☎ 0191 236 2498 Fax 0191 236 2498 **Map 13, G10**
Off A1, 5 miles N of Newcastle, follow signs to Newcastle Race Course.
Founded 1898
A course which has been the venue for a number of professional and important amateur tournaments. The Northumberland is laid out inside, outside, and over the race track. By some way, the 13th is the hardest hole, a 470-yard par 4. Interestingly, the club's winter course is radically different.
18 holes, 6629 yards
par 72, S.S.S 72
Designer Harry Colt, James Braid
Green fees £35
Catering, changing room/showers, bar, practice facilities
Visitors welcome weekdays
Handicap certificate required
Societies welcome by prior arrangement
🏨 Marriott Gosforth Park, High Gosforth Park, Wideopen, Tyne and Wear
☎ 0191 236 4111

PARKLANDS GOLF CLUB

High Gosforth Park, Newcastle-upon-Tyne, Tyne and Wear NE3 5HQ
☎ 0191 236 4480 **Map 13, G10**
Off A1, 3 miles N of Newcastle
Founded 1971
A parkland course with several water holes, becoming increasingly testing as the round progresses.
18 holes, 6060 yards
par 71, S.S.S 69
Green fees £15

Catering, changing room/showers, bar, trolley hire, shop, driving range
Visitors welcome
Societies welcome by prior arrangement

RAVENSWORTH GOLF CLUB

Moss Heaps, Wrekenton, Gateshead, Tyne and Wear NE9 7UU
0191 487 6014 **Map 13, G10**
B1296, 3 miles S of Newcastle
Founded 1906
An upland course with fine views.
18 holes, 5966 yards
par 69, S.S.S 69
Designer J.W. Fraser
Green fees £19
Catering, changing room/showers, bar, trolley hire, shop
Visitors welcome
Handicap certificate required
Societies welcome by prior arrangement

RYTON GOLF CLUB

Doctor Stanners, Clara Vale, Ryton, Tyne and Wear NE40 3TD
0191 413 3253 Fax 0191 413 1642 **Map 13, G10**
Off A695, 7 miles W of Newcastle
Founded 1891
A parkland course.
18 holes, 5950 yards
par 70, S.S.S 69
Green fees £16
Catering, changing room/showers, bar
Visitors welcome weekdays
Societies welcome by prior arrangement

SOUTH SHIELDS GOLF CLUB

Cleadon Hills, South Shields, Tyne and Wear NE34 8EG
0191 456 9842 **Map 13, H10**
thesecretary@south-shields-golf.freeserve.co.uk
www.ssgc.co.uk
Off A1300, SE of town centre
Founded 1893
Lovely coastal views are a bonus from the high ground at South Shields. With a blind approach to the green, the 7th is one of the hardest holes, and the 459-yard 14th is at least its equal. Out-of-bounds and gorse bushes frequently threaten. The greens are firm and swift.
18 holes, 6264 yards
par 71, S.S.S 70
Designer Alister Mackenzie, James Braid.
Green fees £25
Catering, changing room/showers, bar, club and trolley hire, shop
Visitors welcome
Societies welcome by prior arrangement

TYNEMOUTH GOLF CLUB

Spital Dene, Tynemouth, North Shields, Tyne and Wear NE30 2ER
0191 257 4578 Fax 0191 259 5193 **Map 13, H10**
8 miles E of Newcastle
Founded 1913
A parkland course, often affected by seaside winds.
18 holes, 6401 yards
par 70, S.S.S 71
Designer Willie Park
Green fees £20
Catering, changing room/showers, bar, club, trolley and buggy hire, shop
Visitors welcome weekdays – with restrictions
Societies welcome by prior arrangement

TYNESIDE GOLF CLUB

Westfield Lane, Ryton, Tyne and Wear NE40 3QE
0191 413 1600 Fax 0191 413 2742 **Map 13, G10**
edstephenson@tynesdiegolfclub.fsbusinees.co.uk
B8317, 7 miles W of Newcastle
Founded 1879
A Colt-designed, undulating, parkland course.
18 holes, 6033 yards
par 70, S.S.S 69
Designer Harry Colt
Green fees £20
Catering, changing room/showers, bar, trolley and buggy hire, shop, practice facilities
Visitors welcome weekdays – with restrictions
Societies welcome by prior arrangement
Ryton Park Country House Hotel, Holborn Lane, Ryton, Tyne and Wear
0191 413 3535

WALLSEND GOLF COURSE

Rheydt Avenue, Bigges Main, Wallsend, Tyne and Wear NE28 8SU
0191 262 1973 **Map 13, H10**
Off A193, NW of Wallsend
Founded 1973
A parkland course in the Newcastle suburbs.
18 holes, 6608 yards
par 70, S.S.S 71
Designer G. Showball
Green fees £13
Catering, changing room/showers, bar, trolley and buggy hire, shop, driving range
Visitors welcome. Societies welcome by prior arrangement

WEARSIDE GOLF CLUB

Coxgreen, Sunderland, Tyne and Wear SR4 9JT
0191 5342518 Fax 0191 5346186
Map 13, H10
South bank of River Wear, 1 mile W of A19
Founded 1892
Attractive parkland course laid out beside River Wear.
18 holes, 6323 yards
par 71, S.S.S 70
Green fees £26
Catering, changing room/showers, bar, trolley hire, shop, practice facilities
Visitors welcome
Handicap certificate required
Societies welcome by prior arrangement
Lumley Castle, Chester-le-Street, Durham DH3 4NX
0191 389 1111 Fax 0191 389 1881

WESTERHOPE GOLF CLUB

Whorlton Grange, Westerhope, Newcastle-upon-Tyne, Tyne and Wear NE5 1PP
0191 286 9125 **Map 13, G10**
B6324, 5 miles W of Newcastle
Founded 1914
A scenic parkland course with extensive views.
18 holes, 6444 yards
par 72, S.S.S 71
Designer Alex Herd
Green fees £16
Changing room/showers, trolley and buggy hire, shop
Visitors welcome weekdays
Societies welcome by prior arrangement

WHICKHAM GOLF CLUB

Hollinside Park, Fellside Road, Whickham, Newcastle-upon-Tyne, Tyne and Wear NE16 5BA
0191 4881576 Fax 0191 488 1576
Map 13, G10
6 miles SW of Newcastle city centre
Founded 1911
The club moved to this site, part of the Bowes-Lyon family estate in 1938. The views over the Derwent Valley, as far as the Cheviots, are magnificent.
18 holes, 5878 yards
par 68, S.S.S 68
Green fees £20
Catering, changing room/showers, bar, club and trolley hire, shop, practice facilities
Visitors welcome, with restrictions
Handicap certificate required
Societies welcome by prior arrangement

🏨 Marriott Hotel, Metro Centre, Gateshed, Tyne and Wear

WHITBURN GOLF CLUB

Lizard Lane, South Shields, Tyne and Wear NE34 7AF
✆ 0191 529 4210 Fax 0191 5294944
Map 13, H10
www.whitburngolf.co.uk
A183 between Sunderland and South Shields
Founded 1933
A parkland course with an excellent pedigree, with views over Marsden Bay and along the coast further north.
18 holes, 5899 yards
par 70, S.S.S 68
Designer Harry Colt, C.H. Alison, John Morrison.
Green fees £20
Catering, changing room/showers, bar, shop, practice facilities
Visitors welcome with restrictions
Societies welcome by prior arrangement
🏨 Marriott Hotel, Metro Centre, Gateshed, Tyne and Wear

WHITLEY BAY GOLF CLUB

Claremont Road, Whitley Bay, Tyne and Wear NE26 3UF
✆ 0191 252 0180 Fax 0191 297 0030 **Map 13, H10**
secretarywbgolf@netscapeonline.co.uk
www.wbgolf.free-online.co.uk
N of Whitley Bay town centre
Founded 1890
On an elevated site behind the town, this downland course is very exposed to the wind, though the seascapes are a reward. A ravine running through the course must be carried on several holes, especially the demanding 16th. Sweeping, first downhill, then up, the 582-yard 12th is Stroke 1.
18 holes, 6579 yards
par 71, S.S.S 71
Green fees £22
Catering, changing room/showers, bar, club, trolley and buggy hire, shop, practice facilities
Visitors welcome weekdays
Societies welcome by prior arrangement

EAST YORKSHIRE

ALLERTHORPE PARK GOLF CLUB

Allerthorpe, York, East Yorkshire YO4 4RL
✆ 01759 306686 Fax 01759 304308
Map 11, D6
Off A1079, 2 miles W of Pocklington
Founded 1994
A rare 13-hole parkland course.
13 holes, 5634 yards
par 68, S.S.S 67
Designer J.C. Hatcliffe & Partners
Green fees £16
Catering, changing room/showers, bar
Visitors welcome
Societies welcome by prior arrangement

BEVERLEY AND EAST RIDING GOLF CLUB

The Westwood, Beverley, East Yorkshire HU17 8RG
✆ 01482 869519 Fax 01482 868757
Map 11, E7
B1230, 1 miles W of town centre
Founded 1889
Beverley, the second oldest club in Yorkshire, enjoys charming views over the lovely old market town from its windmill clubhouse. The hazards of the common-land Westwood are entirely natural, and, with only two parallel fairways, inaccuracy is severely punished. Having to chip over a herd of bullocks is not unknown!
18 holes, 6017 yards
par 69, S.S.S 69
Designer Alex Herd
Green fees £13
Catering, changing room/showers, bar, club and trolley hire, shop, practice facilities
Visitors welcome
Societies welcome by prior arrangement
🏨 Beverley Arms Hotel, 24 North Bar Within, Beverley, East Yorkshire HU17 8DD
✆ 01482 869241

BOOTHFERRY PARK GOLF CLUB

Spaldington Lane, Spaldington, Near Howden, East Yorkshire DN14 7NG
✆ 01430 430364 **Map 11, D7**
B1228, 3 miles N of Howden, M62 Jct 37
Founded 1982
Very flat, but well designed, course of some length, not overfacing for the beginner yet adequate for the good player. Drainage ditches trap the unwary.
18 holes, 6651 yards
par 73, S.S.S 72
Designer Donald Steel
Green fees £10
Catering, changing room/showers, bar, trolley hire, shop, driving range, practice facilities
Visitors welcome, restricted Saturday
Societies welcome by prior arrangement
🏨 Cave Castle Hotel, South Cave, East Yorkshire HU15 2EU
✆ 01430 422245

BRIDLINGTON GOLF CLUB

Belvedere Road, Bridlington, East Yorkshire YO15 3NA
✆ 01262 606367 Fax 01262 606367
Map 11, F6
golfcrid@aol.com
Off A165, 1½ miles S of Bridlington.
Founded 1905
Bracing clifftop golf with expansive sea views.
18 holes, 6638 yards
par 72, S.S.S 72
Designer James Braid
Green fees £18
Catering, changing room/showers, bar, club, trolley and buggy hire, shop, practice facilities
Visitors welcome, restricted weekends
Societies welcome by prior arrangement

THE BRIDLINGTON LINKS GOLF CLUB

Flamborough Road, Marton, Bridlington, East Yorkshire YO15 1DW
✆ 01262 401584 Fax 01262 401702
Map 11, F5
B1255, 2 miles N of Bridlington
Founded 1993
On the clifftops, with splendid views, and very exposed to the wind.
18 holes, 6720 yards
par 72, S.S.S 72
Designer Howard Swann
Green fees £12
Catering, changing room/showers, bar, club, trolley and buggy hire, shop, driving range, 9-hole course
Visitors welcome
Societies welcome by prior arrangement

BROUGH GOLF CLUB

Cave Road, Brough, East Yorkshire HU15 1HB
✆ 01482 667291 Fax 01482 669873
Map 11, E8
gt@brough-golfclub.co.uk
www.brough-golfclub.co.uk
Off A63, 10 miles W of Hull
Founded 1891
An old club with a pretty parkland course laid out on well-drained land, giving good conditions even in winter. The large Victorian clubhouse gives an air of grandeur, and a good deal of comfort.
18 holes, 6075 yards
par 68, S.S.S 69
Green fees £30

Catering, changing room/showers, bar, club and trolley hire, shop, practice facilities
Visitors welcome but not Wednesdays or weekends
Handicap certificate required
Societies welcome by prior arrangement
Post House, The Marina, Hull, East Yorkshire

CAVE CASTLE GOLF CLUB

South Cave, East Yorkshire HU15 2EU
01430 421286 Fax 01430 421118
Map 11, A7
M62/A63 exit for South Cave, 10 miles W of Hull
Founded 1989
A parkland course on the ouskirts of a charming village at the foot of the Yorkshire Wolds.
18 holes, 6524 yards
par 72, S.S.S 71
Green fees £15
Catering, changing room/showers, bar, accommodation, trolley and buggy hire, shop, practice facilities, conference and function facilities, Leisure complex
Visitors welcome – restrictions weekends
Societies welcome by prior arrangement
Cave Castle Hotel, South Cave, East Yorkshire HU15 2EU
01430 422245

CHERRY BURTON GOLF COURSE

Leconfield Road, Cherry Burton, Beverley, East Yorkshire HU17 7RB
01964 550924 **Map 11, E7**
B1248, 2 miles N of Beverley
Founded 1993
A new course, heading for the Wolds north of Beverley.
9 holes, 4556 yards
par 66, S.S.S 62
Green fees £7
Catering, changing room/showers, bar, shop, driving range, practice facilities
Visitors welcome
Societies welcome by prior arrangement

COTTINGHAM GOLF CLUB

Woodhill Way, Cottingham, East Yorkshire HU16 5RZ
01482 846030 Fax 01482 845932
Map 11, E7
B1233, 3 miles N of Hull
Founded 1994
Water hazards abound on this modern course, with a striking view of Beverley Minster from the 10th tee.
18 holes, 6459 yards
par 72, S.S.S 71
Designer T. Litten, J. Wiles
Green fees £16
Catering, changing room/showers, bar, club and trolley hire, shop, practice facilities, conference and function facilities, health club, swimming pool
Visitors welcome, restricted weekends
Societies welcome by prior arrangement
Jarvis Grange Hotel, Grange Park Lane, Willerby, East Yorkshire HU10 6EA
01482 656488

DRIFFIELD GOLF CLUB

Sunderlandwick, Beverley Road, Driffield, East Yorkshire YO25 9AD
01377 2531116 Fax 01377 240599 **Map 11, E6**
A164, S of Driffield
Founded 1934
A parkland course laid within the grounds of once-grand Sunderlandwick Hall.
18 holes, 6215 yards
par 70, S.S.S 70
Green fees £20
Catering, changing room/showers, bar, trolley hire, shop, practice facilities
Visitors welcome with restrictions
Handicap certificate required
Societies welcome by prior arrangement
The Bell Hotel, Market Place, Driffield, East Yorkshire, East Yorkshire
01377 256661

FLAMBOROUGH HEAD GOLF CLUB

Lighthouse Road, Flamborough, Bridlington, East Yorkshire YO15 1AR
01262 850333 Fax 01262 850277
Map 11, G5
fhgc@cwcom.net
www.fhgc.cwc.net
At Flamborough Head, 5 miles NE of Bridlington
Founded 1931
A windy, clifftop course for those with an appreciation of nautical and natural history. England's oldest surviving lighthouse stands behind the 4th green, and the course overlooks the site of American John Paul Jones's famous victory over British men-of-war in 1779. The cliffs are a very important seabird breeding ground.
18 holes, 6180 yards
par 70, S.S.S 69
Green fees £18
Catering, changing room/showers, bar, trolley and buggy hire, shop, practice facilities
Visitors welcome with restrictions
Societies welcome by prior arrangement
North Star Hotel, Flamborough, Bridlington, East Yorkshire
01262 850379

GANSTEAD PARK GOLF CLUB

Longdales Lane, Coniston, Near Hull, East Yorkshire HU11 4LB
01482 817754 Fax 01482 817754
Map 11, F7
secretary@gansteadpark.co.uk
www.gansteadpark.co.uk
A165 Hull-Bridlington road (signposted)
Founded 1976
As the card implies, there are some lengthy holes at Ganstead Park, but the ground is flat and the course is not physically tiring. Trees, grassy mounds and, particularly, lakes define many holes.
18 holes, 6801 yards
par 72, S.S.S 73
Designer Peter Green
Green fees £18
Catering, changing room/showers, bar, club, trolley and buggy hire, shop, practice facilities
Visitors welcome with restrictions
Societies welcome by prior arrangement
Gardeners Arms, Hull Road, Coniston, East Yorkshire HU11 5AE
01964 562625

HAINSWORTH PARK GOLF CLUB

Brandesburton, Driffield, East Yorkshire YO25 8RT
01964 542362 Fax 01964 542362
Map 11, E7
Off A165 at Brandesburton, 6 miles NW of Beverley
Founded 1983
A parkland course.
18 holes, 6435 yards
par 71, S.S.S 71
Green fees £15
Catering, changing room/showers, bar, accommodation, club, trolley and buggy hire, shop, grass tennis courts, fishing
Visitors welcome
Societies welcome by prior arrangement
Burton Lodge Hotel, Brandesburton, Driffield, East Yorkshire YO25 8RU
01964 542847

HESSLE GOLF CLUB

Westfield Road, Raywell, Cottingham, East Yorkshire HU16

5YL
☎ 01482 650171 Fax 01482 652679
Map 11, E8
Off A164, 3 miles SW of Cottingham
Founded 1898
This is one of the early Thomas/Alliss creations (1975), although the club itself is much older. Over a quarter of a century the trees have grown to enhance the outlook.
18 holes, 6604 yards
par 72, S.S.S 72
Designer Dave Thomas, Peter Alliss
Green fees £23
Catering, changing room/showers, bar, trolley hire, shop
Visitors welcome weekdays
Handicap certificate required
Societies welcome by prior arrangement

HORNSEA GOLF CLUB

Rolston Road, Hornsea, East Yorkshire HU18 1XG
☎ 01964 532020 Fax 01964 532080
Map 11, F7
hornseagolfclub@aol.com
Follow signs for Freeport.
Founded 1898
Although close to the sea, the course is more parkland than links in nature. Hornsea is noted for the strength of its long par 4s, yet it is a two-shotter of only 289 yards which is particularly memorable, the 11th, with a pond and ring of bunkers encircling the green.
18 holes, 6661 yards
par 72, S.S.S 72
Designer Alex Herd, James Braid, Alister Mackenzie
Green fees £22
Catering, changing room/showers, bar, club, trolley and buggy hire, shop, practice facilities, snooker
Visitors welcome – restricted weekends
Societies welcome by prior arrangement
🏨 Burton Lodge Hotel, Brandesburton, Driffield, East Yorkshire YO25 8RU
☎ 01964 542847

HULL GOLF CLUB

The Hall, 27 Packman Lane, Kirk Ella, Hull, East Yorkshire HU10 7TJ
☎ 01482 653026 Fax 01482 658919
Map 11, E8
Off A164, 5 miles W of city centre
Founded 1921
Attractive parkland course, gently undulating.
18 holes, 6246 yards
par 70, S.S.S 70
Designer James Braid
Green fees £26.50
Changing room/showers, trolley hire, shop
Visitors welcome weekdays
Societies welcome by prior arrangement

KILNWICK PERCY GOLF CLUB

Pocklington, York, East Yorkshire YO42 1UF
☎ 01759 303090 **Map 11, D6**
Off B1246, 1 mile E of Pocklington
Founded 1995
It has taken time for the golfing potential of the Yorkshire Wolds to be recognized. John Day's courses are never less than interesting, and this is blessed with gorgeous views.
18 holes, 6214 yards
par 70, S.S.S 70
Designer John Day
Green fees £15
Catering, changing room/showers, bar, club, trolley and buggy hire, shop, practice facilities
Visitors welcome with restrictions
Societies welcome by prior arrangement
🏨 Yorkway Hotel, Hill Road, Pocklington, York, East Yorkshire YO42 2NX
☎ 01759 303071

SPRINGHEAD PARK GOLF CLUB

Willerby Road, Hull, East Yorkshire HU5 5JE
☎ 01482 656309 **Map 11, E8**
Off A164, W of Hull
Founded 1930
A good parkland course which represents excellent value for money.
18 holes, 6402 yards
par 71, S.S.S 71
Green fees £7.50
Club hire, shop
Visitors welcome weekdays
Societies welcome by prior arrangement

SUTTON PARK GOLF CLUB

Salthouse Road, Hull, East Yorkshire HU8 9HF
☎ 01482 374242 Fax 01482 701428
Map 11, F8
A165, 3 miles E of Hull
Founded 1935
A municipal parkland course.
18 holes, 6251 yards
par 70, S.S.S 69
Green fees £7.50
Catering, changing room/showers, bar, club and trolley hire, shop
Visitors welcome
Societies welcome by prior arrangement

WITHERNSEA GOLF CLUB

Chestnut Avenue, Withernsea, East Yorkshire HU19 2PG
☎ 01964 612258 **Map 11, G8**
A1033, 17 miles E of Hull, S side of Withernsea
Founded 1909
A seaside course with expansive views.
9 holes, 6191 yards
par 72, S.S.S 69
Green fees £10
Catering, changing room/showers, bar, shop
Visitors welcome weekdays
Societies welcome by prior arrangement

NORTH YORKSHIRE

ALDWARK MANOR GOLF CLUB

Aldwark, Alne, York, North Yorkshire YO61 1UF
☎ 01347 838353 Fax 01347 830007
Map 11, B6
Off A1, 5 miles SE of Boroughbridge.
Founded 1978
Attractive parkland course in hotel grounds with several interesting holes along the banks of the River Ouse.
18 holes, 6171 yards
par 71, S.S.S 70
Green fees £25
Catering, changing room/showers, bar, accommodation, club and trolley hire, shop, practice facilities
Visitors welcome weekdays
Societies welcome by prior arrangement
🏨 Aldwark Manor, Aldwark, Alne, East Yorkshire
☎ 01347 838353

AMPLEFORTH COLLEGE GOLF CLUB

Castle Drive, Gilling East, York, North Yorkshire YO62 4HP
☎ 01653 628555 **Map 11, B5**
B1363, Gilling East, 18 miles N of York
Founded 1972
Laid out in the grounds of Ampleforth Abbey and College, in a glorious spot surrounded by the Hambleton and Howardian Hills.
9 holes, 5567 yards
par 69, S.S.S 69
Designer Rev. Jerome Lambert OSB
Green fees £12
Visitors welcome with restrictions
Societies welcome by prior arrangement

BEDALE GOLF CLUB

Leyburn Road, Bedale, North Yorkshire DL8 1EZ
✆ 01677 422568 Fax 01677 422451
Map 11, A4
A684, N of Bedale
Founded 1894
A pleasant parkland course on the edge of the Yorkshire Dales.
18 holes, 6610 yards
par 72, S.S.S 72
Green fees £20
Catering, changing room/showers, bar, trolley and buggy hire, shop
Visitors welcome
Handicap certificate required
Societies welcome by prior arrangement

BENTHAM GOLF CLUB

Robin Lane, Bentham, Lancaster LA2 7AG
✆ 015242 61018 **Map 10, E5**
B6480, NE of Lancaster, M6 Jct 34
Founded 1922
A handsome course set off against the backdrop of Ingleborough.
9 holes, 5820 yards
S.S.S 69
Green fees £15
Catering, changing room/showers, bar
Visitors welcome
Societies welcome by prior arrangement

CATTERICK GOLF CLUB

Leyburn Road, Catterick Garrison, North Yorkshire DL9 3QE
✆ 01748 833268 Fax 01748 833268
Map 10, H4
www.cattrickgolfclub.co.uk
A6136, 6 miles S of Scotch Corner
Founded 1930
A particularly testing course, open to the winds, blessed with fine views of the surrounding hills.
18 holes, 6329 yards
par 71, S.S.S 71
Designer Arthur Day
Green fees £24
Catering, changing room/showers, bar, club, trolley and buggy hire, shop, practice facilities
Visitors welcome
Societies welcome by prior arrangement
🏨 Kings Head Hotel, Market Place, Richmond, East Yorkshire
✆ 01748 850220

CLEVELAND GOLF CLUB

Queen Street, Redcar, North Yorkshire TS10 1BT
✆ 01642 471798 Fax 01642 471798
Map 11, C2
peterfletcher@clevelandgolf.f9.co.uk
www.clevelandgolfclub.co.uk
N end of town – follow directions for Esplanade
Founded 1887
Yorkshire's oldest club and its only trational links, with true, firm seaside greens. On the whole, the ground is relatively flat, making judgement of distance all the harder, but holes such as the excellent par-4 4th and endearingly old-fashioned par-5 17th make good use of more substantial undulations.
18 holes, 6746 yards
par 72, S.S.S 72
Green fees £22
Catering, changing room/showers, bar, shop, practice facilities
Visitors welcome
Handicap certificate required
Societies welcome by prior arrangement
🏨 Regency Hotel, Redcar, East Yorkshire

COCKSFORD GOLF CLUB

Stutton, Tadcaster, North Yorkshire LS24 9NG
✆ 01937 834253 Fax 0197 834253
Map 11, B7
www.cocksfordgolfclub.freeserve.co.uk
Off A64
Founded 1991
A short but tight parkland course with the Cock Beck running through the middle.
18 holes, 5679 yards, par 71, S.S.S 69
Green fees £18
Catering, changing room/showers, bar, club and trolley hire, shop, practice facilities
Visitors welcome weekdays
Societies welcome by prior arrangement

CRIMPLE VALLEY GOLF CLUB

Hookstone Wood Road, Harrogate, North Yorkshire HG2 8PN
✆ 01423 883485 Fax 01423 881018
Map 11, A6
Off A61, 1 mile S of Harrogate
Founded 1976
A short course close to the centre of this famous spa town.
9 holes, 5000 yards
S.S.S 66
Designer R. Lumb
Green fees £5
Catering, bar, shop
Visitors welcome
Societies welcome by prior arrangement

DRAX GOLF CLUB

Drax, Selby, North Yorkshire YO8 8PQ
✆ 01405 860533 **Map 11, C8**
Off A1041, 6 miles S of Selby, opposite power station
Founded 1989
A private parkland course.
9 holes, 5644 yards
par 68, S.S.S 67
Designer J.M. Stott
Green fees £6
Visitors welcome only as members' guests

EASINGWOLD GOLF CLUB

Stillington Road, Easingwold, York, North Yorkshire YO61 3ET
✆ 01347 822474 Fax 01347 822474
Map 11, B5
brian@easingwold-golfclub.fsnet.co.uk
www.easingwold-golfclub.co.uk
Off A19, 12 miles N of York
Founded 1930
A handsome and secluded parkland course which has been upgraded and lengthened over the years. There is real charm to the woodland holes, some of which have a feel of Surrey heathland about them, while the 171-yard 13th is a full carry across a lake to an elevated green.
18 holes, 6705 yards
par 73, S.S.S 72
Designer Hawtree
Green fees £25
Catering, changing room/showers, bar, trolley and buggy hire, shop, driving range, practice facilities
Visitors welcome with restrictions
Societies welcome by prior arrangement
🏨 George Hotel, Market Place, Easingwold, North Yorkshire YO61 3ET
✆ 01347 821698

FILEY GOLF CLUB

West Avenue, Filey, North Yorkshire YO14 9BQ
✆ 01723 513293 Fax 01723 514952
Map 11, F5
1 mile S of Filey
Founded 1897
A parkland course, but close enough to the sea for the wind, in particular, to be a frequent factor. Sandy sub-soil gives good playing conditions all year.
18 holes, 6112 yards
par 70, S.S.S 69
Designer James Braid
Green fees £21
Catering, changing room/showers, bar, club, trolley and buggy hire, shop, practice facilities
Visitors welcome
Societies welcome by prior arrangement

FOREST OF GALTRES GOLF CLUB

Skelton Lane, Wigginton, York, North Yorkshire YO32 2RF
☎ 01904 766198 Fax 01904 769400
Map 11, C6
Off A19, 4 miles N of York
Founded 1994
Handsome, contemporary parkland course, enjoying the beauties of an ancient forest and a view towards York Minster from the 8th tee.
18 holes, 6312 yards
par 72, S.S.S 70
Designer Simon Gidman
Green fees £18
Catering, changing room/showers, bar, trolley hire, shop, driving range, practice facilities
Visitors welcome
Societies welcome by prior arrangements (not Saturdays)
Jarvis Fairfield Manor Hotel, Shipton Road, Skelton, York, East Yorkshire
☎ 01904 670222

FOREST PARK GOLF CLUB

Stockton-on-Forest, York, North Yorkshire YO32 9UW
☎ 01904 400425 **Map 11, C6**
Off A64 (1½ miles from E end of York by-pass)
Founded 1991
A parkland course on level ground.
Old Foss Course: 18 holes, 6660 yards, par 71, S.S.S 72
West Course: 9 holes, 3186 yards, par 70, S.S.S 70
Green fees £18
Catering, changing room/showers, bar, club and trolley hire, shop
Visitors welcome
Societies welcome by prior arrangement

FULFORD GOLF CLUB

Heslington Lane, York, North Yorkshire YO10 5DY
☎ 01904 413579 Fax 01904 416918
Map 11, C7
A64, 2 miles S of York
Founded 1906
Norman, Trevino, Weiskopf, and Jacklin are amongst the many distinguished tour winners here. Three strong par 4s in the first five holes provide a searching start. In the heathland, over the road, are the most beautiful holes, including the immense par-5 6th. The condition is never less than immaculate.
18 holes, 6775 yards
par 72, S.S.S 72
Designer Alister Mackenzie
Green fees £35
Changing room/showers, club and trolley hire, shop
Visitors welcome by prior arrangement
Societies welcome by prior arrangement

GANTON GOLF CLUB

Station Road, Ganton, near Scarborough, North Yorkshire YO12 4PA
☎ 01944 710329 Fax 01944 710922
Map 11, E5
secretary@gantongolfclub
A64, 11 miles SW of Scarborough
Founded 1891
See Top 50 Courses, page
18 holes, 6884 yards
par 71, S.S.S 73
Designer Tom Dunn, Harry Vardon, James Braid, Harry Colt, C.K. Cotton
Green fees £55
Catering, changing room/showers, bar, club and trolley hire, shop, practice facilities
Visitors welcome – subject to restrictions
Handicap certificate required – limit: 24
Societies welcome by prior arrangement
The Ganton Greyhound, Ganton, East Yorkshire
☎ 01944 710116

HARROGATE GOLF CLUB

Forest Lane Head, Harrogate, North Yorkshire HG2 7TF
☎ 01423 862999 Fax 01423 860073
Map 11, A6
Hon.secretary@harrogate-gc.co.uk
www.harrogate-gc.co.uk
A59 between Harrogate and Knaresborough
Founded 1892
Set in gentle parkland overlooked by Knaresborough Castle, and always in beautiful condition, Harrogate boasts a particularly fine clubhouse. The overall length may not be long, but there are two par 3s at well over 200 yards, and the finish from the 13th is stern, with five big par 4s.
18 holes, 6241 yards
par 69, S.S.S 70
Designer Sandy Herd, Alister Mackenzie
Catering, changing room/showers, bar, club, trolley and buggy hire, shop, practice facilities
Visitors welcome
Societies welcome by prior arrangement
Majestic Hotel, Ripon Road, Harrogate, East Yorkshire HG1 2HU
☎ 01423 521332

HEWORTH GOLF CLUB

Muncaster House, Muncastergate, York, North Yorkshire YO31 9JY
☎ 01904 422389 Fax 01904 426156
Map 11, C6
golf@heworth-gc.fsnet.co.uk
A1056, 1½ miles from city centre.
Founded 1911
Compact little course almost in the city centre.
12 holes, 6141 yards
par 70, S.S.S 69
Designer E.L. Cheal
Green fees £14
Catering, changing room/showers, bar, trolley hire, shop, practice facilities
Visitors welcome
Societies welcome by prior arrangement
Monkbar Hotel, St Maurice's Road, York, East Yorkshire YO31 7JA
☎ 01904 638086

HUNLEY HALL GOLF CLUB

Ings Lane, Brotton, Saltburn, North Yorkshire TS12 2QQ
☎ 01287 677444 Fax 01287 678250
Map 11, C3
enquiries@hunleyhall.co.uk
www.hunleyhall.co.uk
A174, 15 miles SE of Middlesbrough
Founded 1993
A 27-hole layout on high ground overlooking the sea. The various potential combinations of holes give considerable variety to the overall yardage.
18 holes, 6918 yards
par 73, S.S.S 73
Designer John Morgan
Green fees £20
Catering, changing room/showers, bar, accommodation, club, trolley and buggy hire, shop, driving range, practice facilities, conference facilities, further 9 holes
Visitors welcome
Societies welcome by prior arrangement
The Hunley Hall Hotel, Ings Lane, Brotton, Saltburn, East Yorkshire North Yorkshire
☎ 01287 677444 Fax 01287 678250
enquiries@hunleyhall.co.uk
www.hunleyhall.co.uk

KIRKBYMOORSIDE GOLF CLUB

Manor Vale, Kirkbymoorside, York, North Yorkshire YO62 6EG
☎ 01751 431525 Fax 01751 433190
Map 11, C4
www.kirkbymoorsidegolf.co.uk
A170, N of Kirkbymoorside
Founded 1951
A picturesque course with views

onto the North York Moors.
18 holes, 6112 yards
par 69, S.S.S 69
Green fees £20
Catering, changing room/showers, bar, club and trolley hire, shop
Visitors welcome with restrictions
Societies welcome by prior arrangement

KNARESBOROUGH GOLF CLUB

Butterhills, Boroughbridge Road, Knaresborough, North Yorkshire HG5 0QQ
☎ 01423 862690 Fax 01423 869345
Map 11, A6
knaresboro.golf.club@talk21.com
A6055, 1 mile N of town centre
Founded 1920
Handsome, mature parkland course boasting the longest hole in Yorkshire, the 622-yard par-5 17th.
18 holes, 6413 yards
par 70, S.S.S 71
Designer Hawtree
Green fees £28.50
Catering, changing room/showers, bar, trolley and buggy hire, shop, practice facilities, meeting, conference or function facilities
Visitors welcome, with restrictions
Societies welcome by prior arrangement
🏨 Nidd Hall Hotel, Nidd, Harrogate, East Yorkshire HG3 3BN
☎ 01423 771598

MALTON & NORTON GOLF CLUB

Welham Park, Norton, Malton, North Yorkshire YO17 9QE
☎ 01653 697912 Fax 01653 697912
Map 11, D5
maltonandnorton@golfcl.fsnet.co.uk
www.maltongolfclub.co.uk
Off A64, 18 miles NE of York
Founded 1910
Twenty seven holes can be arranged to make three courses – the modern Derwent with many water hazards, the hillside Welham giving terrific views, and the Park, flatter and gentler.
Derwent: 18 holes, 6286 yards, par 72, S.S.S 70
Park: 18 holes, 6242 yards, par 72, S.S.S 70
Welham: 18 holes, 6456 yards, par 72, S.S.S 71
Green fees £24
Catering, changing room/showers, bar, club and trolley hire, shop, practice facilities, small conference facilities
Visitors welcome – not Saturdays
Handicap certificate required
Societies welcome by prior arrangement
🏨 Talbot Hotel, 45 Yorkersgate, Malton, East Yorkshire
☎ 01653 694031

MASHAM GOLF CLUB

Burnholme, Swinton Road, Masham, Ripon, North Yorkshire HG4 4HT
☎ 01765 689379 Fax 01765 688054
Map 11, A5
Off A6108, 10 miles N of Ripon
Founded 1865
A parkland course in a famous brewing village, with a stream affecting several holes.
9 holes, 6120 yards
par 70, S.S.S 69
Green fees £20
Catering, changing room/showers, bar
Visitors welcome weekdays with restrictions
Societies welcome by prior arrangement

MIDDLESBROUGH GOLF CLUB

Brass Castle Lane, Marton, Middlesbrough, North Yorkshire TS8 9EE
☎ 01642 311515 Fax 01642 319607
Map 11, B3
golf@brass45.fsbusiness.co.uk
www.middlesbroughgolfclub.co.uk
5 miles S of Middlesbrough
Founded 1908
Out in the country, south of Middlesbrough, the course undulates gently, its fairways separated by trees, giving real seclusion to each hole. Recent drainage work and new greens will do much to ensure good conditions even in poor weather.
18 holes, 6278 yards
par 70, S.S.S 70
Designer James Braid
Green fees £14
Catering, changing room/showers, bar, club, trolley and buggy hire, shop, practice facilities, conference facilities
Visitors welcome with handicap – subject to restrictions
Handicap certificate required
🏨 Treebridge, Stokesley Road, Nunthorpe, Middlesbrough, East Yorkshire
☎ 01642 722231

MIDDLESBROUGH MUNICIPAL GOLF COURSE

Ladgate Lane, Middlesbrough, North Yorkshire TS5 7YZ
☎ 01642 315533 Fax 01642 300726
Map 11, B3
A174, 2 miles S of Middlesbrough
Founded 1977
A demanding course, particularly so on the several water holes.
18 holes, 6333 yards
par 71, S.S.S 70
Green fees £9.80
Catering, changing room/showers, bar, club, trolley and buggy hire, shop, driving range
Visitors welcome

Societies welcome by prior arrangement

OAKDALE GOLF CLUB

Oakdale Glen, Harrogate, North Yorkshire HG1 2LN
☎ 01423 567162 Fax 01423 536030
Map 11, A6
secretary@oakdalegc.fsnet.co.uk
www.harrogate-oakdale-golfclub.co.uk
Off A61, N of Harrogate, via Kent Road
Founded 1914
On the outskirts of the spa town of Harrogate, with good views to the moors, Oakdale offers the challenge of a long-established Mackenzie-designed course at a very fair price.
18 holes, 6456 yards
par 71, S.S.S 71
Designer Alister Mackenzie
Green fees £27
Catering, changing room/showers, bar, club, trolley and buggy hire, shop, practice facilities
Visitors welcome weekdays – restricted weekends
Handicap certificate required
Societies welcome by prior arrangement
🏨 Ascot House Hotel, 53 Kings Road, Harrogate, East Yorkshire HG1 5HU

THE OAKS GOLF CLUB

Aughton Common, Aughton, York, North Yorkshire YO42 4PW
☎ 01757 288577 Fax 01757 289029
Map 11, C7
oaksgolfclub@hotmail.com
www.theoaksgolfclub.co.uk
M62 Jct 37, B1228, 1 mile N of Bubwith crossroads
Founded 1996
A welcome, and considerable, addition to the golfing provision in this previously barren area. Close to the Derwent Valley nature reserve, the course is well wooded, with six lakes in play, and boasts excellent greens.
18 holes, 6743 yards
par 72, S.S.S 72
Designer Julian Covey
Green fees £22
Catering, changing room/showers, bar, accommodation, trolley and

buggy hire, shop, driving range, practice facilities
Visitors welcome weekdays
Societies welcome by prior arrangement
The Oaks Golf Club, Aughton, York, East Yorkshire YO42 4PW
01757 288577

PANNAL GOLF CLUB

Follifoot Road, Pannal, Harrogate, North Yorkshire HG3 1ES
01423 872628 Fax 01423 870043
Map 11, A6
pannalgolfclub@btconnect.com
www.pannalgolfclub.cwc.net
A61, 3 miles S of Harrogate
Founded 1906
With expansive views beyond Harrogate to the North York Moors, and many very attractive tree-lined holes on the higher ground, Pannal is charming. The moorland qualities of the fairway turf, plus fine greenkeeping, ensure exemplary conditions all year round. Fine longer par 4s include the 1st, 2nd, 6th and 12th.
18 holes, 6622 yards
par 72, S.S.S 72
Designer Sandy Herd, Charles Mackenzie
Green fees £40
Catering, changing room/showers, bar, club and trolley hire, shop, driving range, practice facilities
Visitors welcome – with restrictions
Handicap certificate required
Societies welcome by prior arrangement
Majestic Hotel, Ripon Road, Harrogate, East Yorkshire HG1 2HU
01423 521332

PIKE HILLS GOLF CLUB

Tadcaster Road, Askham Bryan, York, North Yorkshire YO23 3UW
01904 700797 Fax 01904 700797
Map 11, C7
A64, 3 miles SW of York
Founded 1946
Gently undulating parkland course which surrounds a nature reserve and Site of Special Scientific Interest.
18 holes, 6146 yards
par 71, S.S.S 70
Green fees £20
Catering, changing room/showers, bar, club, trolley and buggy hire, shop, practice facilities
Visitors welcome, subject to restrictions
Societies welcome by prior arrangement
Swallow Chase, Tadcaster Road, York, East Yorkshire

RAVEN HALL HOTEL GOLF CLUB

Ravenscar, North Yorkshire YO13 0ET
01723 870353 **Map 11, E4**
Off A171 between Scarborough and Whitby
Founded 1898
A diminutive course in a stunning location. Not to be missed!
9 holes, 1894 yards
par 32, S.S.S 32
Catering, changing room/showers, bar, accommodation, club hire, full hotel facilities, tennis, swimming pool
Visitors welcome by prior arrangement
Societies welcome by prior arrangement
Raven Hall Country House Hotel, Ravenscar, East Yorkshire
01723 870353

RICHMOND GOLF CLUB

Bend Hagg, Richmond, North Yorkshire DL10 5EX
01748 822457 **Map 10, H4**
A1, 3 miles SW of Scotch Corner
Founded 1892
Richmond is a fascinating old town at the bottom of the Dales, dominated by the ruins of its castle. The views from the golf course delight at every turn.
18 holes, 5779 yards
par 70, S.S.S 68
Designer Frank Pennink
Green fees £20
Catering, changing room/showers, bar, club, trolley and buggy hire, shop, practice facilities
Visitors welcome with restrictions
Societies welcome by prior arrangement
The Turt Hotel, Richmond, East Yorkshire DL10 4DW
01748 829011

RIPON CITY GOLF CLUB

Palace Road, Ripon, North Yorkshire HG4 2LD
01765 603640 Fax 01765 692880
Map 11, A5
office@ripongolf.com
www.ripongolf.com
Off A6108, 1 mile NW of Ripon
Founded 1908
A course extended to 18 holes in recent years, with views of majestic Ripon Cathedral and the Hambleton Hills. The 14th is a challenging water hole.
18 holes, 6084 yards
par 70, S.S.S 69
Designer ADAS
Green fees £20
Catering, changing room/showers, bar, trolley and buggy hire, shop, driving range, practice facilities
Visitors welcome, restricted Saturday
Handicap certificate required
Societies welcome by prior arrangement

ROMANBY GOLF & COUNTRY CLUB

Yafforth Road, Northallerton, North Yorkshire DL7 0PE
01609 779988 Fax 01609 779084
www.romanbygolf.co.uk
Map 11, A4
B6271, 1 mile W of Northallerton
Founded 1993
A river and a number of lakes add to the difficulties on this lengthy parkland course. The 11th, 12th and 13th make up a formidable Amen Corner.
18 holes, 6663 yards
par 72, S.S.S 72
Designer Will Adamson
Green fees £20
Catering, changing room/showers, bar, club, trolley and buggy hire, shop, driving range, function, conference and wedding facilities
Visitors welcome
Societies welcome by prior arrangement

RUDDING PARK HOTEL AND GOLF CLUB

Rudding Park, Follifoot, Harrogate, North Yorkshire HG3 1DJ
01423 871350 Fax 01423 872286
Map 11, A6
sales@ruddingpark.com
www.ruddingpark.com
Off A658, 2 miles SE of Harrogate town centre
Founded 1995
When Martin Hawtree's course in the grounds of this elegant Regency house opened it created quite a stir, for here was an environmentally-friendly course of some quality, mature from the very start, and playable for a very modest fee. Restrained use of water hazards is a feature of the design.
18 holes, 6871 yards
par 72, S.S.S 72
Designer Martin Hawtree
Green fees £19.50
Catering, changing room/showers, bar, accommodation, club, trolley and buggy hire, shop, practice facilities, archery, clay pigeon shooting, 4x4 off-roading, conference facilities
Visitors welcome
Handicap certificate required
Societies welcome by prior arrangement

Rudding Park House & Hotel, Rudding Park, Follifoot, Harrogate, East Yorkshire
01423 871350

SALTBURN GOLF CLUB

Hob Hill, Saltburn-by-the-Sea, North Yorkshire TS12 1NJ
01287 622812 **Map 11, C3**
Off A174, 1 mile from Saltburn
Founded 1894
Although close to the sea, this is a parkland course running alongside woodland. There are delightful seascapes.
18 holes, 5846 yards
par 70, S.S.S 68
Green fees £19
Changing room/showers, trolley hire, shop
Visitors welcome
Handicap certificate required
Societies welcome by prior arrangement

SCARBOROUGH NORTH CLIFF GOLF CLUB

North Cliff Avenue, Burniston Road, Scarborough, North Yorkshire YO12 6PP
01723 360786 Fax 01723 362134
Map 11, E4
www.ncgc.co.uk
On coast road, 2 miles N of Scarborough
Founded 1909
Five holes on the cliffs offer wide seascapes, but the parkland holes over the Whitby road are the more handsome. An exhilarating drive over a valley on the 5th, hilltop greens on the 6th and 7th, inviting par 5s at the 8th and 9th, and the hilly 12th stand out.
18 holes, 6425 yards
par 71, S.S.S 71
Designer James Braid
Green fees £21
Catering, changing room/showers, bar, club and trolley hire
Visitors welcome – restricted weekends
Handicap certificate required
Societies welcome by prior arrangement

SCARBOROUGH SOUTH CLIFF GOLF CLUB

Deepdale Avenue, Scarborough, North Yorkshire YO11 2UE
01723 374737 Fax 01723 374737
Map 11, E4
Off A165, 1 mile S of Scarborough
Founded 1903
Laid out in a valley close to the sea, but generally inland in character.
18 holes, 6039 yards
par 70, S.S.S 69
Designer Alister Mackenzie
Green fees £20
Catering, changing room/showers, bar, club and trolley hire, shop, practice facilities
Visitors welcome
Handicap certificate required
Societies welcome by prior arrangement

SCARTHINGWELL GOLF CLUB

Scarthingwell, Tadcaster, North Yorkshire LS24 9DG
01937 557878 Fax 01937 557909
Map 11, B7
A162, 4 miles S of Tadcaster
Founded 1993
A handsome course with a number of water hazards increasing the challenge.
18 holes, 6759 yards
par 71, S.S.S 72
Designer I. Webster
Green fees £16
Catering, changing room/showers, bar, trolley hire, shop, practice facilities
Visitors welcome
Societies welcome by prior arrangement

SELBY GOLF CLUB

Mill Lane, Brayton, Selby, North Yorkshire YO8 9LD
01757 228622 **Map 11, C8**
Off A19 at Brayton
Founded 1907
Described as 'the course that doesn't close', because of its excellent drainage on a sandy subsoil, Selby is equally good in winter or summer (thanks to fairway irrigation). There are several very long holes – 574-yard par-5 4th, 462-yard par-4 7th – but also several redeeming drive-and-pitch holes.
18 holes, 6374 yards
par 71, S.S.S 71
Designer J H Taylor, Hawtree
Green fees £25
Catering, changing room/showers, bar, club and trolley hire, shop, practice facilities
Visitors welcome weekdays
Handicap certificate required
Societies welcome by prior arrangement

SETTLE GOLF CLUB

Giggleswick, Settle, North Yorkshire BD24 0DH
01729 852288 **Map 10, F6**
A65, 1 mile N of Settle
Founded 1895
A charming course in glorious country.
9 holes, 5414 yards
par 68, S.S.S 66
Designer Tom Vardon
Green fees £10
Changing room/showers
Visitors welcome restricted weekends
Societies welcome by prior arrangement

SKIPTON GOLF CLUB

Off NW Bypass, Skipton, North Yorkshire BD23 3LF
01756 73922 Fax 01756 796665
Map 10, G6
A59, 1 mile N of Skipton
Founded 1893
A hilly parkland course with excellent views.
18 holes, 6049 yards
par 70, S.S.S 69
Green fees £24
Catering, changing room/showers, bar, club hire, shop
Visitors welcome
Societies welcome by prior arrangement

SWALLOW HALL GOLF CLUB

Crockey Hill, York, North Yorkshire YO19 4SG
01904 448889 Fax 01904 448219
Map 11, C7
Off A19, S of York
Founded 1991
An executive length course.
18 holes, 3600 yards
par 56, S.S.S 56
Green fees £7
Catering, changing room/showers, bar, club and trolley hire, shop, driving range, practice facilities, caravan park
Visitors welcome
Societies welcome by prior arrangement

TEESSIDE GOLF CLUB

Acklam Road, Thornaby, North Yorkshire TS17 7JS
01642 676249 Fax 01642 676252
Map 11, B3
A1130, off A19
Founded 1900
A parkland course.
18 holes, 6535 yards
par 72, S.S.S 71
Designer Makepeace, Summerville
Green fees £26
Catering, changing room/showers, bar, trolley hire, shop
Visitors welcome weekdays – with restrictions
Societies welcome by prior arrangement

THIRSK & NORTHALLERTON GOLF CLUB

Thornton-le-Street, Thirsk, North Yorkshire YO7 4AB

01845 522170 Fax 01845 525115
Map 11, B5
A168, 2 miles N of Thirsk
Founded 1914
A friendly club whose good 9-hole course has been expanded in recent years to the full 18.
18 holes, 6495 yards
par 72, S.S.S 71
Green fees £20
Catering, changing room/showers, bar, club, trolley and buggy hire, shop
Visitors welcome weekdays
Handicap certificate required
Societies welcome by prior arrangement

WHITBY GOLF CLUB
Sandsend Road, Whitby, North Yorkshire YO21 3SR
01947 602719 Fax 01947 600660
Map 11, D3
whitby-golf-club@compuserve.com
www.ukgolfer.org
A174, between Whitby and Sandsend
Founded 1892
A very friendly club with two ravine holes on its clifftop course, from which there are good views both to sea and inland.
18 holes, 6134 yards
par 71, S.S.S 71
Green fees £22
Catering, changing room/showers, bar, club, trolley and buggy hire, shop, practice facilities
Visitors welcome
Societies welcome by prior arrangement
White House Hotel, Whitby, East Yorkshire
01947 600469

WILTON GOLF CLUB
Wilton, Redcar, Cleveland, North Yorkshire TS10 4QY
01642 465265 Fax 01642 465463
Map 11, C2
A174, 3 miles W of Redcar
Founded 1952
A parkland course, a total contrast to nearby Cleveland.
18 holes, 6145 yards
par 70, S.S.S 69
Green fees £20
Catering, changing room/showers, bar, trolley hire, shop, practice facilities
Visitors welcome with restrictions
Societies welcome by prior arrangement

THE YORK GOLF CLUB
Lords Moor Lane, Strensall, York, North Yorkshire YO32 5XF
01904 490304 Fax 01904 491852
Map 11, C6
yorkgolfclub@cwcom.net
www.yorkgolfclub.cwc.net
On ring road, 5 miles NE of York.
Founded 1890
Laid out on remarkably level ground on the moorlands adjoining military ranges, York possesses a number of very individual holes such as the short 2nd and 11th, both played from remote tees. The longer holes run along tree-lined avenues giving a glorious sense of privacy, and the greens are praiseworthy.
18 holes, 6301 yards
par 70, S.S.S 70
Designer J.H. Taylor, C.K. Cotton
Green fees £30
Catering, changing room/showers, bar, trolley hire, shop, practice facilities
Visitors welcome, subject to restrictions
Societies welcome by prior arrangement
Dean Court Hotel, Duncombe Place, York, East Yorkshire
01904 625082

SOUTH YORKSHIRE

ABBEYDALE GOLF CLUB
Twentywell Lane, Dore, Sheffield, South Yorkshire S17 4QA
0114 236 0763 Fax 0114 236 0762 **Map 11, A10**
Off A621, 5 miles S of Sheffield
Founded 1895
A well-designed parkland course providing an enjoyable test of golf.
18 holes, 6419 yards
par 72, S.S.S 72
Designer Herbert Fowler
Green fees £35
Catering, changing room/showers, bar, trolley and buggy hire, shop, practice facilities
Visitors welcome with restrictions
Societies welcome by prior arrangement

AUSTERFIELD PARK COUNTRY CLUB
Cross Lane, Austerfield, Doncaster, South Yorkshire DN10 6RF
01302 710841 Fax 01302 710841
Map 11, C10
A614, 2 miles NE of Bawtry
Founded 1974
A long and testing course, with a par 5 exceeding 600-yards.
18 holes, 6900 yards
par 73, S.S.S 73
Designer E & M Baker
Green fees £14
Catering, changing room/showers, bar, trolley and buggy hire, shop, driving range, 9-hole, par-3 course
Visitors welcome
Societies welcome by prior arrangement

BARNSLEY GOLF COURSE
Wakefield Road, Staincross, Barnsley, South Yorkshire S75 6JZ
Map 11, A9
01226 382856
A61, 4 miles N of Barnsley
Founded 1925
A pleasantly undulating parkland course.
18 holes, 5951 yards
par 69, S.S.S 69
Green fees £10
Catering, changing room/showers, bar, club and trolley hire, shop, practice facilities
Visitors welcome
Societies welcome by prior arrangement

BEAUCHIEF PUBLIC GOLF COURSE
Abbey Lane, Sheffield, South Yorkshire S8 0DB
0144 2620040 **Map 11, A10**
M1 Jct 33 to city centre, follow signs to Blackwell
Founded 1925
Very characterful little course with some big holes, such as the 7th and 10th, and a witty short par-3 the 11th.
18 holes, 5452 yards
par 67, S.S.S 66
Green fees £8.50
Catering
Visitors welcome
Societies welcome by prior arrangement

BIRLEY WOOD GOLF CLUB
Birley Lane, Sheffield, South Yorkshire S12 3BP
0114 264 7262 **Map 11, B10**
A616, 4 miles S of Sheffield, M1 Jct 30
Founded 1974
Sheffield is as well provided with municipal golf courses as any English city. Birley Wood is undulating parkland.
18 holes, 5647 yards
par 68, S.S.S 67
Green fees £10
Changing room/showers, bar, club hire, shop, practice facilities
Visitors welcome
Societies welcome by prior arrangement

CONCORD PARK GOLF CLUB
Shiregreen Lane, Sheffield, South Yorkshire S5 6AE
(0114) 2577378 **Map 11, B10**

M1 Jct 34 (for Meadowhall)
Founded 1952
A short but tricky public course with plentiful views of the extensive Meadowhall shopping extravaganza.
18 holes, 4612 yards
par 67, S.S.S 64
Green fees £8
Catering, changing room/showers, bar, club, trolley and buggy hire, shop, driving range
Visitors welcome
Societies welcome by prior arrangement

CROOKHILL PARK GOLF COURSE

Conisborough, Doncater, South Yorkshire DN12 2AH
☎ 01709 862979 **Map 11, A7**
Off A630, 3 miles W of Doncaster
Founded 1974
On hilly ground, with a number of excellent holes (and one or two very testing ones, too).
18 holes, 5849 yards
par 70, S.S.S 68
Green fees £8.75
Catering, changing room/showers, bar, club hire, shop, driving range
Visitors welcome
Societies welcome by prior arrangement

DONCASTER GOLF CLUB

Bawtry Road, Bessacarr, Doncaster, South Yorkshire DN10 6QU
☎ 01302 865632 Fax 01302 865994
Map 11, C9
doncastergolf@aol.com
www.doncastergolfclub.org.uk
A638, S of Doncaster
Founded 1894
An attractive course with tree-lined fairways. The course was redesigned in 1978, the opportunity being taken to bring the challenge up to date.
18 holes, 6220 yards
par 69, S.S.S 70
Designer Hawtree
Green fees £27.50
Catering, changing room/showers, bar, trolley and buggy hire, shop, practice facilities
Visitors welcome – restricted weekends
Societies welcome by prior arrangement
🏨 Mount Pleasant Hotel, Great North Road, Rossington, Doncaster, East Yorkshire
☎ 01302 868696

DONCASTER TOWN MOOR GOLF CLUB

Bawtry Road, Belle Vue, Doncaster, South Yorkshire DN4 5HU
☎ 01302 533778 **Map 11, C9**
A638, inside race course
Founded 1895
A heathland course with plenty of challenge.
18 holes, 6001 yards
par 69, S.S.S 69
Green fees £16
Catering, changing room/showers, bar, trolley hire, shop
Visitors welcome with restrictions
Societies welcome by prior arrangement

DORE & TOTLEY GOLF CLUB

Bradway Road, Sheffield, South Yorkshire S17 4QR
☎ 0114 2369872 Fax 0114 2353436
Map 11, A10
Off A61, SW of Sheffield
Founded 1913
Said to be the least undulating – and, therefore, least exhausting – of the many Sheffield courses, Dore and Totley was founded to facilitate Sunday play, not allowed in the area at that time. The start is formidable, with 467-yard and 444-yard par 4s as the 1st and 3rd holes.
18 holes, 6256 yards
par 70, S.S.S 70
Green fees £26
Catering, changing room/showers, bar, trolley hire, shop
Visitors welcome weekdays with restrictions
Societies welcome by prior arrangement

GRANGE PARK GOLF CLUB

Upper Wortley Road, Kimberworth, Rotherham, South Yorkshire S61 2SJ
☎ 01709 558884 **Map 11, B10**
Off A629, 2 miles W of Rotherham
Founded 1972
A challenging parkland course with fine views.
18 holes, 6461 yards
par 71, S.S.S 71
Designer Fred Hawtree
Green fees £9.50
Catering, changing room/showers, bar, club and trolley hire, shop, driving range
Visitors welcome
Societies welcome by prior arrangement

HALLAMSHIRE GOLF CLUB

Sandygate, Sheffield, South Yorkshire S10 4LA
☎ 0114 230 1007 Fax 0114 230 2153 **Map 11, A10**
Off A57, 3 miles W of Sheffield.
Founded 1897
A very challenging, long, opening par-4 sets the tone for this demanding upland course. Two lively holes, the 10th and 11th, cross a ravine, and, although it is only 345 yards long, the 13th is decidedly tricky. With a backdrop of Peak District moorland, the short 6th is outstanding.
18 holes, 6359 yards
par 71, S.S.S 71
Green fees £38
Catering, changing room/showers, bar, club and trolley hire
Visitors welcome with restrictions
Societies welcome by prior arrangement

HALLOWES GOLF CLUB

Hallowes Lane, Dronfield, Sheffield, South Yorkshire S18 1UR
☎ 01246 411196 Fax 01246 413734
Map 11, A10
M1 Jct 29, A617 to Chesterfield, A61 to Dronfield
Founded 1892
Testing moorland/parkland course with wonderful views over South Yorkshire and North Derbyshire. The 17th-century clubhouse is simply magnificent.
18 holes, 6342 yards
par 71, S.S.S 71
Green fees £30
Catering, changing room/showers, bar, club, trolley and buggy hire, shop, practice facilities
Visitors welcome weekdays
Societies welcome by prior arrangement

HICKLETON GOLF CLUB

Hickleton, Doncaster, South Yorkshire DN5 7BE
☎ 01709 896081 Fax 01709 896083
Map 11, C9
A635, 6 miles W of Doncaster
Founded 1909
A recently designed course at this old club, undulating and scenic.
18 holes, 6434 yards
par 71, S.S.S 71
Designer Brian Huggett, Neil Coles
Green fees £20
Catering, bar, shop
Visitors welcome weekdays
Societies welcome by prior arrangement

HILLSBOROUGH GOLF CLUB

Worrall Road, Sheffield, South Yorkshire S6 4BE
☎ 0114 233 2666 Fax 0114 234 9151 **Map 11, A10**
admin@hillsboroughgolfclub.co.uk
www.hillsboroughgolfclub.co.uk
3 miles from city centre at Wadsley
Founded 1920
Part woodland, part heathland, Hillsborough enjoys good views of the Loxley Valley and the rolling

countryside around Sheffield.
18 holes, 6216 yards
par 71, S.S.S 70
Green fees £30
Catering, changing room/showers, bar, club, trolley and buggy hire, shop, driving range, practice facilities
Visitors welcome – with restrictions
Handicap certificate required
Societies welcome by prior arrangement
Tankersley Manor Hotel, Church Lane, Tankersley, Barnsley, East Yorkshire S75 3DQ
01226 744700

KINGS WOOD GOLF COURSE

Thorne Road, Hatfield, South Yorkshire DN7 6EP
01405 741343 **Map 11, C9**
A614, 2 miles SW of M180 Jct 1
A new pay-and-play facility with much water, from mere ditches to full lakes, to be avoided.
18 holes, 6002 yards
par 70, S.S.S 69
Designer John Hunt
Green fees £7
Club and trolley hire, shop
Visitors welcome
Societies welcome by prior arrangement

LEES HALL GOLF CLUB

Hemsworth Road, Norton, Sheffield, South Yorkshire S8 8LL
0114 255 4402 Fax 0114 255 2900 **Map 11, B10**
Off A6102, 3½ miles S of city centre
Founded 1907
On high ground, giving views over the City of Sheffield.
18 holes, 6171 yards
par 71, S.S.S 70
Green fees £20
Catering, changing room/showers, bar, trolley hire, shop
Visitors welcome
Societies welcome by prior arrangement

LINDRICK GOLF CLUB

Lindrick Common, Worksop, Notts, South Yorkshire S81 8BH
01909 475820 Fax 01909 488685
Map 11, B10
www.lindrickgolf.com
M1 Jct 31, A57 towards Worksop
Founded 1891
A great old course and scene of a (then rare) home victory in the 1957 Ryder Cup, Lindrick is unusual in finishing with a short hole. Its most individual hole is the 4th, with a blind pitch downhill to a green in a dell, while the 13th is quite outstanding.
18 holes, 6606 yards
par 71, S.S.S 72
Designer Tom Dunn, Willie Park, Herbert Fowler
Green fees £48
Catering, changing room/showers, bar, club and trolley hire, shop, driving range, practice facilities
Visitors welcome, not Tuesday
Handicap certificate required
Societies welcome by prior arrangement
Red Lion Hotel, Worksop Road, Todwick, Sheffield, East Yorkshire S26 1DJ
01909 771654

OWSTON PARK GOLF CLUB

Owston Hall, Owston, Doncaster, South Yorkshire DN6 9JF
01302 330821 **Map 11, C9**
A19, 5 miles N of Doncaster
Founded 1988
Trees and ditches come into play on this parkland course on level ground.
9 holes, 6148 yards
par 70, S.S.S 71
Green fees £4.25
Changing room/showers, club and trolley hire, shop, practice facilities
Visitors welcome
Societies welcome by prior arrangement

PHOENIX GOLF CLUB

Pavilion Lane, Brinsworth, Rotherham, South Yorkshire S60 5PA
01709 363788 Fax 01709 3837888 **Map 11, B10**
Off A630, SW of town centre
Founded 1932
A rolling parkland course.
18 holes, 6182 yards
par 71, S.S.S 69
Designer Sir Henry Cotton
Green fees £21
Catering, changing room/showers, bar, club and trolley hire, shop, driving range, tennis courst, squash and fishing
Visitors welcome weekdays
Societies welcome by prior arrangement

RENISHAW PARK GOLF CLUB

Golf House, Mill Lane, Renishaw, Sheffield, South Yorkshire S21 3UZ
01246 432044 Fax 01246 432116
Map 11, B11
M1 Jct 30, A6135
Founded 1911
A relatively flat parkland course by Sheffield standards.
18 holes, 6262 yards
par 71, S.S.S 70
Green fees £24.50
Catering, changing room/showers, bar, trolley hire, shop, practice facilities
Visitors welcome
Handicap certificate required
Societies welcome by prior arrangement

ROBIN HOOD GOLF CLUB

Owston Hall, Askern, Doncaster, South Yorkshire DN6 9JF
01302 722231 Fax 01302 728885
Map 11, C8
www.owstonhall.com
B1220, off A19, 6 miles N of Doncaster
Founded 1996
A golf club existed here from 1923 until 1940, only being re-established in 1996. The lengthy course is one of many facilities of Owston Hall, a Grade II listed building of 1780, a small but comfortable hotel.
18 holes, 6937 yards
par 72, S.S.S 73
Designer W. Adamson
Green fees £12
Catering, changing room/showers, bar, accommodation, club, trolley and buggy hire, shop, practice facilities, conference, function, wedding facilities, gym, sauna
Visitors welcome
Societies welcome by prior arrangement
Owston Hall Hotel, Askern, Doncaster, East Yorkshire DN6 9JF
01302 722800

ROTHER VALLEY GOLF CENTRE

Mansfield Road, Wales Bar, Sheffield, South Yorkshire S31 8PE
0114 247 3000 Fax 0114 247 6000 **Map 11, B10**
2 miles S of M1 Jct 31, Rother Valley Country Park
Founded 1997
The many uncompromising water hazards have been likened to those at Doral in Florida, from which the course derives its nickname, 'The Blue Monster'.
18 holes, 6602 yards
par 72, S.S.S 72
Designer Michael Shattock, Mark Roe
Green fees £12
Catering, changing room/showers, bar, club, trolley and buggy hire, shop, 9-hole, par-3 course
Visitors welcome
Societies welcome by prior arrangement

ROTHERHAM GOLF CLUB

Thrybergh Park, Rotherham, South Yorkshire S65 4NU
01709 850466 Fax 01709 855288
Map 11, B10

A630, 4 miles E of Rotherham
Founded 1902
A long-established parkland course.
18 holes, 6324 yards
par 70, S.S.S 70
Green fees £30
Changing room/showers, trolley and buggy hire, shop
Visitors welcome weekdays
Societies welcome by prior arrangement

ROUNDWOOD GOLF CLUB
Green Lane, Rawmarsh, Rotherham, South Yorkshire S62 6LA
☎ 01709 523471 **Map 11, B10**
Off A633, 2 miles N of Rotherham
Founded 1976
A parkland 9-hole course.
18 holes, 5620 yards
par 67, S.S.S 67
Green fees £12
Catering, bar
Visitors welcome weekdays
Societies welcome by prior arrangement

SANDHILL GOLF CLUB
Little Houghton, Barnsley, South Yorkshire S72 0HW
☎ 01226 753444 Fax 01226 753444
Map 11, B9
Off A635, 6 miles E of Barnsley
Founded 1993
Despite its name, the course is quite flat. A number of holes are distinctive and challenging.
18 holes, 6250 yards
par 71, S.S.S 70
Designer John Royston
Green fees £8.50
Catering, changing room/showers, bar, shop, driving range
Visitors welcome
Societies welcome by prior arrangement

SHEFFIELD TRANSPORT GOLF CLUB
Meadow Head, Sheffield, South Yorkshire S8 7RE
☎ 0114 237 3216 **Map 11, A10**
A61, S of Sheffield
Founded 1923
A private members' club.
18 holes, 3966 yards
S.S.S 62
Visitors welcome only as members' guests

SILKSTONE GOLF CLUB
Field Head, Elmhirst Lane, Silkstone, Barnsley, South Yorkshire S75 4LD
☎ 01226 790328 Fax 01226 792653
Map 11, A9
A628, 1 mile W of M1 Jct 37
Founded 1893
A rolling country course with extensive views.
18 holes, 6069 yards
par 70, S.S.S 70
Green fees £21
Catering, changing room/showers, bar, trolley and buggy hire, shop
Visitors welcome weekdays

Societies welcome by prior arrangement

SITWELL PARK GOLF CLUB
Shrogswood Road, Rotherham, South Yorkshire S60 4BY
☎ 01709 541046 Fax 01709 703637
Map 11, B6410
Off A 631, 2 miles E of Rotherham, M18 Jct 1 or M1 Jct 33
Founded 1913
Sitwell Park's gently undulating ground gives an attractive course of plentiful variety. The five drive-and-pitch holes, ranging from 266 to 357 yards, entice, but they are appropriately tight from the tee. The short holes are engaging, particularly the 5th, threatened by gorse, and the 12th, with its pretty woodland setting.
18 holes, 6229 yards
par 71, S.S.S 70
Designer Alister Mackenzie
Green fees £24
Catering, changing room/showers, bar, club and trolley hire, shop, practice facilities
Visitors welcome, restricted weekends
Handicap certificate required
Societies welcome by prior arrangement
🏨 Consort Hotel, Brampton Road, Thurcroft, Rotherham, East Yorkshire
☎ 01709 530022

STOCKSBRIDGE & DISTRICT GOLF CLUB
Royd Lane, Deepcar, Sheffield, South Yorkshire S36 2RZ
☎ 0114 288 7479 Fax 0114 288 2003 **Map 11, A9**
A616, 9 miles W of Sheffield
Founded 1924
Quite short, but hilly enough to challenge significantly.
18 holes, 5200 yards
par 65, S.S.S 65
Green fees £20
Catering, changing room/showers, bar, shop
Visitors welcome
Societies welcome by prior arrangement

TANKERSLEY PARK GOLF CLUB
Park Lane, High Green, Sheffield, South Yorkshire S35 4LG
☎ 0114 246 8247 Fax 0114 245 7818 **Map 11, A9**
Off A616, Stocksbridge by-pass
Founded 1907
A well-maintained parkland course offering a good challenge.
18 holes, 6212 yards
par 69, S.S.S 70
Designer Hawtree
Green fees £25
Catering, changing room/showers, bar, club and trolley hire, shop, practice facilities
Visitors welcome weekdays
Societies welcome by prior arrangement

THORNE GOLF CLUB
Kirton Lane, Thorne, Doncaster, South Yorkshire DN8 5RJ
☎ 01405 812084 Fax 01405 741899
Map 11, C9
A614, off M180 Jct 1
Founded 1980
Welcome new addition to the facilities in this part of Yorkshire – pretty parkland.
18 holes, 5294 yards
par 68, S.S.S 68
Designer Richard Highfield
Green fees £9
Catering, changing room/showers, bar, club, trolley and buggy hire, shop, practice facilities
Visitors welcome
Societies welcome by prior arrangement
🏨 Belmont Hotel, Horsefair Green, Thorne, East Yorkshire
☎ 01405 812320

THORNHURST PARK GOLF CLUB
Holme Lane, Owston, Doncaster, South Yorkshire DN5 0LR
☎ 01302 237799 Fax 01302 721495
Map 11, C9
A19, between Bentley and Askern
A parkland course with a lake in play on two holes.
18 holes, 6490 yards
par 72, S.S.S 72
Green fees £10
Catering, changing room/showers, bar, trolley hire, shop
Visitors welcome
Societies welcome by prior arrangement

TINSLEY PARK GOLF CLUB
High Hazels Park, Darnall, Sheffield, South Yorkshire S9 4PE
☎ 0114 203 7435 **Map 11, B10**
Off A630, 4 miles E of city centre
Founded 1920
A good quality municipal course.
18 holes, 6084 yards
par 71, S.S.S 69

Green fees £7.50
Catering, changing room/showers, bar, club and trolley hire, shop, hard tennis courts
Visitors welcome
Societies welcome by prior arrangement

WATH-UPON-DEARNE GOLF CLUB

Abdy Lane, Rawmarsh, Rotherham, South Yorkshire S62 7SJ
✆ 01709 872149 Fax 01709 878609
Map 11, B9
Off A633, 7 miles N of Rotherham
Founded 1904
A testing parkland course.
18 holes, 5857 yards
par 68, S.S.S 68
Green fees £21
Catering, changing room/showers, bar, trolley hire, shop
Visitors welcome weekdays
Societies welcome by prior arrangement

WHEATLEY GOLF CLUB

Armthorpe Road, Doncaster, South Yorkshire DN2 5QB
✆ 01302 831655 Fax 01302 812736
Off A18, NE of town centre
Founded 1913 **Map 11, C9**
A well-reputed parkland course, on a base of peat and sand, giving good drainage and excellent fairway grass.
18 holes, 6405 yards
par 71, S.S.S 71
Designer George Duncan
Green fees £27
Catering, changing room/showers, bar, trolley hire, shop
Visitors welcome
Societies welcome by prior arrangement

WOMBWELL (HILLIES) GOLF CLUB

Wentworth View, Wombwell, Barnsley, South Yorkshire S73 0LA
✆ 01226 754433 Fax 01226 758635
Map 11, B9
4 miles SE of Barnsley
Founded 1989
A short public course.
9 holes, 2095 yards
S.S.S 60
Green fees £6.30
Catering, bar
Visitors welcome
Societies welcome by prior arrangement

WORTLEY GOLF CLUB

Hermit Hill Lane, Wortley, Sheffield, South Yorkshire S35 7DF
✆ 0114 2886490 **Map 11, B10**
A616, off M1 Jct 36, ½ mile from Wortley Village
Founded 1894
Gently undulating, well-wooded parkland course.
18 holes, 5866 yards
par 68, S.S.S 69
Green fees £28
Catering, changing room/showers, bar, trolley hire, shop, practice facilities
Visitors welcome with restrictions
Societies welcome by prior arrangement

WEST YORKSHIRE

THE ALWOODLEY GOLF CLUB

Wigton Lane, Alwoodley, Leeds, West Yorkshire LS17 8SA
✆ 0113 268 1680 Fax 0113 268 9458 **Map 11, A7**
julie@alwoodleygolfclub.freeserve.co.uk
www.alwoodley.co.uk
Off A61, 5 miles N of Leeds
Founded 1907
See Top 50 Courses, page
18 holes, 6785 yards
par 71, S.S.S 73
Designer Harry Colt, Alister Mackenzie
Green fees £55
Catering, changing room/showers, bar, club, trolley and buggy hire, shop, practice facilities
Visitors welcome, subject to restrictions
Societies welcome by prior arrangement
🏨 Harewood Arms, Harewood, Leeds, East Yorkshire

BAGDEN HALL HOTEL AND GOLF COURSE

Wakefield Road, Scissett, West Yorkshire HD8 9LE
✆ 01484 864839 Fax 01484 961001
Map 11, A9
On A636 between Denby Dale and Scissett, M1 Jct 39
Founded 1993
A short, but pretty course in pleasant surroundings.
9 holes, 3002 yards
par 56, S.S.S 55
Designer F. O'Donnell, R. Brathwaite
Green fees £10
Catering, changing room/showers, bar, accommodation, club and trolley hire, shop, practice facilities
Visitors welcome
Societies welcome by prior arrangement
🏨 Bagden Hall Hotel, Wakefield Road, Scissett, East Yorkshire
✆ 01484 864839

BAILDON GOLF CLUB

Moorgate, Baildon, Shipley, West Yorkshire BD17 6HZ
✆ 01274 595162 Fax 01274 530551
Map 10, H7
sec@baildongolfclub.freeserve.co.uk
www.baildongolfclub.com
Off A6038, 5 miles N of Bradford
Founded 1896
Wonderful fresh air and stirring views. Moorland rough can be particularly punishing, and the club has established areas of semi-rough to lessen the severity of the course a little. Nevertheless, holes such as the 430-yard dog-leg 3rd are only conquered by courageous and confident play. Wittily written web site.
18 holes, 6231 yards
par 70, S.S.S 70
Designer Tom Morris, James Braid
Green fees £16
Catering, changing room/showers, bar, club and trolley hire, shop, practice facilities
Visitors welcome, restricted weekends
Societies welcome by prior arrangement
🏨 Marriott Hollins Hall Hotel & Country Club, Hollins Hill, Baildon, Shipley, East Yorkshire BD17 7QW
✆ 01274 530053

BEN RHYDDING GOLF CLUB

High Wood, Ben Rhydding, Ilkley, West Yorkshire LS9 8SB
✆ 01943 608759 **Map 10, H7**
Off A65, 2 miles SE of Ilkley
Founded 1947
A short, scenic moorland course.
9 holes, 4711 yards
par 65, S.S.S 64
Designer William Dell
Green fees £12
Changing room/showers, bar
Visitors welcome weekdays
Societies welcome by prior arrangement

BINGLEY ST IVES GOLF CLUB

The Golf Clubhouse, Harden, Bingley, West Yorkshire BD16 1AT
✆ 01274 562506 Fax 01274 511788
Map 10, H7
bingleyst-ives@harden.freeserve.co.uk
www.bingleystivesgc.co.uk
B6429, off A650 SW of Bingley
Founded 1932
Sandy Lyle (twice) and Nick Faldo won the tour events played here in the 1980s. It is a delightful mixture of parkland, woodland and moorland, with lovely views. Among many strong holes, the tight, tree-lined 8th is most appealing, and the 3rd, 5th,

11th and 12th reward the strong player.
18 holes, 6485 yards
par 71, S.S.S 71
Designer Alister Mackenzie
Green fees £25
Catering, changing room/showers, bar, club, trolley and buggy hire, shop, practice facilities
Visitors welcome weekdays
Societies welcome by prior arrangement
Jarvis Bankfield, Bradford Road, Bingley, East Yorkshire BD16 1TV
01274 567123

BRACKEN GHYLL GOLF CLUB

Skipton Road, Addingham, Ilkley, West Yorkshire LS29 0SL
01943 830691 **Map 10, H7**
On old A65, 3 miles W of Ilkley
Founded 1993
An unusually lengthy 9-hole course in the handsome Wharfe Valley.
9 holes, 6560 yards
par 74, S.S.S 71
Green fees £10
Catering, changing room/showers, bar, practice facilities
Visitors welcome weekdays
Societies welcome by prior arrangement

THE BRADFORD GOLF CLUB

Hawksworth Lane, Guiseley, Leeds, West Yorkshire LS20 8NP
01943 873719 Fax 01943 875570
Map 10, H7
Off A6038 NE of Shipley, 10 miles NE of Leeds on A65
Founded 1891
A regular venue for county standard golf events.
18 holes, 6400 yards
par 71, S.S.S 71
Designer Herbert Fowler, Tom Simpson
Green fees £30
Catering, changing room/showers, bar, club and trolley hire, shop, driving range, practice facilities
Visitors welcome – restricted weekends
Handicap certificate required
Societies welcome by prior arrangement
Marriott Hollins Hall Hotel & Country Club, Hollins Hill, Baildon, Shipley, East Yorkshire BD17 7QW
01274 530053

BRADFORD MOOR GOLF CLUB

Scarr Hall, Pollard Lane, Bradford, West Yorkshire BD2 4RW
01274 771716 **Map 10, H7**
2 miles N of city centre
Founded 1906
The name says it all – an upland. moorland course.
9 holes, 5800 yards
par 70, S.S.S 67
Green fees £8
Changing room/showers, bar, trolley hire, shop
Visitors welcome weekdays
Societies welcome by prior arrangement

BRADLEY PARK GOLF CLUB

Bradley Road, Huddersfield, West Yorkshire HD2 1PZ
01484 223772 Fax 01484 451613
Map 10, H8
Off A6107, 2 miles N of Huddersfield, M62 Jct 25
Founded 1978
One of the most challenging of the public courses in Yorkshire, with fine views from its elevated situation.
18 holes, 6284 yards
par 70, S.S.S 70
Designer Donald Steel
Green fees £12
Catering, changing room/showers, bar, club, trolley and buggy hire, shop, driving range, par-3 course
Visitors welcome
Societies welcome by prior arrangement

BRANDON GOLF CLUB

Holywell Lane, Shadwell, Leeds, West Yorkshire LS17 8EZ
0113 273 7471 **Map 11, A7**
1 mile N Leeds ring road, at Roundhay Park
Founded 1967
A short parkland course.
18 holes, 4800 yards
par 68, S.S.S 62
Green fees £6
Catering, club and trolley hire, shop
Visitors welcome
Societies welcome by prior arrangement

BRANSHAW GOLF CLUB

Branshaw Moor, Oakworth, Keighley, West Yorkshire BD22 7ES
01535 647441 Fax 01535 648011
Map 10, G7
B6143, 2 miles SW of Keighley
Founded 1912
A picturesque, undulating moorland course with outstanding views over Haworth and the Brontë country.
18 holes, 5900 yards
par 69, S.S.S 68
Designer James Braid
Green fees £20
Catering, changing room/showers, bar, trolley hire, shop
Visitors welcome – with restrictions
Handicap certificate required
Societies welcome by prior arrangement
Three Sisters Hotel, Brow Top Road, Howarth, East Yorkshire
01535 643458

CALVERLEY GOLF CLUB

Woodhall Lane, Pudsey, West Yorkshire LS28 5QY
0113 256 9244 Fax 0113 256 9244 **Map 11, A7**
Off A647
Founded 1984
A short, undulating parkland course.
18 holes, 5527 yards, par 68, S.S.S 67
9 holes, 2137 yards, par 33,
Green fees £15
Catering, changing room/showers, bar, club, trolley and buggy hire, shop, driving range
Visitors welcome weekdays
Societies welcome by prior arrangement

CASTLEFIELDS GOLF CLUB

Rastrick Common, Brighouse, West Yorkshire HD6 3HL
01484 713276 **Map 11, A8**
A643, 1 mile S of Brighouse
Founded 1903
Unusual 6-hole course on Rastrick Common.
6 holes, 4812 yards
S.S.S 50
Green fees £5
Visitors welcome only as members' guests
Societies welcome by prior arrangement

CITY OF WAKEFIELD GOLF COURSE

Lupset Park, Horbury Road, Wakefield, West Yorkshire WF2 8QS
01924 360282 **Map 11, A8**
A642, 2 miles W of Wakefield
Founded 1936
Genuine public courses of this breeding are few and far between. Morrison's name, alone, should be recommendation enough.
18 holes, 6319 yards
par 72, S.S.S 70
Designer JSF Morrison
Green fees £10
Catering, changing room/showers, bar, club and trolley hire, shop, practice facilities
Visitors welcome with weekend restrictions
Societies welcome by prior arrangement

CLAYTON GOLF CLUB

Thornton View Road, Clayton, Bradford, West Yorkshire BD14 6JX
01274 880047 **Map 10, H7**

A647, 2 miles SW of Bradford
Founded 1906
The 7th, the Kop Hole, has quite a reputation in the Bradford area
9 holes, 5500 yards
par 68, S.S.S 67
Green fees £10
Catering, changing room/showers, bar
Visitors welcome with restrictions
Societies welcome by prior arrangement

CLECKHEATON & DISTRICT GOLF CLUB

483 Bradford Road, Cleckheaton, BD19 6BU, West Yorkshire
✆ 01274 874118 Fax 01274 871382
Map 10, H8
A638, M62 Jct 26
Founded 1900
An undulating parkland course.
18 holes, 5860 yards
par 71, S.S.S 68
Green fees £25
Catering, changing room/showers, bar, club hire, shop
Visitors welcome
Societies welcome by prior arrangement

COOKRIDGE HALL GOLF AND COUNTRY CLUB

Cookridge Lane, Leeds, West Yorkshire LS16 7NL
✆ 0113 203 0002 Fax 0113 285 7115 **Map 11, A7**
Off A660, 3 miles N of Leeds
With plenty of water brought into play, this is very much a contemporary style of course.
18 holes, 6497 yards
par 72, S.S.S 71
Designer Karl Litten
Green fees £25
Catering, changing room/showers, bar, club and trolley hire, shop, driving range, heated indoor swimming pool, sauna & gymnasium
Visitors welcome weekdays
Societies welcome by prior arrangement

CROSLAND HEATH GOLF CLUB

Felk Stile Road, Crosland Heath, Huddersfield, West Yorkshire HD4 7AF
✆ 01484 653216 **Map 10, H8**
Off A62, 3 miles W of Huddersfield
Founded 1914
On high ground with splendid views.
18 holes, 6004 yards
par 70, S.S.S 70
Catering, changing room/showers, bar, trolley hire, shop, practice facilities
Visitors welcome with restrictions
Societies welcome by prior arrangement

CROW NEST PARK GOLF CLUB

Coach Road, Hove Edge, Brighouse, West Yorkshire HD6 2LN
✆ 01484 401121 Fax 01422 203672
Map 10, H8
5 miles E of Halifax, M62 Jct 25
Founded 1995
In the grounds of the one-time home of the philanthropist, Sir Titus Salt, a substantial 9-hole layout with excellent practice facilities.
9 holes, 5956 yards
par 70, S.S.S 69
Designer Will Adamson
Green fees £10
Catering, changing room/showers, bar, trolley hire, shop, driving range, practice facilities, function and wedding facilities
Visitors welcome
Societies welcome by prior arrangement

DEWSBURY DISTRICT GOLF CLUB

The Pinnacle, Sands Lane, Mirfield, West Yorkshire WF14 8HJ
✆ 01924 492399 **Map 11, A8**
Off A644, 2 miles W of Dewsbury
Founded 1891
A hilltop course with some hard climbing early on, but compensatory downhill rewards on the 3rd and 15th (the latter a 430-yard par-4 which can be driven!). The views on a fine day are good.
18 holes, 6360 yards
par 71, S.S.S 71
Designer Tom Morris, Peter Alliss
Green fees £18
Catering, changing room/showers, bar, club and trolley hire, shop
Visitors welcome weekdays
Societies welcome by prior arrangement

EAST BIERLEY GOLF CLUB

South View Road, Bierley, Bradford, West Yorkshire BD4 6PP
✆ 01274 681023 **Map 10, H8**
Off A650, 4 miles SE of city centre
Founded 1928
With narrow fairways and a hilly site the course is more testing than its yardage alone implies.
9 holes, 4700 yards
par 64, S.S.S 63
Green fees £10
Catering, changing room/showers, bar
Visitors welcome with restrictions
Societies welcome by prior arrangement

ELLAND GOLF CLUB

Hammerstones Leach Lane, Hullen Edge, Elland, West Yorkshire HX5 0TA
✆ 01422 372505 **Map 10, H8**
M62 Jct 24 towards Blackley
Founded 1901
A parkland course.
9 holes, 5630 yards
par 66, S.S.S 66
Green fees £15
Catering, changing room/showers, bar, trolley hire, shop
Visitors welcome
Societies welcome by prior arrangement

FARDEW GOLF CLUB

Nursery Farm, Carr Lane, East Morton, Keighley, West Yorkshire BD20 5RY
✆ 01274 561229 Fax 01274 561229
Map 10, G7
A650, 2 miles W of Bingley
Founded 1993
A parkland course in Brontë country.
9 holes, 6208 yards
par 72, S.S.S 70
Green fees £8
Catering, shop, practice facilities
Visitors welcome
Societies welcome by prior arrangement

FERRYBRIDGE 'C' GOLF CLUB

PO Box 39, Stranglands Lane, Knottingley, West Yorkshire WF11 8SQ
✆ 01977 674188 **Map 11, B8**
B6316, off A1
Founded 1976
A private parkland club.
9 holes, 5138 yards
S.S.S 65
Designer N.E. Pugh
Green fees £6
Visitors welcome only as members' guests
Societies welcome by prior arrangement

FULNECK GOLF CLUB

Fulneck, Pudsey, West Yorkshire LS28 8NT
✆ 0113 256 5191 **Map 11, A7**
5 miles W of Leeds
Founded 1892
A rolling parkland course.
9 holes, 5456 yards
par 66, S.S.S 67
Green fees £14
Catering, changing room/showers, bar
Visitors welcome weekdays
Societies welcome by prior arrangement

NORTH/WEST YORKSHIRE

GARFORTH GOLF CLUB

Long Lane, Garforth, Leeds, West Yorkshire LS25 2DS
✆ 0113 286 2021 Fax 0113 286 3308 **Map 11, B7**
Off A642, 9 miles E of Leeds
Founded 1913
A parkland course.
18 holes, 6304 yards
par 69, S.S.S 70
Green fees £28
Catering, changing room/showers, bar, club and trolley hire, shop, driving range
Visitors welcome weekdays
Handicap certificate required
Societies welcome by prior arrangement

GOTTS PARK GOLF COURSE

Armley Ridge Road, Armley, Leeds, West Yorkshire LS12 2QX
✆ 0113 234 2019 **Map 11, A7**
Off A647, 3 miles W of city centre
Founded 1933
Narrow fairways and steep hills make this municipal course quite testing.
18 holes, 4960 yards
par 65, S.S.S 64
Green fees £7.25
Catering, changing room/showers, bar, club hire, shop
Visitors welcome
Societies welcome by prior arrangement

HALIFAX BRADLEY HALL GOLF CLUB

Holywell Green, Halifax, West Yorkshire HX4 9AN
✆ 01422 374108 **Map 11, E7**
B6112, 3 miles S of Halifax
Founded 1907
In fine upland country, and usually influenced by the wind, the course presents a good test right from the start with a drive over a stream and pond. The closing four holes are testing, especially the 17th.
18 holes, 6138 yards
par 70, S.S.S 70
Green fees £18
Catering, changing room/showers, bar, trolley hire, shop, practice facilities
Visitors welcome
Societies welcome by prior arrangement
Premier Lodge, The Quays, Salternebble Hill, Huddersfield Road, Halifax, East Yorkshire HX3 0QT
✆ 01422 347700

HALIFAX GOLF CLUB

Union Lane, Ogden, Halifax, West Yorkshire HX2 8XR
✆ 01422 244171 Fax 01422 241459
Map 10, G8
A629, 4 miles N of Halifax
Founded 1895
Rugged moorland course with rocky mountain streams making the 3rd, 4th and 5th especially exciting. The course gradually climbs onto Ilkley Moor, the fairways mere ribbons in tussocky upland rough. The descent is made in one spectacular plunge down the hillside on the 17th, to a green beyond a stream.
18 holes, 6037 yards
par 70, S.S.S 70
Designer Alex Herd, James Braid
Green fees £20
Catering, changing room/showers, bar, club and trolley hire, shop, practice facilities, conference facilities for 30-100
Visitors welcome
Societies welcome by prior arrangement
Holdsworth House, Holdsworth Road, Holmfield, Halifax, East Yorkshire

HANGING HEATON GOLF CLUB

Whitecross Road, Bennett Lane, Dewsbury, West Yorkshire WF12 7DT
✆ 01924 461606 Fax 01924 430100
Map 11, A8
A653, ¾ mile from Dewsbury
Founded 1922
A gentle parkland course.
9 holes, 5836 yards
par 69, S.S.S 67
Green fees £16
Changing room/showers, shop
Visitors welcome weekdays
Societies welcome by prior arrangement

HEADINGLEY GOLF CLUB

Back Church Lane, Adel, Leeds, West Yorkshire LS16 8DW
✆ 0113 267 9573 Fax 0113 281 7334 **Map 11, A7**
headingley-golf@talk21.com
A660, 5 miles NW of Leeds
Founded 1892
The oldest of the Leeds clubs, Headingley is essentially an out-and-back layout, which results in a constantly changing character as the round progresses. With only one par 5 it is not a long course, but good driving is essential on many holes, not least the 18th, played over a ravine.
18 holes, 6298 yards
par 69, S.S.S 70
Designer Alister Mackenzie
Green fees £30
Catering, changing room/showers, bar, club and trolley hire, shop, practice facilities
Visitors welcome – restricted
Handicap certificate required
Societies welcome by prior arrangement
Jarvis Parkway Hotel, Otley Road, Leeds, East Yorkshire
✆ 0113 267 2551

HEADLEY GOLF CLUB

Headley Lane, Thornton, Bradford, West Yorkshire BD13 3LX
✆ 01274 833481 Fax 01274 670398
Map 10, H7
Off B6145, 5 miles W of Bradford
Founded 1907
Typical of a number of Yorkshire moorland courses, seemingly of no great length, but harder than might be expected.
9 holes, 5140 yards
par 65, S.S.S 65
Green fees £15
Catering, changing room/showers, bar
Visitors welcome weekdays
Societies welcome by prior arrangement

HEBDEN BRIDGE (MOUNT SKIP) GOLF CLUB

Great Mount, Wadworth, Hebden Bridge, West Yorkshire HX7 8PH
✆ 01422 842896 **Map 10, G8**
1 mile from Hebden Bridge
Founded 1930
Superb views of Calderdale from all parts of the course.
9 holes, 5242 yards
par 68, S.S.S 67
Green fees £12
Changing room/showers, bar, conference facilities
Visitors welcome with restrictions
Societies welcome by prior arrangement
Carlton Hotel, Albert Street, Hebden Bridge, East Yorkshire

MARRIOTT HOLLINS HALL HOTEL & COUNTRY CLUB

Hollins Hill, Baildon, Shipley, West Yorkshire BD17 7QW
✆ 01274 534212 Fax 01274 543220
Map 11, A7
A6038, 3 miles from Leeds/Bradford Airport
Founded 1999
Constructing the course to USGA standards ensures good playing surfaces even in winter. With fine views over Baildon Moor and the Aire Valley, the course blends into the locality remarkably well for one so young.
18 holes, 6671 yards
par 71, S.S.S 71

Designer Ross McMurray
Green fees £30
Catering, changing room/showers, bar, accommodation, club, trolley and buggy hire, shop, driving range, practice facilities, extensive conference, function and wedding facilities, leisure complex includes scuba diving
Visitors welcome
Handicap certificate required
Societies welcome by prior arrangement
Marriott Hollins Hall Hotel & Country Club, Hollins Hill, Baildon, Shipley, East Yorkshire BD17 7QW
01274 530053

HORSFORTH GOLF CLUB

Layton Rise, Layton Road, Horsforth, Leeds, West Yorkshire LS18 5EX
0113 258 6819 **Map 11, A7**
Off A65, 6½ miles NW of city centre
Founded 1907
A mixture of moorland and parkland golf.
18 holes, 6293 yards
par 71, S.S.S 70
Green fees £24
Changing room/showers, bar, trolley hire, shop
Visitors welcome
Societies welcome by prior arrangement

HOWLEY HALL GOLF CLUB

Scotchman Lane, Morley, Leeds, West Yorkshire LS27 0NX
01924 350100 Fax 01924 350104
Map 11, A8
office@howleyhall.fsnet.co.uk
www.howleyhall.co.uk
Off B6123, 4 miles SW of Leeds
Founded 1900
Panoramic views of the Pennines are a bonus, although Mackenzie's architectural strengths are what will appeal. at least equally, to the visiting golfer.
18 holes, 6346 yards
par 71, S.S.S 71
Designer Alister Mackenzie
Green fees £33
Catering, changing room/showers, bar, club and trolley hire, shop, practice facilities
Visitors welcome with restrictions
Societies welcome by prior arrangement

HUDDERSFIELD GOLF CLUB

Fixby Hall, Lightridge Road, Huddersfield, West Yorkshire HD2 2EP
01484 420110 Fax 01484 424623
Map 11, E8
www.hudderfield-golf.co.uk
Off A6107, 2 mile N of Huddersfield, M62 Jct 24
Founded 1891
An inspirational moorland course calling for skilful play, with club selection particularly difficult on the hillier holes. The long par 4s, especially the 12th and 16th, call for stout hitting, as does the uphill par-5 5th. Played across a valley, the 13th is a memorable 215-yard par 3.
18 holes, 6447 yards
par 71, S.S.S 71
Designer Herbert Fowler
Green fees £37
Catering, changing room/showers, bar, trolley hire, shop
Visitors welcome weekdays
Societies welcome by prior arrangement

ILKLEY GOLF CLUB

Nesfield Road, Myddleton, Ilkley, West Yorkshire LS29 0BE
01943 600214 Fax 01943 816130
Map 10, H7
ilkleygolfclub@freeuk.com
Off A65 at Ilkley
Founded 1890
One of England's prettiest courses, with the first seven holes laid out along the banks of the River Wharfe, and the 2nd, 3rd, and 4th played on and off an island. With seven par 4s at over 400 yards plenty of strong hitting is required, and the greens are superb.
18 holes, 6262 yards
par 69, S.S.S 70
Designer Harry Colt, Alister Mackenzie
Green fees £37
Catering, changing room/showers, bar, club and trolley hire, shop, practice facilities
Visitors welcome
Handicap certificate required
Societies welcome by prior arrangement

KEIGHLEY GOLF CLUB

Howden Park, Utley, Keighley, West Yorkshire BD20 6DH
01535 604778 Fax 01535 604833
Map 10, G7
golf@keighleygolfclub.fsnet.co.uk
A629, 1 mile W of Keighley
Founded 1904
A breeding ground of past Yorkshire champions, Keighley is a picturesque course with several long par 4s requiring wooden club approaches for most golfers.
18 holes, 6141 yards
par 69, S.S.S 70
Green fees £27
Catering, changing room/showers, bar, trolley hire, shop, practice facilities, snooker
Visitors welcome – restricted weekends
Societies welcome by prior arrangement
Dalesgate Hotel, 406 Skipton Road, Utley, Keighley, East Yorkshire BD20 6HP
01535 664930

LEEDS GOLF CENTRE

Wike Ridge Lane, Shadwell, Leeds, West Yorkshire LS17 9JW
0113 2886000 Fax 0113 2886185
Map 11, A7
www.leedsgolfcentre.co.uk
A58, 5 miles N of Leeds
Founded 1993
An excellent and testing course is supplemented by a 12-hole, par-3 course, driving range etc. Training and provision for juniors is impressive.
18 holes, 6482 yards
par 72, S.S.S 71
Designer Donald Steel
Green fees £14.50
Catering, changing room/showers, bar, club, trolley and buggy hire, shop, driving range, practice facilities, conference & wedding facilities
Visitors welcome
Societies welcome by prior arrangement
Harewood Arms, Harewood, Leeds, East Yorkshire

LEEDS GOLF CLUB

Elmete Road, Roundhay, Leeds, West Yorkshire LS8 2LJ
0113 265 9203 Fax 0113 232 3369 **Map 11, A7**
Off A58, close to Ring Road junction
Founded 1896
Only four miles from the City Centre, yet utterly rural in its setting amidst the trees and rolling country of Roundhay. The 15th is one of the most remarkable holes, a par 3 played through a narrow avenue of trees to a green on a level with the higher branches.
18 holes, 6078 yards
par 69, S.S.S 69
Green fees £25
Changing room/showers, club and trolley hire, shop
Visitors welcome weekdays
Societies welcome by prior arrangement

LIGHTCLIFFE GOLF CLUB

Knowle Top Road, Lightcliffe, Halifax, West Yorkshire HX3 8SW
01422 202459 **Map 10, H8**
A58, 3 miles E of Halifax
Founded 1907

A heathland course.
9 holes, 5826 yards
par 68, S.S.S 68
Green fees £15
Changing room/showers, shop
Visitors welcome with restrictions

Societies welcome by prior arrangement

LOFTHOUSE HILL GOLF CLUB

Leeds Road, Lofthouse Hill, Wakefield, West Yorkshire WF3 3LR
☎ 01924 823703 Fax 01924 823703
Map 11, A8
Off A61, 4 miles from Wakefield
Founded 1994
A floodlit driving range and other practice facilities complement this recent course near Wakefield.
18 holes, 5933 yards
par 70, S.S.S 70
Green fees £15
Catering, changing room/showers, bar, club and trolley hire, shop, driving range, practice facilities
Visitors welcome with restrictions
Societies welcome by prior arrangement

LONGLEY PARK GOLF CLUB

Maple Street, Huddersfield, West Yorkshire HD5 9AX
☎ 01484 426932 **Map 10, H8**
Off A629, SE of town centre
Founded 1911
A parkland course only half a mile from the centre of Huddersfield.
9 holes, 5212 yards
par 66, S.S.S 66
Green fees £13.50
Catering, changing room/showers, bar, club and trolley hire, shop
Visitors welcome weekdays – with restrictions
Societies welcome by prior arrangement

LOW LAITHES GOLF CLUB

Park Mill Lane, Flushdyke, Ossett, West Yorkshire WF5 9AP
☎ 01924 273275 Fax 01924 266067
Map 11, A8
Off M1 Jct 40, 2 miles W of Wakefield
Founded 1925
As might be expected, given a Mackenzie designer label, a course which continues to test all classes of player.
18 holes, 6468 yards
par 72, S.S.S 71
Designer Alister Mackenzie
Green fees £19
Catering, changing room/showers, bar, trolley and buggy hire, shop, practice facilities
Visitors welcome with restrictions
Societies welcome by prior arrangement

THE MANOR GOLF CLUB

Bradford Road, Drighlington, Bradford, West Yorkshire BD11 1AB
☎ 0113 285 2644 **Map 10, H8**
Off A650, 1 mile from M62 Jct 27
A new course conveniently close to the M62.
18 holes, 6508 yards
par 72, S.S.S 71
Designer David Hemstock
Green fees £15
Catering, changing room/showers, bar, club and trolley hire, shop, driving range, pitch & putt
Visitors welcome
Societies welcome by prior arrangement

MARSDEN GOLF CLUB

Hemplow, Marsden, Huddersfield, West Yorkshire HD7 6NN
☎ 01484 844253 **Map 10, G9**
A62, 8 miles W of Huddersfield
Founded 1921
A rarity, a 9-hole course with a Mackenzie designer label. Rugged upland golf.
9 holes, 5702 yards
par 68, S.S.S 68
Designer Alister Mackenzie
Green fees £19
Catering, changing room/showers, bar, shop, practice facilities
Visitors welcome weekdays
Societies welcome by prior arrangement
Hey Green, Waters Road, Marsden, Huddersfield, East Yorkshire
☎ 01484 844235

MELTHAM GOLF CLUB

Thick Hollins Hall, Meltham, Huddersfield, West Yorkshire HD9 4DQ
☎ 01484 851521 Fax 01484 859051
Map 10, H9
meltham@thegolfcourse.co.uk
www.meltham-golf.co.uk
A616 and B6108 to Meltham
Founded 1908
One of the prettiest of Yorkshire's Pennine courses, with wooded, undulating fairways and magnificent views. The 11th is a stern 550-yard par 5 crossed by a stream, and the 13th a delightful lakeside hole.
18 holes, 6396 yards
par 71, S.S.S 70
Designer Sandy Herd
Green fees £22
Catering, changing room/showers, bar, club and trolley hire, shop, practice facilities
Visitors welcome – with restrictions
Handicap certificate required
Societies welcome by prior arrangement
Durker Roods Hotel, Bishops Way, Meltham, East Yorkshire
☎ 01484 851413

MID YORKSHIRE GOLF CLUB

Havercroft Lane, Darrington, Pontefract, West Yorkshire WF8 3BP
☎ 01977 704522 Fax 01977 600823
Map 11, B8
A1 (south), 400 yards from M62/A1 intersection
Founded 1993
A challenging course in a prime spot for road access.
18 holes, 6466 yards
par 72, S.S.S 71
Designer Steve Marnoch
Green fees £15
Catering, changing room/showers, bar, club, trolley and buggy hire, shop, driving range, practice facilities
Visitors welcome with restrictions
Societies welcome by prior arrangement

MIDDLETON PARK GOLF CLUB

Ring Road, Beeston Park, Middleton, West Yorkshire LS10 3TN
☎ 0113 270 9506 **Map 11, A8**
Off A653, 3 miles S of Leeds city centre
Founded 1933
A straightforward parkland course.
18 holes, 5233 yards
par 68, S.S.S 66
Green fees £7.75
Catering, shop
Visitors welcome
Societies welcome by prior arrangement

MOOR ALLERTON GOLF CLUB

Coal Road, Wike, Leeds, West Yorkshire LS17 9NH
☎ 0113 266 1154 Fax 0113 237 1124 **Map 11, A7**
magc@moorallerton.demon.co.uk
Off A61, 5 Miles N of Leeds
Founded 1923
An expansive course in delightfully unspoiled countryside, distinguished by the contemporary challenges of a master architect. The site undulates and there are streams and lakes aplenty, but it is Trent Jones's architectural flair which predominates, with large, extravagantly shaped bunkers, and huge rolling greens. Only thoughtful positional play succeeds here.
Blackmoor: 18 holes, 6673 yards,

par 71, S.S.S 73
High: 18 holes, 6841 yards, par 72, S.S.S 74
Lakes: 18 holes, 6470 yards, par 71, S.S.S 72
Designer Robert Trent Jones
Green fees £45
Catering, changing room/showers, bar, club, trolley and buggy hire, shop, driving range, practice facilities, conference facilities, tennis, bowls, snooker
Visitors' welcome certificate
Handicap certificate required
Societies welcome by prior arrangement, with handicap certificates
Harewood Arms, Harewood, Leeds, East Yorkshire

MOORTOWN GOLF CLUB

Harrogate Road, Leeds, West Yorkshire LS17 7DB
0113 266 1154 Fax 0113 237 1124 **Map 11, A7**
A61, 5½ miles N of Leeds
Founded 1923
One of the great old courses, a Mackenzie prototype which hosted the first Ryder Cup, Moortown has undergone much recent change. The building of housing over the fence has been the principal factor, so now the famous Gibraltar is played as the 10th, but the course's essential character is retained.
18 holes, 6995 yards
par 72, S.S.S 74
Designer Alister Mackenzie
Green fees £45
Catering, changing room/showers, bar, trolley and buggy hire, shop
Visitors welcome
Handicap certificate required
Societies welcome by prior arrangement

NORMANTON GOLF CLUB

Hatfield Hall, Aberford Road, Stanley, Wakefield, West Yorkshire WF3 4JP
01924 377943 Fax 01924 200777
Map 11, B8
A642, 2 miles of Normanton
Founded 1903
The original mulberry bush – that celebrated in the nursery rhyme – is reputedly the one at Normanton Golf Club.
18 holes, 6191 yards
par 72, S.S.S 69
Designer Steven Dawson
Green fees £22
Catering, changing room/showers, bar, club, trolley and buggy hire, shop, driving range, practice facilities, conference & wedding facilities
Visitors welcome with restrictions
Societies welcome by prior arrangement

NORTHCLIFFE GOLF CLUB

High Bank Lane, Shipley, Bradford, West Yorkshire BD18 4LJ
01274 596731 Fax 01274 596731
Map 10, H7
northcliffe@bigfoot.com
www.northcliffegolfclubshipley.co.uk
Off A650 from Bradford
Founded 1921
Good views prevail on this elevated course, which can boast one of the prettiest and most challenging par 3s to close the round.
18 holes, 6113 yards
par 71, S.S.S 70
Designer Harry Varden & James Braid
Green fees £20
Catering, changing room/showers, bar, trolley hire, shop, practice facilities
Visitors welcome, with restrictions
Handicap certificate required
Societies welcome by prior arrangement

OTLEY GOLF CLUB

West Busk Lane, Otley, West Yorkshire LS21 3NG
01943 465329 Fax 01943 850387
Map 10, H7
office@otley-golfclub.co.uk
www.otley-golfclub.co.uk
Off A6038 W of Otley
Founded 1906
Wharfedale provides a verdant backdrop to golf at Otley. The start is serious with the 444-yard 4th the toughest hole on the course. A stream crosses the fairways of the par-5 6th and 8th just in front of the greens, and out-of-bounds is a threat on many holes.
18 holes, 6225 yards
par 70, S.S.S 70
Green fees £26
Catering, changing room/showers, bar, trolley hire, shop, practice facilities
Visitors welcome except Saturday
Societies welcome by prior arrangement
Post House, Leeds Road, Bramhope, Leeds, East Yorkshire Ls16 9JJ
0870 4009049

OULTON PARK GOLF COURSE

Oulton, Rothwell, Leeds, West Yorkshire LS26 8EX
0113 282 3152 Fax 0113 282 6290 **Map 11, B8**
Off A642, 5 miles SE of Leeds, N of M62 Jct 30
Founded 1990
A fine municipal establishment, with three first rate 9-hole loops and exemplary off-course facilities.
Hall Course: 9 holes, 3286 yards, par 36, S.S.S 36
Park Course: 9 holes, 3184 yards, par 35, S.S.S 35
Royds Course: 9 holes, 3169 yards, par 35, S.S.S 35
Green fees £9.90
Catering, changing room/showers, bar, accommodation, club and trolley hire, shop, driving range, practice facilities, heated indoor swimming pool, squash and fishing
Visitors welcome
Societies welcome by prior arrangement
Oulton Hall Hotel, Rothwell Lane, Oulton, Leeds, East Yorkshire

OUTLANE GOLF CLUB

Slack Lane, Outlane, Huddersfield, West Yorkshire HD3 3YL
01422 374762 Fax 01422 311789
Map 10, H8
Off A640, 4 miles W of Huddersfield
Founded 1906
A friendly club with an engaging hillside course, including several memorable holes crossing a ravine.
18 holes, 6010 yards
par 71, S.S.S 70
Green fees £18
Catering, changing room/showers, bar, club and trolley hire, shop
Visitors welcome
Societies welcome by prior arrangement

PAINTHORPE HOUSE GOLF CLUB

Painthorpe Lane, Crigglestone, Wakefield, West Yorkshire WF4 3HE
01924 255083 Fax 01924 252022
Map 11, A8
Off A636, near M1 Jct 39
Founded 1961
A short parkland course.
9 holes, 4544 yards
par 62, S.S.S 62
Green fees £6
Catering, changing room/showers, bar, bowling green
Visitors welcome, restricted Sunday
Societies welcome by prior arrangement

PHOENIX PARK GOLF CLUB

Dick Lane, Thornbury, Bradford, West Yorkshire BD3 7AT
01274 615546 **Map 10, H7**
Off A647, Bradford-Leeds road at Thornbury roundabout
Founded 1922
A rolling parkland course.

9 holes, 4982 yards
par 66, S.S.S 64
Catering
Visitors welcome weekdays
Societies welcome by prior arrangement

PONTEFRACT AND DISTRICT GOLF CLUB

Park Lane, Pontefract, West Yorkshire WF8 4QS
☎ 01977 792241 Fax 01977 792241 **Map 11, B8**
B6134, off M62 Jct 32
Founded 1904
A parkland course located on a gentle hillside.
18 holes, 6227 yards
par 72, S.S.S 70
Green fees £25
Catering, changing room/showers, bar, trolley and buggy hire, shop, practice facilities
Visitors welcome with restrictions
Societies welcome by prior arrangement

PONTEFRACT PARK GOLF CLUB

Park Road, Pontefract, West Yorkshire WF8
☎ 01977 702799 **Map 11, B8**
½ mile from M62, close to Pontefract race course
Founded 1973
A short parkland course on a hilly site, overlooking the Pontefract and District course.
18 holes, 4068 yards
S.S.S 62
Green fees £3
Visitors welcome
Societies welcome by prior arrangement

QUEENSBURY GOLF CLUB

Brighouse Road, Queensbury, Bradford, West Yorkshire BD13 1QF
☎ 01274 816864 **Map 10, H8**
golfwizard66@msn.co.uk
A6036, 4 miles SW of Bradford
Founded 1923
Hilly course, parkland with heathland touches.
9 holes, 5024 yards
par 66, S.S.S 65
Green fees £15
Catering, changing room/showers, bar, shop, practice facilities
Visitors welcome
Handicap certificate required
Societies welcome by prior arrangement

RAWDON GOLF CLUB

Buckstone Drive, Micklefield Lane, Rawdon, West Yorkshire LS19 6BD
☎ 0113 250 6064 Fax 0113 250 5017 **Map 11, A7**
Off A65, S of town.
Founded 1896
A 9-hole parkland course in rolling country.
9 holes, 5980 yards
par 72, S.S.S 69
Green fees £16
Catering, changing room/showers, bar, club and trolley hire, shop, hard & grass tennis courts
Visitors welcome weekdays
Handicap certificate required
Societies welcome by prior arrangement

RIDDLESDEN GOLF CLUB

Howden Rough, Riddlesden, Keighley, West Yorkshire BD20 5QN
☎ 01535 602148 **Map 10, H7**
Off A650, 3 miles N of Keighley
Founded 1927
A moorland course with many interesting short holes, and glorious views over the Aire Valley.
18 holes, 4295 yards
par 63, S.S.S 61
Green fees £16
Catering, changing room/showers, bar
Visitors welcome, with restrictions
Societies welcome by prior arrangement
🏨 Dalesgate Hotel, 406 Skipton Road, Utley, Keighley, East Yorkshire BD20 6HP
☎ 01535 664930

ROUNDHAY GOLF CLUB

Park Lane, Leeds, West Yorkshire LS8 2EJ
☎ 0113 2661686 **Map 11, A7**
A58 from Leeds city centre, turning left at Oakwood Clock Tower
Founded 1926
An attractive parkland course in the portfolio of admirable municipal facilities provided by Leeds City Council – an example to many.
9 holes, 5322 yards
par 70, S.S.S 65
Green fees £9
Changing room/showers, bar, club and trolley hire, shop, practice facilities
Visitors welcome, with restrictions at weekend
Societies welcome by prior arrangement
🏨 Haley's, Shire Oak Road, Headingley, Leeds, East Yorkshire LS6 2DE
☎ 01132 784446 Fax 01132 753342

RYBURN GOLF CLUB

Norland, Sowerby Bridge, Halifax, West Yorkshire HX6 3QP
☎ 01422 831355 **Map 10, G8**
3 miles SW of Halifax
Founded 1910
A moorland course of no great length.
9 holes, 4907 yards
par 66, S.S.S 65
Green fees £15
Catering, changing room/showers, bar
Visitors welcome
Societies welcome by prior arrangement

THE SAND MOOR GOLF CLUB

Alwoodley Lane, Leeds, West Yorkshire LS17 7DJ
☎ 0113 289 2311 Fax 0113 289 3835 **Map 11, A7**
www.sgccwc.net
Off A61, 5 miles N of Leeds
Founded 1926
One of the top courses in Leeds, to be mentioned in the same breath as Alwoodley and Moortown – a formidable trio of neighbouring courses. The 6th and 14th are brutal par 4s.
18 holes, 6429 yards
par 71, S.S.S 71
Designer Alister Mackenzie
Green fees £36
Catering, changing room/showers, bar, club and trolley hire, shop, practice facilities
Visitors welcome weekdays
Handicap certificate required
Societies welcome by prior arrangement

SCARCROFT GOLF CLUB

Syke Lane, Leeds, West Yorkshire LS14 3BQ
☎ 0113 289 2311 Fax 0113 289 3885 **Map 11, B7**
www.sgccwc.net
Off A58, 7 miles N of Leeds
Founded 1937
An attractive course in pleasant countryside north of Leeds.
18 holes, 6426 yards
par 71, S.S.S 69
Green fees £30
Catering, changing room/showers, bar, club and trolley hire, shop, practice facilities
Visitors welcome weekdays
Societies welcome by prior arrangement

THE SHIPLEY GOLF CLUB

Beckfoot, Bingley, West Yorkshire BD16 1LX
☎ 01274 563674 Fax 01274 567739
Map 10, G7
office@shipleygc.co.uk
www.shipleygc.co.uk
A650, 6 miles N of Bradford

Founded 1896
Good value green fees for a long-established parkland course with a Mackenzie pedigree.
18 holes, 6215 yards
par 71, S.S.S 70
Designer Alister Mackenzie
Green fees £25
Catering, changing room/showers, bar, club and trolley hire, shop, practice facilities
Visitors welcome weekdays
Handicap certificate required
Societies welcome by prior arrangement
Jarvis Bankfield, Bradford Road, Bingley, East Yorkshire BD16 1TV
01274 567123

SILSDEN GOLF CLUB

Brunthwaite, Silsden, Keighley, West Yorkshire BD20 0HN
01535 652998 Fax 01535 652998
Map 10, G7
Off A6034, 5 miles N of Keighley
Founded 1913
A compact course of only 14 holes, with good views of the Aire Valley.
14 holes, 4870 yards
par 65, S.S.S 64
Catering, changing room/showers, bar
Visitors welcome, restricted weekends
Societies welcome by prior arrangement

SOUTH BRADFORD GOLF CLUB

Pearson Road, Odsal, Bradford, West Yorkshire BD6 1BH
01274 679195 **Map 10, H8**
Off A638, 2 miles S of city centre
Founded 1906
Only 9 holes, but an interesting course with plenty of variety and much challenge.
9 holes, 6068 yards
par 70, S.S.S 68
Green fees £16
Catering, changing room/showers, bar, trolley hire, shop
Visitors welcome weekdays
Societies welcome by prior arrangement

SOUTH LEEDS GOLF CLUB

Parkside Links, Gipsy Lane, Leeds, West Yorkshire LS11 5TU
0113 2700479 **Map 11, A8**
sec@shac.freeserve.co.uk
www.southleedsgolfclub.co.uk
From M62 at Jct 28 exit A653 to Leeds
Founded 1914
Could this be the hidden gem of Mackenzie's many Leeds courses? What is more, the green fee does not prevent the curious from finding out. Tight and hilly.
18 holes, 5865 yards
par 69, S.S.S 68
Designer Alister Mackenzie
Green fees £18
Catering, changing room/showers, bar, trolley hire, shop, practice facilities
Visitors welcome, with restrictions
Handicap certificate required
Societies welcome by prior arrangement

TEMPLE NEWSAM GOLF COURSES

Temple Newsam Road, Halton, Leeds, West Yorkshire LS15 0LN
0113 264 5624 **Map 11, A7**
Off A63, 5 miles E of Leeds
Founded 1923
Excellent municipal courses breaking out onto heathland occasionally.
Lady Dorothy Course: 18 holes, 6029 yards, par 70, S.S.S 70
Lord Irwin Course: 18 holes, 6448 yards, par 68, S.S.S 71
Green fees £7.50
Catering, changing room/showers, bar, club and trolley hire, shop
Visitors welcome
Societies welcome by prior arrangement

TODMORDEN GOLF CLUB

Rive Rocks, Cross Stone, Todmorden, West Yorkshire OL14 8RD
01706 812986 **Map 10, G8**
1 mile from town centre
Founded 1894
Moorland course in Pennine hill country.
9 holes, 5902 yards
par 68, S.S.S 68
Green fees £15
Catering, changing room/showers, bar
Visitors welcome, restricted Thursday and weekends
Societies welcome by prior arrangement

WAKEFIELD GOLF CLUB

28 Woodthorpe Lane, Sandal, Wakefield, West Yorkshire WF2 6JH
01924 255380 Fax 01924 242752
Map 11, A8
Off A61, 3 miles S of Wakefield
Founded 1891
Right out in the country, with good views, Wakefield is of a good length.
18 holes, 6653 yards
par 72, S.S.S 72
Designer Alex Herd
Green fees £27
Catering, changing room/showers, bar, trolley hire, shop, practice facilities
Visitors welcome
Handicap certificate required
Societies welcome by prior arrangement
Cedar Court Hotel, Denby Dale Road, Calder Grove, Wakefield, East Yorkshire
01924 276310

WATERTON PARK GOLF CLUB

The Balk, Walton, Wakefield, West Yorkshire WF2 6QL
01924 255557 Fax 01924 256969
Map 11, A8
4 miles S of Wakefield city centre, M1 Jct 39
Founded 1995
Charles Waterton was an eccentric 19th-century traveller and naturalist who established the world's first wildfowl reserve in this park, and so, today, golfers enjoy lovely lake views.
18 holes, 6843 yards
par 72, S.S.S 73
Designer Simon Gidman
Green fees £30
Catering, changing room/showers, bar, club, trolley and buggy hire, shop, driving range, practice facilities, conference facilities
Visitors welcome weekdays
Handicap certificate required – limit: 28 men, 45 women
Societies welcome by prior arrangement
Waterton Park Hotel, The Balk, Walton, Wakefield, East Yorkshire WF2 6QL
01924 257911

WEST BOWLING GOLF CLUB

Newall Hall, Rooley Lane, Bradford, West Yorkshire BD5 8LB
01274 724449 Fax 01274 393207
Map 10, H8
Junction of M606 and Bradford ring road
Founded 1898
A parkland course with tree-lined fairways.
18 holes, 5769 yards
par 68, S.S.S 67
Green fees £24
Catering, changing room/showers, bar, trolley hire, shop
Visitors welcome weekdays
Societies welcome by prior arrangement

WEST BRADFORD GOLF CLUB

Chellow Grange, Haworth Road, Bradford, West Yorkshire BD9 6NP
01274 542102 Fax 01274 482079
Map 10, H7

Off B1644, 3 miles W of city centre
Founded 1900
Hilly parkland course.
18 holes, 5738 yards
par 69, S.S.S 68
Green fees £21
Catering, changing room/showers, bar, club and trolley hire, shop, practice facilities
Visitors welcome – restricted weekends
Jarvis Bankfield, Bradford Road, Bingley, East Yorkshire BD16 1TV
01274 567123

WEST END GOLF CLUB (HALIFAX)

Paddock Lane, Highroad Well, Halifax, West Yorkshire HX2 0NT
01422 363293 Fax 01422 341878
Map 10, G8
Off A646, W of Halifax
Founded 1904
Airy course on high ground west of the town centre.
18 holes, 5939 yards
par 69, S.S.S 69
Green fees £21
Catering, changing room/showers, bar, club, trolley and buggy hire, shop, practice facilities
Visitors welcome – not Saturdays
Societies welcome by prior arrangement
Tower House Hotel, Master Lane, Pye Nest, Halifax, East Yorkshire
01422 345000

WETHERBY GOLF CLUB

Linton Lane, Linton, Wetherby, West Yorkshire LS22 4JF
01937 580089 Fax 01937 581915
Map 11, B7
Off A661, 1 mile W of Wetherby
Founded 1910
Attractive parkland course laid out in a valley.
18 holes, 6235 yards
par 71, S.S.S 70
Green fees £28
Catering, changing room/showers, bar, club, trolley and buggy hire, shop
Visitors welcome
Societies welcome by prior arrangement

WHITWOOD GOLF CLUB

Altofts Lane, Whitwood, Castleford, West Yorkshire WF10 5PZ
01977 512835 **Map 11, B8**
Off M62 Jct 31, on Castleford road
Founded 1987
A 9-hole municipal course.
9 holes, 6176 yards
S.S.S 69
Designer Steve Wells
Green fees £9.50
Shop
Visitors welcome weekdays
Societies welcome by prior arrangement

WILLOW VALLEY GOLF & COUNTRY CLUB

Highmoor Valley, Clifton, Brighouse, West Yorkshire HD6 4JB
01274 878624 Fax 01274 852805
Map 10, H8
M62 Jct 25, S of Bradford
Founded 1993
A challenging pair of courses with water features.
18 holes, 6496 yards, par 72, S.S.S 72
Designer Jonathan Gaunt
9 holes, 2039 yards, par 31, S.S.S 69
Green fees £22
Catering, changing room/showers, bar, club, trolley and buggy hire, shop, driving range
Visitors welcome
Societies welcome by prior arrangement

WOODHALL HILLS GOLF CLUB

Woodhall Road, Calverley, Pudsey, West Yorkshire LS28 5UN
0113 256 4771 Fax 0113 295 4594 **Map 10, H7**
Off A647, 4 miles E of Bradford
Founded 1905
A hilly parkland course.
18 holes, 6001 yards
par 70, S.S.S 69
Green fees £20.50
Catering, changing room/showers, bar, club and trolley hire, shop
Visitors welcome with weekend restrictions
Societies welcome by prior arrangement

WOODSOME HALL GOLF CLUB

Woodsome Hall, Fenay Bridge, Huddersfield, West Yorkshire HD8 0LQ
01484 602971 Fax 01484 608260
Map 10, H9
www.woodsomehall.co.uk
A629, 6 miles SE of Huddersfield
Founded 1922
Woodsome Hall is a 16th-century mansion which serves as an aristocratic clubhouse. The opening drive is made downhill from its lawns, but, thereafter, the golf is hilly, especially so on the back nine. Going out, the par-3 3rd, long par-4 8th and par-5 9th command particular respect.
18 holes, 6096 yards
par 70, S.S.S 69
Designer W. Button, James Braid
Green fees £30
Catering, changing room/showers, bar, trolley hire, shop
Visitors welcome with restrictions
Societies welcome by prior arrangement

WOOLLEY PARK GOLF CLUB

Woolley, Wakefield, West Yorkshire WF4 2JS
01226 380144 Fax 01226 390295
Map 11, A9
A61, 5 miles S of Wakefield, 2 mile from M1 Jct 38
Founded 1995
A parkland course of recent provenance.
18 holes, 6591 yards
par 71, S.S.S 71
Designer M. Shattock
Green fees £12
Catering, changing room/showers, bar, shop, practice facilities
Visitors welcome weekdays
Societies welcome by prior arrangement

SOUTH ENGLAND

When compiling a list of the top 100 golf courses in the British Isles it would be all too easy to begin somewhere south-west of London only to find that the list had been completed before even considering the pressing cases of courses in Ireland, Scotland, Wales and the rest of England. That list might start with Sunningdale, Wentworth, Swinley Forest, The Berkshire, Camberley Heath, West Hill, Woking and Worplesdon, a mere mile or two apart and only a few minutes' drive from Heathrow Airport. Alternatively, staying strictly within the confines of the M25, there are The Addington, The Buckinghamshire, Coombe Hill, Royal Blackheath, Royal Mid-Surrey, St George's Hill and Walton Heath. Then there are world-renowned courses of Woburn to the north-west and Royal St George's and its near neighbours Prince's and Royal Cinque Ports to the south-east. The name dropping has only just begun!

At the other end of the scale can be found a number of very good value public and pay-and-play facilities where many a star golfer has begun his or her career, not least Ryder Cup hero, Paul Way. Without these places, golf around the capital city would stagnate, for only the genuinely wealthy and those connected with certain limited trades and professions could engineer their way on to the waiting lists of many of the closed-shop clubs. It must also be said that green fees at most of the big names ensure that for many a round there is something of which they can only dream. Yet there are some courses in the region giving golf of real quality at a fraction of the cost of the great names, Burnham Beeches, Goring & Streatley, Liphook and West Surrey, for example, while, slightly further afield, Crowborough Beacon and (bunkerless) Piltdown give a marvellous introduction to the game in Sussex without breaking the bank. Similarly, in Hampshire, Hayling and Stoneham show that a visitor need not necessarily take out a second mortgage before essaying a brilliant course.

Almost every course mentioned so far has been long established, if not downright ancient. Royal Blackheath, for instance, has been on the go since the beginning of the 17th century. Astonishingly, however, patches of land in this housing developers' paradise do appear, even today, on which new golf courses are built. Nick Faldo's flagship course at Chart Hills and the fine courses at East Sussex National lead the way south of London, while the new Marquess course at Woburn has set fresh standards even for that distinguished venue.

Another group of clubs, such as the The London, Royal Automobile Club, The Oxfordshire, and Swinley Forest, are almost exclusively members-only establishments. The casual visitor simply cannot hope to play, but a limited number of society bookings is taken, and that society is guaranteed something very exclusive and immensely rewarding.

Finally, mention should be made of the glorious golf available in the Channel Islands, and, to, a lesser extent, on the Isle of Wight.

BERKSHIRE

BEARWOOD GOLF CLUB

Mole Road, Sindlesham,
Wokingham, Berkshire RG41 5DB
✆ 0118 976 0060 **Map 4, F3**
B3030 1 mile SW of Winnersh, M4 Jct 10
Founded 1986
Situated within the Bearwood Estate, designated an area of outstanding natural beauty by English Heritage.
9 holes, 5413 yards
par 70, S.S.S 68
Designer B. Tustin
Green fees £18
Catering, changing room/showers, bar, trolley and buggy hire, shop, driving range, practice facilities, riding
Visitors welcome weekdays
Handicap certificate required
Societies welcome Thursdays by prior arrangement
🏨 Reading Moat House, Mill Lane, Sindlesham, Berkshire
✆ 01189 499988

BEARWOOD LAKES GOLF CLUB

Bearwood Road, Sindlesham,
Berkshire RG41 4SJ
✆ 0118 979 7900 Fax 0118 979 2911 **Map 4, F3**
golf@bearwoodlakes.co.uk
www.bearwoodlakes.co.uk
Between B3030 and B3349 W of Wokingham, 1 mile SW M4 Jct 10
Founded 1996
A remarkably mature course for one so young, with the advantage of having been laid out on a well-wooded, gently undulating site. The 13th and 14th may not be the hardest holes on the course, but they are the most dramatic with their nerve-tingling carries over vast expanses of water.
18 holes, 6854 yards
par 72, S.S.S 72
Designer Martin Hawtree
Green fees n/a
Catering, changing room/showers, bar, club, trolley and buggy hire, shop, practice facilities, conference and wedding facilities
Visitors only as members' guests
Societies only as members' party
🏨 Coppid Beech Hotel, John Nike Way, Bracknell, Berkshire RG12 8TF
✆ 01344 303333 Fax 01344 301200
sales@coppid-beech-hotel.co.uk
www.coppidbeech.com

THE BERKSHIRE GOLF CLUB

Swinley Road, Ascot, Berkshire SL5 8AY
✆ 01344 621495 Fax 01334 623328
Map 4, G3
3 miles S of Ascot, M3 Jct 3
Founded 1928
***See* Top 50 Courses, page 14**
Blue Course: 18 holes, 6260 yards
par 71, S.S.S 71
Designer Herbert Fowler
Red Course: 18 holes, 6369 yards
par 72, S.S.S 71
Green fees £60
Catering, changing room/showers, bar, club, trolley and buggy hire, shop
Visitors welcome weekdays – with prior arrangement
Societies welcome by prior arrangement

BILLINGBEAR PARK GOLF CLUB

The Straight Mile, Wokingham, Berkshire RG40 5SJ
✆ 01344 869259 Fax 01344 869259
Map 4, F3
Off B3034 (off A321), near Binfield, 2 miles E of Wokingham, M4 Jct 10
Founded 1994
A parkland course.
9 holes, 5700 yards

par 68, S.S.S 68
Green fees £8
Shop, 9-hole, par-3 course
Visitors welcome
Societies welcome by prior arrangement

BIRD HILLS GOLF CLUB

Drift Road, Hawthorn Hill, Maidenhead, Berkshire SL6 3ST
✆ 01628 771030 Fax 01628 631023
Map 4, G2
A330, 4 miles S of Maidenhead, M4 Jct 8/9
Founded 1985
A parkland course with a number of water hazards.
18 holes, 6176 yards
par 72, S.S.S 69
Designer Clive D. Smith
Green fees £7.50
Catering, changing room/showers, bar, club and trolley hire, shop, driving range, practice facilities
Visitors welcome
Societies welcome by prior arrangement

BLUE MOUNTAIN GOLF CENTRE

Wood Lane, Binfield, Nr Bracknell, Berkshire RG42 4EX
✆ 01344 300220 Fax 01344 360960
Map 4, F3
americangolf@bluemountain.co.uk
B3408, 1 mile W of Bracknell, M4 Jct 10
Founded 1992
Pretty parkland course with water features, able to pride itself on not having lost a day's play to bad weather in two years.
18 holes, 6100 yards
par 70, S.S.S 70
Green fees £18
Catering, changing room/showers, bar, club, trolley and buggy hire, shop, driving range, practice facilities, seven air-conditioned conference rooms
Visitors welcome
Societies welcome by prior arrangement
🏨 Coppid Beech Hotel, John Nike Way, Bracknell, Berkshire RG12 8TF
✆ 01344 303333 Fax 01344 301200
sales@coppid-beech-hotel.co.uk
www.coppidbeech.com

CALCOT PARK GOLF CLUB

Bath Road, Calcot, Reading, Berkshire RG31 7RN
✆ 0118 942 7124 Fax 0118 945 3373 **Map 4, E3**
A4, 3 miles W of Reading, M4 Jct 12
Founded 1930
Calcot Park's beautiful, undulating parkland is home to badgers and deer. Its four short holes are particularly renowned, the 7th, the signature hole, played across a lake to an elevated green, and the 13th across a valley. To open and close the round, there are pairs of long par 4s.
18 holes, 6283 yards
par 70, S.S.S 70
Designer Harry Colt
Green fees £36
Catering, changing room/showers, bar, club and trolley hire, shop, practice facilities
Visitors welcome weekdays
Handicap certificate required
Societies welcome by prior arrangement
🏨 Calcot Hotel, Bath Road, Calcot, Reading, Berkshire
✆ 01189 416423

CASTLE ROYLE GOLF CLUB

Knowl Hill, Reading, Berkshire RG10 9XA
✆ 01628 829252 **Map 4, F2**
M4 Jct 8/9, A4 for 2 miles towards Reading
Founded 1994
A parkland course, almost an inland links.
18 holes, 6828 yards
par 72, S.S.S 73
Designer Neil Coles
Catering, changing room/showers, bar, trolley hire, shop, driving range, practice facilities
Visitors welcome only as members' guests
Societies no

DATCHET GOLF CLUB

Buccleuch Road, Datchet, Berkshire SL3 9BP
✆ 01753 543887 Fax 01753 541872
Map 16, A6
Off B470, M4 Jct 5
Founded 1890
Parkland course in the shadow of Windsor Castle.
9 holes, 5978 yards
par 70, S.S.S 69
Designer J.H. Taylor
Green fees £18
Catering, changing room/showers, bar, trolley hire, shop
Visitors welcome weekdays with restrictions
Societies welcome by prior arrangement

DEANWOOD PARK GOLF COURSE

Stockcross, Newbury, Berkshire RG20 8JS
✆ 01635 48772 Fax 01635 572827
Map 4, D3
deanwood@newburyweb.net
www.newbury.net//deanwood/home.html
A4/B4000 to Stockcross, M4 Jct 13
Founded 1995
A very warm welcome at this parkland course.
9 holes, 2114 yards
par 64, S.S.S 61
Green fees £8.50
Catering, changing room/showers, bar, club and trolley hire, shop, driving range, practice facilities, video tuition
Visitors welcome
Societies welcome by prior arrangement
🏨 Hare and Hounds, Speen, Newbury, Berkshire
✆ 01635 47215

DONNINGTON VALLEY GOLF CLUB

Snelsmore House, Snelsmore Common, Newbury, Berkshire RG14 3BG
✆ 01635 568140 Fax 01635 568141
Map 4, D3
golf@donningtonvaley.co.uk
www.donningtonvalley.co.uk
M4 Jct 13, 1 mile
Founded 1988
A remarkable establishment, not only a challenging golf course but also a vineyard, wine cellars, hotel and more.
18 holes, 6353 yards
par 71, S.S.S 71
Designer Mike Smith
Green fees £18
Catering, changing room/showers, bar, accommodation, club, trolley and buggy hire, shop, practice facilities, conference and wedding facilities
Visitors welcome
Societies welcome by prior arrangement
🏨 Donnington Valley Hotel, Old Oxford Road, Newbury, Berkshire
✆ 01635 551199

DOWNSHIRE GOLF CLUB

Easthampstead Park, Wokingham, Berkshire RG11 3DH
✆ 01344 302030 Fax 01344 301020
Map 4, F3
Off B3430, Nine Mile Ride, between Wokingham and Bracknell
Founded 1973
A fine municipal course with a number of water hazards.
18 holes, 6416 yards
par 73, S.S.S 71
Designer Fred Hawtree
Green fees £13.50
Catering, changing room/showers, bar, club, trolley and buggy hire,

shop, driving range, practice facilities
Visitors welcome
Societies welcome by prior arrangement

EAST BERKSHIRE GOLF CLUB

Ravenswood Avenue, Crowthorne, Berkshire RG45 6BD
01344 772041 Fax 01344 777378
Map 4, F3
Off B3348 near Crowthorne Station, M4 Jct 10, M3 Jct 3
Founded 1903
One of the unsung jewels of heath-and-heather golf. Those in the know compare it with The Berkshire, with its abundant heather and pine trees narrowing many fairways. Par is only 69, but, with seven par 4s over 400 yards long, strong and accurate play is required to play to handicap.
18 holes, 6344 yards
par 69, S.S.S 70
Designer P. Paxton
Green fees £40
Catering, changing room/showers, bar, trolley hire, shop
Visitors welcome weekdays
Handicap certificate required
Societies welcome by prior arrangement
Waterloo Hotel, Crowthorne, Berkshire
01344 777711

GORING & STREATLEY GOLF CLUB

Rectory Road, Streatley-on-Thames, Berkshire RG8 9QA
01491 873229 Fax 01491 875224
Map 4, E2
Off A417, N of Streatley
Founded 1895
A course in three parts with gentle, low-lying holes at the start and finish and expansive holes on top of the downs in mid-round. Joining these together are several somewhat hilly holes, needing puff to climb, but giving much fun on the descent. Fine turf, lovely surroundings, and excellent value.
18 holes, 6320 yards
par 71, S.S.S 70
Designer Tom Dunn
Green fees £28
Catering, changing room/showers, bar, trolley hire, shop, practice facilities
Visitors welcome weekdays
Societies welcome by prior arrangement

HENNERTON GOLF CLUB

Crazies Hill Road, Wargrave, Berkshire RG10 8LT
0118 940 1000/4778 Fax 0118 940 1042 **Map 4, F2**
www.hennertongolfclub.co.uk
Off A321, 2 miles S of Henley
Founded 1992
A parkland course with marvellous views across the Thames Valley.
9 holes, 5460 yards
par 68, S.S.S 67
Designer Dion Beard
Green fees £15
Catering, changing room/showers, bar, club and trolley hire, shop, driving range
Visitors welcome weekdays
Societies welcome by prior arrangement

HURST GOLF CLUB

Sandford Lane, Hurst, Wokingham, Berkshire RG10 OSQ
01734 344355 **Map 4, F3**
Off A327/B3030, E of Reading
Founded 1979
A parkland course.
9 holes, 6030 yards
S.S.S 70
Green fees £6.50
Changing room/showers, bar
Visitors welcome
Societies welcome by prior arrangement

LAVENDER PARK GOLF CLUB

Swinley Road, Ascot, Berkshire SL5 8BD
01344 893344 **Map 4, G3**
A329, 3 miles SW of Ascot
Founded 1974
A par-3 course attached to a 30-bay driving range.
9 holes, 2248 yards
par 54, S.S.S 56
Green fees £5
Catering, changing room/showers, bar, club hire, shop, driving range, practice facilities
Visitors welcome
Societies welcome by prior arrangement

MAIDENHEAD GOLF CLUB

Shoppenhangers Road, Maidenhead, Berkshire SL6 2PZ
01628 624693 **Map 4, G2**
Off A308, S of Maidenhead, M4 Jct 8/9
Founded 1896
A parkland course on level ground.
18 holes, 6360 yards
par 70, S.S.S 70
Green fees £35
Catering, changing room/showers, bar, club and trolley hire, shop, practice facilities
Visitors welcome weekdays
Handicap certificate required
Societies welcome by prior arrangement

MAPLEDURHAM GOLF CLUB

Mapledurham, Reading, Berkshire RG4 7UD
0118 9463353 Fax 0118 9463363
Map 4, F2
A4074, 4 miles NW of Reading
Founded 1992
An undulating, wooded parkland course.
18 holes, 5625 yards
par 69, S.S.S 68
Designer Robert Sandow
Green fees £14
Catering, changing room/showers, bar, club and trolley hire, shop, practice facilities
Visitors welcome
Societies welcome by prior arrangement

MILL RIDE GOLF CLUB

Mill Ride, Ascot, Berkshire SL5 8LT
01344 886777 Fax 01344 886820
Map 4, G3
www.mill-ride.com
Off A329, W of Ascot, M4 Jct 8/9, M3 Jct 3
Founded 1990
A challenging course which mixes parkland and links characteristics in grand gestures with water hazards.
18 holes, 6752 yards
par 72, S.S.S 72
Designer Donald Steel
Green fees £35
Catering, changing room/showers, bar, club and trolley hire, shop, driving range, practice facilities
Visitors welcome only by prior arrangement
Handicap certificate required
Societies welcome by prior arrangement

NEWBURY & CROOKHAM GOLF CLUB

Bury's Bank Road, Greenham Common, Newbury, Berkshire RG19 8BZ
01635 40035 Fax 01635 40045
Map 4, D3
Off A34 2 miles S of Newbury
Founded 1874
Set in handsome woodland, there is much cunning to the design. For instance, the 12th may be only 289 yards on the card, but a line of bunkers cutting across the fairway dictates either a carry of at least 200 yards or a lay-up. Ditches threaten the 7th and 8th.
18 holes, 5940 yards
par 69, S.S.S 68
Designer J.H. Turner
Green fees £25
Catering, changing room/showers, bar, trolley hire, shop, practice facilities

Visitors welcome weekdays
Societies welcome by prior arrangement
Hilton Hotel, Pinchington Lane, Newbury, Berkshire
01635 529000

NEWBURY RACECOURSE GOLF CENTRE

Newbury, Berkshire RG14 7NZ
01635 551464 Fax 01635 528354
Map 4, D3
Off A34, signposted for race course
Founded 1994
Full golfing facilities at one of the most famous race courses in England.
18 holes, 6311 yards
par 70, S.S.S 70
Green fees £13
Catering, changing room/showers, bar, club and trolley hire, shop, driving range, practice facilities
Visitors welcome
Societies welcome by prior arrangement

PARASAMPIA GOLF & COUNTRY CLUB

Donnington Grove, Grove Road, Donnington, Berkshire RG14 2LA
01635 581000 Fax 01635 555259
Map 4, D3
www.parasampia.com
Off Newbury by-pass, M4 Jct 13
Founded 1993
A beautiful and testing course, laid out in the grounds of a Gothic-style 18th-century house (now the clubhouse and hotel), with extensive country views, particularly from the front nine on higher ground. The back nine runs through classic parkland, with a number of lakes.
18 holes, 7108 yards
par 72, S.S.S 74
Designer Dave Thomas
Green fees £30
Catering, changing room/showers, bar, accommodation, club, trolley and buggy hire, shop, driving range, practice facilities, full hotel, conference and function facilities
Visitors welcome weekdays
Societies welcome by prior arrangement
Parasampia Golf and Country Club, Donnington, Newbury, Berkshire
01635 581000

READING GOLF CLUB

Kidmore End Road, Emmer Green, Reading, Berkshire RG4 8SG
0118 9472909 Fax 0118 9464468
Map 4, F2
Off B481, 2 miles N of Reading
Founded 1910
Long-established parkland course across the River Thames from Reading.
18 holes, 6212 yards
par 70, S.S.S 69
Designer James Braid
Green fees £33
Catering, changing room/showers, bar, club and trolley hire, shop, practice facilities
Visitors welcome Monday to Thursday
Societies welcome Tuesday to Thursday by prior arrangement
Holiday Inn, Caversham Road, Reading, Berkshire
01189 59988

ROYAL ASCOT GOLF CLUB

Winkfield Road, Ascot, Berkshire SL57LJ
01344 625175 Fax 01344 872330
Map 4, G3
Inside Ascot race course
Founded 1887
A heathland course within Ascot race course.
18 holes, 5716 yards
par 68, S.S.S 68
Designer J.H. Taylor
Changing room/showers, trolley hire, shop
Visitors welcome only as members' guests
Societies welcome by prior arrangement

THE ROYAL HOUSEHOLD GOLF CLUB

Invergelder Cottage, 53 Red Rose, Binfield, Berkshire RG42 5LJ
020 7930 4832 Fax 020 7839 5950 **Map 16, A6**
Home Park, Windsor Castle.
Founded 1901
A course revitalised with the active participation of the Duke of York.
Visitors strictly by invitation
No societies

SAND MARTINS GOLF CLUB

Finchampstead Road, Wokingham, Berkshire RG40 3RQ
0118 979 2711 Fax 0118 977 0282 **Map 4, F3**
1 mile S of Wokingham, M4 Jct 10, M3 Jct 3
Founded 1993
The front nine plays through wooded parkland with lakes, while the back nine is more open.
18 holes, 6204 yards
par 70, S.S.S 70
Designer E.T. Fox
Green fees £25
Catering, changing room/showers, bar, trolley and buggy hire, shop, driving range
Visitors welcome weekdays
Societies welcome by prior arrangement

SONNING GOLF CLUB

Duffield Road, Sonning, Reading, Berkshire RG4 6GJ
0118 969 3332 Fax 0118 944 8409 **Map 4, F2**
secretary@sonning-golf-club.co.uk
S of A4 at Sonning
Founded 1911
Seven par 4s over 400 yards long and the 542-yard par-5 7th are offset by two very short par 4s (11th and 14th) on this well-kept parkland course. Walking is easy on such level ground, and the fairways are generous. The 175-yard 6th is stroke index 5.
18 holes, 6366 yards
par 70, S.S.S 70
Green fees £40
Catering, changing room/showers, bar, trolley hire, shop, practice facilities, conference, function and wedding facilities
Visitors welcome weekdays
Handicap certificate required – limit: 28
Societies welcome by prior arrangement
The Wee Waif, Charvil roundabout, Charvil, Reading, Berkshire
01189 440066

SULHAM VALLEY GOLF CLUB

Pincents Lane, Calcot, Reading, Berkshire RG3 5UQ
01734 305959 Fax 01734 305002
Map 4, E2
M4 Jct 12, 1 mile
Founded 1992
A parkland course.
18 holes, 6121 yards
par 71
Green fees £20
Catering, changing room/showers, bar, trolley hire, shop, practice facilities
Visitors welcome
Societies welcome by prior arrangement

SWINLEY FOREST GOLF CLUB

Coronation Road, Ascot, Berkshire SL9 5LE
01344 874979 Fax 01344 874733
Map 4, G3
Off B3020, SW of Ascot, M4 Jct 8/9, M3 Jct 3
Founded 1909
It is immediately apparent to those lucky enough to be invited to play at Swinley that this is a classic. The setting, with heather-bound fairways sweeping through an old royal

hunting forest, is incomparable, and the challenge of Colt's layout considerable. The 12th is the pick of many brilliant holes.
18 holes, 6045 yards
par 69, S.S.S 70
Designer Harry Colt
Green fees £70
Catering, changing room/showers, bar, club, trolley and buggy hire, shop, practice facilities
Visitors welcome only as members' guests
Societies welcome by prior arrangement – Wednesdays only

TEMPLE GOLF CLUB
Henley Road, Hurley, Maidenhead, Berkshire SL6 5LH
☎ 01628 824795 Fax 01628 828119 **Map 4, F2**
A 4130 via A404(M), M40 Jct 4, M4 Jct 8/9
Founded 1909
From Temple's clubhouse atop Appletree Hill there are majestic views over the Thames Valley to the Chilterns. Magnificent trees everywhere simply add to the beauty. The two most difficult holes are the strong par-4 2nd and 11th, and the long (and blind) par-3 10th wrecks many a card.
18 holes, 6248 yards
par 70, S.S.S 70
Designer Willie Park Jnr
Green fees £33
Catering, changing room/showers, bar, club and trolley hire, shop, practice facilities
Visitors welcome by prior arrangement
Handicap certificate required
Societies welcome by prior arrangement
🏨 The Compleat Angler, Bisham Road, Marlow, Buckinghamshire
☎ 01628 484444

WEST BERKSHIRE GOLF CLUB
Chaddleworth, Newbury, Berkshire RG20 7DU
☎ 01488 638574 Fax 01488 638781 **Map 4, D2**
Off A338, 6 miles S of Wantage
Founded 1975
A very long course, particularly testing when the wind gets up, and, on this upland site, there is no shelter from it.
18 holes, 7001 yards
par 73, S.S.S 74
Designer Robin Stagg
Green fees £25
Catering, changing room/showers, bar, club, trolley and buggy hire, shop, practice facilities
Visitors welcome weekdays
Societies welcome by prior arrangement

WINTER HILL GOLF CLUB
Grange Lane, Cookham, Berkshire Sl6 9RP
☎ 01628 527613 **Map 4, G2**
Off A415/A4094
Founded 1976
A parkland course overlooking one of the loveliest stretches of the Thames.
18 holes, 6408 yards
par 72, S.S.S 71
Designer Charles Lawrie
Green fees £29
Catering, changing room/showers, bar, club and trolley hire, shop, practice facilities
Visitors welcome weekdays
Societies welcome by prior arrangement

WOKEFIELD PARK GOLF CLUB
Mortimer, Reading, Berkshire RG7 3AE
☎ 0118 933 4018 Fax 0118 933 4162 **Map 4, F3**
wokefieldgolf@initialstyle.co.uk
www.wokefieldgolf.co.uk
Off A33, 8 miles SwW of Reading, M4 Jct 11
Founded 1996
A contemporary parkland course with streams, nine lakes and large bunkers as hazards. The 12th is a par 3 of 194 yards with a full carry over water.
18 holes, 6961 yards
par 72, S.S.S 73
Designer Jonathan Gaunt
Green fees £30
Catering, changing room/showers, bar, accommodation, club, trolley and buggy hire, shop, driving range, practice facilities, full hotel and conference facilities, fishing, croquet, tennis, gym
Visitors welcome
Societies welcome by prior arrangement
🏨 Wokefield Park, Mortimer, Reading, Berkshire RG7 3AE
☎ 01189 334000 Fax 01189 334162
wokefieldgolf@initialstyle.co.uk
www.wokefieldgolf.co.uk

BUCKINGHAMSHIRE

ABBEY HILL GOLF CLUB
Monks Way, Two Mile Ash, Milton Keynes, Buckinghamshire MK8 8AA
☎ 01908 563845 **Map 8, E8**
Off A5, 2 miles S of Stony Stratford
Founded 1975
A public parkland course.
18 holes, 6193 yards
par 71, S.S.S 69
Catering, changing room/showers, bar, club, trolley and buggy hire, shop, driving range, practice facilities
Visitors welcome
Societies welcome by prior arrangement

AYLESBURY GOLF CLUB
Hulcott Lane, Bierton, Aylesbury, Buckinghamshire HP22 5GA
☎ 01296 393644 **Map 8, E10**
A418, 1 mile N of Aylesbury
Founded 1991
A good value parkland course with modern facilities.
18 holes, 5965 yards
par 71, S.S.S 69
Designer T.S. Benwell
Green fees £10
Catering, changing room/showers, bar, club and trolley hire, shop, driving range, practice facilities
Visitors welcome
Societies welcome by prior arrangement
🏨 Posthouse, Tring Road, Aylesbury, Buckinghamshire
☎ 0870 4009002

AYLESBURY PARK GOLF CLUB
Oxford Road, Aylesbury, Buckinghamshire HP17 8QQ
☎ 01296 399166 Fax 01296 336830 **Map 8, E10**
A418, SW of Aylesbury
Founded 1996
A parkland course.
18 holes, 6150 yards
par 70, S.S.S 69
Designer Martin Hawtree
Green fees £12.50
Catering, changing room/showers, bar, club, trolley and buggy hire, shop, practice facilities
Visitors welcome – booking system
Societies welcome by prior arrangement

AYLESBURY VALE GOLF CLUB
Stewkley Road, Wing, Leighton Buzzard, Buckinghamshire LU7 0UJ
☎ 01525 240196 Fax 01525 240848 **Map 8, E9**
2 miles NW of Leighton Buzzard
Founded 1990
A pretty parkland course with a number of water hazards.
18 holes, 6612 yards
par 72, S.S.S 72
Designer D. Wright
Green fees £12
Catering, changing room/showers, bar, club, trolley and buggy hire, shop, driving range, practice facilities

Visitors welcome with prior booking
Societies welcome with prior booking

BEACONSFIELD GOLF CLUB

Seer Green, Beaconsfield, Buckinghamshire HP9 2UR
01494 676545 Fax 01494 681148
Map 4, G2
secretary@beaconsfieldgolfclub.golfagent.co.uk
Seer Green Railway Station – M40 Jct 2
Founded 1902
In many respects a model parkland course, with holes of every kind and length running over immaculately maintained grounds either side of the railway line to Marylebone. A ravine complicates two holes, trees dictate strategy on several of the dog-legs, and the undulations are sufficient to affect club selection widely.
18 holes, 6493 yards
par 72, S.S.S 71
Designer Harry Colt
Green fees £35
Catering, changing room/showers, bar, club and trolley hire, shop, driving range, practice facilities, limited meeting/conference facilities
Visitors welcome weekdays
Handicap certificate required
Societies welcome by prior arrangement
Bell House, Beaconsfield, Buckinghamshire
01494 887211

BUCKINGHAM GOLF CLUB

Tingewick Road, Buckingham, Buckinghamshire MK18 4AE
01280 815566 Fax 01280 821812
Map 8, D9
A421, 2 miles SW of Buckingham
Founded 1914
Undulating parkland course, with frequent encounters with water and lovely views.
18 holes, 6082 yards
par 70, S.S.S 69
Green fees £28
Catering, changing room/showers, bar, trolley and buggy hire, shop, practice facilities, snooker
Visitors welcome weekdays
Handicap certificate required
Societies welcome by prior arrangement
Four Pillars, Buckingham Ring Road South, Buckingham, Buckinghamshire
01280 822622

THE BUCKINGHAMSHIRE GOLF CLUB

Denham Court, Denham Court Drive, Denham, Buckinghamshire UB9 5BG
01895 835777 Fax 01895 835210
Map 16, B5
M40 Jct 1, signposted at A40 roundabout.
Founded 1992
A dignified contemporary design with several exciting water holes, (7th, 8th, 10th and 12th), but also a number of refreshingly simple yet strategic holes, such as the dog-leg 13th and rigorous 17th. Denham Court makes for a noble and gracious clubhouse, with the short 9th charmingly set in its garden.
18 holes, 6880 yards
par 72, S.S.S 73
Designer John Jacobs
Green fees £70
Catering, changing room/showers, bar, club and trolley hire, shop, driving range, practice facilities
Visitors welcome only as members' guests
Societies welcome by prior arrangement

BURNHAM BEECHES GOLF CLUB

Green Lane, Burnham, Slough, Buckinghamshire SL1 8EG
01628 661150 Fax 01628 668968
Map 4, G2
www.bbgc.co.uk
Off A355, 4 miles W of Slough
Founded 1891
Tucked away inside the ancient woodlands of Burnham, sheer beauty complements the many distinctive challenges of this long-established and enchanting course. The six substantial par 4s are not easily tamed, especially the 2nd, 12th, 14th, and 18th, and compulsory carries over treacherous low ground are a feature of several holes.
18 holes, 6449 yards
par 70, S.S.S 71
Green fees £32
Catering, changing room/showers, bar, club, trolley and buggy hire, shop, practice facilities
Visitors welcome weekdays
Societies welcome by prior arrangement

CHARTRIDGE PARK GOLF CLUB

Chartridge, Chesham, Buckinghamshire HP5 2TF
01494 791772 **Map 8, F10**
www.cpgc.co.uk
2 miles NW of Chesham
Founded 1989
Laid out in historic parkland at the highest point in the Chilterns.
18 holes, 5510 yards
par 69, S.S.S 68
Designer John Jacobs
Green fees £25
Catering, changing room/showers, bar, club, trolley and buggy hire, shop, practice facilities
Visitors welcome
Societies welcome by prior arrangement
Hemel Hempsted Travel Inn, Stoney Lane, Bourne End, Hemel Hempsted, Hertfordshire
01442 879149

CHESHAM & LEY HILL GOLF CLUB

Ley Hill, Chesham, HP5 1UZ, Buckinghamshire 01494 784541
01494 785506 **Map 8, F10**
B4504, E of Chesham
Founded 1900
A handsome parkland course on high ground.
9 holes, 5296 yards
par 66, S.S.S 65
Green fees £13
Catering, changing room/showers, bar
Visitors welcome weekdays – with restrictions
Societies welcome by prior arrangement

CHILTERN FOREST GOLF CLUB

Aston Hill, Halton, Aylesbury, Buckinghamshire HP22 5NQ
01296 631267 Fax 01296 632709
Map 8, E10
secretary@chilternforst.co.uk
www.chilternforest.co.uk
Off A4011, SE of Aylesbury
Founded 1900
Visually very attractive with seriously undulating fairways amidst the trees. Decidedly testing!
18 holes, 5765 yards
par 70, S.S.S 70
Green fees £25
Catering, changing room/showers, bar, trolley and buggy hire, shop
Visitors welcome weekdays
Societies welcome by prior arrangement
Red Lion Hotel, High Street, Wendover, Buckinghamshire
01296 622266

DENHAM GOLF CLUB

Tilehouse Lane, Denham, Buckinghamshire UB9 5DE
01895 832022 Fax 01895 835340
Map 16, B5
Off A412, 1 mile NW of Denham

Founded 1910
There are not many courses on which it is possible to slice onto an airfield! It can be done on Denham's 3rd. In fact this is the plainest hole on an otherwise very attractive course. The bunkering gives much food for thought and the many woodland holes are particularly handsome.
18 holes, 6456 yards
par 70, S.S.S 71
Designer Harry Colt
Green fees £40
Catering, changing room/showers, bar, club and trolley hire, shop, practice facilities
Visitors welcome weekdays, with restrictions
Handicap certificate required
Societies welcome by prior arrangement

ELLESBOROUGH GOLF CLUB

Butlers Cross, Aylesbury, Buckinghamshire HP17 OTZ
01296 622114 Fax 01296 622114
Map 8, E10
Off A413, W of Wendover
Founded 1906
Set on the slopes of the Chilterns, on the edge of the Chequers Estate, the views over the surrounding countryside are exceptional. The course is hilly, pleasantly wooded, and with plenty of change of pace. So, a 127-yard par 3 follows a 555-yard par 5, and so on.
18 holes, 6360 yards
par 71, S.S.S 71
Designer James Braid
Green fees £25
Catering, changing room/showers, bar, trolley hire, shop, practice facilities
Visitors welcome weekdays, with restrictions
Handicap certificate required
Societies welcome by prior arrangement

FARNHAM PARK GOLF CLUB

Park Road, Stoke Poges, Slough, Buckinghamshire SL2 4PJ
01753 643332 Fax 01753 647065
Map 4, G2
A355, 2 miles N of Slough
Founded 1977
If only public courses of this quality and standard were available in less enlightened parts of the country! An admirable, and handsome, facility close to famous Stoke Park.
18 holes, 6172 yards
par 71, S.S.S 69
Designer Hawtree
Green fees £15
Catering, changing room/showers, bar, club and trolley hire, shop
Visitors welcome
Societies welcome by prior arrangement
Bell House, Beaconsfield, Buckinghamshire
01494 887211

FLACKWELL HEATH GOLF CLUB

Treadaway Road, Flackwell Heath, High Wycombe, Buckinghamshire HP10 9PE
01628 520929 Fax 01628 530040
Map 4, G2
Close to M40 Jct 3 and 4
Founded 1905
Well-known to travellers on the M40, who get a good view of the run of tricky holes perched on a hillside overlooking High Wycombe.
18 holes, 6211 yards
par 71, S.S.S 70
Green fees £24
Catering, changing room/showers, bar, trolley and buggy hire, shop, practice facilities, conference facility
Visitors welcome, with restrictions.
Handicap certificate required
Societies welcome by prior arrangement

GERRARDS CROSS GOLF CLUB

Chalfont Park, Gerrards Cross, Buckinghamshire SL9 OQA
01753 883263 Fax 01753 883593
Map 16, A4
Off A413, NE of Gerrards Cross
Founded 1921
An undulating parkland course, well wooded, and quite challenging.
18 holes, 6212 yards
par 69, S.S.S 70
Designer B. Pedlar
Green fees £33
Catering, changing room/showers, bar, trolley hire, shop, practice facilities
Visitors welcome weekdays
Handicap certificate required
Societies welcome by prior arrangement

HAREWOOD DOWNS GOLF CLUB

Cokes Lane, Chalfont St Giles, Buckinghamshire HP8 4TA
01494 762308 Fax 01494 766869
Map 4, G1
A413, 2 miles E of Amersham
Founded 1907
An undulating parkland course.
18 holes, 5958 yards
par 69, S.S.S 69
Green fees £30
Catering, changing room/showers, bar, trolley and buggy hire, shop, practice facilities
Visitors welcome
Handicap certificate required
Societies welcome by prior arrangement

HARLEYFORD GOLF CLUB

Harleyford Estate, Henley Road, Marlow, Buckinghamshire SL7 2SP
01628 402300 Fax 01628 478434
Map 4, F2
Off A4155, Marlow-Henley road
Founded 1996
A striking course, as visually satisfying as it is challenging.
18 holes, 6604 yards
par 72, S.S.S 72
Designer Donald Steel
Green fees £40
Catering, changing room/showers, bar, club, trolley and buggy hire, shop, practice facilities
Visitors welcome, with restrictions
Handicap certificate required
Societies welcome by prior arrangement

HAZLEMERE GOLF & COUNTRY CLUB

Penn Road, Hazlemere, High Wycombe, Buckinghamshire HP15 7LR
01494 714722 Fax 01494 713914
Map 4, G2
A404, 2 miles NE of High Wycombe
Founded 1982
A rolling parkland course in delightful countryside.
18 holes, 5807 yards
par 70, S.S.S 69
Designer Terry Murray
Green fees £20
Catering, changing room/showers, bar, club, trolley and buggy hire, shop
Visitors welcome weekdays
Societies welcome by prior arrangement

IVER GOLF CLUB

Hollow Hill, Iver, Buckinghamshire SL0 0JJ
01753 655615 Fax 01753 654225
Map 16, B6
Off B470, SW of Iver
Founded 1983
A challenging pay-and-play course with a number of uncomprising water hazards.
9 holes, 6288 yards
par 72, S.S.S 72
Green fees £11
Catering, changing room/showers, bar, club and trolley hire, shop, driving range
Visitors welcome weekdays
Societies welcome by prior arrangement

IVINGHOE GOLF CLUB

Wellcroft, Ivinghoe, Leighton Buzzard, Buckinghamshire LU7 9EF
☎ 01296 668696 Fax 01296 662755
Map 8, F10
4 miles N of Tring.
Founded 1967
A parkland course.
9 holes, 4508 yards
S.S.S 62
Designer R. Gerrard
Green fees £9
Catering, changing room/showers, bar
Visitors welcome weekdays
Societies welcome by prior arrangement

THE LAMBOURNE CLUB

Dropmore Road, Burnham, Buckinghamshire SL1 8NF
☎ 01628 662936 Fax 01628 663301
Map 4, G2
1 mile N of Burnham, M4 Jct 7, M40 Jct 2
Founded 1992
One of the most notable recent courses in this part of England, a tough parkland course with many lakes.
18 holes, 6771 yards
par 72, S.S.S 73
Designer Donald Steel
Green fees £50
Catering, changing room/showers, bar, club, trolley and buggy hire, shop, practice facilities
Visitors welcome
Handicap certificate required
Societies no societies
🏨 Cliveden House, Buckinghamshire
☎ 01628 605069

LITTLE CHALFONT GOLF CLUB

Lodge Lane, Little Chalfont, Amersham, Buckinghamshire HP8 4AJ
☎ 01494 764877 Fax 01494 762860
Map 16, A4
A404, between Little Chalfont and Chorleywood
Founded 1981
A pretty parkland course.
9 holes, 5852 yards
par 68, S.S.S 68
Designer J.M. Dunne
Green fees £11.50
Catering, changing room/showers, bar, club and trolley hire, shop
Visitors welcome
Societies welcome by prior arrangement

MAGNOLIA PARK GOLF CLUB

Arncott Road, Boarstall, Aylesbury, Buckinghamshire HP18 9XX
☎ 01844 239700 Fax 01844 238991
Map 8, D10
B4011 between Thame and Bicester
Founded 2000
Already rated as one of the best new courses, and immediately acknowledged for the excellence of its greens.
18 holes, 6892 yards
par 73, S.S.S 73
Designer Jonathan Gaunt
Green fees £30
Catering, changing room/showers, bar, club, trolley and buggy hire, shop, practice facilities, conference facilities, wedding and function rooms
Visitors welcome
Societies welcome by prior arrangement
🏨 Studley Priory, Horton Hill, Horton-cum-Studley, Oxford, Oxfordshire OX33 1AZ
☎ 01865 351203 Fax 01865 351613
res@studleypriory.co.uk

MENTMORE GOLF & COUNTRY CLUB

Mentmore, Leighton Buzzard, Buckinghamshire LU7 OUA
☎ 01296 662020 Fax 01296 662592
Map 8, E9
4 miles S of Leighton Buzzard
Founded 1992
Two big, almost American-style, parkland courses with obligatory water hazards in the grounds of this old Rothschild house.
Rosebery Course: 18 holes, 6850 yards
par 72, S.S.S 72
Rothschild Course: 18 holes, 6777 yards
par 72, S.S.S 72
Designer Robert Sandow
Green fees £40
Catering, changing room/showers, club, trolley and buggy hire, shop, driving range, tennis courts, heated indoor swimming pool, fishing, sauna & gymnasium
Visitors welcome weekdays
Handicap certificate required
Societies welcome by prior arrangement

OAKLAND PARK GOLF CLUB

Threehouseholds, Chalfont St Giles, Buckinghamshire HP8 4LW
☎ 01494 877333 Fax 01494 874692
Map 8, F11
1 mile N of Beaconsfield, M40 Jct 2
Founded 1995
Pleasant, well-wooded parkland course.
18 holes, 5230 yards
par 67, S.S.S 66
Designer Jonathan Gaunt
Green fees £25
Catering, changing room/showers, bar, trolley and buggy hire, shop, driving range
Visitors welcome – with restrictions
Handicap certificate required
Societies welcome by prior arrangement
🏨 Bell House, Beaconsfield, Buckinghamshire
☎ 01494 887211

PRINCES RISBOROUGH GOLF CLUB

Lee Road, Saunderton Lee, Princes Risborough, Buckinghamshire HP27 9NX
☎ 01844 346989 Fax 01844 274938
Map 8, E10
A4010, 5 miles NW of High Wycombe
Founded 1990
A parkland course.
9 holes, 5440 yards
par 68, S.S.S 66
Designer Guy Hunt
Green fees £14
Catering, changing room/showers, bar, shop, practice facilities
Visitors welcome
Societies welcome by prior arrangement

RICHINGS PARK GOLF & COUNTRY CLUB

North Park, Iver, Buckinghamshire SL0 9DL
☎ 01753 655352 Fax 01753 655409
Map 16, B6
www.richingspark.co.uk
Off A4, near M4 Jct 5
Founded 1996
A challenging parkland course with much water.
18 holes, 6094 yards
par 70, S.S.S 69
Designer Alan Higgins
Green fees £17
Catering, changing room/showers, bar, club, trolley and buggy hire, shop, driving range, academy course
Visitors welcome weekdays
Societies welcome by prior arrangement

SILVERSTONE GOLF CLUB

Silverstone Road, Stowe, Buckingham, Buckinghamshire MK18 5LH
☎ 01280 850005 Fax 01280 850156
Map 8, D8
A413, S of Towcester
Founded 1992
A parkland course.
18 holes, 6213 yards
S.S.S 71
Designer David Snell

Green fees £14
Catering, changing room/showers, bar, shop, practice facilities
Visitors welcome – booking system
Societies welcome by prior arrangement

STOKE PARK GOLF CLUB

Park Road, Stoke Poges, Buckinghamshire SL2 4PG
✆ 01753 717171 Fax 01753 717181
Map 4, G2
B416, off A4 at Slough
Founded 1908
Stoke's 'wedding cake' mansion is known to all through the James Bond film, Goldfinger, and to those professionals who used to compete here in the News of the World *and Sun Alliance competitions. Recent restoration has worked wonders for condition, but several Colt originals disappeared during expansion to 27 holes.*
18 holes, 6721 yards
par 71, S.S.S 72
Designer Harry Colt
9 holes, 3074 yards
par 36
Green fees £65
Catering, changing room/showers, bar, club, trolley and buggy hire, shop, driving range, practice facilities
Visitors welcome by prior arrangement
Societies welcome by prior arrangement

STOWE GOLF CLUB

Stowe,Buckinghamshire MK18 5EH
✆ 01280 816264 **Map 8, D8**
At Stowe School
Founded 1974
A private course at this renowned public school.
9 holes, 4472 yards
S.S.S 62
Green fees £10
Visitors welcome only as members' guests.
No societies

THORNEY PARK GOLF CLUB

Thorney Mill Road, Iver, Buckinghamshire SL0 9AL
✆ 01895 422095 Fax 01895 431307
Map 16, B6
B470, 3 miles N of M4 Jct 5
Founded 1994
Well conditioned parkland course of some character.
9 holes, 2834 yards
par 34, S.S.S 34
Green fees £8
Catering, changing room/showers, bar, club and trolley hire, shop, conference facilities
Visitors welcome
Societies welcome by prior arrangement

THREE LOCKS GOLF CLUB

Great Brickhill, Milton Keynes, Buckinghamshire MK17 9BH
✆ 01525 270050 Fax 01525 270470
Map 8, F9
info@threelocksgolfclub.co.uk
www.threelocksgolfclub.co.uk
A4146, 3 miles from Leighton Buzzard
Founded 1992
As the name suggests, the course runs beside a canal, but it is the river which runs through the course which adds particular character and challenge.
18 holes, 6036 yards
par 70, S.S.S 68
Designer MRM Sandow, P Critchley
Green fees £15
Catering, changing room/showers, bar, accommodation, club, trolley and buggy hire, shop, practice facilities, conference facilities
Visitors welcome
Societies welcome by prior arrangement
Bell Inn, Woburn, Bedfordshire
✆ 01525 290280

WAVENDON GOLF CENTRE

Lower End Road, Wavendon, Milton Keynes, Buckinghamshire MK17 8DA
✆ 01908 281811 Fax 01908 281257
Map 8, F8
A421 towards Woburn Sands, 2 miles W of M1 Jct 13
Founded 1989
Quite a short pay-and-play course, but the trees and water hazards make it interesting to play and pleasant on the eye.
18 holes, 5479 yards
par 69, S.S.S 69
Designer John Drake
Green fees £12.50
Catering, changing room/showers, bar, accommodation, club, trolley and buggy hire, shop, practice facilities, conference facilities, 2 restaurants, 9-hole course
Visitors welcome
Societies welcome by prior arrangement
Courtyard Marriott, Newport Pagnell, Buckinghamshire
✆ 01908 613688

WESTON TURVILLE GOLF & SQUASH CLUB

New Road, Weston Turville, Aylesbury, Buckinghamshire HP22 5QT
✆ 01296 424084 Fax 01296 395376
Map 8, E10
Off A41, between Aston Clinton and Wendover
Founded 1975
Pleasant parkland course with good views to the Chilterns.
18 holes, 6008 yards
par 69, S.S.S 69
Green fees £20
Catering, changing room/showers, bar, club, trolley and buggy hire, shop, practice facilities, squash
Visitors welcome (restricted Sunday)
Societies welcome by prior arrangement

WEXHAM PARK GOLF COURSE

Wexham Street, Wexham, Buckinghamshire SL3 6NB
✆ 01753 663271 Fax 01753 663318
Map 16, A5
www.wexhamparkgolfcourse.co.uk
2 miles N of Slough, M4 Jct 6, M40 Jct 2
Founded 1977
An 18-hole and two 9-hole courses in charming parkland. Windsor Castle comes into view from the 14th hole on the Blue Course. Water threatens on a number of holes, particularly the 9th and 15th on the Blue.
Blue Course: 18 holes, 5366 yards
par 68, S.S.S 66
Green Course: 9 holes, 2219 yards
par 64, S.S.S 62
Red Course: 9 holes, 2727 yards
par 68, S.S.S 67
Designer E. Lawrence, D. Morgan
Green fees £12.50
Catering, changing room/showers, bar, club, trolley and buggy hire, shop, driving range, practice facilities
Visitors welcome
Societies welcome by prior arrangement

WHITELEAF GOLF CLUB

Whiteleaf, Princes Risborough, Buckinghamshire HP27 OLY
✆ 01844 343097 Fax 01844 275551
Map 8, E10
Off A4010, 1 mile NE of Princes Risborough
Founded 1904
With fine views from high ground, Whiteleaf is a short, but tight, course.
9 holes, 5391 yards
par 66, S.S.S 66
Green fees £18
Catering, changing room/showers, bar, club and trolley hire, shop, practice facilities
Visitors welcome weekdays

Societies welcome by prior arrangement

WINDMILL HILL GOLF CLUB

Tattenhoe Lane, Bletchley, Buckinghamshire MK3 7RB
☎ 01908 631113 Fax 01908 630034
Map 4, E8
Off A421, between Milton Keynes and Buckingham
Founded 1972
Well-wooded parkland course.
18 holes, 6720 yards
par 73, S.S.S 72
Designer Sir Henry Cotton
Green fees £10.75
Catering, changing room/showers, bar, club, trolley and buggy hire, shop, driving range, practice facilities
Visitors welcome
Societies welcome by prior arrangement

WOBURN GOLF CLUB

Little Brickhill, Milton Keynes, Buckinghamshire MK17 9LJ
☎ 01908 370756 Fax 01908 378436
Map 8, F8
M1 Jct 13
Founded 1976
***See* Top 50 Courses, page 58**
Duchess Course: 18 holes, 6651 yards
par 72, S.S.S 72
Duke's Course: 18 holes, 6979 yards
par 72, S.S.S 74
Designer Charles Lawrie
Marquess Course: 18 holes, 7180 yards
par 72
Designer Peter Alliss, Clive Clark, Ross McMurray, Neil Coles, Alex Hay
Green fees by arrangement
Catering, changing room/showers, bar, club, trolley and buggy hire, shop, driving range, practice facilities
Visitors welcome weekdays by prior arrangement
Handicap certificate required
Societies welcome weekdays by prior arrangement

WYCOMBE HEIGHTS GOLF CENTRE

Rayners Avenue, Loudwater, High Wycombe, Buckinghamshire HP10 9SW
☎ 01494 816686 Fax 01494 816728
Map 8, E11
Off A40 (M40 Jct 3)
Founded 1991
A well equipped golf centre on high ground with extensive views.
18 holes, 6253 yards
par 70, S.S.S 72
Designer John Jacobs
Green fees £11
Catering, changing room/showers, bar, club, trolley and buggy hire, shop, driving range, practice facilities
Visitors welcome
Societies welcome by prior arrangement

CHANNEL ISLANDS

ALDERNEY GOLF CLUB

Route des Carrieres, Alderney, Channel Islands GY9 3YD
☎ 01481 822835 Fax 01481 823609
1 mile E of St Anne
Magnificent views everywhere on this delightful, undulating seaside course.
9 holes, 5006 yards
par 64, S.S.S 65
Designer Frank Pennink
Green fees £20
Catering, changing room/showers, bar, club and trolley hire
Visitors welcome
Handicap certificate required
Societies welcome by prior arrangement

LA GRANDE MARE GOLF CLUB

Vazon Bay, Castel, Guernsey, Channel Islands GY5 7LL
☎ 01481 253432 Fax 01481 255194
www.lgm.guernsey.net
Beside Vazon Bay on W coast road.
Founded 1994
Short, but enjoyable parkland course in grounds of luxury hotel, open to green fee visitors as well as hotel guests.
18 holes, 4516 yards
par 64, S.S.S 64
Designer Hawtree
Green fees £27
Catering, changing room/showers, bar, accommodation, club, trolley and buggy hire, shop, practice facilities, health suite, tennis
Visitors welcome
Societies welcome by prior arrangement
🏨 La Grande Mare Hotel, Vazon Bay, Castel, Guernsey, Channel Islands GY5 7LL
☎ 01481 256576 Fax 01481 255194

LES MIELLES GOLF & COUNTRY CLUB

St Ouens Bay, Jersey, Channel Islands JE3 7FQ
☎ 01534 482787 Fax 01534 485414
enquiry@lesmielles.co.je
www.lesmielles.com
St Peter Village
Founded 1994
An American style contemporary course with many water hazards.
18 holes, 5713 yards
par 70, S.S.S 68
Designer J.A. Le Brun
Green fees £22
Catering, changing room/showers, bar, club, trolley and buggy hire, shop, driving range, practice facilities
Visitors welcome
Societies welcome by prior arrangement
🏨 Mermaid Hotel, St Peter, Jersey, Channel Islands JE3 7BN
☎ 01534 741255

LA MOYE GOLF CLUB

La Moye, St Brelade, Jersey, Channel Islands JE3 8GQ
☎ 01534 743401 Fax 01534 747166
Off A13, W side of island.
Founded 1092
For some years a regular European tour venue, La Moye occupies a privileged spot on high ground overlooking the sea. The run of strong par 4s from the 4th is testing, and the more recently constructed 11th, 12th and 13th explore an area of tumbling dunes in quite magnificent fashion.
18 holes, 6664 yards
par 72, S.S.S 72
Designer James Braid
Green fees £40
Catering, changing room/showers, bar, club, trolley and buggy hire, shop, driving range, practice facilities
Visitors welcome by prior arrangement
Societies welcome by prior arrangement

LES ORMES GOLF CLUB

Mont à la Brune, St Brelade, Jersey, Channel Islands JE3 8FL
☎ 01534 497000 Fax 01534 499122
info@lesormes.je
½ mile from airport
Founded 1996
A short seaside course.
9 holes, 2514 yards
par 66, S.S.S 65
Green fees £13
Catering, changing room/showers, bar, club, trolley and buggy hire, shop, driving range, practice facilities, indoor tennis, health and fitness centre
Visitors welcome
Societies welcome by prior arrangement

La Place Hotel, La Route du Coin, St Brelade, Jersey, Channel Islands JE3 8BT
01534 744261

ROYAL GUERNSEY GOLF CLUB

L'Ancresse, Vale, Guernsey, Channel Islands GY3 5BY
01481 245070 Fax 01481 243960
r-g-g-c@lineone.net
3 miles N of St Peter Port
Founded 1890
At no point further than half a mile from the sea, this attractive links is frequently at the mercy of the wind. Five short par 4s offer encouragement but they are counterbalanced by some very strong two-shotters such as the 9th and 11th, and the 2nd, running along the shore.
18 holes, 6215 yards
par 70, S.S.S 70
Designer Mackenzie Ross, F.W. Hawtree
Green fees £38
Catering, changing room/showers, bar, club and trolley hire, shop, driving range
Visitors welcome weekdays
Handicap certificate required – limit: 28 men, 45 ladies
No societies or corporate days
L'Ancresse Bay Hotel, L'Ancresse, Vale, Guernsey, Channel Islands GY3 5AJ
01481 246664

ROYAL JERSEY GOLF CLUB

Le Chemin au Greves, Grouville, Jersey, Channel Islands JE3 9BD
01534 854416 Fax 01534 854416
TheSecretary@royaljersey.com
www.royaljersey.com
Coast road from St Helier towards Gorey
Founded 1878
The oldest of the historic Channel Island clubs, the course runs past the cottage in which Harry Vardon was born. The opening is splendid with four holes alongside the beach, the skyline dominated by the cliff-top Mont Orgeuil. The par 4s are not particularly long, although gorse threatens on many.
18 holes, 6089 yards
par 70, S.S.S 70
Green fees £45
Catering, changing room/showers, bar, club, trolley and buggy hire, shop, practice facilities
Visitors welcome – restricted
Handicap certificate required – limit: 28 men, 36 women
Societies welcome by prior arrangement

Beausite Hotel, La Rue des Pres, Grouville, Jersey, Channel Islands JE3 9DJ
01534 857577 Fax 01534 857211

ST CLEMENTS GOLF CLUB

St Clements, Jersey, Channel Islands JE2 6QN
01534 821938
A5, E of St Helier
Founded 1913
A tight and somewhat unforgiving course, on which, it is said, it is impossible to play to handicap.
9 holes, 2244 yards
par 30
Green fees £10
Catering, changing room/showers, bar
Visitors welcome with restrictions
Societies welcome by prior arrangement

ST PIERRE PARK GOLF COURSE

Rohais, St Peter Port, Guernsey, Channel Islands GY1 1FD
01481 728282
enquiries@stpierrepark.co.uk
www.stpierrepark.co.uk
1 mile W of St Peter Port
In the beautiful grounds of an opulent hotel, a pitch-and-putt course to make competent golfers think, beautifully manicured, with water in store towards the end.
9 holes, 1323 yards
par 27, S.S.S 52
Designer Tony Jacklin
Green fees £15
Catering, bar, accommodation, club and trolley hire, shop, driving range, practice facilities, lavish hotel facilities, including extensive function and conference rooms, health and fitness, tennis, swimming
Visitors welcome
Societies welcome by prior arrangement
St Pierre Park Hotel, Rohais, St Peter Port, Guernsey, Channel Islands GY1 1FD
01481 728282
enquiries@stpierrepark.co.uk
www.stpierrepark.co.uk

HAMPSHIRE

ALRESFORD GOLF CLUB

Cheriton Road, Tichborne Down, Alresford, Hampshire SO24 0PN
01962 733746 Fax 01962 736040
Map 4, E5
secretary@alresford-golf.demon.co.uk
www.alresfordgolf.com
B3046, 1 mile S of Alresford
Founded 1890
With five difficult short holes and narrow fairways the course is more challenging than the yardage alone might suggest.
18 holes, 5905 yards
par 69, S.S.S 68
Green fees £23
Catering, changing room/showers, bar, club and trolley hire, shop, practice facilities
Visitors welcome, subject to restrictions
Societies welcome by prior arrangement
Swan Hotel, 11 West Street, Alresford, Hampshire
01962 732302

ALTON GOLF CLUB

Old Odiham Road, Alton, Hampshire GU34 4BU
01420 82042 **Map 4, F4**
B3349, 2 miles N of Alton
Founded 1908
An undulating parkland course.
9 holes, 5744 yards
par 68, S.S.S 68
Designer James Braid
Green fees £15
Catering, changing room/showers, bar, trolley hire, shop
Visitors welcome weekdays
Societies welcome by prior arrangement

AMPFIELD PAR THREE GOLF CLUB

Winchester Road, Ampfield, Romsey, Hampshire SO51 9BQ
01794 368480 **Map 4, D5**
A3090, 5 miles E of Romsey
Founded 1963
An excellent short course, cleverly designed by Sir Henry Cotton.
18 holes, 2478 yards
par 54, S.S.S 53
Designer Sir Henry Cotton
Green fees £9
Catering, changing room/showers, bar, club and trolley hire, shop
Visitors welcome weekdays
Societies welcome by prior arrangement

ANDOVER GOLF CLUB

51 Winchester Road, Andover, Hampshire SP10 2EF
01264 323980 Fax 01264 358040
Map 4, D4
A3057, off A303
Founded 1907
An attractive and quite testing course with splendid downland views.
9 holes, 6096 yards
par 70, S.S.S 69
Designer J.H. Taylor

Green fees £12
Catering, changing room/showers, bar, trolley hire, shop
Visitors welcome with restrictions
Societies welcome by prior arrangement

ARMY GOLF CLUB

Laffans Road, Aldershot, Hampshire GU11 2HF
✆ 01252 336776 Fax 01252 337562
Map 4, G4
Off A323, 2 miles N of Aldershot
Founded 1883
A very old club with an attractive heathland course.
18 holes, 6579 yards
par 71, S.S.S 71
Green fees £24
Catering, changing room/showers, bar, trolley hire, shop
Visitors welcome weekdays by prior arrangement
Societies welcome by prior arrangement

BARTON-ON-SEA GOLF CLUB

Milford Road, New Milton, Hampshire BH25 5PP
✆ 01425 615308 Fax 01425 612457
Map 4, C7
bosgolfc.uk@mcmail.com
www.barton-on-sea-golf.co.uk
Off B3058, M27 Jct 1
Founded 1897
Magnificent sea views are the order of the day from this cliff-top site with three loops of 9 holes providing a number of playing options. The fresh fish lunch on a Friday is not to be missed.
18 holes, 6521 yards
par 72, S.S.S 71
Designer J. Hamilton Stutt
Green fees £30
Catering, changing room/showers, bar, trolley and buggy hire, shop, practice facilities, 9-hole course
Visitors welcome, with restrictions.
Handicap certificate required
Societies welcome by prior arrangement
🏨 The Chewton Glen Hotel, Christchurch Road, New Milton, Hampshire BH25 6QS
✆ 01425 275341

BASINGSTOKE GOLF CLUB

Kempshott Park, Kempshott, Basingstoke, Hampshire RG23 7LL
✆ 01256 465990 Fax 01256 331793
Map 4, E4
A30, 3 miles W of Basingstoke, M3 Jct 7
Founded 1928
Laid out in an old park with stately trees enhancing the scene and thwarting erratic golf.
18 holes, 6343 yards
par 70, S.S.S 70
Designer James Braid
Green fees £28
Catering, changing room/showers, bar, club, trolley and buggy hire, shop, practice facilities, conference facilities
Visitors welcome weekdays
Handicap certificate required
Societies welcome by prior arrangement
🏨 Audley's Wood Thistle Hotel, Basingstoke, Hampshire
✆ 01256 314769

BISHOPSWOOD GOLF COURSE

Bishopswood Lane, Tadley, Basingstoke, Hampshire RG26 4AT
✆ 0118 9812200 Fax 0118 9408606
Map 4, E3
www.bishopswoodgolfcourse.co.uk
Off A340, 6 miles N of Basingstoke
Founded 1976
The longest 9-hole course in Hampshire, and venue for the 'National Nines' regional final, 2001.
9 holes, 6474 yards
par 72, S.S.S 71
Designer Phillips and Blake
Green fees £16.50
Catering, changing room/showers, bar, club and trolley hire, shop, driving range, conference room
Visitors welcome, with restrictions
Societies welcome by prior arrangement
🏨 Hinds Head, Aldermaston, Berkshire
✆ 01189 712194

BLACKMOOR GOLF CLUB

Firgrove Road, Whitehill, Bordon, Hampshire GU35 9EH
✆ 01420 472775 Fax 01420 487666
Map 4, F5
ctupper@blackmoorgolf.co.uk
www.blackmoorgolf.co.uk
Off A325
Founded 1913
The Selborne Salver, one of the principal tournaments in the amateur calendar always attracts a strong field. By contemporary standards this is not a long course, but with so many manly par 4s, such as the 4th and 10th, strong players are favoured. The 18th is a first class finishing hole.
18 holes, 6164 yards
par 69, S.S.S 69
Designer Harry Colt
Green fees £34
Catering, changing room/showers, bar, trolley hire, shop, practice facilities, conference facilities
Visitors welcome weekdays
Handicap certificate required
Societies welcome by prior arrangement
🏨 The Grange Hotel, London Road, Alton, Hampshire
✆ 01420 86565

BLACKNEST GOLF CLUB

Frith End, Binsted, Hampshire GU34 4QL
✆ 01420 22888 Fax 01420 22001
Map 4, F4
Off A31, at Bentley
Founded 1993
Water is a hazard on many holes of this challenging pay-and-play course.
18 holes, 6019 yards
par 69, S.S.S 69
Green fees £14
Catering, changing room/showers, bar, club and trolley hire, shop, driving range, gymnasium
Visitors welcome
Societies welcome by prior arrangement

BLACKWATER VALLEY GOLF CLUB

Chandlers Lane, Yateley, Surrey GU46 7SZ
✆ 01252 874725 Fax 01252 874725
Map 4, F3
B3272, 5 miles W of Camberley
Founded 1994
A parkland course with a number of lakes.
9 holes, 2365 yards
par 66, S.S.S 66
Designer H.J. Allenby
Green fees £7
Catering, changing room/showers, bar, club and trolley hire, shop, driving range
Visitors welcome
Societies welcome by prior arrangement

BOTLEY PARK HOTEL GOLF & COUNTRY CLUB

Winchester Road, Boorley Green, Botley, Hampshire SO3 2UA
✆ 01489 780888 Fax 01489 789242
Map 4, E6
B3354, 1 mile NW of Botley
Founded 1989
A hotel course with the almost obligatory quota of lakes.
18 holes, 6341 yards
par 70, S.S.S 70
Designer Charles Potterton
Green fees £30
Catering, changing room/showers, bar, accommodation, club, trolley and buggy hire, shop, driving range, practice facilities, extensive leisure and hotel facilities
Visitors welcome weekdays

Handicap certificate required
Societies welcome by prior arrangement
Botley Park Hotel Golf & Country Club, Winchester Road, Boorley Green, Botley, Hampshire
01489 780888

BRAMSHAW GOLF CLUB

Brook, Lyndhurst, Hampshire SO43 7HE
02380 813434 Fax 02380 813460
Map 4, C6
golf@bramshaw.co.uk
www.bramshaw.co.uk
1mile from Jct 1 of M27
Founded 1880
The shorter Forest Course is the oldest in Hampshire, and one of the oldest in England. There are golf-inclusive rates for guests of the Bell Inn.
Forest Course: 18 holes, 5774 yards
par 69, S.S.S 68
Manor Course: 18 holes, 6517 yards
par 71, S.S.S 71
Green fees £18
Catering, changing room/showers, bar, accommodation, club, trolley and buggy hire, shop, practice facilities
Visitors welcome, weekend restrictions
Handicap certificate required
Societies welcome by prior arrangement
The Bell Inn, Brook, Lyndhurst, Hampshire SO43 7HE
02380 812214

BROKENHURST MANOR GOLF CLUB

Sway Road, Brockenhurst, Hampshire SO42 7SG
01590 623332 Fax 01590 624140
Map 4, C7
B3055, 1 mile S of Brockenhurst
Founded 1919
On the edge of the New Forest, with touches of heathland and a meandering stream, Brokenhurst is especially handsome when the trees are in full leaf. Length is at a premium around the turn, with the 8th and 9th very long par 4s, the 10th a 213-yard par 3.
18 holes, 6222 yards
par 70, S.S.S 70
Designer Harry Colt
Green fees £35
Catering, changing room/showers, bar, trolley hire, shop, practice facilities
Visitors welcome by prior arrangement
Handicap certificate required
Societies welcome by prior arrangement

THE BURLEY GOLF CLUB

Cott Lane, Burley, Ringwood, Hampshire BH24 4BB
01425 402431 Fax 01425 402431
Map 4, C6
Off A31 at Picket Post, 4 miles SE
Founded 1905
A little gem in the heart of the New Forest with 18 tees for its nine holes.
9 holes, 6149 yards
par 71, S.S.S 69
Green fees £16
Changing room/showers, bar, trolley hire, practice facilities
Visitors welcome
Handicap certificate required – limit: 28 men, 45 women
No societies
Moorhill House Hotel, Moorhill, Burley, Ringwood, Hampshire BH24 4AH
01425 403285

CAMS HALL ESTATE GOLF CLUB

Cams Hall Estate, Fareham, Hampshire PO16 8UP
01329 827222 Fax 01329 827111
Map 4, E6
A27 (M27 Jct 11)
Founded 1993
The Creek Course is seaside in nature with salt water lakes and dune-like hills. In contrast, the Park Course is more inland in character.
Creek Course: 18 holes, 6244 yards
par 71, S.S.S 70
Park Course: 9 holes, 3247 yards
par 36, S.S.S 36
Designer Peter Alliss, Clive Clark
Green fees £20
Catering, changing room/showers, bar, club, trolley and buggy hire, shop, practice facilities
Visitors welcome
Societies welcome by prior arrangement

CHEWTON GLEN HOTEL GOLF CLUB

Christchurch Road, New Milton, Hampshire BH25 6QS
01425 275341 Fax 01425 272310
Map 4, C7
reservations@chewtonglen.com
www.chewtonglen.com
A35 from Lyndhurst
Founded 1965
A very comfortable hotel with a pretty par-3 course laid out in the beautiful gardens.
9 holes, 854 yards
par 27
Catering, changing room/showers, bar, accommodation, club hire, shop, practice facilities, full conference & hotel facilities
Visitors: open to hotel guests only
The Chewton Glen Hotel, Christchurch Road, New Milton, Hampshire BH25 6QS
01425 275341

CHILWORTH GOLF CLUB

Main Road, Chilworth, Southampton, Hampshire SO16 7JP
023 8074 0544 Fax 023 8073 3166 **Map 4, D6**
A27 between Chilworth and Romsey
Founded 1989
Quite a challenging parkland course with a number of water hazards.
18 holes, 5837 yards
par 69, S.S.S 69
Green fees £12
Catering, changing room/showers, bar, trolley hire, shop, driving range
Visitors welcome with booking system
Societies welcome by prior arrangement
Hilton Hotel, Bracken Place, Chilworth, Hampshire
02380 702700

CORHAMPTON GOLF CLUB

Corhampton, Southampton, Hampshire SO32 3LP
01489 877279 Fax 01489 877680
Map 4, E6
Off B3035, 8 miles E of Southampton
Founded 1891
A handsome course in the Meon Valley.
18 holes, 6444 yards
par 71, S.S.S 71
Green fees £24
Catering, changing room/showers, bar, trolley and buggy hire, shop, practice facilities
Visitors welcome weekdays
Societies welcome by prior arrangement

DEAN FARM GOLF COURSE

Dean Farm, Kingsley, Bordon, Hampshire GU35 9NG
01420 489478 **Map 4, F4**
B3004, between Bordon and Alton
Founded 1984
Useful executive-length course in the Hampshire countryside.
9 holes, 1500 yards
par 29
Green fees £4.50
Bar, club hire, tennis
Visitors welcome
Societies welcome by prior arrangement
The Grange Hotel, London Road,

Alton, Hampshire
✆ 01420 86565

DIBDEN GOLF CENTRE

Main Road, Dibden, Southampton, Hampshire SO45 5TB
✆ 023 8084 5596 Fax 023 8084 5596 **Map 4, D6**
Off A326, at Dibden
Founded 1974
A parkland course looking towards the sea, with all the off-course facilities expected these days.
18 holes, 5986 yards
par 70, S.S.S 69
Designer J. Hamilton Stutt
Green fees £10
Catering, changing room/showers, bar, club and trolley hire, shop, driving range, practice facilities, par-3 course
Visitors welcome
Societies welcome by prior arrangement

DUMMER GOLF CLUB

Dummer, Basingstoke, Hampshire RG25 2AR
✆ 01256 397888 Fax 01256 397889
Map 4, E4
www.dummergc.co.uk
M3 Jct 7
Founded 1992
A scenic course with good facilities.
18 holes, 6377 yards
par 72, S.S.S 70
Designer Peter Alliss, Clive Clark
Green fees £27
Catering, changing room/showers, bar, club, trolley and buggy hire, shop, practice facilities
Visitors welcome
Societies welcome by prior arrangement

DUNWOOD MANOR GOLF CLUB

Danes Road, Awbridge, Near Romsey, Hampshire SO51 0GF
✆ 01794 340549 Fax 01794 341215
Map 4, C5
admin@dunwood-golf.co.uk
www.dunwood-golf.co.uk
Off A27, 4 miles from Romsey
Founded 1970
Set in lovely Hampshire countryside, bordered by ancient woodlands, Dunwood Manor is as pretty as a picture, and is linked with both courses at Bramshaw.
18 holes, 5767 yards
par 69, S.S.S 68
Green fees £24
Catering, changing room/showers, bar, accommodation, club, trolley and buggy hire, shop, practice facilities, self catering lodge accommodation
Visitors welcome weekdays – restricted weekends
Societies welcome by prior arrangement
🏨 The Bell Inn, Brook, Lyndhurst, Hampshire SO43 7HE
✆ 02380 812214

FAREHAM WOODS GOLF CLUB

West Drive, Whiteley, Fareham, Hampshire PO15 6RS
✆ 01329 84441 Fax 01329 84442
Map 4, E6
M27 Jct 9, 6 miles W of Fareham
Founded 1997
A parkland course.
18 holes, 5662 yards
par 70, S.S.S 67
Green fees £15
Catering, changing room/showers, bar, club and trolley hire, shop, practice facilities
Visitors welcome weekdays
Societies welcome by prior arrangement

FLEETLANDS GOLF CLUB

Fareham Road, Gosport, Hampshire PO13 0AW
✆ 023 9254 4492 **Map 4, E6**
Off A32, 2 miles S of Fareham.
Founded 1963
A private members' club.
9 holes, 4852 yards
S.S.S 64
Green fees £5
Visitors welcome only as members' guests
No societies

FLEMING PARK GOLF CLUB

Fleming Park, Magpie Lane, Eastleigh, Hampshire SO50 9LH
✆ 023 8061 2797 **Map 4, E6**
M27/A27, E of Eastleigh
Founded 1973
A parkland course.
18 holes, 4436 yards
par 65, S.S.S 62
Green fees £7.50
Catering, changing room/showers, bar, club, trolley and buggy hire, shop, practice facilities
Visitors welcome
Societies welcome by prior arrangement

FOUR MARKS GOLF CLUB

Headmore Lane, Four Marks, Alton, Hampshire GU34 3ES
✆ 01420 587214 Fax 01420 587313
Map 4, F5
Off A31, 6 miles S of Alton
Founded 1994
With its elevated location there are fine views over the Hampshire countryside, and its free-draining ground contributes to practicable winter golf. An ash tree, 50 yards in front of the 1st tee, is a novel obstacle.
9 holes, 4354 yards
par 62, S.S.S 60
Designer Don Wright
Green fees £7.95
Catering, changing room/showers, bar, club and trolley hire, shop
Visitors welcome
Societies welcome by prior arrangment
🏨 Wykeham Arms, 75 Kingsgate Street, Winchester, Hampshire SO23 9PE
✆ 01962 853834 Fax 01962 854411

FURZELEY GOLF CLUB

Furzeley Road, Denmead, Hampshire PO7 6TX
✆ 023 9223 1180 Fax 023 9223 0921 **Map 4, E6**
2 miles NW of Waterlooville
Founded 1993
A pretty parkland course which plays more challegingly than the statistics alone imply. Lakes come into play on several holes.
18 holes, 4363 yards
par 62, S.S.S 61
Designer Mark Sale
Green fees £10
Catering, changing room/showers, bar, club and trolley hire, shop, practice facilities
Visitors welcome with booking system
Societies welcome by prior arrangement

GOSPORT & STOKES BAY GOLF CLUB

Fort Road, Haslar, Gosport, Hampshire PO12 2AT
✆ 023 9258 1625 Fax 023 9252 7941 **Map 4, E7**
Off A32, 1 mile S of Gosport
Founded 1885
A 9-hole course in a splendid location, overlooking the Solent and Spithead.
9 holes, 5995 yards
par 70, S.S.S 69
Green fees £15
Catering, changing room/showers, bar, club and trolley hire
Visitors welcome with restrictions
Societies welcome by prior arrangement

THE HAMPSHIRE GOLF CLUB

Winchester Road, Goodworth Clatford, Andover, Hampshire SP11 7TB
✆ 01264 357555 Fax 01264 356606
Map 4, D4

A3057, ½ mile S of Andover
Founded 1993
A recent downland course.
18 holes, 6376 yards
S.S.S 70
Designer T. Fiducia, A Mitchell
Green fees £15
Catering, changing room/showers, bar, club and trolley hire, shop, driving range, practice facilities
Visitors welcome
Societies welcome by prior arrangement

HARTLEY WINTNEY GOLF CLUB

London Road, Hartley Wintney, Basingstoke, Hampshire RG27 8PT
☎ 01252 842214 Fax 01252 842214
Map 4, F3
A30, 5 miles W of Camberley
Founded 1891
A parkland course.
9 holes, 6096 yards
par 70, S.S.S 69
Green fees £25
Catering, changing room/showers, bar, trolley hire, shop
Visitors welcome with restrictions
Societies welcome by prior arrangement

HAYLING GOLF CLUB

Links Lane, Hayling Island, Hampshire PO11 0BX
☎ 02392 464491 Fax 02392 464446
Map 4, F7
hgcltd@aol.com
www.haylinggolf.co.uk
SW corner of Hayling Island
Founded 1883
A classic links – one of the oldest in the country – with two famous holes, the 12th (Desert) and 13th (Widow). But the fine qualities of holes such as the 3rd, 6th and 8th, should not be ignored, with their cunningly constricted fairways. The closing stretch is much threatened by gorse.
18 holes, 6531 yards
par 71, S.S.S 71
Designer J.H. Taylor, Tom Simpson
Green fees £32
Catering, changing room/showers, bar, club and trolley hire, shop, practice facilities, conference facilities
Visitors welcome, restricted weekends
Handicap certificate required
Societies welcome by prior arrangement
🏨 Newtown House Hotel, Manor Road, Hayling Island, Hampshire PO11 0QR
☎ 02392 466131

HOCKLEY GOLF CLUB

Twyford, Winchester, Hampshire SO21 1PL
☎ 01962 713165 Fax 01962 713612
Map 4, D5
hockleygolfclub@aol.com
www.hockleygolfclub.org.uk
M3 Jct 11, towards Twyford
Founded 1914
There are superb views of Winchester and the surrounding countryside from these downland fairways. Holes such as the 4th and 7th really stretch the golfer, and the view from the 17th green is magical.
18 holes, 6336 yards
par 71, S.S.S 71
Designer James Braid
Green fees £33
Catering, changing room/showers, bar, trolley and buggy hire, shop, practice facilities
Visitors welcome, with restrictions
Societies welcome by prior arrangement
🏨 Wykeham Arms, 75 Kingsgate Street, Winchester, Hampshire SO23 9PE
☎ 01962 853834 Fax 01962 854411

LECKFORD GOLF CLUB

Leckford, Stockbridge, Hampshire SO20 6JS
☎ 01264 810320 Fax 01264 810429
Map 4, D5
Off A3057, 2 miles N of Stockbridge
Founded 1929
Two courses, part of the facilities available to employees of the John Lewis Partnership.
New Course: 9 holes, 2281 yards
par 66,
Old Course: 9 holes, 3251 yards
par 70, S.S.S 71
Green fees £10
Changing room/showers, shop
Visitors welcome only as members' guests
No societies

LEE-ON-THE-SOLENT GOLF CLUB

Brune Lane, Lee-on-the-Solent, Hampshire PO13 9PB
☎ 023 9255 0207 Fax 023 9255 4233 **Map 4, E7**
www.mod60.com/leegolf
B3385, ½ mile N of Lee-on-the-Solent
Founded 1905
A course with a reputation for difficulty especially over the last six holes.
18 holes, 5933 yards
par 69, S.S.S 69
Green fees £30
Catering, changing room/showers, bar, trolley hire, shop, driving range, practice facilities
Visitors welcome weekdays
Societies welcome by prior arrangement

LIPHOOK GOLF CLUB

Wheatsheaf Enclosure, Liphook, Hampshire GU30 7EH
☎ 01428 723271 Fax 01428 724853
Map 4, G5
liphookgolfclub@btconnect.com
B2030, 1 mile S of Liphook
Founded 1922
For many golfers the perfect heath-and-heather course, with classic holes aplenty, such as the excellent par-4 2nd and 4th. A stream enlivens the parallel 12th and 13th, very attractive holes, while an approach over humps and bumps makes the secretive 9th tricky. All five short holes are first rate.
18 holes, 6167 yards
par 70, S.S.S 69
Designer Arthur Croome
Green fees £35
Catering, changing room/showers, bar, club, trolley and buggy hire, shop, practice facilities
Visitors welcome, restricted weekends
Handicap certificate required– limit: 28 men, 40 women
Societies welcome by prior arrangement

MARRIOTT MEON VALLEY HOTEL GOLF & COUNTRY CLUB

Sandy Lane, Shedfield, Southampton, Hampshire SO32 2HQ
☎ 01329 833455 Fax 01329 834411
Map 4, E6
marriott.com/marriott/sougs
A334 between Wickham and Botley
Founded 1977
Two charming Hamilton Stutt courses in mature parkland with streams, ditches and ponds to thwart the reckless. The 9-hole Valley Course was built around the remains of a Roman village. The 448-yard 2nd on the Meon Course is toughest, but beware the water on the 12th and 17th!
Meon Course: 18 holes, 6520 yards
par 71, S.S.S 71
Designer J Hamilton Stutt
Valley Course: 9 holes, 5758 yards
par 70, S.S.S 66
Green fees £34
Catering, changing room/showers, bar, accommodation, club, trolley and buggy hire, shop, driving range, practice facilities, full hotel & leisure facilities
Visitors welcome by prior

arrangement
Societies welcome by prior arrangement
Marriott Meon Valley Hotel Golf & Country Club, Sandy Lane, Shedfield, Hampshire SO32 2HQ
01329 833455

NEW FOREST GOLF CLUB

Southampton Road, Lyndhurst, Hampshire SO43 7BU
02380 282752 Fax 01380 282484
Map 4, C6
barbera@sagehost.co.uk
www.nfgc.sageweb.co.uk
A35, ½ mile from Lyndhurst
Founded 1888
An attractive course in the heart of the New Forest with ponies and deer roaming free. It may appear short on paper, but note the 585-yard 3rd, and 250-yard par-3 8th.
18 holes, 5772 yards
par 69, S.S.S 68
Green fees £12
Catering, changing room/showers, bar, club and trolley hire, shop, practice facilities
Visitors welcome – restricted Sunday
Societies welcome by prior arrangement
Heather House Hotel, Southampton Road, Lyndhurst, Hampshire
01703 284409

NORTH HANTS GOLF CLUB

Minley Road, Fleet, Hampshire GU51 1RF
01252 616443 Fax 01252 811627
Map 4, F3
secretary@north-hants-fleetgc.co.uk
www.north-hants-fleetgc.co.uk
B3013, 3 miles W of Farnborough, M3 Jct 4A
Founded 1904
Recent changes have introduced a new par-5 water hole, the 3rd. Otherwise this is very much a model heath-and-heather course with several fine strategic par-4s, notably the 11th and 16th. The railway line which threatens the fade on the 16th also induces caution on the par-5 17th.
18 holes, 6519 yards
par 71, S.S.S 72
Designer James Braid, Donald Steel
Green fees £32
Catering, changing room/showers, bar, trolley hire, shop, practice facilities
Visitors welcome weekdays
Handicap certificate required
Societies welcome by prior arrangement
Lismoyne Links, Fleet, Hampshire
01252 628555

OLD THORNS GOLF CLUB

Longmoor Road, Griggs Green, Liphook, Hampshire GU30 7PE
01428 724555 Fax 01428 725036
Map 4, F5
Off A3 at Griggs Green
Founded 1982
A challenging parkland/heathland course with full off-course facilities including Japanese and European restaurants.
18 holes, 6533 yards
par 72, S.S.S 71
Designer John Harris, Peter Alliss, Dave Thomas.
Green fees £35
Catering, changing room/showers, bar, club, trolley and buggy hire, shop, driving range, practice facilities, swimming pool, gymnasium & tennis courts
Visitors welcome by prior arrangement
Societies welcome by prior arrangement

OTTERBOURNE GOLF CENTRE

Poles Lane, Otterbourne, Winchester, Hampshire SO21 2EL
01962 775225 **Map 4, D5**
A31, between Hursley and Otterbourne
Founded 1995
A diminutive public parkland course.
9 holes, 1939 yards
par 30
Green fees £4
Visitors welcome
Societies welcome by prior arrangement

THE PARK GOLF COURSE

Avington, Winchester, Hampshire SO21 1DA
01962 779945 Fax 01962 779530
Map 4, E5
M3 Jct 9, E of Winchester
Founded 1995
Good value 9-hole course.
9 holes, 3808 yards
par 61, S.S.S 58
Designer R. Stent
Green fees £6.80
Club and trolley hire
Visitors welcome
Societies welcome by prior arrangement

PAULTONS GOLF CENTRE

Old Salisbury Road, Ower, Romsey, Hampshire SO51 6AN
023 8081 3992 Fax 023 8081 3993 **Map 4, D6**
M27 Jct 2, towards Ower
Founded 1993
Laid out in an aristocratic old country park, very beautiful.
18 holes, 6238 yards
par 71, S.S.S 70
9 holes, 1324 yards
par 27, S.S.S 27
Green fees £16
Catering, changing room/showers, bar, club, trolley and buggy hire, shop, driving range, practice facilities
Visitors welcome
Societies welcome by prior arrangement

PETERSFIELD GOLF CLUB

Tankerdale Lane, Liss, Hampshire GU33 7QY
01730 895216 Fax 01730 894713
Map 4, F5
richard@petersfieldgolfclub.co.uk
www.petersfieldgolfclub.co.uk
Off A3, after B3006
Founded 1892
An old club which relocated to a new Martin Hawtree course in 1997, in lovely surrounding countryside. the old course is now operated on a pay-and-play basis.
18 holes, 6387 yards
par 72, S.S.S 71
Designer Martin Hawtree
Green fees £25
Catering, changing room/showers, bar, trolley and buggy hire, shop, practice facilities
Visitors welcome, restricted weekends
Societies welcome by prior arrangement
Southdowns Country Hotel, Trotton, Hants, Hampshire
01730 821521

PETERSFIELD SUSSEX ROAD GOLF CLUB

Sussex Road, Petersfield, Hampshire GU31 4EJ
01730 267732 **Map 4, F5**
B214, Sussex Road at Petersfield
Founded 1892
The old Petersfield golf course, run by the club as a pay-and-play facility.
9 holes, 6010 yards
par 72, S.S.S 69
Green fees £6
Changing room/showers, trolley hire, shop
Visitors welcome with booking system
Societies welcome by prior arrangement

PORTSMOUTH GOLF CLUB

Crookhorn Lane, Widley, Waterlooville, Hampshire PO7 5QL
023 9237 2210 Fax 023 9220

0766 **Map 4, E6**
www.portsmouthgc.com
2/3 mile from junction of A3 and B2177
Founded 1972
A public course on a hillside enjoying fine views of Portsmouth Harbour and the Isle of Wight.
18 holes, 6139 yards
par 69, S.S.S 70
Designer Hawtree
Green fees £13.50
Catering, changing room/showers, bar, club and trolley hire, shop, practice facilities, function room
Visitors welcome
Societies welcome by prior arrangement
Bear Hotel, Havant, Hampshire
02392 486501

ROMSEY GOLF CLUB

Nursling, Southampton, Hampshire SO16 0XW
023 8073 2218 Fax 023 8074 1036 **Map 4, D6**
A3057, 2 miles S of Romsey
Founded 1900
A handsome, undulating parkland course overlooking the Test Valley.
18 holes, 5856 yards
par 69, S.S.S 68
Green fees £23
Catering, changing room/showers, bar, trolley hire, shop
Visitors welcome weekdays
Societies welcome by prior arrangement

ROWLANDS CASTLE GOLF CLUB

Links Lane, Rowlands Castle, Hampshire PO9 6AE
023 9241 2785 Fax 023 9241 3649 **Map 4, F6**
B2149 for 2 miles, A3 (M) Jct 2
Founded 1902
A pretty parkland course with many dog-legged fairways curving through the trees and ingeniously bunkered – the 14th is almost an island in sand. The overall length is long, mainly because there are only three short holes, but, of the par 4s, only the 10th, 15th and 18th exceed 400 yards.
18 holes, 6612 yards
par 72, S.S.S 72
Designer Harry Colt
Green fees £30
Catering, trolley and buggy hire, shop, practice facilities
Visitors welcome, except Saturdays
Handicap certificate required
Societies welcome by prior arrangement
Old House, Wickham, Hampshire
01329 833049

ROYAL WINCHESTER GOLF CLUB

Sarum Road, Winchester, Hampshire SO22 5QE
01962 862473 Fax 01962 865048
Map 4, E5
manager@royalwinchestergolfclub.com
www.royalwinchestergolfclub.com
W of Winchester, M3 Jct 11
Founded 1888
Something of a classic, much of the course remaining a J.H. Taylor layout of long-standing, despite the intrusions of the Winchester by-pass.
18 holes, 6204 yards
par 71, S.S.S 70
Designer J.H. Taylor
Green fees £33
Catering, changing room/showers, bar, trolley hire, shop, practice facilities
Visitors welcome weekdays
Handicap certificate required
Societies welcome by prior arrangement

SANDFORD SPRINGS GOLF CLUB

Wolverton, Tadley, Hampshire RG26 5RT
01635 296800 Fax 01635 296801
Map 4, E3
Off A339, between Basingstoke and Newbury
Founded 1988
Three 9-hole courses of very different characters, giving wonderful variety, whatever combination of holes is chosen. Lovely views and beautiful surroundings.
The Lakes Course: 9 holes, 3047 yards
par 35
Designer Hawtree & Son
The Park Course: 9 holes, 2944 yards
par 34
The Woods Course: 9 holes, 3157 yards
par 36
Green fees £23
Catering, changing room/showers, bar, club, trolley and buggy hire, shop, practice facilities
Visitors welcome weekdays with prior booking
Societies welcome by prior arrangement

SOMERLEY PARK GOLF CLUB

Somerley, Ringwood, Hampshire BH24 3PL
01425 461496 **Map 4, B6**
5 miles W of Ringwood
Founded 1995
A private course on the Hampshire/Dorset border.
9 holes, 2155 yards
par 33, S.S.S 62
Designer John Jacobs
Green fees £10
Shop
Visitors welcome only as members' guests
Societies welcome by prior arrangement

SOUTH WINCHESTER GOLF CLUB

Romsey Road, Winchester, Hampshire SO22 5QW
01962 840469 Fax 01962 877900
Map 4, D5
swgc@sw.gcm.co.uk
www.southwinchester.com
Jct 11 (M3) S of City on Romsey Road
Founded 1993
While there is an element of links style in this serious and challenging design, it also features a number of lakes, making it a fitting venue for the Hampshire PGA Championship which takes place here on an annual basis. The underlying chalk ensures excellent golfing conditions all year round.
18 holes, 7086 yards
par 72, S.S.S 74
Designer Dave Thomas
Green fees £25
Catering, changing room/showers, bar, club, trolley and buggy hire, shop, driving range, practice facilities, conference facilities
Visitors welcome with weekend restrictions
Societies welcome by prior arrangement
Lainston House, Sparsholt, Hampshire
01962 863588

SOUTHAMPTON MUNICIPAL GOLF CLUB

Golf Course Road, Bassett, Southampton, Hampshire SO16 7AY
023 8076 8407 **Map 4, D6**
Off A33, 4 miles N of Southampton.
Founded 1935
An excellent municipal facility. Would there were more like it!
18 holes, 6218 yards
par 69, S.S.S 70
Green fees £8.20
Catering, changing room/showers, bar, club and trolley hire, practice facilities, 9-hole course
Visitors welcome with booking system
Societies welcome by prior arrangement

SOUTHSEA GOLF CLUB

The Clubhouse, Burtfields Road, Portsmouth, Hampshire PO3 5HH
✆ 023 9266 4549 Fax 023 9265 0525 **Map 4, E7**
Off M27 Jct 12, 1 mile NE of Southsea
Founded 1914
A public parkland course.
18 holes, 5970 yards
par 71, S.S.S 68
Green fees £10.30
Club and trolley hire, shop, driving range
Visitors welcome
Societies welcome by prior arrangement

SOUTHWICK PARK GOLF CLUB

Pinsley Drive, Southwick, Hampshire PO17 6EL
✆ 023 9238 0131 Fax 023 9221 0289 **Map 4, E6**
B2177, at Southwick
Founded 1977
Principally a club for naval personnel, at which a limited number of visitors can be accepted, with particular emphasis on party bookings.
18 holes, 5992 yards
par 69, S.S.S 69
Designer Charles Lawrie
Green fees £10.20
Catering, changing room/showers, bar, club and trolley hire, shop
Visitors welcome by prior arrangement
Societies welcome by prior arrangement

SOUTHWOOD GOLF CLUB

Ively Road, Farnborough, Hampshire GU14 0LJ
✆ 01252 5487 **Map 4, G3**
½ mile W of town centre
Founded 1977
A public parkland course.
18 holes, 5738 yards
par 69, S.S.S 68
Designer Hawtree & Son
Green fees £14
Changing room/showers, club, trolley and buggy hire, shop
Visitors welcome
Societies welcome by prior arrangement

STONEHAM GOLF CLUB

Monks Wood Close, Bassett, Southampton, Hampshire SO16 3TT
✆ 01703 769272 Fax 01703 766320
Map 4, D6
M27 Jct 5, 3 miles N of Southampton
Founded 1908
A most attractive course, but one on which it is very difficult to play to handicap, a fact confirmed by its hosting of the 1993 Brabazon Trophy. Heather, gorse, trees, and the lie of the land pose the biggest problems, while clever bunkering, streams, and sloping greens complete the picture.
18 holes, 6387 yards
par 72, S.S.S 70
Designer Willie Park
Green fees £29
Catering, changing room/showers, bar, club and trolley hire, shop, practice facilities
Visitors welcome, by prior arrangement
Handicap certificate required
Societies welcome by prior arrangement

TEST VALLEY GOLF CLUB

Micheldever Road, Overton, Basingstoke, Hampshire RG25 3DS
✆ 01256 771137 **Map 4, E4**
Off A303, 2 miles S of Overton.
Founded 1992
A testing downland course which has already hosted important tournaments.
18 holes, 6883 yards
par 72, S.S.S 73
Designer Don Wright, Eamon Darcy.
Green fees £16
Catering, changing room/showers, bar, club, trolley and buggy hire, shop, practice facilities
Visitors welcome – restricted weekends
Societies welcome by prior arrangement

TOURNERBURY GOLF CENTRE

Tournerbury Lane, Hayling Island, Hampshire PO11 9DL
✆ 02392 462266 **Map 4, F7**
A27 to Hayling Island
Founded 1996
From this part of Hayling Island there are extensive views over Chichester Harbour.
9 holes, 3000 yards
par 35, S.S.S 69
Green fees £7
Changing room/showers, club and trolley hire, shop, driving range, practice facilities
Visitors welcome
Societies welcome by prior arrangement
Newtown House Hotel, Manor Road, Hayling Island, Hampshire PO11 0QR
✆ 02392 466131

TYLNEY PARK GOLF CLUB

Rotherwick, Basingstoke, Hampshire RG27 9AY
✆ 01256 762079 Fax 01256 763079
Map 4, E4
Off B3349, 2 miles NW of Hook, M3 Jct 5
Founded 1973
A parkland course with fine trees.
18 holes, 6108 yards
par 70, S.S.S 69
Designer W. Wiltshire
Green fees £22
Catering, changing room/showers, bar, club, trolley and buggy hire, shop, practice facilities
Visitors welcome weekdays
Handicap certificate required
Societies welcome by prior arrangement

WATERLOOVILLE GOLF CLUB

Cherry Tree Avenue, Cowplain, Waterlooville, Hampshire PO8 8AP
✆ 023 9226 3388 Fax 023 9234 7513 **Map 4, E6**
www.waterloovillegolfclub.co.uk
B2150, off A3(M)
Founded 1907
A long, tough course with a number of water hazards and testing par 5s.
18 holes, 6602 yards
par 72, S.S.S 72
Designer Sir Henry Cotton
Green fees £25
Catering, changing room/showers, bar, trolley hire, shop, practice facilities
Visitors welcome weekdays
Handicap certificate required
Societies welcome by prior arrangement

WELLOW GOLF CLUB

Ryedown Lane, East Wellow, Romsey, Hampshire SO51 6BD
✆ 01794 322872 Fax 01794 323832
Map 4, C6
Off A36, 2 miles W of Romsey, M27 Jct 2
Founded 1991
Laid out in the parkland surrounding Florence Nightingale's home, the twenty seven holes can be played in three combinations.
Blackwater and Ryedown Course: 18 holes, 5792 yards
par 70, S.S.S 68
Designer W. Wiltshire
Embley and Blackwater Course: 18 holes, 6295 yards
par 72, S.S.S 70
Ryedown and Embley Course: 18 holes, 5939 yards
par 70, S.S.S 69
Green fees £15
Catering, changing room/showers, bar, trolley and buggy hire, shop,

practice facilities, fitness centre
Visitors welcome – restricted weekends
Societies welcome by prior arrangement
Vine Inn, Romsey Road, Ower, Romsey, Hampshire
02380 814333

WEYBROOK PARK GOLF CLUB

Rooksdown Lane, Basingstoke, Hampshire RG24 9NT
01256 333232 Fax 01256 812973
Map 4, E4
secretary@weybrookpark.fsnet.co.uk
Off A339, 2 miles N of town centre
Founded 1993
A friendly club with a smart clubhouse, gentle parkland course, and delightful views.
18 holes, 6500 yards
par 71, S.S.S 71
Green fees £19.50
Catering, changing room/showers, bar, trolley and buggy hire, shop, practice facilities, small conference room
Visitors welcome – restricted competition days
Societies welcome by prior arrangement
Ringway Hotel, Aldermaston Road, Basingstoke, Hampshire
01256 320212

WICKHAM PARK GOLF CLUB

Titchfield Lane, Wickham, Fareham, Hampshire PO17 5PJ
01329 833342 Fax 01329 834798
Map 4, E6
www.wickhampark.co.uk
Off A27, 2 miles N of Fareham, M27 Jct 9
Founded 1995
Excellent value for money, and good facilities at this parkland course set in the Meon Valley.
18 holes, 5898 yards
par 70, S.S.S 68
Green fees £12
Catering, changing room/showers, bar, club, trolley and buggy hire, shop, practice facilities
Visitors welcome – restricted weekends
Societies welcome by prior arrangement – no company days
Old House, Wickham, Hampshire
01329 833049

WORLDHAM PARK GOLF CLUB

Cakers Lane, Worldham, Alton, Hampshire GU34 3AF
01420 543151 **Map 4, F4**
B3004 near Alton
Founded 1993
Challenging course spiced with bunkers and plentiful water.
18 holes, 6209 yards
par 71, S.S.S 70
Designer F. Whidborne
Green fees £11
Catering, changing room/showers, bar, club, trolley and buggy hire, shop, driving range
Visitors welcome
Societies welcome by prior arrangement
Alton House Hotel, Normandy Street, Alton, Hampshire
01420 80033

ISLE OF WIGHT

COWES GOLF CLUB

Crossfield Avenue, Cowes, Isle of Wight PO31 8HN
01983 292303 **Map 4, D7**
Near Cowes High School
Founded 1909
Compact parkland course with views over the Solent. The 415-yard, dog-leg 4th is Stroke 1, but the short holes are perhaps more unforgiving.
9 holes, 5878 yards
par 70, S.S.S 68
Designer J. Hamilton Stutt
Green fees £15
Catering, changing room/showers, bar, trolley hire
Visitors welcome, with restrictions
Societies welcome by prior arrangement
New Holmwood Hotel, Esplanade, Cowes, Isle of Wight
01983 292508

FRESHWATER BAY GOLF CLUB

Afton Down, Freshwater, Isle of Wight PO40 9TZ
01983 752955 Fax 01983 756704
Map 4, D7
www.isle-of-wight.uk.com/golf
A3055, overlooking Freshwater Bay
Founded 1894
A downland course overlooking the sea with superb views.
18 holes, 5725 yards
par 69, S.S.S 68
Designer J.H. Taylor
Green fees £20
Catering, changing room/showers, bar, club and trolley hire
Visitors welcome with restrictions
Societies welcome by prior arrangement

NEWPORT GOLF CLUB

St George's Down, Shide, Newport, Isle of Wight PO30 3BA
01983 525076 **Map 4, E7**
A3056/A3020, ½ mile S of Newport
Founded 1896
An upland course with extensive views, over the island and out to sea.
9 holes, 5674 yards
par 68, S.S.S 68
Designer Guy Hunt
Green fees £15
Catering, changing room/showers, bar, club hire
Visitors welcome weekdays with restrictions
Societies welcome by prior arrangement

OSBORNE GOLF CLUB

Osborne House Estate, East Cowes, Isle of Wight PO32 6JX
01983 295421 **Map 4, E7**
In grounds of Osborne House, 1 mile from East Cowes ferry terminal
Founded 1904
Delightful parkland course in the grounds of Osborne House. A few holes are known to have existed in Queen Victoria's time. Officers of the Royal Naval College expanded the course to 9 holes, before the then professional at (late lamented) Royal Isle of Wight put the finishing touches to it.
9 holes, 6398 yards
par 70, S.S.S 70
Green fees £20
Catering, changing room/showers, bar, club, trolley and buggy hire, shop, practice facilities
Visitors welcome – restricted weekends
Societies welcome by prior arrangement
Fountain Hotel, Cowes, Isle of Wight
01983 292397

RYDE GOLF CLUB

Binstead Road, Ryde, Isle of Wight PO33 3NF
01983 614809 Fax 01983 567418
Map 4, E7
A3054, 1 mile W of Ryde
Founded 1895
A compact parkland course overlooking the Solent.
9 holes, 5287 yards
par 66, S.S.S 66
Designer J. Hamilton Stutt
Green fees £15
Catering, changing room/showers, bar, club and trolley hire, shop
Visitors welcome weekdays with restrictions
Societies welcome by prior arrangement

SHANKLIN & SANDOWN GOLF CLUB

The Fairway, Lake, Sandown, Isle of Wight PO36 9PR
☎ 01983 404424 Fax 01983 404424
Map 4, E7
At Lake, off main Newport Road to Sandown
Founded 1900
The longer of the two 18-hole layouts on the Isle of Wight, with undulating heathland fairways and more than a touch of links-like quality.
18 holes, 6063 yards
par 70, S.S.S 69
Designer James Braid
Green fees £25
Catering, changing room/showers, bar, club and trolley hire, shop, practice facilities
Visitors welcome – restricted weekends
Handicap certificate required
Societies welcome by prior arrangmenet

VENTNOR GOLF CLUB

Steephill Down Road, Ventnor, Isle of Wight PO38 1BP
☎ 01983 853326 **Map 4, E8**
Off B3327, ½ mile W of Ventnor
Founded 1892
A downland course with magnificent seascapes.
12 holes, 5767 yards
par 70, S.S.S 68
Green fees £15
Catering, changing room/showers, bar, club and trolley hire
Visitors welcome weekdays
Societies welcome by prior arrangement

KENT

AMERICAN GOLF AT ORPINGTON

Sandy Lane, St Paul's Cray, Orpington, Kent BR7 6PT
☎ 01689 839677 Fax 01689 891428
Map 16, G7
orpington@americangolf.co.uk
www.americangolf.com
Off A20 at Ruxley Roundabout at Sidcup
Founded 1972
A complex of two full size courses plus executive golf, range etc.
Cray Valley Course: 18 holes, 5669 yards
par 70, S.S.S 67
Ruxley Park Course: 18 holes, 5712 yards
par 70, S.S.S 68
Green fees £16
Catering, changing room/showers, bar, club, trolley and buggy hire, shop, driving range, practice facilities, bar for hire – parties, weddings, etc
Visitors welcome
Societies welcome by prior arrangement
🏨 Eltham Hotel, 31 Westmount Road, Eltham, London SE9
☎ 02088 508222

AQUARIUS GOLF CLUB

Marmora Road, Honor Oak, London SE22 0RY
☎ 020 8693 1626 **Map 16, E6**
Off A2, at Honor Oak
Founded 1913
An unusual little course laid out over an enclosed reservoir, with novel hazards in the form of pipes and vents.
9 holes, 5246 yards
par 66, S.S.S 66
Changing room/showers, bar
Visitors welcome only as members' guests
No societies

ASHFORD GOLF CLUB

Sandyhurst Lane, Ashford, Kent TN25 4NT
☎ 01233 620180 Fax 01233 622655
Map 5, E4
M20 Jct 9, 2 miles NW of Ashford
Founded 1903
A testing parkland course with expansive views.
18 holes, 6284 yards
par 71, S.S.S 70
Designer C.K. Cotton
Green fees £22
Catering, changing room/showers, bar, trolley hire, shop, practice facilities
Visitors welcome weekdays
Handicap certificate required
Societies welcome by prior arrangement

AUSTIN LODGE GOLF CLUB

Eynsford, Swanley, Kent DA4 0HU
☎ 01322 863000 Fax 01322 862406
Map 16, G7
A225, beside Eynsford Station
Founded 1991
A long (over 7000 yards) parkland course laid out in three separate valleys.
18 holes, 7118 yards
par 73, S.S.S 73
Designer Peter Bevan, Mike Walsh
Green fees £18
Catering, changing room/showers, bar, club, trolley and buggy hire, shop, practice facilities
Visitors welcome
Societies welcome by prior arrangement

BARNEHURST GOLF CLUB

Mayplace Road East, Bexleyheath, Kent DA7 6JU
☎ 01322 551205 Fax 01322 523860
Map 16, G6
Between Bexleyheath and Crayford
Founded 1903
A very old public facility with a James Braid pedigree and good greens.
9 holes, 2535 yards
par 66, S.S.S 66
Designer James Braid
Green fees £11.50
Catering, changing room/showers, bar, club and trolley hire, shop, practice facilities
Visitors welcome
Societies welcome by prior arrangement
🏨 Posthouse Hotel, Southwold Road, Bexley, Kent
☎ 01322 526900

BEARSTED GOLF CLUB

Ware Street, Bearsted, Kent ME14 4PQ
☎ 01622 738198 Fax 01622 735608
Map 5, D3
2½ miles E of Maidstone, M20 Jct 7
Founded 1895
Parkland course within sight of the North Downs.
18 holes, 6439 yards
par 71, S.S.S 71
Green fees £30
Catering, changing room/showers, bar, trolley hire, shop, practice facilities
Visitors welcome weekdays
Handicap certificate required
Societies welcome by prior arrangement
🏨 Hilton Maidstone, Bearsted Road, Maidstone, Kent
☎ 01622 734322

BECKENHAM PLACE PARK GOLF CLUB

Beckenham Hill Road, Beckenham, Kent BR3 2BP
☎ 020 8650 2292 Fax 020 8663 1201 **Map 16, E6**
A222 off A21
Founded 1907
A public course in a pleasant parkland setting, on which the back nine presents a difficult test.
18 holes, 5722 yards
par 68, S.S.S 68
Green fees £7.60
Catering, changing room/showers, bar, club and trolley hire, shop, practice facilities, tennis courts
Visitors welcome
Societies welcome by prior arrangement

BEXLEYHEATH GOLF CLUB

Mount Road, Bexleyheath, Kent BR8 7RJ
✆ 020 8303 6951 **Map 16, G6**
1 mile SW of Bexleyheath, off Upton Road
Founded 1907
Undulating parkland course.
9 holes, 5239 yards
par 66, S.S.S 66
Green fees £20
Catering, changing room/showers, bar
Visitors welcome weekdays
Societies welcome by prior arrangement

BIRCHWOOD PARK GOLF CENTRE

Birchwood Road, Wilmington, Dartford, Kent DA2 7HJ
✆ 01322 660554 Fax 01322 667283
Map 16, G7
B258, between Dartford and Swanley
Founded 1990
The extensive facilities at Birchwood Park include a course of considerable challenge as well as the executive length Orchard Course.
Main: 18 holes, 6364 yards
par 71, S.S.S 70
Orchard Course: 9 holes, 1349 yards
par 29
Green fees £15.50
Catering, changing room/showers, bar, club, trolley and buggy hire, shop, driving range, gymnasium, sauna
Visitors welcome
Societies welcome by prior arrangement

BOUGHTON GOLF CLUB

Brickfield Lane, Boughton, Faversham, Kent ME13 9AJ
✆ 01227 752277 Fax 012277 752361 **Map 5, F3**
M2 Jct 7
Founded 1993
A rolling course with good views over the Kent countryside.
18 holes, 6452 yards
par 72, S.S.S 71
Designer Philip Sparks
Green fees £16
Catering, changing room/showers, bar, club, trolley and buggy hire, shop, driving range, practice facilities
Visitors welcome
Societies welcome by prior arrangement

BROKE HILL GOLF CLUB

Sevenoaks Road, Halstead, Kent TN14 7HR
✆ 01959 5332255 Fax 01959 532680 **Map 5, C3**
www.brokenhillgolf.co.uk
M25 Jct 4, close to Knockholt Station
Founded 1993
Welshman David Williams has designed some of the most interesting courses in the South East of England during the 1990s. This upland course is heavily bunkered and enjoys good views.
18 holes, 6374 yards
par 72, S.S.S 61
Designer David Williams
Green fees £35
Catering, changing room/showers, bar, club, trolley and buggy hire, shop, practice facilities
Visitors welcome weekdays
Societies welcome by prior arrangement

BROMLEY GOLF CLUB

Magpie Hall Lane, Bromley, Kent BR2 8JF
✆ 020 8462 7014 Fax 020 8462 6916 **Map 16, E7**
A21, 2 miles S of Bromley
Founded 1948
A public parkland course.
9 holes, 5490 yards
par 70, S.S.S 67
Green fees £5.15
Changing room/showers, club and trolley hire, shop
Visitors welcome
Societies welcome by prior arrangement

BROOME PARK GOLF CLUB

Broome Park Estate, Barham, Canterbury, Kent CT4 6QX
✆ 01227 830728 Fax 01227 832591
Map 5, G4
www.broomepark.co.uk
A260, off A2 E of Canterbury
Founded 1981
A long and challenging course in the parkland of a 17th-century house.
18 holes, 6610 yards
par 72, S.S.S 72
Designer Donald Steel
Green fees £28
Catering, changing room/showers, bar, club, trolley and buggy hire, shop, driving range, practice facilities
Visitors welcome
Societies welcome by prior arrangement

CANTERBURY GOLF CLUB

Scotland Hills, Littlebourne Road, Canterbury, Kent CT1 1TW
✆ 01227 453532 Fax 01227 784277
Map 5, F3
www.canterburygolfclub.org.uk
A 257 1 mile E of Canterbury
Founded 1927
The perfect foil to the rigours of the famous Kentish links courses a few miles away, Canterbury is a handsome course in undulating, wooded parkland, although, with a 462-yard par 4 to begin, and a 453-yarder to open the back nine, it is not without its own rigours.
18 holes, 6249 yards
par 70, S.S.S 70
Designer Harry Colt
Green fees £27
Catering, changing room/showers, bar, trolley hire, shop, practice facilities
Visitors welcome weekdays
Handicap certificate required
Societies welcome by prior arrangement

CHART HILLS GOLF CLUB

Weeks Lane, Biddenden, Ashford, Kent TN27 8JX
✆ 01580 292222 Fax 01580 292233
Map 5, E4
info@charthills.co.uk
www.charthills.co.uk
Off A 274 between Headcorn and Biddenden
Founded 1993
Nick Faldo's earliest British essay in golf design is immediately incisive with its profuse bunkering and imaginative use of the ponds and streams of this rolling, wooded site. What makes the course so fascinating is that no two holes are alike, the problems to be solved unique to each.
18 holes, 7119 yards
par 72, S.S.S 74
Designer Nick Faldo
Green fees £200 per tee (up to four players)
Catering, changing room/showers, bar, club, trolley and buggy hire, shop, practice facilities, conference, wedding and function facilities, fitness centre
Visitors welcome except Saturday
Societies welcome by prior arrangement
Bell Inn, Smarden, Ashford, Kent TN27 8PW
✆ 01233 770283 Fax01233 820042

CHELSFIELD LAKES GOLF CENTRE

Court Road, Orpington, Kent BR6 9BX
✆ 01689 896266 Fax 01689 824577
Map 16, G7
A224, off M25 Jct 4
Founded 1992
Laid out on downland, with several holes running through an old

orchard. A lake separates the 9th and 18th holes.
18 holes, 6110 yards
par 71, S.S.S 69
Designer Robert Sandow
9 holes, 1188 yards
par 27
Green fees £15
Catering, changing room/showers, bar, club and trolley hire, shop, driving range
Visitors welcome with booking system
Societies welcome by prior arrangement

CHERRY LODGE GOLF CLUB

Jail Lane, Biggin Hill, Westerham, Kent TN16 3AX
✆ 01959 572250 Fax 01959 540672 **Map 16, F8**
Off A233, 3 miles N of Westerham
Founded 1969
A downland course with excellent views, with many challenging holes.
18 holes, 6652 yards
par 72, S.S.S 73
Designer John Day
Green fees £20
Catering, changing room/showers, bar, trolley and buggy hire, shop, practice facilities
Visitors welcome weekdays
Societies welcome by prior arrangement

CHESTFIELD GOLF CLUB

103 Chestfield Road, Chestfield, Whitstable, Kent CT5 3LU
✆ 01227 794411 Fax 01227 794454 **Map 5, F3**
secretary@chestfield-golfclub.co.uk
www.chestfield-golfclub.co.uk
½ mile from Chestfield Station
Founded 1924
Is there a more beautiful clubhouse in the world? Certainly, there are few older. It dates from the 15th century. The course has been updated by Donald Steel. While the 1st and 18th are the most attractive holes, the most challenging are on Shrub Hill, especially the 552-yard 2nd.
18 holes, 6208 yards
par 70, S.S.S 70
Designer Donald Steel
Green fees £22
Catering, changing room/showers, bar, club, trolley and buggy hire, shop, practice facilities
Visitors welcome – restricted weekends
Societies welcome by prior arrangement
🏨 Marine Hotel, 33 Tankerton Road, Whitstable, Kent CT5 2BE
✆ 01227 272672

CHISLEHURST GOLF CLUB

Camden Place, Camden Park Road, Chislehurst, Kent BR7 5HJ
✆ 020 8467 3055 Fax 020 8295 0874 **Map 16, F6**
Off A20/A222, ½ mile from Chilsehurst Station
Founded 1894
A short parkland course with a historic clubhouse.
18 holes, 5106 yards
par 66, S.S.S 65
Designer Willie Park
Green fees £25
Catering, changing room/showers, bar, club and trolley hire, shop, practice facilities
Visitors welcome weekdays
Societies welcome by prior arrangement

COBTREE MANOR PARK GOLF CLUB

Chatham Road, Bexley, Maidstone, Kent ME14 3AZ
✆ 01622 753276 **Map 5, D3**
A229, off M20 Jct 6
Founded 1984
A municipal parkland course of moderate length.
18 holes, 5611 yards
par 69, S.S.S 69
Designer F. Hawtree
Green fees £14
Changing room/showers, club and trolley hire, shop
Visitors welcome
Societies welcome by prior arrangement

DARENTH VALLEY GOLF CLUB

Station Road, Shoreham, Sevenoaks, Kent TN14 7SA
✆ 01959 522944 Fax 01959 525089 **Map 16, G8**
A225, 4 miles N of Sevenoaks
Founded 1973
Undulating parkland course.
18 holes, 6327 yards
par 72, S.S.S 71
Green fees £15
Catering, changing room/showers, bar, club and trolley hire, shop, fishing
Visitors welcome
Societies welcome by prior arrangement

DARTFORD GOLF CLUB

Dartford Heath, Dartford, Kent DA1 2TN
✆ 01322 223616 **Map 16, G6**
Off A2, at Dartford Heath
Founded 1897
One of the few genuine heathland courses in Kent.
18 holes, 5914 yards
par 69, S.S.S 69
Designer James Braid
Green fees £21
Catering, changing room/showers, bar, trolley hire, shop
Visitors welcome weekdays
Handicap certificate required
Societies welcome by prior arrangement

DEANGATE RIDGE GOLF CLUB

Duxcourt Road, Hoo, Rochester, Kent ME3 8RZ
✆ 01634 251950 **Map 5, D3**
Off A228, 4 miles E of Rochester
Founded 1972
A parkland course.
18 holes, 6300 yards
par 71, S.S.S 70
Designer Hawtree & Son
Catering, changing room/showers, bar, club, trolley and buggy hire, shop, driving range, tennis courts, pitch & putt
Visitors welcome
Societies welcome by prior arrangement

EDENBRIDGE GOLF CLUB & TENNIS CENTRE

Crouch House Road, Edenbridge, Kent TN8 5LQ
✆ 01732 867381 Fax 01732 867029 **Map 16, F9**
david@golf-course-management.com
www.edenbridgegolfclub.com
¼ mile W of Edenbridge
Founded 1972
In verdant countryside on the Kent-Surrey border. there are many water holes, and the Old course greens are built to USGA standards.
Old Course: 18 holes, 6577 yards
par 72, S.S.S 72
New Course: 18 holes, 5605 yards
par 67, S.S.S 68
Green fees £20
Catering, changing room/showers, bar, club, trolley and buggy hire, shop, driving range, practice facilities, additional 9-hole course, extensive conference and banqueting facilities, gymnasium and sauna, tennis courts
Visitors welcome – book in advance
Handicap certificate required.
Societies welcome by prior arrangement
🏨 Jarvis Felbridge Hotel, London Road, East Grinstead, East Sussex
✆ 01342 326992

ELTHAM WARREN GOLF CLUB

Bexley Road, Eltham, London SE9 2PE

020 8850 4477 **Map 16, F6**
secretary@elthamwarren.idps.co.uk
www.elthamwarrengolfclub.co.uk
A210, ½ mile from Eltham station
Founded 1890
One of the few James Braid courses remaining as a 9-hole layout, demanding accuracy.
9 holes, 5840 yards
par 69, S.S.S 68
Designer James Braid
Green fees £25
Catering, changing room/showers, bar, trolley hire, shop, practice facilities, snooker
Visitors welcome weekdays
Handicap certificate required
Societies welcome by prior arrangement
Eltham Hotel, 31 Westmount Road, Eltham, London SE9
020 8850 8222

ETCHINGHILL GOLF CLUB

Canterbury Road, Etchinghill, Folkestone, Kent CT18 8FA
01303 863863 Fax 01303 863210
Map 5, F4
M20 Jct 11/12
Founded 1995
An interesting course with plenty of variety, parkland for the first 9 holes, downland for the back nine.
18 holes, 6121 yards
par 70, S.S.S 69
Designer John Sturdy
Green fees £17
Catering, changing room/showers, bar, club, trolley and buggy hire, shop, practice facilities, par-3 course
Visitors welcome
Societies welcome by prior arrangement

FALCON VALLEY GOLF CLUB

Gay Dawn Farm, Fawkham, Dartford, Kent DA3 8LZ
01474 707559 **Map 16, G7**
E of Brands Hatch, 4 miles S of Dartford
Founded 1987
A parkland course once known as Corinthian Golf Course.
9 holes, 6323 yards
par 72, S.S.S 70
Green fees £15
Catering, changing room/showers, bar, shop
Visitors welcome weekdays
Handicap certificate required
Societies welcome by prior arrangement

FAVERSHAM GOLF CLUB

Belmont Park, Throuley, Faversham, Kent ME13 0HB
01795 890561 Fax 01795 890760
Map 5, E3
M2 Jct 6 (2 miles)
Founded 1902
A very attractive course in a beautiful setting in Belmont Park.
18 holes, 6021 yards
par 70, S.S.S 69
Green fees £30
Catering, changing room/showers, bar, trolley and buggy hire, shop, practice facilities
Visitors welcome weekdays
Handicap certificate required – limit: 28
Societies welcome by prior arrangement
Canterbury Hotel, 71 New Dover Road, Canterbury, Kent CT1 3DZ
01227 450551 Fax 01227 780145
canterbury.hotel@btinternet.com

GILLINGHAM GOLF CLUB

Woodlands Road, Gillingham, Kent ME7 2AP
01634 853017 Fax 01634 574749
Map 5, D3
M2 Jct 4, A2 to Chatham
Founded 1905
James Braid course recently amended by Donald Steel. New clubhouse improves facilities.
18 holes, 5522 yards
par 69, S.S.S 67
Designer James Braid, Donald Steel
Green fees £20
Catering, changing room/showers, bar, club and trolley hire, shop, practice facilities
Visitors welcome weekdays
Handicap certificate required
Societies welcome by prior arrangement
The Honourable Pilot Travel Inn, Watling Street, Gillingham, Kent
01634 261500

HAWKHURST GOLF CLUB

High Street, Hawkhurst, Kent TN18 4JS
01580 754074 Fax 01580 754074
Map 5, D5
hawkhead@tesco.net
A268, 14 miles S of Tunbridge Wells
Founded 1968
A gently rolling parkland course.
9 holes, 5791 yards
par 70, S.S.S 68
Designer Rex Baldock
Green fees £18
Catering, changing room/showers, bar, trolley and buggy hire, shop, practice facilities, function rooms, squash
Visitors welcome weekdays
Handicap certificate required
Societies welcome by prior arrangement
Queens Inn, Rye Road, Hawkhurst, Kent, Kent
01580 753577

HEMSTED FOREST GOLF CLUB

Golford Road, Cranbrook, Kent TN17 4AL
01580 712833 Fax 01580 714274
Map 5, D5
karlstevenson@hemstedforest.co.uk
www.hemstedforest.co.uk
M25 Jct 5, A21, then A262 to Sissinghurst
A very attractive parkland course with lakes and mature trees, and domestic buildings laid out around an oast house.
18 holes, 6305 yards
par 70, S.S.S 71
Green fees £27
Catering, changing room/showers, bar, trolley hire, shop, practice facilities
Visitors welcome – restricted weekends
Handicap certificate required
Societies welcome by prior arrangement
Kennel Holt Hotel, Goudhurst Road, Cranbrook, Kent
01580 712032

HERNE BAY GOLF CLUB

Eddington, Herne Bay, Kent CT6 7PG
01227 374097 **Map 5, G3**
Off A299, at Herne Bay/Canterbury Junction
Founded 1895
Parkland course with sea views.
18 holes, 5567 yards
par 68, S.S.S 68
Designer James Braid
Green fees £18
Catering, changing room/showers, bar, club and trolley hire, shop
Visitors welcome, restricted weekends
Societies welcome by prior arrangement

HEVER GOLF CLUB

Hever Road, Hever, Kent TN8 7NP
01732 700771 Fax 01732 700775
Map 16, G10
www.hever.com
Off A21, between Sevenoaks and Edenbridge
Founded 1993
An interesting, newish course, laid out in historic parkland, in which Anne Boleyn roamed as a child. A stream affects some holes, while mature trees (and new ones planted to supplement them) pose many

problems for the inaccurate.
18 holes, 7002 yards
par 72, S.S.S 75
Designer Peter Nicholson
Green fees £35
Catering, changing room/showers, bar, club, trolley and buggy hire, shop, driving range, practice facilities, tennis, swimming, fishing & gymnasium, additional 9-hole course
Visitors welcome
Handicap certificate required
Societies welcome by prior arrangement

HIGH ELMS GOLF CLUB

High Elms Road, Downe, Orpington, Kent BR6 7SZ
✆ 01689 858175 Fax 01689 856326
Map 16, F7
Off A21, 2 miles E of Downe
Founded 1969
Quite a challenging public parkland course.
18 holes, 6221 yards
par 71, S.S.S 70
Designer Fred Hawtree
Green fees £10.80
Catering, changing room/showers, bar, club, trolley and buggy hire, shop, practice facilities
Visitors welcome
Societies welcome by prior arrangement

HOMELANDS BETTER GOLF CENTRE

Ashford Road, Kingsnorth, Ashford, Kent TN26 1NJ
✆ 01233 661620 Fax 01233 720 553
Map 5, F4
isj@bettergolf.co.uk
www.bettergolf.co.uk
M20 Jct 10
Founded 1994
A Donald Steel design to challenge good golfers while encouraging the beginner.
9 holes, 2250 yards
par 64, S.S.S 62
Designer Donald Steel
Green fees £11
Changing room/showers, bar, club, trolley and buggy hire, shop, driving range, practice facilities
Visitors welcome
Societies welcome by prior arrangement

HYTHE IMPERIAL GOLF CLUB

Prince's Parade, Hythe, Kent CT21 6AE
✆ 01303 233745 Fax 01303 267554
Map 5, F4
www.hytheimperialgolfclub.co.uk
On coast at Hythe
Founded 1950
A 9-hole/18-tee course laid out between the Royal Military Canal and the English Channel. The 2nd/11th is a substantial par 5 not easily tamed.
9 holes, 5560 yards
par 68, S.S.S 66
Green fees £15
Catering, changing room/showers, bar, accommodation, club and trolley hire, shop, practice facilities
Visitors welcome
Societies welcome by prior arrangement
Hythe Imperial, Prince's Parade, Hythe, Kent CT21 6AE
✆ 01303 267441

KINGS HILL GOLF CLUB

Kings Hill, West Malling, Kent ME19 4AF
✆ 01732 875040 Fax 01732 875019
Map 5, D3
Off A228, 3 miles from M20 Jct 4
Founded 1996
A challenging parkland course.
18 holes, 6622 yards
par 72, S.S.S 72
Designer David Williams
Green fees £30
Catering, changing room/showers, bar, club and trolley hire, shop, driving range, practice facilities
Visitors welcome weekdays
Societies welcome by prior arrangement

KNOLE PARK GOLF CLUB

Seal Hollow Road, Sevenoaks, Kent TN15 0HJ
✆ 01732 452709 Fax 01732 463159
Map 16, G8
www.kentgolf.co.uk/knolepark
Off B2019, ½ mile from Sevenoaks
Founded 1924
Laid out in the magificent park of Knole House, a testing Abercromby design in an incomparable setting.
18 holes, 6266 yards
par 70, S.S.S 70
Designer J.F. Abercromby
Green fees £25
Catering, changing room/showers, bar, club and trolley hire, shop, practice facilities
Visitors welcome weekdays with restrictions
Societies welcome by prior arrangement

LAMBERHURST GOLF CLUB

Church Road, Lamberhurst, Kent TN3 8DT
✆ 01892 890241 Fax 01892 891140
Map 5, D5
www.kentgolf.co.uk/lamberhurst
B2162, off A21 at Lamberhurst
Founded 1890
A parkland course with a river occasionally adding difficulty.
18 holes, 6345 yards
par 72, S.S.S 70
Designer Frank Pennink
Green fees £25
Catering, changing room/showers, bar, club, trolley and buggy hire, shop, practice facilities
Visitors welcome weekdays
Handicap certificate required
Societies welcome by prior arrangement

LANGLEY PARK GOLF CLUB

Barnfield Wood Road, Beckenham, Kent BR3 6SZ
✆ 020 8650 2090 Fax 020 8658 6310 **Map 16, E6**
B2015, ½ mile N of Beckenham
Founded 1910
A challenging parkland course culminating in a hole played across a lake.
18 holes, 6488 yards
par 69, S.S.S 71
Designer J.H. Taylor
Green fees £35
Catering, changing room/showers, bar, club and trolley hire, shop, practice facilities
Visitors welcome weekday by prior arrangement
Societies welcome by prior arrangement

LEEDS CASTLE GOLF CLUB

Leeds Castle, Hollingbourne, Maidstone, Kent ME17 1PL
✆ 01622 880467 Fax 01622 735616
Map 5, D4
A20, off M20 Jct 8
Founded 1933
An extraordinary place to play golf, in the grounds of imposing Leeds Castle, with the moat in play as a hazard on several holes. The green fee includes admission to the castle and grounds.
9 holes, 2451 yards
par 33, S.S.S 33
Designer Neil Coles
Green fees £11
Catering, changing room/showers, club and trolley hire, shop
Visitors welcome with prior booking
Societies welcome by prior arrangement

LITTLESTONE GOLF CLUB

St Andrews Road, Littlestone, New Romney, Kent TN28 8RB
✆ 01797 363355 Fax 01797 362740
Map 5, F5
www.littlestonegolfclub.co.uk
B2071 to Littlestone
Founded 1888
A delightful links, with superb

greens, of Open Championship qualifying standard. Generally flat, apart from the adventurous 16th and 17th amidst the dunes, there is much challenge in the 4th, 8th, 10th, and 12th, all par 4s. A ditch cutting diagonally across the 11th fairway adds greatly to the excitement.
18 holes, 6470 yards
par 71, S.S.S 72
Designer Dr. Laidlaw Purves, Alister Mackenzie
Green fees £35
Catering, changing room/showers, bar, club and trolley hire, shop, practice facilities
Visitors welcome
Handicap certificate required
Societies welcome by prior arrangement

THE LONDON GOLF CLUB

South Ash Manor Estate, Stansted Lane, Ash, Kent TN15 7EN
01474 879899 Fax 01474 879912
Map 16, H8
golf@londongolf.co.uk
www.londongolf.co.uk
Stansted Lane, off A20 near Brands Hatch
Founded 1993
Two big courses from the Nicklaus design stable. The Golden Bear himself designed the Heritage Course, which displays many of his trade marks, such as gambler's holes on which risk taking on the drive is rewarded with an easier second shot. The International is similarly strategic, on higher, quick-draining chalk.
Heritage Course: 18 holes, 7208 yards
par 72, S.S.S 74
Designer Jack Nicklaus
International Course: 18 holes, 7005 yards
par 72, S.S.S 74
Designer Ron Kirby
Green fees £70
Catering, changing room/showers, bar, club, trolley and buggy hire, shop, driving range, practice facilities, conference and function facilities, Japanese Spa
Visitors:International – welcome by prior arrangement only; Heritage – only as members' guests
Handicap certificate required – limit: 24
Societies welcome by prior arrangement
Brands Hatch Thistle, West Kingsdown, Kent
01474 854900

LULLINGSTONE PARK GOLF CLUB

Parkgate Road, Chelsfield, Orpington, Kent BR6 7PX
01959 533793 **Map 16, G7**
M25 Jct 4
Founded 1967
Impressive facilities and fine main course of considerable length.
18 holes, 6779 yards
par 72, S.S.S 72
Designer Fred Hawtree
9 holes, 2445 yards
par 33, S.S.S 31
Green fees £10.50
Catering, changing room/showers, bar, club, trolley and buggy hire, shop, driving range, practice facilities
Visitors welcome
Societies welcome by prior arrangement

LYDD GOLF CLUB

Romney Road, Lydd, Romney Marsh, Kent TN29 9LS
01797 320808 Fax 01797 321482
Map 5, F5
www.lyddgolfclub.co.uk
B2075, from A259 at New Romney
A seaside course very much exposed to the wind, exploiting the water hazards of Dungeness.
18 holes, 6517 yards
par 71, S.S.S 71
Designer M. Smith
Green fees £17
Catering, changing room/showers, bar, club, trolley and buggy hire, shop, driving range, practice facilities
Visitors welcome
Societies welcome by prior arrangement

MID KENT GOLF CLUB

Singlewell Road, Gravesend, Kent DA11 7RB
01474 560835 Fax 01474 564218
Map 5, C3
Off A227, S of Gravesend
Founded 1908
A good quality downland course, quite testing.
18 holes, 6218 yards
par 69, S.S.S 70
Designer Frank Pennink
Green fees £20
Catering, changing room/showers, bar, club and trolley hire, shop, practice facilities
Visitors welcome weekdays
Handicap certificate required
Societies welcome by prior arrangement

MOATLANDS GOLF CLUB

Watermans Lane, Brenchley, Tonbridge, Kent TN12 6ND
01892 724400 Fax 01892 723300
Map 16, H9
www.moatlands.com
B2160, off A21, 3 miles N of Brenchley
Founded 1993
A big, long, parkland course with extensive views over the Kent countryside.
18 holes, 7060 yards
par 72, S.S.S 74
Designer T. Saito
Green fees £29
Catering, changing room/showers, bar, club, trolley and buggy hire, shop, driving range, tennis, swimming pool & gymnasium
Visitors welcome weekdays
Societies welcome by prior arrangement

NIZELS GOLF CLUB

Nizels Lane, Hildenborough, Tonbridge, Kent TN11 8NX
01732 833833 Fax 01732 833 764
Map 16, H9
www.clubhaus.com
Off B245, from M24 Jct 5, via A21
Founded 1992
A handsome woodland course, with a number of dangerous water holes.
18 holes, 6408 yards
par 72, S.S.S 71
Green fees £40
Catering, changing room/showers, bar, club, trolley and buggy hire, shop, practice facilities
Visitors welcome
Societies welcome by prior arrangement

NORTH FORELAND GOLF CLUB

Convent Road, Broadstairs, Thanet, Kent CT10 3PU
01843 862140 Fax 01843 862663
Map 5, H3
Kingsgate, on B2052 1 mile N of Broadstairs
Founded 1903
A deceptively difficult course, seemingly forgiving because of its open nature on high ground overlooking the sea. Because they play uphill, the 8th, 17th and 18th are particularly demanding, each about 450 yards long. Two of the short holes, the 14th and 16th, are very attractive, playing towards the sea.
18 holes, 6430 yards
par 71, S.S.S 71
Designer Tom Simpson, Herbert Fowler
Green fees £30

Catering, changing room/showers, bar, club, trolley and buggy hire, shop, practice facilities, 9-hole course
Visitors welcome
Handicap certificate required
Societies welcome by prior arrangement

THE OAST GOLF CENTRE

Church Road, Tonge, Sittingbourne, Kent ME9 9AR
☎ 01795 473527 **Map 5, E3**
range@oastgolf.freeserve.co.uk
At Bapchild, 2 miles N of A2
Founded 1989
Par-3 course with driving range
9 holes, 1664 yards
par 54, S.S.S 54
Designer D. Chambers
Green fees £5
Bar, club and trolley hire, shop, driving range, practice facilities, function room
Visitors welcome
Societies welcome by prior arrangement
🏨 Hempstead House, Bapchild, Kent
☎ 01795 428020

OASTPARK GOLF CLUB

Malling Road, Snodland, Kent ME6 5LG
☎ 01634 242661 Fax 01634 240744
Map 5, D3
1 mile E of M20 Jct 4
Founded 1992
The course, in the heart of the Kent orchards, is being redeveloped, reverting to 18 holes. With plenty of water hazards, it is quite challenging.
9 holes, 3133 yards
par 70, S.S.S 70
Green fees £12
Catering, changing room/showers, bar, trolley hire, shop, driving range, function room
Visitors welcome
Societies welcome by prior arrangement
🏨 Larkfield Priory Hotel, London Road, Larkfield, Hever, Kent
☎ 01732 846858

PARKWOOD GOLF CLUB

Chestnut Avenue, Tatsfield, Westerham, Kent TN16 2EG
☎ 01959 577744 Fax 01959 572702
Map 16, F8
Off B2024, Croydon road, from A25
Founded 1993
A long, testing course with fine views over Kent and Surrey and the neighbouring woodland.
18 holes, 6835 yards
par 72, S.S.S 72
Green fees £20
Catering, changing room/showers, bar, trolley and buggy hire, shop, practice facilities
Visitors welcome
Societies welcome by prior arrangement

POULT WOOD GOLF CLUB

Higham Lane, Tonbridge, Kent TN11 9QR
☎ 01732 364039 Fax 01732 353781
Map 5, C4
Off A227, 2 miles N of Tonbridge
Founded 1974
Although laid out on level ground, the woodland setting of these courses makes them particularly attractive.
18 holes, 5569 yards
par 68, S.S.S 67
Designer Fred Hawtree
9 holes, 1218 yards
par 28, S.S.S 28
Green fees £14
Catering, changing room/showers, bar, club and trolley hire, shop, squash
Visitors welcome with booking system
Societies welcome by prior arrangement

PRINCE'S GOLF CLUB

Sandwich Bay, Sandwich, Kent CT13 9QB
☎ 01304 611118 Fax 01304 612000
Map 5, G3
golf@princes-leisure.co.uk
www.princes-leisure.co.uk
Sandwich, follow signs for golf courses
Founded 1906
Three nines of championship quality were constructed in 1949 following the devastation of the old Open Championship course during the War. With restrained bunkering and gentler dunes, Prince's is not as overwhelming to the ordinary player as neighbouring Royal St George's. A warm welcome and excellent facilities await the visitor.
Dunes: 9 holes, 3455 yards
par 36
Himalayas: 9 holes, 3321 yards
par 36
Shore: 9 holes, 3492 yards
par 36
Designer Sir Guy Campbell, John Morrison
Green fees £40
Catering, changing room/showers, bar, club, trolley and buggy hire, shop, driving range, practice facilities
Visitors welcome – restricted Sunday
Societies welcome by prior arrangement
🏨 Bell Hotel, The Quay, Sandwich, Kent CT13 9EF
☎ 01304 613388

REDLIBBETS GOLF CLUB

West Yoke, Ash, Sevenoaks, Kent TN15 7HT
☎ 01474 879190 Fax 01474 879290
Map 16, H8
Off A20, between Fawkham and Ash
Founded 1996
A parkland course close to Brands Hatch.
18 holes, 6651 yards
S.S.S 72
Designer Jonathan Gaunt
Green fees £28.50
Catering, changing room/showers, bar, club and trolley hire, shop, practice facilities
Visitors welcome
Societies welcome by prior arrangement

THE RIDGE GOLF CLUB

Chartway Street, East Sutton, Maidstone, Kent ME17 3DL
☎ 01622 844382 Fax 01622 844168
Map 5, D3
ridge@americangolf.com
Off A274, 3 miles E of Maidstone, M20 Jct 8
Founded 1993
A parkland course giving good views of the orchards and Weald of Kent.
18 holes, 6229 yards
par 71, S.S.S 70
Designer Patrick Dawson
Green fees £20
Catering, changing room/showers, bar, club, trolley and buggy hire, shop, driving range, practice facilities, health club, wedding, functions and conference facilities
Visitors welcome weekdays
Societies welcome by prior arrangement
🏨 Marriott Tudor Park Hotel and CC, Ashford Road, Bearsted, Maidstone, Kent ME14 4NQ
☎ 01622 734334

THE ROCHESTER & COBHAM PARK GOLF CLUB

Park Pale, by Rochester, Kent ME2 3UL
☎ 01474 823411 Fax 01474 824446
Map 5, D3
rcpgc@talk21.com
www.rochesterandcobhamgc.co.uk
Off A2 (Shorne/Higham exit)
Founded 1891
The 16th-century Cobham Hall, home of the Earls of Darnley, overlooks the west of the course, while the family mausoleum of 1783 stands to the south. Charles Dickens

was a frequent visitor to these grounds. Donald Steel's redesigned course is well balanced and sympathetic to the estate's noble character.
18 holes, 6596 yards
par 71, S.S.S 72
Designer Donald Steel
Green fees £32
Catering, changing room/showers, bar, club, trolley and buggy hire, shop, driving range, practice facilities
Visitors welcome weekdays – restricted weekend
Handicap certificate required – limit: 24 men, 30 women
Societies welcome by prior arrangement

ROMNEY WARREN GOLF CLUB

St Andrews Road, Littlestone, New Romney, Kent TN28 8RB
✆ 01797 362231 Fax 01797 362740
Map 5, F5
www.romneywarrengolfclub.co.uk
A2071, off A259 at New Romney*Founded* 1993
A links course laid out alongside the famous championship course at Littlestone. Although much shorter, Romney Warren offers many similar challenges.
18 holes, 5126 yards
par 67, S.S.S 65
Designer J.D. Lewis, B.M. Evans
Green fees £13
Catering, changing room/showers, bar, club, trolley and buggy hire, shop, practice facilities
Visitors welcome by prior arrangement
Societies welcome by prior arrangement

ROYAL BLACKHEATH GOLF CLUB

Court Road, Eltham, London SE9 5AF
✆ 0208 850 1795 Fax 0208 859 0150 **Map 16, F6**
info@rbgc.com
www.rbgc.com
M25 Jct 3, then A20, right at second lights
Founded 1608
Almost certainly the oldest golf club in the world, Royal Blackheath had to abandon its original site in 1923. Even so, its present clubhouse dates from 1664, a beautiful mansion, housing a magnificent collection of golfing memorabilia. Its lawns form the 18th green, which is approached directly over a hedge!
18 holes, 6219 yards
par 70, S.S.S 70
Designer James Braid
Green fees £40
Catering, changing room/showers, bar, club, trolley and buggy hire, shop, practice facilities
Visitors welcome weekdays with letter of introduction or handicap
Handicap certificate required – limit: 28
Societies welcome by prior arrangement
🏨 Eltham Hotel, 31 Westmount Road, Eltham, London SE9
✆ 0208 850 8222

ROYAL CINQUE PORTS GOLF CLUB

Golf Road, Deal, Kent CT14 6RF
✆ 01304 374007 Fax 01304 379530
Map 5, H4
Deal seafront
Founded 1892
A magnificent links of the highest quality, which hosted the Open Championship in 1909 and 1920. Its traditional layout runs out-and-back behind the sea wall with vigorous undulations enlivening play on the stretch from the 3rd to the 7th, and their counterparts on the back nine produce a superb finish.
18 holes, 6754 yards
par 72, S.S.S 72
Designer Tom Dunn, Sir Guy Campbell
Green fees £60
Catering, changing room/showers, bar, club, trolley and buggy hire, shop, practice facilities
Visitors welcome
Handicap certificate required
Societies welcome by prior arrangement

ROYAL ST GEORGE'S GOLF CLUB

Sandwich, Kent CT13 9PB
✆ 01304 613090 Fax 01304 611245
Map 5, G3
Sandwich, follow signs to golf courses
Founded 1887
See Top 50 Courses, page 40
18 holes, 6947 yards
par 70, S.S.S 74
Designer Dr Laidlaw Purves
Green fees £65
Catering, changing room/showers, bar, club and trolley hire, shop, practice facilities
Visitors welcome weekdays only, by prior arrangement
Handicap certificate required – limit: men 18, ladies 15
Societies welcome by prior arrangement

SENE VALLEY GOLF CLUB

Sene, Folkestone, Kent CT18 8BL
✆ 01303 268513 Fax 01303 237513
Map 5, F4
B2065, 2 miles N of Hythe.
Founded 1888
A downland course laid out by Sir Henry Cotton when the Folkestone Club moved from its old home. The course undulates giving occasional seascapes.
18 holes, 6215 yards
par 71, S.S.S 70
Designer Sir Henry Cotton
Green fees £20
Visitors welcome
Handicap certificate required
Societies welcome by prior arrangement

SHEERNESS GOLF CLUB

Power Station Road, Sheerness, Kent ME12 3AE
✆ 01795 662585 Fax 01795 668100
Map 5, E2
thesecretary@sheernessgc.golfagent.co.uk
Off A250 near Sheerness Town
Founded 1903
Described as a semi-links, the course is very exposed to the wind, with many water hazards
18 holes, 6460 yards
par 72, S.S.S 71
Green fees £18
Catering, changing room/showers, bar, trolley and buggy hire, shop, practice facilities
Visitors welcome, with restrictions
Societies welcome by prior arrangement
🏨 Abbey Hotel, The Broadway, Minster-on-Sea, Kent
✆ 01795 872873

SHOOTER'S HILL GOLF CLUB

Lowood, Eaglesfield Road, London SE18 3DA
✆ 020 8854 1216 Fax 020 8854 0469 **Map 16, F6**
A207, Shooter's Hill Road from Blackheath
Founded 1903
A hilly course with plenty of trees. Good views.
18 holes, 5721 yards
par 69, S.S.S 68
Designer Willie Park
Green fees £22
Catering, changing room/showers, bar, trolley and buggy hire, shop
Visitors welcome weekdays
Handicap certificate required
Societies welcome by prior arrangement

SHORTLANDS GOLF CLUB

Meadow Road, Shortlands, Bromley, Kent BR2 0PB
☎ 020 8460 2471 Fax 020 8460 8828 **Map 16, E7**
Off A222, ½ mile W of Shortlands
Founded 1894
A quiet parkland course.
9 holes, 5261 yards
par 65, S.S.S 66
Green fees £10
Catering, changing room/showers, bar, trolley hire, shop
Visitors welcome only as members' guests
Societies welcome by prior arrangement

SIDCUP GOLF CLUB

7 Hurst Road, Sidcup, Kent DA15 9AE
☎ 020 8300 2864 Fax 020 8300 2150 **Map 16, F6**
A222, ½ mile N of Sidcup
Founded 1891
A parkland course.
9 holes, 5722 yards
par 68, S.S.S 68
Designer James Braid
Green fees £18
Changing room/showers
Visitors welcome weekdays
Handicap certificate required
Societies welcome by prior arrangement

SITTINGBOURNE & MILTON REGIS GOLF CLUB

Wormdale, Newington, Sittingbourne, Kent ME9 7PX
☎ 01795 842261 Fax 01795 844117
Map 5, E3
sittingbourne@golfclub.totalserve.co.uk
N of M2 Jct 5
Founded 1929
Donald Steel's new holes have added difficulty to this upland course with fine views.
18 holes, 6291 yards
par 71, S.S.S 70
Designer Donald Steel
Green fees £22
Catering, changing room/showers, bar, trolley and buggy hire, shop, practice facilities
Visitors welcome, with restrictions
Handicap certificate required
Societies welcome by prior arrangement
🏨 Travel Inn, Bobbing Corner, Sheppey Way, Bobbing, Sittingbourne, Kent KE9 8PD
☎ 01795 431890

SOUTHERN VALLEY GOLF CLUB

Thong Lane, Shorne, Gravesend, Kent DA12 4LF
☎ 01474 740026 Fax 01474 360366
Map 5, C3
Off A2 Jct 4, via Thong Lane
Founded 1999
Overlooking the Thames Estuary, with gorse, bracken and hawthorn inducing caution.
18 holes, 6500 yards
par 71, S.S.S 72
Green fees £13.50
Catering, changing room/showers, bar, club, trolley and buggy hire, shop, practice facilities
Visitors welcome
Societies welcome by prior arrangement

ST AUGUSTINE'S GOLF CLUB

Cottington Road, Cliffsend, Ramsgate, Kent CT12 5JN
☎ 01843 590333 Fax 01843 590444
Map 5, G3
B2048, Ramsgate to Sandwich road
Founded 1907
A parkland course intersected by drainage ditches, close enough to the sea to be readily exposed to the wind.
18 holes, 5197 yards
par 69, S.S.S 65
Designer Tom Vardon
Green fees £21.50
Catering, changing room/showers, bar, trolley and buggy hire, shop
Visitors welcome weekdays
Handicap certificate required
Societies welcome by prior arrangement

STAPLEHURST GOLF CENTRE

Craddock Lane, Staplehurst, Kent TN12 0DR
☎ 01580 893362 **Map 5, D4**
A229, 8 miles S of Maidstone
Founded 1993
A parkland course.
9 holes, 6040 yards
par 70, S.S.S 68
Green fees £11
Changing room/showers, bar, driving range
Visitors welcome
Societies welcome by prior arrangement

SUNDRIDGE PARK GOLF CLUB

Garden Road, Bromley, Kent BR1 3NE
☎ 020 8460 1822 Fax 020 8289 3050 **Map 16, E6**
A2212, N of Bromley
Founded 1901
Two fine parkland courses of roughly equal appeal and difficulty.
East Course: 18 holes, 6538 yards
par 71, S.S.S 71
West Course: 18 holes, 6019 yards
par 69, S.S.S 69
Designer Willie Park
Green fees £40
Catering, changing room/showers, bar, trolley hire, shop, practice facilities
Visitors welcome weekdays
Handicap certificate required
Societies welcome by prior arrangement

SWEETWOODS PARK GOLF CLUB

Cowden, Edenbridge, Kent TN8 7JN
☎ 01342 850729 Fax 01342 850866
Map 16, F10
A264, 5 miles E of East Grinstead
Founded 1994
A good test of golf with a number of water hazards, with the additional benefit of fine country views.
18 holes, 6556 yards
par 71, S.S.S 71
Designer P. Strand
Green fees £20
Catering, changing room/showers, bar, club and trolley hire, shop, driving range
Visitors welcome
Societies welcome by prior arrangement

TENTERDEN GOLF CLUB

Woodchurch Road, Tenterden, Kent TN30 7DR
☎ 01580 763987 Fax 01580 763987
Map 5, E5
tenterden-golf-club@lineone.net
www.tenterdengolfclub.co.uk
B2067, 1 mile E of Tenterden
Founded 1905
With glorious views of the Wealden countryside, the course is unusual in opening and closing with par 3s. The 12th, 13th and 15th make formidable contributions to the back nine.
18 holes, 6071 yards
par 70, S.S.S 68
Green fees £22
Catering, changing room/showers, bar, trolley and buggy hire, shop, practice facilities
Visitors welcome weekdays
Handicap certificate required
Societies welcome by prior arrangement
🏨 White Lion, High Street, Tenterden, Kent
☎ 01580 765077

MARRIOTT TUDOR PARK HOTEL GOLF CLUB

Ashford Road, Bearsted, Kent ME14 4NQ

☎ 01622 739412 **Map 5, D3**
A2020, 2 miles E of Maidstone
Founded 1988
Donald Steel's design challenges the good player, yet is still playable by lesser mortals. Fine views extend to the Kentish valleys and North Downs.
18 holes, 5990 yards
par 70, S.S.S 69
Designer Donald Steel
Green fees £35
Catering, changing room/showers, bar, accommodation, club, trolley and buggy hire, shop, driving range, practice facilities, full conference, function and leisure facilities
Visitors welcome, subject to restrictions
Handicap certificate required
Societies welcome by prior arrangement
🏨 Marriott Tudor Park Hotel and CC, Ashford Road, Bearsted, Maidstone, Kent ME14 4NQ
☎ 01622 734334

TUNBRIDGE WELLS GOLF CLUB

Langton Road, Tunbridge Wells, Kent TN4 8XH
☎ 01892 536918 Fax 01892 536918
Map 5, C4
A264, adjoining Spa Hotel
Founded 1889
Very old club, parkland course.
9 holes, 4725 yards
par 65, S.S.S 62
Green fees £15.75
Catering, changing room/showers, bar, club and trolley hire, shop, practice facilities
Visitors welcome
Handicap certificate required
Societies welcome by prior arrangement
🏨 Spa Hotel, Mount Ephraim, Tunbridge Wells, Kent TN4 8XJ
☎ 01892 520331

UPCHURCH RIVER VALLEY GOLF COURSE

Oak Lane, Upchurch, Sittingbourne, Kent ME9 7AY
☎ 01634 360626 **Map 5, E3**
3 miles NE of Rainham (A2)
Founded 1991
Extensive facilities and good value golf with views over the River Medway towards the sea.
18 holes, 6237 yards
par 70, S.S.S 70
Green fees £11.45
Catering, changing room/showers, bar, club and trolley hire, shop, driving range, practice facilities, 9-hole, par-3 course
Visitors welcome
Societies welcome by prior arrangement
🏨 Hempstead House, Bapchild, Kent
☎ 01795 428020

WALMER & KINGSDOWN GOLF CLUB

The Leas, Kingsdown, Deal, Kent CT14 8EP
☎ 01304 363017 Fax 01304 382336
Map 5, H4
kingsdown.golf@gtwiz.co.uk
2 miles S of Deal
Founded 1909
The nearest British mainland course to Europe, Walmer & Kingsdown is set high on the cliffs between Dover and Deal, a wonderful location with magnificent views. With a spectacular situation overlooking the sea, the 450-yard dog-leg 7th is also notably difficult. Sloping and undulating fairways complicate a great many holes.
18 holes, 6444 yards
par 72, S.S.S 71
Designer James Braid, John Lawrie
Green fees £25
Catering, changing room/showers, bar, trolley and buggy hire, shop, practice facilities
Visitors welcome – restricted weekends
Handicap certificate required
Societies welcome by prior arrangement
🏨 Dunkorley's Hotel, 19 Beach Street, Deal, Kent
☎ 01304 375016

WEALD OF KENT GOLF CLUB

Maidstone Road, Headcorn, Kent TN27 9PT
☎ 01622 890866 Fax 01622 891793
Map 5, E4
A274, 7 miles from Maidstone
Founded 1992
A good value test of golf with lakes, ditches and gentle hills to add to the strategy.
18 holes, 6240 yards
par 70, S.S.S 70
Designer John Millen
Green fees £16
Catering, changing room/showers, bar, club, trolley and buggy hire, practice facilities
Visitors welcome
Societies welcome by prior arrangement

WEST KENT GOLF CLUB

Milking Lane, Downe, Orpington, Kent BR6 7LD
☎ 01689 856863 Fax 01689 858693
Map 16, F8
golf@wkgc.co.uk
5 miles S of Orpington, M25 Jct 4
Founded 1916
Close to Down House (home of Charles Darwin) and Biggin Hill, the course is set in a valley with charming surroundings.
18 holes, 6399 yards
par 70, S.S.S 71
Designer R.L. Croft
Green fees £30
Catering, changing room/showers, bar, club, trolley and buggy hire, shop, practice facilities
Visitors welcome weekdays
Societies welcome by prior arrangement
🏨 Kings Arms Hotel, Market Square, Westerham, Kent
☎ 01959 562990

WEST MALLING GOLF CLUB

Addington, Maidstone, Kent ME19 5AR
☎ 01732 844785 Fax 01732 844795
Map 18, E8
www.westmallinggolf.con
Off A20, 1 mile S of Addington
Founded 1974
Two parkland courses whose names recall the famous fighters which roamed Kentish skies during the Battle of Britain.
Hurricane Course: 18 holes, 6240 yards
par 70, S.S.S 70
Designer Max Faulkner
Spitfire Course: 18 holes, 6142 yards
par 70, S.S.S 70
Green fees £25
Catering, changing room/showers, bar, trolley and buggy hire, shop, driving range
Visitors welcome weekdays
Societies welcome by prior arrangement

WESTERHAM GOLF CLUB

Valence Park, Brasted Road, Westerham, Kent TN16 1LJ
☎ 01959 567100 Fax 01959 567101
Map 16, F8
westerham.golfclub@virgin.net
www.golfdirector.com
A25, between M25 Jcts 5 and 6
Founded 1997
Westerham grew out of the great storm of October 1987, felling thousands of trees, and suggesting the routing. The 9th and 18th are spectacular water holes to finish each half.
18 holes, 6272 yards
par 72, S.S.S 72
Designer David Williams

Green fees £25
Catering, changing room/showers, bar, trolley hire, shop, driving range, function room
Visitors welcome with weekend restrictions
Societies welcome by prior arrangement
Donnington Manor, London Road, Dunton Green, Sevenoaks, Kent TN13 2TD
01732 462681

WESTGATE & BIRCHINGTON GOLF CLUB

176 Canterbury Road, Westgate-on-Sea, Kent CT8 8LT
01843 831115 **Map 5, G3**
Off A27, E of Westgate
Founded 1893
A seaside course on which skill is needed to overcome the guile of the design, especially in a wind, the length of the course being in no way proportionate to the fun to be had.
18 holes, 4889 yards
par 64, S.S.S 64
Green fees £13.50
Catering, changing room/showers, bar, trolley hire, shop
Visitors welcome weekdays
Handicap certificate required
Societies welcome by prior arrangement

WHITSTABLE & SEASALTER GOLF CLUB

Collingwood Road, Whitstable, Kent CT5 1EB
01227 272020 Fax 01227 280822
Map 5, F3
Off B2205, W of town centre
Founded 1911
A short links, one of the few on the north coast of Kent.
9 holes, 5357 yards
par 66, S.S.S 63
Green fees £15
Changing room/showers, bar
Visitors welcome – accredited golfers only
No societies

WILDERNESSE CLUB

Park Lane, Seal, Sevenoaks, Kent TN15 0JE
01732 761199 Fax 01732 763809
Map 16, G8
golf@wildernesse.co.uk
www.wildernesse.co.uk
A25, 2 miles E of Sevenoaks
Founded 1890
Wildernesse has been a regular host to regional qualifying rounds for the Open Championship for a number of years. Set off against beautiful woodlands, it is particularly attractive. Trees and bunkers compel straight driving on many holes. The 469-yard par-4 9th easily justifies its rating as Stroke 1.
18 holes, 6440 yards
par 72, S.S.S 71
Green fees £35
Catering, changing room/showers, bar, club and trolley hire, shop, practice facilities
Visitors welcome
Handicap certificate required
Societies welcome by prior arrangement

WOODLANDS MANOR GOLF CLUB

Tinkerpot Lane, Otford, Sevenoaks, Kent TN15 6AB
01959 523806 Fax 01959 524398
Map 16, G8
woodlandsgolfclub@hotmail.com
Off A20 SW of Kingsdown, M25 Jct 3
Founded 1928
Pretty, secluded parkland course with several memorable short holes. Excellent drainage means good conditions winter and summer.
18 holes, 6100 yards
par 68, S.S.S 69
Designer Neil Coles, J. Lyons
Green fees £21
Catering, changing room/showers, bar, trolley and buggy hire, shop, driving range, practice facilities, function/business facilities
Visitors welcome, restricted weekends
Handicap certificate required
Societies welcome by prior arrangement
Brands Hatch Thistle, West Kingsdown, Kent
01474 854900

WROTHAM HEATH GOLF CLUB

Seven Mile Lane, Borough Green, Sevenoaks, Kent TN15 8QZ
01732 884800 Fax 01732 887370
Map 16, G8
B2016, 2 miles E of Borough Green
Founded 1906
A Donald Steel reworking of an older course, wooded heathland with fine views.
18 holes, 5954 yards
par 70, S.S.S 69
Designer Donald Steel
Green fees £25
Catering, changing room/showers, bar, trolley hire, shop
Visitors welcome weekdays
Handicap certificate required
Societies welcome by prior arrangement

OXFORDSHIRE

ASPECT PARK GOLF CLUB

Remenham Hill, Henley-on-Thames, Oxfordshire RG9 3EH
01491 578306 Fax 01491 578306
Map 4, F2
Off A4130 on Remenham Hill
Founded 1988
A parkland course with fine views.
18 holes, 6557 yards
par 72, S.S.S 71
Designer Tim Winsland
Green fees £20
Catering, changing room/showers, bar, club, trolley and buggy hire, shop, driving range, practice facilities, 9-hole pitch-and-putt course, conference facilities
Visitors welcome – restricted weekends
Handicap certificate required
Societies welcome by prior arrangement
Red Lion Hotel, Hart Street, Henley-on-Thames, Oxfordshire
01491 572161

BADGEMORE PARK GOLF CLUB

Henley-on-Thames, Oxfordshire RG9 4NR
01491 574175 Fax 01491 576899
Map 4, F2
info@badgemorepark.com
www.badgemorepark.com
1 mile NW of Henley, M40 Jct 4, M4 Jct 8/9
Founded 1972
Both a members' club and also one of the facilities of the management training centre, which specialises in hosting large events from trade fairs to corporate golf hospitality. Historic, mature parkland.
18 holes, 6129 yards
par 69, S.S.S 69
Designer Robert Sandow
Green fees £19
Catering, changing room/showers, bar, accommodation, club, trolley and buggy hire, shop, driving range, practice facilities, management training centre, function, trade fair, and conference facilities
Visitors welcome, restricted Tuesdays and weekends
Societies welcome
Badgemore Park Management Training Centre, Henley-on-Thames, Oxfordshire RG9 4NR
01491 637300 Fax 01491 637301
info@badgemorepark.com
www.badgemorepark.com

BANBURY GOLF CENTRE

Aynho Road, Adderbury, Banbury, Oxfordshire OX17 3NT
✆ 01295 812880 Fax 01295 810056
Map 8, C8
office@banburygolfcentre.co.uk
www.banburygolfcentre.co.uk
B4100, 6 miles S of Banbury, M40 Jct 10 or 11
Founded 1993
Extensive facilities in the attractive Cherwell Valley, south of Banbury.
18 holes, 6706 yards
par 72, S.S.S 72
Designer Reed, Payn
Green fees £14
Catering, changing room/showers, bar, club, trolley and buggy hire, shop, marquee for functions, additional 9-hole course
Visitors welcome
Societies welcome by prior arrangement
Deddington Arms, Deddington, Banbury, Oxfordshire
✆ 01869 338364

BRAILES GOLF CLUB

Sutton Lane, Lower Brailes, Banbury, Oxfordshire OX15 5BB
✆ 01608 685336 Fax 01608 685205
Map 8, B8
B4035, 4 miles E of Shipston-on-Stour
Founded 1992
An attractive course with glorious Cotswold views.
18 holes, 6310 yards
par 71, S.S.S 70
Designer Brian Hull
Green fees £18
Catering, changing room/showers, bar, club, trolley and buggy hire, shop, practice facilities
Visitors welcome weekdays
Societies welcome by prior arrangement

BURFORD GOLF CLUB

Burford, Oxfordshire OX18 4JG
✆ 01993 822583 Fax 01993 822801
Map 8, B10
A 361, off A40
Founded 1935
Trees give good separation to the many parallel fairways at Burford, one of the few older courses built in the heart of the Cotswolds. Drainage is good on this soil and at this altitude, and the greens are well reputed. Three of the par 4s are over 450 yards long.
18 holes, 6432 yards
par 71, S.S.S 71
Designer J.H. Turner
Green fees £36
Catering, changing room/showers, bar, trolley hire, shop, practice facilities
Visitors welcome
Handicap certificate required
Societies welcome by prior arrangement
Cotswold Gateway, Burford, Oxfordshire OX18 4JG
✆ 01993 822695

CARSWELL GOLF & COUNTRY CLUB

Carswell, Faringdon, Oxfordshire SN7 8PU
✆ 01367 870422 Fax 01367 870592
Map 8, B11
info@carswellcountryclub.co.uk
www.carswellcountryclub.co.uk
A421, 2 miles E of Faringdon
Founded 1994
A welcome addition to the roster of Cotswold courses – an area until recently rather barren.
18 holes, 6800 yards
par 72, S.S.S 72
Green fees £16
Catering, changing room/showers, bar, accommodation, club, trolley and buggy hire, shop, driving range, practice facilities, health and fitness club
Visitors welcome
Handicap certificate required.
Societies welcome by prior arrangement

CHERWELL EDGE GOLF CLUB

Chacombe, Banbury, Oxfordshire OX17 2EN
✆ 01295 711591 Fax 01295 712404
Map 8, C8
B4525, 3 miles E of Banbury, M40 Jct 11
Founded 1983
A well wooded parkland course in undulating country.
18 holes, 5947 yards
par 70, S.S.S 68
Designer Richard Davies
Green fees £12
Catering, changing room/showers, bar, club, trolley and buggy hire, shop, driving range, practice facilities
Visitors welcome
Societies welcome by prior arrangement

CHESTERTON GOLF CLUB

Chesterton, Bicester, Oxfordshire OX26 1TE
✆ 01869 241204 **Map 8, C9**
Off A4095, close to M40 Jct 9
Founded 1973
One of the early farmland conversions, long before the current explosion, which has, therefore, had time to mature admirably.
18 holes, 6229 yards
par 71, S.S.S 70
Designer R.R. Stagg
Green fees £16
Catering, changing room/showers, bar, trolley hire, shop
Visitors welcome weekdays
Societies welcome by prior arrangement

CHIPPING NORTON GOLF CLUB

Southcombe, Chipping Norton, Oxfordshire OX7 5QH
✆ 01608 642383 Fax 01608 645422
Map 8, B9
chipping.nortongc@virginnet.co.uk
Off A44, 2½ miles N of Enstone
Founded 1890
Downland course, 800 feet above sea level, with a lake, pond and stream in the valley of the front nine. The short 3rd involves carrying a lake to an elevated green, and the par-5 6th plays uphill all the way. At the 17th the drive is over a hedge.
18 holes, 6280 yards
par 71, S.S.S 70
Green fees £27
Catering, changing room/showers, bar, club, trolley and buggy hire, shop, practice facilities
Visitors welcome weekdays
Societies welcome by prior arrangement
Crown and Cushion, High Street, Chipping Norton, Oxfordshire
✆ 01608 642533

DRAYTON PARK GOLF CLUB

Steventon Road, Drayton, Abingdon, Oxfordshire OX14 2RR
✆ 01235 550607 Fax 01235 525731
Map 8, C11
Off A34, between Didcot and Abingdon
Founded 1992
A parkland course with rapid greens and many water hazards.
18 holes, 5535 yards
par 67, S.S.S 67
Designer Hawtree
Green fees £12
Catering, changing room/showers, bar, trolley and buggy hire, shop, driving range, 9-hole, par-3 course
Visitors welcome
Societies welcome by prior arrangement

FRILFORD HEATH GOLF CLUB

Frilford Heath, Abingdon, Oxfordshire OX13 5NW
✆ 01865 390864 Fax 01865 390823
Map 8, C11
secretary@frilfordheath.co.uk
www.frilfordheath.co.uk
A338, 3 miles W of Abingdon

Founded 1908
Two excellent heathland courses, the Red and Green, have recently been joined by the challenging Blue Course. Its design is, naturally, more contemporary, with greater use made of water, and it is more parkland in nature. Two- and four-ball play is alternated between the Red and Green Courses, both classics.
Red Course: 18 holes, 6884 yards
par 73, S.S.S 73
Designer J.H. Taylor
Green Course: 18 holes, 6006 yards
par 69, S.S.S 69
Designer J.H. Turner, C.K. Cotton
Blue Course: 18 holes, 6728 yards
par 72, S.S.S 72
Designer Simon Gidman
Green fees £50
Catering, changing room/showers, bar, trolley and buggy hire, shop, practice facilities, limited conference facilities
Visitors welcome
Handicap certificate required
Societies welcome by prior arrangement
Fallowfields, Faringdon Road, Southmoor, Kingston Bagpuize, Abingdon, Oxfordshire OX13 5BH
01865 820416 Fax 01865 821275
stay@fallowfields.com
www.fallowfields.com

HADDEN HILL GOLF CLUB

Wallingford Road, Didcot, Oxfordshire OX11 9BJ
01235 510410 **Map 8, D11**
info@haddenhillgolf.co.uk
www.haddenhillgolf.co.uk
A4130, 1 mile E of Didcot
Founded 1990
With over 30 miles of underground drainage, the course has never been closed because of rain, and the fairways and greens are of high quality. Beautiful views over the Downs. Public driving range.
18 holes, 6563 yards
par 71, S.S.S 71
Designer M.V. Morley
Green fees £14
Catering, changing room/showers, bar, club, trolley and buggy hire, shop, driving range, practice facilities
Visitors welcome
Societies welcome by prior arrangement
The George Hotel, High Street, Wallingford, Oxfordshire OX10 0BS
01491 836665

HENLEY GOLF CLUB

Harpsden, Henley-on-Thames, Oxfordshire RG9 4HG
01491 575742 Fax 01491 412179
Map 4, F2
henleygolfclub@btinternet.com
A4155, 1 mile S of Henley
Founded 1907
A compact course in charming, undulating, woodland surroundings. Six short holes keep the overall length modest, but there are some very solid par 4s, such as the 473-yard 8th. One of the great strengths of the course is the variety of challenges it poses – monotony could never feature here.
18 holes, 6265 yards
par 70, S.S.S 70
Designer James Braid
Green fees £30
Catering, changing room/showers, bar, club, trolley and buggy hire, shop, practice facilities
Visitors welcome weekdays
Handicap certificate required
Societies welcome by prior arrangement

HINKSEY HEIGHTS GOLF COURSE

South Hinksey, Oxford, Oxfordshire OX1 5AB
01865 327775 Fax 01865 736930
Map 8, C10
play@oxford-golf.co.uk
www.oxford-golf.co.uk
A34, W of Oxford
Founded 1994
Overlooking Oxford's 'dreaming spires', the 3rd is arguably one of the best holes in the region.
18 holes, 7023 yards
par 74, S.S.S 74
Designer David Heads
9 holes, 3456 yards
par 27
Green fees £25
Catering, changing room/showers, bar, club, trolley and buggy hire, shop, driving range, practice facilities
Visitors welcome
Societies welcome by prior arrangement
Four Pillars Hotel, Abingdon Road, Oxford, Oxfordshire OX1 4PS
01865 324324

HUNTERCOMBE GOLF CLUB

Nuffield, Henley-on-Thames, RG9 5SL, Oxfordshire
01491 641207 Fax 01491 642060
Map 4, F2
A4130, 6 miles N of Henley
Founded 1901
A wonderful course in a very old-fashioned British way. Heather and gorse are plentiful, and so are extravagantly shaped bunkers, guarding the small greens.
18 holes, 6310 yards
par 70, S.S.S 70
Designer Willie Park
Green fees £27
Catering, changing room/showers, bar, trolley hire, shop, practice facilities
Visitors welcome weekdays, no 3- or 4-balls
Handicap certificate required
Societies welcome by prior arrangement

KIRTLINGTON GOLF CLUB

Kirtlington, Oxfordshire OX5 3JY
01869 351133 Fax 01869 331143
Map 8, C10
A4095, between Woodstock and Bicester.
Founded 1995
A parkland course, as yet open enough to be described as an inland links.
18 holes, 6084 yards
par 70, S.S.S 69
Designer Graham Webster
Green fees £15
Catering, changing room/showers, bar, club, trolley and buggy hire, shop, driving range
Visitors welcome
Societies welcome by prior arrangement

LYNEHAM GOLF CLUB

Lyneham, near Chipping Norton, Oxfordshire OX7 6QQ
01993 831841 Fax 01993 831775
Map 8, B9
golf@lynehamgc.freeserve.co.uk
1 mile off A361 between Burford and Chipping Norton
Founded 1992
Unusually for a Cotswold course, lakes and streams feature widely, coming into play on nine holes, and adding to the already beautiful setting.
18 holes, 6707 yards
par 72, S.S.S 72
Designer D. Carpenter
Green fees £20
Catering, changing room/showers, bar, club, trolley and buggy hire, shop, driving range, practice facilities
Visitors welcome – prior bookings at weekend
Societies welcome by prior arrangement
Mill House Hotel, Kingham, Oxfordshire
01608 658188

NORTH OXFORD GOLF CLUB

Banbury Road, Oxford, Oxfordshire OX2 8EZ
01865 554415 Fax 01865 515921

Map 8, C10
www.nogc.co.uk
A423, 3 miles N of city centre
Founded 1907
Parkland course of modest dimensions on the northern edge of the City.
18 holes, 5805 yards
par 67, S.S.S 67
Green fees £18
Catering, changing room/showers, bar, club and trolley hire, shop
Visitors welcome weekdays
Societies welcome by prior arrangement

THE OXFORDSHIRE GOLF CLUB

Rycote Lane, Milton Common, Thame, Oxfordshire OX9 2PU
✆ 01844 278300 Fax 01844 278003
Map 8, D10
A 329, close to M40 Jct 7
Founded 1993
Extensive earthworks, lavish bunkering and four lakes, make this very much an American-style golf course in the middle of the Oxfordshire countryside. It has already seen European Tour action. For the amateur, the 8th, 11th and 17th are nerve-racking, with water in attendance all the way from tee to green.
18 holes, 7187 yards
par 72, S.S.S 74
Designer Rees Jones
Green fees £80
Catering, changing room/showers, bar, club and trolley hire, shop, driving range, practice facilities, conference and wedding facilities
Visitors welcome only with written application to General Manager.
Handicap certificate required
Societies only those affiliated to EGU
Le Manoir aux Quat' Saisons, Church Road, Great Milton, Oxford, Oxfordshire OX44 7PD
✆ 01844 278881 Fax 01844 278847
lemanoir@blanc.co.uk
www.manoir.co.uk

RAF BENSON GOLF CLUB

Royal Air Force, Benson, Oxfordshire
✆ 01491 837766 **Map 8, D11**
Off A4074, 3 miles NE of Wallingford
Founded 1975
A private course at this famous airfield, once home of the Queen's Flight.
9 holes, 4395 yards
par 63, S.S.S 61
Visitors welcome only as members' guests
No societies

RYE HILL GOLF CLUB

Milcombe, Banbury, Oxfordshire OX15 4RU
✆ 01295 721818 Fax 01295 720089
Map 8, B8
Off A361, at Bloxham
Founded 1993
An expansive course contrasting with neighbouring Tadmarton Heath, although both share wide Cotswold landscapes.
18 holes, 6750 yards
par 72, S.S.S 73
Green fees £14
Catering, changing room/showers, bar, club, trolley and buggy hire, shop, practice facilities, fishing
Visitors welcome – with booking system
Societies welcome by prior arrangement

SOUTHFIELD GOLF CLUB

Hill Top Road, Oxford, Oxfordshire OX4 1PF
✆ 01865 242158 Fax 01865 242158
Map 8, C10
2 miles E of city centre
Founded 1875
Girt about with housing, yet a good test for aspirant Oxford golfing Blues. A stream punctuates the 3rd and 11th, while holes such as the 14th invite tigers to bite off major chunks of the dog-leg. The 12th is a par 3 across a gully, severely punishing the timid shot.
18 holes, 6328 yards
par 70, S.S.S 70
Designer Harry Colt
Green fees £24
Catering, changing room/showers, bar, club, trolley and buggy hire, shop, practice facilities
Visitors welcome weekdays
Societies welcome by prior arrangement

THE SPRINGS HOTEL & GOLF CLUB

Wallingford Road, North Stoke, Wallingford, Oxfordshire OX10 6BE
✆ 01491 827310 Fax 01491 827312
Map 8, D11
info@thespringshotel.co.uk
www.thespringshotel.co.uk
B4009, 2 miles SW of Wallingford, M40 Jct 6
Founded 1998
Beautiful parkland course in a prime location on the banks of the River Thames.
18 holes, 6470 yards
par 72, S.S.S 71
Designer Brian Huggett
Green fees £26
Catering, changing room/showers, bar, accommodation, club, trolley and buggy hire, shop, practice facilities, conference, function and wedding facilities, croquet, fishing, swimming
Visitors welcome
Handicap certificate required
Societies welcome by prior arrangement
The Springs Hotel, North Stoke, Wallingford, Oxfordshire
✆ 01491 836687

STUDLEY WOOD GOLF CLUB

The Straight Mile, Horton-cum-Studley, Oxford, Oxfordshire OX33 1BF
✆ 01865 351144 Fax 01865 351166
Map 8, C10
www.swgc.co.uk
4 miles NE of Oxford, M40 Jct 8
Founded 1996
A remarkable course with a large number of lakes, complementing the noble trees of an ancient deer park.
18 holes, 6811 yards
par 73, S.S.S 73
Designer Simon Gidman
Green fees £30
Catering, changing room/showers, bar, club, trolley and buggy hire, shop, driving range
Visitors welcome
Societies welcome by prior arrangement

TADMARTON HEATH GOLF CLUB

Wigginton, Banbury, Oxfordshire OX15 5HL
✆ 01608 737278 Fax 01608 730548
Map 8, B8
A 361 from Banbury, signposted after Bloxham
Founded 1922
Tadmarton is for the traditionalist, for whom finesse is of greater importance than power. There are big holes – the 9th and 18th, for instance – but it is plotting a way through holes such as the 14th and 15th which gives the connoisseur particular satisfaction. Gorse is a serious threat throughout.
18 holes, 5917 yards
par 69, S.S.S 69
Designer C.K. Hutchison
Green fees £33
Catering, changing room/showers, bar, club and trolley hire, shop, practice facilities, fishing
Visitors welcome weekdays
Handicap certificate required
Societies welcome by prior arrangement

WATERSTOCK GOLF CLUB

Thame Road, Waterstock, Oxford, Oxfordshire OX33 1HT

☎ 01844 338093 Fax 01993778339
Map 8, D10
www.waterstockgolf.co.uk
A4148, M40 Jct 8a
Founded 1994
Built to provide affordable golf on a well-designed course in an area which had been previously starved of golf. As part of an ongoing development plan, a further 9 holes are being added, 14,000 trees planted and two lakes excavated. The 17th is a man-sized par 5 at 565 yards.
18 holes, 6535 yards
par 73, S.S.S 71
Designer Donald Steel
Green fees £15
Catering, changing room/showers, bar, club, trolley and buggy hire, shop, driving range, practice facilities, ballooning, archery, fishing, clay pigeon shooting
Visitors welcome
Societies welcome by prior arrangement
Oxford Belfry Hotel, Milton Common, Great Milton, Oxfordshire
☎ 01844 279381

WITNEY LAKES GOLF CLUB
Downs Road, Witney, Oxfordshire OX8 5SY
☎ 01993 893010 Fax 01193 778866
Map 8, B10
www.witney-lakes.co.uk
B4047, 2 miles W of Witney
Founded 1994
The club's name describes it all – five lakes wreaking havoc on many a scorecard.
18 holes, 6675 yards
par 71, S.S.S 71
Designer Simon Gidman
Green fees £16
Catering, changing room/showers, bar, club, trolley and buggy hire, shop, driving range, swimming pool, gymnasium
Visitors welcome
Societies welcome by prior arrangement

SURREY

ADDINGTON COURT GOLF CLUB
Featherbed Lane, Addington, Croydon, Surrey CR0 9AA
☎ 020 8657 0281 Fax 020 8651 0282 **Map 16, E8**
Off B281, 2 miles E of Croydon
Founded 1931
Four courses, providing extensive public facilities close to Croydon.
Championship Course: 18 holes, 5577 yards
par 68, S.S.S 67
Falconwood Course: 18 holes, 5472 yards
par 68, S.S.S 67
Designer Fred Hawtree
Green fees £12
Catering, changing room/showers, bar, club, trolley and buggy hire, shop, practice facilities, 9-hole & par-3 courses
Visitors welcome
Societies welcome by prior arrangement

THE ADDINGTON GOLF CLUB
205 Shirley Church Road, Croydon, Surrey CR0 5AB
☎ 020 8777 1055 **Map 16, E8**
Between Shirley and New Addington, 2 miles E of Croydon
Founded 1913
Adventurous classic with splendid views over London. The 3rd and 13th are amongst the finest par 3s in the world. Heather, bracken, pines and birches abound, though hilly ground makes the back nine trying for the unfit, and the downhill 12th is one of the most idiosyncratic period pieces imaginable.
18 holes, 6242 yards
par 68, S.S.S 71
Designer J.F. Abercromby
Green fees £35
Catering, changing room/showers, bar
Visitors welcome weekdays
Societies welcome by prior arrangement

ADDINGTON PALACE GOLF CLUB
Addington Park, Gravel Hill, Addington, Surrey CR0 5BB
☎ 020 8654 3061 Fax 020 8655 3632 **Map 16, E8**
A212, 2 miles E of Croydon
Founded 1923
Attractive undulating parkland course roaming the grounds of 18th-century Addington Palace.
18 holes, 6410 yards
par 71, S.S.S 71
Designer J.H. Taylor
Green fees £30
Catering, changing room/showers, bar, trolley hire, shop, practice facilities
Visitors welcome weekdays
Handicap certificate required
Societies welcome by prior arrangement

BANSTEAD DOWNS GOLF CLUB
Burdon Lane, Belmont, Sutton, Surrey SM2 7DD
☎ 020 8642 2284 Fax 020 8642 5252 **Map 16, D8**
bdgc@ukonline.co.uk
Off A217, 1 mile S of Sutton, M25 Jct 8
Founded 1890
The course itself is a Site of Special Scientific Interest, a rare collection of chalkland flora and fauna. The rough is appropriately natural and can be punishing.
18 holes, 6194 yards
par 69, S.S.S 69
Designer J.H. Taylor, James Braid
Green fees £35
Catering, changing room/showers, bar, trolley hire, shop, practice facilities
Visitors welcome weekdays
Handicap certificate required
Societies welcome by prior arrangement
Thatched House Hotel, Cheam Road, Cheam, Surrey
☎ 020 8642 3131

BARROW HILLS GOLF CLUB
Longcross, Chertsey, Surrey KT16 0DS
☎ 01344 635770 **Map 16, B7**
4 miles W of Chertsey
Founded 1970
An executive length private course.
18 holes, 3090 yards
S.S.S 53
Visitors welcome only as members' guests
No societies

BETCHWORTH PARK GOLF CLUB
Reigate Road, Dorking, Surrey RH4 1NZ
☎ 01306 882052 Fax 01306 877462
Map 16, C9
A25, 1 mile E of Dorking
Founded 1911
A very attractive parkland course on the edge of Boxhill.
18 holes, 6266 yards
par 69, S.S.S 70
Designer Harry Colt
Green fees £34
Changing room/showers, club and trolley hire, shop
Visitors welcome weekdays with restrictions
Societies welcome by prior arrangement

BLETCHINGLEY GOLF CLUB
Church Lane, Bletchingley, Surrey RH1 4LP
☎ 01883 744666 Fax 01883 744284
Map 16, E9
www.bletchingleygolfclub.co.uk
A25, 3 miles from M25 Jct 6
Founded 1993

A parkland course.
18 holes, 6531 yards
par 72, S.S.S 71
Designer Paul Wright
Green fees £20
Catering, changing room/showers, bar, club and trolley hire, shop, practice facilities
Visitors welcome weekdays
Societies welcome by prior arrangement

BOWENHURST GOLF CENRE
Mill Lane, Crondall, Farnham, Surrey GU10 5RP
☎ 01252 851695 Fax 01252 852039
Map 4, F4
A287, 4 miles from M3 Jct 5
A short parkland course with attendant driving range.
9 holes, 4014 yards
par 62, S.S.S 60
Green fees £11
Catering, changing room/showers, bar, club and trolley hire, shop, driving range, function facilities
Visitors welcome
Societies welcome by prior arrangement

BRAMLEY GOLF CLUB
Bramley, Guildford, Surrey GU5 0AL
☎ 01483 893685 Fax 01483 894673
Map 16, A9
secretary@bramleygolfclub.co.uk
A281, 2 miles S of Guildford
Founded 1913
A course with quite a pedigree, giving superb views across three counties from its higher parts. The last three holes work their way around an extraordinary lake feature.
18 holes, 5990 yards
par 69, S.S.S 69
Designer James Braid, C.H. Mayo
Green fees £28
Catering, changing room/showers, bar, club, trolley and buggy hire, shop, driving range, practice facilities
Visitors welcome with weekend restrictions
Societies welcome by prior arrangement

BROADWATER PARK GOLF CLUB
Guildford Road, Farncombe, Godalming, Surrey GU7 3BU
☎ 01483 429955 Fax 01483 429955
Map 16, A9
A3100, 4 miles S of Guildford
Founded 1989
Par 3 course with driving range.
9 holes, 2602 yards
par 54
Designer K.D. Milow
Green fees £4.50
Bar, club hire, shop, driving range
Visitors welcome
Societies welcome by prior arrangement, no companies

BURHILL GOLF CLUB
Burwood Road, Walton-on-Thames, Surrey KT12 4BL
☎ 01932 227345 Fax 01932 267159
Map 16, B7
Close to M25 Jct 10
Founded 1907
Famous throughout golf for its annual 'Family Foursomes' tournament, and in miltary history for the achievements of Barnes Wallis who worked at a desk in the dining room during the Second World War, Burhill is a delightful parkland course with a magnificent clubhouse. A second course opened in spring 2001.
New Course: 18 holes, 6597 yards
par 69
Designer Simon Gidman
Old Course: 18 holes, 6479 yards, par 70, S.S.S 71
Designer Willie Park Jnr
Green fees £60
Catering, changing room/showers, bar, club and trolley hire, shop, driving range, practice facilities
Visitors welcome, with restrictions
Handicap certificate required
Societies welcome by prior arrangment
🏨 Oatlands Park Hotel, Oatlands Drive, Weybridge, Surrey
☎ 01932 847242

CAMBERLEY HEATH GOLF CLUB
Golf Drive, Camberley, Surrey GU15 1JG
☎ 01276 23258 Fax 01276 692505
Map 4, G3
www.camberleyheathgolfclub.co.uk
A325 between Bagshot and Frimley
Founded 1913
One of the earlier Surrey heathland courses, highly acclaimed right from its (very expensive) start. A number of short par 4s keep the overall length modest, yet par is not easily matched, such are the effects of the considerable undulations on holes such as the roller-coaster 10th and treacherous 17th.
18 holes, 6326 yards
par 72, S.S.S 71
Designer Harry Colt
Green fees £48
Catering, changing room/showers, bar, club, trolley and buggy hire, shop, driving range, practice facilities, conference and function facilities, Japanese and English cuisine
Visitors welcome weekdays
Handicap certificate required
Societies welcome by prior arrangement
🏨 One Oak Toby, Portsmouth Road, Camberley, Surrey
☎ 01276 691939

CENTRAL LONDON GOLF CENTRE
Burntwood Lane, Wandsworth, London SW17 0AT
☎ 020 8871 2468 Fax 020 8874 7447 **Map 16, E6**
golf@clgc.co.uk
www.clgc.co.uk
Off A3
Founded 1992
A much needed and remarkable facility, the closest to the centre of London.
9 holes, 4664 yards
par 62, S.S.S 62
Designer Patrick Tallack
Green fees £6.50
Catering, changing room/showers, bar, club and trolley hire, shop, driving range, conference and function rooms
Visitors welcome
Societies welcome by prior arrangement
🏨 Travelodge Battersea
☎ 0870 9056343

CHESSINGTON GOLF CENTRE
Garrison Lane, Chessington, Surrey KT9 2LW
☎ 020 8391 0948 Fax 020 8397 2068 **Map 16, C7**
M25 Jct 9 or A3
Founded 1984
Short parkland course with floodlit driving range.
9 holes, 1761 yards
par 60, S.S.S 57
Green fees £7.50
Catering, bar, club, trolley and buggy hire, shop, driving range, practice facilities
Visitors welcome
Societies welcome by prior arrangement
🏨 Travel Inn – Monkey Puzzle, Chessington, Surrey
☎ 01372 744060

CHIDDINGFOLD GOLF CLUB
Petworth Road, Chiddingfold, Surrey GU8 4SL
☎ 01428 685888 Fax 01428 685939
Map 4, G5
A283, S of Godalming
Founded 1994
A parkland course in beautiful country on the Surrey-Sussex border.
18 holes, 5482 yards

par 70, S.S.S 67
Designer Jonathan Gaunt
Green fees £15
Catering, changing room/showers, bar, club, trolley and buggy hire, shop, driving range, practice facilities
Visitors welcome
Societies welcome by prior arrangement

CHIPSTEAD GOLF CLUB

How Lane, Chipstead, Coulsdon, Surrey CR5 3LN
☎ 01737 551053 Fax 01737 55404
Map 16, E8
Off A217, ½ mile N of Chipstead
Founded 1906
A hilly course with glorious views.
18 holes, 5491 yards
par 68, S.S.S 67
Green fees £25
Catering, changing room/showers, bar, club, trolley and buggy hire, shop, practice facilities
Visitors welcome weekdays
Societies welcome by prior arrangement

CHOBHAM GOLF CLUB

Chobham Road, Knaphill, Woking, Surrey GU21 2TZ
☎ 01276 855584 Fax 01276 855663
Map 16, A8
www.chobhamgolfclub.co.uk
A3046, between Chobham and Knaphill
Founded 1994
A young course in mature parkland with a number of lakes.
18 holes, 5959 yards
par 69, S.S.S 67
Designer Peter Alliss, Clive Clark
Green fees £35
Catering, changing room/showers, bar, trolley hire, shop
Visitors welcome only as members' guests
Societies welcome by prior arrangement

CLANDON REGIS GOLF CLUB

Epsom Road, West Clandon, Surrey GU4 7TT
☎ 01483 224888 Fax 01483 211781
Map 16, B8
office@crgc.freeserve.co.uk
A246, 3 miles E of Guildford
Founded 1994
A private club that genuinely welcomes visitors, with a testing design featuring water hazards, in a pretty, rural area of Surrey.
18 holes, 6419 yards
par 72, S.S.S 68
Designer David Williams
Green fees £25
Catering, changing room/showers, bar, club and trolley hire, shop, driving range, practice facilities
Visitors welcome, restricted weekends
Societies welcome by prior arrangement
🏨 Angel Posting House & Livery, 91 High Street, Guildford, Surrey GU1 3DP
☎ 01483 564555 Fax 01483 533770
angelhotel@hotmail.com

COOMBE HILL GOLF CLUB

Golf Club Drive, Coombe Lane West, Kingston, Surrey KT2 7DF
☎ 020 8336 7600 Fax 020 8336 7601 **Map 16, C7**
www.coombehillgolf.com
Off A238, off A3 Kingston bypass
Founded 1911
Very aristocratic course, a favourite of royalty and international celebrities. Each of the short holes is a gem and as pretty as a picture, and those lengthy par 4s which climb to the green are decidedly searching. The 14th is a particularly good example of the testing short par 4.
18 holes, 6293 yards
par 71, S.S.S 71
Designer J.F. Abercromby
Green fees £65
Catering, changing room/showers, bar, club and trolley hire, shop, practice facilities
Visitors welcome weekdays, by prior arrangement
Handicap certificate required
Societies welcome by prior arrangement

COOMBE WOOD GOLF CLUB

George Road, Kingston Hill, Kingston-upon-Thames, Surrey KT2 7NS
☎ 020 8942 3828 Fax 020 8942 0388 **Map 16, C7**
Off A308, 1 mile NE of Kingston
Founded 1904
An attractive course, if somewhat short, and there are some teasing holes, such as the dog-leg 4th.
18 holes, 5299 yards
par 66, S.S.S 66
Designer Tom Williamson
Green fees £23
Catering, changing room/showers, bar, trolley hire, shop
Visitors welcome weekdays
Handicap certificate required
Societies welcome by prior arrangement

COULSDON MANOR GOLF CLUB

Coulsdon Court Road, Coulsdon, Surrey CR5 2LL
☎ 020 8660 6083 Fax 020 8668 3118 **Map 16, E8**
B2030, 5 miles S of Croydon, M25 Jct 7
Founded 1937
A haven of tranquillity, and great value golf in an arboretum boasting one of every kind of tree in Britain.
18 holes, 6037 yards
par 70, S.S.S 68
Designer Harry Colt
Green fees £15.50
Catering, changing room/showers, bar, accommodation, club, trolley and buggy hire, shop, practice facilities, tennis, gym, squash, sauna
Visitors welcome
Societies welcome by prior arrangement
🏨 Coulsdon Manor Hotel, Coulsdon Court Road, Coulsdon, Surrey CR5 2LL
☎ 0208 6680414

THE CRANLEIGH GOLF CLUB

Barhatch Lane, Cranleigh, Surrey GU6 7NG
☎ 01483 268855 Fax 01483 267251
Map 16, B10
Off A281, 1 mile from Cranleigh
Founded 1985
A parkland course.
18 holes, 5648 yards
S.S.S 67
Green fees £24
Shop, driving range
Visitors welcome weekdays
Societies welcome by prior arrangement

CROHAM HURST GOLF CLUB

Croham Road, South Croydon, Surrey CR2 7HJ
☎ 020 8657 5581 Fax 020 8657 3229 **Map 16, E8**
www.crohamhurstgolfclub.co.uk
B269, between South Croydon and Selsdon
Founded 1911
An attractive, undulating parkland course.
18 holes, 6290 yards
par 70, S.S.S 70
Designer James Braid, Hawtree
Green fees £36
Catering, changing room/showers, bar, club and trolley hire, shop, practice facilities, banqueting facilities
Visitors welcome weekdays
Societies welcome by prior arrangement

CUDDINGTON GOLF CLUB

Banstead Road, Banstead, Surrey SM7 1RD
☎ 020 8393 0952 Fax 020 8786 7025 **Map 16, D8**

cuddingtongc@aol.com
A217, M25 Jct 8
Founded 1929
A mature parkland course with a Colt designer tag. In 1999 all greens were reconstructed to USGA specification and have remained in play, however dreadful the weather.
18 holes, 6595 yards
par 71, S.S.S 71
Designer Harry Colt
Green fees £35
Catering, changing room/showers, bar, club and trolley hire, shop, practice facilities, conference facilities
Visitors welcome weekdays
Handicap certificate required
Societies welcome by prior arrangement
Heathside, Brighton Road, Tadworth, Surrey
01737 353355

DORKING GOLF CLUB

Deeplene Avenue, Chart Park, Dorking, Surrey RH5 4BX
01306 886917 Fax 01306 886917
Map 16, C9
A24, 1 mile S of Dorking
Founded 1897
A hilly course with a number of celebrated holes.
9 holes, 5163 yards
par 66, S.S.S 65
Designer James Braid
Green fees £14
Catering, changing room/showers, bar, club and trolley hire, shop
Visitors welcome weekdays
Societies welcome by prior arrangement

DRIFT GOLF CLUB

The Drift, East Horsley, Leatherhead, Surrey KT24 5HD
01483 284772 Fax 01483 284642
Map 16, C9
Off B2039, M25 Jct 10, A3
Founded 1975
Particularly pretty in May and June when the rhododendrons are in full bloom. Good facilities and testing course.
18 holes, 6425 yards
par 73, S.S.S 71
Designer Robert Sandow
Green fees £40
Catering, changing room/showers, bar, club, trolley and buggy hire, shop, driving range, practice facilities, conference/function room
Visitors welcome – restricted weekends
Societies welcome by prior arrangement
Hautboy Hotel, Ockham Road, Ockham, Surrey
01483 225355

DUKE'S DENE GOLF CLUB

Halliloo Valley Road, Woldingham, Surrey CR3 7HA
01883 653501 Fax 01883 653502
Map 16, E8
dukesdene@clubhaus.com
www.clubhaus.com
Off A22
Founded 1996
A course making extensive and sensitive use of the geography of the valley in which it was laid out by American architect Bradford Benz. With USGA specification greens the course plays well in winter.
18 holes, 6393 yards
par 71, S.S.S 70
Designer Bradford Benz
Green fees £25
Catering, changing room/showers, bar, club, trolley and buggy hire, shop, practice facilities, conference facilities and wedding facilities
Visitors welcome with restrictions
Societies welcome by prior arrangement

DULWICH & SYDENHAM HILL GOLF CLUB

Grange Lane, College Road, London SE21 7LH
0208 693 3961 Fax 0208 693 2481 **Map 16, E6**
Off South Circular Road at Dulwich College
Founded 1894
Only 5 miles from the centre of London, with stunning views over the city, and an entertaining course.
18 holes, 6008 yards
par 69, S.S.S 69
Designer Harry Colt
Green fees £25
Catering, changing room/showers, bar, club, trolley and buggy hire, shop, practice facilities
Visitors welcome weekdays
Handicap certificate required
Societies welcome by prior arrangement

DUNSFOLD AERODROME GOLF CLUB

Dunsfold Aerodrome, Godalming, Surrey GU8 4BS
01483 265403 Fax 0183 265670
Map 16, A10
A281, 12 miles S of Guildford
Founded 1965
A private course run by members of British Aerospace staff.
9 holes, 6236 yards
par 72, S.S.S 70
Designer John Sharkey
Green fees £6
Visitors welcome only as members' guests
No societies

EFFINGHAM GOLF CLUB

Guildford Road, Effingham, Surrey KT24 5PZ
01372 452203 Fax 01372 459959
Map 16, B9
secretary@effinghamgolfclub.com
www.effinghamgolfclub.com
A243 between Guildford and Leatherhead
Founded 1927
Rare orchids are amongst the natural delights of Effingham, deer and badger, too. Colt selected a number of outstanding positions for his tees, the 7th, in particular, giving wonderful views deep into Surrey. The 5th is a brute of a par 4, 460 yards long, to a deviously borrowed green.
18 holes, 6534 yards
par 71, S.S.S 71
Designer Harry Colt
Green fees £35
Catering, changing room/showers, bar, trolley and buggy hire, shop, practice facilities, tennis
Visitors welcome weekdays
Handicap certificate required
Societies welcome by prior arrangement
Jarvis Thatcher Hotel, Epsom Road, East Horsley, Surrey
01483 284291

EPSOM GOLF CLUB

Longdown Lane South, Epsom Downs, Epsom, Surrey KT17 4JR
01372 721666 Fax 01372 817183
Map 16, D8
www.epsomgolfclub.co.uk
B288, off A240, 200 yards from Epsom Downs Station
Founded 1889
One of the oldest courses in Surrey, with the oldest puprose-built clubhouse in the county. Short, tight, with excellent greens, and fine views over London.
18 holes, 5658 yards
par 69, S.S.S 68
Designer T.W. Lang
Green fees £26
Catering, changing room/showers, bar, club and trolley hire, shop, practice facilities, conference, function and wedding facilities
Visitors welcome, restricted Tuesday and weekends
Societies welcome by prior arrangement
Travel Inn, St Margarets Drive, Epsom, Surrey
01372 739786

FARLEIGH COURT GOLF CLUB

Old Farleigh Road, Farleigh, Surrey CR6 9PX
0188362 7711 Fax 0188362 7722
Map 16, E8
Off Addington Road, 1½ miles S of Selsdon
Two challenging parkland courses.
18 holes, 6414 yards, par 72, S.S.S 71
9 holes, 6562 yards, par 72, S.S.S 71
Designer John Jacobs.
Catering, changing room/showers, bar, club and trolley hire, shop, driving range, practice facilities
Visitors welcome
Societies welcome by prior arrangement

FARNHAM GOLF CLUB

The Sands, Farnham, Surrey GU10 1PX
01252 782109 Fax 01252 781185
Map 4, G4
Off A31, 3 miles E of Farnham
Founded 1896
Regularly used for PGA Qualifiers, and joint host of the 1995 British Seniors Amateur Open, Farnham is an attractive mixture of parkland and heathland holes, with views over farmland to the Hog's Back. The course has recently been lengthened, emphasising the smallness of the greens, thus testing approach work earnestly.
18 holes, 6447 yards
par 72, S.S.S 71
Green fees £37.50
Catering, changing room/showers, bar, trolley hire, shop, practice facilities
Visitors welcome weekdays
Handicap certificate required
Societies welcome by prior arrangement

FARNHAM PARK PAR THREE GOLF COURSE

Farnham Park, Farnham, Surrey GU9 0AU
01252 715216 **Map 4, F4**
A287, next to Farnham Castle
Founded 1966
A testing little par-3 course.
9 holes, 1163 yards
par 27
Designer Sir Henry Cotton
Green fees £4.50
Catering, changing room/showers, bar, club hire, shop
Visitors welcome
Societies welcome by prior arrangement

FOXHILLS

Stonehill Road, Ottershaw, Surrey KT16 0EL
01932 872050 Fax 01932 875200
Map 16, A7
golf@foxhills.co.uk
www.foxhills.co.uk
B386, 2 miles SW of Chertsey, M25 Jct 11, M
Founded 1975
Bernard Hunt, who played in no fewer than eight Ryder Cups, was associated with Foxhills right from the start, and is honoured by having one of the courses named after him. Both are exceptionally handsome, with pine, beech and birch trees separating the fairways, giving enviable seclusion to players.
Bernard Hunt Course: 18 holes, 6876 yards, par 73, S.S.S 73
Longcross Course: 18 holes, 6743 yards, par 72, S.S.S 72
9 holes, 1400 yards, par 27
Designer Hawtree
Green fees £60
Catering, changing room/showers, bar, accommodation, club, trolley and buggy hire, shop, driving range, practice facilities, leisure club, tennis, swimming, conference facilities, 24-hour service
Visitors welcome weekdays, restricted weekends
Societies welcome by prior arrangement
Foxhills Resort and Club, Stonehill Road, Ottershaw, Surrey KT16 0EL
01932 872050 Fax 01932 874762
www.foxhills.co.uk

GATTON MANOR HOTEL, GOLF & COUNTRY CLUB

Standon Lane, Ockley, Near Dorking, Surrey RH5 5PQ
01306 627555 Fax 01306 627713
Map 16, C10
gattonmanor@enterprise.net
www.gattonmanor.co.uk
Off A29, 1½ miles SW of Ockley, M25 Jct 9
Founded 1969
Exceedingly handsome course with lakes, streams and tall trees to be negotiated, and one of the best finishing holes in the region.
18 holes, 6629 yards
par 72, S.S.S 71
Designer Sir Henry Cotton
Green fees £23
Catering, changing room/showers, bar, accommodation, club, trolley and buggy hire, shop, driving range, practice facilities, tennis, fishing, health club, gym, extensive corporate and function facilities
Visitors welcome, restricted Sundays
Societies welcome by prior arrangement
Gatton Manor Hotel, Golf & Country Club, Standon Lane, Ockley, Nr Dorking, Surrey RH5 5PQ
01306 627555 Fax 01306 627713
gattonmanor@enterprise net
www.gattonmanor.co.uk

GOAL FARM GOLF CLUB

Gole Road, Pirbright, Surrey GU24 0PZ
01483 473183 **Map 16, A8**
Off A322 close to West Hill Golf Club
Founded 1978
One of those very necessary facilities for introducing new players to the game in an area which must seem impenetrable to those without the 'right connections'. It is also a welcome practice facility for those whose connections are of the right sort.
9 holes, 1146 yards
par 27, S.S.S 24
Green fees £4.75
Bar, club hire
Visitors welcome with restrictions
Societies welcome by prior arrangement

GUILDFORD GOLF CLUB

High Path Road, Merrow, Guildford, Surrey GU1 2HL
01483 563941 Fax 01483 453228
Map 16, A9
secretary@guildfordgolfclub.co.uk
A246, 2 miles E of Guildford, M25 Jct 10
Founded 1886
Why Surrey's oldest course is not better known is a mystery, for it is a thoroughly good test, especially in winter, when its excellent drainage sets it apart from the rest.
18 holes, 6090 yards
par 69, S.S.S 70
Green fees £30
Catering, changing room/showers, bar, club and trolley hire, shop, practice facilities
Visitors welcome with restrictions
Societies welcome by prior arrangement

HANKLEY COMMON GOLF CLUB

Tilford, Farnham, Surrey GU10 2DD
01252 792493 Fax 01252 795699
Map 4, F4
Off A287 or B3001, 1 mile SE of Tilford
Founded 1896
There are few plants more unforgiving to erratic golf than heather, and Hankley Common has hundreds of acres of it. This is a

wild, windswept heath, making for a wonderful, if uncompromising, course, and the hilltop 7th green is one of the great places from which to survey it all.
18 holes, 6438 yards
par 71, S.S.S 71
Designer James Braid, Harry Colt
Green fees £50
Catering, changing room/showers, bar, trolley hire, shop, practice facilities
Visitors welcome weekdays
Societies welcome by prior arrangement

HAPPY VALLEY GOLF CLUB

Rook Lane, Chaldon, Caterham, Surrey CR3 5AA
☎ 01883 344555 Fax 01883 344422
Map 16, E8
A22 (M25 Jct 7 or M23 Jct 6).
Founded 1999
A big course with plenty of challenge on rolling country with good views.
18 holes, 6858 yards
par 72, S.S.S 73
Designer David Williams
Green fees £25
Catering, changing room/showers, bar, trolley and buggy hire, shop, driving range, practice facilities, indoor golf school
Visitors welcome weekdays
Societies welcome by prior arrangement

HAZELWOOD GOLF CENTRE

Croysdale Avenue, Green Street, Sunbury-on-Thames, Surrey TW16 6QU
☎ 01932 770932 Fax 01932 770933
Map 16, B7
Off Green Street, M3 Jct 1
A short parkland course.
9 holes, 5660 yards
par 35, S.S.S 67
Designer Jonathan Gaunt
Green fees £7
Club and trolley hire, shop, driving range, golf academy
Visitors welcome
Societies welcome by prior arrangement

HERSHAM VILLAGE GOLF CLUB

Asher Road, Hersham, Walton-on-Thames, Surrey KT12 4RA
☎ 01932 267666 Fax 01932 267146
Map 16, B7
Adjacent to Hersham station, Walton-on-Thames
A parkland course.
9 holes, 2811 yards
par 36
Green fees £18.50
Shop, driving range
Visitors welcome
Societies welcome by prior arrangement

HINDHEAD GOLF CLUB

Churt Road, Hindhead, Surrey GU26 6HX
☎ 01428 604614 Fax 01428 608508
Map 4, G5
A 287, 1½ miles N of Hindhead
Founded 1904
One of the highest courses in Surrey, the front nine is set out along narrow, tree-lined valleys, making these holes very beautiful but treacherous. The back nine is on a flatter plateau, apparently more forgiving, but that is only an illusion. At 441 yards, the 18th is a stern finisher.
18 holes, 6356 yards
par 70, S.S.S 70
Designer J.H. Taylor
Green fees £36
Catering, changing room/showers, bar, club and trolley hire, shop, driving range, practice facilities, small conference facilities
Visitors welcome (restricted weekends)
Handicap certificate required – limit: 20
Societies welcome Wednesday and Thursday by prior arrangement
🏨 Devils Punch Bowl, Hindhead, Surrey
☎ 01428 606565

HOEBRIDGE GOLF CENTRE

Old Woking Road, Old Woking, Surrey GU22 8JH
☎ 01483 722611 Fax 01483 740369
Map 16, A8
www.hoebridge.co.uk
B382 Old Woking Road, E of Woking (via A3, Wisley/Ripley)
Founded 1982
Extensive facilities and a course of John Jacobs pedigree in prime Surrey sand-belt territory. Green fees for the smaller courses are appropriately less.
Hoebridge Course: 18 holes, 6536 yards, par 72, S.S.S 71
Designer John Jacobs
Maybury Course: 18 holes, 2334 yards, par 54
Shey Copse Course: 9 holes, 2294 yards, par 33, S.S.S 31
Green fees £17
Catering, changing room/showers, bar, club, trolley and buggy hire, shop, driving range, practice facilities, function/banquetting facilities, snooker
Visitors welcome
Societies welcome by prior arrangement
🏨 Wheatsheaf Hotel, Chobham Road, Woking, Surrey GU21 4AL
☎ 01483 225188

HOME PARK GOLF CLUB

Hampton Wick, Kingston-upon-Thames, Surrey KT1 4AD
☎ 020 8977 6645 Fax 020 8977 4414 **Map 16, C7**
A308, W side of Kingston Bridge
Founded 1895
Parkland course laid out in the grounds of Hampton Court Palace.
18 holes, 6584 yards
par 71, S.S.S 71
Green fees £22
Catering, changing room/showers, bar, trolley hire, shop, practice facilities
Visitors welcome
Societies welcome by prior arrangement

HORTON PARK GOLF & COUNTRY CLUB

Hook Road, Epsom, Surrey KT19 8QG
☎ 0208 3942626 Fax 0208 3941369
Map 16, D8
hortonparkgc@aol,com
Off A3, 1 mile W of Ewell, M25 Jct 9
Founded 1987
Three challenging par-3 holes – 9th, 10th and 18th – are played over a lake. Excellent value in country park surroundings.
Millennium Course: 18 holes, 6300 yards, par 71, S.S.S 70
Designer P. Nicholson
Green fees £16
Catering, changing room/showers, bar, club, trolley and buggy hire, shop, driving range, function facilities, 9-hole Academy course
Visitors welcome
Societies welcome by prior arrangement
🏨 Travel Inn – Monkey Puzzle, Chessington, Surrey
☎ 01372 744060

HURTMORE GOLF CLUB

Hurtmore Road, Hurtmore, Godalming, Surrey GU7 2RN
☎ 01483 426492 Fax 01483 426121
Map 16, A9
A3, 4 miles S of Guildford
Founded 1992
There may not be great length, but the numerous lakes and prolific bunkering make this quite a challenging course.
18 holes, 5514 yards
par 70, S.S.S 67
Designer Peter Alliss, Clive Clark
Green fees £10
Catering, changing room/showers, bar, club and trolley hire, shop,

practice facilities
Visitors welcome
Societies welcome by prior arrangement

KINGSWOOD GOLF & COUNTRY CLUB

Sandy Lane, Kingswood, Tadworth, Surrey KT20 6NE
01737 832188 Fax 01737 833920
Map 16, D8
sales@kingswood-golf.fsnet.co.uk
B2032, off A217 5 miles S of Sutton
Founded 1928
A near neighbour of Walton Heath, yet different in character, being a flatter, parkland course, playing through avenues of mature trees and rhododendrons, overlooking the Chipstead valley. James Braid's layout of 1928 has been lengthened considerably over the years so that it now approaches 7,000 yards from the medal tees.
18 holes, 6904 yards
par 72, S.S.S 73
Designer James Braid
Green fees £36
Catering, changing room/showers, bar, club, trolley and buggy hire, shop, driving range, practice facilities, squash, snooker, extensive function facilities
Visitors welcome subject to restrictions
Societies welcome by prior arrangement
Bridge House Hotel, Reigate Hill, Reigate, Surrey
01737 244821

LALEHAM GOLF CLUB

Laleham Reach, Chertsey, Surrey KT16 8RP
01932 564211 Fax 01932 564448
Map 16, B7
sec@laleham-golf.co.uk
www.laleham-golf.co.uk
Off A320, 2 miles S of Staines opp Thorpe Park, M25 Jct 11, M3 Jct 2
Founded 1903
A parkland course.
18 holes, 6121 yards
par 70, S.S.S 70
Green fees £22
Catering, changing room/showers, bar, trolley hire, shop
Visitors welcome – restricted weekends
Societies welcome by prior arrangement
Great Fosters, Stroud Road, Egham, Surrey TW20 9UR
01784 433822 Fax 01784 472455
GreatFosters@compuserve.com
www.great-fosters.co.uk

LEATHERHEAD GOLF CLUB

Kingston Raod, Leatherhead, Surrey KT22 0EE
01932 564211 Fax 01932 564448
Map 16, C8
A243, close to M25 Jct 9
Founded 1903
A rolling course in pleasant wooded parkland.
18 holes, 6203 yards
par 71, S.S.S 70
Green fees £35
Catering, changing room/showers, bar, club, trolley and buggy hire, shop, practice facilities
Visitors welcome with prior booking, restricted weekends.
Societies welcome by prior arrangement

LIMPSFIELD CHART GOLF CLUB

Westerham Road, Limpsfield, Surrey RH8 0SL
01883 723405 **Map 16, F9**
A25, between Oxted and Westerham
Founded 1889
A charming heathland course in lovely country.
9 holes, 5718 yards
par 70, S.S.S 68
Green fees £18
Catering, changing room/showers, bar
Visitors welcome weekdays with restrictions
Societies welcome by prior arrangement

LINGFIELD PARK GOLF CLUB

Racecourse Road, Lingfield, Surrey RH7 6PQ
01342 832659 Fax 01342 833066
Map 16, E10
cmorley@lingfieldpark.co.uk
www.lingfieldracecourse.co.uk
M25 Jct 6
Founded 1987
Set in beautiful countryside, this well-wooded course makes good strategic use of rivers, ditches and ponds. Each hole is named after a famous racehorse, and the 15th, Desert Orchid, is a monstrously difficult par 5. Trees closing in at driving range thwart many players on the 5th, Alisya, Stroke 1.
18 holes, 6487 yards
par 72, S.S.S 72
Green fees £36
Catering, changing room/showers, bar, club, trolley and buggy hire, shop, driving range, practice facilities, racecourse facilities – 75 meetings per year, Leisure club
Visitors welcome – restricted weekends
Societies welcome by prior arrangement
Gravetye Manor, Vowels Lane, East Grinstead, East Sussex RH19 4LJ
01342 810567 Fax 01342 810080
gravetye@relaischateaux.fr

MALDEN GOLF CLUB

Traps Lane, New Malden, Surrey KT3 4RS
020 8942 0654 **Map 16, D7**
Off A3, between Wimbledon and Kingston
Founded 1893
A handsome parkland course cut through by a stream which comes into play on a number of holes.
18 holes, 6295 yards
par 71, S.S.S 70
Green fees £27.50
Catering, changing room/showers, bar, trolley and buggy hire, shop, practice facilities
Visitors welcome weekdays
Societies welcome by prior arrangement

MERRIST WOOD GOLF CLUB

Coombe Lane, Worplesdon, Guildford, Surrey GU3 3PE
01483 884050 Fax 01483 884047
Map 16, A8
mwgc@merristwood-golfclub.co.uk
www.merristwood-golfclub.co.uk
NW of Guildford via A322 or A323
Founded 1997
An impressive new course by David Williams, long, and with plenty of water. It is also environmentally important, and the club operates an equal opportunties policy.
18 holes, 6909 yards
par 72, S.S.S 73
Designer David Williams
Green fees £29
Catering, changing room/showers, bar, club, trolley and buggy hire, shop, driving range, practice facilities
Visitors welcome with restrictions
Societies welcome by prior arrangement
Worplesdon Place Hotel, Perry Hill, Worplesdon, Surrey
01483 232407

MILFORD GOLF CLUB

Station Lane, Milford, Near Godalming, Surrey GU8 5HS
01483 416291 Fax 01483 419199
Map 4, G4
milford@americangolf.uk.com
Off A3 at Milford – close to station
Founded 1993
A good example of contemporary design, making the most of a limited area.
18 holes, 5960 yards

par 69, S.S.S 68
Designer Peter Alliss, Clive Clark
Green fees £20
Catering, changing room/showers, bar, club, trolley and buggy hire, shop, driving range, practice facilities, conference facilities
Visitors welcome, with restrictions
Societies welcome by prior arrangement
Inn on the Lake, Ockford road, Godalming, Surrey, Surrey GU7 1RH
01483 419997

MITCHAM GOLF CLUB

Carshalton Road, Mitcham Junction, Mitcham, Surrey CR4 4HN
020 8640 4280 Fax 020 8648 4197 **Map 16, D7**
A237 close to Mitcham Junction Station
Founded 1924
A common-land course with excellent drainage and praiseworthy greens.
18 holes, 5935 yards
par 69, S.S.S 68
Designer Tom Morris, Tom Dunn
Green fees £16
Catering, changing room/showers, bar, trolley hire, shop
Visitors welcome – restricted weekends
Societies welcome by prior arrangement

MOORE PLACE GOLF COURSE

Portsmouth Road, Esher, Surrey KT10 9AL
01372 463533 Fax 01372 469440
Map 16, C8
www.moore-place.co.uk
S of Esher town centre
Founded 1926
Popular public facility on well-drained ground, facilitating good conditions all year round.
9 holes, 2078 yards
par 66, S.S.S 63
Designer Harry Vardon
Green fees £6.30
Catering, bar, club and trolley hire, shop, practice facilities, pub and restaurant, conference suite
Visitors welcome
Societies welcome by prior arrangement
The Bear Inn, High Street, Esher, Surrey
01372 469786

NEW ZEALAND GOLF CLUB

Woodham Lane, Addlestone, Surrey KT15 3QD
01932 345049 Fax 01932 342891
Map 16, B8
A285, 2 miles E of Woking
Founded 1895
New Zealand is one of those high-class courses that does not seek the limelight. On paper it is not a long course, yet six of its par 4s exceed 400 yards, the greens are tiny and tightly bunkered, and acres of heather and avenues of trees await wayward shots.
18 holes, 6012 yards
par 68, S.S.S 69
Designer Tom Simpson
Catering, changing room/showers, bar, club, trolley and buggy hire, shop, practice facilities
Visitors welcome weekdays by prior arrangement
Handicap certificate required
Societies welcome by prior arrangement

NORTH DOWNS GOLF CLUB

Northdown Road, Woldingham, Caterham, Surrey CR3 7AA
01883 653004 Fax 01883 652832
Map 16, E8
info@northdownsgolfclub.co.uk
www.northdownsgolfclub.co.uk
3 miles E of Caterham, M25 Jct 6
Founded 1899
Located 800 feet up, overlooking the London basin. The 462-yard 6th is very difficult, and a pond makes the 14th a hole for big hitters.
18 holes, 5843 yards
par 69, S.S.S 68
Designer Frank Pennink
Green fees £20
Catering, changing room/showers, bar, trolley and buggy hire, shop, practice facilities
Visitors welcome weekdays
Handicap certificate required
Societies welcome by prior arrangement
Travel Inn – Clacket Lane Service Area, M25 Westbound, Westerham, Kent, Kent TN16 2ER
01959 565789

OAK PARK GOLF CLUB

Heath Lane, Crondall, near Farnham, Surrey GU10 5PB
01252 850850 Fax 01252 850851
Map 4, F4
oakpark@americangolf.uk.com
www.americangolf.com
Off A287 Farnham to Odiham road
Founded 1984
The Woodland Course undulates gently through its handsome, tree-lined fairways, giving fine views of the North Hampshire Downs.
Woodland Course: 18 holes, 6352 yards, par 70, S.S.S 70
Designer Patrick Dawson
Village Course: 9 holes, 3279 yards, par 36
Green fees £20
Catering, changing room/showers, bar, club, trolley and buggy hire, shop, driving range, practice facilities, function/wedding facilities, meeting rooms, health club
Visitors welcome
Societies welcome by prior arrangement
George Hotel, 100 High Street, Odiham, Hampshire RG29 1LP
01256 702081 Fax 01256 704213

OAKS SPORTS CENTRE

Woodmansterne Road, Carshalton, Surrey SM5 4AN
020 8643 8363 Fax 0208 770 7303 **Map 16, D8**
golf@oaks.sagehost.co.uk
www.oakssportscentre.co.uk
B278, 1 mile S of Carshalton station, M25 Jct 7
Founded 1973
Useful public facility with floodlit driving range.
18 holes, 6025 yards, par 70, S.S.S 69
9 holes, 1443 yards, par 28, S.S.S 28
Green fees £14.75
Catering, changing room/showers, bar, club, trolley and buggy hire, shop, driving range, conference and function facilities, squash
Visitors welcome – restricted weekend mornings
Societies welcome by prior arrangement
Bridge House Hotel, Reigate Hill, Reigate, Surrey
01737 244821

PACHESHAM PARK GOLF CENTRE

Oaklawn Road, Leatherhead, Surrey KT22 0BT
01372 843453 Fax 01372 844076
Map 16, C8
philktaylor@hotmail.com
Off A244, NW of Leatherhead, M25 Jct 9
Founded 1989
A well-equipped golf centre which can both encourage the beginner and host a professional corporate day. The course is ingeniously laid out, effectively getting harder as the round progresses.
9 holes, 5608 yards
par 70, S.S.S 67
Designer Phil Taylor
Green fees £9
Catering, changing room/showers, bar, club and trolley hire, shop, driving range
Visitors welcome
Societies welcome by prior arrangement

PENNYHILL PARK HOTEL & COUNTRY CLUB

London Road, Bagshot, Surrey GU19 5EU
01276 471774 Fax 01276 473217
Map 4, G3
Off A30, between Camberley and Bagshot
An executive length course in the beautiful grounds of this hotel.
9 holes, 2095 yards
par 32, S.S.S 32
Catering, changing room/showers, bar, accommodation, club and trolley hire
Visitors welcome by prior arrangement
Societies welcome by prior arrangement
Pennyhill Park Hotel & Country Club, London Road, Bagshot, Surrey
01276 471774

PINE RIDGE GOLF CENTRE

Old Bisley Road, Frimley, Camberley, Surrey GU16 5NX
01276 20770 Fax 01276 678837
Map 4, F3
Off B3105, near A30 at Frimley, M3 Jct 3
Founded 1992
The poor man's Camberley Heath? A true heathland course running through undulating pine forest.
18 holes, 6458 yards
par 72, S.S.S 71
Designer Clive D. Smith
Green fees £20
Catering, changing room/showers, bar, club, trolley and buggy hire, shop, driving range, practice facilities
Visitors welcome
Societies welcome by prior arrangement

PURLEY DOWNS GOLF CLUB

106 Purley Downs Road, South Croydon, Surrey CR2 0RB
020 8657 8347 Fax 020 8651 5044 **Map 16, E8**
www.purleydowns.co.uk
A235, 3 miles S of Croydon
Founded 1894
A downland course on hilly land, scenic and testing.
18 holes, 6275 yards
par 70, S.S.S 70
Designer J.H. Taylor, Harry Colt
Green fees £25
Catering, changing room/showers, bar, trolley and buggy hire, shop
Visitors welcome weekdays
Societies welcome by prior arrangement

PUTTENHAM GOLF CLUB

Heath Road, Puttenham, near Guildford, Surrey GU3 1AL
01483 810498 Fax 01483 810988
Map 4, G4
B3000 off A3
Founded 1894
A mixture of heathland and parkland in the Surrey countryside.
18 holes, 6211 yards
par 71, S.S.S 70
Designer Donald Steel
Green fees £25
Catering, changing room/showers, bar, trolley hire, shop, practice facilities
Visitors welcome weekdays
Societies welcome by prior arrangement
Angel Posting House & Livery, 91 High Street, Guildford, Surrey GU1 3DP
01483 564555 Fax 01483 533770
angelhotel@hotmail.com

PYRFORD GOLF CLUB

Warren Lane, Pyrford, Near Woking, Surrey GU22 8XR
01483 751777 Fax 01483 729777
Map 16, B8
www.pyrford@americangolfuk.com
2 miles from A3 at Ripley
Founded 1993
An Alliss/Clark creation with 23 acres of lakes, surrounded by woodlands. Extravagant sculpting of the moundwork gives an inland links feel to the drier parts of the course – of which there are not many, water affecting play on no fewer than 13 holes. Not dissimilar to neighbouring, members-only Wisley.
18 holes, 6230 yards
par 72, S.S.S 70
Designer Peter Alliss, Clive Clark
Green fees £38
Catering, changing room/showers, bar, club, trolley and buggy hire, shop, practice facilities
Visitors welcome, restricted weekends
Societies welcome by prior arrangement
Angel Posting House & Livery, 91 High Street, Guildford, Surrey GU1 3DP
01483 564555 Fax 01483 533770
angelhotel@hotmail.com

REDHILL GOLF COURSE

Canada Avenue, Redhill, Surrey RH1 5BF
01737 770204 Fax 01737 760046
Map 16, D9
A23, 1½ miles S of Redhill
Founded 1993
An executive length pay-and-play course.
9 holes, 1903 yards
par 31, S.S.S 59
Green fees £4.95
Shop, driving range
Visitors welcome
Societies welcome by prior arrangement

REDHILL & REIGATE GOLF CLUB

Clarence Lodge, Pendleton Road, Redhill, Surrey RH1 6LB
01737 244433 Fax 01737 242117
Map 16, D9
Off A23 S of Redhill
Founded 1887
The second oldest, and one of the most deceptive, courses in Surrey. Hardest of all is the 15th, a 469-yard uphill dog-leg, and the short holes range from 136 to 215 yards.
18 holes, 5272 yards
par 68, S.S.S 66
Green fees £15
Catering, changing room/showers, bar, trolley hire, shop, practice facilities, dining room for conferences
Visitors welcome – restricted weekends
Societies welcome by prior arrangement
Reigate Manor Hotel, Reigate Hill, Reigate, Surrey
01737 240125

REIGATE HEATH GOLF CLUB

Flanchford Road, Reigate Heath, Surrey RH2 8QR
01737 242610 **Map 16, D9**
1½ miles W of Reigate, off A25
Founded 1895
With plentiful heather, bracken and gorse there is much trouble for the profligate, although absolution might be found in the recently restored church (once a windmill), adjacent to the clubhouse.
9 holes, 5658 yards
par 67, S.S.S 67
Green fees £20
Catering, changing room/showers, bar, trolley hire, shop, practice facilities
Visitors welcome – restricted weekends
Handicap certificate required
Societies welcome Wednesday and Thursday by prior arrangement
Reigate Manor Hotel, Reigate Hill, Reigate, Surrey
01737 240125

REIGATE HILL GOLF CLUB

Gatton Bottom, Reigate, Surrey RH2 0TU
01737 646070 Fax 01737 642650
Map 16, D9

info@reigatehillgolfclub.co.uk
www.reigatehillgolfclub.co.uk
Off A217, M25 Jct 8
Founded 1995
A club which prides itself on being able to play its USGA specification tees and greens all year round. The design by David Williams features carries over a lake at the 14th and 15th.
18 holes, 6175 yards
par 72, S.S.S 70
Designer David Williams
Green fees £25
Catering, changing room/showers, bar, club, trolley and buggy hire, shop, driving range, practice facilities, conference and function facilities
Visitors welcome weekdays
Societies welcome by prior arrangement
Bridge House Hotel, Reigate Hill, Reigate, Surrey
01737 244821

THE RICHMOND GOLF CLUB

Sudbrook Park, Richmond, Surrey TW10 7AS
020 8940 7792 Fax 020 8332 7914 **Map 16, C6**
Off A307, 2 miles S of Richmond
Founded 1891
A very pretty parkland course with a remarkable 18th-century, Grade 1 listed building as its clubhouse, featuring a 30-foot Baroque Cube Room.
18 holes, 6007 yards
par 70, S.S.S 69
Green fees £32
Catering, changing room/showers, bar, club and trolley hire, shop, driving range, practice facilities
Visitors welcome weekdays
Handicap certificate required
Societies welcome by prior arrangement
Richmond Hill Hotel, Richmond, Surrey
020 8940 2247

RICHMOND PARK GOLF COURSES

Roehampton Gate, Richmond Park, London SW15 5JR
0208 8761795 Fax 0208 8781354
Map 16, C6
rpgc@globalnet.co.uk
www.globalnet.co.uk/rpgc
Within Richmond Park, via Roehampton Gate
Founded 1923
Two busy public courses set in the incomparable surroundings of Richmond Royal Park.
Duke's Course: 18 holes, 6036 yards, par 68, S.S.S 68
Designer F. Hawtree
Prince's Course: 18 holes, 5868 yards, par 68, S.S.S 67
Green fees £15
Catering, bar, club, trolley and buggy hire, shop, driving range, practice facilities
Visitors welcome
Societies welcome by prior arrangement
Richmond Hill Hotel, Richmond, Surrey
020 8940 2247

ROEHAMPTON CLUB

Roehampton Lane, London SW15 5LR
020 8480 4200 Fax 020 8480 4265 **Map 16, D6**
On Roehampton Lane between South Circular Road and A3
Founded 1904
A parkland course, part of the facilities of a much larger members' sports club.
18 holes, 6065 yards
S.S.S 69
Catering, changing room/showers, bar, trolley hire, shop, practice facilities
Visitors welcome only as members' guests
Societies welcome by prior arrangement

ROKER PARK GOLF CLUB

Holy Lane, Aldershot Road, Guildford, Surrey GU3 3PB
01483 236677 **Map 4, G4**
A323, 2 miles W of Guildford
Founded 1992
Quite difficult pay-and-play parkland course.
9 holes, 6074 yards
par 72, S.S.S 72
Designer W.V. Roker
Green fees £7.50
Catering, changing room/showers, bar, club, trolley and buggy hire, shop, practice facilities
Visitors welcome
Societies welcome by prior arrangement

ROYAL MID-SURREY GOLF CLUB

Old Deer Park, Richmond, Surrey TW9 2SB
020 8940 1894 Fax 020 8332 2957 **Map 16, C6**
Off A316 (eastbound), ½ mile N of Richmond
Founded 1892
Familiar to many who fly in to Heathrow, as the approach from the east frequently passes over this historic turf with many royal connections. The Outer Course is one which always seems to play longer than its official yardage, with many big par 4s defended by J.H. Taylor's innovative earthworks.
Outer Course: 18 holes, 6385 yards, par 69, S.S.S 70
Designer J.H. Taylor
Inner Course: 18 holes, 5446 yards, par 68, S.S.S 67
Green fees £65
Catering, changing room/showers, bar, club, trolley and buggy hire, shop, practice facilities
Visitors welcome weekdays
Handicap certificate required
Societies welcome by prior arrangement

ROYAL WIMBLEDON GOLF CLUB

29 Camp Road, Wimbledon Common, London SW19 4UW
020 8946 2125 Fax 020 8944 8652 **Map 16, D7**
secretary@royal-wimbledon-golf.co.uk
www.royal-wimbledon-golf.co.uk
Off Parkside, Wimbledon Common
Founded 1865
One of England's oldest clubs, which moved to its present location in 1907. The 6th and 10th holes play into Caesar's Camp, the site of an old Roman garrison, and the 5th, 13th and 17th are much lauded – strongly defended short holes. Eight par 4s exceed 400 yards in length.
18 holes, 6348 yards
par 70, S.S.S 70
Designer Willie Park, Harry Colt
Green fees £55
Catering, changing room/showers, bar, club and trolley hire, shop, practice facilities
Visitors welcome weekdays
Handicap certificate required
Societies welcome by prior arrangement

RUSPER GOLF CLUB

Rusper Road, Newdigate, Surrey RH5 5BX
01293 871871 Fax 01293 871456
Map 16, D10
TJillth@aol.com
Off A24, 5 miles S of Dorking
Founded 1992
A further 9 holes are under construction to make this a full-length course of some quality, making full use of mature woodlands and natural water features.
9 holes, 6597 yards
par 71, S.S.S 69
Designer Hawtree, AWC Blunden
Green fees £8
Catering, changing room/showers,

bar, club, trolley and buggy hire, shop, driving range
Visitors welcome
Societies welcome by prior arrangement
🏨 Ghyll Manor Hotel, Rusper, West Sussex, East Sussex
☎ 01293 871571

SANDOWN PARK GOLF COURSE

More Lane, Esher, Surrey KT10 8AN
☎ 01372 461234 **Map 16, C7**
In centre of Sandown Park race course.
Founded 1967
A public parkland facility in the middle of the racecourse, with Golf Academy attached.
9 holes, 5658 yards
S.S.S 67
Designer John Jacobs
Green fees £6.25
Catering, changing room/showers, bar, club and trolley hire, shop, practice facilities
Visitors welcome
Societies welcome by prior arrangement

SELSDON PARK HOTEL GOLF CLUB

Addington Road, Sanderstead, South Croydon, Surrey CR2 8YA
☎ 020 8657 8811 Fax 020 8651 6171 **Map 16, E8**
www.principalhotels.co.uk
A2022 Purley-Addington road
Founded 1929
Exceptional value for money for a course of this quality, only 13 miles from central London. Its par of 73 reflects the fact that there are five par 5s. However, the shorter hitter is encouraged, as there is only one par 4 over 400 yards. Strongest hole is the 2nd.
18 holes, 6473 yards
par 73, S.S.S 71
Designer J.H. Taylor
Green fees £27.50
Catering, changing room/showers, bar, accommodation, club, trolley and buggy hire, shop, driving range, practice facilities, many leisure and conference facilities within hotel complex
Visitors welcome
Societies welcome by prior arrangement
🏨 Selsdon Park Hotel, Addington Road, Sanderstead, Croydon, Surrey CR2 8YA
☎ 0208 6578811

SHIRLEY PARK GOLF CLUB

194 Addiscombe Road, Croydon, Surrey CR0 7LB
☎ 0208 654 1143 Fax 0208 654 6733 **Map 16, E8**
info@shirleyparkgolfclub.co.uk
www.shirleyparkgolfclub.co.uk
A232, 1 mile from East Croydon Station
Founded 1914
A parkland course with many good holes, especially the 187-yard 8th, all carry across a valley to an angled, plateau green.
18 holes, 6210 yards
par 71, S.S.S 70
Designer Tom Simpson, Herbert Fowler
Green fees £32
Catering, changing room/showers, bar, club and trolley hire, shop, practice facilities, conference/seminar facilities, snooker
Visitors welcome weekdays
Societies welcome by prior arrangement
🏨 Croydon Park Hotel, 7 Altyre Road, Croydon, Surrey CR9 5AA
☎ 020 840 0900

SILVERMERE GOLF CLUB

Redhill Road, Cobham, Surrey KT11 1EF
☎ 01932 866007 Fax 01932 868259 **Map 16, B8**
sales@silvermere.freeserve.co.uk
www.crowngolf.co.uk
Off B366, M25 Jct 10
Founded 1976
One of the best value courses in Surrey, playing through tree-lined fairways. The 11th is a 605-yard par 5, and the 17th and 18th are played over Silvermere Lake, on which Barnes Wallis first tested the Bouncing Bomb.
18 holes, 6404 yards
par 71, S.S.S 71
Green fees £20
Catering, changing room/showers, bar, club and trolley hire, shop, driving range, conference, wedding, function facilities, Extensive golf teaching/practice facilities
Visitors welcome – restricted weekends
Societies welcome by prior arrangement
🏨 Oatlands Park Hotel, Oatlands Drive, Weybridge, Surrey
☎ 01932 847242

ST GEORGE'S HILL GOLF CLUB

Golf Club Road, St George's Hill, Weybridge, Surrey KT13 0NL
☎ 01932 847758 Fax 01932 821564 **Map 16, B7**
www.stgeorgeshillgolfclub.co.uk
B374, 1 mile from Weybridge, close to Brooklands.
Founded 1912
See Top 50 Courses, page49
Red and Blue Courses: 18 holes, 6496 yards, par 70, S.S.S 71
Green Course: 9 holes, 2897 yards, par 35
Designer Harry Colt
Green fees £65
Catering, changing room/showers, bar, club and trolley hire, shop, practice facilities
Visitors welcome by prior arrangement
Handicap certificate required
Societies welcome by prior arrangement

SUNNINGDALE GOLF CLUB

Ridgemount Road, Sunningdale, Berkshire, Surrey SL5 9RR
☎ 01344 621681 Fax 01344 624154 **Map 4, G3**
Off A30 at Sunningdale
Founded 1900
See Top 50 Courses, page 50
Old Course: 18 holes, 6619 yards, par 72, S.S.S 72
Designer Willie Park, Harry Colt
New Course: 18 holes, 6617 yards, par 71, S.S.S 73
Designer Harry Colt
Green fees £120
Catering, changing room/showers, bar, club and trolley hire, shop, driving range, practice facilities
Visitors welcome weekdays
Handicap certificate required – limit: 18 men, 20 women
Societies welcome by prior arrangement
🏨 Pennyhill Park, Bagshot, Surrey
☎ 01276 471774

SUNNINGDALE LADIES' GOLF CLUB

Cross Road, Sunningdale, Surrey SL5 9RX
☎ 01344 620507 **Map 4, G3**
Off A30 at Sunningdale level crossing
Founded 1902
A little gem of a heathland course, short but exceptionally tight.
18 holes, 3622 yards
par 60, S.S.S 60
Designer Harry Colt
Green fees £18
Catering, changing room/showers, bar, trolley hire
Visitors welcome weekdays
Handicap certificate required
Ladies' societies only welcome by prior arrangement

SURBITON GOLF CLUB

Woodstock Lane, Chessington, Surrey KT9 1UG

☎ 020 8398 3101 Fax 020 8339 0992 **Map 16, C7**
Off A309, off A3 at Hook Junction.
Founded 1895
A parkland course.
18 holes, 6055 yards
par 70, S.S.S 69
Designer Tom Dunn
Green fees £30
Catering, changing room/showers, bar, club and trolley hire, shop
Visitors welcome weekdays
Handicap certificate required
Societies welcome by prior arrangement

SUTTON GREEN GOLF CLUB

New Lane, Sutton Green, Guildford, Surrey GU4 7QF
☎ 01483 766849 Fax 01483 750289
Map 16, A9
admin@suttongreengc.co.uk
www.suttongreengc.co.uk
Off A320 between Woking and Guildford
Founded 1994
A new facility in a prime golfing area with water featuring on nine holes.
18 holes, 6350 yards
par 71, S.S.S 70
Designer David Walker, Laura Davies
Green fees £40
Catering, changing room/showers, bar, club, trolley and buggy hire, shop, practice facilities, conference facilities
Visitors welcome with restrictions
Societies welcome by prior arrangement
🏨 Angel Posting House & Livery, 91 High Street, Guildford, Surrey GU1 3DP
☎ 01483 564555 Fax ☎ 01483 533770
angelhotel@hotmail.com

TANDRIDGE GOLF CLUB

Oxted, Surrey RH8 9NQ
☎ 01883 712274 Fax 01883 730537
Map 16, E9
A25, 2 miles E of Godstone
Founded 1925
Over 300 bunkers were a feature of Colt's original layout. Some have gone, but otherwise the course is very much as he constructed it. The tree-lined fairways give splendid views, and the Tudor-style clubhouse is especially attractive. The start is tough, the first two par 4s stretching over 900 yards.
18 holes, 6250 yards
par 70, S.S.S 70
Designer Harry Colt
Green fees £40
Catering, changing room/showers, bar, club and trolley hire, shop, practice facilities
Visitors welcome weekdays with restrictions
Handicap certificate required
Societies welcome by prior arrangement

THAMES DITTON & ESHER GOLF CLUB

Portsmouth Road, Esher, Surrey KT10 9AL
☎ 020 8398 1551 **Map 16, C8**
A307, off A3 at Scilly Isles roundabout
Founded 1892
A short, but testing, private course on public land.
9 holes, 5149 yards
par 66, S.S.S 65
Green fees £10
Catering, changing room/showers, bar, trolley hire, shop
Visitors welcome weekdays
Societies welcome by prior arrangement

TRADITIONS GOLF COURSE

Pyrford Road, Woking, Surrey GU22 8UE
☎ 01932 350355 Fax 01932 350234
Map 16, A8
tradition@americagolf.uk.com
www.americangolf.com
From A3 follow signs to Wisley
Founded 1999
In Surrey the name 'Traditions' might imply heath-and-heather, but here it is applied to a challenging contemporary course with many lakes and speedy, USGA-specification greens.
18 holes, 6304 yards
par 71, S.S.S 70
Designer Peter Alliss
Green fees £20
Catering, changing room/showers, bar, club, trolley and buggy hire, shop
Visitors welcome
Societies welcome by prior arrangement
🏨 Holiday Inn – Woking, Victoria Way, Woking, Surrey GA21 1AH
☎ 01483 221000

TYRRELLS WOOD GOLF CLUB

The Drive, Leatherhead, Surrey KT22 8QP
☎ 01372 375200 Fax 01372 360836
Map 16 C8
secretary@tyrrellswood-golfclub.co.uk
www.tyrrellswood-golfclub.co.uk
Off A24, 2 miles SE of Leatherhead. M25 Jct 9
Founded 1924
A James Braid course on the Surrey Downs.
18 holes, 6282 yards
par 71, S.S.S 70
Designer James Braid
Green fees £34
Catering, changing room/showers, bar, club and trolley hire, shop, practice facilities
Visitors welcome, restricted weekends
Societies welcome by prior arrangement

WALTON HEATH GOLF CLUB

Deans Lane, Walton-on-the-Hill, Tadworth, Surrey KT20 7TP
☎ 01737 812380 Fax 01737 814225
Map 16, D8
www.whgc.co.uk
Off B2032, A217 18 miles S of London, M25 Jct 8
Founded 1903
See Top 50 Courses, page 53
Old Course: 18 holes, 7019 yards, par 72, S.S.S 74
New Course: 18 holes, 6949 yards, par 72, S.S.S 74
Designer Herbert Fowler
Green fees £76
Catering, changing room/showers, bar, club and trolley hire, shop, practice facilities
Visitors welcome weekdays
Handicap certificate required – limit: 28
Societies welcome by prior arrangement
🏨 Burford Bridge Hotel, London Road, Micklesham, Surrey
☎ 01306 884561

THE WENTWORTH CLUB

Wentworth Drive, Virginia Water, Surrey GU25 4LS
☎ 01344 842201 Fax 01344 842804
Map 4, G4
Off A30, opposite turning for A32
Founded 1924
See Top 50 Courses, page 55
West Course: 18 holes, 7047 yards, par 73, S.S.S 74
East Course: 18 holes, 6201 yards, par 68, S.S.S 70
Designer Harry Colt
Edinburgh Course: 18 holes, 7004 yards, par 72, S.S.S 74
Designer John Jacobs, Gary Player, Bernard Gallagher
Green fees £175
Catering, changing room/showers, bar, club, trolley and buggy hire, shop, driving range, practice facilities
Visitors welcome by prior arrangement
Handicap certificate required
Societies welcome by prior arrangement

WEST BYFLEET GOLF CLUB

Sheerwater Road, West Byfleet, Surrey KT14 6AA
☎ 01932 346584 Fax 01932 340667
Map 16, B8
A245 in West Byfleet
Founded 1906
With six par 4s playing to more than 400 yards, West Byfleet is a good test for the proficient player, with a strong finish. Although the ground is flat there is plenty of character, with gorse and woodlands adding beauty. The 13th is a memorable short hole, played over water.
18 holes, 6211 yards
par 70, S.S.S 70
Designer C.S. Butchart
Green fees £32
Catering, changing room/showers, bar, club, trolley and buggy hire, shop, driving range, practice facilities
Visitors welcome all week
Societies welcome by prior arrangement
🏨 Wickham Hotel, Oakcroft Road, West Byfleet, Surrey
☎ 01932 341627

WEST HILL GOLF CLUB

Bagshot Road, Brookwood, Surrey GU24 0BH
☎ 01483 474365 Fax 01483 474252
Map 16, A8
secretary@westhill-golfclub.co.uk
www.westhill-golfclub.co.uk
A322 at Brookwood
Founded 1909
Along with Woking and Worplesdon, West Hill is one of the three great and handsome Woking clubs almost rubbing shoulders with one another, and home to the famous Father and Son matchplay tournament. The short holes are particularly good, but, then, so are the long par 4s – really invigorating golf.
18 holes, 6368 yards
par 69, S.S.S 70
Designer Willie Park, Jack White, Cuthbert Butchart.
Green fees £45
Catering, changing room/showers, bar, club and trolley hire, shop, practice facilities
Visitors welcome weekdays
Handicap certificate required
Societies welcome by prior arrangement
🏨 Worplesdon Place Hotel, Perry Hill, Worplesdon, Surrey
☎ 01483 232407

WEST SURREY GOLF CLUB

Enton Green, Milford, Godalming, Surrey GU8 5AF
☎ 01483 421275 **Map 4, G4**
½ mile E of Milford station
Founded 1910
Very charming parkland course with lovely views to Hydon Ball and the Hogs Back. Its Fowler pedigree ensures interest and challenge throughout the round, with no score safe until the 17th has been passed, a 385-yard par 4 which climbs through a narrow entrance to a big, rolling green.
18 holes, 6300 yards
par 71, S.S.S 70
Designer W.H. Fowler
Green fees £27
Catering, changing room/showers, bar, trolley hire, shop, practice facilities
Visitors welcome weekdays
Handicap certificate required
Societies welcome by prior arrangement

WILDWOOD GOLF CLUB

Horsham Road, Alfold, Cranleigh, Surrey GU6 8JE
☎ 01403 753255 Fax 01403 752005
Map 16, B11
www.wildwoodgolf.co.uk
A281, between Guildford and Horsham
Founded 1992
A very challenging Hawtree design with a number of lakes and ponds.
18 holes, 6655 yards
par 72, S.S.S 73
Designer Martin Hawtree
Green fees £20
Catering, changing room/showers, bar, club, trolley and buggy hire, shop, practice facilities, fishing
Visitors welcome by prior arrangement
Societies welcome by prior arrangement

WIMBLEDON COMMON GOLF CLUB

19 Camp Road, Wimbledon Common, London SW19 4UW
☎ 020 8946 7571 Fax 020 8947 8697 **Map 16, B7**
secretary@wcgc.co.uk
www.wcgc.co.uk
Wimbledon Common
Founded 1908
Very historic, golf having been played on the common for many years before this club came into being. Brilliant drainage means no temporary greens, and the course itself is full of character. Pillarbox red outer garments must be worn.
18 holes, 5438 yards
par 68, S.S.S 66
Green fees £15
Catering, changing room/showers, bar, club and trolley hire, shop, meeting room
Visitors welcome weekdays
Societies welcome by prior arrangement
🏨 Cannizaro House, West Side, Wimbledon Common, London SW19 4UE
☎ 020 8879 1464 Fax 020 8879 7338
cannizarohouse@thistle.co.uk

WIMBLEDON PARK GOLF CLUB

Home Park Road, London SW19 7HR
☎ 020 8946 1250 Fax 020 8944 8688 **Map 16, D7**
secretary@wpgc.co.uk
www.wpgc.co.uk
Opposite All England Lawn Tennis Club
Founded 1898
Charming old parkland course, short but tricky.
18 holes, 5492 yards
par 66, S.S.S 66
Designer Willie Park Jnr
Green fees £40
Catering, changing room/showers, bar, trolley hire, shop, practice facilities, function, wedding, meeting facilities
Visitors welcome – restricted weekends
Handicap certificate required
Societies welcome by prior arrangement
🏨 Holiday Inn Express, 200 High Street, Colliers Wood, London SW19
☎ 020 8545 7300

WINDLEMERE GOLF CLUB

Windlesham Road, West End, Woking, Surrey GU24 9QL
☎ 01276 858727 Fax 01276 678837
Map 16, A8
Junction of A319 and A322
Founded 1978
A short parkland course with attendant driving range.
9 holes, 2673 yards
par 34, S.S.S 33
Designer Clive D. Smith
Green fees £9
Catering, changing room/showers, bar, club and trolley hire, shop, driving range
Visitors welcome
Societies welcome by prior arrangement

WINDLESHAM GOLF CLUB

Grove End, Bagshot, Surrey GU19 5HY
☎ 01276 452220 Fax 01276 452290
Map 4, G3
www.windleshamgolf.com
Junction of A30 and A322, M3 jct 3

Founded 1994
One of the few courses designed so far by Tommy Horton, promising well for the future, for this is a challenging, but fair, course.
18 holes, 6650 yards
par 72, S.S.S 72
Designer Tommy Horton
Green fees £25
Catering, changing room/showers, bar, club, trolley and buggy hire, shop, driving range, practice facilities
Visitors welcome, restricted weekends
Handicap certificate required
Societies welcome by prior arrangement

THE WISLEY
Mill Lane, Ripley, Nr Woking, Surrey GU23 6QU
☎ 01483 211022 Fax 01483 211662
Map 16, B8
M25 Jct 10
Founded 1991
A spectacular American-style 27-hole creation by Robert Trent Jones Jnr. Six lakes were dug out to add to the golfing challenge and assist with irrigation. The greens are a study in themselves, many of them protected by water or angled across the line, and all of them cunningly contoured.
The Church: 9 holes, 3356 yards, par 36
The Garden: 9 holes, 3385 yards, par 36
The Mill: 9 holes, 3473 yards, par 36
Designer Robert Trent Jones Jnr
Catering, changing room/showers, bar, club and trolley hire, shop, driving range, practice facilities
Visitors welcome only as members' guests
No societies
🏨 Angel Posting House & Livery, 91 High Street, Guildford, Surrey GU1 3DP
☎ 01483 564555 Fax 01483 533770
angelhotel@hotmail.com

WOKING GOLF CLUB
Pond Road, Hook Heath, Woking, Surrey GU22 0JZ
☎ 01483 760053 Fax 01483 772441
Map 16, A8
Off A322/A324, close to St John's village centre
Founded 1893
The earliest heath-and-heather course, which demonstrated the enormous golfing potential of this corner of England. The layout is little changed from Dunn's original, and the longer par 4s continue to stretch low handicap players even to this day. The design of several holes, particularly the 4th, has been much imitated.
18 holes, 6340 yards
par 70, S.S.S 70
Designer Tom Dunn, Stuart Paton, John Low
Green fees £55
Catering, changing room/showers, bar, club, trolley and buggy hire, shop, practice facilities
Visitors welcome weekdays
Handicap certificate required
Societies welcome by prior arrangement

WOODCOTE PARK GOLF CLUB
Meadow Hill, Bridle Way, Coulsdon, Surrey CR5 2QQ
☎ 020 8668 1843 Fax 020 8660 0918 **Map 16, E8**
woodcotepgc@ic24.net
Off A237 from Coulsdon towards Wallington
Founded 1912
A parkland course with a Herbert Fowler pedigree.
18 holes, 6669 yards
par 71, S.S.S 72
Designer Herbert Fowler
Green fees £30
Catering, changing room/showers, bar, trolley hire, shop, practice facilities
Visitors welcome weekdays
Handicap certificate required – limit: 28
Societies welcome by prior arrangement
🏨 Coulsdon Manor Hotel, Coulsdon Court Road, Coulsdon, Surrey CR5 2LL
☎ 020 8668 0414

WORPLESDON GOLF CLUB
Heath House Road, Woking, Surrey GU22 0RA
☎ 01483 472277 **Map 16, A8**
Off A322, 6 miles N of Guildford
Founded 1908
J.F. Abercromby's remarkable first essay in golf architecture, and hardly changed almost a century later. The 13th has been ranked as one of the finest short holes in the land, and the 18th is exceptionally demanding. The short 10th, over a pond, must be one of the earliest signature holes.
18 holes, 6440 yards
par 71, S.S.S 72
Designer J.F. Abercromby
Green fees £45
Catering, changing room/showers, bar, club and trolley hire, shop, practice facilities
Visitors welcome weekdays, by prior arrangement
Handicap certificate required
Societies welcome by prior arrangement

EAST SUSSEX

ASHDOWN FOREST GOLF HOTEL
Chapel Lane, Forest Row, East Sussex RH18 5BB
☎ 01342 824866 Fax 01342 824869
Map 5, B5
Off A22
The second course of Royal Ashdown Forest, running over similar terrain, specialising in society outings and golfing breaks.
18 holes, 5606 yards
par 68, S.S.S 67
Green fees £18
Catering, changing room/showers, bar, accommodation, club and trolley hire, shop, practice facilities
Visitors welcome
Societies welcome by prior arrangement

BRIGHTON & HOVE GOLF CLUB
Devil's Dyke Road, Brighton, East Sussex BN1 8YJ
☎ 01273 556482 Fax 01273 554247
Map 5, A6
A23/A27, 4 miles N of Brighton
Founded 1887
The oldest course in Sussex, built on downland, looking out to sea.
9 holes, 5704 yards
par 68, S.S.S 68
Designer James Braid
Green fees £15
Catering, changing room/showers, bar, club, trolley and buggy hire, shop, practice facilities
Visitors welcome with restrictions
Societies welcome by prior arrangement

COODEN BEACH GOLF CLUB
Cooden Beach, Bexhill-on-Sea, East Sussex TN39 4TR
☎ 01424 842040 Fax 01424 842040
Map 5, D6
Off A259
Founded 1912
Cooden Beach can boast nine holes over 400 yards in length, but, with five par 5s among them, birdies will be on offer at some of them. Ponds and ditches threaten the inaccurate on many holes, and Fowler has supplemented nature with a number of raised greens and deep bunkers.
18 holes, 6500 yards
par 72, S.S.S 71
Designer W. H. Fowler
Green fees £32

Catering, changing room/showers, bar, club, trolley and buggy hire, shop, practice facilities, snooker
Visitors welcome subject to restrictions
Handicap certificate required
Societies welcome by prior arrangement
Jarvis Cooden Beach Hotel, Cooden Beach, Little Common, East Sussex
01424 842281

CROWBOROUGH BEACON GOLF CLUB

Beacon Road, Crowborough, East Sussex TN6 1UJ
01892 661511 Fax 01892 611988
Map 5, C5
cbgc@eastsx.fsnet.co.uk
www.crowboroughbeacongolfclub.co.uk
A26, S of Crowborough
Founded 1895
Crowborough sits 800 feet up on the Downs, giving splendid panoramic views and many an energetic hole. Amongst several serious challenges, the long dog-leg par-4 2nd is about as hard as they come, while the green of the par-3 6th perches on an elusive ledge high above purgatory.
18 holes, 6273 yards
par 71, S.S.S 70
Green fees £27.50
Catering, changing room/showers, bar, club and trolley hire, shop, practice facilities
Visitors welcome certificate
Handicap certificate required
Societies welcome by prior arrangement

DALE HILL HOTEL & GOLF CLUB

Ticehurst, Wadhurst, East Sussex TN5 7DQ
01580 200112 Fax 01580 201249
Map 5, C5
www.dalehill.co.uk
B2087, N of Ticehurst, off A21
Founded 1974
A hotel and leisure centre with two handsome courses.
Dale Hill Course: 18 holes, 6106 yards, par 70, S.S.S 69
Ian Woosnam Course: 18 holes, 6512 yards, par 71, S.S.S 71
Designer Ian Woosnam
Green fees £20
Catering, changing room/showers, bar, accommodation, club, trolley and buggy hire, shop, driving range, practice facilities, full leisure, conference & function facilities
Visitors welcome
Societies welcome by prior arrangement
Dale Hill Hotel, Ticehurst, Wadhurst, East Sussex TN5 7DQ
01580 200112 Fax01580 201249

DEWLANDS MANOR

Cottage Hill, Rotherfield, East Sussex TN6 3JN
01892 852266 Fax 01892 853015
Map 5, C5
Off A267/B2101, ½ mile S of Rotherfield
Founded 1989
A cleverly designed and exceptionally well presented course with excellent facilities. Resident professional, Nick Godin, was the most accurate driver in the world in 1994.
9 holes, 6372 yards
par 72, S.S.S 70
Designer NM & RM Godin
Green fees Phone for details
Catering, changing room/showers, bar, club, trolley and buggy hire, shop
Visitors welcome – book in advance by telephone
Societies welcome by prior arrangement
Spa Hotel, Mount Ephraim, Tunbridge Wells
01892 520331

THE DYKE GOLF CLUB

Devil's Dyke, Devil's Dyke Road, Brighton, East Sussex BN1 8YJ
01273 857296 Fax 01273 857078
Map 5, A6
Off A27 Brighton bypass, 4 miles N of Brighton
Founded 1906
Generally reckoned to be the best course in the Brighton area, high on the Downs with splendid views inland and to sea. Many first rate holes.
18 holes, 6611 yards
par 72, S.S.S 72
Designer Fred Hawtree
Green fees £28
Catering, changing room/showers, bar, club, trolley and buggy hire, shop, practice facilities
Visitors welcome, restricted weekends
Societies welcome by prior arrangement

EAST BRIGHTON GOLF CLUB

Roedean Road, Brighton, East Sussex BN2 5RA
01273 604838 Fax 01273 680277
Map 5, A6
Off A259, behind Brighton Marina
Founded 1893
A downland course with fine sea views.
18 holes, 6346 yards
par 72, S.S.S 70
Designer James Braid
Green fees £22
Catering, changing room/showers, bar, club, trolley and buggy hire, shop, practice facilities
Visitors welcome with restrictions
Societies welcome by prior arrangement

EAST SUSSEX NATIONAL GOLF CLUB

Little Horsted, Uckfield, East Sussex TN22 5ES
01825 880256 Fax 01825 880066
Map 5, B6
golf@eastsussexnational.co.uk
www.eastsussexnational.co.uk
A22, 1½ miles S of Uckfield
Founded 1990
East Sussex has a reputation for looking after its visitors well, allowing them access to the East Course, probably the finer of the two big American-style courses. Water is much in evidence on the 16th and 17th, the former an all-carry short hole, the 17th a formidable long par 4.
East Course: 18 holes, 7138 yards, par 72, S.S.S 74
Designer Bob Cupp
West Course: 18 holes, 7154 yards, par 72, S.S.S 74
Green fees £55
Catering, changing room/showers, bar, accommodation, club, trolley and buggy hire, shop, driving range, practice facilities, function rooms
Visitors welcome
Handicap certificate required – limit: 28
Societies welcome by prior arrangement
Horsted Place, Little Horsted, Uckfield, East Sussex
01825 750581

EASTBOURNE DOWNS GOLF CLUB

East Dean Road, Eastbourne, East Sussex BN20 8ES
01323 720827 Fax 01323 412506
Map 5, C7
A259, W of Eastbourne
Founded 1908
600 feet up on the chalk downs with magnificent views over the sea and inland over Sussex.
18 holes, 6601 yards
par 72, S.S.S 72
Designer J.H. Taylor
Green fees £18
Catering, changing room/showers, bar, club and trolley hire, shop, practice facilities
Visitors welcome with restrictions weekends

Handicap certificate required
Societies welcome by prior arrangement
🏨 Lansdowne Hotel, King Edwards Parade, Eastbourne, East Sussex BN12 4EE
✆ 01323 725174

EASTBOURNE GOLFING PARK

Lottbridge Drove, Eastbourne, East Sussex BN23 6QJ
✆ 01323 520400 Fax 01323 520400
Map 5, C7
½ mile S of Hampden Park off A22
Founded 1992
Probably best described as a lakeland course – water is a feature on 6 of the 9 holes.
9 holes, 4594 yards
par 66, S.S.S 66
Designer Dave Ashton
Green fees £8
Catering, changing room/showers, bar, club, trolley and buggy hire, shop, driving range, large conservatory for private hire
Visitors welcome
Societies welcome by prior arrangement
🏨 Waterfront Lodge, 11-12 Royal Parade, Eastbourne, East Sussex BN22 7AR
✆ 01323 646566

HASTINGS GOLF CLUB

Beauport Park, Battle Road, St Leonards-on-Sea, East Sussex TN37 7BP
✆ 01424 854243 Fax 01424 854244
Map 5, D6
enquiries@hastingsgolfclub.com
www.hastingsgolfclub.com
Off A2100, 3 miles N of Hastings
Founded 1972
A private club playing over municipal facilities, which many, loyally, regard as the most scenic course in Europe. It costs little to adjudicate.
18 holes, 6248 yards
par 71, S.S.S 70
Green fees £14
Catering, changing room/showers, bar, club and trolley hire, shop, driving range, practice facilities, conference facilities
Visitors welcome
Societies welcome by prior arrangement
🏨 Beauport Park Hotel, Beauport Park, Hastings, East Sussex
✆ 01424 851222

HIGHWOODS GOLF CLUB

Ellerslie Lane, Bexhill-on-Sea, East Sussex TN39 4LJ
✆ 01424 212770 Fax 01424 212625
Map 5, D6
A259 between Little Common and Bexhill
Founded 1925
A J.H. Taylor pedigree course allied to a friendly clubhouse atmosphere.
18 holes, 6218 yards
par 70, S.S.S 70
Designer J.H. Taylor
Green fees £28
Catering, changing room/showers, bar, trolley hire, shop, practice facilities
Visitors welcome
Handicap certificate required
Societies welcome by prior arrangement
🏨 Jarvis Cooden Beach Hotel, Cooden Beach, Little Common, East Sussex
✆ 01424 842281

HOLLINGBURY PARK GOLF CLUB

Ditchling Road, Brighton & Hove City, East Sussex BN1 7HS
✆ 01273 500086 Fax 01273 552010
Map 5, A6
enquiries@hollingburygolfclub.co.uk
www.hollingburygolfclub.co.uk
2 miles N of city centre
Founded 1908
A municipal course with fine sea views from its downland site.
18 holes, 6482 yards
par 72, S.S.S 71
Designer James Braid
Green fees £12
Catering, changing room/showers, bar, club, trolley and buggy hire, shop, practice facilities, function room
Visitors welcome, weekend restricted
Societies welcome by prior arrangement

HOLTYE GOLF CLUB

Holtye Common, Cowden, Near Edenbridge, East Sussex TN8 7ED
✆ 01342 850635 Fax 01342 850576
Map 5, B4
J.P.Holmes@holtyegolfclub.fsnet.co.uk
A 264 between Tunbridge Wells and East Grinstead
Founded 1893
Short 9-hole course with traditional heathland hazards.
9 holes, 5325 yards
par 66, S.S.S 66
Green fees £16
Catering, changing room/showers, bar, club and trolley hire, shop, practice facilities
Visitors welcome with restrictions
Societies welcome by prior arrangement

HORAM PARK GOLF COURSE

Chiddingly Road, Horam, Nr Heathfield, East Sussex TN21 0JJ
✆ 01435 813477 Fax 01435 813677
Map 5, C6
angie@horamgolf.freeserve.co.uk
www.horampark.co.uk
Off A267 at Horam
Founded 1984
A 9-hole course with 18 tees to give variety.
9 holes, 6128 yards
par 70, S.S.S 70
Designer G. Johnson
Green fees £15.50
Catering, changing room/showers, bar, club, trolley and buggy hire, shop, practice facilities, pitch-and-putt course, function facilities
Visitors welcome
Societies welcome by prior arrangement
🏨 Boship Farm Hotel, Lower Dicker, near Hailsham, East Sussex BN27 4AT
✆ 01323 844826

LEWES GOLF CLUB

Chapel Hill, Lewes, East Sussex BN7 2BB
✆ 01273 473245 Fax 01273 483474
Map 5, B6
E of Lewes
Founded 1896
Beloved of golfing musicians involved in the Glyndebourne season, a high downland course with spectacular 360-degree views. Main greens in play all year.
18 holes, 6220 yards
par 71, S.S.S 70
Green fees £21
Catering, changing room/showers, bar, club, trolley and buggy hire, shop, driving range, practice facilities
Visitors welcome, restricted weekends
Societies welcome by prior arrangement
🏨 Millers, 134 High Street, Lewes, East Sussex BN7 1XS
✆ 01273 475631 Fax 01273 486226
millers134@aol.com

MID SUSSEX GOLF CLUB

Spatham Lane, Ditchling, East Sussex BN6 8XJ
✆ 01273 846567 Fax 01273 845767
Map 5, B6
admin@midsussexgolfclub.co.uk
www.midsussexgolfclub.co.uk
1 mile E of Ditchling on Lewes road
Founded 1995
A course combining the best of the new (a challenging design by David Williams) with the best of the old (incomparable Sussex countryside).

18 holes, 6462 yards
par 71, S.S.S 71
Designer David Williams
Green fees £22
Catering, changing room/showers, bar, club, trolley and buggy hire, shop, driving range, practice facilities
Visitors welcome, restricted weekends
Societies welcome by prior arrangement

THE NEVILL GOLF CLUB

Benhall Mill Road, Tunbridge Wells, Kent, East Sussex TN2 5JW
☎ 01892 532941 Fax 01892 517861
Map 5, C4
manager@nevillgolfclub.co.uk
www.nevillgolfclub.co.uk
1 mile S of Tunbridge Wells
Founded 1914
Handsome parkland course with good views south over Bayham and Frant. Memorable holes include the 403-yard 14th and 186-yard 15th, both played over a stream.
18 holes, 6349 yards
par 71, S.S.S 70
Green fees £25
Catering, changing room/showers, bar, trolley hire, shop, practice facilities
Visitors welcome weekdays
Handicap certificate required
Societies welcome by prior arrangement
🏨 Spa Hotel, Mount Ephraim, Tunbridge Wells
☎ 01892 520331

PEACEHAVEN GOLF CLUB

Brighton Road, Newhaven, East Sussex BN9 9UH
☎ 01273 514049 Fax 01273 512571
Map 5, B7
A259, 1 mile W of Newhaven
Founded 1895
Only nine holes, but there are several crackers amongst them, and fine views as well.
9 holes, 5488 yards
par 70, S.S.S 67
Designer James Braid
Green fees £12
Catering, changing room/showers, bar, trolley hire, shop
Visitors welcome with restrictions
Societies welcome by prior arrangement

PILTDOWN GOLF CLUB

Piltdown, Uckfield, East Sussex TN22 3XB
☎ 01825 722033 Fax 01825 724192
Map 5, B5
A 272, 1 mile W of Uckfield
Founded 1904
Piltdown is one of those rare courses without a single sand bunker. As with Royal Ashdown and Berkhamsted, that does not imply that the golf will be any easier, for gullies interrupt many fairways just short of the green, and the par 3s are all carry across heather and gorse.
18 holes, 6070 yards
par 68, S.S.S 69
Green fees £33
Catering, changing room/showers, bar, trolley and buggy hire, shop, driving range, practice facilities
Visitors welcome
Handicap certificate required
Societies welcome by prior arrangement
🏨 The Peacock Inn, Shortbridge, Piltdown, East Sussex, East Sussex TN22 3XA
☎ 01825 762463

ROYAL ASHDOWN FOREST GOLF CLUB

Chapel Lane, Forest Row, East Grinstead, East Sussex RH18 5LR
☎ 01342 822018 Fax 01342 825211
Map 5, B5
Off A22 at Forest Row
Founded 1888
A remarkable bunkerless course making brilliant use of the abundant natural hazards of this hilly site. The short 6th is world-famous, and the 11th is a 249-yard par 3 played against a magnificent backdrop. The par-4 7th and 13th both climb relentlessly, though the long 12th descends obligingly.
18 holes, 6477 yards
par 72, S.S.S 71
Designer Archdeacon Scott
Green fees £42
Catering, changing room/showers, bar, club and trolley hire, shop, practice facilities
Visitors welcome, by prior arrangement
Handicap certificate required
Societies welcome by prior arrangement

ROYAL EASTBOURNE GOLF CLUB

Paradise Drive, Eastbourne, East Sussex BN20 8BP
☎ 01323 736986 Fax 01323 729738
Map 5, C7
½ mile from town centre
Founded 1887
An old club, long past its centenary, on a elevated site giving fine views out to sea.
18 holes, 6118 yards, par 70, S.S.S 69
Designer J.H. Taylor, Arthur Croome, Tom Simpson
9 holes, 2147 yards, par 32, S.S.S 61
Green fees £25
Catering, changing room/showers, bar, club, trolley and buggy hire, shop, practice facilities, function room
Visitors welcome
Handicap certificate required – limit: 27
Societies welcome by prior arrangement
🏨 Lansdowne Hotel, King Edwards Parade, Eastbourne, East Sussex BN12 4EE
☎ 01323 725174

RYE GOLF CLUB

New Lydd Road, Camber, Rye, East Sussex TN31 7QS
☎ 01797 225241 Fax 01797 225460
Map 5, E6
ryelinks@btclick.com
B2075, E of Rye
Founded 1894
Rye could almost be described as Royal County Down without the mountains, so brilliantly have the dunes been utilised to create an unrivalled succession of long par 4s and brilliant short holes. The 4th and 18th are amongst the truly great par 4s, and the 7th an outstanding short hole.
Old Course: 18 holes, 6308 yards, par 68, S.S.S 71
Designer Harry Colt
Jubilee Course: 9 holes, 6141 yards, par 71, S.S.S 70
Designer Frank Pennink
Green fees n/a
Catering, changing room/showers, bar, accommodation, club and trolley hire, shop, practice facilities
Visitors welcome only as members' guests
No societies
🏨 Jeake's House, Mermaid Street, Rye, East Sussex TN31 7ET
☎ 01797 222828 Fax 01797 222623
jeakeshouse@btinternet.com
www.s-h-systems.co.uk/hotels/jeakes.html

SEAFORD GOLF CLUB

Firle Road, East Blatchington, East Sussex BN25 2JD
☎ 01323 892442 Fax 01323 894113
Map 5, C7
secretary@seafordgolfclub.co.uk
www.seafordgolfclub.co.uk
A259
Founded 1887
An archetypal downland course with fine views.
18 holes, 6551 yards
par 69, S.S.S 71

Designer J.H. Taylor
Green fees £27
Catering, changing room/showers, bar, accommodation, trolley and buggy hire, shop, driving range, practice facilities
Visitors welcome, with restrictions. Handicap certificate required – limit: 28
Societies welcome by prior arrangement
Seaford Golf Club, Seaford, East Sussex
01323 892442

SEAFORD HEAD GOLF CLUB

Southdown Road, Seaford, East Sussex BN25 4JS
01323 892442 Fax 0323 894113
Map 5, C7
www.seafordgolfclub.co.uk
Off A259
Founded 1907
A public course in spectacular situation on the cliffs overlooking the Seven Sisters and the coast towards Beachy Head. There are a number of renowned holes including one aptly named Hell.
18 holes, 5848 yards
par 71, S.S.S 68
Green fees £12
Catering, changing room/showers, bar, club and trolley hire, shop
Visitors welcome
Societies welcome by prior arrangements

SEDLESCOMBE GOLF CLUB

Kent Street, Sedlescombe, East Sussex TN33 0SD
01424 870898 Fax 01424 870855
Map 5, D6
A21, 4 miles N of Hastings
Founded 1990
A parkland course in beautiful country with plentiful trees and occasional water hazards.
18 holes, 6321 yards
par 71, S.S.S 70
Designer Glen Johnson
Green fees £16
Catering, changing room/showers, bar, club, trolley and buggy hire, shop, driving range, practice facilities
Visitors welcome with advance booking
Societies welcome by prior arrangement

WATERHALL GOLF CLUB

Waterhall Road, Brighton, East Sussex BN1 8YR
01273 508658 **Map 5, A6**
Off A27, 3 miles N of Brighton
Founded 1923
A hilly course on the downs with good views.
18 holes, 5775 yards
par 69, S.S.S 68
Green fees £12
Catering, changing room/showers, bar, club and trolley hire, shop, practice facilities
Visitors welcome
Societies welcome by prior arrangement

WELLSHURST GOLF & COUNTRY CLUB

North Street, Hellingly, East Sussex BN27 4EE
01435 813636 Fax 01435 812444
Map 5, C6
info@wellshurst.com
www.wellshurst.com
A267, 2 miles N of Hailsham
Founded 1991
With beautiful views over the South Downs, a pleasant parkland course with admirable variety of interest.
18 holes, 5771 yards
par 70, S.S.S 68
Designer The Golf Corporation
Green fees £21
Catering, changing room/showers, bar, accommodation, club, trolley and buggy hire, shop, driving range, conference facilities
Visitors welcome
Societies welcome by prior arrangement
Boship Farm Hotel, Lower Dicker, near Hailsham, East Sussex BN27 4AT
01323 844826

WEST HOVE GOLF CLUB

Church Farm, Hangleton, Hove, East Sussex BN3 8AN
01273 413411 Fax 01273 429988
Map 5, A6
A27, Brighton bypass at Hangleton
Founded 1910
A downland course of modern design built when the club relocated to Hangleton in 1990.
18 holes, 6201 yards
par 70, S.S.S 70
Designer Martin Hawtree
Green fees £20
Catering, changing room/showers, bar, trolley and buggy hire, shop, driving range, practice facilities
Visitors welcome
Societies welcome by prior arrangement

WILLINGDON GOLF CLUB

Southdown Road, Eastbourne, East Sussex BN20 9AA
01323 410981 Fax 01323 411510
Map 5, C7
Off A22, 1 mile N of Eastbourne
Founded 1898
Laid out in a valley in the downs, initially by J.H. Taylor and modernised by Alister Mackenzie in 1925, the valley walls giving many hilly lies.
18 holes, 6118 yards
par 69, S.S.S 69
Designer J.H. Taylor, Alister Mackenzie
Green fees £25
Catering, changing room/showers, bar, club, trolley and buggy hire, shop, practice facilities
Visitors welcome weekdays
Societies welcome by prior arrangement

WEST SUSSEX

AVISFORD PARK GOLF CLUB

Yapton Lane, Walberton, Arundel, West Sussex BN18 0LS
01243 554611 **Map 4, G6**
A27, 4 miles W of Arundel
Founded 1990
A parkland course with water in play from the very first hole.
18 holes, 5703 yards
par 68, S.S.S 66
Green fees £12
Catering, changing room/showers, bar, club, trolley and buggy hire, shop, practice facilities, tennis & swimming
Visitors welcome
Societies welcome by prior arrangement

BOGNOR REGIS GOLF CLUB

Downview Road, Felpham, Bognor Regis, West Sussex PO22 8JD
01243 865867 Fax 01243 860719
Map 4, G7
A259, Bognor to Littlehampton road
Founded 1892
Parkland course with a river and ditches to complicate matters.
18 holes, 6238 yards
par 70, S.S.S 70
Designer James Braid
Green fees £25
Catering, changing room/showers, bar, trolley and buggy hire, shop, practice facilities
Visitors welcome
Handicap certificate required
Societies welcome by prior arrangement

BURGESS HILL GOLF CENTRE

Cuckfield Road, Burgess Hill, West Sussex RH15 8RE
01444 258585 Fax 01444 247318
Map 5, B5
www.burgesshillgolfcentre.co.uk
B2036, N of Burgess Hill
Founded 1995

If you are going to have a short course, get a master architect to design it. There is as much challenge in these nine holes as in many an indifferent 18-hole layout. As the venue of the PGA Short Course Championship it can claim genuine championship status – unlike many.
9 holes, 1250 yards
par 27
Designer Donald Steel
Green fees £9
Catering, changing room/showers, bar, club and trolley hire, shop, driving range, practice facilities
Visitors welcome
Societies welcome by prior arrangement
Hickstead Hotel, Jobs Lane, Hickstead, Haywards Heath, East Sussex RH17 5NZ
01444 248023

CHARTHAM PARK GOLF CLUB

Felcourt Road, Felcourt, East Grinstead, West Sussex RH19 2JT
01342 870008 Fax 01342 870719
Map 5, B4
Off A22, 2 miles N of East Grinstead
Founded 1994
One of the new generation of testing courses, designed by Neil Coles.
18 holes, 6680 yards
par 72, S.S.S 72
Designer Neil Coles
Green fees £25
Catering, changing room/showers, bar, club, trolley and buggy hire, shop, driving range, practice facilities
Visitors welcome with weekend restrictions
Societies welcome by prior arrangement
Jarvis Felbridge Hotel, London Road, East Grinstead, East Sussex
01342 326992

CHICHESTER GOLF CENTRE

Hunston Village, Chichester, West Sussex PO20 6AX
10243 533833 Fax 01243 539922
Map 4, G7
B2145, off A27, 3 miles S of Chichester
Founded 1990
Two American-style courses with lots of water in play, with many practice facilities.
Cathederal Course: 18 holes, 6461 yards, par 72, S.S.S 71
Tower Course: 18 holes, 6175 yards, par 72, S.S.S 69
Designer Philip Sanders
Green fees £15
Catering, changing room/showers, bar, club, trolley and buggy hire, shop, driving range, practice facilities, par-3 course
Visitors welcome
Societies welcome by prior arrangement

COPTHORNE GOLF CLUB

Borers Arm Road, Copthorne, West Sussex RH10 3LL
01342 712405 Fax 01342 717682
Map 5, B4
info@copthornegolfclub.co.uk
www.copthornegolfclub.co.uk
Off A264, M23 Jct 10
Founded 1892
A lovely old heathland course in beautiful surroundings.
18 holes, 6505 yards
par 71, S.S.S 71
Designer James Braid, Bill Cox
Green fees £32
Catering, changing room/showers, bar, club and trolley hire, shop, practice facilities
Visitors welcome, with weekend restrictions
Handicap certificate required
Societies welcome by prior arrangement
Copthorne Gatwick, Copthorne Way, Copthorne, East Sussex
01342 714971

COTTESMORE GOLF CLUB

Buchan Hill, Pease Pottage, Crawley, West Sussex RH11 9AT
01293 528256 Fax 01293 522819
Map 5, A5
1 mile W of M23 Jct 11
Founded 1975
Laid out in woodland, with a number of lakes, the Griffin Course is a good challenge. Green fees are very reasonable for the quality of the courses.
Griffin Course: 18 holes, 6248 yards, par 71, S.S.S 70
Designer Michael Rogerson
Phoenix Course: 18 holes, 5514 yards, par 69, S.S.S 67
Green fees £19.50
Catering, changing room/showers, bar, club, trolley and buggy hire, shop, practice facilities, tennis, swimming & gymnasium
Visitors welcome
Societies welcome by prior arrangement

COWDRAY PARK GOLF CLUB

Petworth Road, Midhurst, West Sussex GU29 0BB
01730 813599 Fax 01730 815900
Map 4, G5
A272, 1 mile E of Midhurst
Founded 1920
An elegant course laid out in a Capability Brown parkland.
18 holes, 6212 yards
par 70, S.S.S 70
Designer Tom Simpson
Green fees £26
Catering, changing room/showers, bar, trolley and buggy hire, shop, practice facilities
Visitors welcome
Handicap certificate required
Societies welcome by prior arrangement

EFFINGHAM PARK HOTEL & GOLF CLUB

West Park Road, Copthorne, West Sussex RH10 3EU
01342 716528 Fax 01342 716039
Map 5, B4
B2028, 2 miles E of Copthorne
Founded 1980
A short parkland course attached to this hotel.
9 holes, 1815 yards
par 30, S.S.S 57
Designer Francisco Escario
Green fees £9
Catering, changing room/showers, bar, accommodation, club and trolley hire, shop, practice facilities, full hotel & leisure facilities
Visitors welcome weekdays, with restrictions
Societies welcome by prior arrangement
Copthorne Effingham Park Hotel, West Park Road, Copthorne, East Sussex
01342 714994

FOXBRIDGE GOLF CLUB

Foxbridge Lane, Plaistow, West Sussex RH14 0LB
01403 753303 Fax 01403 753433
Map 4, G5
Off B2133, A281, 15 miles S of Guildford
Founded 1993
Eight lakes feature on the nine holes of this recent parkland course.
9 holes, 6236 yards
par 72, S.S.S 70
Designer Paul Clark
Green fees £18
Catering, changing room/showers, bar, club, trolley and buggy hire, practice facilities
Visitors welcome
Societies welcome by prior arrangement
Old Wharf, Newbridge, Wisborough Green, Billingshurst, East Sussex RH14 0JG
01403 784096 Fax 01403 784096

GOODWOOD GOLF CLUB

Kennel Hill, Goodwood, Chichester, West Sussex PO18 0PN

01243 774968 Fax 01243 781741
Map 4, G6
Off A27, 3 miles N of Chichester
Founded 1892
The description 'Glorious Goodwood' is just as appropriate to this downland golf course as it is to the incomparable racecourse. James Braid is credited with the design, which often runs through avenues of beech trees. At 460 yards, the par-4 7th readily claims top spot in the stroke index.
18 holes, 6434 yards
par 72, S.S.S 71
Designer James Braid
Green fees £32
Catering, changing room/showers, bar, club, trolley and buggy hire, shop, practice facilities
Visitors welcome
Handicap certificate required
Societies welcome by prior arrangment

MARRIOTT GOODWOOD PARK HOTEL & COUNTRY CLUB

Goodwood, Chichester, West Sussex PO18 0QB
01243 775537 Fax 01243 520120
Map 4, G6
www.marriotthotels.co.uk/pmegs
Off A285, 3 miles NE of Chichester
Founded 1988
Very handsome course laid out in the parklands of the Goodwood estate, sheltering beneath the South Downs. The 475-yard 11th features a deer leap and is particularly unforgiving.
18 holes, 6525 yards
par 72, S.S.S 71
Designer Donald Steel
Green fees £28
Catering, changing room/showers, bar, accommodation, club, trolley and buggy hire, shop, driving range, practice facilities, extensive conference, wedding and function facilities, full leisure/health facilities, including gym, tennis, swimming pool, beauty salons
Visitors welcome, restricted weekends
Societies welcome by prior arrangement
Marriott Goodwood Park Hotel and Country Club, Goodwood, Chichester, East Sussex PO18 0QB
01243 775537 Fax 01243 520120
www.marriotthotels.com/pmegs

HAM MANOR GOLF CLUB

West Drive, Angmering, Littlehampton, West Sussex BN16 4JE
01903 783288 Fax 01903 850886
Map 4, H6
secretary.ham.manor@tinyonline.co.uk
www.hammanor.co.uk
Off A259 W of Worthing
Founded 1936
Well reputed upland course with pleasant views.
18 holes, 6267 yards
par 70, S.S.S 70
Designer Harry Colt
Green fees £30
Catering, changing room/showers, bar, club, trolley and buggy hire, shop, practice facilities
Visitors welcome
Handicap certificate required
Societies welcome by prior arrangement
Bailiffscourt, Climping Street, Climping, Littlehampton, East Sussex BN17 5RW
01903 723511 Fax 01903 723107
bailiffscourt@hshotels.co.uk
www.hshotels.co.uk

HASSOCKS GOLF CLUB

London Raod, Hassocks, West Sussex BN6 9NA
01273 846630 Fax 01273 846070
Map 5, A6
jaki@hassocksgc.fsnet.co.uk
www.hassocksgolfclub.co.uk
A273, between Burgess Hill and Hassocks
Founded 1995
Reaping the benefits of investing in sand-based greens right from the start, Hassocks is able to dispense with the dreaded temporary greens. Water hazards seriously threaten scoring, especially on the intimidating opening drive.
18 holes, 5698 yards
par 70, S.S.S 68
Designer Paul Wright
Green fees £14.25
Catering, changing room/showers, bar, club, trolley and buggy hire, shop, practice facilities
Visitors welcome
Societies welcome by prior arrangement
Hickstead Hotel, Jobs Lane, Hickstead, Haywards Heath, East Sussex RH17 5NZ
01444 248023

HAYWARDS HEATH GOLF CLUB

High Beech Lane, Haywards Heath, West Sussex RH16 1SL
01444 414457 Fax 01444 458319
Map 5, B5
1 mile N of Haywards Heath
Founded 1922
Old parkland course upgraded by Donald Steel.
18 holes, 6185 yards
par 71, S.S.S 70
Designer James Braid, Donald Steel
Green fees £26
Catering, changing room/showers, bar, club and trolley hire, shop, driving range, practice facilities
Visitors welcome
Handicap certificate required
Societies welcome by prior arrangement

HILL BARN GOLF CLUB

Hill Barn Lane, Worthing, West Sussex BN14 9QF
01903 237301 Fax 01903 217613
Map 4, H6
NE of A27
Founded 1935
One of the best-known public courses in Britain – especially when it hosted occasional professional tournaments in the 1970s. Short 11th has ten bunkers surrounding the green.
18 holes, 6229 yards
par 70, S.S.S 70
Designer F.G. Hawtree and J.H. Taylor
Green fees £14
Catering, changing room/showers, bar, club, trolley and buggy hire, shop, practice facilities
Visitors welcome
Societies welcome by prior arrangement
Beach Hotel, Marine Parade, Worthing, East Sussex
01903 234001

HORSHAM GOLF COURSE

Worthing Road, Horsham, West Sussex RH13 7AX
01403 271525 Fax 01403 274528
Map 4, H5
Off A24, between Horsham and Southwater
Founded 1993
Quite a challenging short course with several compulsory water carries.
9 holes, 4122 yards
par 33, S.S.S 30
Green fees £7
Catering, changing room/showers, bar, club and trolley hire, shop, driving range, practice facilities
Visitors welcome
Societies welcome by prior arrangement

IFIELD GOLF & COUNTRY CLUB

Rusper Road, Ifield, Crawley, West Sussex RH11 0LN
01293 520222 Fax 01293 612973
Map 5, A4
Off A23, 1 mile W of Crawley

Founded 1927
A parkland course offering a number of inclusive packages for golf societies.
18 holes, 6330 yards
par 70, S.S.S 70
Designer Bernard Darwin
Green fees £23
Catering, changing room/showers, bar, trolley and buggy hire, shop, practice facilities
Visitors welcome weekdays
Societies welcome by prior arrangement

LITTLEHAMPTON GOLF CLUB

170 Rope Walk, Littlehampton, West Sussex BN17 5DL
✆ 01903 717170 Fax 01903 726629
Map 4, H6
Off A259, 1 mile W of Littlehampton
Founded 1898
The only links course on this part of the South Coast.
18 holes, 6244 yards
par 70, S.S.S 70
Designer Hawtree
Green fees £28
Catering, changing room/showers, bar, trolley and buggy hire, shop, practice facilities
Visitors welcome, restricted weekdays
Societies welcome by prior arrangement

MANNINGS HEATH GOLF CLUB

Fullers, Hammerpond Road, Mannings Heath, Horsham, West Sussex RH13 6PG
✆ 01403 210228 Fax 01403 270974
Map 5, A5
manningsheathgolfclubandvenue@msn.com
www.exclusivehotels.co.uk
A281, 2 miles S of Horsham
Founded 1905
Two exceptionally handsome courses deep in the Sussex countryside. Gary Player and Henry Longhurst both included the 11th on the Waterfall as one of their top holes in the world. The 10th is the pick of three lovely short holes on this course. The modern Kingfisher Course demands intelligent play.
Waterfall Course: 18 holes, 6378 yards, par 73, S.S.S 70
Kingfisher Course: 18 holes, 6217 yards, par 70, S.S.S 70
Designer David Williams
Green fees £36
Catering, changing room/showers, bar, club, trolley and buggy hire, shop, driving range, practice facilities, fishing, tennis, conference facilities
Visitors welcome
Societies welcome by prior arrangement

PAXHILL PARK GOLF CLUB

East Mascalls Lane, Lindfield, West Sussex RH16 2QN
✆ 01444 484000 Fax 01444 482709
Map 5, B5
johnbowen@paxhillpark.fs.net.co.uk
www.paxhillpark.co.uk
Off B2028 1 mile N of Lindfield
Founded 1990
The club is proud to describe itself: 'The only sound apart from nature is that of the Bluebell Railway.' It is located in an area of outstanding natural beauty.
18 holes, 6120 yards
par 70, S.S.S 69
Designer P. Tallack
Green fees £16
Catering, changing room/showers, bar, club and trolley hire, shop, driving range, practice facilities
Visitors welcome with restrictions
Societies welcome by prior arrangement
🏨 The Birch Hotel, Lewes Road, Haywards Heath, West Sussex, East Sussex
✆ 01444 451565

PEASE POTTAGE GOLF COURSE

Horsham Road, Pease Pottage, Crawley, West Sussex RH11 9AP
✆ 01293 521706 **Map 5, A5**
M23 Jct 11, S of Crawley
Founded 1986
A public parkland course with driving range.
9 holes, 3511 yards
S.S.S 60
Green fees £8.50
Catering, changing room/showers, bar, club and trolley hire, shop, driving range, practice facilities
Visitors welcome
Societies welcome by prior arrangement

PETWORTH GOLF CLUB

London Road, Petworth, West Sussex GU28 9LX
✆ 01798 344097 Fax 01798 342528
Map 4, G5
A283, 2½ miles N of Petworth
Founded 1989
A parkland course.
18 holes, 6191 yards
par 71, S.S.S 69
Designer C & T. Duncton
Green fees £10
Shop
Visitors welcome
Societies welcome by prior arrangement

PYECOMBE GOLF CLUB

Clayton Hill, Pyecombe, Brighton, West Sussex BN45 7FF
✆ 01273 845372 Fax 01273 843338
Map 5, A6
A273 Hassocks to Brighton road
Founded 1894
Located on the South Downs, blessed with good drainage and lovely country views.
18 holes, 6204 yards
par 71, S.S.S 70
Green fees £25
Catering, changing room/showers, bar, club and trolley hire, shop, practice facilities
Visitors welcome, subject to restrictions
Societies welcome by prior arrangement – no company days
🏨 Arlanda, Brighton, East Sussex
✆ 01273 699300

RUSTINGTON GOLF CENTRE

Golfers Lane, Rustington, West Sussex BN16 4NB
✆ 01903 850790 Fax 01903 850982
Map 4, H6
www.rgcgolf.com
A259, 6 miles W of Worthing
Founded 1992
A well equipped public facility.
18 holes, 5735 yards
par 70, S.S.S 68
Designer David Williams
Green fees £9.50
Catering, changing room/showers, bar, club and trolley hire, shop, driving range, practice facilities, 9-hole, par-3 course
Visitors welcome
Societies welcome by prior arrangement

SELSEY GOLF CLUB

Golf Links Lane, Selsey, West Sussex PO20 9DR
✆ 01243 605716 Fax 01243 602203
Map 4, F7
B2145, 1 mile N of Selsey
Founded 1908
Although inland, there is little shelter from the wind on what is effectively a seaside course.
9 holes, 5834 yards
par 68, S.S.S 68
Designer J.H. Taylor
Green fees £12
Catering, changing room/showers, bar, trolley hire, shop
Visitors welcome
Societies welcome by prior arrangement

SHILLINGLEE PARK GOLF COURSE

Chiddingfold, Godalming, West Sussex GU8 4TA

✆ 01428 653237 Fax 01428 644391
Map 4, G4
Off A283, 5 miles S of Godalming
Founded 1980
A short pay-and-play course, far from easy, with many ponds and a number of compulsory water carries.
9 holes, 5032 yards
par 64, S.S.S 64
Designer Roger Mace
Green fees £11
Catering, changing room/showers, bar, club, trolley and buggy hire, shop, practice facilities
Visitors welcome with restrictions
Societies welcome by prior arrangement

SINGING HILLS GOLF CLUB

Albourne, Brighton, West Sussex BN6 9EB
✆ 01273 835353 Fax 01273 835444
Map 5, A6
Off A23 at Albourne 10 miles N of Brighton
Founded 1992
Various combinations of holes are possible, but, whatever course is played, water is a recurrent feature. Accuracy is at a premium, even when water is not a threat.
Lake/River Course: 18 holes, 6079 yards, par 69, S.S.S 69
River/Valley Course: 18 holes, 6223 yards, par 70, S.S.S 70
Lake/Valley Course: 18 holes, 6562 yards, par 71, S.S.S 72
Designer C. Colllins
Green fees £22
Catering, changing room/showers, bar, club and trolley hire, shop, driving range, practice facilities, conference facilities
Visitors welcome
Societies welcome by prior arrangement
🏨 Hickstead Hotel, Jobs Lane, Hickstead, Haywards Heath, East Sussex RH17 5NZ
✆ 01444 48023

SLINFOLD PARK GOLF & COUNTRY CLUB

Stane Street, Slinfold, Horsham, West Sussex RH13 7RE
✆ 01403 791555 Fax 01403 791465
Map 4, H5
A29, 4 miles W of Horsham
Founded 1993
Although the main beauty of the courses is the fine trees in the parkland, the abiding memory is of the lakes which enhance several spectacular holes.
18 holes, 6432 yards, par 72, S.S.S 71
Designer John Fortune
9 holes, 1315 yards, par 28
Green fees £25
Catering, changing room/showers, bar, club, trolley and buggy hire, shop, driving range, practice facilities
Visitors welcome
Societies welcome by prior arrangement

TILGATE FOREST GOLF CENTRE

Titmus Drive, Tilgate, Crawley, West Sussex RH10 5EU
✆ 01293 530103 Fax 01293 523478
Map 5, A5
Close to M23 Jct 11
Founded 1983
One of the finest public facilities in the country laid out in pine and birch forest, with a thought provoking design capable of challenging all comers.
18 holes, 6359 yards, par 72, S.S.S 69
Designer Neil Coles, Brian Huggett
9 holes, 1936 yards, par 27
Green fees £12.70
Catering, changing room/showers, bar, club and trolley hire, shop, driving range, practice facilities
Visitors welcome
Societies welcome by prior arrangement

WEST CHILTINGTON GOLF CLUB

Broadford Bridge Road, West Chiltington, West Sussex RH20 2YA
✆ 01798 813574 Fax 01798 812631
Map 4, H6
A29, N of West Chiltington
Founded 1988
In the heart of the Sussex countryside, the main course was designed by Ryder Cup star Brian Barnes (who once beat Jack Nicklaus twice in one day, when the great man was at the height of his powers) and his father-in-law Max Faulkner, the only Englishman to win the Open Championship in Ireland.
18 holes, 5877 yards, par 70, S.S.S 69
Designer Max Faulkner, Brian Barnes
9 holes, 1360 yards, par 28
Green fees £15
Catering, changing room/showers, bar, club and trolley hire, shop, practice facilities
Visitors welcome
Societies welcome by prior arrangement

WEST SUSSEX GOLF CLUB

Golf Club Lane, Wiggonholt, Pulborough, West Sussex RH20 2EN
✆ 01798 872563 Fax 01798 872033
Map 4, H6
www.westsussexgolf.co.uk
Off A283 Storrington to Pulborough Road
Founded 1931
See Top 50 Courses, page 56
18 holes, 6223 yards
par 68, S.S.S 70
Designer Sir Guy Campbell, C.K. Hutchison
Green fees £47.50
Catering, changing room/showers, bar, club and trolley hire, shop, driving range, practice facilities
Visitors welcome weekdays except Friday
Handicap certificate required
Societies welcome by prior arrangement – no company days
🏨 The Chequers, Church Place, Pulborough, East Sussex RH20 1AD
✆ 01798 872486

WORTHING GOLF CLUB

Links Road, Worthing, West Sussex BN14 9QZ
✆ 01903 260801 Fax 01903 694664
Map 4, H6
worthinggolf@pavilion.co.uk
Off A27, N of town centre, near junction with A24.
Founded 1905
The easier Upper Course is laid out on the higher ridges of the Downs, and gives stunning views to sea, whereas the Lower Course runs along a valley, enjoying woodland backgrounds, and with some shelter from the wind. Top marks go to the powerful 2nd, a 461-yard par 4.
Lower Course: 18 holes, 6530 yards, par 71, S.S.S 72
Upper Course: 18 holes, 5243 yards, par 66, S.S.S 66
Designer Ha..y Vardon, Harry Colt
Green fees £28
Catering, changing room/showers, bar, trolley and buggy hire, shop, driving range, practice facilities
Visitors welcome – restricted weekends
Handicap certificate required
Societies societies welcome by prior arrangement, not company days.
🏨 Chatsworth Hotel, Worthing, East Sussex
✆ 01903 236103

WEST ENGLAND

Golf in the West Country is to many synonymous with holiday golf. True, tourism is a major industry in the region, and the golf clubs and courses have to be – and are – well geared up to its demands. The visitor will rarely be disappointed.

However, that is to gloss over the intrinsic merit of so many fine courses. Royal North Devon's place in the history of golf is unquestionable: the first English links course (1864), on which the all-conquering games of Horace Hutchinson, Michael Scott and five-times Open Champion, J. H. Taylor, were bred. Following the English Amateur Championship at Saunton in 2001, the loud cry has again been heard that this great links (actually two magnificent courses) must surely be added to the Open Championship roster before long. In Somerset, Burnham & Berrow is of the same quality, with its brilliant and dramatic use of tumbling dunes to provide a stern championship test. David Dixon's sterling play in the 2001 Open Championship, when he kept equal company with the great and good (including Tiger Woods) right up to the end of the final round, did much to remind the world of the high-class amateur golf which has long flourished in the West Country, while bringing the name of his club, Enmore Park, to the attention of many.

A number of the newer courses run to the sort of length seemingly expected today, i.e. somewhere around the 7,000 yard mark: Bowood, Dartmouth, East Dorset and St Mellion certainly fulfil that requirement. Nevertheless, Broadstone, Parkstone, St Enodoc, West Cornwall and Yelverton all display that enviable quality of being able to delight and challenge even the finest players while appearing, on paper, to be anything up to 1,000 yards short of what it, reputedly, takes. The reality is otherwise, and few mid- or high-handicap golfers will come close to playing to their nominal handicap around these – and many other – courses which offer thorough examinations of every department of the game in quite unsurpassed surroundings.

In many respects Gloucestershire is as much Cotswold as it is West Country. So, Broadway (which has a Worcestershire postal address) marches with many a Bristol course (which could just as easily be consigned to Somerset or Wiltshire). As with Devon and Cornwall, length on paper is almost irrelevant, given the undulating nature of the land, and Broadway, Bristol & Clifton, Long Ashton, Minchinhampton and Tracy Park prove the point more than adequately.

Dorset and Wiltshire are atmospheric counties, full of historic monuments and country houses, from Stonehenge to Stourhead. Their golf courses reflect this heritage, with Isle of Purbeck, for instance, laid out between ancient burial mounds and meeting places. Tangling with the heather and gorse bushes, or succumbing to the fabulous view over Poole Harbour and a very large part of Dorset, we may regret our medal score, but the sensitive golfer knows that there is more to golf than mathematics.

CORNWALL

BOWOOD PARK GOLF CLUB

Valley Truckle, Lanteglos,
Camelford, Cornwall PL32 9RT
✆ 01840 213017 Fax 01840 212622
Map 2, F7
Off A39, at Camelford
Founded 1992
A contemporary course laid out in a former royal hunting park.
18 holes, 6692 yards
par 72, S.S.S 72
Green fees £23
Catering, changing room/showers, bar, accommodation, club, trolley and buggy hire, shop, driving range, practice facilities
Visitors welcome, by prior arrangement.
Handicap certificate required
Societies welcome by prior arrangement
🏨 Bowood Park Hotel, Valley Truckle, Lanteglos, Camelford, Cornwall
✆ 01840 213017

BUDE & NORTH CORNWALL GOLF CLUB

Burn View, Bude, Cornwall EX23 8DA
✆ 01288 352006 Fax 01288 356855
Map 2, F6
info@budegolf.co.uk
www.budegolf.co.uk
Bude town centre
Founded 1891
A very natural, Scottish-style links, set in the heart of the town. The ground tumbles about to give some blind shots and uneven stances on tight lies, while the greens are fast and true. There are only two long par 4s, the 16th and 17th. The par 3s are tricky.
18 holes, 6057 yards
par 71, S.S.S 70
Green fees £25
Catering, changing room/showers, bar, club and trolley hire, shop, practice facilities, snooker
Visitors welcome weekdays – restricted weekends
Societies welcome by prior arrangement
🏨 Teeside Hotel, Burn View, Bude, Cornwall
✆ 01288 352351

BUDOCK VEAN HOTEL GOLF CLUB

Mawnan Smith, Falmouth, Cornwall TR11 5LG
✆ 01326 252102 Fax 01326 250892
Map 2, D10
relax@budockvean.co.uk
www.budockvean.co.uk
From A39 follow tourist signs for Trebah Gardens. Hotel ½ mile further on.
Founded 1932
A high ranking hotel with an indoor pool heated by an open log fire! 18 tees add variety to the 9 hole course which is exceptionally well drained.
9 holes, 5227 yards
par 68, S.S.S 65
Designer James Braid
Green fees £18
Catering, changing room/showers, bar, accommodation, club, trolley and buggy hire, shop, practice facilities, full hotel facilities, including private beach, hotel boat, and indoor swimming pool
Visitors welcome.
Handicap certificate required
Societies welcome by prior arrangement
🏨 Budock Vean Hotel, Mawnan Smith, Falmouth, Cornwall TR11 5LG
✆ 01326 250288 Fax 01326 250892
www.budockvean.co.uk

CAPE CORNWALL GOLF & COUNTRY CLUB

St Just, Penzance, Cornwall TR19 7NL
☎ 01736 788611 Fax 01736 788611
Map 2, A10
info@capecornwall.com
www.capecornwall.com
Off A3071, 1 mile W of St Just
Founded 1987
Clinging to the clifftops above the ocean, with many holes affected by old Cornish stone walls. Idiosyncratic perhaps, but full of character.
18 holes, 5004 yards
par 69, S.S.S 68
Designer Bob Hamilton
Green fees £20
Catering, changing room/showers, bar, accommodation, club, trolley and buggy hire, shop, driving range, practice facilities, function room, swimming pool, gymnasium
Visitors welcome
Societies welcome by prior arrangement
🏨 Boswedden Hotel, Cape Cornwall, St Just, Penzance, Cornwall
☎ 01736 788733

CARLYON BAY GOLF CLUB

Beach Road, St Austell, Cornwall PL25 3RD
☎ 01726 814228 Fax 01726 814250
Map 2, E9
info@carlyonbay.co.uk
www.carlyonbay.co.uk
A391 to St Austell
Founded 1926
A luxurious hotel with a scenic golf course which stretches along the cliff tops towards the port of Par. The course is relatively open, and no way discouraging to the less proficient, but designed in such a way that the competent golfer must still play intelligently to match his handicap.
18 holes, 6597 yards
par 72, S.S.S 71
Designer J Hamilton Stutt
Green fees £28
Catering, changing room/showers, bar, accommodation, club, trolley and buggy hire, shop, practice facilities, full leisure facilities at hotel
Visitors welcome – restrictions Saturday
Societies welcome by prior arrangement
🏨 Carlyon Bay Hotel, St Austell, Cornwall PL25 3RD
☎ 01726 812304 Fax 01726 814938

CHINA FLEET COUNTRY CLUB

Saltash, Cornwall
☎ 01752 854666 Fax 01752 848456
Map 2, G8
sales@china-fleet.co.uk
www.china-fleet.co.uk
A38 passing over Tamar Bridge from Devon, take 1st exit left, and 1st turn right (signposted).
Founded 1991
Overlooking the Tamar Estuary and Brunel's famous railway bridge, golf at China Fleet is played in delightful surroundings.
18 holes, 6551 yards
par 72, S.S.S 72
Designer Hawtree
Green fees £25
Catering, changing room/showers, bar, accommodation, club, trolley and buggy hire, shop, driving range, practice facilities, conference, function facilities, Health and beauty suites, swimming, gym, tennis, squash
Visitors welcome
Handicap certificate required
Societies welcome by prior arrangement
🏨 China Fleet Country Club, Saltash, Cornwall PL12 6LJ
☎ 01752 848668

FALMOUTH GOLF CLUB

Swanpool Road, Falmouth, Cornwall TR11 5BQ
☎ 01326 311262 Fax 01326 317783
Map 2, D10
falmouthgolfclub@freezone.co.uk
www.falmouthgolfclub.co.uk
¼ mile W of Swanpool Beach
Founded 1894
Set on a headland, with outstanding views across Falmouth Bay. Excellent greens, and only two substantial par 4s.
18 holes, 5982 yards
par 71, S.S.S 70
Green fees £25
Catering, changing room/showers, bar, club, trolley and buggy hire, shop, driving range, practice facilities
Visitors welcome
Handicap certificate required
Societies welcome by prior arrangement
🏨 Royal Duchy, Cliff Road, Falmouth, Cornwall
☎ 01326 313042

HOLYWELL BAY GOLF CLUB

Holywell Bay, Newquay, Cornwall TR8 5PW
☎ 01637 830095 Fax 01637 831000
Map 2, D8
Off A3075, Newquay to Perranporth road
One of the facilities available at a family fun park, wonderfully sited in the dunes overlooking the Atlantic Ocean.
18 holes, 2784 yards
par 54
Green fees £8
Catering, changing room/showers, club and trolley hire, tennis, swimming, fishing & pitch & putt course
Visitors welcome
Societies welcome by prior arrangement

ISLES OF SCILLY GOLF CLUB

St Mary's, Isles of Scilly, Cornwall TR21 0NF
☎ 01720 422692 Fax 01720 422049
Map 2, A8
At St Mary's
Founded 1904
A lovely course overlooking the sea.
9 holes, 6001 yards
S.S.S 69
Designer Horace Hutchinson
Green fees £16
Catering, changing room/showers, bar
Visitors welcome weekdays
Societies welcome by prior arrangement

KILLIOW PARK GOLF CLUB

Killiow, Kea, Truro, Cornwall TR3 6ET
☎ 01872 270246 Fax 01872 240915
Map 2, D9
office@killiow.co.uk
Off A39 2 miles from Truro
Founded 1987
The course is laid out in the parkland of an 18th-century country house, with attractive mature trees and a lake.
18 holes, 5274 yards
par 69, S.S.S 68
Green fees £17.50
Changing room/showers, bar, club and trolley hire, driving range
Visitors welcome
Societies welcome by prior arrangement
🏨 Alverton Manor, Tregolls Road, Truro, Cornwall TR1 1ZQ
☎ 01872 276633 Fax 01872 222989
alverton@connexions.co.uk

LANHYDROCK GOLF CLUB

Lostwithiel Road, Bodmin, Cornwall PL30 5AQ
☎ 01208 73600 Fax 01208 77325
Map 2, E8
postmaster@lanhydrock-golf.co.uk
www.lanhydrock-golf.co.uk
Off B3268 via A30/A38 1 mile S of Bodmin

Founded 1993
A pretty course with an encouraging number of shorter par 4s. Mature trees, streams, ponds, and the lie of the land have been integrated into the design very effectively to dictate strategy on most holes. Ponds guard the 1st and 6th greens, and bunkering has been kept to a minimum.
18 holes, 6100 yards
par 70, S.S.S 70
Designer J. Hamilton Stutt
Green fees £29
Catering, changing room/showers, bar, accommodation, club, trolley and buggy hire, shop, driving range, practice facilities, conference facilities
Visitors welcome
Societies welcome by prior arrangement
Lanhydrock Golfing Lodge, Lostwithiel Road, Bodmin, Cornwall PL30 5AQ
01208 73600 Fax 01208 77325
postmaster@lanhydrock-golf.co.uk
www.lanhydrock-golf.co.uk

LAUNCESTON GOLF CLUB

St Stephens, Launceston, Cornwall PL15 8HF
01566 773442 Fax 01566 777506
Map 2, G7
Charles.Hicks@tesco.net
www.launcestongolfclub.com
B3254, N of Launceston
Founded 1927
One of the best inland tests in the West Country with superb views to Dartmoor and Bodmin Moor.
18 holes, 6415 yards
par 70, S.S.S 71
Designer J. Hamilton Stutt
Green fees £20
Catering, changing room/showers, bar, club and trolley hire, shop
Visitors welcome – not summer weekends
Handicap certificate required
Societies welcome by prior arrangement
White Hart Hotel, The Square, Launceston, Cornwall
01566 772013

LOOE GOLF CLUB

Bin Down, Looe, Cornwall PL13 1PX
01503 240239 Fax 01503 240864
Map 2, F9
Off B3253, 3 miles E of Looe
Founded 1933
An upland course with fine views over the Cornish countryside and Looe Bay.
18 holes, 5940 yards
par 70, S.S.S 68
Designer Harry Vardon
Green fees £24
Catering, changing room/showers, bar, club, trolley and buggy hire, shop, practice facilities
Visitors welcome
Societies welcome by prior arrangement

LOSTWITHIEL HOTEL GOLF & COUNTRY CLUB

Lower Polscoe, Lostwithiel, Cornwall PL22 OHQ
01208 873822 Fax 01208 873479
Map 2, E8
reception@golf-hotel.co.uk
www.golf-hotel.co.uk
Off A390
Founded 1990
Scenic parkland course alongside River Fowey, overlooked by Restormel Castle.
18 holes, 5984 yards
par 72, S.S.S 70
Green fees £25
Catering, changing room/showers, bar, accommodation, club, trolley and buggy hire, shop, driving range, practice facilities, leisure club, fishing, conference facilities
Visitors welcome
Societies welcome by prior arrangement
Lostwithiel Hotel Golf and Country Club, Lower Polscoe, Lostwithiel, Cornwall PL22 0HQ
01208 873550 Fax 01208 873479
reception@golf-hotel.co.uk
www.golf-hotel.co.uk

MERLIN GOLF CLUB & DRIVING RANGE

Mawgan Porth, Newquay, Cornwall TR8 4DN
01841 540222 Fax 01841 541031
Map 2, D8
Coast road between Newquay and Padstow. Follow signs for St Eval.
Founded 1991
A heathland course with good views of the surrounding countryside and the coastline.
18 holes, 6210 yards
par 71, S.S.S 71
Designer Ross Oliver
Green fees £13
Catering, changing room/showers, bar, club, trolley and buggy hire, shop, driving range, practice facilities, conference facilities
Visitors welcome
Societies welcome by prior arrangement
Watergate Bay Hotel, Watergate Bay, Newquay, Cornwall
01637 860543

MULLION GOLF CLUB

Cury, Helston, Cornwall TR12 7BP
01326 241176 **Map 2, C11**
Off A3083 near Culdrose Naval Air Station.
Founded 1895
The most southerly English course, a habitat for rare flora and fauna, with stunning views across Mount's Bay, Mullion's playing challenge changes with the wind. In such rugged country it is rare to find such extensive bunkering – 8 on the short 16th, 9 on the approach to the 4th green.
18 holes, 6037 yards
par 70, S.S.S 70
Designer W. Sich
Green fees £23
Catering, changing room/showers, bar, club, trolley and buggy hire, shop, practice facilities
Visitors welcome – restrictions weekend
Handicap certificate required
Societies welcome by prior arrangement
Polurrian Hotel, Mullion, Helston, Cornwall TR12 7EN
013262 40421 Fax 013262 40083

NEWQUAY GOLF CLUB

Tower Road, Newquay, Cornwall TR7 1LT
01637 872091 Fax 01637 874066
Map 2, D8
www.newquaygolfclub.com
½ mile W of Newquay
Founded 1890
A links course with magnificent sea views.
18 holes, 6151 yards
par 69, S.S.S 69
Designer Harry Colt
Green fees £25
Catering, changing room/showers, bar, club, trolley and buggy hire, shop, practice facilities
Visitors welcome weekdays
Societies welcome by prior arrangement

PERRANPORTH GOLF CLUB

Budnic Hill, Perranporth, Cornwall TR6 0AB
01872 573701 Fax 01872 573701
Map 2, D8
perranporth@golfclub92.fsnet.co.uk
B3285 off A30
Founded 1927
Vigorous and exacting traditional links with blind shots and all-or-nothing carries. Exceptionally good greens.
18 holes, 6286 yards
par 72, S.S.S 72
Designer James Braid
Green fees £25

Catering, changing room/showers, bar, accommodation, club and trolley hire, shop, driving range, practice facilities
Visitors welcome. Handicap certificate required
Societies welcome by prior arrangement
Crantock Bay Hotel, Crantock, Newquay, Cornwall
01637 830229

PORTHPEAN GOLF CLUB

Porthpean, St Austell, Cornwall PL26 6AY
01726 64613 Fax 01726 71643
Map 2, E9
2 miles from St Austell
Founded 1992
An attractive combination of parkland holes with a number enjoying brilliant views over St Austell Bay.
18 holes, 5210 yards
par 67, S.S.S 66
Green fees £14
Catering, changing room/showers, bar, club and trolley hire, shop, driving range
Visitors welcome
Societies welcome by prior arrangement
Cliff Head Hotel, Sea Road, Carlyon Bay, St Austell, Cornwall PL25 3RB
01726 812125

PRAA SANDS GOLF CLUB

Praa Sands, Penzance, Cornwall TR20 9TQ
01736 763445 Fax 01736 763399
Map 2, C10
A394, 7 miles E of Penzance
Founded 1971
A short but very scenic course on high ground over looking the sea.
9 holes, 4122 yards
par 62, S.S.S 60
Designer R.A. Hamilton
Green fees £14.50
Catering, changing room/showers, bar, club and trolley hire
Visitors welcome
Societies welcome by prior arrangement

RAF CULDROSE GOLF CLUB

Royal Naval Air Station, Culdrose, Cornwall
01326 574121 x 2413 **Map 2, C10**
A3083, 1 mile S of Helston
A lengthy military course.
18 holes, 6432 yards
par 72, S.S.S 71
Green fees £5
Visitors welcome only as members' guests

ROSERROW GOLF & COUNTRY CLUB

Roserrow, St Minver, Cornwall PL27 6QT
01208 863000 Fax 01208 863002
Map 2, E7
roserrow.co.uk
www.roserrow.co.uk
B3314 from Wadebridge to Polzeath, signposted from Polzeath
Founded 1997
An upland course with magnificent sea views across the Camel Estuary. Amongst many facilities, Roserrow can boast its own airstrip.
18 holes, 6551 yards
par 72, S.S.S 72
Green fees £25
Catering, changing room/showers, bar, accommodation, club, trolley and buggy hire, shop, driving range, practice facilities, fitness centre, gym, swimming pool, tennis, bowls, airstrip
Visitors welcome
Handicap certificate required
Societies welcome by prior arrangement
Headland Hotel, Port Gaverne, near Wadebridge, Cornwall
01208 880260

ST AUSTELL GOLF CLUB

Tregongeeves Lane, St Austell, Cornwall PL26 7DS
01726 74756 **Map 2, E9**
office@staustellgolf.fsnet.uk
A390, 1 mile W of St Austell
Founded 1911
St Austell ought to be better known to a wider public. It has the winning combination of a James Braid design in a heathland/parkland setting, great views, and a tin mine in the middle of the course!
18 holes, 6091 yards
par 69, S.S.S 69
Designer James Braid
Green fees £20
Catering, changing room/showers, bar, trolley hire, shop, driving range, practice facilities
Visitors welcome except during competitions
Handicap certificate required
Societies welcome by prior arrangement
Carlyon Bay Hotel, St Austell, Cornwall PL25 3RD
01726 812304 Fax 01726 814938

ST ENODOC GOLF CLUB

Rock, Wadebridge, Cornwall PL27 6LD
01208 863216 Fax 01208 862976
Map 2, E7
In Rock off B3314, 5 miles NW of Wadebridge
Founded 1890
See Top 50 Courses, page 48
Holywell Course: 18 holes, 4165 yards, par 63, S.S.S 61
Designer James Braid
Church Course: 18 holes, 6243 yards, par 69, S.S.S 70
Green fees £35
Catering, changing room/showers, bar, club and trolley hire, shop, practice facilities
Visitors welcome
Handicap certificate required
Societies welcome by prior arrangement

ST KEW GOLF CLUB

St Kew Highway, Wadebridge, Cornwall PL30 3EF
01208 841500 Fax 01208 841500
Map 2, E8
st-kew-golf-club@ic24.net
A39, 2 miles NE of Wadebridge
Founded 1993
Used for the Cornish Professional Short Course Championship, during which the course has been parred only twice in 4 years.
9 holes, 4550 yards
par 64, S.S.S 62
Designer David Derry
Green fees £14
Catering, changing room/showers, bar, club, trolley and buggy hire, shop, driving range, practice facilities
Visitors welcome
Societies welcome by prior arrangement
Lanarth Hotel and Caravan Park, St Kew Highway, Near Bodmin, Cornwall PL30 3EF
01208 841500

ST MELLION HOTEL GOLF & COUNTRY CLUB

St Mellion, Saltash, Cornwall PL12 6SD
01579 351351 Fax 01579 350537
Map 2, G8
www.stmellion.co.uk
A388, 5 miles NW of Saltash
Founded 1976
The Nicklaus Course is not only long, but it is also devilishly tight. With many of the holes laid out in narrow river valleys with steep, wooded sides, tee shots must be strictly on line or the consequences are dire. Nicklaus himself rates it as one of his best designs.
Old Course: 18 holes, 5782 yards, par 68, S.S.S 68
Designer J. Hamilton Stutt
Nicklaus Course: 18 holes, 7019 yards, par 72, S.S.S 74
Designer Jack Nicklaus
Green fees £25

Catering, changing room/showers, bar, accommodation, club, trolley and buggy hire, shop, driving range, practice facilities
Visitors welcome by prior arrangement
Societies welcome by prior arrangement

TEHIDY PARK GOLF CLUB

Camborne, Cornwall TR14 0HH
☎ 01209 842208 Fax 01209 843680
Map 2, C9
Off A30 at Camborne, following signs to Portreath
Founded 1922
A parkland course with many newly planted oaks, an abundance of primroses and daffodils in spring, and a number of irrigation lakes.
18 holes, 6241 yards
par 72, S.S.S 71
Green fees £22
Catering, changing room/showers, bar, club and trolley hire, shop, practice facilities
Visitors welcome
Handicap certificate required
Societies welcome by prior arrangement

TREGANNA CASTLE HOTEL GOLF CLUB

St Ives, Cornwall TR26 2DE
☎ 01736 795254 x 121 **Map 2, B10**
Off A3074, between Hayle and St Ives
Founded 1982
A short parkland course surrounding the hotel with views to St Ives Bay.
18 holes, 3549 yards
par 60, S.S.S 57
Green fees £13.50
Catering, changing room/showers, bar, accommodation, club and trolley hire
Visitors welcome
Societies welcome by prior arrangement

TRELOY GOLF CLUB

Treloy, Newquay, Cornwall TR7 4JN
☎ 01637 878554 Fax 01637 871710
Map 2, D8
golf@treloy.freeserve.co.uk
A3059, 2 miles from Newquay
Founded 1991
A clever design, short but tricky, kept in beautiful condition. Thousands of acres of Cornish countryside are visible from the course.
9 holes, 2143 yards
par 32, S.S.S 31
Designer Bob Sandow
Green fees £8
Catering, changing room/showers, bar, club, trolley and buggy hire, shop, practice facilities
Visitors welcome
Societies welcome by prior arrangement
🏨 Whipsiderry Hotel, Newquay, Cornwall
☎ 01637 874777

TRETHORNE GOLF CLUB

Kennards House, Launceston, Cornwall PL15 8QE
☎ 01566 86903 Fax 01566 86981
Map 2, G7
Off A30, 3 miles W of Launceston
Founded 1993
Young course of some quality, with a devilish, par 3 8th, involving a compulsory 195-yard carry over water.
18 holes, 6432 yards
par 71, S.S.S 71
Designer Frank Frayne
Green fees £24
Catering, changing room/showers, bar, accommodation, club, trolley and buggy hire, shop, driving range, private function room
Visitors welcome
Societies welcome by prior arrangement
🏨 Trethorne Golf Club, Kennards House, Launceston, Cornwall PL15 8QE
☎ 01566 86903

TREVOSE GOLF & COUNTRY CLUB

Constantine Bay, Padstow, Cornwall PL28 8JB
☎ 01841 520208 Fax 01841 521057
Map 2, D7
secretary@trevose-gc.co.uk
www.trevose-gc.co.uk
A30/A39 to Wadebridge, B3274 towards Padstow. After 3 miles turn left for St Merryn, golf signposted.
Founded 1925
With plentiful accommodation available at the club, two supplementary courses, and good value green fees, Trevose is justifiably popular with golfing visitors. Colt's championship course heads straight for the Atlantic, the glorious par-5 4th curving past sand hills before running down to a rolling green above the pounding breakers.
Championship Course: 18 holes, 6608 yards, par 71, S.S.S 72
Designer Harry Colt
New Course: 9 holes, 3031 yards, par 35, S.S.S 35
Designer G. Alliss, P. Gammon
Short Course: 9 holes, 1367 yards, par 29, S.S.S 29
Designer P. Gammon, J. Westlake
Green fees £25
Catering, changing room/showers, bar, accommodation, club, trolley and buggy hire, shop, driving range, practice facilities, conference and function facilities, self-catering and full-board accommodation
Visitors welcome
Handicap certificate required – limit: 28 men, 36 women
Societies welcome by prior arrangement
🏨 Trevose Golf and Country Club, Constantine Bay, Padstow, Cornwall PL28 8JB
☎ 01841 520208

TRURO GOLF CLUB

Treliske, Truro, Cornwall TR1 3LG
☎ 01872 272684 Fax 01872 278684
Map 2, D9
A390, 1 mile W of Truro, on Redruth road
Founded 1937
Truro may not be long, but it has small greens to compensate. There are good views of Truro Cathedral – of 1910 vintage – and its 250-foot spire.
18 holes, 5306 yards
par 66, S.S.S 66
Designer Harry Colt, Hugh Alison, John Morrison
Green fees £20
Catering, changing room/showers, bar, trolley and buggy hire, shop, practice facilities
Visitors welcome
Handicap certificate required
Societies welcome by prior arrangement
🏨 Alverton Manor, Tregolls Road, Truro, Cornwall TR1 1ZQ
☎ 01872 276633 Fax 01872 222989
alverton@connexions.co.uk

WEST CORNWALL GOLF CLUB

Church Lane, Lelant, St Ives, Cornwall TR26 3DZ
☎ 01736 753177 Fax 01736 753401
Map 2, B10
westcornwallgolfclub@fsnet.co.uk
www.westcornwallgolfclub.co.uk
A30, take turning to St. Ives. In Lelant turn right at Badger Inn, course on right past church.
Founded 1889
A picturesque links packed with character. The opening par 3 is far from simple, being long and threatened by out-of-bounds, and it is all too easy to drive into a graveyard on the 4th. Hill climbing on the 9th and mountainous dunes on the 11th make them particularly unforgiving holes.
18 holes, 5884 yards
par 69, S.S.S 69
Designer Rev. F.F. Tyack
Green fees £25

Catering, changing room/showers, bar, club and trolley hire, shop, practice facilities
Visitors welcome
Handicap certificate required
Societies welcome by prior arrangement
🏨 Badger Inn, Lelant, St Ives, Cornwall
✆ 01736 752181

WHITSAND BAY HOTEL GOLF & COUNTRY CLUB

Portwinkle, Torpoint, Cornwall PL11 3BU
✆ 01503 230276 Fax 01503 230339
Map 2, G9
earlehotels@btconnect.com
www.cornish-golf-hotels.co.uk
A374 near Torpoint
Founded 1905
A delightful clifftop course with gorgeous views. Visitors of all abilities are welcomed equally.
18 holes, 6020 yards
par 69, S.S.S 69
Designer Willie Fernie
Green fees £25
Catering, changing room/showers, bar, accommodation, club, trolley and buggy hire, shop, practice facilities, indoor swimming pool and leisure complex, conference facilities
Visitors welcome
Societies welcome by prior arrangement
🏨 Whitsand Bay, Portwinkle, Torpoint, Cornwall PL11 3BU
✆ 01503 230276

DEVON

ASHBURY GOLF CLUB

Fowley Cross, Okehampton, Devon EX20 4NL
✆ 01837 55453 Fax 01837 55468
Map 2, H6
Off A3079, Okehampton to Holsworthy road
Founded 1991
Twenty-seven holes arranged in loops of nine, which, with alternative greens, can give several possible courses.
18 holes, 5623 yards, par 68, S.S.S 67
18 holes, 5563 yards, par 68, S.S.S 66
Green fees £14
Catering, changing room/showers, bar, accommodation, club, trolley and buggy hire, shop, practice facilities, full hotel, leisure & function facilities
Visitors welcome
Societies welcome by prior arrangement
🏨 Ashbury Hotel, Higher Maddaford, Southcott, Okehampton, Devon
✆ 01837 55453

AXE CLIFF GOLF CLUB

Squires Lane, Axmouth, Seaton, Devon EX12 4AB
✆ 01297 24371 **Map 3, D8**
Axmouth Bridge
Founded 1894
With stunning cliff-top views across the Axe Estuary and Lyme Bay.
18 holes, 5969 yards
par 70, S.S.S 70
Designer James Braid
Green fees £20
Catering, changing room/showers, bar, club and trolley hire, shop
Visitors welcome
Handicap certificate required – limit: 28
Societies welcome by prior arrangement
🏨 Seaton Height Motel, Seaton, Devon

BIGBURY GOLF CLUB

Bigbury-on-Sea, Devon TQ7 4BB
✆ 01548 810412 Fax 01548 810207
Map 3, A10
www.bigburygolfclub.com
B3392 off A379 between Kingsbridge and Plymouth
Founded 1923
With outstanding views over the sea to Burgh Island, and inland to Dartmoor, Bigbury also challenges – three short holes are 200 yards or longer.
18 holes, 6061 yards
par 70, S.S.S 69
Designer J.H. Taylor
Green fees £27
Catering, changing room/showers, bar, club, trolley and buggy hire, shop, practice facilities
Visitors welcome – ring first, handicap 'preferred'
Societies welcome by prior arrangement
🏨 Burgh Island, Bigbury-on-Sea, Kingsbridge, Devon TQ7 4BG
✆ 01548 810514 Fax 01548 810243
reception@burghisland.ndirect.co.uk
www.burghisland.ndirect.co.uk

CHULMLEIGH GOLF COURSE

Leigh Road, Chulmleigh, Devon EX18 7BL
✆ 01769 580519 Fax 01769 580519
Map 3, A6
howard@chulmleighgolf.freeserve.co.uk
Off A377 (signposted) between Exeter and Barnstaple
Founded 1976
An 18 hole short course suitable for all abilities.
18 holes, 1450 yards
par 54, S.S.S 54
Designer John Goodban
Green fees £6.50
Changing room/showers, bar, accommodation, club and trolley hire, shop, practice facilities, holiday cottage for rent
Visitors welcome
Societies welcome by prior arrangement – no company days
🏨 Eggesford Country Hotel, Eggesford, Chulmleigh, Devon EX18 7JZ
✆ 01769 580345

CHURSTON GOLF CLUB

Churston, Brixham, Devon TQ5 0LA
✆ 01803 842751 Fax 01803 845738
Map 3, C10
A379, NW of Churston
Founded 1890
A course which rapidly makes its way onto the cliff tops from which there are dramatic views over Tor Bay.
18 holes, 6208 yards
par 70, S.S.S 70
Designer Harry Colt
Green fees £30
Catering, changing room/showers, bar, club and trolley hire, shop, practice facilities, conference facilities
Visitors welcome – with restrictions
Handicap certificate required
Societies welcome by prior arrangement

DAINTON PARK GOLF CLUB

Totnes Road, Ipplepen, Newton Abbot, Devon TQ12 5TN
✆ 01803 815000 Fax 01803 815009
Map 3, B9
A381, 2 miles S of Newton Abbot
Founded 1993
A recent course making full use of the rolling landscape and plentiful water on this parkland site.
18 holes, 6207 yards
par 71, S.S.S 70
Designer Adrian Stiff
Green fees £18
Catering, changing room/showers, bar, club and trolley hire, shop, driving range
Visitors welcome
Societies welcome by prior arrangement

DARTMOUTH GOLF & COUNTRY CLUB

Blackawton, Totnes, Devon TQ9 7DE
✆ 01803 712686 Fax 01803 712628
Map 3, B10
info@dgcc.co.uk

www.dgcc.co.uk
A3122, 4 miles NW of Dartmouth
Founded 1992
Very scenic, in beautiful, rolling Devon countryside with views out to sea, the Championship Course also packs quite a punch. Many streams and lakes, bare rock faces and trees come into play. The 533-yard 4th, water-beset 14th and 15th, and 244-yard all-carry 18th are among the toughest holes.
Championship Course: 18 holes, 7191 yards, par 72, S.S.S 74
Dartmouth Course: 9 holes, 4791 yards, par 66, S.S.S 64
Designer Jeremy Pern
Green fees £27
Catering, changing room/showers, bar, accommodation, club, trolley and buggy hire, shop, driving range, practice facilities, leisure suite
Visitors welcome, but contact club first
Societies welcome by prior arrangement
Dartmouth Golf and Country Club, Blackawton, Totnes, Devon
01803 712686 Fax 01803 712628
info@dgcc.co.uk
www.dgcc.co.uk

DINNATON SPORTING & COUNTRY CLUB

Ivybridge, Devon PL21 9HU
01752 892512 **Map 3, A10**
Off A38, at Ivybridge (signposted).
Founded 1989
Only a short course but, with several lakes, quite challenging.
9 holes, 4089 yards
par 64, S.S.S 60
Designer Cotton/Pink
Green fees £10
Catering, changing room/showers, bar, club and trolley hire, shop
Visitors welcome
Societies welcome by prior arrangement

DOWNES CREDITON GOLF CLUB

Hookway, Crediton, Devon EX17 3PT
01363 773025 Fax 01363 775060
Map 3, B7
downescreditongolfclub@compuserve.com
A377 from Exeter signposted at outskirts of Crediton
Founded 1976
A mixture of hilly and flatter holes.
18 holes, 5954 yards
par 70, S.S.S 69
Green fees £22
Catering, changing room/showers, bar, club and trolley hire, shop, practice facilities
Visitors welcome
Handicap certificate required
Societies welcome by prior arrangement
St Olaves Court, Exeter, Devon
01392 217736

EAST DEVON GOLF CLUB

North View Road, Budleigh Salterton, Devon EX9 6DQ
01395 442018 Fax 01395 445547
Map 3, C8
Off B3179, W of Budleigh Salterton
Founded 1902
Set on the cliffs overlooking the coast, the golfing hazards are very much those of the heath, with gorse and heather prevalent. A number of cunningly sited greens test the approach shot more than adequately.
18 holes, 6239 yards
par 70, S.S.S 70
Green fees £28
Catering, changing room/showers, bar, club and trolley hire, shop, practice facilities
Visitors welcome weekdays
Handicap certificate required
Societies welcome by prior arrangement

ELFORDLEIGH HOTEL GOLF & COUNTRY CLUB

Colebrook, Plympton, Plymouth, Devon PL7 5EB
01752 336428 Fax 01752 344581
Map 2, H9
Off A374, 5 miles E of Plymouth
Founded 1932
A hilly course with plenty of trees and several lakes.
9 holes, 5664 yards
par 68, S.S.S 67
Designer J.H. Taylor
Green fees £15
Catering, changing room/showers, bar, accommodation, club and trolley hire, shop, driving range, full hotel facilities
Visitors welcome, by prior arrangement
Handicap certificate required
Societies welcome by prior arrangement
Elfordleigh Hotel, Colebrook, Plympton, Plymouth, Devon
01752 336428 Fax 01752 344581

EXETER GOLF & COUNTRY CLUB

Countess Wear, Exeter, Devon EX2 7AE
01392 874139 Fax 01392 874139
Map 3, C8
4 miles SE of Exeter, signposted Topsham
Founded 1895
Known affectionately as the flattest course in Devon, an old parkland course with fine trees and good, small greens.
18 holes, 6008 yards
par 69, S.S.S 69
Designer James Braid
Green fees £28
Catering, changing room/showers, bar, trolley hire, shop, practice facilities, tennis, swimming & gymnasium
Visitors welcome weekdays
Handicap certificate required
Societies welcome by prior arrangement

FINGLE GLEN GOLF CLUB

Tedburn St Mary, Exeter, Devon EX6 6AF
01647 61817 Fax 01647 61135
Map 3, B8
Off A30, 4 miles W of Exeter
Founded 1992
A parkland course.
9 holes, 2466 yards
par 33, S.S.S 63
Green fees £11.50
Catering, changing room/showers, bar, club and trolley hire, shop, driving range, practice facilities
Visitors welcome
Societies welcome by prior arrangement

GREAT TORRINGTON GOLF CLUB

Weare Trees, Torrington, Devon EX38 7EZ
01805 622229 Fax 01805 623878
Map 2, H5
theofficeattorringtongolf.co.uk
1 mile W of Torrington
Founded 1895
Panoramic views of the Devon countryside from this 9-hole course of considerable maturity.
9 holes, 4423 yards
par 64, S.S.S 61
Green fees £12
Catering, changing room/showers, bar, club and trolley hire, practice facilities
Visitors welcome – with restrictions
Societies welcome by prior arrangement
Black Horse, The Square, Torrington, Devon
01805 622121

HARTLAND FOREST GOLF & LEISURE PARK

Hartland Forest Leisure Park, Bideford, Devon EX39 5RA
01237 431442 Fax 01237 431734
Map 2, G5
Off A39, 6 miles S of Clovelly
Founded 1980

One of a number of sporting facilities available. On-site accommodation sleeps up to 130.
18 holes, 6015 yards
par 71, S.S.S 69
Designer Allan Cartwright
Green fees £20
Catering, changing room/showers, bar, accommodation, club, trolley and buggy hire, tennis,swimming, fishing
Visitors welcome
Societies welcome by prior arrangement

HELE PARK GOLF CENTRE

Ashburton Road, Newton Abbot, Devon TQ12 6JN
✆ 01626 336060 Fax 01626 332661
Map 3, B9
A383, W of Newton Abbot
Founded 1992
A short parkland course on the outskirts of Newton Abbot.
9 holes, 5168 yards
S.S.S 65
Designer M. Craig
Green fees £7
Catering, changing room/showers, bar, club and trolley hire, shop, driving range, practice facilities
Visitors welcome
Societies welcome by prior arrangement

HIGHBULLEN HOTEL GOLF CLUB

Chittlehamholt, Devon EX37 9HD
✆ 01769 540561 Fax 01769 540492
Map 3, A6
A361, S of Chittlehamholt
Founded 1960
A luxurious hotel with a very scenic parkland course, with views as far as Dartmoor and Exmoor. Golf is free for hotel guests.
18 holes, 5755 yards
par 68, S.S.S 67
Green fees £14
Catering, changing room/showers, bar, accommodation, club, trolley and buggy hire, shop, practice facilities
Visitors welcome with reservation
Societies welcome by prior arrangement
🏨 Highbullen Hotel, Chittlehamholt, Devon
✆ 01769 540561

HOLSWORTHY GOLF CLUB

Killatree, Holsworthy, Devon EX22 6LP
✆ 01409 253177 Fax 01409 253177
Map 2, G6
hgcsecretary.co.uk
www.holsworthygolfclub.co.uk
A3072, W of Holsworthy
Founded 1937
Tree-lined, gently sloping fairways give views over the Devon countryside extending to Dartmoor in the east and Bodmin moor in the west.
18 holes, 6100 yards
par 70, S.S.S 69
Green fees £20
Catering, changing room/showers, bar, club and trolley hire, shop, practice facilities
Visitors welcome
Societies welcome by prior arrangement
🏨 Court Barn Hotel, Clawton, near Holsworthy, Devon
✆ 01409 271219

HONITON GOLF CLUB

Middlehills, Honiton, Devon EX14 9TR
✆ 01404 44422 Fax 01404 46383
Map 3, D7
A35, 2 miles S of Honiton
Founded 1896
Gentle parkland, despite being at an altitude of c. 800 feet.
18 holes, 5940 yards
par 69, S.S.S 68
Green fees £23
Catering, changing room/showers, bar, club and trolley hire, shop, practice facilities, caravan site
Visitors welcome
Handicap certificate required – limit: 28 men, 40 ladies
Societies welcome by prior arrangement
🏨 Lea Hill Hotel, Membury, Axminster, Devon EX13 7AQ
✆ 01404 881881 Fax 01404 881890

HURDWICK GOLF COURSE & CLUB

Tavistock, Devon PL19 0LL
✆ 01822 612746 Fax 01822 612746
Map 2, H8
1 mile N of Tavistock on Brentor Road
Founded 1990
Lovely views to Dartmoor and Bodmin Moor from this executive length parkland course with, it is believed, the longest par 5 in Devon.
18 holes, 5300 yards
par 68, S.S.S 67
Designer Hawtree, Bartlet
Green fees £15
Catering, changing room/showers, bar, club, trolley and buggy hire
Visitors welcome
Societies welcome by prior arrangement
🏨 Bedford Hotel, Bedford Square, Tavistock, Devon
✆ 01822 613221

ILFRACOMBE GOLF CLUB

Hele Bay, Ilfracombe, Devon EX34 9RT
✆ 01271 863328 Fax 01271 867731
Map 2, H3
ilfracombegolfclub@virgin.net
www.ilfracombegolfclub.com
Off A399, 1 mile E of Ilfracombe
Founded 1892
The sea is visible from every tee, giving views well into Wales across the Bristol Channel. The Quarry may well be the shortest hole in Devon – only 75 yards.
18 holes, 5795 yards
par 69, S.S.S 68
Designer T.K.Weir, Harry Colt, Hugh Alison, John Morrison
Green fees £20
Catering, changing room/showers, bar, club and trolley hire, shop, practice facilities, restaurant available for outside bookings during winter
Visitors welcome
Societies welcome by prior arrangement
🏨 Collingdale Hotel, Larkstone Terrace, Ilfracombe, Devon EX34 9NU
✆ 01271 863770

LIBBATON GOLF CLUB

High Bickington, Umberleigh, Devon EX37 9BS
✆ 01769 560269 **Map 3, A6**
B3217, off A377
Founded 1990
An undulating parkland course with floodlit driving range.
18 holes, 6494 yards
par 73, S.S.S 72
Designer Col. P. Badham
Green fees £15
Catering, changing room/showers, bar, club, trolley and buggy hire, shop, driving range, practice facilities, fishing
Visitors welcome
Societies welcome by prior arrangement

MANOR HOUSE HOTEL GOLF CLUB

Moretonhampstead, Devon TQ13 8RE
✆ 01647 440998 Fax 01647 440961
Map 3, B8
manortee@aol.com
B3213, 2 miles from Moretonhampstead
Founded 1929
An extremely pretty course on the edge of Dartmoor. The River Bovey adds greatly to the beauty as it winds through the woods, but it also enters play on no fewer than eight holes, often dramatically. There is

more freedom on the upland back nine, the 11th its strongest hole.
18 holes, 6016 yards
par 69, S.S.S 69
Designer J.F. Abercromby
Green fees £25
Catering, changing room/showers, bar, accommodation, club, trolley and buggy hire, shop, practice facilities, tennis, snooker, croquet, wedding licence, award winning chef
Visitors welcome
Handicap certificate required
Societies welcome by prior arrangement
Manor House Hotel, Moretonhampstead, Devon TQ13 8RE
01647 440355

MORTEHOE & WOOLACOMBE GOLF CLUB

Easewell, Mortehoe, Ilfracombe, Devon EX34 7EH
01271 870225 **Map 2, H4**
B3343, E of Mortehoe
Founded 1992
A short course with quite magnificent views across Morte Bay to Lundy Island.
9 holes, 4852 yards
par 66, S.S.S 63
Designer David Hoare
Green fees £7
Catering, changing room/showers, bar, club and trolley hire
Visitors welcome
Societies welcome by prior arrangement

NEWTON ABBOT (STONER) GOLF CLUB

Bovey Road, Newton Abbot, Devon TQ12 6QQ
01626 352460 Fax 01626 330210
Map 3, B9
A 382, 3 miles N of Newton Abbot
Founded 1930
Gentle parkland, well wooded, making full use of streams as hazards.
18 holes, 5764 yards
par 69, S.S.S 68
Designer James Braid
Green fees £25
Catering, changing room/showers, bar, trolley hire, shop
Visitors welcome. Handicap certificate required
Societies welcome Thursday by prior arrangement
Dolphin Hotel, Station Road, Bovey Tracey, Devon TQ13 9AL
01626 832413

OKEHAMPTON GOLF CLUB

Okehampton, Devon EX20 1EF
01837 52113 Fax 01837 52734
Map 2, H7
Off A31, 1 mile S of Okehampton
Founded 1913
A very charming course, combining elements of woodland and moorland, with a river thrown in for good measure.
18 holes, 5243 yards
par 68, S.S.S 67
Designer J.H. Taylor
Green fees £20
Changing room/showers, bar, club and trolley hire, shop
Visitors welcome by prior arrangement
Societies welcome by prior arrangement

OTTER VALLEY GOLF CENTRE

Upottery, Honiton, Devon EX14 9QP
01404 861266 **Map 3, D7**
andrewthompson@otter-golf.co.uk
www.otter-golf.co.uk
Off A303 near Monkton, 4 miles N of Honiton
Founded 1989
An enterprising venture, based around extensive indoor and outdoor teaching facilities. The rural views from the course are a delight.
9 holes, 1499 yards
par 29, S.S.S 29
Designer Andrew Thompson
Green fees £7.50
Accommodation, club and trolley hire, shop, practice facilities, extensive indoor and outdoor teaching facilities, self-catering accommodation
Visitors welcome
Societies welcome by prior arrangement
Monkton Court, Monkton, Honiton, Devon EX14 9QH
01404 42309

PADBROOK PARK GOLF CLUB

Cullompton, Devon EX15 1RU
01884 38286 Fax 01884 34359
Map 3, D7
M5 Jct 28, at southern end of Cullompton
Founded 1992
A scenic course, which also challenges with its use of woodland and water.
9 holes, 6108 yards
par 70, S.S.S 69
Designer Bob Sandow
Green fees £13
Catering, changing room/showers, bar, club, trolley and buggy hire, shop, practice facilities, indoor bowls, health and fitness studio, fishing, conference and function facilities
Visitors welcome
Societies welcome by prior arrangement
Travelodge, Sampford Peverell, near Tiverton, Devon EX16 7HD
01884 821087

PORTMORE GOLF PARK

Landkey Road, Barnstaple, Devon EX32 9LB
01271 378378 Fax 01271 378378
Map 3, A5
Off A361, 1 mile E of Barnstaple
Founded 1993
A parkland pay-and-play course.
9 holes, 3048 yards
par 70, S.S.S 68
Designer Hawtree, Cox
Green fees £10
Shop, driving range, 9-hole par-3 course
Visitors welcome
Societies welcome by prior arrangement

ROYAL NORTH DEVON GOLF CLUB

Golf Links Road, Westward Ho!, Bideford, Devon EX39 1HD
01237 473817 Fax 01237 423456
Map 2, G4
info@royalnorthdevongolfclub.co.uk
www.royalnorthdevongolfclub.co.uk
M5 Jct 27, via A361 to Westward Ho!/Appledore. In Westward Ho! take Beach Road and Golf Links Road
Founded 1864
The oldest links club in England, its course laid out on common land grazed by sheep and ponies. Tall sea rushes are an extremely punitive hazard towards the middle of the round, and the monumental Cape Bunker, necessitating a carry of 170 yards, still terrifies many players on the 4th.
18 holes, 6665 yards
par 72, S.S.S 72
Designer Tom Morris, Herbert Fowler
Green fees £30
Catering, changing room/showers, bar, club and trolley hire, shop, practice facilities, golf museum
Visitors welcome
Handicap certificate required
Societies welcome by prior arrangement
Culloden House Hotel, Fosketh Hill, Westward Ho!, Bideford, Devon
01237 479421

SAUNTON GOLF CLUB

Saunton, Braunton, Devon EX33 1LG
01271 812436 Fax 01271 814241
Map 2, G4

www.sauntongolf.co.uk
B3231, off A361, 6 miles NW of Barnstaple.
Founded 1897
See Top 50 Courses, page 44
East Course: 18 holes, 6729 yards, par 71, S.S.S 73
Designer Herbert Fowler
West Course: 18 holes, 6403 yards, par 71, S.S.S 72
Designer Frank Pennink
Green fees £40
Catering, changing room/showers, bar, club and trolley hire, shop, practice facilities
Visitors welcome. Handicap certificate required
Societies welcome by prior arrangement

SIDMOUTH GOLF CLUB

Cotmaton Road, Sidmouth, Devon EX10 8SX
✆ 01395 513023 Fax 01395 514661
Map 3, D8
M5 Jct 30, ½ mile W of Sidmouth
Founded 1889
There are brilliant sea views from the course, built on a hill side.
18 holes, 5068 yards
par 66, S.S.S 65
Designer J.H. Taylor
Green fees £20
Catering, changing room/showers, bar, club and trolley hire, shop
Visitors welcome
Societies welcome by prior arrangement

SPARKWELL GOLF COURSE

Blacklands, Sparkwell, Plymouth, Devon PL7 5DF
✆ 01752 837219 **Map 2, H9**
Close to A38 Plympton junction
Founded 1993
A simple pay-and-play layout close to Plymouth.
9 holes, 5498 yards
par 68, S.S.S 68
Designer John Gabb
Green fees £7
Catering, changing room/showers, bar, club and trolley hire, shop
Visitors welcome
Societies welcome by prior arrangement

STADDON HEIGHTS GOLF CLUB

Plymstock, Plymouth, Devon PL9 9SP
✆ 01752 402475 Fax 01752 401998
Map 2, H9
SE Plymouth, via Plymstock
Founded 1904
A cliff top course with fine views over Plymouth Sound.
18 holes, 5845 yards
par 68, S.S.S 70
Green fees £18
Catering, changing room/showers, bar, club and trolley hire, shop
Visitors welcome – weekend restrictions
Handicap certificate required
Societies welcome by prior arrangement

TAVISTOCK GOLF CLUB

Down Road, Tavistock, Devon PL19 9AQ
✆ 01822 612344 Fax 01822 612344
Map 2, H8
1 mile SE of Tavistock on Whitchurch Down
Founded 1890
A downland course with lovely turf and excellent views towards Dartmoor.
18 holes, 6250 yards
par 70, S.S.S 70
Designer Herbert Fowler
Green fees £22
Catering, changing room/showers, bar, trolley hire, shop
Visitors welcome
Societies welcome by prior arrangement

TEIGN VALLEY GOLF CLUB

Christow, Exeter, Devon EX6 7PA
✆ 01647 253026 Fax 01647 253026
Map 3, B8
B3193, off A38 at Teign Valley exit
Founded 1995
A testing parkland course whose intrinsic beauties are outshone by the imposing Dartmoor hills surrounding it.
18 holes, 5913 yards
par 70, S.S.S 68
Designer Peter Nicholson
Green fees £15
Catering, changing room/showers, bar, club, trolley and buggy hire, shop, practice facilities
Visitors welcome
Societies welcome by prior arrangement

TEIGNMOUTH GOLF CLUB

Exeter Road, Teignmouth, Devon TQ14 9NY
✆ 01626 773614 Fax 01626 777070
Map 3, C9
B3192, 2 miles NW of Teignmouth
Founded 1924
A heathland course with a cunning design giving a good test to players of all abilities, with the added bonus of superb views.
18 holes, 6227 yards
par 71, S.S.S 70
Designer Alister Mackenzie
Green fees £25
Catering, changing room/showers, bar, club and trolley hire, shop, practice facilities
Visitors welcome
Handicap certificate required
Societies welcome by prior arrangement

THURLESTONE GOLF CLUB

Thurlestone, Kingsbridge, Devon TQ7 3NZ
✆ 01548 560405 Fax 01548 562149
Map 3, A10
Off A379/B3193, 2 miles W of Kingsbridge
Founded 1897
After an extraordinary opening hole the course climbs onto the clifftops to give magnificent seascapes and many an exciting hole. Played directly towards the sea, the appealing 5th is, nevertheless, a tough par 3 at 226 yards, and the run of par 4s from the 8th calls for powerful striking.
18 holes, 6340 yards
par 71, S.S.S 70
Designer Harry Colt
Green fees £28
Catering, changing room/showers, bar, club and trolley hire, shop, practice facilities, tennis
Visitors welcome and prior reservation
Handicap certificate required
No societies

TIVERTON GOLF CLUB

Post Hill, Tiverton, Devon EX16 4NE
✆ 01884 252114 Fax 01884 251607
Map 3, C6
Off A361, between Tiverton and M5 Jct 27
Founded 1932
Unlike many Devon courses, Tiverton is lush parkland with magnificent trees. A good test of golf.
18 holes, 6236 yards
par 71, S.S.S 71
Designer James Braid, Sir Henry Cotton
Green fees £2
Catering, changing room/showers, bar, trolley hire, shop
Visitors welcome
Handicap certificate required
Societies welcome by prior arrangement

TORQUAY GOLF CLUB

Petitor Road, St Marychurch, Torquay, Devon TQ1 4QF
✆ 01803 327471 Fax 01803 316116
Map 3, C9
A379, 1 ½ miles of Torquay
Founded 1909
A parkland course which climbs to offer fine views over the sea.

18 holes, 6198 yards
par 69, S.S.S 70
Green fees £24
Catering, changing room/showers, bar, club, trolley and buggy hire, shop, practice facilities
Visitors welcome
Handicap certificate required
Societies welcome by prior arrangement

WARREN GOLF CLUB

Dawlish Warren, Devon EX7 0NF
✆ 01626 862255 Fax 01626 888005
Map 3, C8
M5 Jct 30, follow signs to Dawlish, under railway bridge at Dawlish Warren
Founded 1892
A true links situated on a spit of land which is an important nature reserve. Golf, flora, fauna and marvellous views.
18 holes, 5965 yards
par 69, S.S.S 69
Designer James Braid
Green fees £21.50
Catering, changing room/showers, bar, trolley hire, shop, practice facilities
Visitors welcome
Handicap certificate required
Societies welcome by prior arrangement
🏨 Langstone Cliff Hotel, Mount Pleasant Road, Dawlish Warren, Devon EX7 0NA
✆ 01626 868000

WATERBRIDGE GOLF COURSE

Down St Mary, Crediton, Devon EX17 5LG
✆ 01363 85111 **Map 3, B7**
A337, 7 miles NW of Crediton
Founded 1992
Short but quite testing parkland layout.
9 holes, 1955 yards
par 32, S.S.S 32
Designer David Taylor
Green fees £6
Club and trolley hire
Visitors welcome
Societies welcome by prior arrangement
🏨 New Inn, Coleford, Crediton, Devon EX17 5BZ
✆ 01363 84242
www.reallyreal-group.com

WOODBURY PARK HOTEL GOLF & COUNTRY CLUB

Woodbury Castle, Woodbury, Devon EX5 1JJ
✆ 01395 233382 Fax 01395 234701
Map 3, C8
Off B3180, via A3052 from M5 Jct 30
Founded 1992
Owned by racing driver Nigel Mansell, a parkland course with water in play on seven holes and well-protected greens.
Oaks Course: 18 holes, 6707 yards, par 72, S.S.S 72
Designer J. Hamilton Stutt
Acorn Course: 9 holes, 6000 yards, par 70, S.S.S 70
Green fees £35
Catering, changing room/showers, bar, accommodation, club, trolley and buggy hire, shop, driving range, practice facilities, full hotel, leisure and conference facilities
Visitors welcome
Societies welcome by prior arrangement
🏨 Woodbury Park Hotel, Woodbury Castle, Woodbury, Exeter, Devon EX5 1JJ
✆ 01395 233382 Fax 01395 233384

WRANGATON (SOUTH DEVON) GOLF CLUB

Golf Links Road, Wrangaton, South Brent, Devon TQ10 9HJ
✆ 01364 72161 Fax 01364 73229
Map 3, A10
Off A38 between South Brent and Ivybridge
Founded 1895
The front nine is moorland, giving fine views of the South Hams, while the back nine is gentler parkland.
18 holes, 6083 yards
par 70, S.S.S 69
Green fees £18
Catering, changing room/showers, bar, club, trolley and buggy hire, shop, practice facilities
Visitors welcome
Societies welcome by prior arrangement
🏨 Dartbridge Hotel, Totnes Road, Buckfastleigh, Devon
✆ 01364 642214

YELVERTON GOLF CLUB

Golf Links Road, Yelverton, Devon PL20 6BN
✆ 01822 852824 Fax 01822 852824
Map 2, H8
A386, 1 mile S of Yelverton
Founded 1904
Yelverton rejoices in bracing upland golf on crisp turf and fast greens with expansive views onto Dartmoor. Gorse in profusion is an unforgiving hazard and the architect, Herbert Fowler, made good use of the mounds and craters of the old tin workings here, also bringing 18th-century drainage ditches into play.
18 holes, 6351 yards
par 71, S.S.S 72
Designer Herbert Fowler
Green fees £30
Catering, changing room/showers, bar, club and trolley hire, shop, practice facilities
Visitors welcome
Handicap certificate required
Societies welcome by prior arrangement

DORSET

THE ASHLEY WOOD GOLF CLUB

Wimborne Road, Blandford Forum, Dorset DT11 9HN
✆ 01258 422253 Fax 01258 450590
Map 3, H7
B3082 ½ mile S of Blandford
Founded 1896
Blessed with excellent drainage and wonderful views over the Stour and Tarrant Valleys, and recently extended to 18 holes.
18 holes, 6276 yards
par 70, S.S.S 70
Designer Patrick Tallack
Green fees Telephone for details
Catering, changing room/showers, bar, club, trolley and buggy hire, shop, practice facilities
Visitors welcome
Handicap certificate required at weekends
Societies welcome by prior arrangement
🏨 Anvil Hotel, Pimperne, Dorset DT11 8UQ
✆ 01258 452431

BRIDPORT & WEST DORSET GOLF CLUB

East Cliff, West Bay, Bridport, Dorset DT6 4EP
✆ 01308 421491 Fax 01308 421095
Map 3, F8
1 ½ miles S of Bridport
Founded 1891
A links, set on the clifftops, giving stunning views over Chesil Beach, Lyme Bay, and the Dorset countryside. The short 'Port Coombe' hole is 'as pretty as it is deceptive'.
18 holes, 6028 yards
par 73, S.S.S 69
Designer F.W. Hawtree
Green fees £22
Catering, changing room/showers, bar, trolley hire, shop, 9 hole pitch and putt
Visitors welcome
Societies welcome by prior arrangement
🏨 Haddon House Hotel, West Bay, Bridport, Dorset DT6 4EL
✆ 01308 423626

BROADSTONE GOLF CLUB

Wentworth Drive, Broadstone, Dorset BH18 8DQ
✆ 01202 692595 Fax 01202 692595
Map 4, B7
Admin@BroadstoneGolfClub.Com
BroadstoneGolfClub.com
A349, between Poole and Wimborne
Founded 1898
An exceptionally beautiful heathland course, with marvellous views from the high ground over a wide area of Dorset – a haven for wildlife, too. The 7th and 13th are candidates for any list of the finest holes in Britain, exceedingly tough par 4s, and the 16th is almost in their league.
18 holes, 6315 yards
par 70, S.S.S 70
Designer Tom Dunn, Harry Colt
Green fees £32
Catering, changing room/showers, bar, club and trolley hire, shop, practice facilities
Visitors welcome – restricted weekends
Handicap certificate required – limit: 22
Societies welcome by prior arrangement
🏨 Haven Hotel, Sandbanks, Dorset
✆ 01202 707333

THE BULBURY GOLF CLUB

Bulbury Lane, Lytchett Matravers, Poole, Dorset BH16 6EP
✆ 01929 459574 Fax 01929 459000
Map 4, B7
A35, 3 miles NW of Poole
Founded 1989
A course born out of the frustration of a golfer fed up with queueing at a municipal facility. Hardly surprisingly, visitors are well looked after. Lakes and trees have been added to the basic design.
18 holes, 6313 yards
par 72, S.S.S 70
Green fees £20
Catering, changing room/showers, bar, trolley hire, shop, practice facilities
Visitors welcome
Societies welcome by prior arrangement

CAME DOWN GOLF CLUB

Came Down, Dorchester, Dorset DT2 8NR
✆ 01305 812531 Fax 01305 813 494
Map 3, G8
A354, 2 miles S of Dorchester
Founded 1896
It seems that golf may have been played at Came Down as long ago as 1886. J.H. Taylor's course opened in 1906 and was substantially revised by Colt in 1927. Little change has taken place since. Situated on the Ridgeway, 400 feet up, the views are fine, the golf challenging.
18 holes, 6244 yards
par 71
Designer J.H Taylor, Harry Colt
Green fees £24
Catering, changing room/showers, bar, club, trolley and buggy hire, shop, practice facilities
Visitors welcome with restrictions
Societies welcome by prior arrangement, Wednesdays only

CANFORD MAGNA GOLF CLUB

Knighton Lane, Wimborne, Dorset BH21 3AS
✆ 01202 592552 Fax 01202 595550
Map 4, B7
www.canfordmagnagc.co.uk
Off A341, 2 miles E of Wimborne
An ambitious project giving 45 holes of contrasting golf.
Parkland Course: 18 holes, 6495 yards, par 71, S.S.S 71
Riverside Course: 18 holes, 6214 yards, par 70, S.S.S 70
Designer Howard Swann
Knighton Course: 9 holes, 1377 yards, par 27
Green fees £20
Catering, changing room/showers, bar, club, trolley and buggy hire, shop, driving range, practice facilities
Visitors welcome
Societies welcome by prior arrangement

CANFORD SCHOOL GOLF CLUB

Canford School, Wimborne, Dorset BH21 3AD
✆ 01202 841254 Fax 01202 881009
Map 4, B7
msb@canford.com
2 miles SE of Wimborne
Founded 1984
Essentially, an enormously valuable school asset, but enquiries by societies and companies are welcome. Plentiful trees and numerous water hazards.
9 holes, 5934 yards
par 67, S.S.S 69
Designer Peter Boult
Green fees £10
Changing room/showers, practice facilities
Visitors welcome only as members' guests
Societies welcome by prior arrangement

CHEDINGTON COURT GOLF CLUB

South Perrott, Beaminster, Dorset DT8 3HU
✆ 01935 891413 Fax 01935 891217
Map 3, F7
A356, 4 miles SE of Crewkerne
Founded 1991
A hotel course in beautiful rolling countryside on the Dorset-Somerset border.
18 holes, 5950 yards
par 70, S.S.S 70
Designer Chapman, Hemstock, Astill
Green fees £16
Catering, changing room/showers, bar, accommodation, club, trolley and buggy hire, shop, driving range, practice facilities, full hotel facilities
Visitors welcome
Societies welcome by prior arrangement
🏨 Chedington Park Hotel, South Perrott, Beaminster, Dorset DT8 3HU
✆ 01935 891413

CHRISTCHURCH GOLF CLUB

Barrack Road, Iford, Christchurch, Dorset BH23 2BA
✆ 01202 888016 **Map 4, C7**
Eastern boundary of Bournemouth
Founded 1977
An excellent pay-and-play course dominated by the River Stour which 'exerts a baleful influence on most of the holes'.
9 holes, 4330 yards
par 68, S.S.S 66
Green fees £7
Catering, changing room/showers, club, trolley and buggy hire, practice facilities, tennis & bowls
Visitors welcome
Societies welcome by prior arrangement

THE CLUB AT MEYRICK PARK

Central Drive, Meyrick Park, Bournemouth, Dorset BH2 6LH
✆ 01202 786000 Fax 01202 786020
Map 4, B7
www.clubhaus.com
From A347, Wimborne road, take Braidley Road. At T-junction turn right. Club on left.
Founded 1894
Meyrick Park was the first golf club in England to play over a municipal course, in the manner then prevalent in Scotland. It is now privately managed, but it still opens with a monster par 3 of 244 yards.
18 holes, 5411 yards
par 69, S.S.S 69
Designer Tom Dunn, Harry Colt
Green fees £15.15

Catering, changing room/showers, bar, accommodation, club and trolley hire, shop, practice facilities
Visitors welcome
Societies welcome by prior arrangement
The Club at Meyrick Park, Meyrick Park, Bournemouth, Dorset BH2 6LH
01202 786000

CRANE VALLEY GOLF CLUB

The Clubhouse, Verwood, Dorset BH317LE
01202 814088 Fax 1202 813407
Map 4, B6
B3081 on outskirts of Verwood
Founded 1992
The Valley course is shaping up to become one of the best tests in the south-west. Donald Steel has made dramatic use of the river which runs through the course, dominating the 5th, 6th and 11th holes. The 9-hole Woodland Course is open to players without a handicap certificate.
Valley Course: 18 holes, 6421 yards, par 72, S.S.S 71
Designer Donald Steel
Woodland Course: 9 holes, 2030 yards, par 66, S.S.S 60
Green fees £22.50
Catering, changing room/showers, bar, club, trolley and buggy hire, shop, driving range, practice facilities
Visitors welcome
Handicap certificate required
Societies welcome by prior arrangement

DORSET HEIGHTS GOLF CLUB

Belchalwell, Blandford Forum, Dorset DT11 0EG
01258 861386 Fax 01258 860900
Map 3, H7
A357 near Blandford Forum
Founded 1991
As the name suggests, the course is elevated and undulating, giving fine views of the countryside.
18 holes, 6138 yards
par 70, S.S.S 70
Designer D.W. Astill
Catering, changing room/showers, bar, club, trolley and buggy hire, shop, driving range, practice facilities
Visitors welcome
Societies welcome by prior arrangement

DUDMOOR FARM GOLF CLUB

Dudmoor Farm Road, Christchurch, Dorset BH23 6AQ
01202 473826 Fax 01202 480207
Map 4, C7
Off B3073
An executive-length course.
9 holes, 1428 yards
par 31
Green fees £6
Catering, changing room/showers, club hire, squash and fishing
Visitors welcome
Societies welcome by prior arrangement

DUDSBURY GOLF CLUB

64 Christchurch Road, Ferndown, Dorset BH22 8ST
01202 593499 Fax 01202 594555
Map 4, B7
duds@dudsbury.demon.co.uk
B3073, 3 miles N of Bournemouth
Founded 1992
A very challenging course with water in play on 14 holes, and some big carries required to match par on holes such as the 16th.
18 holes, 6904 yards
par 71, S.S.S 73
Designer Donald Steel
Green fees £32
Catering, changing room/showers, bar, club, trolley and buggy hire, shop, driving range, practice facilities, conference, function, and wedding facilities, 6 hole academy course
Visitors welcome
Handicap certificate required
Societies welcome by prior arrangement
St Leonards Hotel, 185 Ringwood Road, St Leonards, Dorset BH24 2NP
01202 578828

EAST DORSET GOLF CLUB

Bere Regis, Wareham, Dorset BH20 7NT
01929 472244 Fax 011929 471294 **Map 3, H8**
5 miles S of Bere Regis
Founded 1978
Martin Hawtree transformed an existing course to create the very challenging Lakeland Course and the gentler Woodland Course, which runs through a rhododendron wood.
Lakeland Course: 18 holes, 7027 yards, par 72, S.S.S 75
Designer Martin Hawtree
Woodland Course: 9 holes, 4887 yards, par 66, S.S.S 64
Green fees £30
Catering, changing room/showers, bar, club, trolley and buggy hire, shop, driving range, practice facilities
Visitors welcome
Handicap certificate required
Societies welcome by prior arrangement

FERNDOWN FOREST GOLF CLUB

Forest Links Road, Ferndown, Dorset BH22 9QE
01202 876096 Fax 01202 894095
Map 4, B7
golfingpleasure@supernet.com
www.ferndown-forest-leisure.co.uk
Off A31 Ferndown bypass
Founded 1993
A short, flat, but handsome course running through a conservation area.
18 holes, 5068 yards
par 68, S.S.S 65
Green fees £11
Catering, changing room/showers, bar, club and trolley hire, shop, driving range, small conference room
Visitors welcome
Societies welcome by prior arrangement
Ferndown Forest Inn, Forest Links Road, Ferndown, Dorset BH22 9QE
01202 899990

FERNDOWN GOLF CLUB

119 Golf Links Road, Ferndown, Dorset BH228BU
Map 4, B7
Off A347, 6 miles N of Bournemouth
Founded 1912
Ferndown's Old Course has staged many professional tournaments over the years. Nowadays it would be too short to trouble the modern professional, but, for the handicap golfer, it remains a fine challenge in a glorious woodland setting. Gentle hills, eight dog-legs. imaginative bunkering, and thick heather complement ingeniously contoured greens.
Old Course: 18 holes, 6452 yards, par 71, S.S.S 71
Designer Harold Hilton
President's Course: 9 holes, 5604 yards, par 70, S.S.S 68
Green fees £45
Catering, changing room/showers, bar, club, trolley and buggy hire, shop, practice facilities
Visitors welcome weekdays, not Thursday
Handicap certificate required
Societies welcome by prior arrangement

HALSTOCK GOLF ENTERPRISES

Common Lane, Halstock, Near Yeovil, Dorset BA22 9SF
01935 891689 Fax 01935 891839
Map 3, F7

halstock-golf@freeuk.com
At Halstock, 6 miles S of Yeovil
Founded 1987
The earliest facility in the area designed specifically to help those wishing to take up the game to get started.
18 holes, 4481 yards
par 66, S.S.S 63
Green fees £11
Changing room/showers, bar, club and trolley hire, shop, driving range
Visitors welcome, restricted Sunday
No societies
Little Barwick House, Barwick, near Yeovil, Somerset BA22 9TD
01935 423902 Fax 01935 420908

HIGHCLIFFE CASTLE GOLF CLUB

107 Lymington Road, Highcliffe-on-Sea, Christchurch, Dorset BH23 4LA
01425 272210 Fax 01425 272210
Map 4, C4
A337, 1 mile W of Highcliffe
Founded 1913
To score well on this course the eight short holes must be parred, and they are far from easy.
18 holes, 4778 yards
par 64, S.S.S 63
Designer Leslie Green, Cecil Sargent
Green fees £25.50
Catering, changing room/showers, bar
Visitors welcome
Handicap certificate required
Societies welcome by prior arrangement
Gordleton Mill, Lymington, Dorset
01590 682219

ISLE OF PURBECK GOLF CLUB

Studland, Dorset BH19 3AB
01929 450361 Fax 01929 450501
Map 4, B8
www.purbeckgolf.co.uk
B3351, 3 miles N of Swanage
Founded 1892
The views over the whole of Dorset, Poole Harbour, Bournemouth and the sea are amongst the finest in British golf. With gorse and heather in profusion, the penalties for inaccuracy can be severe and there are several outstanding holes, such as the breathtaking 5th, and the 8th, 11th and 12th.
Purbeck Course: 18 holes, 6283 yards, par 70, S.S.S 71
Designer Harry Colt
Dene Course: 9 holes, 2022 yards, par 30, S.S.S 30
Green fees £30
Catering, changing room/showers, bar, club and trolley hire, shop, practice facilities
Visitors welcome
Societies welcome by prior arrangement

KNIGHTON HEATH GOLF CLUB

Francis Avenue, West Howe, Bournemouth, Dorset BH11 8NX
01202 572633 Fax 01202 590774
Map 4, B7
A348/A3049 Jct, 3 miles N of Poole
Founded 1976
A club which lived through a number of financial crises until the members bought it in 1976, raising its condition superbly thereafter. Heather and pine trees line the fairways, the greens are fast and true. A number of dog-legs and hilly lies ensure that the golf will always be testing.
18 holes, 6094 yards
par 70, S.S.S 69
Green fees £20.25
Catering, changing room/showers, bar, trolley hire, practice facilities
Visitors welcome
Societies welcome by prior arrangement

LYME REGIS GOLF CLUB

Timber Hill, Lyme Regis, Dorset DT7 3HQ
01297 442963 Fax 01297 442963
Map 3, E8
www.lymeregis.com/golfclub.htm
Off A35 signposted from A3052
Founded 1893
Stunning views across Lyme Bay are but one of the charms of this delightful course, very much at the mercy of the wind. The 15th, 600 feet up, is one of the most spectacular holes in the country, and the 16th, a long par 4, the most difficult against par.
18 holes, 6264 yards
par 71, S.S.S 70
Designer R.D. Nichols
Green fees £23
Catering, changing room/showers, bar, shop, practice facilities
Visitors welcome – not Thursday or Sunday
Handicap certificate required
Societies welcome by prior arrangement

LYONS GATE GOLF CLUB

Lyons Gate Farm, Lyons Gate, Dorchester, Dorset DT2 7AZ
01300 345239 **Map 3, G7**
A352, 12 miles N of Dorchester
Founded 1991
A short course, deep in the country, with marvellous views and a host of wild flowers. The longest hole is just over 300 yards, but there are plans to expand.
9 holes, 1943 yards
S.S.S 60
Designer Ken Abel
Green fees £8.50
Club and trolley hire, shop
Visitors welcome
Societies welcome by prior arrangement

MOORS VALLEY GOLF CLUB

Horton Road, Ringwood, Dorset BH24 2ET
01425 480448 Fax 01425 480779
Map 4, B6
Off A31, 4 miles SW of Ringwood
Founded 1988
An oasis on the edge of Verwood Forest, one of the many attractions in a country park offering great variety for visitors. The course is far from easy, with an island short hole and several long par 4s.
18 holes, 6270 yards
par 72, S.S.S 70
Designer Martin Hawtree
Green fees £11.50
Catering, changing room/showers, bar, club and trolley hire, shop, practice facilities
Visitors welcome
Societies welcome by prior arrangement

PARKSTONE GOLF CLUB

49a Links Road, Parkestone, Poole, Dorset BH14 9QS
01202 707138 Fax 01202 706027
Map 4, B7
www.parkestonegolfclub.co.uk
Off A35 between Bournemouth and Poole
Founded 1910
A lovingly maintained heathland course amidst the pines and birches of Parkstone. The rolling hills of this nature conservation area add to the beauty and contribute greatly to the strategy. With five short holes and five par 5s the card is slightly unusual, but there are many quality par 4s.
18 holes, 6263 yards
par 72, S.S.S 70
Designer Willie Park, James Braid
Green fees £35
Catering, changing room/showers, bar, club and trolley hire, shop, driving range, practice facilities
Visitors welcome
Handicap certificate required – limit: 22 men, 36 women
Societies welcome by prior arrangement
Salterns Hotel, 38 Salterns Way, Lillput, Poole, Dorset
01202 707321

PARLEY GOLF CENTRE

Parley Green Lane, Hurn, Dorset BH23 6BB
✆ 01202 591600 **Map 4, B7**
Opposite Bournemouth airport
Founded 1992
Short parkland course opposite Bournemouth airport.
9 holes, 4584 yards
par 66, S.S.S 64
Designer Paul Goodfellow
Green fees £5
Catering, changing room/showers, bar, trolley hire, shop, driving range
Visitors welcome
Societies welcome by prior arrangement

QUEEN'S PARK

Queens Park West Drive, Bournemouth, Dorset BH8 9BY
✆ 01202 396198 **Map 4, B7**
2 miles NE Bournemouth
Founded 1905
In its heyday, Queen's Park was good enough to host professional tournaments. It is not quite so difficult nowadays, but it remains one of the best municipal courses in the country. Narrow fairways are bordered by heather and pines.
18 holes, 6305 yards
par 72, S.S.S 70
Green fees £13.50
Catering, changing room/showers, bar, club and trolley hire, shop, practice facilities
Visitors welcome
Societies welcome by prior arrangement

RIVERSMEET PAR THREE GOLF CLUB

Stony Lane South, Christchurch, Dorset BH23 1HW
✆ 01202 477987 Fax 01202 470853
Map 4, C7
2 miles W of Christchurch
A par 3 course with good views of Hengistbury Head.
18 holes, 1650 yards
par 54
Green fees £4.90
Club hire, shop, practice facilities
Visitors welcome
Societies welcome by prior arrangement

SHERBORNE GOLF CLUB

Higher Clatcombe, Sherborne, Dorset DT9 4RN
✆ 01935 814431 Fax 01935 814218
Map 3, G6
enquiries@sherbornegolfclub.fsnet.co.uk
Off B3145, 1 mile N of Sherborne
Founded 1894
In one of the loveliest parts of Dorset, Sherborne's quality is a testament to the members who restored James Braid's layout – literally by hand – after the war. Development has continued over the years to give a short course which, nevertheless, can challenge the best players. The surroundings are exceptionally beautiful.
18 holes, 5882 yards
par 70, S.S.S 68
Designer James Braid
Green fees £20
Catering, changing room/showers, bar, trolley hire, shop, practice facilities
Visitors welcome
Handicap certificate required
Societies welcome by prior arrangement, Tuesdays and Wednesdays only

SOLENT MEADS PAR THREE GOLF CLUB

Rolls Drive, Hengistbury Head, Bournemouth, Dorset
✆ 01202 420795 **Map 4, C7**
Off Broadway at Hengistbury Head
A short course in a brilliant location by the sea.
18 holes, 2325 yards
par 54
Green fees £7
Changing room/showers, club hire, shop, driving range, practice facilities
Visitors welcome
Societies welcome by prior arrangement

STURMINSTER MARSHALL GOLF CLUB

Moor Lane, Sturminster Marshall, Dorset BH21 4AH
✆ 01258 854444 Fax 01258 858262
Map 4, A7
A350, 8 miles NW of Poole
Founded 1992
A course which has enabled many Dorset residents to take up golf on a pay-and-play basis before graduating to one of the old-established clubs, and therefore a very valuable and successful endeavour.
9 holes, 5026 yards
par 68, S.S.S 65
Designer John Sharkey
Green fees £11
Changing room/showers, trolley and buggy hire, shop, practice facilities
Visitors welcome
Societies welcome by prior arrangement

WAREHAM GOLF CLUB

Sandford Road, Wareham, Dorset BH20 4DH
✆ 01929 554147 Fax 01929 554147
Map 4, A7
admin@warehamgolfclub.com
www.warehamgolfclub.com
A351, ½ mile N of Wareham
Founded 1908
Set on the edge of Wareham Forest with lovely views of the Purbeck Hills and Poole Harbour. Excellent (and good value) catering in the modern clubhouse.
18 holes, 5753 yards
par 69, S.S.S 68
Green fees £22
Catering, changing room/showers, bar, club and trolley hire, shop, practice facilities
Visitors welcome – handicap preferred
Societies welcome by prior arrangement
Priory Hotel, Church Green, Wareham, Dorset BH20 4ND
✆ 01929 551666 Fax 01929 554519

WEYMOUTH GOLF CLUB

Links Road, Weymouth, Dorset DT4 0PF
✆ 01305 773981 Fax 01305 788029
Map 3, G8
weymouthgolfclub@aol.com
www.weymouthgc.co.uk
Off A354 W of town centre
Founded 1909
Pretty parkland course with lovely views of the Dorset Downs and the coast. A new road forced important changes in 1983, for the better, as it turned out.
18 holes, 5981 yards
par 70, S.S.S 69
Designer James Braid, J Hamilton Stutt
Green fees £24
Catering, changing room/showers, bar, club and trolley hire, shop, practice facilities
Visitors welcome
Handicap certificate required
Societies welcome by prior arrangement
Prince Regent Hotel, 139 The Esplanade, Weymouth, Dorset
✆ 01305 771313

GLOUCESTERSHIRE

BRICKHAMPTON COURT GOLF CLUB

Cheltenham Road, Churchdown, Gloucester GL2 9QF
✆ 01452 859444 Fax 01452 859333
Map 7, G9
info@brickhampton.co.uk
www.brickhampton
M5 Jct 11 B4063 between Gloucester and Cheltenham

Founded 1995
A full length 18-hole course with prominent water features and 9-hole executive course head many facilities at this comprehensive golf complex.
18 holes, 6449 yards, par 71, S.S.S 71
Designer Simon Gidman
9 holes, 1859 yards, par 31, S.S.S 31
Green fees £19
Catering, changing room/showers, bar, trolley and buggy hire, shop, driving range, conference facilities
Visitors welcome
Societies welcome by prior arrangement
Hatherley Manor Hotel, Down Hatherley Lane, Gloucester GL2 9QA
01452 731032

BRISTOL & CLIFTON GOLF CLUB

Beggar Bush Lane, Failand, Bristol, Gloucester BS8 3TH
01275 393474 Fax 01275 394611
Map 3, F3
mansec@bristolgolf.co.uk
www.bristolgolf.co.uk
M5 Jct 19, towards Bristol. At first traffic lights turn right into Beggar Bush Lane.
Founded 1891
A course which frequently calls for accurately placed shots to overcome the many dog-legged holes. On the front nine there are a number of lengthy par 4s. The stretch from the 13th to the 16th, in and out of a valley and through a quarry, appeals greatly – when successfully negotiated.
18 holes, 6316 yards
par 70, S.S.S 70
Green fees £32
Catering, changing room/showers, bar, club and trolley hire, shop, driving range, practice facilities
Visitors welcome
Handicap certificate required
Societies welcome by prior arrangement
Redwood Lodge, Beggar Bush Lane, Failand, Bristol, Gloucester BS8 3TG
01275 393901

BROADWAY GOLF CLUB

Willersey Hill, Broadway, Worcs WR12 7LG
01386 853683 Fax 01386 858643
Map 7, H8
Off A44, 1½ miles E of Broadway
Founded 1895
A delightful course with sweeping views, almost 1,000 feet up on the edge of the Cotswolds. The 177-yard 5th and 370-yard 6th are celebrated in these parts, the hilliness of the ground rendering yardages redundant, club selection depending to a great extent on the strength of the wind.
18 holes, 6228 yards
par 72, S.S.S 70
Designer Alister Mackenzie, Tom Simpson, James Braid
Green fees £30
Catering, changing room/showers, bar, club, trolley and buggy hire, shop, practice facilities
Visitors welcome – restricted Saturdays
Handicap certificate required
Societies welcome by prior arrangement
Dormy House Hotel, Willersey Hill, Broadway, Worcestershire
01386 852711

CANONS COURT GOLF CLUB

Bradley Green, Wotton-under-Edge, Gloucester GL12 7PN
01453 843128 Fax 01453 844151
Map 3, G2
Off B4060, NW of Wotton-under-Edge
Founded 1982
A parkland pay-and-play course close to the M5.
9 holes, 5724 yards
S.S.S 68
Green fees £10
Changing room/showers, bar, shop
Visitors welcome
Societies welcome by prior arrangement

CHIPPING SODBURY GOLF CLUB

Chipping Sodbury, Bristol, Gloucester BS37 6PU
01454 314087 Fax 01454 320052
Map 3, G2
M4 Jct 18, 4 miles N
Founded 1905
The New Course is of championship length (it can be extended to around 7000 yards) and is distinctive for the two huge drainage ditches which cut through more than half the holes.
New Course: 18 holes, 6786 yards, par 72, S.S.S 72
Designer Hawtree
Old Course: 9 holes, 6194 yards, par 70, S.S.S 69
Green fees £24
Catering, changing room/showers, bar, club, trolley and buggy hire, shop, driving range, practice facilities
Visitors welcome
Handicap certificate required
Societies welcome by prior arrangement

CIRENCESTER GOLF CLUB

Cheltenham Road, Bagendon, Cirencester, Gloucester GL7 7BH
01285 653939 Fax 01285 650665
Map 7, H10
Off A435, 2 miles N of Cirencester
Founded 1893
A rolling parkland course with pleasant Cotswold views.
18 holes, 6055 yards
par 70, S.S.S 69
Designer James Braid
Green fees £25
Catering, changing room/showers, bar, trolley and buggy hire, shop, practice facilities, 6-hole academy course
Visitors welcome – weekend restrictions
Societies welcome by prior arrangement

CLEEVE HILL GOLF CLUB

Cleeve Hill, Cheltenham, Gloucester GL52 3PW
01242 672025 **Map 7, G9**
B4632, 2 miles NE of Cheltenham
Founded 1976
A rolling heathland course with many good views.
18 holes, 6441 yards
par 72, S.S.S 71
Green fees £11
Catering, changing room/showers, bar, club and trolley hire, shop
Visitors welcome – weekend restrictions
Societies welcome by prior arrangement

COTSWOLD EDGE GOLF CLUB

Upper Rushmire, Wotton-under-Edge, Gloucester GL12 7PT
01453 844167 Fax 0153 845120
Map 3, G2
B4058, 1 mile NE of Wotton-under-Edge
Founded 1980
Situated in a quiet valley on the western fringes of the Cotswolds.
18 holes, 6170 yards
par 71, S.S.S 71
Green fees £15
Catering, changing room/showers, bar, club, trolley and buggy hire, shop, practice facilities
Visitors welcome weekdays
Societies welcome by prior arrangement

COTSWOLD HILLS GOLF CLUB

Ullenwood, Cheltenham, Gloucester GL53 9QT

✆ 01242 515263 Fax 01242 515317
Map 7, G10
M5 Jct 11a, A417. Then A436 for ½ mile. Turn left at cross-roads signed National Star Centre.
Founded 1902
A hilltop course with extensive views. Played from the blue tees the length rises to 6801 yards, including a 601-yard par 5 (the 16th).
18 holes, 6565 yards
par 72, S.S.S 71
Designer Maurice Little
Green fees £26
Catering, changing room/showers, bar, club and trolley hire, shop, practice facilities
Visitors welcome
Handicap certificate required
Societies welcome by prior arrangement
🏨 Moat House Hotel, Shurdington Road, Brockworth, Gloucester, Gloucester GL3 4PB
✆ 01452 519988

DYMOCK GRANGE GOLF CLUB

The Old Grange, Leominster Road, Dymock, Gloucester GL18 2AN
✆ 01531 890840 Fax 01531 890852
Map 7, E9
Off A449, between Ledbury and Ross-on-Wye
Founded 1995
Short parkland courses in a beautiful and remote part of the county.
9 holes, 2696 yards, par 36
9 holes, 1695 yards, par 30
Green fees £12
Catering, changing room/showers, bar, shop, fitness centre
Visitors welcome
Societies welcome by prior arrangement

FILTON GOLF CLUB

Golf Course Lane, Bristol, Gloucester BS34 7QS
✆ 01179 694169 Fax 01179 314359
Map 3, F3
M5 Jct 16 off A38, 2½ miles N of Bristol
Founded 1909
A well respected course on high ground north of Bristol, giving views from the clubhouse as far as the Brecon Beacons and the Cotswolds.
18 holes, 6318 yards
par 70, S.S.S 70
Green fees £22
Catering, changing room/showers, bar, club, trolley and buggy hire, shop, practice facilities
Visitors welcome weekdays
Handicap certificate required
Societies welcome by prior arrangement
🏨 Premier Lodge, Gloucester Road, Filton, Gloucester
✆ 01179 791011

FOREST HILLS GOLF CLUB

Mile End Road, Coleford, Gloucester GL16 7BY
✆ 01594 810620 **Map 7, E10**
B4028, 1 mile E of Coleford
Founded 1992
A number of water hazards affect play on this parkland course with splendid views over the Forest of Dean.
18 holes, 5724 yards
par 68, S.S.S 68
Designer Adrian Stiff
Green fees £13
Catering, changing room/showers, bar, club, trolley and buggy hire, shop, driving range, practice facilities
Visitors welcome
Societies welcome by prior arrangement

FOREST OF DEAN GOLF CLUB & BELLS HOTEL

Lords Hill, Coleford, Gloucester GL16 8BE
✆ 01594 832583 Fax 01594 832584
Map 7, E10
B4431, ½ mile from Coleford
Founded 1973
An undulating parkland course with good views and a number of water holes.
18 holes, 6033 yards
par 70, S.S.S 69
Designer John Day
Green fees £18
Catering, changing room/showers, bar, accommodation, club, trolley and buggy hire, shop, driving range, practice facilities
Visitors welcome
Societies welcome by prior arrangement
🏨 Bells Hotel, Lords Hill, Coleford, Gloucester GL16 8BE
✆ 01594 832583

JARVIS GLOUCESTER HOTEL & COUNTRY CLUB

Matson Lane, Gloucester, Gloucester GL4 9EA
✆ 01452 525653 **Map 7, F10**
B4073, 2 miles S of Gloucester
Founded 1976
A hilly parkland course with good views of Gloucester Cathedral (which should be visited by all golf historians, as there is a window showing a golfer taking part in the Battle of Crecy in 1346!).
18 holes, 6170 yards
par 70, S.S.S 69
Designer Donald Steel
Green fees £19
Catering, changing room/showers, bar, accommodation, club, trolley and buggy hire, shop, driving range, practice facilities, full hotel & leisure facilities
Visitors welcome
Societies welcome by prior arrangement

HENBURY GOLF CLUB

Henbury Road, Westbury-on-Trym, Bristol, Gloucester BS10 7QB
✆ 01179 500044 Fax 01179 591928
Map 3, F3
thesecretary@henburygolfclub.co.uk
www.henburygolfclub.co.uk
M5 Jct 17, A4018 to Westbury. 2½ miles, at first set of road traffic lights, turn right into Henbury Road.
Founded 1891
A popular course, attractive, too, with the River Trym and woodlands adding visual delight.
18 holes, 6007 yards
par 69, S.S.S 70
Green fees £25
Catering, changing room/showers, bar, club, trolley and buggy hire, shop, practice facilities, small conference/function room
Visitors welcome weekdays
Handicap certificate required
Societies welcome by prior arrangement
🏨 Henbury Lodge Hotel, Station Road, Henbury, Gloucester
✆ 01179 502615

THE KENDLESHIRE GOLF CLUB

Henfield Road, Coalpit Heath, Bristol, Gloucester BS36 2TG
✆ 01179 567000 Fax 011795 73433
Map 3, G3
info@kendleshire.co.uk
www.kendleshire.co.uk
Close to M32, Jct 1
Founded 1996
One of the up-and-coming new courses, recognised as such in the golfing press.
18 holes, 6500 yards
par 71, S.S.S 71
Designer Adrian Stiff
Green fees £25
Catering, changing room/showers, bar, club, trolley and buggy hire, shop, driving range, practice facilities, conference facilities
Visitors welcome
Societies welcome by prior arrangement
🏨 Emerson Green Travelodge, The Emersons Green Beefeater, 200/202 Westerleigh Road, Emersons Green, Gloucester BS16 7AN
✆ 01179 564755

KNOWLE GOLF CLUB

Fairway, West Town Lane, Brislington, Bristol, Gloucester BS4 5DF
☎ 01179 770660 Fax 01179 720615
Map 3, F3
mikeharrington5@excite.co.uk
www.knowlegolfclub.co.uk
Off A4, 3 miles S of Bristol
Founded 1905
Knowle's long-established parkland course offers a well-varied challenge in handsome surroundings. A short par 4 makes a welcoming opener, but the 471-yard par-4 2nd brings an immediate contrast. The back nine is longer, with strong par 4s at the 14th, 16th and 17th, and a 551-yard 18th.
18 holes, 6016 yards
par 69, S.S.S 69
Designer J.H. Taylor
Green fees £22
Catering, changing room/showers, bar, trolley hire, shop, practice facilities
Visitors welcome
Handicap certificate required
Societies welcome by prior arrangement

LILLEY BROOK GOLF CLUB

Cirencester Road, Charlton Kings, Cheltenham, Gloucester GL53 8EG
☎ 01242 526785 Fax 01242 256880
Map 7, G10
secretary@lilleybrookgc.fsnet.co.uk
A435, 2 miles SE of Cheltenham
Founded 1992
A fine old Mackenzie course on high ground overlooking Cheltenham.
18 holes, 6212 yards
par 69, S.S.S 70
Designer Alister Mackenzie
Green fees £25
Catering, changing room/showers, bar, club, trolley and buggy hire, shop, practice facilities, conference facilities
Visitors welcome – weekend restrictions
Handicap certificate required
Societies welcome by prior arrangement
🏨 Cheltenham Park Hotel, Cirencester Road, Charlton Kings, Cheltenham, Gloucester
☎ 01242 222021

LONG ASHTON GOLF CLUB

Clarken Coombe, Long Ashton, Bristol, Gloucester BS41 9DW
☎ 01275 392229 Fax 01275 394395
Map 3, F3
secretary@longashtongolfclub.co.uk
www.longashtongolfclub.co.uk
On B3128 via M5 Jct 19, A369, and B3129
Founded 1893
Host to the 1966 Martini International and 1972 Coca-Cola Young Professionals' tournaments, Long Ashton is a course of two distinct halves, with most of the longer holes coming on the back nine. From its high ground there are good views of the city of Bristol and the more distant Mendips.
18 holes, 6077 yards
par 70, S.S.S 70
Designer F.W. Hawtree, J.H. Taylor
Green fees £30
Catering, changing room/showers, bar, trolley hire, shop, practice facilities
Visitors welcome weekdays
Handicap certificate required
Societies welcome by prior arrangement
🏨 Redwood Lodge, Beggar Bush Lane, Failand, Bristol, Gloucester BS8 3TG
☎ 01275 393901

LYDNEY GOLF CLUB

Lakeside Avenue, Lydney, Gloucester GL15 5QA
☎ 01594 843940 **Map 3, G1**
Off A48, SE of Lydney
Founded 1909
Flat parkland course overlooking the Severn Estuary.
9 holes, 5468 yards
par 66, S.S.S 66
Green fees £10
Catering, changing room/showers, bar, practice facilities
Visitors welcome
Societies welcome by prior arrangement (maximum 36)
🏨 Cinderhill House, St Briavels, Lydney, Gloucester GL15 6RH
☎ 01594 530393 Fax 01594 530098

MANGOTSFIELD GOLF CLUB

Carsons Road, Mangotsfield, Bristol, Gloucester BS17 3LW
☎ 0117 956 5501 **Map 3, G3**
Off B4465, 6 miles NE of Bristol
Founded 1975
A short, hilly parkland course.
18 holes, 5337 yards
par 68, S.S.S 66
Green fees £10
Catering, changing room/showers, bar, club, trolley and buggy hire, shop
Visitors welcome
Societies welcome by prior arrangement

MINCHINHAMPTON GOLF CLUB

Minchinhampton, Stroud, Gloucester GL6 9BE
☎ 01453 832642 Fax 01453 837360
Map 7, G11
Old Course on Minchinhampton Common. Cherington and Avening courses off B4104, 3 miles SE of Minchinhampton
Founded 1889
The Old Course provided an exacting test on common land for many years before the dangers of injuring walkers and motorists caused two new courses to be built 3 miles away. They are parkland, in a more international style.
Old Course: 18 holes, 6019 yards, par 71, S.S.S 69
Avening Course: 18 holes, 6263 yards, par 70, S.S.S 70
Designer F. Hawtree
Cherington Course: 18 holes, 6387 yards, par 71, S.S.S 70
Designer M. Hawtree
Green fees £26
Catering, changing room/showers, bar, club and trolley hire, shop, practice facilities
Visitors welcome
Handicap certificate required
Societies welcome by prior arrangement

NAUNTON DOWNS GOLF CLUB

Naunton, Cheltenham, Gloucester GL54 3AE
☎ 01451 850090 Fax 01451 850091
Map 7, H9
B4068, between Stow-on-the-Wold and Cheltenham
Founded 1993
A downland course with wonderful views of the Cotswold scenery close to beautiful Bourton-on-the-Water.
18 holes, 6078 yards
par 71, S.S.S 70
Designer Jacob Pott
Green fees £19
Catering, changing room/showers, bar, club, trolley and buggy hire, shop, practice facilities, conference facilities and tennis
Visitors welcome by prior arrangement
Societies welcome by prior arrangement

NEWENT GOLF CLUB

Coldharbour Lane, Newent, Gloucester GL18 1DJ
☎ 01531 820478 Fax 01531 820478
Map 7, F9
B4215, at Newent
Founded 1994
A short pay and play course.
9 holes, 4200 yards
par 66, S.S.S 59
Green fees £10
Club and trolley hire, shop
Visitors welcome

Societies welcome by prior arrangement

PAINSWICK GOLF CLUB

Painswick, Stroud, Gloucester GL6 6TL
☎ 01452 812180 Fax 01452 612622
Map 7, F10
A46, 1 mile N of Painswick
Founded 1891
A commonland course, hilly with good views.
18 holes, 4780 yards
par 67, S.S.S 65
Designer David Brown
Green fees £15
Catering, changing room/showers, bar, club and trolley hire
Visitors welcome weekdays
Societies welcome by prior arrangement

HILTON PUCKRUP HALL HOTEL & GOLF CLUB

Puckrup, Tewkesbury, Gloucester GL20 6EL
☎ 01684 271591 Fax 01684 271550
Map 7, G8
puckruphall@hotmail.com
www.tewkesbury.hilton.com
A38, 3 miles N of Tewkesbury M50 Jct 1
Founded 1992
Puckrup Hall is a modern luxury hotel, so it comes as a pleasant surprise to find that excessive length has not been forced onto the course artificially. Gidman's design provides subtler challenges, with the lakeside par-5 5th particularly attractive, and the 18th a full-shot par 3 played over water.
18 holes, 6189 yards
par 70, S.S.S 70
Designer Simon Gidman
Green fees £25
Catering, changing room/showers, bar, accommodation, club, trolley and buggy hire, shop, practice facilities, full hotel conference, function and leisure facilities
Visitors welcome
Handicap certificate required
Societies welcome by prior arrangement
🏨 Hilton Puckrup Hall Hotel, Tewkesbury, Gloucester GL20 6EL
☎ 01684 296200
puckruphall@hotmail.com
www.tewkesbury.hilton.com

RODWAY HILL GOLF COURSE

Newent Road, Highnam, Gloucester, Gloucester GL2 8DN
☎ 01452 384222 **Map 7, F9**
B4215, 2 miles from Gloucester
Founded 1990
Until recently Gloucester had little to offer in the way of golf. This pay-and-play course is the best value of the new facilities, quite challenging, too.
18 holes, 6070 yards
par 70, S.S.S 69
Designer John Gabb
Green fees £11
Catering, changing room/showers, bar, club and trolley hire, shop, practice facilities
Visitors welcome
Societies welcome by prior arrangement
🏨 Jarvis Gloucester Hotel and Country Club, Matson Lane, Gloucester, Gloucester
☎ 01452 411331

SHERDONS GOLF CENTRE

Tredington, Tewkesbury, Gloucester GL20 7BP
☎ 01684 274782 Fax 01684 275358
Map 7, G9
Off A38, 2 miles S of Tewkesbury
Founded 1995
A parkland play and pay course.
9 holes, 2654 yards
par 34, S.S.S 33
Green fees £6
Catering, changing room/showers, shop, driving range, practice facilities
Visitors welcome
Societies welcome by prior arrangement

SHIPTON GOLF CLUB

Near Frogmill Hotel, Andoversford, Gloucester GL54 4HT
☎ 01242 890237 Fax 01242 820336
Map 7, G10
¼ mile S of A40/A436 junction, 1 mile from Andoversford
Founded 1995
Short pay-and-play facility in the Cotswolds.
9 holes, 4866 yards
par 68, S.S.S 62
Designer Paul Worcester
Green fees £6
Changing room/showers, club and trolley hire
Visitors welcome
Societies welcome by prior arrangement

SHIREHAMPTON PARK GOLF CLUB

Park Hill, Shirehampton, Bristol, Gloucester BS11 0UL
☎ 0117 982 3059 Fax 0117 982 2083 **Map 3, F3**
B4054, 2 miles E of M5 Jct 18
Founded 1907
On the western edge of Bristol overlooking the Avon Gorge.
18 holes, 5430 yards
par 67, S.S.S 66
Green fees £20
Catering, changing room/showers, bar, club and trolley hire, shop, practice facilities
Visitors welcome
Handicap certificate required
Societies welcome by prior arrangement

STINCHCOMBE HILL GOLF CLUB

Stinchcombe Hill, Dursley, Gloucester GL11 6AQ
☎ 01453 542015 Fax 01453 549545
Map 3, G2
Off A4135, 1 mile NW of Dursley
Founded 1889
With magnificent views across the Severn Estuary to the hills of South Wales, fine turf and hilly lies make this an enjoyable but challenging course.
18 holes, 5734 yards
par 68, S.S.S 68
Designer Arthur Hoare
Green fees £20
Catering, changing room/showers, bar, trolley hire, shop, practice facilities
Visitors welcome
Societies welcome by prior arrangement

TEWKESBURY PARK HOTEL GOLF CLUB

Lincoln Green Lane, Tewkesbury, Gloucester GL20 7DN
☎ 01684 295405 Fax 01684 292386
Map 7, G9
www.corushotels.com/tewkesbury park
Off A38, 1 mile S of Tewkesbury
Founded 1976
A pretty parkland course with lovely views of the Avon and Severn, as well as enchanting Tewkesbury Abbey.
18 holes, 6533 yards
par 73, S.S.S 72
Designer Frank Pennink
Green fees £25
Catering, changing room/showers, bar, accommodation, club, trolley and buggy hire, shop, practice facilities, pitch & putt course, full hotel leisure, conference and function facilities
Visitors welcome with prior booking
Societies welcome by prior arrangement
🏨 Tewkesbury Park Hotel, Lincoln Green Lane, Tewkesbury, Gloucester
☎ 01684 295405

THORNBURY GOLF CENTRE

Bristol Road, Thornbury, Gloucester BS35 3XL

✆ 01454 281144 Fax 01454 281177
Map 3, G2
A38, at Thornbury
Founded 1992
In the gently rolling country adjoining the Severn Estuary, two interesting parkland courses. Even the Low Course, all par 3s, will still test the accomplished golfer.
High Course: 18 holes, 6154 yards, par 71, S.S.S 69
Designer Hawtree
Low Course: 18 holes, 2195 yards, par 54, S.S.S 54
Green fees £16
Catering, changing room/showers, bar, accommodation, club, trolley and buggy hire, shop, driving range, conference facilities
Visitors welcome
Societies welcome by prior arrangement
Thornbury Golf Lodge, Bristol Road, Thornbury, Gloucester
✆ 01454 281144

TRACY PARK GOLF CLUB

Bath Road, Wick, Gloucester BS30 5RN
✆ 0117 937 2251 Fax 0117 937 4288 **Map 3, G3**
golf@tracypark.com
www.tracypark.com
M4 Jct 18, A46 and A420 (well signposted)
Founded 1976
Two handsome courses laid out on the site of one of the bloodiest battles of the Civil War, both making full use of the magnificent 400-year old trees and many water hazards in the park. The Crown Course features several demanding par 4s and a 562-yard opening hole.
Crown Course: 18 holes, 6443 yards, par 70, S.S.S 71
Cromwell Course: 18 holes, 6011 yards, par 70, S.S.S 69
Designer Golf Design
Green fees £30
Catering, changing room/showers, bar, accommodation, club, trolley and buggy hire, shop, driving range, practice facilities, full hotel, conference and function facilities
Visitors welcome
Societies welcome by prior arrangement
Tracy Park Hotel, Bath Road, Wick, Gloucester BS30 5RN
✆ 01179 372251

WESTONBIRT GOLF CLUB

c/o Westonbirt School, Tetbury, Gloucester GL8 8QG
✆ 01666 880242 Fax 01666 880385
Map 7, G11
From A433 follow signs to Westonbirt Arboretum. Drive through Westonbirt Village. Car park is shared with church.
Founded 1930
Laid out in the beautiful parkland which was once part of the Holfords' estate.
9 holes, 4505 yards
par 64, S.S.S 60
Green fees £9
Changing room/showers, practice facilities, conference and wedding facilities at main house
Visitors welcome
Societies welcome by prior arrangement – limited availability
Hare and Hounds, Westonbirt, Tetbury, Gloucester GL8 8QL
✆ 01666 880233 Fax 01666 880221

WOODLANDS GOLF & COUNTRY CLUB

Trench Lane, Almondsbury, Bristol, Gloucester BS32 4JZ
✆ 01454 619319 Fax 01454 619397
Map 3, F2
golf@woodlands-golf.com
www.woodlands-golf.com
M5 Jct 16, A38 towards Bradley Stoke. 1st roundabout turn left towards Almondsbury Bus Park. 2nd roundabout turn left.
Founded 1985
With several lakes, water comes into play on many holes of this scenic course.
18 holes, 6068 yards
par 70, S.S.S 69
Designer Golf Design
Green fees £12
Catering, changing room/showers, bar, club, trolley and buggy hire, shop, practice facilities, fishing
Visitors welcome
Societies welcome by prior arrangement
Tracy Park Hotel, Bath Road, Wick, Gloucester BS30 5RN
✆ 01179 372251

WOODSPRING GOLF & COUNTRY CLUB

Yanley Lane, Long Ashton, Bristol, Gloucester BS41 9LR
✆ 01275 394378 Fax 01275 394473
Map 3, F3
A38, near Bristol Airport
Founded 1994
Three 9-hole loops of challenging parkland golf with water hazards, hills and a natural gorge. Every hole gives cause for thought.
Avon Course: 9 holes, 2960 yards, par 35, S.S.S 34
Brunel Course: 9 holes, 3320 yards, par 37, S.S.S 35
Severn Course: 9 holes, 3267 yards, par 36, S.S.S 35
Designer Peter Alliss, Clive Clark, Donald Steel
Green fees £25
Catering, changing room/showers, bar, club, trolley and buggy hire, shop, driving range, practice facilities
Visitors welcome
Handicap certificate required
Societies welcome by prior arrangement

SOMERSET

BATH GOLF CLUB

Sham Castle, North Road, Bath, Somerset BA2 6JG
✆ 01225 425182 Fax 01225 331027
Map 3, G4
www.bathgolfclub.org.uk
Off A36, 1½ miles SE of Bath
Founded 1880
A historic site on which golf is played on lovely turf over and past ancient earthworks. From this high ground the views over Bath are to be savoured. The 3rd and 5th are demanding par 4s threatened by out-of-bounds, and the 12th is only in reach of two fine shots.
18 holes, 6442 yards
par 71, S.S.S 71
Designer Harry Colt
Green fees £27
Catering, changing room/showers, bar, club and trolley hire, shop, practice facilities
Visitors welcome
Handicap certificate required
Societies welcome by prior arrangement

BREAN GOLF CLUB

Coast Road, Brean, Burnham-on-Sea, Somerset TA8 2QY
✆ 01278 752111 Fax 01278 752111
Map 3, E4
admin@brean.com
www.brean.com
M5 Jct 22 follow signs to Brean Leisure Park
Founded 1971
An admirable development from a simple pitch-and-putt into a full 18-hole layout. Water hazards enter play on many holes, with the ever-present threat of wind on a coastal course.
18 holes, 5565 yards
par 69, S.S.S 67
Green fees £15
Catering, changing room/showers, bar, accommodation, club, trolley and buggy hire, shop, practice facilities
Visitors welcome – restricted weekends
Societies welcome by prior

arrangement
Brean Golf Club, Coast Road, Brean Sands, Somerset
01278 751595

BURNHAM & BERROW GOLF CLUB

St Christopher's Way, Burnham-on-Sea, Somerset TA8 2PE
01278 785760 Fax 01278 795440
Map 3, E4
Secretary@BurnhamandBerrowGC.2-golf.com
www.BurnhamandBerrowGC.2-golf.com
M5 Jct 22, follow B3140 for 2½ miles, St Christopher's Way is on left
Founded 1890
Magnificent championship links brilliantly exploiting the dunes to complicate driving and test approach work seriously. Bunkering need only be sparing, for there is some awful scrambling to be done if any of these greens is missed. Around the turn the character changes, being flatter, but troubled with ditches and marshes.
18 holes, 6759 yards, par 71, S.S.S 73
9 holes, 6332 yards, par 70, S.S.S 69
Green fees £40
Catering, changing room/showers, bar, accommodation, club and trolley hire, shop, practice facilities, Dormy House accommodation on site
Visitors welcome
Handicap certificate required – limit: 22 men, 30 women
Societies welcome by prior arrangement
Batch Country Hotel, Lympsham, Somerset
01934 750371

CANNINGTON COUNTRYSIDE GOLF CENTRE

Cannington College, Bridgewater, Somerset TA5 2LS
01278 655050 Fax 01278 655055
Map 3, E5
golf@cannington.ac.uk
www.cannington.ac.uk
M5 Jct 23, A38 to Bridgewater, A39 to Cannington
Founded 1993
A 9-hole course with 18 tees, giving views of the River Parrot and Bristol Channel. Extensive teaching facilities.
9 holes, 6072 yards
par 68, S.S.S 70
Designer Martin Hawtree
Green fees £8.50
Changing room/showers, club and trolley hire, shop, driving range, practice facilities, full conference facilities within college
Visitors welcome
Societies welcome by prior arrangement
Kings Head, High Street, Cannington, Bridgewater, Somerset
01278 652293

CLEVEDON GOLF CLUB

Castle Road, Clevedon, Somerset BS21 7AA
01275 874057 Fax 01275 341228
Map 3, E3
B3124, 1 mile N of Clevedon
Founded 1908
On a hill top overlooking the Severn Estuary with terrific views and several splendid holes.
18 holes, 6117 yards
par 70, S.S.S 69
Designer J.H. Taylor
Green fees £25
Catering, changing room/showers, bar, club and trolley hire, shop, practice facilities
Visitors welcome weekdays
Handicap certificate required
Societies welcome by prior arrangement

ENMORE PARK GOLF CLUB

Enmore, Bridgewater, Somerset TA5 2AN
01278 671519 Fax 01278 671740
Map 3, D5
golfclub@enmore.fsnet.co.uk
www.golfdirector.com/enmore
A39 from Bridgewater towards Minehead, left for Spaxton, left for Enmore
Founded 1906
Set in lovely rolling country with extensive views of the Quantocks. The Hawtree design implies thoughtful golf.
18 holes, 6411 yards
par 71, S.S.S 71
Designer Hawtree
Green fees £20
Catering, changing room/showers, bar, club, trolley and buggy hire, shop, practice facilities
Visitors welcome – restricted weekends
Societies welcome by prior arrangement

ENTRY HILL GOLF CLUB

Entry Hill, Bath, Somerset BA2 5NA
01225 834248 **Map 3, G4**
Off A367, Wells road
Founded 1985
A hilly public course.
9 holes, 4206 yards
par 66, S.S.S 61
Green fees £8.25
Changing room/showers, club and trolley hire, shop
Visitors welcome with booking system
Societies welcome by prior arrangement

FARRINGTON GOLF CLUB

Marsh Lane, Farrington Gurney, Somerset BS39 6TS
01760 241274 Fax 01761 451021
Map 3, G4
info@farringtongolfclub.net
www.farringtongolfclub.net
Off A37, 12 miles S of Bristol
Founded 1992
Hidden away from the bustle of everyday life in rural Somerset, yet challenging in a contemporary way, with several treacherous water holes, excellent practice facilities, and a serious executive course.
18 holes, 6693 yards
par 72, S.S.S 72
Green fees £20
Catering, changing room/showers, bar, club, trolley and buggy hire, shop, driving range, practice facilities, 9-hole executive course, function/wedding suite
Visitors welcome
Handicap certificate required
Societies welcome by prior arrangement
Ston Easton Park, Ston Easton, Bath, Somerset
01761 241631

FOSSEWAY COUNTRY CLUB

Charlton Lane, Midsomer Norton, Bath, Somerset BA3 4BD
017161 412214 Fax 01761 418357 **Map 3, G4**
A367, SE of Midsomer Norton
Founded 1970
A pretty parkland course with views towards the Mendips.
9 holes, 4608 yards
par 67, S.S.S 65
Designer C.K. Cotton, Frank Pennink
Green fees £10
Catering, changing room/showers, bar, trolley hire, swimming pool and squash
Visitors welcome with restrictions
Societies welcome by prior arrangement

FROME GOLF CLUB

Critchill Manor, Frome, Somerset BA11 4LJ
01373 453410 Fax 01373 453410
Map 3, G4
A361, close to Nunney Catch roundabout
Founded 1993
Good facilities at this attractive parkland course.

18 holes, 5466 yards
par 69, S.S.S 67
Green fees £13
Catering, changing room/showers, bar, club and trolley hire, shop, driving range, practice facilities
Visitors welcome
Societies welcome by prior arrangement – no company days

ISLE OF WEDMORE GOLF CLUB

Lascot Hill, Wedmore, Somerset BS28 4QT
☎ 01934 712452 Fax 01934 713554
Map 3, E4
www.wedmoregolfclub.com
M5 Jct 22, A38 northbound, club signposted in Lower Weare
Founded 1992
There are delightful views over the Cheddar Valley and Mendip Hills from this environmentally-friendly parkland course.
18 holes, 6057 yards
par 70, S.S.S 69
Designer Terry Murray
Green fees £18
Catering, changing room/showers, bar, accommodation, club and trolley hire, shop, practice facilities, wedding, function facilities
Visitors welcome with restrictions
Societies welcome by prior arrangement
🏨 Sidcot Hotel, Bridgwater Road, Winscombe, Somerset
☎ 01934 742497

KINGWESTON GOLF CLUB

Millfield School, Street, near Glastonbury, Somerset BA16 0YD
☎ 01458 448300 **Map 3, F5**
Off B3153, 2 miles SE of Glastonbury
Founded 1983
A private course, part of the extensive sport facilities available at Millfield School.
9 holes, 4516 yards
S.S.S 62
Visitors welcome only as members' guests
No societies

LANSDOWN GOLF CLUB

Lansdown, Bath, Somerset BA1 9BT
☎ 01225 420242 Fax 01225 339252
Map 3, G3
admin@lansdowngolfclub.co.uk
www.lansdowngolfclub.co.uk
M4 Jct 18, A46 towards Bath, then A420 towards Bristol. 1st left at Toghill House Farm, left at T-junction. Course 1 mile further on.
Founded 1894
Superb views across the Bristol Channel towards the Black Mountains of Wales are a bonus on this most southerly of the Cotswold courses.
18 holes, 6316 yards
par 71, S.S.S 70
Green fees £22
Catering, changing room/showers, bar, trolley and buggy hire, shop, practice facilities, private dining room available for functions and conferences
Visitors welcome – with restrictions
Handicap certificate required
Societies welcome by prior arrangement
🏨 Lansdown Grove Hotel, Lansdown Road, Bath, Somerset
☎ 01225 483888

LONG SUTTON GOLF CLUB

Long Load, Langport, Somerset TA10 9JU
☎ 01458 241017 Fax 01458 241022
Map 3, F6
B3165, 6 miles NW of Yeovil
Founded 1991
A rolling parkland course in the Somerset countryside.
18 holes, 6367 yards
par 71, S.S.S 70
Designer Patrick Dawson
Green fees £16
Catering, changing room/showers, bar, club, trolley and buggy hire, shop, driving range, practice facilities
Visitors welcome weekdays
Societies welcome by prior arrangement

THE MENDIP GOLF CLUB

Gurney Slade, Bath, Somerset BA3 4UT
☎ 01749 840570 Fax 01749 841439
Map 3, F4
www.mendipgolfclub.co.uk
Off A37, 3 miles N of Shepton Mallett
Founded 1908
At an altitude of 1,000 feet above sea level, the views are far reaching. The course itself has much to commend it, with gently undulating fairways posing many problems, and constantly varied greens.
18 holes, 6383 yards
par 71, S.S.S 70
Designer Harry Vardon, Frank Pennink
Green fees £21
Catering, changing room/showers, bar, club and trolley hire, shop, practice facilities
Visitors welcome (handicap required at weekends)
Handicap certificate required
Societies welcome by prior arrangement

MENDIP SPRING GOLF CLUB

Honeyhall Lane, Congresbury, Somerset BS49 5JT
☎ 01934 852322 Fax 01934 853021
Map 3, F4
mendipspring@lineone.net
www.mendipspring.co.uk
M5 Jct 21 and A370, 12 miles S of Bristol
Founded 1992
Both courses make considerable use of water in their defensive armament, with the 452-yard 11th on Brinsea troubled on both sides as it describes a gigantic arc.
Brinsea Course: 18 holes, 6334 yards, par 71, S.S.S 70
Lakeside Course: 9 holes, 4784 yards, par 68, S.S.S 66
Green fees £23
Catering, changing room/showers, bar, club, trolley and buggy hire, shop, driving range, practice facilities, full conference, function and wedding facilities
Visitors welcome – prior booking on Brinsea
Handicap certificate required
Societies welcome by prior arrangement
🏨 Daneswood House, Cuck Hill, Shipham, Near Cheddar, Somerset BS25 1RD
☎ 01934 843145 Fax 01934 843824
daneswoodhousehotel@compuserve.com

MINEHEAD & WEST SOMERSET GOLF CLUB

The Warren, Warren Road, Minehead, Somerset TA24 5SJ
☎ 01643 702057 Fax 01643 705095
Map 3, C5
secretary@mineheadgolf.co.uk
www.mineheadgolf.co.uk
At E end of Esplanade
Founded 1882
The second oldest course in the southwest, with a renowned closing stretch beside the sea.
18 holes, 6228 yards
par 71, S.S.S 71
Green fees £24.50
Catering, changing room/showers, bar, club and trolley hire, shop, practice facilities
Visitors welcome
Societies welcome by prior arrangement
🏨 The York House, 48 The Avenue, Minehead, Somerset TA24 5AN
☎ 01643 705151

OAKE MANOR GOLF CLUB

Oake, Taunton, Somerset TA4 1BA
☎ 01823 461993 Fax 01823 461995
Map 3, D6
www.oakemanor.com

Off A38, close to M5 Jct 26
Founded 1993
A stiff test with lakes and streams on many holes. The views to the surrounding hills are inspiring.
18 holes, 6109 yards
par 70, S.S.S 69
Designer Adrian Stiff
Green fees £17.50
Catering, changing room/showers, bar, club and trolley hire, shop, driving range, practice facilities
Visitors welcome by prior arrangement
Societies welcome by prior arrangement

ORCHARDLEIGH GOLF CLUB

Frome, Somerset BA11 2PH
✆ 01373 454200 Fax 01373 454202
Map 3, G4
A362 Frome-Radstock road
Founded 1995
With water coming into play on seven holes, this long, mature parkland course is as hard on erratic play as it is easy on the eye.
18 holes, 6831 yards
par 72, S.S.S 73
Designer Brian Huggett
Green fees £22
Catering, changing room/showers, bar, club, trolley and buggy hire, shop, driving range, practice facilities
Visitors welcome – restricted weekends
Societies welcome by prior arrangement
Bowlish House, Wells Road, Shepton Mallet, Somerset BA4 5JD
✆ 01749 342022 Fax 01749 342022

PUXTON PARK GOLF CLUB

Puxton, Weston-super-Mare, Somerset BS24 6TA
✆ 01934 876942 **Map 3, E4**
A370, 2 miles E of M5 Jct 21
Founded 1992
A pay and play course of good length, just inland from Weston-super-Mare and therefore vulnerable to the winds which whip up the Severn Estuary.
18 holes, 6600 yards
par 72
Green fees £8
Shop
Visitors welcome
Societies welcome by prior arrangement

SALTFORD GOLF CLUB

Golf Club Lane, Saltford, Bristol, Somerset BS18 3AA
✆ 01225 873220 Fax 01225 873525
Map 3, G3
Off A4, between Bath and Bristol
Founded 1904
A parkland course in the rolling country west of Bath with extensive views.
18 holes, 6225 yards
par 71, S.S.S 71
Designer Harry Vardon
Green fees £24
Catering, changing room/showers, bar, club, trolley and buggy hire, shop, practice facilities
Visitors welcome weekdays
Societies welcome by prior arrangement

STOCKWOOD VALE GOLF CLUB

Stockwood Lane, Keynsham, Bristol, Somerset BS31 2ER
✆ 0117 986 6505 Fax 0117 986 8974 **Map , G3**
Off A4174, 1 mile SE of Bristol
Founded 1991
A difficult public course, undulating and with good views.
18 holes, 6031 yards
par 71, S.S.S 71
Designer M. Ramsay
Green fees £15
Catering, changing room/showers, bar, trolley hire, shop, driving range
Visitors welcome
Societies welcome by prior arrangement

TALL PINES GOLF CLUB

Cooks Bridle Path, Downside, Backwell, Bristol, Somerset BS48 3DJ
✆ 01275 472076 Fax 01275 474869
Map 3, F3
Off A38, close to Bristol Airport
Founded 1991
A parkland course with good views.
18 holes, 6100 yards
par 70, S.S.S 69
Designer Terry Murray
Green fees £16
Catering, changing room/showers, trolley and buggy hire, shop, practice facilities
Visitors welcome with reservations
Societies welcome by prior arrangement

TAUNTON & PICKERIDGE GOLF CLUB

Corfe, Taunton, Somerset TA3 7BY
✆ 01823 421537 Fax 01823 421742
Map 3, D6
sec@taunt-pickgolfclub.sagehost.co.uk
B3170, 5 miles S of Taunton
Founded 1892
A lovely course with delightful views over the Vale of Taunton. The holes utilise the natural features admirably, without being imposed on them.
18 holes, 5880 yards
par 69, S.S.S 68
Green fees £22
Catering, changing room/showers, bar, trolley hire, shop, practice facilities
Visitors welcome
Handicap certificate required
Societies welcome by prior arrangement
The Falcon Hotel, Henlade, Taunton, Somerset
✆ 01823 442502

TAUNTON VALE GOLF CLUB

Creech Heathfield, Taunton, Somerset TA3 5EY
✆ 01823 412220 Fax 01823 413583
Map 3, E6
A38/A361 Jct, NE of Taunton
Founded 1991
Two parkland courses plus driving range give full facilities.
18 holes, 6167 yards, par 70, S.S.S 69
Designer John Payne
9 holes, 2004 yards, par 64, S.S.S 60
Green fees £16
Catering, changing room/showers, bar, club, trolley and buggy hire, shop, driving range, practice facilities
Visitors welcome with prior booking
Societies welcome by prior arrangement

TICKENHAM GOLF CLUB

Clevedon Road, Tickenham, Bristol, Somerset BS21 6RY
✆ 01275 856626 **Map 3, F3**
info@tickenhamgolf.co.uk
www.tickenhamgolf.co.uk
M5 Jct 20, follow signs for Nailsea and Bristol, golf on left in Tickenham
Founded 1994
With fine views from its site on the side of ancient Cadbury Camp, Tickenham offers a good test of the approach game with well-protected USGA-specification greens.
9 holes, 4000 yards
par 60, S.S.S 58
Designer A. Sutcliffe
Green fees £6
Bar, club and trolley hire, shop, driving range, practice facilities, game improvement centre
Visitors welcome
Societies welcome by prior arrangement
Star Inn, Tickenham, Somerset BS21 6SE
✆ 01275 858836

VIVARY GOLF COURSE

Vivary Park, Taunton, Somerset TA1 3JW

☎ 01823 289274 **Map 3, D6**
Off A38, S of Taunton
Founded 1928
Despite the diminutive length, Fowler's guile ensures a tricky round.
18 holes, 4620 yards
par 63, S.S.S 63
Designer Herbert Fowler
Green fees £8.50
Catering, changing room/showers, bar, club and trolley hire, shop, tennis
Visitors welcome
Societies welcome by prior arrangement

WELLS GOLF CLUB

East Horrington Road, Wells, Somerset BA5 3DS
☎ 01749 675005 Fax 01749 675005
Map 3, F5
secretary@wellsgolfclub99.freeserve.co.uk
Off B3139 of Wells
Founded 1893
Very pretty parkland course close to one of England's most beautiful cathedrals.
18 holes, 6015 yards
par 70, S.S.S 69
Green fees £20
Catering, changing room/showers, bar, club, trolley and buggy hire, shop, driving range
Visitors welcome
Handicap certificate required
Societies welcome by prior arrangement
White Hart Hotel, Sadler Street, Wells, Somerset
☎ 01749 672056

WESTON-SUPER-MARE GOLF CLUB

Uphill Road North, Weston-super-Mare, Somerset BS23 4NQ
☎ 01934 626968 **Map 3, E4**
Off A 370 south of town centre
Founded 1892
Renowned for its fine seaside turf and greens, Weston-super-Mare displays many of the qualities of traditional seaside golf, not least on the famous 15th, a long par 4 often compared to the Road Hole at St Andrews. Only 355 yards long, the 1st is, nevertheless, a fine, tight, opening hole.
18 holes, 6208 yards
par 70, S.S.S 70
Designer Tom Dunn, Alister Mackenzie
Green fees £35
Visitors welcome – handicap certificate required at weekends
Societies welcome by prior arrangement

WHEATHILL GOLF CLUB

Wheathill, Somerton, Somerset TA11 7HG
☎ 01963 240667 Fax 01963 240230
Map 3, F5
Off B3153, 5 miles E of Somerton
Founded 1993
A pretty parkland course laid out besides a river.
18 holes, 5362 yards
par 68, S.S.S 66
Designer John Payne
Green fees £10
Catering, changing room/showers, bar, club, trolley and buggy hire, shop, practice facilities, academy course
Visitors welcome
Societies welcome by prior arrangement

WINDWHISTLE GOLF, SQUASH & COUNTRY CLUB

Cricket St Thomas, Chard, Somerset TA20 4DG
☎ 01460 30231 Fax 01460 30055
Map 3, E7
A30, 3 miles E of Chard
Founded 1932
J.H. Taylor's 9 hole course of 1932 was extended to 18 holes in 1992. At over 700 feet above sea level the views are splendid.
18 holes, 6470 yards
par 71, S.S.S 71
Designer J.H. Taylor, Leonard Fisher
Green fees £15
Catering, changing room/showers, bar, club and trolley hire, shop, driving range, squash
Visitors welcome by prior arrangement
Societies welcome by prior arrangement

WORLEBURY GOLF CLUB

Monks Hill, Worlebury, Weston-super-Mare, Somerset BS22 9SX
☎ 01934 625789 Fax 01934 621935
Map 3, E4
secretary@worleburygc.co.uk
www.worleburygc.co.uk
M5 Jct 21, follow signs for Worlebury
Founded 1908
The views alone, both inland to the hills, and towards the Bristol Channel, would make a visit worthwhile. However, there is plenty of golfing challenge, not least the very opening drive.
18 holes, 5956 yards
par 70, S.S.S 69
Designer Harry Vardon
Green fees £20
Catering, changing room/showers, bar, trolley hire, shop, practice facilities
Visitors welcome
Handicap certificate required
Societies welcome by prior arrangement
Commodore Hotel, Beach Road, Kewstoke, Weston-super-Mare, Somerset BS22 9UZ
☎ 01934 415778

YEOVIL GOLF CLUB

Sherborne Road, Yeovil, Somerset BA21 5BW
☎ 01935 422965 Fax 01935 411283
Map 3, F6
yeovilgolfclub@yeovilgc.fsnet.co.uk
A30 E of Yeovil
Founded 1907
Yeovil charms, running through very pretty countryside on the edge of the town. With only one par 4 over 400 yards it does not overface those of modest power, although there is a 232-yard par 3 at the 15th. Handicap certificates are not required for the 9-hole course.
Old Course: 18 holes, 6144 yards, par 72, S.S.S 70
Designer Herbert Fowler, Tom Simpson
Newton Course: 9 holes, 4876 yards, par 68, S.S.S 65
Green fees £25
Catering, changing room/showers, bar, club and trolley hire, shop, driving range, practice facilities
Visitors welcome
Handicap certificate required
Societies welcome by prior arrangement
Little Barwick House, Barwick, Near Yeovil, Somerset BA22 9TD
☎ 01935 423902 Fax 01935 420908

WILTSHIRE

BOWOOD GOLF & COUNTRY CLUB

Derry Hill, Calne, Wiltshire SN11 9PQ
☎ 01249 822228 Fax 01249 822218
Map 4, A3
golfclub@bowood-estate.co.uk
www.bowood-estate.co.uk
A4, between Chippenham and Calne, signposted from M4 Jct 17
Founded 1992
Golf on the grand scale in a Capability Brown estate. Even from the yellow tees two of the par fives exceed 560 yards, the 4th and 10th, and the approach to the 4th green must flirt with water. Several two-shotters stand out for their severity, notably the 7th and 8th.
18 holes, 7317 yards
par 72, S.S.S 74
Designer Dave Thomas

Green fees £34
Catering, changing room/showers, bar, accommodation, club, trolley and buggy hire, shop, driving range, practice facilities, luxurious Queenwood Lodge available for guests, academy course, conference, wedding and function facilities
Visitors welcome afternoons only
Societies welcome by prior arrangement
Angel Hotel, Market Place, Chippenham, Wiltshire
01249 652615 Fax 01249 443210

BRADFORD-ON-AVON GOLF CLUB

Trowbridge Road, Bradford-on-Avon, Wiltshire
01225 868268 **Map 3, H4**
A636, S of Bradford
Founded 1991
A handsome little course beside the river, on the outskirts of one of the most striking towns in England.
9 holes, 2109 yards
S.S.S 61
Green fees £6
Visitors welcome weekdays
Societies welcome by prior arrangement

BRINKWORTH GOLF CLUB

Longmans Farm, Brinkworth, Chippenham, Wiltshire SN15 5DG
01225 868268 **Map 4, B2**
Off B4042, between Swindon and Malmesbury
Founded 1984
An attractive parkland course with a number of water hazards.
18 holes, 5884 yards
par 70, S.S.S 70
Green fees £8
Catering, changing room/showers, bar, club and trolley hire
Visitors welcome
Societies welcome by prior arrangement

BROOME MANOR GOLF CLUB

Pipers Way, Swindon, Wiltshire SN3 1RG
01793 532403 Fax 01793 433255
Map 4, C2
Off B4006, 2 miles SE of Swindon
Founded 1976
The main course is well respected, and is backed up by excellent additional facilities.
18 holes, 6283 yards, par 71, S.S.S 70
Designer Hawtree
9 holes, 2690 yards, S.S.S 30
Green fees £12
Catering, changing room/showers, bar, club and trolley hire, shop, driving range, practice facilities
Visitors welcome
Societies welcome by prior arrangement

CHIPPENHAM GOLF CLUB

Malmesbury Road, Chippenham, Wiltshire SN15 5LT
01249 652040 Fax 01249 446681
Map 4, A2
A350, 1 mile N of Chippenham, M4 Jct 17
Founded 1896
A downland course with good turf.
18 holes, 5540 yards
par 69, S.S.S 67
Green fees £20
Catering, changing room/showers, bar, club and trolley hire, shop, practice facilities
Visitors welcome
Societies welcome by prior arrangement

THE CRICKLADE HOTEL & COUNTRY CLUB

Common Hill, Cricklade, Wiltshire SN6 6HA
01793 750751 Fax 01793 751767
Map 4, B2
jane@crickladehotel.fsnet.co.uk
www.crickladehotel.co.uk
B4040 ½ mile W of Cricklade, M4 Jct 15/16
Founded 1991
An executive-length course with several entertaining short par 4s, notably the 5th, on which a ditch, 160 yards out, frequently causes disastrous indecision.
9 holes, 3660 yards
par 62, S.S.S 57
Designer Ian Bolt
Green fees £16
Catering, changing room/showers, bar, accommodation, club and trolley hire, full hotel and conference facilities, swimming pool, gym, beauty room
Visitors welcome weekdays only
Societies welcome by prior arrangement
Cricklade Hotel and Country Club, Common Hill, Cricklade, Wiltshire SN6 6HA
01793 750751 Fax 01793 751767

CUMBERWELL PARK GOLF CLUB

Bradford-on-Avon, Wiltshire BA15 2PQ
01225 863322 Fax 01225 868160
Map 3, H4
www.cumberwellpark.co.uk
A363, between Bradford-on-Avon and Bath
Founded 1994
Three loops of 9 holes with a good deal of water, particularly on the Blue nine. The first hole on that Blue 9 is an extreme dog-leg of 579 yards, and the Red 9 finishes with a monster of a par 5 at 606 yards.
Lakeland Course: 18 holes, 6922 yards, par 71, S.S.S 73
Parkland Course: 18 holes, 6727 yards, par 71, S.S.S 72
Woodland Course: 18 holes, 6749 yards, par 72, S.S.S 72
Green fees £22.50
Catering, changing room/showers, bar, club, trolley and buggy hire, shop, practice facilities
Visitors welcome
Societies welcome by prior arrangement

ERLESTOKE SANDS GOLF CLUB

Erlestoke, Devizes, Wiltshire SN10 5UB
01380 830300 Fax 01380 831284
Map 4, A4
info@erlestokesands.co.uk
www.erlestokesands.co.uk
B3098 between Westbury and West Lavington
Founded 1992
An important recent addition to the golfing provision in Wiltshire. Built on two levels, the course plunges down spectacularly on the 168-yard 7th, to a green set off against a lake and the distant hills.
18 holes, 6705 yards
par 73, S.S.S 72
Designer Adrian Stiff
Green fees £18
Catering, changing room/showers, bar, club, trolley and buggy hire, shop, driving range, practice facilities
Visitors welcome
Societies welcome by prior arrangement
The Bear Hotel, The Market Place, Devizes, Wiltshire SN10 1HS
01380 722444 Fax 01380 722450

HAMPTWORTH GOLF & COUNTRY CLUB

Hamptworth Road, Landford, Wiltshire SP5 2DU
01794 390155 Fax 01794 390022
Map 4, C6
info@hamptworthgolf.co.uk
www.hamptworthgolf.co.uk
On A36 (signposted) between M27 Jct 2 and Salisbury
Founded 1993
Hamptworth's fairways curve through beautiful countryside, mostly a 150-year old forest, and many holes are punctuated by streams and ponds. The most

difficult hole, unusually, is a par 5 of only 468 yards, the 7th, but it really is treacherous.
18 holes, 6443 yards
par 72, S.S.S 71
Designer P.Sanders
Green fees £30
Catering, changing room/showers, bar, club, trolley and buggy hire, shop, driving range, conference facilities, croquet, 4X4 driving
Visitors welcome – restricted weekends
Societies welcome by prior arrangement
New Forest Lodge, Southampton Road, Landford, Wiltshire SP5 2ED
01794 390999

HIGH POST GOLF CLUB
Great Durnford, Salisbury, Wiltshire SP4 6AT
01722 782356 Fax 01722 782674
Map 4, C5
highpostgolfclub@lineone.net
A345 4 miles N of Salisbury
Founded 1922
Overlooking Salisbury Plain and the Boscombe Down airfield, High Post enjoys a chalk base, giving excellent all-year-round conditions. The bunkerless 9th, a 384-yard dog-leg, has been highly praised by Peter Alliss and Sir Henry Cotton. Alliss also commends the 12th, a substantial par 4 with cross-bunkers short of the green.
18 holes, 6305 yards
par 70, S.S.S 70
Designer Hawtree
Green fees £25
Visitors welcome – handicap certificate required at weekends
Handicap certificate required
Societies welcome by prior arrangement

HIGHWORTH COMMUNITY GOLF CENTRE
Swindon Road, Highworth, Wiltshire SN6 7SJ
01793 766014 **Map 4, C1**
A361, N of Swindon
Founded 1990
A downland course giving fine views.
9 holes, 3120 yards
par 35, S.S.S 35
Green fees £7.20
Club and trolley hire, shop, pitch-and-putt course
Visitors welcome
Societies welcome by prior arrangement

KINGSDOWN GOLF CLUB
Kingsdown, Corsham, Wiltshire SN13 8BS
01225 742530 Fax 01225 743472
Map 3, H4
kingsdowngc@genie.co.uk
S of A4 between Bathford and Ashley
Founded 1880
Fine turf and excellent conditioning are almost inevitable on the upland courses of Wiltshire. Kingsdown delivers the goods, and a fair challenge.
18 holes, 6445 yards
par 72, S.S.S 71
Green fees £24
Catering, changing room/showers, bar, club and trolley hire, shop, practice facilities
Visitors welcome, with restrictions
Handicap certificate required – limit: men 28, women 36
Societies welcome by prior arrangement
Leigh Park Hotel, Leigh Park Road, Bradford-on-Avon, Wiltshire BA15 2RA
01225 864885

THE MANOR HOUSE GOLF CLUB AT CASTLE COMBE
Castle Combe, Near Chippenham, Wiltshire SN14 7JW
01249 782982 Fax 01249 782992
Map 3, H3
enquiries@manorhousegolfclub.co.uk
www.exclusivehotels.co.uk
B4039 at Castle Combe, M4 Jct 17/18
Founded 1992
Laid out in the undulating parkland of the 14th Century Manor House, this is one of the most attractive of the courses built in the 1990s. A number of lakes, the Bybrook River and its tributaries affect play on many holes, giving a breathtaking par-3 17th and gorgeous 18th.
18 holes, 6286 yards
par 72, S.S.S 71
Designer Peter Alliss, Clive Clark
Green fees £40
Catering, changing room/showers, bar, accommodation, club, trolley and buggy hire, shop, driving range, practice facilities, meeting, function, board rooms, Grand Saxon Hall, private dining suites
Visitors welcome
Handicap certificate required
Societies welcome by prior arrangement
The Manor House, Castle Combe, Near Chippenham, Wiltshire SN14 7HR
01249 782206 Fax 01249 782159
enquiries@manor-house.co.uk

MARLBOROUGH GOLF CLUB
The Common, Marlborough, Wiltshire SN8 1DU
01672 512147 Fax 01672 513164
Map 4, C3
M4 Jct 15, A346 south
Founded 1888
Rolling downland fairways give wide views of the Marlborough Downs and Og Valley. Invitingly, the restaurant and bar are open all day, every day.
18 holes, 6491 yards
par 72, S.S.S 71
Green fees £25
Catering, changing room/showers, bar, trolley and buggy hire, shop, practice facilities, full conference facilities
Visitors welcome, with restrictions – handicap certificate required at weekends
Handicap certificate required
Societies welcome by prior arrangement
Castle and Ball Hotel, High Street, Marlborough, Wiltshire
01672 515201

MONKTON PARK PAR THREE GOLF COURSE
Monkton Park, Chippenham, Wiltshire SN15 3PE
01249 653928 Fax 01249 653928
Map 4, A2
Centre of Chippenham, M4 Jct 17, 4 miles
Founded 1960
A pitch-and-putt course open to all.
9 holes, 1000 yards
par 27, S.S.S 27
Designer M. Dawson
Green fees £4
Club hire, shop, crazy golf
Visitors welcome
Societies welcome by prior arrangement
Angel Hotel, Market Place, Chippenham, Wiltshire
01249 652615 Fax 01249 443210

NORTH WILTS GOLF CLUB
Bishops Cannings, Near Devizes, Wiltshire SN10 2LP
01380 860330 Fax 01380 860877
Map 4, B3
secretary@northwiltsgolfclub.fsnet.co.uk
Between A4 and A361
Founded 1890
An elevated downland course with fine views, and, at its highest point, a cockfighting pit.
18 holes, 6400 yards
par 71, S.S.S 71
Green fees £21
Catering, changing room/showers, bar, club, trolley and buggy hire,

shop, practice facilities, indoor video golf clinic
Visitors welcome
Societies welcome by prior arrangement
The Bear Hotel, The Market Place, Devizes, Wiltshire SN10 1HS
01380 722444 Fax 01380 722450

OAKSEY PARK GOLF CLUB

Oaksey, Malmesbury, Wiltshire SN16 9SB
01666 577995 Fax 01666 577174
Map 4, B1
Off A419/A429 at Oaksey
Founded 1991
Parkland course laid out beside Cotswold Water Parks.
9 holes, 2904 yards
par 70, S.S.S 69
Green fees £10
Catering, changing room/showers, bar, shop, driving range, fishing, shooting, riding, water sports
Visitors welcome
Societies welcome by prior arrangement

OGBOURNE DOWNS GOLF CLUB

Ogbourne St George, Marlborough, Wiltshire SN8 1TB
01672 841327 Fax 01672 841327
Map 4, C2
M4 Jct 15, A346 towards Marlborough
Founded 1907
Set on the wide-open spaces of the chalk downs south of Swindon, Ogbourne is renowned for the quality of its turf and excellence of its greens. Sloping lies and approaches played to ledge greens are a feature of many holes. Star billing for the 202-yard 15th across a ravine.
18 holes, 6363 yards
par 71, S.S.S 70
Designer J.H. Taylor
Green fees £25
Catering, changing room/showers, bar, club, trolley and buggy hire, shop, driving range, practice facilities
Visitors welcome weekdays
Handicap certificate required – limit: 28
Societies welcome by prior arrangement
Parkland Hotel, Ogbourne St George, Marlborough, Wiltshire SN8 1SL
01672 841555

ROYAL MILITARY COLLEGE OF SCIENCE GOLF CLUB

RMCS, Shrivenham, Swindon, Wiltshire SN6 8LA
01793 785725 **Map 4, C2**
r.humphrey@rmcs.cranfield.ac.uk
Off A420
Founded 1956
A private club on a secure military site, open to staff, students and their guests only.
18 holes, 5684 yards
par 70, S.S.S 69
Green fees £8
Changing room/showers, driving range, practice facilities
Visitors welcome only as members' guests
No societies

RUSHMORE PARK GOLF CLUB

Tollard Royal, Salisbury, Wiltshire SP5 5QB
01725 516326 Fax 01725 516466
Map 4, B5
B3081, between Sixpenny Handley and Tollard Royal, 16 miles SW of Salisbury
Founded 1994
An expanding establishment in rolling Cranborne Chase country.
18 holes, 5585 yards
par 71, S.S.S 67
Green fees £13
Catering, changing room/showers, bar, club and trolley hire, shop, driving range, practice facilities
Visitors welcome with prior booking
Societies welcome by prior arrangement

SALISBURY & SOUTH WILTS GOLF CLUB

Netherhampton, Salisbury, Wiltshire SP2 8PR
01722 742645 Fax 01722 742645
Map 4, B5
mail@salisburygolf.co.uk
www.salisburygolf.co.uk.
A3094, near Salisbury Race Course
Founded 1888
The availability of an extra nine holes, which weave in and out of Salisbury race course, gives the club considerable flexibility. There are fine views of Salisbury Cathedral, and the trees on J.H. Taylor's main course have matured over the years to add to the beauty of this charming spot.
18 holes, 6485 yards, par 71, S.S.S 71
Bibury Course: 9 holes, 66 yards, par 66, S.S.S 68
Designer J.H. Taylor, Simon Gidman
Green fees £25
Catering, changing room/showers, bar, club, trolley and buggy hire, shop, practice facilities, banqueting/function facilities
Visitors welcome
Societies welcome by prior arrangement
Rose and Crown, Harnham Road, Salisbury, Wiltshire SP2 8JQ
01722 399955

SHRIVENHAM PARK GOLF CLUB

Penny Hooks, Shrivenham, Swindon, Wiltshire SN6 8EX
01793 783853 Fax 01793 782999
Map 4, C2
A420, between Oxford and Swindon
Founded 1967
A rolling course with the good drainage of downland subsoil, with marked benefits during a wet winter.
18 holes, 5769 yards
par 69, S.S.S 69
Designer Glen Johnson
Green fees £15
Catering, changing room/showers, bar, trolley and buggy hire, shop, practice facilities
Visitors welcome with advance booking
Societies welcome by prior arrangement

THOULSTONE PARK GOLF CLUB

Chapmanslade, North Westbury, Wiltshire BA13 4AQ
01373 832825 Fax 01373 832821
Map 4, A4
On A36 outside Warminster
Founded 1993
A gentle parkland course featuring water on the 4th, 7th and 18th.
18 holes, 6248 yards
par 70, S.S.S 70
Designer M.R.M. Sandow
Green fees £15
Catering, changing room/showers, bar, club and trolley hire, shop, driving range, practice facilities, conference facilities
Visitors welcome
Societies welcome by prior arrangement

TIDWORTH GARRISON GOLF CLUB

Bulford Road, Tidworth, Wiltshire SP9 7AF
01980 842301 Fax 01980 842301
Map 4, C4
A338, Salisbury to Marlborough Road, 1 mile SW of Tidworth
Founded 1908
Tidworth's downland turf gives good golfing conditions all year round. From the high ground there are fine views over Salisbury Plain.
18 holes, 6320 yards
par 70, S.S.S 70
Designer Donald Steel
Green fees £27.50

Catering, changing room/showers, bar, club, trolley and buggy hire, shop, practice facilities
Visitors welcome – restrictions
Handicap certificate required
Societies welcome by prior arrangement
The Red House Hotel and Conference Centre, Cholderton, Wiltshire SP4 0EG
01980 629542

UPAVON GOLF CLUB

Douglas Avenue, Upavon, Wiltshire SN9 6BQ
01980 630281 Fax 01980 630787
Map 4, B4
A342, 1½ miles SE of Upavon Village
Founded 1918
Situated on free-draining chalk downland, conditions are admirable even in winter. The inspiring sound of skylarks soaring complements the admirable views of Pewsey Vale. The 13th is a 602-yard par 5 from the back tee, and the closing hole is a par 3 of 160 yards across a valley.
18 holes, 6402 yards
par 71, S.S.S 71
Designer R. Blake
Green fees £22
Catering, changing room/showers, bar, club, trolley and buggy hire, shop, practice facilities
Visitors welcome with restrictions
Societies welcome by prior arrangement

THE WEST WILTS GOLF CLUB

Elm Hill, Warminster, Wiltshire BA12 0AU
01985 212110 Fax 01985 219809
Map 4, A4
Off A36, signposted on Westbury road
Founded 1891
The chalky downland earth on which most of the early Wiltshire courses were built means that, to this day, they enjoy brilliantly drained springy turf and excellent greens. West Wilts is a case in point. The views simply add to the joy. Not a long course, perhaps, but tricky enough.
18 holes, 5709 yards
par 70, S.S.S 68
Designer J.H. Taylor
Green fees £20
Catering, changing room/showers, bar, club and trolley hire, shop, practice facilities
Visitors welcome – weekend restrictions
Handicap certificate required
Societies welcome by prior arrangement
Bishopstrow House Hotel, Bishopstrow, Warminster, Wiltshire
0198 5216769

WHITLEY GOLF COURSE

Corsham Road, Whitley, Melksham, Wiltshire SN12 7QE
01225 790099 **Map 4, A3**
2 miles from centre of Melksham
Founded 1993
A useful pay-and-play facility within striking distance of Bath.
9 holes, 2300 yards
par 66, S.S.S 61
Designer Laurance Ross
Green fees £7
Catering, changing room/showers, bar, club and trolley hire, driving range
Visitors welcome
Societies welcome by prior arrangement
Beechfield House Hotel, Beanacre, Melksham, Wiltshire SN12 7PU
01225 703700

THE WILTSHIRE GOLF CLUB

Vastern, Wootton Bassett, Swindon, Wiltshire SN4 7PB
01793 849999 Fax 01793 849988
Map 4, B2
A3102, 1 mile S of Wootton Bassett
Founded 1992
Water comes into play on 8 holes of what is essentially a rolling downland course.
18 holes, 6522 yards
par 72, S.S.S 72
Designer Peter Alliss, Clive Clark
Green fees £30
Catering, changing room/showers, bar, club, trolley and buggy hire, shop, driving range, practice facilities
Visitors welcome by prior arrangement
Societies welcome by prior arrangement

WRAG BARN GOLF & COUNTRY CLUB

Shrivenham Road, Highworth, Swindon, Wiltshire SN6 7QQ
01793 861327 Fax 01793 861325
Map 4, C2
www.wragbarn.com
B4000, Shrivenham road from Highworth
Founded 1990
A rolling parkland course which has received much praise in the golfing press.
18 holes, 6600 yards
par 72, S.S.S 71
Designer Martin Hawtree
Green fees £25
Catering, changing room/showers, bar, club, trolley and buggy hire, shop, driving range, practice facilities, academy course
Visitors welcome with restrictions
Societies welcome by prior arrangement

IRELAND

In 2005 the Ryder Cup matches will be held on Irish soil for the very first time, at the K Club, in the heart of Irish racing country. It is a fine course designed by Arnold Palmer, just one of the extensive and lavish facilities on offer at this luxurious 5-star country hotel. It is symbolic of the new Republic of Ireland, a country which has blossomed and hugely prospered within the European Union. New millionaires are created almost daily, and new golf courses are springing up at a similar rate. What is more, a large number of these courses are impressively good. Of ten Republic of Ireland courses selected for our top 50, half are recent designs, and there were at least half-a-dozen more seriously pressing for inclusion.

Tom Morris, Harry Colt and James Braid were amongst those who crossed the water to lay out most of the best of Ireland's early golf courses, and some of these are still amongst the country's finest. But the unsung hero of Irish golf design was one of its own sons, the quiet, unassuming Eddie Hackett. He designed a remarkable number of courses, many of them to a very limited budget, yet the standard was enormously impressive. Tom Craddock and Pat Ruddy were his natural successors, again displaying vivid imagination and flair. Now two of Ireland's finest golfers, Des Smyth and Christie O'Connor Jnr., are proving also to be in the top flight of golf architects. With Arnold Palmer, Jack Nicklaus and Bernhard Langer also constructing major courses in Ireland the visitor is spoiled for choice. Not without reason do Tiger Woods, Tom Watson and a host of other notables usually spend the week before the Open Championship in Ireland, acclimatising themselves once more to links golf, and enjoying the best of Irish fishing, food and *craic*.

Poor old Northern Ireland has not had it so good, with political unrest festering for eighty years since the north and south were separated in 1920. Its finest golf courses are amongst the best in the world, yet rarely has a top class professional field been assembled in the province. Until recently the one notable exception was the 1951 Open Championship when Max Faulkner triumphed at Royal Portrush. Now, happily, the Senior British Open has brought many great names to Royal County Down, with Jack Nicklaus amongst the converts to this noble course.

Golfers travel to Ireland from the farthest corners of the world, making pilgrimages to Ballybunion, Ballyliffin, Killarney, Portmarnock and the rest, but it is still possible to find quiet courses where the weekday green fee is well under £20, some even within a half-hour's drive from the centre of Dublin or Belfast. So, if a green fee approaching £200 to play Old Head or the K Club is just outside the budget, have a crack at Skibbereen or Youghal, The Curragh or Woodlands and you'll have plenty of change left over for a glass or two of the 'black stuff' after the round.

CO ANTRIM

ALLEN PARK GOLF CENTRE

Allen Park Golf Centre, 45 Castle Road, Antrim, Antrim BT41 4NA
☎ 028 9442 9001 Fax 028 9442 9001 **Map 1, G3**
allenpask@antrim.gov.uk
www.antrim.gov.uk
2 miles from Antrim on Randalstown Road
Founded 1996
Designed by Ulsterman Tom MacAuley, who was one of the first golf architects to utilise computers for design purposes.
18 holes, 6683 yards
par 72, S.S.S 72
Designer Tom MacAuley
Green fees £14
Changing room/showers, club and trolley hire, shop, driving range, practice facilities
Visitors welcome with restrictions
Societies welcome by prior arrangement
Dunadry Inn, Dunadry, Muckamore, Antrim
☎ 028 9443 4343

BALLYCASTLE GOLF CLUB

2 Cushendall Road, Ballycastle, Antrim BT64 6QP
☎ 028 207 62536
Fax 028 207 69909 **Map 1, G2**
A2, Antrim coast road
Founded 1890
Starting off in parkland beside the Margy and Carey rivers, Ballycastle suddenly changes character to true links as the course follows the shore from the 6th. The 9th and 11th, both to elevated greens, are fine holes. There are superb seascapes from much of the course.
18 holes, 5927 yards
par 71, S.S.S 70
Green fees £20
Catering, changing room/showers, bar, club and trolley hire, shop
Visitors welcome – with restrictions
Societies welcome by prior arrangement
Marine Hotel, North Street, Ballycastle, Antrim
☎ 028 207 62222

BALLYCLARE GOLF CLUB

25 Springvale Road, Ballyclare, Antrim BT39 9JW
☎ 028 9332 2696 Fax 028 9332 2696 **Map 1, H3**
ballyclaregolfclub@supanet.com
1½ miles N of Ballyclare
Founded 1923
Quite a difficult parkland course with plentiful water hazards.
18 holes, 5840 yards
par 71, S.S.S 71
Designer Tom MacAuley
Green fees £18
Catering, changing room/showers, bar, trolley and buggy hire, shop, practice facilities
Visitors welcome with restrictions
Societies welcome by prior arrangement
Ross Park Hotel, 20 Doagh Road, Kells, Antrim
☎ 028 258 91663

BALLYMENA GOLF CLUB

128 Raceview Road, Ballymena, Antrim BT42 4HY
☎ 028 2586 1207 Fax 028 2586 1487 **Map 1, G3**
A42, 2 miles E of Ballymena
Founded 1902
A parkland course with heathland elements.
18 holes, 5299 metres
par 68, S.S.S 67
Green fees £17
Catering, changing room/showers, bar, club, trolley and buggy hire, shop
Visitors welcome – with restrictions
Societies welcome by prior arrangement

BENTRA GOLF COURSE

Slaughterford Road, Whitehead, Antrim BT38 9TG
☎ 028 93378996 **Map 1, H3**
A2 Larne road, 4 miles N of Carrickfergus
A short parkland course with good facilities.
9 holes, 2885 metres
par 37, S.S.S 35
Designer James Braid
Green fees £7.70
Catering, changing room/showers, bar, club and trolley hire, shop, driving range, practice facilities
Visitors welcome
Societies welcome by prior arrangement

BUSHFOOT GOLF CLUB

50 Bushfoot Road, Portballintrae, Antrim BT37 8RR
☎ 028 207 31317 Fax 028 207 31852 **Map 3, G2**
Bushmills to Portballintrae Road
Founded 1890
In an incomparable situation besides the famous Bushmills Distillery, a tricky 9-hole course.
9 holes, 5999 yards
par 70, S.S.S 67
Green fees £14
Catering, changing room/showers, bar, club and trolley hire
Visitors welcome
Handicap certificate required
Societies welcome by prior arrangement
🏨 Royal Court Hotel, Dunluce Road, Portrush, Antrim BT56 8JQ
☎ 027 808 22236

CAIRNDHU GOLF CLUB

192 Coast Road, Ballygally, Larne, Antrim BT40 2QC
☎ 01574 583324 **Map 1, H3**
On coast road, 4 miles N of Larne
Founded 1928
A marvellously scenic course, set on high ground with views over the sea to Scotland, and inland to the Antrim glens. Going out, the par-4 3rd needs a 175-yard carry simply to reach the fairway, while the tee shots at the 10th, 11th, and 12th are particularly demanding.
18 holes, 6385 yards
par 70, S.S.S 69
Designer John Morrison
Green fees £20
Catering, changing room/showers, bar, club, trolley and buggy hire, shop, driving range, practice facilities
Visitors welcome
Societies welcome by prior arrangement
🏨 Highways Hotel, Ballyloran, Larne, Antrim BT40 2SU
☎ 028 2827 2272

CARRICKFERGUS GOLF CLUB

35 North Road, Carrickfergus, Antrim BT38 8LP
☎ 028 9336 3713 Fax 028 9336 3023 **Map 1, H3**
Off M5, 7 miles E of Belfast
Founded 1926
A beautifully situated parkland course with fine views over Belfast Lough.
18 holes, 5752 yards
par 68, S.S.S 68
Green fees £15
Catering, changing room/showers, bar, trolley hire, shop
Visitors welcome – with weekend restrictions
Societies welcome by prior arrangement

CUSHENDALL GOLF CLUB

21 Shore Road, Cushendall, Antrim BT44 0NG
☎ 028 217 71318 Fax 028 217 71318 **Map 1, H2**
Antrim coast road, 25 miles N of Larne
Founded 1937
It would be worth driving to Cushendall simply to experience the magic of the Antrim coast road, and the golf course, short though it is, shares these spectacular views across the sea to Scotland.
9 holes, 4384 metres
par 66, S.S.S 63
Designer Daniel Delargy
Green fees £13
Catering, changing room/showers, bar, practice facilities
Visitors welcome – with restrictions
Societies welcome by prior arrangement

DOWN ROYAL PARK GOLF COURSE

Dunygarton Road, Lisburn, Antrim BT27 5RT
☎ 02892 621339 Fax 02892 621339
Map 1, G4
M1 Sprucefield Junction, signposted
Founded 1989
A rare heathland course in this part of Ireland, with the 2nd on the Down Royal course reckoned to be one of the best par 5s in Ireland – over 600 yards long.
Down Royal Course: 18 holes, 6824 yards, par 72, S.S.S 72
Designer Golf Associates
Valley Course: 9 holes, 2019 yards, par 33
Green fees £17
Catering, changing room/showers, bar, accommodation, club, trolley and buggy hire, shop, driving range, practice facilities, conference and exhibition facilities
Visitors welcome
Societies welcome by prior arrangement
🏨 Down Royal Park, Dunygarton Road, Lisburn, Antrim BT27 5RT
☎ 02892 621339 Fax 02892 621339

GALGORM CASTLE GOLF CLUB

Galgorm Castle, Ballymena, Antrim BT42 1HL
☎ 028 25646161 Fax 028 25651157
Map 1, G3
golf@galgormcastle.com
www.galgormcastle.com
A42, 1mile SW of Ballymena
Founded 1997
A very recent course, laid out in the grounds of one of Ireland's great historic castles.
18 holes, 6736 yards
par 72, S.S.S 72
Designer Simon Gidman
Green fees £20
Catering, changing room/showers, bar, club and trolley hire, shop, driving range, practice facilities, conference facilities
Visitors welcome
Societies welcome by prior arrangement
🏨 Tullygass House, Sourhill Road, Ballymena, Antrim
☎ 028 256 52639

GRACEHILL GOLF CLUB

141 Ballinlea Road, Stranocum, Ballymoney, Antrim BT53 8PX
☎ 028 207 51209 Fax 028 207 51074 **Map 1, G2**
info@gracehillgolfclub.co.uk
www.gracehillgolfclub.co.uk
7 miles SW of Ballymoney
Founded 1995
A fine addition to Ireland's roster of parkland courses, with lakes and trees giving beauty and, in many cases, considerable challenge. Green fees are reduced on Mondays and Tuesdays, and on all days of the week represent excellent value.
18 holes, 6540 yards
par 72, S.S.S 73
Designer F. Ainsworth
Green fees £15
Catering, changing room/showers, bar, trolley hire, practice facilities, disabled facilities
Visitors welcome, subject to timesheet
Societies welcome by prior arrangement
🏨 Causeway Hotel, 40 Causeway Road, Bushmills, Antrim
☎ 028 207 31226

GREENACRES GOLF CLUB

153 Ballyrobert Road, Ballyclare, Antrim BT39 9RT
✆ 028 9335 4111 Fax 028 9335 4166 **Map 1, H3**
M2, 6 miles N of Belfast, on B56 signposted to Ballyclare
Founded 1995
Gently undulating parkland, with lakes in play at 5 holes.
18 holes, 5819 yards
par 71, S.S.S 69
Green fees £12
Catering, changing room/showers, bar, club and trolley hire, driving range, practice facilities
Visitors welcome – weekend restrictions
Societies welcome by prior arrangement
Corr's Corner, 315 Ballyclare Road, Newtownabbey, Antrim
✆ 028 9084 9221

GREENISLAND GOLF CLUB

156 Upper Road, Greenisland, Carrickfergus, Antrim BT38 8RW
✆ 028 90862236 **Map 1, H3**
2 miles from Carrickfergus
Founded 1894
A parkland course set beneath the Knocagh Monument, enjoying majestic views over Belfast Lough and the coast of County Down.
9 holes, 6045 yards
par 71, S.S.S 69
Green fees £12
Catering, changing room/showers, bar
Visitors welcome with restrictions
Societies welcome by prior arrangement
Glenavana Hotel, 588 Shore Road, Whiteabbey, Newtownabbey, Antrim BT37 0SN
✆ 028 90864461

HILTON TEMPLEPATRICK GOLF CLUB

Castle Upton Estate, Paradise Walk, Templepatrick, Antrim BT39 0DD
✆ 028 9443 5542 Fax 028 94 435511 **Map 1, G3**
golf.manages@parkstatus.co.uk
M2 from Belfast towards International Airport – signposted Templepatrick.
Founded 1999
A serious and challenging parkland course, host to the 2001 Ulster PGA Championship.
18 holes, 7012 yards
par 72, S.S.S 71
Designer David Feherty, David Jones
Green fees £35
Catering, changing room/showers, bar, accommodation, club, trolley and buggy hire, shop, driving range, practice facilities
Visitors welcome
Societies welcome by prior arrangement
Hilton Templepatrick, Templepatrick, Antrim
✆ 028 9443 5542

LAMBEG GOLF CLUB

Bells Lane, Lambeg, Lisburn, Antrim BT27 4QH
✆ 028 9266 2738 Fax 028 9260 3432 **Map 1, G3**
Off Lisburn road, SW of Belfast
Founded 1986
A parkland course.
18 holes, 4139 metres
par 66, S.S.S 62
Green fees £7.40
Bar, shop
Visitors welcome with restrictions
Societies welcome by prior arrangement

LARNE GOLF CLUB

54 Ferris Bay Road, Islandmagee, Larne, Antrim BT40 3RJ
✆ 028 9338 2288 **Map 1, H3**
Between Larne and Whitehead
Founded 1894
A parkland course which runs down to the sea shore.
9 holes, 6288 yards
par 70, S.S.S 70
Designer George Baillie
Green fees £8
Catering, changing room/showers, bar
Visitors welcome with restrictions
Societies welcome by prior arrangement

LISBURN GOLF CLUB

68 Eglantine Road, Lisburn, Antrim BT27 5RQ
✆ 028 9267 7216 Fax 028 9260 3608 **Map 1, H4**
A1, 3 miles S of Lisburn
Founded 1891
A well-wooded parkland course with a testing finish, with a blind shot on the 17th and a downhill par 3 to end.
18 holes, 6647 yards
par 72, S.S.S 72
Designer Fred Hawtree
Green fees £25
Changing room/showers, club and trolley hire, shop
Visitors welcome – with restrictions
Societies welcome by prior arrangement

MALLUSK GOLF CLUB

Mallusk, Newtownabbey, Antrim BT36 2RF
✆ 028 9084 3799 **Map 1, G3**
A8, Antrim road from Belfast
Founded 1992
A short parkland course with a number of water hazards.
9 holes, 4444 metres
par 62, S.S.S 62
Designer David Fitzgerald
Green fees £6.50
Changing room/showers, club hire, shop
Visitors welcome
Societies welcome by prior arrangement

MASSEREENE GOLF CLUB

51 Lough Road, Antrim, Antrim BT41 4DQ
✆ 028 9442 9293 Fax 028 9448 7661 **Map 1, G3**
2 miles SW of Antrim
Founded 1895
A parkland course on which the back nine runs along the shores of Lough Neagh.
18 holes, 6559 yards
par 72, S.S.S 71
Designer Fred Hawtree
Green fees £25
Changing room/showers, club and trolley hire, shop
Visitors welcome
Societies welcome by prior arrangement

ROYAL PORTRUSH GOLF CLUB

Dunluce Road, Portrush, Antrim BT56 8JQ
✆ 02870 822311 Fax 012870 823139 **Map 1, G2**
info@royalportrushgolfclub.com
www.royalportrushgolfclub.com
On coast road ½ mile from Portrush
Founded 1888
See Top 50 Courses, page 38
Dunluce Links: 18 holes, 6772 yards, par 73, S.S.S 73
Designer Harry Colt
Valley Links: 18 holes, 6818 yards, par 70, S.S.S 71
Green fees £80
Catering, changing room/showers, bar, club, trolley and buggy hire, shop, practice facilities
Visitors welcome – restricted weekends
Handicap certificate required – limit: 18 men, 24 women
Societies welcome by prior arrangement
Royal Court Hotel, Dunluce Road, Portrush, Antrim BT56 8JQ
✆ 02780 822236

WHITEHEAD GOLF CLUB

McCrea's Brae, Whitehead, Antrim BT38 9NZ
✆ 02893 370820 Fax 02893 370825 **Map 1, H3**
robin@whiteheadgc.fsnet.co.uk

On coast road between Larne and Carrickfergus
Founded 1904
A parkland course, yet overlooking the Irish Sea in spectacular fashion.
18 holes, 6050 yards
par 70, S.S.S 69
Designer A.B. Armstrong
Green fees £15
Catering, changing room/showers, bar, trolley hire, shop, conference facilities
Visitors welcome – with restrictions
Societies welcome by prior arrangement

CO ARMAGH

ASHFIELD GOLF CLUB

Freeduff, Cullybanna, Newry, Armagh BT35 0JJ
✆ 028 3086 8180 Fax 028 3086 8111 **Map 1, G4**
Off B30, 2 miles NE of Crossmaglen
Founded 1990
A parkland course in hilly country near Crossmaglen.
18 holes, 5616 yards
par 69, S.S.S 70
Designer Frank Ainsworth
Green fees £10
Catering, changing room/showers, bar, club and trolley hire, shop, driving range
Visitors welcome
Societies welcome by prior arrangement

COUNTY ARMAGH GOLF CLUB

Newry Road, Armagh, Armagh BT60 1EN
✆ 028 3752 2501 Fax 028 3752 5861 **Map 1, G4**
Off A28, ½ mile from city centre
Founded 1893
A parkland course dominated by a 100-ft obelisk erected in 1770 which stands between the 10th and 13th greens.
18 holes, 6212 yards
par 70, S.S.S 69
Designer Alan Rankin
Green fees £15
Catering, changing room/showers, bar, club and trolley hire, shop, practice facilities
Visitors welcome – with weekend restrictions
Societies welcome by prior arrangement

EDENMORE GOLF CLUB

Drumnabreeze Road, Magheralin, Craigavon, Armagh BT67 0RH
✆ 028 9261 1310 Fax 028 9261 3310 **Map 1, G4**
A3, 4 miles E of Lurgan
Founded 1992
A rolling parkland course.
18 holes, 6244 yards
par 71, S.S.S 70
Designer Frank Ainsworth
Green fees £12
Catering, changing room/showers, bar, club, trolley and buggy hire, shop
Visitors welcome
Societies welcome by prior arrangement

LURGAN GOLF CLUB

The Demesne, Lurgan, Armagh BT67 9BN
✆ 028 3832 2087 Fax 028 3832 5306 **Map 1, G4**
½ mile from town centre beside Castle
Founded 1893
A challenging parkland course overlooking a lake.
18 holes, 6257 yards
par 70, S.S.S 70
Designer Frank Pennink
Green fees £15
Catering, changing room/showers, bar, trolley hire, shop
Visitors welcome with restrictions
Societies welcome by prior arrangement

PORTADOWN GOLF CLUB

192 Gilford Road, Portadown, Armagh BT63 5LF
✆ 028 3833 4655 Fax 028 3839 1394 **Map 1, G4**
Off A50, 2 miles SE of Portadown
Founded 1900
A parkland course laid out alongside and over the River Bann.
18 holes, 6130 yards
par 70, S.S.S 69
Green fees £17
Catering, changing room/showers, bar, club and trolley hire, shop, bowls and snooker
Visitors welcome weekdays – with restrictions
Societies welcome by prior arrangement

SILVERWOOD GOLF & SKI CENTRE

Turmoyra Lane, Silverwood, Lurgan, Armagh BT66 6NG
✆ 028 3832 6606 Fax 028 3834 7272 **Map 1, G4**
M1 Jct 10
Founded 1983
A parkland course with a number of water hazards.
18 holes, 6496 yards
par 72, S.S.S 72
Green fees £12
Catering, changing room/showers, bar, club and trolley hire, shop, driving range, practice facilities
Visitors welcome
Societies welcome by prior arrangement

TANDRAGEE GOLF CLUB

Markethill Road, Tandragee, Armagh BT62 2ER
✆ 028 3884 0727 Fax 028 3884 0664 **Map 1, G4**
www.tandragee.co.uk
Off B3, 1 mile SW of Tandragee
Founded 1922
A testing parkland course renowned for its short holes.
18 holes, 5747 metres
par 71, S.S.S 70
Designer F. Hawtree
Green fees £15
Catering, changing room/showers, bar, club and trolley hire, shop, gymnasium, sauna
Visitors welcome
Societies welcome by prior arrangement

BELFAST

BALLYEARL GOLF & LEISURE CENTRE

585 Doagh Road, Newtownabbey, Belfast BT36 5RZ
✆ 028 9084 8287 Fax 028 9084 4896 **Map 1, H3**
Via A8, N of Mossley on B59
A public parkland course.
9 holes, 2306 metres
Green fees £4.90
Changing room/showers, club hire, shop, driving range, squash, gymnasium
Visitors welcome
Societies welcome by prior arrangement

BALMORAL GOLF CLUB

518 Lisburn Road, Belfast, Belfast BT9 6GX
✆ 028 9038 1514 Fax 028 9066 6759 **Map 1, H3**
Off Lisburn Road, 2 miles S of city centre
Founded 1914
A well-wooded parkland course.
18 holes, 6276 yards
par 69, S.S.S 70
Green fees £20
Catering, changing room/showers, bar, club and trolley hire, shop, practice facilities
Visitors welcome – with restrictions
Societies welcome by prior arrangement

BELVOIR PARK GOLF CLUB
73 Church Road, Newtownbreda, Belfast, Belfast BT8 4AN
✆ 028 9049 1693 **Map 1, H3**
info@belvoirparkgolfclub.com
belvoirparkgolfclub.com
Off Ormeau road, 4 miles from Belfast
Founded 1927
From the terrace of Belvoir Park's white clubhouse the eye is drawn down the avenue of trees framing the 10th fairway to the distant hills. Many fairways undulate beguilingly, and streams cross them from time to time. Yet this idyllic scene is only two miles from the centre of Belfast.
18 holes, 6516 yards
par 71, S.S.S 71
Designer Harry Colt
Green fees £33
Catering, changing room/showers, bar, club, trolley and buggy hire, shop, practice facilities
Visitors welcome with restrictions
Societies welcome by prior arrangement

CLIFTONVILLE GOLF CLUB
Westland Road, Belfast, Belfast BT8 4AN
✆ 028 9074 4158 **Map 1, H3**
Between Cavehill Road and Cliftonville Circus
Founded 1911
A parkland course with water hazards.
9 holes, 6242 yards
par 70, S.S.S 70
Green fees £13
Catering, changing room/showers, bar, trolley hire, shop
Visitors welcome with restrictions
Societies welcome by prior arrangement

DUNMURRY GOLF CLUB
91 Dunmurry Lane, Dunmurry, Belfast, Belfast BT17 9JS
✆ 028 9061 0834 Fax 028 9060 2540 **Map 1, H3**
Off M1 following signs to Dunmurry
Founded 1905
A characterful parkland course.
18 holes, 5832 yards
par 69, S.S.S 68
Designer Tom MacAuley
Green fees £20
Catering, changing room/showers, bar, club and trolley hire, shop, practice facilities
Visitors welcome with restrictions
Societies welcome by prior arrangement

FORTWILLIAM GOLF CLUB
Downview Avenue, Belfast, Belfast B15 4EZ
✆ 028 9037 0770 Fax 028 9078 1891 **Map 1, H3**
M2 Jct 3, Antrim road southbound for 1 mile
Founded 1891
A handsome parkland course.
18 holes, 5973 yards
par 70, S.S.S 69
Green fees £22
Catering, changing room/showers, bar, club and trolley hire, shop, practice facilities
Visitors welcome
Societies welcome by prior arrangement

GILNAHIRK GOLF CLUB
Manns Corner, Upper Braniel Road, Belfast, Belfast BT5 7TX
✆ 028 9044 8477 **Map 1, H3**
Off Ballygowan Road, 3 miles SE of Belfast
Founded 1983
A moorland course.
9 holes, 2699 metres
S.S.S 68
Green fees £8.50
Shop
Visitors welcome
Societies welcome by prior arrangement

THE KNOCK GOLF CLUB
Summerfield, Dundonald, Belfast, Belfast BT16 0QX
✆ 028 90 483251 Fax 028 90 483251 **Map 1, H3**
Off A20, 1 mile E of Stormont
Founded 1895
A challenging golf course, overlooked by Stormont Castle, and blessed with a magnificent collection of stately trees, including what is thought to be the oldest monkey-puzzle in the British Isles. Accurate driving is essential. Streams guard a number of greens, not least the daunting 447-yard 14th, Stroke 1.
18 holes, 6402 yards
par 70, S.S.S 71
Designer Harry Colt, Hugh Alison, Alister Mackenzie
Green fees £20
Catering, changing room/showers, bar, club, trolley and buggy hire, shop, practice facilities
Visitors welcome – except Saturdays
Societies welcome by prior arrangement

MALONE GOLF CLUB
240 Upper Malone Road, Dunmurry, Belfast, Belfast BT17 9LB
✆ (028) 9061 2758 Fax (028) 9043 1394 **Map 1, H3**
manager@malonegolfclub.co.uk
www.malonegolfclub.co.uk
5 miles S of the City centre
Founded 1895
Two distinguished course set in mature wooded parkland and renowned for their standard of presentation: often referred to as the 'Augusta of Northern Ireland', not without reason, given the waterside setting of many greens.
Main Course: 18 holes, 6599 yards, par 71, S.S.S 71
Edenderry Course: 9 holes, 6320 yards, par 72, S.S.S 70
Green fees £35
Catering, changing room/showers, bar, club, trolley and buggy hire, shop, practice facilities, fly fishing, squash, bowls
Visitors welcome – with restrictions
Societies welcome by prior arrangement
Wellington Park Hotel, 21 Malone Road, Belfast BT9 6RU
✆ 028 381111

ORMEAU GOLF CLUB
50 Park Road, Belfast, Belfast BT7 2FX
✆ 028 9064 1069 Fax 028 9064 6250 **Map 1, H3**
Between Ravenhill Road and Ormeau Road, S of city centre
Founded 1892
A parkland course.
9 holes, 5308 yards
par 68, S.S.S 65
Green fees £9
Catering, changing room/showers, bar, club and trolley hire, shop
Visitors welcome – except Saturdays
Societies welcome by prior arrangement

SHANDON PARK GOLF CLUB
73 Shandon Park, Belfast, Belfast BT5 6NY
✆ 028 9079 3730 Fax 028 9040 2773 **Map 1, H3**
Off A55, 3 miles from city centre
Founded 1926
A parkland course.
18 holes, 6282 yards
par 70, S.S.S 70
Green fees £22
Catering, changing room/showers, bar, club and trolley hire, shop, practice facilities
Visitors welcome with restrictions
Societies welcome by prior arrangement

CO DOWN

ARDGLASS GOLF CLUB
Castle Place, Ardglass, Down BT30 7PP
✆ 02844 841219 Fax 02844 841841
Map 1, H4

golfclub@ardglass.force9.co.uk
www.ardglass.force9.co.uk
B1, 7 miles E of Downpatrick
Founded 1896
With the first five holes on the edge of the cliffs above the Irish Sea, it is clear from the outset that this is a remarkable course. The short 2nd, for instance, is an all-or-nothing carry across a deep gorge. Later, the 11th is almost a mirror image. Spectacular views.
18 holes, 6065 yards
par 70, S.S.S 69
Designer David Jones
Green fees £20
Catering, changing room/showers, bar, club and trolley hire, shop
Visitors welcome – ring first
Societies welcome by prior arrangement
Margaret's Cottage, Ardglass, Down
02844 841080

ARDMINNAN GOLF CLUB

15 Ardminnan Road, Portaferry, Down BT22 1QJ
028 9177 1321 Fax 028 9177 1321 **Map 1, H4**
A20, 18 miles SE of Newtownards
Founded 1995
A new course on the Ards Peninsula.
9 holes, 2766 metres
par 70, S.S.S 69
Designer Frank Ainsworth
Green fees £10
Shop
Visitors welcome
Societies welcome by prior arrangement

BANBRIDGE GOLF CLUB

116 Huntly Road, Banbridge, Down BT32 3UR
028 4062 6189 Fax 028 4066 9400 **Map 1, G4**
info@banbridge-golf.freeserve.co.uk
www.banbridge-golf.freeserve.co.uk
½ mile from Banbridge, off main Belfast-Dublin road
Founded 1912
A parkland course with delightful views towards the Mourne Mountains. The 6th and 10th are the most menacing holes.
18 holes, 5590 yards
par 69, S.S.S 67
Green fees £15
Catering, changing room/showers, bar, trolley hire, shop, practice facilities, conference facilities
Visitors welcome – with restrictions
Handicap certificate required
Societies welcome by prior arrangement
Bannville House Hotel, Lurgan Road, Banbridge, Down
028 406 28884 Fax 028 406 270777
reception@BannvilleHouse.co.uk

BANGOR GOLF CLUB

Broadway, Bangor, Down BT20 4RH
02891 270922 Fax 02891 453394
Map 1, H3
bgcsecretary@aol.com
In central Bangor
Founded 1903
Well regarded, and challenging, parkland course close to the sea, with a number of fine dog-legs calling for good positional play.
18 holes, 6410 yards
par 71, S.S.S 71
Designer James Braid
Green fees £20
Catering, changing room/showers, bar, club and trolley hire, shop, practice facilities
Visitors welcome – not Saturday
Societies welcome by prior arrangements
Marine Court Hotel, Quay Street, Bangor, Down BT20 5ED
028 9145 1100

BLACKWOOD GOLF CENTRE

150 Crawfordsburn Road, Bangor, Down BT19 1GB
028 9185 2706 Fax 028 9185 3785 **Map 1, H3**
B170, off A2 signposted Clandeboye
Founded 1995
An impressive pair of courses, part heathland, part parkland.
Hamilton Course: 18 holes, 6392 yards, par 71, S.S.S 70
Designer Simon Gidman
Temple Course: 18 holes, 2492 yards, par 54, S.S.S 54
Green fees £15
Catering, changing room/showers, bar, club and trolley hire, shop, driving range, practice facilities
Visitors welcome
Societies welcome by prior arrangement

BRIGHT CASTLE GOLF CLUB

14 Coniamstown Road, Bright, Downpatrick, Down BT30 8LU
028 4484 1319 **Map 1, H4**
Off B1, 4 miles S of Downpatrick
Founded 1970
A parkland course of heroic dimensions, the 16th hole stretching to more than 700 yards from the very back tee. The Mourne Mountains provide a glorious backdrop.
18 holes, 7143 yards
par 73, S.S.S 74
Green fees £10
Catering, changing room/showers, bar, trolley and buggy hire
Visitors welcome
Societies welcome by prior arrangement

CARNALEA GOLF CLUB

Station Road, Bangor, Down BT19 1EZ
028 91 270368 Fax 028 91 273989 **Map 1, H3**
Bangor, off Crawfordsburn Road
Founded 1927
A mixture of links and parkland on the shores of Belfast Lough.
18 holes, 5647 yards
par 69, S.S.S 67
Green fees £16
Catering, changing room/showers, bar, club and trolley hire, shop
Visitors welcome except Saturdays
Societies welcome by prior arrangement

CLANDEBOYE GOLF CLUB

Conlig, Newtownards, Down BT23 3PN
028 9127 1767 Fax 028 9147 3711 **Map 1, H3**
Off A21, near Bangor
Founded 1933
Clandeboye sprang to international notice in 1984 when one of the finest fields of women golfers was assembled for the Irish Open, for once attracting all the top American players. The strength of the Dufferin Course is its long par 4s particularly the 467-yard 8th and 427-yard 18th.
Dufferin Course: 18 holes, 6469 yards, par 71, S.S.S 71
Ava Course: 18 holes, 5755 yards, par 71, S.S.S 68
Designer Bernhard von Limburger
Green fees £25
Catering, changing room/showers, bar, club, trolley and buggy hire, shop, driving range, practice facilities
Visitors welcome weekdays
Societies welcome by prior arrangement

CROSSGAR GOLF CLUB

231 Derryboye Road, Crossgar, Down BT30 9DL
028 4483 1523 **Map 1, H4**
A7, between Downpatrick and Saintfield
Founded 1993
A parkland course.
9 holes, 4580 yards
par 64, S.S.S 63
Green fees £10
Catering, changing room/showers, bar, shop
Visitors welcome
Societies welcome by prior arrangement

DONAGHADEE GOLF CLUB
84 Warren Road, Donaghadee, Down BT21 0PQ
☎ 02891 883624 Fax 02891 888891 **Map 1, H3**
donaghadee@golf-club.fsnet.co.uk
On coast road, 6 miles from Bangor
Founded 1899
A mixture of links and parkland, with attractive seascapes.
18 holes, 5570 metres
par 71, S.S.S 69
Green fees £22
Catering, changing room/showers, bar, club, trolley and buggy hire, shop, practice facilities
Visitors welcome – restricted weekends
Societies welcome by prior arrangement
Copelands, 60 Warren Road, Donaghadee, Down BT21 0PD
☎ 02891 888189

DOWNPATRICK GOLF CLUB
Saul Road, Downpatrick, Down BT30 6PA
☎ 028 4461 2152 Fax 028 4461 7506 **Map 1, H4**
www.downpatrickgolfclub.com
1 mile E of Downpatrick – signposted.
Founded 1930
An undulating parkland course.
18 holes, 6100 yards
par 69, S.S.S 69
Designer Hawtree
Green fees £15
Catering, changing room/showers, bar, club, trolley and buggy hire, shop, practice facilities
Visitors welcome
Societies welcome by prior arrangement

HELEN'S BAY GOLF CLUB
Golf Road, Helen's Bay, Bangor, Down BT19 1TL
☎ 028 9185 2601 Fax 028 9185 2815 **Map 1, H3**
Off B20, 4 miles W of Bangor
Founded 1896
A very beautiful parkland course on the shores of Belfast Lough, with glorious views.
9 holes, 5261 metres
par 68, S.S.S 67
Green fees £12
Catering, changing room/showers, bar, trolley hire
Visitors welcome with restrictions
Societies welcome by prior arrangement

HOLYWOOD GOLF CLUB
Nuns Walk, Demesne Road, Holywood, Down BT18 9LE
☎ 028 9042 2138 Fax 028 9042 5040 **Map 1, H3**
Off A2, 1 mile S of Holywood
Founded 1904
A hilly course with a number of tricky holes and fine views.
18 holes, 5932 yards
par 69, S.S.S 68
Green fees £16
Catering, changing room/showers, club, trolley and buggy hire, shop, practice facilities
Visitors welcome weekdays
Societies welcome by prior arrangement

KILKEEL GOLF CLUB
Mourne Park, Kilkeel, Down BT34 4LB
☎ 028417 65095 **Map 1, H5**
Off A2, 3 miles W of Kilkeel
Founded 1948
Kilkeel's joint hosting of the Amateur Championship with Royal County Down in 1999 alerted many first-time visitors to the golfing challenges and outstanding beauty of this lovely parkland course. Backed by the Mourne Mountains, Eddie Hackett's modern layout demands long, straight driving through avenues of oak, beech and chestnut trees.
18 holes, 6579 yards
par 72, S.S.S 72
Designer Eddie Hackett
Green fees £16
Catering, changing room/showers, bar, trolley and buggy hire, shop, driving range, practice facilities
Visitors welcome
Societies welcome by prior arrangement
Kilmorey Arms Hotel, Kilkeel, Down
☎ 028417 62220

KIRKISTOWN CASTLE GOLF CLUB
142 Main Road, Cloughey, Newtownards, Down BT22 1JA
☎ 028 4277 1233 Fax 028 4277 1699 **Map 1, H4**
kirkistown@aol.com
www.kcgc.org
A2, in the village of Cloughey
Founded 1902
When James Braid arrived to advise on alterations, he remarked, 'If only I had this within fifty miles of London.' Kirkistown Castle is still remote enough that visitors have little difficulty in getting a game, other than on busy Saturdays. Brilliant drainage means good playing conditions whatever the recent weather.
18 holes, 5596 metres
par 69, S.S.S 70
Designer James Braid
Green fees £18.75
Catering, changing room/showers, bar, shop
Visitors welcome – restricted Friday and Saturday mornings
Societies welcome by prior arrangement

MAHEE ISLAND GOLF CLUB
Comber, Belfast, Down BT23 6ET
☎ 028 9754 1234 **Map 1, H3**
½ mile from Comber, 14 miles SE of Belfast
Founded 1929
A parkland course situated on an island in Strangford Lough, beside the remains of Verdrum Abbey.
9 holes, 5590 yards
par 68, S.S.S 68
Green fees £10
Changing room/showers, club and trolley hire, shop
Visitors welcome with restrictions
Societies welcome by prior arrangement
Strangford Arms, 92 Church Street, Newtownards, Down
☎ 028 9181 4141

MOUNT OBER GOLF CLUB
24 Ballymaconachy Road, Knockbracken, Belfast, Down BT8 4SB
☎ 02890 792108 Fax 02890 705862 **Map 1, H3**
mt-ober@ukonline.co.uk
SW of Belfast city centre, near Four Winds roundabout
Founded 1985
Undulating parkland course with views over Belfast.
18 holes, 5448 yards
par 67, S.S.S 66
Green fees £13
Catering, changing room/showers, bar, club, trolley and buggy hire, shop, driving range, practice facilities, dry ski slope
Visitors welcome – restricted weekends
Societies welcome by prior arrangement
La Mon House, Gransha Road, Gransha, Belfast, Down
☎ 02890 448631

RINGDUFFERIN GOLF CLUB
Ringdufferin Road, Toye, Killyleagh, Down BT30 9PH
☎ 028 4482 8812 **Map 1, H4**
Off A22, 3 miles N of Killyleagh
Founded 1993
A parkland course overlooking Strangford Lough.
18 holes, 4652 metres
par 68, S.S.S 66
Designer Frank Ainsworth
Green fees £20

Catering, changing room/showers, bar, club and trolley hire, shop, driving range, practice facilities, fishing
Visitors welcome
Societies welcome by prior arrangement

ROCKMOUNT GOLF CLUB

28 Drumalig Road, Carryduff, Belfast, Down BT8 8EQ
☎ 028 90812279 Fax 02890 815851
Map 1, H3
www.rockmountgolfclub.co.uk
A24, 5 miles from Belfast
Founded 1995
Only a few minutes from the centre of Belfast, yet right out in the country. The course design utilises the undulating nature of the ground strategically, and there is an exciting approach to the 11th green over a lake.
18 holes, 6373 yards
par 72, S.S.S 71
Green fees £20
Catering, changing room/showers, bar, trolley and buggy hire, shop, practice facilities, private dining/function room
Visitors welcome – restricted Saturdays
Societies welcome by prior arrangement
Ivanhoe Hotel, 556 Saintfield Road, Belfast 8, Down BT8 8EU
☎ 028 9081 2240

ROYAL BELFAST GOLF CLUB

Station Road, Craigavad, Holywood, Down BT18 0BP
☎ 028 9042 8165 Fax 028 9042 1404 **Map 1, H3**
royalbelfastgc@btclick.com
A2 at Holywood
Founded 1881
Ireland's oldest club moved to this site in 1925, at the same time taking over the former residence of Belfast's Lord Mayor as its dignified clubhouse. The ground slopes down to the shores of Belfast Lough, giving many tricky holes and ravishing views. The 1st is one of Ulster's best.
18 holes, 6306 yards
par 70, S.S.S 71
Designer Harry Colt
Green fees £40
Catering, changing room/showers, bar, club and trolley hire, shop, driving range, practice facilities, tennis, squash
Visitors welcome – with restrictions, phone first
Societies welcome by prior arrangement

ROYAL COUNTY DOWN GOLF CLUB

Newcastle, Down BT33 0AN
☎ 028 4372 3314 Fax 028 4372 6281 **Map 1, H4**
Newcastle, behind Slieve Donard Hotel.
Founded 1889
See Top 50 Courses, page 33
Championship Course: 18 holes, 7037 yards, par 71, S.S.S 74
Designer Tom Morris
Annesley Course: 18 holes, 4681 yards, par 63, S.S.S 63
Green fees £70
Catering, changing room/showers, bar, club and trolley hire, shop, practice facilities
Visitors welcome by prior arrangement
Societies welcome by prior arrangement

SCRABO GOLF CLUB

233 Scrabo Road, Newtownards, Down BT23 4SL
☎ 028 9756 2365 Fax 028 9182 2919 **Map 1, H3**
Off A21, 1 mile S of Newtownards
Founded 1907
A hilly parkland course with good views.
18 holes, 6232 yards
par 71, S.S.S 71
Green fees £15
Catering, changing room/showers, bar, club and trolley hire, shop, practice facilities
Visitors welcome with restrictions
Societies welcome by prior arrangement

THE SPA GOLF CLUB

Grove Road, Ballynahinch, Down BT24 8BR
☎ 028 9756 2365 Fax 028 9756 4158 **Map 1, H4**
Off B175, 1 mile S of Ballynahinch
Founded 1907
An undulating parkland course with fine views over the Mourne Mountains.
18 holes, 6564 yards
par 72, S.S.S 72
Designer Frank Ainsworth
Green fees £15
Catering, changing room/showers, bar, club, trolley and buggy hire, shop, practice facilities
Visitors welcome by prior arrangement
Societies welcome by prior arrangement

TEMPLE GOLF & COUNTRY CLUB

60 Church Road, Boardmills, Lisburn, Down BT27 6UP
☎ 028 9263 9213 Fax 028 9263 8637 **Map 1, H4**
5 miles S of Belfast on Ballynahinch road
Founded 1994
A parkland course.
9 holes, 5451 yards
par 68, S.S.S 66
Green fees £10
Catering, changing room/showers, bar, shop
Visitors welcome
Societies welcome by prior arrangement

WARRENPOINT GOLF CLUB

Lower Dromore Road, Warrenpoint, Down BT34 3LN
☎ 028 4175 3695 Fax 028 4175 2918 **Map 1, G5**
warrenpointgolfclub@talk21.com
On outskirts of Warrenpoint (6 miles S of Newry)
Founded 1893
A parkland course in rolling country with a number of seaside touches on those holes which lead down towards a tidal estuary.
18 holes, 6173 yards
par 71, S.S.S 70
Designer Tom Craddock
Green fees £20
Catering, changing room/showers, bar, club and trolley hire, shop, practice facilities, conference room
Visitors welcome
Societies welcome by prior arrangement
Canal Court Hotel, Merchants Way, Newry, Down BT34 2LR
☎ 028 3025 1234

CO FERMANAGH

CASTLE HUME GOLF CLUB

Belleek Road, Enniskillen, Fermanagh BT93 7ED
☎ 028 66 327077 Fax 028 66 327076 **Map 1, E4**
www.castlehumegolf.com
A46 Enniskillen to Donegah/Belleek Road
Founded 1991
Castle Hume has established itself as one of the more challenging of recent courses built in Northern Ireland. It has hosted the Ulster PGA Championships of 1996, '97, and '98. Excessive length is not a consideration, but the views over Lough Erne more than compensate. Green fees reflect its remoteness.
18 holes, 5932 metres
par 72, S.S.S 71
Designer Tony Carroll
Green fees £15
Catering, changing room/showers,

bar, club, trolley and buggy hire, shop, driving range, practice facilities
Visitors welcome
Societies welcome by prior arrangement
Manor House, Killadeas, Enniskillen, Fermanagh
028 6862 1561

ENNISKILLEN GOLF CLUB

Castlecoole, Enniskillen, Fermanagh BT74 6HZ
028 66 325250 Fax 028 66 326510 **Map 1, E4**
enniskillen.golf@btclick.com
home.btclick.com/enniskillen.golf
Signposted from A4, 1 mile from Enniskillen
Founded 1896
Great value golf away from Ireland's main tourist areas. Enniskillen's golf course occupies gentle, rolling parkland alongside the estate of historic Castlecoole House, giving fine views over Fermanagh's Lakeland from the higher ground. On the whole, outright length is not critical, with only two par 4s measuring over 400 yards.
18 holes, 6189 yards
par 71, S.S.S 69
Green fees £15
Catering, changing room/showers, bar, club, trolley and buggy hire
Visitors welcome
Societies welcome by prior arrangement
Killyhelvin Hotel, Dublin Road, Enniskillen, Fermanagh
028 66 323481

CO LONDONDERRY

BENONE PAR THREE GOLF CLUB

53 Benone Avenue, Benone, Limavady, Londonderry BT49 0LQ
028 7775 0555 **Map 1, F2**
A2 coast road, 12 miles N of Limavady
A short parkland course on the Londonderry coast.
9 holes, 1447 yards
par 27
Green fees £4
Visitors welcome
Societies welcome by prior arrangement

BROWN TROUT GOLF & COUNTRY INN

209 Agivey Road, Aghadowey, Coleraine, Londonderry BT51 4AD
028 7086 8209 Fax 028 7086 8878 **Map 1, G2**
bill@browntroutinn.com
www.browntroutinn.com
A54, 7 miles S of Coleraine
Founded 1984
Given the club's name it comes as no surprise to find that golfers cross water seven times in 9 holes.
9 holes, 5488 yards
par 70, S.S.S 68
Designer Bill O'Hara
Green fees £10
Catering, changing room/showers, bar, club and trolley hire, shop, practice facilities
Visitors welcome
Societies welcome by prior arrangement
Brown Trout Golf and Country Inn, 209 Agivey Road, Aghadowey, Londonderry
028 7086 8209

CASTLEROCK GOLF CLUB

65 Circular Road, Castlerock, Londonderry BT51 4TJ
02870 848314 Fax 02870 848314 **Map 1, G2**
A2, 5 miles W of Coleraine
Founded 1901
A fine, true links with splendid views along the Causeway Coast. There is plenty of movement in the sandhills, and the best holes are full of individual character and visual attraction. However, Castlerock's most famous hole, the par-3 'Leg-of-Mutton' 4th, is plainer – and vicious, with out-of-bounds on both sides.
Mussenden Course: 18 holes, 6687 yards, par 73, S.S.S 72
Designer Ben Sayers
Bann Course: 9 holes, 2938 yards, par 34, S.S.S 33
Green fees £30
Catering, changing room/showers, bar, club and trolley hire, shop, practice facilities, snooker
Visitors welcome – restricted at weekends
Handicap certificate required
Societies welcome by prior arrangement

CITY OF DERRY GOLF CLUB

49 Victoria Road, Londonderry, Londonderry BT47 2PU
02871 346369 Fax 02871 310008 **Map 1, F2**
cityofderry@aol.com
2 miles W of Londonderry on main Strabane road
Founded 1912
Parkland courses with splendid views over the River Foyle.
Prehen: 18 holes, 5877 metres, par 71, S.S.S 70
Designer Willie Park Jnr
Dunhugh: 9 holes, 4708 metres, par 66, S.S.S 66
Green fees £20
Catering, changing room/showers, bar, club and trolley hire, shop, practice facilities
Visitors welcome
Handicap certificate required
Societies welcome by prior arrangement
Everglades Hotel, Victoria Road, Prehen, Londonderry, Londonderry
028 71 346722

FOYLE INTERNATIONAL GOLF CENTRE

12 Alder Road, Londonderry, Londonderry BT48 8DB
012871 352222 Fax 028 71353967 **Map 1, F2**
mail@foylegolf.club24.co.uk
www.foylegolfcentre.co.uk
1½ miles from Foyle Bridge, in direction of Moville
Founded 1994
Golf here is played under the shadow of Donegal's famous purple hills, and the Grianan of Aileach, the historic seat of the former kings of Ulster. The course is adjacent to the Amelia Earhart Museum, the famous aviatrix having landed at this very spot on her historic flight from America.
Championship Course: 18 holes, 6678 yards, par 72, S.S.S 71
Woodlands Course: 9 holes, 2698 yards, par 54,
Green fees £15
Catering, changing room/showers, bar, club, trolley and buggy hire, shop, driving range, practice facilities, private function, meeting, dining rooms, Indoor driving range
Visitors welcome
Societies welcome by prior arrangement
Waterfoot Hotel and Country Club, Clooney Road, Londonderry, Londonderry
028 7145 500

KILREA GOLF CLUB

Drumagarner Road, Kilrea, Londonderry BT51 5TB
028 2582 1048 **Map 1, F3**
½ mile from Kilrea on Maghera road
Founded 1920
A parkland course.
9 holes, 4514 yards
S.S.S 62
Green fees £10
Catering, changing room/showers
Visitors welcome with restrictions
Societies welcome by prior arrangement

MOYOLA PARK GOLF CLUB

15 Curran Road, Castledawson, Magherafelt, Londonderry BT45

8DG
✆ 028 7946 8468 Fax 028 7946 8468 **Map 1, G3**
Off M2, at Magherafelt roundabout
Founded 1976
A parkland course on which the Moyola River plays a strategic role.
18 holes, 6062 yards
par 71, S.S.S 71
Designer Don Patterson
Green fees £17
Catering, changing room/showers, bar, club, trolley and buggy hire, shop, practice facilities
Visitors welcome
Societies welcome by prior arrangement

PORTSTEWART GOLF CLUB
117 Strand Road, Portstewart, Londonderry BT55 7PG
✆ 028 7083 2015 Fax 028 7083 4097 **Map 1, G2**
Off A2, 3 miles NW of Coleraine
Founded 1894
For many years Portstewart's magnificent sand hills were only partly exploited for golf. A recent expansion has given the Strand Course access to these, making it one of the finest and most testing links in Ireland. There are superb views of the Atlantic Ocean and mouth of the River Bann.
Strand Course: 18 holes, 6784 yards, par 72, S.S.S 73
Old Course: 18 holes, 4733 yards, par 64, S.S.S 62
Riverside Course: 9 holes, 2662 yards, par 32,
Green fees £10
Catering, changing room/showers, bar, club and trolley hire, shop, practice facilities
Visitors welcome
Societies welcome by prior arrangement

RADISSON ROE PARK HOTEL & GOLF RESORT
Limavady, Londonderry BT49 9LB
✆ 028 7172 2212 **Map 1, F2**
Off B192, 1 mile W of Limavady
Founded 1993
A parkland course backed by the Sperrin Mountains and the Eagle Rock.
18 holes, 6318 yards
par 70, S.S.S 71
Designer Frank Ainsworth
Green fees £20
Catering, changing room/showers, bar, accommodation, club, trolley and buggy hire, shop, driving range, practice facilities, golf Academy, full hotel, leisure & function facilities
Visitors welcome
Societies welcome by prior arrangement
🏨 Radisson Roe Park Hotel, Limavady, Londonderry
✆ 028 7772 2222

CO TYRONE

AUCHNACLOY GOLF CLUB
99 Tullyvar Road, Auchnacloy, Tyrone
✆ 028 8255 7050 **Map 1, F4**
B35, 12 miles SW of Dungannon
Founded 1995
A parkland course close to the Monaghan border.
9 holes, 5017 metres
par 70, S.S.S 68
Green fees £10
Driving range
Visitors welcome
Societies welcome by prior arrangement

DUNGANNON GOLF CLUB
34 Springfield Lane, Mullaghmore, Dungannon, Tyrone BT70 1QX
✆ (028) 8772 2098 Fax (028) 8772 7338 **Map 1, F3**
¼ mile from Dungannon on Donaghmore Road
Founded 1890
A parkland course on which the 9th hole is a full carry over water and named Darren Clarke.
18 holes, 6046 yards
par 72, S.S.S 72
Green fees £18
Catering, changing room/showers, bar, club hire, shop, practice facilities, small meeting rooms
Visitors welcome – restricted weekends
Handicap certificate required
Societies welcome by prior arrangement

FINTONA GOLF CLUB
Eccleville Demesne, 1 Kiln Street, Fintona, Tyrone BT78 2BJ
✆ 028 8284 1480 Fax 028 8284 1480 **Map 1, F3**
9 miles S of Omagh
Founded 1904
A trout stream is a significant hazard on this pretty parkland course.
9 holes, 5765 metres
par 72, S.S.S 70
Green fees £15
Catering, changing room/showers, bar, shop
Visitors welcome weekdays
Societies welcome by prior arrangement

KILLYMOON GOLF CLUB
200 Killymoon Road, Cookstown, Tyrone BT80 8TW
✆ 028 8676 3762 Fax 028 8676 3762 **Map 1, G3**
S of Cookstown
Founded 1889
Killymoon was one of the founder members of the Golfing Union of Ireland, having a pretty course in rolling, well-wooded parkland close to Cookstown, and an extensive modern clubhouse. Only one two-shot hole exceeds 400 yards, but there is good length in several par 3s, and two of the par 5s.
18 holes, 5496 metres
par 70, S.S.S 69
Green fees £18
Catering, changing room/showers, bar, trolley hire, shop, practice facilities
Visitors welcome – not Thursdays or Saturdays
Societies welcome by prior arrangement
🏨 Tullylagan Country House, Sandholes, Cookstown, Tyrone
✆ 028 8676 5100

NEWTOWNSTEWART GOLF CLUB
38 Golf Course Road, Newtownstewart, Tyrone BT78 4HU
✆ 028 8166 1466 Fax 028 8166 2506 **Map 1, F3**
www.globalgolf.com/newtownstewart
Off A84, 2 miles SW of Newtownstewart
Founded 1914
A quiet parkland course with abundant wildlife.
18 holes, 5840 metres
par 70, S.S.S 69
Designer Frank Pennink
Green fees £12
Catering, changing room/showers, bar, club, trolley and buggy hire, shop, driving range, practice facilities
Visitors welcome
Societies welcome by prior arrangement

OMAGH GOLF CLUB
83A Dublin Road, Omagh, Tyrone BT78 1HQ
✆ 028 8224 3160 Fax 028 8224 3160 **Map 1, F3**
www.omaghgolfclub.fsnet.co.uk
1 mile from Omagh on Belfast to Dublin road
Founded 1910
The River Drumnagh comes into play on a number of holes as well as adding to the beauty of the course.
18 holes, 5683 metres
par 71, S.S.S 70
Green fees £10
Catering, changing room/showers,

bar, trolley hire
Visitors welcome – not Saturdays
Societies welcome by prior arrangement
Silverbirch Hotel, 5 Gortin Road, Omagh, Tyrone
028 8224 2520 Fax 028 82249061
info@silverbirchhotel.com
www.silverbirchhotel.com

STRABANE GOLF CLUB

Ballycolman, Strabane, Tyrone BT82 9PH
028 7138 2271 Fax 028 7188 6514 **Map 1, F3**
A5, 1 mile S of Strabane
Founded 1908
A challenging parkland course.
18 holes, 6135 yards
par 69, S.S.S 69
Designer Eddie Hackett
Green fees £15
Catering, changing room/showers, bar, trolley and buggy hire, shop, practice facilities
Visitors welcome
Societies welcome by prior arrangement

CO CARLOW

BORRIS GOLF CLUB

Deerpark, Borris, Carlow
0503 73310 Fax 0503 73750
Map 1, F8
Borris, 16 miles from Carlow
Founded 1907
A parkland course with Mount Leinster as a backdrop.
9 holes, 6120 metres
par 70, S.S.S 69
Green fees £12
Catering, changing room/showers, bar, trolley hire
Visitors welcome – with restrictions
Societies welcome by prior arrangement

CARLOW GOLF CLUB

Deer Park, Dublin Road, Carlow
0503 31695 Fax 0503 40065
Map 1, F7
info@carlowgolfclub.ie
www.carlowgolfclub.com
On main Dublin to Carlow road, 1 mile from Carlow
Founded 1899
A lovely, mature parkland course which attracts the top amateurs to its famous Midland Scratch Cup. Winner of six, Joe Carr, rates the 7th highly, while Peter McEvoy favours the 12th. Christy O'Connor plumped for the 16th, and the par 3s are splendid. Such are the varied strengths of Carlow.
18 holes, 5974 yards
par 70, S.S.S 71
Designer Cecil Barcroft, Tom Simpson, Molly Gourlay
Green fees £35
Catering, changing room/showers, bar, club, trolley and buggy hire, shop, practice facilities, small conference facilities
Visitors welcome – not Sundays
Societies welcome by prior arrangement
Courthouse Hotel, Dublin Street, Carlow, Carlow
0503 33243

MOUNT WOLSELEY GOLF CLUB

Tullow, Carlow
0503 51674 Fax 0503 52123
Map 1, F8
wolseley@iol.ie
Off N81, ½ mile S of Tullow
Founded 1996
One of the new generation of Irish parkland courses on which Christy O'Connor's design skills are clearly apparent. Water hazards threaten, especially going out, and fairway bunkers penalise unthinking driving.
18 holes, 7106 yards
par 72, S.S.S 74
Designer Christy O'Connor Jnr
Green fees £35
Catering, changing room/showers, bar, club, trolley and buggy hire, shop, practice facilities, board and conference rooms, health and fitness club
Visitors welcome
Societies welcome by prior arrangement
Seven Oaks Hotel, Athy Road, Carlow
0503 31308 Fax 0503 32155
sevenoak@tinet.ie

CO CAVAN

BELTURBET GOLF CLUB

Erne Hill, Belturbet, Cavan
049 22287 **Map 1, F4**
½ mile from Belturbet on Cavan road
Founded 1950
A short parkland course, renowned for its condition.
9 holes, 5347 yards
par 68, S.S.S 65
Green fees £10
Catering, changing room/showers, bar, club and trolley hire
Visitors welcome
Societies welcome by prior arrangement

BLACKLION GOLF CLUB

Tuam, Blacklion, via Sligo, Cavan
072 53024 **Map 1, E4**
Off Sligo to Enniskillen road at Blacklion
Founded 1962
A very handsome parkland course laid out beside a lake.
9 holes, 5716 metres
par 72, S.S.S 69
Designer Eddie Hackett
Green fees £8
Catering, changing room/showers, bar, trolley hire, fishing
Visitors welcome
Societies welcome by prior arrangement

CABRA CASTLE GOLF CLUB

Kingscourt, Cavan
04296 67030 **Map 1, F5**
2 miles E of Kingscourt
Founded 1978
A parkland course.
9 holes, 5308 metres
par 70, S.S.S 68
Catering, changing room/showers, bar
Visitors welcome with restrictions
Societies welcome by prior arrangement

COUNTY CAVAN GOLF CLUB

Arnmore House, Drumelis, Cavan
049 43 31541 Fax 049 43 31541
Map 1, F5
info@cavangolf.ie
www.cavangolf.ie
70 miles NW of Dublin on N3 and B4
Founded 1894
Parkland course in a quiet part of the Irish countryside.
18 holes, 5634 yards
par 70, S.S.S 69
Green fees £16
Catering, changing room/showers, bar, club, trolley and buggy hire, shop, driving range, practice facilities
Visitors welcome – with restrictions
Societies welcome by prior arrangement
Farnham Arms Hotel, Main Street, Cavan
049 32577

SLIEVE RUSSELL HOTEL GOLF & COUNTRY CLUB

Ballyconnell, Cavan
049 9526458 Fax 049 9526640
Map 1, E4
www.quinnhotels.com
90 miles NW of Dublin, N3 via Navan and Cavan
Founded 1992
Despite hosting the 1996 Irish PGA, Slieve Russell remains one of the slumbering giants of the exciting new generation of Irish golf courses. In attractive, rolling country the course winds its way past ancient

drumlins, lakes and streams in dramatic fashion. The 2nd, 12th and 13th curve around lakes treacherously.
18 holes, 7053 yards
par 72, S.S.S 72
Designer Patrick Merrigan
Green fees £36
Catering, changing room/showers, bar, accommodation, club, trolley and buggy hire, shop, driving range, practice facilities, full hotel, leisure, conference and function facilities, 9-hole par-3 course
Visitors welcome – except Saturdays
Societies welcome by prior arrangement
Slieve Russell Hotel Golf and Country Club, Ballyconnell, Cavan
049 952 6458

VIRGINIA GOLF CLUB

Park Hotel, Virginia, Cavan
049 854 8066 **Map 1, F5**
Off main Dublin to Cavan road
Founded 1945
A short meadowland course.
9 holes, 4139 metres
par 64, S.S.S 62
Green fees £8
Changing room/showers, club hire, fishing
Visitors welcome
Societies welcome by prior arrangement

CO CLARE

CLONLARA GOLF & LEISURE CLUB

Clonlara, Clare
061 354141 **Map 1, D8**
7 miles NE of Limerick
Founded 1993
A parkland course, part of extensive leisure facilities.
12 holes, 5289 metres
par 70, S.S.S 69
Green fees £7
Catering, changing room/showers, bar, club, trolley and buggy hire, tennis, fishing, self catering accommodation
Visitors welcome
Societies welcome by prior arrangement

DROMOLAND GOLF & COUNTRY CLUB

Newmarket-on-Fergus, Clare
061 368444 Fax 061 368498
Map 1, C7
dromolandgc@tinet.ie
N18, 2½ miles from Shannon Airport
Founded 1963
The scene is dominated by Dromoland Castle, dating from the 16th Century, and now a very luxurious hotel. The parkland course is handsome rather than excessively testing, with the short 7th and par-5 11th particularly attractive, the latter teasing the overambitious as it dog-legs around Drumoland Lough.
18 holes, 6098 yards
par 71, S.S.S 71
Designer Wigginton
Green fees £35
Catering, changing room/showers, bar, accommodation, club, trolley and buggy hire, shop, practice facilities, full 5-star hotel facilities, conference centre, and most outdoor sports including fishing and archery
Visitors welcome
Handicap certificate required – limit: 24 men, 40 women
Societies welcome by prior arrangement
Dromoland Castle Hotel, Newmarket on Fergus, Clare
061 368144

EAST CLARE GOLF CLUB

Bodyke, Clare
061 921322 **Map 1, D7**
R352, between Ennis and Scarrif
Founded 1992
A very challenging course, with no fewer than 11 lakes, in delightful rolling countryside.
18 holes, 6476 yards
par 71, S.S.S 71
Designer Arthur Springs
Green fees £15
Catering, changing room/showers, club, trolley and buggy hire, practice facilities
Visitors welcome
Societies welcome by prior arrangement

ENNIS GOLF CLUB

Drumbiggle, Ennis, Clare
065 24074 Fax 065 41848
Map 1, C7
egc@eircom.net
golfclub.ennis.ie
Off N18, ½ mile NW of Ennis – signposted from town centre
Founded 1907
Tree-lined fairways and tightly-defended greens are a feature of this charming parkland course, less than a mile from the centre of one of Ireland's oldest towns.
18 holes, 5592 metres
par 71, S.S.S 69
Green fees £20
Catering, changing room/showers, bar, club, trolley and buggy hire, shop, driving range
Visitors welcome – some restrictions
Societies welcome by prior arrangement

KILKEE GOLF CLUB

East End, Kilkee, Clare
065 9056048 Fax 065 9056977
Map 1, B8
kilkeegolfclub@eircom.net
½ mile NW of Kilkee
Founded 1896
A parkland course straying onto the cliff tops from which there are stunning views over the Atlantic Ocean.
18 holes, 5331 metres
par 69, S.S.S 68
Designer Eddie Hackett
Green fees £20
Catering, changing room/showers, bar, club, trolley and buggy hire, shop
Visitors welcome
Handicap certificate required
Societies welcome by prior arrangement
Ocean Cove Hotel, East End, Kilkee, Clare
065 9083111

KILRUSH GOLF CLUB

Parknamoney, Kilrush, Clare
065 905 1138 Fax 065 905 2633
Map 1, B8
www.westclare.com/golf
Off N68, ½ mile NE of Kilrush
Founded 1934
A parkland course recently extended to 18 holes.
18 holes, 5986 metres
par 70, S.S.S 70
Designer Arthur Spring
Green fees £18
Catering, changing room/showers, bar, club and trolley hire, shop, practice facilities
Visitors welcome
Societies welcome by prior arrangement

LAHINCH GOLF CLUB

Lahinch, Clare
065 708 1003 Fax 065 708 1592
Map 1, B7
Off N67, 2 miles W of Ennistimon
Founded 1893
See Top 50 Courses, page 28
Old Course: 18 holes, 6720 yards, par 72, S.S.S 73
Designer Tom Morris, Alister Mackenzie
Castle Course: 18 holes, 5620 yards, par 70, S.S.S 70
Green fees £50
Catering, changing room/showers, bar, club and trolley hire, shop, practice facilities
Visitors welcome by prior arrangement

Societies welcome by prior arrangement

SHANNON GOLF CLUB
Shannon Airport, Clare
061 471020 Fax 061 471507
Map 1, C8
½ mile S of Shannon Airport
Founded 1966
With many trans-Atlantic flights calling at Shannon, the best place to loosen up after a long inter-continental journey. A tree-lined parkland course of some length, with a number of water hazards and well-positioned bunkers.
18 holes, 6874 yards
par 72, S.S.S 74
Designer John Harris
Green fees £22
Catering, changing room/showers, bar, club, trolley and buggy hire, shop, practice facilities
Visitors welcome
Societies welcome by prior arrangement

SPANISH POINT GOLF CLUB
Spanish Point, Miltown Malbay, Clare
065 7084198 **Map 1, B7**
www.spanish-point.com
N67, 2 miles S of Miltown Malbay
Founded 1896
A very short links course with lovely views, especially from the 8th and 9th tees, overlooking Spanish Point beach.
9 holes, 4624 metres
par 64, S.S.S 63
Green fees £15
Catering, changing room/showers, bar, club and trolley hire
Visitors welcome
Societies welcome by prior arrangement
Burke's Armada Hotel, Spanish Point, Miltown Malbay, Clare
065 7084110 Fax 065 7084632
armada@iol.ie

WOODSTOCK GOLF CLUB
Shanaway Road, Ennis, Clare
065 682 9463 Fax 065 682 0304
Map 1, C7
N85, 2 miles from Ennis
Founded 1993
A young course with water affecting many holes, notably the par-4 7th and three short holes, the 6th, 8th and 11th.
18 holes, 5879 metres
par 71, S.S.S 71
Designer Arthur Spring
Green fees £25
Catering, changing room/showers, bar, club, trolley and buggy hire, practice facilities
Visitors welcome
Societies welcome by prior arrangement

CO CORK

BANDON GOLF CLUB
Castlebernard, Bandon, Cork
023 41111 Fax 023 44690
Map 1, C10
Off N71, 1 mile SW of Bandon
Founded 1909
A very charming country course.
18 holes, 6191 yards
par 70, S.S.S 70
Green fees £20
Catering, changing room/showers, bar, club and trolley hire, shop, practice facilities
Visitors welcome – with restrictions
Societies welcome by prior arrangement

BANTRY BAY GOLF CLUB
Donemark, Bantry, West Cork, Cork
027 50579 Fax 027 50579
Map 1, B10
www.bantrygolf.com
Off N71, 2 miles N of Bantry
Founded 1975
An exceptionally beautiful course, parkland in nature, overlooking the Atlantic, backed by the mountains of West Cork.
18 holes, 5910 metres
par 71, S.S.S 72
Designer Eddie Hackett, Christy O'Connor Jnr.
Green fees £20
Catering, changing room/showers, bar, club, trolley and buggy hire
Visitors welcome with restrictions
Societies welcome by prior arrangement

BEREHAVEN GOLF CLUB
Millcove, Castletownbere, Cork
027 70700 Fax 027 70700
Map 1, A10
bearagolfclub@eircom.net
3 miles from Castletownbere, towards Glengarriff
Founded 1908
A scenic course overlooking Bantry Bay – one of the very few with its own caravan and camping site.
9 holes, 2369 metres
par 68, S.S.S 64
Designer Members of the Royal Navy
Green fees £15
Catering, changing room/showers, bar, club and trolley hire, caravan and camping site, tennis, sauna
Visitors welcome – with restrictions
Societies welcome by prior arrangement

CHARLEVILLE GOLF CLUB
Charleville, Cork
063 81257 Fax 063 81274
Map 1, C9
Off R515, 2 miles W of Charleville
Founded 1909
Two parkland courses on level ground with many trees. Situated in the Golden Vale at the foot of the Ballyhoura Mountains, they are scenic courses.
West Course: 18 holes, 6212 yards, par 71, S.S.S 69
East Course: 9 holes, 6702 yards, par 72, S.S.S 72
Designer Eddie Connaughton
Green fees £18
Catering, changing room/showers, bar, club, trolley and buggy hire, driving range
Visitors welcome weekdays
Societies welcome by prior arrangement

COBH GOLF CLUB
Ballywilliam, Cobh, Cork
021 812399 Fax 021 812615
Map 1, D10
1 mile NE of Cobh
Founded 1987
A public parkland course.
9 holes, 4576 metres
S.S.S 64
Designer Eddie Hackett
Green fees £8
Bar
Visitors welcome
Societies welcome by prior arrangment

COOSHEEN GOLF CLUB
Coosheen, Schull, Cork
028 28182 **Map 1, B10**
1 mile E of Schull
Founded 1989
A parkland course overlooking the sea.
9 holes, 4001 metres
par 60, S.S.S 61
Green fees £10
Catering, changing room/showers, bar
Visitors welcome
Societies welcome by prior arrangement

CORK GOLF CLUB
Little Island, Cork
021 4353451 Fax 021 4353410
Map 1, D10
Little Island, off N25 – signposted
Founded 1888
At Cork beauty and an unforgiving nature are combined to produce a fine, but testing course. The 3rd, 4th and 5th run along the shores of the River Lee, before the course enters a quarry at the fascinating 6th. Cork's

closing stretch from the 14th provides a rigorous final examination.
18 holes, 6119 metres
par 72, S.S.S 72
Designer Alister Mackenzie
Green fees £50
Catering, changing room/showers, bar, club and trolley hire, shop, practice facilities
Visitors welcome – with restrictions
Handicap certificate required – limit: 28 men, 48 women
Societies welcome by prior arrangement
Morans Silversprings, Tivoli, Cork, Cork
021 450 7533

DONERAILE GOLF CLUB

Doneraile, Cork
022 24137 **Map 1, C9**
Off T11, 9 miles from Mallow
Founded 1927
A parkland course.
9 holes, 5528 yards
S.S.S 66
Green fees £15
Catering, changing room/showers, bar, trolley hire
Visitors welcome
Societies welcome by prior arrangement

DOUGLAS GOLF CLUB

Douglas, Cork
353 21 4895297 Fax 353 21 4895297 **Map 1, D10**
admin@douglasgolfclub.ie
www.douglasgolfclub.ie/
Cork 3 miles
Founded 1909
A handsome parkland course, not unduly long, but quite tricky, with out-of-bounds threatening on many holes, and a number of raised, undulating greens. Peter McEvoy has recast the course, using the slopes of the land to good strategic effect, supplementing nature where necessary, to put an emphasis on intelligent play.
18 holes, 5972 metres
par 72, S.S.S 71
Designer Peter McEvoy
Green fees IR£32
Catering, changing room/showers, bar, club and trolley hire, shop, practice facilities
Visitors welcome except Tuesday
Societies welcome by prior arrangement

DUNMORE GOLF CLUB

Dunmore House, Muckross, Clonakilty, Cork
023 33352 **Map 1, C10**
3 miles S of Clonakilty
Founded 1967
An undulating course overlooking the Atlantic.
9 holes, 4464 yards
par 64, S.S.S 61
Designer Eddie Hackett
Green fees £10
Catering, changing room/showers, bar, club and trolley hire
Visitors welcome weekdays with restrictions
Societies welcome by prior arrangement

EAST CORK GOLF CLUB

Gortacrue, Midleton, Cork
021 631687 Fax 021 613695
Map 1, D10
Off R626, 2 miles N of Midleton
Founded 1970
A wooded parkland course.
18 holes, 5744 yards
par 69, S.S.S 67
Designer Eddie Hackett
Green fees £15
Catering, changing room/showers, bar, club, trolley and buggy hire, shop, driving range, practice facilities
Visitors welcome – restricted weekends
Societies welcome by prior arrangement

FERMOY GOLF CLUB

Corrin, Fermoy, Cork
025 32694 Fax 025 33072
Map 1, D9
fermoygolfclub@eircom.net
Off N8, signposted from Fermoy
Founded 1892
An old club which moved to its present, hillside site in 1972. From its sunny, south-facing slopes there are good views over the plains of Cork. Heather and gorse are profuse.
18 holes, 5831 metres
par 70, S.S.S 69
Designer John Harris
Green fees £20
Catering, changing room/showers, bar, club and trolley hire, shop, practice facilities
Visitors welcome
Societies welcome by prior arrangement

FERNHILL GOLF HOTEL & COUNTRY CLUB

Carrigaline, Cork
021 437 2226 Fax 021 437 1011
Map 1, D10
www.fernhillgolfhotel.com
Off N28, 3 miles W of Ringaskiddy
Founded 1994
A parkland course attached to a country hotel.
18 holes, 5766 metres
par 69, S.S.S 69
Designer M.L Bowes
Green fees £14
Catering, changing room/showers, bar, accommodation, club, trolley and buggy hire, shop, practice facilities
Visitors welcome
Societies welcome by prior arrangement
Fernhill Golf Hotel & Country Club, Carrigaline, Cork
021 372226

FOTA ISLAND GOLF CLUB

Carrigtwohill, Cork
021 4883700 Fax 021 4883713
Map 1, D10
reservations@fotaisland.ie
www.fotaisland.com
N25 from Cork (towards Waterford), exit for Carrigtwohill and Cobh, take R624 towards Cobh, course on right
Founded 1992
Venue for the 2001 and 2002 Murphy's Irish Open, Fota Island has risen to prominence rapidly. Many of its fairways are lined with the tall trees of a deer park, and water features prominently in the design. The final hole, a 507-yard par 5, plays to a minuscule island green.
18 holes, 6925 yards
par 71, S.S.S 73
Designer Jeff Howes
Green fees £55
Catering, changing room/showers, bar, club, trolley and buggy hire, shop, driving range, practice facilities
Visitors welcome
Societies welcome by prior arrangement
Middleton Park Hotel, Old Cork Road, Middleton, Cork
021 4631767

FRANKFIELD GOLF CLUB

Frankfield, Douglas, Cork
021 363124 **Map 1, D10**
Douglas, S of Cork.
Founded 1984
A parkland course.
9 holes, 4621 metres
S.S.S 65
Green fees £5
Catering, changing room/showers, driving range
Visitors welcome
Societies welcome by prior arrangement

GLENGARRIFF GOLF CLUB

Glengarriff, Cork
027 63150 **Map 1, B10**
N71, 55 mile W of Cork
Founded 1934

A seaside course overlooking Bantry Bay.
9 holes, 4514 yards
par 66, S.S.S 61
Green fees £15
Catering, changing room/showers, bar, club and trolley hire
Visitors welcome
Societies welcome by prior arrangement

HARBOUR POINT GOLF COMPLEX

Clash, Little Island, Cork
☎ 021 4353094 Fax 021 4354408
Map 1, D10
N25 exit for Little Island
Founded 1991
An endearing feature of Harbour Point's pricing is reduced green fees for those teeing off early, and even lower fees for the clergy. The gently undulating fairways roam pretty country, with pleasant views to the sea. Beware the short holes! They are notoriously tricky, as reflected by the stroke index.
18 holes, 6163 metres
par 72, S.S.S 72
Designer Patrick Merrigan
Green fees £24
Catering, changing room/showers, bar, club, trolley and buggy hire, shop, driving range, practice facilities
Visitors welcome
Societies welcome by prior arrangement

KANTURK GOLF CLUB

Fairy Hill, Kanturk, Cork
☎ 029 50534 **Map 1, C9**
Off R579, 1 mile S of Kanturk
Founded 1971
An undulating parkland course with fine mountain views.
18 holes, 6262 yards
par 72, S.S.S 70
Designer R. Barry
Green fees £12
Catering, changing room/showers, bar, trolley hire, practice facilities
Visitors welcome
Societies welcome by prior arrangement

KINSALE GOLF CLUB

Farrangalway, Kinsale, Cork
☎ 021 477 4722 Fax 021 477 3114
Map 1, C10
Off R600, 2 miles from Kinsale
Founded 1912
The Farrangalway Course was added in 1994 and built in gentle rolling farmland.
Farrangalway Course: 18 holes, 6609 yards, par 71, S.S.S 72
Designer Jack Kenneally
Ringenane Course: 9 holes, 5332 yards, par 70, S.S.S 68
Green fees £22
Catering, changing room/showers, bar, club, trolley and buggy hire, shop, practice facilities
Visitors welcome
Societies welcome by prior arrangement

LEE VALLEY GOLF & COUNTRY CLUB

Clashanure, Ovens, Cork
☎ 021 733 1721 Fax 021 733 1695
Map 1, C10
N22, 10 miles W of Cork
Founded 1993
An important course designed by Christy O'Connor, the 8th being much troubled by water and spoken of as one of Ireland's finest holes. Other tricky holes include the 10th, 15th and 18th.
18 holes, 6725 yards
par 72, S.S.S 72
Designer Christy O'Connor Jr.
Green fees £29
Catering, changing room/showers, bar, club, trolley and buggy hire, shop, driving range, practice facilities
Visitors welcome
Societies welcome by prior arrangement

MACROOM GOLF CLUB

Macroom, Cork
☎ 026 41072 Fax 026 41391
Map 1, C9
macroomgc@iol.ie
Centre of Macroom town, through castle arch
Founded 1921
A fascinating course, handsomely backed by the Kerry Mountains. Of the many interesting features, the 3rd tee adjoins the Double Rank, a historic falconry.
18 holes, 5574 metres
par 72, S.S.S 68
Green fees £20
Catering, changing room/showers, bar, club, trolley and buggy hire, practice facilities
Visitors welcome – with restrictions
Societies welcome by prior arrangement
🏨 Castle Hotel, Macroom, Cork
☎ 026 41074

MAHON GOLF CLUB

Cloverhill, Blackrock, Cork
☎ 021 294280 **Map 1, D10**
Off N28, 1 mile from Douglas
Founded 1980
A municipal parkland course.
18 holes, 4818 metres
par 68, S.S.S 66
Green fees £10
Bar, club hire, practice facilities
Visitors welcome
Societies welcome by prior arrangement

MALLOW GOLF CLUB

Ballyellis, Mallow, Cork
☎ 022 21145 Fax 022 42501
Map 1, C9
golfmall@gcfree.indigo.ie
On Killavullen Road, 1 mile from town centre
Founded 1947
Well-reputed parkland course overlooking the Blackwater valley. The front nine is decidedly long. However the 200-yard par-3 finishing hole is much harder than it looks.
18 holes, 5960 metres
par 72, S.S.S 72
Designer Eddie Hackett
Green fees £20
Catering, changing room/showers, bar, club, trolley and buggy hire, shop, practice facilities, tennis, squash
Visitors welcome – with restrictions
Societies welcome by prior arrangement
🏨 Hibernian Hotel, Main Street, Mallow, Cork
☎ 022 21588

MITCHELSTOWN GOLF CLUB

Gurrane, Mitchelstown, Cork
☎ 025 24072 **Map 1, D9**
1½ miles from Mitchelstown, off main Cork to Dublin road
Founded 1908
Backed by the Galtee Mountains, a pretty parkland course in a peaceful situation.
18 holes, 5600 yards
par 67, S.S.S 68
Designer David Jones
Green fees £15
Changing room/showers, bar, trolley hire, practice facilities
Visitors welcome – not Sundays
Societies welcome by prior arrangement

MONKSTOWN GOLF CLUB

Parkgarriff, Monkstown, Cork
☎ 021 4841376 Fax 021 4841722
Map 1, D10
office@monkstowngolfclub.com
Monkstown, near Cork
Founded 1908
Parkland course with fine views over Cork Harbour from the front nine. An old castle looks on, and the greens are highly spoken of.
18 holes, 5669 metres
par 70, S.S.S 69
Green fees £28

Catering, changing room/showers, bar, club and trolley hire, shop, practice facilities
Visitors welcome
Societies welcome by prior arrangement
Rockestown Park Hotel, Rockestown Road, Cork, Cork
021 4892233

MUSKERRY GOLF CLUB

Carrigrohane, Cork
021 385297 Fax 021 385297
Map 1, C10
Off R617, 3 miles SW of Blarney
Founded 1897
An undulating parkland course with trees and water in abundance.
18 holes, 6327 yards
par 71, S.S.S 70
Designer Alister Mackenzie
Green fees £12.50
Catering, changing room/showers, bar, club and trolley hire, shop, practice facilities
Visitors welcome with restrictions
Societies welcome by prior arrangement

OLD HEAD GOLF CLUB

Kinsale, Cork
021 4778444 Fax 021 4778022
Map 1, C10
info@oldheadgolf.ie
www.oldheadgolflilnks.com
Off R600 at Kinsale
Founded 1997
For one of the most expensive green fees in Europe visitors are entitled to expect something exceptional. What they get is a stunning course in a breathtaking location, high on the cliffs overlooking the ocean. The condition is remarkable in a course so young and the facilities are quite superb.
18 holes, 7300 yards
par 72, S.S.S 72
Designer Eddie Hackett, Paddy Merrigan, Ron Kirby, Joe Carr & Liam Higgins
Green fees £190
Catering, changing room/showers, bar, club and buggy hire, shop, driving range, practice facilities
Visitors welcome
Handicap certificate required – limit: 24 men, 36 women
Societies welcome by prior arrangement
Blindgate House, Kinsale, Cork
021 4777858

RAFFEEN CREEK GOLF CLUB

Ringaskiddy, Cork
021 378430 **Map 1, C10**
1 mile from Ringaskiddy
Founded 1989
A parkland course overlooking the sea.
9 holes, 5098 metres
par 70, S.S.S 67
Designer Eddie Hackett
Green fees £12
Catering, changing room/showers, bar
Visitors welcome weekdays
Societies welcome by prior arrangement

SKIBBEREEN GOLF CLUB

Licknavar, Skibbereen, Cork
028 21227 Fax 028 22994
Map 1, B10
www.westcorkweb.ie/skibbereen/skibgolf
Off R595, 2 miles W of Skibbereen
Founded 1931
A parkland course in beautiful country in the far south west of the county.
18 holes, 5474 metres
par 71, S.S.S 69
Designer Eddie Hackett
Green fees £18
Catering, changing room/showers, bar, club, trolley and buggy hire, driving range, practice facilities
Visitors welcome
Societies welcome by prior arrangement

YOUGHAL GOLF CLUB

Knockaverry, Youghal, Cork
024 92787 Fax 024 92641
Map 1, D10
N25, 1 mile from Youghal
Founded 1898
A testing parkland course with fine sea views.
18 holes, 6174 yards
par 70, S.S.S 69
Designer John Harris
Green fees £18
Catering, changing room/showers, bar, club, trolley and buggy hire, shop, practice facilities
Visitors welcome
Societies welcome by prior arrangement

CO DONEGAL

BALLBOFEY & STRANORLAR GOLF CLUB

The Glebe, Stranorlar, Donegal
074 31093 Fax 074 31058
Map 1, E3
Off N13, between Ballbofey and Stranorlar
Founded 1957
A parkland course running in and out of valleys, with a mountain backdrop.
18 holes, 5922 yards
par 68, S.S.S 68
Designer P.C. Carr
Green fees £15
Changing room/showers, bar, club and trolley hire, practice facilities
Visitors welcome weekdays – restricted weekends
Societies welcome by prior arrangement

BALLYLIFFIN GOLF CLUB

Inishowen, Ballyliffin, Donegal
077 76119 Fax 077 76672
Map 1, F2
R238, 6 miles from Cardonagh
Founded 1947
See Top 50 Courses, page 14
Glashedy Links: 18 holes, 7135 yards, par 72, S.S.S 75
Designer Pat Ruddy, Tom Craddock.
Old Links: 18 holes, 6612 yards, par 71, S.S.S 72
Green fees £30
Catering, changing room/showers, bar, club, trolley and buggy hire, driving range, practice facilities
Visitors welcome by prior arrangement
Societies welcome by prior arrangement
Ballyliffin Hotel, Inishowen, Donegal
077 76106

BUNCRANA GOLF CLUB

Ballymacara, Buncrana, Donegal
077 62279 **Map 1, F2**
At Buncrana pass 'Fruit of the Loom' factory and Inishowen Gateway Hotel, then 1st left
Founded 1951
Overlooking the beautiful White Strand, on the shores of Lough Swilly, a rugged and enjoyable links.
9 holes, 4250 yards
par 62, S.S.S 64
Green fees £10
Changing room/showers
Visitors welcome
Societies welcome by prior arrangement
Inishowen Gateway Hotel, Buncrana, Donegal
077 61144 Fax 077 62278
inigatho@iol.ie

BUNDORAN GOLF CLUB

Bundoran, Donegal
072 41302 Fax 072 42014
Map 1, D3
www.bundorangolfclub.com
N15, in town of Bundoran
Founded 1894
A famous old course, linked with the great Christy O'Connor, whose home club this was for some years. Set on the shores of Donegal Bay, there are wonderful views both to

sea and of the Blue Stack Mountains. The long par 3s and par-4 17th are notably testing.
18 holes, 5688 metres
par 70, S.S.S 70
Designer Harry Vardon
Green fees £20
Changing room/showers, bar, accommodation, club, trolley and buggy hire, shop, practice facilities, conference and leisure facilities at hotel
Visitors welcome – with restrictions
Societies welcome by prior arrangement
Great Northern Hotel, Bundoran, Donegal
072 41204

CRUIT ISLAND GOLF CLUB

Kincasslagh, Dungloe, Donegal
075 43296 Fax 075 48028
Map 1, D2
www.eirecom.net/~cruitisland
On Cruit Island, 6 miles N of Dungloe
Founded 1985
An astonishing little course on the cliffs above the crashing breakers of the Atlantic Ocean. An incomparable experience.
9 holes, 5297 yards
par 68, S.S.S 64
Green fees £7
Catering, changing room/showers, bar, practice facilities
Visitors welcome
Societies welcome by prior arrangement

DONEGAL GOLF CLUB

Murvagh, Donegal
073 34054 Fax 073 34377
Map 1, E3
info@donegalgolfclub.ie
www.donegalgolfclub.ie
Off N15, 6 miles S of Donegal
Founded 1960
A links on the grand scale, in keeping with the might of the Atlantic Ocean and the majesty of the Blue Stack mountains which form a glorious backdrop. The wickedly-bunkered, par-3 5th leads to a sequence of three panoramic holes along the shore with length always at a premium.
18 holes, 6621 metres
par 73, S.S.S 75
Designer Eddie Hackett, Pat Ruddy
Green fees £30
Catering, changing room/showers, bar, club, trolley and buggy hire, shop, practice facilities
Visitors welcome – with restrictions
Handicap certificate required
Societies welcome by prior arrangement
Sandhouse Hotel, Rossnowlagh, Donegal
072 51777

DUNFANAGHY GOLF CLUB

Kill, Dunfanaghy, Letterkenny, Donegal
074 36335 Fax 074 36335
Map 1, E2
www.golfdunfanaghy.com
Off N56, 1 mile S of Dunfanaghy
Founded 1906
A short but utterly enchanting seaside course, with a number of mischievous holes and beautiful views across Sheephaven Bay.
18 holes, 5540 yards
par 68, S.S.S 66
Designer Harry Vardon
Green fees £14
Catering, changing room/showers, bar, club, trolley and buggy hire, practice facilities
Visitors welcome
Societies welcome by prior arrangement

GREENCASTLE GOLF CLUB

Greencastle, Donegal
077 81013 Fax 077 81015
Map 1, F2
b-mc-caul@yahoo.com
www.derry.net/greencastle
23 miles NE of Londonderry on shore of Lough Foyle
Founded 1892
An old club, which expanded to 18 holes in 1991, noted for the warmth of its welcome. Its splendid location on the banks of Lough Foyle, gives wonderful views, and some very entertaining holes along the shore.
18 holes, 5211 metres
par 69, S.S.S 66
Designer Eddie Hackett
Green fees £20
Catering, changing room/showers, bar
Visitors welcome
Handicap certificate required
Societies welcome by prior arrangement
McNamara's Hotel, Moville, Donegal
077 82010 Fax 077 82564

GWEEDORE GOLF CLUB

Magheragallon, Derrybeg, Letterkenny, Donegal
075 31140 **Map 1, E2**
T72 from Donegal
Founded 1926
A far from easy 9-hole course, known for its good short holes.
9 holes, 6201 yards
par 71, S.S.S 69
Green fees £8
Catering, changing room/showers, bar, trolley hire
Visitors welcome
Societies welcome by prior arrangement

LETTERKENNY GOLF & SOCIAL CLUB

Barnhill, Letterkenny, Donegal
074 21150 Fax 074 21175
Map 1, E2
Off R245, 3 miles from Letterkenny
Founded 1913
A tree-lined course giving beautiful views over Lough Swilly.
18 holes, 6293 yards
par 70, S.S.S 71
Designer Eddie Hackett
Green fees £17
Changing room/showers, bar, club, trolley and buggy hire, shop, practice facilities, small conference room
Visitors welcome – timesheet in operation
Societies welcome by prior arrangement
Holiday Inn, Derry Road, Letterkenny, Donegal
074 24369 Fax 074 25389

NARIN & PORTNOO GOLF CLUB

Narin, Portnoo, Donegal
075 45107 Fax 074 45107
Map 1, D3
6 miles N of Glenties, keeping left at Maas
Founded 1930
One of the gems of the Donegal coast, and a very brute when the wind whistles in off the Atlantic. A very natural course, the fairways heave over bumpy dunes to small greens. The six short holes demand precision, with the shortest of them, the 16th, perhaps the least forgiving.
18 holes, 5396 metres
par 69, S.S.S 69
Green fees £20
Catering, changing room/showers, bar, trolley and buggy hire, shop
Visitors welcome – with restrictions
Societies welcome by prior arrangement
Narin Inn, Narin, Portnoo, Donegal
07545108

NORTH WEST GOLF CLUB

Lisfannon, Fahan, Donegal
077 61715 Fax 077 61844
Map 1, F2
R238, 1 mile S of Buncrana
Founded 1892
A testing links course on moderately level ground.
18 holes, 5759 metres
par 70, S.S.S 70

Green fees £17
Catering, changing room/showers, bar, trolley hire, shop, practice facilities
Visitors welcome
Societies welcome by prior arrangement
Inishowen Gateway Hotel, Buncrana, Donegal

OTWAY GOLF CLUB
Saltpans, Rathmullan, Letterkenny, Donegal
074 58319 **Map 1, F2**
15 miles NE of Letterkenny
Founded 1893
A very short seaside course overlooking Lough Swilly.
9 holes, 4234 yards
par 64, S.S.S 60
Green fees £10
Changing room/showers
Visitors welcome
Societies welcome by prior arrangement

PORTSALON GOLF CLUB
Portsalon, Fanad, Donegal
074 59459 **Map 1, E2**
Off R246, 20 miles N of Letterkenny
Founded 1891
A natural links overlooking the deep blue waters of Lough Swilly. It is not a long course – in fact there are only two par 4s over 400 yards and two par 5s – but the greens are small, the rough is dangerous and great skill is required to overcome the wind.
18 holes, 5878 yards
par 69, S.S.S 68
Green fees £12
Catering, changing room/showers, bar, trolley and buggy hire
Visitors welcome
Societies welcome by prior arrangement

REDCASTLE GOLF CLUB
Redcastle, Moville, Donegal
077 82073 **Map 1, F3**
On Londonderry to Moville road
Founded 1983
In a glorious spot overlooking Lough Foyle – the short holes are highly respected.
9 holes, 6146 yards
par 72, S.S.S 70
Green fees £10
Catering, changing room/showers, bar, club and trolley hire, tennis, swimming & fishing
Visitors welcome
Societies welcome by prior arrangement

ROSAPENNA GOLF CLUB
Downings, Rosapenna, Donegal
074 55301 Fax 074 55128
Map 1, E2
Off R245, 2 miles W of Carrickart, 25 miles N of Letterkenny
Founded 1894
Rosapenna was one of the unsung glories of Donegal golf, loved by those who visited, but they were few in number. Since the expansion of the golf hotel the story has changed, and not only are visitors arriving in greater strength but also a further 18 holes are under construction.
18 holes, 6254 yards
par 70, S.S.S 71
Designer Tom Morris, Harry Vardon, James Braid.
Green fees £22
Catering, changing room/showers, bar, accommodation, club, trolley and buggy hire, shop, driving range, practice facilities, tennis, swimming and gymnasium
Visitors welcome
Societies welcome by prior arrangement
Rosapenna Golf Hotel, Downings, Donegal
074 55301

CO DUBLIN

BALBRIGGAN GOLF CLUB
Blackhall, Balbriggan, Dublin
(01) 841 2173 Fax (01) 841 3927
Map 1, G6
ww.balbriggangolfclub.com
Off N1, Dublin to Belfast road, 1 mile S of Balbriggan
Founded 1945
A parkland course with far reaching views.
18 holes, 6476 yards
par 71, S.S.S 71
Green fees £16
Catering, changing room/showers, bar, trolley and buggy hire, practice facilities
Visitors welcome
Societies welcome by prior arrangement

BALCARRICK GOLF CLUB
Corballis, Donabate, Dublin
(01) 843 6228 Fax (01) 843 6957
Map 1, G6
Off R126, at Donabate – signposted
Founded 1972
A parkland course close to the sea and very much exposed to the wind. Good views.
18 holes, 5940 metres
par 73, S.S.S 72
Green fees £20
Catering, changing room/showers, bar, trolley hire, shop, practice facilities
Visitors welcome – with weekend restrictions
Societies welcome by prior arrangement

BALLINASCORNEY GOLF CLUB
Ballinascorney, Tallaght, Dublin
(01) 451 6430 **Map 1, G7**
9 miles SW of Dublin
Founded 1971
A very attractive parkland course set in a valley.
18 holes, 5464 metres
par 71, S.S.S 67
Green fees £15
Catering, changing room/showers, bar, club, trolley and buggy hire, fishing
Visitors welcome weekdays
Societies welcome by prior arrangement

BEAVERSTOWN GOLF CLUB
Beaverstown, Donabate, Dublin
(01) 843 6439 Fax (01) 843 5059
Map 1, G6
www.beaverstown.com
Off R126, at Donabate – signposted
Founded 1985
A parkland course close to Dublin Airport.
18 holes, 5874 metres
par 71, S.S.S 70
Designer Eddie Hackett
Green fees £20
Catering, changing room/showers, bar, trolley hire, practice facilities
Visitors welcome weekdays
Societies welcome by prior arrangement

BEECH PARK GOLF CLUB
Johnstown, Rathcoole, Dublin
(01) 458 0522 Fax (01) 458 8365
Map 1, G7
2 miles from Rathcoole on road to Kilkeel
Founded 1974
A parkland course, heavily wooded.
18 holes, 5730 metres
par 72, S.S.S 70
Designer Eddie Hackett
Green fees £25
Catering, changing room/showers, bar, trolley hire, practice facilities
Visitors welcome weekdays – with restrictions
Societies welcome by prior arrangement

CARRICKMINES GOLF CLUB
Golf Lane, Carrickmines, Dublin 18
(01) 295 5972 **Map 1, G6**
6 miles S of Dublin

Founded 1900
A 9-hole course in the southern suburbs of Dublin with scenic views of the City and Bay of Dublin.
9 holes, 6063 yards
par 71, S.S.S 69
Green fees £23
Changing room/showers, bar, trolley hire
Visitors welcome with restrictions
No societies

CASTLE GOLF CLUB
Woodside Drive, Rathfarnham, Dublin 14
(01) 490 4207 Fax (01) 492 0264
Map 1, G6
Off N81, 2 miles S of Dublin
Founded 1913
A parkland course which favours the intelligent golfer.
18 holes, 6270 yards
par 70, S.S.S 70
Designer Harry Colt
Green fees £35
Catering, changing room/showers, bar, trolley hire, shop, practice facilities
Visitors welcome with restrictions
Societies welcome by prior arrangement

CITY WEST HOTEL, CONFERENCE CENTRE & GOLF RESORT
Saggart, Dublin
(01) 458 8566 Fax (01) 831 5779
Map 1, G7
N82, off N7, at Saggart
Founded 1994
A parkland layout making much use of lakes, not least on the 18th, where the approach to the angled green is all carry and very substantial at that.
18 holes, 6441 yards
par 71, S.S.S 71
Designer Christy O'Connor Jnr.
Green fees £29
Catering, changing room/showers, bar, accommodation, club, trolley and buggy hire, shop, driving range, practice facilities
Visitors welcome
Societies welcome by prior arrangement

CLONTARF GOLF CLUB
Donnycarney House, Malahide Road, Dublin 3
(01) 833 1892 Fax (01) 833 1933
Map 1, G6
From city centre follow signs to Clontarf and Howth
Founded 1912
The closest course to Dublin city centre, a Colt gem with many tight holes.
18 holes, 5317 metres
par 69, S.S.S 68
Designer Harry Colt
Green fees £26
Catering, changing room/showers, bar, club and trolley hire, shop
Visitors welcome
Societies welcome by prior arrangement

COLDWINTERS GOLF CLUB
Newtown House, St Margaret's, Dublin
(01) 864 0324 Fax (01) 834 1400
Map 1, G6
2 miles from Dublin Airport
Founded 1994
Two inexpensive parkland courses.
18 holes, 5973 metres, S.S.S 71
9 holes, 2163 metres, S.S.S 31
Green fees £8.50
Catering, changing room/showers, bar, shop, driving range
Visitors welcome
Societies welcome by prior arrangement

CORRSTOWN GOLF CLUB
Corrstown, Killsallaghan, Dublin
(01) 8640533 Fax (01) 8640537
Map 1, G6
info@corrstown.com
www.corrstown.com
6 miles N of Dublin Airport (close to St Margarets Golf Club)
Founded 1993
Even the 9-hole Orchard Course challenges engagingly, with its tree-lined fairways and the pond on the dog-leg 5th. Water is a rather more significant factor on the main River Course. The 13th is a wicked, water-threatened par 4, while the 9th and 18th both play to uncompromising island greens.
River Course: 18 holes, 6298 metres, par 72, S.S.S 71
Orchard Course: 9 holes, 2792 metres, par 35
Designer E.B. Connaughton
Green fees £25
Catering, changing room/showers, bar, trolley and buggy hire, shop, practice facilities
Visitors welcome – with restrictions
Societies welcome by prior arrangement
Great Southern Hotel, Dublin Airport, Dublin
(01) 844 6000 Fax (01) 844 6001
res@dubairport.gsh.ie

DEER PARK HOTEL & GOLF COURSES
Deer Park Hotel, Howth Castle, Howth, Dublin
(01) 8222624 Fax (01) 8392405
Map 1, G6
From city centre follow signs for Howth
Founded 1974
Laid out in the grounds of Howth Castle, two busy parkland courses with hotel guests frequently having priority.
Grace O'Malley Course: 18 holes, 6770 yards, par 72, S.S.S 71
Deer Park Course: 18 holes, 6830 yards, par 72, S.S.S 73
Designer Fred Hawtree
Green fees £9.90
Catering, changing room/showers, bar, accommodation, club, trolley and buggy hire, shop, full hotel facilities
Visitors welcome with restrictions
Societies welcome by prior arrangement
Deer Park Hotel, Howth, Dublin
(01) 8322624

DONABATE GOLF CLUB
Balcarrick, Donabate, Dublin
(01) 843 6059 Fax (01) 843 5012
Map 1, G6
Off R126 at Donabate – signposted
Founded 1925
A parkland course.
18 holes, 5784 yards
par 70, S.S.S 69
Green fees £25
Catering, changing room/showers, bar, club, trolley and buggy hire, practice facilities
Visitors welcome restricted weekends
Societies welcome by prior arrangement

DUBLIN MOUNTAIN GOLF CLUB
Gortlum, Brittas, Dublin
(01) 458 2622 **Map 1, G7**
Off R114, 1 mile E of Brittas
Founded 1993
An undulating parkland course.
18 holes, 5635 metres
par 70, S.S.S 69
Green fees £9
Trolley hire, practice facilities
Visitors welcome
Societies welcome by prior arrangement

DUN LAOGHAIRE GOLF CLUB
Eglinton Park, Tivoli Road, Dun Laoghaire, Dublin
(01) 2803916 Fax (01) 2804868
Map 1, G6
dlgc@iol.ie
www.dunlaoghairegolfclub.ie
1 mile from ferry port, 7 miles S of Dublin
Founded 1910
Peaceful parkland course, once the scene of a 392-yard drive on the

18th, by Tommie Campbell.
18 holes, 5298 yards
par 69, S.S.S 68
Designer Harry Colt
Green fees £35
Catering, changing room/showers, bar, club and trolley hire, shop, conference and function facilities
Visitors welcome weekdays
Handicap certificate required
Societies welcome by prior arrangement
Royal Marine, Marine Road, Dun Laoghaire, Dublin
(01) 2801911

EDMONDSTOWN GOLF CLUB

Edmondstown Road, Rathfarnham, Dublin 16
(01) 4931082 Fax (01) 4933152
Map 1, G6
info@edmondstowngolfclub.ie
www.edmondstowngolfclub.ie
5 miles S of Dublin
Founded 1944
In the suburbs of Dublin, but there are beautiful views of the Dublin Mountains, especially from the back nine.
18 holes, 6113 metres
par 71, S.S.S 71
Designer McEvoy & Cooke
Green fees £35
Catering, changing room/showers, bar, club, trolley and buggy hire, shop
Visitors welcome – with restrictions
Societies welcome by prior arrangement
The Plaza Hotel, Belyard Road, Dublin
(01) 850 566566

ELM GREEN GOLF CLUB

Castleknock, Dublin 15
(01) 820 0797 Fax (01) 822 6668
Map 1, G6
Off Navan road beside Phoenix Park
Founded 1996
A public course testing all levels of golfer.
18 holes, 5796 yards
par 71, S.S.S 66
Designer Eddie Hackett
Green fees £12
Catering, changing room/showers, bar, club, trolley and buggy hire, driving range, pitch and putt
Visitors welcome
Societies welcome by prior arrangement

ELM PARK GOLF CLUB

Nutley House, Donnybrook, Dublin 4, Dublin
(01) 269 3438 Fax (01) 269 4505
Map 1, G6
3 miles from city centre, turning off Dun Laoghaire road at Merrion, just S of Holyhead ferry terminal
Founded 1924
A testing, if short, parkland course frequently interrupted by streams. There is little rough, but the design is such that thoughtful play is rewarded. The par-3 1st is typical, with two streams in attendance.
18 holes, 5374 metres
par 69, S.S.S 69
Green fees £40
Catering, changing room/showers, bar, club, trolley and buggy hire, shop, driving range, practice facilities
Visitors welcome by prior arrangement
Societies welcome by prior arrangement

FINNSTOWN COUNTRY HOUSE HOTEL & GOLF COURSE

Finnstown House Hotel, Lucan, Dublin
(01) 628 0644 Fax (01) 628 1088
Map 1, G6
Off N4, 8 miles W of Dublin
A parkland course in the long-established grounds of what is now a country house hotel, the course operated on a pay-and-play basis.
9 holes, 5172 yards
par 66, S.S.S 64
Designer Robert Browne
Green fees £12
Catering, changing room/showers, bar, accommodation, trolley and buggy hire, shop, tennis, swimming & hotel facilities
Visitors welcome with prior booking
Societies welcome by prior arrangement
Finnstown Country House Hotel & Golf Course, Newcastle Road, Lucan, Dublin
(01) 628 0644

FORREST LITTLE GOLF CLUB

Forrest Little, Cloghran, Dublin
(01) 840 1183 Fax (01) 840 1000
Map 1, G6
N1, 6 miles N of Dublin, near Dublin Airport
Founded 1972
Near Dublin Airport, so near in fact that the 8th tee is directly under the flight path. Nevertheless a good parkland course with a river causing many problems.
18 holes, 5865 metres
par 70, S.S.S 70
Designer F. Hawtree
Green fees £20
Bar, club hire, shop
Visitors welcome weekdays
Societies welcome by prior arrangement

FOXROCK GOLF CLUB

Torquay Road, Foxrock, Dublin 18
(01) 289 5668 Fax (01) 289 4943
Map 1, G6
5 miles S of Dublin, off Leopardstown road
Founded 1893
A charming 9 holer with a splendid club house. Former tour star John O'Leary began his golfing career here.
9 holes, 5667 metres
par 70, S.S.S 68
Green fees £30
Changing room/showers, bar, trolley hire, shop
Visitors welcome weekdays with restrictions
Societies welcome by prior arrangement

GRANGE GOLF CLUB

Whitechurch Road, Rathfarnham, Dublin 16
(01) 493 2832 Fax (01) 493 9490
Map 1, G6
M50 Jct 11, to Ballyboden, Taylors Lane than Whitechurch Road
Founded 1911
An unusual parkland course, in that it begins with two par 3s, but that first hole is over 200 metres long, uphill, well-wooded and seriously bunkered, and, thus, uncommonly challenging. The Kilmashogue hills form a lovely backdrop and the final hole is crossed by a stream just before the green.
18 holes, 5517 metres
par 70, S.S.S 69
Designer James Braid
Green fees £35
Catering, changing room/showers, bar, shop
Visitors welcome weekdays
Societies welcome by prior arrangement

HAZEL GROVE GOLF CLUB

Mount Seskin Road, Jobstown, Tallaght, Dublin 24
(01) 452 0911 **Map 1, G6**
Off Blessington road, 3 miles from Tallaght
Founded 1988
A parkland course with plans to extend to 18 holes.
9 holes, 5300 metres
S.S.S 67
Designer Eddie Hackett
Green fees £9
Catering, changing room/showers, bar, practice facilities, function room
Visitors welcome – with restrictions

Societies welcome by prior arrangement

HERMITAGE GOLF CLUB

Lucan, Dublin
(01) 6268491 Fax (01) 6268491
Map 1, G6
8 miles NW of Dublin City centre
Founded 1905
A course which has seen international championship action, is only a few minutes' from the centre of Dublin, and yet is totally secluded. The layout is on two levels, plunging down spectacularly on the par-3 10th towards the River Liffey and the much praised, long par-5 11th.
18 holes, 6051 metres
par 71, S.S.S 71
Green fees £40
Catering, changing room/showers, bar, club, trolley and buggy hire, shop, practice facilities
Visitors welcome weekdays
Societies welcome by prior arrangement
Spa Hotel, Lucan, Dublin
(01) 6280494

HOLLYWOOD LAKES GOLF CLUB

Ballyboughal, Dublin
(01) 8433407 Fax (01) 8433002
Map 1, G6
austinbrogan@hotmail.com
R129 to Ballboughal
Founded 1990
The 14th is said to be the longest par 5 in Ireland. A long and challenging course.
18 holes, 6688 yards
par 72, S.S.S 72
Designer Mel Flanagan
Green fees £20
Catering, changing room/showers, bar, club, trolley and buggy hire, practice facilities
Visitors welcome, restricted weekends
Societies welcome by prior arrangement
Carriage House, Lusk, Dublin
(353) 18438857

HOWTH GOLF CLUB

St Fintan's, Carrickbrack Road, Sutton, Dublin
(01) 8323055 Fax (01) 8321793
Map 1, G6
Secretary@howthgolfclub.ie
www.howthgolfclub.ie
2km from Sutton Dart Station, taking road to Howth at Sutton Cross
Founded 1916
The hilly site implies good views and relatively meaningless yardages – guile is of more value than brawn.
18 holes, 5466 metres
par 72, S.S.S 69
Green fees £35
Catering, changing room/showers, bar, trolley and buggy hire, shop, practice facilities
Visitors welcome – restricted weekends
Societies welcome by prior arrangement
Marine Hotel, Sutton Gross, Dublin 13
(01) 8390000 Fax (01) 8390442

THE ISLAND GOLF CLUB

Corballis, Donabate, Dublin
(01) 843 340 Fax (01) 843 6860
Map 1, G6
Off main Dublin to Belfast Road, 3 miles N of Swords
Founded 1890
A remarkable course with narrow bumpy fairways, which has been revised to reduce the number of blind shots, yet retains the best features of towering dunes, wicked pot bunkers, grasping seaside rough, and occasional patches of gorse. The 11th, named Cricket Field, commemorates a 19th-century visit by W.G. Grace.
18 holes, 6078 metres
par 71, S.S.S 72
Designer F. Hawtree, E. Hackett
Green fees £60
Catering, changing room/showers, bar, club, trolley and buggy hire, shop
Visitors welcome by prior arrangement
Societies welcome by prior arrangement

KILLINEY GOLF CLUB

Ballinclea Road, Killiney, Dublin
(01) 285 1983 Fax (01) 285 2823
Map 1, G7
Off Castlecorner Road, 1 mile NW of Kilkenny
Founded 1903
A parkland course with splendid views over Dublin and towards the Wicklow Mountains.
9 holes, 6220 yards
S.S.S 70
Designer E. Connaughton
Green fees £20
Catering, changing room/showers, bar, club, trolley and buggy hire, shop
Visitors welcome
Societies welcome by prior arrangement

KILMASHOGUE GOLF CLUB

College Road, Whitechurch, Dublin 16
(087) 2749844 **Map 1, G6**
5 miles S of Dublin
Founded 1994
A parkland course in the southern suburbs of Dublin.
9 holes, 5320 metres
par 70, S.S.S 70
Green fees £10
Shop
Visitors welcome
Societies welcome by prior arrangement

KILTERNAN GOLF & COUNTRY CLUB HOTEL

Enniskerry Road, Kilternan, Dublin
(01) 295 5559 Fax (01) 295 5670
Map 1, G7
Off R117, near Kilternan, 4 miles NW of Bray
Founded 1987
A parkland course with good views over Dublin Bay.
18 holes, 5906 yards
par 68, S.S.S 67
Designer Eddie Connaughton
Green fees £18
Catering, changing room/showers, bar, accommodation, club, trolley and buggy hire, shop, driving range, practice facilities, full hotel facilities
Visitors welcome – weekend restrictions
Societies welcome by prior arrangements

LUCAN GOLF CLUB

Celbridge Road, Lucan, Dublin
(01) 628 0246 Fax (01) 628 2929
Map 1, G6
N4, 14 miles W of Dublin, near Lucan
Founded 1897
A parkland course, gently undulating, with a number of water hazards.
18 holes, 5958 metres
par 71, S.S.S 70
Designer Eddie Hackett
Green fees £25
Catering, changing room/showers, bar, club, trolley and buggy hire
Visitors welcome weekdays with restrictions
Societies welcome by prior arrangement

LUTTRELSTOWN CASTLE GOLF & COUNTRY CLUB

Castleknock, Dublin 15
(01) 808 9988 Fax (01) 808 9989
Map 1, G6
www.luttrellstown.ie
1 mile W of Carpenterstown, off M50 Jct 6
Founded 1993
Perhaps Luttrelstown's fame owes more to the David Beckham/Posh Spice wedding, part of the celebrations for which took place in

the castle, than to the challenge of the course, but it has already hosted the Irish Women's Open.
18 holes, 6420 metres
par 72, S.S.S 73
Designer Nick Bielenberg, Edward Connaughton
Green fees £50
Catering, changing room/showers, bar, club, trolley and buggy hire, shop, driving range, practice facilities
Visitors welcome by prior arrangement
Societies welcome by prior arrangement

MALAHIDE GOLF CLUB

Beechwood, The Grange, Malahide, Dublin
(01) 846 1611 Fax (01) 846 1270
Map 1, G6
malgc@clubi.ie
www,malahidegolfclub.ie
Off R124, 3 miles from Malahide Village, 1 mile from Portmarnock
Founded 1892
Fine views of Dublin City, Mountain and Bay are obtained from this parkland/seaside course on which water features on many holes. The hills are not steep, but there are one or two blind or semi-blind shots.
18 holes, 6066 metres
par 71, S.S.S 72
Designer Eddie Hackett
Green fees £35
Catering, changing room/showers, bar, club, trolley and buggy hire, shop, driving range, practice facilities, small conference facilities
Visitors welcome
Societies welcome by prior arrangement
Grand Hotel, Malahide, Dublin
(01) 8450000

MILLTOWN GOLF CLUB

Lower Churchtown Road, Milltown, Dublin 14
(01) 497 6090 Fax (01) 497 6008
Map 1, G6
3 miles S of Dublin city
Founded 1907
A parkland course.
18 holes, 5638 metres
par 71, S.S.S 69
Designer Freddie Davis
Green fees £35
Catering, changing room/showers, bar, club and trolley hire, shop
Visitors welcome weekdays with restrictions
Societies welcome by prior arrangement

NEWLANDS GOLF CLUB

Clondalkin, Dublin 22
(01) 459 2903 Fax (01) 459 3498
Map 1, G6
N7, 6 miles SW of Dublin at Newlands
Founded 1926
A parkland course in South West Dublin.
18 holes, 6184 yards
par 71, S.S.S 70
Designer James Braid
Green fees £35
Catering, changing room/showers, bar, club, trolley and buggy hire, shop, practice facilities
Visitors welcome weekdays
Societies welcome by prior arrangement

PORTMARNOCK GOLF CLUB

Portmarnock, Dublin
(01) 846 2968 Fax (01) 846 2601
Map 1, G6
1 mile S of Portmarnock on private road
Founded 1894
See Top 50 Courses, page 31
Old Course: 18 holes, 7282 yards, par 72, S.S.S 75
New Course: 9 holes, 3370 yards, par 37
Green fees £100
Catering, changing room/showers, bar, club, trolley and buggy hire, shop, driving range, practice facilities
Handicap certificate required
Visitors welcome – restricted weekends
Societies welcome by prior arrangement

PORTMARNOCK HOTEL & GOLF LINKS

Strand Road, Portmarnock, Dublin
(01) 846 0611 Fax (01) 846 1077
Map 1, G6
www.portmarnock.com
At Portmarnock, via Malahide from Dublin city centre
Founded 1995
It was always clear that there was room for at least one further course in the wild dunes of Portmarnock. It took Mark McCormack's business acumen to bring it to fruition. Although less than ten years old, the course plays in every respect like its noble neighbour, a magnificent, testing links.
18 holes, 6260 metres
par 71, S.S.S 73
Designer Bernhard Langer
Green fees £75
Catering, changing room/showers, bar, accommodation, club and trolley hire, shop, practice facilities
Visitors welcome by prior arrangement
Societies welcome by prior arrangement
Portmarnock Hotel & Golf Links, Strand Road, Portmarnock, Dublin
(01) 8461800

RATHFARNHAM GOLF CLUB

Newtown, Dublin 16
(01) 493 1201 Fax (01) 493 1561
Map 1, G7
M50 Jct 11, 6 miles S of Dublin
Founded 1899
A parkland course.
9 holes, 5815 metres
par 71, S.S.S 70
Designer John Jacobs.
Green fees £22.50
Catering, changing room/showers, bar, trolley hire, shop
Visitors welcome weekdays – with restrictions
Societies welcome by prior arrangement

ROYAL DUBLIN GOLF CLUB

North Bull Island, Dollymount, Dublin 3
(01) 833 6346 Fax (01) 833 6504
Map 1, G6
info@theroyaldublin.com
www.theroyaldublin.com
3½ miles NE of Dublin, on coast road to Howth
Founded 1885
One of Ireland's great old links, rebuilt in this form by Harry Colt in 1920. Langer and Ballesteros (twice) won the most recent Irish Opens played here, continuing a long tradition of distinguished champions. Coming home, usually into the wind, the 10th and 13th are stiff, the 18th nail-biting.
18 holes, 6309 metres
par 72, S.S.S 73
Designer Harry Colt
Green fees £75
Catering, changing room/showers, bar, club and trolley hire, shop, practice facilities, important nature conservation site, small conference facility
Visitors welcome – restricted on competition days
Handicap certificate required – limit: 24 men, 36 women
Societies welcome weekdays by prior arrangement
Clontarf Castle Hotel, Castle Avenue, Clontarf, Dublin 3
(01) 8332321

RUSH GOLF CLUB

Rush, Dublin
(01) 843 7548 Fax (01) 843 8177
Map 1, G6

Off R127, 16 miles N of Dublin
Founded 1943
A charming and quite testing 9-hole course.
9 holes, 5598 metres
par 70, S.S.S 69
Green fees £18
Catering, changing room/showers, bar, trolley hire
Visitors welcome – with restrictions
Societies welcome by prior arrangement

SKERRIES GOLF CLUB

Hacketstown, Skerries, Dublin
(01) 8491567 Fax (01) 8491591
Map 1, G6
skerriesgolfclub@eircom.net
www.skerriesgolfclub.ie
3 miles N of Swords, 6 miles E of main Dublin to Belfast road
Founded 1905
The title, Skerries, might suggest a course on a rocky coast, but, in fact, this is a tree-lined parkland layout, although, in fairness, there are distant sea views.
18 holes, 6107 metres
par 73, S.S.S 72
Green fees £30
Catering, changing room/showers, bar, trolley and buggy hire, shop, practice facilities
Visitors welcome – with restrictions
Handicap certificate required
Societies welcome by prior arrangement

SLADE VALLEY GOLF CLUB

Lynch Park, Brittas, Dublin
(01) 458 2739 Fax (01) 458 2784
Map 1, G6
Off N4, 8 miles W of Dublin
Founded 1970
A parkland course surrounded by beautiful scenery.
18 holes, 5337 metres
par 69, S.S.S 68
Designer W. Sullivan, D. O'Brien
Green fees £17
Changing room/showers, club and trolley hire, shop
Visitors welcome weekdays
Societies welcome by prior arrangement

ST ANNE'S GOLF CLUB

North Bull Island, Dollymount, Dublin 5
(01) 833 6471 Fax (01) 833 4618
Map 1, G6
www.stanneslinksgolf.com
From Dublin city centre, follow signs for Howth turning onto Causeway Road at Dollymount
Founded 1921
Backing onto Royal Dublin, St Anne's was for many years only a 9-hole course. Happily, enough of this fecund links land was available for Eddie Hackett to extend the course, which is a very enjoyable test.
18 holes, 5669 metres
par 70, S.S.S 69
Designer Eddie Hackett
Green fees £30
Catering, changing room/showers, bar, trolley and buggy hire, shop
Visitors welcome
Societies welcome by prior arrangement

ST MARGARET'S GOLF & COUNTRY CLUB

St Margaret's, Dublin
(01) 864 0400 Fax (01) 864 0289
Map 1, G6
Off R122, 1 mile N of St Margaret's
Founded 1993
A big course with grand gestures, making full use of water hazards and mound work, very challenging from the back tees.
18 holes, 6917 yards
par 73, S.S.S 73
Designer Tom Craddock, Pat Ruddy
Green fees £45
Catering, changing room/showers, bar, club, trolley and buggy hire, driving range, practice facilities
Visitors welcome
Societies welcome by prior arrangement
Grand Hotel, Malahide, Dublin
(01) 8450000

STACKSTOWN GOLF CLUB

Kellystown Road, Rathfarnham, Dublin 16
(01) 494 1993 Fax (01) 493 3934
Map 1, G6
Close to M50 Jct 11
Founded 1975
A hilly parkland course with fine views over Dublin.
18 holes, 6494 metres
par 72, S.S.S 72
Green fees £20
Catering, changing room/showers, bar, trolley and buggy hire, shop
Visitors welcome weekdays
Societies welcome by prior arrangement

SUTTON GOLF CLUB

Cush Point, Sutton, Dublin 13
(01) 832 3013 Fax (01) 832 1603
Map 1, G6
7 miles NE of city centre
Founded 1890
A 9-hole links course.
9 holes, 5624 metres
par 70, S.S.S 67
Green fees £20
Catering, changing room/showers, bar, shop
Visitors welcome – with restrictions
Societies welcome by prior arrangement

SWORDS OPEN GOLF COURSE

Balheary Avenue, Swords, Dublin
(01) 8409819 **Map 1, G6**
swordsgs@indigo.ie
Off N1, at "Estuary" roundabout
Founded 1992
Parkland course laid out either side of the Broadmeadow River.
18 holes, 5600 metres
par 71, S.S.S 70
Designer Tommy Halpin
Green fees £15
Changing room/showers, club and trolley hire, practice facilities
Visitors welcome
Societies welcome by prior arrangement
White Sands Hotel, Portmarnock, Dublin
(01) 8960003

TURVEY GOLF CLUB

Turvey Avenue, Donabate, Dublin
(01) 843 5169 **Map 1, G6**
Off R126, E of Donabate
Founded 1994
A parkland course.
18 holes, 6600 yards
par 71, S.S.S 72
Designer Paddy McGuirk
Green fees £20
Catering, changing room/showers, bar, trolley hire, practice facilities
Visitors welcome
Societies welcome by prior arrangement

WESTMANSTOWN GOLF CLUB

Clonsilla, Dublin 15
(01) 820 5817 Fax (01) 820 5858
Map 1, G6
2 miles NE of Lucan
Founded 1988
A parkland course.
18 holes, 6395 yards
par 71, S.S.S 70
Designer Eddie Hackett
Green fees £25
Catering, changing room/showers, bar, trolley and buggy hire, practice facilities
Visitors welcome
Societies welcome by prior arrangement

WOODBROOK GOLF CLUB

Dublin Road, Bray, Dublin
01282 4799 Fax 01282 1950
Map 1, G7
woodbrook@internet-ireland.ie
www.woodbrook.ie

Off N11, 10 miles S of Dublin
Founded 1926
Christy O'Connor Jnr won the 1975 Irish Open played at Woodbrook. But, by modern standards, the course was too short for the contemporary game, so Peter McEvoy was brought in to redesign the course and lengthen it. Although the course is perched on the cliffs it is actually pure parkland.
18 holes, 6956 yards
par 72, S.S.S 74
Designer Peter McEvoy
Green fees £55
Catering, changing room/showers, bar, club, trolley and buggy hire, shop, driving range, practice facilities
Visitors welcome
Societies welcome by prior arrangement

CO GALWAY

ATHENRY GOLF CLUB

Palmerstown, Oranmore, Galway
(091) 794466 Fax (091) 794971
Map 1, C6
Jct N6 and R348, 5 miles W of Athenry
Founded 1902
A parkland course with plenty of trees.
18 holes, 5552 metres
par 70, S.S.S 70
Designer Eddie Hackett
Green fees £18
Catering, changing room/showers, bar, club, trolley and buggy hire, shop, driving range, practice facilities
Visitors welcome weekdays
Societies welcome by prior arrangement

BALLINASLOE GOLF CLUB

Moher, Ballinasloe, Galway
(0905) 42126 Fax (0905) 42538
Map 1, D6
Portumna road from Ballinasloe
Founded 1894
A recently lengthened parkland course.
18 holes, 5865 metres
par 72, S.S.S 70
Designer Eddie Hackett
Green fees £15
Catering, changing room/showers, bar, trolley hire, practice facilities
Visitors welcome
Societies welcome by prior arrangement
Haydens Gateway Hotel, Dunlo Street, Ballinasloe, Galway
(0905) 42347

BEARNA GOLF & COUNTRY CLUB

Corboley, Barna, Galway
(091) 592677 Fax (091) 592674
Map 1, C6
bearnagc@tinet.ie
www.bearnagolfmembers.com
Coast road from Galway, via Salthill, turn right in Barna Village
Founded 1996
Good value golf on a lengthy and testing new course, with splendid views of the Aran Islands, The Burren, and Galway Bay from the 16th and 17th tees.
18 holes, 6174 metres
par 72, S.S.S 73
Designer Bobby Brown
Green fees £25
Catering, changing room/showers, bar, club, trolley and buggy hire, shop, conference facilities
Visitors welcome
Societies welcome by prior arrangement
Twelve Pins Lodge, Barna, Galway
(091) 592368

CONNEMARA GOLF CLUB

Ballyconneely, Clifden, Galway
(095) 23502 Fax (095) 23662
email: links@iol.ie
www.westcoastlinks.com
Map 1, A6
Off R341, 4 miles W of Ballyconneely
Founded 1973
If every hole were as rigorous as those on the back nine, Connemara might have claim to Pine Valley's status as the world's hardest course. The golf is, undoubtedly, muscular, but it is put into perspective by the might of the Atlantic Ocean and mountain backdrop of the Twelve Bens.
Old: 18 holes, 6263 metres
par 72, S.S.S 75
Designer Eddie Hackett
New: 9 holes, 2712 metres par 35
Green fees £35
Catering, changing room/showers, bar, club, trolley and buggy hire, shop, practice facilities
Visitors welcome
Societies welcome by prior arrangement

CONNEMARA ISLES GOLF CLUB

Annaghvane, Lettermore, Connemara, Galway
(091) 572498 Fax (091) 572214
Map 1, B5
3 miles W of Costello
A parkland course.
9 holes, 5168 yards
par 70, S.S.S 67
Designer Craddock/Ruddy
Green fees £10
Visitors welcome
Societies welcome by prior arrangement

CURRA WEST GOLF CLUB

Curra, Kylebrack, Loughrea, Galway
(091) 45121 **Map 1, D6**
20 miles SE of Galway
Founded 1996
A parkland course.
9 holes, 5113 metres
par 70, S.S.S 67
Green fees £7
Visitors welcome
Societies welcome by prior arrangement

GALWAY BAY GOLF & COUNTRY CLUB

Renville, Oranmore, Galway
(091) 790503 Fax (091) 792510
Map 1, C6
gbay@iol.ie
www.gbaygolf.com
3 miles W of Galway City
Founded 1993
Perhaps best described as parkland by the ocean, Galway Bay features lakes and streams, wooden bridges, and the sort of moundwork which characterizes late 20th-century golf architecture. It has already witnessed European Tour action, when Costantino Rocca's winning score of 12-under demonstrated the sound defences of the design.
18 holes, 6537 metres
par 72, S.S.S 75
Designer Christy O'Connor Jnr.
Green fees £40
Catering, changing room/showers, bar, accommodation, club, trolley and buggy hire, shop, practice facilities, full hotel and conference facilities
Visitors welcome
Handicap certificate required
Societies welcome by prior arrangement
Galway Bay Golf and Country Club Hotel, Renville, Oranmore, Galway
(091) 790500

GALWAY GOLF CLUB

Blackrock, Salthill, Galway, Galway
(091) 790500 Fax (091) 529783
Map 1, C6
3 miles W of Galway
Founded 1895
A parkland course of some standing running out towards the ocean, although never quite taking on links characteristics. Trees narrow many fairways, calling for precision tee

shots.
18 holes, 6376 yards
par 70, S.S.S 71
Designer Alister Mackenzie
Green fees £20
Catering, changing room/showers, bar, club and trolley hire, shop
Visitors welcome with restrictions
Societies welcome by prior arrangement

GORT GOLF CLUB
Castlequarter, Gort, Galway
☎ (091) 632244 Fax (091) 632387
Map 1, C7
gortgolf@eircom.net
20 miles S of Galway
Founded 1924
The club dates back to 1924, but this is a new course, and every bit as challenging as might be expected from a Christy O'Connor design.
18 holes, 5979 metres
par 71, S.S.S 71
Designer Christy O'Connor Jnr
Green fees £17
Catering, changing room/showers, bar, club, trolley and buggy hire, shop
Visitors welcome – restricted weekends
Societies welcome by prior arrangement
Lady Gregory Hotel, Ennis Road, Gort, Galway
☎ (091) 632333

LOUGHREA GOLF CLUB
Graigue, Loughrea, Galway
☎ (091) 41049 **Map 1, D6**
R350, 1 mile N of Loughrea
Founded 1924
A parkland course extended to 18 holes ten years ago and now nicely grown in.
18 holes, 5261 metres
par 69, S.S.S 67
Designer Eddie Hackett
Green fees £12
Catering, changing room/showers, bar, trolley hire, practice facilities
Visitors welcome
Societies welcome by prior arrangement

MOUNTBELLOW GOLF CLUB
Mountbellow, Ballinasloe, Galway
☎ (0905) 79259 **Map 1, D6**
Off N63, between Roscommon and Galway
Founded 1929
A parkland course with two quarries.
9 holes, 5143 metres
par 69, S.S.S 66
Green fees £8
Catering, changing room/showers, bar, trolley hire
Visitors welcome
Societies welcome by prior arrangement

OUGHTERARD GOLF CLUB
Gortreevagh, Oughterard, Galway
☎ (091) 552131 Fax (091) 552733
Map 1, C6
Off N59, 15 miles NW of Galway
Founded 1973
A parkland course, well-wooded.
18 holes, 6752 yards, S.S.S. 69
Green fees £20
Catering, changing room/showers, bar, club, trolley and buggy hire, shop, driving range, practice facilities, fishing
Visitors welcome
Societies welcome by prior arrangement

PORTUMNA GOLF CLUB
Ennis Road, Portumna, Galway
☎ (0509) 41059 **Map 1, D7**
Off R352, 2 miles W of Portumna
Founded 1913
A wooded parkland course.
18 holes, 5474 metres
par 68, S.S.S 67
Designer E. Connaughton
Green fees £15
Catering, changing room/showers, bar, club, trolley and buggy hire, shop, practice facilities
Visitors welcome
Societies welcome by prior arrangement

TUAM GOLF CLUB
Barnacurragh, Tuam, Galway
☎ (093) 28993 Fax (093) 26003
Map 1, C6
Off R347, 2 miles S of Tuam
Founded 1904
Laid out in a forestry park.
18 holes, 5944 metres
par 72, S.S.S 70
Designer Eddie Hackett
Green fees £15
Catering, changing room/showers, bar, club, trolley and buggy hire, shop, practice facilities
Visitors welcome – with restrictions
Societies welcome by prior arrangement

CO KERRY

ARDFERT GOLF CLUB
Sackville, Ardfert, Tralee, Kerry
☎ (066) 34744 Fax (066) 34744
Map 1, B8
R551, 15 miles NW of Tralee
Founded 1993
A parkland course.
9 holes, 4754 metres
par 66
Designer James Healy
Green fees £9
Shop
Visitors welcome
Societies welcome by prior arrangement

BALLYBUNION GOLF CLUB
Sandhill Road, Ballybunion, Kerry
☎ (068) 27146 Fax (068) 27387
Map 1, B8
R551, ½ mile S of Ballybunion
Founded 1893
See Top 50 Courses, page 11
Old Course: 18 holes, 6651 yards, par 71, S.S.S 72
Designer Tom Simpson
Cashen Course: 18 holes, 6477 yards, par 72, S.S.S 72
Designer Robert Trent Jones
Green fees £60
Catering, changing room/showers, bar, club and trolley hire, shop, driving range, practice facilities
Visitors welcome by prior arrangement
Societies welcome by prior arrangement

BALLYHEIGUE CASTLE GOLF CLUB
Ballyheigue, Tralee, Kerry
☎ (066) 713 3555 Fax (066) 713 3147 **Map 1, B9**
Tralee
Founded 1995
A 9-hole parkland course.
9 holes, 6292 metres
par 72, S.S.S 74
Designer Roger Jones
Green fees £15
Visitors welcome
Societies welcome by prior arrangement

BEAUFORT GOLF CLUB
Churchtown, Beaufort, Kerry
☎ (064) 44440 Fax (064) 44752
Map 1, B9
beaufortgc@eircom.net
www.globalgolf.com
Off N72, 7 miles W of Killarney
Founded 1994
With the McGillycuddy Reeks as a magnificent backcloth, the ruins of Core Castle standing by the 13th green, and 200-year-old trees adorning the parkland, Beaufort is as satisfying to behold as it is to play.
18 holes, 6587 yards
par 71, S.S.S 72
Designer Arthur Spring
Green fees £30
Catering, changing room/showers, bar, club, trolley and buggy hire, shop, practice facilities
Visitors welcome
Societies welcome by prior arrangement

Castlerosse Hotel, Killarney, Kerry
(064) 31144

CASTLEGREGORY GOLF & FISHING CLUB

Stradbally, Castlegregory, Kerry
(066) 39444 **Map 1, A9**
2 miles W of Castlegregory
Founded 1989
An extraordinary little links which has been squeezed between a lake and the sea with a noble mountain background.
9 holes, 2569 metres
par 68, S.S.S 68
Designer Arthur Spring
Green fees £15
Catering, changing room/showers, club and trolley hire, fishing
Visitors welcome
Societies welcome by prior arrangement

CEANN SIBÉAL GOLF CLUB

Ballyferriter, Dingle, Kerry
(066) 9156255 Fax (066) 9156409
Map 1, A9
dinglegc@iol.ie
www.dingle-golf.com
Dingle peninsula, 9 miles from Dingle
Founded 1924
The westernmost golf course in Europe, it is still blessedly remote, despite the escalating number of tourists visiting County Kerry. Traditional seaside hazards of unpredictable rough, serious bunkers, and fast, undulating greens are surpassed for mischief by the little stream which frequently affects play. It makes the 479-yard par-5 13th decidedly exciting.
18 holes, 6691 yards
par 72, S.S.S 71
Designer Eddie Hackett, Christie O'Connor Jnr
Green fees £35
Catering, changing room/showers, bar, club, trolley and buggy hire, shop
Visitors welcome
Handicap certificate required
Societies welcome by prior arrangement
Skellig Hotel, Dingle, Kerry
(066) 9151144

DOOKS GOLF CLUB

Glenbeigh, Kerry
(066) 9768205 Fax (066) 9768476
Map 1, A9
office@dooks.com
www.dooks.com
Ring of Kerry road between Killorglin and Glenbeigh
Founded 1889
Laid out on remote sand dunes overlooking Dingle Bay, with a backdrop of Ireland's highest mountains, Dooks is a classic links. It is neither as dramatic nor as long as Tralee or Waterville, but the rough is tenacious, the greens are elusive, and the ravishing scenery is bound to distract.
18 holes, 6071 yards
par 70, S.S.S 68
Green fees £30
Catering, changing room/showers, bar, club and trolley hire, shop
Visitors welcome – with restrictions
Societies welcome by prior arrangement
Towers Hotel, Glenbeigh, Kerry
(066) 9768212

KENMARE GOLF CLUB

Kenmare, Kerry
(064) 41291 Fax (064) 42061
Map 1, B10
Off N71, S of Kenmare
Founded 1903
Enjoying a glorious setting at the head of Kenmare Bay, the course was extended in 1994, the new holes playing up and down a steep valley.
18 holes, 6053 yards
par 71, S.S.S 69
Designer Eddie Hackett
Green fees £20
Catering, changing room/showers, bar, club and trolley hire, practice facilities
Visitors welcome by prior arrangement
Societies welcome by prior arrangement

KILLARNEY GOLF & FISHING CLUB

Mahony's Point, Killarney, Kerry
(064) 31034 Fax (064) 33065
Map 1, B9
reservations@killarney-golf.com
www.killarney-golf.com
N72, 4km W of Killarney
Founded 1893
See Top 50 Courses, page 27
Mahony's Point Course: 18 holes, 6164 metres, par 72, S.S.S 72
Designer Sir Guy Campbell, Henry Longhurst, Lord Castlerosse
Killeen Course: 18 holes, 6474 metres, par 72, S.S.S 73
Designer Dr Sullivan, Eddie Hackett
Lackabane Course: 18 holes, 6140 metres, par 72, S.S.S 73
Designer Donald Steel
Green fees £50
Catering, changing room/showers, bar, club, trolley and buggy hire, shop, driving range, practice facilities, sauna and fitness suite
Visitors welcome
Handicap certificate required – limit: 28 men, 36 women
Societies welcome by prior arrangement
Castlerosse Hotel, Killarney, Kerry
(064) 31144

KILLORGLIN GOLF CLUB

Stealroe, Killorglin, Kerry
(066) 976 1979 Fax (066) 97 61437 **Map 1, B9**
kilgolf@iol.ie
N70, 2km from Killorglin
Founded 1992
One of the most scenic courses, even in this richly blessed part of Ireland. Set on a hillside overlooking Castlemain Harbour, Dingle Bay, the Slieve Mish Mountains and the imposing Macgillicuddy's Reeks.
18 holes, 6470 metres
par 72, S.S.S 71
Designer Eddie Hackett
Green fees £18
Catering, changing room/showers, bar, club, trolley and buggy hire, shop
Visitors welcome
Handicap certificate required
Societies welcome by prior arrangement
Bianconi Inn, Main Street, Killorglin, Kerry
(066) 9761146

LISTOWEL GOLF CLUB

Feale View, Listowel, Kerry
(068) 21592 Fax (068) 23387
Map 1, B8
In the village of Listowel
Founded 1993
A parkland course.
9 holes, 5728 yards
par 70, S.S.S 68
Designer Eddie Hackett
Green fees £10
Bar
Visitors welcome
Societies welcome by prior arrangement

PARKNASILLA GOLF CLUB

Parknasilla, Sneem, Kerry
(064) 45122 Fax (064) 45323
Map 1, A10
2 miles E of Sneem on Ring of Kerry Road
Founded 1974
An undulating seaside course with a number of stunning holes on the edge of the water.
12 holes, 5284 metres
par 69, S.S.S 67
Designer Arthur Spring
Green fees £18

Changing room/showers, club and trolley hire, tennis and swimming pool
Visitors welcome
Societies welcome by prior arrangement

RING OF KERRY GOLF & COUNTRY CLUB

Templenoe, Kenmare, Kerry
(064) 6442000 Fax (064) 6442533
Map 1, B10
www.ringofkerrygolf.com
Off N70, 4 miles W of Kenmare
Founded 1999
A very new course, of considerable length and difficulty, a mixture of parkland and links, with the wonderful Kerry scenery ever present.
18 holes, 6923 yards
par 72, S.S.S 73
Designer Eddie Hackett, Jonathon Gaunt, Steve Marnoch
Green fees £50
Catering, changing room/showers, bar, club, trolley and buggy hire, practice facilities
Visitors welcome
Societies welcome by prior arrangement

ROSS GOLF CLUB

Ross Road, Killarney, Kerry
(064) 31125 Fax (064) 31860
Map 1, B9
½ mile from Killarney
Founded 1995
A parkland course with a number of water hazards backed by the ravishing Killarney scenery of lakes and mountains.
9 holes, 5674 metres
par 72, S.S.S 72
Designer Rodger Jones
Catering, changing room/showers, bar, shop
Visitors welcome
Societies welcome by prior arrangement

TRALEE GOLF CLUB

West Barrow, Ardfert, Kerry
(066) 713 6379 Fax (066) 713 6008 **Map 1, B8**
Off R558, 7 miles NW of Tralee
Founded 1896
See 50 Top Courses, page 51
18 holes, 6799 yards
par 71, S.S.S 73
Designer Arnold Palmer
Green fees £60
Catering, changing room/showers, bar, club and trolley hire, shop, practice facilities
Visitors welcome by prior arrangement
Handicap certificate required
Societies welcome by prior arrangement

WATERVILLE HOUSE & GOLF LINKS

Waterville, Kerry
(066) 9474102 Fax (066) 9474482
Map 1, A10
wvgolf@iol.ie
www.watervillegolf.com
Off N70, 1 mile NW of Waterville
Founded 1889
See 50 Top Courses, page 54
18 holes, 7225 yards
par 72, S.S.S 74
Designer Eddie Hackett, John A. Mulcahy
Green fees £100
Catering, changing room/showers, bar, accommodation, club, trolley and buggy hire, shop, driving range, practice facilities, salmon and lake fishing
Visitors welcome
Handicap certificate required – limit: 28 men, 36 women
Societies welcome by prior arrangement
Waterville House, Waterville, Kerry
(066) 9474102

CO KILDARE

ATHY GOLF CLUB

Geraldine, Athy, Kildare
(0507) 31729 **Map 1, F7**
Off N78, 1 mile N of Athy
Founded 1906
A rolling parkland course.
18 holes, 6340 yards
par 71, S.S.S 71
Green fees £13
Catering, changing room/showers, bar, trolley hire, practice facilities
Visitors welcome weekdays
Societies welcome by prior arrangement

BODENSTOWN GOLF CLUB

Bodenstown, Sallins, Kildare
(045) 97096 **Map 1, F7**
Off R407, 4 miles N of Naas
Founded 1983
Two parkland courses, the Ladyhill Course making up for its shorter length by being somewhat tighter.
Old Course: 18 holes, 6132 metres, par 72, S.S.S 71
Ladyhill Course: 18 holes, 5278 metres, par 72, S.S.S 69
Green fees £12
Catering, changing room/showers, bar, club, trolley and buggy hire, practice facilities
Visitors welcome weekdays
Societies welcome by prior arrangement

CASTLEWARDEN GOLF & COUNTRY CLUB

Straffan, Kildare
(01) 458 9254 Fax (01) 458 9254
Map 1, G6
www.castlewardengolfclub.com
Off N7, 6 miles NE of Naas
Founded 1990
A parkland course of good length and difficulty which will appeal to the pockets of those who can only dream of affording to play at the K Club, almost next door.
18 holes, 6624 yards
par 72, S.S.S 72
Designer Tommy Halpin, R.J. Browne
Green fees £17
Catering, changing room/showers, bar, trolley hire, shop, practice facilities
Visitors welcome weekdays – except Tuesday
Societies welcome by prior arrangement

CILL DARA GOLF CLUB

Little Curragh, Kildare Town, Kildare
(045) 521433 **Map 1, F7**
1 mile E of Kildare
Founded 1920
A parkland course with crisp, well-drained turf, giving excellent lies.
9 holes, 5842 metres
par 71, S.S.S 70
Green fees £10
Catering, changing room/showers, bar, shop
Visitors welcome with restrictions
Societies welcome by prior arrangement

CRADDOCKSTOWN GOLF CLUB

Blessington Road, Naas, Kildare
(045) 897610 Fax (045) 896968
Map 1, F7
From southbound N7/N9 take 1st left turn towards Naas
Founded 1991
There is a fine panoramic view of this testing course from the clubhouse.
18 holes, 6700 yards
par 71, S.S.S 70
Designer Arthur Spring
Green fees £15
Catering, changing room/showers, bar, trolley hire, practice facilities
Visitors welcome – restricted weekends
Societies welcome by prior arrangement
Ambassador Hotel, Kill, Kildare
(045) 877064

THE CURRAGH GOLF CLUB

Curragh, Kildare
☎ (045) 441238 Fax (045) 442476
Map 1, F7
Off N7, between Newbridge and Kildare
Founded 1883
Quite possibly the oldest golf club in Ireland, established in 1883 but, certainly, golf was played here as early as 1857. The heathland course stands on a hillside amongst the pines over the road from the world famous Curragh race course, with the back nine reckoned to contain the better holes.
18 holes, 6035 metres
par 72, S.S.S 71
Green fees £18
Catering, changing room/showers, bar, club and trolley hire, shop, practice facilities
Visitors welcome weekdays
Societies welcome by prior arrangement

HIGHFIELD GOLF COURSE

Carbury, Kildare
☎ (0405) 31021 Fax (0405) 31021
Map 1, F6
hgc@indigo.ie
www.highfield-golf.ie
M4 from Dublin, 6 miles after Enfield turn left, following signs for Highfield
Founded 1992
Located in a quiet country area, with water affecting a number of holes, especially the difficult 7th and 9th.
18 holes, 5720 metres
par 72, S.S.S 70
Designer Alan Duggan
Green fees £14
Catering, changing room/showers, bar, club, trolley and buggy hire, shop, driving range, practice facilities
Visitors welcome – restricted weekends
Societies welcome by prior arrangement

THE K CLUB

Kildare Hotel and CC, Straffan, Kildare
☎ (01) 601 7300 Fax (01) 601 7399
Map 1, G6
At Straffan, off R403
Founded 1991
See 50 Top Courses, page 26
18 holes, 7178 yards
par 72, S.S.S 74
Designer Arnold Palmer
Green fees £160
Catering, changing room/showers, bar, accommodation, club, trolley and buggy hire, shop, driving range, practice facilities, fishing, shooting, riding and full hotel facilities
Visitors welcome
Handicap certificate required
Societies welcome by prior arrangement
🏨 The Kildare Hotel & Country Club, Straffan, Kildare
☎ (01) 601 7200
hotel@kclub.ie

KILKEA CASTLE GOLF CLUB

Castledermot, Kildare
☎ (0503) 45555 Fax (0503) 45505
Map 1, F7
Off R418, 3½ miles NW of Castledermot
Founded 1995
The castle, the oldest inhabited building in Ireland, is visible from every hole on the course. However, it is the River Griese which occupies a greater part of the golfer's mind, a major threat throughout the round. It contributes to what many regard as the toughest finish in Irish golf.
18 holes, 6200 metres
par 71, S.S.S 71
Designer David Cassidy
Green fees £30
Catering, changing room/showers, bar, club and trolley hire, shop, practice facilities
Visitors welcome
Societies welcome by prior arrangement
🏨 Kilkea Castle Hotel, Castledermot, Kildare
☎ (0503) 45156 Fax (0503) 45187

KILLEEN GOLF CLUB

Killeenbeg, Kill, Kildare
☎ (045) 866003 Fax (045) 875881
Map 1, G6
Off N7, 1½ miles NW of Kill
Founded 1986
A parkland course with many lakes.
18 holes, 5815 metres
par 71, S.S.S 71
Designer Pat Ruddy, Michael Kelly
Green fees £17
Catering, changing room/showers, bar, trolley hire, practice facilities
Visitors welcome weekdays
Societies welcome by prior arrangement

KNOCKANALLY GOLF & COUNTRY CLUB

Donadea, North Kildare, Kildare
☎ (045) 869322 Fax (045) 869322
Map 1, F6
Off N4, near Newtown
Founded 1985
A parkland course of championship status in a former country house estate.
18 holes, 6424 yards
par 72, S.S.S 72
Designer Noel Lyons
Green fees £18
Catering, changing room/showers, bar, club, trolley and buggy hire, shop, practice facilities
Visitors welcome
Societies welcome by prior arrangement

LEIXLIP GOLF CLUB

Leixlip, Kildare
☎ (01) 624 4978 Fax (01) 624 6185
Map 1, G6
Off N4, 10 miles W of Dublin
Founded 1994
A parkland course.
9 holes, 6030 yards
par 72, S.S.S 70
Designer Eddie Hackett
Green fees £13
Catering, changing room/showers, bar
Visitors welcome
Societies welcome by prior arrangement

NAAS GOLF CLUB

Kerdiffstown, Naas, Kildare
☎ (045) 874644 Fax (045) 896109
Map 1, F7
Off N7, 1 mile N of Johnstone
Founded 1896
A rolling parkland course, well-wooded.
18 holes, 5660 metres
par 71, S.S.S 69
Designer Arthur Spring
Green fees £18
Catering, changing room/showers, bar, trolley hire, practice facilities
Visitors welcome – with restrictions
Societies welcome by prior arrangement

NEWBRIDGE GOLF CLUB

Tankardsgarden, Newbridge, Kildare
☎ (045) 431289 Fax (045) 431289
Map 1, F7
Off M7, 8 miles SW of Naas
Founded 1997
A parkland course.
18 holes, 5956 metres
par 72, S.S.S 72
Designer Pat Suttle
Green fees £9
Catering, changing room/showers, bar, club and trolley hire
Visitors welcome
Societies welcome by prior arrangement

WOODLANDS GOLF CLUB

Coill Dubh, Naas, Kildare
☎ (045) 860777 Fax (045) 860988
Map 1, F7
Off Dublin to Naas main road at Naas
Founded 1991
A recently extended parkland course

with water hazards and well placed fairway bunkers.
18 holes, 6020 metres
par 72, S.S.S 71
Designer T. Halpin
Green fees £12
Catering, changing room/showers, bar, trolley hire, 9-hole pitch and putt course
Visitors welcome with restrictions
Societies welcome by prior arrangement

CO KILKENNY

CALLAN GOLF CLUB

Geraldine, Callan, Kilkenny
(056) 25136 Fax (056) 55155
Map 1, E8
Off R699, 1 mile SE of Callan
Founded 1929
A pleasant parkland course with occasional water hazards.
18 holes, 6383 yards
par 72, S.S.S 70
Designer Bryan Moore
Green fees £15
Catering, changing room/showers, bar, club and trolley hire, shop, driving range, practice facilities, fishing
Visitors welcome
Societies welcome by prior arrangement

CASTLECOMER GOLF CLUB

Dromgoole, Castlecomer, Kilkenny
(056) 41139 Fax (056) 41139
Map 1, F8
www.homepage.eirecom.net/~castlecomergolfclub
N7, 10 miles N of Kilkenny
Founded 1935
A parkland course.
9 holes, 5923 yards
par 71, S.S.S 71
Designer Pat Ruddy
Green fees £12
Visitors welcome by prior arrangement
Societies welcome by prior arrangement

KILKENNY GOLF CLUB

Glendine, Kilkenny, Kilkenny
(056) 65400 Fax (056) 23593
Map 1, F8
Off N77, 2 miles N of Kilkenny
Founded 1896
The 10th tee of this handsome, rolling parkland course is on the site of an ancient bronze-age kitchen.
18 holes, 6510 yards
par 71, S.S.S 70
Green fees £25
Catering, changing room/showers, bar, club, trolley and buggy hire, shop, practice facilities
Visitors welcome – with restrictions
Societies welcome by prior arrangement
Newpark Hotel, Castlecomer Road, Kilkenny, Kilkenny
(056) 22122

MOUNT JULIET GOLF CLUB

Thomastown, Kilkenny
(056) 73000 Fax (056) 73019
Map 1, F8
Off N10, 10 miles S of Kilkenny
Founded 1991
Nick Faldo, Bernhard Langer and Sam Torrance won the three Irish Opens played at Mount Juliet in the mid-1990s. It is almost an American course transported to Kilkenny, relying on a number of artificially created lakes and mounds for its character, but there is no denying its considerable challenge.
18 holes, 7143 yards
par 72, S.S.S 74
Designer Jack Nicklaus
Green fees £75
Catering, changing room/showers, bar, accommodation, club, trolley and buggy hire, shop, driving range, practice facilities
Visitors welcome
Societies welcome by prior arrangement
Mount Juliet Hotel, Thomastown, Kilkenny
(056) 22122

MOUNTAIN VIEW GOLF CLUB

Kiltorcan, Ballyhale, Kilkenny
(056) 68122 **Map 1, F8**
info@mviewgolf.com
www.mviewgolf.com
Off A9 Dublin to Waterford Road at Ballyhale
Founded 1997
A rolling parkland course only recently extended to its full 18 holes. Water hazards are plentiful, and there are extensive views over three counties from the 1st tee.
18 holes, 6000 yards
par 70, S.S.S 70
Designer John O'Sullivan
Green fees £12
Catering, changing room/showers, bar, club and trolley hire
Visitors welcome
Societies welcome by prior arrangement
Carroll Hotel, Knoltopher, Kilkenny
(056) 68082

CO LAOIS

ABBEYLEIX GOLF CLUB

Rathmoyle, Abbeyleix, Laois
(0502) 31450 **Map 1, E7**
Off M7, 10 miles S of Portlaoise
Founded 1895
A 9-hole parkland course.
9 holes, 5626 metres
par 70, S.S.S 69
Designer Mel Flanaghan
Green fees £10
Changing room/showers, bar, trolley hire
Visitors welcome weekdays
Societies welcome by prior arrangement

HEATH (PORTLAOISE) GOLF CLUB

The Heath, Portlaoise, Laois
(0502) 46533 Fax (0502) 46866
Map 1, F7
Off M7, 3 miles NE of Portlaoise
Founded 1930
Golf was played on the heath in the 1880s when the ground was shared with race horses. Today the golf is shared with sheep, which roam the course freely. As the name suggests, heather and gorse are frequently encountered, but there are also three lakes. The surrounding scenery is attractive.
18 holes, 6422 yards
par 71, S.S.S 70
Green fees £10
Catering, changing room/showers, bar, club, trolley and buggy hire, shop, driving range, practice facilities
Visitors welcome
Societies welcome by prior arrangement

MOUNTRATH GOLF CLUB

Knockinina, Mountrath, Laois
(0502) 32643 Fax (0502) 32643
Map 1, E7
Off N7, Dublin to Limerick road
Founded 1929
Parkland course in the heart of the lush Irish countryside.
18 holes, 6100 yards
par 71, S.S.S 69
Green fees £12
Catering, changing room/showers, bar, trolley and buggy hire, practice facilities
Visitors welcome – with restrictions
Societies welcome by prior arrangement
Killeshin Hotel, Portlaoise, Laois
(0502) 21663

PORTARLINGTON GOLF CLUB

Garryhinch, Portarlington, Laois
✆ (0502) 23115 Fax (0502) 23044
Map 1, F7
Off R419, 2 miles SW of Portarlington
Founded 1909
A picturesque parkland course set off against woodland. A river makes the back nine testing.
18 holes, 5872 metres
par 71, S.S.S 71
Designer Eddie Hackett
Green fees £14
Catering, changing room/showers, bar, trolley and buggy hire, practice facilities
Visitors welcome weekdays
Societies welcome by prior arrangement

RATHDOWNEY GOLF CLUB

Coolnaboul West, Rathdowney, Portlaoise, Laois
✆ (0505) 46170 Fax (0505) 46065
Map 1, E7
1 mile from Rathdowney Square, via Johnstown Road
Founded 1930
Recently expanded to 18 holes, there are now several distinctly challenging holes, including the 6th (par 5), 12th (par 4) and 17th (par 3). Excellent value for money.
18 holes, 6408 yards
par 71, S.S.S 70
Designer Eddie Hackett, Pat Suttle
Green fees £12
Changing room/showers, bar, trolley hire
Visitors welcome – restricted weekends
Societies welcome by prior arrangement
🏨 Foxrock Inn, Clough, Ballacolla, Portlaoise, Laois
✆ (0502) 38637

CO LEITRIM

BALLINAMORE GOLF CLUB

Creevy, Ballinamore, Leitrim
✆ (078) 44346 **Map 1, E5**
Ballinamore@eirecom.net
www.ballinamore.com
1½ miles outside Ballinamore
Founded 1941
The club and course were redeveloped recently, making it one of the best 9-hole courses in the country. Water affects play on the first two holes.
9 holes, 5514 metres
par 70, S.S.S 68
Designer Arthur Spring
Green fees £10
Catering, changing room/showers, bar, club hire
Visitors welcome
Societies welcome by prior arrangement
🏨 Commercial Hotel, Ballinamore, Leitrim
✆ (078) 44675

CARRICK-ON-SHANNON GOLF CLUB

Woodbrook, Carrick-on-Shannon, Leitrim
✆ (079) 67015 **Map 1, E5**
N4, 3 miles W of Carrick-on-Shannon
Founded 1910
A parkland course overlooking the River Shannon.
9 holes, 5584 metres
par 70, S.S.S 68
Designer Eddie Hackett
Green fees £12
Catering, changing room/showers, bar, club hire
Visitors welcome
Societies welcome by prior arrangement

CO LIMERICK

ABBEYFEALE GOLF CLUB

Dromtrasna Collins, Abbeyfeale, Limerick
✆ (068) 31454 **Map 1, C8**
abbeyfealegolf@hotmail.com
On N21, main Limerick to Killarney road
Founded 1993
Only nine holes, but with a particularly venomous opening hole – water everywhere.
9 holes, 4962 yards
par 32, S.S.S 39
Designer Arthur Spring, Maurice Riorden
Green fees £8
Catering, club, trolley and buggy hire, shop, driving range
Visitors welcome – restricted Sunday mornings
Societies welcome by prior arrangement
🏨 Devon Inn Hotel, Templeglentine, Abbeyfeale, Limerick
✆ (069) 84122 Fax (069) 84255

ADARE GOLF CLUB

Adare Manor, Adare, Limerick
✆ (061) 395044 Fax (061) 396987
Map 1, C8
golf@adaremanor.com
www.adaremanor.ie
South of Limerick on Tralee Road
Founded 1995
Not to be confused with Adare Manor, this is a Trent Jones creation on the grand scale. Jones described the 18th as, 'the finest finishing hole in world golf.' The course, with its three lakes, is laid out in the grounds of the striking Adare Manor, resembling a Loire chateau.
18 holes, 7138 yards
par 72
Designer Robert Trent Jones Snr
Green fees £75
Catering, changing room/showers, bar, accommodation, club, trolley and buggy hire, shop, driving range, practice facilities, full conference, leisure and equestrian facilities
Visitors welcome
Societies welcome by prior arrangement
🏨 Adare Manor, Adare, Limerick
✆ (061) 396566 Fax (061) 396124
reservations@adaremanor.com

ADARE MANOR GOLF CLUB

Adare, Limerick
✆ (061) 396204 Fax (061) 396800
Map 1, C8
N21, 10 miles SW of Limerick
Founded 1900
A charming little course in incomparable surroundings, with the short 1st hole playing directly towards the keep of Desmond Castle, built around 1200. Much of the rest of the layout weaves its way around a 15th-century Franciscan Abbey and its graveyard. One of the most atmospheric courses in Ireland.
18 holes, 5764 yards
par 69, S.S.S 69
Designer Ben Sayers, Eddie Hackett
Visitors welcome weekdays
Societies welcome by prior arrangement
🏨 Adare Manor, Adare, Limerick
✆ (061) 396566 Fax (061) 396124
reservations@adaremanor.com

CASTLETROY GOLF CLUB

Castletroy, Limerick, Limerick
✆ (061) 335261 Fax (061) 335373
Map 1, D8
Off N7, 2 miles from Limerick city centre
Founded 1937
A high-quality course beginning and ending with particularly testing holes.
18 holes, 5802 metres
par 71, S.S.S 71
Green fees £24
Catering, changing room/showers, bar, club, trolley and buggy hire, practice facilities
Visitors welcome weekdays
Societies welcome by prior arrangement

KILLELINE PARK GOLF & COUNTRY CLUB

Newcastle West, Limerick
✆ (069) 61600 Fax (069) 62853
Map 1, C8
Off R522, ½ mile S of Newcastle West
Founded 1993
A pretty parkland course backed by the Galtee Mountains.
18 holes, 6500 yards
par 71, S.S.S 71
Green fees £12
Catering, changing room/showers, bar, club and trolley hire, shop, practice facilities
Visitors welcome
Societies welcome by prior arrangement

LIMERICK COUNTY GOLF & COUNTRY CLUB

Ballyneety, Limerick
✆ (061) 351881 Fax (061) 351384
Map 1, D8
www.limerickcounty.com
Off R512, 5 miles S of Limerick city centre
Founded 1994
There are extensive views from the higher ground of this rolling parkland course. Six lakes and imaginative contouring provide a considerable test.
18 holes, 6137 metres
par 72, S.S.S 74
Designer Des Smyth
Green fees £20
Catering, changing room/showers, bar, club, trolley and buggy hire, shop, driving range, practice facilities
Visitors welcome
Societies welcome by prior arrangement

LIMERICK GOLF CLUB

Ballyclough, Limerick, Limerick
✆ (061) 414083 Fax (061) 415146
Map 1, C8
Off R511, 3 miles S of Limerick
Founded 1891
A tree-lined parkland course with a stream interrupting the 6th hole – twice!
18 holes, 6487 yards
par 72, S.S.S 71
Designer Alister Mackenzie
Green fees £30
Catering, changing room/showers, bar, club, trolley and buggy hire, shop, practice facilities
Visitors welcome weekdays
Societies welcome by prior arrangement

NEWCASTLE WEST GOLF CLUB

Ardagh, Limerick
✆ (069) 76500 Fax (069) 76511
Map 1, C8
Off N20/R521, 3 miles SW of Rathkeale
Founded 1938
A new course (1994) for a much older club, constructed on sandy, quick drying soil, in a beautiful setting with lakes, streams and trees.
18 holes, 5905 metres
par 71, S.S.S 72
Designer Arthur Spring
Green fees £18
Catering, changing room/showers, bar, club and trolley hire, shop, driving range, practice facilities
Visitors welcome
Societies welcome by prior arrangement

CO LONGFORD

COUNTY LONGFORD GOLF CLUB

Glack, Dublin Road, Longford, Longford
✆ (043) 46310 Fax (043) 47082
Map 1, E5
Off N4, SE of Longford
Founded 1900
Expansion is in train at County Longford with the acquisition of 14 acres of new land and a much improved club house. Eddie Hackett's current course, on free-draining rolling ground, makes much use of a stream which crosses five holes on the outward nine, as well as the 18th.
18 holes, 6348 yards
par 70, S.S.S 71
Designer Eddie Hackett
Green fees £12
Catering, changing room/showers, bar, club, trolley and buggy hire, practice facilities
Visitors welcome
Societies welcome by prior arrangement

CO LOUTH

ARDEE GOLF CLUB

Ardee, Louth
✆ (041) 685 3227 Fax (041) 685 6137 **Map 1, G5**
Off N52, ½ mile NW of Ardee
Founded 1911
A pretty parkland course featuring a stream on a number of holes.
18 holes, 6348 yards
par 70, S.S.S 71
Designer Eddie Hackett
Green fees £25
Catering, changing room/showers, bar, club, trolley and buggy hire
Visitors welcome
Societies welcome by prior arrangement

COUNTY LOUTH GOLF CLUB

Baltray, Drogheda, Louth
✆ (041) 982 2329 Fax (04) 982 2969
Map 1, G5
Off R167, 5 miles NE of Drogheda
Founded 1892
See 50 Top Courses, page 17
18 holes, 6783 yards
par 73, S.S.S 72
Designer Tom Simpson
Green fees £50
Catering, changing room/showers, bar, club, trolley and buggy hire, shop, practice facilities, tennis
Visitors welcome by prior arrangement
Societies welcome by prior arrangement

DUNDALK GOLF CLUB

Blackrock, Dundalk, Louth
✆ (042) 9321731 Fax (042) 9322022
Map 1, G5
dkgc@iol.ie
www.eiresoft.com/dundalkgc
3 km S of Dundalk
Founded 1905
A championship course which has been expanded and refined over many years and is renowned for the standard of its green keeping. Although the course lies close to the sea, trees are a significant factor, and the land rolls gently. Dundalk hosted the All Ireland Finals in 1997 and 2000.
18 holes, 6160 metres
par 72, S.S.S 72
Designer Peter Alliss, Dave Thomas
Green fees £35
Catering, changing room/showers, bar, club and trolley hire, shop, practice facilities
Visitors welcome with restrictions
Societies welcome by prior arrangement

GREENORE GOLF CLUB

Greenore, Louth
✆ (042) 937 3212 Fax (042) 937 2022 **Map 1, G5**
Off R173, 11 miles NE of Dundalk
Founded 1886
The shores of Carlingford Lough are beautiful, and Greenore's golf course looks out from amidst the pine trees over its waters to the imposing Mourne Mountains in County Down. Greenore's standing has grown over the years, as,

indeed, the course has grown longer, with tight fairways and firm, swift greens.
18 holes, 6514 yards
par 71, S.S.S 71
Designer Eddie Hackett
Green fees £18
Catering, changing room/showers, bar, trolley hire, practice facilities
Visitors welcome
Societies welcome by prior arrangement

KILLINBEG PARK GOLF CLUB
Killin Park, Killin, Dundalk, Louth
✆ (042) 39303 **Map 1, G5**
Off N53, 2 miles W of Dundalk
Founded 1991
A short parkland course, well-wooded and with occasional water hazards.
18 holes, 4717 metres
par 69, S.S.S 65
Designer Eddie Hackett
Green fees £10
Catering, changing room/showers, bar, club and trolley hire
Visitors welcome
Societies welcome by prior arrangement

SEAPOINT GOLF CLUB
Termonfeckin, Drogheda, Louth
✆ (041) 9822333 Fax (041) 9822331
Map 1, G5
golflink@seapoint.ie
www.seapointgolfclub.com
R166 5 miles E of Drogheda
Founded 1993
An exciting new links course with fine views up the Irish Sea coast to the Mourne Mountains from the closing holes beside the beach. The most difficult holes for the visitor are likely to prove to be the 4th and 5th, part of an inland sequence much troubled by water.
18 holes, 6420 metres
par 72, S.S.S 74
Designer Des Smyth
Green fees £25
Catering, changing room/showers, bar, club, trolley and buggy hire, shop, driving range, practice facilities
Visitors welcome – with reservations
Societies welcome by prior arrangement
Ballymascanlon Hotel, Dundalk, Louth
✆ (042) 9371124

TOWNELEY HALL GOLF CLUB
Tullyallen, Drogheda, Louth
✆ (041) 42229 Fax (041) 31762
Map 1, G5
Off R168, 5 miles NW of Drogheda
Founded 1994
A parkland course.
9 holes, 5221 metres
par 71, S.S.S 69
Green fees £6
Visitors welcome
Societies welcome by prior arrangement

CO MAYO

ACHILL ISLAND GOLF CLUB
Keel, Achill, Mayo
✆ (098) 43456 **Map 1, B4**
R391, at Keel
Founded 1951
A seaside links with outstanding views, situated on the stunning Achill Island off the coast of County Mayo.
9 holes, 2689 metres
par 70, S.S.S 67
Designer P. Skerritt
Green fees £7
Catering, changing room/showers, bar, club and trolley hire
Visitors welcome
Handicap certificate required
Societies welcome by prior arrangement

ASHFORD CASTLE GOLF CLUB
Cong, Mayo
✆ (092) 46003 **Map 1, C6**
R345, 25 miles N of Galway on Lough Corrib
A parkland course overlooking the vast expanse of Lough Corrib.
9 holes, 4500 yards
S.S.S 68
Designer Eddie Hackett
Green fees £15
Bar
Visitors welcome
Societies welcome by prior arrangement

BALLINA GOLF CLUB
Mossgrove, Shanaghy, Ballina, Mayo
✆ (096) 21050 Fax (096) 21050
Map 1, C4
1 km from town centre
Founded 1910
A scenic course on which every single hole is overlooked by the Ox Mountains. At 560 yards, the 12th is a very substantial par 5.
18 holes, 5851 metres
par 71, S.S.S 69
Designer Eddie Hackett
Green fees £16
Changing room/showers, bar, club, trolley and buggy hire, practice facilities
Visitors welcome – restricted Saturdays
Societies welcome by prior arrangement

BALLINROBE GOLF CLUB
Clooncastle, Ballinrobe, Mayo
✆ (092) 41118 Fax (096) 41889
Map 1, C5
Off N84, 1 mile NW of Ballinrobe
Founded 1895
A parkland course close to Lough Mask, with many lakes and a river incorporated into the design. Old woodlands add to the beauty.
18 holes, 6043 metres
par 73, S.S.S 72
Designer Eddie Hackett
Green fees £15
Catering, changing room/showers, bar, club, trolley and buggy hire, shop, driving range
Visitors welcome – with restrictions
Societies welcome by prior arrangement

BALLYHAUNIS GOLF CLUB
Coolnaha, Ballyhaunis, Mayo
✆ (0907) 30014 **Map 1, B5**
N83, 2 miles N of Ballyhaunis
Founded 1929
A rolling parkland course in the east of the county.
9 holes, 5413 yards
par 70, S.S.S 68
Green fees £10
Changing room/showers, bar, club hire, practice facilities
Visitors welcome – with restrictions
Societies welcome by prior arrangement

CARNE GOLF LINKS
Carne, Belmullet, Mayo
✆ (097) 82292 Fax (097) 81477
Map 1, B4
www.carnegolflinks.com
Off R313, on the Mullet Peninsula, 3 miles SW of Belmullet
Founded 1925
One of the great Eddie Hackett's last designs, on which he let nature dictate the architecture. So, there are some blind shots, as might be encountered at Lahinch or Newcastle, but the golfer is rewarded by playing through dunes up to 70 feet high. One of Ireland's great links courses.
18 holes, 6119 metres
par 72, S.S.S 72
Designer Eddie Hackett
Green fees £25
Catering, changing room/showers, bar, club, trolley and buggy hire, practice facilities
Visitors welcome
Societies welcome by prior arrangement

CASTLEBAR GOLF CLUB
Hawthorn Avenue, Rocklands, Castlebar, Mayo
(094) 21649 Fax (094) 26088
Map 1, C5
Off N84, 2 miles SE of Castlebar
Founded 1910
A well-wooded parkland course.
18 holes, 6500 yards
par 71, S.S.S 72
Designer Peter McEvoy
Green fees £20
Catering, changing room/showers, bar, club, trolley and buggy hire, practice facilities
Visitors welcome weekdays
Societies welcome by prior arrangement

CLAREMORRIS GOLF CLUB
Castlemagaret, Claremorris, Mayo
(094) 71527 **Map 1, C5**
claremorrisgc@ebookireland.com
www.ebookireland.com
N17, 2 miles from Claremorris
Founded 1924
What was, until recently, a simple 9-hole course has now been extended to a long and notably testing course by Tom Craddock.
18 holes, 6136 metres
par 73, S.S.S 73
Designer Tom Craddock
Green fees £18
Catering, changing room/showers, bar, club, trolley and buggy hire, driving range, practice facilities
Visitors welcome – with restrictions on Sundays
Societies welcome by prior arrangement
The Belmont Hotel, Knock, Mayo
(094)

MULRANNY GOLF CLUB
Mulranny, Westport, Mayo
(098) 36262 **Map 1, B5**
N59, 15 miles NW of Westport
Founded 1968
A links course with fine views over Clew Bay.
9 holes, 6255 yards
par 71, S.S.S 69
Green fees £8
Catering, changing room/showers, bar
Visitors welcome
Societies welcome by prior arrangement

SWINFORD GOLF CLUB
Brabazon Park, Swinford, Mayo
(094) 51378 **Map 1, C5**
R320, 1 mile S of Swinford
Founded 1922
A parkland course with views towards the Ox Mountains.
9 holes, 5542 metres
par 70, S.S.S 68
Green fees £10
Catering, changing room/showers, bar, trolley hire
Visitors welcome – with restrictions
Societies welcome by prior arrangement

WESTPORT GOLF CLUB
Carrowholly, Westport, Mayo
(098) 28262 Fax (098) 27217
Map 1, B5
wpgolf@iol.ie
www.golfwestport.com
Off N59, 2 miles N of Westport
Founded 1908
The course lies beside Clew Bay, with Croagh Patrick forming an imposing backdrop. It dates from 1973, when the club relocated, and is essentially parkland in nature, although adjoining the bay on the back nine, the drive at the 15th being made over its tranquil waters.
18 holes, 7072 yards
par 73, S.S.S 74
Designer Fred Hawtree
Green fees £25
Catering, changing room/showers, bar, club, trolley and buggy hire, shop, driving range, practice facilities
Visitors welcome
Societies welcome with prior reservation
Knockranny House Hotel, Knockranny, Westport, Mayo
(098) 28600

CO MEATH

ASHBOURNE GOLF CLUB
Archerstown, Ashbourne, Meath
(01) 835 2005 Fax (01) 835 2561
Map 1, G6
Off N2, 1 mile SE of Ashbourne
Founded 1991
A parkland course making good strategic use of water hazards.
18 holes, 5778 metres
par 71, S.S.S 70
Designer Des Smyth
Green fees £20
Catering, changing room/showers, bar, club, trolley and buggy hire, shop, driving range, practice facilities
Visitors welcome weekdays – with restrictions
Societies welcome by prior arrangement

BLACK BUSH GOLF CLUB
Thomastown, Dunshaughlin, Meath
(01) 8250021 Fax (01) 8250400
Map 1, G6
golf@blackbush.iol.ie
www.iol.ie/~bbush
N3,1 mile E of Dunshaughlin.
Founded 1987
27 holes of parkland golf in the suburbs of Dublin, pleasantly rural, with wildlife abounding. Water hazards feature prominently.
18 holes, 6849 yards
par 73, S.S.S 72
Designer Robert Browne
Green fees £n/a
Catering, changing room/showers, bar, club, trolley and buggy hire, shop, practice facilities, 9-hole course
Visitors welcome – restrictions weekends
Societies welcome by prior arrangement

COUNTY MEATH GOLF CLUB
Newtownmoynagh, Trim, Meath
(046) 31463 Fax (046) 37554
Map 1, F6
sec@trimgolff.net
www.trimgolf.net
R160, from Trim towards Longwood
Founded 1898
The names of the architects, Eddie Hackett and Tom Craddock, should be sufficient to commend this recently expanded course, which is rapidly gaining more than a local reputation for the consistency of its challenge.
18 holes, 6136 metres
par 73, S.S.S 72
Designer Eddie Hackett, Tom Craddock
Green fees £20
Catering, changing room/showers, bar, trolley hire, shop, practice facilities
Visitors welcome – with restrictions
Societies welcome by prior arrangement
Wellington Court Hotel, Trim, Meath
(046) 31516

GORMANSTON COLLEGE GOLF CLUB
Franciscan College, Gormanston, Meath
(01) 841 2203 Fax (01) 841 2874
Map 1, G6
22 miles N of Dublin
Founded 1961
A private parkland course.
9 holes, 1973 metres
Visitors welcome only as members' guests
No societies

HEADFORT GOLF CLUB
Kells, Meath
(046) 40857 Fax (01) 841 2874
Map 1, F5

Off N3, 1 mile E of Kells
Founded 1928
A recent expansion to 36 holes has established Headfort as one of the premier inland clubs in Ireland. The parkland in which both courses are located is part of the estate of the Marquis of Headfort, full of beautiful old trees and wooded islands. Both courses are of championship standard.
18 holes, 6487 metres, par 72, S.S.S 75
Designer Christy O'Connor Jr.
18 holes, 6007 metres, par 72, S.S.S 71
Green fees £21
Catering, changing room/showers, bar, club and trolley hire, shop, practice facilities
Visitors welcome
Societies welcome by prior arrangement

KILCOCK GOLF CLUB
Gallow, Kilcock, Meath
☎ (01) 6287592 Fax (01) 6287283
Map 1, G6
Off R125, 4 miles W of Maynooth
Founded 1985
Gentle parkland course.
18 holes, 5812 metres
par 72, S.S.S 70
Designer Eddie Hackett
Green fees £14
Catering, changing room/showers, bar, trolley and buggy hire, practice facilities
Visitors welcome – with restrictions
Societies welcome by prior arrangement

LAYTOWN & BETTYSTOWN GOLF CLUB
Bettystown, Meath
☎ (041) 982 7170 Fax (041) 982 8506 **Map 1, G5**
Off R151, 4 miles E of Drogheda
Founded 1909
The home course of tour star Des Smyth, who has made recent alterations to the front nine, further strengthening this testing links course. With small greens and tight bunkering the course will challenge even the best players, as was witnessed when Mary McKenna took the 1981 Irish Ladies' Amateur Championship.
18 holes, 6454 yards
par 71, S.S.S 72
Designer Des Smyth
Green fees £25
Catering, changing room/showers, bar, club and trolley hire, shop, practice facilities
Visitors welcome – with restrictions
Societies welcome by prior arrangement

MOOR PARK GOLF CLUB
The Manor, Mooretown, Navan, Meath
☎ (046) 27661 Fax (046) 27661
Map 1, G6
Off N3, 3 miles SE of Navan
Founded 1993
A parkland course on which no fewer than nine counties are visible from the 9th tee.
18 holes, 5852 yards
par 72, S.S.S 69
Designer Eddie Hackett
Green fees £8
Changing room/showers, club and trolley hire
Visitors welcome
Societies welcome by prior arrangement
Ardboyne Hotel, Navan, Meath
☎ (046) 23119

NAVAN GOLF CLUB
Proudstown, Navan, Meath
☎ (046) 72888 **Map 1, F6**
Off R162, 2 miles N of Navan
Founded 1997
A new parkland course of good length, offering good value for money.
18 holes, 6035 metres
par 72, S.S.S 70
Green fees £15
Catering, changing room/showers, bar, club, trolley and buggy hire, shop, driving range, practice facilities
Visitors welcome
Societies welcome by prior arrangement

ROYAL TARA GOLF CLUB
Bellinter, Navan, Meath
☎ (046) 25244 Fax (046) 25508
Map 1, G6
www.royaltaragolfclub.com
Off N3, 4 miles S of Navan
Founded 1906
One of only two clubs in the Irish Republic with a royal title, in this case referring to the Hill of Tara, seat of the ancient Kings of Ireland. The parkland courses are pleasantly challenging.
18 holes, 5757 metres, par 71, S.S.S 70
Designer Des Smyth
9 holes, 3184 metres, par 35, S.S.S 35
Green fees £20
Catering, changing room/showers, club, trolley and buggy hire, practice facilities
Visitors welcome
Societies welcome by prior arrangement

CO MONAGHAN

CASTLEBLAYNEY GOLF CLUB
Onomy, Castleblayney, Monaghan
☎ (042) 974 9485 **Map 1, F4**
N2, in Castleblayney
Founded 1985
A pretty parkland course overlooking Muckno Lake.
9 holes, 5378 yards
par 68, S.S.S 66
Designer R. Browne
Green fees £8
Catering, changing room/showers, bar, fishing
Visitors welcome
Societies welcome by prior arrangement

CLONES GOLF CLUB
Hilton Park, Clones, Monaghan
☎ (049) 56017 Fax (042) 974 2333
Map 1, F4
3 miles from Clones
Founded 1913
A rolling parkland course built on free-draining limestone.
9 holes, 5790 yards
par 68, S.S.S 67
Green fees £10
Catering, changing room/showers, bar
Visitors welcome weekdays
Societies welcome by prior arrangement

MANNAN CASTLE GOLF CLUB
Donaghmoyne, Carrickmacross, Monaghan
☎ (042) 966 3308 Fax (042) 966 3195 **Map 1, G5**
R179, 4 miles E of Carrickmacross
Founded 1993
A testing parkland course with a number of water hazards.
18 holes, 6020 yards
par 70, S.S.S 69
Green fees £15
Catering, changing room/showers, bar
Visitors welcome
Societies welcome by prior arrangement

NUREMORE GOLF CLUB
Nuremore, Carrickmacross, Monaghan
☎ (042) 64016 **Map 1, G5**
Off N2, 2 miles SE of Carrickmacross
Founded 1964
One of the most testing inland layouts in this part of Ireland, so

testing in fact that David Jones was called in to make Eddie Hackett's course just a little less daunting. It has been host to the Ulster Professional Championship.
18 holes, 5870 metres
par 71, S.S.S 69
Designer Eddie Hackett, David Jones
Green fees £20
Catering, changing room/showers, bar, club, trolley and buggy hire, shop, practice facilities
Visitors welcome
Societies welcome by prior arrangement

ROSSMORE GOLF CLUB
Rossmore Park, Monaghan, Monaghan
✆ (047) 71222 **Map 1, F4**
mark@mcnicgolflimited.com
www.mcnicgolflimited.com
Off R118, 2½ miles from Monaghan
Founded 1916
The views build as the round proceeds at Rossmore, until five counties are visible from the 16th tee.
18 holes, 5590 metres
par 70, S.S.S 69
Designer Des Smyth
Green fees £20
Catering, changing room/showers, bar, club and trolley hire, shop, driving range, conference, management, team building facilities, some in partnership with outside bodies
Visitors welcome
Societies welcome by prior arrangement
Four Seasons Hotel, Monaghan Town, Monaghan
✆ (047) 81888

CO OFFALY

BIRR GOLF CLUB
The Glenns, Birr, Offaly
✆ (0509) 20082 Fax (0509) 22155
Map 1, E7
Off R432, 2 miles NW of Birr
Founded 1893
A parkland course in gentle rolling country.
18 holes, 5754 metres
par 70, S.S.S 70
Designer Eddie Connaughton
Green fees £12
Catering, changing room/showers, bar, club and trolley hire, driving range, practice facilities
Visitors welcome – with restrictions
Societies welcome by prior arrangement

CASTLE BARNA GOLF CLUB
Castlebarnagh, Daingean, Offaly
✆ (0506) 53384 Fax (0506) 53077
Map 1, F6
Off R402, 10 miles E of Tullamore
Founded 1992
A recent parkland course.
18 holes, 5669 metres
par 72, S.S.S 66
Designer Alan Duggan
Green fees £10
Catering, changing room/showers, bar, club, trolley and buggy hire, practice facilities
Visitors welcome
Societies welcome by prior arrangement

EDENDERRY GOLF CLUB
Kishavanna, Edenderry, Offaly
✆ (0405) 31072 **Map 1, F6**
Off R402, 1½ miles NE of Edenderry
Founded 1910
A parkland course extended to 18 holes ten years ago in the far east of the county.
18 holes, 6029 metres
par 72, S.S.S 72
Designer Arthur Havers, Eddie Hackett
Green fees £15
Catering, changing room/showers, bar, trolley hire
Visitors welcome weekdays – with restrictions
Societies welcome by prior arrangement

ESKER HILLS GOLF & COUNTRY CLUB
Ballykilmurray, Tullamore, Offaly
✆ (0506) 55999 Fax (0506) 55021
Map 1, E6
eskerhills@eircom.ie
www.globalgolf.com
Off N80, 3 miles NW of Tullamore
Founded 1996
A remarkably undulating course for a county that is generally flat and boggy. O'Connor had little earth moving to do, yet this is a course on which nature governs strategy. Lakes and trees enhance the beauty and increase the challenge. As is customary, O'Connor has incorporated teasing short par 4s.
18 holes, 6669 yards
par 71, S.S.S 71
Designer Christy O'Connor Jnr.
Green fees £18
Catering, changing room/showers, bar, club, trolley and buggy hire, practice facilities
Visitors welcome by prior arrangement
Societies welcome by prior arrangement

TULLAMORE GOLF CLUB
Brookfield, Tullamore, Offaly
✆ (0506) 21439 Fax (0506) 41806
Map 1, E7
www.tullamoregolfclub.com
Off R421, 3 miles S of Tullamore
Founded 1896
For 70 years James Braid's layout gave good service, but in 1996 Patrick Merrigan was instructed to undertake a partial rebuild, in the process adding three lakes. The course looks much the same, in beautiful parkland with the Slieve Bloom Mountains as a backdrop, but the defences are now tighter.
18 holes, 6428 yards
par 70, S.S.S 71
Designer James Braid, Patrick Merrigan
Green fees £25
Catering, changing room/showers, bar, club, trolley and buggy hire, shop, practice facilities
Visitors welcome weekdays – with restrictions
Societies welcome by prior arrangement

CO ROSCOMMON

ATHLONE GOLF CLUB
Hodson Bay, Athlone, Roscommon
✆ (0902) 92073 Fax (0902) 94080
Map 1, E6
Roscommon Road, 3 miles N of Athlone
Founded 1892
An old club with a military background, which moved to its present home on the shores of Lough Ree in 1938. Adjoining the lough, there are delightful holes at the 6th, 11th, and 16th. The wooded holes are equally handsome, and many are significantly dog-legged, such as the remarkable 12th.
18 holes, 5973 metres
par 71, S.S.S 72
Designer J. McAllister
Green fees £18
Catering, changing room/showers, bar, accommodation, club and trolley hire, shop, practice facilities
Visitors welcome
Societies welcome with prior notice
Hodson Bay Hotel, Athlone, Roscommon
✆ (0902) 92444 Fax (0902) 92688

BALLAGHADERREEN GOLF CLUB
Aughalustia, Ballaghaderreen, Roscommon
✆ (0907) 60295 **Map 1, D5**
corki@iol.ie
www.ballaghaderreen

Signposted from Ballaghaderreen
Founded 1936
A 9-hole course with separate tees on several holes to give considerable variety. A pleasant, tree-lined, parkland course.
9 holes, 5339 metres
par 70, S.S.S 67
Designer Paddy Skerret
Green fees £10
Catering, changing room/showers, bar, driving range, practice facilities
Visitors welcome
Handicap certificate required – limit: men 24, women 30
Societies welcome by prior arrangement
Durkins, The Square, Ballaghaderreen, Roscommon
(0907) 60051

BOYLE GOLF CLUB

Knockadoobrusna, Roscommon Road, Boyle, Roscommon
(079) 62192 **Map 1, D5**
N61, 2 miles S of Boyle
Founded 1911
A gently rolling parkland course with a beautiful mountain background.
9 holes, 4914 metres
par 67, S.S.S 64
Designer Eddie Hackett
Green fees £10
Catering, changing room/showers, bar, club hire
Visitors welcome
Societies welcome by prior arrangement

CASTLEREA GOLF CLUB

Clonallis, Castlerea, Roscommon
0907 20068 **Map 1, D5**
1km outside Castlerea on the Knock Road
Founded 1905
A pleasant parkland course with a river in play.
9 holes, 2196 metres
par 68, S.S.S 67
Green fees £10
Changing room/showers, bar, trolley hire, practice facilities
Visitors welcome – restricted Sundays
Handicap certificate required
Societies welcome by prior arrangement
Tullys Hotel, Main Street, Castlerea, Roscommon

ROSCOMMON GOLF CLUB

Mote Park, Roscommon, Roscommon
(0903) 26382 Fax (0903) 26043
Map 1, D6
South edge of Roscommon town.
Founded 1904
Recently extended to 18 holes, and with a comfortable new clubhouse, Roscommon offers relaxed golf in the heart of the Irish countryside. A number of demanding holes – the 425-metre 8th, and 404-metre 10th – are balanced against charming holes, such as the 137-metre 13th, all carry over water.
18 holes, 6059 metres
par 72, S.S.S 71
Designer Eddie Connaughton
Green fees £15
Catering, changing room/showers, bar, trolley and buggy hire, practice facilities
Visitors welcome – restricted weekends
Societies welcome by prior arrangement
Abbey Hotel, Abbeytown, Roscommon, Roscommon
(0903) 26240

STROKESTOWN GOLF CLUB

Cloonfinlough, Strokestown, Roscommon
(078) 33084 **Map 1, E5**
R368, 2 miles from Strokestown
Founded 1992
A parkland course with pleasant lake views.
9 holes, 5230 metres
par 68, S.S.S 67
Green fees £5
Changing room/showers
Visitors welcome
Societies welcome by prior arrangement

CO SLIGO

BALLYMOTE GOLF CLUB

Ballinascarrow, Ballymote, Sligo
(071) 83158 **Map 1, D4**
Off N4, 15 miles S of Sligo
Founded 1943
A club founded in the 1940s with a new parkland course, built in the 1990s.
9 holes, 5302 metres
par 68, S.S.S 67
Green fees £7
Changing room/showers, club and trolley hire
Visitors welcome
Societies welcome by prior arrangement

COUNTY SLIGO GOLF CLUB

Rosses Point, Sligo
(071) 77134 Fax (071) 77460
Map 1, D4
cosligo@iol.ie
www.countysligogolfclub.ie
Off R291, 5 miles NW of Sligo
Founded 1894
One of the most romantic of Irish links courses, in the heart of Yeats country, overlooked by Ben Bulben, Rosses Point starts slowly, but the view from the 3rd tee raises expectations, and there will be no disappointment, with the dog-leg 14th rated as one of Ireland's greatest par 4s.
18 holes, 6611 yards, par 71, S.S.S 72
Designer Harry Colt, C.H. Alison
9 holes, 5588 yards, par 70, S.S.S 69
Green fees £35
Catering, changing room/showers, bar, club, trolley and buggy hire, shop, practice facilities
Visitors welcome by prior arrangement – restricted weekends
Handicap certificate required
Societies welcome by prior arrangement
Sligo Park Hotel, Pearce Road, Sligo, Sligo
(071) 60291

ENNISCRONE GOLF CLUB

Ballina Road, Enniscrone, Sligo
(096) 36297 Fax (096) 36657
Map 1, C4
enniscronegolf@eircom.net
homepage.eircom.net/~enniscrone
On Killala Bay, close to Enniscrone village
Founded 1931
A wonderfully situated links, on a peninsula with the waters of Killala Bay on three sides. The greens, inventively designed by Eddie Hackett, are a study in themselves, and invariably in excellent condition. A favourite of many is the 16th, a right-angled dog-leg threatened by out-of-bounds, with an elevated green.
18 holes, 6857 yards
par 73, S.S.S 73
Designer Eddie Hackett, Donald Steel
Green fees £30
Catering, changing room/showers, bar, club, trolley and buggy hire, shop, practice facilities, 9-hole course
Visitors welcome
Societies welcome by prior arrangement

STRANDHILL GOLF CLUB

Strandhill, Sligo
(071) 68188 Fax (071) 68811
Map 1, D4
R292, 5 miles W of Sligo
Founded 1931
A charming links course overlooking the Atlantic, backed by the mountains.
18 holes, 5635 metres

par 69, S.S.S 68
Green fees £25
Catering, changing room/showers, bar, club, trolley and buggy hire, practice facilities
Visitors welcome weekdays
Societies welcome by prior arrangement

TUBBERCURRY GOLF CLUB

Ballymote Road, Tubbercurry, Sligo
✆ (071) 85849 **Map 1, D4**
N17, main Galway to Sligo road
Founded 1991
Nestling at the foot of the Ox Mountains, with great views of Muckelty, Knocknashee and Croagh Patrick.
9 holes, 6200 yards
par 70, S.S.S 67
Designer Eddie Hackett
Green fees £10
Catering, changing room/showers, bar, trolley hire, driving range, practice facilities
Visitors welcome – restricted Sundays
Societies welcome by prior arrangement
🏨 Cowleys Hotel, Emmet Street, Tubbercurry, Sligo
✆ (071) 85025

CO TIPPERARY

BALLYKISTEEN GOLF & COUNTRY CLUB

Monard, Tipperary
✆ (052) 51439 **Map 1, D8**
M24, 2 miles NW of Tipperary
Founded 1994
Breathing new life into a former stud farm, Ballykisteen is a handsome parkland course with thoughtful finishing touches such as the stone walls which line the lakes and streams which are such a feature.
18 holes, 6765 yards
par 72, S.S.S 73
Designer Des Smyth
Green fees £20
Catering, changing room/showers, bar, club, trolley and buggy hire, shop, driving range, practice facilities
Visitors welcome by prior arrangement
Societies welcome by prior arrangement

CAHIR PARK GOLF CLUB

Kilcommon, Cahir, Tipperary
✆ (052) 41474 Fax (052) 42717
Map 1, D9
1 mile from Cahir, on Clogheen road
Founded 1967
Water is in play on six holes, and two holes are actually played over the River Suir.
18 holes, 6348 yards
par 71, S.S.S 71
Designer Eddie Hackett
Green fees £18
Catering, changing room/showers, bar, trolley and buggy hire, shop, driving range, practice facilities
Visitors welcome – with restrictions
Societies welcome by prior arrangement
🏨 Cahir House Hotel, The Square, Cahir, Tipperary
✆ (052) 42727

CARRICK-ON-SUIR GOLF CLUB

Garravoone, Carrick-on-Suir, Tipperary
✆ (051) 640047 Fax (051) 640558
Map 1, E9
R676, 1 mile S of Carrick-on-Suir
Founded 1939
A handsomely situated parkland course overlooking the Suir Valley, backed by mountains.
18 holes, 6061 metres
par 72, S.S.S 70
Designer Eddie Hackett
Green fees £12
Catering, changing room/showers, bar, club, trolley and buggy hire
Visitors welcome – with weekend restrictions
Societies welcome by prior arrangement

CLONMEL GOLF CLUB

Lyreanearla, Mountain Road, Clonmel, Tipperary
✆ (052) 21138 Fax (052) 24050
Map 1, E9
Off R768, 2½ miles SE of Clonmel
Founded 1911
An exceptionally handsome course, backed by the Comeragh Mountains, on which hilly lies complicate club selection.
18 holes, 6392 yards
par 72, S.S.S 71
Designer Eddie Hackett
Green fees £18
Catering, changing room/showers, bar, club, trolley and buggy hire, shop, practice facilities
Visitors welcome weekdays
Societies welcome by prior arrangement

COUNTY TIPPERARY GOLF CLUB

Dundrum, Cashel, Tipperary
✆ (062) 71116 Fax (062) 71366
Map 1, D8
Off R505, 6 miles NW of Cashel
Founded 1993
A parkland course, well-wooded and with a stream running through it, built in the estate of an old country house.
18 holes, 6682 yards
par 72, S.S.S 72
Designer Philip Walton
Green fees £20
Catering, changing room/showers, bar, accommodation, club, trolley and buggy hire, shop, practice facilities
Visitors welcome
Societies welcome by prior arrangement
🏨 Dundrum House Hotel, Dundrum, Tipperary
✆ (062) 71116 Fax (062) 71366

NENAGH GOLF CLUB

Beechwood, Nenagh, Tipperary
✆ (067) 31476 Fax (067) 34808
Map 1, D7
N7 from Dublin
Founded 1929
Recently redeveloped into an 18-hole course on free-draining soil giving good playing conditions all year round.
18 holes, 6009 metres
par 72, S.S.S 70
Designer Patrick Merrigan
Green fees £25
Catering, changing room/showers, bar, club and trolley hire, shop, practice facilities
Visitors welcome
Societies welcome by prior arrangement
🏨 Abbey Court Hotel, Dublin Road, Nenaeh, Tipperary
✆ (067) 41111

ROSCREA GOLF CLUB

Derryvale, Roscrea, Tipperary
✆ (0505) 21130 Fax (0505) 23410
Map 1, E7
Off N7, 2 miles E of Roscrea
Founded 1892
An old 9 hole parkland course revitalised by extension to 18 holes. The gently rolling fairways are lined with mature trees and there are a number of water features.
18 holes, 6323 yards
par 71, S.S.S 70
Designer Arthur Spring
Green fees £14
Catering, changing room/showers, bar, club and trolley hire, practice facilities
Visitors welcome
Societies welcome by prior arrangement

TEMPLEMORE GOLF CLUB

Manna South, Templemore, Tipperary
✆ (0504) 32923 **Map 1, E7**

johnkm@tinet.ie
½ mile S of Templemore
Founded 1971
Laid out under the shadow of the Devil's Bit mountain, beside the Irish Police Training College.
9 holes, 5443 metres
par 70, S.S.S 68
Designer Eddie Hackett
Green fees £10
Catering, changing room/showers, bar, tennis
Visitors welcome – restricted Sundays
Societies welcome by prior arrangement
Templemore Arms, Main Street, Templemore, Tipperary

THURLES GOLF CLUB

Turtulla, Thurles, Tipperary
(0504) 21983 Fax (0504) 24647
Map 1, E8
½ mile from Thurles on Cork Road
Founded 1945
Very beautiful parkland course on the banks of the River Suir.
18 holes, 6465 yards
par 72, S.S.S 71
Green fees £20
Catering, changing room/showers, bar, club and trolley hire, shop, driving range, practice facilities
Visitors welcome – with restrictions on Sundays
Societies welcome by prior arrangement

TIPPERARY GOLF CLUB

Rathanny, Tipperary, Tipperary
(062) 51119 **Map 1, D8**
Off R664, 1 mile S of Tipperary
Founded 1896
A parkland course with water hazards and mature woodlands.
18 holes, 5843 metres
par 71, S.S.S 71
Green fees £15
Catering, changing room/showers, bar, club, trolley and buggy hire
Visitors welcome
Societies welcome by prior arrangement

CO WATERFORD

DUNGARVAN GOLF CLUB

Knocknagranagh, Dungarvan, Waterford
(058) 43310 Fax (058) 44113
Map 1, E9
N25, 2 miles NE of Dungarvan
Founded 1924
A parkland course with many water hazards overlooking Dungarvan Bay, a new course built when the club abandoned its old home in 1993.
18 holes, 6134 metres
par 72, S.S.S 73
Designer Maurice Fives
Green fees £20
Catering, changing room/showers, bar, club, trolley and buggy hire, shop, practice facilities
Visitors welcome
Societies welcome by prior arrangement

DUNMORE EAST GOLF CLUB

Dunmore East, Waterford
(051) 383151 Fax (051) 383151
Map 1, F9
mskehan@waterford-dunmore.com
www.waterford-dunmore.com
Signposted from Dunmore Strand
Founded 1993
From its elevated position there are fine views, and on the 15th the tee shot must cross the sea to reach the fairway.
18 holes, 6655 yards
par 72, S.S.S 70
Designer W.H. Jones
Green fees £18
Catering, changing room/showers, bar, club, trolley and buggy hire, shop
Visitors welcome
Societies welcome by prior arrangment
The Strand Hotel, Dunmore East, Waterford
(051) 383174

FAITHLEGG GOLF CLUB

Faithlegg, Waterford
(051) 382241 Fax (051) 382664
Map 1, F9
fgc@eircom.net
www.faithlegg.com
6 miles E of Waterford
Founded 1993
Faithlegg's setting in lovely rolling country, alongside the River Suir, is sufficient to commend it. The design of the course demands intelligent play to negotiate the dog-legs and rapid greens. There is an extraordinary disparity between the lengths of the front and back nines, 2903 yards out, 3771 yards in.
18 holes, 6674 yards
par 72, S.S.S 72
Designer Patrick Merrigan
Green fees £25
Catering, changing room/showers, bar, accommodation, club, trolley and buggy hire, shop, practice facilities, full hotel facilities
Visitors welcome
Societies welcome by prior arrangement
Faithlegg House Hotel, Faithlegg, Waterford
(051) 382000

GOLD COAST GOLF CLUB

Ballinacourty, Dungarvan, Waterford
(058) 42249 Fax (058) 43378
Map 1, E9
www.clonea.com
Off R675, 4 miles E of Dungarvan
Founded 1993
Dungarvan Golf Club left its old 9-hole course on this site because there seemed little prospect of ever expanding to 18 holes. Fate contrived to make 54 acres of adjoining land available almost immediately! The site is magnificent, with stunning views past the lighthouse over Dungarvan Bay and beyond.
18 holes, 6749 yards
par 72, S.S.S 72
Designer Maurice Fives.
Green fees £20
Catering, changing room/showers, bar, club, trolley and buggy hire, practice facilities, swimming, tennis, gymnasium
Visitors welcome
Societies welcome by prior arrangement
Gold Coast Golf Hotel, Dungarvan, Waterford
(058) 42249

LISMORE GOLF CLUB

Ballyin, Lismore, Waterford
(058) 54026 Fax (058) 53338
Map 1, D9
Off N72, ½ mile W of Lismore
Founded 1965
A parkland course overlooking the Blackwater River.
9 holes, 5790 yards
par 69, S.S.S 67
Designer Eddie Hackett
Green fees £12
Catering, changing room/showers, bar, trolley hire
Visitors welcome weekdays – with restrictions
Societies welcome by prior arrangement

TRAMORE GOLF CLUB

Newtown Hill, Tramore, Waterford
(051) 386170 Fax (051) 390961
Map 1, F9
tragolf@iol.ie
www.tramoregolfclub.com
7 miles S of Waterford, 1 mile from Tramore on Dungarvan coast road
Founded 1894
Sir Henry Cotton rated the dog-leg 17th as one of the best holes in the British Isles, a hole of no great length but considerable challenge. The same could be said of the immensely tight 11th. Gorse and streams add to the difficulties of many holes, such as the brilliant 4th.

18 holes, 6055 metres
par 72, S.S.S 72
Designer H.C. Tippett
Green fees £30
Catering, changing room/showers, bar, club, trolley and buggy hire, shop, practice facilities
Visitors welcome – with restrictions
Handicap certificate required
Societies welcome by prior arrangement
Grand Hotel, Tramore, Waterford
(051) 381414

WATERFORD CASTLE GOLF CLUB

The Island, Ballinakill, Waterford, Waterford
(051) 871633 Fax (051) 871634
Map 1, F9
On Little Island reached by ferry from R683.
Founded 1991
Everything about Waterford Castle is remarkable, from the castle, dating back to the 11th century, to the Des Smyth golf course. Located on an island in the River Suir, it can only be reached by ferry. Five thousand trees have been planted, and it goes without saying that water features strongly.
18 holes, 6231 metres
par 72, S.S.S 73
Designer Des Smyth
Green fees £27
Catering, changing room/showers, bar, club, trolley and buggy hire, driving range, practice facilities
Visitors welcome
Handicap certificate required
Societies welcome by prior arrangement
Waterford Castle, The Island, Waterford, Waterford
(051) 878203

WATERFORD GOLF CLUB

Newrath, Waterford, Waterford
(051) 874182 Fax (051) 853405
Map 1, F9
N9, in northern outskirts of Waterford
Founded 1912
A gentle parkland course, yet one on which scoring is far from easy, with a lovely sweeping, downhill par 4 to finish, leaving pleasant memories in the vistor's mind.
18 holes, 5722 metres
par 71, S.S.S 70
Designer Willie Park, James Braid, J. Hamilton Stutt.
Green fees £22
Catering, changing room/showers, bar, club, trolley and buggy hire, practice facilities
Visitors welcome
Societies welcome by prior arrangement

WATERFORD MUNICIPAL GOLF COURSE

Williamstown, Waterford, Waterford
(051) 853131 **Map 1, F9**
Off R708, 2 miles S of Waterford
Founded 1997
The last full 18-hole course designed by Eddie Hackett before he died in 1996. Despite a minimal construction budget, the course design makes golfers of all abilities think.
18 holes, 6700 yards
par 72, S.S.S 71
Designer Eddie Hackett
Green fees £12
Club and trolley hire
Visitors welcome by prior arrangement
Societies welcome by prior arrangement

WEST WATERFORD GOLF & COUNTRY CLUB

Dungarvan, Waterford
(058) 43216 Fax (058) 44343
Map 1, E9
info@westwaterfordgolf.com
www.westwaterfordgolf.com
Off N25, 4km W of Dungarvan
Founded 1993
Set in rolling parkland against a backdrop of the Comeragh Mountians, Knockmealdowns and the Drum Hills, and with streams affecting play on seven holes, West Waterford is both handsome and testing. Toughest of all is the 459-yard 12th, part of a sequence of holes threatened by the Brickey River.
18 holes, 6802 yards
par 72, S.S.S 74
Designer Eddie Hackett
Green fees £18
Catering, changing room/showers, bar, club, trolley and buggy hire, shop, practice facilities
Visitors welcome
Societies welcome by prior arrangement
Gold Coast Golf Hotel, Dungarvan, Waterford
(058) 42249

CO WESTMEATH

DELVIN CASTLE GOLF CLUB

Clonyn, Delvin, Westmeath
(044) 64315 **Map 1, F6**
Off N52, 1 mile SW of Delvin
Founded 1992
Set in the parkland of a 19th-century castle, and running past a 16th-century ruin.
18 holes, 5818 metres
par 70, S.S.S 68
Designer John Day
Green fees £10
Catering, changing room/showers, bar, club and trolley hire, shop, practice facilities
Visitors welcome

Societies welcome by prior arrangement

GLASSON GOLF HOTEL & COUNTRY CLUB

Glasson, Athlone, Westmeath
(0902) 85120 Fax (0902) 85444
Map 1, E6
info@glassongolf.ie
www.glassongolf.ie
N55, 6 miles N of Athlone
Founded 1993
With Lough Ree providing a glorious backdrop to proceedings – and private moorings are available for those who arrive by boat – Glasson is especially handsome. It is a fine test which builds towards a signature hole at the 15th, on which both tee and green are set out into the Lough.
18 holes, 7120 yards
par 72, S.S.S 74
Designer Christy O'Connor Jnr
Green fees £32
Catering, changing room/showers, bar, accommodation, club, trolley and buggy hire, shop, practice facilities, full hotel and extensive conference facilities
Visitors welcome
Societies welcome by prior arrangement
Glasson Golf Hotel, Glasson, Athlone, Westmeath
(0902) 85120 Fax (0902) 85444

MOATE GOLF CLUB

Aghanargit, Moate, Westmeath
(0902) 85120 Fax (0902) 85444
Map 1, E6
N6, 7 miles E of Athlone
Founded 1900
Recently extended to 18 holes incorporating lakes.
18 holes, 5784 metres
par 72, S.S.S 70
Designer Bobby Browne
Green fees £12
Catering, changing room/showers, bar, trolley hire
Visitors welcome
Societies welcome by prior arrangement

MOUNT TEMPLE GOLF CLUB

Mount Temple, Moate, Westmeath
(0902) 81271 Fax (0902) 81267

Map 1, E6
Off N6, 5 miles E of Athlone
Founded 1991
A parkland course reputed for the excellence of its greens.
18 holes, 6481 yards
par 72, S.S.S 72
Designer Michael Dolan
Green fees £14
Catering, changing room/showers, bar, club, trolley and buggy hire, shop, practice facilities
Visitors welcome weekdays
Societies welcome by prior arrangement

MULLINGAR GOLF CLUB
Belvedere, Mullingar, Westmeath
(044) 48366 Fax (044) 41499
Map 1, E6
N52, 3 miles S of Mullingar
Founded 1894
One of James Braid's later creations, highly respected by the top amateurs who come here annually for the Open Scratch Trophy. Christy O'Connor rated the 189-yard par-3 2nd as one of the best short holes in Ireland. Astonishingly, Braid took only a single day to plan the course.
18 holes, 6468 yards
par 72, S.S.S 71
Designer James Braid
Green fees £20
Catering, changing room/showers, bar, club hire, shop, practice facilities
Visitors welcome
Societies welcome by prior arrangement
Bloomfield House Hotel, Kilbeggan Road, Mullingar, Westmeath
(044) 40894 Fax (044) 43767
bloomfieldhouse@eircom.ie
www.bloomfieldhouse.com

CO WEXFORD

COURTOWN GOLF CLUB
Kiltennel, Gorey, Wexford
(055) 25166 Fax (055) 25553
Map 1, G8
courtown@iol.ie
L31, off N11 at Gorey
Founded 1936
A pleasant (and far cheaper) alternative to the many lavish new courses south of Dublin. This well-wooded, parkland course, near the sea, has an interesting collection of short holes, with water on hand at the 148-metre 18th. Two of the par 5s, the 9th and 12th, exceed 515 metres.
18 holes, 5878 metres
par 71, S.S.S 71
Designer John Harris
Green fees £22
Catering, changing room/showers, bar, club, trolley and buggy hire, shop, practice facilities
Visitors welcome
Societies welcome with prior booking

ENNISCORTHY GOLF CLUB
Knockmarshall, Enniscorthy, Wexford
(054) 33191 Fax (054) 36736
Map 1, F8
N30, 2 miles SW of Enniscorthy
Founded 1908
A lengthy parkland course with good facilities.
18 holes, 6115 metres
par 72, S.S.S 72
Designer Eddie Hackett
Green fees £16
Catering, changing room/showers, bar, club, trolley and buggy hire, shop, driving range, practice facilities
Visitors welcome – with restrictions
Societies welcome by prior arrangement

NEW ROSS GOLF CLUB
Tinneranny, New Ross, Wexford
(051) 421433 Fax (051) 420098
Map 1, F8
R704, 1 mile W of New Ross
Founded 1905
Recently extended to 18 holes by Des Smyth, providing a considerable challenge.
18 holes, 5751 yards
par 71, S.S.S 70
Designer Des Smyth
Green fees £14
Catering, changing room/showers, bar, trolley hire
Visitors welcome
Societies welcome by prior arrangement

ROSSLARE GOLF CLUB
Rosslare Strand, Rosslare, Wexford
(053) 32203 Fax (053) 32263
Map 1, G9
office@rosslaregolf.com
www.iol.ie/~rgolfclb/
6 miles from Rosslare ferry terminal
Founded 1905
On a narrow strip of linksland overlooking the treacherous sandbanks of this part of the Irish Sea coast, Rosslare has long been renowned for its condition, especially its greens. With plenty of natural movement in the ground there is abundant challenge on the approach shot to many greens, some semi-hidden.
18 holes, 6740 yards, par 72, S.S.S 72
Designer F.G. Hawtree, J.H. Taylor, Christy O'Connor, Jnr.
12 holes, 3956 yards, par 46
Green fees £25
Catering, changing room/showers, bar, club, trolley and buggy hire, shop, practice facilities
Visitors welcome
Societies welcome by prior arrangement
Kelly's Resort Hotel, Rosslare Strand, Wexford
(053) 32114

ST HELEN'S BAY GOLF CLUB
St Helen's, Kilrane, Rosslare Harbour, Wexford
(053) 33234 Fax (053) 33803
Map 1, G9
www.sthelensbay.com
Off N25, 2 miles S of Rosslare Harbour
Founded 1993
Situated in the dunes overlooking the beach, a links course might be predicted. In fact, only the last few holes are of that kind, most of the rest of the course running through parkland with trees and water. The short holes are particularly good, with the seaside 17th the pick.
18 holes, 6091 metres
par 72, S.S.S 72
Designer Philip Walton
Green fees £22
Catering, changing room/showers, bar, club, trolley and buggy hire, practice facilities
Visitors welcome
Societies welcome by prior arrangement
Kelly's Resort Hotel, Rosslare Strand, Wexford
(053) 32114

TARA GLEN GOLF CLUB
Ballymoney, Gorey, Wexford
(055) 25413 Fax (055) 25612
Map 1, G8
4 miles E of Gorey
Founded 1993
A parkland course.
9 holes, 5826 metres
par 72, S.S.S 70
Green fees £14
Bar
Visitors welcome
Societies welcome by prior arrangement

WEXFORD GOLF CLUB
Mulgannon, Wexford, Wexford
(053) 42238 **Map 1, G9**
In Wexford, alongside Talbot Hotel
Founded 1960
A parkland course with views

towards the sea.
18 holes, 6306 yards
par 72, S.S.S 71
Designer J. Hamilton Stutt, Des Smyth
Green fees £18
Catering, changing room/showers, bar, club, trolley and buggy hire, practice facilities
Visitors welcome
Societies welcome by prior arrangement

CO WICKLOW

ARKLOW GOLF CLUB

Abbeylands, Arklow, Wicklow
☎ (0402) 32492 Fax (0402) 32971
Map 1, G8
N11, ½ mile S of Arklow
Founded 1927
A links course with a number of sea inlets, remarkably little known for such an interesting course.
18 holes, 5770 yards
par 69, S.S.S 67
Designer Eddie Hackett
Green fees £18
Catering, changing room/showers, bar, club, trolley and buggy hire, driving range, practice facilities
Visitors welcome weekdays
Societies welcome by prior arrangement

BALTINGLASS GOLF CLUB

Baltinglass, Wicklow
☎ (0508) 81350 Fax (0508) 81350
Map 1, F7
½ mile, N of Baltinglass
Founded 1928
A parkland course on the banks of the River Slaney.
9 holes, 6070 yards
par 68, S.S.S 69
Green fees £10
Catering, changing room/showers, bar, trolley hire
Visitors welcome
Societies welcome by prior arrangement

BLAINROE GOLF CLUB

Blainroe, Wicklow
☎ (0404) 68168 Fax (0404) 69369
Map 1, G7
R750, 2½ miles S of Wicklow
Founded 1978
A hilly parkland course overlooking the sea with a number of tough holes such as the 228-yard par-3 15th and 458-yard 16th.
18 holes, 6175 metres
S.S.S 72
Designer Hawtree
Green fees £30
Catering, changing room/showers, bar, club and trolley hire, shop, practice facilities
Visitors welcome
Societies welcome by prior arrangement

BRAY GOLF CLUB

Ravenswell Road, Bray, Wicklow
☎ (01) 286 2484 Fax (01) 286 2484
Map 1, G7
Off N29 from Dublin
Founded 1897
A parkland course.
9 holes, 5671 metres
par 70, S.S.S 70
Green fees £17
Catering, changing room/showers, bar, club and trolley hire, shop
Visitors welcome weekdays – with restrictions
Societies welcome by prior arrangement

CHARLESLAND GOLF & COUNTRY CLUB HOTEL

Charlesland, Greystones, Wicklow
☎ (01) 287 4350 Fax (01) 287 4360
Map 1, G7
teetimes@charlesland.com
www.charlesland.com
S of Greystones, 22 miles from Dublin via N11
Founded 1992
Parkland by the sea, rather than pure links, there are good views to sea and inland towards the Sugarloaf Mountains. Good value for a course so handy for Dublin.
18 holes, 6800 yards
par 72, S.S.S 72
Designer Eddie Hackett
Green fees £25
Catering, changing room/showers, bar, accommodation, club, trolley and buggy hire, shop, driving range, practice facilities, full hotel, conference, function and wedding facilities
Visitors welcome
Societies welcome by prior arrangement
🏨 Charlesland Golf and Country Club Hotel, Charlesland, Greystones, Wicklow
☎ (01) 2878200

COOLLATTIN GOLF CLUB

Coollattin, Shillelagh, Wicklow
☎ (055) 29125 Fax (055) 29125
Map 1, G8
R749, 4 miles SW of Tinahely
Founded 1960
A parkland course extended to 18 holes by Peter McEvoy.
18 holes, 6148 yards
par 70, S.S.S 69
Designer Peter McEvoy
Green fees £20
Catering, changing room/showers, bar, club, trolley and buggy hire, shop, practice facilities
Visitors welcome
Societies welcome by prior arrangement

DELGANY GOLF CLUB

Delgany, Wicklow
☎ (01) 287 4697 Fax (01) 287 3977
Map 1, G7
delganygolf@sircomm.net
Off N11 near Delgany
Founded 1908
A wonderful old course, bouncing around on undulating ground amidst magnificent scenery.
18 holes, 5480 metres
par 69, S.S.S 68
Designer Harry Vardon
Green fees £30
Catering, changing room/showers, bar, club, trolley and buggy hire, shop, practice facilities
Visitors welcome – with restrictions
Handicap certificate required – limit: 24 men, 36 women
Societies welcome by prior arrangement
🏨 Glenview Hotel, Delgany, Wicklow
☎ (01) 287 3399

DJOUCE MOUNTAIN GOLF CLUB

Roundwood, Wicklow
☎ (01) 281 8585 Fax (01) 281 8585
Map 1, G7
Off N11, 15 miles NW of Wicklow
Founded 1997
A 9-hole course in the foothills of the Wicklow Mountains.
9 holes, 5636 metres
par 71, S.S.S 69
Designer Eddie Hackett
Green fees £10
Visitors welcome
Societies welcome by prior arrangement

DRUID'S GLEN GOLF CLUB

Newtownmountkennedy, Wicklow
☎ (01) 287 3600 Fax (01) 287 3699
Map 1, G7
N11, 20 miles S of Dublin
Founded 1995
Pat Ruddy and Tom Craddock were instructed to design 'the most beautiful parkland course in Ireland, and never mind the expense.' The jury is out on whether or not it is the most beautiful, but it is certainly expensive. Colin Montgomerie won two of the four Irish Opens played there.
18 holes, 7026 yards
par 71, S.S.S 74
Designer Tom Craddock, Pat Ruddy

Green fees £85
Catering, changing room/showers, bar, club, trolley and buggy hire, shop, driving range, practice facilities
Visitors welcome
Societies welcome by prior arrangement

THE EUROPEAN CLUB

Brittas Bay, Wicklow, Wicklow
(0404) 47415 Fax (0404) 47449
Map 1, G8
info@theeuropeanclub.com
www.theeuropeanclub.com
Off N11, 25 miles S of Dublin
Founded 1989
See Top 50 Courses, page 19
18 holes, 7209 yards
par 71, S.S.S 72
Designer Pat Ruddy
Green fees £80
Catering, changing room/showers, club, trolley and buggy hire, shop, practice facilities, 2 extra holes
Visitors welcome – advisable to pre-book
Societies welcome by prior arrangement

GLEN OF THE DOWNS GOLF CLUB

Coolnaskeagh, Delgany, Wicklow
(01) 2876240 Fax (01) 2870063
Map 1, G7
Off N11, 10 miles S of Bray
Founded 1998
An upland course with expansive views to the Wicklow Mountains as well as over the Irish Sea. Not as over-designed as some of the more recent Irish courses, the natural contours being used to good effect.
18 holes, 6443 yards
par 71, S.S.S 71
Designer Peter McEvoy
Green fees £30
Catering, changing room/showers, bar, club, trolley and buggy hire, shop, practice facilities
Visitors welcome – with restrictions
Societies welcome by prior arrangement

GLENMALURE GOLF CLUB

Greenane, Rathdrum, Wicklow
(0404) 46679 Fax (0404) 46783
Map 1, G7
R759, 3 miles W of Rathdrum
Founded 1993
A moorland course in the heart of the beautiful Wicklow Mountains.
18 holes, 5237 metres
par 71, S.S.S 66
Designer Pat Suttle, Peter McEvoy
Green fees £15
Catering, changing room/showers, bar, club and trolley hire
Visitors welcome
Societies welcome by prior arrangement

GREYSTONES GOLF CLUB

Whitshed Road, Greystones, Wicklow
(01) 2874136 Fax (01) 2873749
Map 1, G7
secretary@greystonesgc.com
www.greystonesgc.com
20 miles S of Dublin on N/M11
Founded 1895
A short parkland course laid out with two completely separate halves, with the 13th, 14th and 17th played across water.
18 holes, 5322 metres
par 69, S.S.S 68
Designer Patrick Merrigan
Green fees £30
Catering, changing room/showers, bar, club, trolley and buggy hire, shop, practice facilities
Visitors welcome weekdays – with restrictions
Societies welcome by prior arrangement
La Touche Hotel, Greystones, Wicklow
(01) 2874401

KILCOOLE GOLF CLUB

Kilcoole, Wicklow
(01) 287 2066 Fax (01) 287 1803
Map 1, G7
Off N11, S of Kilcoole on Newcastle road
Founded 1992
A parkland course close to the sea.
9 holes, 5506 metres
par 70, S.S.S 69
Designer Brian Williams
Green fees £15
Catering, changing room/showers, trolley hire
Visitors welcome weekdays – with restrictions
Societies welcome by prior arrangement

OLD CONNA GOLF CLUB

Ferndale Road, Bray, Wicklow
(01) 2826055 Fax (01) 2825611
Map 1, G7
info@oldconna.com
2 miles from Bray
Founded 1987
A parkland course enjoying fine mountain views and glimpses of the Irish Sea.
18 holes, 6553 yards
par 72, S.S.S 72
Designer Eddie Hackett
Green fees £35
Catering, changing room/showers, bar, club, trolley and buggy hire, shop, practice facilities
Visitors welcome – with restrictions
Societies welcome by prior arrangement
Glenview Hotel, Delgany, Wicklow
(01) 287 3399

POWERSCOURT GOLF CLUB

Powerscourt Estate, Enniskerry, Wicklow
(01) 204 6033 Fax (01) 276 1303
Map 1, G7
golfclub@powerscourt.ie
www.powerscourt.ie
Off N11, 12 miles S of Dublin
Founded 1996
Powerscourt is one of Ireland's great estates, its house and gardens now one of the country's top visitor attractions. In its parkland, Peter McEvoy has created an appropriately grand course, made the more spectacular by its backdrop of Sugar Loaf Mountain. The par-3 16th evokes the 12th at Augusta.
18 holes, 6421 metres
par 72, S.S.S 74
Designer Peter McEvoy
Green fees £75
Catering, changing room/showers, bar, accommodation, club, trolley and buggy hire, shop, driving range, practice facilities, luxury apartments available on site
Visitors welcome – with restrictions
Handicap certificate required – limit: 28 men, 40 women
Societies welcome by prior arrangement
Powerscourt Golf Club Apartments, Enniskerry, Wicklow
(01) 204 6033 Fax (01) 276 1303
golfclub@powerscourt.ie
www.powerscourt.ie

RATHSALLAGH HOUSE GOLF & COUNTRY CLUB

Dunlavin, Wicklow
(045) 403316 Fax (045) 403295
Map 1, F7
info@rathsallagh.com
www.rathsallagh.com
From Dublin, M7/M9 towards Carlow, left at exit for Dunlavin, Rathsallagh (signposted) 3 miles from Dunlavin
Founded 1995
In the heart of Irish racing country, close to the Wicklow Mountains, Rathsallagh House was voted Irish Country House of the Year for 2000. Its golf course, although clearly of championship standard, nevertheless manages to capture the

relaxed warmth of the hotel, blending perfectly with the charm of its surroundings.
18 holes, 6916 yards
par 72, S.S.S 72
Designer Christy O'Connor Jnr, Peter McEvoy
Green fees £45
Catering, changing room/showers, bar, accommodation, club, trolley and buggy hire, shop, driving range, practice facilities, full hotel, function and conference facilities, field sports
Visitors welcome
Societies welcome by prior arrangement
Rathsallagh House Golf and Country Club, Dunlavin, Wicklow
(045) 403112

ROUNDWOOD GOLF CLUB

Newtownmountkennedy, Wicklow
(01) 281 8488 Fax (01) 284 3642
Map 1, G7
Off R765, off N11, 2½ miles W of Newtownmountkennedy
Founded 1995
A mixture of heathland and parkland with woods and lakes. There are fine views of the Wicklow Mountains and to the sea.
18 holes, 6685 yards
par 72, S.S.S 72
Green fees £22.50
Changing room/showers, bar, club, trolley and buggy hire, practice facilities
Visitors welcome
Societies welcome by prior arrangement

TULFARRIS GOLF & COUNTRY CLUB

Blessington Lakes, Wicklow
(045) 867644 Fax (045) 867561
Map 1, G7
Off N81, 5 miles S of Blessington
Founded 1987
A stunning location on the shores of Blessington Lake, already hailed as Merrigan's finest design to date.
18 holes, 7116 yards
par 72, S.S.S 74
Designer Patrick Merrigan
Green fees £50
Catering, changing room/showers, bar, club, trolley and buggy hire, driving range, practice facilities
Visitors welcome
Societies welcome by prior arrangement
Tulfarris House, Blessington, Wicklow
(045) 867555

WICKLOW GOLF CLUB

Dunbur Road, Wicklow, Wicklow
(0404) 67379 **Map 1, G7**
Off R750, S of Wicklow on the coast
Founded 1904
A parkland course on exposed high ground overlooking the sea.
18 holes, 5695 metres
par 71, S.S.S 70
Designer Tom Craddock, Pat Ruddy
Green fees £20
Catering, changing room/showers, bar, club and trolley hire, shop
Visitors welcome weekdays
Societies welcome by prior arrangement

WOODENBRIDGE GOLF CLUB

Woodenbridge, Arklow, Wicklow
(0402) 35202 Fax (0402) 35202
Map 1, G8
Off R747, 4 miles NW of Arklow
Founded 1884
A parkland course in pretty country on the road to the famous Vale of Avoca. The River Avoca is an occasional threat, and the surrounding woodlands add beauty.
18 holes, 6400 yards
par 71, S.S.S 70
Designer Patrick Merrigan
Green fees £27
Catering, changing room/showers, bar, trolley hire, practice facilities
Visitors welcome – with restrictions
Societies welcome by prior arrangement

SCOTLAND

There are some who challenge Scotland's claim to its being the 'home of golf'. It is quite possible that the game, as we know it, began on the frozen waterways of the Netherlands or amongst the Indians of North America. Scottish golfers, however, established the ground rules. The principles of the ancient Scottish game prevail throughout the world today, with the Royal & Ancient and USGA in general, but not quite universal, agreement about how the game should be conducted. Historians are, at least, agreed that a game resembling golf was played in Scotland as far back as the Middle Ages, with Dornoch, St Andrews and Montrose amongst those documented in ancient history.

We have the Scots to thank for exporting the game to every corner of the world. Scottish merchants established a course in Calcutta in 1829, the first outside the British Isles. Two one-time Dunfermline schoolmates took golf across the Atlantic. Robert Lockhart brought clubs and balls from Scotland when he made a visit to his homeland, giving them to his friend John Reid, who was instrumental in the establishment of the first American club at Yonkers, New York, in 1888. Charles Blair Macdonald, America's first great amateur golfer, had learned to play while a student at St Andrews. He was the first major American golf architect, embracing Scottish design features at the National Golf Links on Long Island, and introducing golf to the mid-west, establishing the first 18-hole course in the USA at Chicago. From Dornoch the young Donald Ross emigrated to the USA, taking with him a sound understanding of the subtlety of the best golf architecture. His influence on the development of American course design is felt even today.

Within living memory, Scottish green fees were second to none in terms of value for money. Today, unfortunately, they reflect the tourism potential of their heritage and location. Helicopter pads and landing strips have put Macrihanish, Nairn, Cruden Bay and Islay within easy reach of golfers from all over the world, while even the most remote club with a simple 9-hole course has now recognized that it can obtain in a single visit what it recently charged for a whole week. The Open Championship venues at Carnoustie, Muirfield, Royal Troon, Turnberry and St Andrews are surrounded by scores of other first-rate courses, so it is hardly surprising that green fees more or less anywhere on the coasts of Angus, Ayrshire, East Lothian and Fife will be substantial.

Scotland is not just about traditional seaside courses. There are at least as many fine inland courses with Gleneagles, Blairgowrie, Dalmahoy, Elgin, Lanark and Ladybank setting a formidable standard, to name but a few. Everywhere the scenery is magnificent. Even within the city boundaries of Glasgow and Edinburgh there are superb views from their many admirable courses, although it should be noted that a number of clubs in both cities are strictly private, on which the only visitors permitted are those who are members' guests.

ABERDEENSHIRE

ABOYNE GOLF CLUB

Formaston Park, Aboyne,
Aberdeenshire AB34 5HP
✆ 013398 87078 Fax 013398 87078
Map 14, G9
Off A93, E of Aboyne
Founded 1883
A course in two halves, part parkland, part hilly. The finish is unusual – two par 3s.
18 holes, 5910 yards
par 69, S.S.S 68
Green fees £19
Catering, changing room/showers, bar, trolley hire, shop, practice facilities
Visitors welcome
Societies welcome by prior arrangement

ALFORD GOLF CLUB

Montgarrie Road, Alford,
Aberdeenshire AB33 8AE
✆ 019755 62178 Fax 019755 62178
Map 14, G9
www.golfalford.co.uk
A944, 25 miles W of Aberdeen
A parkland course divided by a narrow-gauge railway.
18 holes, 5843 yards
par 69, S.S.S 66
Green fees £13
Catering, changing room/showers, bar, trolley hire, shop, practice facilities
Visitors welcome
Societies welcome by prior arrangement

AUCHENBLAE GOLF CLUB

Auchenblae, Laurencekirk,
Aberdeenshire AB30 1BU
✆ 01561 320331 **Map 14, G10**
½ mile NE of Auchenblae
Founded 1894
A scenic public course.
9 holes, 2208 yards
par 33, S.S.S 32
Green fees £6
Trolley hire
Visitors welcome
Societies welcome by prior arrangement

AUCHMILL GOLF CLUB

Bonnyview Road, West Heatheryfold, Aberdeen AB2 7FQ
✆ 01224 71214 **Map 14, H9**
A96
Founded 1975
A very tough proposition by public golf standards with narrow fairways and unforgiving rough.
18 holes, 5833 yards
par 70, S.S.S 68
Designer Brian Huggett, Neil Coles
Green fees £6.95
Catering, changing room/showers, bar, practice facilities
Visitors welcome
Societies welcome by prior arrangement

BALLATER GOLF CLUB

Victoria Road, Ballater,
Aberdeenshire AB35 5QX
✆ 013397 55567 Fax 013397 55057
Map 14, F9
sec@ballatergolfclub.co.uk
www.ballatergolfclub.co.uk
A93, 42 miles W of Aberdeen
Founded 1892
A charming heathland course on the banks of the Dee, only 11 miles from Balmoral, surrounded by the most wonderful mountain scenery.
18 holes, 6112 yards
par 70, S.S.S 69
Green fees £19
Catering, changing room/showers, bar, club, trolley and buggy hire, shop, practice facilities, conference facilities, bowling and tennis, Fishing can be arranged
Visitors welcome – booking advisable

Societies welcome by prior arrangement
Westbank House, Albert Road, Ballater, Aberdeenshire
01339 55305

BALNAGASK GOLF COURSE

St Fitticks Road, Aberdeen, Aberdeenshire
01224 871286 Fax 01224 873418
Map 14, H9
2 miles E of Aberdeen
Founded 1955
A public links course, played over by the Nigg Bay Club.
18 holes, 5986 yards
par 70, S.S.S 69
Green fees £9
Club hire
Visitors welcome
Societies welcome by prior arrangement

BANCHORY GOLF CLUB

Kinneskie, Banchory, Aberdeenshire AB31 5TA
01330 822365 Fax 01330 822491
Map 14, G9
Off A93, at W end of High Street
Founded 1904
A parkland course in lovely scenery beside the River Dee.
18 holes, 5775 yards
par 69, S.S.S 68
Green fees £18
Catering, changing room/showers, bar, trolley hire, shop, practice facilities
Visitors welcome weekdays except Thursdays
Societies welcome weekdays by prior arrangement

BRAEMAR GOLF CLUB

Cluniebank Road, Braemar, Aberdeenshire AB35 5XX
013397 41618 **Map 14, F10**
½ mile from Braemar
Founded 1902
Said to be the highest 18-hole course in Scotland, but in fact it is relatively easy walking beside the River Clunie. The 2nd plays alongside the river and is most unforgiving.
18 holes, 4916 yards
par 65, S.S.S 64
Designer Joe Anderson
Green fees £16
Catering, changing room/showers, bar, trolley hire
Visitors welcome
Societies welcome by prior arrangement

CRUDEN BAY GOLF CLUB

Aulton Road, Cruden Bay, Peterhead, Aberdeenshire AB42 0NN
01779 812285 Fax 01779 812945
Map 14, H8
cbaygc@aol.com
www.crudenbaygolfclub.co.uk
Off A90, 22 miles NE of Aberdeen
Founded 1899
See Top 50 Courses, page 18
Main Course: 18 holes, 6395 yards, par 70, S.S.S 72
Designer Tom Simpson
St Olaf Course: 9 holes, 4710 yards, par 64, S.S.S 62
Green fees £50
Catering, changing room/showers, bar, club, trolley and buggy hire, shop, driving range, practice facilities
Visitors welcome – subject to restrictions
Handicap certificate required
Societies welcome by prior arrangement
Kilmarnock Arms Hotel, Bridge Street, Cruden Bay, Peterhead, Aberdeenshire AB42 0HD
01779 812213

CULLEN GOLF CLUB

The Links, Cullen, Buckie, Aberdeenshire AB56 4WB
01542 840174 Fax 01548 841977
Map 14, G7
Off A98, ½ mile W of Cullen
Founded 1879
A short links, but no easy task with rocks and the beach threatening on several holes. The 3rd, 7th and 11th are all par 3s over 230 yards long.
18 holes, 4610 yards
par 63, S.S.S 62
Designer Tom Morris
Green fees £12
Catering, changing room/showers, bar, practice facilities
Visitors welcome
Societies welcome by prior arrangement

DEESIDE GOLF CLUB

Bieldside, Aberdeen AB15 9DL
01224 869457 Fax 01224 869457
Map 14, F9
A93, 3 miles W of Aberdeen
Founded 1903
Two riverside courses with a stream very much in play on many holes on the main course.
18 holes, 6264 yards, par 71, S.S.S 70
9 holes, 3316 yards, S.S.S 36
Green fees £25
Catering, changing room/showers, bar, trolley and buggy hire, shop, practice facilities
Visitors welcome
Handicap certificate required
Societies welcome by prior arrangement

DUFF HOUSE ROYAL GOLF CLUB

The Barnyards, Banff, Aberdeenshire AB45 3SX
01261 812062 Fax 01261 812224
Map 14, G8
A98, in centre of Banff
Founded 1910
A fascinating, beautifully maintained course, parkland although almost on the sea, short on paper, but with three par 4s at 460 yards or more, and a 242-yard par 3. The typical Mackenzie greens are big but trickily contoured, and the River Deveron adds beauty and danger on several holes.
18 holes, 6161 yards
par 68, S.S.S 70
Designer James Braid, Alister Mackenzie
Green fees £24
Catering, changing room/showers, bar, trolley and buggy hire, shop, practice facilities
Visitors welcome with restrictions
Societies welcome by prior arrangement

DUNECHT HOUSE

Dunecht, Skene, Aberdeenshire AB3 7AX
01330 860223 **Map 14, H9**
A944, 12 miles W of Aberdeen
Founded 1925
A private wooded course.
9 holes, 3135 yards
S.S.S 70
Green fees £8
Visitors welcome only as members' guest.

FRASERBURGH GOLF CLUB

Philorth Road, Fraserburgh, Aberdeenshire AB4 8TL
01346 516616 Fax 01346 516616
Map 14, H7
1 mile SE of Fraserburgh
Founded 1881
A true links with serious sand hills. The course opens and closes with substantial par 4s.
Corbie Course: 18 holes, 6278 yards, par 70, S.S.S 70
Designer James Braid
Rosehill Course: 9 holes, 2400 yards, par 66, S.S.S 66
Green fees £15
Catering, changing room/showers, bar, trolley hire, shop, practice facilities
Visitors welcome
Societies welcome by prior arrangement

HAZLEHEAD GOLF CLUB

Hazlehead Park, Aberdeen
AB15 8DD
01224 321830 **Map 14, H9**
Off A944, 4 miles W of Aberdeen
Founded 1927
The No. 1 course can be unforgiving with its well-wooded fairways and good length. No. 2 is partially wooded, while the 9 hole course is quite open.
No. 1 Course: 18 holes, 6204 yards, par 71, S.S.S 70
No. 2 Course: 18 holes, 5801 yards, par 67, S.S.S 68
No. 3 Course: 9 holes, 5540 yards, par 70, S.S.S 68
Green fees £9
Catering, changing room/showers, bar, trolley and buggy hire, shop, practice facilities
Visitors welcome
Societies welcome by prior arrangement

HUNTLY GOLF CLUB

Cooper Park, Huntly, Aberdeenshire
AB54 4SH
01466 792360 Fax 01466 792643
Map 14, G8
www.huntlygc.com
A96, N of Huntly
Founded 1892
There are many drive-and-pitch holes, rewarding accurate approach work. Only the 8th exceeds 400 yards.
18 holes, 5933 yards
par 67, S.S.S 66
Green fees £12
Catering, changing room/showers, bar, trolley hire, shop, practice facilities
Visitors welcome
Societies welcome by prior arrangement

INSCH GOLF CLUB

Golf Terrace, Insch, Aberdeenshire
AB52 6JY
01464 820363 Fax 01464 820363
Map 14, G8
inschgolf@euphony.net
Off A96 in village of Insch
Founded 1906
With panoramic views of the beautiful surrounding hills and the village of Insch, this parkland course has recently been expanded to 18 holes. With natural woodland, water hazards, and rolling greens, the golf is entertaining.
18 holes, 5414 yards
par 69, S.S.S 66
Green fees £16
Catering, changing room/showers, bar, trolley and buggy hire, practice facilities
Visitors welcome, with restrictions
Societies welcome by prior arrangement
Commercial Hotel, Commercial Street, Insch, Aberdeenshire
01464 820209

INVERALLOCHY GOLF CLUB

Whitelink, Inverallochy, Fraserburgh, Aberdeenshire AB43 8XY
01346 582000 **Map 14, H7**
Off A92, 4 miles E of Fraserburgh
Running alongside the beach, the course plays somewhat longer than its card length, because of no fewer than 8 par 3s.
18 holes, 5300 yards
par 66, S.S.S 66
Green fees £12
Changing room/showers, bar, practice facilities
Visitors welcome
Societies welcome by prior arrangement

INVERURIE GOLF CLUB

Backhall Road, Inverurie, Aberdeenshire AB51 5JB
01467 620193 Fax 01467 621051
Map 14, G9
administrator@inveruriegc.co.uk
www.inveruriegc.co.uk
Off A96, 16 miles from Aberdeen
Founded 1923
The front nine is relatively open, whereas the back nine runs through gorse and woodland, with the 14th, 15th and 16th wrecking many promising cards.
18 holes, 5711 yards
par 69, S.S.S 68
Green fees £14
Catering, changing room/showers, bar, club and trolley hire, shop, practice facilities
Visitors welcome, with restrictions
Societies welcome by prior arrangement
Kintore Arms Hotel, 83 High Street, Inverurie, Aberdeenshire AB51 3QJ
01467 621367 Fax 01467 625620

KEITH GOLF CLUB

Fife Park, Keith, Aberdeenshire
AB55 5DF
01542 882469 Fax 01542 888176
Map 14, F8
B9014, off A96, W side of Keith
Founded 1963
The 232-yard 7th hole is probably the most difficult on the course. Out of bounds threatens on the left, to which the hole leans. Lovely views over surrounding countryside.
18 holes, 5802 yards
par 69, S.S.S 68
Green fees £13
Changing room/showers, trolley hire
Visitors welcome
Societies welcome by prior arrangement

KEMNAY GOLF CLUB

Monymusk Road, Kemnay, Aberdeenshire AB51 5RA
01467 643746 Fax 01467 643746
Map 14, G9
B994, off A96
Founded 1908
As so often in Scotland, the views threaten to distract from the golfing task in hand, which in particular is to avoid the stream which crosses four holes.
18 holes, 6342 yards
par 71, S.S.S 71
Green fees £16
Catering, changing room/showers, bar, trolley and buggy hire, shop
Visitors welcome
Societies welcome by prior arrangement

KING'S LINKS GOLF CLUB

Golf Road, King's Links, Aberdeen, Aberdeenshire AB24 5QB
01224 632269 **Map 14, H9**
1 mile N of Aberdeen
A testing links course with no shelter from the wind. The greens can play very fast.
18 holes, 6384 yards
par 72, S.S.S 71
Green fees £9.50
Changing room/showers
Visitors welcome
Societies welcome by prior arrangement

KINTORE GOLF CLUB

Balbithan Road, Kintore, Aberdeenshire AB51 0UR
01467 632631 Fax 01467 632631
Map 14, H9
A96, 16 miles NW of Aberdeen
Founded 1911
A mixture of woodland and wilder moorland, with splendid views across the surrounding Aberdeenshire countryside and River Don Valley.
18 holes, 6019 yards
par 70, S.S.S 69
Green fees £13
Catering, changing room/showers, bar, club, trolley and buggy hire, practice facilities
Visitors welcome
Societies welcome by prior arrangement

LONGSIDE GOLF CLUB

West End, Longside, Peterhead, Aberdeenshire AB42 4XJ
01779 821549 **Map 14, H8**

A590, 5 miles W of Peterhead
Recently extended to 18 holes, a relatively short and flat parkland course.
18 holes, 5215 yards
par 66, S.S.S 66
Green fees £12
Catering, changing room/showers, bar
Visitors welcome restricted weekends
Societies welcome by prior arrangement

McDONALD GOLF CLUB

Hospital Road, Ellon, Aberdeenshire AB41 9AW
☎ 01358 722891 Fax 01358 720001
Map 14, H8
mcdonald.golf@virgin.net
http:
A948 (off A90) from Ellon towards Auchnagatt
Founded 1927
A well-wooded parkland course with streams and a pond.
18 holes, 5991 yards
par 70, S.S.S 70
Green fees £14
Catering, changing room/showers, bar, trolley hire, shop, practice facilities
Visitors welcome, with restrictions
Societies welcome by prior arrangement

MELDRUM HOUSE GOLF CLUB

Meldrum House Estate, Oldmeldrum, Aberdeenshire AB51 0AE
☎ 01651 873553 Fax 01651 873635VH9 **Map 14, H9**
www.meldrumhouse.co.uk
A947, 11 miles N of Aberdeen
Founded 1998
An impressive new course which can boast past Open Champion, Paul Lawrie, as its attached professional. Water features prominently in the design, with a brief respite only on the back nine.
18 holes, 6379 yards
par 70, S.S.S 72
Designer Graeme Webster
Green fees £35
Catering, changing room/showers, bar, accommodation, club, trolley and buggy hire, shop, driving range, practice facilities
Visitors welcome only as members' guests, or as hotel resident.
Societies welcome by prior arrangement
🏨 Meldrum House Hotel, Oldmeldrum, Aberdeenshire
☎ 01651 872294 Fax 01651 872464

MURCAR GOLF CLUB

Bridge of Don, Aberdeen AB23 8BD
☎ 01224 704354 Fax 01224 704354
Map 14, H9
Off A90, 5 miles N of Aberdeen
Founded 1909
The increased world-wide awareness of Royal Aberdeen has brought with it recognition of the considerable golfing merits of its immediate neighbour, Murcar. It has similarly narrow fairways running through the dunes and the same fine views of Aberdeen. The most challenging hole is the undulating 439-yard par 4 4th.
Murcar Course: 18 holes, 6287 yards, par 71, S.S.S 71
Designer A. Simpson
Strabathie Course: 9 holes, 5392 yards, par 70, S.S.S 67
Green fees £28
Catering, changing room/showers, bar, trolley hire, shop, practice facilities
Visitors welcome, with restrictions
Handicap certificate required
Societies welcome by prior arrangement

NEWBURGH-ON-YTHAN GOLF CLUB

Beach Road, Newburgh, Aberdeenshire AB41 6BE
☎ 01358 789084 Fax 01358 789956VH9
secretary@newburgh-on-ythan.co.uk
www.newburgh-onythan.co.uk
12 miles N of Aberdeen on the coast
Founded 1888
Little-known links course alongside a bird sanctuary.
18 holes, 6162 yards
par 72, S.S.S 71
Designer McAndrew & Greens of Scotland
Green fees £16
Catering, changing room/showers, bar, club and trolley hire, shop, practice facilities, tennis, bird watching
Visitors welcome, with restrictions
Societies welcome by prior arrangement
🏨 Lady Arms Hotel, Main Street, Newburgh, Aberdeenshire
☎ 01358 789444

NEWMACHAR GOLF CLUB

Swailend, Newmachar, Aberdeen, Aberdeenshire AB21 7UU
☎ 01651 863002 Fax 01651 863055
Map 14, H9
newmachargolfclub@compuserve.com
www.newmachargolfclub.co.uk
A947 between Dyce and Newmachar
Founded 1989
It was while he was attached to Newmachar that Paul Lawrie triumphed in the 1999 Open at Carnoustie. The Hawkshill Course is one of the toughest in the region, with water threatening on seven holes, and abundant pine and birch. Rolling country gives the gentler Swailend Course a different feel.
Hawkshill Course: 18 holes, 6623 yards, par 72, S.S.S 74
Swailend Course: 18 holes, 6388 yards, par 72, S.S.S 71
Designer Dave Thomas
Green fees £30
Catering, changing room/showers, bar, club, trolley and buggy hire, driving range, practice facilities, range open to general public
Visitors welcome
Handicap certificate required
Societies welcome by prior arrangement
🏨 Dunavon House Hotel, Victoria Street, Dyce, Aberdeenshire
☎ 01224 722483

OLDMELDRUM GOLF CLUB

Kirk Brae, Oldmeldrum, Aberdeenshire AB51 0DJ
☎ 01651 873555 Fax 01651 873555
Map 14, H9
www.oldmeldrumgolf.freeserve.co.uk
A947, 17 miles N of Aberdeen
Founded 1885
The 'Groaner Stone', dating back to the days of Robert the Bruce, catches the eye on the 14th hole of this parkland course, but it will be the water threatening the par-3 11th which may grab the attention more alarmingly.
18 holes, 5988 yards
par 70, S.S.S 69
Green fees £14
Catering, changing room/showers, bar, club, trolley and buggy hire, shop, practice facilities
Visitors welcome by prior arrangement
Handicap certificate required
Societies welcome by prior arrangement
🏨 Meldrum Arms Hotel, The Square, Oldmeldrum, Aberdeenshire AB51 ODS
☎ 01651 872238

PETERCULTER GOLF CLUB

Oldtown, Burnside Road, Peterculter, Aberdeenshire AB14 0LN
☎ 01224 735245 Fax 01224 735580
Map 14, H9
www.petercultergolfclub.co.uk

A93, 8 miles W of Aberdeen
Founded 1989
A course whose many difficulties are counter-balanced by the splendid views up the Dee Valley and the abundance of wildlife.
18 holes, 5924 yards
par 68, S.S.S 69
Green fees £12
Visitors welcome
Societies welcome by prior arrangement

PETERHEAD GOLF CLUB

Craigewan Links, Peterhead, Aberdeenshire AB42 1LT
✆ 01779 472149 Fax 01779 480725
Map 14, H8
Off A952, N of town
Founded 1841
A classic links course which has so far eluded the main mass of travelling golfers. Park and Braid utilised the natural features to create quite a testing course, especially in a stiff breeze. Characteristic features include long carries from a number of tees, notably on the 11th, 12th and 13th.
Old Course: 18 holes, 6173 yards, par 70, S.S.S 71
Designer Willie Park, James Braid
New Course: 9 holes, 2237 yards, par 62, S.S.S 62
Green fees £16
Catering, changing room/showers, bar, trolley hire, practice facilities
Visitors welcome
Societies welcome by prior arrangement

PORTLETHEN GOLF CLUB

Badentoy Road, Portlethen, Aberdeen AB12 4YA
✆ 01224 782571 Fax 01224 781090
Map 14, H9
info@portlethengc.fsnet.co.uk
Off A90, 6 miles S of Aberdeen
Founded 1980
The longest course in the area, with a good mixture of different kinds of hole, from the charming par-3 5th over a pond to a brute of a finishing hole.
18 holes, 6670 yards
par 72, S.S.S 72
Designer Donald Steel
Green fees £15
Catering, changing room/showers, bar, trolley and buggy hire, shop, practice facilities, conference room
Visitors welcome – not Saturdays
Societies welcome by prior arrangement
🏨 Travel Inn, Mains of Balquarn, Portlethen, Aberdeen, Aberdeenshire
✆ 01224 783856

ROSEHEARTY GOLF CLUB

c/o Mason's Arms, Rosehearty, Fraserburgh, Aberdeenshire AB43 7JJ
✆ 01346 571250 **Map 14, H7**
(B9031) 4 miles W of Fraserburgh
A short course, but a genuine links, nonetheless.
9 holes, 2197 yards
S.S.S 62
Green fees £7
Visitors welcome
Societies welcome by prior arrangement

ROTHES GOLF CLUB

Blackhall, Rothes, Aberlour, Aberdeenshire AB38 7AN
✆ 01340 831443 Fax 01340 831443
Map 14, F8
A941, 9 miles S of Elgin
Founded 1990
From the fairways of this recently constructed course there are brilliant views of the River Spey and Rothes Castle, in the heart of malt whisky country.
9 holes, 4972 yards
par 68, S.S.S 64
Designer John Souter
Green fees £12
Changing room/showers
Visitors welcome – restricted weekends
Societies welcome by prior arrangement

ROYAL ABERDEEN GOLF CLUB

Balgownie, Bridge of Don, Aberdeen AB23 8AT
✆ 01224 702571 Fax 01224 826591
Map 14, H9
reservations@royal-aberdeen.demon.co.uk
Off A90, N of Aberdeen
Founded 1780
The world's sixth oldest golf club moved to its present home in 1887, running out and back along a thin strip of majestic dunesland beside the shore. Elevated tees and raised greens give fine seascapes, and the bunkering and rough leave no doubt as to the seriousness of the challenge.
18 holes, 6415 yards
par 70, S.S.S 73
Designer Robert Simpson
Green fees £60
Catering, changing room/showers, bar, club and trolley hire, shop, practice facilities
Visitors welcome, subject to restrictions
Handicap certificate required – limit: 24
Societies small parties welcome by prior arrangement.
🏨 Marcliffe at Pitfodels, North Deeside Road, Aberdeen, Aberdeenshire
✆ 01224 861000

ROYAL TARLAIR GOLF CLUB

Buchan Street, Macduff, Aberdeenshire AB44 1TA
✆ 01261 832897 Fax 01261 833455
Map 14, G8
info@royaltarlair.co.uk
www.royaltarlair.co.uk
4 miles E of Banff
Founded 1926
A parkland course perched on top of the cliffs, giving many magnificent views and one frightener – the sight of the 13th green on the far side of a gully, and, beyond, tumbling down the rocks to the sea. Everything is just as nature left it, including greens to die for.
18 holes, 5866 yards
par 71, S.S.S 68
Green fees £10
Catering, changing room/showers, bar, trolley hire, shop
Visitors welcome
Handicap certificate required
Societies welcome by prior arrangement
🏨 The Knowes Hotel, 78 Market Street, Macduff, Aberdeenshire
✆ 01261 832229

STONEHAVEN GOLF CLUB

Cowie, Stonehaven, Aberdeenshire AB39 3RH
✆ 01569 762124 Fax 01569 765973
Map 14, H10
Off A92, N of town centre
Founded 1888
A clifftop course overlooking Stonehaven Bay. The par-3 15th is a wicked compulsory carry over an abyss.
18 holes, 5128 yards
par 66, S.S.S 65
Designer A. Simpson
Green fees £15
Catering, changing room/showers, bar, trolley and buggy hire, practice facilities
Visitors welcome – restricted weekends
Societies welcome by prior arrangement

STRATHLENE GOLF CLUB

Portessie, Buckie, Aberdeenshire AB56 2DJ
✆ 01542 831798 Fax 01542 831798
Map 14, G7
www.scottishholidays.net/strathlene
A942, 2 miles E of Buckie
Founded 1877
Strathlene requires approach shots

to be played to a number of raised greens. The views are magnificent, but the wind can wreak havoc with the high-flown pitch.
18 holes, 5977 yards
par 69, S.S.S 69
Designer G. Smith
Green fees £12
Catering, changing room/showers, bar, trolley hire
Visitors welcome
Societies welcome by prior arrangement

TARLAND GOLF CLUB
Aberdeen Road, Tarland, Aboyne, Aberdeenshire AB34 4TB
✆ 013398 81000 **Map 14, G9**
B9119, 30 miles NW of Aberdeen
Founded 1908
A remarkably challenging little course in the heart of Deeside, surrounded by wonderful countryside (most particularly the view from the 8th fairway). Wildlife abounds, and the 4th, 5th and 6th test the best.
9 holes, 5875 yards
par 67, S.S.S 67
Designer Tom Morris
Green fees £15
Catering, changing room/showers, bar, trolley hire, shop, practice facilities
Visitors welcome – restricted some weekends
Societies welcome by prior arrangement
The Commercial Hotel, The Square, Tarland, Aboyne, Aberdeenshire AB34 4TX
✆ 013398 81922

TORPHINS GOLF CLUB
Torphins, Aberdeenshire AB31 4JU
✆ 013398 82402 Fax 013398 82402
Map 14, G9
stuart@macgregor5.fsnet.co.uk
A980, 6 miles NW of Banchory
Founded 1896
Parkland course with Highland views.
9 holes, 4738 yards
par 64, S.S.S 64
Green fees £12
Changing room/showers
Visitors welcome, except competition days
Societies welcome by prior arrangement
Learney Arms Hotel, Torphins, Aberdeenshire
✆ 013398 82202

TURRIFF GOLF CLUB
Rosehall, Turriff, Aberdeenshire AB53 4HD
✆ 01888 562982 Fax 01888 568050
Map 14, G8
grace@turiffgolf.sol.co.uk
www.turiffgolfclub.free-online.co.uk
Approximately 35 miles N from Aberdeen
Founded 1896
Situated on the banks of the River Deveron, with lovely views of the river valley.
18 holes, 6095 yards
par 70, S.S.S 69
Designer G.M. Fraser
Green fees £18
Catering, changing room/showers, bar, trolley hire, shop, practice facilities
Visitors welcome, with restrictions.
Handicap certificate required
Societies welcome by prior arrangement
The Fife Hotel, The Square, Turriff, Aberdeenshire
✆ 01888 563124

WESTHILL GOLF CLUB
Westhill Heights, Westhill, Aberdeenshire AB32 6RY
✆ 01224 742567 Fax 01224 749124
Map 14, H9
A944, 8 miles W of Aberdeen
Founded 1977
A course on which the parkland holes give way to a stretch of genuine moorland.
18 holes, 5849 yards
par 69, S.S.S 69
Designer Charles Lawrie
Green fees £14
Catering, changing room/showers, bar, club and trolley hire, shop, practice facilities
Visitors welcome, except Saturdays
Societies welcome by prior arrangement

ANGUS

ARBROATH ARTISAN GOLF CLUB
Elliot, Arbroath, Angus DD11 2PE
✆ 01241 875837 Fax 01241 875837
Map 14, G11
A92, 1 mile SW of Arbroath
Founded 1903
A municipal links of some quality, heavily bunkered and with the additional hazards of a burn and the railway line.
18 holes, 6185 yards
par 70, S.S.S 69
Designer James Braid
Green fees £16
Catering, changing room/showers, bar, club and trolley hire, shop, practice facilities
Visitors welcome
Societies welcome by prior arrangement

BRECHIN GOLF CLUB
Trinity, by Brechin, Angus DD9 7PD
✆ 01356 622383 Fax 01356 626925
Map 14, G10
1 mile outside Brechin on Aberdeen road
Founded 1893
A rolling parkland course, on which six short par 4s are offset by the more demanding 1st, 9th and 15th (all about 430 yards) and the 215-yard 13th.
18 holes, 6096 yards
par 72, S.S.S 70
Green fees £17
Catering, changing room/showers, bar, club, trolley and buggy hire, shop, practice facilities, squash
Visitors welcome
Societies welcome by prior arrangement
Glenesk Hotel, High St, Edzell, Angus
✆ 01356 648319

CAIRD PARK GOLF CLUB
Mains Loan, Caird Park, Dundee, Angus DD4 9BX
✆ 01382 438871 **Map 14, F11**
Off A972, N of Dundee
Founded 1926
The main course, well-wooded parkland, has been extended to make it quite a tough par 72 layout.
18 holes, 6303 yards, par 72, S.S.S 70
9 holes, 1692 yards, S.S.S 29
9 holes, 1983 yards, S.S.S 29
Green fees £15
Changing room/showers, bar, club and trolley hire, shop
Visitors welcome
Societies welcome by prior arrangement

CAMPERDOWN GOLF CLUB
Camperdown Park, Dundee, Angus DD4 9BX
✆ 01382 623398 **Map 14, G11**
Off A923, 3 miles NW of Dundee
Founded 1960
A first-rate public facility with lovely views across the River Tay to Fife. A seriously challenging course.
18 holes, 6561 yards
par 71, S.S.S 72
Green fees £15
Changing room/showers, trolley hire, shop, practice facilities
Visitors welcome
Societies welcome by prior arrangement

CARNOUSTIE GOLF COURSES

Links Parade, Carnoustie, Angus DD7 7JE
✆ 01241 853249 Fax 01241 853720
Map 14, G11
Off A930, SW of Carnoustie
Founded 16th century
See Top 50 Courses, page 15
Championship Links: 18 holes, 7361 yards, par 71
Designer James Braid
Burnside Links: 18 holes, 6020 yards, par 68, S.S.S. 69
Buddon Links: 18 holes, 5420 yards, par 66, S.S.S 66
Green fees £70
Catering, changing room/showers, bar, club, trolley and buggy hire, shop, driving range, practice facilities
Visitors welcome
Handicap certificate required
Societies welcome by prior arrangement

DOWNFIELD GOLF CLUB

Turnberry Avenue, Dundee, Angus DD2 3QP
✆ 01382 825595 Fax 01382 813111
Map 14, F11
downfieldgc@ukonline.co.uk
www.downfieldgolf.com
Off A923 N of Dundee ring road
Founded 1932
One of the four final qualifying courses for the 1999 Open, and a frequent host of prestigious Scottish championships, Downfield is one of Scotland's finest parkland courses, highly praised by Peter Thomson and Peter Alliss. The start is testing, with two tough par 4s and a 228-yard par 3.
18 holes, 6820 yards
par 73, S.S.S 73
Designer C.K. Cotton
Green fees £31
Catering, changing room/showers, bar, club, trolley and buggy hire, shop, practice facilities
Visitors welcome, with restrictions
Societies welcome by prior arrangement
🏨 Swallow Hotel, Kingsway West, Invergowrie, Dundee, Angus
✆ 01382 641122

EDZELL GOLF CLUB

High St, Edzell, Angus DD9 7TF
✆ 01356 647283 Fax 01356 648094
Map 14, G10
secretary@edzellgolfclub.demon.co.uk
B966, S of village
Founded 1895
A pretty course, surrounded by glorious scenery. The 446-yard 2nd is a handful early on, but, on the whole, length is of less significance than accuracy. A cool head helps to overcome the treachery of the 15th, only 338 yards, but with out-of-bounds on both sides, plus devilish cross-bunkers.
18 holes, 6348 yards
par 71, S.S.S 71
Designer Bob Simpson
Green fees £23
Catering, changing room/showers, bar, club, trolley and buggy hire, shop, driving range, practice facilities
Visitors welcome
Handicap certificate required
Societies welcome by prior arrangement
🏨 Glenesk Hotel, High St, Edzell, Angus
✆ 01356 648319

FORFAR GOLF CLUB

Cunninghill, Arbroath Road, Forfar, Angus DD8 2RL
✆ 01307 463773 Fax 01307 468495
Map 14, G11
A932, E of Forfar
Founded 1871
A mix of links, parkland and heathland with several memorable holes, but pride of place is usually given to the long par-4 15th 'Braid's Best'.
18 holes, 6052 yards
par 69, S.S.S 70
Designer Tom Morris, James Braid
Green fees £17
Catering, changing room/showers, bar, trolley hire, shop, driving range, practice facilities
Visitors welcome
Societies welcome by prior arrangement

KIRRIEMUIR GOLF CLUB

Northmuir, Kirriemuir, Angus DD8 4PN
✆ 01575 573317 Fax 01575 574608
Map 14, F10
Off B955, 1 mile N of Kirriemuir
Founded 1884
Accuracy is a requirement here, with narrow fairways and tiny greens.
18 holes, 5510 yards
par 68, S.S.S 67
Designer James Braid
Green fees £20
Catering, changing room/showers, bar, trolley hire, shop, practice facilities
Visitors welcome weekdays, restrictions at weekends
Societies welcome by prior arrangement

LETHAM GRANGE GOLF CLUB

Letham Grange, Colliston, By Arbroath, Angus DD11 4RL
✆ 01241 890373 Fax 01241 890725
Map 14, G11
lethamgrange@sol.co.uk
www.lethamgrange.co.uk
A993, 4 miles N of Arbroath
Founded 1987
The perfect pick-me-up for those suffering from an excess of links golf. While it would be extravagant to describe it (as it sometimes is) as the Augusta of Scotland, it does give a fair impression of the nature of the challenge, with water in play on 13 highly individual holes.
Old Course: 18 holes, 6632 yards, par 73, S.S.S 73
Designer Donald Steel
Glen's Course: 18 holes, 5528 yards, par 68, S.S.S 68
Designer Tom MacAuley
Green fees £35
Catering, changing room/showers, bar, accommodation, club, trolley and buggy hire, shop, practice facilities, conference facilities
Visitors welcome
Societies welcome by prior arrangement
🏨 Letham Grange Resort, Colliston, By Arbroath, Angus DD11 4RL
✆ 01241 890373 Fax 01241 890725
lethamgrange@sol.co.uk
www.lethamgrange.co.uk

MONIFIETH GOLF LINKS

Medal Starter's Box, Princes Street, Monifieth, Angus DD5 4AW
✆ 01382 532767 Fax 01382 535553
Map 14, G11
monifiethgolf@freeuk.com
www.monifiethgolf.co.uk
6 miles E of Dundee
Founded 1850
The Medal Course has been a regular final qualifying venue each time the Open Championship has been played at Carnoustie. The course opens alongside the main railway line, with the 4th perhaps the pick of the opening sequence. A burn dominates the excellent 7th, and pine trees line several fairways.
Medal Course: 18 holes, 6655 yards, par 71, S.S.S 72
Ashludie Course: 18 holes, 5123 yards, par 68, S.S.S 67
Designer James Braid
Green fees £30
Catering, changing room/showers, bar, trolley hire, shop, practice facilities
Visitors welcome – restricted weekends
Handicap certificate required

Societies welcome by prior arrangement
Panmure Hotel, Princes Street, Monifieth, Angus
01382 532911

MONTROSE GOLF CLUB

Montrose Links Trust, Traill Drive, Montrose, Angus DD10 8SW
01674 672932 Fax 01674 671800
Map 14, G10
secretary@montroselinks.co.uk
www.montroselinks.co.uk
Well signposted in town
Founded 1562
Golf was recorded as having taken place at Montrose as early as 1562, making it the 5th oldest course in the world. By 1866 it had developed into a 25-hole course. Today's championship links is mostly the work of Willie Park in 1903, a classic, exploiting the dunes inspiringly.
Medal Course: 18 holes, 6496 yards, par 71, S.S.S 72
Designer Tom Morris, Willie Park Jnr.
Broomfield Course: 18 holes, 4830 yards, par 66, S.S.S 63
Green fees £28
Catering, changing room/showers, bar, club and trolley hire, shop, practice facilities
Visitors welcome
Handicap certificate required
Societies welcome by prior arrangement
Park Hotel, John Street, Montrose, Angus DD10 8RJ
01674 673415

PANMURE GOLF CLUB

Barry, Carnoustie, Angus DD7 7RT
01241 853120 Fax 01241 859737
Map 14, G11
Off A930, W of Carnoustie
Founded 1845
A first-rate links, despite being some distance inland, used for Open Championship final qualifying. There is hardly a level piece of ground on the fairways, greens or rough (which can be unmerciful). Arguably, the 6th, 12th and 13th are the pick of the holes – not overlong, but searching par 4s.
18 holes, 6317 yards
par 70, S.S.S 71
Green fees £35
Catering, changing room/showers, bar, trolley hire, shop, practice facilities
Visitors welcome weekdays
Societies welcome by prior arrangement

ARGYLL & BUTE

BLAIRMORE & STRONE GOLF CLUB

High Road, Strone, Dunoon, Argyll & Bute PA23 8JJ
01369 860307 **Map 12, D3**
A880, off A815 at Cothouse Jct
Founded 1896
A short but tricky course with wonderful views of the Forth of Clyde.
9 holes, 2112 yards
par 62, S.S.S 62
Designer James Braid
Green fees £10
Changing room/showers, bar
Visitors welcome with restrictions
Societies welcome by prior arrangement
Kilmun Hotel, Shore Road, Kilmun, Dunoon, Argyll & Bute
01369 840418

BUTE GOLF CLUB

Sithean, Academy Road, Rothesay, Isle of Bute, Argyll & Bute PA20 0BG
01700 504369 **Map 12, C4**
Off A844, S of Rothesay
Founded 1888
A natural links, with hazardous gorse bushes.
9 holes, 2497 yards
par 68, S.S.S 65
Green fees £8
Changing room/showers
Visitors welcome
Societies welcome by prior arrangement

CARRADALE GOLF CLUB

Airds, Carradale, Argyll & Bute PA28 6RY
01583 431378 **Map 12, B6**
B842, 15 miles N of Campbeltown
Founded 1906
Seals and dolphins, wild goats and rocky outcrops, and magnificent seascapes may distract the golfer from the earnest task of scoring on this short, but most demanding, jewel of a course.
9 holes, 4694 yards
par 64, S.S.S 64
Green fees £10
Changing room/showers, trolley hire
Visitors welcome
Societies welcome by prior arrangement
Carradale Hotel, Airds, Carradale, Argyll & Bute
01583 431233

COLONSAY GOLF CLUB

Isle of Colonsay, Argyll & Bute PA61 7YP
019512 316 **Map 15, C9**
A870, on Colonsay
A remarkable little course, with turf quite unlike that found anywhere else.
18 holes, 4775 yards
par 72, S.S.S 72
Green fees £5
Visitors welcome
Societies welcome by prior arrangement

COWAL GOLF CLUB

Ardenslate Road, Dunoon, Argyll & Bute PA23 8LT
01369 705673 Fax 01369 705673
Map 12, D4
info@cowalgolfclub.co.uk
www.cowalgolfclub.co.uk
1 mile N of Dunoon
Founded 1891
Set on high ground overlooking the Firth of Clyde, with magnificent views to Arran and Ailsa Craig, Cowal is a charming course and friendly club. A burn threatens on the 376-yard 3rd, and the 191-yard 5th is a tricky proposition with a dyke running diagonally beside the green.
18 holes, 6063 yards
par 70, S.S.S 70
Designer James Braid
Green fees £23
Catering, changing room/showers, bar, club and trolley hire, shop, practice facilities
Visitors welcome
Societies welcome by prior arrangement
Enmore Hotel, Marine Parade, Dunoon, Argyll & Bute PA23 8HH
01369 702230 Fax 01369 702148
enmorehotel@btinternet.com

CRAIGNURE GOLF CLUB

Scallastle, Craignure, Isle of Mull, Argyll & Bute PA64 5AP
01680 812416 Fax 01680 300402
Map 15, D8
mullair@btinternet.com
Isle of Mull 1 mile from ferry terminal
Founded 1895
Recent alterations and the construction of 18 separate tees have added to the difficulties of this attractive seaside course.
9 holes, 5351 yards
par 69, S.S.S 66
Designer Howitt, Phillips
Green fees £11
Changing room/showers, club and trolley hire
Visitors welcome
Societies welcome by prior arrangement
Craignure Inn, Craignure, Argyll & Bute
01680 812305

DALMALLY GOLF COURSE
c/o Orchy Bank, Dalmally, Argyll & Bute PA33 1AS
01838 200370 **Map 12, D1**
A85, 2 miles W of Dalmally
Founded 1987
Easy walking on this level parkland course beside the River Orchy, surrounded by the mountains. The 3rd involves a compulsory 150-yard carry over the river.
9 holes, 4528 yards
par 64, S.S.S 63
Designer C. Macfarlane Barrow
Green fees £10
Changing room/showers, bar, club and trolley hire, practice facilities
Visitors welcome
Societies welcome by prior arrangement
Glen Orchy Lodge, Dalmally, Argyll & Bute PA33 1AS
01838 200312

DUNAVERTY GOLF CLUB
Southend, Campbeltown, Argyll & Bute PA28 6RF
01586 830677 **Map 12, A8**
www.redrival.com/dunaverty
B842, 10 miles S of Campbeltown
Founded 1889
A remote and beguiling links on the southern tip of the Mull of Kintyre, with impressive seascapes.
18 holes, 4799 yards
par 66, S.S.S 63
Green fees £12
Changing room/showers, trolley hire, shop, fishing
Visitors welcome – restricted on Saturdays
Societies welcome by prior arrangement

GLENCRUITTEN GOLF CLUB
Glencruitten Road, Oban, Argyll & Bute PA34 4PU
01631 562868 **Map 12, B1**
Off A816, NE of town centre
Founded 1908
With rocky outcrops, thick rough, several blind par 3s, and hills which make yardages sometimes impossible to judge, this might seem, at first glance, a course to avoid. Yet there is great charm, the condition is excellent, and James Braid's routing cleverly utilises the natural features to considerable golfing effect.
18 holes, 4452 yards
par 61, S.S.S 63
Designer James Braid
Green fees £16
Catering, changing room/showers, bar, club, trolley and buggy hire, shop, practice facilities
Visitors welcome with restrictions
Societies welcome by prior arrangement

INNELLAN GOLF CLUB
Knockamillie Road, Innellan, Dunoon, Argyll & Bute
01369 702573 **Map 12, C4**
A815, S of Dunoon
Founded 1891
Excellent views over the Forth of Clyde from this hilltop course.
9 holes, 4878 yards
par 64, S.S.S 64
Green fees £12
Catering, bar, club hire
Visitors welcome
Societies welcome by prior arrangement

INVERARAY GOLF CLUB
North Cromalt, Inveraray, Argyll & Bute
01499 302508 **Map 12, C2**
A83, S of Inveraray
Founded 1893
A parkland course, overlooking handsome Loch Fyne.
9 holes, 5790 yards
par 70, S.S.S 68
Green fees £10
Changing room/showers, practice facilities
Visitors welcome
Societies welcome by priror arrangement

ISLAY GOLF CLUB
Western Cottage, Port Ellen, Isle of Islay, Argyll & Bute PA42 7AT
01496 302409 **Map 15, C11**
islaygolf@btinternet.com
www.islay.golf.btinternet
2 miles from Port Ellen Ferry terminal
Founded 1891
One of the most natural links, created in an era when earth-moving was unheard of. Inevitably there are blind shots, but in this environment they seem completely in keeping. A blind approach makes the 7th, Scotland's Maiden, particularly hard. The 14th and 16th stand out, as does the short 10th.
18 holes, 6226 yards
par 71, S.S.S 70
Designer Willie Campbell
Green fees £30
Catering, changing room/showers, bar, accommodation, club and trolley hire, shop, practice facilities
Visitors welcome
Societies welcome by prior arrangement
The Machrie Hotel, Machrie, Port Ellen, Isle of Islay, Argyll & Bute
01496 302310 Fax 01496 302404

ISLE OF GIGHA GOLF CLUB
Isle of Gigha, Argyll & Bute PA41 7AA
01538 505242 **Map 12, A5**
10 minute walk from Tayinloan ferry terminal
Founded 1986
The views over the Sound of Gigha, and of the Kintyre and Knapdale peninsulas, provide a magnificent backdrop to golf on these meadowland fairways.
9 holes, 5042 yards
par 66, S.S.S 65
Designer Members of the Committee
Green fees £10
Changing room/showers, club and trolley hire
Visitors welcome
Societies welcome by prior arrangement
Isle of Gigha Hotel, Isle of Gigha, Argyll & Bute
01538 505254

KYLES OF BUTE GOLF CLUB
The Moss, Kames, Tighnabruaich, Argyll & Bute PA21 2EE
01700 811603 **Map 12, B4**
26 miles W of Dunoon
Founded 1907
A rocky, heathery course with superb views of the Kyles of Bute, and potentially dreadful trouble in the serious rough.
9 holes, 4814 yards
par 66, S.S.S 64
Green fees £8
Changing room/showers, club and trolley hire
Visitors welcome – restricted weekends
Societies welcome by prior arrangement
Kames Hotel, Kames, Tighnabruaich, Argyll & Bute
01700 811489

LOCHGILPHEAD GOLF CLUB
Blarbuie Road, Lochgilphead, Argyll & Bute PA31 8LE
01546 602340 **Map 12, D2**
½ mile N of Lochgilphead
Founded 1963
Water hazards on five holes are the main threats on this parkland course in a very beautiful part of the country.
9 holes, 4484 yards
par 64, S.S.S 63
Green fees £10
Changing room/showers, trolley hire, practice facilities
Visitors welcome
Societies welcome by prior arrangement

MACHRIHANISH GOLF CLUB

Machrihanish, Campbeltown, Argyll & Bute PA28 6PT
☎ 01586 810213 Fax 01586 810221
Map 12, A7
B843, 5 miles W of Campbeltown
Founded 1876
Machrihanish's fame has now spread to the extent that pilgrims come from all over the world simply to take on one of the most intimidating opening drives in golf, a 200-yard carry over the beach. The rest of this classic course is no less challenging, if, thankfully, less uncompromising.
18 holes, 6225 yards
par 70, S.S.S 71
Green fees £25
Catering, changing room/showers, bar, club, trolley and buggy hire, shop, practice facilities, 9-hole course
Visitors welcome – pre-booking advisable
Societies welcome by prior arrangement

MILLPORT GOLF CLUB

Millport, Isle of Cumbrae, Argyll & Bute KA28 0HB
☎ 01475 530306 Fax 01475 530306
Map 12, D5
Close to ferry terminal
Founded 1888
Millport's heathland course tests thoroughly, as well as giving great views from its island site.
18 holes, 5828 yards
par 68, S.S.S 69
Designer James Braid
Green fees £20
Catering, changing room/showers, bar, trolley hire, shop, practice facilities
Visitors welcome
Societies welcome by prior arrangement

PORT BANNATYNE GOLF CLUB

Bannatyne Mains Road, Port Bannatyne, Isle of Bute, Argyll & Bute PA20 0PH
☎ 01700 502009 **Map 12, C4**
www.geocities.com/~golftraveler/whats-new.htm
2 miles N of Rothesay Pier.
Founded 1912
A very scenic course, on a hillside, but not over energetic. The magnificent views take in Kames Bay, Cowal Hills, Kyles of Bute, Loch Striven, Loch Fyne and the Kintyre Peninsula.
13 holes, 5085 yards
par 68, S.S.S 65
Designer Peter Morrison
Green fees £11
Catering, changing room/showers, bar
Visitors welcome
Societies welcome by prior arrangement
🏨 Ardbeg Lodge Hotel, 23 Marine Place, Rothesay, Isle of Bute, Argyll & Bute
☎ 01700 505448

ROTHESAY GOLF CLUB

Canada Hill, Rothesay, Argyll & Bute PA20 9HN
☎ 01700 502244 Fax 01700 503554
Map 12, C4
On Isle of Bute – well signposted from ferry pier
Founded 1892
The breathtaking 360-degree land- and sea-scape from the 12th green is one of the finest in all British golf. It comes at a price – there is some steep hillclimbing to be done – but there are many golfing pleasures, too.
18 holes, 5395 yards
par 69, S.S.S 66
Designer James Braid, Ben Sayers
Green fees £10
Catering, changing room/showers, bar, club and trolley hire, shop, practice facilities
Visitors welcome
Societies welcome by prior arrangement

TARBERT GOLF CLUB

Kilberry Road, Tarbert, Argyll & Bute PA29 6XX
☎ 01880 820565 **Map 12, B4**
B8024, 1 mile W of Tarbert
Founded 1910
Hills, woods and streams add to the character of this essentially heathland course.
9 holes, 4460 yards
par 66, S.S.S 63
Green fees £5
Visitors welcome – restricted Sunday.
Societies welcome by prior arrangement

TAYNUILT GOLF CLUB

Taynuilt, Laroch, Argyll, Argyll & Bute PA35 1JH
☎ 01866 822429 Fax 01866 822255
Map 12, C1
murray_sim@msn.com
A85, 12 miles E of Oban
Founded 1987
Surrounded by mountains and overlooking Loch Etive.
9 holes, 4510 yards
par 64, S.S.S 63
Green fees £10
Visitors welcome
Societies welcome by prior arrangement

TOBERMORY GOLF CLUB

Tobermory, Isle of Mull, Argyll & Bute PA75 6PG
☎ 01688 302338 Fax 01688 302338
Map 15, D7
tobgolf@fsbusiness.co.uk
www.tobermory.co.uk/golf/tobermory.htm
Well signposted in Tobermory
Founded 1896
A scenically spectacular clifftop course offering a rare challenge: it has never yet (at the time of writing) been played to par.
9 holes, 4890 yards
par 64, S.S.S 64
Designer David Adams
Green fees £13
Changing room/showers, bar, accommodation, club and trolley hire, practice facilities
Visitors welcome
Societies welcome by prior arrangement
🏨 Fairways Lodge, Tobermory, Argyll & Bute
☎ 01688 302238

VAUL GOLF CLUB

Scarinish, Isle of Tiree, Argyll & Bute PA77 6TP
☎ 01879 220334 **Map 15, B8**
2 miles from Scarinish
Founded 1920
Golf at its most primæval, with natural bunkers created by animals sheltering from the wind, fenced greens, and an uplifting sense of remoteness.
9 holes, 5674 yards
par 72, S.S.S 68
Green fees £5
Changing room/showers
Visitors welcome
Course closed Sundays.
Societies welcome by prior arrangement

AYRSHIRE

ANNANHILL GOLF CLUB

Irvine Road, Kilmarnock, Ayrshire KA3 2RT
☎ 01563 521512 **Map 12, E6**
A71, 1 mile W of Kilmarnock
Founded 1957
A municipal parkland course of a decent length.
18 holes, 6269 yards
par 71, S.S.S 70
Designer Jack McLean
Green fees £10
Changing room/showers, bar, practice facilities

Visitors welcome
Societies welcome by prior arrangement

ARDEER GOLF CLUB
Greenhead, Stevenston, Ayrshire KA20 4JX
01294 464542 Fax 01294 465316
Map 12, D6
Off A78
Founded 1880
Ardeer's parkland course is unusual in starting and finishing with a short hole. Trees line the undulating fairways, and there is a pleasing sense of seclusion from the everyday world. The attractive 9th is only a drive and pitch, but the green is cunningly contoured and just beyond a burn.
18 holes, 6409 yards
par 72, S.S.S 71
Designer Hamilton Stutt
Green fees £18
Catering, changing room/showers, bar, trolley hire, shop, practice facilities
Visitors welcome weekdays – restricted Sunday
Societies welcome by prior arrangement

AUCHENHARVIE GOLF CLUB
Moor Park Road West, Stevenston, Ayrshire KA20 3HU
01294 603103 **Map 12, D6**
Off A738
Founded 1982
A well-equipped municipal course, close to the sea, although not a true links.
9 holes, 5300 yards
par 66, S.S.S 65
Green fees £5.50
Catering, changing room/showers, bar, club and trolley hire, shop, driving range
Visitors welcome – advance booking system
Societies welcome by prior arrangement

BALLOCHMYLE GOLF CLUB
Ballochmyle, Mauchline, Ayrshire KA5 6LE
01290 550469 Fax 01290 553657
Map 12, E7
secretary@ballochmyle.freeserve.co.uk
Off A76, Kilmarnock to Dumfries road
Founded 1937
With lovely views of the surrounding countryside, this wooded parkland course has small, well-defended greens.
18 holes, 5972 yards
par 70, S.S.S 69
Green fees £20
Catering, changing room/showers, bar, trolley hire, practice facilities
Visitors welcome, not Sundays
Societies welcome by prior arrangement
South Beach Hotel, 73 South Beach, Troon, Ayrshire
01292 312033

BEITH GOLF CLUB
Threepwood Road, Beith, Ayrshire KA15 2JR
01505 503166 **Map 12, E5**
Off A737, 1 mile N of Beith
Founded 1896
Hilly in parts, extensive views.
18 holes, 5616 yards
par 68, S.S.S 68
Green fees £18
Catering, changing room/showers, bar
Visitors welcome, with restrictions
Societies welcome by prior arrangement

BELLISLE GOLF CLUB
Bellisle Park, Doonfoot Road, Ayr, Ayrshire KA7 4DU
01292 441258 Fax 01292 442632
Map 12, E7
Bellisle Park, S of Ayr
Founded 1927
Full marks to South Ayrshire Council for maintaining the public courses in its care to the highest standards. Indeed, Bellisle is good enough to have hosted professional tournaments and Final Qualifying for the Open. Of the par 4s, only the 8th and 9th are under 400 yards. A serious course.
18 holes, 6431 yards
par 71, S.S.S 72
Designer James Braid
Green fees £18
Catering, changing room/showers, bar, club and trolley hire, shop, practice facilities
Visitors welcome
Societies welcome by prior arrangement

BRODICK GOLF CLUB
Brodick, Isle of Arran, Ayrshire KA27 8DL
01770 302349 Fax 01772 302349
Map 12, C6
½ mile from ferry pier
Founded 1897
Laid out alongside the beach.
18 holes, 4405 yards
par 62, S.S.S 62
Green fees £18
Changing room/showers, bar, trolley hire, shop, practice facilities
Visitors welcome, except competition days
Societies welcome by prior arrangement

BRUNSTON CASTLE GOLF CLUB
Golf Course Road, Dailly, Girvan, Ayrshire KA26 9GD
01465 811471 Fax 01465 811545
Map 12, D8
golf@brunston.freeserve.co.uk
www.brunstoncastle.co.uk
B741 to Dailly
Founded 1992
An important recent course laid out in the valley of the River Girvan, made the more taxing by the river's presence and by the lake which almost surrounds the 17th green.
18 holes, 6792 yards
par 72, S.S.S 72
Designer Donald Steel
Green fees £26
Catering, changing room/showers, bar, club, trolley and buggy hire, shop, driving range, practice facilities
Visitors welcome – booking advised.
Societies welcome by prior arrangement

CAPRINGTON GOLF CLUB
Ayr Road, Caprington, Kilmarnock, Ayrshire KA1 4UW
01563 521915 **Map 12, E6**
B7038, 1½ miles S of Kilmarnock
A gentle parkland course.
18 holes, 5810 yards
par 69, S.S.S 68
Green fees £9.25
Changing room/showers, bar, trolley hire, shop
Visitors welcome – restricted on Saturday
Societies welcome by prior arrangement

CORRIE GOLF CLUB
Corrie, Sannox, Isle of Arran, Ayrshire KA27 8JD
01770 810223 Fax 01770 810268
Map 12, C6
A841, 6 miles N of Brodick
Founded 1892
Five short and four drive-and-pitch holes make up this characterful heathland course beside the sea.
9 holes, 3896 yards
par 62, S.S.S 61
Green fees £10
Catering, shop
Visitors welcome with restrictions
Societies welcome by prior arrangement

DALMILLING GOLF CLUB
Westwood Avenue, Ayr KA8 0QY
01292 263893 Fax 01292 610543
Map 12, E7

Off A719, 1½ miles E of town
Founded 1961
Open parkland course, with burns to contend with early in the round.
18 holes, 5724 yards
par 69, S.S.S 67
Green fees £14
Catering, changing room/showers, bar, club and trolley hire, shop
Visitors welcome
Societies welcome by prior arrangement

DOON VALLEY GOLF CLUB

1 Hillside, Patna, Ayrshire KA6 7JT
✆ 01292 531607 Fax 01292 532489
Map 12, D7
A713, Ayr to Castle Douglas road, 10 miles S of Ayr
Founded 1927
A hilly course giving pleasant views of the River Doon, the village of Patna, and the woodlands beyond.
9 holes, 5856 yards
par 70, S.S.S 69
Green fees £8
Changing room/showers, bar
Visitors welcome
Societies welcome – no company days
Kirkton Hotel, 1 Main Street, Dalrymple, Ayrshire
✆ 01292 560241

GIRVAN GOLF CLUB

Golf Course Road, Girvan, Ayrshire KA26 9HW
✆ 01465 714346 Fax 01465 714346
Map 12, D8
Off A77, N of town
Founded 1860
The 'poor man's Turnberry', with the first eight holes played along the shore with views to Ailsa Craig.
18 holes, 5064 yards
S.S.S 64
Designer James Braid
Green fees £12
Catering, changing room/showers, trolley hire
Visitors welcome
Societies welcome by prior arrangement

GLASGOW GAILES GOLF CLUB

Gailes, Irvine, Ayrshire KA11 5AE
✆ 0141 942 2011 Fax 0141 942 0770 **Map 12, D6**
secretary@glasgow-golf.com
www.glasgowgailes-golf.com
Off A78, 1 mile S of Irvine
Founded 1892
Gailes is the seaside course of the Glasgow Golf Club, and, unlike its parkland senior partner, is open to visitors. Heather and gorse can wreck a score on almost any hole. The greens, too, require intuition and skill to overcome them. The 14th, 15th and 18th are the back nine's stars.
18 holes, 6539 yards
par 71, S.S.S 72
Designer Willie Park
Green fees £42
Catering, changing room/showers, bar, club, trolley and buggy hire, shop, practice facilities
Visitors welcome with weekend restrictions
Societies welcome by prior arrangement

IRVINE GOLF CLUB

Bogside, Irvine, Ayrshire KA8 8SN
✆ 01294 275979 **Map 12, D6**
N of Irvine, towards Kilwinning
Founded 1887
Recognition of Irvine's credentials has been its elevation to the role of a Final Qualifying course for the Open Championship when it is held at Royal Troon or Turnberry. Gorse and heather take a terrible toll on inaccurate golf, and there only two par 3s, and a single par 5.
18 holes, 6408 yards
par 71, S.S.S 73
Green fees £30
Catering, changing room/showers, bar, shop, practice facilities
Visitors welcome
Societies welcome by prior arrangement

IRVINE RAVENSPARK GOLF CLUB

Kidsneuk Lane, Irvine, Ayrshire KA12 8SR
✆ 01294 271 293 **Map 12, D6**
Off A737, N of Irvine
Founded 1907
A high class municipal course, good enough to have hosted significant championships.
18 holes, 6429 yards
par 71, S.S.S 71
Green fees £4
Catering, changing room/showers, bar, shop, practice facilities
Visitors welcome
Societies welcome by prior arrangement

KILBIRNIE PLACE GOLF CLUB

Largs Road, Kilbirnie, Ayrshire KA25 7AT
✆ 01505 683398 **Map 12, D5**
A760, 1 mile W of town
Founded 1922
A gentle parkland course.
18 holes, 5411 yards
par 69, S.S.S 67
Green fees £10
Changing room/showers, bar
Visitors welcome – restricted Saturdays
Societies welcome by prior arrangement

KILMARNOCK (BARASSIE) GOLF CLUB

29 Hillhouse Road, Barassie, Troon, Ayrshire KA10 6SY
✆ 01292 313920 Fax 01292 313920
Map 12, D6
secretarykbgc@lineone.net
www.kbgc.co.uk
B746, 2 miles N of Troon
Founded 1887
Barassie has long had a reputation as a first-rate links, maintained to perfection. The one doubt used to be its slightly tame ending. A recent expansion to 27 holes has enabled the creation of a main course of modern championship dimensions, with the redundant holes now the 9-hole course.
Barassie Links: 18 holes, 6817 yards, par 72, S.S.S 74
Hillhouse: 9 holes, 2888 yards, par 34, S.S.S 34
Green fees £40
Catering, changing room/showers, bar, club and trolley hire, shop, practice facilities
Visitors monday, Tuesday, Thursday, Friday with prior booking
Societies welcome by prior arrangement

LAMLASH GOLF CLUB

Lamlash, Isle of Arran, Ayrshire KA27 8JU
✆ 01770 100196 Fax 01770600296
Map 12, C6
www.arrangolf.uk.co
3 miles S of Brodick ferry terminal
Founded 1889
From the very first drive, looking out onto Holy Island, invigoration will be the order of the day. The course is trickier than its length alone might suggest.
18 holes, 4640 yards
par 64, S.S.S 64
Designer Auchterlonie, Fernie
Green fees £16
Catering, changing room/showers, bar, club, trolley and buggy hire, shop
Visitors welcome
Societies welcome by prior arrangement
Glenisle Hotel, Lamlash, Isle of Arran, Ayrshire
✆ 01770 600258

LARGS GOLF CLUB

Irvine Road, Largs, Ayrshire KA30 8EW
✆ 01475 673594 Fax 01475 673594

Map 12, D5
secretary@largsgolfclub.co.uk
www.largsgolfclub.co.uk
A78, 1 mile S of town centre
Founded 1891
A parkland course with glorious views over the water to Arran and Cumbrae. The tree-lined fairways demand good placement, notably from the 8th to 12th.
18 holes, 6115 yards
par 70, S.S.S 71
Designer J Hamilton Stutt
Green fees £30
Catering, changing room/showers, bar, club and trolley hire, shop
Visitors welcome – restricted weekends
Societies welcome by prior arrangment
Moorings Hotel, May Street, Largs, Ayrshire
01475 672672

LOCHRANZA GOLF COURSE

Lochranza, Isle of Arran, Ayrshire KA27 8HL
01770 830273 Fax 01770 830600
Map 12, B5
office@lochgolf.demon.co.uk
www.arran.net
Via Ardrossan-Arran ferry or Claonaig-Lochranza ferry
Founded 1899
The present course was relaid in 1991, an ingenious layout with 18 tees playing to 6 double- and 6 single-greens. Lochranza is the longest of the Arran courses, and has the island's longest holes. A distillery just over the road surely adds to the spirit of the game played here!
18 holes, 5487 yards
par 70, S.S.S 67
Designer I.M. Robertson
Green fees £13
Changing room/showers, club and trolley hire, shop, practice facilities
Visitors welcome
Societies welcome by prior arrangement

LOUDOUN GOWF CLUB

Galston, Ayrshire KA4 8PA
01563 821993 Fax 01563 820011
Map 12, E6
secretary@loudgowf.sol.co.uk
A71, ½ mile E of Galston
Founded 1909
The only 'Gowf' club in the world, using the old Scots spelling – appropriate for a spot on which golf has been played since 1773.
18 holes, 6016 yards
par 68, S.S.S 69
Designer Hyde Prestwick
Green fees £20
Catering, changing room/showers, bar, trolley hire, shop, driving range, practice facilities
Visitors welcome weekdays
Societies welcome by prior arrangement
Loudoun Mains, Newmilns, Ayrshire
01560 321246

MACHRIE BAY GOLF CLUB

Machrie Bay, Brodick, Isle of Arran, Ayrshire KA27 8DZ
01770 850232 Fax 01770 850247
Map 12, B6
9 miles W of Brodick
Founded 1900
A short links course, with only one hole longer than 300 yards. The great Walter Hagen is reputed to have gone round in a mere 53 shots!
9 holes, 4400 yards
par 66, S.S.S 62
Designer Willie Fernie
Green fees £8
Catering, changing room/showers, club and trolley hire, practice facilities
Visitors welcome
Societies welcome by prior arrangement

MAYBOLE GOLF CLUB

Memorial Park, Maybole, Ayrshire KA19
01655 889770 **Map 12, D8**
Off A77, S of Ayr
Founded 1970
Short parkland course with lovely views of Carrick Hills.
9 holes, 5304 yards
S.S.S 66
Green fees £8
heated swimming pool
Visitors welcome
Societies welcome by prior arrangement

MUIRKIRK GOLF CLUB

c/o 65 Main Street, Muirkirk, Cumnock, Ayrshire KA18 3QR
01290 660184 **Map 12, F7**
A70, Edinburgh to Ayr road
Founded 1991
An inland pay-and-play facility with views as far as the Isle of Arran on a clear day.
9 holes, 3640 yards
par 68, S.S.S 67
Green fees £8
Changing room/showers
Visitors welcome
Societies welcome by prior arrangement
Coach House Hotel, Main Street, Muirkirk, Cumnock, Ayrshire
01290 661257

NEW CUMNOCK GOLF CLUB

Lochill, Cumnock Road, New Cumnock, Ayrshire KA18 4BQ
01290 423659 **Map 12, F7**
A76, NW of New Cumnock
Founded 1902
A parkland course, overlooking the Loch, beginning with a treacherous road hole.
9 holes, 5176 yards
par 68, S.S.S 68
Designer Willie Fernie
Green fees £5
Catering, changing room/showers, bar, accommodation, fishing
Visitors welcome, except Sundays
Societies welcome by prior arrangement
Lochside House Hotel, Lochill, New Cumnock, Ayrshire
01290 333000

PRESTWICK GOLF CLUB

2 Links Road, Prestwick, Ayrshire KA9 1QG
01292 477404 Fax 01292 477255
Map 12, E7
bookings@prestwickgc.co.uk
www.prestwickgc.co.uk
Next to Prestwick railway station
Founded 1851
Prestwick was host to the first twelve Open Championships, and twenty-four in all. Add eleven Amateur Championships and some measure of Prestwick's importance is apparent. The original course was of twelve holes, but today's 18-holer retains many ancient features, not least the Cardinal bunker, dominating the par-5 3rd.
18 holes, 6700 yards
par 71, S.S.S 73
Designer Tom Morris
Green fees £80
Catering, changing room/showers, bar, club, trolley and buggy hire, shop, practice facilities
Visitors welcome, subject to restrictions
Handicap certificate required – limit: 28 men, 36 women
Societies welcome by prior arrangement
South Beach Hotel, 73 South Beach, Troon, Ayrshire
01292 312033

PRESTWICK ST CUTHBERT GOLF CLUB

East Road, Prestwick, Ayrshire KA9 2SX
01292 477101 Fax 01292 671730
Map 12, E7
prestwick.stcuthbertgc@virgin.net
www.stcuthbert.co.uk
Off A77 at Heathfield Roundabout
Founded 1899

Easy walking on this parkland/heathland course, quite different in nature from Old Prestwick and St Nicholas.
18 holes, 6133 yards
par 71, S.S.S 71
Designer Tutt & Co
Green fees £24
Catering, changing room/showers, bar, trolley hire
Visitors welcome weekdays. Handicap certificate required
Societies welcome by prior arrangement
South Beach Hotel, 73 South Beach, Troon, Ayrshire
01292 312033

PRESTWICK ST NICHOLAS GOLF CLUB

Grangemuir Road, Prestwick, Ayrshire KA9 1SN
01292 477608 Fax 01292 473900
Map 12, E7
Off A79, S of town centre
Founded 1851
A deceptively tricky course, worthy of its status as a final qualifying course for Turnberry Opens. The quarry holes (7th to 10th) are noteworthy, and the 227-yard par-3 18th makes a formidable finisher. It is quite possible to slice into the sea on the 1st, 11th and 12th.
18 holes, 5952 yards
par 69, S.S.S 69
Designer James Allan, Charles Hunter
Green fees £30.50
Catering, changing room/showers, bar, club and trolley hire, shop
Visitors welcome weekdays – restricted Sunday
Societies welcome by prior arrangement
Parkstone Hotel, Ardayre Road, Prestwick, Ayrshire
01292 477286

ROUTENBURN GOLF CLUB

Routenburn Road, Largs, Ayrshire KA30 8QA
01475 687240 **Map 12, D5**
From Greenock, turn left on entering town
Founded 1914
Inexpensive golf by the generally pricey standards of Ayrshire. New water features have been added to this course which enjoys marvellous views over the Firth of Clyde.
18 holes, 5604 yards
par 68, S.S.S 68
Designer James Braid
Green fees £11
Catering, changing room/showers, bar, trolley hire, shop, practice facilities
Visitors welcome
Societies welcome by prior arrangement
Willowbank Hotel, Greenock Road, Largs, Ayrshire
01475 672311

ROYAL TROON GOLF CLUB

Craigend Road, Troon, Ayrshire KA10 6EP
01292 311555 Fax 01292 318204
Map 12, D6
bookings@royaltroon.com
www.royaltroon.com
Southern outskirts of Troon
Founded 1878
See Top 50 Courses, page 41
Championship Course: 18 holes, 7101 yards, par 71, S.S.S 74
Designer Willie Fernie, James Braid
Portland Course: 18 holes, 6289 yards, par 71, S.S.S 71
Green fees £135
Catering, changing room/showers, bar, club and trolley hire, shop, driving range, practice facilities
Visitors welcome – restrictions. Handicap certificate required – limit: 20
Societies welcome by prior arrangement, limited to 24
Lochgreen House, Monktonhill Road, Southwood, Troon, Ayrshire KA10 7EN
01292 313343 Fax 01292 318661

SEAFIELD GOLF CLUB

Bellisle Park, Doonfoot Road, Ayr, Ayrshire KA7 4DU
01292 441258 Fax 01292 442632
Map 12, E7
Bellisle Park, S of Ayr
Founded 1930
A beautifully presented little gem, part linksland, with a demanding finish troubled by a burn.
18 holes, 5481 yards
par 68, S.S.S 67
Green fees £12
Catering, changing room/showers, bar, club and trolley hire, shop, practice facilities
Visitors welcome
Societies welcome by prior arrangement

SHISKINE GOLF CLUB & TENNIS CLUB

Shiskine, Blackwaterfoot, Isle of Arran, Ayrshire KA27 8HA
01770 860226 Fax 01770 860205
Map 12, B6
www.shiskinnegolf.com
Off B880 on Blackwaterfoot
Founded 1896
Unusual 12-hole links which has generated almost cult status, following high rankings in the league tables currently so fashionable in the golfing press. Tiny greens and tight fairways reward accurate play, and the views are incomparable.
12 holes, 2990 yards
par 42, S.S.S 41
Designer Willie Fernie
Green fees £13
Catering, changing room/showers, bar, club, trolley and buggy hire, shop, tennis
Visitors welcome
Handicap certificate required
Societies welcome by prior arrangement
Kinloch Hotel, Blackwaterfoot, Isle of Arran, Ayrshire KA27 8ET
01770 860444

SKELMORLIE GOLF CLUB

Beithglass Road, Skelmorlie, Ayrshire PA17 5ES
01475 520152 **Map 12, D4**
A78 S from Greenock
Founded 1891
Hilly moorland course with spectacular views across Firth of Clyde.
18 holes, 5030 yards
par 65, S.S.S 65
Designer James Braid
Green fees £16
Catering, changing room/showers, bar, club and trolley hire, practice facilities
Visitors welcome – restricted Saturdays
Societies welcome by prior arrangements
Heywood Hotel, 13 Shore Road, Skelmorlie, Ayrshire, Ayrshire
01475 520258

TROON MUNICIPAL GOLF COURSES

Harling Drive, Troon, Ayrshire KA10 6NF
01292 312464 Fax 01292 312578
Map 12, D6
In centre of Troon
Lochgreen is a serious challenge – Jack Nicklaus qualifying here for the 1962 Open.
Lochgreen: 18 holes, 6822 yards, par 74, S.S.S 73
Darley: 18 holes, 6360 yards, par 71, S.S.S 72
Fullarton: 18 holes, 4869 yards, S.S.S 63
Green fees £18
Changing room/showers, bar, club hire, shop
Visitors welcome
Societies welcome by prior arrangement

TURNBERRY HOTEL & GOLF COURSES

Turnberry, Ayrshire KA26 9LT
☎ 01655 331000 Fax 01655 331706
Map 12, D8
turnberry@westin.com
www.turnberry.co.uk
Off A77, 15 miles S of Ayr
Founded 1906
See Top 50 Courses, page 52
Ailsa Course: 18 holes, 6976 yards, par 70, S.S.S 72
Designer Mackenzie Ross
Kintyre Course: 18 holes, 6853 yards, par 72, S.S.S 71
Designer Mackenzie Ross, Donald Steel
Green fees £95
Catering, changing room/showers, bar, accommodation, club and trolley hire, shop, driving range, practice facilities, full luxury hotel facilities, extensive indoor and outdoor sporting pursuits available, conference and banqueting facilities, Colin Montgomerie Golf Academy
Visitors welcome – hotel guests have first priority
Societies welcome by prior arrangement
🏨 Turnberry Hotel, Golf Courses and Spa, Turnberry, Ayrshire KA26 9LT
☎ 01655 331000

WEST KILBRIDE GOLF CLUB

33-35 Fullerton Drive, Seamill, West Kilbride, Ayrshire KA23 9HT
☎ 01294 823911 Fax 01294 823042
Map 12, D5
A78, W Kilbride
Founded 1893
West Kilbride is a serious test of golf, and has hosted the Scottish Boys' Championship. It has all the hallmarks of a traditional links with an invasive burn and even a stone wall reminiscent of North Berwick.
18 holes, 6452 yards
par 71, S.S.S 71
Designer Tom Morris, James Braid
Green fees £21
Catering, changing room/showers, bar, club and trolley hire, shop, driving range, practice facilities
Visitors welcome with weekend restrictions
Societies welcome by prior arrangement

WESTERN GAILES GOLF CLUB

Gailes, Irvine, Ayrshire KA11 5AE
☎ 01294 311649 Fax 01294 312 312
Map 12, D6
enquiries@westerngailes.com
www.westerngailes.com
Off A78, 3 miles N of Troon
Founded 1897
See Top 50 Courses, page 57
18 holes, 6637 yards
par 71, S.S.S 73
Green fees £75
Catering, changing room/showers, bar, trolley hire
Visitors welcome, with restrictions
Handicap certificate required
Societies welcome by prior arrangement
🏨 Marine Hotel, Troon, Ayrshire KA10 6HE
☎ 01292 314444

WHITING BAY GOLF CLUB

Golf Course Road, Whiting Bay, Isle of Arran, Ayrshire KA27 8PR
☎ 01770 700775 **Map 12, C7**
Off A841, NW of village
Founded 1895
One of the hillier courses on Arran, quite testing.
18 holes, 4405 yards
par 63, S.S.S 63
Green fees £10
Catering, changing room/showers, bar, club, trolley and buggy hire, shop
Visitors welcome
Societies welcome by prior arrangement

BORDERS

DUNS GOLF CLUB

Hardens Road, Duns, Berwickshire, Borders TD11 3NR
☎ 01361 882194 **Map 13, E5**
Off A6105, 1 mile W of Duns
Founded 1894
Recently extended, today's course offers good views of the Cheviots and Lammermuirs. The 2nd and 6th are strong holes on the way out, but the worst trouble may well occur on the 15th, only 116 yards long, but with water front and back of the green.
18 holes, 6209 yards
par 70, S.S.S 70
Green fees £16
Catering, changing room/showers, bar, trolley hire, practice facilities
Visitors welcome
Societies welcome by prior arrangement
🏨 Barniken Hotel, Murray Street, Duns, Borders
☎ 01361 882466

EYEMOUTH GOLF CLUB

Gunsgreen House, Eyemouth, Borders TD14 5DX
☎ 018907 50004 **Map 13, F5**
Off A1, 6 miles N of town
Founded 1894
Wholescale disruption was caused to the old course when a new harbour was constructed. Advantage was taken to build what is effectively a completely fresh course, of considerable length, with a superb clubhouse. The course begins gently, running along the rocky shore, inexorably building to a climax at the 15th.
18 holes, 6472 yards
par 72, S.S.S 72
Designer J.R. Bain
Green fees £20
Catering, changing room/showers, bar, club, trolley and buggy hire, shop, practice facilities
Visitors welcome
Societies welcome by prior arrangement
🏨 Churches Hotel, Harbour Road, Eyemouth, Borders
☎ 01890 750401

GALASHIELS GOLF CLUB

Ladhope Recreation Ground, Galashiels, Borders TD1 2NJ
☎ 01896 753724 **Map 13, C6**
Off A7, ½ mile from town centre
Founded 1884
A steep climb joins the two separate halves of this parkland course, which gives fine views from the higher ground.
18 holes, 5309 yards
par 67, S.S.S 66
Designer James Braid
Green fees £15
Catering, changing room/showers, bar, trolley hire
Visitors welcome
Societies welcome by prior arrangement

HAWICK GOLF CLUB

Vertish Hill, Hawick, Borders TD9 0NY
☎ 01450 372293 **Map 13, C7**
Off A7, 1 mile SW of Hawick
Founded 1877
The start is difficult, with three tight holes climbing steeply. Thereafter the views over the surrounding countryside are superb, with a fine panorama of the town from the 15th green. The final hole, a downhill par 3, can be merciless. Tony Jacklin, Colin Montgomerie, and Nick Faldo are honorary members.
18 holes, 5933 yards
par 68, S.S.S 69
Green fees £21
Catering, changing room/showers, bar, trolley and buggy hire, practice facilities, function suite
Visitors welcome – restricted weekends
Societies welcome by prior

arrangement
Elm House Hotel, 17 North Bridge Street, Hawick, Borders
01450 372866

THE HIRSEL GOLF CLUB
Kelso Road, Coldstream, Borders TD12 4NJ
01890 882678 Fax 01890 882233
Map 13, E6
A697, W of Coldstream
Founded 1948
A course which derives its atmosphere from the noble estate in which it is laid out. It becomes increasingly difficult as the round proceeds.
18 holes, 6111 yards
par 70, S.S.S 70
Green fees £20
Catering, changing room/showers, bar, club, trolley and buggy hire, shop, practice facilities
Visitors welcome
Societies welcome by prior arrangement

INNERLEITHEN GOLF CLUB
Leithen Water, Leithen Road, Innerleithen, Borders EH44 6NL
01896 830951 **Map 13, B6**
Off A72, 3/4 mile from Innerleithen
Founded 1886
A pretty course set in the Tweed Valley, the river coming into play on several holes.
9 holes, 6066 yards
par 70, S.S.S 69
Designer Willie Park
Green fees £11
Practice facilities
Visitors welcome
Societies welcome by prior arrangement

JEDBURGH GOLF CLUB
Dunion Road, Jedburgh, Roxburghshire, Borders TD8 6LA
01835 863587 Fax 01835 862360
Map 13, D7
www.tweedalepress.co.uk/jedburgh golfclub.html
B6358, 1 mile W of Jedburgh
Founded 1889
From its undulating fairways there are engaging views over the surrounding countryside to the Cheviots.
9 holes, 5555 yards
par 68, S.S.S 67
Designer Willie Park Jnr
Green fees £16
Catering, changing room/showers, bar, trolley hire, practice facilities
Visitors welcome – restricted competition days.
Societies welcome by prior arrangement

Spread Eagle Hotel, 20 High Street, Jedburgh, Borders
01835 862870

KELSO GOLF CLUB
Golf Course Road, Kelso, Borders TD5 7SL
01573 223009 Fax 01573 228490
Map 13, D6
Off B6461
Founded 1887
Parkland course within Kelso race course.
18 holes, 6066 yards
par 70, S.S.S 69
Designer James Braid
Green fees £16
Catering, changing room/showers, bar, trolley and buggy hire, practice facilities
Visitors welcome
Societies welcome by prior arrangement

LANGHOLM GOLF CLUB
Langholm, Borders DG13 0JR
013873 80673 **Map 13, B9**
Off A7, in Langholm
Founded 1892
Hilly course with fine views extending as far as the Lake District.
9 holes, 6180 yards
par 70, S.S.S 70
Green fees £10
Practice facilities
Visitors welcome – restricted weekends
Societies welcome by prior arrangement

MELROSE GOLF CLUB
Dingleton, Melrose, Borders
01896 822855 **Map 13, C6**
Off A68, S of Melrose
Founded 1880
A course which climbs gently onto the hills above Melrose to give fine views of Scott country.
9 holes, 5579 yards
par 70, S.S.S 68
Green fees £16
Changing room/showers, bar, practice facilities
Visitors welcome
Societies welcome

MINTO GOLF CLUB
Denholm, Hawick, Borders TD9 8SH
01450 870220 Fax 01450 870126
Map 13, D7
Off A698, at Denholm
Founded 1928
A pretty woodland course with fine views.
18 holes, 5542 yards
par 68, S.S.S 67
Green fees £18
Catering, changing room/showers, bar, trolley and buggy hire, practice facilities
Visitors welcome
Societies welcome by prior arrangement

NEWCASTLETON GOLF CLUB
Holm Hill, Newcastleton, Borders TD9 0QD
01387 375257 **Map 13, C9**
B9357, off A7 from Carlisle to Hawick
Founded 1894
From its hilly fairways, Newcastleton gives fine views of the Liddesdale Hills.
9 holes, 5503 yards
par 69, S.S.S 70
Designer J. Shade
Green fees £10
Changing room/showers
Visitors welcome
Societies welcome by prior arrangement
Liddesdale Hotel, Douglas Square, Newcastleton, Borders
01387 375255

PEEBLES GOLF CLUB
Kirkland Street, Peebles, Borders EH45 8EU
01721 720197 **Map 13, B6**
www.peeblesgolfclub.co.uk
Off A72 W of town
Founded 1892
Set in glorious surroundings on the hills above the town, Peebles offers a good balance between challenging and gentler holes. The latter come in mid round, giving an opportunity to retrench – and enjoy the scenery – before the rigours of the finish from the 377-yard 14th, which plays deceptively long.
18 holes, 6160 yards
par 70, S.S.S 70
Designer James Braid, Harry Colt
Green fees £20
Catering, changing room/showers, bar, club and trolley hire, shop, practice facilities
Visitors welcome. Handicap certificate required
Societies welcome by prior arrangement

THE ROXBURGHE HOTEL & GOLF COURSE
Heiton, By Kelso, Borders TD5 8JZ
01573 450331 Fax 01573 450611
Map 13, D6
hotel@roxburghe.net
www.roxburghe.net
A698 at Heiton
Founded 1997
One of the top-rated new courses in Britain, The Roxburghe has set new standards in the Borders. The most

photographed hole is the 14th, a 571-yard par 5 playing alongside the River Teviot towards a viaduct. At 469 yards, the 10th is toughest of the two-shotters, favouring a fade.
18 holes, 7111 yards
par 72, S.S.S 75
Designer Dave Thomas
Green fees £40
Catering, changing room/showers, bar, accommodation, club, trolley and buggy hire, shop, driving range, practice facilities
Visitors welcome – restrictions
Handicap certificate required
Societies welcome by prior arrangement
Roxburghe Hotel, Heiton, Kelso, Borders TD5 8JZ
01573 450331

ROYAL BURGH OF LAUDER GOLF CLUB

Galashiels Road, Lauder, Borders TD2 6QD
01578 722240 **Map 13, C5**
From A68 in Lauder, take Galashiels Road at Town Hall
Founded 1896
The fine views over Lauderdale will comfort the golfer who has come to grief on either of Lauder's favourite holes, the dog-leg Wood Hole and par-3 Quarry Hole.
9 holes, 6050 yards
par 72, S.S.S 69
Designer Willie Park Jnr
Green fees £10
Changing room/showers, practice facilities
Visitors welcome – with restrictions
Societies welcome by prior arrangement
Lauderdale Hotel, Edinburgh Road, Lauder, Borders
01578 722231

RUTHERFORD CASTLE GOLF CLUB

West Linton, Borders EH46 7AS
01968 661233 Fax 01968 661233
Map 13, A5
info@ruth-castlegc.co.uk
www.ruth-castlegc.co.uk
A702, S of Edinburgh
Founded 1996
Plentiful water hazards and tall trees add to the difficulties of this new course, just 15 minutes from the Edinburgh bypass. Backed by the Pentland Hills, there are dramatic views from the higher ground.
18 holes, 6525 yards
par 72, S.S.S 71
Designer OCM
Green fees £15
Changing room/showers, bar, trolley and buggy hire
Visitors welcome
Societies welcome by prior arrangement
Allan Ramsay Hotel, Carlops, Peeblesshire, West Lothian
01968 660258

SELKIRK GOLF CLUB

The Hill, Selkirk, Borders TD7 4NW
01750 20621 **Map 13, C6**
A7, ½ mile S of Selkirk
Founded 1883
A typical Borders moorland course, climbing onto the hills to give glorious views.
9 holes, 5560 yards
par 68, S.S.S 67
Designer Willie Park
Green fees £16
Trolley and buggy hire
Visitors welcome restricted weekends
Societies welcome by prior arrangement

ST BOSWELLS GOLF CLUB

Braeheads, St Boswells, Near Melrose, Borders TD6 0DE
01835 823527 **Map 13, D6**
Off B6404 (off A68) in St Boswells
Founded 1899
A remarkably flat parkland course in a marvellous spot, with the salmon-filled River Tweed running alongside, and the impressive ruins of Dryburgh Abbey on the opposite bank.
9 holes, 5274 yards
par 68, S.S.S 66
Green fees £15
Changing room/showers, bar, trolley hire
Visitors welcome
Societies welcome by prior arrangement
Dunfermline House, Buccleuch Street, Melrose, Borders TD6 9LB
01896 882148

TORWOODLEE GOLF CLUB

Edinburgh Road, Galashiels, Borders TD1 2NE
01896 752260 Fax 01896 752260
Map 13, C6
One mile N of Galashiels on A7
Founded 1895
Recently extended to 18 holes to give a course of much contrast. The old holes are well wooded beside the River Gala, whereas the new holes break out onto a hillside.
18 holes, 6021 yards
par 69, S.S.S 70
Designer Willie Park
Green fees £18
Catering, changing room/showers, bar, trolley and buggy hire
Visitors welcome
Societies welcome by prior arrangement
Abbotsford Arms Hotel, Stirling Street, Galashiels, Borders
01896 752517

WEST LINTON GOLF CLUB

West Linton, Borders EH46 7HN
01968 660970 Fax 01968 660970
Map 13, A5
A702, 18 miles SW of Edinburgh
Founded 1890
A remarkable course sitting on a plateau 1000 feet above sea level. The star hole is the 14th, which entails a 200-yard carry over an abyss from the tee. Another good hole is the 18th, an uncompromising par 3.
18 holes, 6132 yards
par 68, S.S.S 67
Green fees £20
Catering, changing room/showers, bar, trolley and buggy hire, shop, practice facilities
Visitors welcome weekdays
Societies welcome by prior arrangement

CAITHNESS & SUTHERLAND

BONAR BRIDGE/ARDGAY GOLF CLUB

Migdale Road, Bonar Bridge, Caithness & Sutherland IV24 3EJ
01863 766199 **Map 14, D7**
secbbagc@aol.com
www.bonarbrigdegolfclub.co.uk
Off A836 at Bonar Bridge
Founded 1904
The smell of the pine trees and views over Loch Migdale to the surrounding mountains add to the delights of this charming golf course.
9 holes, 5284 yards
par 68, S.S.S 66
Designer Donald Steel
Green fees £12
Catering, changing room/showers, club and trolley hire
Visitors welcome
Societies welcome by prior arrangement

BRORA GOLF CLUB

43 Golf Road, Brora, Caithness & Sutherland KW9 6QS
01408 621417 Fax 01408 622157
Map 14, E6
secretary@broragolf.co.uk
www.highlandescape.com
A9, 18 miles N of Dornoch
Founded 1891
James Braid's most northerly course is a traditional links in the best

sense, with small, fast greens protected by electric fences from the sheep and cattle which roam freely. The short holes are arranged to face the wind from every quarter, with the 9th and 13th standing out, justly famed.
18 holes, 6110 yards
par 69, S.S.S 69
Designer Tom Morris, James Braid
Green fees £25
Catering, changing room/showers, bar, club and trolley hire, shop, practice facilities, snooker, fishing
Visitors welcome
Societies welcome by prior arrangement
The Royal Marine Hotel, Golf Road, Brora, Caithness & Sutherland KW9 6QS
01408 621252 Fax 01408 621181
highlandescape@btinternet.com

THE CARNEGIE CLUB

Skibo Castle, Clashmore, Dornoch, Caithness & Sutherland IV25 3RQ
01862 894600 Fax 01862 894601
Map 14, E7
Off A9, SW of Dornoch
Founded 1995
One of the most opulent developments of recent years, much more than simply a castle and a golf course. This is more a way of life for the seriously wealthy. For those lucky enough to play it, the golf course is an absolute joy, with all the traditional links attributes.
18 holes, 6671 yards
par 71, S.S.S 72
Designer Donald Steel
Green fees £130
Catering, changing room/showers, bar, accommodation, club, trolley and buggy hire, shop, driving range, practice facilities
Visitors welcome, very restricted
Handicap certificate required
Societies welcome by prior arrangement

DURNESS GOLF CLUB

Balnakeil, Durness, Caithness & Sutherland IV27 4PN
01971 511364 **Map 14, D5**
A838, in the far NW of Scotland
Founded 1988
9 holes with 18 tees ending with one of the most spectacular holes in British golf, an all-or-nothing carry across 100 yards of the Atlantic Ocean to an ungenerous green. The most northerly course on mainland Britain.
9 holes, 5555 yards
par 70, S.S.S 69
Green fees £15
Trolley hire, practice facilities
Visitors welcome – restricted weekends
Societies welcome by prior arrangement

GOLSPIE GOLF CLUB

Ferry Road, Golspie, Caithness & Sutherland KW10 6ST
01408 633266 Fax 01408 633393
Map 14, E6
info@golspie-golf-club.co.uk
www.golspie-golf-club.co.uk
A9, 10 miles N of Dornoch
Founded 1889
At Golspie golf is possible almost to midnight in summer. The course is a mixture of true links, heath-and-heather, and simple parkland. From the 3rd, the course skirts the shore, while the 8th and 9th could almost have been translated from Surrey. The mountain and sea views are quite outstanding.
18 holes, 5890 yards
par 68, S.S.S 68
Designer James Braid
Green fees £25
Catering, changing room/showers, bar, club and trolley hire, shop, practice facilities
Visitors welcome
Societies welcome by prior arrangement

HELMSDALE GOLF CLUB

Golf Road, Helmsdale, Caithness & Sutherland KW8 6JA
01431 821650 **Map 14, E6**
A9, N of Dornoch
Founded 1895
A tight heathland course with plenty of gorse and bracken.
9 holes, 3720 yards
par 62, S.S.S 61
Green fees £5
Visitors welcome
Societies welcome by prior arrangement

LYBSTER GOLF CLUB

Main Street, Lybster, Caithness & Sutherland KW1 6BL
01593 721201 **Map 14, F5**
On A99, S of Wick
Founded 1926
A gentle heathland course.
9 holes, 1896 yards
par 62, S.S.S 61
Green fees £7
Visitors welcome
Societies welcome by prior arrangement

REAY GOLF CLUB

Reay, Thurso, Caithness & Sutherland KW14 7RE
01847 894189 Fax 01847 894189
Map 14, E5
info@reaygolfclub.co.uk
www.reaygolfclub.co.uk
A 836, 11 miles W of Thurso
Founded 1893
The most northerly 18-hole links on the British mainland, which would be far better known if it were not quite so remote. It is unusual in opening and closing with par 3s, the 1st a monster of 235 yards. The 7th, across a burn, is another exacting par 3.
18 holes, 5831 yards
par 69, S.S.S 69
Designer James Braid
Green fees £20
Changing room/showers, bar, club and trolley hire, practice facilities
Visitors welcome
Societies welcome by prior arrangement

ROYAL DORNOCH GOLF CLUB

Golf Road, Dornoch, Caithness & Sutherland IV25 3LW
01862 810219 Fax 01862 810792
Map 14, E7
rdgc@royaldorncoh.com
www.royaldornoch.com
From Dornoch Square take Golf Road – signposted from A9.
Founded 1877
See Top 50 Courses, page 34
Championship Course: 18 holes, 6732 yards, par 72, S.S.S 74
Designer Tom Morris, John Sutherland, George Duncam
Struie Course: 18 holes, 5438 yards, par 69, S.S.S 66
Green fees £60
Catering, changing room/showers, bar, club and trolley hire, shop, practice facilities, conference facilities during winter months
Visitors welcome – restricted Saturdays
Handicap certificate required – limit: 24 men, 39 ladies
Societies welcome by prior arrangement
Castle Hotel, Castle Street, Dornoch, Caithness & Sutherland
01862 810216

THURSO GOLF CLUB

Newlands of Geise, Thurso, Caithness & Sutherland KW14 7XD
01847 892575 **Map 14, F5**
www.eurogolf.com
2 miles W of Thurso
Founded 1898
A parkland course overlooking the Pentland Firth towards Orkney.
18 holes, 5853 yards
par 69, S.S.S 69
Designer W. Stewart, R. Waugh
Green fees £15

Catering, bar, club hire
Visitors welcome
Societies welcome by prior arrangement
Pentland Hotel, Princes Street, Thurso, Caithness & Sutherland
01847 893202

WICK GOLF CLUB
Reiss, Wick, KW1 5LJ, Caithness & Sutherland
01955 602726 **Map 14, F5**
On A99, N of Wick
Founded 1870
A traditional links, out and back, with undulating fairways and absolutely no shelter from the wind.
18 holes, 5976 yards
par 69, S.S.S 70
Designer James Braid
Green fees £15
Changing room/showers, bar, club and trolley hire
Visitors welcome
Societies welcome by prior arrangement

CLACKMANNANSHIRE

ALLOA GOLF CLUB
Schawpark, Sauchie, Alloa, Clackmannanshire FK10 3AX
01259 724476 Fax 01259 724476
Map 12, H3
bellville51@hotmail.com
www.alloagolfpage.co.uk
A908 N of Alloa
Founded 1891
Set in a beautiful 150-acre estate, backed by the Ochil Hills, Alloa is most attractive. The closing holes, from the 15th, constitute quite a challenge.
18 holes, 6229 yards
par 70, S.S.S 71
Designer James Braid
Green fees £24
Catering, changing room/showers, bar, trolley hire, shop, practice facilities
Visitors welcome – with restrictions
Societies welcome by prior arrangement
Dunmar House Hotel, Tullibody Road, Alloa, Clackmannanshire
01259 214339

ALVA GOLF CLUB
Beauclerc Street, Alva, Clackmannanshire FK12 5LH
01259 760431 **Map 12, G3**
A91, 7 miles from Stirling
Short course at the foot of the Ochil Hills.
9 holes, 4846 yards
par 66, S.S.S 64
Green fees £10
Changing room/showers, bar
Visitors welcome, except club competitions
Societies welcome by prior arrangement

BRAEHEAD GOLF CLUB
Cambus, Alloa, Clackmannanshire FK10 2NT
01259 725766 Fax 01259 214070
Map 12, G3
A706, 1 mile W of Alloa
Founded 1891
Excellent views are obtained on this testing parkland course, which ends with a couple of stern par 4s.
18 holes, 6086 yards
par 70, S.S.S 69
Green fees £16
Catering, changing room/showers, bar, club, trolley and buggy hire, shop, practice facilities
Visitors welcome – prior booking required
Societies welcome by prior arrangement

DOLLAR GOLF CLUB
Brewlands House, Dollar, Clackmannanshire FK14 7EA
01259 742400 Fax 01259 743497
Map 12, H3
www.dollargolfclub.co.uk.
Off A91, N of Dollar
Founded 1890
Dollar is great fun, and the splendour of its mountain surroundings adds to the delight. Twelve drive-and-pitch holes, all bunkerless, might seem to herald a low score, but that is to neglect the effects of sloping lies, mountain streams, and cunningly sited greens, none moreso than the 97-yard 2nd.
18 holes, 5242 yards
par 69, S.S.S 66
Designer Ben Sayers
Green fees £13.50
Catering, changing room/showers, bar, club and trolley hire
Visitors welcome – with restrictions
Societies welcome by prior arrangement

TILLICOULTRY GOLF CLUB
Alva Road, Tillicoultry, Clackmannanshire FK13 6BL
01259 750124 Fax 01259 752934
Map 12, H3
A91, 9 miles E of Stirling
Founded 1899
A hilly course in the Ochil Hills.
9 holes, 5365 yards
par 68, S.S.S 66
Green fees £10.50
Catering, changing room/showers, bar
Visitors welcome
Societies welcome by prior arrangement

TULLIALLAN GOLF CLUB
Alloa Road, Kincardine on Forth, Clackmannanshire FK10 4BB
01259 730798 Fax 01259 733750
Map 12, H3
enquiries@tulliallangc.f9.co.uk
www.tulliallan-golf-club.co.uk
A908, N of Kincardine Bridge, adjacent to Scottish Police College
Founded 1902
A hilly parkland course on which it is possible to slice out-of-bounds on eight holes, and a burn affects seven.
18 holes, 5965 yards
par 69, S.S.S 69
Green fees £16
Catering, changing room/showers, bar, club and trolley hire, shop, practice facilities
Visitors welcome, except competition days
Societies welcome by prior arrangement
Powfoulis Hotel, Bothkennar, By Falkirk, Stirlingshire FK2 8PR
01324 831267

DUMFRIES & GALLOWAY

CASTLE DOUGLAS GOLF CLUB
Abercromby Road, Castle Douglas, Dumfries and Galloway DG7 1BA
01556 502801 **Map 12, G10**
Off A75/A713, NE of Castle Douglas
Founded 1905
A parkland course with two lengthy par 4s, the 6th and 8th, and one very steep hill.
9 holes, 5408 yards
par 68, S.S.S 66
Green fees £12
Catering, changing room/showers, bar, club and trolley hire
Visitors welcome
Societies welcome by prior arrangement

COLVEND GOLF CLUB
Sandyhills, Colvend, Dalbeattie, Dumfries and Galloway DG5 4PY
01556 630398 Fax 01556 630495
Map 12, G10
thesecretary@colvendgolfclub.co.uk
www.colvendgolfclub.co.uk
A710, 6 miles from Dalbeattie
Founded 1905
Recently expanded from 9 holes to 18, there are superb views over the Solway Firth (even to the Isle of Man on a clear day). The new holes

extend into woodland at the 14th.
18 holes, 5220 yards
par 68, S.S.S 67
Designer Willie Fernie, John Soutar
Green fees £20
Catering, changing room/showers, bar, club, trolley and buggy hire, practice facilities
Visitors welcome
Societies welcome by prior arrangement
Clonyard House Hotel, Colvend, Dalbeattie, Dumfries and Galloway DG5 4QW
01556 630372

CRICHTON GOLF CLUB

Bankend Road, Dumfries, Dumfries and Galloway DG1 4TH
01387 247894 **Map 12, H9**
1 mile from Dumfries
Founded 1884
A parkland course with a difficult 200-yard par 3 at the 5th.
9 holes, 6168 yards
par 70, S.S.S 69
Green fees £12
Catering, changing room/showers, bar, shop, practice facilities
Visitors welcome weekdays
Societies welcome by prior arrangement

DALBEATTIE GOLF CLUB

Maxwell Park, Dalbeattie, Dumfries and Galloway
01556 611421 **Map 12, G10**
Off B794, SW of Dumfries
Founded 1897
An interesting parkland course with lovely views along a river valley.
9 holes, 5710 yards
par 68, S.S.S 68
Green fees £12
Changing room/showers
Visitors welcome
Societies welcome by prior arrangement

DUMFRIES & COUNTY GOLF CLUB

Nunfield, Edinburgh Road, Dumfries, Dumfries and Galloway DG1 1JX
01387 268918 Fax 01387 253585
Map 12, H9
dumfriescounty@netscapeonline.co.uk
www.dumfriesandcounty-ge.tsnet
Off A75, via A701
Founded 1912
A highly reputed course, undulating, and with fine views over the surrounding countryside.
18 holes, 5928 yards
par 69, S.S.S 69
Designer Willie Fernie
Green fees £26
Catering, changing room/showers, bar, club and trolley hire, shop, practice facilities
Visitors welcome – restricted weekends
Societies welcome by prior arrangement

DUMFRIES & GALLOWAY GOLF CLUB

2 Laurieston Avenue, Maxwelltown, Dumfries, Dumfries and Galloway DG2 7NY
01387 263848 Fax 01387 263848
Map 12, H9
A75, W of Dumfries
Founded 1888
An old club, strongly linked with 1883 Open Champion, Willie Fernie. A recent land purchase has enabled the club to extend the course with two strong par 4s at the 9th and 10th. Other demanding holes include 3rd, 7th and 11th (par 4s) and the 564-yard par-5 5th.
18 holes, 6309 yards
par 70, S.S.S 71
Designer Willie Fernie
Green fees £26
Catering, changing room/showers, bar, club and trolley hire, shop, practice facilities, snooker
Visitors welcome – restrictions
Handicap certificate required
Societies welcome by prior arrangement
Cairndale Hotel, English Street, Dumfries, Dumfries and Galloway
01387 254111

GATEHOUSE GOLF CLUB

c/o Innisfree, Laurieston, Castle Douglas, Dumfries and Galloway DG7 2PW
01644 450260 Fax 01644 450260
Map 12, F11
From Gatehouse of Fleet (A75) take road to Laurieston
Founded 1921
A wonderful spot with superb views inland to the mountains as well as to sea over Wigtown Bay. Admirable condition.
9 holes, 5042 yards
par 66, S.S.S 66
Green fees £10
Changing room/showers, meals by arrangement
Visitors welcome, except Sunday morning
Societies welcome by prior arrangement
Murray Arms Hotel, Gatehouse of Fleet, Dumfries and Galloway DG7 2HY
01557 814207

GRETNA GOLF CLUB

Kirtle View, Gretna, Dumfries and Galloway DG16 5HD
01461 338464 **Map 13, B10**
Off M74 and A75, W of Gretna
Founded 1991
A good place to break the journey close to the Scottish border, with its testing 9-hole course and fine views.
9 holes, 6430 yards
par 72, S.S.S 71
Designer Nigel Williams
Green fees £8
Changing room/showers, trolley hire, driving range
Visitors welcome
Societies welcome by prior arrangement

HODDOM CASTLE GOLF CLUB

Hoddom Bridge, Ecclefechan, Dumfries and Galloway DG11 1AS
01576 300251 Fax 01576 300757
Map 13, A9
B725, 2 miles SW of Ecclefechan, M74 Jct 19
Founded 1973
The River Annan is a persistent threat, and handsome companion, throughout the round.
9 holes, 4558 yards
par 68, S.S.S 66
Green fees £7
Visitors welcome
Societies welcome by prior arrangement

KIRKCUDBRIGHT GOLF CLUB

Stirling Crescent, Kirkcudbright, Dumfries and Galloway DG6 4EZ
01557 330314 Fax 01557 330314
Map 12, F11
kbtgolfclub@lineone.net
A711, off A75
Founded 1893
There are fine views of the town and Dee Estuary (particularly from the 3rd and 11th) on this surprisingly hilly parkland course.
18 holes, 5717 yards
par 69, S.S.S 69
Green fees £18
Catering, changing room/showers, bar, trolley and buggy hire, practice facilities
Visitors welcome
Handicap certificate required
Societies welcome by prior arrangement
Royal Hotel, St Cuthbert Street, Kirkcudbright, Dumfries and Galloway
01557 331213

LOCHMABEN GOLF CLUB

Castlehill Gate, Lochmaben, Dumfries and Galloway DG11 1NT

☎ 01387 810552 **Map 12, A9**
Off A709, 4 miles from Lockerbie
Founded 1926
A particularly attractive course, laid out many years ago by James Braid, between two lochs.
18 holes, 5357 yards
par 67, S.S.S 66
Designer James Braid
Green fees £16
Catering, changing room/showers, bar, trolley hire, practice facilities
Visitors welcome
Societies welcome by prior arrangement

LOCKERBIE GOLF CLUB

Corrie Road, Lockerbie, Dumfries and Galloway DG11 2ND
☎ 01576 203363 Fax 01576 203363
Map 12, A9
www.lockerbiegolf.com
Off M74 at Lockerbie
Founded 1889
Pleasantly situated to give excellent views as far as the Lakeland Fells and the Annandale Valley. A pond comes into play on three holes.
18 holes, 5493 yards
par 67, S.S.S 67
Designer James Braid
Green fees £16
Catering, changing room/showers, bar, club, trolley and buggy hire, practice facilities
Visitors welcome
Societies welcome by prior arrangement
Queens Hotel, Annan Road, Lockerbie, Dumfries and Galloway
☎ 01756 202415

MOFFAT GOLF CLUB

Coatshill, Moffat, Dumfries and Galloway DG10 9SB
☎ 01683 220020 **Map 12, A8**
A701, off M74
Founded 1884
In the hills above Moffat, giving magnificent views, and an outrageous 9th hole, played over a rock face to an elevated green.
18 holes, 5263 yards
par 69, S.S.S 67
Designer Ben Sayers
Green fees £18.50
Catering, changing room/showers, bar, club and trolley hire
Visitors welcome with restrictions
Societies welcome by prior arrangement

NEW GALLOWAY GOLF CLUB

New Galloway, Castle Douglas, Dumfries and Galloway DG7 2NL
☎ 01644 450685 Fax 01644 450685
Map 12, F9
secretary@nggc.co.uk
Off A713, turning left at Ken Bridge Hotel. Course through village.
Founded 1902
The first two holes climb onto a plateau from which there are magnificent views of Loch Ken and the surrounding hills. Well-reputed greens.
9 holes, 5006 yards
par 68, S.S.S 67
Designer George Baillie
Green fees £12.50
Changing room/showers, bar, club and trolley hire, practice facilities
Visitors welcome
Societies welcome by prior arrangement
Ken Bridge Hotel, New Galloway, Dumfries and Galloway
☎ 01644 420211

NEWTON STEWART GOLF CLUB

Kirroughtree Avenue, Minnigaff, Newton Stewart, Dumfries and Galloway DG8 6PF
☎ 01671 402172 **Map 12, E10**
A75, N of Newton Stewart
Founded 1981
A parkland course with many subtle humps and hollows to give character to almost every fairway. A stream crosses several holes and there are occasional patches of gorse, but, otherwise, golfers are free to enjoy themselves relatively unfettered, surrounded by lovely scenery.
18 holes, 5903 yards
par 69, S.S.S 70
Green fees £20
Catering, changing room/showers, bar, club, trolley and buggy hire
Visitors welcome
Handicap certificate required
Societies welcome by prior arrangement

PORTPATRICK (DUNSKEY) GOLF CLUB

Golf Course Road, Portpatrick, Dumfries and Galloway DG9 8TB
☎ 01776 810273 Fax 01776 810811
Map 12, C11
portpatrickgolf@aol.com
www.scottishgolf.com
8 miles SW of Stranraer
Founded 1903
Perched on top of the cliffs, with views over the sea to the Mull of Kintyre and Ireland. Most memorable is the 13th, Sandeel, a 293-yard par 4, downhill to a green by the pounding waves – and eminently driveable. The short holes are good, especially the 7th and 11th.
Dunskey Course: 18 holes, 5908 yards, par 70, S.S.S 69
Designer William Hunter
Dinvin Course: 9 holes, 1504 yards, par 27, S.S.S 27
Green fees £22
Catering, changing room/showers, bar, club, trolley and buggy hire, shop, practice facilities
Visitors welcome, with restrictions
Handicap certificate required – limit: 24 men, 36 women
Societies welcome by prior arrangement
Fernhill Hotel, Heugh Road, Portpatrick, Dumfries and Galloway
☎ 01776 810220

POWFOOT GOLF CLUB

Cummertrees, Annan, Dumfries and Galloway DG12 5QE
☎ 01461 700276 Fax 01461 700276
Map 13, A10
Off B724, 4 miles W of Annan, A75
Founded 1903
Powfoot's championship status has been further enhanced with a number of recent ladies' and girls' championships. In spring and summer it is a picture, with the gorse and heather in full bloom, but both can destroy a good score. Of many fine holes, the 3rd is toughest, alongside the shore.
18 holes, 6255 yards
par 71, S.S.S 71
Designer James Braid
Green fees £24
Catering, changing room/showers, bar, club and trolley hire, shop, practice facilities
Visitors welcome – not Saturdays
Societies welcome by prior arrangement
Powfoot Golf Hotel, Links Avenue, Powfoot, Dumfries and Galloway DG12 5PN
☎ 01461 700254

SANQUHAR GOLF CLUB

Blackaddie Road, Sanquhar, Dumfries, Dumfries and Galloway DG4 6JZ
☎ 01659 50577 Map 12, G7
www.scottishgolf.com
A76, 30 miles S of Ayr
Founded 1894
A parkland course with fine views and a particularly testing 2nd hole.
9 holes, 5630 yards
par 70, S.S.S 68
Designer Willie Fernie
Green fees £12
Changing room/showers
Visitors welcome
Societies welcome by prior arrangement

SOUTHERNESS GOLF CLUB
Southerness, Dumfries, Dumfries and Galloway DG2 9AZ
☎ 01387 880677 Fax 01387 880644
Map 12, H11
admin@southernessgc.sol.co
www.southernessgolfclub.com
A710 (Solway Coast Road), 15 miles from Dumfries
Founded 1947
See Top 50 Courses, page 46
18 holes, 6566 yards
par 69, S.S.S 73
Designer Mackenzie Ross
Green fees £35
Catering, changing room/showers, bar, trolley hire, shop, practice facilities
Visitors welcome
Handicap certificate required
Societies welcome by prior arrangement
Clonyard House Hotel, Colvend, Dalbeattie, Dumfries and Galloway DG5 4QW
☎ 01556 630372

ST MEDAN GOLF CLUB
Monreith, Port William, Newton Stewart, Dumfries and Galloway DG8 8NJ
☎ 01988 700358 **Map 12, E11**
Off A747, 3 miles S of Port William
Founded 1905
Idyllically situated on Monrieth Bay, with ravishing views of the Mull of Galloway and Isle of Man, St Medan is Scotland's most southerly course, and a real charmer!
9 holes, 4454 yards
par 64, S.S.S 63
Green fees £15
Catering, changing room/showers, bar, club and trolley hire
Visitors welcome
Societies welcome by prior arrangement
Corsemalzie House Hotel, Mochrum, Port William, Newton Stewart, Dumfries and Galloway
☎ 01988 860254

STRANRAER GOLF CLUB
Creachmore, Leswalt, Stranraer, Dumfries and Galloway DG9 0LF
☎ 01776 870245 Fax 01776 870445
Map 12, C10
A 718, 2 miles N of Stranraer
Founded 1905
Essentially a mixture of attractive parkland and heathland holes overlooking Loch Ryan, but with a memorable excursion to the beach on the 5th, a glorious hole. The 9th, 16th and 17th are par 4s to stretch any golfer, and three appearances of a burn make the 3rd far from easy.
18 holes, 6308 yards
par 70, S.S.S 72
Designer James Braid
Green fees £20
Catering, changing room/showers, bar, club, trolley and buggy hire, practice facilities
Visitors welcome
Societies welcome by prior arrangement
North West Castle Hotel, Port Rodie, Stranraer, Dumfries and Galloway
☎ 01776 704413

THORNHILL GOLF CLUB
Blacknest, Thornhill, Dumfries and Galloway DG3 5DW
☎ 01848 330546 **Map 12, H8**
A76, 1 mile E of Thornhill
Founded 1893
Suurounded by the entrancing scenery of the southern uplands, Thornhill is a mixture of parkland and heathland. The par-4 4th is intimidating, with a burn threatening the drive, and a green on two levels, well protected on a hummock. The dog-leg 15th is handsomely set off against a loch.
18 holes, 6085 yards
par 71, S.S.S. 70
Green fees £16
Catering, changing room/showers, bar, club and trolley hire, shop, practice facilities
Visitors welcome – restricted competition days
Societies welcome by prior arrangement
Trigony House Hotel, Closeburn, Thornhill, Dumfries and Galloway DG3 5EZ
☎ 01848 331212

WIGTOWN & BLADNOCH GOLF CLUB
Lightlands Terrace, Wigtown, Dumfries and Galloway DG8 9EF
☎ 01988 403354 **Map 12, E11**
Off A714, between Wigtown and Bladnoch
Founded 1960
The views over the sea and surrounding countryside are attractive, the course itself surprising tricky.
9 holes, 5462 yards
par 68, S.S.S 67
Designer J. Muir
Green fees £15
Catering, changing room/showers
Visitors welcome – restricted weekends
Societies welcome by prior arrangement

WIGTOWNSHIRE COUNTY GOLF CLUB
Mains of Park, Glenluce, Newton Stewart, Dumfries and Galloway DG8 0NN
☎ 01581 300420 **Map 12, D11**
wgx@glenluce.org.uk
www.glenluce.org.uk/countygolfclub.html
A75, 8 miles SE of Stranraer
Founded 1894
Set on the shores of Luce Bay, Wigtownshire County must be the only true links on the Scottish coast between Southerness and Turnberry. It is not unduly long, with only one par 4 over 400 yards and a single par 5, but there is mischief in the subtly sloping greens.
18 holes, 5843 yards
par 70, S.S.S 68
Designer C. Hunter, Gordon Cunningham
Green fees £19
Catering, changing room/showers, bar, club, trolley and buggy hire, practice facilities
Visitors welcome
Societies welcome by prior arrangement
North West Castle Hotel, port Rodie, Stranraer, Dumfries and Galloway
☎ 01776 704413

DUNBARTONSHIRE

BALMORE GOLF CLUB
Balmore, Torrance, Dunbartonshire G64 4AW
☎ 01360 620123 Fax 01360 620284
Map 12, F4
www.balmoregolfclub.co.uk
Off A807, N of Glasgow
Founded 1894
As with many courses in the Glasgow suburbs, there are fine views of the surrounding hills from these pleasant parkland fairways.
18 holes, 5542 yards
par 66, S.S.S 67
Designer James Braid
Green fees £25
Catering, changing room/showers, bar, club, trolley and buggy hire, shop, practice facilities
Visitors welcome, with restrictions
Societies welcome by prior arrangement

BEARSDEN GOLF CLUB
Thorn Road, Bearsden, Glasgow, Dunbartonshire G61 4BP
☎ 0141 942 2351 **Map 12, F4**
Off A809, NW of Glasgow
Founded 1891
A 9-hole course arranged so that 11

tees play to 16 greens.
9 holes, 6014 yards
par 68, S.S.S 69
Green fees £12
Catering, changing room/showers, bar, practice facilities
Visitors welcome as members' guest
Societies restricted

CARDROSS GOLF CLUB

Main Road, Cardross, Dumbarton, Dunbartonshire G82 5LB
✆ 01389 8411213 Fax 01389 842162 **Map 12, E4**
www.cardross.com
A814, W of Dumbarton
Founded 1895
A testing parkland course in handsome surroundings.
18 holes, 6469 yards
par 71, S.S.S 72
Designer Willie Fernie, James Braid
Green fees £25
Catering, changing room/showers, bar, club and trolley hire, shop, practice facilities
Visitors welcome – restricted weekends
Societies welcome by prior arrangement

CLOBER GOLF CLUB

Craighton Road, Milngavie, Glasgow, Dunbartonshire G62 7HP
✆ 0141 956 1685 Fax 0141 955 1416 **Map 12, F4**
NW of Milngavie
Founded 1951
A parkland course with a high proportion of par 3s, of which the 119-yard 5th is notorious, with out-of-bounds on both sides and a stream in front.
18 holes, 4963 yards
par 66, S.S.S 65
Green fees £15
Catering, changing room/showers, trolley hire, shop
Visitors welcome with restrictions
Societies welcome by prior arrangement

CLYDEBANK & DISTRICT GOLF CLUB

Hardgate, Clydebank, Dunbartonshire G81 5QY
✆ 01389 38333 Fax 01389 383831
Map 12, F4
N of Clydebank, 2 miles E of Erskine Bridge
Founded 1905
A parkland course with pleasant views over the Clyde.
18 holes, 5823 yards
par 68, S.S.S 68
Green fees £13
Changing room/showers, trolley hire, shop
Visitors welcome
Handicap certificate required
Societies welcome by prior arrangement

CLYDEBANK MUNICIPAL GOLF CLUB

Overtown Road, Dalmuir, Clydebank, Dunbartonshire G81 3RE
✆ 0141 9528698 Fax 0141 952 632
Map 12, F4
2 miles NW of town centre
Founded 1927
A hilly parkland course.
18 holes, 5349 yards
par 67, S.S.S 66
Green fees £7
Club and trolley hire, shop
Visitors welcome
Societies welcome by prior arrangement

DOUGALSTON GOLF CLUB

Strathblane Raod, Milngavie, Glasgow, Dunbartonshire G62 8HJ
✆ 0141 955 2434 Fax 0141 955 2406 **Map 12, F4**
A81, at Milngavie
Founded 1977
A pretty parkland course, well wooded, with ponds.
18 holes, 6225 yards
par 71, S.S.S 71
Designer J. Harris
Green fees £20
Catering, changing room/showers, bar, club and trolley hire, shop, practice facilities
Visitors welcome
Societies welcome by prior arrangement

DOUGLAS PARK GOLF CLUB

Hillfoot, Bearsden, Glasgow, Dunbartonshire G61 2TJ
✆ 0141 942 0985 Fax 0141 942 0985 **Map 12, F4**
A81, E of Bearsden
Founded 1897
The views to the Campsie Fells are an added attraction on this undulating parkland course.
18 holes, 5962 yards
par 69, S.S.S 69
Designer Willie Fernie
Green fees £22
Catering, changing room/showers, bar, trolley and buggy hire, shop
Visitors welcome only by prior arrangement with secretary
Societies welcome by prior arrangement – no company days

DULLATUR GOLF CLUB

Dullatur, Glasgow, Dunbartonshire G68 0AR
✆ 01236 723230 **Map 12, G4**
2 miles N of Cumbernauld
Founded 1896
A parkland course.
18 holes, 6253 yards
par 70, S.S.S 70
Green fees £25
Catering, changing room/showers, bar, trolley and buggy hire, shop, practice facilities
Visitors welcome – restricted weekends
Societies welcome by prior arrangement

DUMBARTON GOLF CLUB

Broadmeadow, Dumbarton, Dunbartonshire G82 2BQ
✆ 01389 732830 Fax 01389 765995
Map 12, E4
Off A814, N of Dumbarton
Founded 1888
A course with character, the 7th green being sunken in a punchbowl, and the final green on the far side of water.
18 holes, 5969 yards
par 71, S.S.S 69
Green fees £22
Catering, changing room/showers, bar, practice facilities
Visitors welcome weekdays
Societies welcome by prior arrangement

HAYSTON GOLF CLUB

Campsie Road, Kirkintilloch, Glasgow, Dunbartonshire G66 1RN
✆ 0141 775 0723 Fax 0141 776 9030 **Map 12, F4**
7 miles N of Glasgow
Founded 1926
An undulating James Braid course with splendid views of the Campsie Hills.
18 holes, 6052 yards
par 70, S.S.S 70
Designer James Braid
Green fees £20
Catering, changing room/showers, bar, trolley hire, shop, practice facilities
Visitors welcome only as members' guests
Societies welcome by prior arrangement Tuesday and Thursday – no company days
Smiths Hotel, Broadcroft, Kirkintilloch, Dunbartonshire
✆ 0141 775 0398

HELENSBURGH GOLF CLUB

25 East Abercromby Street, Helensburgh, Dunbartonshire G84 9HZ
✆ 01436 674173 Fax 01436 671170
Map 12, D3
Off A82, signposted in Helensburgh
Founded 1893

A club which has been part of town life since its foundation. The views south over the Clyde and north over Loch Lomond are impressive. Ditches are a feature of many holes, and there are six par 4s over 400 yards in length. The par-3 3rd is particularly unforgiving.
18 holes, 6104 yards
par 69, S.S.S 70
Designer Tom Morris
Green fees £25
Catering, changing room/showers, bar, club and trolley hire, shop, practice facilities
Visitors welcome weekdays
Societies welcome by prior arrangement

HILTON PARK GOLF CLUB

Auldmarroch Estate, Stockiemuir Road, Milngavie, Dunbartonshire G62 7HB
✆ 0141 956 4657 Fax 0141 956 4657 **Map 12, F4**
info@hiltonparkgolfclub.fsnet.co.uk
B809, 8 miles NW of Glasgow
Founded 1927
A club with the luxury of two enjoyable moorland courses, surrounded by lovely scenery.
Hilton Course: 18 holes, 6054 yards, par 70, S.S.S 70
Allander Course: 18 holes, 5487 yards, par 69, S.S.S 67
Designer James Braid
Green fees £25
Catering, changing room/showers, bar, club and trolley hire, shop, practice facilities
Visitors welcome weekdays
Handicap certificate required
Societies welcome by prior arrangement

KIRKINTILLOCH GOLF CLUB

Todhill, Campsie Road, Kirkintilloch, Dunbartonshire G66 1RN
✆ 0141 776 1256 **Map 12, F4**
Off A803, 1 mile NW of Kirkintilloch
Founded 1895
A pleasantly wooded country course.
18 holes, 5860 yards
par 70, S.S.S 68
Designer James Braid
Catering, changing room/showers, bar, shop
Visitors welcome only as members' guests
Societies welcome by prior arrangement

LENZIE GOLF CLUB

19 Crosshill Road, Lenzie, Dunbartonshire G66 5DA
✆ 0141 777 7748 Fax 0141 812 3018 **Map 12, F4**
scottdavidson@lenziegolfclub.demon.co.uk
www.lenziegolfclub
M80 Jct 2
Founded 1889
Trees are a major hazard on this parkland course which gives extensive views north to the Campsie Hills and Ben Lomond.
18 holes, 5984 yards
par 69, S.S.S 69
Green fees £24
Catering, changing room/showers, bar, trolley hire, shop, practice facilities, seminar rooms
Visitors welcome weekdays
Handicap certificate required
Societies welcome by prior arrangement

LOCH LOMOND GOLF CLUB

Rossdhu House, Luss, Dunbartonshire G83 8NT
✆ 01436 655555 Fax 01436 655500
Map 12, E3
www.lochlomond.com
A82 at Luss
Founded 1994
Television coverage of the Solheim Cup and Standard Life Loch Lomond tour events have made the course familiar to many – from a distance, that is, because it is strictly members only. The site is ravishingly beautiful, the design brilliant, and Tom Weiskopf reckons it is his masterpiece. The case rests.
18 holes, 7060 yards
par 71
Designer Tom Weiskopf, Jay Morrish
Catering, changing room/showers, bar, trolley and buggy hire, shop, driving range, practice facilities
Visitors welcome only as members' guests
No societies

MILNGAVIE GOLF CLUB

Laighpark, Milngavie, Glasgow, Dunbartonshire G62 8HE
✆ 0141 956 1619 Fax 0141 956 4252 **Map 12, F4**
Off A809 at Craigton Village
Founded 1895
A short, but scenic, course which is always said to play its full length.
18 holes, 5818 yards
par 68, S.S.S 68
Designer Auchterlonie Brothers
Green fees £22
Catering, changing room/showers, bar, practice facilities
Visitors welcome by prior arrangement
Handicap certificate required
Societies welcome by prior arrangement
🏨 West Highland Gate, Main Street, Milngavie, Dunbartonshire
✆ 0141 956 7835

PALACERIGG GOLF CLUB

Palacerigg Country Park, Cumbernauld, Dunbartonshire G67 3HU
✆ 01236 734969 Fax 01236 721461
Map 12, G4
Off B8054, 2 miles S of Cumbernauld
Founded 1975
One of Sir Henry Cotton's very few designs in Scotland, a parkland course with a cunning 15th, a par 4 on which indecision on the tee invariably leads to driving into a burn.
18 holes, 6444 yards
par 72, S.S.S 71
Designer Sir Henry Cotton
Green fees £8
Catering, changing room/showers, bar, shop, practice facilities
Visitors welcome
Societies welcome by prior arrangement

VALE OF LEVEN GOLF CLUB

Northfield Road, Bonhill, Alexandria, Dunbartonshire G83 9ET
✆ 01389 752351 Fax 01389 752351
Map 12, E4
richardbarclay@valeoflevengolfclub.org.uk
www.valeoflevengolfclub.org.uk
From A82 at Dumbarton follow signs for Bonhill
Founded 1907
As so often is the case with long-established Scottish courses, the golf will be trickier than the yardage suggests. Fine views of Loch Lomond are a bonus.
18 holes, 5167 yards
par 67, S.S.S 66
Green fees £16
Catering, changing room/showers, bar, trolley hire, shop
Visitors welcome
Handicap certificate required
Societies welcome by prior arrangement
🏨 Cameron House Hotel, Loch Lomond, Dunbartonshire G84 9SF
✆ 01389 755565

WESTERWOOD HOTEL GOLF & COUNTRY CLUB

St Andrews Drive, Cumbernauld, Dunbartonshire G68 0EW
✆ 01236 457171 Fax 01236 738478
Map 12, G4
westerwood@morton-hotels.com
www.morton-hotels.com
Off A80, midway between Glasgow and Stirling
Founded 1989

The green fee represents good value for a course designed by Thomas and Ballesteros. Naturally, it is full of individuality, with many heathland touches. Two of the par 5s exceed 550 yards, but it is the 165-yard 15th, with its green below a 50-foot quarry, which stands out.
18 holes, 6616 yards
par 72, S.S.S 72
Designer Dave Thomas, Severiano Ballesteros
Green fees £22.50
Catering, changing room/showers, bar, accommodation, club, trolley and buggy hire, shop, practice facilities, full hotel, conference, wedding and function facilities
Visitors welcome
Societies welcome by prior arrangement
Westerwood Hotel, Golf & Country Club, St Andrews Drive, Cumbernauld, Glasgow, Dunbartonshire G68 0EW
01236 457171 Fax 01236 738478
westerwood@morton-hotels.com
www.morton-hotels.com

WINDYHILL GOLF CLUB
Windyhill, Bearsden, Dunbartonshire G61 4QQ
0141 942 2349 Fax 0141 942 5874 **Map 12, F4**
A809 to Baljaffray roundabout, then B8050
Founded 1908
Part parkland, part moorland, only 7 miles from the centre of Glasgow, yet wild and rugged. The par-3 14th, for instance, plays to a green nestling between rocky crags, with fine mountain views beyond.
18 holes, 6616 yards
par 71, S.S.S 70
Designer James Braid
Green fees £20
Catering, changing room/showers, bar, club and trolley hire, shop, practice facilities
Visitors welcome – restricted Sunday
Societies welcome by prior arrangement

EAST LOTHIAN

CASTLE PARK GOLF COURSE
Gifford, Haddington, East Lothian EH41 4PL
01620 810733 Fax 01620 810723
Map 13, C4
stuartfortune@aol.com
www.castleparkgolfclub.co.uk
On Longyester road, 2 miles S of Gifford
Founded 1994
Not unreasonably, Castle Park has been described as a mini Gleneagles. Set in the former Deer Park of Yester Castle, with the Lammermuir Hills as background, this good value course is expanding to 18 holes.
9 holes, 5744 yards
par 68, S.S.S 68
Designer Archie Baird
Green fees £12
Catering, changing room/showers, bar, club, trolley and buggy hire, driving range, practice facilities
Visitors welcome
Societies welcome by prior arrangement
Goblin Ha' Hotel, Gifford, Haddington, East Lothian
01620 810244

DUNBAR GOLF CLUB
East Links, Dunbar, East Lothian EH42 1LL
01368 862317 Fax 01368 865202
Map 13, D4
enquiries@dunbargolfclub.sol.co.uk
www.dunbar-golfclub.co.uk
½ mile E of Dunbar
Founded 1856
Most easterly of the famous Lothian links, Dunbar occupies a narrow strip of land, often no more than two fairways wide, alongside the open sea. The toughest hole, the 12th, is a long par 4 playing to a green set on a headland, almost equalled by the 7th and 14th.
18 holes, 6404 yards
par 71, S.S.S 71
Designer Tom Morris
Green fees £30
Catering, changing room/showers, bar, club and trolley hire, shop, practice facilities
Visitors welcome
Societies welcome by prior arrangement
Nether Abbey Hotel, Direlton Avenue, North Berwick, East Lothian
01620 892802

GIFFORD GOLF CLUB
Edinburgh Road, Gifford, East Lothian EH41 4JE
01620 810591 **Map 13, C4**
Off B6355
Founded 1904
A fine 9-hole course set in the foothills of the Lammermuirs, with excellent greens, and the Speedyburn running through the course, coming into play on four holes.
9 holes, 6256 yards
par 71, S.S.S 70
Designer Willlie Watt
Green fees £13
Catering, changing room/showers, trolley hire
Visitors welcome
Societies welcome by prior arrangement

THE GLEN GOLF CLUB
East Links, Tantallon Terrace, North Berwick, East Lothian EH39 4LE
01620 892726 Fax 01620 895447
Map 13, D4
secretary@glengolfclub.co.uk
www.glengolfclub.co.uk
North Berwick, east of harbour
Founded 1906
Less famous than the West Links, but very entertaining in its own right, and fairly easy on the purse. After a stiff climb at the 1st, the views from the higher part of the course are breathtaking, past Bass Rock, over the Firth of Forth. The short 13th is brilliant.
18 holes, 6043 yards
par 69, S.S.S 69
Designer James Braid, Ben Sayers, Mackenzie Ross
Green fees £20
Catering, changing room/showers, bar, club and trolley hire, shop, practice facilities, function room
Visitors welcome – restrictions
Handicap certificate required – limit: 28 men, 40 women
Societies welcome by prior arrangement
Nether Abbey Hotel, Direlton Avenue, North Berwick, East Lothian
01620 892802

GULLANE GOLF CLUB
West Links Road, Gullane, East Lothian EH31 2BB
01620 842255 Fax 01620 842327
Map 13, C3
bookings@gullanegolfclub.com
www.gullanegolfclub.com
A198, E of Edinburgh
Founded 1882
***See* Top 50 Courses, page 23**
No.1 Course: 18 holes, 6466 yards, par 71, S.S.S 72
No.2 Course: 18 holes, 6223 yards, par 71, S.S.S 70
No.3 Course: 18 holes, 5252 yards, par 68, S.S.S 66
Green fees £60
Catering, changing room/showers, bar, club, trolley and buggy hire, shop, driving range, practice facilities
Visitors welcome – booking advisable
Handicap certificate required.
Societies welcome by prior arrangement
Golf Hotel, Main Street, Gullane,

East Lothian
☎ 01620 843259

HADDINGTON GOLF CLUB

Amisfield Park, Haddington, East Lothian EH41 4PT
☎ 01620 822727 Fax 01620 826580
Map 13, C4
hadd.golf1@tesco.net
www.haddingtongolf.co.golf
15 miles E of Edinburgh off A1
Founded 1865
Set in the parkland grounds of a historic house, with the River Tyne running through it.
18 holes, 6317 yards
par 71, S.S.S 70
Green fees £18
Catering, changing room/showers, bar, club, trolley and buggy hire, shop, practice facilities, meeting room facilities
Visitors welcome, with restrictions
Societies welcome by prior arrangement
🏨 Maitlandfield Hotel, 24 Sidegate, Haddington, East Lothian EH41 4B2
☎ 01620 826513

THE HONOURABLE COMPANY OF EDINBURGH GOLFERS

Muirfield, Gullane, East Lothian EH31 2EG
☎ 01620 842123 Fax 01620 842977
Map 13, C3
hce@byinternet
Off A198, NE of village
Founded 1744
See Top 50 Courses, page 29
18 holes, 6801 yards
par 70, S.S.S 73
Designer James Braid, H. Cotton
Green fees £80
Catering, changing room/showers, bar, trolley and buggy hire, practice facilities
Visitors welcome Tuesday and Thursday
Handicap certificate required – limit: 18 men, 24 women
Societies welcome by prior arrangement

KILSPINDIE GOLF CLUB

Aberlady, East Lothian EH32 0QD
☎ 01875 870358 Fax 01875 870358
Map 13, C4
A198, 17 miles E of Edinburgh
Founded 1867
Shorter than its illustrious neighbours, but a genuine links with tight, well-bunkered fairways. Overlooking Aberlady Bay and nature reserve.
18 holes, 5480 yards
par 69, S.S.S 66
Green fees £25
Catering, changing room/showers, bar, club and trolley hire, shop, practice facilities
Visitors welcome
Handicap certificate required
Societies welcome by prior arrangement
🏨 The Old Aberlady Inn, Main Street, Aberlady, East Lothian
☎ 01875 870503

LONGNIDDRY GOLF CLUB

Links Road, Longniddry, East Lothian EH32 0NL
☎ 01875 852228 Fax 01875 853371
Map 13, C4
secretary@longniddrygolfclub.co.uk
www.longniddrygolfclub.co.uk
A1/A198 to Longniddry Village
Founded 1921
Essentially parkland, but there are many links touches, as well as superb views across the Firth of Forth. It is a course without a par 5, but, as Christie O'Connor put it, 'you've a lot of very good four and seven eighths.' Eight par 4s exceed 400 yards in length.
18 holes, 6260 yards
par 68, S.S.S 70
Designer Harry Colt, James Braid, Mackenzie Ross, Donald Steel
Green fees £32
Catering, changing room/showers, bar, club, trolley and buggy hire, shop, practice facilities
Visitors welcome
Handicap certificate required
Societies welcome by prior arrangement
🏨 Kilspindie House Hotel, Aberlady, East Lothian
☎ 01875 870682

LUFFNESS NEW GOLF CLUB

Aberlady, East Lothian EH32 0QA
☎ 01620 843336 Fax 01620 842933
Map 13, C3
A198 between Aberlady and Gullane
Founded 1894
With springy fairways and some of the finest greens in the land, Luffness is always a pleasure to play. Those greens are generally small, and not easily found from long range. Luffness rough can be savage, and the plentiful bunkering is serious. Accuracy is the key here, not outright length.
18 holes, 6122 yards
par 69, S.S.S 70
Designer Tom Morris, James Braid
Green fees £37.50
Catering, changing room/showers, bar, trolley hire, practice facilities
Visitors welcome weekdays
Handicap certificate required – limit: 24 men, 36 women
Societies welcome by prior arrangement
🏨 Golf Hotel, Main Street, Gullane, East Lothian
☎ 01620 843259

THE MUSSELBURGH GOLF CLUB

Monktonhall, Musselburgh, East Lothian EH21 6SA
☎ 0131 665 2005 **Map 13, B4**
B6415, 1 mile S of Musselburgh
Founded 1938
Not to be confused with the Old Links, this course is parkland in nature, and a serious examination of technique, reflected in a Standard Scratch Score two shots above par.
18 holes, 6725 yards
par 71, S.S.S 73
Designer James Braid
Green fees £22
Catering, changing room/showers, bar, accommodation, club, trolley and buggy hire, shop
Visitors welcome – restricted weekends
Societies welcome by prior arrangement

MUSSELBURGH OLD COURSE

10 Balcarres Road, Musselburgh, East Lothian EH21 7SD
☎ 0131 665 6981 **Map 13, B4**
info@musselburgholdlinks.co.uk
www.musselburgholdlinks.co.uk
A1, 5 miles E of Edinburgh
Founded 1672
An absolute must for all golfers with a sense of history: the oldest playing course in the world (back to at least 1672), host to six Open Championships (1874–1889), five Musselburgh players taking 11 Open titles between them, and original home to The Honourable Company, Royal Burgess, and Bruntsfield.
9 holes, 2808 yards
par 34, S.S.S 34
Green fees £8
Changing room/showers, club and trolley hire, original hickory clubs for hire
Visitors welcome, but phone first
Societies welcome by prior arrangement
🏨 Donmaree Hotel, Musselburgh, East Lothian

NORTH BERWICK GOLF CLUB

West Links, Beach Road, North Berwick, East Lothian EH39 4BB
☎ 01620 892135 Fax 01620 893274
Map 13, C3
Off A198, just W of town centre
Founded 1832
One of the great traditional links courses, full of character – some of it

undoubtedly capricious, with stone walls and blind shots, for instance. The 192-yard 15th 'Redan' has been copied all over the world, and, apparently, the 11th was the model for the famous 18th at Seminole in Florida.
18 holes, 6420 yards
par 71, S.S.S 71
Green fees £40
Catering, changing room/showers, bar, club and trolley hire, shop
Visitors welcome
Handicap certificate required
Societies welcome by prior arrangement
Marine Hotel, Cromwell Road, North Berwick, East Lothian
01620 892406

ROYAL MUSSELBURGH GOLF CLUB

Prestongrange House, Prestonpans, East Lothian EH32 9RP
01875 810276 Fax 01875 810276
Map 13, B4
www.royalmusselburgh.co.uk
Off A59, W of Prestonpans
Founded 1774
A parkland course with pleasant views over the Firth of Forth.
18 holes, 6237 yards
par 70, S.S.S 70
Designer James Braid
Green fees £20
Catering, changing room/showers, bar, club, trolley and buggy hire, shop, practice facilities
Visitors welcome
Societies welcome by prior arrangement

WHITEKIRK GOLF COURSE

Whitekirk, near North Berwick, East Lothian EH39 5PR
01620 870300 Fax 01620 870330
Map 13, D3
golf@whitekirk.u-net.com
www.whitekirk.com
A198, 3 miles SE of North Berwick
Founded 1995
One of the more affordable of the exciting new golfing developments in Scotland. Rocky outcrops, links-like humps and bumps, and deep grassy hollows give this heathland course considerable character, and there are fine sea views, too. The opening of a leisure club and hotel will make this a complete resort.
18 holes, 6526 yards
par 72, S.S.S 72
Designer Cameron Sinclair
Green fees £20
Catering, changing room/showers, bar, club, trolley and buggy hire, shop, driving range, practice facilities
Visitors welcome
Societies welcome by prior arrangement
Nether Abbey Hotel, Direlton Avenue, North Berwick, East Lothian
01620 892802

WINTERFIELD GOLF CLUB

St Margaret's, North Road, Dunbar, East Lothian EH42 1AU
01368 862280 **Map 13, D4**
Off A1087, W of Dunbar
Founded 1935
A short seaside course on paper, but the 1st hole is a long par 3 with a 220-yard carry to the green.
18 holes, 5155 yards
par 65, S.S.S 65
Green fees £15
Catering, changing room/showers, bar, club, trolley and buggy hire, shop, practice facilities
Visitors welcome with restrictions
Societies welcome by prior arrangement
Bayswell Hotel, Bayswell Park, Dunbar, East Lothian
01368 860044

FIFE

ABERDOUR GOLF CLUB

Seaside Place, Aberdour, Fife KY3 0TX
01383 860688 Fax 01383 860050
Map 13, A3
6 miles SE of Dunfermline
Founded 1896
Although running along the shores of the Firth of Forth, it is, in fact, parkland in kind.
18 holes, 5460 yards
par 67, S.S.S 66
Designer Robertson/Anderson
Green fees £17
Catering, changing room/showers, bar, club and trolley hire, shop
Visitors welcome – restricted Saturday
Societies welcome by prior arrangement

ANSTRUTHER GOLF CLUB

Marsfield, Shore Road, Anstruther, Fife KY10 2QG
01333 312283 Fax 01333 312283
Map 13, D2
Off A917
Founded 1890
A course short in length but high on character, with fine panoramas across the Firth of Forth to the Isle of May.
9 holes, 4532 yards
par 62, S.S.S 63
Green fees £12
Catering, changing room/showers, bar, trolley hire
Visitors welcome, with restrictions
Societies welcome by prior arrangement
Craws Nest Hotel, Pittenweem Road, Anstruther, Fife
01333 310691

AUCHTERDERRAN GOLF CLUB

Woodend Road, Cardenden, Fife KY5 0NH
01592 721579 **Map 13, B3**
N of Cardenden
Founded 1904
Although reasonably flat, the course is still interesting to the good player.
9 holes, 5400 yards
par 66, S.S.S 66
Green fees £9
Changing room/showers, bar
Visitors welcome with restrictions
Societies welcome by prior arrangement

BALBIRNIE PARK GOLF CLUB

Balbirnie Park, Markinch, Glenrothes, Fife KY7 6NR
01592 612095 **Map 13, B2**
Off A92, 2 miles E of Glenrothes
Founded 1983
A parkland course of some quality in handsome surroundings.
18 holes, 6210 yards
par 71, S.S.S 70
Designer Fraser Middleton
Green fees £25
Catering, changing room/showers, bar, club, trolley and buggy hire, shop, practice facilities
Visitors welcome with restrictions
Societies welcome by prior arrangement

BALLINGRY GOLF CLUB

Lochore Meadows Country Park, Crosshill, Lochgelly, Fife KY5 8BA
01592 860086 **Map 13, A3**
B920, 2 miles N of Lochgelly
One of a number of outdoor activities available at this country park, the course being set, prettily, beside a loch.
9 holes, 6482 yards
par 72, S.S.S 71
Green fees £7.50
Changing room/showers, swimming, fishing, riding, water sports
Visitors welcome
Societies welcome by prior arrangement

BURNTISLAND GOLF HOUSE CLUB

Dodhead, Burntisland, Fife KY3 9EY
01592 874093 Fax 01592 874093
Map 13, B3
wktbghc@aol.com

B923, 1 mile E of Burntisland
Founded 1898
Attractively situated, backed by a wooded hill, and enjoying fine seascapes, this course is quite difficult, especially when the wind blows, when there is little relief from it.
18 holes, 5965 yards
par 70, S.S.S 70
Designer Willie Park, James Braid
Green fees £17
Catering, changing room/showers, bar, club and trolley hire, shop, driving range, practice facilities
Visitors welcome – restricted weekends
Societies welcome by prior arrangement

CANMORE GOLF CLUB

Venturefair Avenue, Dunfermline, Fife KY12 0PE
☎ 01383 7281416 **Map 13, A3**
Off Pilmuir Street, N of Dunfermline town centre
Founded 1897
Far from long, and generally flat, but a decent test of accuracy, none the less.
18 holes, 5376 yards
par 67, S.S.S 66
Designer Ben Sayers
Green fees £15
Catering, changing room/showers, bar, club and trolley hire, shop, practice facilities
Visitors welcome, weekend restricted
Societies welcome by prior arrangement
Garvock House Hotel, Transy, Dunfermline, Fife
☎ 01383 621067

CHARLETON GOLF COURSE

Charleton, Colinsburgh, Fife KY9 1HG
☎ 01333 340505 Fax 01333 340583
Map 13, C2
www.charleton.co.uk
Off A917/B942 W of Colinsburgh
Founded 1992
One of Scotland's premier pay-and-play facilities, handily placed to give a good workout to those about to essay the great Fife links. Amongst favourable comments from visitors is one from former US President, George Bush.
18 holes, 6149 yards
par 72, S.S.S 70
Designer John Salvesen
Green fees £18
Catering, changing room/showers, bar, accommodation, club, trolley and buggy hire, shop, driving range, practice facilities, 9-hole pitch-and-putt, conference facilities
Visitors welcome
Societies welcome by prior arrangement
Charleton House, Charleton, Colinsburgh, Fife

COWDENBEATH GOLF CLUB

Seco Place, Cowdenbeath, Fife KY4 8PD
☎ 0183 511918 **Map 13, A3**
6 miles E of Dunfermline
Founded 1991
A parkland course.
18 holes, 6100 yards
S.S.S 69
Green fees £5
Bar, practice facilities
Visitors welcome
Societies welcome by prior arrangement

CRAIL GOLFING SOCIETY

Balcomie Clubhouse, Fifeness, Crail, Fife KY10 3XN
☎ 01333 450686 Fax 01333 450416
Map 13, D2
crailgolfs@aol.com
www.golfagent.com/clubsites/crail
10 miles SE of St Andrews
Founded 1786
The famous old Balcomie Links has recently been joined by a second, bigger course, designed by Gil Hanse of Pennsylvania. Balcomie may be idiosyncratic but it is a classic, with the first five holes hugging the shoreline in magnificent splendour. Craighead puts a similar premium on accuracy from the tee.
Balcomie Links: 18 holes, 5922 yards, par 69, S.S.S 69
Designer Tom Morris
Craighead Links: 18 holes, 6728 yards, par 71, S.S.S 73
Designer Gil Hanse
Green fees £25
Catering, changing room/showers, bar, club and trolley hire, shop, practice facilities
Visitors welcome – advisable to book well in advance
Societies welcome by prior arrangement
The Golf Hotel, 4 High Street, Crail, Fife KY10 3TD
☎ 01333 450206 Fax 01333 450795
thegolfhotel@ibm.net

CUPAR GOLF CLUB

Hilltarvit, Cupar, Fife KY15 5JT
☎ 01334 653549 **Map 13, B2**
secretary@cupargolfclub.freeserve.co.uk
S of town centre
Founded 1855
Probably the oldest continuous 9-hole club in the U.K. with a tricky hilly course.
9 holes, 5074 yards
par 68, S.S.S 66
Green fees £15
Catering, changing room/showers, bar, club and trolley hire
Visitors welcome – restricted Saturdays
Societies welcome by prior arrangement
Eden House Hotel, Pitscottie Road, Cupar, Fife
☎ 01334 652510

DUNFERMLINE GOLF CLUB

Pitfirrane, Crossford, Dunfermline, Fife KY12 8QW
☎ 01383 723534 **Map 13, A3**
pitfirrane@aol.com
A994, 2 miles W of Dunfermline
Founded 1887
A historic club with a 600-year old clubhouse, and the knowledge that past members established the St Andrews Club at Yonkers in New York. The course is unusual in having five par 5s and five par 3s, and the short holes are reckoned to be the key to success.
18 holes, 6121 yards
par 72, S.S.S 70
Designer J.R. Stutt
Green fees £21
Catering, changing room/showers, bar, trolley hire, shop, practice facilities
Visitors welcome weekdays
Societies welcome by prior arrangement
Keavil House Hotel, Crossford, Dunfermline, Fife KY12 8QW
☎ 01383 723534

DUNNIKIER PARK GOLF CLUB

Dunnikier Way, Kirkcaldy, Fife KY1 3LP
☎ 01592 261599 Fax 01592 642541
Map 13, B3
B981, off A92
Founded 1963
A parkland course with views of the Firth of Forth and Lomond Hills.
18 holes, 6601 yards
par 72, S.S.S 72
Designer R. Stutt
Green fees £11.50
Catering, changing room/showers, bar, club, trolley and buggy hire, shop, practice facilities
Visitors welcome
Societies welcome by prior arrangement

FALKLAND GOLF CLUB

The Myre, Falkland, Fife KY15 7AA
☎ 01337 857404 **Map 13, B2**
A192, N of Falkland

Founded 1976
A short public course with well-regarded, speedy greens.
9 holes, 5216 yards
par 68, S.S.S 65
Green fees £8
Catering, changing room/showers, bar, trolley hire
Visitors welcome
Societies welcome by prior arrangement

GLENROTHES GOLF CLUB

Golf Course Road, Glenrothes, Fife KY6 2LA
01592 75461 **Map 13, B2**
Off B921, W of Glenrothes
Founded 1958
A stream comes into play on 4 holes on the back nine of this good quality public course.
18 holes, 6444 yards
par 71, S.S.S 71
Designer J.R. Stutt
Green fees £11
Catering, changing room/showers, bar, practice facilities
Visitors welcome – restricted weekends
Societies welcome by prior arrangement

GOLF HOUSE CLUB

Elie, Fife KY9 1AS
01333 330301 Fax 01333 330895
Map 13, C2
sandy@golfhouseclub.freeserve.co.uk
A917, 12 miles S of St Andrews
Founded 1875
Elie displays all the virtues of links golf, with fine seascapes. Unusually, under modern par ratings it has no par 5s, and only two short holes. The shore holes are outstanding, and James Braid (who was brought up here) declared the 13th, Croupie, to be the finest hole in Scotland.
18 holes, 6273 yards, par 70, S.S.S 70
Designer James Braid
9 holes, 2277 yards, S.S.S 32
Green fees £38
Catering, changing room/showers, bar, club and trolley hire, shop, practice facilities
Visitors welcome, Monday to Saturday
Daily ballot in summer
Handicap certificate required– limit: 28 men, 36 women.
Societies welcome by prior arrangement
Victoria Hotel, Victoria Road, Kirkcaldy, Fife
01592 260117

KINGHORN MUNICIPAL GOLF CLUB

McDuff Crescent, Kinghorn, Fife KY3 9RE
01592 890345 **Map 13, B3**
A921, S of Kinghorn
Founded 1887
On an elevated site with views over the Firth of Forth, a surprisingly testing course.
18 holes, 5629 yards
par 65, S.S.S 67
Designer Tom Morris
Green fees £11
Changing room/showers
Visitors welcome
Societies welcome by prior arrangement

KINGSBARNS GOLF LINKS

Kingsbarns, St Andrews, Fife KY16 8QD
01334 460860 **Map 13, D2**
A917, SE of St Andrews
Founded 2000
A spectacular new development destined for the top. Farmland was skilfully turned into linksland to give all the features of traditional seaside golf. Holes on both nines skirt the sea gloriously, with the gorgeous 3rd, 15th and 16th just pipped for pride of place by the stunning 606-yard 12th.
18 holes, 7126 yards
par 72, S.S.S. 74
Designer Kyle Phillips
Green fees £105
Catering, changing room/showers, bar, club and trolley hire, shop
Visitors welcome – advance booking
Handicap certificate required
Societies welcome by prior arrangement

KIRKCALDY GOLF CLUB

Balwearie Road, Kirkcaldy, Fife KY2 5LT
01592 205240 Fax 01592 205240
Map 13, B3
enquiries@kirkcaldygolfclub.sol.co.uk
Off A92
Founded 1804
Despite a proliferation of drive-and-pitch holes this is quite a tricky parkland course with a renowned 17th hole.
18 holes, 6038 yards
par 71, S.S.S 69
Designer Tom Morris
Green fees £22
Catering, changing room/showers, bar, club, trolley and buggy hire, shop, practice facilities
Visitors welcome
Societies welcome by prior arrangement
Victoria Hotel, Victoria Road, Kirkcaldy, Fife
01592 260117

LADYBANK GOLF CLUB

Annsmuir, Ladybank, Fife KY15 7RA
01337 830814 Fax 01337 831505
Map 13, B2
ladybankgc@aol.com
A92 SW of Cupar
Founded 1879
Since 1978 many great players have qualified here for Opens at St Andrews, including Langer, Torrance, Newton, and Woosnam. Its velvet fairways are lined with heather and broom, and run through avenues of pine trees. Accuracy from the tee is rewarded, especially on the mischievous dog-legs, such as the 16th.
18 holes, 6754 yards
par 71, S.S.S 72
Designer Tom Morris
Green fees £35
Catering, changing room/showers, bar, club, trolley and buggy hire, shop, driving range, practice facilities
Visitors must be members of a recognised golf club
Handicap certificate required
Societies welcome by prior arrangement (not weekend)
Fernie Castle Hotel, Letham, nr Cupar, Fife KY15 7RU
01337 810381 Fax 1337810522

LESLIE GOLF CLUB

Balsillie Laws, Leslie, Glenrothes, Fife KY6 3EZ
01592 620040 **Map 13, B2**
Off A911, N of Leslie
Founded 1898
A parkland course.
9 holes, 4940 yards
par 63, S.S.S 64
Green fees £5
Changing room/showers
Visitors welcome by prior arrangement
Societies welcome by prior arrangement

LEVEN LINKS GOLF CLUB

The Promenade, Leven, Fife KY8 4HS
01333 421390 Fax 01333 428859
Map 13, B2
Off A955, at E end of Leven
Founded 1846
Leven adjoins Lundin and shares with it fast running links fairways and views across the Firth of Forth to East Lothian. The most famous hole is the 18th, a very long par 4 with its green, sleeper faced, raised up above a burn. The 5th and 6th are

also outstanding.
18 holes, 6436 yards
par 71, S.S.S 70
Green fees £24
Catering, changing room/showers, bar, club and trolley hire, shop, practice facilities
Visitors welcome with restrictions
Societies welcome by prior arrangement

LOCHGELLY GOLF CLUB

Cartmore Road, Lochgelly, Kirkaldy, Fife KY5 9PB
✆ 01592 780174 **Map 13, B3**
Off A910, W of Lochgelly
Founded 1895
A gentle parkland course.
18 holes, 5454 yards
par 68, S.S.S 67
Green fees £12
Catering, changing room/showers, bar, shop
Visitors welcome
Societies welcome by prior arrangement

LUNDIN GOLF CLUB

Golf Road, Lundin Links, Fife KY8 6BA
✆ 01333 320202 Fax 01333 329743
Map 13, C2
secretary@lundingolfclub.co.uk
www.lundingolfclub.co.uk
1 mile E of Leven on Leven/St Andrews Road
Founded 1868
A regular qualifying course for St Andrews Opens, Lundin opens and closes with strong links holes, while there is an excursion inland in mid-round. The hardest hole is probably the 4th, a 450-yard par 4 with a demanding stroke over a stream. The short 14th is aptly named Perfection.
18 holes, 6394 yards
par 71, S.S.S 71
Designer James Braid
Green fees £32
Catering, changing room/showers, bar, club and trolley hire, shop, practice facilities
Visitors welcome with restrictions
Societies welcome by prior arrangement
🏨 The Old Manor, Lundin Links, Fife KY8 6AJ
✆ 01333 320368 Fax 01333 320911

PITREAVIE (DUNFERMLINE) GOLF CLUB

Queensferry Road, Dunfermline, Fife KY11 8PR
✆ 01383 722591 Fax 01383 722591
Map 13, A3
M90 Jct 2
Founded 1922
A wooded course, heathland in character, giving pleasant views over the Forth Valley.
18 holes, 6032 yards
par 70, S.S.S 69
Designer Alister Mackenzie
Green fees £19.50
Catering, changing room/showers, bar, club and trolley hire, shop, practice facilities
Visitors welcome
Societies welcome by prior arrangement
🏨 Pitbauchlie Hotel, Aberdour Road, Dunfermline, Fife
✆ 0383 722282

SALINE GOLF CLUB

Kinneddar Hill, Saline, Fife KY12 9LT
✆ 01383 852591 **Map 13, A3**
5 miles NW of Dunfermline
Founded 1912
Remarkably, although the course is in the East of Scotland, with the Forth Valley plainly visible, it is possible also to see the West Coast from this hilly site!
9 holes, 5302 yards
par 68, S.S.S 66
Green fees £10
Catering, changing room/showers, bar, practice facilities, function room
Visitors welcome, not Saturdays
Societies welcome by prior arrangement
🏨 Saline Hotel, Main Street, Saline, Fife
✆ 01383 852798

SCOONIE GOLF CLUB

North Links, Leven, Fife KY8 4SP
✆ 01333 307007 Fax 01333 307008
Map 13, B2
manager@scooniegolfclub.com
www.scooniegolfclub.com
Near central Leven
Founded 1951
A gentle parkland course contrasting with the rigours of its famous links neighbours.
18 holes, 4979 yards
par 67, S.S.S 65
Green fees $11.50
Catering, changing room/showers, bar, trolley hire
Visitors welcome with restrictions
Societies welcome by prior arrangement
🏨 Caledonian Hotel, High Street, Leven, Fife
✆ 01333 424101

SCOTSCRAIG GOLF CLUB

Golf Road, Tayport, Fife DD6 9DZ
✆ 01382 552515 Fax 01382 553130
Map 13, C1
scotscraig@scottishgolf.com
www.scottishgolf.com/scotscraig
Tayport, 10 miles N of St Andrews
Founded 1817
Highly-regarded Scotscraig plays over undulating, links-like turf with the added hazards of trees, gorse and heather. The course is a regular Open Championship final qualifying venue, with holes such as the strategic 4th and 7th giving even the best players cause for thought. Out-of-bounds threatens several of the closing holes.
18 holes, 6669 yards
par 71, S.S.S 72
Designer James Braid
Green fees £35
Catering, changing room/showers, bar, shop, practice facilities
Visitors welcome weekdays – restricted weekends
Societies welcome by prior arrangement

ST ANDREWS BALGOVE COURSE

St Andrews Links Trust, Pilmour House, St Andrews, Fife KY16 9SF
✆ 01334 466666 Fax 01334 479555
Map 13, C1
www.standrews.org.uk
On A91
Founded 1993
A very basic course to encourage beginners, and, indeed, allowing even non-golfers the opportunity of saying that they have played at St Andrews!
9 holes, 1520 yards
Designer Donald Steel
Green fees £7
Driving range
Visitors welcome
Societies welcome by prior arrangement

ST ANDREWS DUKE'S COURSE

Old Course Hotel, Golf Resort & Spa, St Andrews, Fife KY16 9SP
✆ 01334 474371 Fax 01334 477668
Map 13, C2
info@oldcoursehotel.co.uk
www.oldcoursehotel.co.uk
Course located at Craigtoun Park, 3 miles S of St Andrews
Founded 1995
Peter Thomson, five-times Open Champion, has applied links philsophy to this inland design. Interestingly, for him, golf is meant to be played along the ground, not in the air. Pot bunkers and gorse are supplemented by stands of trees and a number of streams, which cross several fairways and greens.
18 holes, 7271 yards
par 72, S.S.S 75
Designer Peter Thomson

Green fees £60
Catering, changing room/showers, bar, accommodation, club, trolley and buggy hire, shop, driving range, practice facilities
Visitors welcome
Handicap certificate required
Societies welcome by prior arrangement
Old Course Hotel, St Andrews, Fife KY16 9SP
01334 474371 Fax 01334 477668
info@oldcoursehotel.co.uk
www.oldcoursehotel.co.uk

ST ANDREWS EDEN COURSE

St Andrews Links Trust, Pilmour House, St Andrews, Fife KY16 9SF
01334 466666 Fax 01344 479555
Map 13, C1
enquires@standrews.org.uk
www.standrews.org.uk
In St Andrews
Founded 1914
There were terrible mutterings when the closing holes of Colt's Eden Course were ploughed up to allow proper visitor facilities at St Andrews, but the truth is that they were never the best holes, and the Eden's trump card remains its proximity to the sea on the 4th and 7th.
18 holes, 6162 yards
par 70, S.S.S 73
Designer Harry Colt
Green fees £22
Catering, changing room/showers, bar, club and trolley hire, shop, driving range, practice facilities
Visitors welcome
Societies welcome by prior arrangement

ST ANDREWS JUBILEE COURSE

St Andrews Links Trust, Pilmour House, St Andrews, Fife KY16 9SF
01334 466666 Fax 01334 479555
Map 13, C1
enquiries@standrews.org.uk
www.standrews.org.uk
In St Andrews
Founded 1897
For many years the Jubilee was the least attractive of the courses at St Andrews, the nearest to the sea, but simply slotted in where there was nothing else of interest. Donald Steel's upgrading keeps the basic out-and-back layout and occasional double-greens, but introduces several wicked holes, particularly coming home.
18 holes, 6805 yards
par 72, S.S.S 73
Designer Donald Steel
Green fees £28
Catering, changing room/showers, bar, club and trolley hire, shop, driving range, practice facilities
Visitors welcome
Handicap certificate required
Societies welcome by prior arrangement

ST ANDREWS NEW COURSE

St Andrews Links Trust, Pilmour House, St Andrews, Fife KY16 9SF
01334 466666 Fax 01334 479555
Map 13, C1
enquiries@standrews.org.uk
www.standrews.org.uk
In St Andrews
Founded 1895
From the visitors' tees, the New Course is probably harder than the Old. Here the greens are single, the fairways narrower, and the rough more serious. At the same time, there is even less feature by which to evaluate distance and angle, making the approach shot one of utter commitment.
18 holes, 6604 yards
par 71, S.S.S 75
Designer Tom Morris
Green fees £31
Catering, changing room/showers, bar, club, trolley and buggy hire, shop, driving range, practice facilities
Visitors welcome
Societies welcome by prior arrangements

ST ANDREWS OLD COURSE

St Andrews Links Trust, Pilmour House, St Andrews, Fife KY16 9SF
01334 466666 Fax 01334 479555
Map 13, C1
enquiries@standrews.org.uk
www.standrews.org.uk
In St Andrews
Founded 1400
See Top 50 Courses, page 47
18 holes, 7115 yards
par 72, S.S.S 75
Green fees £85
Catering, changing room/showers, bar, club and trolley hire, shop, driving range, practice facilities
Visitors welcome, not Sundays
Handicap certificate required – limit: 24 men, 36 women
Societies welcome by prior arrangement – book through Old Course Experience tel: 01334 479050

ST ANDREWS STRATHTYRUM COURSE

St Andrews Links Trust, Pilmour House, St Andrews, Fife KY16 9SF
01334 466666 Fax 01334 479555
Map 13, C1
www.standrews.org.uk
On A91, St Andrews Links
Founded 1993
Plugging the gap between the Balgove and Eden Courses in terms of length and difficulty.
18 holes, 5094 yards
par 69, S.S.S 64
Designer Donald Steel
Green fees £17
Driving range
Visitors welcome
Societies welcome by prior arrangement

ST MICHAELS GOLF CLUB

Leuchars, Fife KY16 0DX
01334 839365 Fax 01334 838666
Map 13, C1
stmichaelsgc@btclick.com
www.stmichaelsgc.co.uk
A919, ½ mile from Leuchars
Founded 1903
An excellent place for final honing of the game before tackling St Andrews, with generous fairways and few daunting hazards.
18 holes, 5802 yards
par 70, S.S.S 68
Green fees £20
Catering, changing room/showers, bar, club and trolley hire
Visitors welcome – restricted weekends
Societies welcome by prior arrangement
St Michaels Inn, St Michaels, Fife KY16 0DU
01334 839220

THORNTON GOLF CLUB

Station Road, Thornton, Fife KY1 4DW
01592 771173 Fax 01592 774955
Map 13, B3
www.thorntongolfclubfife.co.uk
Off A92, 5 miles N of Kirkcaldy
Founded 1921
The River Ore, frequently forming the club boundary, enters play on the back nine, part of a testing closing stretch.
18 holes, 6155 yards
par 70, S.S.S 69
Green fees £15
Catering, changing room/showers, bar, trolley hire
Visitors welcome
Societies welcome by prior arrangement

GLASGOW

ALEXANDRA PARK GOLF CLUB

Alexandra Park, Dennistown, Glasgow G31 8SE

✆ 0141 556 1294 **Map 12, F4**
M8, ½ mile E of Glasgow
Founded 1880
Trees are a feature of this hilly parkland course with three par-3s over 200 yards in length.
9 holes, 4562 yards
par 62
Designer Graham McArthur
Changing room/showers, practice facilities
Visitors welcome
Societies welcome by prior arrangement

BISHOPBRIGGS GOLF CLUB

Brackenbrae Road, Bishopbriggs, Glasgow G64 2DX
✆ 0141 772 1810 Fax 0141 762 2532 **Map 12, F4**
Off A803, 6 miles N of Glasgow
Founded 1907
Parkland course.
18 holes, 6041 yards
par 69, S.S.S 69
Designer James Braid
Catering, changing room/showers, bar, shop
Visitors welcome only as members' guests
Societies welcome by prior arrangement

CATHCART CASTLE GOLF CLUB

Mearns Road, Clarkston, Glasgow G76 7YL
✆ 0141 638 0082 Fax 0141 638 1201 **Map 12, F5**
Off A726, 1 mile from Clarkston
Founded 1895
Undulating parkland course.
18 holes, 5832 yards
par 68, S.S.S 68
Green fees £28
Catering, changing room/showers, bar, club and trolley hire, shop
Visitors welcome weekdays with letter of introduction
Handicap certificate required
Societies welcome by prior arrangement

CAWDER GOLF CLUB

Cadder Road, Bishopbriggs, Glasgow G64 3QD
✆ 0141 772 7101 Fax 0141 772 4463 **Map 12, F4**
Off A803, 1 mile NE of Bishopbriggs
Founded 1933
Two contrasting courses, the Cawder hilly, the Keir flat.
Cawder Course: 18 holes, 6295 yards, par 70, S.S.S 71
Keir Course: 18 holes, 5877 yards, par 68, S.S.S 68
Designer James Braid, Donald Steel
Green fees £31
Catering, changing room/showers, bar, club and trolley hire, shop
Visitors welcome weekdays
Societies welcome by prior arrangement

COWGLEN GOLF CLUB

301 Barrhead Road, Glasgow G43 1EU
✆ 0141 632 0556 Fax 01505 503000 **Map 12, E5**
M77, S of Glasgow, following signs for Pollok and Barrhead
Founded 1906
A rather charming course, which builds, from the 8th tee, to a view across Glasgow and onwards to the Trossachs.
18 holes, 6053 yards
par 70, S.S.S 69
Designer James Braid
Green fees £25
Catering, changing room/showers, bar, club and trolley hire, shop, driving range, practice facilities
Visitors welcome – restricted weekends
Handicap certificate required
Societies welcome by prior arrangement
🏨 Tinto Firs, Kilmarnock Road, Glasgow
✆ 0141 637 2353

GLASGOW GOLF CLUB

Killermont, Bearsden, Glasgow G61 2TW
✆ 0141 942 1713 **Map 12, F5**
Off A81, NE of Glasgow
Founded 1787
The 8th oldest club in the world, with a magnificent clubhouse and fine parkland course.
18 holes, 5977 yards
par 70, S.S.S 69
Designer Tom Morris
Catering, changing room/showers, bar, trolley hire, shop, practice facilities
Visitors welcome only as members' guests
Handicap certificate required
No societies

HAGGS CASTLE GOLF CLUB

70 Dumbreck Road, Dumbreck, Glasgow G41 4SN
✆ 0141 427 3355 Fax 0141 427 1157 **Map 12, F5**
haggscastlegc@lineone.net
Close to M77 Jct 1
Founded 1910
Haggs Castle is the nearest course to Glasgow City Centre, and a former home to the Scottish Open European Tour event. The course is well defended with small greens, narrow, dog-legged fairways, and strategically significant trees, as typified by the Stroke 1 14th, needing a long approach through the trees.
18 holes, 6426 yards
par 72, S.S.S 71
Designer Dave Thomas
Green fees £35
Catering, changing room/showers, bar, club, trolley and buggy hire, shop, practice facilities
Visitors welcome weekdays
Handicap certificate required
Societies welcome by prior arrangement

KING'S PARK GOLF CLUB

150A Croftpark Avenue, Croftfoot, Glasgow G54
✆ 0141 630 1597 **Map 12, F5**
Croftfoot, 3 miles S of Glasgow
Founded 1934
A municipal parkland course.
9 holes, 4236 yards
par 64, S.S.S 60
Green fees £5
Club hire
Visitors welcome
Societies welcome by prior arrangement

KNIGHTSWOOD GOLF COURSE

Lincoln Avenue, Knightswood, Glasgow G13 3DN
✆ 0141 959 6358 **Map 12, F4**
S of A82, 4 miles NW of Glasgow
Founded 1929
A flat parkland course with long par 4s at the 1st and 3rd, and two short holes over 200 yards.
9 holes, 5586 yards
par 70, S.S.S 69
Green fees £7.50
Changing room/showers
Visitors welcome – restricted Wednesday and Friday mornings
Societies welcome by prior arrangement
🏨 Jury's Pond Hotel, Great Western Road, Glasgow

LETHAMHILL GOLF CLUB

Cumbernauld Road, Glasgow G33 1AH
✆ 0141 770 6220 Fax 0141 770 0520 **Map 12, F4**
A80, 3 mile NE of Glasgow
Founded 1933
Municipal parkland course.
18 holes, 5946 yards
par 70, S.S.S 68
Green fees £7.20
Changing room/showers
Visitors welcome
Societies welcome by prior arrangement

LINN PARK GOLF CLUB

Simshill Road, Glasgow G44 5TA
✆ 0141 637 5871 **Map 12, F5**
Off B766, 4 miles S of Glasgow
Founded 1924
A parkland course with a high proportion of short holes towards the beginning of the round.
18 holes, 4952 yards
par 66, S.S.S 65
Green fees £5.50
Changing room/showers
Visitors welcome
Societies welcome by prior arrangement

LITTLEHILL GOLF CLUB

Auchinairn Road, Glasgow G64 1UT
✆ 0141 772 1916 **Map 12, F4**
A803, 3 miles N of Glasgow
Founded 1926
Municipal course with rather greater length than most Glasgow public facilities.
18 holes, 6228 yards
par 70, S.S.S 70
Green fees £6
Changing room/showers
Visitors welcome
Societies welcome by prior arrangement

POLLOK GOLF CLUB

90 Barrhead Road, Glasgow G43 1BG
✆ 0141 649 0977 Fax 0141 649 1398 **Map 12, F5**
M77 Jct 2, head E for 1 mile.
Founded 1892
Set amidst the stately trees of the Pollock Estate (which also contains the world-famous Burrell Collection and Pollock House). The White Cart Water is a significant threat on the 14th.
18 holes, 6358 yards
par 71, S.S.S 70
Green fees £32
Catering, changing room/showers, bar, practice facilities
Visitors welcome – restricted weekends
Societies welcome by prior arrangement
🏨 Tinto Firs, Kilmarnock Road, Glasgow
✆ 0141 637 2353

ROUKEN GLEN GOLF CLUB

Stewarton Road, Thornliebank, Glasgow G46 7UZ
✆ 0141 638 7044 **Map 12, F5**
Off A77, 5 miles S of Glasgow
Founded 1922
Short public course.
18 holes, 4800 yards
S.S.S 63
Green fees £5
Driving range
Visitors welcome
Societies welcome by prior arrangement

RUCHILL GOLF CLUB

Ruchil Park, Brassey Street, Maryhill, Glasgow G20
✆ 0141 946 7676 **Map 12, F4**
Off A879, 2 miles N of Glasgow
Founded 1928
A public executive-length course.
9 holes, 2240 yards
S.S.S 31
Green fees £5
Visitors welcome
Societies welcome by prior arrangement

SANDYHILLS GOLF CLUB

223 Sandyhills Road Glasgow G32 9NA
✆ 0141 778 1179 **Map 12, F5**
Off A74, 4 miles SE of Glasgow
Founded 1905
Undulating parkland course.
18 holes, 6253 yards
par 71, S.S.S 71
Green fees £17.50
Catering, changing room/showers, bar
Visitors welcome weekdays
Societies welcome by prior arrangement

WILLIAMWOOD GOLF CLUB

Clarkston Road, Netherlee, Glasgow G44 3YR
✆ 0141 637 1783 Fax 0141 571 0166 **Map 12, F5**
B767, 5 miles S of Glasgow
Founded 1906
Interesting parkland course, somewhat hilly, with a lake and pond in addition to wooded areas.
18 holes, 5878 yards
par 68, S.S.S 69
Designer James Braid
Green fees £25
Catering, changing room/showers, bar, trolley hire, shop, practice facilities
Visitors welcome weekdays
Societies welcome by prior arrangement

INVERNESS

ABERNETHY GOLF CLUB

Nethy Bridge, Inverness PH25 3EB
✆ 01479 821305 Fax 01479 821305 **Map 14, E9**
abernethy-golfclub@lineone.net
nethybridge.com/golfclub.htm
B970, 1/4 mile N of Nethy Bridge
Founded 1893
A natural moorland course alongside the Abernethy Forest, with glorious views of the Strathspey Valley.
9 holes, 5038 yards
par 66, S.S.S 66
Green fees £13
Catering, changing room/showers, club and trolley hire
Visitors welcome
Societies welcome by prior arrangement
🏨 Heatherbrae Hotel, Dell Road, Nethy Bridge, Inverness
✆ 01479 821345

ALNESS GOLF CLUB

Ardross Road, Alness, Ross-shire, Inverness IV17 0QA
✆ 01349 88 3877 **Map 14, D7**
info@alnessgolfclub.co.uk
www.alness.com
A9 at Alness
Founded 1904
A tricky, hilly course with good views of the Cromarty Firth.
18 holes, 4886 yards
par 67, S.S.S 64
Designer Cassells
Green fees £13
Catering, changing room/showers, bar, club and trolley hire
Visitors welcome except during competitions
Societies welcome by prior arrangement

BOAT-OF-GARTEN GOLF & TENNIS CLUB

Boat-of-Garten, Inverness PH24 3BQ
✆ 01479 831282 Fax 01479 831523 **Map 14, E9**
boatgolf@enterprise.net
www.boatgolf.com
6 miles NE of Aviemore
Founded 1898
Beside the River Spey in the heart of the Cairngorms, "The Boat" is ravishingly beautiful. Deer and the occasional osprey may distract the golfer – the scenery is bound to – and the course itself is trickier than the yardage alone might indicate, with a number of dog-legs curving through the birches.
18 holes, 5866 yards
par 69, S.S.S 69
Designer James Braid
Green fees £23
Catering, changing room/showers, bar, club, trolley and buggy hire, shop, practice facilities, tennis
Visitors welcome
Handicap certificate required
Societies welcome by prior arrangement
🏨 The Boat Hotel, Boat-of-Garten, Inverness
✆ 01479 831258

CARRBRIDGE GOLF CLUB

Inverness Road, Carrbridge, Inverness PH23 3AU
☎ 01479 841623 **Map 14, E9**
enquiries@carrbridgegolf.com
www.carrbridgegolf.com
Off A9, 7 miles N of Aviemore
Founded 1980
Set in the glorious Strathspey countryside, Carrbridge is a pretty – and surprisingly challenging – 9-hole course with water in some form on every single hole. Carrbridge was the first Scottish ski village.
9 holes, 5402 yards
par 71, S.S.S 68
Green fees £12
Changing room/showers, club and trolley hire
Visitors welcome – restricted Sundays
Small societies welcome – no company days
Carrbridge Hotel, Carrbridge, Inverness
☎ 01479 841202

FORT AUGUSTUS GOLF CLUB

Markethill, Fort Augustus, Inverness PH32 4AU
☎ 01320 366309 **Map 14, D9**
A82, 1 mile W of Fort Augustus
Founded 1926
A pretty moorland course alongside the Caledonian Canal, with a dangerous 321-yard opening hole and a 550-yard par-5 6th.
9 holes, 5454 yards
par 67, S.S.S 67
Green fees £10
Changing room/showers, bar, club and trolley hire
Visitors welcome – restricted weekends
Societies welcome by prior arrangement

FORT WILLIAM GOLF CLUB

North Road, Fort William, Inverness PH33 6SW
☎ 01397 704464 **Map 14, C10**
A82, 2 miles N of Fort William
Founded 1974
Major improvements were made to the course in 1995, ensuring good playing conditions. Situated at the foot of Ben Nevis, the scenery is stunning.
18 holes, 6217 yards
par 72, S.S.S 71
Designer Hamilton Stutt
Green fees £15
Catering, changing room/showers, bar, club and trolley hire
Visitors welcome
Societies welcome by prior arrangement

FORTROSE & ROSEMARKIE GOLF CLUB

Ness Road East, Fortrose, Ross-shire IV10 8SE
☎ 01381 620529 Fax 01381 620529
Map 14, E8
A832, off A9 N of Inverness
Founded 1888
Charming old links course overlooking the Moray Firth. Keep an eye out for dolphins.
18 holes, 5875 yards
par 71, S.S.S 69
Designer James Braid
Green fees £20
Catering, changing room/showers, bar, club, trolley and buggy hire, shop, driving range, practice facilities
Visitors welcome, with restrictions
Societies welcome by prior arrangement

GRANTOWN-ON-SPEY GOLF CLUB

Golf Course Road, Grantown-on-Spey, Moray PH26 3HY
☎ 01479 872079 Fax 01479 873725
Map 14, E8
secretary@grantownonspeygolfclub.co.uk
www.grantownonspeygolfclub.co.uk
At Grantown, turning opposite police station.
Founded 1890
Well-wooded parkland in lovely scenery, reckoned to be a fair test for every calibre of golfer.
18 holes, 5710 yards
par 70, S.S.S 68
Designer A.C. Brown, Willie Park, James Braid
Green fees £20
Catering, changing room/showers, bar, club, trolley and buggy hire, shop, practice facilities
Visitors welcome – restricted weekends
Societies welcome by prior arrangement
Garth Hotel, Castle Road, Grantown-on-Spey, Inverness PH26 3HN
☎ 01479 872836

INVERGORDON GOLF CLUB

King George Street, Invergordon, Inverness IV18 0BD
☎ 01349 852715 **Map 14, E7**
Off B817 in Invergordon
Founded 1893
Extended to 18 holes in 1994, the new holes are relatively open, while the old ones are bordered by trees and rhododendrons.
18 holes, 6030 yards
par 69, S.S.S 69
Designer A Rae
Green fees £15
Catering, changing room/showers, bar, trolley hire, practice facilities
Visitors welcome, except during club competitions
Societies welcome by prior arrangement

INVERNESS GOLF CLUB

Culcabock Road Inverness IV2 3XQ
☎ 01463 231989 Fax 01463 239882
Map 14, D8
clubmanager@invernessgolfclub.co.uk
www.invernessgolfclub.co.uk
Off A9, 1 mile S of Inverness
Founded 1883
A parkland course with pleasant views over the sea to the Black Isle, perhaps the strongest hole being the 14th, a long par 4 threatened by a burn.
18 holes, 6256 yards
par 70, S.S.S 69
Designer James Braid
Green fees £29
Catering, changing room/showers, bar, club and trolley hire, shop, practice facilities
Visitors welcome, with restrictionsHandicap certificate required
Societies welcome by prior arrangement
Marriott Hotel, Damfield Road, Inverness, Inverness
☎ 01463 237166

KINGUSSIE GOLF CLUB

Gynack Road, Kingussie, Inverness PH21 1LR
☎ 01540 661600 Fax 01540 662066
Map 14, E9
kinggolf@globalnet.co.uk
www.kingussie-golf.co.uk
Off A86, at Duke of Gordon Hotel
Founded 1891
There are magnificent views from this upland course, 1000 feet above sea level. A river enters play on 5 holes.
18 holes, 5411 yards
par 73, S.S.S 68
Designer Harry Vardon, Sandy Herd
Green fees £18
Catering, changing room/showers, bar, club, trolley and buggy hire, shop, practice facilities
Visitors welcome
Societies welcome by prior arrangement
Scot House Hotel, Newtonmore Road, Kinggussie, Inverness
☎ 01540 661351

LOCH NESS GOLF CLUB

Fairways Leisure Group Ltd, Castle Heather, Inverness, Inverness

IV2 6AA
✆ 01463 713335 Fax 01463 712695
Map 14, D8
info@golflochness.com
www.golflochness.com
Off A9
Founded 1996
Despite the considerable length of this course. the shortest hole is a mere 76 yards, and totally unforgiving. Fine views over the Moray Firth.
18 holes, 6772 yards
par 73, S.S.S 72
Green fees £20
Catering, changing room/showers, bar, club, trolley and buggy hire, shop, driving range, practice facilities, function Suite
Visitors welcome
Societies welcome by prior arrangement

MUIR OF ORD GOLF CLUB

Great North Road, Muir of Ord, Inverness IV6 7SX
✆ 01463 870825 Fax 01463 871867
Map 14, D8
muirgolf@supanet.com
www.golfhighland.co.uk
Off A862, 15 miles N of Inverness
Founded 1875
The 219-yard par-3 12th is reckoned to be one of the toughest holes in the Highlands, with no margin for error.
18 holes, 5596 yards
par 68, S.S.S 68
Designer James Braid
Green fees £16
Catering, changing room/showers, bar, club, trolley and buggy hire, shop, practice facilities
Visitors welcome with weekend restrictions
Societies welcome by prior arrangement
🏨 The Priory Hotel, The Square, Beauly, Inverness
✆ 01463 782309

NAIRN DUNBAR GOLF CLUB

Lochloy Road, Nairn, Inverness IV12 5AE
✆ 01667 452741 Fax 01667 456897
Map 14, E8
secretary@nairndunbar.com
www.nairndunbar.com
Off A96, E of Nairn
Founded 1899
A championship links made all the harder by ditches, gorse, birch, willows, and the rough and tumble of the dunes. Among many strong par 4s, the 7th, King Steps, is a favourite of many, with the Minister's Loch awaiting a pulled drive. The par-5 13th, Long Peter, is formidable.
18 holes, 6720 yards
par 72, S.S.S 73
Green fees £30
Catering, changing room/showers, bar, club and trolley hire, shop, practice facilities
Visitors welcome
Societies welcome by prior arrangement
🏨 Golf View Hotel, Seabank Road, Nairn, Inverness
✆ 01667 452301

NAIRN GOLF CLUB

Seabank Road, Nairn, Inverness IV12 4HB
✆ 01667 453208 Fax 01667 456328
Map 14, E8
bookings@nairngolfclub.prestel.co.uk
www.nairngolfclub.co.uk
A96, 15 miles E of Inverness
Founded 1887
See Top 50 Courses, page 30
18 holes, 6705 yards
par 72, S.S.S 74
Designer Archie Simpson, Tom Morris, James Braid
Green fees £70
Catering, changing room/showers, bar, club and trolley hire, shop, driving range, practice facilities, 9-hole course, snooker
Visitors welcome – restrictions
Handicap certificate required – limit: 28 men, 36 women
Societies welcome by prior arrangement – no company days
🏨 Golf View Hotel, Seabank Road, Nairn, Inverness
✆ 01667 452301

NEWTONMORE GOLF CLUB

Golf Course Road, Newtonmore, Inverness PH20 1AT
✆ 01540 673328 Fax 01540 673878
Map 14, D9
newtonmoregolf@btinternet.com
www.newtonmoregolf.com
Close to centre of village
Founded 1893
The club can claim to be only 1½ miles from the centre of Scotland, and reckons to have more left-handed golfers than any other club. It is remarkably level, considering its surroundings, the Grampians, Cairngorms and Lochaber.
18 holes, 6041 yards
par 70, S.S.S 69
Designer James Braid
Green fees £16
Catering, changing room/showers, bar, club, trolley and buggy hire, shop, practice facilities
Visitors welcome
Societies welcome by prior arrangement

SPEAN BRIDGE GOLF CLUB

Spean Bridge, Fort William, Inverness PH33
✆ 01397 704954 **Map 14, B10**
A82, 9 miles N of Fort William
A short 9-hole course at the foot of Glen Spean, dominated by the mass of Ben Nevis.
9 holes

STRATHPEFFER SPA GOLF CLUB

Strathpeffer Spa, Inverness IV14 9AS
✆ 01997 421219 Fax 01997 421011
Map 14, D8
www.strathpeffer42.freeserve.co.uk
Off A834, N of village
Founded 1888
One of the most challenging Highland courses, despite its diminutive length. There are seven par 3s and a number of short par 4s, yet no hole is easy, because of the hilly nature of the site. Glorious mountain views are a bonus.
18 holes, 4792 yards
par 65, S.S.S 64
Designer Willie Park, Tom Morris
Green fees £14
Catering, changing room/showers, bar, club and trolley hire, shop, practice facilities
Visitors welcome
Societies welcome by prior arrangement

TAIN GOLF CLUB

Chapel Road, Tain, Ross-shire, Inverness IV19 1JE
✆ 01862 892314 Fax 01862 892099
Map 14, E7
info@tain-golfclub.co.uk
www.tain-golfclub.co.uk
35 miles N of Inverness
Founded 1890
Tom Morris's northern jewel, part links, part inland, is but a stone's throw from the famous Glenmorangie Distillery. Many fairways are tight between gorse and broom, and a burn comes into play.
18 holes, 6404 yards
par 70, S.S.S 71
Designer Tom Morris
Green fees £30
Catering, changing room/showers, bar, club, trolley and buggy hire, shop, practice facilities
Visitors welcome
Societies welcome by prior arrangement
🏨 Morangie House Hotel, Morangie Road, Tain, Inverness IV19 1PY
✆ 01862 892281

TARBAT GOLF CLUB
Portmahomack, Tain, Inverness IV20 1YB
☎ 01862 871598 Fax 01862 871598
Map 14, E7
E of Portmahomack, 10 miles NE of Tain
Founded 1909
Wonderfully remote links set on a peninsula overlooking the Dornoch and Moray Firths.
9 holes, 5082 yards
par 67, S.S.S 65
Green fees £10
Practice facilities
Visitors welcome – restricted Saturday
Societies welcome by prior arrangement

TORVEAN GOLF CLUB
Glenurquhart Road, Inverness IV3 6JN
☎ 01463 711434 Fax 01463 225651
Map 14, D8
torveangolfclub@btinternet.com
A82 Fort William road, 1 mile from city centre
Founded 1962
Four par 4s may be under 300 yards in length, but they are balanced by a 565-yard par 5, a 220-yard par 3, and a 471-yard par 4.
18 holes, 5784 yards
par 69, S.S.S 68
Designer Hamilton
Green fees £13.70
Catering, changing room/showers, bar, club and trolley hire
Visitors welcome
Societies welcome by prior arrangement
Loch Ness House Hotel, Glenurquhart Road, Inverness
☎ 01463 231248

LANARKSHIRE

AIRDRIE GOLF CLUB
Rochsoles, Airdrie, Lanarkshire ML6 0PQ
☎ 01236 762195 **Map 12, G4**
B802, 1 mile N of Airdrie
Founded 1877
A well wooded parkland course.
18 holes, 6004 yards
par 69, S.S.S 69
Designer James Braid
Green fees £15
Catering, changing room/showers, bar, trolley hire, shop, practice facilities
Visitors welcome weekdays with advance booking
Societies welcome by prior arrangement

BELLSHILL GOLF CLUB
Orbiston, Bellshill, Lanarkshire ML4 2RZ
☎ 01698 745124 Fax 01698 292576
Map 12, F5
B7070 (M74 Jct 5)
Founded 1905
Over the years the course has been refined to make it thoroughly testing, well bunkered and with strategic use of clumps of trees.
18 holes, 6264 yards
par 70, S.S.S 71
Green fees £20
Catering, changing room/showers, bar, practice facilities
Visitors welcome with weekend restrictions
Societies welcome by prior arrangement

BIGGAR GOLF CLUB
The Park, Broughton Road, Biggar, Lanarkshire ML12 6AH
☎ 01899 220319 **Map 13, A6**
Off A702, signposted
Founded 1895
Paul Lawrie holds the professional course record of 63, but the amateur record is a remarkable 61. The surrounding counrtryside makes an impressive backdrop.
18 holes, 5537 yards
par 68, S.S.S 67
Designer Willie Park
Green fees £10
Catering, changing room/showers, bar, trolley hire
Visitors welcome
Societies welcome by prior arrangement

BLAIRBETH GOLF CLUB
Burnside, Rutherglen, Lanarkshire G73 4SF
☎ 0141 634 3355 **Map 12, F5**
1 mile of S of Rutherglen
Founded 1910
A hilly parkland course.
18 holes, 5518 yards
par 70, S.S.S 68
Green fees £15
Catering, changing room/showers, bar
Visitors welcome by prior arrangement
Societies welcome by prior arrangement

BOTHWELL CASTLE GOLF CLUB
Blantyre Road, Bothwell, Lanarkshire G71 8PS
☎ 01698 853177 Fax 01698 854052
Map 12, G5
Off B7071, NW of Bothwell
Founded 1922
A flat parkland course which builds to a 5-5-4 finish stretching 4/5 of a mile.
18 holes, 6243 yards
par 71, S.S.S 70
Green fees £20
Catering, changing room/showers, bar, trolley and buggy hire, shop, practice facilities
Visitors welcome weekdays, many restrictions
No societies

CALDERBRAES GOLF CLUB
57 Roundknowe Road, Uddingston, Lanarkshire G71 7TS
☎ 01698 813425 **Map 12, F5**
At start of M74 and M73, next to Glasgow Zoo
Founded 1891
Narrow fairways contribute to the difficulty of this deceptively tricky course.
9 holes, 5186 yards
par 66, S.S.S 67
Green fees £18
Catering, changing room/showers, bar, trolley hire, practice facilities
Visitors welcome with restrictions
Societies welcome by prior arrangement
Black Bear Travel Lodge, Uddingston, Lanarkshire

CAMBUSLANG GOLF CLUB
30 Westburn Drive, Cambuslang, Lanarkshire G72 7NA
☎ 0141 641 3130 **Map 12, F5**
Near Cambuslang Station
Founded 1892
A private members' club with a 9-hole parkland course.
9 holes, 5942 yards
S.S.S 69
Catering, changing room/showers, bar
Visitors welcome only as members' guests
No societies

CARLUKE GOLF CLUB
Hallcraig, Mauldslie Road, Carluke, Lanarkshire ML8 5HG
☎ 01555 771070 **Map 12, G5**
Off A73, 1 mile S of Carluke
Founded 1894
A hilly parkland course with good views over the Clyde Valley.
18 holes, 5805 yards
par 70, S.S.S 68
Green fees £20
Catering, changing room/showers, bar, trolley hire, shop
Visitors welcome weekdays
Societies welcome by prior arangement

CARNWATH GOLF CLUB
1 Main Street, Carnwath, Lanarkshire ML11 8JX
✆ 01555 840251 Fax 01555 841070
Map 12, H6
A721, 7 miles E of Lanark
Founded 1907
Quite undulating parkland course with fine views.
18 holes, 5953 yards
par 70, S.S.S 69
Green fees £15
Catering, changing room/showers, bar, trolley hire
Visitors welcome, with restrictions
Societies welcome by prior arrangement
🏨 Nestlers, Newbiggin, Carnwath, Lanarkshire
✆ 01555 840680

CATHKIN BRAES GOLF CLUB
Cathkin Road, Rutherglen, Lanarkshire G73 4SE
✆ 0141 634 06605 Fax 0141 6309186 **Map 12, F5**
B759, 1 mile S of Burnside
Founded 1888
A moorland course which features a small loch at the 5th hole.
18 holes, 6208 yards
par 71, S.S.S 71
Designer James Braid
Green fees £25
Catering, changing room/showers, bar, trolley and buggy hire, shop, practice facilities
Visitors welcome weekdays
Handicap certificate required
Societies welcome by prior arrangement

COATBRIDGE GOLF CLUB
Townhead Road, Coatbridge, Lanarkshire ML52 2HX
✆ 01236 28975 **Map 12, G4**
1½ miles W of Coatbridge
Founded 1971
An attractive public course with plenty of trees.
18 holes, 6020 yards
S.S.S 69
Green fees £5
Catering, changing room/showers, shop, driving range
Visitors welcome
Societies welcome by prior arrangement

COLVILLE PARK GOLF CLUB
Jerviston Estate, Motherwell, Lanarkshire ML1 4UG
✆ 01698 263017 Fax 01698 230418
Map 12, G5
A723, 1 mile NE of Motherwell
Founded 1923
The first nine runs through tree lined fairways while the back nine is more open. The hardest hole is the 444-yard 16th.
18 holes, 6301 yards
par 71, S.S.S 70
Designer James Braid
Green fees £25
Catering, changing room/showers, bar, shop, practice facilities
Visitors welcome weekdays by prior arrangement
Societies welcome by prior arrangement

CROW WOOD GOLF CLUB
Cumbernauld Road, Muirhead, Lanarkshire G69 9JF
✆ 0141 779 4954 Fax 0141 779 1943 **Map 12, F4**
A80, 6 miles NE of Glasgow
Founded 1925
A tree-lined parkland course at the foot of the Campsie Fells, with the short par-4 10th perhaps the most beautiful hole.
18 holes, 6261 yards
par 71, S.S.S 71
Designer James Braid
Green fees £23
Catering, changing room/showers, bar, club and trolley hire, practice facilities
Visitors welcome, with restrictions
Societies welcome by prior arrangement
🏨 Crow Wood House Hotel, Cumbernauld Road, Muirhead, Lanarkshire
✆ 01417 793861

DALZIEL PARK GOLF & COUNTRY CLUB
100 Hagen Drive, Motherwell, Lanarkshire ML1 5RZ
✆ 01698 862444 Fax 01688 862863
Map 12, G5
information@dalzielpark.co.uk
www.dalzielpark.co.uk
B7029, A723, 5 miles E of Motherwell
Founded 1997
Accuracy off the tee is required to find the tight fairways of this recently extended parkland course.
18 holes, 6137 yards
par 70, S.S.S 69
Green fees £20
Catering, changing room/showers, bar, accommodation, shop, driving range, conference, wedding and function facilities
Visitors welcome with restrictions
Societies welcome by prior arrangement
🏨 Dalziel Park Golf and Country Club, 100 Hagen Drive, Motherwell, Lanarkshire ML1 5RZ
✆ 01698 862862

DOUGLAS WATER GOLF CLUB
Rigside, Lanark, Lanarkshire ML11 9NB
✆ 01555 880361 **Map 12, G6**
M74, Jct 11
Founded 1922
There are fine views from the undulating fairways and a 560-yard par 5 encourages long hitters.
9 holes, 5894 yards
par 72, S.S.S 69
Green fees £8
Catering, changing room/showers, bar
Visitors welcome – restricted weekends
Societies welcome by prior arrangement

DRUMPELLIER GOLF CLUB
Drumpellier Avenue, Coatbridge, Lanarkshire ML5 1RX
✆ 01236 424139 Fax 01236 428723
Map 12, G4
A89, 8 miles E of Glasgow
Founded 1894
A parkland course which opens with a 464-yard par 4, although the most individual hole is probably the 12th, a short par 3 protected by a copse.
18 holes, 6227 yards
par 71, S.S.S 70
Designer James Braid
Green fees £22
Catering, changing room/showers, bar, club and trolley hire, shop
Visitors welcome weekdays
Societies welcome by prior arrangement

EAST KILBRIDE GOLF CLUB
Chapelside Road, Nerston, East Kilbride, Lanarkshire G74 4PF
✆ 01355 220913 **Map 12, F5**
8 miles S of Glasgow
Founded 1900
A testing parkland course.
18 holes, 6419 yards
par 71, S.S.S 71
Green fees £25
Catering, changing room/showers, bar, club and trolley hire, shop
Visitors welcome weekdays by prior arrangement. Handicap certificate required
Societies welcome by prior arrangement

EASTER MOFFAT GOLF CLUB
Mansion House, Plains, Airdrie, Lanarkshire ML6 8NP
✆ 01236 842878 Fax 01236 842904
Map 12, G4
A89, 3 miles E of Airdrie
Founded 1922
An intriguing mix of moorland and parkland holes.

18 holes, 6221 yards
par 72, S.S.S 70
Green fees £15
Catering, changing room/showers, bar, trolley hire, shop
Visitors welcome weekdays
Societies welcome by prior arrangement

HAMILTON GOLF CLUB

Riccarton, Ferniegair, Hamilton, Lanarkshire ML3 7UE
☎ 01698 282872 **Map 12, G5**
A72, 1 mile S of Hamilton
Founded 1892
The mature trees lining many fairways make this a particularly handsome parkland course.
18 holes, 6255 yards
par 70, S.S.S 71
Designer James Braid
Catering, changing room/showers, bar, trolley hire, shop
Visitors welcome weekdays by prior arrangement
Societies welcome by prior arrangement

HOLLANDBUSH GOLF CLUB

Acre Tophead, Lesmahagow, Coalburn, Lanarkshire ML11 0JS
☎ 01555 893646 **Map 12, G6**
A74, between Lesmahagow and Coalburn
Founded 1954
A mixture of parkland and moorland holes, the back nine playing over hilly ground.
18 holes, 6246 yards
par 71, S.S.S 70
Green fees £8.20
Catering, changing room/showers, bar, club and trolley hire, shop, practice facilities
Visitors welcome
Societies welcome by prior arrangement

THE KAMES GOLF CLUB

East End, Cleghorn, Lanarkshire ML11 8NR
☎ Fax 01555 870022 **Map 12, H5**
A721 between Carluke and Carnwath
Founded 1993
A host of varied packages is available for members and visitors, from a quick dash round the 9-hole course to a bumper weekend package of almost endless golf and restorative meals.
Mouse Valley: 18 holes, 6226 yards, par 70, S.S.S 72
Kames Course: 9 holes, 5076 yards, par 65, S.S.S 65
Designer Graham Taylor
Green fees £14
Catering, changing room/showers, bar, club, trolley and buggy hire, shop, practice facilities, clay pigeon shooting
Visitors welcome
Societies welcome by prior arrangement

KIRKHILL GOLF CLUB

Greenlees Road, Cambuslang, Lanarkshire G72 8YN
☎ 0141 641 3083 Fax 0141 641 8499 **Map 12, F5**
A749, Rutherglen to E Kilbride Road
Founded 1910
The 1st makes a difficult opening with the need to drive clear of a burn and yet avoid the out-of-bounds which is close on the right. A challenging parkland course.
18 holes, 6030 yards
par 70, S.S.S 70
Designer James Braid
Green fees £22
Catering, changing room/showers, bar, shop, practice facilities
Visitors welcome weekdays
Societies welcome by prior arrangement

LANARK GOLF CLUB

The Moor, Whitelees Road, Lanark, Lanarkshire ML11 7RX
☎ 01555 663219 Fax 01555 663219
Map 12, H6
lanarkgolfclub@talk21.com
Off A73
Founded 1851
Lanark's remarkable geology provides turf of best links quality at an altitude of 600 feet. With Tinto Hill as an omnipresent backdrop and pine trees and a lake nearer at hand, it is an attractive, scenic course. Strong par 4s abound, with the 2nd, 4th and 15th hardest of all.
18 holes, 6306 yards
par 70, S.S.S 71
Designer Tom Morris, Ben Sayers, James Braid
Green fees £26
Catering, changing room/showers, bar, trolley and buggy hire, shop, practice facilities
Visitors welcome with restrictions
Societies welcome by prior arrangement
Cartland Bridge Hotel, Glasgow Road, Lanark, Lanarkshire
☎ 01555 664426

LANGLANDS GOLF CLUB

Hurlawcrook Road, Nr Auldhouse, East Kilbride, Lanarkshire G75 0QQ
☎ 01355 248173 Fax 01355 248121
Map 12, F5
2 miles S of E Kilbride
Founded 1985
A challenging moorland course designed by Fred Hawtree, good value.
18 holes, 6201 yards
par 70, S.S.S 70
Designer F. Hawtree
Green fees £8.40
Shop
Visitors welcome
Societies welcome by prior arrangement

LARKHALL GOLF CLUB

Burnhead Road, Larkhall, Lanarkshire ML9 3AA
☎ 01698 881113 **Map 12, G5**
B7109 SW of Larkhall
Founded 1909
A useful public facility of good length, 10 miles SE of Glasgow.
9 holes, 3216 yards
par 36, S.S.S 35
Green fees £4
Catering, changing room/showers, bar
Visitors welcome – restricted Saturday
Societies welcome by prior arrangement

LEADHILLS GOLF CLUB

Leadhills, Biggar, Lanarkshire ML12 6XR
☎ 01659 74456 **Map 12, H7**
Off B797
Founded 1935
The highest course in Scotland at 1500 feet above sea level (although one or two Highland courses make a similar claim). Invigorating, rugged, moorland golf played over a hilly site where yardages are largely irrelevant.
9 holes, 4354 yards
par 66, S.S.S 64
Green fees £5
Visitors welcome
Societies welcome by prior arrangement

MOUNT ELLEN GOLF CLUB

Johnson Road, Gartcosh, Lanarkshire G69 9EY
☎ 01236 78 2632 **Map 12, G4**
W of M73, 8 miles NE of Glasgow
Founded 1904
Four substantial par 4s and a 233-yard par 3 provide a significant challenge on this tricky course.
18 holes, 5525 yards
par 68, S.S.S 67
Green fees £18
Changing room/showers, bar, trolley and buggy hire, shop
Visitors welcome with restrictions
Societies welcome by prior arrangement

SHOTTS GOLF CLUB
Blairhead, Benhar Road, Shotts, Lanarkshire ML7 5BJ
✆ 01501 820431 **Map 12, H5**
B7057, 2 miles from M8
Founded 1895
With a James Braid pedigree, a good examination of golf with fine views.
18 holes, 6205 yards
par 70, S.S.S 70
Designer James Braid
Green fees £20
Catering, changing room/showers, bar, trolley and buggy hire, shop, practice facilities
Visitors welcome – restricted weekends
Societies welcome by prior arrangement

STRATHAVEN GOLF CLUB
Overton Avenue, Glasgow Road, Strathaven, Lanarkshire ML10 6NL
✆ 01357 520421 Fax 01357 520539
Map 12, G6
manager@strathavengolfclub.fsbusiness.co.uk
A74 southbound Jct 9, A726 to Off A726, N of Strathaven
Founded 1908
A very scenic course, 700 feet up, with tree-lined, undulating fairways. A good test.
18 holes, 6250 yards
par 71, S.S.S 71
Designer Willie Fernie, J.R. Stutt
Green fees £25
Catering, changing room/showers, bar, trolley and buggy hire, shop, practice facilities, small meeting room
Visitors welcome – restrictions
Handicap certificate required
Societies welcome by prior arrangement
🏨 Strathaven Hotel, Hamilton Road, Strathaven, Lanarkshire
✆ 01357 520789

STRATHCLYDE PARK GOLF CLUB
Mote Hill, Hamilton, Lanarkshire ML3 6BY
✆ 01698 429350 **Map 12, G5**
Hamilton/Motherwell exit from M74
An attractive municipal course set between a race course and a nature reserve.
9 holes, 6350 yards
par 72, S.S.S 70
Green fees £3.40
Catering, changing room/showers, bar, shop, driving range, practice facilities
Visitors welcome
Societies welcome by prior arrangement

TORRANCE HOUSE GOLF COURSE
Strathaven Road, East Kilbride, Lanarkshire G75 0QZ
✆ 01355 248638 **Map 12, F5**
Off A726, 1½ miles S of East Kilbride
Founded 1969
A public parkland course of good length and decent challenge.
18 holes, 6415 yards
par 72, S.S.S 71
Green fees £8.20
Catering, changing room/showers, bar, club and trolley hire, shop, practice facilities
Visitors welcome
Societies welcome by prior arrangement

WISHAW GOLF CLUB
55 Cleland Road, Wishaw, Lanarkshire ML2 7PH
✆ 01698 372869 **Map 12, G5**
Off A721,N of Wishaw town centre
Founded 1897
A well-bunkered parkland course.
18 holes, 5999 yards
par 69, S.S.S 69
Designer James Braid
Green fees £15
Catering, changing room/showers, bar, trolley and buggy hire, shop, practice facilities
Visitors welcome weekdays
Societies welcome by prior arrangement

MIDLOTHIAN

BABERTON GOLF CLUB
50 Baberton Avenue, Juniper Green, Edinburgh, Midlothian EH14 5DU
✆ 0131 453 4911 Fax 0131 453 4678 **Map 13, B4**
babertongolfclub@btinternet.com
www.baberton.co.uk
Off A70 at Juniper Green
Founded 1893
Handsome, rolling parkland course with fine views of Pentland Hills, Forth Bridges, Edinburgh Castle and the Edinburgh sky line. The par 3s, particularly those on the way out, are quite demanding.
18 holes, 6129 yards
par 69, S.S.S 70
Designer Willie Park,
Green fees £22
Catering, changing room/showers, bar, trolley hire, shop, practice facilities
Visitors welcome with restrictions
Societies welcome by prior arrangement

BRAID HILLS GOLF COURSE
Braid Hills Road, Edinburgh, Midlothian EH10 6JY
✆ 0131 447 6666 **Map 13, B4**
A702, 3 miles S of Edinburgh
Founded 1893
There are stunning views over Edinburgh from these public courses. Gorse and the hilly nature of the site means that the golf is often remarkably testing.
No 1: 18 holes, 5692 yards, par 70, S.S.S 68
No 2: 18 holes, 4832 yards, par 65, S.S.S 63
Green fees £9.20
Changing room/showers, club and trolley hire
Visitors welcome
Societies welcome by prior arrangement

BROOMIEKNOWE GOLF CLUB
36 Golf Course Raod, Bonnyrigg, Midlothian EH19 2HZ
✆ 0131 663 9317 Fax 0131 663 2152 **Map 13, B4**
www.broomieknowe.com
A7/A6094, 7 miles SE of Edinburgh
Founded 1905
On an upland site, there are good views from the course.
18 holes, 6200 yards
par 70, S.S.S 70
Designer James Braid
Green fees £17
Catering, changing room/showers, bar, club and trolley hire, shop, driving range, practice facilities
Visitors welcome
Societies welcome by prior arrangement

THE BRUNTSFIELD LINKS GOLFING SOCIETY
The Clubhouse, 32 Barnton Avenue, Edinburgh, Midlothian EH4 6JH
✆ 0131 336 1479 Fax 0131 336 5538 **Map 13, B4**
secretary@bruntsfield.sol.co.uk
www.sol.co.uk/bruntsfieldlinks/
3 miles NW of Edinburgh, off A90 (Forth Bridge), A7
Founded 1761
A very old club, which moved to this site, overlooking the Firth of Forth, at the end of the 19th century. The course has seen a number of championships, such as the British Seniors, British Boys, and Scottish Mid Amateur. Subtle borrows are a feature of the well-protected greens.
18 holes, 6407 yards
par 71, S.S.S 71
Designer Willie Park, Alister Mackenzie, Fred Hawtree
Green fees £40

Catering, changing room/showers, bar, club, trolley and buggy hire, shop, driving range, practice facilities, meeting room
Visitors welcome – restricted competition days
Handicap certificate required – limit: 28 men, 36 women
Societies welcome by prior arrangement
Drummond House, 17 Drummond Place, Edinburgh, Midlothian EH3 6PL
0131 557 9189

CARRICK KNOWE GOLF COURSE

Glendevon Park, Edinburgh, Midlothian EH12 5VZ
0131 337 1096 **Map 13, B4**
Off A8, 3 miles W of Edinburgh
Founded 1930
A flat parkland course close to the city centre.
18 holes, 6299 yards
par 71, S.S.S 70
Green fees £8.80
Changing room/showers, club and trolley hire
Visitors welcome – restricted weekends
Societies welcome by prior arrangement

CRAIGENTINNY GOLF CLUB

Fillyside Road, Edinburgh, Midlothian EH7 6RG
0131 554 7501 **Map 13, B4**
2½ miles NE of Edinburgh
Founded 1891
A flat parkland course dominated by the backdrop of Arthur's Seat.
18 holes, 5418 yards
par 67, S.S.S 65
Green fees £8.80
Changing room/showers, club and trolley hire
Visitors welcome
Societies welcome by prior arrangement

CRAIGMILLAR PARK GOLF CLUB

1 Observatory Road, Edinburgh, Midlothian EH9 3HG
0131 667 2837 **Map 12, B4**
Off A7, 2 miles S of city centre
Founded 1895
Laid out on a wonderful site running around Blackford Hill, where the Royal Observatory stands, with superb views over Edinburgh. Demanding holes include the 4th, 5th, 12th and 16th, all par 4s over 400 yards in length.
18 holes, 5859 yards
par 70, S.S.S 69
Designer James Braid
Green fees £20
Catering, changing room/showers, bar, club, trolley and buggy hire, shop, practice facilities
Visitors welcome weekdays by prior arrangement
Handicap certificate required
Societies welcome by prior arrangement

MARRIOTT DALMAHOY HOTEL & COUNTRY CLUB

Dalmahoy, Kirknewton, Midlothian EH27 8EB
0131 333 1845 Fax 0131 335 3203 **Map 13, A4**
www.marriott.com
A71, 7 miles W of Edinburgh
Founded 1927
Two fine courses maintained immaculately. The East is the championship course, the lakeside 16th being one of the best holes. Here Catrin Nilsmark sealed victory for Europe in the 1992 Solheim Cup. It is part of a sequence of very strong par 4s, interrupted by the wicked par-3 15th.
East Course: 18 holes, 6638 yards, par 72, S.S.S 72
West Course: 18 holes, 5168 yards, par 68, S.S.S 66
Designer James Braid
Green fees £45
Catering, changing room/showers, bar, accommodation, club, trolley and buggy hire, shop, driving range, practice facilities, conference facilities
Visitors welcome, with restrictions.
Handicap certificate required – limit: 28
Societies welcome by prior arrangement
Dalmahoy Marriott Hotel, Kirknewton, near Edinburgh, Midlothian
0131 333 1845 Fax 0131 333 1433
www.marriott.com/marriott/edigs

DUDDINGSTON GOLF CLUB

Duddingston Road West, Edinburgh, Midlothian EH15 3QD
0131 661 7688 Fax 0131 652 6057 **Map 13, B4**
Off A1, 2 miles S of city centre
Founded 1895
One of the best of the Edinburgh parkland courses with the 4th and 11th being very demanding par 4s and a mischievous short hole at the 14th, which is surrounded by water.
18 holes, 6438 yards
par 71, S.S.S 71
Designer Willie Park
Green fees £28
Catering, changing room/showers, bar, club, trolley and buggy hire, shop, practice facilities
Visitors welcome weekdays
Societies welcome by prior arrangement

GLENCORSE GOLF CLUB

Milton Bridge, Penicuik, Midlothian EH26 0RD
01968 677189 Fax 01968 674399 **Map 13, B4**
glencorsegc@glencorsepenicuik.fsnet.co.uk
A701, 9 miles S of Edinburgh
Founded 1890
A remarkable little course with eight par 3s, only one of which is under 200 yards, and the 237-yard 5th is one of hardest par 3s in Scotland. A stream enters play on ten holes.
18 holes, 5217 yards
par 64, S.S.S 66
Designer Willie Park Jnr
Green fees £20
Catering, changing room/showers, bar, club and trolley hire, shop, practice facilities
Visitors welcome, subject to restrictions
Societies welcome by prior arrangement
Drummond House, 17 Drummond Place, Edinburgh, Midlothian EH3 6PL
0131 557 9189

KINGS ACRE GOLF COURSE

Lasswade, Midlothian EH18 1AU
0131 663 3456 Fax 0131 663 7076 **Map 13, B4**
info@kings-acregolf.com
www.kings-acregolf.com
At Lasswade, between City By-Pass and A7
Founded 1997
Over 50 bunkers and a number of water hazards punctuate the course which ends with a hole appropriately named 'The Last Splash'.
18 holes, 5935 yards
par 70, S.S.S 68
Designer Graeme Webster
Green fees £17
Catering, changing room/showers, bar, accommodation, club, trolley and buggy hire, shop, practice facilities, seminar room, golf academy
Visitors welcome
Societies welcome by prior arrangement
Dalhousie Castle Hotel, Bonnyrigg, Midlothian EH18 1AU
0131 663 3456

KINGSKNOWE GOLF CLUB

326 Lanark Road, Edinburgh, Midlothian EH14 2JD

☎ 0131 441 1144 Fax 0131 441 2079 **Map 13, B4**
A70, 4 miles SW of Edinburgh
Founded 1907
An undulating parkland course with a number of strong two-shot holes, especially the 460-yard 16th.
18 holes, 5981 yards
par 69, S.S.S 69
Designer Alex Herd, James Braid
Green fees £22
Catering, changing room/showers, bar, club, trolley and buggy hire, shop, practice facilities
Visitors welcome with restrictions
Societies welcome by prior arrangement

LIBERTON GOLF CLUB

297 Gilmerton Road, Edinburgh, Midlothian EH16 5UJ
☎ 0131 664 3009 Fax 0131 666 0853 **Map 13, B4**
A7, 3 miles SE of city centre
Founded 1920
An undulating parkland course.
18 holes, 5299 yards
par 67, S.S.S 66
Green fees £20
Catering, changing room/showers, bar, trolley hire, shop, practice facilities
Visitors welcome
Societies welcome by prior arrangement

LOTHIANBURN GOLF CLUB

106a Biggar Road, Edinburgh, Midlothian EH10 7DU
☎ 0131 445 2206 **Map 13, B4**
www.golfers.net
A702, 4½ miles S of city centre
Founded 1893
Pleasantly rural course in the Pentland foothills.
18 holes, 5662 yards
par 71, S.S.S 68
Designer James Braid
Green fees £16
Catering, changing room/showers, bar, club and trolley hire, shop, practice facilities
Visitors welcome weekdays with restrictions
Societies welcome by prior arrangement

MELVILLE GOLF CENTRE

Lasswade, Midlothian EH18 1AN
☎ 0131 6540224 Fax 0131 654 0814 **Map 13, B4**
A7, S of Edinburgh
Founded 1995
The shape of many holes puts a premium on thoughtful golf.
9 holes, 4604 yards
par 66, S.S.S 62
Designer G. Webster
Green fees £8
Changing room/showers, trolley hire, shop, driving range, practice facilities
Visitors welcome
Societies welcome by prior arrangement

MERCHANTS OF EDINBURGH GOLF CLUB

10 Craighill Gardens, Morningside, Edinburgh, Midlothian EH10 5PY
☎ 0131 447 1219 **Map 13, B4**
Off A702, SW of Edinburgh
Founded 1907
Although short on paper, there are many testing holes including a 244-yard par 3 to open. There are good views of Edinburgh throughout the round and particularly on the difficult par-3 13th.
18 holes, 4889 yards
par 65, S.S.S 64
Green fees £15
Catering, changing room/showers, bar, club and trolley hire, shop
Visitors welcome weekdays with restrictions
Societies welcome by prior arrangement

MORTONHALL GOLF CLUB

231 Braid Road, Edinburgh, Midlothian EH10 6PB
☎ 0131 447 6974 Fax 0131 447 8712 **Map 13, B4**
clubhouse@mortonhallgc.sagehost.co.uk
www.mortonhallgc.co.uk
Off A702
Founded 1892
Parkland course with unrivalled views across Edinburgh to the Firth of Forth and the Pentland Hills.
18 holes, 6502 yards
par 72, S.S.S 72
Green fees £30
Catering, changing room/showers, bar, trolley hire, shop, practice facilities
Visitors welcome weekdays
Handicap certificate required
Societies welcome by prior arrangment
Braids Hill Hotel, Braid Road, Edinburgh, Midlothian

MURRAYFIELD GOLF CLUB

43 Murrayfield Road, Edinburgh, Midlothian EH12 6EU
☎ 0131 337 1009 Fax 0131 313 0721 **Map 13, B4**
Off A8, 2 miles W of city centre
Founded 1896
A parkland course with good views of Edinburgh.
18 holes, 5742 yards
par 70, S.S.S 69
Green fees £30
Catering, changing room/showers, bar, club and trolley hire, shop
Visitors welcome only by prior arrangement
Societies welcome by prior arrangement

NEWBATTLE GOLF CLUB

Abbey Road, Eskbank, Dalkeith, Midlothian EH22 3AD
☎ 0131 663 2123 Fax 0131 654 1810 **Map 13, B4**
Off A68, SW of Dalkeith
Founded 1896
A wooded parkland course on which the River Esk comes into play.
18 holes, 6012 yards
par 69, S.S.S 70
Designer Harry Colt
Green fees £18
Catering, changing room/showers, bar, trolley hire, shop, practice facilities
Visitors welcome weekdays with restrictions
Societies welcome by prior arrangement

PORTOBELLO GOLF CLUB

Stanley Street, Portobello, Edinburgh, Midlothian EH15 1JJ
☎ 0131 669 4361 **Map 13, B4**
Off A1, 4 miles E of Edinburgh
Founded 1853
A flat parkland course.
9 holes, 4810 yards
par 64, S.S.S 64
Green fees £8.80
Changing room/showers, club and trolley hire
Visitors welcome – restricted weekends
Societies welcome by prior arrangement

PRESTONFIELD GOLF CLUB

6 Priestfield Road North, Edinburgh, Midlothian EH16 5HS
☎ 0131 667 9665 Fax 0131 667 9665 **Map 13, B4**
A7, 1 mile S of city centre
Founded 1920
A parkland course having an unusual back nine consisting of eight par 4s and a lone par 3.
18 holes, 6214 yards
par 70, S.S.S 70
Designer Peter Robertson
Green fees £20
Catering, changing room/showers, bar, club, trolley and buggy hire, shop
Visitors welcome – restricted weekends
Societies welcome by prior arrangement

RATHO PARK GOLF CLUB

Ratho, Newbridge, Midlothian EH28 8NX
✆ 0131 335 0069 Fax 0131 333 1752 **Map 13, A4**
A71, adjacent to Edinburgh airport
Founded 1928
A parkland course, on a windswept level site alongside the airport.
18 holes, 5932 yards
par 69, S.S.S 68
Designer James Braid
Green fees £25
Catering, changing room/showers, bar, trolley hire, shop, practice facilities
Visitors welcome
Societies welcome by prior arrangement

RAVELSTON GOLF CLUB

24 Ravelston Dykes Road, Edinburgh, Midlothian EH4 5NZ
✆ 0131 315 2486 **Map 13, B4**
Off A90, 3 miles NW of city centre
Founded 1912
A rare 9-hole Braid design, with a demanding 2nd hole, a long uphill par 3.
9 holes, 5218 yards
par 66, S.S.S 65
Designer James Braid
Green fees £15
Catering, changing room/showers, bar
Visitors welcome weekdays
Handicap certificate required
Societies welcome by prior arrangement

ROYAL BURGESS GOLFING SOCIETY OF EDINBURGH

181 Whitehouse Road, Barnton, Edinburgh, Midlothian EH4 6BY
✆ 0131 339 2075 Fax 0131 339 3712 **Map 13, B4**
www.royalburgess.co.uk
Off A90, 5 miles W of city centre
Founded 1735
The club with the longest continuous history, dating back to 1735. It moved to its present site in 1896. The course is beautifully maintained in wooded parkland. There are strong challenges on the 4th, 7th and the par-3 13th.
18 holes, 6494 yards
par 71, S.S.S 71
Designer Tom Morris
Green fees £40
Catering, changing room/showers, bar, club and trolley hire, shop, practice facilities
Visitors welcome weekdays with prior booking
Societies welcome by prior arrangement

SILVERKNOWES GOLF CLUB

Silverknowes Parkway, Edinburgh, Midlothian EH4 5ET
✆ 0131 336 3843 **Map 13, B4**
4 miles N of Edinburgh, close to city bypass
Founded 1947
A parkland course overlooking the Firth of Forth with well defended greens.
18 holes, 6214 yards
par 71, S.S.S 70
Green fees £8.80
Changing room/showers, club and trolley hire, practice facilities
Visitors welcome
Societies welcome by prior arrangement

SWANSTON GOLF CLUB

111 Swanston Road, Fairmilehead, Edinburgh, Midlothian EH10 7DS
✆ 0131 445 2239 Fax 0131 445 2239 **Map 13, B4**
www.swanstongolfclub.com
Off B701, 4 miles S of Edinburgh
Founded 1927
A hilly course with some steep climbing to be done.
18 holes, 5004 yards
par 66, S.S.S 65
Green fees £15
Catering, changing room/showers, bar, club, trolley and buggy hire, shop
Visitors welcome
Societies welcome by prior arrangement

TORPHIN HILL GOLF CLUB

Torphin Road, Edinburgh, Midlothian EH13 0PG
✆ 0131 441 1100 Fax 0131 441 7166 **Map 13, A4**
Off A720, 5 miles SW of city centre
Founded 1895
A heathland course with good views over Edinburgh.
18 holes, 5025 yards
par 67, S.S.S 66
Green fees £12
Catering, changing room/showers, bar, trolley hire, shop, practice facilities
Visitors welcome weekdays
Societies welcome by prior arrangement

TURNHOUSE GOLF CLUB

154 Turnhouse Road, Corstorphine, Edinburgh, Midlothian EH12 0AD
✆ 0131 339 1014 Fax 0131 338 1844 **Map 13, A4**
www.turnhousegolfclub.co.uk
A9080, W of Edinburgh (Maybury Roundabout)
Founded 1897
An undulating parkland course, with a demanding stretch beginning at the 234-yard 5th (on which there is a fine view of the Forth Road Bridge). On the back nine, the par-4 10th and 12th both stretch to more than 450 yards.
18 holes, 6153 yards
par 69, S.S.S 70
Designer James Braid
Green fees £22
Catering, changing room/showers, bar, club and trolley hire, shop, practice facilities
Visitors welcome – restricted
Handicap certificate required – limit: 24
Societies welcome by prior arrangement
Royal Scot Hotel, 111 Glasgow Road, Edinburgh, Midlothian EH12 8NP
✆ 0131 334 9191

VOGRIE COUNTRY PARK GOLF CLUB

Vogrie Estate Country Park, Gorebridge, Midlothian EH23 4NU
✆ 01875 821716 **Map 13, B5**
Off B6372
Founded 1990
A municipal course located in a country park.
9 holes, 5060 yards
par 66
Green fees £5.70
Changing room/showers
Visitors welcome
Societies welcome by prior arrangement

MORAY

BUCKPOOL GOLF CLUB

Barhill Road, Buckie, Moray AB56 1DU
✆ 01542 832236 Fax 01542 832236 **Map 14, F7**
A942, off A98
Founded 1933
A very attractive course with magnificent sea views. The 444-yard 5th is played directly on Morven, the mountain which dominates the skyline despite being miles away on the far side of the Moray Firth.
18 holes, 6257 yards
par 70, S.S.S 70
Designer F. Hawtree, J.H. Taylor
Green fees £15
Catering, changing room/showers, bar, club and trolley hire, practice facilities, squash, snooker
Visitors welcome
Handicap certificate required
Societies welcome by prior arrangement
Cluny Hotel, Cluny Square,

Buckie, Moray
☎ 01542 832922

DUFFTOWN GOLF CLUB

Tomintoul Road, Dufftown, Moray
AB55 4BS
☎ 01340 820325 Fax 01340 820325
Map 14, F8
www.speyside.moray.org/dufftowngolfclub
B9009, 1 mile S of Dufftown
Founded 1896
At 1000 ft up in the mountains the views are magnificent, particularly on the 10th tee, almost the highest point on the course, and the start of a 462-yard daunting hole. The 67-yard 7th is one of the shortest holes in golf.
18 holes, 5308 yards
par 67, S.S.S 67
Green fees £12
Changing room/showers, bar, club and trolley hire
Visitors welcome
Societies welcome by prior arrangement

ELGIN GOLF CLUB

Hardhillock, Birnie Road, Elgin, Moray IV30 8SX
☎ 01343 542338 Fax 01343 542341
Map 14, F8
secretary@elgingolfclub.com
www.elgingolfclub.com
Southern boundary of Elgin, off A941
Founded 1906
The finest inland course in the north of Scotland, with velvet fairways sweeping through noble avenues of trees. Having eight par 4s over 400 yards (indeed, four over 440 yards), Elgin presents a stiff challenge to all golfers, a challenge maintained to the very end, the 18th being particularly demanding.
18 holes, 6411 yards
par 69, S.S.S 71
Designer John MacPherson
Green fees £24
Catering, changing room/showers, bar, club and trolley hire, shop, driving range, practice facilities
Visitors welcome weekdays
Societies welcome by prior arrangment
🏨 Eight Acres Hotel, Sheriffmill, Moriston Road, Elgin, Moray IV30 3UN
☎ 01343 543077

FORRES GOLF CLUB

Muiryshade, Forres, Moray
IV36 0RD
☎ 0139 672250 Fax 01309 672250
Map 14, E8
sandy@forresgolfclub.fsnet.co.uk
www.forresgolfclub.fsnet.co.uk
A96 between Inverness and Aberdeen
Founded 1889
A long-established parkland course with many tree-lined holes particularly in midround. The 5th green is very tricky to putt, but the notorious hole is the 16th, aptly named The Pond, where many cards are ruined.
18 holes, 6236 yards
par 70, S.S.S 70
Designer James Braid
Green fees £19
Catering, changing room/showers, bar, club, trolley and buggy hire, shop, practice facilities
Visitors welcome
Societies welcome by prior arrangement

GARMOUTH & KINGSTON GOLF CLUB

Spey Street, Garmouth, Moray
IV32 7NJ
☎ 01343 870388 Fax 01343 870388
Map 14, F7
garmouthgolfclub@aol.com
Off A96 at Mosstodloch, at mouth of River Spey
Founded 1932
The course includes both links and parkland holes and is handsomely situated at the mouth of River Spey.
18 holes, 5935 yards
par 69, S.S.S 69
Designer G.Smith, Moray
Green fees £16
Catering, changing room/showers, bar, club, trolley and buggy hire, shop, practice facilities
Visitors welcome
Societies welcome by prior arrangement
🏨 Garmouth Hotel, South Road, Garmouth, Moray
☎ 01343 870226

HOPEMAN GOLF CLUB

Hopeman, Moray IV30 5YA
☎ 01343 830578 Fax 01343 830152
Map 14, F7
hopemangc@aol.com
www.hopeman-golf-club.co.uk
B912, E of Hopeman, 7 miles NE of Elgin
Founded 1909
Hopeman boasts one of the most engaging holes in Scotland. The 12th is 100 ft plunge down to a tiny green on the beach.
18 holes, 5590 yards
par 68, S.S.S 67
Designer Charles Neaves
Green fees £13
Catering, changing room/showers, bar, trolley and buggy hire
Visitors welcome – restricted weekends
Societies welcome by prior arrangement
🏨 Burnside House, Duffus, Elgin, Moray
☎ 01343 835165

MORAY GOLF CLUB

Stotfield Road, Lossiemouth, Moray
IV31 6QS
☎ 01343 812018 Fax 01343 815102
Map 14, F7
secretary@moraygolf.co.uk
www.moraygolf.co.uk
A96 to Elgin, then follow signs to Lossiemouth. Course at West Beach.
Founded 1889
Two first rate links courses in a region with an unusually benign climate. The longer, and older, course saves one of its best holes for last, the 406-yard 18th being recognised as one of the finest finishing holes in Scotland. A further six par 4s measure over 400 yards.
Old Course: 18 holes, 6578 yards, par 71, S.S.S 73
Designer Tom Morris
New Course: 18 holes, 6004 yards, par 69, S.S.S 69
Designer Sir Henry Cotton
Green fees £30
Catering, changing room/showers, bar, club, trolley and buggy hire, shop, practice facilities
Visitors welcome – restrictions
Handicap certificate required – limit: 24
Societies welcome by prior arrangement
🏨 The Stotfield Hotel, Stotfield Road, Lossiemouth, Moray
☎ 01343 812011

SPEY BAY GOLF CLUB

Spey Bay Hotel, Spey Bay, Fochabers, Moray IV32 7PJ
☎ 01343 820424 Fax 01343 829282
Map 14, F7
info@speybay.com
www.speybay.com
Leave A96 at Fochabers, following road to Spey Bay
Founded 1907
One of the few courses designed by Ben Sayers – originally with square greens. The views across the Moray Firth are rewarding, but there is little shelter if the wind blows.
18 holes, 6200 yards
par 70, S.S.S 69
Designer Ben Sayers
Green fees £25
Catering, changing room/showers, bar, accommodation, club, trolley and buggy hire, driving range,

driving range, self-catering cottages, conference facilities
Visitors welcome.
Handicap certificate required
Societies welcome by prior arrangement
Spey Bay Hotel, Spey Bay, Fochabers, Moray IV32 7PJ
01343 820424

ORKNEY & SHETLAND

ORKNEY GOLF CLUB

Grainbank, Kirkwall, Orkney KW15 1RD
01856 872457 Fax 01856 872457
Map 15, G8
W of Kirkwall
Founded 1889
Given that the sea is such a major factor in the life and geography of Orkney, it comes as a surprise to find that this is an inland parkland course.
18 holes, 5411 yards
par 70, S.S.S 67
Green fees £15
Catering, changing room/showers, bar, club and trolley hire, practice facilities
Visitors welcome
Societies welcome by prior arrangement

SANDAY GOLF CLUB

c/o Nearhouse, Sanday, Orkney KW17 2BW
01857 600 341 Fax 01857 600 341 **Map 15, H7**
nearhouse@zetnet.co.uk
B9069, 2 miles NE of Lady Village
Founded 1977
With both the North Sea and Atlantic Ocean visible, and play possible until midnight in summer, this charming links is also a haven for wild flowers and Arctic Skuas.
9 holes, 2426 yards
par 34, S.S.S 36
Green fees £10
Club hire
Visitors welcome
Societies welcome by prior arrangement
Kettletoft Hotel, Sanday, Orkney, Orkney and Shetland
01857 600217

SHETLAND GOLF CLUB

Dale, Gott, Shetland ZE2 9SB
01595 840369 Fax 01595 840369
Map 15, G3
clubmanager@shetlandgolfclub.co.uk
www.shetlandgolfclub.co.uk
A970, 4 miles N of Lerwick
Founded 1891
Set in a valley, every single hole is visible from the clubhouse. The hazards are mostly natural, not least an omnipresent burn, but length should not be a problem, with only the 17th exceeding 400 yards.
18 holes, 5776 yards
par 68, S.S.S 68
Designer F. Middleton
Green fees £15
Catering, changing room/showers, bar, club and trolley hire
Visitors welcome, subject to restrictions
Societies welcome by prior arrangement
Herrislea House Hotel, Vensgarth, Tingwall, Shetland, Orkney and Shetland
01595 840208

STROMNESS GOLF CLUB

Stromness, Orkney KW16 3DU
01856 850772 **Map 15, F8**
www.stromnessgc.co.uk
A965, S of Stromness
Founded 1890
Seaside parkland course with fine views over Scapa Flow, and an intriguing par 3 which is played over wartime gun emplacements.
18 holes, 4762 yards
par 65, S.S.S 63
Green fees £12
Catering, changing room/showers, bar, club hire
Visitors welcome
Societies welcome by prior arrangement

WHALSAY GOLF CLUB

Skaw Taing, Whalsay, Shetland ZE2 9AL
01806 566737 **Map 15, G3**
On Whalsay Island (by ferry from Lerwick)
Founded 1976
Britain's most northerly course is an extraordinary affair with no proper fairways, the route being indicated by a series of marker posts. Perferred lies are, therefore, played all year round. The views from the cliff tops are breath taking.
18 holes, 6009 yards
par 70, S.S.S 68
Green fees £10
Catering, changing room/showers, bar
Visitors welcome
Societies welcome by prior arrangement

PERTH & KINROSS

ABERFELDY GOLF CLUB

Taybridge Road, Aberfeldy, Perth & Kinross PH15 2BH
01887 820535 Fax 01887 820535
Map 14, D11
abergc@supanet.co.uk
www.aberfeldygolf.co.uk
A827, off A9, on northern edge of Aberfeldy
Founded 1895
A pretty course, surrounded by pleasing scenery, either side of the River Tay. The river is crossed by the world's longest single span reinforced plastic bridge!
18 holes, 5283 yards
par 68, S.S.S 66
Green fees £16
Catering, changing room/showers, bar, club, trolley and buggy hire
Visitors welcome
Societies welcome by prior arrangement
Killiecrankie Hotel, Killiecrankie, by Pitlochry, Perth & Kinross PH16 5LG
01796 473220

THE ALYTH GOLF CLUB

Pitcrocknie, Alyth, Perth & Kinross PH11 8HF
01828 632268 Fax 01828 633491
Map 14, F11
admin@alythgolf.co.uk
www.alythgolfclub.co.uk
B854, 1 mile S of Alyth
Founded 1894
Very charming parkland course with the emphasis on precision golf. The 5th, 9th, 10th and 11th stand out.
18 holes, 6205 yards
par 70, S.S.S 71
Designer Tom Morris, James Braid
Green fees £22
Catering, changing room/showers, bar, club, trolley and buggy hire, shop, practice facilities
Visitors welcome
Handicap certificate required
Societies welcome by prior arrangement

AUCHTERARDER GOLF CLUB

Ochil Road, Auchterarder, Perth & Kinross PH3 1LS
01764 662804 Fax 01764 662804
Map 12, H2
A9, SW of Auchterarder
Founded 1892
A wooded parkland course with four short holes on the back nine.
18 holes, 5775 yards
par 69, S.S.S 68
Green fees £20
Catering, changing room/showers,

bar, club and trolley hire, shop, practice facilities
Visitors welcome
Societies welcome by prior arrangement

BISHOPSHIRE GOLF CLUB

Kinneswood, Kinross, Perth & Kinross KY13
☎ 01592 780203 **Map 13, A2**
M90, Jct 7, 3 miles E of Kinross
Founded 1903
A pay-and-play facility.
10 holes, 4700 yards
S.S.S 64
Designer Willie Park
Green fees £5
Visitors welcome
Societies welcome by prior arrangement

BLAIR ATHOLL GOLF CLUB

Invertilt Road, Blair Atholl, Perth & Kinross PH18 5TG
☎ 01796 481 407 **Map 14, E10**
Off A9, 35 miles N of Perth
Founded 1896
A pretty parkland course with a stream.
9 holes, 5710 yards
par 70, S.S.S 68
Green fees £14
Catering, changing room/showers, bar, club and trolley hire, practice facilities
Visitors welcome
Societies welcome by prior arrangement

THE BLAIRGOWRIE GOLF CLUB

Rosemount, Blairgowrie, Perth & Kinross PH10 6LG
☎ 01250 872622 Fax 01250 875451
Map 14, F11
admin@blairgowrie-golf.co.uk
www.blairgowrie-golf.co.uk
Off A93, 1 mile SW of Blairgowrie
Founded 1889
World-famous for its glorious heathland fairways which wind through pine and birch, heather and gorse. Tom Morris's original 9-hole course of 1889 is still playable today. The Lansdowne Course from the 1970s is long and testing, but it is James Braid's Rosemount Course that beguiles memorably and examines thoroughly.
Rosemount Course: 18 holes, 6590 yards, par 72, S.S.S 73
Designer James Braid
Lansdowne Course: 18 holes, 6802 yards, par 72, S.S.S 74
Designer Peter Alliss, Dave Thomas
Wee Course: 9 holes, 4654 yards, par 64, S.S.S 63
Designer Tom Morris
Green fees £50
Catering, changing room/showers, bar, club and trolley hire, shop, practice facilities
Visitors welcome with letter of introduction and handicap, with restrictions Wednesday, Friday and weekends
Handicap certificate required – limit: 28 men, 36 women
Societies welcome by prior arrangement, with restrictions.
🏨 Rosemount Golf Hotel, Blairgowrie, Perth & Kinross
☎ 01250 872604

CALLANDER GOLF CLUB

Aveland Road, Callander, Perth & Kinross FK17 8EN
☎ 01877 330090 Fax 01877 330062
Map 12, F2
callandergc@nextcall.net
M9 Jct 9 and A84 to Callander
Founded 1890
Callander, the village known to television audiences as the Tannochbrae of 'Dr Finlay's Casebook', is surrounded by the wonderful scenery of the Trossachs. The course is a gem of a period piece, with the 6th and 15th tricky, even today.
18 holes, 5151 yards
par 66, S.S.S 66
Designer Tom Morris, Willie Fernie
Green fees £18
Catering, changing room/showers, bar, club and trolley hire, shop, practice facilities
Visitors welcome – handicap required on Sunday
Societies welcome by prior arrangement
🏨 Abbotsford Lodge, Stirling Road, Callander, Perth & Kinross FK17 8DA
☎ 01877 330066

COMRIE GOLF CLUB

Laggan Braes, Comrie, Perth & Kinross PH6 2LR
☎ 01764 670055 **Map 12, G1**
A85, E of town centre
Founded 1891
A heathland course amidst glorious scenery, with a couple of par 3s which are tricky, demanding considerable accuracy from the tee.
9 holes, 6040 yards
par 70, S.S.S 70
Green fees £15
Catering, changing room/showers, club and trolley hire
Visitors welcome
Societies welcome by prior arrangement
🏨 Royal Hotel, Drummond Street, Comrie, Perth & Kinross
☎ 01764 679200

CRAIGIE HILL GOLF CLUB

Cherrybank, Perth, Perth & Kinross PH2 0NE
☎ 01738 622644 Fax 01738 620829
Map 14, F11
www.craigiehill.scottishgolf.com
West end of Perth, easily reached from M90 and A9
Founded 1911
There are panoramic views over Perth to the Highlands from this short, slightly hilly course.
18 holes, 5386 yards
par 66, S.S.S 67
Green fees £18
Catering, changing room/showers, bar, trolley hire, shop, practice facilities, small meeting room
Visitors welcome – restricted Saturdays
Societies welcome by prior arrangement
🏨 Lovat Hotel, Glasgow Road, Perth, Perth & Kinross
☎ 01738 636555

CRIEFF GOLF CLUB

Perth Road, Crieff, Perth & Kinross PH7 3LR
☎ 01764 652909 Fax 01764 655096
Map 12, G1
A85, between Stirling and Perth
Founded 1891
A beautifully maintained course with fine views over the Strathearn Valley, with the 7th and 12th perhaps the pick of the holes.
Ferntower Course: 18 holes, 6402 yards, par 71, S.S.S 71
Designer James Braid
Dornock Course: 9 holes, 4772 yards, par 64, S.S.S 63
Green fees £25
Catering, changing room/showers, bar, club and trolley hire, shop, practice facilities
Visitors welcome – restricted weekends
Societies welcome by prior arrangement

DALMUNZIE GOLF COURSE

Dalmunzie Hotel, Spittal of Glenshee, Blairgowrie, Perth & Kinross PH10 7QG
☎ 01250 885224 Fax 01250 885225
Map 14, F10
dalmunzie@aol.com
A93 at Spittal of Glenshee – follow signs to Dalmunzie Hotel
Founded 1920
Surrounded by majestic mountains and split by a burn, Dalmunzie is far more challenging than the bald figures suggest. A 235-yard par-3 is

no easy opener, for example.
9 holes, 2099 yards
par 30, S.S.S 31
Designer Alister Mackenzie
Green fees £10
Catering, bar, accommodation, club hire, tennis, fishing, shooting, mountain biking
Visitors welcome
Societies welcome by prior arrangement
Dalmunzie House Hotel, Spittal of Glenshee, Blairgowrie, Perth & Kinross PH10 7QG
01250 885224

DUNKELD & BIRNAM GOLF CLUB

Fungarth, Dunkeld, Perth & Kinross PH8 0HU
01350 727524 Fax 01350 728660
Map 14, E11
A923, 1 mile S of Dunkeld
Founded 1892
The original 9-hole, heathland course, overlooking the Tay Valley and the Loch of Lowes is much loved. Nine further lochside holes have been added, promising to be every bit as entertaining as the others.
18 holes, 5551 yards
par 70, S.S.S 67
Designer D.A. Tod, John Souter
Green fees £18
Catering, changing room/showers, bar, club and trolley hire, practice facilities
Visitors welcome
Societies welcome by prior arrangement
Royal Dunkeld Hotel, Atholl Street, Dunkeld, Perth & Kinross
01350 727771

DUNNING GOLF CLUB

Rollo Park, Dunning, Perth & Kinross PH2 0QX
01764 684747 **Map 13, A1**
Off A9, 9 miles SW of Perth
Founded 1953
A parkland layout with a stream persistently crossing the course.
9 holes, 4885 yards
par 66, S.S.S 63
Green fees £14
Changing room/showers, trolley hire
Visitors welcome – restricted weekends
Societies welcome by prior arrangement

GLENALMOND GOLF CLUB

Trinity College, Glenalmond, Perth & Kinross
01738 880275 **Map 14, E11**
10 miles NW of Perth
One of the few public schools running to its own golf course.
9 holes, 5812 yards
S.S.S 68
Designer James Braid
Visitors welcome only as members' guests
No societies

THE GLENEAGLES HOTEL

Auchterarder, Perth & Kinross PH3 1NF
01764 662231 Fax 01764 662134
Map 12, H2
resort.sales@gleneagles.com
www.gleneagles.com
A823, off A9 Stirling-Perth road
Founded 1919
See Top 50 Courses, page 22
King's Course: 18 holes, 6471 yards, par 70, S.S.S 73
Designer James Braid
Queen's Course: 18 holes, 5969 yards, par 68, S.S.S 70
Designer James Braid
PGA Centenary Course: 18 holes, 7081 yards, par 72, S.S.S 73
Designer Jack Nicklaus
Wee Course: 9 holes, 1418 yards, par 27
Green fees £100
Catering, changing room/showers, bar, accommodation, club, trolley and buggy hire, shop, driving range, practice facilities
Visitors welcome
Societies welcome by prior arrangement
Gleneagles Hotel, Auchterarder, Perth & Kinross PH3 1NF
01764 662231

GREEN HOTEL GOLF COURSES

2 The Muirs, Kinross, Perth & Kinross KY13 8AS
01577 863407 Fax 01577 863180
Map 13, A2
M90, Jct 6
Founded 1900
Two scenic hotel courses open also to the public.
Blue: 18 holes, 6456 yards, par 71, S.S.S 71
Red: 18 holes, 6257 yards, par 72, S.S.S 70
Green fees £15
Catering, changing room/showers, bar, accommodation, club, trolley and buggy hire, shop, practice facilities, full hotel facilities, swimming pool, fishing
Visitors welcome
Societies welcome by prior arrangement
Green Hotel, 2 The Muirs, Kinross, Perth & Kinross KY13 8AS
01577 863467

KENMORE GOLF CLUB

Kenmore, Aberfeldy, Perth & Kinross PH15 2HN
01887 830226 Fax 01887 830211
Map 14, E11
info@taymouth.co.uk
www.taymouth.co.uk
A9 to Ballinluig, A827 to Kenmore
Founded 1992
The Highland setting is stunning, the course testing, with exemplary greenkeeping.
9 holes, 6052 yards
par 70, S.S.S 69
Designer R. Menzies
Green fees £14
Catering, changing room/showers, bar, accommodation, club, trolley and buggy hire, shop, practice facilities, self-catering cottage and caravan for hire on course
Visitors welcome
Societies welcome by prior arrangement
Kenmore Hotel, Kenmore, Aberfeldy, Perth & Kinross
01887 830205

KILLIN GOLF CLUB

Killin, Perth & Kinross FK21 8TX
01567 820312 **Map 14, D11**
www.kingolfclub.co.uk
A827, W of Loch Tay
Founded 1913
Exceptionally scenic course with one of the prettiest of all finishing holes. The 5th is an impish short hole, only 97 yards long, but the green is located just behind a stone wall.
9 holes, 5016 yards
par 66, S.S.S 65
Designer John Duncan
Green fees £12
Catering, changing room/showers, bar, club, trolley and buggy hire, shop
Visitors welcome
Societies welcome by prior arrangement

KING JAMES VI GOLF CLUB

Moncrieffe Island, Perth, Perth & Kinross PH2 8NR
01738 632460 Fax 01738 445132
Map 13, A1
On Moncrieffe Island in the centre of Perth, accessed by footbridge
Founded 1858
A tranquil haven in the middle of Perth, with tree-lined fairways on an island. It is easy to hit the ball into the River Tay on the 11th and 13th, and other strong holes include the long 4th.
18 holes, 6038 yards
par 70, S.S.S 69
Designer Tom Morris
Green fees £18

Catering, changing room/showers, bar, trolley hire, shop
Visitors welcome – restricted weekends
Societies welcome by prior arrangement

MILNATHORT GOLF CLUB

South Street, Milnathort, Kinross, Perth & Kinross KY13 9XA
01577 864069 **Map 13, A2**
M90, Jct 6, 1 mile N of Kinross
Founded 1910
A parkland course on which clumps of trees increase the difficulty on several holes.
9 holes, 5985 yards
par 71, S.S.S 69
Green fees £12
Changing room/showers, bar, practice facilities
Visitors welcome
Societies welcome by prior arrangement

MUCKHART GOLF CLUB

Muckart, Dollar, Perth & Kinross FK14 7JH
01259 781423 **Map 12, H2**
A91, SW of Muckhart
Founded 1908
The Ochil Hills form an impressive backdrop to golf here. Pleasantly undulating, the original course finishes with a fine par 5. The new course is most impressive, bringing into play swampy ground, which can be very penal indeed.
Muckhart Course: 18 holes, 6034 yards, par 71, S.S.S 70
Naemoor Course: 9 holes, 3234 yards, par 35,
Green fees £15
Catering, changing room/showers, bar, trolley hire, shop, practice facilities
Visitors welcome with restrictions
Societies welcome by prior arrangement

MURRAYSHALL COUNTRY HOUSE HOTEL & GOLF CLUB

Murrayshall, New Scone, Perth, Perth & Kinross PH2 7PH
01738 551171 Fax 01738 552595
Map 14, F11
Off A94, 3 miles NE of Perth
Founded 1981
An elegant parkland course on which lines of trees define most fairways. The dogleg 7th is one of the best holes, needing pinpoint accuracy to find the green in a thicket, fronted by a stream.
18 holes, 6441 yards
par 73, S.S.S 72
Designer Hamilton Stutt
Green fees £22
Catering, changing room/showers, bar, accommodation, club, trolley and buggy hire, shop, driving range, practice facilities
Visitors welcome
Societies welcome by prior arrangement
Murrayshall Country House Hotel, New Scone, Perth & Kinross
01738 551171

MUTHILL GOLF CLUB

Peat Road, Muthill, Perth & Kinross PH5 2DA
01764 681523 Fax 01764 681557
Map 12, G1
muthillgolfclub@lineone.net
A822, 2 miles S of Crieff
Founded 1911
A fairly level parkland course giving lovely views of the surrounding countryside and of the more distant Grampians.
9 holes, 4700 yards
par 66, S.S.S 63
Green fees £13
Catering, changing room/showers, club and trolley hire
Visitors welcome
Societies welcome by prior arrangement
Muthill Inn, Willoughby Street, Muthill, Perth & Kinross

NORTH INCH GOLF CLUB

c/o Perth & Kinross Council, 5 High Street, Perth, Perth & Kinross PH1 5JS
01738 636481 **Map 13, A1**
Central Perth
Alongside the River Tay, a parkland course with easy walking and fine views.
18 holes, 5178 yards
par 65, S.S.S 65
Green fees £7.50
Catering, bar, trolley hire
Visitors welcome
Societies welcome by prior arrangement

PITLOCHRY GOLF CLUB

Golf Course Road, Pitlochry, Perth & Kinross PH16 5QY
01796 472792 Fax 01796 473599
Map 14, E10
pitlochrygolfcourse@pitlochryestate.sagehost.co.uk
28 miles NW of Perth
Founded 1909
The first five holes climb inexorably, but the views from the top are breathtaking.
18 holes, 5811 yards
par 69, S.S.S 69
Designer Willie Fernie, C.K. Hutchison
Green fees £18
Catering, changing room/showers, bar, club and trolley hire, shop, practice facilities
Visitors welcome, with restrictions
Societies welcome by prior arrangement
Killiecrankie Hotel, Killiecrankie, by Pitlochry, Perth & Kinross PH16 5LG
01796 473220

ST FILLANS GOLF CLUB

South Lochearn Road, St Fillans, Perth & Kinross PH26 2NJ
01764 685312 **Map 12, G1**
A85, 12 miles W of Crieff
Founded 1903
A lovely parkland course surrounded by impressive mountain scenery.
9 holes, 5766 yards
par 68, S.S.S 67
Designer Willie Auchterlonie
Green fees £12
Catering, changing room/showers, bar, club and trolley hire
Visitors welcome
Societies welcome by prior arrangement

STRATHMORE GOLF CENTRE

Leroch, Alyth, Perth & Kinross PH11 8NZ
01828 633322 Fax 01828 633533
Map 14, F11
enquiries@strathmoregolf.com
Off A926, 5 miles E of Blairgowrie
Founded 1996
Challenging parkland course with views over Strathmore.
18 holes, 6454 yards
par 72, S.S.S 72
Designer John Salvesen
Green fees £20
Catering, changing room/showers, bar, club, trolley and buggy hire, shop, driving range, practice facilities
Visitors welcome
Societies welcome by prior arrangement
Rosemount Golf Hotel, Blairgowrie, Perth & Kinross
01250 872604

STRATHTAY GOLF CLUB

Lyon Cottage, Strathtay, Pitlochry, Perth & Kinross PH9 0PG
01887 840211 **Map 14, E11**
Off A827, towards Aberfeldy
Founded 1909
A hilly course with delightful views and an idiosyncratic 5th hole, on which the green is hidden behind a vast hill.
9 holes, 4082 yards
par 63, S.S.S 63
Green fees £10
Changing room/showers

Visitors welcome with restrictions
Societies welcome by prior arrangement

TAYMOUTH CASTLE GOLF CLUB

Kenmore, Aberfeldy, Perth & Kinross PH15 2NT
✆ 01887 830228 Fax 01887 830765
Map 14, E11
A827, 6 miles W of Aberfeldy
Founded 1923
Taymouth Castle gives visitors the best of both worlds, spectacular mountain scenery, yet easy walking on a level parkland course. (The castle itself resembles a wedding cake). James Braid's layout starts gently with a couple of short par 4s, before testing the resolve with a water hole at the 4th.
18 holes, 6066 yards
par 69, S.S.S 69
Designer James Braid
Green fees £16
Catering, changing room/showers, bar, trolley hire, shop, practice facilities
Visitors welcome
Societies welcome by prior arrangement

WHITEMOSS GOLF CLUB

Whitemoss Road, Dunning, Perth, Perth & Kinross PH2 0QX
✆ 01738 730300 **Map 13, A1**
Off A9, SW of Perth
Founded 1994
A welcome new course in the beautiful Strathearn Valley.
18 holes, 6200 yards
par 69, S.S.S 69
Green fees £15
Catering, changing room/showers, bar, club and trolley hire, practice facilities
Visitors welcome
Societies welcome by prior arrangement

RENFREWSHIRE

BARSHAW GOLF CLUB

Barshaw Park, Glasgow Road, Paisley, Renfrewshire PA2
✆ 0141 889 2908 Fax 0141 840 2148 **Map 12, E4**
Off A737, 1 mile E of Paisley Cross
Founded 1920
A municipal course with a good mixture of flat and hilly holes.
18 holes, 5703 yards
par 68, S.S.S 67
Green fees £8.50
Changing room/showers, trolley hire
Visitors welcome
Societies welcome by prior arrangement

BONNYTON GOLF CLUB

Eaglesham, Renfrewshire G76 0QA
✆ 01355 302781 Fax 01355 303151
Map 12, F5
Off B764, 1 mile SW of Glasgow
Dramatic moorland course offering spectacular views over Glasgow and the surrounding countryside as far as Ben Lomond.
18 holes, 6255 yards
par 72, S.S.S 71
Green fees £38
Catering, changing room/showers, bar, club, trolley and buggy hire, shop, practice facilities
Visitors welcome, with restrictions
Societies welcome by prior arrangement

CALDWELL GOLF CLUB

Caldwell, Uplawmoor, Renfrewshire G78 4AU
✆ 01505 850329 Fax 01505 850604
Map 12, E5
A736, 5 miles SW of Barrhead
Founded 1903
A rolling parkland course on which the short 3rd is named 'Risk an' Hope', with out-of-bounds threatening on the right, all the way to the green.
18 holes, 6195 yards
par 71, S.S.S 70
Green fees £23
Catering, changing room/showers, bar, trolley hire, shop, practice facilities
Visitors welcome – restricted weekends
Societies welcome by prior arrangement

COCHRANE CASTLE GOLF CLUB

Scott Avenue, Craigston, Johnstone, Renfrewshire PA5 0HF
✆ 01505 320146 Fax 01505 325338
Map 12, E5
5 miles W of Paisley
Founded 1895
Although the amateur course record stands at 65, the course has been remarkably resistant to professional scoring. No professional has broken par.
18 holes, 6226 yards
par 71, S.S.S 71
Designer Charles Hunter
Green fees £17
Catering, changing room/showers, bar, trolley hire, shop, practice facilities
Visitors welcome – restricted weekends
Societies welcome by prior arrangement

EAST RENFREWSHIRE GOLF CLUB

Pilmuir, Newton Mearns, Renfrewshire G77 6RT
✆ 01355 500256 Fax 01355 500323
Map 12, F5
A77, 2 miles S of Newton Mearns
Founded 1922
Sometimes described as the 'Gleneagles of Glasgow', East Renfrewshire gives extensive views over Glasgow towards the hills north of the Clyde Valley. Its undulating fairways, cleverly raised greens and many evergreen copses provide the main golfing challenge. Out-of-bounds makes the 9th very dangerous, and a loch adds to the beauty.
18 holes, 6097 yards
par 70, S.S.S 70
Designer James Braid
Green fees £30
Catering, changing room/showers, bar, club and trolley hire, shop, driving range, practice facilities, function facilities
Visitors welcome, subject to restrictions
Handicap certificate required
Societies welcome by prior arrangement
🏨 McDonald Thistle Hotel, Eastwood Toll, Giffnock, Glasgow, Renfrewshire

EASTWOOD GOLF CLUB

Muirshield, Loganwell, Newton Mearns, Renfrewshire G77 6RX
✆ 01355 500282 **Map 12, F5**
A77, 3 miles S of Newton Mearns
Founded 1893
Moorland course in lovely scenery. The par-5 8th is reckoned to be the hardest hole on the course.
18 holes, 5666 yards
par 68, S.S.S 68
Designer Theodore Moone
Green fees £24
Catering, changing room/showers, bar, trolley hire, shop, practice facilities
Visitors welcome weekdays
Societies welcome by prior arrangement

ELDERSLIE GOLF CLUB

63 Main Road, Elderslie, Renfrewshire PA5 9AZ
✆ 01505 323956 Fax 01505 340346
Map 12, E4
A737, 2 miles from M8 Jct 29
Founded 1908
An undulating parkland course.
18 holes, 6165 yards

par 70, S.S.S 70
Designer James Braid
Green fees £21
Catering, changing room/showers, bar, trolley hire, shop, practice facilities
Visitors welcome, weekdays by prior arrangement
Handicap certificate required
Societies welcome by prior arrangement

ERSKINE GOLF CLUB

Bishopton, Renfrewshire PA7 5PH
✆ 01505 862302 **Map 12, E4**
5 miles NW of Paisley
Founded 1904
A charming course which runs down to the shores of the River Clyde. Unusually there are only two par 3s, the 6th and 11th.
18 holes, 6287 yards
par 71, S.S.S 70
Green fees £25
Catering, changing room/showers, bar, trolley and buggy hire, shop
Visitors welcome – restricted weekends
Handicap certificate required
Societies welcome by prior arrangement

FERENEZE GOLF CLUB

Fereneze Avenue, Barrhead, Renfrewshire G78 1HJ
✆ 0141 881 1519 **Map 12, E5**
Off B744, 9 miles SW of Glasgow
Founded 1904
A steep climb over the first 3 holes leads to gentler ground, from which there are fine panoramas. The front nine is unusual in having three par 3s, three par 4s and three par 5s.
18 holes, 5962 yards
par 71, S.S.S 70
Green fees £20
Catering, changing room/showers, bar, club and trolley hire, shop, practice facilities
Visitors welcome weekdays, by prior arrangement
Societies welcome by prior arrangement

GLEDDOCH GOLF CLUB

Langbank, Renfrewshire PA14 6YE
✆ 01475 540304 Fax 01475 540459
Map 12, E4
B789 Old Greenock Road
Founded 1974
With good views over the Firth of Clyde, a mixture of parkland and heathland holes.
18 holes, 6375 yards
par 71, S.S.S 71
Designer J Hamilton Stutt
Green fees £30
Catering, changing room/showers, bar, club, trolley and buggy hire, shop, driving range, practice facilities, squash, horse riding
Visitors welcome weekdays
Societies welcome by prior arrangement

GOUROCK GOLF CLUB

Cowal View, Gourock, Renfrewshire PA19 1HD
✆ 01475 631001 Fax 01475 631001
Map 12, D4
Off A770, 7 miles W of Port Glasgow
Founded 1896
There is considerable movement in the land, giving the architects plenty of scope for cunning green locations. The views across the River Clyde are outstanding.
18 holes, 6512 yards
par 73, S.S.S 73
Designer James Braid, Sir Henry Cotton
Green fees £20
Catering, changing room/showers, bar, club and trolley hire, shop, practice facilities
Visitors welcome
Handicap certificate required
Societies welcome by prior arrangement

GREENOCK GOLF CLUB

Forsyth Street, Greenock, Renfrewshire PA16 8RE
✆ 01475 720793 Fax 01475 791912
Map 12, D4
www.greenockgolfclub.co.uk
Forsyth Street, off A8 at Greenock
Founded 1890
27 holes of James Braid golf in a remarkable setting, with terrific views over the Clyde to the mountains beyond. The 7th tee gives the most spectacular views, at the start of the most difficult section of the course. Beware the 91-yard 8th on the little course – devilish stuff!
18 holes, 5838 yards, par 68, S.S.S 69
Designer James Braid
9 holes, 2160 yards, par 32, S.S.S 32
Green fees £25
Catering, changing room/showers, bar, trolley hire, shop, practice facilities
Visitors welcome weekdays
Societies welcome by prior arrangement

KILMALCOLM GOLF CLUB

Porterfield Road, Kilmalcolm, Renfrewshire PA13 4PD
✆ 01505 872139 Fax 01505 874007
Map 12, E4
Off A761, E of Kilmalcolm
Founded 1891
A moorland course 400 feet above sea level giving excellent views. Two testing holes follow each other at the 6th and 7th, a 230-yard par 3 and 472-yard par 4.
18 holes, 5961 yards
par 69, S.S.S 69
Designer Willie Campbell
Green fees £20
Catering, changing room/showers, bar, trolley and buggy hire, shop, practice facilities
Visitors welcome weekdays
Societies welcome by prior arrangement

LOCHWINNOCH GOLF CLUB

Burnfoot Road, Lochwinnoch, Renfrewshire PA12 4AN
✆ 01505 842153 Fax 01505 843668
Map 12, E5
Off A760, 9 miles SW of Paisley
Founded 1897
Overlooking a bird sanctuary, a well presented parkland course with tricky greens and the occasional stream.
18 holes, 6243 yards
par 71, S.S.S 71
Green fees £20
Visitors welcome weekdays
Societies welcome by prior arrangement

THE OLD COURSE RANFURLY GOLF CLUB

Ranfurly Place, Bridge of Weir, Renfrewshire PA11 3DE
✆ 01505 613612 Fax 01505 613214
Map 12, E4
secretary@oldranfurly.com
www.oldranfurly.com
7 miles W of Paisley, M8 Jct 29
Founded 1905
From the higher parts of this undulating course there are fine views over the Clyde to Ben Lomond. Of several technically challenging holes, the 1st and 9th demand strong play, and the 16th is a blind par 3.
18 holes, 6061 yards
par 70, S.S.S 70
Designer Willie Park Jnr
Green fees £20
Catering, changing room/showers, bar, practice facilities
Visitors welcome – with restrictions
Societies welcome by prior arrangement

PAISLEY GOLF CLUB

Braehead, Paisley, Renfrewshire PA2 8TZ
✆ 0141 884 3903 Fax 0141 884 3903 **Map 12, E5**
paisleygc@onetel.net.uk
Off B774, S of Paisley

Founded 1895
There are superb views over the Clyde Valley towards Ben Lomond, but the golfer's attention must be given to the gorse and heather which punishes the wayward shot, especially on the harder front nine. Nevertheless, on the homeward nine, the 200-yard 15th and 443-yard 18th are especially challenging.
18 holes, 6466 yards
par 71, S.S.S 72
Designer J Hamilton Stutt
Green fees £24
Catering, changing room/showers, bar, shop, practice facilities
Visitors welcome weekdays, subject to restrictions
Handicap certificate required
Societies welcome by prior arrangement

PORT GLASGOW GOLF CLUB
Devol Road, Port Glasgow, Renfrewshire PA14 5XE
☎ 01475 704181/700334 **Map 12, E4**
www.portglasgowgolfclub.co.uk
1 mile Port Glasgow
Founded 1895
A hilltop course giving fine views over the Clyde to the Cowal Hills.
18 holes, 5712 yards
par 68, S.S.S 68
Designer J.J. Braid
Green fees £20
Catering, changing room/showers, bar, practice facilities
Visitors welcome
Societies welcome by prior arrangement

RALSTON GOLF CLUB
Strathmore Avenue, Paisley, Renfrewshire PA1 3DT
☎ 0141 882 1349 Fax 0141 883 9837 **Map 12, E4**
A737, 2 miles E of Paisley Cross (off Glasgow Road)
Founded 1904
Long-established parkland course near Paisley.
18 holes, 6105 yards
par 71, S.S.S 70
Designer James Braid
Green fees £28
Catering, changing room/showers, bar, trolley hire, shop, practice facilities
Visitors on application to Secretary
Societies welcome by prior arrangement

RANFURLY CASTLE GOLF CLUB
Golf Road, Bridge of Weir, Renfrewshire PA11 3HN
☎ 01505 612609 Fax 01505 610406 **Map 12, E4**
www.ranfurlycastle.com
M8, Jct 29, follow Bridge of Weir signs, turning left on entering village
Founded 1889
One of the best courses in the area, a mixture of heathland and moorland holes. The 8th and 11th are both very demanding par 4s, but there are a number of compensatory drive-and-pitch holes.
18 holes, 6284 yards
par 70, S.S.S 71
Green fees £25
Catering, changing room/showers, bar, trolley hire, shop, practice facilities
Visitors welcome weekdays
Handicap certificate required
Societies welcome by prior arrangement

RENFREW GOLF CLUB
Blythswood Estate, Inchinnan Road, Renfrew, Renfrewshire PA4 9EG
☎ 0141 886 6692 Fax 0141 886 1808 **Map 12, E4**
secretary@renfrew.scottishgolg.com
www.renfrew.scottishgolf.com
M8 Jcts 26 or 27, following signs for Renfrew
Founded 1894
The present parkland course dates from the early 1970s, and is well fitted to the contemporary game, hosting many important tournaments and Open Championship qualifying. Interestingly, some of the shorter par 4s are amongst the best holes, such as the 315-yard 12th with an all-or-nothing approach across a pond.
18 holes, 6818 yards
par 72, S.S.S 72
Designer John D Harris
Green fees £30
Catering, changing room/showers, bar, trolley hire, shop, practice facilities
Visitors welcome – restricted
Handicap certificate required
Societies welcome by prior arrangement
🏨 Normandy Hotel, Inchinnan Road, Renfrew, Renfrewshire PA4 9EJ
☎ 0141 886 4100

WHINHILL GOLF CLUB
Beith Road, Greenock, Renfrewshire PA16
☎ 01475 24694 **Map 12, D4**
On Greenock-Largs road
Founded 1911
A short course designed by Willie Fernie, inland from Greenock.
18 holes, 5504 yards
S.S.S 68
Designer Willie Fernie
Visitors welcome
Societies welcome by prior arrangement

WHITECRAIGS GOLF CLUB
72 Ayr Road, Newton Mearns, Glasgow, Renfrewshire G46 6SW
☎ 0141 639 4530 Fax 0141 639 4530 **Map 12, F5**
www.thewhitecraigsgolfclub.co.uk
A77, 1 mile N of Newton Mearns
Founded 1905
A handsome parkland course.
18 holes, 6230 yards
par 70, S.S.S 70
Catering, changing room/showers, bar, club and trolley hire, shop, practice facilities
Visitors welcome weekdays
Handicap certificate required
Societies welcome by prior arrangement

STIRLINGSHIRE

ABERFOYLE GOLF CLUB
Braeval, Aberfoyle, Stirlingshire FK8 3UY
☎ 01877 383 493 **Map 12, F2**
1 mile from Aberfoyle Village
Founded 1890
A parkland course with inspirational views of Ben Lomond and the Trossachs.
18 holes, 5158 yards
par 66, S.S.S 66
Green fees £15
Catering, changing room/showers, bar, trolley hire, practice facilities
Visitors welcome with restrictions
Societies welcome by prior arrangement

BALFRON GOLF SOCIETY
Kepculloch Road, Balfron, Stirlingshire G63 0QP
☎ 01360 440037 **Map 12, F3**
golfbalfron@aol.com
Off A875
Founded 1994
From this newly extended upland course there are fine views of the Campsie Fells and Endrick Water.
18 holes, 5950 yards
par 71, S.S.S 69
Designer R. Hiseman
Green fees £10
Changing room/showers
Visitors welcome – restricted weekends
Societies welcome by prior arrangement – no company days

BONNYBRIDGE GOLF CLUB
Larbert Road, Bonnybridge, Falkirk, Stirlingshire FK4 1NY
☎ 01324 812822 **Map 12, G4**

Off A883, NE of Bonnybridge
Founded 1924
A heathland course.
9 holes, 6058 yards
par 72, S.S.S 69
Shop
Visitors welcome only as members' guests
Societies welcome by prior arrangement

BRIDGE OF ALLAN GOLF CLUB

Sunnylaw, Bridge of Allan, Stirling, Stirlingshire FK9 4LY
☎ 01786 832332 **Map 12, G3**
Off M9
Founded 1895
A hilly parkland course with good views and a monster opening hole, a 223-yard uphill par 3, with a mound to be crossed just before the green.
9 holes, 4932 yards
par 66, S.S.S 65
Designer Tom Morris
Green fees £10
Changing room/showers, trolley hire
Visitors welcome – restricted weekends
Societies welcome by prior arrangement

BUCHANAN CASTLE GOLF CLUB

Drymen, Stirlingshire G63 0HY
☎ 01360 660307 Fax 01360 870383
Map 12, E3
Off A811, 1 mile W of Drymen
Founded 1936
An elegant parkland course on the Duke of Montrose's estate.
18 holes, 6015 yards
par 70, S.S.S 69
Designer James Braid
Green fees £30
Catering, changing room/showers, bar, club and trolley hire, shop, practice facilities
Visitors welcome by prior arrangement
Societies welcome by prior arrangement

CAMPSIE GOLF CLUB

Crow Road, Lennoxtown, Glasgow, Stirlingshire G66 7HX
☎ 01360 312249 **Map 12, F4**
B822, N of Lennoxtown
Founded 1897
Set on a hillside with extensive views, the short par 4 is a feature – there are six under 300 yards – none more capricious than the 278-yard 13th.
18 holes, 5517 yards
par 70, S.S.S 68
Designer Aucterlonie/Stark
Green fees £15
Catering, changing room/showers, bar, club hire, shop, practice facilities
Visitors welcome weekdays
Societies welcome by prior arrangement

DUNBLANE NEW GOLF CLUB

Perth Road, Dunblane, Stirlingshire FK15 0LJ
☎ 01786 821521 Fax 01786 821522
Map 12, G2
A9, off M9, E of Dunblane
Founded 1923
A hilly parkland course with a number of strong holes. Left-handers fear the par-3 11th, on which it is all too easy for them to slice out of bounds.
18 holes, 5957 yards
par 70, S.S.S 69
Green fees £20
Catering, changing room/showers, bar, club and trolley hire, shop
Visitors welcome weekdays
Societies welcome by prior arrangement

FALKIRK GOLF CLUB

136 Stirling Road, Camelon, Falkirk, Stirlingshire FK2 7YP
☎ 01324 612219 Fax 01324 639573
Map 12, G4
carmuirs.fgc@virgin.net
A9, 1½ miles NW of Falkirk
Founded 1922
Streams and gorse add to the difficulties of this cunningly designed course, on which a number of Roman burial sites have been discovered.
18 holes, 6230 yards
par 71, S.S.S 70
Designer James Braid
Green fees £15
Catering, changing room/showers, bar, trolley hire, shop, practice facilities
Visitors welcome weekdays
Inchyra Grange, Polmont, Stirlingshire
☎ 01324 711911

FALKIRK TRYST GOLF CLUB

86 Burnhead Road, Larbert, Stirlingshire FK5 4BD
☎ 01324 562415 **Map 12, G3**
A88, W of Stenhousemuir
Founded 1885
A heathland course which plays much like a links, with hole lengths varied in such a way that every club in the bag will be needed.
18 holes, 6053 yards
par 70, S.S.S 69
Green fees £18
Catering, changing room/showers, bar, club and trolley hire, shop, practice facilities
Visitors welcome weekdays
Societies welcome by prior arrangement

GLENBERVIE GOLF CLUB

Stirling Road, Larbert, Stirlingshire FK5 4SJ
☎ 01324 562605 Fax 01324 551054
Map 12, G3
A9, NW of Larbert
Founded 1932
Glenbervie's wooded, parkland course has seen the Scottish Professional Golfers' Championship, British Boys' Championship (twice), and been used for regional qualifying for the Open Championship. Although the course is fairly level, the Ochil Hills make a fine background. There is a good change of pace and balance during the round.
18 holes, 6423 yards
par 71, S.S.S 71
Designer James Braid
Green fees £30
Catering, changing room/showers, bar, trolley hire, shop, practice facilities
Visitors welcome weekdays with restrictions
Societies welcome by prior arrangement

GRANGEMOUTH GOLF CLUB

Polmonthill, Polmont, Stirlingshire FK2 0YA
☎ 01324 711500 Fax 01324 717907
Map 12, H3
M9 Jct 4
Founded 1973
A long testing course on which the 7th calls for a 216-yard shot, all carry across a reservoir.
18 holes, 6314 yards
par 71, S.S.S 71
Green fees £12.50
Catering, changing room/showers, bar, trolley hire, shop
Visitors welcome with prior booking
Societies welcome by prior arrangement

KILSYTH LENNOX GOLF CLUB

Tak-Ma-Doon Road, Kilsyth, Stirlingshire G65 0RS
☎ 01236 823525 **Map 12, G4**
Off A803, N of Kilsyth
Founded 1900
A testing moorland course, fairly undulating.
18 holes, 5930 yards
par 70, S.S.S 70
Green fees £10
Catering, changing room/showers, bar, buggy hire, shop

Visitors welcome weekdays
Societies welcome by prior arrangement

POLMONT GOLF CLUB
Manuelrigg, Maddiston, Falkirk, Stirlingshire FK2 0LS
☎ 01324 711277 Fax 01324 712504
Map 12, H4
B805, 4 miles SE of Falkirk
Founded 1901
Somewhat hilly, tree-lined fairways give panoramic views of the Forth Valley and Ochil Hills. Par-3 3rd is particularly unforgiving.
9 holes, 6092 yards
par 72, S.S.S 70
Designer John Panton
Green fees £8
Catering, changing room/showers, bar, club and trolley hire, practice facilities, conference facilities
Visitors welcome, not Saturdays
Handicap certificate required
Societies welcome by prior arrangement
Inchyra Grange, Polmont, Stirlingshire
☎ 01324 711911

STIRLING GOLF CLUB
Queen's Road, Stirling, Stirlingshire FK8 3AA
☎ 01786 473801 Fax 01786 450748
Map 12, G3
B8051, 1 mile W of Stirling
Founded 1869
A fine course in a magnificent setting under the walls of Stirling Castle. The 15th is probably the hardest hole, an uphill dog-leg on which the approach shot must be played across an expanse of rough, with no alternative for the faint hearted.
18 holes, 6409 yards
par 72, S.S.S 71
Designer James Braid, Sir Henry Cotton
Green fees £25
Catering, changing room/showers, bar, club, trolley and buggy hire, shop, practice facilities
Visitors welcome weekdays
Societies welcome by prior arrangement

STRATHENDRICK GOLF CLUB
Glasgow Road, Drymen, Stirlingshire G63 0AA
☎ 01360 660695 **Map 12, E3**
Off A811, W of Stirling
Founded 1901
A hilly course designed by Willie Fernie.
9 holes, 5116 yards
S.S.S 64
Designer Willie Fernie
Green fees £12
Visitors welcome weekdays
Societies welcome by prior arrangement

WEST COAST

ASKERNISH GOLF CLUB
Lochboisedale, Askernish, South Uist HS81 5ST
☎ 01878 700298 **Map 15, B5**
Off A865, NW of Loch Boisdale
Founded 1891
On the shores of the Atlantic Ocean, with terrific views, the golf here is played on an uncommon grass, machair.
9 holes, 5114 yards
par 68, S.S.S 67
Designer Tom Morris
Green fees £10
Club hire
Visitors welcome
Societies welcome by prior arrangement

GAIRLOCH GOLF CLUB
Gairloch, Ross-Shire IV21 2BQ
☎ 01445 712407 **Map 14, B7**
secretary@gairlochgc@freeserve.uk
A832, 60 miles W of Inverness
Founded 1898
A jewel in the crown of Wester Ross, a testing links with magnificent views of the spectacular mountain scenery and wide sea scapes.
9 holes, 4093 yards
par 63, S.S.S 64
Green fees £15
Catering, changing room/showers, bar, club and trolley hire, practice facilities
Visitors welcome
Societies welcome by prior arrangement
Gairloch Hotel, Gairloch, Ross-Shire, West Coast IV21 2BL
☎ 01445 712001

ISLE OF BARRA GOLF COURSE
Cleat, Castlebay, Isle of Barra HS9 5YX
☎ 01871 810419 Fax 01871 810418
Map 15, A6
www.ofbarra.com/golf
On Isle of Barra
Founded 1992
The most Westerly course in Scotland, in the Outer Hebrides.
9 holes, 5032 yards
par 68
Green fees £10
Club and trolley hire
Visitors welcome
Societies welcome by prior arrangment
Castlebay Hotel, Castlebay, Barra, West Coast HS9 5XD
☎ 01871 810223

ISLE OF HARRIS GOLF CLUB
Scarista, Isle of Harris HS3 3HX
☎ 01859 550331 Fax 01859 550226
Map 15, C4
harrisgolf@ic14.net
www.harrisgolf.com
A859, 10 miles S of Tarbert, 40 miles S of Stornoway
Founded 1983
An astonishing course, clinging to the hillside above the Atlantic Ocean, requiring inventive golf simply to survive. The website, with mouth-watering pictures, gives details of a brilliant, worldwide life membership scheme.
9 holes, 4864 yards
par 68, S.S.S 64
Green fees £10
Changing room/showers, club hire, practice facilities
Visitors welcome
Societies welcome by prior arrangement
Scarista House, Scarista, Isle of Harris, West Coast HS3 3HX
☎ 01859 550238

ISLE OF SKYE GOLF CLUB
Sconser, Isle of Skye IV48 8TD
☎ 01478 650414 Fax 01478 613025
Map 14, A8
isleofskye.golfclub@btinternet.com
www.uk-golf.com/clubs/isleofskye
On A87, from Skye Bridge to Portree
Founded 1964
With the mountains of Skye on one hand and the sea on the other, this is a magical spot. The course is essentially parkland and manages to incorporate a substantial par 4, the 2nd, into its short length.
9 holes, 4677 yards
par 66, S.S.S 64
Green fees £15
Catering, changing room/showers, club and trolley hire, shop, practice facilities
Visitors welcome
Societies welcome by prior arrangement
Cuillin Hills Hotel, Portree, Isle of Skye, West Coast IV51 9LU
☎ 01478 612003

LOCHCARRON GOLF CLUB
Lochcarron, Strathcarront IV54 8YU
☎ 01520 722257 **Map 14, B8**
www.lochcarrongolf.co.uk
A896, W of junction with A890 at Lochcarron
Founded 1908
In a magnificent location at the head of a sea loch, surrounded by

mountains, Lochcarron is a short, but far from easy, course, the challenge varying with the tide. Part parkland, part seashore.
9 holes, 3578 yards
par 62, S.S.S 60
Green fees £10
Club hire
Visitors welcome – restricted Saturdays
Societies welcome by prior arrangement
Strathcarron Hotel, Strathcarron, West Coast
01520 722227

SKEABOST GOLF CLUB

Skeabost Bridge, Isle of Skye IV51 9NR
01470 532202 Fax 01470 532454
Map 14, A8
6 miles NW of Portree on Dunvegan road
Founded 1982
A very pretty little course, part of it running through woodland, the rest overlooking the sea.
9 holes, 3224 yards
par 62, S.S.S 59
Designer John Stuart
Green fees £6
Catering, changing room/showers, bar, accommodation, trolley hire, shop, practice facilities
Visitors welcome
Societies welcome by prior arrangement
Skeabost House Hotel, Isle of Skye, West Coast
01470 532202

STORNOWAY GOLF CLUB

Lady Lever Park, Stornoway, Isle of Lewist HS2 0EA
01851 702240 **Map 15, D2**
admin@stornoway-golfclub.co.uk
www.stornoway-golfclub.co.uk
West edge of town
Founded 1890
With panoramic views across the Minch to the Scottish mainland and the Isle of Skye. The 11th is a notoriously difficult par 5.
18 holes, 5252 yards
par 68, S.S.S 66
Green fees £15
Catering, changing room/showers, bar, club and trolley hire, shop, practice facilities
Visitors welcome – closed Sundays
Societies welcome by prior arrangement
Caberfeidh Hotel, Stornoway, West Coast

TRAIGH GOLF CLUB

c/o Camusdarach, Arisaig PH39 4NT
01687 450337 **Map 14, B10**
A830, 10 miles S of Mallaig
A spectacular setting with breath taking views to the islands of Eigg, Rhum and Skye. The course was redesigned in the 1990s and plays over a grassy ridge, 60 feet high.
9 holes, 4912 yards
par 68, S.S.S 65
Designer John Salvesen
Green fees £10
Catering, changing room/showers, bar, club and trolley hire
Visitors welcome
Societies welcome by prior arrangement

WEST LOTHIAN

BATHGATE GOLF CLUB

Edinburgh Road, Bathgate, West Lothian EH48 1BA
01506 630505 Fax 01506 636775
Map 12, H4
bathgate.golfclub@lineone.net
In Bathgate town centre, 2 miles from M8 Jcts 3A and 4
Founded 1892
Almost certainly the only club to have produced two Ryder Cup Captains, Eric Brown and Bernard Gallagher. Another, Sam Torrance, holds the course record of 58.
18 holes, 6328 yards
par 71, S.S.S 70
Designer Willie Park Jnr, James Braid
Green fees £17
Catering, changing room/showers, bar, club, trolley and buggy hire, shop, practice facilities
Visitors welcome, except competition days
Societies welcome by prior arrangement
Dreadnought Hotel, 17/19 Whitburn Road, Bathgate, West Lothian
01506 653194

DEER PARK GOLF & COUNTRY CLUB

Golf Course Road, Livingston, West Lothian EH54 8AB
01506 431037 Fax 01506 435608
Map 13, A4
dpsales@muir-group.co.uk
M8 Jct 3
Founded 1978
Championship standard course which is good enough to have hosted qualifying rounds for the Open Championship and Scottish PGA.
18 holes, 6688 yards
par 72, S.S.S 72
Green fees £24
Catering, changing room/showers, bar, trolley and buggy hire, shop, practice facilities, conference & function facilities, ten-pin bowling, swimming pool and gym
Visitors welcome
Societies welcome by prior arrangement
Deer Park Travel Inn, Deer Park Avenue, Knightsbridge, Livingstone, West Lothian
01506 439202

DUNDAS PARKS GOLF CLUB

South Queensferry, West Lothian EH30 9SS
0131 319 1347 **Map 13, A4**
M8/9, take A8000 to Forth Road Bridge
Founded 1974
Situated beside Dundas Castle.
9 holes, 6024 yards
par 70, S.S.S 69
Green fees £10
Changing room/showers, practice facilities
Visitors welcome, with restrictions
Societies welcome by prior arrangement
Forth Bridges Hotel, Ferrymuir Gate, South Queensferry, West Lothian
0131 499 9955

GREENBURN GOLF CLUB

6 Greenburn Road, Fauldhouse, West Lothian EH47 9HG
01501 771187 Fax 01501 772615
Map 13, A4
secretary@greenburngolfclub.fsnet.co.uk
M8, 4 miles S of Jct 3
Founded 1953
An interesting moorland course with a number of water hazards, divided by a railway line.
18 holes, 6046 yards
par 71, S.S.S 71
Green fees £17
Catering, changing room/showers, bar, trolley hire, shop, practice facilities
Visitors welcome, with restrictions
Societies welcome by prior arrangement

HARBURN GOLF CLUB

West Calder, West Lothian EH55 8RS
01506 871256 Fax 01506 870286
Map 13, A4
B7008, 2 miles S of West Calder
Founded 1921
At an altitude of 600 feet, Harburn is exposed to the wind, but there is some shelter afforded by the beeches, oaks and pines which line most fairways. There are many

challenging holes, with the narrow 16th somewhat intimidating.
18 holes, 5921 yards
par 69, S.S.S 69
Green fees £18
Catering, changing room/showers, bar, trolley and buggy hire, shop, driving range, practice facilities
Visitors welcome, except Wednesdays – restricted weekends
Societies welcome by prior arrangement

LINLITHGOW GOLF CLUB

Braehead, Linlithgow, West Lothian EH49 6QF
☎ 01506 844356 Fax 01506 842764
Map 12, H4
linlithgowgolf@talk21.com
www.linlithgowgolf.co.uk
From M9 follow A706, Lanark Road
Founded 1913
A good number of drive-and-pitch par 4s keeps the overall yardage low, but the undulating land complicates club selection, and the quick greens are tricky. Panoramic views.
18 holes, 5729 yards
par 70, S.S.S 68
Green fees £20
Catering, changing room/showers, bar, trolley hire, shop, practice facilities
Visitors welcome – restricted weekends
Societies welcome by prior arrangement

NIDDRY CASTLE GOLF CLUB

Castle Road, Winchburgh, West Lothian EH52 2RQ
☎ 01506 891097 **Map 13, A4**
B9080, W of Edinburgh
Founded 1982
A challenging little course with compact greens.
9 holes, 5476 yards
par 70, S.S.S 67
Green fees £13
Changing room/showers
Visitors welcome
Societies welcome by prior arrangement

POLKEMMET COUNTRY PARK

Whitburn, Bathgate, West Lothian EH47 0AD
☎ 01501 743905 **Map 12, H4**
M8 Jct 4
Founded 1981
A long course laid out in a country park, surrounded by woodland and intersected by the River Almond.
9 holes, 6496 yards
par 74, S.S.S 74
Green fees £4.75
Catering, changing room/showers, bar, trolley hire, driving range
Visitors welcome
Societies welcome by prior arrangement

PUMPHERSTON GOLF CLUB

Drumshoreland Road, Pumpherston, West Lothian EH53 0LF
☎ 01506 432869 **Map 13, A4**
M8 Jct 3, W of Edinburgh
Founded 1895
A parkland course dominated by a pond, which encircles the 6th green.
9 holes, 4950 yards
par 66, S.S.S 64
Catering, changing room/showers, bar
Visitors welcome only as members' guests
Societies welcome by prior arrangement

UPHALL GOLF CLUB

Houston Mains, Uphall, West Lothian EH52 6JT
☎ 01506 856404 Fax 01506 855358
Map 13, A4
M8 Jct 3, 10 miles W of Edinburgh
Founded 1895
A short course with plenty of character. The club specialises in golf outings and functions, and is warmly welcoming to visitors.
18 holes, 5588 yards
par 69, S.S.S 67
Green fees £14
Catering, changing room/showers, bar, club and trolley hire, shop, practice facilities
Visitors welcome
Societies welcome by prior arrangement

WEST LOTHIAN GOLF CLUB

Airngath Hill, Linlithgow, West Lothian EH49 7RH
☎ 01506 826030 Fax 01506 826030
Map 12, H4
Off A706, 1 mile S
Founded 1892
There are fine views over the Forth Valley from this parkland course.
18 holes, 6406 yards
par 71, S.S.S 71
Designer Willie Park, Adams, Middleton
Green fees £20
Catering, changing room/showers, bar, club and trolley hire, shop, practice facilities
Visitors welcome weekdays by arrangement
Societies welcome by prior arrangement

WALES

At present, Wales offers the best value in British golf. A round at one of its top courses, such as Royal Porthcawl or Royal St David's, will set the visitor back about half what it would cost to play a course of equal distinction on the coasts of Lancashire or Ayrshire. As a consequence, golf at the lesser Welsh courses is proportionately cheaper, too. It is hard to understand why this should be, for the quality is high, and access to the majority of courses is absurdly simple, with fast roads and adequate railways serving the North and South Wales coasts very effectively.

The long Welsh coastline has many fine links courses, with Tenby generally reckoned to be the oldest established club in the province, although golf was certainly played in Wales before 1888 when Tenby came into being. Other links gems include Aberdovey, Ashburnham, Borth & Ynyslas, Conwy, North Wales, Prestatyn and Pyle & Kenfig. Their greens are amongst the truest in existence. However, some of the other seaside courses, not strictly true links, are amongst its most spectacular, such as the dramatic cliff-top Nefyn & District, and the glorious Southerndown. Neither should you miss Bull Bay, which scrambles over hilly ground on the north coast of Anglesey.

Only sporadically has the big-time professional game visited Wales, although, in recent years, St Pierre near Chepstow has hosted a number of very successful European Tour events. Now Celtic Manor has entered the frame, staging its own Wales Open for the first time in 2000. The requirements of a bid to stage the Ryder Cup in Wales may cause wholescale rebuilding of the remarkable Wentwood Hills course at Celtic Manor, so adventurous golfers are encouraged to pit their wits against its formidable challenges now, for it may become even more demanding in the future.

Wales being a mountainous country, the surrounding scenery on almost every course is at least uplifting, if not downright distracting. Mid-Wales remains disarmingly quiet and unspoiled and a round of golf at Cradoc, Llandrindod Wells or Welshpool, for instance, is to be enjoyed as much for the clear mountain air, abundant wildlife and glorious mountain backdrops, as it is for the charm and guile of the course architecture. For the golfer looking for 'something different' there are unique experiences available at mountain-top Festiniog, the notably tricky par-3 course at Llanfairfechan with its majestic seacapes, or delightful Bala, on a rocky hill overlooking the famous lake. The only problem is the 1st hole, a monstrous par 3, arguably the hardest short hole in Wales!

It is inevitable that seaside and mountain courses predominate in Wales, for there is not a great deal of flat ground inland, but there are parkland courses of some distinction, such as The Glamorganshire, The Rolls of Monmouth, Vale of Llangollen and Wrexham. Indeed, Vale of Llangollen offers the best of all worlds, running on level ground alongside the salmon-filled River Dee, yet surrounded by rhododendron-clad mountains.

ANGLESEY

ANGLESEY GOLF CLUB

Station Road, Rhosneigr, Anglesey LL64 5QX
✆ 01407 811202 Fax 01407 811202
Map 6, E2
A4080 NE of Rhosneigr
Founded 1914
Unspoiled natural linksland with sheep for company. The best hole is probably the last, with both the drive and approach threatened by a winding river. Despite the overall flatness of the site, level lies are few, and ridges, mounds, craters and clumps of marram grass provide the main physical obstacles.
18 holes, 6300 yards
par 70, S.S.S 70
Designer Harold Hilton
Green fees £15
Catering, changing room/showers, bar, club, trolley and buggy hire, shop, practice facilities
Visitors welcome, but phone first
Societies by prior arrangement

BARON HILL GOLF CLUB

Beaumaris, Anglesey LL58 8YW
✆ 01248 810231 Fax 01248 810231
Map 6, G1
1 mile SW of Beaumaris, signposted from A545
Founded 1895
Quite tricky with rocky outcrops, gorse and a stream. Severe dog-leg 6th can be troublesome.
9 holes, 5596 yards
par 68, S.S.S 69
Green fees £12
Catering, changing room/showers, bar, trolley hire
Visitors welcome, except competition days and ladies have priority Tuesdays
Societies welcome by prior arrangement

BULL BAY GOLF CLUB

Bull Bay Road, Amlwch, Anglesey LL68 9RY
✆ 01407 831188 Fax 01407 832612
On coast road 1 mile beyond Amlwch towards Cemaes Bay
Founded 1913
Excellent heathland course on Anglesey's northern coast. Fowler's cunning use of the rolling land means that most greens are approached uphill, with many drives encouragingly downhill. The rough and gorse are severely punishing, the course fully exposed to the wind, and holes such as the 7th challenge even the best.
18 holes, 6217 yards
par 70, S.S.S 70
Designer Herbert Fowler
Green fees £20
Catering, changing room/showers, bar, club, trolley and buggy hire, shop, practice facilities
Visitors welcome – restrictions weekends
Handicap certificate required
Societies welcome by prior arrangement
Bull Bay Hotel, Bull Bay, Amlwch, Anglesey
✆ 01407 830223

HOLYHEAD GOLF CLUB

Lon Garreg Fawr, Trearddur Bay, Holyhead, Anglesey LL65 2YL
✆ 01407 763279 Fax 01407 763279
Map 6, E1
www.holyheadgolfclub.co.uk
B4245 2 miles south of Holyhead
Founded 1912
With Dublin only 90 minutes away by 'Superferry' many Irish golfers are discovering this fine links with its convenient dormy house. Rocky outcrops and thick gorse punish waywardness, and though a number of the par 4s are quite short they are appropriately tight. Putting on these greens is a joy.

18 holes, 6058 yards
par 71, S.S.S 70
Designer James Braid
Green fees £19
Catering, changing room/showers, bar, accommodation, club and trolley hire, shop, practice facilities
Visitors welcome, but phone first
Societies welcome by prior arrangement

LLANGEFNI GOLF CLUB

Llangefni, Anglesey LL77 8YQ
✆ 01248 722193 **Map 6, F1**
Off A5111 at south end of Llangefni
Founded 1983
Eight par 3s and a single par 4 make up this public facility divided by hedgerows.
9 holes, 1487 yards
par 28
Designer Hawtree
Green fees £3
Catering, changing room/showers, bar, club hire, shop
Visitors welcome

STORWS WEN GOLF CLUB

Brynteg, Benllech, Anglesey LL78 8JY
✆ 01248 852673 Fax 01248 852673
Map 6, F1
B5108 2 miles from Benllech
Founded 1996
Handsome new 9-holer with fine panoramas and attractive water holes.
9 holes, 5002 yards
par 68, S.S.S 64
Designer K Jones
Green fees £10
Catering, changing room/showers, bar, club, trolley and buggy hire
Visitors welcome
Societies welcome by prior arrangement

CARDIGANSHIRE

ABERYSTWYTH GOLF CLUB

Brynmor Road, Aberystwyth, Cardiganshire SY23 2HY
✆ 01970 615104 Fax 01970 626622
Map 6, G7
aberystwythgolf@talk21.com
½ mile from centre of town on north side
Founded 1911
A very scenic parkland course overlooking the town and the broad sweep of Cardigan Bay, and with views inland to the mountains. Two long par 4s open the round, and the revamped par-5 10th plays to a green surrounded by water. The course is remarkably resistant to low scoring.
18 holes, 6119 yards
par 70, S.S.S 71
Designer Harry Vardon
Green fees £18.50
Catering, changing room/showers, bar, trolley hire, shop, practice facilities
Visitors welcome – advisable to book in advance
Societies by prior arrangement
Conrah Country House, Chancery, Aberystwyth, Cardiganshire SY23 4DF
✆ 01970 617941 Fax 01970 624546
hotel@conrahfreeserve.co.uk

BORTH & YNYSLAS GOLF CLUB

Borth, Cardiganshire SY24 5JS
✆ 01870 871202 Fax 01870 871202
Map 6, G6
On B4353 coast road north of Borth
Founded 1885
One of the oldest clubs in Wales and a regular host to Welsh Golf Union championships, Borth has that admirable quality of being able to test good players while not being impossible for those with less ability. Traditional links turf gives excellent winter golf and there are special winter packages.
18 holes, 6116 yards
par 70, S.S.S 70
Designer Harry Colt
Green fees £20
Catering, changing room/showers, bar, club, trolley and buggy hire, shop, practice facilities
Visitors welcome weekdays and some weekends but phone first
Societies welcome by prior arrangement

CARDIGAN GOLF CLUB

Gwbert-on-Sea, Cardigan, Cardiganshire SA43 1PR
✆ 01239 615359 Fax 01239 621775
Map 6, D9
golf@cardigan.fsnet.co.uk
www.cardigangolf.sagenet.co.uk
3 miles N of Cardigan
Founded 1895
Part meadowland, part links, the course is built on high ground overlooking the Teifi Estuary with the sea visible from every single hole. The linksland finish is particularly attractive, with the view from the 16th tee to be savoured. One of the longer Welsh courses, but most fairways are generous.
18 holes, 6687 yards
par 72, S.S.S 73
Designer Hawtree
Green fees £20
Catering, changing room/showers, bar, club, trolley and buggy hire, shop, practice facilities, squash
Visitors welcome – with restrictions
Societies welcome by prior arrangement
Gwbert Hotel, Gwbert-on-Sea, Cardiganshire SA43 1PP
✆ 01239 612638

CILGWYN GOLF CLUB

Llangybi, Lampeter, Cardiganshire SA48 8NN
✆ 01570 493286 **Map 6, G9**
Off A485 at Llangybi, 5 miles N of Lampeter
Founded 1977
Pretty 9-hole layout in peaceful valley.
9 holes, 5327 yards
par 68, S.S.S 66
Green fees £10
Visitors welcome
Societies welcome by prior arrangement

PENRHOS GOLF & COUNTRY CLUB

Llanrhystud, Nr. Aberystwyth, Cardiganshire SY23 5AY
✆ 01974 202999 Fax 01974 202100
Map 6, G7
www.penrhosgolf.co.uk
B4337, off A487 in Llanrhystud
Founded 1991
New course with impressive facilities in delightful countryside with extensive views over Cardigan Bay.
Penrhos: 18 holes, 6641 yards, par 72, S.S.S 73
Designer Jim Walters
Academy: 9 holes, 1827 yards, par 31
Green fees £18
Catering, changing room/showers, bar, accommodation, club, trolley and buggy hire, shop, driving range, gym, sauna, swimming pool, tennis etc, and full conference facilities
Visitors welcome
Societies welcome by prior arrangement
Penrhos Golf and Country Club, Llanrhystud, Cardiganshire SY23 5AY
✆ 01974 202999 Fax 01974 202100
www.penrhosgolf.co.uk

CARMARTHENSHIRE

ASHBURRNHAM GOLF CLUB

Cliffe Terrace, Burry Port, Carmarthenshire SA16 0HN
✆ 01554 832269 Fax 01554 832466
Map 6, F11
A484, 5 miles west of Llanelli
Founded 1894
A famous, if undeniably flat, old course, one of Harry Vardon's.

favourites, on which both Bernard Gallagher and Sam Torrance won their first professional tournament. The bunkering, especially around the greens, is plentiful, and a number of fairways are interrupted by ridges, adding to their strategic defences. Always well presented.
18 holes, 6916 yards
par 72, S.S.S 74
Designer J.H. Taylor
Green fees £27
Catering, changing room/showers, bar, club and trolley hire, shop, practice facilities
Visitors welcome on production of handicap certificate
Handicap certificate required
Societies welcome by prior arrangement

CARMARTHEN GOLF CLUB
Blaenycoed Road, Carmarthen, Carmarthenshire SA33 6EH
☎ 01267 281588 **Map 6, F10**
4 miles NW of town
Founded 1907
Splendid views over lovely countryside from this challenging upland course with a fine clubhouse.
18 holes, 6245 yards
par 71, S.S.S 70
Designer J.H. Taylor
Green fees £20
Catering, changing room/showers, bar, club and trolley hire, shop, practice facilities
Visitors welcome, but phone for weekend starting times
Handicap certificate required
Societies welcome by prior arrangement

DERLLYS GOLF CLUB
Derllys Court, Llysonnen Road, Carmarthen, Carmarthenshire SA33 5DT
☎ 01267 211575 Fax 01267 211575
Map 6, E10
Off A40 4 miles W of Carmarthen
Founded 1993
Parkland course with a par-5 lake hole.
9 holes, 2859 yards
par 70, S.S.S 66
Designer P Johnson
Green fees £10
Catering, changing room/showers, bar, club and trolley hire
Visitors welcome at all times
Societies welcome by prior arrangement

GLYN ABBEY GOLF CLUB
Trimsaran, Kidwelly, Carmarthenshire SA17 4LB
☎ 01554 810278 Fax 01554 810889
Map 6, F11
course-enquiries@glynabbey.co.uk
www.glynabbey.co.uk
B4317 between Trimsaran and Carway
Founded 1992
Set out on the wooded slopes of the beautiful Gwendraeth Valley, and constructed to a Hawtree design, Glyn Abbey is both handsome and challenging. The 447-yard 7th clearly fits both categories.
18 holes, 6173 yards
par 70, S.S.S 70
Designer Hawtree
Green fees £12
Catering, changing room/showers, bar, accommodation, club, trolley and buggy hire, shop, driving range, practice facilities, 9-hole academy course, gym/fitness suite
Visitors welcome
Societies welcome by prior arrangement
🏨 Gwellian Court Hotel, Mynydd y Garreg, Kidwelly, Carmarthenshire
☎ 01554 890217

GLYNHIR GOLF CLUB
Glynhir Road, Llandybie, Ammanford, Carmarthenshire SA18 2TF
☎ 01269 851365 Fax 01269 851365
Map 6, G10
3 miles N of Ammanford
Founded 1909
Pretty parkland course in the delightful Loughor Valley.
18 holes, 6000 yards
par 69, S.S.S 70
Designer F Hawtree
Green fees £16
Catering, changing room/showers, bar, club, trolley and buggy hire, shop, practice facilities
Visitors welcome, but not Sundays – phone first
Handicap certificate required
Societies welcome weekdays by prior arrangement

SARON GOLF COURSE
Penwern, Saron, Llandysul, Carmarthenshire SA44 4EL
☎ 01559 370705 **Map 6, E9**
On A484 between Newcastle Emlyn and Cardigan
Founded 1994
Short course in handsome Teifi Valley countryside.
9 holes, 2300 yards
par 32
Green fees £7
Club and trolley hire, fishing
Visitors welcome
Societies welcome by prior arrangement

CONWY

ABERGELE GOLF CLUB
Tan-y-Gopa Road, Abergele, Conwy
☎ 01745 824034 Fax 01745 824034
Map 10, A11
At west end of town
Founded 1910
Laid out beneath the towers and turrets of Gwrych Castle, most of the course is on the flat with a number of big par 4s and 5s. There is a sting in the tail with the short 17th climbing steeply, and an intriguing downhill par 5 returning to the clubhouse.
18 holes, 6520 yards
par 72, S.S.S 71
Designer Hawtree
Green fees £25
Catering, changing room/showers, bar, trolley hire, shop, practice facilities
Visitors welcome, but phone first
Societies welcome by prior arrangement

BETWS-Y-COED GOLF CLUB
Clubhouse, Betws-y-Coed, Conwy LL24 0AL
☎ 01690 710556 **Map 6, H2**
N of village centre, off main A5
Founded 1977
Charming parkland course on the banks of the Conwy River.
9 holes, 4996 yards
par 64, S.S.S 63
Green fees £15
Catering, changing room/showers, bar, club hire
Visitors welcome, but phone first
Societies welcome by prior arrangement

CONWY (CAERNARVONSHIRE) GOLF CLUB
Morfa, Conwy, Conwy LL32 8ER
☎ 01492 592423 Fax 01492 593363
Map 6, H1
A55 coast road at west end of Conwy Tunnel – follow signs for Marina
Founded 1890
Magnificent championship links in incomparable setting between the mountains and the sea. Very challenging when the wind is up (and it usually is), with a nail-biting finish as narrow fairways run through impenetrable gorse. The 17th is a notorious card-wrecker, and much gorse must be carried on the final drive.
18 holes, 6936 yards
par 72, S.S.S 74
Green fees £25

Catering, changing room/showers, bar, club, trolley and buggy hire, shop, practice facilities
Visitors welcome weekdays, very limited availability at weekends, phone to book starting time
Handicap certificate required
Societies welcome by prior arrangement

LLANDUDNO (MAESDU) GOLF CLUB

Hospital Road, Llandudno, Conwy LL30 1HU
☎ 01492 876450 Fax 01492 871570
Map 6, H1
A55 exit for Conwy/Deganwy, follow A456 through Deganwy – club on right
Founded 1915
Blessed with magnificent views along the North Wales coast, this is a challenging mixture of parkland and links golf. The uphill par-4 2nd is not easily reached in two, and there are other big par 4s at the 7th, 13th and 14th. The 16th is a particularly demanding hole.
18 holes, 6545 yards
par 72, S.S.S 72
Designer Harry Colt, Tom Jones
Green fees £25
Catering, changing room/showers, bar, club, trolley and buggy hire, shop, practice facilities
Visitors welcome subject to club commitments
Societies welcome by prior arrangement
🏨 Royal Hotel, Church Walks, Llandudno, Conwy LL30 2HW
☎ 01492 876476

LLANFAIRFECHAN GOLF CLUB

Llannerch Road, Llanfairfechan, Conwy LL33 0EB
☎ 01248 680524 **Map 6, G2**
West end of Llanfairfechan
Founded 1972
Remarkably challenging par-3 course with seven holes over 200 yards. Great coastal views.
9 holes, 3119 yards
par 54, S.S.S 57
Green fees £10
Catering, changing room/showers, bar
Visitors welcome except competition days
Societies welcome by prior arrangement

NORTH WALES GOLF CLUB

72 Bryniau Road, West Shore, Llandudno, Conwy LL30 2DZ
☎ 01492 875325 Fax 01492 875355
Map 6, H1
golf@nwgc.freeserve.co.uk
www.northwales.uk.com
A546, W of Llandudno at West Shore
Founded 1894
Described by Sir Henry Cotton as a gem, North Wales boasts three famous short holes on the back nine, extraordinary, old-fashioned affairs and utterly unique. With billowing seaside fairways there are, inevitably, a few blind shots, but there is such individual character to so many holes that they seem entirely appropriate.
18 holes, 6287 yards
par 71, S.S.S 71
Designer Tancred Cummins, Harold Hilton
Green fees £25
Catering, changing room/showers, bar, club, trolley and buggy hire, shop, practice facilities
Visitors welcome
Handicap certificate required
Societies welcome by prior arrangement
🏨 Esplanade Hotel, Promenade, Llandudno, Conwy LL30 2LL
☎ 01492 860300

OLD COLWYN GOLF CLUB

Woodland Avenue, Old Colwyn, Conwy LL29 9DL
☎ 01492 515581 **Map 10, A11**
Off B5383 in Old Colwyn
Founded 1907
Entertaining meadowland course, quite hilly in parts, giving splendid views and the chance to drive several downhill par 4s.
9 holes, 5243 yards
par 68, S.S.S 66
Green fees £10
Catering, changing room/showers, bar
Visitors welcome, but not Saturdays
Societies welcome by prior arrangement

PENMAENMAWR GOLF CLUB

Conway Old Road, Penmaenmawr, Conwy LL34 6RD
☎ 01492 623330 Fax 01492 622105
Map 6, H1
A55 to Dwygfylchi, 1st left, 1st right, then left
Founded 1910
Alternative tees give considerable variety second time round on this tricky, hilly course, featuring several stone walls. Superb scenery.
9 holes, 5361 yards
par 67, S.S.S 66
Green fees £12
Catering, changing room/showers, bar, trolley hire, practice facilities
Visitors welcome, not Saturdays
Handicap certificate required
Societies welcome by prior arrangement.
🏨 Caerlyr Hall Hotel, Conwy Old Road, Penmaenmawr, Conwy LL34 6SW
☎ 01492 623518

RHOS-ON-SEA GOLF CLUB

Penrhyn Bay, Llandudno, Conwy LL30 3PU
☎ 01492 549100 Fax 01492 549100
Map 6, H1
On coast road W of Rhos-on-Sea
Founded 1899
Low lying, very flat course with many greens defended by dry moats. Several water hazards.
18 holes, 6064 yards
par 69, S.S.S 69
Designer Tom Simpson
Green fees £20
Catering, changing room/showers, bar, accommodation, club, trolley and buggy hire, shop, practice facilities
Visitors welcome, but phone first to obtain starting time
Societies welcome by prior arrangement

DENBIGHSHIRE

BRYN MORFYDD HOTEL GOLF CLUB

Llanrhaedr, Denbigh, Denbighshire LL16 4 NP
☎ 01745 890280 Fax 01745 890488
Map 7, B1
www.bryn.morfydd.co.uk
A525 between Denbigh and Ruthin
Founded 1982
Beautiful views of the Vale of Clwyd from this hilly course with a number of tricky holes. The older par-3 course is by Alliss and Thomas.
Dukes Course: 18 holes, 5753 yards, par 70, S.S.S 67
Designer Duncan Muirhead, Colin Henderson
Duchess Course: 9 holes, 1049 yards, par 27
Designer Peter Alliss, Dave Thomas
Green fees £15
Catering, changing room/showers, bar, accommodation, club and trolley hire, shop, practice facilities
Visitors welcome, but book in advance
Societies welcome by prior arrangement

DENBIGH GOLF CLUB

Henllan Road, Denbigh, Denbighshire LL16 5AA
☎ 01745 816669 Fax 01745 814888
Map 7, B1

secretary@denbighgolfclub.fs business.co.uk
www.ukgolfer.org
B5382, 1 mile NW of Denbigh
Founded 1922
Set on high ground above Denbigh, there are fine views from the course. Accuracy is essential as there are a great many old oaks lining the fairways, and safe passage through them calls for skill and intelligence. Two pairs of back-to-back par 3s are an unusual feature of the layout.
18 holes, 5712 yards
par 69, S.S.S 68
Designer John Stockton
Green fees £24.50
Catering, changing room/showers, bar, club and trolley hire, shop, practice facilities
Visitors welcome
Handicap certificate required
Societies welcome by prior arrangement
Esplanade Hotel, Promenade, Llandudno, Conwy LL30 2LL
01492 860300

KINMEL PARK GOLF CLUB

Bodelwyddan, Denbighshire LL18 5SR
01745 833548 Fax 01745 824861
Map 10, A11
Off A55 at Bodelwyddan, on old A55
Founded 1989
Short course attached to driving range.
9 holes, 1550 yards
par 29
Designer Peter Stebbings
Green fees £3.50
Club hire, shop, driving range, practice facilities
Visitors welcome
Societies welcome by prior arrangement

PRESTATYN GOLF CLUB

Marine Road East, Prestatyn, Denbighshire LL19 7HS
01745 854320 Fax 01745 888327
Map 10, B10
manager@prestatyngc.co.uk
www.prestatyngc.co.uk
A548 North Wales coast road, golf course is at north east end of Prestatyn town
Founded 1905
Long, flat, and windswept championship links. Water hazards affect a number of early holes with the wide Prestatyn Gutter a serious threat on the challenging 9th and 10th. Thereafter play moves to more undulating ground beside the railway, with the 16th the sternest of an excellent run of strong holes.
18 holes, 6808 yards

par 72, S.S.S 73
Designer J. Collins
Green fees £22
Catering, changing room/showers, bar, club, trolley and buggy hire, shop, practice facilities, snooker
Visitors welcome, but not Saturday
Handicap certificate required
Societies welcome by prior arrangement
Esplanade Hotel, Promenade, Llandudno, Conwy LL30 2LL
01492 860300

RHUDDLAN GOLF CLUB

Meliden Road, Rhuddlan, Denbighshire LL18 6LB
01745 590217 Fax 01745 590472
Map 10, B10
golf@rhuddlangolfclub.fsnet.co.uk
www.rhuddlangolfclub.co.uk
A547 on east side of town
Founded 1930
A number of lengthy par 4s make this a good test for the low-handicap player, while the charm of the shorter par 4s will endear Rhuddlan to all golfers. Upgraded over the years by the Hawtree family, a major tree-planting programme brings welcome environmental benefits.
18 holes, 6471 yards
par 70, S.S.S 71
Designer F Hawtree
Green fees £20
Catering, changing room/showers, bar, club, trolley and buggy hire, shop, practice facilities, snooker
Visitors welcome – with restrictions
Handicap certificate required
Societies welcome by prior arrangement
Plas Elwy Hotel, St Asaph, Denbighshire
01745 582263

RHYL GOLF CLUB

Coast Road, Rhyl, Denbighshire LL18 3RE
01745 353171 Fax 01745 353171
Map 10, A10
A548 between Rhyl and Prestatyn
Founded 1890
The remaining nine holes of a once-renowned links denuded by years of coastal erosion and property development. It is the real thing, though.
9 holes, 6165 yards
par 70, S.S.S 70
Designer James Braid
Green fees £15
Catering, changing room/showers, bar, club and trolley hire, shop
Visitors welcome, but limited at weekends, phone in advance
Societies welcome by prior arrangement

RUTHIN-PWLLGLAS GOLF CLUB

Pwllglas, Ruthin, Denbighshire LL15 2PE
01978 790692 Fax 01978 790692
Map 7, B2
Off A494 2 miles S of Ruthin
Founded 1920
A very charming little course in an idyllic setting, on high ground overlooking the Clwyd Valley and Hills. Completely separate 9th and 18th holes mean that there are ten genuine holes. The 419-yard 8th is the toughest on paper, but such hilly fairways readily magnify errors on any hole.
10 holes, 5362 yards
par 66, S.S.S 66
Green fees £12.50
Catering, changing room/showers, bar, club hire
Visitors welcome, except competition days
Societies welcome by prior arrangement

ST MELYD GOLF CLUB

The Paddock, Meliden Road, Prestatyn, Denbighshire LL19 8NB
01745 854405 Fax 01745 856908
Map 10, B10
www.stmelydgolf.co.uk
A547 ½ mile S of Prestatyn
Founded 1922
Only nine holes, but the 1st, 2nd and 5th sort the good golfers from the mere pretenders.
9 holes, 5839 yards
par 68, S.S.S 68
Green fees £16
Catering, changing room/showers, bar
Visitors welcome, phone in advance
Societies welcome by prior arrangement

VALE OF LLANGOLLEN GOLF CLUB

Holyhead Road, Llangollen, Denbighshire LL20 7PR
01978 860906 Fax 01978 860906
Map 7, C3
A5, 2 miles E of Llangollen
Founded 1908
Flat parkland course surrounded by engaging mountain scenery. The best holes keep close company with the River Dee, especially the wicked 9th, a 425-yard tester demanding a long drive along the river's edge if there is to be any chance of finding the green, perched above the fast-flowing waters.
18 holes, 6656 yards
par 72, S.S.S 73
Green fees £20
Catering, changing room/showers,

bar, club and trolley hire, shop, practice facilities
Visitors welcome – restricted competition days
Handicap certificate required
Societies welcome by prior arrangement
Tyn-y-Wern Hotel, Holyhead Raod, Llangollen, Denbighshire LL20 7PR
01978 860252

FLINTSHIRE

CAERWYS (NINE OF CLUBS) GOLF CLUB

Caerwys, Nr. Mold, Flintshire CH7 5AQ
01352 720692 **Map 10, B11**
West side of village, 1½ miles S of A55 between Holywell and St Asaph
Founded 1989
Far from easy short course in lovely surroundings.
9 holes, 3080 yards
par 60, S.S.S 60
Designer Eleanor Barlow
Green fees £4.50
Catering, changing room/showers, bar, club and trolley hire
Visitors welcome
Societies welcome by prior arrangement

FLINT GOLF CLUB

Cornist Park, Flint, Flintshire CH6 5HJ
01244 812974 Fax 01244 811885
Map 10, C11
1 mile SW of Flint, follow signs for hospital
Founded 1966
Several notably searching holes on this compact course with pleasant views. The clubhouse is reputed to be haunted!
9 holes, 5980 yards
par 70, S.S.S 69
Designer H G Griffith
Green fees £10
Catering, changing room/showers, bar
Visitors welcome weekdays
Societies welcome by prior arrangement

HAWARDEN GOLF CLUB

Groomsdale Lane, Hawarden, Flintshire CH5 3EH
01244 531447 Fax 01244 536901
Map 7, C1
Off B5125 beyond station
Founded 1911
Recent extension has brought several water holes into play on this entertaining parkland course.
18 holes, 5842 yards
par 69, S.S.S 68
Green fees £16
Catering, changing room/showers, bar
Visitors welcome, but book in advance
Handicap certificate required
Societies welcome by prior arrangement

HOLYWELL GOLF CLUB

Brynford, Holywell, Flintshire CH8 8LQ
01352 713937 Fax 01352 713937
Map 10, B11
holywell_golf_club@lineone.net
B5121, W of Holywell
Founded 1906
Wonderfully springy, links-like turf at almost 800 feet above sea level. Old mine workings provide unorthodox hazards in the form of grassy craters, while gorse bushes and bracken punish wild driving. On the whole, the greens are tiny and cleverly defended by natural breaks and borrows. Few bunkers needed.
18 holes, 6091 yards
par 70, S.S.S 70
Green fees £18
Catering, changing room/showers, bar, club and trolley hire, shop, practice facilities
Visitors welcome, but advisable to book in advance
Societies welcome by prior arrangement
Stamford Gate Hotel, Halkyn Road, Holywell, Flintshire
01352 712942

KINSALE GOLF CLUB

Llanerchymor, Holywell, Flintshire CH8 9DX
01745 561080 Fax 01745 561079
Map 10, B11
Off A458 coast road (signposted)
Overlooking Dee estuary, the most challenging holes are those dropping to lower ground and climbing back.
9 holes, 6005 yards
par 71, S.S.S 70
Designer K Smith
Green fees £9.90
Catering, changing room/showers, bar, accommodation, club and trolley hire, driving range
Visitors welcome
Societies welcome by prior arrangement

MOLD GOLF CLUB

Cilcain Road, Pantymwyn, Mold, Flintshire CH7 5EH
01352 741513 Fax 01352 741517
Map 7, C1
At Pantymwyn 3 miles W of Mold
Founded 1909
With several tough par 4s on the back nine this undulating course plays somewhat longer than the yardage suggests.
18 holes, 5512 yards
par 67, S.S.S 67
Designer Hawtree
Green fees £18
Catering, changing room/showers, bar, club and trolley hire, shop, practice facilities
Visitors welcome, but phone first
Restricted at weekends
Societies welcome by prior arrangement

NORTHOP COUNTRY PARK GOLF CLUB

Northop, Chester, Flintshire CH7 6WA
01352 840440 Fax 01352 840445
Map 7, C1
A55, at Connah's Quay turnoff west end of Northop
Founded 1994
A North Wales rarity, a country-club style course linked to a hotel and housing development. Early on, the 3rd is testing, its drive pinched between ditches, and the dog-leg 4th invites all out attack, while the 8th is a charming downhill par 5. Water dominates all stages of the 16th.
18 holes, 6735 yards
par 72, S.S.S 73
Designer John Jacobs
Green fees £30
Catering, changing room/showers, bar, club, trolley and buggy hire, shop, driving range, practice facilities, tennis courts, gym/sauna, linked with nearby St David's Park Hotel
Visitors welcome – phone first
Societies welcome by prior arrangement

OLD PADESWOOD GOLF CLUB

Station Road, Padeswood, Mold, Flintshire CH7 4JL
01244 547701 Fax 01244 545082
Map 7, C1
oldpad@par72-fsbusiness.uk
A5118, 3 miles from Mold
Founded 1978
Newer than adjoining Padeswood and Buckley, this is a mixture of holes on flat ground frequently intersected by ditches and streams, and others on undulating land close to the clubhouse. So, the start and finish is characterized by tumbling holes, not least the roller coaster par-5 2nd and 17th.
18 holes, 6710 yards

par 72, S.S.S 72
Designer Jarvis
Green fees £20
Catering, changing room/showers, bar, club, trolley and buggy hire, shop, practice facilities, 9-hole par-3 course, function and conference facilities
Visitors welcome, but phone in advance
Societies welcome by prior arrangement
Castle House, 23 Castle Street, Chester, Cheshire CH1 2DS
01244 350354 Fax 01244 350354

PADESWOOD & BUCKLEY GOLF CLUB

The Caia, Station Lane, Padeswood, Mold, Flintshire CH7 4JD
01244 550537 Fax 01244 541600
Map 7, C1
A5118, 8 miles W of Chester – past entrance to Old Padeswood Golf Club
Founded 1933
Gently undulating in well-wooded parkland with pleasant views to the surrounding hills. Water is a frequent hazard, especially on the 5th where two lakes enter play. Running alongside the River Alyn, the 9th is a particularly testing hole, and the 16th is a substantial par 5 at 562 yards.
18 holes, 5982 yards
par 70, S.S.S 69
Designer David Williams
Green fees £20
Catering, changing room/showers, bar, club and trolley hire, shop, practice facilities
Visitors welcome weekdays – phone in advance
Societies welcome by prior arrangement

GWYNEDD

ABERDOVEY GOLF CLUB

Aberdovey, Gwynedd LL35 0RT
01654 767493 Fax 01654 767027
Map 6, G6
www.aberdoveygolf.co.uk
A493, W of town centre
Founded 1892
A classic links with superb greens. There is a wonderfully traditional feel to the golf, sensitively retained throughout alterations. The par-3 3rd, Cader, is magical, and the two-shot 16th, although under 300 yards, is mischievous, close to the railway, with its tiny, raised green hardly more than a pimple.
18 holes, 6445 yards
par 71, S.S.S 71
Designer James Braid, Herbert Fowler, Howard Swan
Green fees £20
Catering, changing room/showers, bar, trolley and buggy hire, shop, practice facilities, snooker, small conference room
Visitors welcome, subject to restrictions
Handicap certificate required – limit: 24 men, 36 women
Societies welcome by prior arrangement
Trefeddian Hotel, Aberdovey, Gwynedd
01654 767213

ABERSOCH GOLF CLUB

Golf Road, Abersoch, Gwynedd LL53 7EY
01758 712622 Fax 01758 712777
Map 6, E4
½ mile S Abersoch
Founded 1907
The nine original links holes – seaside gems – remain, despite a course extension to 18 holes.
18 holes, 5819 yards
par 69, S.S.S 68
Designer Harry Vardon
Green fees £18
Catering, changing room/showers, bar, club and trolley hire, shop, practice facilities
Visitors welcome
Handicap certificate required
Societies welcome by prior arrangement

BALA GOLF CLUB

Penlan, Bala, Gwynedd LL23 7YD
01678 520359 Fax 01678 521361
Map 7, A3
Off A494 Dolgellau road – c. 1 mile from Bala
Founded 1972
Adventurous mountain golf with brilliant views, and one of the toughest of all opening holes.
10 holes, 4980 yards
par 66, S.S.S 64
Designer Local enthusiasts
Green fees £12
Catering, changing room/showers, bar, club and trolley hire, shop, snooker, pool
Visitors welcome –restricted weekends
Societies welcome by prior arrangement
Plas Coch Hotel, High Street, Bala, Gwynedd
01678 520309

BALA LAKE HOTEL GOLF CLUB

Bala, Gwynedd LL23 7YF
01678 520344 Fax 01678 521193
Map 7, A3
B4403 1 mile S of Bala
Short parkland course laid out in hotel grounds on the shores of Lake Bala.
9 holes, 4280 yards
S.S.S 61
Catering, changing room/showers, bar, accommodation
Visitors welcome
Societies welcome by prior arrangement
Bala Lake Hotel, Bala, Gwynedd
01678 520344

CAERNARFON GOLF CLUB

Aberforeshore, Llanfaglan, Caernarfon, Gwynedd LL54 5RP
01286 678359 Fax 01286 672535
Map 6, F2
www.northwales.uk.com/golf/caernarfon
Off A487, SW of Caernarfon
Founded 1909
Gentle meadowland course made trickier by a number of water hazards. Lovely views across the Menai Strait to Anglesey and also into Snowdonia.
18 holes, 5891 yards
par 69, S.S.S 68
Green fees £15
Catering, changing room/showers, bar, trolley and buggy hire, shop, practice facilities
Visitors welcome – with restrictions
Societies welcome by prior arrangement
Stables Hotel, Llanwnda, Caernarfon, Gwynedd LL54 5SD
01286 830711

CRICCIETH GOLF CLUB

Ednyfed Hill, Criccieth, Gwynedd LL52 0PH
01766 522154 **Map 6, A4**
Off main coast road above town
Founded 1905
Undulating meadowland course with splendid views past the castle to the sea.
18 holes, 5787 yards
par 69, S.S.S 68
Green fees £12
Catering, changing room/showers, bar, trolley hire
Visitors welcome, but phone in advance
Societies welcome by prior arrangement

DOLGELLAU GOLF CLUB

Hengwrt Estate, Pencefn Road, Llanelltyd, Dolgellau, Gwynedd LL40 2ES
01341 422603 Fax 01341 422603
Map 6, H5
dolgellaugolf@netscapeonline.co.uk

www.dolgellaugolf.co.uk
½ mile north of Dolgellau, signposted
Founded 1910
Engaging and scenic short course, with sloping greens and fairways compounding the slightest error.
9 holes, 4152 yards
par 66, S.S.S 63
Designer J Medway
Green fees £20
Catering, accommodation, club and trolley hire, practice facilities
Visitors welcome
Societies welcome by prior arrangement
Plas Dolmylenin, Ganllwyd, Gwynedd

FFESTINIOG GOLF CLUB

Y Cefn, Ffestiniog, Gwynedd
01766 831829 **Map 6, G3**
B4391 Bala road, 1 mile E of Ffestiniog
Founded 1893
Extraordinary golf played in the wildest country – primitive, but uplifting, and very far from easy.
9 holes, 5022 yards
par 68, S.S.S 66
Green fees £10
Catering, changing room/showers, bar
Visitors welcome
Societies welcome by prior arrangement

NEFYN & DISTRICT GOLF CLUB

Lon Golf, Morfa Nefyn, Gwynedd LL53 6DA
01758 720966 Fax 01758 720476
Map 6, E3
nefyngolf@tesco.net
www.nefyn-golf-club.com
1 mile W of Nefyn
Founded 1907
One of the most spectacularly sited golf courses in the world, clinging to the cliff edge high above the sea and the pretty beach hamlet of Porthdinllaen. Such beauty easily distracts from the seriousness of the golfing challenge. It took all Ian Woosnam's skills to set the course record 67.
Nefyn Old Course: 18 holes, 6201 yards, par 71, S.S.S 71
Nefyn New Course: 18 holes, 6548 yards, par 71, S.S.S 71
Green fees £26
Catering, changing room/showers, bar, club, trolley and buggy hire, shop, driving range, practice facilities, private dining/conference room
Visitors welcome – with restrictions
Societies welcome by prior arrangement
Nanhoran Arms Hotel, St Davids Road, Nefyn, Gwynedd
01758 720203

PORTHMADOG GOLF CLUB

Morfa Bychan, Porthmadog, Gwynedd LL49 9UU
01766 514124 Fax 01766 514638
Map 6, G4
S of Porthmadog towards Black Rock Sands
Founded 1905
The back nine is one of the finest sequences of links holes in Wales, with the dangerous 14th, Himalayas, as the centrepiece. In contrast the early holes are more heathland in character, involving several water hazards. The views from the high ground over Tremadog Bay and into Snowdonia are magical.
18 holes, 6363 yards
par 71, S.S.S 71
Designer James Braid
Green fees £25
Catering, changing room/showers, bar, club, trolley and buggy hire, shop, practice facilities
Visitors welcome by prior arrangement
Handicap certificate required
Societies welcome by prior arrangement

PWLLHELI GOLF CLUB

Golf Road, Pwllheli, Gwynedd LL53 5PS
01758 701644 Fax 01758 701644
Map 6, E4
www.pwllheligolf.co.uk
½ mile SW of town centre
Founded 1900
A happy combination of rugged links golf and gentler inland holes, with fine panoramas. Gorse, savage rough, thoughtful bunkering, and natural seaside humps and hollows give the links holes from the 8th considerable character and, as play moves inland towards the finish, water hazards and trees constitute the principal problems.
18 holes, 6091 yards
par 69, S.S.S 69
Green fees £22
Catering, changing room/showers, bar, shop, practice facilities
Visitors welcome, but restricted Tuesdays, Thursdays and weekends
Societies welcome by prior arrangement

ROYAL ST DAVID'S GOLF CLUB

Harlech, Gwynedd LL46 2UB
01766 780361 Fax 01766 781110
Map 6, G4
secretary@royalstdavids.co.uk
www.royalstdavids.co.uk
A496 W of Harlech
Founded 1894
See Top 50 Courses, page 39
18 holes, 6571 yards
par 69, S.S.S 73
Designer W.H. More, H. Finch-Hatton, Harry Colt, Charles Lawrie
Green fees £30
Catering, changing room/showers, bar, trolley and buggy hire, shop, practice facilities
Visitors welcome
Handicap certificate required
Societies welcome by prior arrangement
St David's Hotel, Harlech, Gwynedd
01766 780366

ST DEINIOL GOLF CLUB

Penybryn, Bangor, Gwynedd LL57 1PX
01248 353098 **Map 6, G2**
East side of town centre off B5122
Founded 1906
With gorse and trees narrowing many fairways and plenty of movement in the ground on this upland site, this is far from the gentle stroll the card length might at first suggest. Waywardness is disastrous. The views – high into Snowdonia, far along the coast, over the rooftops of Bangor – impress.
18 holes, 5654 yards
par 68, S.S.S 67
Designer James Braid
Green fees £14
Catering, changing room/showers, bar, club and trolley hire, shop, snooker
Visitors welcome – with restrictions
Handicap certificate required
Societies welcome by prior arrangement
Eryl Mor Hotel, Garth, Bangor, Gwynedd
01248 353789

MID GLAMORGAN

ABERDARE GOLF CLUB

Abernant, Aberdare, Mid Glamorgan CF44 0RY
01685 872797 Fax 01685 872797
Map 7, B10
Aberdare – follow signs to hospital
Founded 1921
Scenic golf, with a backdrop of the Brecon Beacons.
18 holes, 5875 yards
par 69, S.S.S 69
Green fees £16
Catering, changing room/showers, bar, trolley hire, shop
Visitors welcome

Handicap certificate required
Societies welcome by prior arrangement
Aberdare Country Park Hotel, Aberdare, Mid Glamorgan
01685874672

BARGOED GOLF CLUB

Heolddu, Bargoed, Mid Glamorgan CF81 9GF
01443 830143 **Map 3, D2**
A469, 8 miles N of Caerphilly
Founded 1912
A tough course in the mountains, with superb views.
18 holes, 6233 yards
par 70, S.S.S 70
Green fees £18.50
Catering, changing room/showers, bar, trolley and buggy hire, shop, practice facilities
Visitors welcome
Societies welcome by prior arrangement

BRYN MEADOWS GOLF & COUNTRY HOTEL

Maesycwmmer, Nr Ystrad Mynach, Caerphilly, Mid Glamorgan CF8 7SN
01495 225590 Fax 01495 228272
Map 3, D2
information@brynmeadows.co.uk
www.brynmeadows.co.uk
M4 Jct 28, then A467/A472 towards Ystrad Mynach
Founded 1973
A warm welcome and extensive facilities for visitors at this scenic parkland course overlooking five valleys.
18 holes, 6200 yards
par 72, S.S.S 69
Designer Craig Defoy
Green fees £17.50
Catering, changing room/showers, bar, accommodation, club, trolley and buggy hire, shop, practice facilities, leisure club, conference and wedding facilities
Visitors welcome – with restrictions
Societies welcome by prior arrangement

CAERPHILLY GOLF CLUB

Pencapel, Mountain Road, Caerphilly, Mid Glamorgan CF83 1HJ
029 2086 3441 Fax 029 2086 3441 **Map 3, D2**
A469, 7 miles N of Cardiff
Founded 1905
Mountainside course expanding to 18 holes. Good views.
13 holes, 5944 yards
par 71, S.S.S 70
Green fees £20
Catering, changing room/showers, bar, trolley hire, shop, practice facilities
Visitors welcome weekdays.
Handicap certificate required
Societies welcome by prior arrangement
Greenhill Hotel, 48 Mountain Road, Caerphilly, Mid Glamorgan CF83 1HL
029 2088 3164

CASTELL HEIGHTS GOLF CLUB

Blaengwynlais, Caerphilly, CF8 1NG, Mid Glamorgan
029 2088 666 Fax 029 2086 9030
Map 3, D2
Caerphilly, 4 miles from M4 Jct 32
Founded 1982
A short pay-and-play course.
9 holes, 5376 yards
S.S.S 66
Green fees £4.50
Visitors welcome
Societies welcome by prior arrangement

COED-Y-MWSTWR GOLF CLUB

Coychurch, Bridgend, Mid Glamorgan CF35 6AF
01656 862121 Fax 01656 864934
Map 3, B3
M4 Jct 35, A473 towards Bridgend, right into Coychurch village, follow sign for Coed-y-Mwstwr Hotel
Founded 1994
A challenging parkland course on the outskirts of Bridgend.
12 holes, 6144 yards
par 70, S.S.S 70
Green fees £16
Catering, changing room/showers, bar, trolley hire, shop, driving range, practice facilities
Visitors welcome – restricted weekends
Handicap certificate required
Societies welcome by prior arrangement
Coed-y-Mwstwr Hotel, Coed-y-Mwstwr, Coychurch, Bridgend, Mid Glamorgan
01656 860621

CREIGIAU GOLF CLUB

Llanwit Road, Creigiau, Cardiff, Mid Glamorgan CF4 8NN
02920 890263 Fax 02920 890706
Map 3, C3
manager@creigiaugolf.co.uk
www.creigiaugolf.co.uk
M4 Jct 34, A4119, signposted
Founded 1921
A testing parkland/downland course with a number of water hazards.
18 holes, 6015 yards
par 71, S.S.S 70
Green fees £30
Catering, changing room/showers, bar, trolley hire, shop, practice facilities
Visitors welcome weekdays.
Handicap certificate required
Societies welcome by prior arrangement

LLANTRISANT & PONTYCLUN GOLF CLUB

Off Ely Valley Road, Talbot Green, Mid Glamorgan CF72 8AL
01443 228169 Fax 01443 224601
Map 3, C2
2 miles N of M4 Jct 34
Founded 1927
A parkland course.
18 holes, 5328 yards
par 68, S.S.S 66
Green fees £20
Catering, changing room/showers, bar, club and trolley hire, shop
Visitors welcome weekdays
Handicap certificate required
Societies welcome by prior arrangement
Miskin Manor, Pendoylan Road, Groesfaen, Mid Glamorgan
01443 224204

MAESTEG GOLF CLUB

Mount Pleasant, Neath Road, Maesteg, Mid Glamorgan CF34 9PR
01656 732037 Fax 01656 734106
Map 3, C2
B4282, 1 mile W of Maesteg
Founded 1912
High on a hill top with expansive views.
18 holes, 5929 yards
par 70, S.S.S 69
Green fees £17
Catering, changing room/showers, bar, club and trolley hire, shop, practice facilities
Visitors welcome
Handicap certificate required
Societies welcome by prior arrangement

MERTHYR TYDFIL GOLF CLUB

Cilsanws Mountain, Cefn Coed, Merthyr Tydfil, Mid Glamorgan CF48 2NU
01685 723 308 **Map 3, C1**
Off A470, Cefn Coed
Founded 1809
Wonderful views from this tricky highland course.
18 holes, 5622 yards
par 69, S.S.S 68
Green fees £10
Catering, changing room/showers
Visitors welcome not Sunday
Societies welcome by prior arrangement

MORLAIS CASTLE GOLF CLUB

Pant, Dowlais, Merthyr Tydfil, Mid Glamorgan CF48 2UY
☎ 01685 722822 Fax 01685 388700
Map 3, C1
meorig.price@lineone.net
A465/A470 to Merthyr Tydfil, follow signs for Brecon Mountain Railway
Founded 1900
Situated on the edge of the Brecon Beacons National Park, with outstanding views.
18 holes, 6320 yards
par 71, S.S.S 71
Designer James Braid
Green fees £16
Catering, changing room/showers, bar, club, trolley and buggy hire, shop, driving range, practice facilities
Visitors welcome – restricted weekends
Handicap certificate required
Societies welcome by prior arrangement
🏨 Tregenna Hotel, Park Terrace, Merthyr Tydfil, Mid Glamorgan
☎ 01685 723627

MOUNTAIN ASH GOLF CLUB

Cefnpennar, Mountain Ash, Mid Glamorgan CF45 4DT
☎ 01443 479628 Fax 01443 479628
Map 3, C2
From Mountain Ash follow signs to Cefnpennar
Founded 1907
An elevated course overlooking the Brecon Beacons.
18 holes, 5553 yards
par 69, S.S.S 67
Green fees £15
Catering, changing room/showers, bar, trolley hire, shop, practice facilities
Visitors welcome
Handicap certificate required
Societies welcome by prior arrangement

MOUNTAIN LAKES GOLF CLUB

Heol Penbryn, Blaengwynlais, Caerphilly, Mid Glamorgan CF83 1NG
☎ 029 2086 1128 Fax 029 2086 3243 **Map 3, D2**
Near Black Cock Inn, Caerphilly Mountain
Founded 1988
A combination of mountain and parkland golf with no fewer than 20 lakes.
18 holes, 6046 yards
par 74, S.S.S 73
Designer Robert Sandow
Green fees £18
Catering, changing room/showers, bar, club, trolley and buggy hire, shop, driving range, practice facilities
Visitors welcome by prior arrangement
Societies welcome by prior arrangement

PONTYPRIDD GOLF CLUB

Ty Gwyn Road, Pontypridd, Mid Glamorgan CF37 4DJ
☎ 01443 402359 Fax 01443 491622
Map 3, D2
Off A470, E of town centre
Founded 1905
A new clubhouse has improved the facilities at this entertaining upland course.
18 holes, 5721 yards
par 69, S.S.S 68
Green fees £20
Catering, changing room/showers, bar, club, trolley and buggy hire, shop, practice facilities
Visitors welcome weekdays
Handicap certificate required
Societies welcome by prior arrangement

PYLE & KENFIG GOLF CLUB

Waun-y-Mer, Kenfig, Bridgend, Mid Glamorgan CF33 4PU
☎ 01656 783093 Fax 01656 772822
Map 3, B3
M4 Jct 37, off A4229
Founded 1922
The early holes, on flatter ground, are more downland in character, but on the back nine the fairways run through an area of wild dunes, with the dog-leg 13th and 14th exploiting them particularly. A muscular par 3, the 15th, leads to three long and tough par 4s to close.
18 holes, 6688 yards
par 71, S.S.S 73
Designer Harry Colt
Green fees £30
Catering, changing room/showers, bar, club, trolley and buggy hire, shop, practice facilities
Visitors welcome weekdays.
Handicap certificate required
Societies welcome by prior arrangement

RHONDDA GOLF CLUB

Penrhys, Ferndale, Rhondda, Mid Glamorgan CF43 3PW
☎ 01443 441384 Fax 01443 441384
Map 3, C2
Off B4512, 6 miles W of Pontypridd
Founded 1910
A hilly upland course with splendid views.
18 holes, 6205 yards
par 70, S.S.S 71
Green fees £15
Catering, changing room/showers, bar, club, trolley and buggy hire, shop, driving range, practice facilities
Visitors welcome
Handicap certificate required
Societies welcome by prior arrangement

ROYAL PORTHCAWL GOLF CLUB

Rest Bay, Porthcawl, Mid Glamorgan CF36 3UW
☎ 01656 782251 Fax 01656 771687
Map 3, B3
www.royalporthcawl
M4 Jct 37, NW of Porthcawl on the coast
Founded 1891
See Top 50 Courses, page 37
18 holes, 6740 yards
par 72, S.S.S 74
Designer Charles Gibson, Harry Colt, Tom Simpson
Green fees £40
Catering, changing room/showers, bar, club, trolley and buggy hire, shop, practice facilities
Visitors welcome and prior booking
Handicap certificate required – limit: 20 men, 30 women
Societies welcome by prior arrangement

SOUTHERNDOWN GOLF CLUB

Ogmore-by-Sea, Bridgend, Mid Glamorgan CF32 0QP
☎ 01656 880476 Fax 01656 880317
Map 3, B3
southerndowngolf@btconnect.com
www.southerndowngolfclub.com
M4 Jct 35/A48/B4265. At Ewenny turn right, course on left – 2 miles
Founded 1905
Earth and sky seemingly touch at Southerndown, and nowhere more than on the 1st, which climbs relentlessly, but lovely coastal views are the reward. With eight par 4s over 400 yards in length, undulating fairways, gorse and bracken aplenty, and the skilled bunkering of many notable architects, Southerndown tests persistently.
18 holes, 6590 yards
par 70, S.S.S 73
Designer Willie Fernie, Harry Vardon, James Braid, Herbert Fowler, Willie Park, Harry Colt, Donald Steel
Green fees £25
Catering, changing room/showers, bar, club, trolley and buggy hire, shop, practice facilities
Visitors welcome
Handicap certificate required
Societies welcome by prior arrangement

Heronston Hotel, Bridgend, Mid Glamorgan
01656 668811

VIRGINIA PARK GOLF CLUB
Virginia Park, Caerphilly, Mid Glamorgan CF83 3SW
024 2086 3919 **Map 3, D2**
At Caerphilly Leisure Centre
Founded 1993
Quite a challenging layout, with lakes and trees.
9 holes, 5622 yards
par 66, S.S.S 65
Green fees £6
Catering, changing room/showers, bar, club and trolley hire, shop, driving range
Visitors welcome
Societies welcome by prior arrangement

WHITEHALL GOLF CLUB
The Pavilion, Nelson, Treharris, Mid Glamorgan CF46 6ST
01443 740245 **Map 3, D2**
A4054 from Nelson
Founded 1922
Fine views add to the delights of this tricky mountain course.
9 holes, 5666 yards
par 69, S.S.S 68
Green fees £15
Catering, changing room/showers, bar
Visitors welcome
Handicap certificate required
Societies welcome by prior arrangement

MONMOUTHSHIRE

ALICE SPRINGS GOLF CLUB
Bettws Newydd, Usk, Monmouthshire NP5 1JY
01873 880244 Fax 01873 880838
Map 7, D11
B4598, N of Usk
Founded 1989
Two parkland courses and excellent off-course facilities, only a 35 minute drive from Cardiff, make this a popular venue for corporate and society events.
Green Course: 18 holes, 6438 yards, S.S.S 72
Red Course: 18 holes, 5870 yards, S.S.S 69
Green fees £16
Catering, changing room/showers, bar, club, trolley and buggy hire, shop, driving range, practice facilities
Visitors welcome
Societies welcome by prior arrangement

BLACKWOOD GOLF CLUB
Cwmgelli, Blackwood, Monmouthshire NP12 1BR
01495 223152 **Map 7, C1**
A4048, ¼ mile N of Blackwood
Founded 1914
A parkland course in delightful scenery. The long par-4 2nd is searching.
9 holes, 5332 yards
par 66, S.S.S 66
Green fees £14
Catering, changing room/showers, bar, accommodation
Visitors welcome weekdays
Handicap certificate required
Societies no societies
Maes Manor Hotel, Blackwood, Monmouthshire
01495 220011

CAERLEON GOLF CLUB
Broadway, Caerleon, Monmouthshire NP6 1AY
01633 420342 **Map 7, D1**
At Caerleon, 3 miles from M4 Jct 25
Founded 1974
A well equipped pay-and-play establishment close to Wales's prime Roman remains.
9 holes, 5800 yards
par 68, S.S.S 68
Designer Donald Steel
Green fees £5
Catering, changing room/showers, bar, club and trolley hire, shop, driving range, practice facilities
Visitors welcome
Societies welcome by prior arrangement

CELTIC MANOR HOTEL GOLF & COUNTRY CLUB
Coldra Woods, Newport, Monmouthshire NP6 1JQ
01633 413000 **Map 7, D11**
A48, close to M4 Jct 24
Founded 1995
See Top 50 Courses, page 16
Wentwood Hills :18 holes, 7403 yards, par 72, S.S.S 77
Designer Robert Trent Jones Snr, Robert Trent Jones Jnr.
Roman Road: 18 holes, 7001 yards, par 70, S.S.S 74
Coldra Woods: 18 holes, 4094 yards, par 61, S.S.S 60
Designer Robert Trent Jones Snr
Green fees £45
Catering, changing room/showers, bar, accommodation, club, trolley and buggy hire, shop, driving range, practice facilities
Visitors welcome, by prior arrangement
Handicap certificate required
Societies welcome by prior arrangement

Celtic Manor Hotel, Newport, Monmouthshire
01633 413000 Fax 01633 412910

DEWSTOW GOLF CLUB
Caerwent, Monmouthshire NP26 4AH
01291 430444 Fax 01291 425816
Map 3, F2
Off A48 at Caerwent
Founded 1988
Two parkland courses with views across the Bristol Channel. The Park Course, uniquely, incorporates a totem pole on one of its holes.
Park Course: 18 holes, 6226 yards, par 69, S.S.S 69
Valley Course: 18 holes, 6091 yards, par 72, S.S.S 70
Green fees £14
Catering, changing room/showers, bar, club, trolley and buggy hire, shop, driving range, practice facilities
Visitors welcome – advance booking system
Societies welcome by prior arrangement

GREENMEADOW GOLF CLUB
Treherbert Road, Croesyceiliog, Cwmbran, Monmouthshire NP44 2BZ
01633 862626 **Map 7, C11**
A4042, 4 miles N of Newport
Founded 1980
With tight, tree-lined fairways, water hazards and well-defended greens, this is quite a testing course, with good views, and good off-course facilities.
18 holes, 6078 yards
par 70, S.S.S 70
Green fees £17
Catering, changing room/showers, bar, club, trolley and buggy hire, shop, driving range, practice facilities
Visitors welcome
Societies welcome by prior arrangement

LLANWERN GOLF CLUB
Tennyson Avenue, Llanwern, Newport, Monmouthshire NP18 2DW
01633 412029 Fax 01633 412029
Map 3, E2
secretaryllanwerngc@hotmail.com
www.llanwerngolfclub.co.uk
M4 Jct 24
Founded 1928
A parkland course on the outskirts of Newport.
18 holes, 6177 yards
par 70, S.S.S 69
Green fees £20
Catering, changing room/showers,

bar, club hire, shop, practice facilities
Visitors welcome – restricted weekends
Handicap certificate required
Societies welcome by prior arrangement
Stakis Hotel, Newport, Monmouthshire
01633 413737

MONMOUTH GOLF CLUB

Leasebrook Lane, Monmouth, Monmouthshire NP25 3SN
01600 772399 Fax 01600 772399
Map 7, E10
A40, 100 yards from Monmouth roundabout
Founded 1896
A notably friendly club with a very scenic course.
18 holes, 5698 yards
par 69, S.S.S 69
Green fees £16
Catering, changing room/showers, bar, club, trolley and buggy hire, shop, practice facilities
Visitors welcome
Societies welcome by prior arrangement
Riverside Hotel, Monmouth, Monmouthshire
01600 715577

MONMOUTHSHIRE GOLF CLUB

Llanfoist, Abergavenny, Monmouthshire NP7 9HE
01873 852606 Fax 01873 852606
Map 7, C10
B4269, 2 miles SW of Abergavenny, off A4042 or A465
Founded 1892
Laid out beside the River Usk, with exceptionally beautiful mountain scenery all around, the Monmouthshire, unusually, has six short holes. Of these, the 12th and 16th are both about 230 yards long, and tough, too. The River Usk threatens the slightest pulled shot on the 490-yard par-5 6th.
18 holes, 5978 yards
par 70, S.S.S 70
Designer James Braid
Green fees £25
Catering, changing room/showers, bar, club and trolley hire, shop, practice facilities
Visitors welcome
Handicap certificate required
Societies welcome by prior arrangement
The Bear Hotel, Crickhowell, Powys NP8 1BW
01873 810408

THE NEWPORT GOLF CLUB

Great Oak, Rogerstone, Newport, Monmouthshire NP10 9FX
01633 892643 Fax 01633 896676
Map 3, E2
B4591, 1 mile NW of M4 Jct 27
Founded 1903
In 1913, three Rogerstone golfers appeared in court for playing golf on a Sunday. Happily, in the 21st Century, members may enjoy the delights of the course on a Sunday without fear of the law's long arm. Situated 300 feet above sea level, there are excellent views from the course.
18 holes, 6460 yards
par 72, S.S.S 71
Designer Willie Fernie
Green fees £30
Catering, changing room/showers, bar, club, trolley and buggy hire, shop, practice facilities
Visitors welcome weekdays
Handicap certificate required
Societies welcome by prior arrangement

OAKDALE GOLF COURSE

Llwynon Lane, Oakdale, Blackwood, Monmouthshire NP2 0NF
01495 220044 **Map 3, D2**
B4251 near Blackwood
Founded 1990
An executive-length pay-and-play course with floodlit driving range.
9 holes, 2470 yards
par 56
Green fees £2.50
Catering, changing room/showers, club and trolley hire, shop, driving range
Visitors welcome
Societies welcome by prior arrangement

PARC GOLF CENTRE

Church Lane, Coedkernew, Newport, Monmouthshire NP1 9TU
01633 680933 Fax 01633 681011
Map 3, E2
Off A48, 3 miles S of Newport
Founded 1990
A 38-bay floodlit driving range heads the off-course facilities, while the course itself makes use of water hazards.
18 holes, 5619 yards
par 70, S.S.S 68
Designer B. Thomas
Green fees £12
Catering, changing room/showers, bar, club, trolley and buggy hire, shop, driving range, practice facilities
Visitors welcome
Societies welcome by prior arrangement

PONTNEWYDD GOLF CLUB

Maesgwyn Farm, Upper Cwmbran, Monmouthshire NP44 1AB
01633 482170 **Map 3, E2**
W of Pontnewydd
A mountain course with fine views.
10 holes, 5353 yards
par 67, S.S.S 67
Green fees £15
Changing room/showers, bar
Visitors welcome weekdays
Societies welcome by prior arrangement

PONTYPOOL GOLF CLUB

Lasgarn Lane, Trevethin, Pontypool, Monmouthshire NP4 8TR
01495 763 655 **Map 3, E2**
Trevethin, N of Pontypool on the A4043, Church Avenue, then Lasfarn Lane
Founded 1903
Very scenic highland course on far from level ground.
18 holes, 5963 yards
par 69, S.S.S 69
Green fees £20
Catering, changing room/showers, bar, club, trolley and buggy hire, shop, practice facilities
Visitors welcome – restricted weekends
Handicap certificate required
Societies welcome by prior arrangement
Parkway Hotel, Cumbran Drive, Cumbran, Monmouthshire
01633 871199

RAGLAN PARC GOLF CLUB

Parc Lodge, Raglan, Monmouthshire NP5 2ER
01291 690077 **Map 3, E1**
A40/A449 junction, 6 miles W of Monmouth
Founded 1994
A long course offering a serious challenge.
18 holes, 6604 yards
par 72, S.S.S 73
Green fees £15
Catering, changing room/showers, bar, club, trolley and buggy hire, shop, practice facilities
Visitors welcome
Societies welcome by prior arrangement

THE ROLLS OF MONMOUTH GOLF CLUB

The Hendre, Monmouth, Monmouthshire NP25 5HG
01600 715353 Fax 01600 713115
Map 7, D10
B 4233, 3 miles W of Monmouth
Founded 1982
Laid out in the spacious park of the one-time home of Charles Rolls, of

Rolls-Royce fame. With magnificent specimen trees, deer, waterfowl, and glorious surrounding scenery enhancing the experience, this modern course is also a fine test. Star holes include the water-beset 6th, gambling 7th, tough 15th, and all-or-nothing 18th.
18 holes, 6733 yards
par 72, S.S.S 73
Green fees £34
Catering, changing room/showers, bar, club and trolley hire, shop
Visitors welcome by prior arrangement
Societies welcome by prior arrangement
Crown at Whitebrook, Whitebrook, Monmouth, Monmouthshire NP25 4TX
01600 860254 Fax 01600 860607
crown@whitebrook.demon.co.uk

SHIRENEWTON GOLF & COUNTRY CLUB

Shirenewton, Chepstow, Monmouthshire NP16 6RL
01291 641642 Fax 01291 641472
Map 3, F2
A48, 2 miles N of Crick
Founded 1995
Fine views of the Severn Estuary from this good value, modern, parkland course.
18 holes, 6607 yards
par 72, S.S.S 72
Green fees £16
Catering, changing room/showers, bar, club, trolley and buggy hire, shop, practice facilities, snooker, function room
Visitors welcome at all times
Societies welcome by prior arrangement

MARRIOTT ST PIERRE HOTEL & COUNTRY CLUB

St Pierre Park, Chepstow, Monmouthshire NP16 6YA
01291 625261 Fax 01291 629975
Map 3, F2
A48, 2 miles W of Chepstow
Founded 1962
The history of St Pierre goes back to Norman times, and the majority of the championship course runs through the estate's beautiful wooded parkland, with several greens set out into lakes. But there are contrasting holes on high ground, the recently remodelled par-4 5th being quite a card wrecker.
Old Course: 18 holes, 6818 yards, par 71, S.S.S 74
Designer C.K.Cotton
Mathern Course: 18 holes, 5732 yards, par 68, S.S.S 68
Green fees £40
Catering, changing room/showers, bar, accommodation, club, trolley and buggy hire, shop, driving range, practice facilities, full hotel, function and conference facilities
Visitors welcome, by prior arrangement
Handicap certificate required
Societies welcome by prior arrangement
Marriott St Pierre, Chepstow, Monmouthshire
01291 626261

TREDEGAR PARK GOLF CLUB

Parc-y-Brain Road, Rogerstone, Newport, Monmouthshire NP10 9TG
01633 894433 Fax 01633 897152
Map 3, E2
Tpgc@btinternet.com
B4591, M4, W of Jct 27
Founded 1925
An old club with a brand new course.
18 holes, 6564 yards
par 72, S.S.S 71
Designer Robert Sandow
Green fees £15
Catering, changing room/showers, bar, club, trolley and buggy hire, shop, practice facilities, function rooms
Visitors welcome – with restrictions
Handicap certificate required
Societies welcome by prior arrangement
The Post House Hotel, Church Road, Pentwyn, Cardiff, Monmouthshire CF23 8XA
01222 731212

TREDEGAR & RHYMNEY GOLF CLUB

Tredegar, Rhymney, Monmouthshire NP2 3BQ
01685 840743 Fax 01685 843440
Map 3, D1
B4256, W of Tredegar
Founded 1921
An upland course with fine views.
9 holes, 5564 yards
par 68, S.S.S 67
Green fees £10
Catering, changing room/showers, bar
Visitors welcome, not Sundays
Societies welcome by prior arrangement

WERNDDU GOLF CLUB

Old Ross Road, Abergavenny, Monmouthshire NP7 8NG
01873 856223 Fax 01873 852177
Map 3, E1
enquiries@wernddugolfclub.co.uk
www.wernddugolfclub.co.uk
B4521, 1 mile E of Abergavenny
Founded 1993
With superb views of the Usk valley and Black Mountains, this is a well-equipped golf centre.
18 holes, 5413 yards
par 68, S.S.S 67
Designer J. Watkins
Green fees £15
Catering, changing room/showers, bar, club and trolley hire, shop, driving range, practice facilities, 9-hole pitch-and-putt, coarse fishing
Visitors welcome
Societies welcome by prior arrangement
Angel Hotel, Cross Street, Abergavenny, Monmouthshire
01873 857121

WEST MONMOUTHSHIRE GOLF CLUB

Golf Road, Pond Road, Nantyglo, Monmouthshire NP3 4QT
01495 310233 Fax 01495 311361
Map 3, D1
Off A467, towards Winchestown
Founded 1906
Officially recognized as the highest golf course in Britain, although the members of one or two Scottish clubs, such as Leadhills, might challenge that. Hardly surprisingly, there are majestic views and some hill climbing to be done. The 14th tee is the highest point, at 1513 feet above sea level.
18 holes, 6118 yards
par 71, S.S.S 69
Designer Ben Sayers
Green fees £18
Catering, changing room/showers, bar, trolley hire, shop
Visitors welcome – restricted weekends
Societies welcome by prior arrangement

WOODLAKE PARK GOLF CLUB

Glascoed, Near Usk, Monmouthshire NP4 0TE
01291 673933 Fax 01291 673811
Map 3, E1
golf@woodlake.co.uk
www.woodlake.co.uk
3 miles W of Usk
Founded 1993
In a remarkable setting, overlooking Llandegfedd Reservoir, the views are magnificent, with five counties visible from the 6th tee. The par-4 15th is rated Stroke 1, a bogey five to most players.
18 holes, 6284 yards
par 71, S.S.S 72
Green fees £20
Catering, changing room/showers, bar, trolley and buggy hire, shop, practice facilities, indoor practice

area
Visitors welcome
Handicap certificate required
Societies welcome by prior arrangement
Clytha Arms, Clytha, Abergavenny, Monmouthshire NP7 9BW
01873 840206 Fax 01873 840206
one.bev@lineone.net
www.website.lineone.net/-one.bev

PEMBROKESHIRE

HAVERFORDWEST GOLF CLUB

Arnolds Down, Haverfordwest, Pembrokeshire SA61 2XQ
01437 763565 Fax 01291 673811
Map 6, C10
A40, 1 mile E of Haverfordwest
Founded 1904
A parkland course in attractive countryside.
18 holes, 6005 yards
par 70, S.S.S 69
Green fees £19
Catering, changing room/showers, bar, club, trolley and buggy hire, shop
Visitors welcome
Societies welcome by prior arrangement

MILFORD HAVEN GOLF CLUB

Hubberston, Milford Haven, Pembrokeshire SA72 3RX
01646 697762 Fax 01646 697870
Map 6, C11
www.mhgc.co.uk
W of Milford Haven
Founded 1913
Overlooking Milford Haven and its busy shipping lanes.
18 holes, 6071 yards
par 71, S.S.S 70
Green fees £15
Catering, changing room/showers, bar, club, trolley and buggy hire, shop
Visitors welcome
Societies welcome by prior arrangement

NEWPORT (PEMBS) GOLF CLUB

Newport, Pembrokeshire SA42 0NR
01239 820244 Fax 01239 820244
Map 6, D9
2½ miles NW of Newport
Founded 1925
A links course overlooking Newport Bay.
9 holes, 5815 yards
par 70, S.S.S 68
Designer James Braid
Green fees £15
Catering, changing room/showers, bar, club, trolley and buggy hire, shop
Visitors welcome
Societies welcome by prior arrangement

PRISKILLY FOREST GOLF CLUB

Castle Morris, Haverfordwest, Pembrokeshire SA62 5EH
01348 840276 Fax 01348 840276
Map 6, C10
www.priskilly-forest.co.uk
Off A40, at Letterston
Founded 1992
A challenging course with expansive rural views.
9 holes, 5874 yards
par 70, S.S.S 69
Designer J. Walters
Green fees £14
Catering, changing room/showers, bar, club, trolley and buggy hire, shop, fishing
Visitors welcome
Societies welcome by prior arrangement

SOUTH PEMBROKESHIRE GOLF CLUB

Military Road, Pembroke Dock, Pembrokeshire SA72 6SE
01646 621453 **Map 6, C11**
Off B4322, SW of town centre
Founded 1970
A parkland course with some seaside characteristics overlooking Pembroke Dock.
18 holes, 6100 yards
par 71, S.S.S 70
Green fees £13
Catering, changing room/showers, bar, club hire
Visitors welcome – with restrictions
Societies welcome by prior arrangement

ST DAVIDS CITY GOLF CLUB

Whitesands Bay, St Davids, Pembrokeshire SA62 6PT
01437 720751 **Map 6, B10**
2 miles W of St Davids
Founded 1903
The golf course of this tiny Cathedral city is located on the coast almost at St David's Head, and rejoices in stunning sea views.
9 holes, 6117 yards
par 70, S.S.S 70
Green fees £13
Changing room/showers, trolley hire
Visitors welcome
Societies welcome by prior arrangement

TENBY GOLF CLUB

The Burrows, Tenby, Pembrokeshire SA70 7NP
01834 842978 Fax 01834 842978
Map 6, D11
Tenby, South Beach
Founded 1888
The oldest club in Wales, with a wonderful links course. There is great movement in the land which implies very few level stances and occasional blind and semi-blind shots. One of the great holes is the 3rd with an uncompromising approach to an elevated green. The sea views are inspirational.
18 holes, 6450 yards
par 69, S.S.S 71
Designer James Braid
Green fees £25
Catering, changing room/showers, bar, club and trolley hire, shop
Visitors welcome
Handicap certificate required
Societies welcome by prior arrangement

TREFLOYNE GOLF COURSE

Trefloyne Park, Penally, Tenby, Pembrokeshire SA70 7RG
01834 842165 Fax 01834 842165
Map 6, D11
enquiries@trefloynegolfcourse.co.uk
www.trefloynegolfcourse.co.uk
Off A4139, 1½ miles W of Tenby
Founded 1996
Trefloyne's impressive parkland course will be further enhanced when a new clubhouse is completed. Par-4 13th across a quarry is testing.
18 holes, 6635 yards
par 71, S.S.S 73
Designer F.H. Gilman
Green fees £20
Catering, changing room/showers, bar, club, trolley and buggy hire, shop, practice facilities
Visitors welcome
Societies welcome by prior arrangement
Penally Abbey, Penally, Tenby, Pembrokeshire SA70 7PY
01834 843033 Fax 01834 844714
penally.abbey@btinternet.com

POWYS

BRECON GOLF CLUB

Newton Park, Llanfaes, Brecon, Powys LD3 8PA
01874 622004 **Map 7, B9**
A40, W of town centre
Founded 1902
Surrounded by magnificent mountain scenery, the views are wonderful, yet the walking is easy as

the course is remarkably flat.
9 holes, 5256 yards
par 66, S.S.S 66
Designer James Braid
Green fees £10
Catering, changing room/showers, bar
Visitors welcome
Societies welcome by prior arrangement

BUILTH WELLS GOLF CLUB

Golf Club Road, Builth Wells, Powys LD2 3NF
✆ 01982 553296 Fax 01982 551064
Map 7, B8
builthwellsgolfclub1@btinternet.com
www.builthwellsgolfclub.com.uk
A 483 Builth-Llandovery Road, opposite Caer Beris Manor Hotel
Founded 1923
One of the prettiest courses in Mid-Wales, and trickier than its yardage suggests. Its 15th-century clubhouse is very welcoming to visitors.
18 holes, 5376 yards
par 66, S.S.S 67
Green fees £16
Catering, changing room/showers, bar, club and trolley hire, shop, practice facilities
Visitors welcome
Handicap certificate required
Societies welcome by prior arrangement
🏨 Caer Beris Manor Hotel, Builth Wells, Powys
✆ 01982 552607

CRADOC GOLF CLUB

Penoyre Park, Cradoc, Brecon, Powys LD3 9LP
✆ 01874 623658 Fax 01874 611711
Map 7, B9
secretary@cradoc.co.uk
www.cradoc.co.uk
Off B4520, 2 miles N of Brecon
Founded 1974
With the majestic backdrop of the Brecon Beacons and Black Mountains, this would be an idyllic spot, even without a golf course. Equally beautiful are the trees framing many holes. The 456-yard par-4 6th is Stroke 1, and even the shorter par 4s offer plenty to think about.
18 holes, 6331 yards
par 72, S.S.S 71
Designer C.K. Cotton
Green fees £20
Catering, changing room/showers, bar, club, trolley and buggy hire, shop, driving range, practice facilities
Visitors welcome – with restrictions weekends
Societies welcome by prior arrangement
🏨 George Hotel, George Street, Brecon, Powys LD39 7LD
✆ 01874 623421

KNIGHTON GOLF CLUB

Ffrydd Wood, Knighton, Powys LD7 1EF
✆ 01547 528646 Fax 01547 529284
Map 7, C7
On A488
Founded 1906
Great value – £10 to play a Harry Vardon course in some of the least spoiled countryside in Britain – and Offa's Dyke croses the course, as well.
9 holes, 5362 yards
par 68, S.S.S 66
Designer Harry Vardon
Green fees £10
Catering, changing room/showers, bar, trolley hire, practice facilities
Visitors welcome – competitions have priority at weekends
Societies welcome by prior arrangement
🏨 Red Lion Hotel, West Street, Knighton, Powys LD7 1EW
✆ 01547 528231

LLANDRINDOD WELLS GOLF CLUB

The Clubhouse, Llandrindod Wells, Powys LD1 5NY
✆ 01597 823873 Fax 01597 823873
Map 7, B7
A483, S of Llandrindod – signposted
Founded 1905
Golf is played at Llandrindod in the company of buzzard and red kite, on what is best described as an upland links. The turf is fine and the greens fast, but the natural hazards can be penal. Yardages mean little up here, witness the 297-yard 'Death or Glory' 18th.
18 holes, 5759 yards
par 69, S.S.S 69
Designer Harry Vardon, James Braid
Green fees £15
Catering, changing room/showers, bar, club, trolley and buggy hire, shop
Visitors welcome
Societies welcome by prior arrangement
🏨 Metropole Hotel, Temple Street, Llandrindod Wells, Powys LD1 5DY
✆ 01597 823700

MACHYNLLETH GOLF CLUB

Ffordd Drenewydd, Machynlleth, Powys SY20 8UH
✆ 01654 702000 **Map 6, H6**
Off A489, 1 mile E of Machynlleth
Founded 1904
A 9-hole course in a very unspoiled part of Mid Wales, with enough difficulty to make it a good warm up for Aberdovey and Borth.
9 holes, 5726 yards
par 68, S.S.S 68
Designer James Braid
Green fees £12
Catering, changing room/showers, bar, trolley hire
Visitors welcome – restricted Sundays
Societies welcome by prior arrangement

NEWTOWN ST GILES GOLF CLUB

Pool Road, Newtown, Powys SY16 3AJ
✆ 01686 625844 Fax 01686 625844
Map 7, B5
www.st-giles.org.uk
E of Newtown on A483 Welshpool Road
Founded 1895
Charming countryside course on the banks of the River Severn.
9 holes, 6012 yards
par 70, S.S.S 70
Green fees £12.50
Catering, changing room/showers, bar, club and trolley hire, shop, practice facilities
Visitors welcome – restricted at weekends
Societies welcome by prior arrangement
🏨 Garthmyl Hall, Garthmyl, Montgomery, Powys SY15 6RS
✆ 01686 640550

RHOSGOCH GOLF CLUB

Rhosgoch, Builth Wells, Powys LD2 3JY
✆ 01497 851251 **Map 7, B8**
N of Hay-on-Wye
Founded 1991
The shorter of the two courses near Builth Wells.
9 holes, 5078 yards
par 70, S.S.S 65
Green fees £7
Catering, club hire
Visitors welcome
Societies welcome by prior arrangement

ST IDLOES GOLF CLUB

Penrhallt, Llanidloes, Powys SY18 6LG
✆ 01686 412559 Fax 01926 889536
Map 7, A6
Off B4569, ½ mile from Llanidloes
Founded 1920
An undulating course with good views of the handsome surrounding countryside.
9 holes, 5540 yards

par 66, S.S.S 66
Green fees £10
Catering, changing room/showers, bar, club and trolley hire, shop
Visitors welcome – restricted Sundays
Handicap certificate required
Societies welcome by prior arrangment

WELSH BORDER GOLF COMPLEX

Bulthy Farm, Bulthy, Middletown, Powys SY21 8ER
✆ 01743 884247 **Map 7, C4**
A458, between Shrewsbury and Welshpool
Founded 1991
Rather a good 9-hole course in wonderful countryside, with several entertaining water holes.
9 holes, 3050 yards
S.S.S 69
Designer A. Griffiths
Green fees £14
Catering, club hire
Visitors welcome
Societies welcome by prior arrangement

WELSHPOOL GOLF CLUB

Golfa Hill, Welshpool, Powys SY21 9AQ
✆ 01938 850249 **Map 7, C5**
welshpool.golfclub@virginnet.co.uk
www.welshpoolgolfclub.co.uk
Off A458, W of Welshpool
Founded 1894
1,000 feet up, with stunning mountain views in all directions and the freshest air, there is much golfing challenge at Welshpool. Admittedly, some holes climb punishingly, and there are many short par 4s, but the best holes are excellent, such as the two-shot 12th and 18th, and par-3 14th.
18 holes, 5708 yards
par 70, S.S.S 68
Designer James Braid
Green fees £12.50
Catering, changing room/showers, bar, club and trolley hire, shop
Visitors welcome
Societies welcome by prior arrangement
Golfa Hall Hotel, Golfa Hill, Welshpool, Powys
✆ 01938 553399

SOUTH GLAMORGAN

BRYNHILL (BARRY) GOLF CLUB

Port Road, Barry, South Glamorgan CF62 8PN
✆ 01446 720277 Ext 100 Fax 01446 740422 **Map 3, D3**
A4050, from M4 Jct 33
Founded 1923
Quite a hilly parkland course.
18 holes, 6352 yards
par 72, S.S.S 71
Designer Dave Thomas
Green fees £20
Catering, changing room/showers, bar, club and trolley hire, shop, practice facilities
Visitors welcome – with restrictions
Handicap certificate required
Societies welcome by prior arrangement
The Olives Guest House, Pont Road, Barry, South Glamorgan
✆ 01446 730891

CARDIFF GOLF CLUB

Sherborne Avenue, Cyncoed, Cardiff, South Glamorgan CF23 6SJ
✆ 029 2075 3067 Fax 029 2068 0011 **Map 3, D3**
3 miles N of Cardiff
Founded 1921
A well-wooded, parkland course in a leafy suburb of Cardiff. Over the years the trees have grown to define fairways, greenside bunkering is tight, and there are a few water hazards.
18 holes, 6015 yards
par 70, S.S.S 70
Green fees £35
Catering, changing room/showers, bar, trolley hire, shop
Visitors welcome – restricted weekends
Handicap certificate required
Societies welcome by prior arrangement

COTTRELL PARK GOLF CLUB

St Nicholas, Cardiff, South Glamorgan CF5 6JY
✆ 01446 781781 Fax 01446 781187 **Map 3, D3**
admin@cottrell-park.co.uk
www.cottrell-park.co.uk
M4 Jct 33, A4232 to Culverhouse Cross, A48 to St Nicholas
Founded 1996
A parkland course on an estate steeped in history, with particularly fine views from the 9-hole Button Course.
Mackintosh Course: 18 holes, 6606 yards, par 72, S.S.S 73
Designer Robert Sandow
Button Course: 9 holes, 2807 yards, par 70, S.S.S 67
Green fees £25
Catering, changing room/showers, bar, club, trolley and buggy hire, shop, driving range, practice facilities, conference, wedding and function facilities
Visitors welcome
Handicap certificate required on 18-hole course
Societies welcome by prior arrangement
Copthorne Hotel, Culverhouse Cross, Cardiff, South Glamorgan
✆ 02920 599100

DINAS POWIS GOLF CLUB

Old Highwalls, Dinas Powis, South Glamorgan CF64 4AJ
✆ 029 2051 2727 Fax 029 2051 2727 **Map 3, D3**
A4055, SW of Cardiff
Founded 1914
An upland course with pleasant sea views.
18 holes, 5486 yards
par 67, S.S.S 67
Green fees £25
Catering, changing room/showers, bar, trolley hire, shop
Visitors welcome
Handicap certificate required
Societies welcome by prior arrangement

GLAMORGANSHIRE GOLF CLUB

Lavernock Road, Penarth, Vale of Glamorgan, South Glamorgan CF64 5UP
✆ 029 20701185 Fax 029 20701185 **Map 3, D3**
glamgolf@BTConnect.Com
www.glamorganshiregolfclub.com
B4267 to Lower Penarth
Founded 1890
The birthplace of the Stableford scoring system, and the first inland course in Wales. This historic club was influential in the early days of Welsh golf, introducing the first professional to the country and holding early Welsh Championships. From the high ground the views across the Bristol Channel are extensive.
18 holes, 6091 yards
par 70, S.S.S 70
Green fees £30
Changing room/showers, bar, club, trolley and buggy hire, shop, practice facilities
Visitors welcome with handicap – with restrictions
Societies welcome by prior arrangement
Copthorne Hotel, Culverhouse Cross, Cardiff, South Glamorgan
✆ 02920 599100

LLANISHEN GOLF CLUB

Heol Hir, Cardiff, South Glamorgan CF14 9UD
✆ 02920 755076 Fax 02920 755078 **Map 3, D3**

M4 Jct 32, A470, via Whitchurch, Pantmawr, Hoel Llanishen Fach
Founded 1905
From this upland course there are good views over Cardiff and the Bristol Channel.
18 holes, 5327 yards
par 68, S.S.S 66
Green fees £30
Catering, changing room/showers, bar, club and trolley hire, shop, practice facilities
Visitors welcome weekdays
Handicap certificate required
Societies welcome by prior arrangement
🏨 Newhouse Hotel, Thornhill Road, Cardiff, South Glamorgan
✆ 01222 520280 Fax 01222 520324

PETERSTONE GOLF CLUB

Peterstone, Wentloog, Cardiff, South Glamorgan CF3 8TN
✆ 01633 680563 Fax 01633 680563
Map 3, D3
peterstone@vapro.net
B4239, off M4 Jct 28
Founded 1990
One of the more recent additions to the Cardiff golfing scene, the course overlooks the Severn Estuary. It is well geared to society and corporate golf.
18 holes, 6555 yards
par 72, S.S.S 72
Designer Robert Sandow
Green fees £18
Catering, changing room/showers, bar, trolley and buggy hire, shop
Visitors welcome weekdays
Societies welcome by prior arrangement

RADYR GOLF CLUB

Drysgol Road, Radyr, Cardiff, South Glamorgan CF15 8BS
✆ 029 2084 2408 Fax 029 2084 3914 **Map 3, D3**
www.radyrgolf.co.uk
Off A470, M4 Jct 32
Founded 1902
More testing than its card length implies and good enough to have hosted matches at county level.
18 holes, 6031 yards
par 69, S.S.S 70
Green fees £36
Changing room/showers, club, trolley and buggy hire, shop
Visitors welcome – restricted weekends
Societies welcome by prior arrangement

RAF ST ATHAN GOLF CLUB

St Athan, Barry, South Glamorgan CF62 4WA
✆ 01446 751043 Fax 01446 751862
Map 3, C3
B4265, near Llantwit Major
Founded 1977
One of the few RAF courses on which visitors may play with relatively few restrictions.
9 holes, 6452 yards
par 72, S.S.S 72
Green fees £12
Catering, changing room/showers, bar, shop
Visitors welcome – restricted Sundays
Handicap certificate required
Societies welcome by prior arrangement

ST ANDREWS MAJOR GOLF CLUB

Coldbrook Road, Cadoxton, Barry, South Glamorgan CF6 3BB
✆ 01446 722227 **Map 3, D3**
M4 Jct 33
Founded 1993
A Welsh course honouring a Scottish saint! Extension and expansion is hoped for.
9 holes, 3000 yards
par 70, S.S.S 68
Designer Richard Hund
Green fees £8
Catering, changing room/showers, bar, club and trolley hire, shop
Visitors welcome
Societies welcome by prior arrangement

ST MARY'S HOTEL GOLF & COUNTRY CLUB

St Mary's Hill, Pencoed, South Glamorgan CF35 5EA
✆ 01656 861100 Fax 01656 863400
Map 3, C3
Off M4 Jct 35
Founded 1990
The hotel is a handsome 17th-century coach house, with two courses overlooking the wooded, rolling hills of the Vale of Glamorgan.
18 holes, 5291 yards, par 69, S.S.S 66
9 holes, 2426 yards, par 35,
Green fees £15
Catering, changing room/showers, bar, accommodation, trolley and buggy hire, shop, driving range, conference and function facilities
Visitors welcome weekdays
Handicap certificate required
Societies welcome by prior arrangement
🏨 St Mary's Hotel & Country Club, St Mary Hill, Pencoed, South Glamorgan
✆ 01656 861100 Fax 01656 863400

ST MELLONS GOLF CLUB

St Mellons, Cardiff, South Glamorgan CF7 8JY
✆ 01633 680401 Fax 01633 681219
Map 3, D3
Off A48, E of Cardiff
Founded 1937
Not an easy course to tame, and a past venue for occasional professional tournaments.
18 holes, 6225 yards
par 70, S.S.S 70
Green fees £32
Catering, changing room/showers, bar, club, trolley and buggy hire, shop
Visitors welcome weekdays
Societies welcome by prior arrangement

VALE OF GLAMORGAN HOTEL GOLF & COUNTRY CLUB

Hensol Park, Hensol, South Glamorgan CF7 8JY
✆ 01443 665899 Fax 01443 222220
Map 3, C3
M4 Jct 34
Founded 1994
An ambitious project of golf courses, hotel and other leisure pursuits in the attractive parkland grounds of Hensol Castle. A 20-acre lake and a number of streams are utilized strategically.
Lake Course: 18 holes, 6507 yards, par 72, S.S.S 71
Designer Peter Johnson
Hensol Course: 9 holes, 3115 yards, par 36
Green fees £25
Catering, changing room/showers, bar, accommodation, club, trolley and buggy hire, shop, driving range, extensive leisure, conference and function facilities
Visitors welcome – restricted weekends
Handicap certificate required
Societies welcome by prior arrangement
🏨 Vale of Glamorgan Hotel, Hensol Park, South Glamorgan CF7 8JY
✆ 01443 665899 Fax 01443 222220

WENVOE CASTLE GOLF CLUB

Wenvoe, Cardiff, South Glamorgan CF5 6BE
✆ 029 2059 4371 Fax 029 2059 4371 **Map 3, D3**
Off A4050, W of Cardiff
Founded 1936
A hilly parkland course with good views.
18 holes, 6422 yards
par 72, S.S.S 71
Green fees £32
Catering, changing room/showers,

bar, trolley hire, shop
Visitors welcome – restricted weekends
Handicap certificate required
Societies welcome by prior arrangement

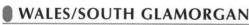

WHITCHURCH GOLF CLUB

Pantmawr Road, Whitchurch, Cardiff, South Glamorgan CF14 7TD
☎ 029 20620985 Fax 029 20529860
Map 3, D3
M4 Jct 32, take A470 towards Cardiff – turn left at lights (400 yards)
Founded 1915
A genuine championship course (including Welsh PGA, British Girls, Welsh Ladies) with views across the Bristol Channel to Somerset.
18 holes, 6212 yards
par 71, S.S.S 70
Designer Fred Johns
Green fees £35
Catering, changing room/showers, bar, club and trolley hire, shop, practice facilities
Visitors welcome
Handicap certificate required
Societies welcome by prior arrangement
🏨 Village Hotel, 29 Pendwyallt Road, Coyton, Whitchurch, Cardiff, South Glamorgan CF14 7EF
☎ 02920 524300

WEST GLAMORGAN

ALLT-Y-GRABAN GOLF CLUB

Allt-y-Graban Road, Pontlliw, Swansea, West Glamorgan SA4 1DT
☎ 01792 885757 **Map 3, A2**
M4 Jct 47, A48 towards Pontlliw, Allt-y-Graban road on left *c.* 2½ miles
Founded 1993
Quite a challenging 9-hole course, on undulating parkland, with good views.
9 holes, 4480 yards
par 66, S.S.S 63
Designer G. Thomas
Green fees £12
Catering, changing room/showers, bar, club and trolley hire
Visitors welcome
Societies welcome by prior arrangement
🏨 Fountain Inn, Bolgoed Road, Pontardulais, West Glamorgan
☎ 01792 882501

CLYNE GOLF CLUB

120 Owls Lodge Lane, Mayals, Swansea, West Glamorgan SA3 5DP
☎ 01792 401989 Fax 01792 401078
Map 3, A2
SW of Swansea
Founded 1920
With many fairways bounded by gorse and ferns, accurate driving is called for, and often allowance must be made for the effect of side-slopes. The turf is springy and fast running, the greens have a high reputation, and from the high ground the views to sea and inland are splendid.
18 holes, 6334 yards
par 70, S.S.S 71
Designer Harry Colt
Green fees £25
Catering, changing room/showers, bar, club and trolley hire, shop, driving range
Visitors welcome
Handicap certificate required
Societies welcome by prior arrangement

EARLSWOOD GOLF CLUB

Jersey Marine, Neath, West Glamorgan SA10 6JP
☎ 01792 812198 **Map 3, A2**
Off A483 (B4290), 5 miles E of Swansea
Founded 1993
From its site on a hillside there are expansive seascapes, and downland turf gives some of the best lies in golf.
18 holes, 5174 yards
par 68, S.S.S 68
Green fees £8
Changing room/showers, club and trolley hire, shop
Visitors welcome
Societies welcome by prior arrangement

FAIRWOOD PARK GOLF CLUB

Blackhills Lane, Upper Killay, Swansea, West Glamorgan SA2 7JN
☎ 01792 297849 Fax 01792 297849
Map 3, A2
Swansea Airport – opposite entrance
Founded 1969
Ponds and ditches threaten, particularly on the closing stretch. Several substantial par 4s, and a 563-yard par 5 at the 5th.
18 holes, 6754 yards
par 73, S.S.S 73
Designer Hawtree & Co
Green fees £25
Catering, changing room/showers, bar, club, trolley and buggy hire, shop, practice facilities
Visitors welcome with handicap certificate
Societies welcome by prior arrangement
🏨 Langrove Lodge, Kittle, Swansea, West Glamorgan
☎ 01792 232410

GLYNNEATH GOLF CLUB

Penygraig, Pontneathvaughan, Glynneath, West Glamorgan SA11 5UH
☎ 01639 720452 Fax 01639 720452
Map 3, B1
www.glynneathgolfclub.co.uk
B4242 (off A465)
Founded 1931
Nestling in the Brecon Beacons National Park, a pretty parkland course. The 6th is an interesting par 3 played across a ravine.
18 holes, 5656 yards
par 69, S.S.S 68
Green fees £17
Catering, changing room/showers, bar, club and trolley hire, shop, practice facilities, snooker
Visitors welcome
Handicap certificate required
Societies welcome weekdays by prior arrangement
🏨 Ty Newydd Country Hotel, Penderyn Road, Hirwaun, West Glamorgan CF44 9SX
☎ 01685 813433

THE GOWER GOLF CLUB

Cefn Goleu, Three Crosses, Gowerton, Swansea, West Glamorgan SA4 3HS
☎ 01792 879905 Fax 01792 872480
Map 3, A2
www.gower-golf.co.uk
A4118 follow signs to Upper Killay, then North Gower and Three Crosses
Founded 1995
An impressive new course which has already hosted county matches. Fine views, and excellent value for money.
18 holes, 6441 yards
par 71, S.S.S 72
Designer Donald Steel
Green fees £17
Catering, changing room/showers, bar, accommodation, club, trolley and buggy hire, shop, practice facilities, conference facilities
Visitors welcome – restricted weekends
Societies welcome by prior arrangement

INCO GOLF CLUB

Clydach, Swansea, West Glamorgan SA6 5EU
☎ 01792 844216 **Map 3, A1**
A4067, N of Swansea
Founded 1965
A parkland course recently extended to 18 holes.
18 holes, 6064 yards

par 70, S.S.S 69
Green fees £10
Catering, changing room/showers, bar
Visitors welcome
Societies welcome by prior arrangement

LAKESIDE GOLF CLUB

Water Street, Margam, Port Talbot, West Glamorgan SA13 2PA
☎ 01639 899959 **Map 3, B2**
M4 Jct 38, follow signs for Margam Park
Founded 1992
Parkland course with a good many par 3s. Margam Castle is visible from the 12th tee.
18 holes, 5000 yards
par 63, S.S.S 63
Designer M. Wootton
Green fees £9.50
Catering, changing room/showers, bar, club and trolley hire, shop, driving range
Visitors welcome
Societies welcome by prior arrangement
🏨 The Twelve Knights, Margam Road, Margam, Port Talbot, West Glamorgan
☎ 01639 882381

LANGLAND BAY GOLF CLUB

Langland Bay Road, Mumbles, Swansea, West Glamorgan SA3 4QR
☎ 01792 361721 Fax 01792 361082
Map 3, A2
golf@langlandbay.sagehost.co.uk
M4 Jct 43, through Swansea, then follow signs for Mumbles
Founded 1904
A meadowland course running down to the cliffs overlooking Langland and Caswell Bays. The views are stunning, with holes such as the 8th and 16th standing out. At 449 and 453 yards respectively, the 6th and 7th are formidable holes in mid-round, but there are many compensatory short par 4s.
18 holes, 5857 yards
par 70, S.S.S 69
Designer James Braid
Green fees £28
Catering, changing room/showers, bar, trolley hire, shop, practice facilities
Visitors welcome – with restrictions
Handicap certificate required
Societies welcome by prior arrangement
🏨 Langland Court, Langland, Swansea, West Glamorgan
☎ 01792 361545

MORRISTON GOLF CLUB

160 Clasemont Road, Morriston, Swansea, West Glamorgan SA6 6AJ
☎ 01792 796528 Fax 01792 796528
Map 3, A2
M4 Jct 46, 1 mile S
Founded 1919
Friendly club with an enjoyable parkland course in the northern suburbs of Swansea.
18 holes, 5755 yards
par 68, S.S.S 68
Green fees £18
Catering, changing room/showers, bar, trolley hire, shop, practice facilities, lounge may be hired for company training, christenings etc
Visitors welcome – restricted weekends
Societies welcome by prior arrangement
🏨 Jarvis International, Phoenix Way, Swansea Enterprise Park, Morriston, Swansea, West Glamorgan
☎ 01792 310330

NEATH GOLF CLUB

Cadoxton, Neath, West Glamorgan SA10 8AH
☎ 01639 632759 Fax 01639 632759
Map 3, B2
2 miles NE of Neath
Founded 1934
As James Braid said, 'The situation is superb...the views from every part of the course are magnificent, whilst the air is most exhilarating.' He was in the process of creating a cleverly varied course, with long, medium and short examples of par 3s, 4s, and 5s, enjoying marvellous vistas.
18 holes, 6490 yards
par 72, S.S.S 72
Designer James Braid
Green fees £20
Catering, changing room/showers, bar, club and trolley hire, shop, practice facilities, snooker
Visitors welcome weekdays
Handicap certificate required
Societies welcome by prior arrangement
🏨 Castle Hotel, The Parade, Neath, West Glamorgan
☎ 01639 641119

PALLEG GOLF CLUB

Palleg Road, Lower Cwmtwrch, Swansea Valley, West Glamorgan SA9 2QQ
☎ 01639 842193 **Map 3, B1**
A4067, M4 Jct 45
Founded 1930
A 9-hole parkland course of some length and challenge.
9 holes, 6418 yards
par 72, S.S.S 72
Green fees £18
Catering, changing room/showers, bar, club hire, shop
Visitors welcome weekdays – restricted weekends
Societies welcome by prior arrangement

PENNARD GOLF CLUB

2 Southgate Road, Southgate, Swansea, West Glamorgan SA3 2BT
☎ 01792 233131 Fax 01792 234 797
Map 2, H1
pigeon01@globalnet.co.uk
www.golfagent.com/clubsites/pennard
8 miles W of Swansea, via A4067 and B4436
Founded 1896
A remarkable course, a genuine links yet set high on the cliffs overlooking the Gower coastline. The 7th and 16th play to spectacularly sited greens above the shore, the 7th beside the ruins of an old castle, too. Gorse affects the early holes, returning later to threaten the fine 17th.
18 holes, 6265 yards
par 71, S.S.S 72
Designer James Braid
Green fees £27
Catering, changing room/showers, bar, club and trolley hire, shop, practice facilities
Visitors welcome – with restrictions.
Handicap certificate required
Societies welcome by prior arrangement

PONTARDAWE GOLF CLUB

Cefn Llan, Pontardawe, Swansea, West Glamorgan SA8 4SH
☎ 01792 863118 Fax 01792 830041
Map 3, B1
A4067 to Pontardawe Cross, 4th left, 6th right
Founded 1924
Panoramic views of the Swansea Valley and Gower Coast from this elevated course, especially from the 16th tee.
18 holes, 6003 yards
par 70, S.S.S 70
Green fees £22
Catering, changing room/showers, bar, trolley hire, shop, practice facilities, snooker
Visitors welcome – restricted weekends
Handicap certificate required
Societies welcome by prior arrangement
🏨 Pen yr Allt Hotel, Alltwen, Pontardawe, Swansea, West Glamorgan
☎ 01792 863320

SWANSEA BAY GOLF CLUB
Jersey Marine, Neath, West Glamorgan SA10 6JP
☎ 01792 812198 **Map 3, A2**
Off A483, E of Swansea
Founded 1892
A seaside course overlooking, as its name suggests, Swansea Bay.
18 holes, 6605 yards
par 72, S.S.S 72
Green fees £16
Catering, changing room/showers, bar, club and trolley hire, shop, practice facilities
Visitors welcome
Societies welcome by prior arrangement

WREXHAM

CHIRK GOLF CLUB
Chirk, Wrexham LL14 5AD
☎ 01691 774407 Fax 01691 773878
Map 7, C3
A483, off A5 at Chirk
Founded 1990
A big course with three of the par 5s enormous, the dog-leg 9th being well over 650 yards long, one of the longest holes in Europe. Water carries on the 1st, 10th and 18th drives are daunting, and the streams which affect the 16th and 17th make them particularly challenging.
18 holes, 7045 yards
par 72, S.S.S 73
Green fees £18
Catering, changing room/showers, bar, club, trolley and buggy hire, shop, driving range, practice facilities
Visitors welcome – with restrictions
Societies welcome by prior arrangement

CLAYS FARM GOLF CENTRE
Bryn Estyn Road, Wrexham LL13 9UB
☎ 01978 661406 **Map 7, D2**
Off A534 (signposted)
Founded 1992
Recent meadowland course, mostly straightforward, but hedges and out-of-bounds are frequent hazards.
18 holes, 5908 yards
par 69, S.S.S 69
Green fees £14
Changing room/showers, club, trolley and buggy hire, shop, driving range, practice facilities
Visitors welcome
Societies welcome by prior arrangement

MOSS VALLEY GOLF CLUB
Moss Road, Wrexham LL11 4UR
☎ 01978 720518 **Map 7, C2**
Off A541, NW of Wrexham follow signs for Summerhill (Brynhyfryd)
Founded 1988
Set in a gorgeous wooded valley, there is some strenuous climbing to be done – but great fun for the fit!
9 holes, 5582 yards
par 68, S.S.S. 67
Green fees £6
Catering, changing rooms/ showers, bar and club and trolley hire
Visitors welcome
Societies welcome by prior arrangement

PEN-Y-CAE GOLF CLUB
Ruabon Road, Pen-y-Cae, Wrexham LL14 1TW
☎ 01978 810108 **Map 7, C2**
A483/A539 at Ruabon, off A5
Founded 1993
Executive-length course in wooded parkland with several stiff challenges, especially the 2nd and 8th.
9 holes, 4280 yards
par 64, S.S.S 62
Green fees £7.50
Catering, changing room/showers, bar, club and trolley hire, shop
Visitors welcome
Societies welcome by prior arrangement

PLASSEY GOLF CLUB
Plassey Caravan Site & Leisure Park, Eyton, Wrexham LL13 0SP
☎ 01978 780020 **Map 7, D2**
Off A483, signposted Plassey and Bangor-on-Dee
Founded 1992
The best holes on this short course in pretty parkland play along a river valley. There is a brewery on site.
9 holes, 4761 yards
par 64, S.S.S 62
Designer K Williams
Green fees £9
Catering, changing room/showers, bar, club and trolley hire, shop, practice facilities, squash, swimming, country craft shops
Visitors welcome
Societies welcome by prior arrangement

WREXHAM GOLF CLUB
Holt Road, Wrexham LL13 9SB
☎ 01978 261033 Fax 01978 364268
Map 7, D2
A534, 2 miles NE of Wrexham
Founded 1904
With no two holes alike, this is one of the best parkland courses in North Wales, with several first class holes on each half. The 3rd, 5th and 7th are searching par 4s, and the 4th a rogue of a short hole. A mid-fairway tree complicates the par-5 12th.
18 holes, 6233 yards
par 70, S.S.S 70
Designer James Braid
Green fees £20
Catering, changing room/showers, bar, trolley hire, shop, practice facilities
Visitors welcome weekdays
Handicap certificate required
Societies welcome by prior arrangement

FRANCE, PORTUGAL & SPAIN

The courses in this section have been chosen with holiday golf in mind. The French courses are those within easy reach of the ferry ports on the Channel coast and the Spanish courses are confined to those along the Mediterranean coast with easy access from airports at Barcelona, Valencia, Malaga and Seville. Portuguese courses, too, have been limited to those within striking distance of the Algarve or Lisbon.

Spain and Portugal have long been popular winter destinations for British golfers. Now, with many from snowbound Scandinavia and Germany, cold and wet Holland and Belgium also flocking to these idyllic parts in huge numbers, it is wise to book starting times well in advance. Good deals are available through specialist golf tour operators who offer comprehensive packages with guaranteed starting times, competitions and so on.

Golf in Portugal is a recent phenomenon, almost an explosion, which followed the successful opening of its first golf resort, Penina, in 1966. The oldest club, Oporto, dates back to the 19th century, when it offered a retreat for those British who worked in the port wine trade. The modest course of the Lisbon Sporting Club served the capital from 1922, and Estoril acquired its charming course in 1945, but these were all there were on the mainland until Penina. Now there are about fifty courses, with almost as many again in the pipeline. On the whole the Portuguese do not themselves play, with only around 12,000 active golfers, so the courses are very much geared up for visitors.

Spain is another matter. A golf club in the Canaries was set up as long ago as 1891. Wealthy Spaniards, diplomats and visiting businessmen played at the magnificent Puerta de Hierro in Madrid from 1904. Several Royal golf clubs followed, mainly along the north coast (including Real Pedreña where Severiano Ballesteros learned his trade), and Saint Cugat brought the game to Barcelona in 1914. The coming of Sotogrande in 1964, soon followed by Las Brisas, put the Costa del Sol on the golfing map (although Guadalmina actually predated Sotogrande by five years). Advance booking is essential in this region, with many tee times reserved for members, time-share residents and so on. Better still, leave these arrangements to a tour operator.

The first golf course in continental Europe was established in France, at Pau, in 1856. But golf in France remained the preserve of the wealthy and aristocratic for well over a hundred years, and only now is golf tourism beginning to emerge. Our selected courses are restricted to those close to the Channel ferry ports, but those with time to spare should also consider some of the excellent (if expensive) golf courses available around Paris, such as Chantilly, Le Golf National, Fontainebleau and St Cloud. There is also first-rate golf nearby across the border in Belgium with a dozen Royal courses of real distinction, especially Royal Belgique, Royal Zoute, Royal Sart-Tilman, Royal Antwerp and Royal GC des Fagnes.

FRANCE

GOLF CLUB DE L'AMIRAUTE

Tourgéville, F-14800 Deauville, France
✆ 02 31 88 38 00
Fax 02 31 88 32 00
D278, 10 km S of Deauville
Founded 1993
In the countryside near Pont-l'Evêque, a challenging course designed by Bill Baker. The bunkering is not too penal and the fairways generous, but there are plentiful water hazards, and even a statue or two, from which there is relief in the form of a free drop.
18 holes, 6017 metres
par 73, S.S.S 73
Designer Bill Baker
Green fees 250 F
Catering, changing room/showers, bar, club, trolley and buggy hire, shop, driving range, practice facilities
Visitors welcome
Societies welcome by prior arrangement

GOLF CLUB D'ARRAS

Rue Briquet Taillander, F-62223 Anzin-Saint-Aubin, France
✆ 03.21.50.24.24
Fax 03.21.50.27.22
www.arras-golfclub.com
4 km NW of Arras, via A1 or A26, 100 km SE of Calais
Founded 1990
A championship course which has already hosted the Ladies' French Open twice. Much of the course is laid out in marshland with water affecting play on the first ten holes. Later the course moves onto hillier ground, more heathland in nature, before water returns with a vengeance on the 18th.
La Vallée: 18 holes, 6150 metres, par 72
Designer Jean-Claude Cornillot
Les Aubépines: 9 holes, 1550 metres, par 30
Green fees 190 F
Catering, changing room/showers, bar, accommodation, club and buggy hire, shop, driving range, practice facilities
Visitors welcome
Handicap certificate required – limit: 35
Societies welcome by prior arrangement

GOLF DE BELLE DUNE

Promenade de Marquenterre, F-80790 Fort-Mahon-Plage, France
✆ 03.22.23.45.50
Fax 03.22.23.93.41
20 km S of Le Touquet
Founded 1993
There are shades of Formby about Belle Dune as it emerges from the pine woods into the dunes. Built in collaboration with the Picardy Coastal Devlopment planners, with environmental considerations always a priority, it is exceptionally natural, with tight winding fairways and swift greens, demanding accurate and thoughtful play throughout.
18 holes, 5909 metres
par 72, S.S.S 71
Designer Jean Manuel Rossi
Green fees 160 F
Catering, changing room/showers, bar, club and trolley hire, shop, practice facilities
Visitors welcome with handicap certificate or Green Card
Societies welcome by prior arrangement

GOLF CLUB DE BEUZEVAL-HOULGATE

Route de Gonneville, 14510 Houlgate, France
✆ 02.31.24.80.49
Fax 02.31.28.04.48
Off D513, 2 km SE of Houlgate

Founded 1981
Country estate golf at its best, with the Château de Beuzeval overlooking proceedings. There are views towards the English Channel, but the golfer's mind will be on the traditional parkland hazards of trees and hedges. The Alliss/Thomas 9-hole course of 1980 was extended to 18 holes in 1986.
18 holes, 6225 metres
par 73, S.S.S 72
Designer Peter Alliss, Dave Thomas
Green fees 130 F
Catering, changing room/showers, bar, club, trolley and buggy hire, shop, practice facilities
Visitors welcome
Societies welcome by prior arrangement

GOLF DU BOIS DE RUMINGHEM

1613 Rue St Antione, 62370 Ruminghem, France
✆ 03.21.85.30.33
Fax 03.21.36.38.38
Off N43, 15 km SE of Calais
Founded 1991
One can be teeing off at Ruminghem, on the edge of the Forêt d'Eperlecques, within half an hour of disembarking at Calais. The front nine runs over relatively open parkland, while the back nine is woodland golf at its best, utterly secluded and peaceful, apart from the delights of birdsong.
18 holes, 6115 metres
par 73
Designer Bill Baker
Green fees 250 F
Catering, changing room/showers, bar, club, trolley and buggy hire, shop, driving range, practice facilities
Visitors welcome
Societies welcome by prior arrangement

GOLF DE BONDUES

Château de la Vigne, F-59910 Bondues, France
✆ 03.20.23.20.62
Fax 03.20.23.24.11
10 km NE of Lille
Founded 1967
Two big, demanding courses in contrasting styles. The White Course displays its American parentage in the extensive strategic use made of water – it comes into play on 12 holes. Fred Hawtree's course is more wooded, a little longer, and certainly no easier. The elegant clubhouse is an 18th-century château.
Parcours Jaune: 18 holes, 6260 metres, par 73
Designer Fred Hawtree
Parcours Blanc: 18 holes, 6012 metres, par 72
Designer Robert Trent Jones Snr & Jnr
Green fees 200 F
Catering, changing room/showers, bar, buggy hire, driving range, practice facilities
Visitors welcome, except Tuesdays
Handicap certificate required – limit: 34
Societies welcome by prior arrangement

GOLF DE BREST IROISE

Parc de Lann-Rohou, Saint Urbain, F-29800 Landernau, France
✆ 02.98.85.16.17
Fax 02.98.85.19.39
25 km E of Brest, via N12 and D170
Founded 1976
Gorse, heather, trees and even rocky outcrops contribute to the ruggedness of this upland course, which has been voted the best in Brittany, and ranked 13th in all France. In the past its condition was sometimes questionable, but recent reports are very favourable, as they are of the hotel/clubhouse.
18 holes, 5672 metres, par 71
Designer Michael Fenn
9 holes, 3329 metres, par 37
Green fees 230 F
Catering, changing room/showers, bar, accommodation, club and buggy hire, shop, driving range, practice facilities
Visitors welcome
Societies welcome by prior arrangement

GOLF DE BRIGODE

36 Avenue du Golf, F-59650 Villeneuve-d'Ascq, France
✆ 03.20.91.17.86
Fax 03.20.05.96.36
D506, 10 km NE of Lille
Founded 1967
A past host to a number of French PGA Championships, Brigode has an English feel to its wooded, parkland course, mostly on level ground. The most nerve-wracking hole is undoubtedly the 4th, a par 3 played through the trees, over a lake, and immediately below the clubhouse dining room window.
18 holes, 6182 metres
par 72
Designer Bill Baker
Green fees 200 F
Catering, changing room/showers, bar, club and buggy hire, driving range, practice facilities
Visitors welcome (not Tuesdays)
Handicap certificate required – limit: 30
Societies welcome by prior arrangement

GOLF DU CHAMP DE BATAILLE

Château du Champ-de-Bataille, F-27110 Le Neubourg, France
✆ 02.32.35.03.72
Fax 02.32.35.83.10
Off N13 (between Lisieux and Evreux) at Le Neubourg
Founded 1988
Built around a 17th-century château, Champ de Bataille opens and closes with somewhat artificial formal holes, as if trying to imitate the château's classical style. Otherwise, this is a magnificent, long, hilly, woodland course, cut through a pine forest, with a number of lakes adding increased hazards and beauty.
18 holes, 6575 metres
par 72, S.S.S 74
Designer Robin Nelson
Green fees 220 F
Catering, changing room/showers, bar, buggy hire, shop, practice facilities
Visitors welcome
Societies welcome by prior arrangement

GOLF DU CHATEAU DES ORMES

Château des Ormes, Epiniac, F-35120 Dol-de-Bretagne, France
✆ 02.99.73.54.44
Off D705, between Dol-de-Bretagne and Combourg
Founded 1988
The 16th-century château, formerly the home of the Bishop of Dol, provides an elegant focal point for this heavily-wooded, rolling course. Narrow fairways, a number of dog-legs, and occasional ponds feature. Bring the camera for the view back from the 3rd green, over a pond to the château.
18 holes, 6070 metres
par 72
Green fees 200F
Catering, changing room/showers, bar, accommodation, club, trolley and buggy hire, shop, practice facilities
Visitors welcome
Handicap certificate required
Societies welcome by prior arrangement

DIEPPE-POURVILLE GOLF CLUB

51 Route de Pourville, F-76200 Dieppe, France
✆ 02.35.84.25.05

Fax 02.35.84.97.11
Off D75, 2 km W of Dieppe
Founded 1897
An old course, the 4th oldest in France, which once ran to 27 holes. Only 18 now remain, but they have been upgraded over the years. The site is undulating, more parkland than links, with trees and water hazards providing strategic obstacles. From the high ground the views are superb.
18 holes, 5763 metres
par 70
Designer Willie Park
Green fees 190 F
Catering, changing room/showers, bar, club and buggy hire, shop, driving range, practice facilities
Visitors welcome
Societies welcome by prior arrangement

GOLF DE DINARD

Boulevard de la Houle, F-35800 Saint-Briac-sur-Mer, France
☎ 02.99.88.32.07
Fax 02.99.88.04.53
8 km W of Dinard on coast road
Founded 1887
The second oldest golf club in France (after Pau), with a classic seaside course. True, there is an excursion inland, and there is little length, but when the course reaches the cliff tops on the 6th the views become quite magical. Fast, firm, wind-dried greens call for deft pitching skills.
18 holes, 5137 metres
par 68
Designer Willie Dunn
Green fees 300 F
Catering, changing room/showers, bar, club and buggy hire, shop, practice facilities
Visitors welcome
Handicap certificate required – limit: 35
Societies welcome by prior arrangement

GOLF D'ETRETAT

BP No 7, Route du Havre, F-76790 Etretat, France
☎ 02.35.27.04.89
Fax 02.35.29.49.02
D940, 1 km W of Etretat
Founded 1908
Arnaud Massy (the only Frenchman to win the Open Championship) was professional here for a few years after the Second World War. He chose a glorious spot for his twilight years, a clifftop course of great beauty with one of the loveliest of all seaside holes in the 10th.
18 holes, 6072 metres
par 72, S.S.S 72
Designer M. Chantepie, D. Fruchet
Green fees 200 F
Catering, changing room/showers, bar, buggy hire, shop, driving range, practice facilities
Visitors welcome
Handicap certificate required
Societies welcome by prior arrangement

GOLF DE GRANVILLE

Bréville, F-50290 Bréhal, France
☎ 02.33.50.23.06 Fax 02.33.61.91.87
5 km N of Granville
Founded 1912
A true links, with many of the characteristics of an old Scottish course. Subtle humps and bumps affect most approach shots to the generally small greens, roads cross several holes, and a burn fronts the 14th green. The clubhouse is remarkable, all towers and turrets in a quasi half-timbered style.
18 holes, 5854 metres, par 71
Designer Harry Colt, C.H. Alison, Hawtree
9 holes, 2323 metres, par 33
Green fees 200 F
Catering, changing room/showers, bar, club, trolley and buggy hire, shop, driving range, practice facilities
Visitors welcome
Handicap certificate required
Societies welcome by prior arrangement

GOLF D'HARDELOT-LES-DUNES

3 Avenue du Golf, F-62152 Hardelot, France
☎ 03.21.91.90.90
Fax 03.21.83.28.71
15 km S of Boulogne
Founded 1991
A contrasting modern partner for Les Pins, longer and hillier. In fact there are a number of blind tee shots – not to everyone's taste – and it is easy to be cut out by the pine trees which line the fairways if the wrong line is taken on the many dog-legs.
18 holes, 6031 metres
par 73, S.S.S 73
Designer Paul Rolin
Green fees 240 F
Catering, changing room/showers, bar, club, trolley and buggy hire, shop, driving range, practice facilities
Visitors welcome – with restrictions
Societies welcome by prior arrangement

GOLF D'HARDELOT-LES-PINS

3 Avenue du Golf, F-62152 Hardelot, France
☎ 03.21.83.73.10
Fax 03.21.83.24.33
15 km S of Boulogne
Founded 1931
A comparison is often made between Les Pins and the Red Course at The Berkshire, quite reasonably, for the setting and distribution of the holes are very similar. There are five par 5s and five par 3s, although the most remarkable hole is the 355-metre 9th, a double dog-leg.
18 holes, 5871 metres
par 72, S.S.S 72
Designer Tom Simpson
Green fees 240 F
Catering, changing room/showers, bar, club, trolley and buggy hire, shop, practice facilities
Visitors welcome – with restrictions
Societies welcome

GOLF DE NAMPONT-ST-MARTIN

Maison Forte, F-80120 Nampont-St-Martin, France
☎ 03.22.29.92.90
Fax 03.22.29.97.54
Off N1 between Montreuil and Abbeville
Founded 1978
A 15th-century moated castle forms part of the clubhouse facilities at this expanding club near the historic battlefield of Crécy. On the practice range golfers hit balls into a lake, and water is a recurring feature on some parts of the course. However, many holes also penetrate charming woodland.
Parcours Les Cygnes: 18 holes, 6051 metres, par 72
Parcours Belvedere: 18 holes, 5145 metres, par 72
Designer Thomas Chatterton
Green fees 150 F
Catering, changing room/showers, bar, club, trolley and buggy hire, shop, driving range, practice facilities
Visitors welcome
Societies welcome by prior arrangement

NEW GOLF DE DEAUVILLE

Saint Arnoult, F-14800 Deauville, France
☎ 02.31.14.24.24
Fax 02.31.14.24.25
At St Arnoult, 3 km S of Deauville
Founded 1929
Simpson's original course of 1929 is something of an object lesson in understatement, its skilful design

luring the unwary into thinking the course is very much easier than it actually is. Sir Henry Cotton's 9-hole course runs on higher ground, both giving admirable views over the town to the sea.
18 holes, 5951 metres, par 71, S.S.S 71
Designer Tom Simpson
9 holes, 6066 metres, par 72, S.S.S 72
Designer Sir Henry Cotton
Green fees 300 F
Catering, changing room/showers, bar, accommodation, trolley and buggy hire, shop, driving range, practice facilities
Visitors welcome by prior arrangement
Handicap certificate required – limit: 24 men, 28 women
Societies welcome by prior arrangement

OMAHA BEACH GOLF CLUB

Ferme Saint Sauveur, F-14520 Port-en-Bessin, France
☎ 02.31.22.12.12
Fax 02,31.22.12.13
www.best-channel-golfs.com
8 km N of Bayeux
Founded 1986
The much photographed 6th on the Sea Nine, clinging to the cliff edge, high above Port-en-Bessin, is the most spectacular of many good holes at this famous Second World War landing site. With woodland, moorland and lake holes also part of the mix, almost every kind of golf is represented.
Mer & Bocage: 18 holes, 6216 metres, S.S.S 72
Etang: 9 holes, 2693 metres, S.S.S 35
Designer Yves Bureau
Green fees 160 F
Catering, changing room/showers, bar, club, trolley and buggy hire, shop, driving range, practice facilities
Visitors welcome
Handicap certificate required
Societies welcome by prior arrangement

GOLF DE PLENEUF-VAL-ANDRE

Rue de la Plage des Vallées, F-22370 Pléneuf-Val-André, France
☎ 02.96.63.01.12
Fax 02.96.63.01.06
D 786 coast road, 60 km W of Saint-Malo
Founded 1992
A first-rate seaside course with excellent facilities, including an enormous driving range. The holes nearest the beach are true links holes, while on the higher ground (where the views along the Emerald Coast are magnificent) there is more of a heathland feel, while yet further inland meadowland qualities prevail.
18 holes, 6052 metres
par 72
Designer Alain Prat
Green fees 270 F
Catering, changing room/showers, bar, club and buggy hire, shop, driving range, practice facilities
Visitors welcome
Societies welcome by prior arrangement

GOLF DE ST JULIEN

St Julien-sur-Calonne, 14130 Pont-l'Evêque, France
☎ 02.31.64.30.30
Fax 02.31.64.12.43
3 km SE of Pont-l'Evêque
Gastronomes revere Pont-l'Evêque for its world-famous cheese, and food-loving golfers are beginning to appreciate the merits of these nearby courses, the big one dominated by seven lakes, waterfalls, and 90 bunkers. The countryside is gently rolling pastureland, the views pleasant, rather than spectacular, but the golfing challenge is serious enough.
18 holes, 6291 metres, par 73, S.S.S 72
Designer Alain Prat, Bill Baker
9 holes, 2133 metres, par 33, S.S.S 64
Green fees 140 F
Catering, changing room/showers, bar, club, trolley and buggy hire, shop, practice facilities, tennis
Visitors welcome
Societies welcome by prior arrangement

ST MALO-LE TRONCHET GOLF CLUB

Le Tronchet, F-35540 Miniac-Morvan, France
☎ 02.99.58.96.69
Fax 02.99.58.10.39
Off N 137/N176, 6 km SW of Dol-de-Bretagne
Founded 1986
Laid out around Lake Mirloup, the course explores gentle valleys and copses. The par-3 6th is the signature hole, all carry across water, and there are a number of long par 4s, but, on the whole, the fairways are generous. An old 17th-century priory serves as the clubhouse.
18 holes, 6212 metres, par 72
9 holes, 2684 metres, par 36
Designer Hubert Chesneau
Green fees 260 F
Catering, changing room/showers, bar, club, trolley and buggy hire, shop, driving range, practice facilities
Visitors welcome
Societies welcome by prior arrangement

ST OMER GOLF CLUB

Chenin des Bois, Acquin-Westbécourt, F-62380 Lumbres, France
☎ 03.21.38.59. 90
Fax 03.21.93.02.47
Off N42, 10 km W of St Omer
Founded 1990
Often referred to as Aa St Omer, after the River Aa in whose valley the course is laid out. On the main course, nine holes rise and fall quite steeply, with water coming into play, though not alarmingly. The remaining holes contrast nicely, running through a beech and oak wood.
18 holes, 6294 metres, par 73
9 holes, 2038 metres, par 31
Green fees 170 F
Catering, changing room/showers, bar, club, trolley and buggy hire, shop, driving range, practice facilities
Visitors welcome
Societies welcome by prior arrangement

GOLF DU TOUQUET

Avenue de Golf, BP41, F-62520 Le Touquet, France
☎ 03.21.06.28.00
Fax 03.21.06.28.01
2 km S of Le Touquet
Founded 1904
For long a favourite of the British – indeed, P.G. Wodehouse had a villa here – much work has been put in to restore the courses to their former glory, including the reconstruction of holes lost during the war. La Mer is the jewel in the crown, a long and magnificent links.
La Mer: 18 holes, 6275 metres, S.S.S 74
Designer Harry Colt
La Forêt: 18 holes, 5659 metres, par 70, S.S.S 70
Designer Horace Hutchinson
Le Manoir: 9 holes, 2817 metres, par 35
Designer H.J. Baker
Green fees 300 F
Catering, changing room/showers, bar, club, trolley and buggy hire, shop, driving range, practice facilities
Visitors welcome
Handicap certificate required
Societies welcome by prior arrangement

GOLF DE WIMEREUX

Route d'Ambletouse, F-62930 Wimereux, France
✆ 03.21.32.43.20
Fax 03.21.33.62.21
D940, 6 km N of Boulogne
Founded 1907
One of the few genuine links courses on the Channel coast south of Holland and Belgium. A bleak course, very much at the mercy of the wind, it has devastating rough if the summer is damp enough to grow it. Deep bunkers and swift, wind-dried, greens are the main defences.
18 holes, 6150 metres
par 72
Green fees 230 F
Catering, changing room/showers, bar, club and buggy hire, shop, driving range, practice facilities
Visitors welcome
Societies welcome by prior arrangement

PORTUGAL

AROEIRA 1

Herdade da Aroeira, Fonte da Telha 2815-207 Charneca da Caparica, Portugal
✆ (21) 297 1345 Fax (21) 297 1238
Off N377, 15 km S of Lisbon
Founded 1972
Aroeira's class was recognized by its hosting of the Portuguese Open from 1996 to 1999. It shows many of the qualities of Vilamoura and Palmares (other Pennink Portuguese courses), in the individuality of each hole. Natural undulations and forest trees are utilized to perfection along with artificially created water hazards.
18 holes, 6040 metres
par 72, S.S.S 72
Designer Frank Pennink
Green fees 9000 esc
Catering, changing room/showers, bar, club, trolley and buggy hire, shop, driving range, practice facilities
Visitors welcome
Handicap certificate required
Societies by arrangement

AROEIRA 2

Herdade da Aroeira, Fonte da Telha 2815-207 Charneca da Caparica, Portugal
✆ (21) 297 1345 Fax (21) 297 1238
Off N377, 15 km S of Lisbon
Founded 2000
Donald Steel is as much a historian of golf architecture as he is an innovator. His task at Aroeira was to match the challenge of Frank Pennink's original, and this he has achieved by the employment of tall pine trees in the strategic defence of the course. Breeding always shows.
18 holes, 6113 metres
par 72, S.S.S 72
Designer Donald Steel
Green fees 9000 esc
Catering, changing room/showers, bar, club, trolley and buggy hire, shop, driving range, practice facilities
Visitors welcome
Handicap certificate required
Societies by arrangement

BELAS

Alameda do Aqueduto, 2745 Belas, Portugal
✆ (21) 962 6130 Fax (21) 962 6131
belas.golf@mail.telepac.pt
Off N117, 10 km NW of Lisbon
Founded 1997
Across the road from the old Lisbon Sporting Club, Belas is a technically demanding course running over barren hillsides, with immaculate fairways and greens in an otherwise inhospitable landscape. The 501-metre 2nd replicates the challenge of the 13th at Augusta, while the 18th runs the gauntlet of a lake.
18 holes, 6380 metres
par 72, S.S.S 72
Designer Rocky Roquemore
Green fees 9000 esc
Catering, changing room/showers, bar, club, trolley and buggy hire, shop, driving range, practice facilities
Visitors welcome
Societies by arrangement

BENAMOR

8800-067 Conceição, Tavira, Algarve, Portugal
✆ (281) 320880 Fax (281) 320888
On EN125, 22 miles E of Faro
Just as Sir Henry Cotton perceived the golfing potential in the Algarve at Penina, so he realized what might be on offer east of Faro. In 1986 he sketched a design at Benamor, which has only just been developed, revealing the golfing challenge of this undulating site, abounding with wildlife.
18 holes, 5440 metres
par 71, S.S.S 71
Designer Sir Henry Cotton
Changing room/showers, bar, club and trolley hire, shop, driving range
Visitors welcome
Handicap certificate required
Societies welcome by prior arrangement

ESTORIL

Avenida de República, 2765 Estoril, Portugal
✆ (21) 468 0054 Fax (21) 468 2796
cge@mail.telepac.pt
N9, 2 km N of Estoril
Founded 1928
One of the most captivating of all Portuguese courses, and host to twenty early Portuguese Opens. It is not a long course, with only two par 4s over 400 yards, but Mackenzie Ross's design is a masterpiece, calling for intelligent play. The greens are a delight, the fairways like velvet.
Championship Course: 18 holes, 5262 metres, par 69, S.S.S 69
Designer Mackenzie Ross
Blue Course: 9 holes, 2585 metres, par 68, S.S.S 65
Green fees 9000 Esc
Catering, changing room/showers, bar, club and trolley hire, shop, driving range, practice facilities
Visitors welcome
Handicap certificate required
Societies by arrangement

PALMARES

Meia Praia, Apartado 74, 8601-901 Lagos, Algarve, Portugal
✆ (282) 762953 Fax (282) 762534
Off EN125, 6km NE of Lagos
Founded 1975
One of the older courses in the Algarve, and all the better for it, being beautifully conditioned and run by a caring management. The views from the hilltop holes are quite magnificent, especially that from the 17th tee. Five early holes run through true linksland, giving the round considerable variety.
18 holes, 5961 metres
par 71, S.S.S 72
Designer Frank Pennink
Green fees 11000 esc
Catering, changing room/showers, bar, club, trolley and buggy hire, shop, driving range, practice facilities
Visitors welcome
Handicap certificate required
Societies by arrangement

PARQUE DA FLORESTA

Budens, 8650-060 Vila do Bispo, Algarve, Portugal
✆ (282) 690054 Fax (282) 695157
EN125, W of Lagos
Founded 1987
Pepe Gancedo has designed some of the most spectacular (and frequently controversial) clubs in continental Europe. He makes bold statements and expects golfers to have the ability and nerve to overcome the problems set. Parque

da Floresta, climbing over steep hills and plunging into deep valleys, is stunning and uncompromising.
18 holes, 5670 metres
par 72, S.S.S 72
Designer Pepe Gancedo
Green fees 7900 esc
Catering, changing room/showers, bar, club and trolley hire, shop, driving range
Visitors welcome
Societies welcome by prior arrangement

CAESAR PARK PENHA LONGA

Estrada de Lagoa Azul, Linhó, 2710 Sintra, Portugal
✆ (21) 924 9011 Fax (21) 924 9024
N9, 4 km NW of Estoril
Founded 1992
Host to the 1994 and 1995 Portuguese Opens, Penha Longa roams a hilly, wooded site alongside the remains of a monastery and royal lodge. An ancient aqueduct features on the 6th and 7th, but, from the golfing point of view, it is the finish from the 15th which challenges most.
Penha Longa: 18 holes, 6290 metres, par 72, S.S.S 73
Mostiero: 9 holes, 2588 metres, par 35, S.S.S 35
Designer Robert Trent Jones Jnr
Green fees 14500 esc
Catering, changing room/showers, bar, accommodation, club, trolley and buggy hire, shop, driving range, practice facilities
Visitors welcome
Handicap certificate required
Societies by arrangement

LE MERIDIAN PENINA GOLF & RESORT

PO Box 146, Penina, 8501-952 Portimão, Algarve, Portugal, Codex
✆ (282) 420200 Fax (282) 420300
EN 125 5 km W of Portimão
Founded 1966
The first resort course in Portugal, immediately revealing the enormous tourism potential of golf in the Algarve. It is hard to imagine that the beautiful, tree-lined fairways were once a boggy paddy field. Recent upgrading has enhanced the Championship Course's status as a very tough test even for the stars.
Championship Course: 18 holes, 6343 metres, par 73, S.S.S 73
Designer Sir Henry Cotton
Academy Course: 9 holes, 2035 metres, par 30
Resort Course: 9 holes, 2987 metres, par 70, S.S.S 71
Green fees 12000 esc
Catering, changing room/showers, bar, accommodation, club, trolley and buggy hire, shop, driving range, practice facilities, swimming, tennis
Visitors welcome
Handicap certificate required for Championship Course – limit: 28 men, 36 ladies
Societies by arrangement
🏨 Le Meridien-Penina Golf and Resort, Portugal
✆ (066) 9761146

PESTANA GOLF

Apartado 1011, 8400-908 Carvoeiro, Lagoa, Algarve, Portugal
✆ (282) 340900 Fax (282) 340901
g.pestana@mail.telepac.pt
www.pestana.com
EN125 S of Lagoa, 9 km E of Portimão
Founded 1992
It is said that one of the olive trees alongside the 581-metre 18th is all of 1,200 years old. Many others date back to the 15th century. Vale da Pinta is one of the least spoiled of Portugal's recent courses, a rural retreat full of handsome – and testing – holes.
Pinta Course: 18 holes, 6151 metres, par 71, S.S.S 72
Gramacho Course: 18 holes, 5919 metres, par 72, S.S.S 71
Designer Ronald Fream
Green fees 10000 esc
Catering, changing room/showers, bar, club, trolley and buggy hire, shop, driving range, practice facilities, David Leadbetter Teaching Academy
Visitors welcome
Handicap certificate required – limit: 27 men, 35 ladies
Societies by arrangement

PINHEIROS ALTOS

Apartado 2168, Quinta do Lago, 8135 Almancil, Algarve, Portugal
✆ (289) 359910 Fax (289) 394392
EN125, W of Faro on Quinta do Lago estate
Founded 1992
In addition to the challenges set by Ronald Fream's design, Pinheiros Altos appeals with its great variety. The front nine runs over hilly ground covered in pine woods. For the back nine the course moves to the banks of the Ria Formosa nature reserve. The short 5th and 17th excel.
18 holes, 6186 metres
par 72, S.S.S 73
Designer Ronald Fream
Green fees 20.000 esc
Catering, changing room/showers, bar, club, trolley and buggy hire, shop, driving range, practice facilities
Visitors welcome
Handicap certificate required – limit: 28 men, 45 women
Societies welcome by prior arrangement

PRAIA D'EL REY GOLF & COUNTRY CLUB

Vale de Janelas, Apartado 2, 2510 Obidos, Portugal
✆ (262) 905005 Fax (262) 905009
educla@mail.telepac.pt
www.praia-del-rey.com
IC1 Lisbon to Obidos, N114 to Peniche, following signs for Serra d'El Rey
Founded 1997
In a remarkably short time this stunning course has been acclaimed as one of the best – and most testing – links in Europe. The rough (gorse, tough grasses and sandy wastes) can be vicious, and the wind will almost always play a significant role. The finish from the 15th probes relentlessly.
18 holes, 6467 metres
par 72, S.S.S 72
Designer Cabell Robinson
Green fees 9500 esc
Catering, changing room/showers, bar, club, trolley and buggy hire, shop, practice facilities
Visitors welcome
Handicap certificate required
Societies by arrangement

QUINTA DA MARINHA HOTEL VILLAGE RESORT

Casa 36, 2750 Cascais, Portugal
✆ (21) 486 9881 Fax (21) 486 9032
marinhagolf@mail.telepac.pt
N247, 5m W of Cascais
Founded 1984
Only now is this Trent Jones course, in a magnificent site overlooking the sea, beginning to deliver its potential. The 13th, working down to a green hanging above the sea, is perhaps the signature hole, but the double dog-leg 6th and 10th demand fullest attention.
18 holes, 6014 metres
par 71, S.S.S 71
Designer Robert Trent Jones
Green fees 8500 ecs
Catering, changing room/showers, bar, club, trolley and buggy hire, shop, driving range, practice facilities
Visitors welcome – handicap certificate required weekends and holidays
Handicap certificate required
Societies by arrangement

QUINTA DO LAGO

Campo de Golfe, Quinta do Lago, 8135 Almancil, Algarve, Portugal
(289) 390700 Fax (289) 394013
Quinta Do Lago Estate 20 Km W Of Faro
Founded 1974
Laid out on undulating, sandy ground, and shaded by umbrella pines, this is a frequent host to the Portuguese Open. The 15th, a 200-metre par-3, stands out, but the 10th and 18th are also splendid par 4s on a high quality course.
18 holes, 6488 metres
par 72, S.S.S 73
Designer William Mitchell
Green fees 13000 esc
Catering, changing room/showers, bar, club, trolley and buggy hire, shop, driving range, practice facilities, riding, watersports, tennis
Visitors welcome
Handicap certificate required

QUINTA DO PERU

2830 Quinta do Conde, Portugal
(21) 213 4320 Fax (21) 213 4321
golf@quinta-do-peru.com
N10, 10km W of Setubal
Founded 1994
Showing admirable restraint, Rocky Roquemore has made maximum strategic use of the old pines and rolling hills of this handsome site. He has supplemented nature with a number of lakes and plentiful sand. Many sloping greens deceive, and the par-3 8th and 16th both demand all-or-nothing carries over water.
18 holes, 6036 metres
par 72, S.S.S 72
Designer Rocky Roquemore
Green fees 12000 esc
Catering, changing room/showers, bar, club, trolley and buggy hire, shop, driving range, practice facilities
Visitors welcome
Handicap certificate required – limit: 28 men, 36 women
Societies by arrangement

RIA FORMOSA

Quinta do Lago, 8135 Almancil, Algarve, Portugal
(289) 390700 Fax (289) 394013
Quinta Do Lago Estate 20 Km W of Faro
Founded 19741989
Originally part of a 36-hole complex at Quinta do Lago, but now established as a separate course, Ria Formosa enjoys a similar rolling, wooded terrain. A lake forms the angle of the dog-leg on the 12th, and the final drive must be made over water to a sloping fairway.
18 holes, 6205 metres
par 72, S.S.S 73
Designer William Mitchell, Joseph Lee
Green fees 13000 esc
Catering, changing room/showers, bar, club, trolley and buggy hire, shop, driving range, practice facilities, riding, watersports, tennis
Visitors welcome
Handicap certificate required
Societies by arrangement

SAN LORENZO

Quinta do Lago, 8135 Almancil, Algarve, Portugal
(289) 396522 Fax (289) 396908
Quinta do Lago Estate, 20 km W of Faro
Founded 1988
One of Europe's great courses, roaming pine-clad, sandy hills, yet breaking out for a stunning run of holes along the banks of the Ria Formosa: the 6th, 7th and 8th are breathtaking. The finish, alongside a lagoon, is magical, with the final approach made over water to an island green.
18 holes, 6238 metres
par 72, S.S.S 73
Designer Joseph Lee
Green fees 24500 esc
Catering, changing room/showers, bar, club, trolley and buggy hire, shop, driving range, practice facilities
Visitors – priority for Meridien Hotel guests, other vistors restricted
Handicap certificate required – limit: 28 men, 36 ladies

TROIA GOLF

Complexo Turistica de Tróia, 7570 Grândola, Portugal
(265) 499335 Fax (265) 494315
15 km S of Setubal
Founded 1980
Thought by many to be Portugal's toughest course, but known to only a few because it lies away from the main tourist haunts. New management promises to restore the course to peak condition. With pine-lined fairways running through wild dunes Tróia has much in common with Formby – a high commendation.
18 holes, 6337 metres
par 72, S.S.S 74
Designer Robert Trent Jones
Green fees 5500 esc
Catering, changing room/showers, bar, club and trolley hire, shop, driving range, practice facilities
Visitors welcome
Societies by arrangement

GOLDEN EAGLE GOLF & COUNTRY CLUB

Quinta do Brinçal, Arrouquelas, 2040 Rio Maior, Portugal
(243) 908148 Fax (243) 908149
60km N of Lisbon on IC2
Founded 1994
For several years after its foundation, the club maintained a policy of exclusivity, which meant that few visitors were able to sample the many delights of this extremely beautiful course in rolling woodland – quite unlike the brasher resort courses of the Algarve. Now the situation has changed, and a visit is warmly recommended.
18 holes, 5997 metres, par 72, S.S.S.72
Designer Rocky Roquemore
Green fees 8000 esc
Catering, changing room/showers, bar, club and trolley hire, shop, driving range
Visitors welcome with prior reservation
Societies by arrangement

VALE DO LOBO OCEAN COURSE

Parque do Golfe, 8135-864 Vale do Lobo Codex, Algarve, Portugal
(289) 393939 Fax (289) 353003
golf@etvdla.pt
www.valedolobo.pt
6 km SW of Almancil
Founded 1968
Sir Henry Cotton's original Vale de Lobo course was split into two in 1987, with his back nine surviving as the back nine of the new Ocean course. It is particularly handsome, with pines and figs lining the fairways, two of which tumble down to beach-side greens. Bring the camera!
18 holes, 5424 metres
par 71, S.S.S 71
Designer Sir Henry Cotton
Green fees 18000 esc
Catering, changing room/showers, bar, club, trolley and buggy hire, shop, driving range, practice facilities
Visitors welcome – strict dress code
Handicap certificate required
Societies by arrangement

VALE DO LOBO ROYAL COURSE

Parque do Golfe, 8135-864 Vale do Lobo Codex, Algarve, Portugal
(289) 393939 Fax (289) 353003
golf@etvdlo.pt
www.valedolobo.pt
6 km SW of Almancil
Founded 1968
The 205-metre 16th is, without

question, the best-known hole in Portugal, played along the cliff-tops with a series of ravines plunging to the beach if the carry to the green is unsuccessful. But the rest of the course is less spectacular and hemmed in by a sprawling housing development.
18 holes, 6050 metres
par 72, S.S.S 72
Designer Sir Henry Cotton, Rocky Roquemore
Green fees 22000 esc
Catering, changing room/showers, bar, club, trolley and buggy hire, shop, driving range, practice facilities
Visitors welcome – strict dress code
Handicap certificate required – limit: 27 men, 35 ladies
Societies by arrangement

VILA SOL

Alto do Semino, 8125 Quarteira, Algarve, Portugal
✆ (289) 300505 Fax (289) 300592
20 km W of Faro via EN125 and N396
Founded 1991
The professionals who contested the 1992 and 1993 Portuguese Opens here were full of praise for the strength of the design and the excellence of the greens. Water hazards are plentiful and the fairways are narrow, bordered by pines, figs, oaks and almonds. The first four holes are particularly demanding.
18 holes, 6267 metres
par 72, S.S.S 72
Designer Donald Steel
Green fees 15000 esc
Catering, changing room/showers, bar, club, trolley and buggy hire, shop, driving range, practice facilities, tennis and beach club
Visitors welcome
Handicap certificate required – limit: 27 men, 35 ladies
Societies by arrangement

VILAMOURA LAGUNA COURSE

Vilamoura, 8125 Quarteira, Algarve, Portugal
✆ (289) 310180 Fax (289) 310183
www.vilamoura.net
20 km W of Faro via EN125
Founded 1990
Recently assembled from part of a previous 27-hole complex at Vilamoura, the Laguna course is quite different from its neighbours, with lake and marshland holes near the sea, and inland holes of a more heathland nature. Heroics are required on the 4th, 5th, 14th and 15th – treacherous water holes.
18 holes, 6133 metres
par 72, S.S.S 73
Designer Joseph Lee, Rocky Roquemore
Green fees 11500 esc
Catering, changing room/showers, bar, club, trolley and buggy hire, shop, driving range, practice facilities
Visitors welcome
Handicap certificate required – limit: 28 men, 36 ladies
Societies by arrangement

VILAMOURA OLD COURSE

Vilamoura, 8125 Quarteira, Algarve, Portugal
✆ (289) 310341 Fax (289) 310321
www.vilamoura.net
20 km W of Faro via EN125
Founded 1969
The grand old lady of the Algarve, a classic of restrained design, recently refurbished to peak condition. Frank Pennink employed individual trees brilliantly to block out the second shots of those who have driven thoughtlessly. All four short holes are first-rate, with the beautiful 4th played across water and sand.
18 holes, 6254 metres
par 73, S.S.S 72
Designer Frank Pennink, Martin Hawtree
Green fees 20000 esc
Catering, changing room/showers, bar, club, trolley and buggy hire, shop, driving range, practice facilities
Visitors welcome
Handicap certificate required – limit: 24 men, 28 ladies
Societies by arrangement

VILAMOURA PINHAL COURSE

Vilamoura, 8125 Quarteira, Algarve, Portugal
✆ (289) 310390 Fax (289) 310393
www.vilamoura.net
20 km W of Faro via EN125
Founded 1976
With input from three architects at varying stages of its development, Pinhal is a mixture of two quite different styles. The surviving Pennink holes are woodland in character, not unlike Vilamoura's Old Course. The newer holes are in a more blatant, American style with plentiful moundwork, and open, rolling fairways.
18 holes, 6206 metres
par 72, S.S.S 71
Designer Frank Pennink, Robert Trent Jones, Martin Hawtree
Green fees 12500 esc
Catering, changing room/showers, bar, club, trolley and buggy hire, shop, driving range, practice facilities
Visitors welcome
Handicap certificate required – limit: 28 men, 36 ladies
Societies by arrangement

SPAIN

ALCAIDESA LINKS GOLF COURSE

Apdo de Correos 125, E–11360 San Roque, Cadiz, Spain
✆ 956 791 040 Fax 956 791 041
15km E of Gibraltar
Founded 1991
The nearest thing to a links course to be found in southern Spain, Alcaidesa enjoys fabulous views along the curving Mediterranean shoreline to the Rock of Gibraltar, with the sea visible from all parts of the course. Many greens are raised up, as at Dornoch, and deep, pot bunkers abound.
18 holes, 6158 metres
par 72, S.S.S 71
Designer Peter Alliss, Clive Clark
Green fees 9000 P
Catering, changing room/showers, bar, club, trolley and buggy hire, shop, driving range, practice facilities
Visitors welcome by prior arrangement
Handicap certificate required – limit: 28 men, 36 women
Societies welcome by prior arrangement

CLUB DE GOLF ALOHA

Nueva Andalucia, E-29660 Marbella, Malaga, Spain
✆ 952 813 750 Fax 952 812 389
7 km NW of Marbella
Founded 1975
Aloha was the last course designed by the great Javier Araña, very much a members' club for the wealthy of Marbella and Puerto Banus. The substantial green fee reflects this, but the condition is commensurate. Backed by the mountains, Aloha is visually attractive, with tight, hilly fairways and wicked greens.
18 holes, 6242 metres
par 72, S.S.S 72
Designer Javier Araña
Green fees 18000 P
Catering, changing room/showers, bar, club, trolley and buggy hire, shop, driving range, 9-hole short course
Visitors welcome, with booking

system
Handicap certificate required

ARO-MAS NOU

Apdo 429, E-17250 Playa de Aro, Spain
☎ 972 816 727 Fax 972 826 906
Off C250, 35 km SE of Girona
Founded 1990
325 metres up, on the mountain tops overlooking the Costa Brava, Mas Nou gives spectacular views in every direction, without being excessively hilly. The design is controversial, with a number of sharp dog-legs and big drops into oblivion. Generally, it is an advantage to be able to fade the ball.
18 holes, 6218 metres
par 72
Designer Ramón Espinosa
Green fees 6500 P
Catering, changing room/showers, bar, club, trolley and buggy hire, shop, driving range, practice facilities, 9-hole par-3 course
Visitors welcome
Handicap certificate required

EL BOSQUE GOLF & COUNTRY CLUB

Carretera de Godelleta, E-46370 Chiva, Valencia, Spain
☎ 961 808 000 Fax 961 808 001
Off N111, 24 km W of Valencia
Founded 1975
El Bosque figured briefly on the European Tour schedule in the 1990s, with Vijay Singh amongst the winners. It is an American-style layout with big, heavily sculpted bunkers and multiple tees, allowing the course to be played at many different lengths. Hilly fairways, dog-legs and lakes contribute to the difficulty.
18 holes, 6367 metres
par 72, S.S.S 74
Designer Robert Trent Jones Sr
Green fees 8000 P
Catering, changing room/showers, bar, club, trolley and buggy hire, shop, driving range
Visitors welcome
Handicap certificate required – limit: 28 men, 36 women
Societies welcome by prior arrangement

REAL CLUB DE GOLF EL PRAT

Apdo 10, E-08820 El Prat de Llobregat, Barcelona, Spain
☎ 933 790 278 Fax 933 705 102
15 km S of Barcelona, beside Barcelona Airport
Founded 1954
The procession of noisy airliners overhead can be distracting, but there is no gainsaying the high quality of the golf. Araña's lovely old course is the one used for Spanish Opens, still held here from time to time. The best holes, such as Araña's 14th, call for precisely shaped shots.
Recorrido Amarillo: 18 holes, 6172 metres, par 72, S.S.S 73
Designer Dave Thomas
Recorrido Verde: 18 holes, 6224 metres, par 73, S.S.S 74
Designer Javier Araña
Green fees 12380 P
Catering, changing room/showers, bar, club, trolley and buggy hire, shop, driving range, practice facilities
Visitors welcome
Handicap certificate required – limit: 28 men, 36 ladies

CAMPO DE GOLF EL SALER

Parador Nacional Luis Vivès, E-46012 El Saler, Valencia, Spain
☎ 961 610 384 Fax 961 627 016
V15, 18 km SE of Valencia
Founded 1968
Javier Araña's masterpiece, one of Europe's great courses, is a brilliant combination of links and woodland holes on the shores of the Mediterranean. Good course management is required to negotiate the dog-legs of the fragrant pine forest, while, on the links holes, savage rough, billowing dunes and undulating fairways prevail.
18 holes, 6485 metres
par 72, S.S.S 75
Designer Javier Araña
Green fees 8000 P
Catering, changing room/showers, bar, club, trolley and buggy hire, shop, practice facilities
Visitors welcome
Societies welcome by prior arrangement

EMPORDA

Ctra de Palafrugell a Torroella, E-17257 Gualta, Girona, Spain
☎ 972 760 450 Fax 972 757 100
Off C255, 40 km E of Girona
Founded 1991
A full 36 holes will soon be on offer at this continuing development near much-loved Pals. Robert von Hagge's design skills are in evidence, with moundwork, water, and his characteristic long, rolling greens. The condition is first rate, and the course length can be varied by more than 1000 metres.
18 holes, 6160 metres
par 71, S.S.S 71
Designer Robert von Hagge
Green fees 9000 P
Catering, changing room/showers, bar, club, trolley and buggy hire, shop, driving range, additional 9-hole course
Visitors welcome
Handicap certificate required – limit: 28 men, 36 women

ESCORPION

Apartado de Correos No 1, E-46117 Betera, Valencia, Spain
☎ 961 601 211 Fax 961 690 187
Off C 234, 20 km NW of Valencia
Founded 1975
Escorpión is an unusual course in that almost every hole, apart from the par 3s, is a dog-leg, a consequence of routing the fairways through orange groves laid out geometrically. Water is a factor on many holes, although the bunkering is less penal than on some of the newer courses.
18 holes, 6345 metres
par 72, S.S.S 73
Designer Ron Kirby
Green fees 8000 P
Catering, changing room/showers, bar, club, trolley and buggy hire, shop, driving range
Visitors welcome
Handicap certificate required – limit: 28 men, 36 women

GRANADA CLUB DE GOLF

Avda de los Corsarios, 1, E-18110 Las Gabias, Granada, Spain
☎ 958 584 436 Fax 958 584 060
8 km SW of Granada
Founded 1986
Newly improved roads have put the Alhambra and Granada's Moorish quarter of Albaicin within easy reach of the airport at Malaga. Ramón Espinosa's course here is now as accessible as Sotogrande. Set off against the high mountains of the Sierra Nevada, the course provides a complete test at all levels.
18 holes, 6037 metres
par 71, S.S.S 73
Designer Ramón Espinosa
Green fees 5000 P
Catering, changing room/showers, bar, club and buggy hire, shop, driving range
Visitors welcome

CLUB DE GOLF GUADALMINA

Urb. Guadalmina Alta, E-29678 San Pedro De Alcántara, Malaga, Spain
☎ 952 886 522 Fax 952 883 483
N340, 12 km SW of Marbella
Founded 1959
The South was one of the earliest championship courses south of Madrid. It charms, where more

challenging courses might not, with the 10th green right by the water's edge, giving glorious views to Gibraltar. The shorter North Course follows the Arroyo del Chapo, with tighter fairways in more parkland style.
North Course: 18 holes, 5825 metres, S.S.S 70
Designer Falco Nardi
South Course: 18 holes, 6075 metres, par 72, S.S.S 72
Designer Javier Araña
Green fees 8000 P
Catering, changing room/showers, bar, club, trolley and buggy hire, shop, driving range, practice facilities, 9-hole par-3 course
Visitors welcome
Handicap certificate required – limit: 28 men, 36 women

LA CALA RESORT

La Cala de Mijas, E-29647 Mijas Costa, Malaga, Spain
☎ 952 669 033 Fax 952 669 039
Off N340, 10 km from Mijas
Founded 1990
La Cala is a gem for those fit enough to play the two courses here, up in the mountains, a short distance inland from Fuengirola. True, buggies are available for hire, but, to be at one with the buzzards and eagles, one should walk. The shorter South Course is tougher.
North Course: 18 holes, 6187 metres, par 72
South Course: 18 holes, 5960 metres, par 71
Designer Cabell Robinson
Green fees 8000 P
Catering, changing room/showers, bar, accommodation, club and buggy hire, shop, practice facilities
Visitors welcome
Handicap certificate required – limit: 28 men, 36 women

GOLF & COUNTRY CLUB LA DUQUESA

Urb El Hacho, E-29691 Manilva, Malaga, Spain
☎ 952 890 425 Fax 952 890 057
Off N340, 15 km SW of Estepona
Founded 1987
On the hillsides of La Duquesa, Robert Trent Jones could have built a forbidding course, playable only by the great. Instead, he tempered the bunkering and greens, for few approaches here are made from level ground. Nevertheless, a strong nerve is frequently called for to drive to angled, sloping fairways.
18 holes, 6142 metres
par 72
Designer Robert Trent Jones
Green fees 6000 P
Catering, changing room/showers, bar, club and buggy hire, shop, driving range, practice facilities
Visitors welcome
Handicap certificate required – limit: 28 men, 36 women

HYATT LA MANGA CLUB GOLF RESORT

Los Belones, E-30385 Cartagena, Murcia, Spain
☎ 968 331 234 Fax 968 331 235
30 km E of Cartagena
Founded 1970
Three golf courses, five-star hotel, real estate, and every imaginable sporting facility from tennis courts to horse riding are just some of the features of this self-contained resort. It was the South Course, in its early days, which hosted five Spanish Opens in succession, with the great Arnold Palmer triumphing in 1975.
South Course: 18 holes, 6361 metres, par 72, S.S.S 73
Designer Robert Dean Puttnam
West Course: 18 holes, 5971 metres, par 71, S.S.S 72
Designer Dave Thomas
North Course: 18 holes, 5780 metres, par 71, S.S.S 70
Designer Robert Dean Puttnam
Green fees 20000 P
Catering, changing room/showers, bar, accommodation, club, trolley and buggy hire, shop, driving range, practice facilities
Visitors welcome
Handicap certificate required for South Course

REAL CLUB DE GOLF LAS BRISAS

Apartado 147, E-29660 Nueva Andalucia, Marbella, Spain
☎ 952 810 875 Fax 952 815 518
15 km W of Marbella
Founded 1968
One of the earliest courses to introduce American-style target golf to Europe, Las Brisas follows a valley running down from the Sierra Blanca mountains towards the sea. Water is used to telling effect, especially on the par-5 12th, on which only the strongest might risk a do-or-die eagle attempt.
18 holes, 6163 metres
par 72, S.S.S 72
Designer Robert Trent Jones
Green fees 18000 P
Catering, changing room/showers, bar, club, trolley and buggy hire, shop, driving range, practice facilities
Visitors welcome – with restrictions
Handicap certificate required – limit: 28 men, 36 women

CLUB DE CAMPO MEDITERRANEO

Urb La Coma, E-12190 Borriol, Castellón de la Plana, Spain
☎ 964 321 227 Fax 964 321 357
5 km NW of Castellon de la Plana
Founded 1978
Castellón is a busy working town of little visual interest. It would hardly attract holiday vistors. That is why Mediterraneo remains one of the least celebrated of the excellent courses on this part of the Mediterranean coast. Its par 4s may be short, but beware the par 3s and 5s!
18 holes, 6239 metres
par 72, S.S.S 73
Designer Ramon Espinosa
Green fees 6000 P
Catering, changing room/showers, bar, club, trolley and buggy hire, shop, practice facilities
Visitors welcome
Handicap certificate required – limit: 28 men, 36 women

MIJAS GOLF INTERNATIONAL

Apdo de Coreos 145, E-29640 Fuengirola, Malaga, Spain
☎ 952 476 843 Fax 952 467 943
MA 426, 4 km NW of Fuengirola
Founded 1976
Probably the busiest courses on the Costa del Sol, which is more a tribute to their popularity, efficient management, and high standards of green-keeping than potential criticism. Los Lagos lives up to its name, with eight lakes and abundant wildlife, while the shorter Los Olivos is hillier, with smaller greens.
Los Lagos: 18 holes, 6367 metres, par 71, S.S.S 74
Los Olivos: 18 holes, 6009 metres, par 72, S.S.S 72
Designer Robert Trent Jones
Green fees 8000 P
Catering, changing room/showers, bar, club, trolley and buggy hire, shop, practice facilities
Visitors welcome, booking required
Handicap certificate required – limit: 28 men, 36 women

MONTECASTILLO HOTEL & GOLF RESORT

Carratera de Arcos, E-11406 Jérez de la Frontera, Cadiz, Spain
☎ 956 151 200 Fax 956 151 209
N342, 10 km NE of Jérez de la Frontera
Founded 1992
The Volvo Masters, one of the big money tournaments at the end of

the European professional season has been held at Montecastillo since 1997, when Lee Westwood won. Here, in sherry country, the scenery is unspectacular, but there is plenty of undulation in the ground, Nicklaus's design taking full advantage.
18 holes, 6494 metres
par 72, S.S.S 72
Designer Jack Nicklaus
Green fees 9000 P
Catering, changing room/showers, bar, accommodation, club and buggy hire, shop, driving range, practice facilities
Visitors welcome – hotel guests have priority
Handicap certificate required – limit: 28 men, 36 women

GOLF NOVO SANCTI PETRI

Urb Novo Sancti Petri, E-11139 Chiclana de la Frontera, Cadiz, Spain
✆ 956 494 005 Fax 956 494 350
www.golf-novosancti.es
24 km SW of Cadiz, between Novo Sancti Petri and La Barrosa
Founded 1991
The first course in Spain designed by its greatest golfer, Severiano Ballesteros. A further nine holes will open soon to give two full courses of equal length and difficulty. Ballesteros has created tight fairways, bordered by new plantations and water, putting a premium on driving accuracy. The greens are expansive.
18 holes, 6510 metres, par 72, S.S.S 74
Designer Severiano Ballesteros
9 holes, 3250 metres, par 36, S.S.S 37
Green fees 8500 P
Catering, changing room/showers, bar, club and buggy hire, shop, practice facilities
Visitors welcome
Handicap certificate required – limit: 28 men, 36 women

OLIVA NOVA GOLF

E-46780 Oliva, Valencia, Spain
✆ 962 855 975 Fax 962 857 667
www.olivanovagolf.es
N 322, 8 km SE of Gandia
Founded 1997
Oliva Nova is one of the more recent designs by Severiano Ballesteros, on the Mediterranean coast, roughly half-way between Valencia and Alicante. Early indications are that the greens present the biggest problem, often borrowing in more than one direction on the same green. Water, of course, is a recurrent feature.
18 holes, 6270 metres
par 72, S.S.S 73
Designer Severiano Ballesteros
Green fees 6500 P
Catering, changing room/showers, bar, club, trolley and buggy hire, shop, practice facilities, academy course
Visitors welcome
Handicap certificate required – limit: 28 men, 36 women

PALS

Carretera de Pals, E-17256 Pals, Girona, Spain
✆ 972 636 006 Fax 972 637 009
Off C255, 40 km E of Girona
Founded 1966
Pals has been established so long in Spanish golfing folklore that it has acquired something of the status of Sunningdale – undoubtedly great, but not quite long enough for the contemporary professional. The Spanish and Girona Opens have been played here, but, for the amateur, it remains a great value jewel.
18 holes, 6222 metres
par 73, S.S.S 73
Designer Fred Hawtree
Green fees 6000 P
Catering, changing room/showers, bar, club and buggy hire, shop, driving range, practice facilities
Visitors welcome
Handicap certificate required – limit: 28 men, 36 women

PANORAMICA GOLF & COUNTRY CLUB

Urb Panoramica, E-12320 San Jorge, Castellón, Spain
✆ 964 493 072 Fax 964 493 063
A7 Jct 42/43, exit Vinaros, 7 km NW of Vinaros
Founded 1995
Bernhard Langer has made many friends with this superb course, half-way between Valencia and Tarragona. In many ways it looks nothing, with stumpy trees and occasional lakes to hinder progress. The plain fact is that it provides one of Spain's best tests, and costs a fraction of those more fashionable.
18 holes, 6429 metres
par 72, S.S.S 74
Designer Bernhard Langer
Green fees 5500 P
Catering, changing room/showers, bar, club, trolley and buggy hire, shop, practice facilities
Visitors welcome
Handicap certificate required – limit: 28 men, 36 women

SAN ROQUE CLUB

CN 340, E-11360 San Roque, Cadiz, Spain
✆ 956 613 030 Fax 956 613 013
www.sanroque.com
N 340 between Sotogrande (3 km) and Gibraltar (15km)
Founded 1990
For aspiring European Tour Professionals, events at San Roque can make or break them, for it is one of two final qualifying venues. Its luxurious Suites Hotel housed the members and families of both teams during the 1997 Ryder Cup matches. Immaculately maintained, not too troubled by real estate development.
18 holes, 6440 metres
par 72, S.S.S 74
Designer Dave Thomas, Tony Jacklin
Green fees 10000 P
Catering, changing room/showers, bar, accommodation, club and buggy hire, shop, practice facilities
Visitors welcome
Handicap certificate required – limit: 28 men, 36 women

REAL CLUB DE GOLF SOTOGRANDE

Paseo de Parque, E-11310 Sotogrande, Cadiz, Spain
✆ 956 795 050 Fax 956 795 029
Off N340, Between Estepona (30 km) and Gibraltar (20 km)
Founded 1964
The earlier of two great Trent Jones courses at Sotogrande – the other was developed into Valderrama – and, for many, still the yardstick by which other Costa del Sol courses are measured. Rough is almost non-existent, with the main strategic problems plainly visible: cork oaks, three lakes and perfectly positioned bunkers.
18 holes, 6224 metres, par 72, S.S.S 74
Designer Robert Trent Jones
9 holes, 1299 metres, par 29
Green fees 18,000 P
Catering, changing room/showers, bar, club, trolley and buggy hire, shop, practice facilities
Visitors welcome
Handicap certificate required – limit: 28 men, 36 women

GOLF TORREQUEBRADA

Apdo de Correos 120, E-29630 Benalmadena, Malaga, Spain
✆ 952 561 102 Fax 952 561 129
5 km NE of Fuengirola
Founded 1977
Sandwiched between the mountains and the sea, Torrequebrada is visually magnificent. All Gancedo's

courses are full of character, and Torrequebrada is no exception, with its many uncompromising tee shots to palm-lined fairways, and uplifting seascapes. Torrequebrada hosted the 1979 Spanish Open, when Dale Hayes won with a score of 278.
18 holes, 5806 metres
par 72, S.S.S 71
Designer Pepe Gancedo
Green fees 9500 P
Catering, changing room/showers, bar, club and buggy hire, shop, practice facilities
Visitors welcome
Handicap certificate required – limit: 28 men, 36 women

CLUB DE GOLF VALDERRAMA

Avda de los Cortijos, E-11310 Sotogrande, Cadiz, Spain
✆ 956 791 200 Fax 956 796 292
www.valderrama.com
Off N 340 at Sotogrande, between Estepona (30 km) and Gibraltar (18 km)
Founded 1975
It was its proprietor, Jaime Ortiz-Patino, who developed Valderrama from being simply the second course at Sotogrande into a Ryder Cup venue and the scene of the end of season multi-tour showdown, the American Express Stroke Play. Valderrama's design attracts controversy, especially the 17th, notorious for its terrifyingly treacherous green.
18 holes, 6311 metres
par 71, S.S.S 72
Designer Robert Trent Jones
Green fees 30,000 P
Catering, changing room/showers, bar, club and buggy hire, shop, practice facilities, 9-hole par-3 course
Visitors welcome – with restrictions
Handicap certificate required – limit: 28 men, 36 women

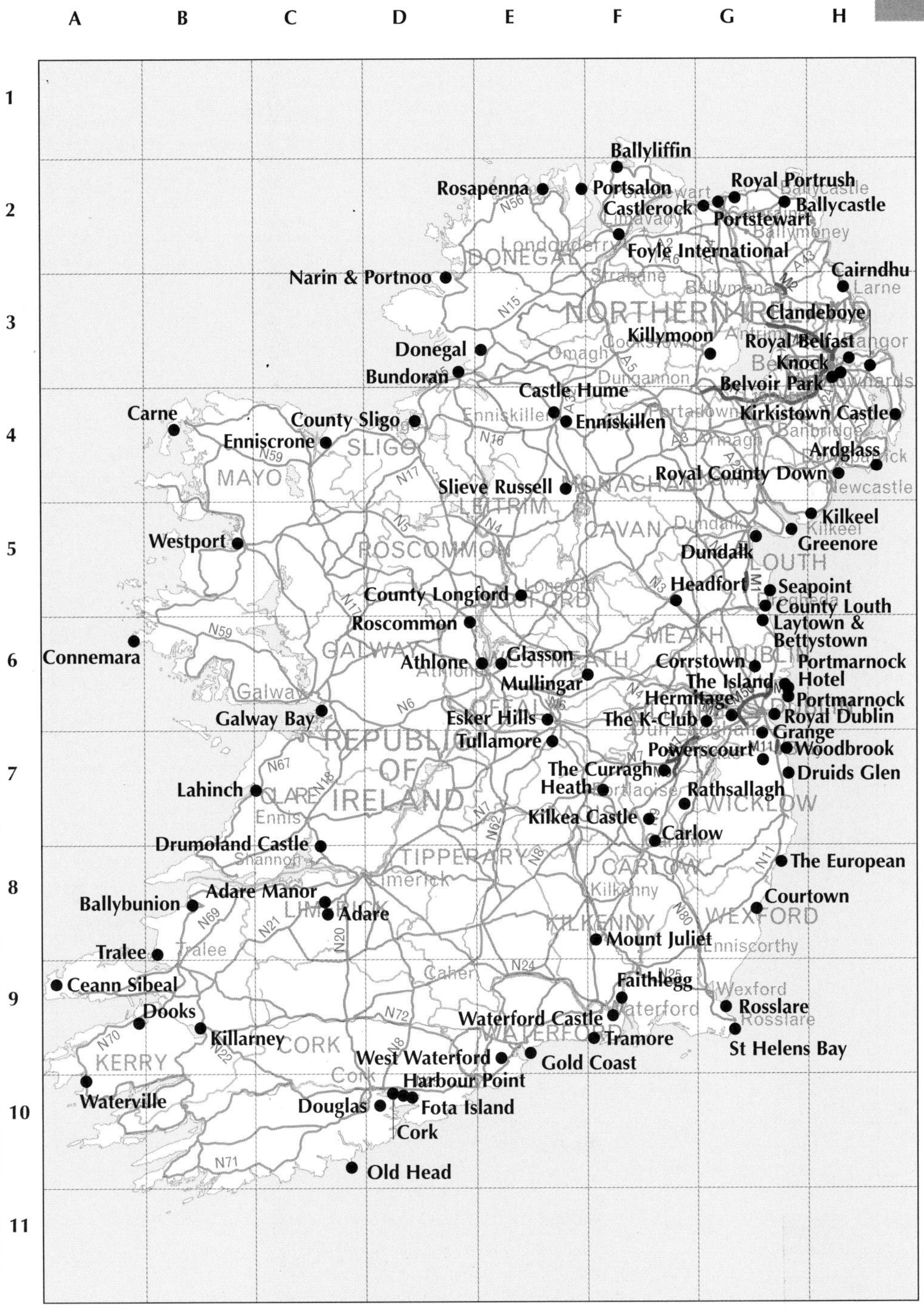

1

A B C D E F G H

1 2 3 4 5 6 7 8 9 10 11

Ballyliffin
Rosapenna
Portsalon
Royal Portrush
Castlerock
Ballycastle
Portstewart
Foyle International
Narin & Portnoo
Cairndhu
Clandeboye
Killymoon
Royal Belfast
Donegal
Knock
Bundoran
Belvoir Park
Castle Hume
Carne
County Sligo
Kirkistown Castle
Enniscrone
Enniskillen
Ardglass
Royal County Down
Slieve Russell
Kilkeel
Greenore
Westport
Dundalk
Headfort
Seapoint
County Longford
County Louth
Roscommon
Laytown & Bettystown
Connemara
Athlone
Glasson
Corrstown
Portmarnock Hotel
Mullingar
The Island
Hermitage
Portmarnock
Royal Dublin
Galway Bay
Esker Hills
The K-Club
Grange
Tullamore
Powerscourt
Woodbrook
The Curragh
Druids Glen
Lahinch
Heath
Rathsallagh
Kilkea Castle
Carlow
Drumoland Castle
The European
Adare Manor
Courtown
Ballybunion
Adare
Mount Juliet
Tralee
Ceann Sibeal
Faithlegg
Rosslare
Dooks
Waterford Castle
Killarney
Tramore
St Helens Bay
West Waterford
Gold Coast
Waterville
Harbour Point
Douglas
Fota Island
Cork
Old Head

2

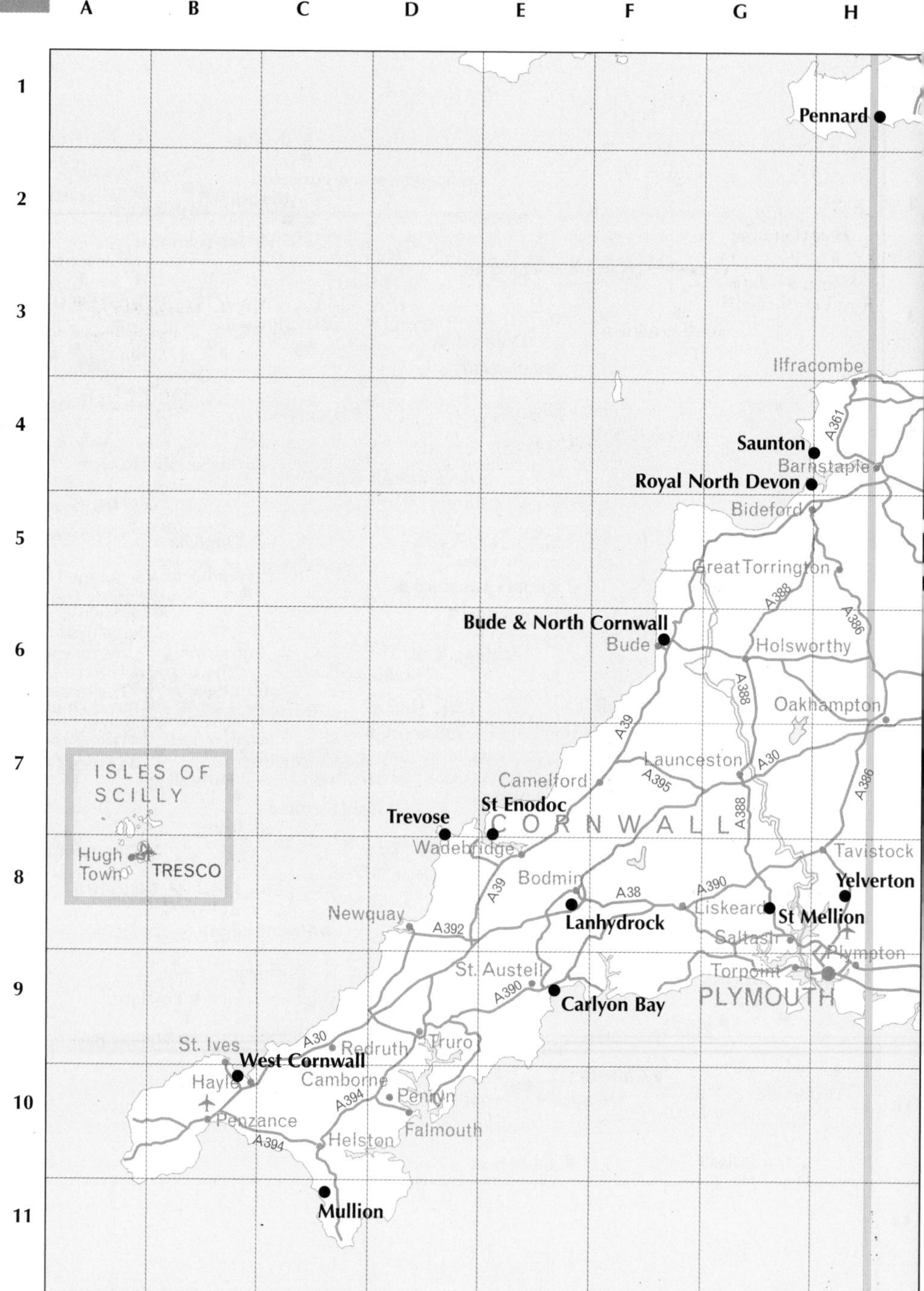
A
B
C
D
E
F
G
H
1
2
3
4
5
6
7
8
9
10
11
Pennard
Ilfracombe
A361
Saunton
Barnstaple
Royal North Devon
Bideford
Great Torrington
A388
A386
Bude & North Cornwall
Bude
Holsworthy
A388
Oakhampton
A39
Launceston
A30
A395
Camelford
A386
St Enodoc
Trevose
CORNWALL
A388
Wadebridge
Tavistock
Bodmin
Yelverton
A39
A38
A390
Lanhydrock
Liskeard
St Mellion
Newquay
A392
Saltash
Plympton
St. Austell
Torpoint
A390
Carlyon Bay
PLYMOUTH
ISLES OF SCILLY
Hugh Town
TRESCO
St. Ives
A30
Redruth
Truro
West Cornwall
Hayle
Camborne
A394
Penryn
Penzance
Falmouth
A394
Helston
Mullion

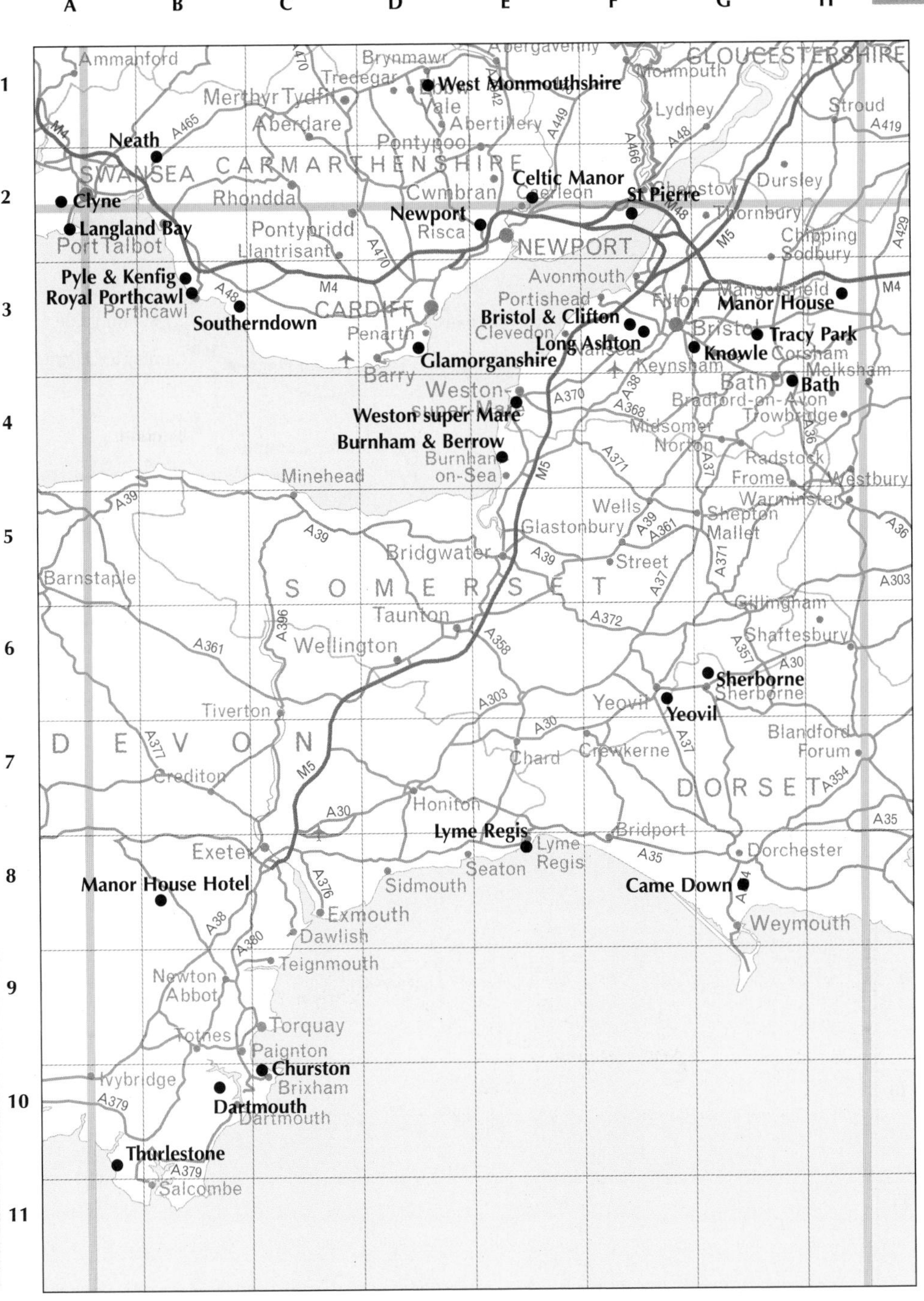
A
B
C
D
E
F
G
H
1
2
3
4
5
6
7
8
9
10
11
West Monmouthshire
Neath
Clyne
Langland Bay
Pyle & Kenfig
Royal Porthcawl
Southerndown
Celtic Manor
Newport
St Pierre
Glamorganshire
Bristol & Clifton
Long Ashton
Knowle
Manor House
Tracy Park
Bath
Weston super Mare
Burnham & Berrow
Sherborne
Yeovil
Lyme Regis
Came Down
Manor House Hotel
Churston
Dartmouth
Thurlestone
Ammanford
Brynmawr
Abergavenny
Tredegar
Merthyr Tydfil
Aberdare
Abertillery
Pontypool
Monmouth
Lydney
Stroud
Dursley
Chepstow
Thornbury
Chipping Sodbury
Mangotsfield
SWANSEA
CARMARTHENSHIRE
GLOUCESTERSHIRE
Rhondda
Cwmbran
Caerleon
Pontypridd
Risca
Llantrisant
Port Talbot
Porthcawl
NEWPORT
Avonmouth
Portishead
Filton
Bristol
CARDIFF
Penarth
Barry
Clevedon
Keynsham
Corsham
Melksham
Weston-super-Mare
Bradford-on-Avon
Trowbridge
Midsomer Norton
Radstock
Frome
Westbury
Burnham-on-Sea
Minehead
Wells
Warminster
Shepton Mallet
Glastonbury
Bridgwater
Street
Barnstaple
SOMERSET
Gillingham
Shaftesbury
Taunton
Wellington
Tiverton
Yeovil
Sherborne
DEVON
Crewkerne
Chard
Blandford Forum
Crediton
Honiton
DORSET
Bridport
Exeter
Lyme Regis
Seaton
Dorchester
Sidmouth
Exmouth
Weymouth
Dawlish
Teignmouth
Newton Abbot
Torquay
Totnes
Paignton
Ivybridge
Brixham
Dartmouth
Salcombe
M4
M5
M48
A465
A470
A48
A449
A466
A419
A429
A442
A38
A370
A368
A371
A37
A36
A39
A361
A303
A372
A358
A396
A30
A357
A377
A354
A35
A376
A380
A379

4

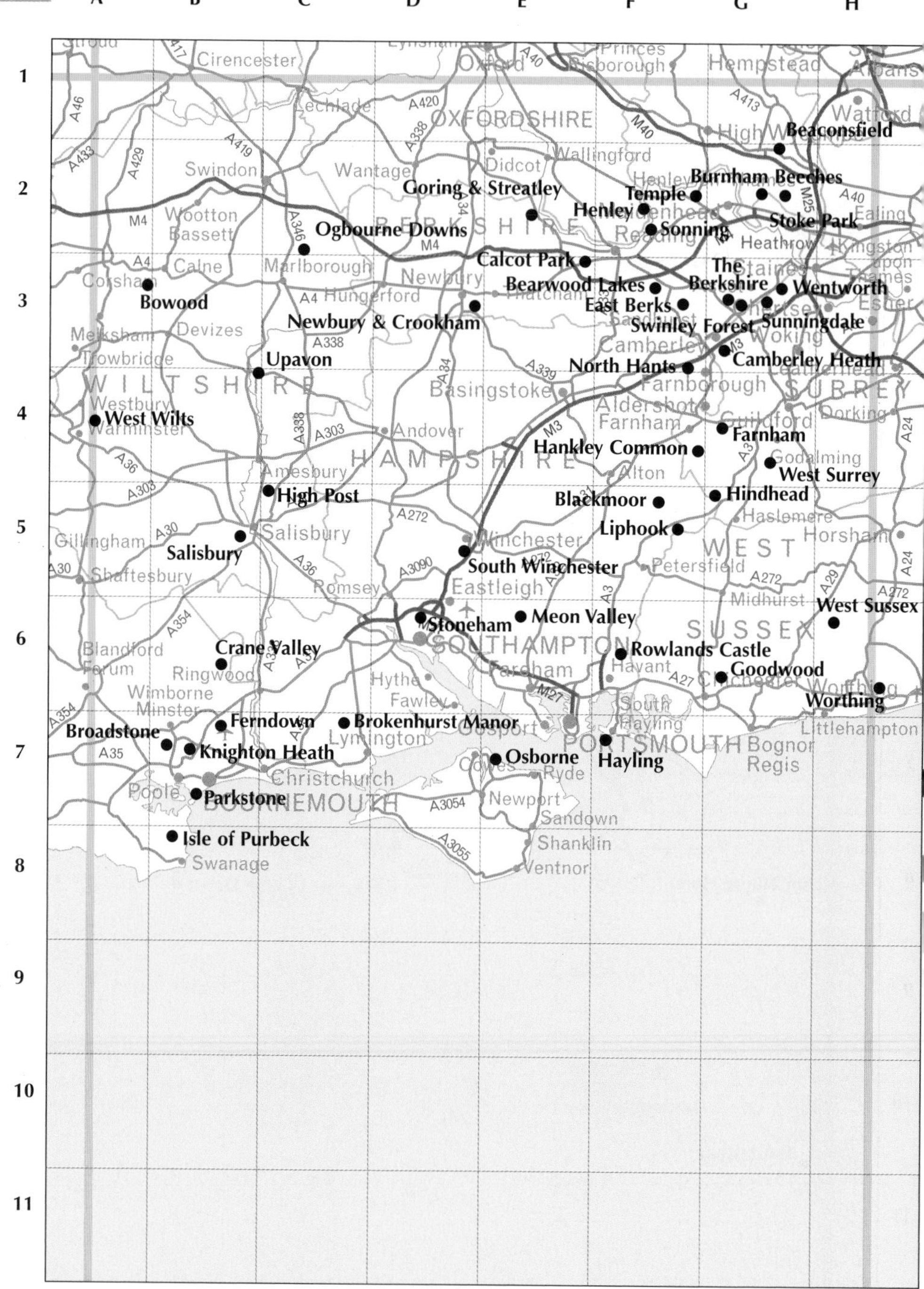

A
B
C
D
E
F
G
H
1
2
3
4
5
6
7
8
9
10
11
Beaconsfield
Goring & Streatley
Burnham Beeches
Temple
Henley
Stoke Park
Ogbourne Downs
Sonning
Calcot Park
The Berkshire
Wentworth
Bowood
Bearwood Lakes
East Berks
Newbury & Crookham
Swinley Forest
Sunningdale
Upavon
North Hants
Camberley Heath
West Wilts
Farnham
Hankley Common
West Surrey
High Post
Blackmoor
Hindhead
Liphook
Salisbury
South Winchester
Stoneham
Meon Valley
West Sussex
Crane Valley
Rowlands Castle
Goodwood
Worthing
Broadstone
Ferndown
Brokenhurst Manor
Knighton Heath
Osborne
Hayling
Parkstone
Isle of Purbeck

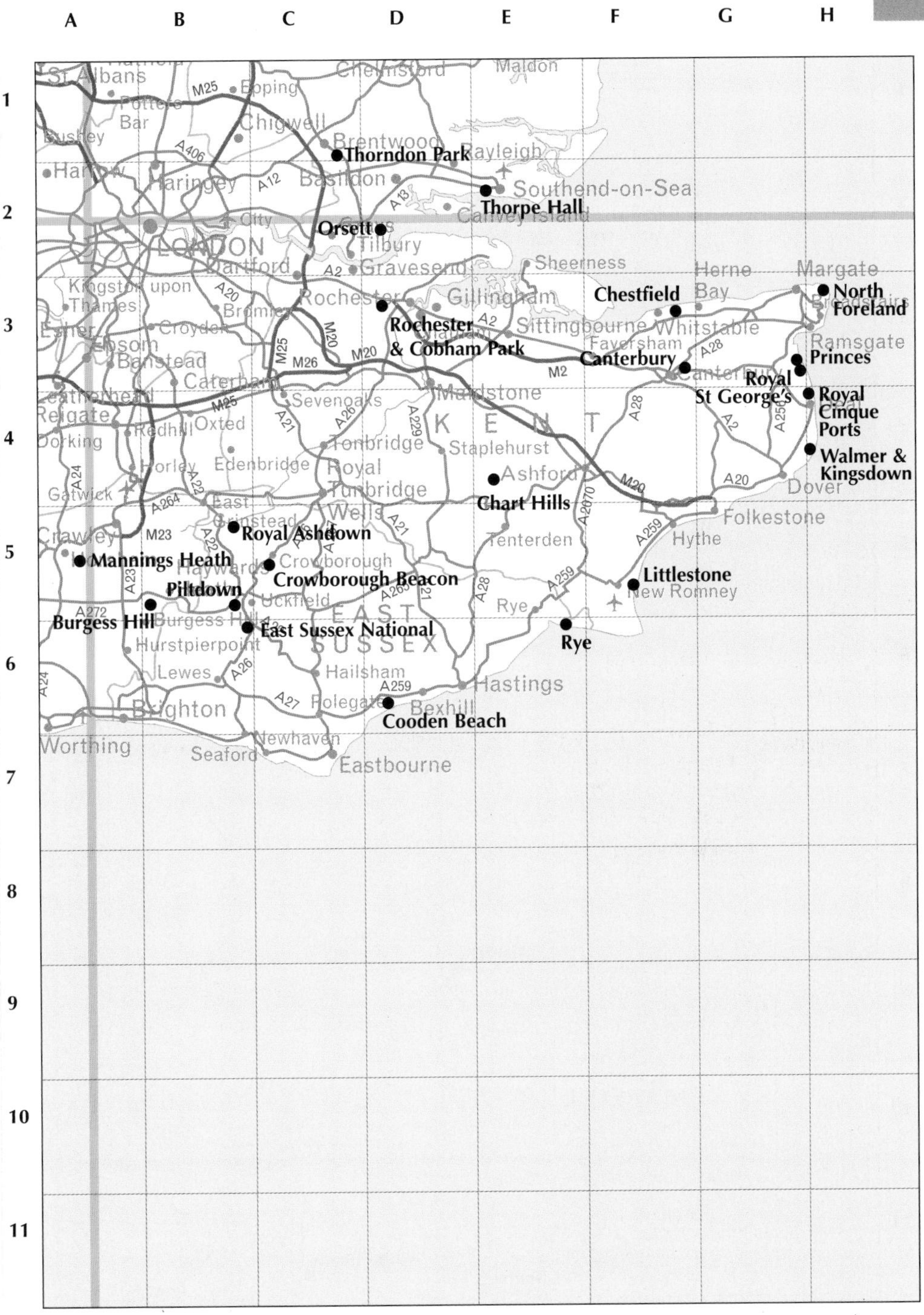

A B C D E F G H

1 2 3 4 5 6 7 8 9 10 11

Thorndon Park
Thorpe Hall
Orsett
Rochester & Cobham Park
Chestfield
North Foreland
Princes
Canterbury
Royal St George's
Royal Cinque Ports
Walmer & Kingsdown
Chart Hills
Royal Ashdown
Mannings Heath
Crowborough Beacon
Littlestone
Piltdown
Burgess Hill
East Sussex National
Rye
Cooden Beach

St Albans
Epping
Potters Bar
Chigwell
Bushey
Brentwood
Rayleigh
Maldon
Chelmsford
Harrow
Haringey
Basildon
Southend-on-Sea
Canvey Island
City
LONDON
Tilbury
Dartford
Gravesend
Sheerness
Herne Bay
Margate
Kingston upon Thames
Rochester
Gillingham
Broadstairs
Esher
Croydon
Bromley
Sittingbourne
Whitstable
Epsom
Faversham
Ramsgate
Banstead
Caterham
Canterbury
Leatherhead
Maidstone
Reigate
Sevenoaks
KENT
Dorking
Redhill
Oxted
Tonbridge
Staplehurst
Horley
Edenbridge
Royal Tunbridge Wells
Ashford
Gatwick
East Grinstead
Dover
Folkestone
Crawley
Hythe
Tenterden
Crowborough
Haywards Heath
New Romney
Uckfield
Rye
Burgess Hill
EAST SUSSEX
Hurstpierpoint
Hailsham
Hastings
Lewes
Brighton
Polegate
Bexhill
Worthing
Seaford
Newhaven
Eastbourne

M25 A406 A12 A13 A2 A20 M20 M25 M26 M2 A28 A256 A26 A229 A21 A24 A22 A264 M23 A2070 A259 A23 A272 A26 A27 A28

6

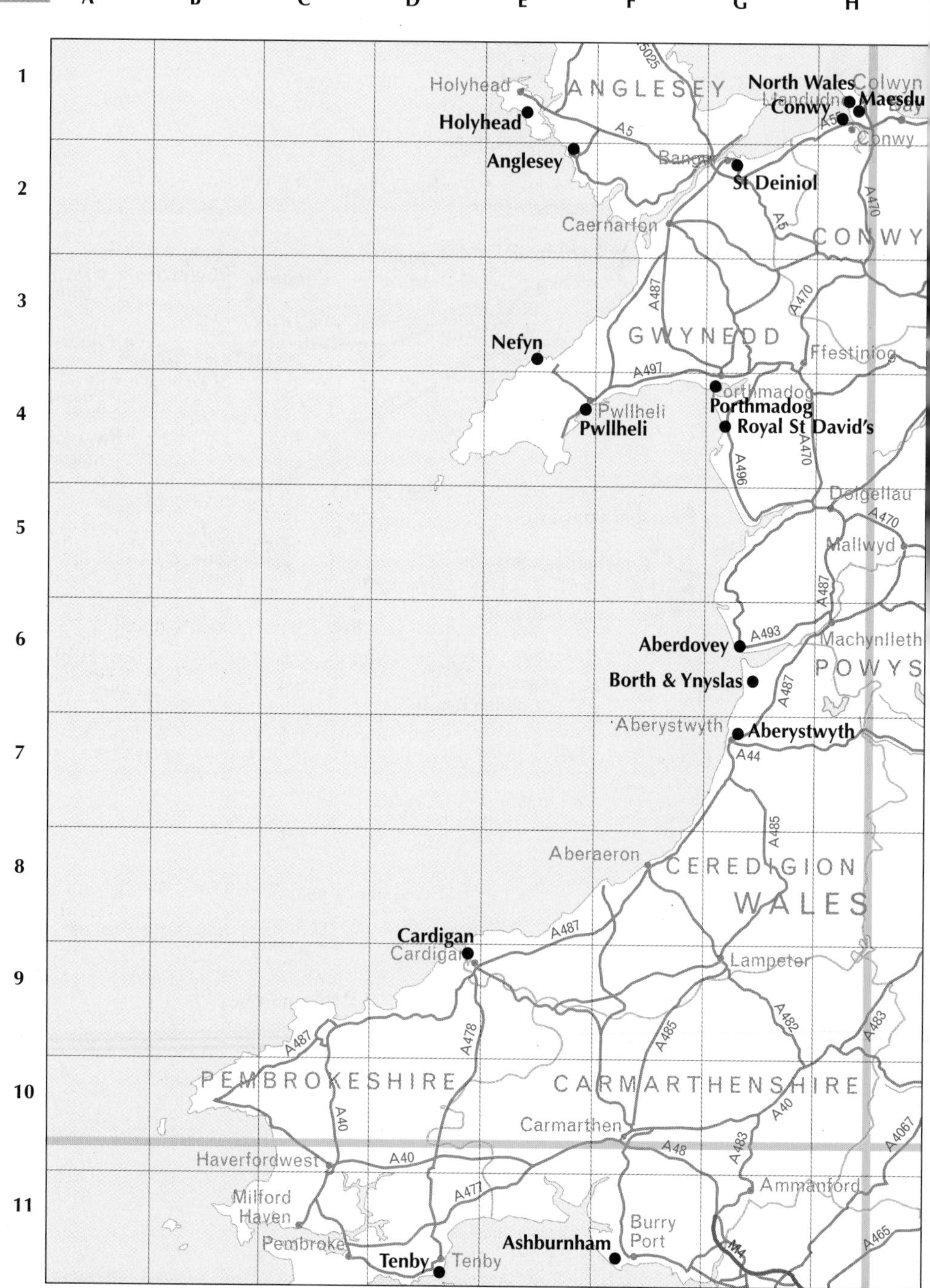
A
B
C
D
E
F
G
H
1
2
3
4
5
6
7
8
9
10
11
ANGLESEY
Holyhead
Holyhead
Anglesey
North Wales
Colwyn Bay
Maesdu
Conwy
Llandudno
Conwy
Bangor
St Deiniol
Caernarfon
CONWY
GWYNEDD
Nefyn
Ffestiniog
Porthmadog
Porthmadog
Royal St David's
Pwllheli
Pwllheli
A5
A470
A487
A497
A496
Dolgellau
Mallwyd
A493
Aberdovey
Machynlleth
POWYS
Borth & Ynyslas
Aberystwyth
Aberystwyth
A44
A485
Aberaeron
CEREDIGION
WALES
Cardigan
Cardigan
Lampeter
A482
A483
A478
PEMBROKESHIRE
CARMARTHENSHIRE
Carmarthen
A40
A48
A4067
Haverfordwest
Milford Haven
Pembroke
A477
Ammanford
Burry Port
Ashburnham
Tenby
Tenby
M4
A465

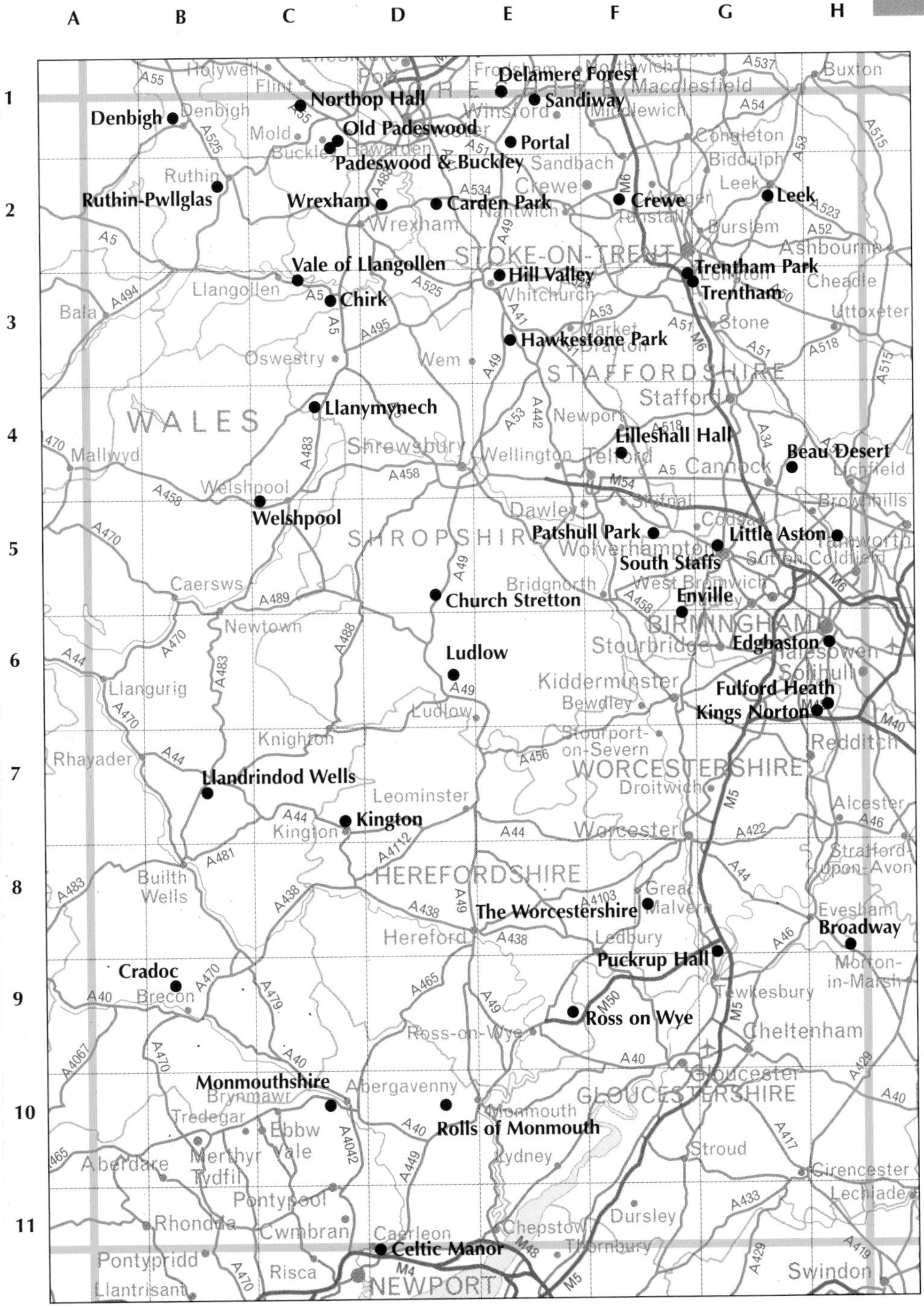
A B C D E F G H
1 2 3 4 5 6 7 8 9 10 11
Delamere Forest
Sandiway
Northop Hall
Denbigh
Old Padeswood
Portal
Padeswood & Buckley
Ruthin-Pwllglas
Wrexham
Carden Park
Crewe
Leek
Vale of Llangollen
Hill Valley
Trentham Park
Trentham
Chirk
Hawkestone Park
Llanymynech
Lilleshall Hall
Beau Desert
Welshpool
Patshull Park
Little Aston
South Staffs
Church Stretton
Enville
Edgbaston
Ludlow
Fulford Heath
Kings Norton
Llandrindod Wells
Kington
The Worcestershire
Broadway
Puckrup Hall
Cradoc
Ross on Wye
Monmouthshire
Rolls of Monmouth
Celtic Manor
WALES
SHROPSHIRE
STAFFORDSHIRE
STOKE-ON-TRENT
BIRMINGHAM
WORCESTERSHIRE
HEREFORDSHIRE
GLOUCESTERSHIRE
NEWPORT

8

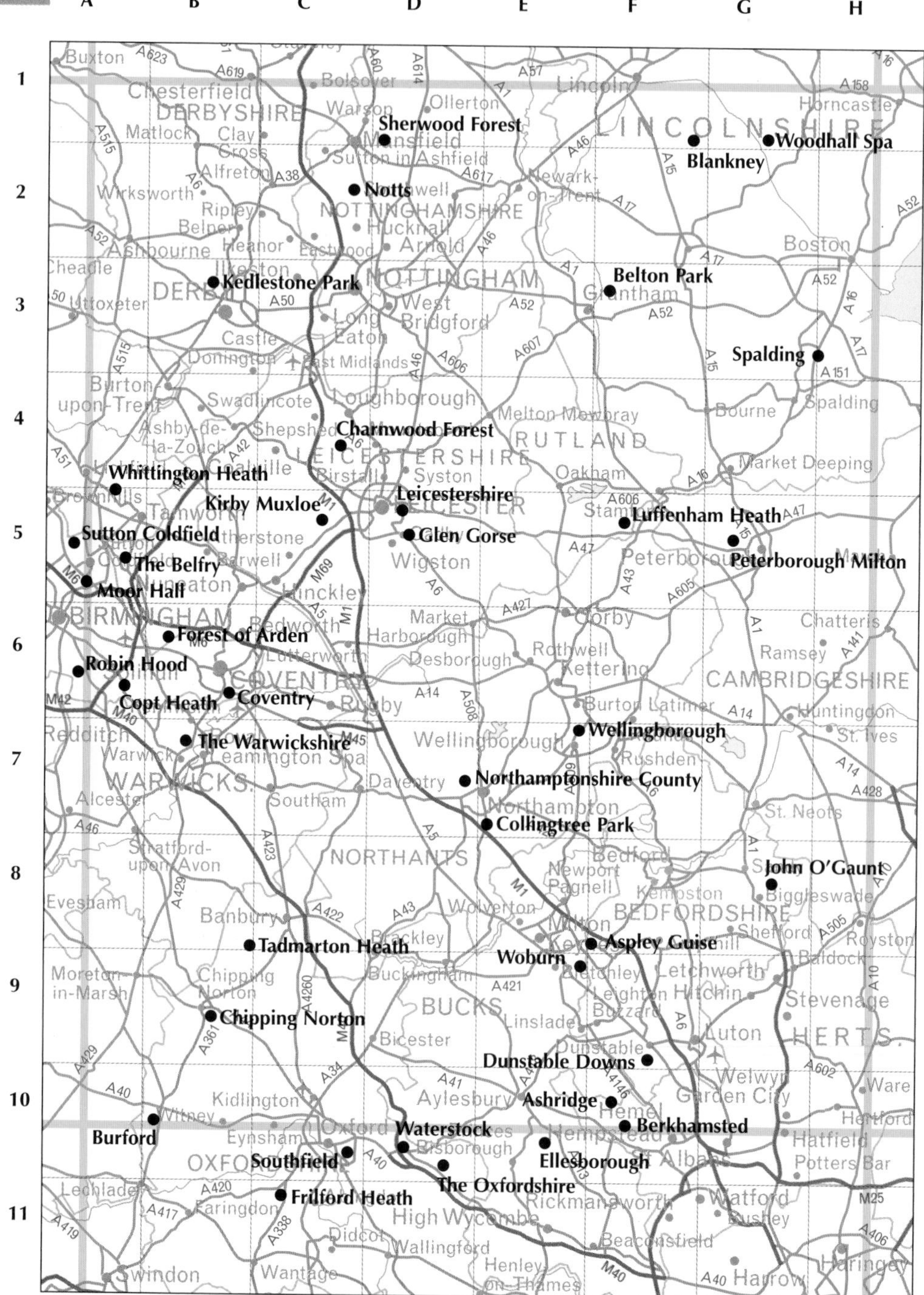
A
B
C
D
E
F
G
H
1
2
3
4
5
6
7
8
9
10
11
Sherwood Forest
Woodhall Spa
Blankney
Notts
Belton Park
Kedlestone Park
Spalding
Charnwood Forest
Whittington Heath
Leicestershire
Kirby Muxloe
Luffenham Heath
Sutton Coldfield
Glen Gorse
The Belfry
Peterborough Milton
Moor Hall
Forest of Arden
Robin Hood
Copt Heath
Coventry
Wellingborough
The Warwickshire
Northamptonshire County
Collingtree Park
John O'Gaunt
Tadmarton Heath
Aspley Guise
Woburn
Chipping Norton
Dunstable Downs
Ashridge
Burford
Waterstock
Berkhamsted
Southfield
Ellesborough
The Oxfordshire
Frilford Heath
DERBYSHIRE
LINCOLNSHIRE
NOTTINGHAMSHIRE
LEICESTERSHIRE
RUTLAND
CAMBRIDGESHIRE
WARWICKS.
NORTHANTS
BEDFORDSHIRE
BUCKS
HERTS.
OXFORDSHIRE

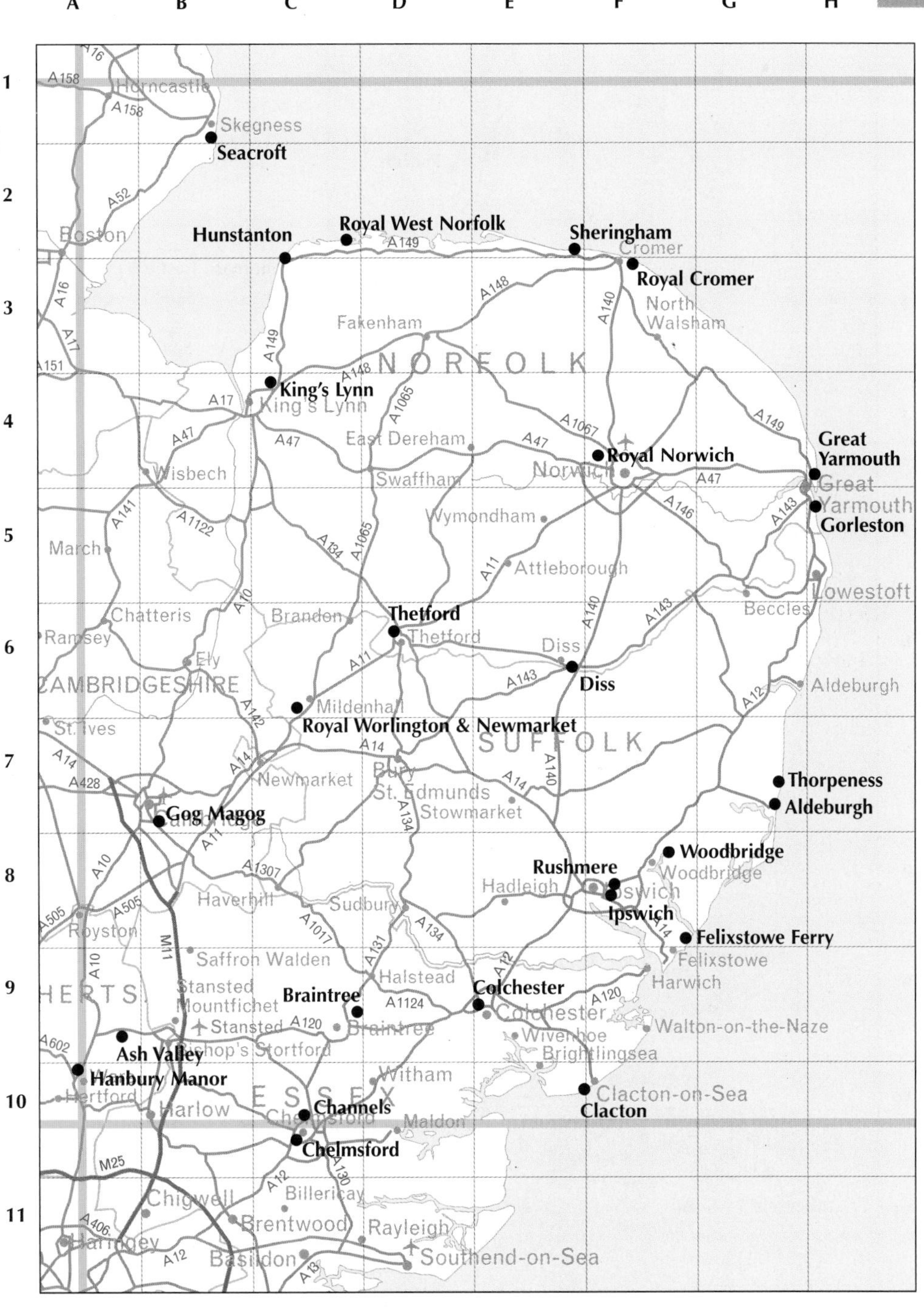
A B C D E F G H
1 2 3 4 5 6 7 8 9 10 11
Seacroft
Hunstanton
Royal West Norfolk
Sheringham
Royal Cromer
King's Lynn
Royal Norwich
Great Yarmouth
Gorleston
Thetford
Diss
Royal Worlington & Newmarket
Thorpeness
Aldeburgh
Gog Magog
Woodbridge
Rushmere
Ipswich
Felixstowe Ferry
Colchester
Braintree
Ash Valley
Hanbury Manor
Channels
Chelmsford
Clacton
NORFOLK
SUFFOLK
CAMBRIDGESHIRE
HERTS.
ESSEX
Horncastle
Skegness
Boston
Cromer
North Walsham
Fakenham
East Dereham
Swaffham
Norwich
Wisbech
March
Wymondham
Attleborough
Lowestoft
Beccles
Chatteris
Brandon
Ramsey
Ely
Mildenhall
Aldeburgh
St. Ives
Newmarket
Bury St. Edmunds
Stowmarket
Hadleigh
Haverhill
Sudbury
Royston
Saffron Walden
Halstead
Harwich
Stansted Mountfitchet
Stansted
Bishop's Stortford
Walton-on-the-Naze
Wivenhoe
Brightlingsea
Witham
Clacton-on-Sea
Hertford
Harlow
Maldon
Billericay
Chigwell
Brentwood
Rayleigh
Basildon
Southend-on-Sea
Haringey
Felixstowe
A16
A158
A52
A17
A151
A149
A148
A1065
A47
A1067
A140
A141
A1122
A134
A10
A11
A143
A146
A12
A142
A14
A428
A1307
A505
A1017
A131
A120
A1124
M11
A602
M25
A406
A130
A13

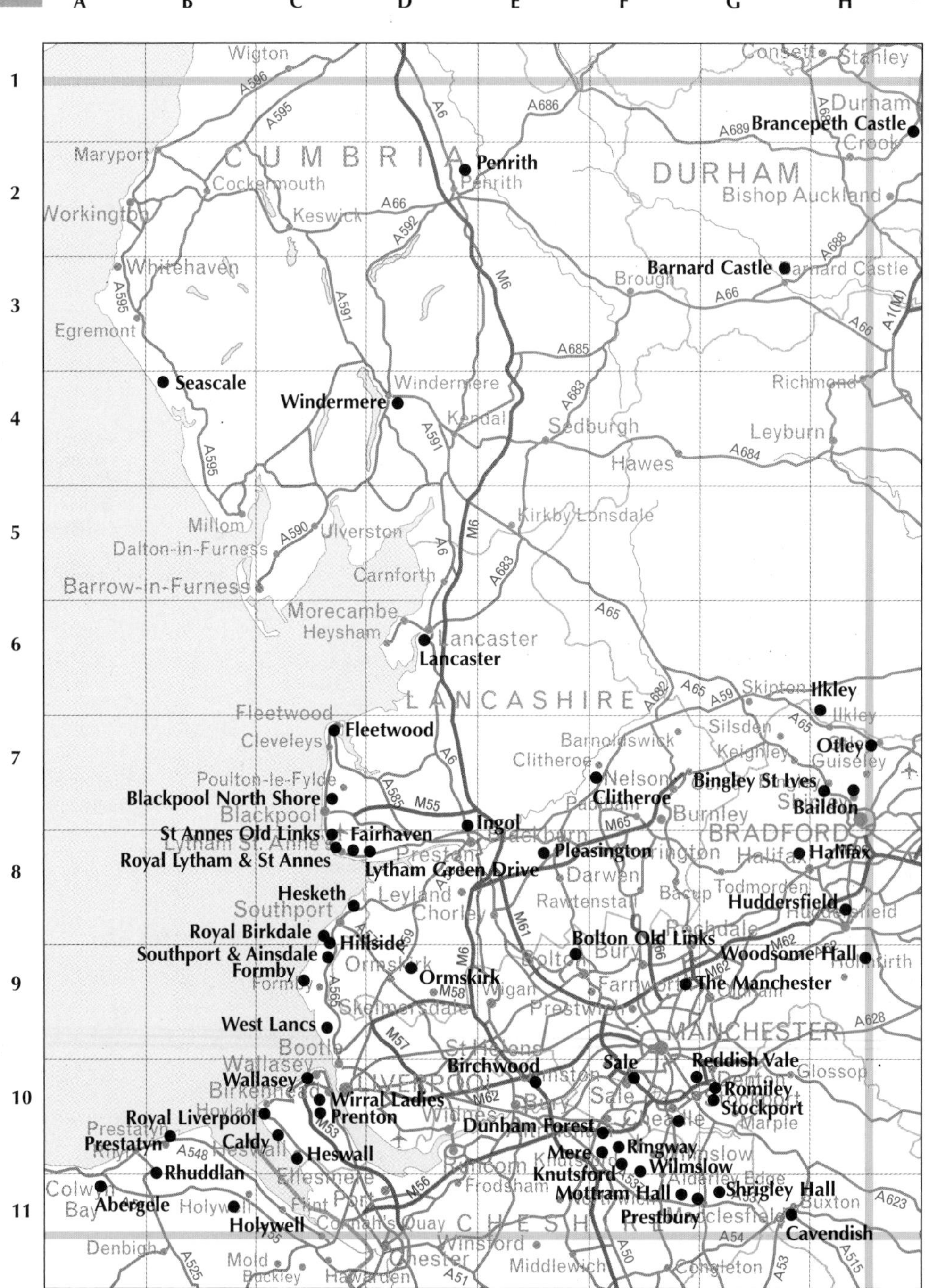
A
B
C
D
E
F
G
H
1
2
3
4
5
6
7
8
9
10
11
CUMBRIA
DURHAM
LANCASHIRE
BRADFORD
MANCHESTER
LIVERPOOL
Brancepeth Castle
Penrith
Barnard Castle
Seascale
Windermere
Lancaster
Ilkley
Fleetwood
Otley
Bingley St Ives
Clitheroe
Baildon
Blackpool North Shore
Ingol
St Annes Old Links
Fairhaven
Pleasington
Halifax
Royal Lytham & St Annes
Lytham Green Drive
Hesketh
Huddersfield
Royal Birkdale
Hillside
Bolton Old Links
Southport & Ainsdale
Woodsome Hall
Formby
Ormskirk
The Manchester
West Lancs
Birchwood
Sale
Reddish Vale
Wallasey
Wirral Ladies
Romiley
Prenton
Stockport
Royal Liverpool
Dunham Forest
Prestatyn
Caldy
Ringway
Mere
Heswall
Wilmslow
Rhuddlan
Knutsford
Shrigley Hall
Mottram Hall
Abergele
Holywell
Prestbury
Cavendish
Wigton
Maryport
Workington
Whitehaven
Egremont
Cockermouth
Keswick
Millom
Dalton-in-Furness
Barrow-in-Furness
Ulverston
Carnforth
Morecambe
Heysham
Kendal
Sedburgh
Kirkby Lonsdale
Hawes
Leyburn
Richmond
Brough
Bishop Auckland
Durham
Stanley
Skipton
Silsden
Keighley
Guiseley
Barnoldswick
Nelson
Burnley
Blackburn
Preston
Leyland
Chorley
Darwen
Rawtenstall
Bacup
Todmorden
Rochdale
Bury
Bolton
Wigan
Farnworth
Prestwich
Oldham
Glossop
Denton
Marple
Cheadle
Alderley Edge
Buxton
Macclesfield
Congleton
Middlewich
Winsford
Northwich
Frodsham
Runcorn
Widnes
St Helens
Skelmersdale
Bootle
Birkenhead
Hoylake
Ellesmere Port
Flint
Connah's Quay
Chester
Hawarden
Mold
Buckley
Denbigh
Colwyn Bay
A596
A595
A6
A686
A689
A66
A592
M6
A688
A591
A685
A683
A684
A590
A65
A682
A59
A585
M55
M65
M61
A566
A565
M58
M57
M62
A628
M53
A548
M56
A623
A54
A515
A53
A50
A51
A525
A1(M)

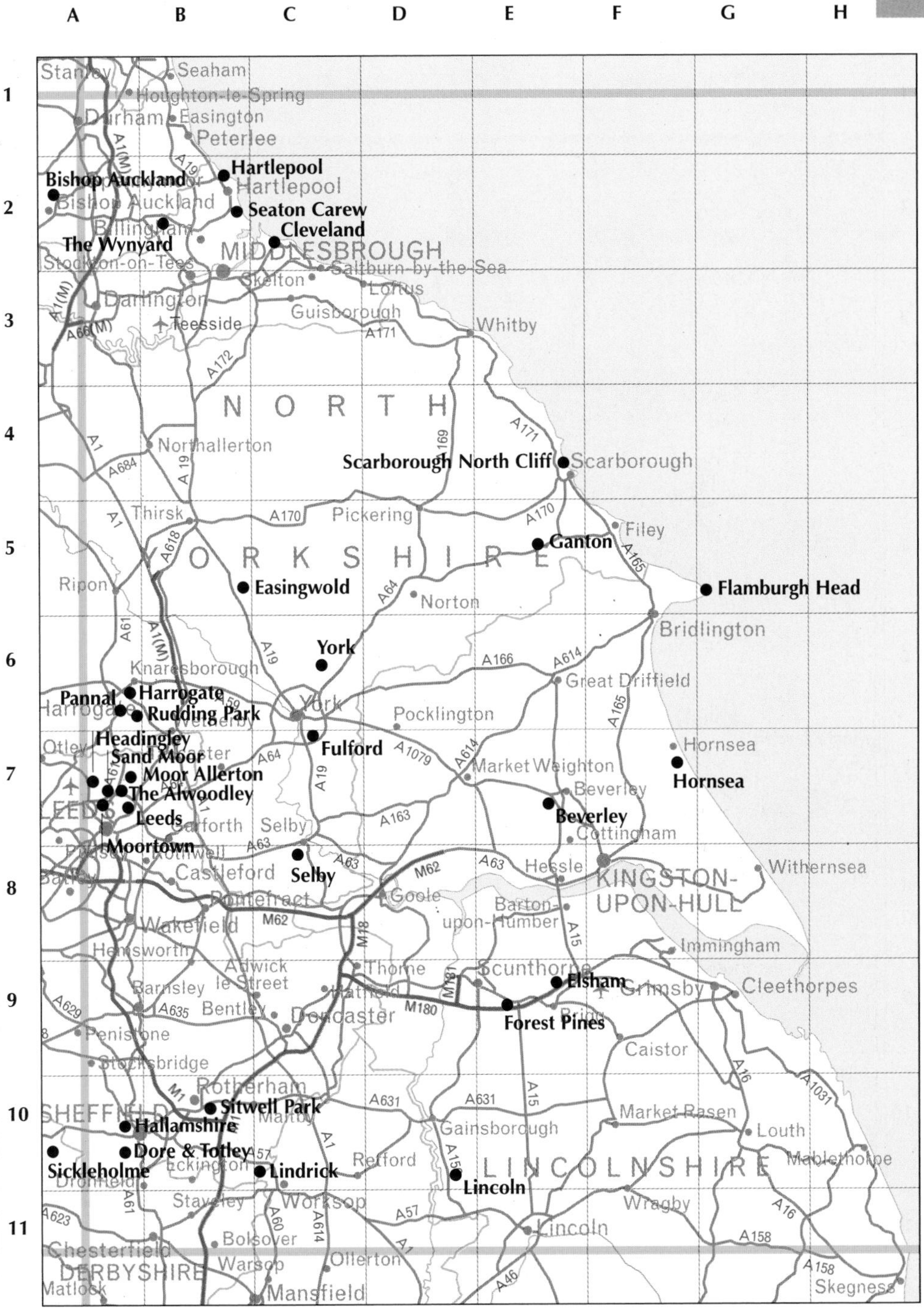

A B C D E F G H

1 2 3 4 5 6 7 8 9 10 11

Bishop Auckland
Hartlepool
Seaton Carew
Cleveland
The Wynyard
Scarborough North Cliff
Ganton
Flamburgh Head
Easingwold
York
Pannal
Harrogate
Rudding Park
Headingley
Sand Moor
Moor Allerton
The Alwoodley
Leeds
Moortown
Fulford
Hornsea
Beverley
Selby
Elsham
Forest Pines
Sitwell Park
Hallamshire
Dore & Totley
Sickleholme
Lindrick
Lincoln

Stanley
Seaham
Houghton-le-Spring
Durham
Easington
Peterlee
Hartlepool
Bishop Auckland
Billingham
MIDDLESBROUGH
Stockton-on-Tees
Saltburn-by-the-Sea
Skelton
Loftus
Darlington
Teesside
Guisborough
Whitby
NORTH
Northallerton
Scarborough
Thirsk
Pickering
Filey
YORKSHIRE
Ripon
Norton
Bridlington
Knaresborough
Great Driffield
Harrogate
Wetherby
York
Pocklington
Otley
Hornsea
Market Weighton
Beverley
LEEDS
Garforth
Selby
Cottingham
Rothwell
Castleford
Hessle
KINGSTON-UPON-HULL
Withernsea
Pontefract
Goole
Barton-upon-Humber
Wakefield
Hemsworth
Immingham
Adwick le Street
Thorne
Scunthorpe
Barnsley
Hatfield
Grimsby
Cleethorpes
Bentley
Doncaster
Brigg
Penistone
Caistor
Stocksbridge
Rotherham
SHEFFIELD
Maltby
Market Rasen
Gainsborough
Louth
Eckington
Retford
LINCOLNSHIRE
Mablethorpe
Dronfield
Staveley
Worksop
Wragby
Lincoln
Chesterfield
Bolsover
DERBYSHIRE
Warsop
Ollerton
Matlock
Mansfield
Skegness

A1(M) A19 A1 A66(M) A172 A171 A684 A170 169 A618 A64 A165 A61 A59 A166 A614 A1079 A63 A163 M62 M18 A15 M181 M180 A629 A635 M1 A631 A16 A1031 A57 A158 A623 A60 A46

12

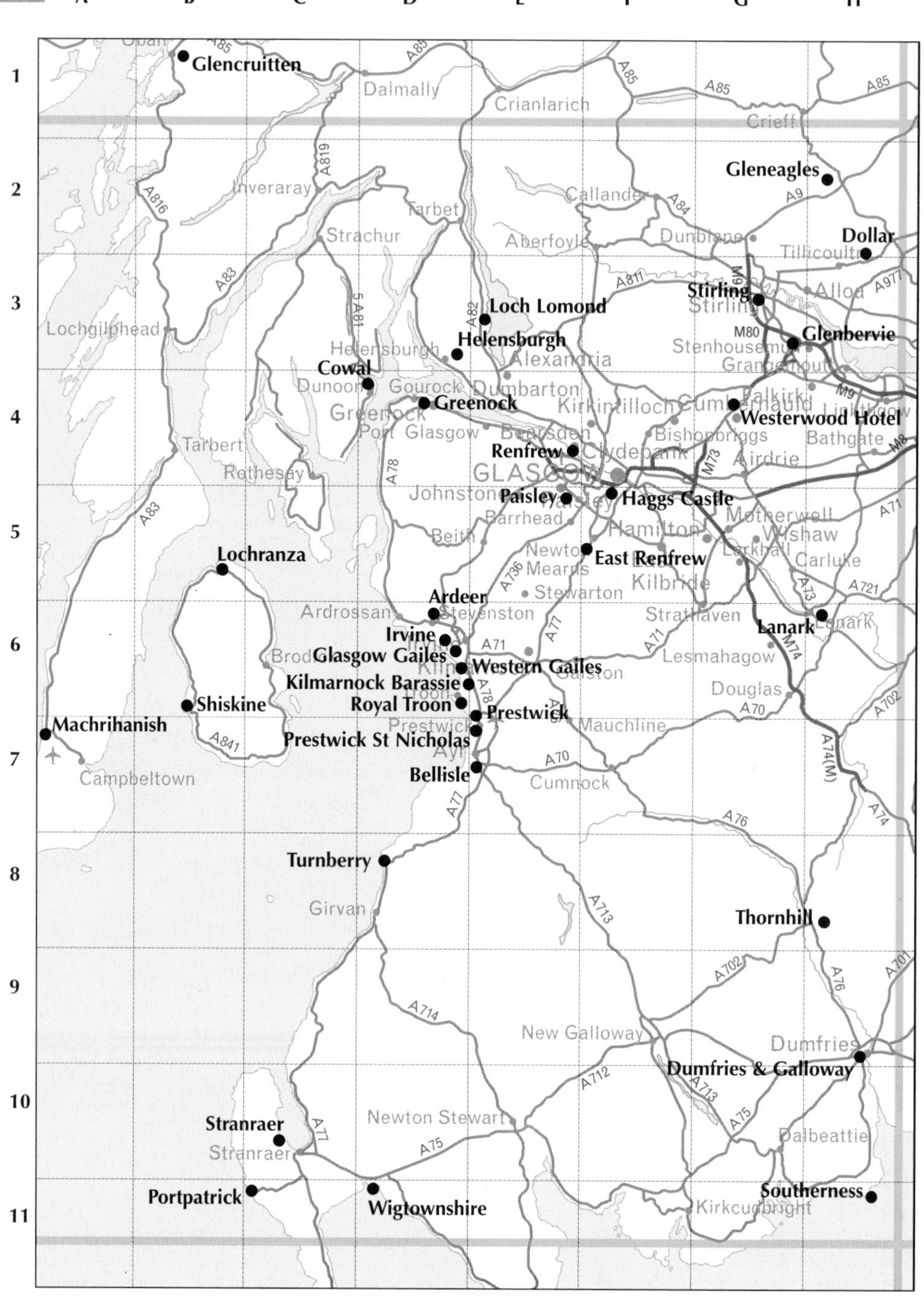

A
B
C
D
E
F
G
H
1
2
3
4
5
6
7
8
9
10
11
Glencruitten
Dalmally
Crianlarich
Crieff
Gleneagles
Inveraray
Tarbet
Callander
Strachur
Aberfoyle
Dunblane
Dollar
Stirling
Loch Lomond
Lochgilphead
Helensburgh
Glenbervie
Cowal
Alexandria
Greenock
Dumbarton
Westerwood Hotel
Port Glasgow
Bishopbriggs
Bathgate
Tarbert
Renfrew
Airdrie
Rothesay
GLASGOW
Paisley
Haggs Castle
Barrhead
Motherwell
Beith
Wishaw
Lochranza
East Renfrew
Carluke
Stewarton
Ardeer
Ardrossan
Strathaven
Irvine
Lanark
Glasgow Gailes
Lesmahagow
Western Gailes
Kilmarnock Barassie
Douglas
Shiskine
Royal Troon
Machrihanish
Prestwick
Mauchline
Prestwick St Nicholas
Bellisle
Campbeltown
Cumnock
Turnberry
Girvan
Thornhill
New Galloway
Dumfries
Dumfries & Galloway
Newton Stewart
Stranraer
Dalbeattie
Portpatrick
Wigtownshire
Southerness
Kirkcudbright
A85
A816
A819
A83
A84
A9
A811
A82
A81
M9
M80
A977
M73
M8
A78
A71
A736
A77
A721
A73
M74
A70
A702
A74(M)
A74
A76
A713
A714
A712
A701
A75
A841

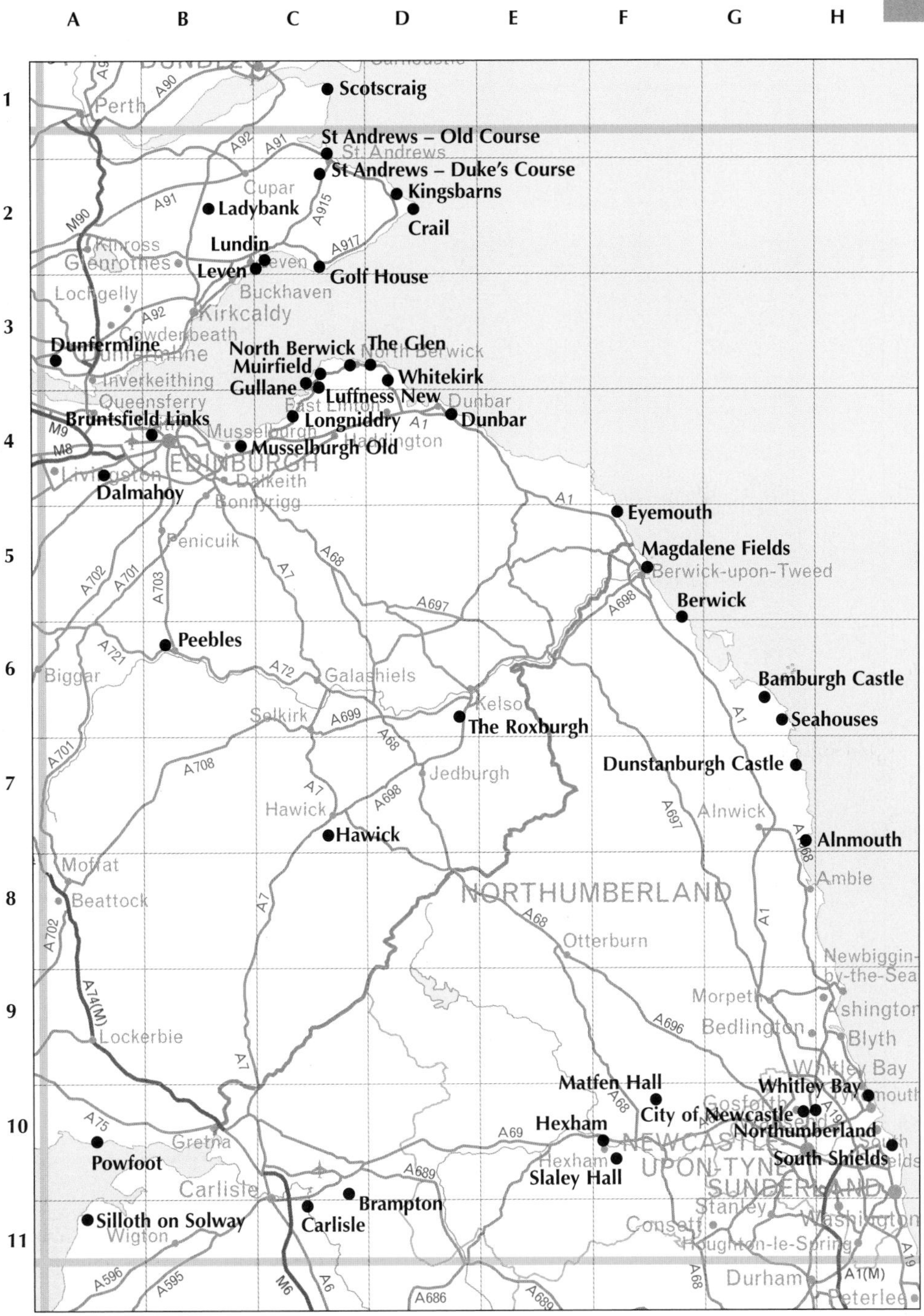

A B C D E F G H

1 2 3 4 5 6 7 8 9 10 11

Scotscraig
St Andrews – Old Course
St Andrews – Duke's Course
Kingsbarns
Crail
Ladybank
Lundin
Leven
Golf House
Dunfermline
North Berwick
The Glen
Muirfield
Gullane
Whitekirk
Luffness New
Dunbar
Bruntsfield Links
Longniddry
Musselburgh Old
Dalmahoy
Eyemouth
Magdalene Fields
Berwick
Peebles
Bamburgh Castle
Seahouses
The Roxburgh
Dunstanburgh Castle
Hawick
Alnmouth
Matfen Hall
Whitley Bay
City of Newcastle
Northumberland
Hexham
Slaley Hall
South Shields
Powfoot
Brampton
Silloth on Solway
Carlisle

Perth
St Andrews
Cupar
Kinross
Glenrothes
Leven
Buckhaven
Lochgelly
Kirkcaldy
Cowdenbeath
Dunfermline
North Berwick
Inverkeithing
Queensferry
East Linton
Dunbar
Musselburgh
Haddington
EDINBURGH
Livingston
Dalkeith
Bonnyrigg
Penicuik
Berwick-upon-Tweed
Biggar
Galashiels
Selkirk
Kelso
Jedburgh
Hawick
Alnwick
Moffat
Amble
Beattock
NORTHUMBERLAND
Otterburn
Newbiggin-by-the-Sea
Morpeth
Ashington
Lockerbie
Bedlington
Blyth
Whitley Bay
Tynemouth
Gosforth
NEWCASTLE UPON TYNE
Gretna
Hexham
SUNDERLAND
Carlisle
Stanley
Consett
Washington
Wigton
Houghton-le-Spring
Durham
Peterlee

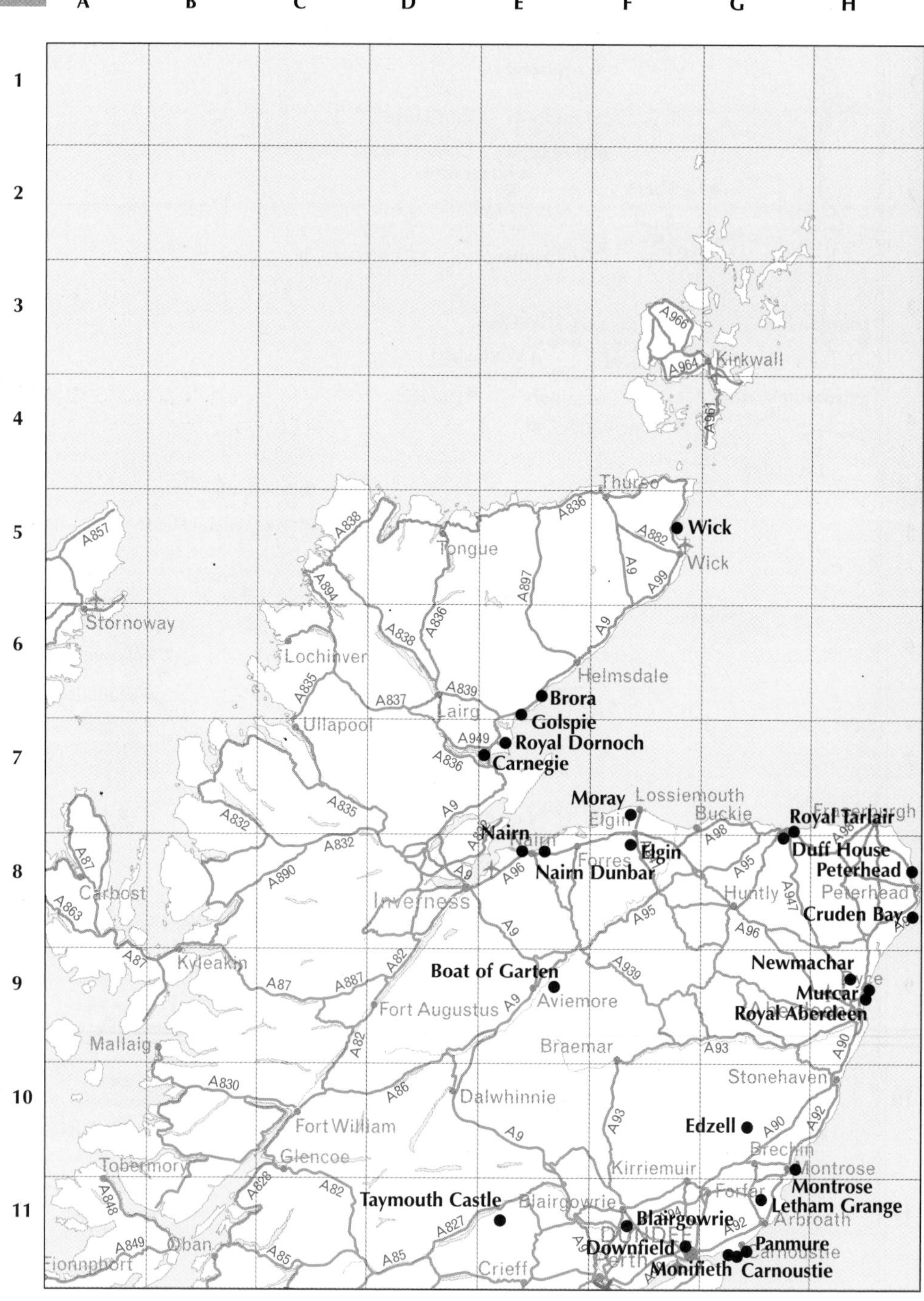

A
B
C
D
E
F
G
H
1
2
3
4
5
6
7
8
9
10
11
Kirkwall
Thurso
Wick
Wick
Tongue
Stornoway
Lochinver
Helmsdale
Brora
Golspie
Lairg
Ullapool
Royal Dornoch
Carnegie
Moray
Lossiemouth
Buckie
Royal Tarlair
Fraserburgh
Nairn
Elgin
Elgin
Duff House
Peterhead
Nairn Dunbar
Forres
Carbost
Inverness
Huntly
Peterhead
Cruden Bay
Kyleakin
Newmachar
Boat of Garten
Dyce
Murcar
Fort Augustus
Aviemore
Royal Aberdeen
Mallaig
Braemar
Stonehaven
Dalwhinnie
Edzell
Fort William
Brechin
Tobermory
Glencoe
Kirriemuir
Montrose
Montrose
Forfar
Taymouth Castle
Blairgowrie
Letham Grange
Blairgowrie
Arbroath
Dundee
Panmure
Downfield
Carnoustie
Oban
Crieff
Perth
Monifieth
Carnoustie
Fionnphort

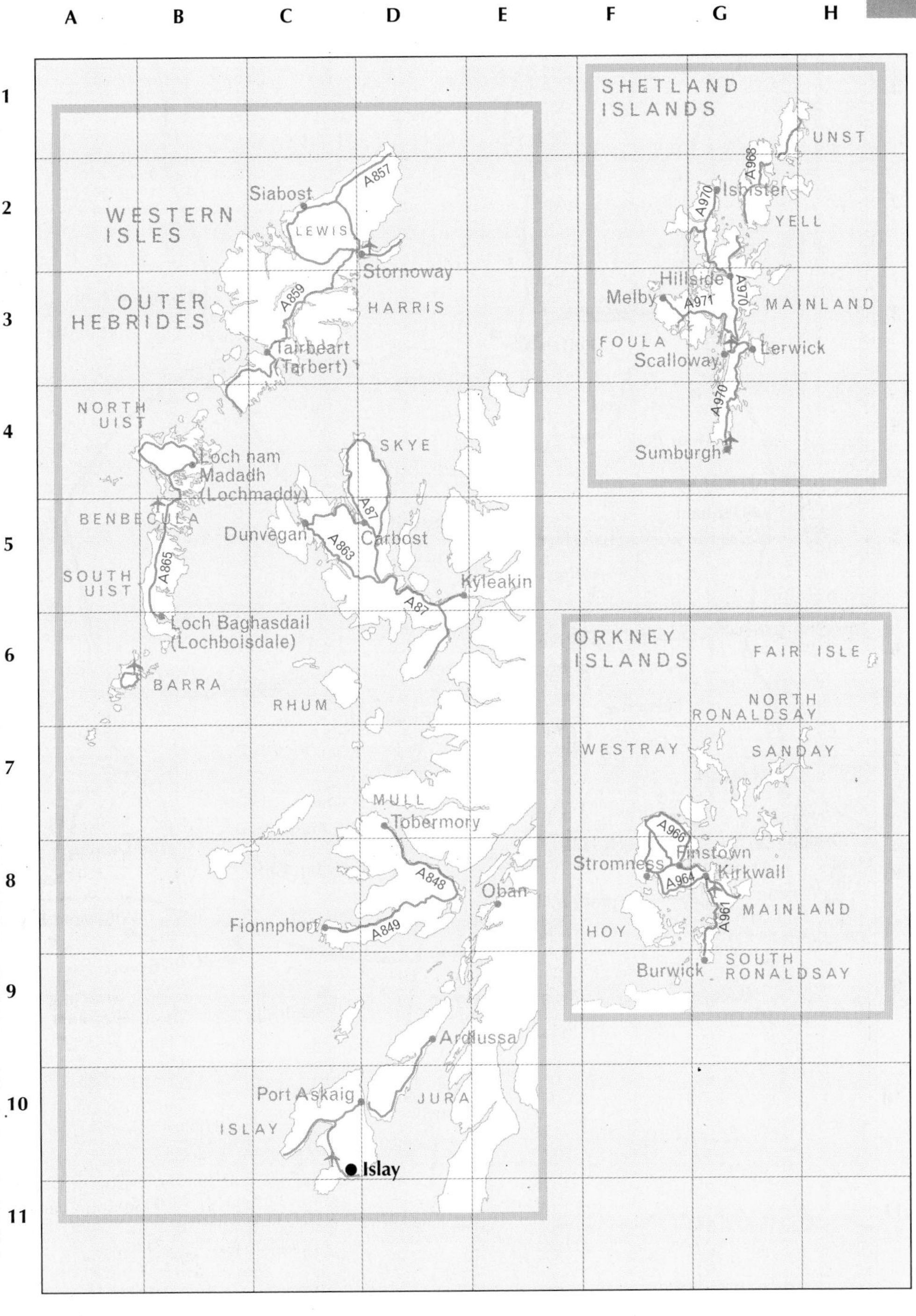

A B C D E F G H

1 2 3 4 5 6 7 8 9 10 11

WESTERN ISLES

OUTER HEBRIDES

Siabost
LEWIS
A857
Stornoway
A859
HARRIS
Tairbeart (Tarbert)
NORTH UIST
Loch nam Madadh (Lochmaddy)
BENBECULA
A865
SOUTH UIST
Loch Baghasdail (Lochboisdale)
BARRA
SKYE
A87
Dunvegan
A863
Carbost
Kyleakin
RHUM
MULL
Tobermory
A848
Oban
Fionnphort
A849
Ardlussa
Port Askaig
JURA
ISLAY
Islay

SHETLAND ISLANDS

UNST
A968
Isbister
A970
YELL
Hillside
A970
Melby
A971
MAINLAND
FOULA
Lerwick
Scalloway
A970
Sumburgh

ORKNEY ISLANDS

FAIR ISLE
NORTH RONALDSAY
WESTRAY
SANDAY
A966
Finstown
Stromness
A964
Kirkwall
MAINLAND
A961
HOY
SOUTH RONALDSAY
Burwick

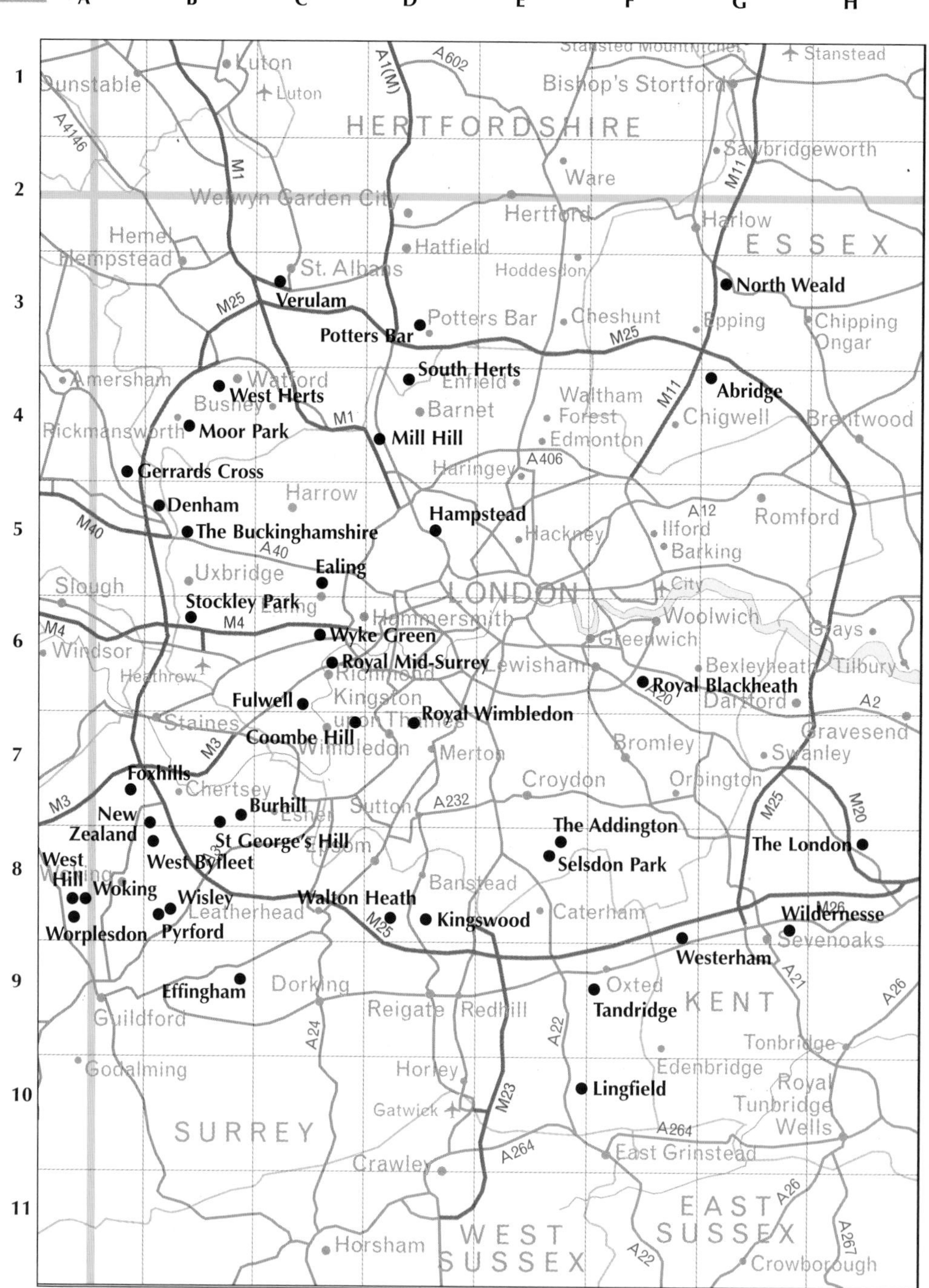
A
B
C
D
E
F
G
H
1
2
3
4
5
6
7
8
9
10
11
HERTFORDSHIRE
ESSEX
LONDON
SURREY
KENT
WEST SUSSEX
EAST SUSSEX
Verulam
Potters Bar
North Weald
South Herts
West Herts
Abridge
Moor Park
Mill Hill
Gerrards Cross
Denham
Hampstead
The Buckinghamshire
Ealing
Stockley Park
Wyke Green
Royal Mid-Surrey
Royal Blackheath
Fulwell
Royal Wimbledon
Coombe Hill
Foxhills
New Zealand
Burhill
St George's Hill
The Addington
The London
West Byfleet
Selsdon Park
West Hill
Woking
Wisley
Walton Heath
Kingswood
Wildernesse
Worplesdon
Pyrford
Westerham
Effingham
Tandridge
Lingfield
Dunstable
Luton
Stanstead
Bishop's Stortford
Sawbridgeworth
Ware
Welwyn Garden City
Hertford
Harlow
Hemel Hempstead
Hatfield
St. Albans
Hoddesdon
Cheshunt
Epping
Chipping Ongar
Amersham
Watford
Enfield
Waltham Forest
Bushey
Barnet
Chigwell
Brentwood
Rickmansworth
Edmonton
Haringey
Harrow
Romford
Ilford
Hackney
Barking
Uxbridge
Slough
City
Hammersmith
Woolwich
Grays
Windsor
Greenwich
Heathrow
Richmond
Lewisham
Bexleyheath
Tilbury
Kingston upon Thames
Dartford
Staines
Gravesend
Wimbledon
Merton
Bromley
Swanley
Chertsey
Croydon
Orpington
Esher
Sutton
Epsom
Banstead
Caterham
Leatherhead
Sevenoaks
Dorking
Oxted
Guildford
Reigate
Redhill
Tonbridge
Godalming
Horley
Edenbridge
Royal Tunbridge Wells
Gatwick
East Grinstead
Crawley
Horsham
Crowborough
M1
M25
M11
M40
M4
M3
M20
M26
M23
A1(M)
A602
A4146
A406
A12
A40
A2
A20
A232
A21
A26
A22
A24
A264
A267

INDEX

C

INDEX

INDEX

INDEX

Acknowledgements

Executive Editor Trevor Davies

Editor Sharon Ashman

Senior Designer Jo Bennett

Production Controller Jo Sim

Maps Line & Line

Database Hardwater Associates

Index Alan Thatcher